CONSTITUTIONAL LAW

WEST LEGAL STUDIES

Options.
Over 300 products in every area of the law: textbooks, CD-ROMs, reference books, test banks, online companions, and more – helping you succeed in the classroom and on the job.

Support.
We offer unparalleled, practical support: robust instructor and student supplements to ensure the best learning experience, custom publishing to meet your unique needs, and other benefits such as West's Student Achievement Award. And our sales representatives are always ready to provide you with dependable service.

Feedback.
As always, we want to hear from you! Your feedback is our best resource for improving the quality of our products. Contact your sales representative or write us at the address below if you have any comments about our materials or if you have a product proposal.

Accounting and Financials for the Law Office • Administrative Law • Alternative Dispute Resolution Bankruptcy • Business Organizations/Corporations • Careers and Employment • Civil Litigation and Procedure • CLA Exam Preparation • Computer Applications in the Law Office • Contract Law Court Reporting • Criminal Law and Procedure • Document Preparation • Elder Law • Employment Law • Environmental Law • Ethics • Evidence Law • Family Law • Intellectual Property • Interviewing and Investigation • Introduction to Law • Introduction to Paralegalism • Law Office Management Law Office Procedures • Legal Nurse Consulting • Legal Research, Writing, and Analysis • Legal Terminology • Paralegal Internship • Product Liability • Real Estate Law • Reference Materials Social Security • Sports Law • Torts and Personal Injury Law • Wills, Trusts, and Estate Administration

---

West Legal Studies
5 Maxwell Drive
Clifton Park, New York 12065-2919

For additional information, find us online at:
www.westlegalstudies.com

THOMSON
DELMAR LEARNING

CONSTITUTIONAL LAW

C. Suzanne Bailey, J.D.
Chana Barron, J.D., M.S.

THOMSON
DELMAR LEARNING

Australia Canada Mexico Singapore Spain United Kingdom United States

THOMSON
DELMAR LEARNING

WEST LEGAL STUDIES

CONSTITUTIONAL LAW
C. Suzanne Bailey, J.D.
Chana Barron, J.D., M.S.

Career Education Strategic Business Unit:
Vice President:
Dawn Gerrain

Director of Editorial:
Sherry Dickinson

Editor:
Shelley Esposito

Developmental Editor:
Melissa Riveglia

Editorial Assistant:
Brian Banks

Director of Production:
Wendy A. Troeger

Production Editor:
Betty L. Dickson

Director of Marketing:
Wendy Mapstone

Marketing Manager:
Gerard McAvey

Cover Design:
Rose Design

Cover Image
©Corel Corporation

Library of Congress Cataloging-in-
Publication Data
Bailey, C. Suzanne.
  Constitutional law / C. Suzanne Bailey,
Chana Barron.—1st ed.
      p. cm.—(West legal studies)
  Includes bibliographical references
and index.
    ISBN 0-7668-4014-X (alk. paper)
  1. Constitutional law—United States.
I. Barron, Chana. II. Title. III. West legal
studies series
    KF4550.B255 2005
    342.73—dc22
                                    2005029342

NOTICE TO THE READER

Publisher does not warrant or guarantee any of the products described herein or perform any independent analysis in connection with any of the product information contained herein. Publisher does not assume, and expressly disclaims, any obligation to obtain and include information other than that provided to it by the manufacturer.

The reader is notified that this text is an educational tool, not a practice book. Since the law is in constant change, no rule or statement of law in this book should be relied upon for any service to any client. The reader should always refer to standard legal sources for the current rule or law. If legal advice or other expert assistance is required, the services of the appropriate professional should be sought.

The Publisher makes no representation or warranties of any kind, including but not limited to, the warranties of fitness for particular purpose or merchantability, nor are any such representations implied with respect to the material set forth herein, and the publisher takes no responsibility with respect to such material. The publisher shall not be liable for any special, consequential, or exemplary damages resulting, in whole or part, from the readers' use of, or reliance upon, this material.

CONTENTS

TABLE OF CASES

Cases cited in excerpted cases and within other quoted materials are not included. The cases bolded in this table are the cases excerpted in the text.

PREFACE

The writing of this book has been, in many ways, a significant learning experience. The process of writing a book was unknown territory for us, and while there have been some real frustrations, the experience has been very rewarding. Attempting to write a comprehensive but concise constitutional law textbook meant that we had to carefully consider how best to organize and present the materials without making it so concise that it didn't give the student the background in the very basic laws of this country that we felt was necessary. We hope we have achieved that goal.

We wanted to write a constitutional law textbook designed specifically for undergraduate students. This was important to us because, having taught constitutional law, it was apparent that undergraduate students needed something different from the traditional casebook that is used in law schools throughout the country and something more than a recitation from a particular academic perspective. We felt it was not enough just to have the undergraduate student read cases and try to understand what the Court was doing; there was a true need to have explanatory material to introduce and supplement the case law. At the same time we wanted the students to understand the Constitution and its interpretation in the context of history, sociology, and politics. This book was designed to convey to the student the essential principles, tests, and history of constitutional law, with cases to demonstrate and reinforce the discussion.

FEATURES OF THE TEXT

All of the chapters in this book contain some key features worth noting. Each chapter begins with a quote that relates to the topic covered by the chapter and represents a perspective that we thought was important for the student to consider. In addition, we have included marginal definitions of legal terms used for the first time in that particular chapter. Perhaps one of the most unique aspects of this textbook, however, is the inclusion of historical sidebars. These sidebars discuss historical events and people that tie in with the issues raised in the chapters or cases that are included in the chapters as well. These historical sidebars are designed to give the student some context for the constitutional issues, as well as give the student insight into some of the individuals involved in the cases they will be reading. At the end of each chapter are Review Questions designed to provoke discussion and help the student absorb the lessons of the chapter. In addition to the Review Questions, each chapter also has a segment called Internet Connections that gives the students Web sites that will allow them to access more information on the issues raised in the chapter. Lists of Key Terms also appear at the end of each chapter, as well as the End Notes that support the information found in the chapter. At the end of the book, the student will find several appendices. The appendices include a copy of the U.S. Constitution, selected federal statutes, advice on reading and briefing cases, researching the Constitution, a list of Supreme Court Justices throughout the years, and the Supreme Court timetable. A glossary of terms is also included.

ORGANIZATION OF THE TEXT

Chapter 1 begins the discussion with an overview of the historical background and events leading to the writing of the Constitution. To do this, the chapter begins with a discussion of the Articles of Confederation and the failure of the loose confederation of states that existed in the earliest days of this country's history. The chapter then moves forward to discuss the Constitutional Convention, focusing on the different proposals made and the compromises reached, which led to the drafting of the body of the U.S. Constitution. A discussion of the debate, much of which is found in the Federalist Papers, which preceded the ratification process follows, along with information regarding the writing of the Bill of Rights and the reasoning behind having a separate, second ratification process for those important amendments to the Constitution. Lastly, Chapter 1 looks at the Constitution itself and its ability to change as our society changes. It is the ability to amend this Constitution, through a rigorous amendment process, which has kept it a viable document that is still relevant to today's society.

Chapter 2 focuses on the major divisions the Framers set for our constitutional scheme of government and the reasons underlying the scheme. Following a brief introduction, the chapter discusses the horizontal division of our government into three separate branches—Executive (law-enforcing), Legislative (lawmaking), and Judicial (law-interpreting). The division of power of the Separation of Powers doctrine was to prevent any one branch from becoming too powerful by providing checks by each branch on the actions of the other branches. Each of the five constitutional issues arising from the horizontal division is discussed and illustrative cases are provided for each issue. The discussion and cases address the ways in which conflicts between branches arise, the social, historical, and political factors upon which they are based, and the constitutional principles and legal reasoning used by the Supreme Court in resolving them. The chapter then turns to the vertical division of government in America—that between the national government and the state governments—known as the system of federalism. This section addresses the differences in the powers held by the state and federal governments as set out in the Constitution and how the Court has gone about determining the extent of those boundaries. It also provides a historical perspective on how the Supreme Court has interpreted federalism throughout our history.

Chapter 3 contains information on the structuring of the federal court system and the important concept of judicial review. The discussion begins with the historical and political forces that shaped the early courts. While the Constitution itself said little about how the court system was to be structured, there were statutes enacted which gave form and substance to the system. The early section of this chapter not only discusses these statutes, it also discusses attempts to change the structure of the system in later years, and the political reasons for the proposal of some of these changes. After this historical perspective the discussion in the chapter turns to the U.S. Supreme Court and the jurisdictional powers that court holds. There are many jurisdictional requirements to be met before the Court can hear a case and these are discussed at length, followed by a discussion of the limits on the Court's jurisdiction. The next section discusses the court rules that impact taking a case to the Supreme Court, as well as the process used by the Court to determine which cases they will hear. The subsequent section discusses the standards of review the Court uses in making its decisions, followed by a lengthy discussion on the theories explaining how the Court makes its decisions. The chapter is completed by discussing the crucial concept of Judicial Review and the Court's role as the final arbiter of the constitutionality of the laws passed and judicial opinions handed down.

Chapter 4, Congress and Its Powers, focuses on the many powers that are given to the federal legislature by the Constitution. After a brief introduction, the bulk of the chapter is devoted to discussing, one by one, these congressional powers, which include the power to regulate commerce, the power to declare war, the power to coin money, the power to legislate and investigate, the power to enter into treaties with foreign countries, the power to tax and spend, the power to engage in foreign affairs, the power to establish post offices and regulate immigration. Many relevant cases are included in the discussion to enable the student to see the extent of the powers held by Congress and the Court's interpretation of those powers. The chapter concludes with a discussion of the Tenth Amendment and the limits it places on Congressional power.

Chapter 5 discusses the Presidency and the powers of the President as set out in the Constitution. In addition, the Court's interpretation of that power is considered over time and in particular situations with attention paid to the distinction between the executive's power in regard to domestic affairs and foreign affairs. The President's power to veto legislation and to appoint other executive officers of the government is also included in the chapter. Finally, the circumstances under which the President may be removed from office and how the Court has defined the constitutional limitations on removal and the background for these decisions are set forth.

The focus in Chapter 6 is on fundamental rights. There are three major fundamental rights that are most strongly protected by the Constitution. This chapter discusses the right to vote, the right to travel, and the right a citizen has to access the court system. After discussing these three rights, including cases that illustrate how the Court has interpreted these rights and applied the law, the chapter concludes with a discussion of the reluctance, if not the outright refusal, of the Court to expand the concept of fundamental rights to include other rights that society may consider to be crucial. The discussion includes cases in which the Court explains its refusal to expand the number of rights to be considered fundamental.

Due Process and Equal Protection are discussed in Chapter 7. The Due Process Clauses of the Fifth and Fourteenth Amendments, as well as the Equal Protection Clause of the Fourteenth Amendment have provided the underpinnings for a significant portion of the Supreme Court's constitutional analysis. It was through the Court's use of the Fourteenth Amendment Due Process Clause that the guarantees the federal government granted citizens in the Bill of Rights were made applicable to the states, thereby requiring each state government to recognize and protect these same rights. The chapter discusses the incorporation of these rights. Also included in the chapter is a discussion of what constitutes due process both substantively and procedurally, and how the Court, through its interpretation of the Constitution, has, over time, changed the boundaries for these protections. The Equal Protection Clause, passed after the Civil War, was intended to prevent the states from treating citizens of color differently from white citizens. The chapter discusses how the Court has expanded that purpose over time to preclude disparate treatment of other groups; the standards that are used in analyzing equal protection claims and the reasoning supporting these decisions.

Chapter 8 discusses discrimination. It begins with a general discussion of discrimination and how discrimination can be proven. The chapter then moves to discussing discrimination in the public school system, as well as segregation in public universities and colleges. The discussion then turns to desegregation, the end of the doctrine of separate but equal, and the historical and political pressures that came to bear when the school systems were becoming integrated. Gender discrimination and discrimination based on alienage are also discussed in this chapter. The chapter concludes with a discussion of affirmative action and the many perspectives on this interesting topic.

The right to privacy and the numerous rights claimed under the privacy umbrella are discussed in Chapter 9. The discussion begins with an overview of the constitutional basis for this claimed right, and then moves on to discuss specific topics that are included in privacy. These include the right to marry, procreate, procure an abortion, and raise your children, as well as issues regarding sex and sexuality and the claimed right to die.

Chapter 10 focuses on one of our most basic freedoms—the freedom of expression. Protection of expression ensures wide-ranging public debate—the very basis of a representative democracy. The First Amendment guarantee of freedom of expression is far more complicated than it appears from the simple words of the amendment. This chapter examines the complexity of the issues surrounding the guarantee. Initially, the principles underlying First Amendment expression analysis are set forth along with a discussion of how these have evolved and changed. These principles include the issue of content of expression, where the expression occurs, the parameters of the regulation, and the distinction between speech and conduct. Also considered is symbolic expression, for example, draft-card burning or flag burning as a means of political expression. The chapter also addresses the regulation of expression in special contexts such as the school and in the political process by placing limits on campaign financing. As you will see from the chapter, freedom of expression, during the twentieth century changed from an area that was rarely addressed by the Court to one occupying a great deal of the Justices' time.

Change was not only occurring in the area of freedom of expression. Chapter 11 focuses on the changes in constitutional protections for speech that had traditionally been considered unprotected by First Amendment speech guarantees. Speech that was deemed to be harmful or without value was not entitled to the same freedom from regulation by the government as that which was associated with the free exchange of ideas. The interpretation and analysis of regulations surrounding these traditionally unprotected areas—advocacy of illegal conduct; fighting words; obscenity; defamation and commercial speech—has changed over the course of the twentieth century and the changing social and political environment across that time. Chapter 11 discusses these changing conditions, interpretations, and analyses in each of these five traditionally unprotected areas.

The freedom we have to freely associate with others is the topic discussed in Chapter 12. This First Amendment right is the basis for our belief that we can freely associate with whomever we choose. This chapter includes a discussion of the basic right, as well as challenges to this right that have arisen over our country's history; a history that includes attempts by the government to interfere with this right.

The last of the rights surrounding expression found in the First Amendment is discussed in Chapter 13, which addresses freedom of the press. In an era where we often hear the claim that the press is protecting the public's right to know, this is often the center of much debate. Chapter 13 begins with an introduction and a history of freedom of the press and then moves into the special privileges enjoyed by the press under the First Amendment. The chapter then discusses several types of governmental actions that have led to challenges that the government was attempting to unconstitutionally interfere with the freedom of the press. Included in the discussion are the use of gag orders, prior restraints, closure orders, and the balance necessary at times to provide a fair trial for a defendant while giving deference to freedom of the press.

Also prized among our rights granted by the Constitution and the Bill of Rights is freedom of religion. Chapter 14 discusses in detail one of the two provisions of the Constitution designed to protect citizens against government encroachment on one's religion—the Free Exercise Clause. The reasons underlying inclusion of this clause were to limit the government's ability to burden the practice of citizens' chosen religion and to prevent the government from restricting religious belief. The first subject addressed in this chapter concerns how and what the Court has determined to constitute religious belief. Once that issue is settled, we turn to the thornier issue of when the government may regulate conduct that is intimately tied to the practice of one's religious beliefs. One of the central concerns here is the government's intent in passing the regulation. If the intent is to burden religious practice, the Court employs a different standard of analysis. The chapter contains a discussion of the standards employed, as well as the expanding and contracting nature of the Court's pronouncements regarding the constraints government may impose on the exercise of the right to religious freedom.

The final chapter involves the second provision found in the Constitution regarding religion. The Establishment Clause is introduced in this chapter, followed by a discussion of the crucial Lemon Test. This test, coming from the case of *Lemon v. Kurtzman*, is a three-prong test to determine whether the government action is in violation of the Establishment Clause. This three-prong test is generally the test used to evaluate government involvement with religious organizations or endeavors. After discussion of the Lemon Test, the discussion turns to topics such as Sunday Closing Laws, government involvement in ceremonies and displays, and financial aid to private schools and universities. This discussion includes prayer in school, religious education in public schools, and religious beliefs included in school curriculum.

By now it may be clear to the reader that this book is also an attempt to share our love of the Constitution and the law. We believe our Constitution has proven to be a successful outline for the governance of a democratic nation and a guardian of personal rights and liberties. We are excited to share our knowledge of, insight into, and love of that living document with others and hope that they will gain a greater appreciation of its importance through a greater understanding of it. We believe that understanding of the Constitution and the rights it bestows on us is important to being good citizens and guardians of the constitutional heritage that we benefit from daily in this country. Hopefully, this book reflects the excitement that we feel in discussing these rights and privileges.

SUPPLEMENTAL TEACHING MATERIALS

- The **Instructor's Manual** is available on-line at *www.westlegalstudies.com* in the Instructor's Lounge under Resource. Written by the authors of the text, the *Instructor's Manual* contains the following:
  - Chapter Outlines
  - Answers to the questions within the text
  - Essay questions to be used on exams
- **On-line Companion**™—The On-line Companion™ Web site can be found at *www.westlegalstudies.com* in the resource section of the Web site.
- **Web Page**—Come visit our Web site at *www.westlegalstudies.com*, where you will find valuable information such as hot links and sample materials to download, as well as other West legal Studies products.
- **Westlaw**—West's on-line computerized legal research system offers students "hands-on" experience with a system commonly used in law offices. Qualified adopters can receive ten free hours of Westlaw®. Westlaw® can be accessed with Macintosh and IBM PC and compatibles. A modem is required.

ACKNOWLEDGMENTS

We would like to take this opportunity to acknowledge the assistance and support we have received during this endeavor. We would like to extend our thanks to Kristi S. Mindrup for her assistance in researching the case law used in this textbook and to Stacia S. Benoy for her assistance in proofreading the manuscript and pointing out inconsistencies and typographical errors. We would also like to thank family and friends for their unwavering support and willingness to listen to our complaints and frustrations. Finally, we would like to thank the reviewers who provided very valuable comments and suggestions for the text.

Hank Arnold
Aiken Technical College
Aiken, South Carolina

Deborah Kottel
University of Great Falls
Great Falls, Montana

Sally Bisson
College of Saint Mary
Omaha, Nebraska

Rachel Margules
Oakland University
Rochester, Michigan

Chelsea Campbell
Lehman College
Bronx, New York

Anne Geraghty Rathert
Webster University
St. Louis, Missouri

John DeLeo
Central Pennsylvania College
Summerdale, Pennsylvania

Michael Rayboun
University of West Florida
Pensacola, Florida

Robert Diotalevi
Florida Gulf Coast University
Fort Myers, Florida

Jacqueline Spielman
Villa Julie College
Stevenson, Maryland

David Hallett
Pioneer Pacific College
Wilsonville, Oregon

Christopher Whaley
Roane State Community College
Harriman, Tennessee

Timothy Hart
College of Sequoias
Visalia, California

Oran's Dictionary of the Law
(3d ed. 2000). For definitions
of legal terms.

Please note the Internet resources are of a time-sensitive nature and URL addresses may often change or be deleted.
Contact us at westlegalstudies@delmar.com

ABOUT THE AUTHORS

C. Suzanne Bailey is an associate professor in the Department of Law Enforcement & Justice Administration at Western Illinois University. She teaches a variety of classes, including Criminal Procedure, Evidence, Civil law, Criminal and Civil Liability, White Collar Crime, Organized Crime and Current Issues in the Courts. She is a graduate of the University of Michigan and Thomas M. Cooley Law School in Lansing, Michigan. She practiced law for eight years before she began teaching in Lansing Community College's Legal Assistant Program. She also taught at Auburn University, Montgomery, Alabama where she was director of the Legal Assistant Program.

Chana Barron is a former Deputy Attorney General for the State of New Jersey where she handled criminal appeals. She was an Assistant Professor in the Department of Justice & Public Safety at Auburn University—Montgomery where she served as prelaw advisor before entering the Ph.D program in Sociology at the University of Iowa. Ms. Barron is currently completing her program there. She acquired her B.A at Rutgers University, her J.D. at the Benjamin N. Cardozo School of Law and her M.S. at American University.

CHAPTER 1

THE CONSTITUTION AND ITS HISTORY

"If men were angels, no government would be necessary. If angels were to govern men, neither external nor internal controls on government would be necessary. In framing a government which is to be administered by men over men, the great difficulty lies in this: You must first enable the government to control the governed; and in the next place, oblige it to control itself. A dependence on the people is, no doubt, the primary control on the government; but experience has taught mankind the necessity of auxiliary precautions."

—James Madison,
The Federalist, No. 51

INTRODUCTION

If you were to ask many people about the early days of this country and the **Constitution**, the document that outlines the structure of the government, most people would probably state that the Constitution and the form of government we still enjoy today were the natural consequences of the Revolutionary War. However, the Constitution and the federal government were the result of a failed first attempt at forming a new, democratic government for the United States.

This chapter will briefly explore the history of the Constitution, its roots, the people involved in its writing, the process followed to write the Constitution, and a discussion of why this document has survived and is the oldest written national constitution in the world.

constitution a document that sets out the basic principles and most general laws of a country, state, or organization.

THE CONTINENTAL CONGRESS AND THE ARTICLES OF CONFEDERATION

In 1774 the British-controlled North American colonies, in response to perceived tyranny by the King of England, joined together to fight against the injustices they believed had been committed against them by England.[1] They came together to form the United States of America,[2] a confederation of states or a "firm league of friendship" that resulted in a written document outlining the rights and responsibilities of the states, known as the **Articles of Confederation**.[3] See the highlights from the Articles of Confederation in Exhibit 1–1.

In this confederation the states were to retain their sovereign, independent status, while participating in a Continental Congress that was to be the bureaucratic agent of the United States. There was no executive or system of federal courts in this government, and the reality was that the Continental Congress was weak and had few real powers. This legislative body was given the power to raise a Continental Army to fight the British for independence and was given permission by the states to raise money through loans to this end. However, throughout the Revolutionary War, the Continental Army suffered from low recruitment, supply shortages, and morale problems.[4] Even when the Revolutionary War ended with the Treaty of Paris in 1783, the relationship between the Continental Congress and the states did not improve, if anything, it continued to deteriorate.[5]

Articles of Confederation the document that held together the 13 original American colonies before the adoption of the Constitution.

Exhibit 1–1 Highlights from the Articles of Confederation

States Involved: New Hampshire, Massachusetts, Rhode Island, Connecticut, New York, New Jersey, Pennsylvania, Delaware, Maryland, Virginia, North Carolina, South Carolina and Georgia

Name of the Confederacy:	**The United States of America**
Sovereignty:	**Each state retained sovereignty**
Common goals:	**Defense, Security of Liberty, Mutual and general welfare, to stand together against force**
Civil Rights:	**All citizens entitled to all privileges and immunities; all citizens shall have free egress to and from other states**
Trade & Commerce:	**All shall enjoy the privileges of trade and commerce**
Extradition:	**Each state shall cooperate and return fugitives**
Full Faith & Credit:	**Each state must recognize the records, acts and judicial proceedings of the courts or magistrates of other states**
Continental Congress:	**Each state shall elect delegates; each state shall have between 2 and 7 delegates**
Congressional Votes:	**Each state was allotted one**
Foreign Affairs:	**No state, without the consent of the Continental Congress, shall interfere in foreign affairs; nor shall any state grant titles of nobility**
War:	**No state shall engage in war without the consent of the Continental Congress; The United States had the sole power to determine peace and war**
Disputes between States:	**The United States Supreme Court was the last resort in deciding such disputes**
Coining Money:	**This power belonged to the United States, not the individual states; it included the power to fix standards of weights and measures**
Post Offices:	**The United States had the power to establish post offices and set postage rates**
Debts Owed by the Country:	**Burden of country's debt was shared by all states; included a pledge to honor the debts incurred during the Revolutionary War**
Observation of the Agreement:	**The perpetual union of the states shall be honored by all the states**

The Continental Congress faced the daunting task of paying off the debts incurred because of the war without much cooperation from the states. It did not help that this legislative body could only regulate trade or conduct foreign policy if the states voluntarily agreed. The states, who jealously guarded their sovereignty, often failed to send delegates to attend a meeting of the Continental Congress, so conducting business was often futile.[6]

As a result of this form of government, many economic and political problems developed. States could often not agree on state boundaries, states often levied duties on goods coming from other states, many states minted their own money, and piracy reigned on the high seas.[7] In addition to the problems caused by state action, the Continental Congress could not enforce the tax powers given to it by the 13 states or take any real action to protect itself from further state action.[8] Many leading citizens of the day believed that the country was bound to fail unless action was taken. Numerous pleas to the states for reform were ignored.

Against this background, ordinary citizens began to believe that the current state governments were taking too much control over their liberties and day-to-day activities. This led to rebellion. One notable example was an event called Shays' Rebellion. This rebellion did not break out spontaneously; it began with the farmers of Western Massachusetts petitioning the state government for reforms. Specifically they wanted the state to adopt paper currency, lower taxes, and judicial reform.[9] The state did not act on the farmers' petition, and the farmers organized for rebellion. Captain Daniel Shays, one of the farmers and a veteran of the Revolution, led the group as they occupied the Springfield, Massachusetts Courthouse for three days during September 1786.

Captain Shays began this occupation with 1,500 followers, but the numbers grew to 2,000 when, in early 1787, Shays and his followers attacked an arsenal in Springfield, Massachusetts.[10] While the state militia was able to defend against the attacks, it was not able at first to defeat the rebellion. A short time later, in Petersham, Massachusetts, the rebellion was quashed and many of its leaders were arrested. These leaders were tried and convicted, but before their death sentences could be carried out, they were pardoned.[11] Even though the rebellion ended, its effect was to pressure the Massachusetts legislature to reform. Many scholars credit Shays' Rebellion as one of the seminal events that led to the writing of the United States Constitution.[12]

There are two reasons why the government founded on the Articles of Confederation failed. One reason was the individuals who drafted the Articles of Confederation were mistaken to put their trust in the character of the politicians who would be serving the state governments.[13] As history has shown, these state legislators were often more concerned with maintaining their own power and local interests than with the future of the country. The second reason was the drafters' optimistic belief that the states would work together for the good of the entire new nation.[14] The state officials were often corrupt and this, coupled with a weak Continental Congress, meant that the chances of the states coordinating their efforts for the greater good were slim.

These two reasons, along with the fact that the Articles of Confederation could only be amended if all 13 states agreed, virtually ensured that the Continental Congress would be ineffective.

All of the events and discord eventually led several of the states to meet at the convention at Annapolis. However, only 5 of the 13 states were represented. Representatives from New York, New Jersey, Pennsylvania, Delaware, and Virginia met to discuss the possibility of amending the Articles of Confederation. By the end of that convention, however, the representatives agreed that rather than amend the existing Articles, a convention in Philadelphia with all of the state representatives should be held in May 1787 to discuss this matter of national concern. The convention at Annapolis ended with those present reporting back to their respective states and working to convince others of the need to revise the federal system.

THE CONSTITUTIONAL CONVENTION

The purpose of the **Constitutional Convention**, also known as the Philadelphia Convention, was ostensibly to revise the Articles of Confederation. The convention was held from May to September of 1787, with delegates attending from all states except Rhode Island.[15] The 55 delegates in attendance quickly and unanimously chose General George Washington as President of the convention and the convention proceeded behind guarded, closed doors.[16] The governor of Virginia, Edmund Randolph, began the formal discussions with a speech in which he stressed the need for a strong, centralized national government. He then summarized a plan for a new national government.[17] The plan called for a national government consisting of three branches. A **bicameral** (or two-chamber) legislature, an executive branch, and a judicial branch were designed to embody certain national powers and to act as a check against one another.[18] This original plan came to be known as the Virginia Plan.[19] It called for an enlargement of the powers of the central government for the best interest of the country as a whole.[20] For 10 days the delegates discussed the terms of that plan. For many, the plan contained some revolutionary and frightening ideas. Even though the idea of a centralized sovereign government that shared power with the sovereign states as well as a federal judiciary seems innocuous today, this was revolutionary thinking at the time of the convention. While the Virginia Plan was being debated the New Jersey delegates proposed their own plan, known as the New Jersey Plan, which proposed a union of states that came together to form a federal government,[21] and called for a revision of the

constitutional convention
representatives of the people of a country who meet to write or change a constitution.

bicameral (two chambers) a two-part legislature, such as the U.S. Congress, is bicameral: composed of the Senate (the "upper house" or "upper chamber") and the House of Representatives (the "lower house" or "lower chamber").

Articles of Confederation to allow Congress to raise revenue and regulate commerce. The plan did not create a different form for the centralized government. The New Jersey Plan was debated for three days before a vote was taken and the plan was rejected.[22]

Alexander Hamilton (see Exhibit 1–2) proposed a third plan, but this too was rejected because it too closely resembled the British form of government that had been rejected by the Colonies.[23] Some delegates went so far as to suggest that a monarchy would be appropriate.[24]

S I D E B A R

Hamilton was born in 1757 on the island of Nevis, in the Leeward group, British West Indies. He was the illegitimate son of a common-law marriage between a poor itinerant Scottish merchant of aristocratic descent and an English-French Huguenot mother who was a planter's daughter. In 1766, after the father had moved his family elsewhere in the Leewards to St. Croix in the Danish (now United States) Virgin Islands, he returned to St. Kitts while his wife and two sons remained on St. Croix.

The mother, who opened a small store to make ends meet, and a Presbyterian clergyman provided Hamilton with a basic education, and he learned to speak fluent French. About the time of his mother's death in 1768, he became an apprentice clerk at Christiansted in a mercantile establishment, whose proprietor became one of his benefactors. Recognizing his ambition and superior intelligence, they raised a fund for his education.

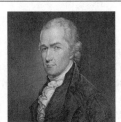

Exhibit 1–2
Alexander Hamilton, New York (courtesy of © Stapleton Collection/Corbis)

In 1772, bearing letters of introduction, Hamilton traveled to New York City. Patrons he met there arranged for him to attend Barber's Academy at Elizabethtown (present Elizabeth), NJ. During this time, he met and stayed for a while at the home of William Livingston, who would one day be a fellow signer of the Constitution. Late the next year, 1773, Hamilton entered King's College (later Columbia College and University) in New York City, but the Revolution interrupted his studies.

Although not yet 20 years of age, in 1774–75 Hamilton wrote several widely read pro-Whig pamphlets. Right after the war broke out, he accepted an artillery captaincy and fought in the principal campaigns of 1776–77. In the latter year, winning the rank of lieutenant colonel, he joined the staff of General Washington as secretary and aide-de-camp and soon became his close confidant as well.

In 1780 Hamilton wed New Yorker Elizabeth Schuyler, whose family was rich and politically powerful; they were to have eight children. In 1781, after some disagreements with Washington, he took a command position under Lafayette in the Yorktown, VA, campaign (1781). He resigned his commission that November.

Hamilton then read law at Albany and quickly entered practice, but public service soon attracted him. He was elected to the Continental Congress in 1782–83. In the latter year, he established a law office in New York City. Because of his interest in strengthening the central government, he represented his state at the Annapolis Convention in 1786, where he urged the calling of the Constitutional Convention.

In 1787 Hamilton served in the legislature, which appointed him as a delegate to the convention. He played a surprisingly small part in the debates, because he was frequently absent on legal business, his extreme nationalism put him at odds with most of the delegates, and he was frustrated by the conservative views of his two fellow delegates from New York. He did, however, sit on the Committee of Style, and he was the only one of the three delegates from his state that signed the finished document. Hamilton's part in New York's ratification the next year was substantial, though he felt the Constitution was deficient in many respects. Against determined opposition, he waged a strenuous and successful campaign, including collaboration with John Jay and James Madison in writing *The Federalist*. In 1787 Hamilton was again elected to the Continental Congress.

When the new government got under way in 1789, Hamilton won the position of Secretary of the Treasury. He began at once to place the nation's disorganized finances on a sound footing. In a series of reports (1790–91), he presented a program not only to stabilize national finances but also to shape the future of the country as a powerful, industrial nation. He proposed establishment of a national bank, funding of the national debt, assumption of state war debts, and the encouragement of manufacturing.

Hamilton's policies soon brought him into conflict with Jefferson and Madison. Their disputes with him over his pro-business economic program, sympathies for Great Britain, disdain for the common man, and opposition to the principles and excesses of the French revolution contributed to the formation of the first U.S. party system. It pitted Hamilton and the Federalists against Jefferson and Madison and the Democratic-Republicans.

During most of the Washington administration, Hamilton's views usually prevailed with the President, especially after 1793 when Jefferson left the government. In 1795 family and financial needs forced Hamilton to resign from the Treasury Department and resume his law practice in New York City. Except for a stint as inspector-general of the Army (1798–1800) during the undeclared war with France, he never again held public office.

While gaining stature in the law, Hamilton continued to exert a powerful impact on New York and national politics. Always an opponent of fellow-Federalist John Adams, he sought to prevent his election to the presidency in 1796. When that failed, he continued to use his influence secretly within Adams' cabinet. The bitterness between the two men became public knowledge in 1800 when Hamilton denounced Adams in a letter that was published through the efforts of the Democratic-Republicans.

Continued

In 1802 Hamilton and his family moved into The Grange, a country home he had built in a rural part of Manhattan not far north of New York City. But the expenses involved and investments in northern land speculations seriously strained his finances.

Meanwhile, when Jefferson and Aaron Burr tied in Presidential electoral votes in 1800, Hamilton threw valuable support to Jefferson. In 1804, when Burr sought the governorship of New York, Hamilton again managed to defeat him. That same year, Burr, taking offense at remarks he believed to have originated with Hamilton, challenged him to a duel, which took place at present Weehawken, NJ, on July 11. Mortally wounded, Hamilton died the next day. He was in his late forties at death. He was buried in Trinity Churchyard in New York City.[25]

After the New Jersey and Hamilton plans were rejected, the delegates were back to considering the Virginia Plan. There were two major areas of disagreement with this plan. First, how was representation to be decided and once it had been decided, if representation were to be based on population, how were slaves to be counted? The first issue led to many heated debates. The larger states were adamant that the representation should be by population; the larger the state's population, the greater the representation in the legislature. The smaller states were equally determined that there be equality in representation and favored a set number of representatives from each state and insisted that without this equality the larger states would have an unfair advantage in representation. The debate raged on for 17 weeks until the delegates reached what is now called the Great Compromise.[26] In this compromise a new centralized government was formed with the three previously mentioned branches. The legislative branch was to be bicameral, as the Virginia Plan had proposed, with the House of Representatives, or the lower house, having representation based on a state's population.[27] As such, the small states lost the battle over representation when it came to the House of Representatives.

However, when it came to the upper house, or the Senate, the compromise called for equal representation. Each state, regardless of its size would have two Senators representing it in the upper house.[28]

To further settle the issue of representation, the delegates had to determine how the population was to be counted for determining the number of representatives each state would send to serve in the House of Representatives. Oliver Ellsworth (see Exhibit 1–3) of Connecticut proposed the three-fifths compromise. The number of representatives in the lower house would be determined by the number of free persons and three-fifths of all other individuals residing in the state, or, in other words, the number of slaves within the boundaries of a state.[29] With this

Oliver Ellsworth was born on April 29, 1745, in Windsor, CT, to Capt. David and Jemima Ellsworth. He entered Yale in 1762 but transferred to the College of New Jersey (later Princeton) at the end of his second year. He continued to study theology and received his A.B. degree after 2 years. Soon afterward, however, Ellsworth turned to the law. After 4 years of study, he was admitted to the bar in 1771. The next year Ellsworth married Abigail Wolcott.

From a slow start Ellsworth managed to build a prosperous law practice. His reputation as an able and industrious jurist grew, and in 1777 Ellsworth became Connecticut's state attorney for Hartford County. That same year he was chosen as one of Connecticut's representatives in the Continental Congress. He served on various committees during six annual terms until 1783. Ellsworth was also active in his state's efforts during the Revolution. As a member of the Committee of the Pay Table, Oliver Ellsworth was one of the five men who supervised Connecticut's war expenditures. In 1779 he assumed greater duties as a member of the council of safety, which, with the governor, controlled all military measures for the state.

Exhibit 1–3 Oliver Ellsworth, Connecticut (courtesy of © Stapleton Collection/Corbis)

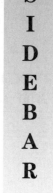

S I D E B A R

When the Constitutional Convention met in Philadelphia in 1787 Ellsworth once again represented Connecticut and took an active part in the proceedings. During debate on the Great Compromise, Ellsworth proposed that the basis of representation in the legislative branch remain by state, as under the Articles of Confederation. He also left his mark through an amendment to change the word 'national' to 'United States' in a resolution. Thereafter, 'United States' was the title used in the convention to designate the government.

Ellsworth also served on the Committee of Five that prepared the first draft of the Constitution. Ellsworth favored the three-fifths compromise on the enumeration of slaves but opposed the abolition of the foreign slave trade. Though he left

Continued

the convention near the end of August and did not sign the final document, he urged its adoption upon his return to Connecticut and wrote Letters of a Landholder to promote its ratification.

Ellsworth served as one of Connecticut's first two senators in the new federal government between 1789 and 1796. In the Senate he chaired the committee that framed the bill organizing the federal judiciary and helped to work out the practical details necessary to run a new government. Ellsworth's other achievements in Congress included framing the measure that admitted North Carolina to the Union, devising the non-intercourse act that forced Rhode Island to join, drawing up the bill to regulate the consular service, and serving on the committee that considered Alexander Hamilton's plan for funding the national debt and for incorporating the Bank of the United States.

In the spring of 1796 he was appointed Chief Justice of the Supreme Court and also served as commissioner to France in 1799 and 1800. Upon his return to America in early 1801, Ellsworth retired from public life and lived in Windsor, CT. He died there on November 26, 1807, and was buried in the cemetery of the First Church of Windsor.[30]

compromise, the delegates seemed to understand that without the willingness to look for alternatives, the Constitutional Convention would have failed.

A few days after the Great Compromise was reached, the delegates voted to appoint a Committee of Detail to draw up a draft of the proposed constitution. This committee, comprised of Nathaniel Gorham, John Rutledge, Edmund Randolph, James Wilson, and Oliver Ellsworth, worked for days, and finally, on August 6, 1787, presented the convention with a draft of the Constitution.[31] For five weeks the delegates continued to debate various issues raised by the draft.[32] The issue of commerce was the source of much discussion. Perhaps the most difficult of the commerce issues for the delegates to settle was the issue of slavery. It looked as though this difficult issue might manage to derail the writing of the Constitution. Again, however, a compromise was found. Delegates from Georgia and South Carolina reached an agreement with the New England states. The New England states would agree to support continuing slave importation for a period of 20 years and in return, the southern states would accept "a clause that required only a simple majority vote on navigation laws, a crippling blow to southern economic interests."[33]

One of the last major obstacles to completing the Constitution was the method to be used to elect the President. Several different methods were proposed, but another major compromise was reached in which the **electoral college** was created.[34] The electoral college is a group of individuals who are elected by the general population to cast a final, deciding vote for the presidency of the United States. There were three reasons why this compromise was appealing to the delegates. First, the larger states were given delegate representation that was proportionate to their size and population; second, the state legislatures had the power to select delegates; and third, the House of Representatives was given the power to choose the president if no candidate received a majority of electoral votes.[35]

The Constitutional Convention ended on September 17, 1787 with a vote to send the new Constitution to the Continental Congress so that they, in turn, could send it out to the states for ratification[36] (see Exhibit 1–4).

electoral college   a name for the persons chosen by voters to elect the president and vice president of the United States. The *electoral college* is now almost a formality, and the vote of the general public in each state directly controls the election.

THE RATIFICATION PROCESS, THE FEDERALIST PAPERS, AND THE BILL OF RIGHTS

When it came to ratifying the new proposed Constitution, the question was whether this process was an amendment of the Articles of confederation that required the unanimous consent of all 13 states, or was there a different vote requirement for ratification? The drafters of the Constitution believed that this document was not an amendment to the Articles of Confederation in that it created a new form of government. The drafters agreed that ratification of this new form of government, and the document that formed it, required

EXHIBIT 1–4 The Letter from George Washington to the Continental Congress[37]

IN CONVENTION, *September 17, 1787*

SIR:

We have now the honor to submit to the consideration of the United States in Congress assembled, that Constitution which has appeared to us the most advisable.

The friends of our country have long seen and desired that the power of making war, peace, and treaties, that of levying money, and regulating commerce, and the correspondent executive and judicial authorities, should be fully and effectually vested in the General Government of the Union; but the impropriety of delegating such extensive trust to one body of men is evidence: hence results in the necessity of a different organization.

It is obviously impracticable in the Federal Government of these States to secure all rights of independent sovereignty to each, and yet provide for the interest and safety of all. Individuals entering into society must give up a share of liberty to preserve the rest. The magnitude of the sacrifice must depend as well on situation and circumstance, as on the object to be obtained. It is at all times difficult to draw with precision the line between those rights which must be surrendered, and those which may be preserved; and, on the present occasion, this difficulty was increased by a difference among the several States as to their situation, extent, habits, and particular interests.

In all our deliberations on this subject, we kept steadily in our view that which appears to us the greatest interest of every true American, the consolidation of our Union, in which is involved our prosperity, felicity, safety—perhaps our national existence. This important consideration, seriously and deeply impressed on our minds, led each State in the Convention to be less rigid on points of inferior magnitude than might have been otherwise expected; and thus, the constitution which we now present is the result of a spirit of amity, and of that mutual deference and concession, which the peculiarity of our political situation rendered indispensable.

That it will meet the full and entire approbation of every State is not, perhaps, to be expected; but each will, doubtless, consider, that had her interest alone been consulted, the consequences might have been particularly disagreeable or injurious to others; that it is liable to as few exceptions as could reasonably have been expected, we hope and believe; that it may promote the lasting welfare of that Country so dear to us all, and secure her freedom and happiness, is our most ardent wish.

With great respect, we have the honor to be, sir, your excellency's most obedient and humble servants. By the unanimous order of the convention.

GEO. WASHINGTON, President,

His Excellency the President of Congress.

approval by two-thirds of the states (nine states at that time).[38] Each state held ratification conventions and the voters in each state chose the delegates that attended.[39] This was important because the newly proposed government was one that had power because its citizens had granted it, not because the states or the state politicians had given it.[40]

The ratification process did not happen quickly, however. There was opposition to the formation of this new, centralized government. Some individuals, called Anti-Federalists, opposed the new form of government because of the broad powers it granted, some objected because they saw it as a challenge to the sovereignty of the states, while others were concerned because there was no guarantee of individual rights.[41]

Pennsylvania was the first state to hold a ratifying convention. The Anti-Federalists and the supporters of the Constitution, the Federalists, exchanged a spirited debate on the merits and drawbacks of the proposed federal government. When the vote was taken on December 12, 1787, the Federalists had won. Pennsylvania ratified the Constitution by a 46 to 23 vote.[42]

This was just the first of the state conventions and battles between the Federalists and Anti-Federalists. In late December 1787 feelings about the formation of the new federal government became so intense that Anti-Federalists arrived uninvited to a Federalist gathering. The event, in Carlisle, Pennsylvania, was a ratification celebration, but when the Anti-Federalists arrived, they hung two Federalists in effigy and burned a copy of the Constitution.[43]

The Anti-Federalist feelings were not unique to Pennsylvania. Other states undergoing the ratification process were also experiencing resistance. Anti-Federalists wrote essays designed to persuade citizens to vote against ratification, and the Federalists countered with a series of essays that have come to be known as the Federalist Papers. These 85 essays discussed the weaknesses of the Articles of Confederation and promoted the positive changes that would come about with the ratification of the Constitution and the implementation of the new federal government.[44] The Federalist Papers have been called the "best commentary on the principles of government ever written,"[45] and cover a variety of topics and arguments in favor of the new centralized form of government.

Ultimately, the Federalists prevailed in the battle for ratification and on July 2, 1788, word was received that New Hampshire, the ninth state required for ratification, had voted to ratify the Constitution.[46] Once the Confederation Congress got word of the ratification, they appointed a committee to assist in the transition from the Confederation of States to the constitutionally based United States.[47]

Ratification did not end the debate about the Constitution. During the ratification debates, many citizens were concerned that the Constitution did not contain guarantees of individual civil rights. The Federalists addressed this with promises that a Bill of Rights would become a part of the Constitution through the amendment process once the new government was in place. These promises were kept and on September 25, 1789, the United States' First Congress proposed a 12-amendment Bill of Rights to the state legislatures.[48] The Congress agreed with Thomas Jefferson who said, "A bill of rights is what the people are entitled to against every government on earth, general or particular, and what no just government should refuse, or rest on inference"[49] (see Exhibit 1–5).

floor more than 150 times, third only after Gouverneur Morris and James Wilson. Madison was also a member of numerous committees, the most important of which were those on postponed matters and style. His journal of the convention is the best single record of the event. He also played a key part in guiding the Constitution through the Continental Congress.

While taking a lead in the ratification process in Virginia, Madison defended the document against such powerful opponents as Patrick Henry, George Mason, and Richard Henry Lee. In New York, where Madison was serving in the Continental Congress, he collaborated with Alexander Hamilton and John Jay in a series of essays that in 1787–88 appeared in the newspapers and were soon published in book form as *The Federalist* (1788). This set of essays is a classic of political theory and a lucid exposition of the republican principles that dominated the framing of the Constitution.

In the U.S. House of Representatives (1789–97), Madison helped frame and ensure passage of the Bill of Rights. He also assisted in organizing the executive department and creating a system of federal taxation. As leaders of the opposition to Hamilton's policies, he and Jefferson founded the Democratic-Republican Party.

In 1794 Madison married a vivacious widow who was 16 years his junior, Dolley Payne Todd, who had a son; they were to raise no children of their own. Madison spent the period 1797–1801 in semiretirement, but in 1798 he wrote the Virginia Resolutions, which attacked the Alien and Sedition Acts. While he served as Secretary of State (1801–9), his wife often served as President Jefferson's hostess.

In 1809 Madison succeeded Jefferson. Like the first three Presidents, Madison was enmeshed in the ramifications of European wars. Diplomacy had failed to prevent the seizure of U.S. ships, goods, and men on the high seas, and a depression wracked the country. Madison continued to apply diplomatic techniques and economic sanctions that were eventually effective to some degree against France, but British interference with shipping continued, as well as other grievances. This led to the War of 1812.

The war, for which the young nation was ill prepared, ended in stalemate in December 1814 when the inconclusive Treaty of Ghent, which nearly restored prewar conditions, was signed. However, thanks to Andrew Jackson's spectacular victory at the Battle of New Orleans (Chalmette) in January 1815, most Americans believed they had won. Twice tested, independence had survived, and an ebullient nationalism marked Madison's last years in office, during which period the Democratic-Republicans held virtually uncontested sway.

In retirement after his second term, Madison managed Montpelier but continued to be active in public affairs. He devoted long hours to editing his journal of the Constitutional Convention, which the government was to publish 4 years after his death. He served as co-chairman of the Virginia constitutional convention of 1829–30 and as rector of the University of Virginia during the period 1826–36. Writing newspaper articles defending the administration of Monroe, he also acted as his foreign policy adviser.

Madison spoke out, too, against the emerging sectional controversy that threatened the existence of the Union. Although a slaveholder all his life, he was active during his later years in the American Colonization Society, whose mission was the resettlement of slaves in Africa.

Madison died at the age of 85 in 1836, survived by his wife and stepson.[50]

The **ratification** of these amendments took almost four years. While the first two proposed amendments were rejected, proposed amendments 3–12 were ratified and became the first 10 amendments to the U.S. Constitution,[51] known now as the **Bill of Rights** (see Exhibit 1–6). Early Americans viewed the rights protected by the Bill of Rights to be natural rights or inalienable rights, and included such rights as freedom of religion, freedom of speech, freedom of the press, freedom of assembly, right to counsel, right against self-incrimination, right against unreasonable searches and seizures, privacy, right of confrontation, and many others.

ratification confirmation and acceptance of a previous act done by you or by another person.

Bill of Rights the first 10 amendments (changes or additions) to the U.S. Constitution.

EXHIBIT 1–6	Amendments to the United States Constitution	
Number	**Subject**	**Year of Ratification**
Amendment I	Religion, Speech, Press, Assembly and Petition	1791
Amendment II	Right to Bear Arms	1791
Amendment III	Quartering of Troops	1791
Amendment IV	Search and Seizure	1791
Amendment V	Grand Jury, Double Jeopardy, Self-Incrimination, Due Process	1791
Amendment VI	Criminal Trials, Jury Trial, Right to Confrontation, Right to Counsel	1791
Amendment VII	Civil Suits and Jury Trial	1791

Continued

EXHIBIT 1–6 Continued		
Amendment VIII	Excessive Bail or Fines, Cruel and Unusual Punishment	1791
Amendment IX	Non-Enumerated Rights	1791
Amendment X	Rights Reserved to the States	1791
Amendment XI	Lawsuits against a State	1795
Amendment XII	Election of the President and Vice President	1804
Amendment XIII	Abolition of Slavery	1865
Amendment XIV	Privilege and Immunities, Due Process, Equal Protection, Apportionment of Representatives, Civil War Disqualification and Debt	1868
Amendment XV	Right Protected Regardless of Race	1870
Amendment XVI	Income Tax	1913
Amendment XVII	Election of Senators	1913
Amendment XVIII	Prohibition of Alcohol	1919
Amendment XIX	Women's Right to Vote	1920
Amendment XX	Presidential Terms and Succession to Office	1933
Amendment XXI	Repeal of Prohibition	1933
Amendment XXII	Presidency Term Limits	1951
Amendment XXIII	Washington D.C. Presidential Voting	1961
Amendment XXIV	Poll Tax	1964
Amendment XXV	Presidential Succession	1967
Amendment XXVI	Right to Vote Age Qualification	1971
Amendment XXVII	Compensation of Congressional Members	1992

THE CONSTITUTION AS A LIVING DOCUMENT

The U.S. Constitution has been a viable document for more than 200 years and is the longest existing constitution in history. What is so unique about this document that allows it to continue and be viable when so many other constitutions have either been rewritten or have been discarded entirely? It is the ability of this Constitution to be amended to reflect changing social mores and values that has allowed the United States to remain stable and productive throughout the years.

Amendment one of the provisions of the U.S. Constitution enacted since the original Constitution became law.

The **amendment** process is found in the Constitution itself. Article V of the Constitution creates the process by which it can be amended. The amendment process requires several steps, as outlined in Article V:

The Congress, whenever two thirds of both Houses shall deem it necessary, shall propose Amendment to this Constitution, or, on the Application of the Legislatures of two thirds of the several States, shall call a Convention for proposing Amendments, which, in each Case, shall be valid to all Intents and Purposes, as Part of this Constitution, when ratified by the Legislatures of three fourths of the several States, or by Convention in three fourths thereof, as the one or the other Mode of Ratification may be proposed by the Congress ...[52]

Congress has brought all 33 proposed constitutional amendments forward, and the convention alternative has never been successfully used to generate a proposed amendment. While Congressional proposals certainly are in keeping with Article V, there have been two major questions posed by this method. The first question raised by the amendment process arose when the Bill of Rights was proposed. While some members of the two Houses assumed that these proposed amendments would be integrated into the text of the Constitution, they were actually proposed as additions to the text.[53] Ultimately, the decision was made that these proposed amendments would supplement the text, and that practice has remained to the present.

The second question brought up by the congressional proposals has been the two-thirds vote requirement. There were those who argued that this requirement mandated a two-thirds vote of the entire membership of both Houses of Congress while others argued that the requirement was met by a two-thirds vote of the quorum of members in attendance at the time the proposal was made. *Rhode Island v. Palmer*,[54] also known as the National Prohibition Cases, answered this question. In that case, the Court held that a two-thirds vote of the appropriate quorum was appropriate for determining whether the proposed amendment would be sent to the states for ratification.[55]

In addition to these two questions, other steps in the process have been challenged. Specifically, the ratification process has been challenged on numerous grounds. One of the questions is whether Congress can prescribe a

---

DILLON V. GLOSS
256 U.S. 368 (1921)

Mr. Justice VAN DEVANTER delivered the opinion of the Court.

This is an appeal from an order denying a petition for a writ of habeas corpus. [Citation omitted]. The petitioner was in custody under section 26 of title 2 of the National Prohibition Act, c. 85, 41 Stat. 305, on a charge of transporting intoxicating liquor in violation of section 3 of that title, and by his petition sought to be discharged on several grounds, all but two of which were abandoned after the decision in National Prohibition Cases, 253 U. S. 350, 40 Sup. Ct. 486, 588, 64 L. Ed. 946. The remaining grounds are, first, that the Eighteenth Amendment to the Constitution, to enforce which title 2 of the act was adopted, is invalid, because the congressional resolution proposing the amendment declared that it should be inoperative unless ratified within seven years; and, secondly, that, in any event, the provisions of the act which the petitioner was charged with violating, and under which he was arrested, had not gone into effect at the time of the asserted violation nor at the time of the arrest.

The power to amend the Constitution and the mode of exerting it are dealt with in article 5, which reads:

'The Congress, whenever two thirds of both houses shall deem it necessary, shall propose amendments to this Constitution, or, on the application of the Legislatures of two thirds of the several states, shall call a convention for proposing amendments, which, in either case, shall be valid to all intents and purposes, as part of this Constitution,

when ratified by the Legislatures of three fourths of the several states, or by conventions in three fourths thereof, as the one or the other mode of ratification may be proposed by the Congress: Provided that no amendment which may be made prior to the year one thousand eight hundred and eight shall in any manner affect the first and fourth clauses in the ninth section of the first article; and that no state, without its consent, shall be deprived of its equal suffrage in the Senate.'

It will be seen that this article says nothing about the time within which ratification may be had—neither that it shall be unlimited nor that it shall be fixed by Congress. What then is the reasonable inference or implication? Is it that ratification may be had at any time, as within a few years, a century or even a longer period, or that it must be had within some reasonable period which Congress is left free to define? Neither the debates in the federal convention which framed the Constitution nor those in state conventions which ratified it shed any light on the question.

The proposal for the Eighteenth Amendment is the first in which a definite period for ratification was fixed. Theretofore 21 amendments had been proposed by Congress and seventeen of these had been ratified by the Legislatures of three fourths of the states—some within a single year after their proposal and all within four years. Each of the remaining 4 had been ratified in some of the states, but not in a sufficient number. Eighty years after the partial ratification of one, an effort was made to complete its

Continued

ratification, and the Legislature of Ohio passed a joint resolution to that end, after which the effort was abandoned. Two, after ratification in one less than the required number of states had lain dormant for a century. The other, proposed March 2, 1861, declared:

> 'No amendment shall be made to the Constitution which will authorize or give to Congress the power to abolish or interfere, within any state, with the domestic institutions thereof, including that of persons held to labor or service by the laws of said state.'

Its principal purpose was to protect slavery and at the time of its proposal and partial ratification it was a subject of absorbing interest, but after the adoption of the Thirteenth Amendment it was generally forgotten. Whether an amendment proposed without fixing any time for ratification, and which after favorable action in less than the required number of states had lain dormant for many years, could be resurrected and its ratification completed had been mooted on several occasions, but was still an open question.

These were the circumstances in the light of which Congress in proposing the Eighteenth Amendment fixed seven years as the period for ratification. Whether this could be done was questioned at the time and debated at length, but the prevailing view in both houses was that some limitation was intended and that seven years was a reasonable period.

That the Constitution contains no express provision on the subject is not in itself controlling; for with the Constitution, as with a statute or other written instrument, what is reasonably implied is as much a part of it as what is expressed. An examination of article 5 discloses that it is intended to invest Congress with a wide range of power in proposing amendments. Passing a provision long since expired, it subjects this power to only two restrictions: one that the proposal shall have the approval of two-thirds of both houses, and the other excluding any amendment which will deprive any state, without its consent, of its equal suffrage in the Senate. A further mode of proposal—as yet never invoked—is provided, which is, that on the application of two-thirds of the states Congress shall call a convention for the purpose. When proposed in either mode amendments to be effective must be ratified by the Legislatures, or by conventions, in three-fourths of the states, 'as the one or the other mode of ratification may be proposed by

the Congress.' Thus the people of the United States, by whom the Constitution was ordained and established, have made it a condition to amending that instrument that the amendment be submitted to representative assemblies in the several states and be ratified in three-fourths of them. The plain meaning of this is (a) that all amendments must have the sanction of the people of the United States, the original fountain of power, acting through representative assemblies, and (b) that ratification by these assemblies in three-fourths of the states shall be taken as a decisive expression of the people's will and be binding on all.

We do not find anything in the article which suggests that an amendment once proposed is to be open to ratification for all time, or that ratification in some of the states may be separated from that in others by many years and yet be effective. We do find that which strongly suggests the contrary. First, proposal and ratification are not treated as unrelated acts, but as succeeding steps in a single endeavor, the natural inference being that they are not to be widely separated in time. Secondly, it is only when there is deemed to be a necessity therefore that amendments are to be proposed, the reasonable implication being that when proposed they are to be considered and disposed of presently. Thirdly, as ratification is but the expression of the approbation of the people and is to be effective when had in three-fourths of the states, there is a fair implication that it must be sufficiently contemporaneous in that number of states to reflect the will of the people in all sections at relatively the same period, which of course ratification scattered through a long series of years would not do. These considerations and the general purport and spirit of the article lead to the conclusion expressed by Judge Jameson 'that an alteration of the Constitution proposed to-day has relation to the sentiment and the felt needs of to-day, and that, if not ratified early while that sentiment may fairly be supposed to exist, it ought to be regarded as waived, and not again to be voted upon, unless a second time proposed by Congress.' That this is the better conclusion becomes even more manifest when what is comprehended in the other view is considered; for, according to it, four amendments proposed long ago—two in 1789, one in 1810 and one in 1861— are still pending and in a situation where their ratification in some of the states many years since by representatives of generations now largely forgotten may be effectively

Continued

supplemented in enough more states to make three-fourths by representatives of the present or some future generation.

To that view few would be able to subscribe, and in our opinion it is quite untenable. We conclude that the fair inference or implication from article 5 is that the ratification must be within some reasonable time after the proposal.

Of the power of Congress, keeping within reasonable limits, to fix a definite period for the ratification we entertain no doubt. As a rule the Constitution speaks in general terms, leaving Congress to deal with subsidiary matters of detail as the public interests and changing conditions may require; and article 5 is no exception to the rule. Whether a definite period for ratification shall be fixed, so that all may know what it is and speculation on what is a reasonable time may be avoided, is, in our opinion, a matter of detail which Congress may determine as an incident of its power to designate the mode of ratification. It is not questioned that seven years, the period fixed in this instance, was reasonable, if power existed to fix a definite time; nor could it well be

questioned considering the periods within which prior amendments were ratified.

The provisions of the act which the petitioner was charged with violating and under which he was arrested (title 2, §§ 3, 26) were by the terms of the act (title 3, § 21) to be in force from and after the date when the Eighteenth Amendment should go into effect, and the latter by its own terms was to go into effect one year after being ratified. Its ratification, of which we take judicial notice, was consummated January 16, 1919. That the Secretary of State did not proclaim its ratification until January 29, 1919, is not material, for the date of its consummation, and not that on which it is proclaimed, controls. It follows that the provisions of the act with which the petitioner is concerned went into effect January 16, 1920. His alleged offense and his arrest were on the following day; so his claim that those provisions had not gone into effect at the time is not well grounded.

Final order affirmed.

time limit for state ratification. In 1921 the Court decided *Dillon v. Gloss*[56] in which the petitioner challenged the seven-year limit for ratification that had been written into the Eighteenth Amendment. Petitioner claimed this time limit rendered the Eighteenth Amendment invalid.

While the Eighteenth Amendment was the first one to have a specific time limit written into it for ratification, and Article V was silent with regard to whether Congress could impose such a time limit, the Court looked to the intent of the Framers. It believed that the Framers intended to give Congress a "wide range of power in proposing amendments" and this included the ability of Congress to set a reasonable time for ratification. Ultimately, the Court held the seven-year time period to be reasonable. The Court noted that it was not deciding the question of whether a dormant proposed amendment could be resurrected and its ratification completed years later. This question was left open.

This question became more crucial when, in 1992, the long-standing Twenty-Seventh Amendment was ratified by New Jersey. The Twenty-Seventh Amendment concerned congressional pay, and had been proposed on September 25, 1789.[57] It had been ratified by many states, beginning with Maryland in December 1789, but then lay without complete ratification for almost 200 years. There were those who argued that this was not a reasonable time and that the ratification should not be certified and the amendment deemed effective. However, Congress accepted the final ratification of the Twenty-Seventh Amendment upon official notice from the New Jersey legislature and once this ratification had been authenticated, it was certified by the Archivist of the United States and it became official as mandated by statute.[58] This acceptance leaves the question posed open, still. One could argue that it indicates that a proposed amendment, unless a time limit is written into the proposal, is viable indefinitely. However, the question still remains unanswered by the Court.

Another question that has arisen in the ratification process is whether Congress can extend the time period for ratification without conferring with those states that ratified the amendment during the original time period. This issue became the subject of much debate when Congress wanted to extend the time period for ratification of the Equal Rights Amendment. Those opposed challenged Congress' ability to make such an extension, and the question was taken to a federal district court in *Idaho v. Freeman*.[59] That court held that Congress did not have the power to make such an extension. However, before the appeal could be taken to the Supreme Court, the time period of the proposed extension expired and the matter became moot.

The Equal Rights Amendment debates also raised another significant issue. The question was whether states that had already ratified could withdraw ratification so that their vote could not be counted toward the overall ratification count. The states argued that it was within their authority to do so, but Congress argued that once a state had voted for ratification, that vote could not be changed. This was not the first time this issue had been discussed. The Court had confronted this issue earlier in 1939 with the case of *Coleman v. Miller*.[60] In this case, the Court was confronted with questions regarding the ability of a state to withdraw its ratification vote. The amendment in question was the Child Labor Amendment, and the Legislature of Kansas wanted to withdraw its ratification of that amendment. The Court ultimately held,

> We think that in accordance with this historic precedent the question of the efficacy of ratifications by state legislatures, in the light of previous rejection or attempted withdrawal, should be regarded as a political question pertaining to the political departments, with the ultimate authority in Congress in the exercise of its control over the promulgation of the adoption of the amendment.[61]

Once the Court determined that this was a political question to be decided by Congress, the Court did not determine the substantive question, but left it to congressional determination. Not only did the Court not decide the issue, any determination made by Congress was also not subject to judicial review. This view was supported by one of the Framers of the Constitution. James Madison's response to the suggestion that the Constitution could be conditionally ratified was that "the Constitution requires an adoption in toto and forever. It has been so adopted by the other States. An adoption for a limited time would be as defective as an adoption of some of the articles only. In short any condition whatever must viciate [sic] the ratification."[62] This all seems to lead to the conclusion that Congress is the branch of government to determine these matters, and the Court will not intervene.

Summary

The history of the Constitution is an interesting and colorful one. Intertwined with this history are legal issues that give the reader some hints of the types of issues and Court decisions to come. The reader should always keep this history in mind reading the upcoming chapters and cases since the discussion of the Framers and their intent often relates back to the earliest days of the judicial history of the United States.

Key Terms

Amendment
Articles of Confederation
bicameral

Bill of Rights
constitution
constitutional convention

electroal college
ratification

Review Questions

1. There are similarities and differences between the Articles of Confederation and the U.S. Constitution. What are the similarities shared in these two historic documents and what are the differences?

2. What historic events or stimuli prompted the Framers of the Constitution to make the changes that reflect the differences between the Articles of Confederation and the U.S. Constitution?

3. What was the Great Compromise and why was it so important in the drafting of the Constitution?

4. Who were the Federalists and what role did they play in the ratification of the Constitution?

5. Should the states be allowed to rescind a ratification vote if the majority of the representatives from that state decide that the previous decision to ratify was incorrect? Why or why not?

Internet Connections

1. For more historical information on the U.S. Constitution, see The Constitution of the United States, Thomas, Legislative Information on the Internet, The Library of Congress at *http://memory.loc.gov.*

2. To read the Bill of Rights and learn more about its history, visit The Bill of Rights, Thomas, Legislative Information on the Internet, The Library of Congress at *http://memory.loc.gov.*

3. To view the Federalist Papers, see The Federalist Papers, Thomas, Legislative Information on the Internet, The Library of Congress at *http://memory.loc.gov.*

4. To learn more about the debates that took place during the Constitutional Convention, see the Avalon Project at Yale Law School, The Madison Debates, The Debates in the Federal Convention of 1787 at *http://www.yale.edu.*

End Notes

[1] The Continental Congress wrote a manifesto issued on October 13, 1778, protesting the threats from Great Britain. It began with these words, "**THESE** United States, having been driven to hostilities by the oppressive and tyrannous measures of Great-Britain; having been compelled to commit the essential rights of man to the decision of arms; and having been at length forced to shake off a yoke which had grown too burthensome to bear, they declared themselves free and independent." This was a unanimously declared manifesto and can be found at http://memory.loc.gov.

[2] *The Articles of Confederation*, p. 1, November 15, 1777, at http://www.law.ou.edu.

[3] *Id.* at 1.

[4] "To Form a More Perfect Union: The Work of the Continental Congress and the Constitutional Convention," *American Memory: Documents from the Continental Congress and the Constitutional Convention 1774–1789*, The Library of Congress, at http://memory.loc.gov (July 11, 2003).

[5] *Id.*

[6] *The Articles of Confederation*, p. 1, November 15, 1777, at http://www.law.ou.edu.

[7] "A History of the Constitution," The Constitutional Law Center, at http://www.supreme.lp.findlaw.com (July 11, 2003).

[8] *Id.*

[9] Stephen C. O'Neill, *Shays' Rebellion*, Supreme Judicial Court Historical Society, 1998, at http://www.sjchs.history.org (July 13, 2003).

[10] *Id.*

[11] *Id.*

[12] *Id.*

[13] Marci Hamilton, "Finding the Right Government for Iraq: U.S. History Shows That It May Take Time, Patience, Rethinking and Amendment," Findlaw's Legal Commentary, April 26, 2003, at http://www.findlaw.com (July 12, 2003).

[14] *Id.*

[15] *The Making of the U.S. Constitution*, Transcription of the Introduction from the First Volume of the Annals of Congress, 1 Annals of Cong. 5 (Joseph Gales ed., 1790).

[16] *Id.* at 6.

[17] "A More Perfect Union: The Creation of the U.S. Constitution," The National Archives and Records Administration, at http://www.archives.gov (July 12, 2003).

[18] *Id.*

[19] *Id.*

[20]James Madison, "The Debates in the Federal Convention of 1787, Tuesday May 29," at http://www.constitution.org (July 11, 2003).

[21]"A More Perfect Union: The Creation of the U.S. Constitution," The National Archives and Records Administration, at http://www.archives.gov (July 12, 2003).

[22]*Id.*

[23]*Id.*

[24]*Id.*

[25]This biography is from "The Founding Fathers, Delegates to the Constitutional Convention," The National Archives and Records Administration, at http://www.archives.gov (July 15, 2003).

[26]"A History of the Constitution," The Constitutional Law Center, at http://www.supreme.lp.findlaw.com (July 11, 2003).

[27]*Id.*

[28]*Id.*

[29]"A More Perfect Union: The Creation of the U.S. Constitution," The National Archives and Records Administration, at http://www.archives.gov (July 12, 2003).

[30]This biography is from "The Founding Fathers, Delegates to the Constitutional Convention," The National Archives and Records Administration, at http://www.archives.gov (July 15, 2003).

[31]"A More Perfect Union: The Creation of the U.S. Constitution," The National Archives and Records Administration, at http://www.archives.gov (July 12, 2003).

[32]*Id.*

[33]*Id.*

[34]*Id.*

[35]"A More Perfect Union: The Creation of the U.S. Constitution," The National Archives and Records Administration, at http://www.archives.gov (July 12, 2003).

[36]*Id.*

[37]"The Letter from George Washington to the Continental Congress," The Library of Congress, American Memory at http://memory.loc.gov/amman/today/Sep17.html (July 25, 2005).

[38]"A History of the Constitution," The Constitutional Law Center, at http://www .supreme.lp.findlaw.com (July 11, 2003).

[39]*Id.*

[40]*Id.*

[41]"A More Perfect Union: The Creation of the U.S. Constitution," The National Archives and Records Administration, at http://www.archives.gov (July 12, 2003).

[42]*Id.*

[43]*Id.*

[44]*Id.*

[45]*Id.* quoting Thomas Jefferson.

[46]*Id.*

[47]*Id.*

[48]"A More Perfect Union: The Creation of the U.S. Constitution, The Bill of Rights," The National Archives and Records Administration, at http://www.archives.gov (July 23, 2003).

[49]"The Bill of Rights: A Brief History," ACLU Briefing Paper, at http://www.archives.aclu.org (July 23, 2003).

[50]This biography is from "The Founding Fathers, Delegates to the Constitutional Convention," The National Archives and Records Administration, at http://www.archives.gov (July 29, 2003).

[51]"A More Perfect Union: The Creation of the U.S. Constituiton, The Bill of Rights," The National Archives and Records Administration, at http://www.archives.gov (July 23, 2003).

[52]U.S. Const. art.V.

[53]Annals of Cong., 433–436 (1789).

[54]*Rhode Island v. Palmer*, 253 U.S. 350 (1920).

[55]*Id.* at 386.

[56]*Dillon v. Gloss*, 256 U.S. 368 (1921).

[57]U.S. Const. amend. XXVII.

[58]National Archives and Records Administration Act of 1984, 1 U.S.C. § 106b.

[59]*Idaho v. Freeman*, 529 F. Supp. 1107 (D. C. D. Idaho, 1981).

[60]*Coleman v. Miller*, 307 U.S. 433 (1939).

[61]*Id.* at 450.

[62]5 The Papers of Alexander Hamilton, 184 (H. Syrett ed., 1962).

ONLINE   For additional resources, go to *http://www.westlegalstudies.com*

DIVIDING GOVERNMENT HORIZONTALLY AND VERTICALLY

[T]he Framers . . . adopted . . . "a plan not merely to amend the Articles of confederation but to create an entirely new National Government with a National Executive, National Judiciary, and a National Legislature." In adopting that plan, the Framers envisioned a uniform national system, rejecting the notion that the Nation was a collection of States, and instead creating a direct link between the national Government and the people of the United States.

—*Justice John Paul Stevens*
U.S. Term Limits, Inc. v. Thornton

INTRODUCTION

The Framers of the Constitution were afraid of the concentration of power in the hands of a single institution or power-holder and sought to ensure that the American system of government would prevent consolidation of power. To accomplish this goal, the power of the federal government was divided among three branches in a way that would allocate different powers to each branch. This is known as horizontal division of government and is called the **separation of powers** doctrine. Moreover, the powers assigned to each branch also included checks on the power of the other branches. Thus, the American system of government is described as one of checks and balances.

This same concern about the potential concentration of power also explains the vertical division of government evidenced by the system of **federalism**. Under federalism the power is split between the federal government and the governments of the individual states. The federal government is assigned certain specific tasks that pertain to problems that must be addressed by the nation, acting through the executive, legislative, and judicial branches of the federal government. These are called **enumerated powers**.

There are situations, however, where the problems of a particular state and the means by which they are handled are more amenable to more local solutions. Thus, the powers not explicitly designated in the Constitution to the federal government remain in the hands of the states. These are called **police powers**.

This chapter addresses the issues raised by these horizontal and vertical divisions. Both have given rise to conflicts. Challenges have been made to decisions taken by one or another branch of the federal government for violating the separation of powers doctrine. Similarly, there have been conflicts between the federal and state governments over which is the proper branch to be acting in regard to specific areas. The chapters that follow will cover in depth the powers assigned to the branches of the federal government by the Constitution and the questions that arise in each of these areas. Here, the discussion will mostly concern the conflicts that arise specifically from the divisions, rather than the interpretation of particular grants of power.

separation of powers the division of the federal government (and the state governments) into legislative (lawmaking), judicial (law interpreting), and executive (law carrying-out) branches; each acts to prevent the others from becoming powerful.

federalism a system of political organization with several different levels of government (for example, city, state, and national) coexisting in the same area with the lower levels having some independent powers.

enumerated powers those powers specifically granted to the three branches of government in the U.S. Constitution.

police powers the government's right and power to set up and enforce laws to provide for the safety, health, and general welfare of the people.

17

THE SEPARATION OF POWERS DOCTRINE

As noted, the Framers of our Constitution were concerned about the concentration of power because they saw it as the root cause of tyranny. This is the reason why the Constitution was structured in the way it was and the Framers used the language they did. While the Constitution contains neither provision nor express language setting forth the principle of separation of powers, it does, through its structure and language, make clear the intention that the powers of the three branches of the government be separate.

In his first draft of what would later become the Bill of Rights, James Madison included an amendment that would make the separation of powers explicit. Members of Congress rejected this proposed amendment. The general belief was that the separation of powers doctrine is implicit in the Constitution. Therefore, an amendment such as that proposed by Madison would be redundant.

The Constitution outlines the powers of each branch of the government. In addition, the language makes clear that these powers are exclusive to the particular branch. Article I of the Constitution states, "All legislative Powers herein granted shall be vested in a Congress of the United States, which shall consist of a Senate and House of Representatives."[1] Article II vests executive power in "a President of the United States of America."[2] Article III provides that, "the judicial Power of the United States, shall be vested in one Supreme Court, and in such inferior Courts as the Congress may from time to time ordain and establish."[3] Thus, it is clear that each branch has its own sphere within which to exercise power. While this scheme may not ensure that our government is the most efficient, it was, however, designed to ensure and maximize the freedom of its citizens.

This scheme raises a concern about the extent to which power granted specifically to one branch can be exercised in a way that prevents interference with the power of another branch. Consequently, the issues, which the Supreme Court addresses in the context of the separation of powers doctrine, speak to those concerns. There are five separate issues that arise from the separation of powers. They are:

1. Executive Encroachment on Legislative Powers
2. Congressional Encroachment on Executive Power
3. Executive Privilege and Immunities
4. Congressional Immunity
5. Congressional Encroachment on Judicial Powers

Cases have arisen that required the Court to define and interpret the constitutional provisions giving rise to these issues and the conflicts between the branches of the federal government. However, the low numbers of these cases show that the language and structure imposed by the Framers has achieved the goal of separating federal powers by clearly delineating the roles of each branch.

Executive Encroachment on Legislative Powers

As we will see, the President's power is far less detailed or delineated in the Constitution than that of Congress' (see Chapter 5). Rather, a significant portion of executive power is implied. While the Court supported a broad interpretation of Presidential power overall, it has been particularly emphatic about limiting that power when it comes to lawmaking. The Court has made it clear that the President may not make laws. The President may only carry out the law. *Youngstown Sheet and Tube Co. v. Sawyer*[4] best demonstrates the Court's position on this issue.

President Truman, in an effort to avoid a national steel strike during the Korean War, issued an executive order to the Secretary of Commerce to seize the nation's steel mills and operate them under federal direction. The President did not seek congressional approval of his action. In response to the seizure, the steel companies sought an **injunction**, or a court order, to prevent effectuation of the President's order.

The government set forth multiple arguments in support of the President's actions. Among these were the President's authority as Commander in Chief, and his oath to see that the laws of the United States are "faithfully" executed. The Court rejected the government's arguments and struck down the seizure order. In a 6 to 3 decision, with multiple concurring and dissenting opinions, Justice Black, in his majority opinion, concluded that the President's action, undertaken without Congress' assent, was an improper exercise of the lawmaking power explicitly granted to Congress by the Constitution. The concurring opinions relied primarily on the fact that Congress had specifically rejected seizure as an option for handling labor disputes when it debated, and then enacted, the **Taft-Hartley Act**.[5] Accordingly, the President's action was a clear usurpation of Congress' power and will.

The dissenting Justices maintained that given the nature of the circumstances, the President's actions were justified. Moreover, they asserted that the seizure maintained the status quo until Congress could act.

> **injunction**   a judge's order to a person to do or to refrain from doing a particular thing.

> **Taft-Hartley Act** (29 U.S.C. § 141)   a 1947 federal law that added several employers' rights to the union rights in the Wagner Act; it established several union "unfair labor practices" (such as attempting to force an employee to join a union).

YOUNGSTOWN SHEET & TUBE COMPANY V. SAWYER
343 U.S. 579 (1952)

Justice BLACK delivered the opinion of the Court.

We are asked to decide whether the President was acting within his constitutional power when he issued an order directing the Secretary of Commerce to take possession of and operate most of the Nation's steel mills. The mill owners argued that the President's order amounts to lawmaking, a legislative function which the Constitution has expressly, confided to the Congress and not to the President. The Government's position is that the order was made on findings of the President that his action was necessary to avert a national catastrophe which would inevitably result from a stoppage of steel production, and that in meeting this grave emergency the President was acting within the aggregate of his constitutional powers as the Nation's Chief Executive and the Commander in Chief of the Armed Forces of the United States.

II.

The President's power, if any, to issue the order must stem either from an act of Congress or from the Constitution itself. There is no statute that expressly authorizes the President to take possession of property as he did here. Nor is there any act of Congress to which our attention has been directed from which such a power can fairly be implied. Indeed, we do not understand the Government to rely on statutory authorization for this seizure. There are two statutes which do authorize the President to take both personal and real property, under certain conditions. However, the Government admits that these conditions were not met and that the President's order was not rooted in either of the statutes.

Moreover, the use of the seizure technique to solve labor disputes in order to prevent work stoppages was not only unauthorized by any congressional enactment prior to this controversy, Congress had refused to adopt that method of settling labor disputes. When the Taft-Hartley Act was under consideration in 1947, Congress rejected an amendment which would have authorized such governmental seizures in cases of emergency. Apparently it was thought that the technique of seizure like that of compulsory arbitration, would interfere with the process of collective bargaining. Consequently, the plan Congress adopted in that Act did not provide for seizure under any circumstances. Instead, the plan sought to bring about settlements by use of the customary devices of mediation, conciliation, investigation by boards of inquiry, and public reports. In some instances temporary injunctions were authorized to provide cooling-off periods. All this failing, unions were left free to strike after a secret vote by

Continued

employees as to whether they wished to accept their employers' final settlement offer.

Particular reliance is placed [by the government] on provisions in Article II which say that "The executive Power shall be vested in a President. . ."; that "he shall take Care that the Laws be faithfully executed"; and that he "shall be Commander in Chief of the Army and Navy of the United States."

The order cannot properly be sustained as an exercise of the President's military power as Commander in Chief of the Armed Forces. [W]e cannot with faithfulness to our constitutional system hold that the Commander in Chief of the Armed Forces has the ultimate power as such to take possession of private property in order to keep labor disputes from stopping production. This is a job for the Nation's lawmakers, not for its military authorities.

Nor can the seizure order be sustained because of the several constitutional provisions that grant executive power to the President. In the framework of our Constitution, the President's power to see that the laws are faithfully executed refutes the idea that he is to be a lawmaker. The Constitution limits his functions in the law-making process to recommending of laws he thinks wise and vetoing of laws he thinks bad. And the Constitution is neither silent nor equivocal about who shall make laws which the President is to execute.

It is said that other Presidents without congressional authority have taken possession of private business enterprises in order to settle labor disputes. But even if this be true, Congress has not thereby lost its exclusive constitutional authority to make laws necessary and proper to carry out the powers vested by the Constitution "in the Government of the United States, or any Department or Officer thereof."

The Founders of this Nation entrusted the law-making power to the Congress alone in both good and bad times. It would do no good to recall the historical events, the fears of power and the hopes for freedom that lay behind their choice. Such a review would but confirm our holding that this seizure order cannot stand.

Affirmed.

Justice FRANKFURTER, concurring.

Although the considerations relevant to the legal enforcement of the principle of separation of powers seem to me more complicated and flexible than may appear from what MR. JUSTICE BLACK has written, I join his opinion because I thoroughly agree with the application of the principle to the circumstances of this case. Even though such differences in attitude toward this principle may be merely differences in emphasis and nuance, they can hardly be reflected by a single opinion for the Court. Individual expression of views in reaching a common result is therefore important.

A constitutional democracy like ours is perhaps the most difficult of man's social arrangements to manage successfully. Our scheme of society is more dependent than any other form of government on knowledge and wisdom and self-discipline for the achievement of its aims. For our democracy implies the reign of reason on the most extensive scale. The Founders of this Nation were not imbued with the modern cynicism that the only thing that history teaches is that it teaches nothing. They acted on the conviction that the experience of man sheds a good deal of light on his nature. It sheds a good deal of light not merely on the need for effective power, if a society is to be at once cohesive and civilized, but also on the need for limitations on the power of governors over the governed.

To that end they rested the structure of our central government on the system of checks and balances. For them the doctrine of separation of powers was not mere theory; it was a felt necessity. Not so long ago it was fashionable to find our system of checks and balances obstructive to effective government. It was easy to ridicule that system as outmoded—too easy. The experience through which the world has passed in our own day has made vivid the realization that the Framers of our Constitution were not inexperienced doctrinaires. These long-headed statesmen had no illusion that our people enjoyed biological or psychological or sociological immunities from the hazards of concentrated power. It is absurd to see a dictator in a representative product of the sturdy democratic traditions of the Mississippi Valley. The accretion of dangerous power does not come in a day. It does come, however slowly, from the generative force of unchecked disregard of the restrictions that fence in even the most disinterested assertion of authority.

Continued

Congress made a conscious choice of policy in a field full of perplexity and peculiarly within legislative responsibility for choice. In formulating legislation for dealing with industrial conflicts, Congress could not more clearly and emphatically have withheld authority than it did in 1947. Perhaps as much so as is true of any piece of modern legislation. Congress acted with full consciousness of what it was doing and in the light of much recent history. Previous seizure legislation had subjected the powers granted to the President to restrictions of varying degrees of stringency. Instead of giving him even limited powers, Congress in 1947 deemed it wise to require the President, upon failure of attempts to reach a voluntary settlement, to report to Congress if he deemed the power of seizure a needed shot for his locker. The President could not ignore the specific limitations of prior seizure statutes. No more could he act in disregard of the limitation put upon seizure by the 1947 Act.

It cannot be contended that the President would have had power to issue this order had Congress explicitly negated such authority in formal legislation. Congress has expressed its will to withhold this power from the President as though it had said so in so many words. The authoritatively expressed purpose of Congress to disallow such power to the President and to require him, when in his mind the occasion arose for such a seizure, to put the matter to Congress and ask for specific authority from it, could not be more decisive if it had been written into [the] Act of 1947.

No authority that has since been given to the President can by any fair process of statutory construction be deemed to withdraw the restriction or change the will of Congress as expressed by a body of enactments, culminating in the Labor Management Relations Act of 1947.

Apart from his vast share of responsibility for the conduct of our foreign relations, the embracing function of the President is that "he shall take Care that the Laws be faithfully executed. . . ." The nature of that authority has for me been comprehensively indicated by Mr. Justice Holmes. "The duty of the President is to see that the laws be executed is a duty that does not go beyond the laws or require him to achieve more than Congress sees fit to leave within his power." *Meyers v. United States, 272 U.S. 52,177 (1926)* The powers of the President are not as particularized as are those of Congress. But unenumerated powers do not mean undefined powers. The separation of powers built into our Constitution gives essential content to undefined provisions in the frame of our government.

It is not a pleasant judicial duty to find that the President has exceeded his powers and still less so when his purposes were dictated by concern for the Nation's well being, in the assured conviction that he acted to avert danger. But it would stultify one's faith in our people to entertain even a momentary fear that the patriotism and the wisdom of the President and the Congress, as well as the long view of the immediate parties in interest, will not find ready accommodation for differences on matters which, however close to the concern and however intrinsically important, are overshadowed by the awesome issues which confront the world.

In reaching the conclusion that conscience compels, I . . . derive consolation from the reflection that the President and the Congress between them will continue to safeguard the heritage which came to them straight from George Washington.

Justice DOUGLAS, concurring.

There can be no doubt that the emergency which caused the President to seize these steel plants was one that bore heavily on the country. But the emergency did not create power; it merely marked an occasion when power should be exercised. And the fact that it was necessary that measures be taken to keep steel in production does not mean that the President, rather than the Congress, had the constitutional authority to act. The Congress, as well as the President, is trustee of the national welfare. The President can act more quickly than the Congress. The President with the armed services at his disposal can move with force as well as with speed. All executive power—from the reign of ancient kings to the rule of modern dictators—has the outward appearance of efficiency.

Legislative power, by contrast, is slower to exercise. There must be delay while the ponderous machinery of committees, hearings, and debates is put into motion. That takes time; and while the Congress slowly moves into action, the emergency may take its toll in wages, consumer goods, war production, the standard of living of the people, and perhaps even lives. Legislative

Continued

action may indeed often be cumbersome, time-consuming, and apparently inefficient. But as Mr. Justice Brandeis stated in his dissent in *Meyers V. United States, 272 U.S. 52,293:*

"The doctrine of the separation of powers was adopted by the Convention of 1787, not to promote efficiency but to preclude the exercise of arbitrary power. The purpose was, not to avoid friction, but by means of the inevitable friction incident to the distribution of the governmental powers among three departments, to save the people from autocracy."

If we sanctioned the present exercise of power by the President, we would be expanding Article II of the Constitution, and rewriting it to suit the political conveniences of the present emergency. Article II which vests the "executive Power" in the President defines that power with particularity.

The great office of President is not a weak and powerless one. The President represents the people and is their spokesman in domestic and foreign affairs. The office is respected more than any other in the land. It gives a position of leadership that is unique. The power to formulate policies and mould opinion inheres in the Presidency and conditions our national life. The impact of the man and the philosophy he represents may at times be thwarted by the Congress. Stalemates may occur when emergencies mount and the Nation suffers for lack of harmonious, reciprocal action between the White House and Capitol Hill. That is a risk inherent in our system of separation of powers. The tragedy of such stalemates might be avoided by allowing the President the use of some legislative authority. The Framers with memories of the tyrannies produced by a blending of executive and legislative power rejected that political arrangement. Some future generation may, however, deem it so urgent that the President have legislative authority that the Constitution will be amended. We could not sanction the seizures and condemnations of the steel plants in this case without reading Article II as giving the President not only the power to execute the laws but to make some. Such a step would most assuredly alter the pattern of the Constitution.

We pay a price for our system of checks and balances, for the distribution of power among the three branches of government. It is a price that today may seem exorbitant to many. Today a kindly President uses the seizure power to effect a wage increase and to keep the steel furnaces in production. Yet tomorrow another President might use the same power to prevent a wage increase, to curb trade unionists, to regiment labor as oppressively as industry thinks it has been regimented by this seizure.

The actual art of governing under our Constitution does not and cannot conform to judicial definitions of the power of any of its branches based on isolated clauses or even single Articles torn from context. While the Constitution diffuses powers the better to secure liberty, it also contemplates that practice will integrate the interdependence, autonomy and reciprocity.

The appeal, . . . that we declare the existence of inherent powers . . . to meet an emergency asks us to do what many think would be wise, although it is something the forefathers omitted. They knew what emergencies were, knew the pressures they engender for authoritative action, knew, too, how they afford a ready pretext for usurpation. We may also suspect that they suspected that emergency powers would tend to kindle emergencies. Aside from suspension of the privilege of the writ of habeas corpus in time of rebellion or invasion, when the public safety may require it, they made no express provision for exercise of extraordinary authority because of a crisis. I do not think we rightfully may so amend their work, and, if we could, I am not convinced it would be wise to do so, although many modern nations have forthrightly recognized that war and economic crises may upset the normal balance between liberty and authority. Their experience with emergency powers may not be irrelevant to the argument here that we should say that the Executive, of his own volition, can invest himself with undefined emergency powers.

In the practical working of our Government we already have evolved a technique within the framework of the Constitution by which normal executive powers may be considerably expanded to meet an emergency. Congress may and has granted extraordinary authorities which lie dormant in normal times but may be called into play by the Executive in war or upon proclamation of a national emergency.

In view of the ease, expedition and safety with which Congress can grant and has granted large emergency powers, certainly ample to embrace

Continued

this crisis, I am quite unimpressed with the argument that we should affirm possession of them without statute. Such power either has no beginning or it has no end. If it exists, it is at least a step in that wrong direction.

The controlling fact here is that Congress, within its constitutionally delegated power, has prescribed for the President specific procedures, exclusive of seizure, for his use in meeting the present type of emergency. Congress has reserved to itself the right to determine where and when to authorize the seizure of property in meeting such an emergency. Under these circumstances the President's order . . . invaded the jurisdiction of Congress. It violated the essence of the principle of the separation of governmental powers. Accordingly, the injunction against its effectiveness should be sustained.

Justice CLARK, concurring.

The limits of presidential power are obscure. However, Article II, no less than Article I, is part of "a constitution intended to endure for ages to come, and, consequently, to be adapted to the various crises of human affairs."

In my view . . . the Constitution does grant to the President extensive authority in times of grave and imperative national emergency. In fact, to my thinking, such a grant may well be necessary to the very existence of the Constitution itself.

I conclude that where Congress has laid down specific procedures to deal with the type of crisis confronting the President, he must follow those procedures in meeting the crisis; but that in the absence of such action by Congress, the President's independent power to act depends upon the gravity of the situation confronting the nation. I cannot sustain the seizure in question because here, . . . Congress had prescribed methods to be followed by the President in meeting the emergency at hand.

Chief Justice VINSON, with whom Justices REED and MINTON, join, dissenting.

Some members of the Court are of the view that the President is without power to act in a time of crisis in the absence of express statutory authorization. Other members of the Court affirm on the basis of their reading of certain statutes. Because we cannot agree that affirmance is proper on any ground, and because of the transcending importance of the questions presented not only in this critical litigation but also to the powers of the President and of future Presidents to act in time of crisis, we are compelled to register this dissent.

I.

In passing upon the question of Presidential powers in this case, we must first consider the context in which those powers were exercised.

Those who suggest that this is a case involving extraordinary powers should be mindful that these are extraordinary times. A world not yet recovered from the devastation of World War II has been forced to face the threat of another and more terrifying global conflict.

[I]f the President has any power under the Constitution to meet a critical situation in the absence of express statutory authorization, there is no basis whatever for criticizing the exercise of such power in this case.

II.

Admitting that the Government could seize the mills, plaintiffs claim that the implied power to eminent domain can be exercised only under an Act of Congress; under no circumstances, they say, can that power be exercised by the President unless he can point to an express provision in enabling legislation. This was the view adopted by the District Judge when he granted the preliminary injunction.

Under this view, the President is left powerless at the very moment when the need for action may be most pressing and when no one, other than he, is immediately capable of action. Under this view, he is left powerless because a power not expressly given to Congress is nevertheless found to rest exclusively with Congress.

Consideration of this view of executive impotence calls for further examination of the nature of the separation of powers under our tripartite system of Government.

[T]he comprehensive grant of the executive power to a single person was bestowed soon after the country had thrown the yoke of monarchy. Only by instilling initiative and vigor in all of the three departments of Government, declared Madison, could tyranny in any form be avoided. Hamilton added: "Energy in the Executive is a leading character in the definition of good government. It is essential to the

Continued

protection of the community against foreign attacks; it is not less essential to the steady administration of the laws; to the protection of property against those irregular and high-handed combinations which sometimes interrupt the ordinary course of Justice; to the security of liberty against the enterprises and assaults of ambition, of faction, and of anarchy." It is thus apparent that the Presidency was deliberately fashioned as an office of power and independence. Of course, the Framers created no autocrat capable of arrogating any power unto himself at any time. But neither did they create an automaton impotent to exercise the powers of Government at a time when the survival of the Republic itself may be at stake.

[W]e are not called upon today to expand the Constitution to meet a new situation. For, in this case, we need only look at history and time-honored principles of constitutional law—principles that have been applied consistently by all branches of the Government throughout our history. It is those who assert the invalidity of the Executive Order who seek to amend the Constitution in this case.

III.

Presidents have taken prompt action to enforce the laws and protect the country whether or not Congress happened to prove in advance for the particular method of execution. At the minimum, the executive actions reviewed herein sustain the action of the President in this case. And many of the cited examples of Presidential practice go far beyond the extent of power necessary to sustain the President's order to seize the steel mills. The fact that temporary executive seizures of industrial plants to meet an emergency have not been directly tested in this Court furnishes not the slightest suggestion that such actions have been illegal. Rather, the fact that Congress and the courts have consistently recognized and given their support to such executive action indicates that such a power of seizure has been accepted throughout our history.

History bears out the genius of the Founding Fathers, who created a Government subject to law but not left subject to inertia when vigor and initiative are required.

IV.

Focusing now on the situation confronting the President [here], we cannot but conclude that the President was performing his duty under the Constitution to "take Care that the Laws be faithfully executed"—a duty described by President Benjamin Harrison as "the central idea of the office."

Whatever the extent of Presidential power on more tranquil occasions, and whatever the right of the President to execute legislative programs as he sees fit without reporting the mode of execution to Congress, the single Presidential purpose disclosed on this record is to faithfully execute the laws by acting in an emergency to maintain the status quo, thereby preventing collapse of the legislative programs until Congress could act. The President's action served the same purposes as a judicial stay entered to maintain the status quo in order to preserve the jurisdiction of a court. In his Message to Congress immediately following the seizure the President explained the necessity of his action in executing the military procurement and anti-inflation legislative programs and expressed his desire to cooperate with any legislative proposals approving, regulating or rejecting the seizure of the steel mills. Consequently, there is no evidence whatever of any Presidential purpose to defy Congress or act in any way inconsistent with the legislative will.

* * *

VI.

The diversity of views expressed in the six opinions of the majority, the lack of reference to authoritative precedent, the repeated reliance upon prior dissenting opinions, the complete disregard of the uncontroverted facts showing the gravity of the emergency and the temporary nature of the taking all serve to demonstrate how far afield one must go to affirm the order of the District Court.

The broad executive power granted by Article II to an officer on duty 365 days a year cannot, it is said be invoked to avert disaster. Instead, the President must confine himself to sending a message to Congress recommending action. Under this messenger-boy concept of the Office, the President cannot even act to preserve legislative programs from destruction so that Congress will have something left to act upon. There is no judicial finding that the executive action was unwarranted because there was in fact no basis for the President's finding of the existence

Continued

of an emergency for, under this view, the gravity of the emergency and the immediacy of the threatened disaster are considered irrelevant as a matter of law.

Seizure of plaintiffs' property is not a pleasant undertaking. Similarly unpleasant to a free country are the draft which disrupts the home and military procurement which causes economic dislocation and compels adoption of price controls, wage stabilization and allocation of materials. The President informed Congress that even a temporary Government operation of plaintiffs' properties was "thoroughly distasteful" to him, but was necessary to prevent immediate paralysis of the mobilization program. Presidents have been in the past, and any man worthy of the Office should be in the future, free to take at least interim action necessary to execute legislative programs essential to survival of the Nation. A sturdy judiciary should not be swayed by the unpleasantness or unpopularity of necessary executive action, but must independently determine for itself whether the President was acting, as required by the Constitution, to "take Care that the Laws be faithfully executed."

As we have seen, those concurring in the Court's decision placed a great deal of emphasis on the fact that Congress had rejected seizure as an option in handling labor disputes. This raises another issue for consideration in determining whether a President's exercise of power encroaches upon Congress' lawmaking power. Does the limitation the Court places on the President's implied powers extend to those situations in which Congress impliedly acquiesces to the President's action? This question was raised in *Dames & Moore v. Reagan*.[6] The Court found that where Congress appears to have assented to the President's exercise of power, the President would be deemed to have acted within the scope of his authority.

Dames & Moore arose out of Iran's seizure of the United States Embassy in Tehran and the capture of our diplomatic personnel. In response to these actions President Carter, pursuant to the International Emergency Economic Powers Act,[7] declared a national emergency and prevented the removal or transfer of all Iran's properties and interests that were, or would become, subject to United States jurisdiction. Pursuant to President Carter's order, the Department of Treasury then issued regulations, which included one allowing for prejudgment **attachment**.

attachment formally seizing property (or a person) in order to bring it under the control of the court; this is usually done by getting a court order to have a law enforcement officer take control of the property.

Dames & Moore filed suit against the government of Iran among others claiming it was owed money for services performed for the Atomic Energy Organization of Iran. The District Court ordered attachment against defendant's property and the property of Iranian banks to secure a judgment in the event of Dames & Moore's success in the lawsuit. When the hostages were released the United States was obliged to nullify all attachments and judgments obtained under President Carter's action as agreed to in order to obtain the hostages release. The claims were suspended and were later to be arbitrated by an international tribunal.

The Court heard the constitutional challenge to the suspension of the contractual claim. The Court found that the President had the constitutional authority to suspend the claims. Recognizing that Congress had not explicitly delegated such power to the President, his action was implicitly authorized in light of Congress' long history of agreeing to similar presidential conduct. For example, Congress had approved of the use of executive agreements between the President and foreign powers in settling other claims. The Court, however, stressed the limited scope of its ruling. The holding was limited to situations where suspension was a "necessary incident to the resolution of a major foreign policy dispute,"[8] and Congress acquiesced in this sort of presidential action. Congress' approval alone would be insufficient, it was just one of the factors to be considered.

Congressional Encroachment on Presidential Power

Executive encroachment on Congress' power is not the only way in which the separation of powers doctrine may be violated. Congress may sometimes encroach upon the President's powers. This may, in fact, occur in the context within which Congress is monitoring executive branch acts including those of federal administrative agencies. The device by which Congress can monitor those actions is known as a legislative veto. The provision for a legislative veto is included in a statute that delegates certain powers to a federal agency. When such provision is made, and the agency acts in a manner that Congress disagrees with, the provision allows one or both houses to cancel the action by resolution.

An important Supreme Court decision concerned the use of the legislative veto and its constitutionality. In *Immigration and Naturalization Service v. Chadha*,[9] the Court held that the legislative veto violated the Constitution in two ways: (1) it violated the President's veto power and (2) it violated the bicameral structure of Congress. More importantly, however, was the question whether the veto constituted an exercise of legislative power that was impermissible under the Constitution.

At issue was whether the House of Representatives alone could veto a decision by the Attorney General to suspend deportation of Chadha, an alien. When the House was informed of the Attorney General's action pursuant to the legislative veto provision in the Immigration and Nationality Act,[10] it, in accordance with the Act, vetoed the decision in Chadha's case as well as those of several others by resolution.

Addressing the question of whether the veto was in fact an exercise of the legislative power, the Court recognized that not all acts of Congress constitute such an exercise. In this case, however, it found that to overrule the Attorney General on a deportation question was such an exercise of legislative power since it had the "purpose and effect of altering the legal rights, duties and relations of persons . . . outside the legislative branch."[11] Since the action constituted an exercise of legislative power it was necessary that it conform to the criteria necessary for passing legislation. Accordingly, the measure needed to pass both houses of the legislature as prescribed in the Constitution and could not be done by using a unilateral resolution of the House. It was clear that it was irrelevant whether the legislative veto was a more efficient means of monitoring/controlling administrative action.

Justices White and Rehnquist dissented. Justice White asserted that a legislative veto failed to constitute the functional equivalent of passing a law. He argued that if Congress could delegate law-making powers to administrative agencies, it could reserve to itself a means of checking on how that authority was being used. Justice White maintained that the legislative veto need not comply with the requirements of Article I so long as the original grant of authority comported with the Constitution's requirements.

The Court has also found that the separation of powers doctrine can be violated by Congress when it delegates responsibility for enforcement of the laws into the hands of one who is subject to removal only by the Congress itself. In *Bowsher v. Synar*,[12] the Court found that Congress' delegation of power to the Comptroller General to make automatic reductions in spending and to submit a report on such to the President was unconstitutional. The provision was part of the Gramm-Rudman-Hollings Act, known as the Balanced Budget and Emergency Deficit Control Act of 1985,[13] which was designed to set a limit on federal spending from 1985 to 1991. The provision was challenged as an unconstitutional violation of the delegation of legislative powers and that the Comptroller General's role in the reduction of the deficit infringed the separation of powers doctrine.

The Court held that the powers delegated to the Comptroller General by the Act were executive in nature. In other words, the power delegated was for the enforcement of a legislative act, and because Congress could remove the Comptroller General, it retained control over the enforcement of the law. Accordingly, Congress had retained for itself an action delegated by the Constitution to the executive branch of the government and this was unconstitutional.

Justice Stevens, joined by Justice Marshall, concurred in the result. Justice Stevens maintained that Congress could delegate legislative power to the executive branch or independent agencies. When, however, Congress sought to retain power and exercise that power it could not authorize a lesser representative of the legislative branch to act on its behalf. Justice Stevens determined that the Comptroller General was just such a lesser representative.

The separation of powers issue was again raised in *Morrison v. Olson.*[14] The central issue was the constitutionality of the independent counsel provisions of the Ethics in Government Act of 1978.[15] It was challenged on the basis of infringing not just the President's authority, but also the limitations imposed on the judiciary in Article III of the Constitution.

Chief Justice Rehnquist, writing for the majority, rejected the separation of powers argument finding that the Act did not unduly interfere with the President's role. Congress was not attempting to limit presidential power and increase its own. The Court went on to find that the Act did not constitute a usurpation of executive functions by the judiciary. Simply because the independent counsel was free from the executive branch supervision, it continued to retain sufficient control to ensure that the President could perform his constitutional duties.

Justice Scalia dissented vigorously. It was his position that the separation of powers doctrine required the President to maintain complete control over the investigation and prosecution of law violations. The appointment of an independent counsel with power to investigate and prosecute cases against wrongdoing by members of the executive branch was, he argued, a clear violation of the Constitution.

Executive Privilege and Immunities

In an attempt to ensure the goal of independence of the three branches of the government, the Framers sought to protect our leaders from constraints, which might impinge on that independence. Consequently, the President is safe from criminal prosecution during his tenure in office. He is subject only to the Senate, which sits in judgment in an impeachment trial. The federal judiciary is protected against removal for unpopular decisions by a guarantee of tenure for life once appointed and a measure that prevents salaries from being reduced. Finally, Congress is immune from liability for statements made during debate. This provision was designed to promote free and full discussion in arriving at Congressional determinations.

In this section the civil and criminal immunity for members of the Congress and members of the executive branch will be considered. This will be followed by a brief examination of the doctrine of executive privilege, which will be more thoroughly discussed in Chapter 5.

Congressional Immunity

The Constitution directly provides **immunity,** or protection from prosecution or arrest for our representatives in Congress who are engaged in their official duties. Article I, § 6 states that, "for any Speech or Debate in either House, [members of Congress] shall not be questioned in any other Place." While questions regarding the Speech and Debate Clause, as it is known, have not often come before the Supreme Court, in *Hutchinson v. Proxmire*[16] the Court was asked whether the clause protected information originally presented on the floor of the Senate or in the *Congressional Record* and then disseminated by a senator in press releases and newsletters.

immunity the freedom of national, state, and local government officials from prosecution for, or arrest during, most official acts, and their freedom from most tort lawsuits resulting from their official duties.

Wisconsin Senator William Proxmire awarded his "Golden Fleece of the Month Award" for egregious, wasteful government spending to a behavioral scientist who used the funding to research the behavior patterns of monkeys. Specifically included in the research was whether the monkeys clenched their jaws when exposed to aggravating, stressful stimuli. Senator Proxmire was sued by the scientist for defamation when the information about the award was distributed in press releases and included in the Senator's newsletters. The Senator's motion for summary judgment was granted by the District Court, which found that the Speech and Debate Clause granted absolute immunity to the Senator. The Seventh Circuit Court of Appeals affirmed this decision, and the Supreme Court granted certiorari.

After a long recitation on the history of the clause and its meaning, the Court concluded that the Speech and Debate Clause did not grant such absolute immunity.

HUTCHINSON V. PROXMIRE
443 U.S. 111 (1979)

Chief Justice BURGER delivered the opinion of the Court.

* * *

III

The purpose of the Speech or Debate Clause is to protect Members of Congress "not only from the consequences of litigation's results but also from the burden of defending themselves." *Dombrowski v. Eastland, 387 U.S. 82,85(1967)* If the respondents have immunity under the Clause, no other questions need be considered for they may "not be questioned in any other Place."

IV

In support of the Court of Appeals holding that newsletters and press releases are protected by the Speech or Debate Clause, respondents rely upon both historical precedent and present-day congressional practices. They contend that the impetus for the Speech or Debate Clause privilege in our constitution came from the history of parliamentary efforts to protect the right of members to criticize the spending of the Crown and from the prosecution of a Speaker of the House of Commons for publication of a report outside of Parliament. Respondents also contend that in the modern day very little speech or debate occurs on the floor of either House; from this they argue that press releases and newsletters are necessary for Members of Congress to communicate with other Members.

The Speech or Debate Clause has been directly passed on by this Court relatively few times in 190 years. Literal reading of the Clause would, of course, confine its protection narrowly to a "Speech or Debate *in* either House." But the Court has given the Clause a practical rather than a strictly literal reading which would limit the protection to utterances made within the four walls of either Chamber. Thus, we have held that committee hearings are protected, even if held outside the Chambers; committee reports are also protected.

The gloss going beyond a strictly literal reading of the Clause has not, however, departed from the objective of protecting only legislative activities. In Thomas Jefferson's view:

"[The privilege] is restrained to things done in the House in a Parliamentary course. . . . For [the Member] is not to have privilege contra morem parliamentarium, to exceed the bounds and limits of his place and duty."

One of the draftsmen of the Constitution, James Wilson, expressed a similar thought in lectures delivered between 1790 and 1792 while he was a Justice of this Court. He rejected Blackstone's statement that the Parliament's privileges were preserved by keeping them indefinite:

"Very different is the case with regard to the legislature of the United States. . . . The great maxims upon which our law of parliament is founded, are defined and ascertained in our constitutions. The arcana of privilege, and the

Continued

arcana of prerogative, are equally unknown to our system of jurisprudence."

In this respect, Wilson was underscoring the very purpose of our Constitution—*inter alia*, to provide written definitions of the powers, privileges, and immunities granted rather than rely on evolving constitutional concepts identified from diverse sources as in English law. Like thoughts were expressed by Joseph Story, writing in the first edition of his Commentaries on the Constitution in 1833:

> "But this privilege is strictly confined to things done in the course of parliamentary proceedings, and does not cover things done beyond the place and limits of duty."

In *United States v. Brewster*, we acknowledged the historical roots of the Clause going back to the long struggle between the English House of Commons and the Tudor and Stuart monarchs when both criminal and civil processes were employed by Crown authority to intimidate legislators. Yet we cautioned that the Clause "must be interpreted in light of the American experience, and in the context of the American constitutional scheme of government rather than the English parliamentary system . . . [Their] Parliament is the supreme authority, not a coordinate branch. Our speech or debate privilege was designed to preserve legislative independence, not supremacy."

Nearly a century ago in *Kilbourn v. Thompson*, this Court held that the Clause extended "to things generally done in a session of the House by one of its members *in relation to the business before it*." More recently we expressed a similar definition of the scope of the Clause:

> "Legislative acts are not all-encompassing. The heart of the Clause is speech or debate in either House. Insofar as the Clause is construed to reach other matters, *they must be an integral part of the deliberative and communicative processes* by which members participate *in committee and House proceedings* with respect to the consideration and passage or rejection of proposed legislation or with respect to other matters which the Constitution places within the jurisdiction of either House. As the Court of Appeals put it, the courts have extended the privilege to matters beyond pure speech or debate in either House, but 'only when

necessary to prevent indirect impairment of such deliberations.'"

Whatever imprecision there may be in the term "legislative activities," it is clear that nothing in history or in the explicit language of the Clause suggests any intention to create an absolute privilege from liability or suit for defamatory statements made outside the Chamber. In *Brewster* we observed:

> "The immunities of the Speech or Debate Clause were not written into the Constitution simply for the personal or private benefit of members of Congress, but to protect the integrity of the legislative process by insuring the independence of individual legislators."

Claims under the Clause going beyond what is needed to protect legislative independence are to be closely scrutinized. In *Brewster* we took note of this:

> "The authors of our Constitution were well aware of the history of both the need for the privilege and *the abuses that could flow from too sweeping safeguards*. In order to preserve other values, they wrote the privilege so that it tolerates and protects behavior on the part of Members not tolerated and protected when done by other citizens, *but the shield does not extend beyond what is necessary to preserve the integrity of the legislative process*."

Indeed, the precedents abundantly support the conclusion that a Member may be held liable for republishing defamatory statements originally made in either House. We perceive no basis for departing from that long-established rule.

Mr. Justice Story, in his Commentaries, for example, explained that there was no immunity for republication of a speech first delivered in Congress:

> "Therefore, although a speech delivered in the House of Commons is privileged, and the member cannot be questioned respecting it elsewhere; *yet if he publishes his speech, and it contains libelous matter, he is liable to an action and prosecution therefore, as in common cases of libel*. And the same principles seem applicable to the privilege of debate and speech in Congress. No man ought to have a right to defame others

Continued

under colour of a performance of the duties of his office. And if he does so *in the actual discharge of his duties in Congress, that furnishes no reason, why he should be enabled through the medium of the press to destroy the reputation, and invade the repose of other citizens*. It is neither within the scope of his duty, nor in furtherance of public rights, or public policy. Every citizen has as good a right to be protected by the laws from malignant scandal, and false charges, and defamatory imputations, as a member of Congress has to utter them in his seat."

In *Gravel v. United States*, we recognized that the doctrine denying immunity for republication had been accepted in the United States "[Private] publication by Senator Gravel . . . was in no way essential to the deliberations of the Senate; nor does questioning as to private publication threaten the integrity or independence of the Senate by impermissibly exposing its deliberations to executive influence."

We reaffirmed that principle in *Doe v. McMillan:* "A member of Congress may not with impunity publish a libel from the speaker's stand in his home district, and clearly the Speech or Debate Clause would not protect such an act even though the libel was read from an official committee report. The reason is that republishing a libel under such circumstances is not an essential part of the legislative process and is not part of that deliberative process 'by which Members participate in committee and house proceedings.' "

We reach a similar conclusion here. A speech by Proxmire in the Senate would be wholly immune and would be available to other members of Congress and the public in the Congressional Record. But neither the newsletters nor the press release was "essential to the deliberations of the Senate" and neither was part of the diliberative process.

Respondents, however, argue that newsletters and press releases are essential to the functioning of the Senate; without them, they assert, a Senator cannot have a significant impact on the other Senators. We may assume that a Member's published statements exert some influence on other votes in the Congress and therefore have a relationship to the legislative and deliberative process. But in *Brewster*, we rejected respondents' expansive reading of the Clause: "It is

well known, of course, that Members of the Congress engage in many activities other than the purely legislative activities protected by the Speech or Debate Clause. These include . . . preparing so-called 'news letters' to constituents, news releases, and speeches delivered outside the Congress."

There we went on to note that *United States v. Johnson*, had carefully distinguished between what is only "related to the due functioning of the legislative process," and what constitutes the legislative process entitled to immunity under the Clause: "In stating that those things [Johnson's attempts to influence the Department of Justice] 'in no wise related to the due functioning of the legislative process' were *not* covered by the privilege, the Court did not in any sense imply as a corollary that everything that 'related' to the office of a Member was shielded by the Clause. Quite the contrary, in *Johnson* we held, citing *Kilbourn v. Thompson*, that only acts generally done in the course of the process of enacting legislation were protected.

"In no case has this Court ever treated the Clause as protecting all conduct *relating* to the legislative process."

Respondents also argue that the newsletters and press releases are privileged as part of the "informing function" of Congress. Advocates of a broad reading of the "informing function" sometimes tend to confuse two uses of the term "informing." In one sense, Congress informs itself collectively by way of hearings of its committees. It was in that sense that Woodrow Wilson used "informing" in a statement quoted by respondents. In reality, Wilson's statement related to congressional efforts to learn of the activities of the Executive Branch and administrative agencies; he did not include wide-ranging inquiries by individual Members on subjects of their choice. Moreover, Wilson's statement itself clearly implies a distinction between the *informing* function and the *legislative* function:

"Unless Congress have and use every means of acquainting itself with the acts and the disposition of the administrative agents of the government, the country must be helpless to learn how it is being served; and unless Congress both scrutinize these things and sift them by every form of discussion, the country must remain in

Continued

embarrassing, crippling ignorance of the very affairs which it is most important that it should understand and direct. The informing function of Congress should be preferred even to its legislative function. . . . [The] only really self-governing people is that people which discusses and interrogates its administration."

It is in this narrower Wilsonian sense that this Court has employed "informing" in previous cases holding that congressional efforts to inform itself through committee hearings are part of the legislative function. The other sense of the term, and the one relied upon by respondents, perceives it to be the duty of Members to tell the public about their activities. Valuable and desirable as it may be in broad terms, the transmittal of such information by individual Members in order to inform the public and other Members is not a part of the legislative function or the deliberations that make up the legislative process. As a result, transmittal of such information by press releases and newsletters is not protected by the Speech or Debate Clause.

Justice BRENNAN, dissenting.

I disagree with the Court's conclusion that Senator Proxmire's newsletters and press releases fall outside the protection of the speech-or-debate immunity. In my view, public criticism by legislators of unnecessary governmental expenditures, whatever its form, is a legislative act shielded by the Speech or Debate Clause. I would affirm the judgment below. . .

Thus, it is clear where the line has been drawn. Members of Congress are shielded from civil and criminal liability for comments made as an integral part of the deliberations and communications they take part in both in committee and legislative proceedings. Comments outside of this role, or outside these activities, are not covered by the privilege and may subject the member to liability. The intent of the Framers to protect the legislative process is guaranteed by these boundaries.

Executive Branch Immunity

There is no provision similar to the Speech and Debate Clause granting immunity to members of the executive branch. The Court has, however, acknowledged that there exists some immunity. While it appears that there has been no general acceptance of immunity from judicial process (e.g., subpoenas) for the President and other executive branch officials, in *Nixon v. Fitzgerald*[17] the Court found that the President has absolute immunity from civil liability for official acts.

Fitzgerald, a management analyst with the Department of the Air Force, filed suit against President Nixon and two of his aides after he was fired from his job. Fitzgerald maintained that he was fired in retaliation for testimony he gave before a congressional subcommittee about cost overruns and unexpected technical problems with an airplane that was in development.

The Court began by reciting its recognition of the principle that government officials were not entirely without some immunity from civil suits. In its decisions about immunity for government officials the Court noted that those decisions were "guided by the Constitution, federal statutes, and history" and also considered the common law and public policy.[18] Employing these tools, the Court concluded that under our system "mandat[ing] separation of powers" the President was entitled to absolute immunity from damages arising from his public acts.[19] This conclusion was based on the importance of the President as the Chief Executive Officer of the United States, which would or could be diverted by concern over private lawsuits and interfere in the effective functioning of the government. The Court balanced these interests against the exercise of jurisdiction over the President in cases of private suits for damages premised on official acts. The Court found that a grant of absolute immunity did not leave the nation without a remedy for presidential misconduct. Such a remedy existed in the Constitution in the form of impeachment.[20]

Accordingly, President Nixon was immune from liability for Fitzgerald's firing even if he was responsible for either causing it maliciously or in an illegal manner. Justice White energetically dissented in an opinion joined by Justices Brennan, Marshall, and Blackmun. He opposed the Court's finding that immunity attached to a particular office, that of the President, rather than, as had been the case until that time, to a particular function.[21] White argued that the Court's holding "clothe[d] the Office of President with sovereign immunity, placing it beyond law."[22]

In the companion case in which the President's aides were being sued, *Harlow v. Fitzgerald*,[23] the Court found that absolute immunity did not pertain to executive officials in general. Absolute immunity extended only to certain officials in the executive branch, such as prosecutors and the President. Only qualified immunity for high officials in general was available. The Court claimed that this preserved a balance between the importance of damages as a remedy to protect citizens' rights and the need to protect officials who act in the public interest.[24] The Court rejected the argument that public policy necessitated a blanket grant of absolute immunity to presidential aides and asserted that those officials who sought absolute immunity for their acts had the burden of proving that public policy required such a grant of immunity.[25] Hence, the Court recognized a distinction between the extent of immunity for a President and that for his aides based generally on the centrality of the President in the government structure.

It must be remembered, however, that *Nixon v. Fitzgerald* provides absolute immunity only for official acts. In *Clinton v. Jones*,[26] the Court found that no immunity extends to the President for acts that are not related to his office.

President Clinton was being sued for acts committed while he was Governor of Arkansas. He sought temporary immunity from the suit during his term of office as President. He argued that in the absence of a grant of immunity there remained the possibility that there would be interference by the judiciary in the executive branch that would violate the separation of powers doctrine.

In response to his arguments, the Court found temporary immunity during the President's term of office was not required by the Constitution. The Court, in essence, adopted Justice White's dissent in *Nixon v. Fitzgerald* noting that immunity for acts within the President's official capacity has its basis in the function of the acts rather than the identity of the actor.[27] The Court also found there was no separation of powers violation. There was no evidence that the judiciary would perform any executive function, nor was there evidence that the litigation would in any way place undue burdens on the President's ability to perform his constitutional duties.[28] Finally, the Court noted that since the judiciary had the power to review the legality of the President's official conduct, citing *Youngstown Sheet and Tube*,

> *The federal courts ha[d] the power to determine the legality of his unofficial conduct. The burden on the President's time and energy that is a mere by-product of such review surely cannot be considered as onerous as the direct burden imposed by judicial review and the occasional invalidation of his official actions. We therefore hold that the doctrine of separation of powers does not require federal courts To stay all private action against the President until he leaves office.[29]*

executive privilege the right of the President of the United States and subordinates to keep some information (primarily documents) from public disclosure. The privilege is used most often for military and diplomatic secrets.

Over time, Presidents have asserted their right to withhold particular information requested by another branch of government by claiming an **executive privilege** to keep some information confidential. President Jefferson was the first to make a claim of executive privilege in response to a subpoena from

Chief Justice Marshall in the treason trial of Aaron Burr.[30] The Supreme Court, however, did not address the issue until 1974 in *United States v. Nixon*,[31] when President Nixon refused to turn over Oval Office tapes to the Special Prosecutor investigating the Watergate break-in and cover-up (discussed more fully in Chapters 3 and 5).

In that case, the Court affirmed its recognition that the Constitution does provide for an executive privilege, but found that privilege was not absolute and did not extend to the materials at issue in the case.[32] In addition, the unanimous Court, in an opinion by Chief Justice Burger, asserted that neither the separation of powers doctrine, nor a "valid need for protection of communications between high government officials and those who advise and assist them in the performance of their manifold duties" could alone, or together, sustain an absolute claim of immunity from judicial process.[33] To sustain such a claim, it would be necessary to demonstrate that national security would be impaired.

UNITED STATES v. NIXON
418 U.S. 683 (1974)

Chief Justice BURGER delivered the opinion of the Court.

* * *

IV

THE CLAIM OF PRIVILEGE

A

[W]e turn to the claim that the subpoena should be quashed because it demands "confidential conversations between a President and his close advisors that it would be inconsistent with the public interest to produce." The first contention is a broad claim that the separation of powers doctrine precludes judicial review of a President's claim of privilege. The second contention is that if he does not prevail on the claim of absolute privilege, the court should hold as a matter of constitutional law that the privilege prevails over the subpoena *duces tecum*.

In the performance of assigned constitutional duties each branch of the Government must initially interpret the Constitution, and the interpretation of its powers by any branch is due great respect from the others. The President's counsel, as we have noted, reads the Constitution as providing an absolute privilege of confidentiality for all Presidential communications. Many decisions of this Court, however, have unequivocally reaffirmed the holding of *Marbury v. Madison*, 1 Cranch 137 (1803), that "[it] is emphatically the province and duty of the judicial department to say what the law is."

No holding of the Court has defined the scope of judicial power specifically relating to the enforcement of a subpoena for confidential Presidential communications for use in a criminal prosecution, but other exercises of power by the Executive Branch and the Legislative Branch have been found invalid as in conflict with the Constitution. In a series of cases, the Court interpreted the explicit immunity conferred by express provisions of the Constitution on Members of the House and Senate by the Speech or Debate Clause. Since this Court has consistently exercised the power to construe and delineate claims arising under express powers, it must follow that the Court has authority to interpret claims with respect to powers alleged to derive from enumerated powers.

Our system of government "requires that federal courts on occasion interpret the Constitution in a manner at variance with the construction given the document by another branch."

"Deciding whether a matter has in any measure been committed by the Constitution to another branch of government, or whether the action of that branch exceeds whatever authority has been committed, is itself a delicate exercise in constitutional interpretation, and is a responsibility of this Court as ultimate interpreter of the Constitution."

Notwithstanding the deference each branch must accord the others, the "judicial Power of the United States" vested in the federal courts by Art. III, sec.1, of the Constitution can no more

Continued

be shared with the Executive Branch than the Chief Executive, for example, can share with the Judiciary the veto power, or the Congress share with the Judiciary the power to override a Presidential veto. Any other conclusion would be contrary to the basic concept of separation of powers and the checks and balances that flow from the scheme of a tripartite government. We therefore reaffirm that it is the province and duty of this Court "to say what the law is" with respect to the claim of privilege presented in this case.

B

In support of his claim of absolute privilege, the President's counsel urges two grounds, one of which is common to all governments and one of which is peculiar to our system of separation of powers. The first ground is the valid need for protection of communications between high Government officials and those who advise and assist them in the performance of their manifold duties; the importance of this confidentiality is too plain to require further discussion. Human experience teaches that those who expect public dissemination of their remarks may well temper candor with a concern for appearances and for their own interests to the detriment of the decision making process. Whatever the nature of the privilege of confidentiality of Presidential communication in the exercise of Art. II powers, the privilege can be said to derive from the supremacy of each branch within its own assigned area of constitutional duties. Certain powers and privileges flow from the nature of enumerated powers; the protection of the confidentiality of Presidential communications has similar constitutional underpinnings.

The second ground asserted by the President's counsel in support of the claim of absolute privilege rests on the doctrine of separation of powers. Here it is argued that the independence of the Executive Branch within its own sphere, insulates a President from a judicial subpoena in an ongoing criminal prosecution, and thereby protects confidential Presidential communications.

However, neither the doctrine of separation of powers, nor the need for confidentiality of high-level communications, without more, can sustain an absolute unqualified Presidential privilege of immunity from judicial process under all circumstances. The President's need for complete candor and objectivity from advisors calls for great deference from the courts. However, when the privilege depends solely on the broad, undifferentiated claim of public interest in the confidentiality of such conversations, a confrontation with other values arises. Absent a claim of need to protect military, diplomatic, or sensitive national security secrets, we find it difficult to accept the argument that even the very important interest in confidentiality of Presidential communications is significantly diminished by production of such material for *in camera* inspection with the protection that a district court will be obliged to provide.

The impediment that an absolute, unqualified privilege would place in the way of the primary constitutional duty of the Judicial Branch to do justice in criminal prosecutions would plainly conflict with the function of the courts under Art. III. In designing the structure of our Government and dividing and allocating the sovereign power among three co-equal branches, the Framers of the Constitution sought to provide a comprehensive system, but the separate powers were not intended to operate with absolute independence.

"While the Constitution diffuses power the better to secure liberty, it also contemplates that practice will integrate the dispersed powers into a workable government. It enjoins upon its branches separateness but interdependence, autonomy but reciprocity." *Youngstown Sheet & Tube Co. v. Sawyer*, 343 U.S. at 635.

To read Art. II powers of the {President} as providing an absolute privilege as against a subpoena essential to enforcement of criminal statutes on no more than a generalized claim of the public interest in confidentiality of nonmilitary and nondiplomatic discussion would upset the constitutional balance of "a workable government" and gravely impair the role of the courts under Art. III.

Encroachment on Judicial Powers

Separation of powers issues relating to the judicial branch arise very infrequently. The same general rules that are applicable to encroachments on the other branches also apply when the judicial branch is involved. The other branches may not appropriate the functions assigned to the judiciary, nor may the judiciary take to itself those functions designated by the Constitution to belong to Congress or the executive branches. Congress may, however, assign to the judicial branch actions that could be considered lawmaking provided the subject of such actions relates to the role of the courts. *Mistretta v. United States*,[34] illustrates this principle very well.

Mistretta arose from the congressional passage of the Sentencing Reform Act of 1984.[35] Until passage of the Act, an **indeterminate** or indefinite sentencing scheme was employed for federal crimes. That scheme was believed to result in disproportionate sentences among similarly situated offenders for similar crimes. Additionally, there was a lack of certainty about when an offender would be released. To remedy these problems, Congress set up the United States Sentencing Commission to develop mandatory statutory guidelines for judges to apply in sentencing federal offenders. The Commission was to consist of seven members, at least three of whom would be federal judges. The members of the Commission were to be appointed by the President with the advice and consent of the Senate. Mistretta, who pleaded guilty, was sentenced under the Commission's guidelines and challenged their constitutionality claiming the guidelines were an unconstitutional delegation of Congress' lawmaking power to the judicial branch. The argument was, in essence, that the judges on the Commission were making sentencing policy, which was a legislative function.

The Court rejected Mistretta's argument and found the guidelines constitutional. The separation of powers doctrine was not violated since the Commission was not made part of the judicial branch of government. Similarly separation of powers was not violated by either requiring federal judges to sit on the Commission or by empowering the President to appoint Commission members. The Court determined that Congress was not proscribed from delegating power to experts to formulate policy and that no constitutional violation resulted from doing so, particularly in light of the statutory directions provided in the Act.

indeterminate with the exact time period not set; for example, an indeterminate sentence is a criminal sentence with a maximum or minimum set, but not the exact amount of time.

MISTRETTA V. UNITED STATES
488 U.S. 361 (1989)

Justice BLACKMUN delivered the opinion of the Court.

* * *

IV

Separation of Powers

[W]e turn to Mistretta's claim that the Act violates the constitutional principle of separation of powers.

This Court consistently has given voice to, and has reaffirmed, the central judgment of the Framers of the Constitution that, within our political scheme, the separation of governmental powers into three coordinate Branches is essential to the preservation of liberty. Madison, in writing about the principle of separated powers said, "No political truth is certainly of greater in-

trinsic value or is stamped with the authority of more enlightened patrons of liberty."

In applying the principle of separated powers in our jurisprudence, we have sought to give life to Madison's view of the appropriate relationship among the three coequal Branches. Accordingly, we have recognized, as Madison admonished at the founding, that while our Constitution mandates that "each of the three general departments of government [must remain] entirely free from the control or coercive influence, direct or indirect, of either of the others," the Framers did not require—and indeed rejected— the notion that the three Branches must be entirely separate and distinct.

In adopting this flexible understanding of separation of powers, we simply have recognized Madison's teaching that the greatest security against tyranny—the accumulation of excessive

Continued

authority in a single Branch—lies not in a hermetic division among the Branches, but in a carefully crafted system of checked and balanced power within each Branch. Accordingly, as we have noted many times, the Framers "built into the tripartite Federal Government . . . a self-executing safeguard against the encroachment or aggrandizement of one branch at the expense of the other."

Mistretta . . . argues that Congress, in constituting the Commission as it did, effected an unconstitutional accumulation of power within the Judicial Branch. . . .

At the same time, petitioner asserts, Congress unconstitutionally eroded the integrity and independence of the Judiciary by requiring Article III judges to sit on the Commission, by requiring that those judges share their rulemaking authority with non-judges, and by subjecting the Commission's members to appointment and removal by the President. According to petitioner, Congress, consistent with the separation of powers, may not upset the balance among the Branches by co-opting federal judges into the quintessentially political work of establishing sentencing guidelines, by subjecting those judges to the political whims of the Chief Executive, and by forcing judges to share their power with non-judges.

A

Location of the Commission

We observe that Congress' decision to create an independent rulemaking body to promulgate sentencing guidelines and to locate that body within the Judicial Branch is not unconstitutional unless Congress has vested in the Commission powers that are more appropriately performed by the other Branches or that undermine the integrity of the Judiciary.

Nonetheless, . . . significant exceptions to this general rule have approved the assumption of some nonadjudicatory activities of the Judicial Branch. In keeping with Justice Jackson's *Youngstown* admonition that the separation of powers contemplates the integration of dispersed powers into a workable Government, we have recognized the constitutionality of a "twilight area" in which the activities of the separate Branches merge. In his dissent in *Meyers v. United States*, 272 U.S. 52 (1926), Justice Brandeis

explained that the separation of powers "left to each [Branch] power to exercise, in some respects, functions in their nature executive, legislative and judicial."

That judicial rulemaking, at least with respect to some subjects, falls within this twilight area is no longer an issue for dispute. None of our cases indicate that rulemaking *per se* is a function that may not be performed by an entity within the Judicial Branch, either because rulemaking is inherently nonjudicial or because it is a function exclusively committed to the Executive Branch. On the contrary, we specifically have held that Congress, in some circumstances, may confer rulemaking authority on the Judicial Branch.

Our approach to other nonadjudicatory activities that Congress has vested either in federal courts or in auxiliary bodies within the Judicial Branch has been identical to our approach to judicial rulemaking: consistent with the separation of powers, Congress may delegate to the Judicial Branch nonadjudicatory functions that do not trench upon the prerogatives of another Branch and that are appropriate to the central mission of the Judiciary.

In light of this precedent and practice, we can discern no separation-of-powers impediment to the placement of the Sentencing Commission within the Judicial Branch. As we described at the outset, the sentencing function long has been a peculiarly shared responsibility among the Branches of Government, and has never been thought of as the exclusive constitutional province of any one Branch. For more than a century, federal judges have enjoyed wide discretion to determine the appropriate sentence in individual cases and have exercised special authority to determine the sentencing factors to be applied in any given case. Indeed, the legislative history of the Act makes clear that Congress' decision to place the Commission within the Judicial Branch reflected Congress' "strong feeling" that sentencing has been and should remain "primarily a judicial function." That Congress should vest such rulemaking in the Judicial Branch, far from being "incongruous" or vesting within the Judiciary responsibilities that more appropriately belong to another Branch, simply acknowledges the role that the Judiciary always has played, and continues to play, in sentencing.

Continued

First, although the Commission is located in the Judicial Branch, its powers are not united with the powers of the Judiciary in a way that has meaning for separation-of-powers analysis. Whatever constitutional problems might arise if the powers of the Commission were vested in a court, the Commission is not a court, does not exercise judicial power, and is not controlled by or accountable to members of the Judicial Branch. The Commission, on which members of the Judiciary may be a minority, is an independent agency in every relevant sense. In contrast to a court's exercising judicial power, the Commission is fully accountable to Congress, which can revoke or amend any or all of the Guidelines as it sees fit either within the 180-day waiting period, or at any time. In contrast to a court, the Commission's members are subject to the President's limited powers of removal. In contrast to a court, its rulemaking is subject to the notice and comment requirements of the Administrative Procedure Act . . .

Nor do the Guidelines, though substantive, involve a degree of political authority inappropriate for a nonpolitical Branch. Although the Guidelines are intended to have substantive effects on public behavior, they do not bind or regulate the primary conduct of the public or vest in the Judicial Branch the legislative responsibility for establishing minimum and maximum penalties for every crime. They do no more than fetter the discretion of sentencing judges to do what they have done for generations—impose sentences within the broad limits established by Congress. Given their limited reach, the special role of the Judicial Branch in the field of sentencing, and the fact that the Guidelines are promulgated by an independent agency and not a court, it follows that as a matter of "practical consequences" the location of the Sentencing Commission within the Judicial Branch simply leaves with the Judiciary what long has belonged to it.

B

Composition of the Commission

We now turn to petitioner's claim that Congress' decision to require at least three federal judges to serve on the Commission and to require those judges to share their authority with non-judges undermines the integrity of the Judicial Branch.

In our view, petitioner significantly overstates the mandatory nature of Congress' directive that at least three members of the Commission shall be federal judges, as well as the effect of this service on the practical operation of the Judicial Branch. Service on the Commission by any particular judge is voluntary. The Act does not conscript judges for the Commission. No Commission member to date has been appointed without his consent and we have no reason to believe that the Act confers upon the President any authority to force a judge to serve on the Commission against his will. Accordingly, we simply do not face the question whether Congress may require a particular judge to undertake the extrajudicial duty of serving on the Commission. Congress has created numerous nonadjudicatory bodies, such as the Judicial Conference, that are composed entirely, or in part, of federal judges. Accordingly, absent a more specific threat to judicial independence, the fact that Congress has included federal judges on the Commission does not itself threaten the integrity of the Judicial Branch.

Moreover, we cannot see how the service of federal judges on the Commission will have a constitutionally significant practical effect on the operation of the Judicial Branch. We see no reason why service on the Commission should result in widespread judicial recusals.

We are somewhat more troubled by petitioner's argument that the Judiciary's entanglement in the political work of the Commission undermines public confidence in the disinterestedness of the Judicial Branch. While the problem of individual bias is usually cured through recusal, no such mechanism can overcome the appearance of institutional partiality that may arise from judiciary involvement in the making of policy. The legitimacy of the Judicial Branch ultimately depends on its reputation for impartiality and nonpartisanship. That reputation may not be borrowed by the political Branches to cloak their work in the neutral colors of judicial action.

Although it is a judgment that is not without difficulty, we conclude that the participation of federal judges on the Sentencing Commission does not threaten, either in fact or in appearance, the impartiality of the Judicial Branch. We are drawn to this conclusion by one paramount consideration: that the Sentencing Commission is devoted exclusively to the development of rules to rationalize a process that has been and will continue to be performed exclusively by the

Continued

Judicial Branch. In our view this is an essentially neutral endeavor and one in which judicial participation is peculiarly appropriate. [J]udicial participation on the Commission ensures that judicial experience and expertise will inform the promulgation of rules for the exercise of the Judicial Branch's own business—that of passing sentence on every criminal defendant. To this end, Congress has provided, not inappropriately, for a significant judicial voice on the Commission.

Finally, we reject petitioner's argument that the mixed nature of the Commission violates the Constitution by requiring Article III judges to share judicial power with non-judges. As noted earlier, the Commission is not a court and exercises no judicial power. Thus, the Act does not vest Article III power in nonjudges or require Article III judges to share their power with non-judges.

C

Presidential Control

Mistretta argues that this power of Presidential appointment and removal prevents the Judicial Branch from performing its constitutionally assigned functions. Although we agree with petitioner that the independence of the Judicial Branch must be "jealously guarded" against outside interference, and that, as Madision admonished at the founding, "neither of [the Branches] ought to possess directly or indirectly, an overruling influence over the others in the administration of their respective powers," we do not believe that the President's appointment and removal powers over the Commission afford him influence over the functions of the Judicial Branch or undue sway over its members.

We have never considered it incompatible with the functioning of the Judicial Branch that the President has the power to elevate federal judges from one level to another or to tempt judges away from the bench with Executive Branch positions. The mere fact that the President within his appointment portfolio has positions that may be attractive to federal judges does not of itself, corrupt the integrity of the Judiciary. Were the impartiality of the Judicial Branch so easily subverted, our constitutional system of tripartite

Government would have failed long ago. We simply cannot imagine that federal judges will comport their actions to the wishes of the President for the purpose of receiving an appointment to the Sentencing Commission.

The President's removal power over Commission members poses a similarly negligible threat to judicial independence. The Act does not, and could not under the Constitution, authorize the President to remove, or in any way diminish the status of Article III judges, as judges.

In other words, since the President has no power to affect the tenure or compensation of Article III judges, even if the Act authorized him to remove judges from the Commission at will, he would have no power to coerce the judges in the exercise of their judicial duties. In any case, Congress did not grant the President unfettered authority to remove Commission members. Instead, precisely to ensure that they would not be subject to coercion even in the exercise of their nonjudicial duties, Congress insulated the members from Presidential removal except for good cause. Under these circumstances, we see no risk that the President's limited removal power will compromise the impartiality of Article III judges serving on the Commission and, consequently, no risk that the Act's removal provision will prevent the Judicial Branch from performing its constitutionally assigned function of fairly adjudicating cases and controversies.

We conclude that in creating the Sentencing Commission—an unusual hybrid in structure and authority—Congress neither delegated excessive legislative power nor upset the constitutionally mandated balance of powers among the coordinate Branches. The Constitution's structural protections do not prohibit Congress from delegating to an expert body located within the Judicial Branch the intricate task of formulating sentencing guidelines consistent with such significant statutory direction as is present here. Nor does our system of checked and balanced authority prohibit Congress from calling upon the accumulated wisdom and experience of the Judicial Branch in creating policy on a matter uniquely within the ken of judges. Accordingly, we hold that the Act is constitutional.

As he did in *Chadha*, Justice Scalia dissented vigorously. He argued that there is "no place within our constitutional system for an agency created by Congress to exercise no governmental power other than making of laws."[36]

Justice SCALIA, dissenting.

* * *

II

The delegation of lawmaking authority to the Commission is, in short, unsupported by a legitimating theory to explain why it is not a delegation of legislative power. To disregard structural legitimacy is wrong in itself—but since structure has purpose, the disregard also has adverse practical consequences. In this case, as suggested earlier, the consequence is to facilitate and encourage judicially uncontrollable delegation. Until our decision last Term in *Morrison v. Olson*, 487 U.S. 654 (1988), it could have been said that Congress could delegate lawmaking authority only at the expense of increasing the power of either the President or the courts. Most often, as a practical matter, it would be the President, since the judicial process is unable to conduct the investigations and make the political assessments essential for most policymaking. Thus, the need for delegation would have to be important enough to induce Congress to aggrandize its primary competitor for political power, and the recipient of the policymaking authority, while not Congress itself, would at least be politically accountable. But even after it has been accepted, pursuant to *Morrison*, that those exercising executive power need not be subject to the control of the President, Congress would still be more reluctant to augment the power of even an independent executive agency than to create an otherwise powerless repository for its delegation. Moreover, assembling the full-time senior personnel for an agency exercising executive powers is more difficult than borrowing other officials (or employing new officers on a short-term basis) to head an organization such as the Sentencing Commission.

By reason of today's decision, I anticipate that Congress will find delegation of its lawmaking powers much more attractive in the future. If rulemaking can be entirely unrelated to the exercise of judicial or executive powers, I foresee all manner of "expert" bodies, insulated from the political process, to which Congress will delegate various portions of its lawmaking responsibility. How tempting to create an expert Medical Commission (mostly M.D.'s, with perhaps a few Ph.D.'s in moral philosophy) to dispose of such thorny, "no win" political issues as the withholding of life-support systems in federally funded hospitals, or the use of fetal tissue for research. This is an undemocratic precedent that we set—not because of the scope of the delegated power, but because its recipient is not one of the three Branches of Government. The only governmental power the Commission possesses is the power to make law; and it is not the Congress.

* * *

III

Today's decision follows the regrettable tendency of our recent separation-of powers jurisprudence, to treat the Constitution as though it were no more than a generalized prescription that the functions of the Branches should not be commingled too much—how much is too much to be determined, case-by-case, by this Court. The Constitution is not that. Rather, as its name suggests, it is a prescribed structure, a framework, for the conduct of government. In designing that structure, the Framers *themselves* considered how much commingling was, in the generality of things, acceptable, and set forth their conclusions in the document. That is the meaning of the statements concerning acceptable commingling made by Madison in defense of the proposed Constitution, and now routinely used as an excuse for disregarding it. When he said, . . . that separation of powers "d[oes] not mean that these [three] departments ought to have no *partial agency* in , or no *controul* over the acts of each other" his point was that the commingling specifically provided for in the structure that he and his colleagues had designed—the Presidential veto over legislation, the Senate's confirmation of executive and judicial officers, the Senate's ratification of treaties, the Congress' power to impeach and remove executive and judicial officers—did not violate a proper understanding of separation of powers. He would be aghast, I think, to hear those words used as justification for ignoring that carefully designed structure so long as, in the changing view of the Supreme Court from time to time, "too much commingling" does not occur. Consideration of the degree of commingling that a particular disposition produces may be appropriate at the margins, where the outline of the framework itself is not clear; but it seems to me far from a marginal question whether our constitutional structure allows for a body which is not the Congress, and yet exercises no

Continued

governmental powers except the making of rules that have the effect of laws.

I think the Court errs, in other words, not so much because it mistakes the degree of commingling, but because it fails to recognize that this case is not about commingling, but about the creation of a new Branch altogether, a sort of junior varsity Congress. It may well be that in some circumstances such a Branch would be desirable; perhaps the agency before us here will prove to be so. But there are many desirable dispositions that do not accord with the constitutional structure we live under. And in the long run the improvisation of a constitutional structure on the basis of currently perceived utility will be disastrous.

It appears that Justice Scalia sees no opportunity for any overlap of functions among the branches of the federal government, which does not appear to be true of the Court in general. The Court has been careful to limit any overlap, taking seriously the Framers' determination that to ensure a government of limited powers, the separation of powers doctrine must not be given a broad interpretation. Nevertheless, the Court has seen fit to allow some play in the definition.

FEDERALISM

Under our system of federalism, the governments of the states and the federal government coexist. The system imposes limits on each, in favor of the other. The limits on the federal government result from the constitutional mandate that proscribes action by the federal government unless such action is specifically granted to it by the Constitution. This limitation is different from that placed on state governments. State governments, unlike the federal government, have a general police power permitting them to legislate for the protection of the health, safety, and welfare of their citizens. As a result, state government actions are considered legitimate pursuant to federal law so long as they do not infringe on the specific limitations imposed by the Constitution. This is made manifest by the Tenth Amendment which states that "[t]he powers not delegated to the United States by the Constitution, nor prohibited by it to the States, are reserved to the States respectively. . . ."[37]

The federal government is without a general police power. Consequently, the federal government cannot act for the health, safety, and welfare of its citizens. The actions the federal government takes must fall within one of the constitutionally specified powers. For an action of the federal government to be valid it must, therefore, fall within one of the enumerated powers and not violate any constitutional limitations. Both of these requirements must be met.

The Court has played a significant role in defining federalism and setting its boundaries. The Court has had to determine whether the actions of federal or state governments exceed the boundaries set by the Constitution or trespass upon the powers of one another. The Court's decisions are intimately intertwined with the history, politics, and economics of their time. At the same time it should be noted that because precedent binds the Court, it often appears to be moving more slowly than the society within which it exists. For this reason, President Franklin D. Roosevelt attempted to increase the number of justices on the Court in 1937 to gain a new majority that would be less amenable to state and business interests. (See the sidebar in Chapter 3.) The Court's decisions have also demonstrated the changing nature of the relationship between the national and state governments, expanding and contracting the role of each first set forth in the Constitution.

Exhibit 2.1	Chronological History of the U.S. Supreme Court's Changing Concept of Federalism

Years	Historical Period
1770–1820	The Birth of Our Nation
1820–1860	The Years Leading to the Civil War
1880–1900	Post–Civil War Growth
1900–1920	The Progressive Era
1930–1960	The New Deal, World War II, and Postwar Prosperity
1960–1970	The Great Society and the Vietnam War
1970–2003	The New Federalism

Most of the cases have arisen in the context of the Commerce Clause, and, as such, the discussion of that provision in Chapter 4 will provide the most complete picture of this relationship. This section, however, will provide a broad historical perspective within which to place that discussion. Following the chronological path the Court has taken will assist in defining and interpreting the relationship between the federal and state governments (see Exhibit 2.1).

Historical Perspective on Federalism

During the first part of the birth of this nation, the Founding Fathers were debating the structure of the new nation's government. From the beginning there was tension between those who desired a strong federal government and those who wanted the states to retain the major share of power for directing growth. This becomes clear when looking at the scope of the Articles of Confederation, the first attempt to establish a government for the United States. Under the Articles of Confederation the federal government consisted solely of Congress and its powers were strictly limited. (For a more complete discussion see Chapter 1.) Limited congressional powers and the tension between the central government and the states led to the writing of the Constitution.

The tension, however, did not abate with the writing of the Constitution. During the ratification process, the Federalists, favoring the new Constitution and led, among others, by such as Alexander Hamilton, George Washington, and Benjamin Franklin, engaged in vigorous debate, both in speeches and writings, with those who became known as the Anti-Federalists. The Anti-Federalists included Thomas Paine and Patrick Henry. The Anti-Federalists opposed the Constitution, at least in part, because they believed the republican form of government it enacted could not work on a national scale.

Even after the ratification of the Constitution, the issue of which government, state or federal, retained what power had not been settled. Hamilton became the head of the Federalists and the Anti-Federalists coalesced around Thomas Jefferson who favored a greater role for the states than that advocated by Hamilton and the Federalists. The balance of power between the states and the federal government centered on economic development and regulation as it does today.

The federal government took an increasingly larger role in economic development in the early nineteenth century. In 1819, with the case of *McCulloch v. Maryland*[38] (discussed more fully in Chapter 4), the Supreme Court was asked to delineate the extent of the federal government's power. In essence, the Court was being asked whether that power was to be given the narrow reading advocated by Jefferson or a broader construction as urged by the Federalists.

The case specifically addressed the question whether the federal government had the authority to establish a national bank under the constitutional provision which allowed Congress "[t]o make all Laws which shall be necessary and proper for carrying into Execution the . . . Powers . . . vested by [the] Constitution in the Government of the United States . . . ."[39] Chief Justice Marshall, seemingly prescient, stated that:

> *The government is acknowledged by all to be one of Enumerated powers. The principle that it can exercise only the powers granted to it . . . is now universally admitted. But the question respecting the extent of the powers actually granted is perpetually arising and will probably continue to arise, as long as our system shall exist.*[40]

The Court construed "necessary and proper" broadly, finding that the national government could act to implement its prescribed powers. Thus the doctrine of implied powers came into being, allowing the federal government to exercise powers that are ancillary to those explicitly enumerated. The Court concluded that the act of chartering the bank was valid because it bore a reasonable relationship to an enumerated government power.

As the 1800s progressed, clashes between the state and federal governments over the power to regulate commerce increased, particularly leading up to the Civil War. During this time, the states were clashing over tariffs and then South Carolina claimed the right of states to nullify federal laws. This doctrine of state power was buried with the bodies of all those citizens who fought for and against it. Federal law could not be nullified by the states.

Throughout the post–Civil War years and the Progressive Era, the power of the federal government expanded. The national government played a more active role in regulating and reforming the economic system as the effects of industrialization changed the American economy and social structure. The federal government also took the central role in regulating commerce. That role was largely one of protecting large commercial interests.

At the beginning of the twentieth century, the emergence of the Progressive Era brought with it a move by state governments to cope with the problems associated with industrialization, urbanization, and immigration, which were seen to be increased by the federal government's support of big business. The progressive reforms, at this time, moved from the state level to a national level, rather than from the national to state level, as had been the case with other economic reform. In 1916, the Sixteenth Amendment to the Constitution, imposing a federal income tax, was adopted and thereafter declared constitutional. This provided the federal government with increased revenues and led to revenue sharing between the federal and state governments. It also provided the federal government with additional power to direct the national agenda, which continues today.

With the election of Franklin Roosevelt, during the Great Depression, the power of the federal government was secured. Toward the end of the Great Depression there was cooperation between the state and federal governments brought about by World War II and the period directly following it. This was a time when both state and federal authorities worked together to achieve common goals.

Later, during Lyndon Johnson's presidency in the 1960s, the federal government took an active role in solving the nation's social problems. Congress passed the Civil Rights Act of 1964 and funded programs such as Head Start, which were associated with eliminating poverty. Grants to the states increased. As time went by, however, conflict between state and federal regulators increased. Programs overlapped and conflicted. State regulators wanted greater control over the programs administered in their jurisdictions.

The war in Vietnam and the oil crisis of the 1970s marked the beginning of a change in the balance of power between the state and federal governments. Economic growth slowed and confidence in the federal government was undermined both by the war and, somewhat later, the Watergate scandal.

With Richard Nixon's ascension to the presidency, efforts to reduce the role of the federal government's control over grant programs were introduced. Along with this, the Nixon administration sought to reform the welfare system. During the 1970s and 1980s there was a shift away from the idea that the federal government could solve the nation's social problems in reaction to Congress' use of its power to achieve policy objectives.

In the 1990s, the Court became increasingly willing to strike down federal legislation that it found more properly within the states' police power. The Court's decision in *United States v. Lopez*[41] set down the first limits on the extent of the federal government's power under the Commerce Clause in 60 years.

Lopez concerned Congress' passage of the Gun-Free School Zones Act of 1990,[42] prohibiting the knowing possession of a firearm in areas known to be school zones, or where there was reasonable cause to believe it was such a zone. In a 5 to 4 decision, the Court found the Act to be unconstitutional because it exceeded the power of Congress to regulate under the Commerce Clause. Chief Justice Rehnquist, writing for the majority, reached this conclusion based on the fact that the Act was criminal in nature, having nothing to do with commerce, and the Court refused to

> *[p]ile inference upon inference in a manner that would convert congressional authority under the Commerce Clause to a general police power of the sort retained by the States. To do so would require us to conclude that the Constitution's enumeration of powers does not presuppose something not enumerated, and that there will never be a distinction between what is truly national and what is truly local.*[43]

In a concurrence, Justice Thomas expressed the view that the Constitution could not support the contention that Congress has power over all activities substantially affecting interstate commerce. As such, he advocated an even narrower view of federal authority under the Constitution than the majority.[44]

Justice Breyer, joined in dissent by Justices Stevens, Souter, and Ginsburg, maintained that the Court's decision did not comport with modern precedent and could potentially undermine legal certainty in this area of the law.[45]

This trend toward narrowing the power of the federal government in matters involving the Commerce Clause has continued (see Chapter 4) and the Court offers no evidence of retreat from its march toward a new federalism that will seek a new balance of power between the governments of the states and the nation.

Federalism—State Oversight of the Federal Government

Before concluding the consideration of federalism, the power individual states have to restrict the actions of the federal government must be examined. States may not nullify federal laws, that is a power vested in the Supreme Court by our Constitution,[46] but just where the line is drawn dividing authority between the states and the federal government was raised in *United States Term Limits, Inc. v. Thornton*.[47] The issue in this case revolved around the states' ability to restrict the number of terms that an individual could serve in Congress and demonstrated a deep division among the members of the Court.

The case specifically involved an amendment to Arkansas' Constitution that denied congressional candidates who had served in the House for three terms or the Senate for two terms, access to the ballot. This change was similar to term limit provisions adopted by 22 other states.

In another 5 to 4 decision, the Court struck down the term limits provision as unconstitutional. The majority relied on the Constitutional provision setting forth the specific requirements for congressional membership.[48] The specific question that Justice Stevens was concerned with was whether these constitutional clauses set forth the exclusive requirements for membership or whether they merely constituted the minimum requirements. He found that the individual states were without the power to modify the constitutional requirements.

U.S. TERM LIMITS, INC. v. THORNTON
514 U.S. 779 (1995)

Justice STEVENS delivered the opinion of the Court.

The Constitution sets forth qualifications for membership in the Congress of the United States

Today's cases present a challenge to an amendment to the Arkansas State Constitution that prohibits the name of an otherwise eligible candidate for Congress from appearing on the general election ballot if that candidate has already served three terms in the House of Representatives or two terms in the Senate. The Arkansas Supreme Court held that the amendment violates the Federal Constitution. We agree with that holding. Such a state-imposed restriction is contrary to the "fundamental principle of our representative democracy," embodied in the Constitution, that "the people should choose whom they please to govern them." *Powell v. Mc-Cormack*, 395 U.S. 486 (1969). Allowing individual States to adopt their own qualifications for congressional service would be inconsistent with the Framers' vision of a uniform National Legislature representing the people of the United States. If the qualifications set forth in the text of the Constitution are to be changed, the text must be amended.

II

Powell's Holding

Petitioners argue somewhat half-heartedly that the narrow holding in *Powell*, which involved the power of the House to exclude a member pursuant to Art. I sec. 5, does not control the more general question whether Congress has the power to add qualifications. *Powell*, however, is not susceptible to such a narrow reading. Our conclusion that Congress may not alter or add to the qualifications in the Constitution was integral to our analysis and outcome.

Unsurprisingly, the state courts and lower federal courts have similarly concluded that *Powell* conclusively resolved the issue whether Congress has the power to impose additional qualifications.

In sum, after examining *Powell's* historical analysis and its articulation of the "basic principles of our democratic system," we reaffirm that the qualifications for service in Congress set forth in the text of the Constitution are "fixed" at least in the sense that they may not be supplemented by Congress.

III

Our reaffirmation of *Powell* does not necessarily resolve the specific questions presented in these cases. For petitioners argue that whatever the constitutionality of additional qualifications for membership imposed by Congress, the historical and textual materials discussed in *Powell* do not support the conclusion that the Constitution prohibits additional qualifications imposed by States. In the absence of such a constitutional prohibition, petitioners argue, the Tenth Amendment and the principle of reserved powers require that States be allowed to add such qualifications.

Petitioners argue that the Constitution contains no express prohibition against state-added qualifications, and that Amendment 73 is therefore an appropriate exercise of a State's reserved power to place additional restrictions on the choices that its own voters may make. We disagree for two independent reasons. First, we conclude that the power to add qualifications is not within the "original powers" of the States, and thus is not reserved to the States by the Tenth Amendment. Second, even if States possessed some original power in this area, we conclude that the Framers intended the Constitution to be the exclusive source of qualifications for members of Congress, and that the Framers thereby "divested" States of any power to add qualifications.

As we have frequently noted, "the States unquestionably do retain a significant measure of sovereign authority. They do so, however, only to the extent the Constitution has not divested them of their original powers and transferred those powers to the Federal Government.

Continued

Contrary to petitioners' assertions, power to add qualifications is not part of the original powers of sovereignty that the Tenth Amendment reserved to the States. Petitioners' Tenth Amendment argument misconceives the nature of the right at issue because that Amendment could only "reserve" that which existed before. As Justice Story recognized, "the states can exercise no powers whatsoever, which exclusively spring out of the existence of the national government, which the constitution does not delegate to them. . . . No state can say, that it has reserved, what it never possessed."

With respect to qualifications for service in Congress, no such right existed before the Constitution was ratified. The contrary argument overlooks the revolutionary character of the Government that the Framers conceived. After the Constitutional Convention convened, the Framers were presented with, and eventually adopted a variation of, "a plan not merely to amend the Articles of Confederation but to create an entirely new National Government with a National Executive, National Judiciary, and a National Legislature." In adopting that plan, the Framers envisioned a uniform national system, rejecting the notion that the Nation was a collection of States, and instead creating a direct link between the National Government and the people of the United States. In that National Government, representatives owe primary allegiance not to the people of a State, but to the people of the Nation.

We believe that the Constitution reflects the Framers' general agreement with the approach later articulated by Justice Story.

This conclusion is consistent with our previous recognition that, in certain limited contexts, the power to regulate the incidents of the federal system is not a reserved power of the States, but rather is delegated by the Constitution.

In short, as the Framers recognized, electing representatives to the national Legislature was a new right, arising from the Constitution itself. The Tenth Amendment thus provides no basis for concluding that the States possess reserved congressional qualifications, the text and structure of the Constitution, the relevant historical materials, and, most importantly, the "basic principles of our democratic system" all demonstrate that the Qualifications Clauses were intended to preclude the States from exercising

any such power and to fix as exclusive the qualifications in the Constitution.

The Convention and Ratification Debates

The provisions in the Constitution governing federal elections confirm the Framers' intent that States lack power to add qualifications to those that are fixed in the Constitution. Instead, any state power to set the qualifications for membership in Congress must derive not from the reserved powers of state sovereignty, but rather from the delegated powers of national sovereignty. In the absence of any constitutional delegation to the States of power to add qualifications to those enumerated in the Constitution, such a power does not exist.

The Preclusion of State Power

Even if we believed that States possessed as part of their original powers some control over congressional qualifications, the text and structure of the Constitution, the relevant historical materials, and, most importantly, the "basic principles of our democratic system" all demonstrate that the Qualifications Clauses were intended to preclude the States from possessing any such power to fix as exclusive the qualifications in the Constitution.

Framers feared that the diverse interests of the States would undermine the National Legislature, and thus they adopted provisions intended to minimize the possibility of state interference with federal elections.

In light of the Framers' evident concern that States would try to undermine the National Government, they could not have intended States to have the power to set qualifications. Indeed, one of the more anomalous consequences of petitioners' argument is that it accepts federal supremacy over the procedural aspects of determining the times, places and manner of elections while allowing the States *carte blanche* with respect to the substantive qualifications for membership in Congress.

Democratic Principles

Similarly, we believe that state-imposed qualifications, as much as congressionally imposed qualifications, would undermine the second critical idea recognized in *Powell;* that an aspect of sovereignty is the right of the people to vote for whom they wish. Again, the source of the

Continued

qualification is of little moment in assessing the qualification's restrictive impact.

In sum, the available historical and textual evidence, read in light of the basic principles of democracy underlying the Constitution and recognized by this Court in *Powell* reveal the Framers' intent that neither Congress nor the States should possess the power to supplement the exclusive qualifications set forth in the text of the Constitution.

* * *

V

We are . . . firmly convinced that allowing the several States to adopt term limits for congressional service would effect a fundamental change in the constitutional framework. Any such change must come not by legislation adopted either by Congress or by an individual State, but rather—as have other important changes in the elective process—through the amendment procedures set forth in Article V. The Framers decided that the qualifications for service in the Congress of the United States be fixed in the Constitution and be uniform throughout the Nation. That decision reflects the Framers' understanding that Members of Congress are chosen by separate constituencies, but that they become, when elected, servants of the people of the United States. They are not merely delegates appointed by separate, sovereign States; they occupy offices that are integral and essential components of a single National Government. In the absence of a properly passed constitutional amendment, allowing individual States to craft their own qualifications for Congress would thus erode the structure envisioned by the Framers, a structure that was designed, in the word of the Preamble to our Constitution, to form a "more perfect Union."

The dissenters, in an opinion by Justice Thomas, claimed that the Constitution did not prevent the people of each state from imposing additional requirements on congressional candidates. The requirements set forth in the Constitution only restricted the states from abolishing all eligibility requirements for congressional membership.

The Court's decision reaffirmed the holding in *Powell v. McCormack*,[49] and brought a halt to the movement for term limits through imposing qualifications on candidates for Congress. Supporters, however, turned to a new strategy in *Cook v. Gralike*.[50]

In *Cook*, Missouri voters approved a state constitutional amendment requiring that the ballot in congressional elections point out candidates who declined to support term limits. The designation, next to the candidate's name would read, "DISREGARDED VOTERS' INSTRUCTIONS ON TERM LIMITS." The Court again held the provision unconstitutional and in a unanimous decision found that it far exceeded the power given the states by the Constitution that allowed only issuance of procedural requirements by the states. The Court concluded that the Election Clauses did not permit the states to engage in actions that might well dictate the outcome of elections.[51]

Summary

In their desire to ensure against the concentration of power at a single source, the Framers structured a government that divided power horizontally among the branches of the federal government and vertically between the federal and state governments.

It is clear that the Court has taken seriously the Constitution's restrictions designed to prevent encroachments by one branch on another, as well as keeping any branch from assuming major control over governmental functions. Despite Justice Scalia's attempt to restrict any overlap among the functions assigned to each branch and his claim that the Court has not enforced the separation of powers doctrine as the Framers intended, the Court has consistently interpreted that doctrine narrowly.

This consistency in interpretation is not nearly so clear when we turn to the Court's interpretation of federalism. There, the Court has been much more subject to the vagaries of the historical, social, and economic factors in reaching its decisions. This is particularly true when it is the interpretation of the Commerce Clause that is at issue. The Court has moved from an expansion of federal power to its more recent stance of limiting the national government's role.

Key Terms

attachment
enumerated powers
executive privilege
indeterminate

injunction
separation of powers
federalism
immunity

police powers
Taft-Hartley Act

Review Questions

1. Justice Scalia's position on the separation of powers seems to be at odds with the majority in *Mistretta*. What are the differences between his position and the Court's position in that case?

2. What was the purpose of dividing the powers of the federal government among the 3 branches? What areas of conflict emerge from the separation of powers?

3. Compare and contrast the federal government's power under the "Necessary and Proper" Clause with the state governments' police power.

4. What distinction was drawn between the grant of absolute immunity for the President and immunity for those who worked closely with the President in *Nixon v. Fitzgerald*?

5. Discuss the economic, political and social forces that affected the balance of power between the state and federal governments from colonial times to the present.

Internet Connections

1. For more information on the Framers' intentions regarding the horizontal and vertical division of power, visit The United States Constitution Online at *http://www.USConstitution.net*.

2. To learn more about federalism, visit the home page for *Publius: The Journal of Federalism*, a scholarly journal devoted to issues of federalism, at *http://www.lafayette.edu/publius*.

End Notes

[1] U.S. Const. art. I, § 1.

[2] U.S. Const. art. II, § 1.

[3] U.S. Const. art. III, § 1.

[4] *Youngstown Sheet and Tube Co. v. Sawyer*, 343 U.S. 579 (1952).

[5] 29 U.S.C. § 141 (1947).

[6] *Dames & Moore v. Regan*, 453 U.S. 654 (1981).

[7] 50 U.S.C. § 1701–1707.

[8] *Dames & Moore v. Regan*, 453 U.S. 654 (1981).

[9] *Immigration and Naturalization Service v. Chadha*, 462 U.S. 919 (1982).

[10] 8 U.S.C. § 1254 (1).

[11] *Immigration and Naturalization Service v. Chadha*, 462 U.S. 919 (1982).

[12] *Bowsher v. Synar*, 478 U.S. 714 (1986).

[13] 2 U.S.C. § 901–909.

[14] *Morrison v. Olson*, 487 U.S. 654 (1988).

[15] 28 U.S.C. § 49.

[16] *Hutchinson v. Proxmire*, 443 U.S. 111 (1979).

[17] *Nixon v. Fitzgerald*, 457 U.S. 731 (1982).

[18] *Id.* at 747.

[19] *Id.* at 748–749.

[20] *Id.* at 757.

[21] *Id.* at 766.

[22] *Id.* at 767.

[23] *Harlow v. Fitzgerald,* 457 U.S. 800 (1982).

[24] *Id.* at 807.

[25] *Id.* at 808–809.

[26] *Clinton v. Jones,* 520 U.S. 681 (1997).

[27] *Id.* at 709.

[28] *Id.* at 702–703.

[29] *Id.* at 705–706.

[30] *United States v. Burr,* 25 F. Cas. 187 (CC Va. 1807).

[31] *United States v. Nixon* 418 U.S. 683 (1974).

[32] *Id.* at 707, 715.

[33] *Id.* at 706.

[34] *Mistretta v. U.S.* 488 U.S. 361 (1989).

[35] 18 U.S.C. § 3551-3559; 28 U.S.C. §§ 991–998 (1984).

[36] *Mistretta,* 488 U.S. at 420–421.

[37] U.S. Const. amend. X.

[38] *McCulloch v. Maryland,* 17 U.S. 316 (1819).

[39] U.S. Const. art. I, § 8.

[40] *McCulloch,* 17 U.S. at 405.

[41] *U.S. v. Lopez,* 514 U.S. 549 (1995).

[42] 18 U.S.C. § 922 (q) (1) (A).

[43] *Lopez,* 514 U.S. at, 567–568.

[44] *Id.* at 567.

[45] *Id.* at 625, 630.

[46] *Marbury v. Madision,* 5 U.S. 137 (1803); *see also,* Chapter 3.

[47] *U.S. Term Limits, Inc. v. Thornton,* 514 U.S. 779 (1995).

[48] U.S. Const. art. I, § 2.

[49] *Powell v. McCormack,* 395 U.S. 486 (1969); *see also,* Chapter 4.

[50] *Cook v. Gralike,* 531 U.S. 510 (2001).

[51] *Id.* at 525–526.

ONLINE   For additional resources, go to *http://www.westlegalstudies.com*

THE COURTS—JURISDICTION AND JUDICIAL REVIEW

"It is emphatically the province and duty of the judicial department to say what the law is. Those who apply the rule to particular cases, must of necessity expound and interpret that rule. If two laws conflict with each other, the courts must decide on the operation of each."

—*Mr. Chief Justice John Marshall*
Marbury v. Madison

INTRODUCTION

The United States Constitution says little about the actual structure of the federal court system. When reading Article III, § 1, it becomes apparent that the Framers of the Constitution left the details of the structure of the federal courts to Congress. That portion of the Constitution says:

"The judicial Power of the United States, shall be vested in one supreme Court, and in such inferior Courts as the Congress may from time to time ordain and establish."[1]

While that constitutional provision goes on to give a few details, the Framers of the Constitution believed an independent federal court system was essential to the future of the United States.[2] The Constitution does provide two specific protections for the federal judiciary. First, as will be discussed below, judges and justices in the federal system are appointed for life, and second, judicial compensation cannot, by Constitutional mandate, be reduced during a judge's or justice's time in office.[3] In spite of this, however, the federal court system, by far, is the branch of the federal government left to be detailed by an entity other than the Framers of the Constitution.

Early History

The first organization of the federal court system was outlined in the Judiciary Act of 1789.[4] While some things have changed, the basic design consisted of the Supreme Court and a system of lower federal courts whose location was based on state boundaries. Six justices sat on the U.S. Supreme Court bench under this scheme[5] and while the number of justices changed from time to time, the current number of nine justices has been in place since 1869.[6] This is not to say that no attempt has been made to increase the number of justices, but such attempts have been unsuccessful as seen in the sidebar regarding the Court-Packing Plan of 1937 (Exhibit 3.1).

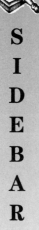

EXHIBIT 3.1 He Just Ain't Fast Enough
(2/9/37, by Homan in the Brooklyn Citizen)

THE COURT-PACKING PLAN OF 1937

President Franklin Delano Roosevelt came into office in 1932 during the Great Depression. Throughout his first term President Roosevelt began restructuring the American economy through a series of new laws collectively called the New Deal. While there was much support for the New Deal initially, a growing number of critics began to challenge some of its legislation. After the Supreme Court struck down the Agricultural Adjustment Act saying that the states, not the federal government, had the power to regulate agriculture,[7] FDR began to worry that if the Supreme Court continued to use this line of reasoning the New Deal would soon fall apart. With this in mind, and with a reelection mandate showing overwhelming support for FDR and the New Deal, he announced his court-packing plan in early 1937.[8] What did FDR propose? He proposed that when a judge or justice reached his/her 70th birthday and did not retire, the president would appoint a new member of the court subject to approval by the Senate.[9] The two purposes of FDR's proposal were to bring the judicial system new and younger blood and to have these younger men make decisions based on personal experience and contact with the average citizen.[10] The reaction to the court-packing plan was negative, and many felt that the executive branch was attempting to assume too much power and would lead to the other two branches becoming dependent on the executive branch.[11] Before the Senate could vote on the plan, two things happened which effectively stopped the plan. The Supreme Court upheld both the Wagner Act and the Social Security Act and Justice Van Devanter announced his retirement. These two events signaled Supreme Court support for FDR's policies and the retirement gave him an opportunity to make a Supreme Court appointment. With these two events, the plan was allowed to die in committee.[12] FDR had a Court he could live with and ultimately, he was able to appoint eight justices to the Court during his tenure in office.[13] The damage he did to his relationship with Congress, however, was not easily mended. The court-packing plan had energized FDR's opponents and by the end of the decade, the New Deal was a thing of the past.

The organization of the federal courts was not without controversy. When the original states discussed ratification of the Constitution many of them were concerned that the federal court system was a potential danger to the power of the states.[14] In light of the experiences many new Americans had with the British legal system and the states under the Articles of Confederation, these individuals wanted four changes to the judiciary provisions of the Constitution. These four changes included: "guaranteeing civil as well as criminal trial juries, restricting federal appellate jurisdiction to questions of law, eliminating or radically curtailing congressional authority to establish lower federal courts, and eliminating the authorization for federal diversity jurisdiction."[15] These concerns were taken into consideration as James Madison put together the proposed legislation to create the federal court system. The legislation was passed and signed into law on September 24, 1789.[16]

Not only did the Judiciary Act of 1789 set the number of Supreme Court justices, it did several other noteworthy things. First, it spelled out the Court's appellate jurisdiction that included the power to review federal circuit court decisions in civil cases and the state supreme court decisions that invalidated federal statutes or treaties.[17] In addition, this Act also created a system of lower federal courts that consisted of two types of trial courts. The plan created 13 district courts that were to be presided over by one district judge. These district courts were to hold four sessions a year in locations designated in each district.[18] The Act further provided for three circuit courts—an Eastern, a Middle, and a Southern circuit. These courts were instructed to meet in one of two specified cities within the circuit twice a year and decisions were to be made by panels of three judges, one district judge and two Supreme Court justices assigned to each circuit.[19] The circuit courts' jurisdiction included **diversity of citizenship** cases, major federal crimes, cases involving the United States as a plaintiff, and some limited appellate jurisdiction.[20] The federal courts were not given a general federal question jurisdiction until many decades later with the Judiciary Act of 1875.[21]

The Judiciary Act of 1875 had two effects. "It established the federal courts' preeminent role as protectors of constitutional and statutory rights and liberties and

diversity of citizenship
the situation that occurs when persons on one side of a case in federal court come from a different state from persons on the other side.

as interpreters of the growing mass of federal statutes and administrative regulations."[22] In doing so, the Act also gave the district courts some of the circuit courts' original jurisdiction and enlarged the circuit courts' appellate jurisdiction.[23]

The Judiciary Act of 1875 did not, however, end the controversy over the structure of the federal court system, nor did it change the structure into its present form. That occurred with the Circuit Court of Appeals Act of 1891.[24] This Act created new circuit courts of appeals and "made the federal district courts the system's primary trial courts."[25] Since 1891 the Supreme Court's limited certiorari jurisdiction has been legislatively enlarged and this has created the Court as it is today.[26]

Structure of the Federal Courts

In addition to the U.S. Supreme Court with its nine justices, the federal system also includes 13 Circuit Courts of Appeal and 94 district courts. The Circuit Courts of Appeal include 12 regional circuits and one U.S. Court of Appeals for the Federal Circuit "that has nationwide jurisdiction to hear appeals in specialized cases, such as those involving patent laws and cases decided by the Court of International Trade and the Court of Federal Claims."[27] A panel of three judges typically hears the cases in these courts and the decision is made by majority vote.

Each state has at least one federal district court and some states have two or more. The district courts are presided over by one judge and as this is the trial court or the court of general jurisdiction, this is where the majority of cases begin in the federal system. These courts have jurisdiction to hear all cases involving **federal** (or constitutional) **questions**, federal criminal matters, and civil matters so long as the amount in controversy is at least $75,000 and there is diversity of citizenship between the litigants. There are 13 Federal Circuit Courts of Appeal and the country is divided into circuits as shown in Exhibit 3.2.

federal question a legal issue directly involving the U.S. Constitution, statutes, or treaties. Federal courts have jurisdiction in cases involving a *federal question*.

| **EXHIBIT 3.2** | Federal Circuit Courts of Appeal |

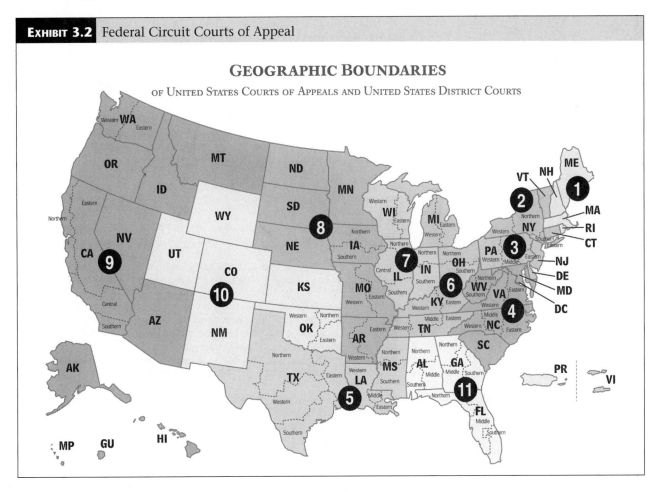

GEOGRAPHIC BOUNDARIES

OF UNITED STATES COURTS OF APPEALS AND UNITED STATES DISTRICT COURTS

All of the judges and justices in the federal system are appointed for life. This is not to say that they can never be removed from office, but so long as a judge or justice is competent, performs his or her duties appropriately, and is not found guilty of treason, bribery, or other high crimes and misdemeanors, that individual's term of office continues until retirement or death. It is Article III, Section 1 of the Constitution that specifically provides judges with life tenure predicated on good behavior. If it becomes necessary to remove a judge or justice from office, the House of Representatives institutes the impeachment process[28] and the judge or justice is tried by the Senate.[29]

In addition to having a lifetime appointment, federal judges and Supreme Court justices (see Exhibit 3.3) also are protected by Article III, § 1, which mandates that the federal justices and judges will not have their compensation reduced during their term in office.[30] By giving judges and justices the assurance that Congress cannot lower their salaries as a weapon to force the courts to make decisions according to congressional wishes, the Framers of the Consti-

SIDEBAR

EXHIBIT 3.3   The Current Supreme Court

Front row from left to right: Antonin Scalia, John Paul Stevens, William H. Rehnquist, Sandra Day O'Connor, and Anthony Kennedy. Back row from left to right: Ruth Bader Ginsburg, David H. Souter, Clarence Thomas, and Stephen G. Breyer (Courtesy of Reuters/Newsmedia, Inc./Corbis)

U.S. SUPREME COURT
THE CURRENT SUPREME COURT

The Court is currently made up of nine justices; it consists of one Chief Justice and eight associate justices. In 2004, the Chief Justice is William H. Rehnquist, appointed to the bench in 1971 and who became Chief Justice in 1986. Chief Justice Rehnquist earned his law degree from Stanford University and practiced law for many years prior to his appointment. Chief Justice Rehnquist died September 4, 2005 and was replaced by John G. Roberts, Jr. on September 29, 2005. Chief Justice Roberts is a graduate of Harvard Law School, and served on the U.S. Court of Appeals bench prior to his appointment to the Supreme Court.

The oldest member of the Court is Justice John Paul Stevens. Justice Stevens earned his law degree from Northwestern University, clerked for Justice Rutledge of the Court following graduation and practiced law for many years in Illinois. President Ford appointed him to the Supreme Court bench in 1975.

The first woman to be appointed to the Court was Sandra Day O'Connor. She graduated from Stanford Law School and after law school she served as Deputy County Attorney of San Mateo County, California, practiced in her own firm and held many government offices prior to her nomination to the Court by President Reagan in 1981. Justice O'Connor tendered her resignation at the end of the 2004 term and a new justice will be appointed to take her place.

In 1986 President Reagan appointed Antonin Scalia to the Court. Justice Scalia earned his law degree from Harvard Law School, and then practiced law for a few years before entering into government service. Prior to serving on the Supreme Court, Justice Scalia served on the Court of Appeals.

Anthony Kennedy earned his law degree from Harvard Law School in 1961, then practiced and taught law prior to his service on the U.S. Court of Appeals. After 12 years of service on the federal bench, President Reagan nominated him to the Supreme Court. He was confirmed by the Senate and took office in 1988.

David H. Souter was serving as a Judge for the U.S. Court of Appeals when nominated by President George H.W. Bush for the Supreme Court bench. Justice Souter had a great deal of judicial experience as he had served in various courts since 1978. He was sworn into office in 1990.

President George H.W. Bush nominated Clarence Thomas to the Supreme Court in 1991. This nomination was one of the most controversial in recent history. After a contentious confirmation process, he was confirmed. Justice Thomas came to the Court from the U.S. Court of Appeals and earned his law degree from Yale Law School in 1974.

The second woman to serve on the Supreme Court is Ruth Bader Ginsburg. Justice Ginsburg earned her law degree from Columbia Law School and taught and practiced law before she was nominated by President Carter to the U.S. Court of Appeals in 1980. She served on that bench until 1993 when she was nominated by President Clinton and confirmed by the Senate.

Stephen G. Breyer was the second associate justice nominated by President Clinton. Justice Breyer came to the Supreme Court after serving as a Judge on the U.S. Court of Appeals. He attended Harvard Law School where he graduated magna cum laude. After law school, Justice Breyer clerked for Supreme Court Justice Arthur Goldberg, taught law at Harvard University, and served in various capacities in the Department of Justice.[31]

tution have ensured the neutrality and independence of the courts. This means the judges and justices are free to follow the law and not the whims of the other branches of the government.

THE JURISDICTION OF THE COURT

The jurisdiction of the Supreme Court is spelled out in Article III, Section 2 of the U.S. Constitution. It says:

> *"The judicial Power shall extend to all Cases, in Law and Equity, arising under this Constitution, the Laws of the United States, and Treaties made, or which shall be made, under their Authority;—to all Cases affecting Ambassadors, other public ministers and Consuls;—to all Cases of admiralty and maritime Jurisdiction;—to Controversies to which the United States shall be a Party;— to Controversies between two or more States;—between a State and Citizens of another State;—between Citizens of different States;—between Citizens of the same State claiming Lands under Grants of different States, and between a State, or the Citizens thereof, and foreign States, Citizens or Subjects.*
>
> *In all Cases affecting Ambassadors, other public Ministers and Consuls, and those in which a State shall be Party, the supreme Court shall have original Jurisdiction. In all the other Cases before mentioned, the supreme Court shall have appellate Jurisdiction, both as to Law and Fact, with such Exceptions, and under such Regulations as the Congress shall make.*
>
> *The Trial of all Crimes, except in Cases of Impeachment, shall be by Jury; and such Trial shall be held in the State where the said Crimes shall have been committed; but when not committed within any State, the Trial shall be at such Place or Places as the Congress may by Law have directed."*[32]

original jurisdiction the power of a court to take a case, try it, and decide it (as opposed to appellate jurisdiction, the power of a court to hear and decide an appeal).

While this section discusses the **original jurisdiction** of the Court, it does not address the Court's appellate jurisdiction. Originally, the Supreme Court had jurisdiction to hear the types of cases spelled out in the Constitution, as discussed above, but had limited appellate jurisdiction to review circuit court decisions in civil cases concerning matters over $2000.[33] The Supreme Court and other federal courts were not given a general federal question jurisdiction until 1875 and were not granted general appellate jurisdiction until the 1890s.

Cases and Controversies

appellate jurisdiction the power and authority of a higher court to take up cases that have already been in a lower court and the power to make decisions about these cases.

When the Supreme Court or the circuit courts of appeals exercise their **appellate jurisdiction**, there are some basic requirements and restrictions that must be met and respected. The first of these requirements is that these courts must not give advisory opinions. This is what has commonly been called the **"case and controversy"** requirement and is derived from Article III, § 2 quoted above. This means that these courts cannot give advisory opinions or answer questions regarding a hypothetical situation. It is clear from the early writings of the Framers of the Constitution that they never intended for federal judges and justices to decide issues of law without an actual dispute. This intent was honored very early when the Justices of the Supreme Court declined to give President Washington advice about the legal issues arising out of a decision for the United States to remain neutral in a dispute between England and France in the late 1700s.[34]

case and controversy real (not hypothetical or faked) disputes that turn into lawsuits. The U.S. Constitution gives the federal courts the power to decide certain "cases and controversies."

The case and controversy requirement gives rise to two general groups of cases. In the case of *Cohens v. Virginia*,[35] Chief Justice Marshall wrote of these two groups:

> *In the first, jurisdiction depends on the character of the cause, whoever may be the parties. This class comprehends 'all cases in law and equity arising*

under this constitution, the laws of the United States, and treaties made, or which shall be made, under their authority.' This cause extends the jurisdiction of the Court to all the cases described, without making in its terms any exception whatever, and without any regard to the condition of the party. If there be any exception, it is to be implied, against the express words of the article. In the second class, the jurisdiction depends entirely on the character of the parties. In this are comprehended controversies between 'two or more States, between a State and citizens of another State,' and 'between State and foreign States, citizens or subject.' If these be the parties, it is entirely unimportant, what may be the subject of the controversy. Be it what it may, these parties have a constitutional right to come into the courts of the Union.[36]

While this quote clearly demonstrates the types of cases that are considered to fall within the "case and controversy" requirement, it was not the last word from the Supreme Court on the subject. In *Aetna Life Insurance Company v. Haworth*,[37] Chief Justice Hughes provided more insight into what is a controversy and what is a case when he wrote:

*A 'controversy' in this sense must be one that is appropriate for judicial determination. A **justiciable** [emphasis added] controversy is thus distinguished from a difference or dispute of a hypothetical character; from one that is academic or moot. The controversy must be definite and concrete, touching the legal relations of parties having adverse legal interests. It must be a real and substantial controversy admitting of specific relief through a degree of a conclusive character, as distinguished from, an opinion advising what the law would be upon a hypothetical state of facts.[38]*

The Court's words demonstrate that the phrase "case and controversy" limits the jurisdiction of the federal courts to those situations involving adversarial legal positions that traditionally can be resolved only through access to the courts. On the other hand, this term gives definition to the role of the federal judiciary within the three branches of the federal government. The judicial role does not include intrusion into the activities assigned to the legislative or executive branches of the federal government.

Additionally, the case and controversy requirement demands adverse litigants[39] and as the Court has written, the power of the courts should only be used "in the last resort, and as a necessity in the determination of real, earnest and vital controversy between individuals. It never was thought that, by means of a friendly suit, a party beaten in the legislature could transfer to the courts an inquiry as to the constitutionality of the legislative act."[40]

The rule that the Court may not provide advisory opinions is not without an exception. Sometimes declaratory judgments are allowed. This is a judicial action in which the court is not asked to give a monetary award, but is asked to determine the legal effect of the conduct of the parties involved in the dispute. However, a **declaratory judgment** also requires a concrete controversy.

Standing

The second requirement for the Court to have jurisdiction is **standing**. This simply means that the court must determine whether the individual bringing the action has "alleged such a personal stake in the outcome of the controversy"[41] to make it actionable. There are four requirements for standing, and they are: (1) injury in fact, (2) individual harm, (3) causation, and (4) a "substantial likelihood" that the relief the moving party is seeking will remedy the harm claimed.

To demonstrate an injury in fact, a party could show either economic or noneconomic harm. "[A]t an irreducible minimum"[42] the party suing must have suffered a real, personal, or anticipated injury that can be attributed to the defendant's action.

justiciable   proper to be decided by a particular court; for example, a *justiciable controversy* is a real, rather than hypothetical, dispute. Federal courts may handle only cases that present a justiciable controversy.

declaratory judgment   a judicial opinion that states the rights of the parties or answers a legal question without awarding any damages or ordering that anything be done.

standing   a person's right to bring (start) or join a lawsuit because he or she is directly affected by the issues raised. This is called *standing to sue*.

The second element of standing involves an injury that is individualized to the party bringing the action. The Court has been reluctant to allow individuals to come to it with general grievances that are shared with the community at large. An example of this would be an individual taxpayer who brings an action to keep the government from using tax dollars for a program that the individual taxpayer does not support. The Court will refuse to hear this case, as the individual does not have a grievance that is sufficiently personal to establish standing. The grievance is one that is probably shared by a number of other taxpayers. The only exception to this idea that taxpayers generally do not have standing to challenge the government's use of tax dollars occurs when a taxpayer is suing to overturn a federal tax program that allegedly violates the Establishment Clause of the First Amendment.

Another example of a lack of standing due to the absence of individualized harm is an individual asserting legal rights on behalf of another. The courts have consistently dismissed lawsuits for a lack of standing when someone is asserting a third party's rights. This general rule will be followed unless there is a special relationship recognized by the courts. For example, an individual who has been appointed another's guardian does have the right to assert legal rights on behalf of that individual.

The third element of standing is causation. In order for an individual to successfully bring a lawsuit, that individual must be able to show a direct causal link between the alleged injury and the conduct alleged to give rise to the injury. In other words, the injury would not have occurred except for the defendant's action.

Lastly, the Court also requires that the party bringing the lawsuit must also be able to demonstrate that the relief being sought will remedy the harm created by the defendant.[43] If this element, as well as the other three is met, then a party has standing and will be allowed to proceed with the lawsuit.

One last issue regarding standing should be discussed. This issue involves the standing of an organization to either bring a lawsuit or assert rights on behalf of its members. Organizations do have standing to bring an action on behalf of its own members when "(a) its members would otherwise have standing to sue in their own right; (b) the interests it seeks to protect are germane to the organization's purpose; and (c) neither the claim asserted [n]or the relief requested, requires the participation of individual members in the lawsuit."[44]

In spite of the rules discussed, it has long been recognized that the Court may choose to disregard the principles of standing in cases involving exceptional circumstances.[45] The Court has also held that Congress may choose to pass legislation that gives standing in situations where the plaintiff might not otherwise have it. As the Court stated in *Warth v. Seldin,*

> *Congress may grant an express right of action to persons who otherwise would be barred by prudential standing rules. Of course, Article III's requirement remains: the plaintiff still must allege a distinct and palpable injury to himself, even if it is an injury shared by a large class of other possible litigants.*[46]

Mootness

The third requirement for jurisdiction involves the concept of mootness. A case becomes **moot** when an issue that is viable at the time the case is resolved or becomes so before the case can be heard and decided. The general rule is that the case and controversy requirement not only has to be met at the beginning of the lawsuit, but must exist throughout the entire time of litigation.[47] If this controversy ends, or the individual bringing the lawsuit no longer has a personal stake in the outcome of the lawsuit, the case is deemed to be moot and will be dismissed.

moot *moot* has several conflicting and overlapping definitions, including: no longer important or no longer needing a decision because already decided . . .; abstract; not a real case involving a real dispute.

There are several ways a case can become moot during litigation, including a change in the law,[48] a change in the status of the parties involved in the litigation,[49] or because one of the parties undertakes an action that dissolves or resolves the controversy.[50] Theoretically, if any of these three things happen, the case will be dismissed. There are, however, three exceptions that can be used to avoid dismissal.

The first exception applies in criminal cases. In some circumstances, a case is not moot even if a convicted defendant has served his sentence, as there may still be collateral legal issues to be resolved. The Court has said that a case "is moot only if it is shown that there is no possibility that any collateral legal consequences will be imposed on the basis of the challenged conviction."[51]

The second exception is the "voluntary cessation" exception. "Voluntary cessation" deals with situations in which the offending party has voluntarily stopped doing the offending behavior or action. Just because the activity has stopped does not mean that the offending party may not decide to resume the activity in the future. A case can only be moot in this situation when "there is no reasonable expectation that the wrong will be repeated."[52]

The last exception is one used in the famous case of *Roe v. Wade*.[53] While there was a challenge that the case was moot and should be dismissed, the Court declined to do so, relying on the exception made when the challenged action is too short in duration to allow the matter to be litigated before the issue becomes moot. The Court has referred to this type of dispute as "capable of repetition, but evading review."[54] In order for this exception to apply, it must be shown that the challenged action stopped or expired before there was time to litigate the matter and there is a reasonable expectation that the same complaining party will experience the same injurious action in the future.[55]

In summary, the federal courts will not hear moot cases. They require that the issues to be litigated be ongoing disputes and unless one of the above exceptions applies, the federal courts will dismiss any case that has become moot.

Ripeness

ripe a case is ripe for selection and decision by the U.S. Supreme Court if the legal issues involved are clear enough and well enough evolved and presented so that a clear decision can come out of the case. Any court or agency that has the power to turn down cases may use ripeness as a way of deciding whether to take the case. Ripeness also includes the idea that the case involves a real controversy, not merely potential harm.

While the other jurisdictional requirements address the issue and parties to the action, ripeness concerns the time frame when the lawsuit can be brought or will be heard. If a case is not **ripe**, the Court will refuse to hear it. In general, a challenge to a law will fail if the litigation is brought prior to enforcement of that law. This is because until the law is enforced, the litigant can only assert a belief that the law will cause an injury or violate a right[56] rather than an actual injury. The Court is unwilling to litigate an issue that has not yet arisen. This ties in closely with the requirement that an actual controversy must exist before the Court will hear a case. Again this underlines the Court's unwillingness to answer a hypothetical question.

In early cases regarding ripeness, the Court required that plaintiffs actually suffer injury in order to have their cases reviewed in the federal system. This was demonstrated in the case of *United Public Workers v. Mitchell*,[57] which involved a group of government employees who were forbidden, under the Hatch Act, to participate in various political activities. Only one individual in the group of plaintiffs had actually undertaken a political activity, but the rest of the group asserted a claim based on their desire to engage in such activity. The Court held that the issue was ripe only for the plaintiff who had actually engaged in prohibited political activity.

The Court has relaxed its rules regarding ripeness in recent years. Now, the ripeness requirement is met if the plaintiff can demonstrate a reasonable danger that an injury will occur as a result of a statute or rule's enforcement.

Nonjusticiable Political Questions

This concept has its origins in the famous case of *Marbury v. Madison*,[58] which will be discussed at length later in this chapter, but the doctrine was not presented as a separate doctrine until the 1849 case of *Luther v. Borden*.[59] This case involved competing political factions when the State of Rhode Island was forming its government. These two factions each wanted to be the lawful government of Rhode Island and went to the Court for a decision as to their respective legitimacy. The Court held that this was a state matter that should be decided within the state courts, however, Chief Justice Taney, who wrote the opinion, went on to discuss the nonjusticiability of this political question. He wrote that as far as the U.S. Constitution was concerned, Article IV, § 4 empowers the federal government to guarantee to each state a republican form of government and the clause further gives the power to do so to Congress.[60] Thus, it is Congress' power to determine which political faction was the legitimate state government. In *Luther*, the Court said:

> Under this article of the Constitution it rests with Congress to decide what government is the established one in a State. For as the United States guarantee to each State a republican government, Congress must necessarily decide what government is established in the State before it can determine whether it is republican or not. And when the senators and representatives of a State are admitted into the councils of the Union, the authority of the government under which they are appointed, as well as its republican character, is recognized by the proper constitutional authority. And its decision is binding on every other department of the government, and could not be questioned in a judicial tribunal.[61]

The Court also noted that when implementing this clause, Congress had given the executive branch the authority to protect the states against domestic violence by use of federal troops. The President had not actually sent troops into Rhode Island, but had pledged support to one of the political factions. Since the President pledged support if it were needed, the President had made a decision about the legitimacy of this political faction, and the Court held that this made the decision binding on them and therefore, nonjusticiable.

The current view of the political questions doctrine is found in the 1962 case of *Baker v. Carr*.[62] Justice Brennan wrote for the majority in that case and he said that the political questions doctrine denotes "[t]he relationship between the judiciary and the coordinate branches of the Federal Government, and not the federal judiciary's relationship to the States. . . ."[63] In doing so, the Court has now made the political questions doctrine "a function of the separation of powers."[64] Now when deciding whether an issue involves a nonjusticiable political question, the Court looks at the Constitution to determine whether the matter has been committed or given to another branch of the federal government. If it has been so committed, the Court will then look beyond the initial question to determine "whether the action of that branch exceeds whatever authority has been committed,"[65] and thus is subject to constitutional interpretation. Justice Brennan noted that there are several formulations for determining whether an issue is a political question, but then identified common elements of each formulation:

> Prominent on the surface of any case held to involve a political question is found a textually demonstrable constitutional commitment of the issue to a coordinate political department; or a lack of judicially discoverable and manageable standards for resolving it; or the impossibility of deciding without an initial policy determination of a kind clearly for nonjudicial discretion; or the

impossibility of a court's undertaking independent resolution without express-
ing lack of the respect due coordinate branches of government; or an unusual
need for unquestioning adherence to a political decision already made; or the
potentiality of embarrassment from multifarious pronouncements by various
departments on the question.[66]

In that particular case, none of these factors applied and the Court was left with a nonjusticiable political question.

The political questions doctrine came up again in the subsequent case of *Powell v. McCormack.*[67] In this case, the United States House of Representatives refused to seat Powell, a member-elect, because of his political views. The elected individual challenged the House's action and on its surface, this would appear to be a nonjusticiable political question. Chief Justice Warren wrote for the majority that held that the only factor to be used to determine whether this was a political question was whether there was a "textually demonstrable constitutional commitment"[68] to the House that allowed it the absolute or sole power to determine the qualifications of its members. After looking at the constitutional provision in question, the Court determined that the political questions doctrine did not bar review of the challenge to the House's action. While the Court agreed that the House had the constitutionally vested power to look at the age, residency, and citizenship of its members and exclude those who did not meet the requirements, the Court held that the House had exceeded its authority when it excluded a duly elected representative based on that individual's beliefs, conduct, or character. It now appears that the use of the political questions doctrine depends on whether the governmental body has exceeded the powers given to it under the Constitution.

The Court continues to use the political questions doctrine in a restrictive manner. It is now applied narrowly. The Court has consistently held that its job is to interpret statutes, treaties, executive agreements, and administrative rules and, while a case may have political overtones the Court has said, "we cannot shirk this responsibility merely because our decision may have significant political overtones."[69]

In summary, the Court currently will use the political questions doctrine to refuse review of a case if, first, it appears that the issue is one that has been committed to another branch of the federal government under the Constitution. In addition, the Court will also look to see if there are manageable standards that could be used by the Court to resolve the issue. If there are none, the Court will use the political questions doctrine and find the case nonjusticiable.

LIMITS ON JURISDICTION

habeas corpus (Latin) "You have the body." A judicial order to someone holding a person to bring that person to court. It is most often used to get a person out of unlawful imprisonment by forcing the captor and the person being held to come to court for a decision on the legality of the imprisonment or other holding (such as keeping a child when someone else claims custody).

Congress does have the power to limit the federal courts' jurisdiction. While there are limits on this power, Congress has exercised it in the past. An example of Congress' power to limit the Court's jurisdiction was found in the early case of *Ex Parte McCardle.*[70] This case involved a newspaper publisher who had been imprisoned for sedition during the post–Civil War era. His **habeas corpus** action was brought to the Court under an 1867 act of Congress that authorized the federal courts to grant habeas corpus to anyone imprisoned in violation of the Constitution. Before the Court could rule on this, however, Congress passed another act that revoked the federal courts' appellate jurisdiction over these types of cases. In doing so, Congress revoked the jurisdiction it had previously given the federal courts. The issue in this case is whether Congress has the authority to revoke such jurisdiction.

Ex Parte McCardle
74 U.S. 506 (1868)

The CHIEF JUSTICE delivered the opinion of the court.

The first question necessarily is that of jurisdiction; for, if the act of March 1868, takes away the jurisdiction defined by the act of February 1867, it is useless, if not improper, to enter into the discussion of other questions.

It is quite true, as was argued by the counsel for the petitioner, that the appellate jurisdiction of this court is not derived from acts of Congress. It is, strictly speaking, conferred by the Constitution. But it is conferred 'with such exceptions and under such regulations as Congress shall make.'

It is unnecessary to consider whether, if Congress had made no exceptions and no regulations, this court might not have exercised general appellate jurisdiction under rules prescribed by itself. For among the earliest acts of the first congress, at its first session, was the act of September 24th, 1789, to establish the judicial courts of the United States. That act provided for the organization of this court, and prescribed regulations for the exercise of its jurisdiction.

The source of that jurisdiction, and the limitations of it by the Constitution and by statute, have been on several occasions subjects of consideration here. In the case of *Durousseau v. The United States*, particularly, the whole matter was carefully examined, and the court held, that while 'the appellate powers of this court are not given by the judicial act, but are given by the Constitution,' they are nevertheless, 'limited and regulated by that act, and by such other acts as have been passed on the subject.' The court said, further, that the judicial act was an exercise of the power given by the Constitution to Congress 'of making exceptions to the appellate jurisdiction of the Supreme Court.' 'They have described affirmatively,' said the court, 'its jurisdiction, and this affirmative description has been understood to imply a negation of the exercise of such appellate power as is not comprehended within it.'

The principle that the affirmation of appellate jurisdiction implies the negation of all such jurisdiction not affirmed having been thus established, it was an almost necessary consequence that acts of Congress, providing for the exercise of jurisdiction should come to be spoken of as acts granting jurisdiction, and not as acts making exceptions to the constitutional grant of it.

The exception to appellate jurisdiction in the case before us, however, is not an inference from the affirmation of other appellate jurisdiction. It is made in terms. The provision of the act of 1867, affirming the appellate jurisdiction of this court in cases of *habeas corpus* is expressly repealed. It is hardly possible to imagine a plainer instance of positive exception.

We are not at liberty to inquire into the motives of the legislature. We can only examine into its power under the Constitution; and the power to make exceptions to the appellate jurisdiction of this court is given by express words.

What, then, is the effect of the repealing act upon the case before us? We cannot doubt as to this. Without jurisdiction the court cannot proceed at all in any cause. Jurisdiction is the power to declare the law, and when it ceases to exist, the only function remaining to the court is that of announcing the fact and dismissing the cause. And this is not less clear upon authority than upon principle.

Several cases were cited by the counsel for the petitioner in support of the position that jurisdiction of this case is not affected by the repealing act. But none of them, in our judgment, afforded any support to it. They are all cases of the exercise of judicial power by the legislature, or of legislative interference with courts in the exercising of continuing jurisdiction.

On the other hand, the general rule, supported by the best elementary writers, is, that 'when an act of the legislature is repealed, it must be considered, except as to transactions past and closed, as if it never existed.' And the effect of repealing acts upon suits under acts repealed, has been determined by the adjudications of this court. The subject was fully considered in *Norris v. Crecker*, and more recently in *Insurance Company v. Ritchie*. In both of these cases it was held that no judgment could be rendered in a suit after the repeal of the act under which it was brought and prosecuted.

Continued

It is quite clear, therefore, that this court cannot proceed to pronounce judgment in this case, for it has no longer jurisdiction of the appeal; and judicial duty is not less fitly performed by declining ungranted jurisdiction than in exercising firmly that which the Constitution and the laws confer.

Counsel seem to have supposed, if effect be given to the repealing act in question, that the whole appellate power of the court, in cases of *habeas corpus*, is denied. But this is an error. The act of 1868 does not except from that jurisdiction any cases but appeals from Circuit Courts under the act of 1867. It does not affect the jurisdiction which was previously exercised.

The appeal of the petitioner in this case must be

DISMISSED FOR WANT OF JURISDICTION.

The Court held that Congress did have the authority to revoke or withdraw jurisdiction previously granted. Congress does have the power to limit or expand the appellate jurisdiction of the federal courts as Article III, § 2 not only grants the courts the power of appellate jurisdiction, it also makes this power subject to any exception or regulation Congress may make. This case did not impact the federal courts' original jurisdiction or affect the courts' appellate jurisdiction in other types of cases.

Congress' ability to limit the federal courts' jurisdiction is not without limits. This is demonstrated in the case of *United States v. Klein*[71] in which the Court was asked to decide whether Congress had the constitutional power to enact a statute that limits the jurisdiction of the federal courts when in doing so, Congress dictates the outcome of a particular case.

UNITED STATES V. KLEIN

December Term, 1871

The CHIEF JUSTICE delivered the opinion of the court.

The general question in this case is whether or not the proviso relating to suits for the proceeds of abandoned and captured property in the Court of Claims, contained in the appropriation act of July 12th, 1870, debars the defendant in error from recovering, as administrator of V.F. Wilson, deceased, the proceeds of certain cotton belonging to the decedent, which came into the possession of the agents of the Treasury Department as captured or abandoned property, and the proceeds of which were paid by them according to law into the Treasury of the United States.

The answer to this question requires a consideration of the rights of property, as affected by the late civil war, in the hands of citizens engaged in hostilities against the United States.

It may be said in general terms that property in the insurgent States may be distributed into four classes:

1st. That which belonged to the hostile organizations or was employed in actual hostilities on land.
2d. That which at sea became lawful subject of capture and prize.
3d. That which became the subject of confiscation.
4th. A peculiar description, known only in the recent war, called captured and abandoned property.

The first of these descriptions of property, like property of other like kind in ordinary international wars, became, wherever taken, *ipso facto*, the property of the United States.

The second of these descriptions comprehends ships and vessels with their cargoes belonging to the insurgents or employed in aid of them; but property in these was not changed by capture alone but by regular judicial proceeding and sentence.

Accordingly it was provided in the Abandoned and Captured Property Act of March 12th, 1863, that the property to be collected under it 'shall not include any kind or description used or intended to be used for carrying on war against the

Continued

United States, such as arms, ordnance, ships, steamboats and their furniture, forage, military supplies, or munitions of war.'

Almost all the property of the people in the insurgent States was included in the third description, for after sixty days from the date of the President's proclamation of July 25th, 1862, all the estates and property of those who did not cease to aid, countenance, and abet the rebellion became liable to seizure and confiscation, and it was made the duty of the President to cause the same to be seized and applied, either specifically or in the proceeds thereof, to the support of the army. But it is to be observed that tribunals and proceedings were provided, by which alone such property could be condemned, and without which it remained unaffected in the possession of the proprietors.

It is thus seen that, except to property used in actual hostilities, as mentioned in the first section of the act of March 12th, 1863, no titles were divested in the insurgent States unless in pursuance of a judgment rendered after due legal proceedings. The government recognized to the fullest extent the humane maxims of the modern law of nations, which exempt private property of non-combatant enemies from capture as booty of war. Even the law of confiscation was sparingly applied. The cases were few indeed in which the property of any not engaged in actual hostilities was subjected to seizure and sale.

The spirit which animated the government received special illustration from the act under which the present case arose. We have called the property taken into the custody of public officers under that act a peculiar species, and it was so. There is, so far as we are aware, no similar legislation mentioned in history.

The act directs the officers of the Treasury Department to take into their possession and make sale of all property abandoned by its owners or captured by the national forces, and to pay the proceeds into the national treasury.

That it was not the intention of Congress that the title to these proceeds should be divested absolutely out of the original owners of the property seems clear upon a comparison of different parts of the act.

[I]t is reasonable to infer that it was the purpose of Congress that the proceeds of the property for which the special provision of the act was made should go into the treasury without change of ownership. Certainly such was the intention in respect to the property of loyal men. That the same intention prevailed in regard to the property of owners who, though then hostile, might subsequently become loyal, appears probable from the circumstance that no provision is anywhere made for confiscation of it; while there is no trace in the statute book of intention to divest ownership of private property not excepted from the effect of this act, otherwise than by proceedings for confiscation.

* * *

This language makes the right to the remedy dependent upon proof of loyalty, but implies that there may be proof of ownership without proof of loyalty. The property of the original owner is, in no case, absolutely divested. There is, as we have already observed, no confiscation, but the proceeds of the property have passed into the possession of the government, and restoration of the property is pledged to none except to those who have continually adhered to the government. Whether restoration will be made to others, or confiscation will be enforced, is left to be determined by considerations of public policy subsequently to be developed.

* * *

The proclamation of pardon, by a qualifying proclamation issued on the 26th of March, 1864, was limited to those persons only who, being yet at large and free from confinement or duress, shall voluntarily come forward and take the said oath with the purpose of restoring peace and establishing the national authority.

On the 29th of May, 1865, amnesty and pardon, with the restoration of the rights of property except as to slaves, and that as to which legal proceedings had been instituted under laws of the United States, were again offered to all who had, directly or indirectly, participated in the rebellion, except certain persons included in fourteen classes. All who embraced this offer were required to take and subscribe an oath of like tenor with that required by the first proclamation.

On the 7th of September, 1867, still another proclamation was issued, offering pardon and amnesty, with restoration of property, as before and on the same oath, to all but three excepted classes.

Continued

And finally, on the 4th of July, 1868, a full pardon and amnesty was granted, with some exceptions, and on the 25th of December, 1868, without exception, unconditionally and without reservation, to all who had participated in the rebellion, with restoration of rights of property as before. No oath was required.

It is true that the section of the act of Congress which purported to authorize the proclamation of pardon and amnesty by the President was repealed on the 21st of January, 1867; but this was after the close of the war, when the act had ceased to be important as an expression of the legislative disposition to carry into effect the clemency of the Executive, and after the decision of this court that the President's power of pardon 'is not subject to legislation;' that 'Congress can neither limit the effect of his pardon, nor exclude from its exercise any class of offenders . . .' The repeal of the section in no respect changes the national obligation, for it does not alter at all the operation of the pardon, or reduce in any degree the obligations of Congress under the Constitution to give full effect to it, if necessary, by legislation.

We conclude, therefore, that the title to the proceeds of the property which came to the possession of the government by capture or abandonment, with the exceptions already noticed, was in no case divested out of the original owner. It was for the government itself to determine whether these proceeds should be restored to the owner or not. The promise of the restoration of all rights of property decides that question affirmatively as to all persons who availed themselves of the proffered pardon.

✳ ✳ ✳

What, then, was the effect of the provision of the act of 1870 upon the right of the owner of the cotton in this case? He had done certain acts which this court has adjudged to be acts in aid of the rebellion; but he abandoned the cotton to the agent of the Treasury Department, by whom it has been sold and the proceeds paid into the Treasury of the United States; and he took, and has not violated, the amnesty oath under the President's proclamation. Upon this case the Court of Claims pronounced him entitled to a judgment for the net proceeds in the treasury. This decree was rendered on the 26th of May, 1869; the appeal to this court made on the 3d of June, and was filed here on the 11th of December, 1869.

✳ ✳ ✳

Soon afterwards the provision in question was introduced as a proviso to the clause in the general appropriation bill, appropriating a sum of money for the payment of judgments of the Court of Claims, and became a part of the act, with perhaps little consideration in either House of Congress.

This proviso declares in substance that no pardon, acceptance, oath, or other act performed in pursuance, or as a condition of pardon, shall be admissible in evidence in support of any claim against the United States in the Court of Claims . . . Proof of loyalty is required to be made according to the provisions of certain statutes, irrespective of the effect of any executive proclamation, pardon, or amnesty, or act of oblivion; and when judgment has been already rendered on other proof of loyalty, the Supreme Court, on appeal, shall have no further jurisdiction of the cause, and shall dismiss the same for want of jurisdiction.

✳ ✳ ✳

The substance of this enactment is that an acceptance of a pardon, without disclaimer, shall be conclusive evidence of the acts pardoned, but shall be null and void as evidence of the rights conferred by it, both in the Court of Claims and in this court on appeal.

It was urged in argument that the right to sue the government in the Court of Claims is a matter of favor; but this seems not entirely accurate. It is as much the duty of the government as of individuals to fulfill its obligations. Before the establishment of the Court of Claims claimants could only be heard by Congress. That court was established in 1855 for the triple purpose of relieving Congress, and of protecting the government by regular investigation, and of benefitting the claimants by affording them a certain mode of examining and adjudicating upon their claims. It was required to hear and determine upon claims founded upon any law of Congress, or upon any regulation of an executive department, or upon any contract, express or implied, with the government of the United States. Originally it was a court merely in name, for its power extended only to the preparation of bills to be submitted to Congress.

In 1863 the number of judges was increased from three to five, its jurisdiction was enlarged, and, instead of being required to prepare bills for

Continued

Congress, it was authorized to render final judgment, subject to appeal to this court and to an estimate by the Secretary of the Treasury of the amount required to pay each claimant. This court being of opinion that the provision for an estimate was inconsistent with the finality essential to judicial decisions, Congress repealed that provision. Since then the Court of Claims has exercised all the functions of a court, and this court has taken full jurisdiction on appeal.

The Court of Claims is thus constituted one of those inferior courts which Congress authorizes, and has jurisdiction of contracts between the government and the citizen, from which appeal regularly lies to this court.

Undoubtedly the legislature has complete control over the organization and existence of that court and may confer or withhold the right of appeal from its decisions. And if this act did nothing more, it would be our duty to give it effect. If it simply denied the right of appeal in a particular class of cases, there could be no doubt that it must be regarded as an exercise of the power of Congress to make 'such exceptions from the appellate jurisdiction' as should seem to it expedient.

But the language of the proviso shows plainly that it does not intend to withhold appellate jurisdiction except as a means to an end. Its great and controlling purpose is to deny to pardons granted by the President the effect which this court had adjudged them to have. The proviso declares that pardons shall not be considered by this court on appeal. We had already decided that it was our duty to consider them and give them effect, in cases like the present, as equivalent to proof of loyalty. It provides that whenever it shall appear that any judgment of the Court of Claims shall have been founded on such pardons, without other proof of loyalty, the Supreme Court shall have no further jurisdiction of the case and shall dismiss the same for want of jurisdiction. The proviso further declares that every pardon granted to any suitor in the Court of Claims and reciting that the person pardoned has been guilty of any act of rebellion or disloyalty, shall, if accepted in writing without disclaimer of the fact recited, be taken as conclusive evidence in that court and on appeal, of the act recited; and on proof of pardon or acceptance, summarily made on motion or otherwise, the jurisdiction of the court shall cease and the suit shall be forthwith dismissed.

* * *

It seems to us that this is not an exercise of the acknowledged power of Congress to make exceptions and prescribe regulations to the appellate power.

The court is required to ascertain the existence of certain facts and thereupon to declare that its jurisdiction on appeal has ceased, by dismissing the bill. What is this but to prescribe a rule for the decision of a cause in a particular way? In the case before us, the Court of Claims has rendered judgment for the claimant and an appeal has been taken to this court. We are directed to dismiss the appeal, if we find that the judgment must be affirmed, because of a pardon granted to the intestate of the claimants. Can we do so without allowing one party to the controversy to decide it in its own favor? Can we do so without allowing that the legislature may prescribe rules of decision to the Judicial Department of the government in cases pending before it?

We think not; and thus thinking, we do not at all question what was decided in the case of *Pennsylvania v. Wheeling Bridge Company*. In that case, after a decree in this court that the bridge, in the then state of the law, was a nuisance and must be abated as such, Congress passed an act legalizing the structure and making it a post-road; and the court, on a motion for process to enforce the decree, held that the bridge had ceased to be a nuisance by the exercise of the constitutional powers of Congress, and denied the motion. No arbitrary rule of decision was prescribed in that case, but the court was left to apply its ordinary rules to the new circumstances created by the act. In the case before us no new circumstances have been created by legislation. But the court is forbidden to give the effect to evidence which, in its own judgment, such evidence should have, and is directed to give it an effect precisely contrary.

We must think that Congress has inadvertently passed the limit which separates the legislative from the judicial power.

It is of vital importance that these powers be kept distinct. The Constitution provides that the judicial power of the United States shall be vested in one Supreme Court and such inferior courts as the Congress shall from time to time ordain and establish. The same instrument, in the last clause of the same article, provides that in all cases other than those of original jurisdiction, 'the Supreme Court shall have appellate

Continued

jurisdiction both as to law and fact, with such exceptions and under such regulations as the Congress shall make.'

Congress has already provided that the Supreme Court shall have jurisdiction of the judgments of the Court of Claims on appeal. Can it prescribe a rule in conformity with which the court must deny to itself the jurisdiction thus conferred, because and only because its decision, in accordance with settled law, must be adverse to the government and favorable to the suitor? This question seems to us to answer itself.

The rule prescribed is also liable to just exception as impairing the effect of a pardon, and thus infringing the constitutional power of the Executive.

It is the intention of the Constitution that each of the great co-ordinate departments of the government—the Legislative, the Executive, and the Judicial—shall be, in its sphere, independent of the others. To the executive alone is intrusted [sic] the power of pardon; and it is granted without limit. Pardon includes amnesty. It blots out the offence pardoned and removes all its penal consequences. It may be granted on conditions. In these particular pardons, that no doubt might exist as to their character, restoration of property was expressly pledged, and the pardon was granted on condition that the person who availed himself of it should take and keep a prescribed oath.

Now it is clear that the legislature cannot change the effect of such a pardon any more than the executive can change a law. Yet this is attempted by the provision under consideration. The court is required to receive special pardons as evidence of guilt and to treat them as null and void. It is required to disregard pardons granted by proclamation on condition, though the condition has been fulfilled, and to deny them their legal effect. This certainly impairs the executive authority and directs the court to be instrumental to that end.

We think it unnecessary to enlarge. The simplest statement is the best.

We repeat that it is impossible to believe that this provision was not inserted in the appropriation bill through inadvertence; and that we shall not best fulfill the deliberate will of the legislature by DENYING the motion to dismiss and AFFIRMING the judgment of the Court of Claims; which is

ACCORDINGLY DONE.

In deciding the case in this manner, the Court reinforced the separation of powers concept and rejected Congress' attempt to dictate the outcome of this case. If the Court had upheld the congressional action it would have, in effect, allowed Congress to dictate the judgments of the Court.

The lesson to be learned from these two cases is that in order for Congress to limit the federal courts' jurisdiction, it must do so in a neutral manner. If the manner is neutral, as demonstrated in *Ex parte McCardle*, the Court will allow the limitation, but if it is intended to produce a particular outcome, the limitation will not be upheld.

The current view of the congressional power to limit the federal courts' jurisdiction includes not only the above principles, but also allows for congressional acts that restrict the federal courts' jurisdiction to hear particular types of cases, so long as the congressional acts leave the state court option available to the prospective plaintiffs. It is also worth noting that if Congress attempted to eliminate any type of jurisdiction in all courts, this would be unconstitutional.

TAKING THE CASE TO THE SUPREME COURT

Often people are overheard declaring "I'm going to take my case all the way to the Supreme Court." While many would like to do so, it is not as easy as the declaration makes it seem. The first step to perfecting an appeal to the Court is to file a petition for a Writ of Certiorari. The Court receives hundreds of these petitions a year, and it must sort through the petitions and determine which are worthy of review. It is not possible for the Court to hear each and every one of these cases, and so it has developed criteria for making the decision. Supreme Court Rule 10 states "Review on a writ of certiorari is not a matter of right, but of judicial discretion. A petition for a writ of certiorari will be granted only for compelling reasons."[72] This rule goes on to outline reasons why the Court would consider granting a petition for a Writ of Certiorari. They include:

(a) a United States court of appeals has entered a decision in conflict with the decision of another United States court of appeals on the same important matter; has decided an important federal question in a way that conflicts with a decision by a state court of last resort; or has so far departed from the accepted and usual course of judicial proceedings, or sanctioned such a departure by a lower court, as to call for an exercise of this Court's supervisory power;

(b) a state court of last resort has decided an important federal question in a way that conflicts with the decision of another state court of last resort or of a United States court of appeals;

(c) a state court or a United States court of appeals has decided an important question of federal law that has not been, but should be, settled by this Court, or has decided an important federal question in a way that conflicts with relevant decisions of this Court.[73]

The Court will decide if the petition meets any of these criteria by reviewing it. To qualify for this review, however, Supreme Court Rules require a petitioner to file the petition for Writ of Certiorari with the Supreme Court Clerk within 90 days after the entry of judgment by a lower court,[74] unless an extension for an additional 60 days is granted by one of the Justices. A Justice will only do so for good cause. A petitioner must file 40 copies of the petition with the Clerk and once the Clerk determines that the petition is in compliance with the rules, the case will be placed on the docket for consideration.[75]

The Clerk will review the contents of the petition when making this determination. Supreme Court Rule 14 outlines what the petition must contain. The list includes the questions presented for review, a list of all the parties to the proceedings, a table of contents if the petition exceeds five pages in length, citations of the official and unofficial reports of the opinions and orders entered in the case by a lower court or administrative agency, a concise statement of the jurisdictional basis for Supreme Court review, the constitutional provisions, treaties, or ordinances involved in the case, a concise statement of the facts of the case, a concise statement of the arguments or reasons relied on for the allowance of the Writ of Certiorari, and any other materials essential to understand the petition.[76]

Once the Clerk determines that the petition is in compliance with the rules and places it on the docket, the justices will review the petition and vote on whether to accept the case for review by using the **rule of four**. This rule dictates that if four of the nine justices vote in favor of reviewing the case, the Clerk of the Court will prepare, sign, and enter an order granting the Writ of **Certiorari** and notify counsel of record as well as the court whose judgment is being reviewed.[77] If three or fewer justices vote in favor of review, the Court will deny the petition and the Clerk will prepare an order to that effect and notify the same parties as noted above. Once the parties and the lower court have been notified, the Clerk will request that the clerk of the lower court certify and transmit the record of the case and the case will be scheduled for briefing and oral argument.[78]

rule of four the principle that if at least four of the nine U.S. Supreme Court Justices vote to take a case, the court will hear the case; the Court uses the *rule of four* for cases that reach the Court by certiorari.

certiorari (Latin) "To make sure." A request for *certiorari* (or "cert." for short) is like an appeal, but one which the higher court is not required to take for decision; it is literally a writ from the higher court asking the lower court for the record of the case.

STANDARDS OF REVIEW

Once the Court has issued the Writ of Certiorari and agreed to review the case, the next question to be asked is what standard will the Court use to decide the issues presented. There are three potential standards of review and these standards will be found throughout the course of this textbook as well as any other discussion of constitutional issues. The easiest of the three standards is the

rational basis test   the principle that a court should not second-guess a legislature (or an administrative agency) about the wisdom of a law (or of an administrative decision) if the law (or decision) has some *rational basis*.

mere rationality standard, often called the **rational basis test**. This standard requires the Court to uphold the government action if two criteria are met. First, the Court will look to see if the government is pursuing a legitimate government interest. In most instances, if the government is regulating on the basis of health, safety, or public welfare, the Court will find a legitimate government interest. Second, there must be a rational relationship between the means chosen by the government to regulate and the stated objective of the regulation. This rational relationship will be found barring a government action that is arbitrary or capricious. The types of cases when this standard will be used include Dormant Commerce Clause cases, substantive due process cases, equal protection cases, and Contract Clause cases.

When deciding a Dormant Commerce Clause case, the Court will determine whether the state regulation affects interstate commerce and thus violates the Commerce Clause. To do so, the Court determines whether the state regulation serves a legitimate state interest and if there is a rational relationship between the regulation and the goal of that regulation.

With substantive due process cases, the Court first looks to see if there is a fundamental right being affected by the state regulation. If there is, one of the other two standards of review will be used. If not, as in the case of most economic regulations, the Court will use the mere rationality standard to review the state regulation.

Equal protection cases will be reviewed by the mere rationality standard so long as the case does not involve a suspect or quasi-suspect classification as part of the state regulation. The Court looks carefully to be sure that there is no impact on a fundamental right by the state regulation, and if not, as in the case of most economic regulations and nonfundamental rights cases, the Court will use the mere rationality standard of review. Lastly, Contract Clause cases traditionally use the mere rationality standard.

The second standard of review is middle-level, or mid-level review. With this standard, the government action or regulation has to be in place to meet an important governmental objective. This requirement is halfway between a legitimate governmental interest involved in the mere rationality standard and the compelling governmental interest required by the third standard of review, strict scrutiny. The middle-level standard requires that the governmental interest being promoted must be substantially related to an important governmental interest. This standard will be used in some kinds of equal protection cases, Contract Clause cases, and free expression, noncontent-based regulations. The types of equal protections cases using this standard involve semi-suspect classifications such as gender and illegitimacy. The free expression cases using this standard involve time, place, and manner regulations that are not based on the message the speaker is conveying. An example of this is the requirement of a parade permit. The permit is required not to regulate the message of the parade, but to ensure that traffic is not unduly obstructed, that there is a sufficient police presence for crowd control and directing traffic, and a for variety of other legitimate enforcement issues.

strict scrutiny   the principle that a state law (or an administrative agency regulation) that affects fundamental individual rights is valid only if it accomplishes compelling state objectives in the least restrictive way possible.

The third standard of review used by the Court is the **strict scrutiny** standard. This is the hardest of the standards to meet and is composed of two requirements. In order for a government action or regulation to pass the strict scrutiny standard, the government must show that there is a compelling government interest promoted by the action or regulation and that this action or regulation is necessary to accomplish the compelling goal. This means that a less restrictive means is not available to accomplish the same governmental goal. This standard will be used in cases involving substantive due process issues, cases involving fundamental rights, equal protection reviews, content-based freedom of expression cases, and freedom of religion cases.

THE WAYS THE COURT MAKES DECISIONS

There are three models of approaches used by the Court to make its decisions. These three models include the legally relevant model, the attitudinal model and the strategic model. Judges and justices are to leave their own personal views and political beliefs outside the courtroom, but then how do they make decisions? These three models will assist in understanding this process.

Legally Relevant Model Approaches

The legally relevant model emphasizes that the role of the judge or justice is to leave his or her personal beliefs out of any decisions he or she makes. There are six legally relevant approaches in this model. The first legally relevant approach is the concept of **stare decisis**. This Latin term is used interchangeably with the term *precedent*, and stands for the proposition that judges ought to look to previous decisions to decide cases that are similar in facts and issues. The value of this approach is that by using previous decisions, stability, predictability, and accountability to the law is promoted. By using this approach, those individuals in the justice system know how certain issues will be decided, how to draft an effective argument based on past decisions, and what laws will, in all likelihood, pass constitutional examination.

> **stare decisis** (Latin) "Let the decision stand." The rule that when a court has decided a case by applying a legal principle to a set of facts, the court should stick by the principle and apply it to all later cases with clearly similar facts unless there is a strong reason not to, and that courts below *must* apply the principle in similar cases.

While this seems to be ideal, there are critics of the concept of *stare decisis*. So many cases have been decided during the course of the country's judicial history that it is possible to find precedent to support almost any argument put forth by the litigants. Many would argue that this diminishes the value of precedent and makes the public skeptical of the value of court decisions.

Another interesting criticism of this approach comes from the Court itself. Justice Black, in *Green v. United States*,[79] criticized *stare decisis* in his dissent, saying:

> Ordinarily it is sound policy to adhere to prior decisions but this practice has quite properly never been a blind, inflexible rule. Courts are not omniscient. Like every other human agency, they too can profit from trial and error, from experience and reflection. As others have demonstrated, the principle commonly referred to as stare decisis has never been thought to extend so far as to prevent the courts from correcting their own errors. Accordingly, this Court has time and time again from the very beginning reconsidered the merits of its earlier decisions even though they claimed great longevity and repeated reaffirmation. Indeed, the Court has a special responsibility where questions of constitutional law are involved to review its decisions from time to time and where compelling reasons present themselves to refuse to follow erroneous precedents; otherwise its mistakes in interpreting the Constitution are extremely difficult to alleviate and needlessly so.[80]

Justice Black makes a point, and in fact, the Court has reversed its prior decisions when it has felt that such an outcome was warranted. While this may not happen with regularity, it is a tool in the Court's arsenal.

Another legally relevant approach is the *doctrine of original intent*. The idea behind this approach is that the judges should look to the intent of the Framers of the Constitution to make decisions. One of the most notorious cases using this approach is *Barron v. Baltimore*.[81] In this case, three individuals were challenging the taking of property by the City of Baltimore. They challenged the action using the Fifth Amendment to the Constitution that prohibits the taking of property without just compensation. The City of Baltimore claimed that the Fifth Amendment did not apply to state actions. Chief Justice Marshall wrote for the majority and noted that "[t]he constitution was ordained and established by the people of the United States for themselves, for their own government, and not for the government of the individual states."[82] Marshall then continued on to discuss the fact that some of the provisions of the constitution are couched in terms that show that they are applicable to the congress and others in more general terms indicate that they apply to the federal government in general. Ultimately, Marshall concluded, "These amendments contain no expression indicating an intention to apply them to state government. This court cannot so apply them."[83] In so holding, Marshall demonstrated a desire to follow the original intent of the Framers of the Constitution. The thought is that it is appropriate to follow the authors of the Constitution because these gentlemen acted in a thoughtful manner with every indication that they knew precisely what they were doing. With this in mind, there is no need to look for a means of making a decision using a method other than looking to the intent of the Framers. If an issue is such that it appears that the Framers may not have contemplated it, this point of view advocates that the decision-maker carefully look at the intent of the Framers and the appropriate decision will become apparent. The key here is to keep the decision-making process "value-free" as the Framers intended. In looking at the original intent when making decisions, the law remains stable.

This is not to say that there are not reasons to be critical of the original intent doctrine. Some legal scholars insist that the Constitution becomes useless if judges and justices adhere strictly to the original intent of the Framers. Many feel that the true genius of the Constitution is the fact that it is adaptable to current issues and societal problems. If a judge doggedly looks to the intent of the Framers, it is possible that this adaptability will be lost.

Another criticism of the original intent doctrine is the fact that it is often difficult to discern the intentions of the Framers. How can we discern this after two centuries? Of course one can always look to the writings of the Framers, the record of the debates that took place during the writing of the Constitution and other such documents, but taken as a whole, the intent of this group of individuals seems inconsistent. Justice Jackson in the case of *Youngstown Sheet & Tube Company v. Sawyer* noted this inconsistency.[84] In his concurring opinion he wrote:

> *Just what our forefathers did envision, or would have envisioned had they foreseen modern conditions, must be divined from materials almost as enigmatic as the dreams Joseph was called upon to interpret for Pharaoh. A century and a half of partisan debate and scholarly specification yields no net result but only supplies more or less apt quotations from respected sources on each side of any question. They largely cancel each other.*[85]

So, while the original intent doctrine may seem attractive, it does have its detractors and its limits. This may explain why there are other legally relevant approaches promoted by other legal scholars.

Literalism is another legally relevant approach to decision-making. This approach emphasizes the words of the Constitution itself, rather than the intent of the Constitution's Framers. The supporters of this approach believe judges and justices should consider only the meaning of the words of the Constitution when applying them to disputes. This can lead to inconsistent decisions and if taken to the extreme, lead to opinions that most would find to be unacceptable. For example, if one were to look at the Fourth Amendment language "no Warrants shall issue, but upon probable cause . . ."[86] and used the literalist approach to decision-making, one might conclude that none of the recognized search warrant exceptions could ever apply, however, this is just not so. There are several well-established exceptions to the warrant requirement that have withstood the Court's scrutiny.

While literalism is promoted as a value-free means of making important judicial decisions, this view has its critics as well. The first criticism is that English is an imprecise language at best. Words often have more than one meaning, there are idioms used in English that say one thing when they actually mean another, and a few words even have multiple meanings that may seem conflicting. To use literalism effectively, words could only have one precise meaning and would have to be used in a consistent manner. Otherwise, it would lead to inconsistent or even confusing decisions.

Another legally relevant approach is a combination of original intent and literalism. This approach, *meaning of the words*, asks decision-makers to look at the words found in the Constitution and interpret them according to their meaning at the time the Framers wrote them. Unlike the literalists, individuals adhering to the meaning of the words doctrine emphasize the common meaning of the words. This approach, too, is thought to be unbiased and untainted by an individual judge's or justice's personal values or opinions. Chief Justice Rehnquist provides an example of the meaning of the words approach in *Nixon v. United States*,[87] in which the Court was asked to rule on some procedural matters used by the Senate during Judge Walter Nixon's impeachment hearings. Nixon claimed that the Senate had violated the Impeachment Trial Clause of Article I, § 3, cl.6 of the Constitution, which grants the Senate the power to try all impeachments. The Senate had appointed a small committee to hear the impeachment matter, rather than submitting it to the entire Senate. Chief Justice Rehnquist examined the meaning of the word "try" when deciding whether the matter was properly before the Court. He wrote:

> Petitioner argues that the word "try" in the first sentence imposes by implication an additional requirement on the Senate in that the proceedings must be in the nature of a judicial trial. From there petitioner goes on to argue that this limitation precludes the Senate from delegating to a select committee the task of hearing the testimony of witnesses, as was done pursuant to Senate Rule XI. " '[T]ry' means more than simply 'vote on' or 'review' or 'judge.' In 1787 and today, trying a case means hearing the evidence, not scanning a cold record." Petitioner concludes from this that courts may review whether or not the Senate "tried" him before convicting him.

> There are several difficulties with this position which lead us ultimately to reject it. The word "try," both in 1787 and later, has considerably broader meanings than those to which petitioner would limit it. Older dictionaries define try as "[t]o examine" or "[t]o examine as a judge." In more modern usage the term has various meanings. For example, try can mean "to examine or investigate judicially," "to conduct the trial of," or "to put to the test by experiment, investigation, or trial."[88]

The Court ultimately held that the case was not justiciable, and reaffirmed the lower court's decision dismissing Nixon's action.

The fifth legally relevant approach is the *logical reasoning* approach, which promotes a reasoned or logical analysis as necessary in making a judicial decision. This approach is again designed to take the judge's or justice's own values, biases, and beliefs out of the decision-making process. The case of *Marbury v. Madison*[89] demonstrates the logical reasoning approach. If a decision is based on the logic-based analysis of a major premise, followed by a minor premise that leads to a conclusion, as was the situation in *Marbury*, the decision appears to be the result of a rational, almost scientific analysis. Chief Justice Marshall applied this analysis in *Marbury* when he used the major premise that "an act of the legislature, repugnant to the constitution, is void,"[90] and followed with the minor premise that the statutory act in question was "repugnant to the constitution." This led Chief Justice Marshall to the conclusion that the law in question was void or unconstitutional. Unfortunately, if the major premise is false or unsound, the rest of the argument and the conclusion will be false or unsound as well. This is the major criticism of the approach.

The last legally relevant approach is the **balancing approach**. Its advocates argue that because each case is unique, the method for deciding should not be based on the past or on a philosophical basis, but rather, the interests

balancing approach a doctrine in constitutional law that says a court should balance constitutional rights such as free speech against the right of the government to control conduct it calls harmful; any judicial decision-making principle that "balances rights and responsibilities."

of the individual should be weighed against the interests of the government. Whichever party can demonstrate that their interests are more important than the other will prevail. The problem with this approach is that there is conflict as to how this balancing ought to begin. There are those who would begin the balancing process by putting the individual on an equal footing with the government. Others would give preference to the individual and make the government begin at a disadvantage. Still others would give the advantage to the government and put the individual in an inferior position. Until this conflict can be resolved, the balancing approach remains unsettled.

Attitudinal Model Approaches

The second model of approaches to decision-making is, as noted, the attitudinal approaches or extralegal approaches. The attitudinal approaches exist because some believe that the legally relevant approaches do not fully explain the decision-making process. Those who argue for these approaches believe that the judges and justices cannot leave their personal beliefs and values aside when making a decision. Furthermore, under this approach public opinion plays a role in how cases are decided.

Two of the leading experts on this model, Jeffrey Segal and Harold Spaeth, claim "attitudinal factors are all that systematically explain the votes of the justices. With the exception of the solicitor General our empirical analyses find no other extra-attitudinal influences operating on a systematic level."[91] Thus, if a case is presented to the Court with two competing policy alternatives, a judge or justice will vote for the position that more closely matches his or her ideals or values. Studies by legal scholars suggest that individual justices are consistent in deciding cases according to their preferences. This is called the *preference-based approach*. Some scholars would go so far as to suggest that these preferences not only control the judge's or justice's decision, but that the only question left to be answered in most cases is exactly to what extent these preferences control the decision.

Some of the factors that seem to affect these preferences include political party affiliation, social background, other branches of the federal government, public opinion, and special interest groups. One scholar, Stuart S. Nagel, did a study in 1961 that indicated that there is a relationship between the judge's or justice's political party affiliation and the kinds of decisions made by that individual.[92] Another study done in 1970 by S. Sidney Ulmer found that a judge's or justice's social background could have an impact on the preference or attitudes when it comes to decision-making.[93]

Other branches of the federal government also play a role in the decisions made using the attitudinal model. The executive branch has an impact on decision-making by appointing judges to the federal bench who reflect the President's own ideology and agenda.

The legislative branch also plays a role in determining which appointees actually get confirmed to the bench. The Senate, or a majority of the Senators, can vote to confirm an individual who most closely reflects the ideology they find desirable. Congress as a whole also can influence the attitudes and preferences of the justices or judges from the standpoint that Congress can overrule Court decisions through the legislative process. Lastly, Congress has the power to set the salaries of the judges and justices in the federal system. Although Congress may not, according to the Constitution, lower a judge's or justice's salary during his or her tenure, Congress may choose not to give the judiciary a raise. Because of these things, the judges and justices in the federal system must take note of the preferences, values, and attitudes of the Congress.

Public opinion also influences the attitudes and preferences of the federal judiciary. Several studies suggest that the Court does pay attention to public opinion and the mood of the country.[94] So public opinion, no matter what the legally relevant advocates assert, does seem to have an impact on Supreme Court decisions.

When it comes to special interest groups, some scholars suggest that without these groups, there would be no cases or controversies for the courts to decide. Not only are special interest groups significant in that they often can be party to the action, but they also influence the courts through **amicus curiae** briefs. Caldeira and Wright's 1988 study shows that the greater number of *amicus curiae* briefs filed prior to a certiorari decision, the more likely that certiorari will be granted by the Court.[95]

Strategic Model

The strategic model combines elements of both the legally relevant model and the attitudinal model. With this model, the judges and justices use both the internal and external factors in the system to reach decisions.[96] This would suggest that, while the Court is not an isolated institution, it would allow for elements of both models to be relevant in the decision-making process.

Another view of the strategic model is that in addition to using both internal and external factors, the judges and justices also recognize that they are not reaching a decision in a vacuum. A justice of the Supreme Court must work with eight other justices in reaching a decision. The preferences of the other justices and the reality that these individuals will continue to work with one another must be taken into account when a justice takes a position on a particular matter.

Whichever model is used to explain the decision-making process of the Court, the important conclusion is that no one theory seems to explain all decisions. It is possible that the judges and justices use a variety of approaches in reaching decisions.

TYPES OF SUPREME COURT DECISIONS

Once the federal appellate courts (the federal circuit courts of appeal and the U.S. Supreme Court) have made a decision, the **opinions** of the courts are published. These published opinions fall into several categories, but four types of opinions typically are found in the published collections.

One type of opinion is binding on all lower courts and contains the **ratio decidendi** or rule of law on which a court's decision is founded, and is called the majority opinion. A judge or justice is assigned to author the opinion by the chief judge or the Chief Justice writes the **majority opinion**.

A judge or justice who disagrees with the decision reflected in the majority opinion writes the **dissenting opinion**. It is possible for a U.S. Supreme Court decision to have more than one dissenting opinion. **Concurring opinions** are opinions that agree with either the majority or the dissenting opinion's outcome, but for different reasons. As with the dissenting opinion, there can be more than one concurring opinion. A **per curiam opinion** is one that is written anonymously, but is unanimous.

JUDICIAL REVIEW

One of the most significant events in the judicial history of the United States is the decision in *Marbury v. Madison*,[97] in which the Court initially used the concept of **judicial review**. For the first time, the Court asserted that it was the final arbiter of what was or was not constitutional. The facts of this case involve Marbury, who was appointed to a judgeship by a lame-duck president. The outgoing President had made the appointment and the commission had been signed by the outgoing Secretary of State, but not delivered to Marbury

---

amicus curiae (Latin) "Friend of the court." A person allowed to give argument or appear in a lawsuit who is not a party to the lawsuit.

opinion a judge's statement of the decision he or she has reached in a case.

ratio decidendi (Latin) "Reason for decision." The *rationale* for a judge's holding; the basic ideas a judge uses to come to a decision in a case.

majority opinion written when over half of the judges in a case agree about both the result and the reasoning used to reach that result.

dissenting opinion a judge's formal disagreement (in writing) with the decision of the majority of the judges in a lawsuit.

concurring opinion opinion in which a judge agrees with the result reached in an opinion by another judge in the same case but not necessarily with the reasoning that the other judge used to reach the conclusion.

per curiam opinion "By the Court." Describes an opinion backed by all the judges in a particular court and usually with no one judge's name on it.

judicial review a court's power to declare a statute unconstitutional and to interpret laws; . . . A higher court's examination of a lower court's decision.

or any of the other "midnight judges." After President Jefferson had taken office, Marbury demanded that his Secretary of State, Madison, deliver the already signed commission. Madison refused to do so, and Marbury took his case directly to the U.S. Supreme Court.

WILLIAM MARBURY v. JAMES MADISON, SECRETARY OF STATE OF THE UNITED STATES
1 U.S. 137 [CRANCH] (1803)

February Term, 1803

Mr. Chief Justice MARSHALL delivered the opinion of the court.

At the last term, on the affidavits then read and filed with the clerk, a rule was granted in this case, requiring the secretary of state to show cause why a mandamus should not issue, directing him to deliver to William Marbury his commission as a justice of the peace for the county of Washington, in the district of Columbia.

No cause has been shown, and the present motion is for a mandamus. The peculiar delicacy of this case, the novelty of some of its circumstances, and the real difficulty attending the points which occur in it, require a complete exposition of the principles on which the opinion to be given by the court is founded.

＊ ＊ ＊

The government of the United States has been emphatically termed a government of laws, and not of men. It will certainly cease to deserve this high appellation, if the laws furnish no remedy for the violation of a vested legal right.

If this obloquy is to be cast on the jurisprudence of our country, it must arise from the peculiar character of the case.

It behoves [sic] us then to inquire whether there be in its composition any ingredient which shall exempt from legal investigation, or exclude the injured party from legal redress. In pursuing this inquiry the first question which presents itself, is, whether this can be arranged with that class of cases which come under the description of damnum absque injuria—a loss without an injury.

This description of cases never has been considered, and it is believed never can be considered as comprehending offices of trust, of honour [sic] or of profit. The office of justice of peace in the district of Columbia is such an office; it is therefore worthy of the attention and guardianship of the laws. It has received that attention and guardianship. It has been created by special act of congress, and has been secured, so far as the laws can give security to the person appointed to fill it, for five years. It is not then on account of the worthlessness of the thing pursued, that the injured party can be alleged to be without remedy.

＊ ＊ ＊

It follows then that the question, whether the legality of an act of the head of a department be examinable in a court of justice or not, must always depend on the nature of that act.

If some acts be examinable, and others not, there must be some rule of law to guide the court in the exercise of its jurisdiction.

In some instances there may be difficulty in applying the rule to particular cases; but there cannot, it is believed, be much difficulty in laying down the rule.

By the constitution of the United States, the president is invested with certain important political powers, in the exercise of which he is to use his own discretion, and is accountable only to his country in his political character, and to his own conscience. To aid him in the performance of these duties, he is authorized to appoint certain officers, who act by his authority and in conformity with his orders.

In such cases, their acts are his acts; and whatever opinion may be entertained of the manner in which executive discretion may be used, still there exists, and can exist, no power to control that discretion. The subjects are political. They respect the nation, not individual rights, and being entrusted to the executive, the decision of

Continued

the executive is conclusive. The application of this remark will be perceived by adverting to the act of congress for establishing the department of foreign affairs. This officer, as his duties were prescribed by that act, is to conform precisely to the will of the president. He is the mere organ by whom that will is communicated. The acts of such an officer, as an officer, can never be examinable by the courts.

But when the legislature proceeds to impose on that officer other duties; when he is directed peremptorily to perform certain acts; when the rights of individuals are dependent on the performance of those acts; he is so far the officer of the law; is amenable to the laws for his conduct; and cannot at his discretion sport away the vested rights of others.

The conclusion from this reasoning is, that where the heads of departments are the political or confidential agents of the executive, merely to execute the will of the president, or rather to act in cases in which the executive possesses a constitutional or legal discretion, nothing can be more perfectly clear than that their acts are only politically examinable. But where a specific duty is assigned by law, and individual rights depend upon the performance of that duty, it seems equally clear that the individual who considers himself injured has a right to resort to the laws of his country for a remedy.

If this be the rule, let us inquire how it applies to the case under the consideration of the court.

The power of nominating to the senate, and the power of appointing the person nominated, are political powers, to be exercised by the president according to his own discretion. When he has made an appointment, he has exercised his whole power, and his discretion has been completely applied to the case. If, by law, the officer be removable at the will of the president, then a new appointment may be immediately made, and the rights of the officer are terminated. But as a fact which has existed cannot be made never to have existed, the appointment cannot be annihilated; and consequently if the officer is by law not removable at the will of the president, the rights he has acquired are protected by the law, and are not resumable [sic] by the president. They cannot be extinguished by executive authority, and he has the privilege of asserting them in like manner as if they had been derived from any other source.

The question whether a right has vested or not, is, in its nature, judicial, and must be tried by the judicial authority, If, for example, Mr. Marbury had taken the oaths of a magistrate, and proceeded to act as one; in consequence of which a suit had been instituted against him, in which his defence [sic] had depended on his being a magistrate; the validity of his appointment must have been determined by judicial authority.

So, if he conceives that by virtue of his appointment he has a legal right either to the commission which has been made out for him or to a copy of that commission, it is equally a question examinable in a court, and the decision of the court upon it must depend on the opinion entertained of his appointment.

That question has been discussed, and the opinion is, that the latest point of time which can be taken as that at which the appointment was complete, and evidenced, was when, after the signature of the president, the seal of the United States was affixed to the commission.

It is then the opinion of the court,

1. That by signing the commission of Mr. Marbury, the president of the United States appointed him a justice of peace for the county of Washington in the district of Columbia; and that the seal of the United States, affixed thereto by the secretary of state, is conclusive testimony of the verity of the signature, and of the completion of the appointment; and that the appointment conferred on him a legal right to the office for the space of five years.
2. That, having this legal title to the office, he has a consequent right to the commission; a refusal to deliver which is a plain violation of that right, for which the laws of his country afford him a remedy.

It remains to be inquired whether,

3. He is entitled to the remedy for which he applies. This depends on,
   1. The nature of the writ applied for. And,
   2. The power of this court.

1. The nature of the writ.

Blackstone, in the third volume of his Commentaries, page 110, defines a mandamus to be, 'a command issuing in the king's name from the court of king's bench, and directed to any person, corporation, or inferior court of judicature within the king's dominions, requiring them to

Continued

do some particular thing therein specified which appertains to their office and duty, and which the court of king's bench has previously determined, or at least supposes, to be consonant to right and justice.'

* * *

This writ, if awarded, would be directed to an officer of government, and its mandate to him would be, to use the words of Blackstone, 'to do a particular thing therein specified, which appertains to his office and duty, and which the court has previously determined or at least supposes to be consonant to right and justice.' Or, in the words of Lord Mansfield, the applicant, in this case, has a right to execute an office of public concern, and is kept out of possession of that right.

These circumstances certainly concur in this case.

Still, to render the mandamus a proper remedy, the officer to whom it is to be directed, must be one to whom, on legal principles, such writ may be directed; and the person applying for it must be without any other specific and legal remedy.

* * *

It is scarcely necessary for the court to disclaim all pretensions to such a jurisdiction. An extravagance, so absurd and excessive, could not have been entertained for a moment. The province of the court is, solely, to decide on the rights of individuals, not to inquire how the executive, or executive officers, perform duties in which they have a discretion. Questions, in their nature political, or which are, by the constitution and laws, submitted to the executive, can never be made in this court.

* * *

But where he is directed by law to do a certain act affecting the absolute rights of individuals, in the performance of which he is not placed under the particular direction of the president, and the performance of which the president cannot lawfully forbid, and therefore is never presumed to have forbidden; as for example, to record a commission, or a patent for land, which has received all the legal solemnities; or to give a copy of such record; in such cases, it is not perceived on what ground the courts of the country are further excused from the duty of giving judgment, that right to be done to an injured individual, than if the same services were to be performed by a person not the head of a department.

This opinion seems not now for the first time to be taken up in this country.

It must be well recollected that in 1792 an act passed, directing the secretary at war to place on the pension list such disabled officers and soldiers as should be reported to him by the circuit courts, which act, so far as the duty was imposed on the courts, was deemed unconstitutional; but some of the judges, thinking that the law might be executed by them in the character of commissioners, proceeded to act and to report in that character.

This law being deemed unconstitutional at the circuits, was repealed, and a different system was established; but the question whether those persons, who had been reported by the judges, as commissioners, were entitled, in consequence of that report, to be placed on the pension list, was a legal question, properly determinable in the courts, although the act of placing such persons on the list was to be performed by the head of a department.

* * *

There is, therefore, much reason to believe, that this mode of trying the legal right of the complainant, was deemed by the head of a department, and by the highest law officer of the United States, the most proper which could be selected for the purpose.

When the subject was brought before the court the decision was, not, that a mandamus would not lie to the head of a department, directing him to perform an act, enjoined by law, in the performance of which an individual had a vested interest; but that a mandamus ought not to issue in that case—the decision necessarily to be made if the report of the commissioners did not confer on the applicant a legal right.

The judgment in that case is understood to have decided the merits of all claims of that description; and the persons, on the report of the commissioners, found it necessary to pursue the mode prescribed by the law subsequent to that which had been deemed unconstitutional, in order to place themselves on the pension list.

The doctrine, therefore, now advanced is by no means a novel one.

Continued

* * *

The constitution vests the whole judicial power of the United States in one supreme court, and such inferior courts as congress shall, from time to time, ordain and establish. This power is expressly extended to all cases arising under the laws of the United States; and consequently, in some form, may be exercised over the present case; because the right claimed is given by a law of the United States.

In the distribution of this power it is declared that 'the supreme court shall have original jurisdiction in all cases affecting ambassadors, other public ministers and consuls, and those in which a state shall be a party. In all other cases, the supreme court shall have appellate jurisdiction.'

It has been insisted at the bar, that as the original grant of jurisdiction to the supreme and inferior courts is general, and the clause, assigning original jurisdiction to the supreme court, contains no negative or restrictive words; the power remains to the legislature to assign original jurisdiction to that court in other cases than those specified in the article which has been recited; provided those cases belong to the judicial power of the United States.

If it had been intended to leave it in the discretion of the legislature to apportion the judicial power between the supreme and inferior courts according to the will of that body, it would certainly have been useless to have proceeded further than to have defined the judicial power, and the tribunals in which it should be vested. The subsequent part of the section is mere surplusage, is entirely without meaning, if such is to be the construction. If congress remains at liberty to give this court appellate jurisdiction, where the constitution has declared their jurisdiction shall be original; and original jurisdiction where the constitution has declared it shall be appellate; the distribution of jurisdiction made in the constitution, is form without substance.

Affirmative words are often, in their operation, negative of other objects than those affirmed; and in this case, a negative or exclusive sense must be given to them or they have no operation at all.

It cannot be presumed that any clause in the constitution is intended to be without effect; and therefore such construction is inadmissible, unless the words require it.

* * *

When an instrument organizing fundamentally a judicial system, divides it into one supreme, and so many inferior courts as the legislature may ordain and establish; then enumerates its powers, and proceeds so far to distribute them, as to define the jurisdiction of the supreme court by declaring the cases in which it shall take original jurisdiction, and that in others it shall take appellate jurisdiction, the plain import of the words seems to be, that in one class of cases its jurisdiction is original, and not appellate; in the other it is appellate, and not original. If any other construction would render the clause inoperative, that is an additional reason for rejecting such other construction, and for adhering to the obvious meaning.

To enable this court then to issue a mandamus, it must be shown to be an exercise of appellate jurisdiction, or to be necessary to enable them to exercise appellate jurisdiction.

It has been stated at the bar that the appellate jurisdiction may be exercised in a variety of forms, and that if it be the will of the legislature that a mandamus should be used for that purpose, that will must be obeyed. This is true; yet the jurisdiction must be appellate, not original.

It is the essential criterion of appellate jurisdiction, that it revises and corrects the proceedings in a cause already instituted, and does not create that case. Although, therefore, a mandamus may be directed to courts, yet to issue such a writ to an officer for the delivery of a paper, is in effect the same as to sustain an original action for that paper, and therefore seems not to belong to appellate, but to original jurisdiction. Neither is it necessary in such a case as this, to enable the court to exercise its appellate jurisdiction.

The authority, therefore, given to the supreme court, by the act establishing the judicial courts of the United States, to issue writs of mandamus to public officers, appears not to be warranted by the constitution; and it becomes necessary to inquire whether a jurisdiction, so conferred, can be exercised.

The question, whether an act, repugnant to the constitution, can become the law of the land, is a question deeply interesting to the United States; but, happily, not of an intricacy proportioned to its interest. It seems only necessary to

Continued

recognise [sic] certain principles, supposed to have been long and well established, to decide it.

That the people have an original right to establish, for their future government, such principles as, in their opinion, shall most conduce to their own happiness, is the basis on which the whole American fabric has been erected. The exercise of this original right is a very great exertion; nor can it nor ought it to be frequently repeated. The principles, therefore, so established are deemed fundamental. And as the authority, from which they proceed, is supreme, and can seldom act, they are designed to be permanent.

This original and supreme will organizes the government, and assigns to different departments their respective powers. It may either stop here; or establish certain limits not to be transcended by those departments.

The government of the United States is of the latter description. The powers of the legislature are defined and limited; and that those limits may not be mistaken or forgotten, the constitution is written. To what purpose are powers limited, and to what purpose is that limitation committed to writing; if these limits may, at any time, be passed by those intended to be restrained? The distinction between a government with limited and unlimited powers is abolished, if those limits do not confine the persons on whom they are imposed, and if acts prohibited and acts allowed are of equal obligation. It is a proposition too plain to be contested, that the constitution controls any legislative act repugnant to it; or, that the legislature may alter the constitution by an ordinary act.

Between these alternatives there is no middle ground. The constitution is either a superior, paramount law, unchangeable by ordinary means, or it is on a level with ordinary legislative acts, and like other acts, is alterable when the legislature shall please to alter it.

If the former part of the alternative be true, then a legislative act contrary to the constitution is not law: if the latter part be true, then written constitutions are absurd attempts, on the part of the people, to limit a power in its own nature illimitable.

Certainly all those who have framed written constitutions contemplate them as forming the fundamental and paramount law of the nation, and consequently the theory of every such government must be, that an act of the legislature repugnant to the constitution is void.

This theory is essentially attached to a written constitution, and is consequently to be considered by this court as one of the fundamental principles of our society. It is not therefore to be lost sight of in the further consideration of this subject.

If an act of the legislature, repugnant to the constitution, is void, does it, notwithstanding its invalidity, bind the courts and oblige them to give it effect? Or, in other words, though it be not law, does it constitute a rule as operative as if it was a law? This would be to overthrow in fact what was established in theory; and would seem, at first view, an absurdity too gross to be insisted on. It shall, however, receive a more attentive consideration.

It is emphatically the province and duty of the judicial department to say what the law is. Those who apply the rule to particular cases, must of necessity expound and interpret that rule. If two laws conflict with each other, the courts must decide on the operation of each.

So if a law be in opposition to the constitution: if both the law and the constitution apply to a particular case, so that the court must either decide that case conformably to the law, disregarding the constitution; or conformably to the constitution, disregarding the law: the court must determine which of these conflicting rules governs the case. This is of the very essence of judicial duty.

* * *

Thus, the particular phraseology of the constitution of the United States confirms and strengthens the principle, supposed to be essential to all written constitutions, that a law repugnant to the constitution is void, and that courts, as well as other departments, are bound by that instrument.

The rule must be discharged.

It is apparent from the Court's discussion that the Court struggled with exactly how far its power extended. But, after reviewing the Judiciary Act of 1789 and the remedy it seemed to afford Marbury, and then looking at Article III, § 2 of the Constitution, the Court concluded that these two were in conflict and a determination had to be made as to which of these conflicting laws would prevail. Ultimately, the Court held that since the Constitution was the supreme will of the people of the United States, Congress could not simply change the Constitution by passing legislation. With this part of the decision made, the Court next made the statement discussed, *supra*, "an act of the legislature, repugnant to the constitution, is void."[98] The Court then went on to discuss the authority to make the decision as to what laws are repugnant and which are constitutionally permissible. The Court held "It is emphatically the province and duty of the judicial department to say what the law is. Those who apply the rule to particular cases, must of necessity expound and interpret that rule. If two laws conflict with each other, the courts must decide on the operation of each."[99] With this decision, the Court espoused the concept of judicial review for the first time and claimed its role in the federal government.

This, however, is not the last word on the concept of judicial review. The *Marbury* case spoke to the Court's power to review federal legislative acts, and there is little question about the Court's power to hear appeals from lower federal courts. However, that case did not talk about the Court's power to review state legislation or state court decisions or acts by the executive branch of the federal government. The question about the Court's power to review state legislation was answered in the 1810 case of *Fletcher v. Peck*.[100] This case involved a deed between John Peck and Robert Fletcher. Peck had purchased the property from James Gunn who had purchased it from the State of Georgia. Fletcher had, in turn, purchased the property from Peck, but found that there were several questions about the property title and a challenge that Georgia did not have the authority to sell the property. The Court began by acknowledging that Georgia had the power to dispose of unappropriated lands within its own borders. However, since the question alleged that the act was in violation of the Constitution, the Court had to examine the matter to decide if the law was "repugnant" to the Constitution and therefore, void. While the Court acknowledged its power to review this matter, it acknowledged that it was "a question of much delicacy, which ought seldom, if ever to be affirmative, in a doubtful case."[101] Ultimately, the Court held that the state constitution had not restricted the Georgia legislature's power to sell and convey this land, but this did not change the fact that the Court exercised its power of judicial review.

The power the Court used in *Fletcher* was extended within a few short years in the case of *Martin v. Hunter's Lessee*[102] in 1816. In this case, the Court was asked to review a state court decision regarding a Virginia statute. While the Court's appellate jurisdiction allows it to review federal questions or claims that a state law conflicts with the U.S. Constitution, the Court cannot adjudicate state issues. In the *Martin* case, the question before the Court was whether a Virginia statute conflicted with a federal treaty. Virginia argued that it was the state court's job to determine whether the state action violated the U.S. Constitution, but the Supreme Court disagreed.

MARTIN, *HEIR AT LAW AND DEVISEE OF* FAIRFAX V. HUNTER'S *LESSEE* 14 U.S. 304 (1816)

March 20, 1816

STORY, J., delivered the opinion of the court.

This is a writ of error from the court of appeals of Virginia, founded upon the refusal of that court to obey the mandate of this court, requiring the judgment rendered in this very cause, at February term, 1813, to be carried into due execution. The following is the judgment of the court of appeals rendered on the mandate: 'The court is unanimously of opinion, that the appellate power of the supreme court of the United States does not extend to this court, under a sound construction of the constitution of the United States; that so much of the 25th section of the act of congress to establish the judicial courts of the United States, as extends the appellate jurisdiction of the supreme court to this court, is not in pursuance of the constitution of the United States; that the writ of error, in this cause, was improvidently allowed under the authority of that act; that the proceedings thereon in the supreme court were, *coram non judice*, in relation to this court, and that obedience to its mandate be declined by the court.'

The questions involved in this judgment are of great importance and delicacy. Perhaps it is not too much to affirm, that, upon their right decision, rest some of the most solid principles which have hitherto been supposed to sustain and protect the constitution itself. The great respectability, too, of the court whose decisions we are called upon to review, and the entire deference which we entertain for the learning and ability of that court, add much to the difficulty of the task which has so unwelcomely fallen upon us. It is, however, a source of consolation, that we have had the assistance of most able and learned arguments to aid our inquiries; and that the opinion which is now to be pronounced has been weighed with every solicitude to come to a correct result, and matured after solemn deliberation.

Before proceeding to the principal questions, it may not be unfit to dispose of some preliminary considerations which have grown out of the arguments at the bar.

The constitution of the United States was ordained and established, not by the states in their sovereign capacities, but emphatically, as the preamble of the constitution declares, by 'the people of the United States.' There can be no doubt that it was competent to the people to invest the general government with all the powers which they might deem proper and necessary; to extend or restrain these powers according to their own good pleasure, and to give them a paramount and supreme authority. As little doubt can there be, that the people had a right to prohibit to the states the exercise of any powers which were, in their judgment, incompatible with the objects of the general compact; to make the powers of the state governments, in given cases, subordinate to those of the nation, or to reserve to themselves those sovereign authorities which they might not choose to delegate to either. The constitution was not, therefore, necessarily carved out of existing state sovereignties, nor a surrender of powers already existing in state institutions, for the powers of the states depend upon their own constitutions; and the people of every state had the right to modify and restrain them, according to their own views of the policy or principle. On the other hand, it is perfectly clear that the sovereign powers vested in the state governments, by their respective constitutions, remained unaltered and unimpaired, except so far as they were granted to the government of the United States.

* * *

The government, then, of the United States, can claim no powers which are not granted to it by the constitution, and the powers actually granted, must be such as are expressly given, or given by necessary implication. On the other hand, this instrument, like every other grant, is to have a reasonable construction, according to the import of its terms; and where a power is expressly given in general terms, it is not to be restrained to particular cases, unless that construction grow out of the context expressly, or by necessary implication. The words are to be taken in their natural and obvious sense, and not in a sense unreasonably restricted or enlarged.

The constitution unavoidably deals in general language. It did not suit the purposes of the people, in framing this great charter of our liberties, to provide for minute specifications of its powers, or to declare the means by which those

Continued

powers should be carried into execution. It was foreseen that this would be a perilous and difficult, if not an impracticable, task. The instrument was not intended to provide merely for the exigencies of a few years, but was to endure through a long lapse of ages, the events of which were locked up in the inscrutable purposes of Providence. It could not be foreseen what new changes and modifications of power might be indispensable to effectuate the general objects of the charter; and restrictions and specifications, which, at the present, might seem salutary, might, in the end, prove the overthrow of the system itself. Hence its powers are expressed in genetal [sic] terms, leaving to the legislature, from time to time, to adopt its own means to effectuate legitimate objects, and to mould and model the exercise of its powers, as its own wisdom, and the public interests, should require.

* * *

The third article of the constitution is that which must principally attract our attention. The 1st. section declares, 'the judicial power of the United States shall be vested in one supreme court, and in such other inferior courts as the congress may, from time to time, ordain and establish.' The 2d section declares, that 'the judicial power shall extend to all cases in law or equity, arising under this constitution, the laws of the United States, and the treaties made, or which shall be made, under their authority; to all cases affecting ambassadors, other public ministers and consuls; to all cases of admiralty and maritime jurisdiction; to controversies to which the United States shall be a party; to controversies between two or more states; between a state and citizens of another state; between citizens of different states; between citizens of the same state, claiming lands under the grants of different states; and between a state or the citizens thereof, and foreign states, citizens, or subjects.' It then proceeds to declare, that 'in all cases affecting ambassadors, other public ministers and consuls, and those in which a state shall be a party, the supreme court shall have *original jurisdiction*. In all the other cases before mentioned the supreme court shall have *appellate jurisdiction*, both as to law and fact, with such exceptions, and under such regulations, as the congress shall make.'

* * *

Let this article be carefully weighed and considered. The language of the article throughout is manifestly designed to be mandatory upon the legislature. Its obligatory force is so imperative, that congress could not, without a violation of its duty, have refused to carry it into operation. The judicial power of the United States *shall be vested* (not may be vested) in one supreme court, and in such inferior courts as congress may, from time to time, ordain and establish.

* * *

The object of the constitution was to establish three great departments of government; the legislative, the executive, and the judicial departments. The first was to pass laws, the second to approve and execute them, and the third to expound and enforce them. Without the latter, it would be impossible to carry into effect some of the express provisions of the constitution.

* * *

The judicial power must, therefore, be vested in some court, by congress; and to suppose that it was not an obligation binding on them, but might, at their pleasure, be omited [sic] or declined, is to suppose that, under the sanction of the constitution, they might defeat the constitution itself; a construction which would lead to such a result cannot be sound.

* * *

If, then, it is a duty of congress to vest the judicial power of the United States, it is a duty to vest the *whole judicial power*. The language, if imperative as to one part, is imperative as to all. If it were otherwise, this anomaly would exist, that congress might successively refuse to vest the jurisdiction in any one class of cases enumerated in the constitution, and thereby defeat the jurisdiction as to all; for the constitution has not singled out any class on which congress are bound to act in preference to others.

The next consideration is as to the courts in which the judicial power shall be vested. It is manifest that a supreme court must be established; but whether it be equally obligatory to establish inferior courts, is a question of some difficulty. If congress may lawfully omit to establish inferior courts, it might follow, that in some of the enumerated cases the judicial power could nowhere exist. The supreme court can have original jurisdiction in two classes of cases only, viz. in cases affecting ambassadors, other public ministers and consuls, and in cases in which a state is a party. Congress cannot vest any portion of the

Continued

judicial power of the United States, except in courts ordained and established by itself; and if in any of the cases enumerated in the constitution, the state courts did not then possess jurisdiction, the appellate jurisdiction of the supreme court (admitting that it could act on state courts) could not reach those cases, and, consequently, the injunction of the constitution, that the judicial power 'shall be vested,' would be disobeyed. It would seem, therefore, to follow, that congress are bound to create some inferior courts, in which to vest all that jurisdiction which, under the constitution, is *exclusively* vested in the United States, and of which the supreme court cannot take original cognizance. They might establish one or more inferior courts; they might parcel out the jurisdiction among such courts, from time to time, at their own pleasure. But the whole judicial power of the United States should be, at all times, vested either in an original or appellate form, in some courts created under its authority.

[W]e are of opinion that the words are used in an imperative sense. They import an absolute grant of judicial power. They cannot have a relative signification applicable to powers already granted; for the American *people* had not made any previous grant. The constitution was for a new government, organized with new substantive powers, and not a mere supplementary charter to a government already existing. The confederation was a compact between states; and its structure and powers were wholly unlike those of the national government. The constitution was an act of the people of the United States to supercede the confederation, and not to be ingrafted [sic] on it, as a stock through which it was to receive life and nourishment.

* * *

It being, then, established that the language of this clause is imperative, the next question is as to the cases to which it shall apply. The answer is found in the constitution itself. The judicial power shall extend to all the cases enumerated in the constitution. As the mode is not limited, it may extend to all such cases, in any form, in which judicial power may be exercised. It may, therefore, extend to them in the shape of original or appellate jurisdiction, or both; for there is nothing in the nature of the cases which binds to the exercise of the one in preference to the other.

In what cases (if any) is this judicial power exclusive, or exclusive at the election of congress? It will be observed that there are two classes of cases enumerated in the constitution, between which a distinction seems to be drawn. The first class includes cases arising under the constitution, laws, and treaties of the United States; cases affecting ambassadors, other public ministers and consuls, and cases of admiralty and maritime jurisdiction. In this class the expression is, and that the judicial power shall extend to *all cases;* but in the subsequent part of the clause which embraces all the other cases of national cognizance, and forms the second class, the word '*all*' is dropped seemingly *ex industria*. Here the judicial authority is to extend to controversies (not to *all* controversies) to which the United States shall be a party, &c. From this difference of phraseology, perhaps, a difference of constitutional intention may, with propriety, be inferred. It is hardly to be presumed that the variation in the language could have been accidental. It must have been the result of some determinate reason; and it is not very difficult to find a reason sufficient to support the apparent change of intention. In respect to the first class, it may well have been the intention of the framers of the constitution imperatively to extend the judicial power either in an original or appellate form to *all cases;* and in the latter class to leave it to congress to qualify the jurisdiction, original or appellate, in such manner as public policy might dictate.

* * *

This leads us to the consideration of the great question as to the nature and extent of the appellate jurisdiction of the United States. We have already seen that appellate jurisdiction is given by the constitution to the supreme court in all cases where it has not original jurisdiction; subject, however, to such exceptions and regulations as congress may prescribe. It is, therefore, capable of embracing every case enumerated in the constitution, which is not exclusively to be decided by way of original jurisdiction. But the exercise of appellate jurisdiction is far from being limited by the terms of the constitution to the supreme court. There can be no doubt that congress may create a succession of inferior tribunals, in each of which it may vest appellate as well as original jurisdiction. The judicial power is delegated by the constitution in the most general terms, and may, therefore, be exercised by congress under every variety of form, of appellate or original jurisdiction. And as there is nothing in the constitution which restrains or limits this power, it must, therefore, in all other cases, subsist in the utmost latitude of which, in its own nature, it is susceptible.

Continued

* * *

It is the *case*, then, and not *the court*, that gives the jurisdiction. If the judicial power extends to the case, it will be in vain to search in the letter of the constitution for any qualification as to the tribunal where it depends. It is incumbent, then, upon those who assert such a qualification to show its existence by necessary implication. If the text be clear and distinct, no restriction upon its plain and obvious import ought to be admitted, unless the inference be irresistible.

* * *

But it is plain that the framers of the constitution did contemplate that cases within the judicial cognizance of the United States not only might but would arise in the state courts, in the exercise of their ordinary jurisdiction. With this view the sixth article declares, that 'this constitution, and the laws of the United States which shall be made in pursuance thereof, and all treaties made, or which shall be made, under the authority of the United States, shall be the supreme law of the land, and the judges in every state shall be bound thereby, any thing in the constitution or laws of any state to the contrary notwithstanding.' It is obvious that this obligation is imperative upon the state judges in their official, and not merely in their private, capacities. From the very nature of their judicial duties they would be called upon to pronounce the law applicable to the case in judgment. They were not to decide merely according to the laws or constitution of the state, but according to the constitution, laws and treaties of the United States—'the supreme law of the land.'

* * *

It must, therefore, be conceded that the constitution not only contemplated, but meant to provide for cases within the scope of the judicial power of the United States, which might yet depend before state tribunals. It was foreseen that in the exercise of their ordinary jurisdiction, state courts would incidentally take cognizance of cases arising under the constitution, the laws, and treaties of the United States. Yet to all these cases the judicial power, by the very terms of the constitution, is to extend. It cannot extend by original jurisdiction if that was already rightfully and exclusively attached in the state courts, which (as has been already shown) may occur; it must, therefore, extend by appellate jurisdiction, or not at all. It would seem to follow that the appellate power of the United States must, in such cases, extend to state tribunals; and if in such cases, there is no reason why it should not equally attach upon all others within the purview of the constitution.

It has been argued that such an appellate jurisdiction over state courts is inconsistent with the genius of our governments, and the spirit of the constitution. That the latter was never designed to act upon state sovereignties, but only upon the people, and that if the power exists, it will materially impair the sovereignty of the states, and the independence of their courts. We cannot yield to the force of this reasoning; it assumes principles which we cannot admit, and draws conclusions to which we do not yield our assent.

It is a mistake that the constitution was not designed to operate upon states, in their corporate capacities. It is crowded with provisions which restrain or annul the sovereignty of the states in some of the highest branches of their prerogatives. The tenth section of the first article contains a long list of disabilities and prohibitions imposed upon the states. Surely, when such essential portions of state sovereignty are taken away, or prohibited to be exercised, it cannot be correctly asserted that the constitution does not act upon the states.

* * *

It is assuming the very ground in controversy to assert that they possess an absolute independence of the United States. In respect to the powers granted to the United States, they are not independent; they are expressly bound to obedience by the letter of the constitution; and if they should unintentionally transcend their authority, or misconstrue the constitution, there is no more reason for giving their judgments an absolute and irresistible force, than for giving it to the acts of the other co-ordinate departments of state sovereignty.

* * *

There is an additional consideration, which is entitled to great weight. The constitution of the United States was designed for the common and equal benefit of all the people of the United States. The judicial power was granted for the same benign and salutary purposes. It was not to be exercised exclusively for the benefit of parties who might be plaintiffs, and would elect the national forum, but also for the protection of

Continued

defendants who might be entitled to try their rights, or assert their privileges [sic], before the same forum. Yet, if the construction contended for be correct, it will follow, that as the plaintiff may always elect the state court, the defendant may be deprived of all the security which the constitution intended in aid of his rights. Such a state of things can, in no respect, be considered as giving equal rights. To obviate this difficulty, we are referred to the power which it is admitted congress possess to remove suits from state courts to the national courts; and this forms the second ground upon which the argument we are considering has been attempted to be sustained.

* * *

On the whole, the court are of opinion, that the appellate power of the United States does extend to cases pending in the state courts; and that the 25th section of the judiciary act, which authorizes the exercise of this jurisdiction in the specified cases, by a writ of error, is supported by the letter and spirit of the constitution. We find no clause in that instrument which limits this power; and we dare not interpose a limitation where the people have not been disposed to create one.

Strong as this conclusion stands upon the general language of the constitution, it may still derive support from other sources. It is an historical fact, that this exposition of the constitution, extending its appellate power to state courts, was, previous to its adoption, uniformly and publicly avowed by its friends, and admitted by its enemies, as the basis of their respective reasonings, both in and out of the state conventions. It is an historical fact, that at the time when the judiciary act was submitted to the deliberations of the first congress, composed, as it was, not only of men of great learning and ability, but of men who had acted a principal part in framing, supporting, or opposing that constitution, the same exposition was explicitly declared and admitted by the friends and by the opponents of that system. It is an historical fact, that the supreme court of the United States have, from time to time, sustained this appellate jurisdiction in a great variety of cases, brought from the tribunals of many of the most important states in the union, and that no state tribunal has ever breathed a judicial doubt on the subject, or declined to obey the mandate of the supreme court, until the present occasion. This weight of contemporaneous exposition by all parties, this acquiescence of enlightened state courts, and these judicial decisions of the supreme court through so long a period, do, as we think, place the doctrine upon a foundation of authority which cannot be shaken, without delivering over the subject to perpetual and irremediable doubts.

* * *

We have thus gone over all the principal questions in the cause, and we deliver our judgment with entire confidence, that it is consistent with the constitution and laws of the land.

We have not thought it incumbent on us to give any opinion upon the question, whether this court have authority to issue a writ of mandamus to the court of appeals to enforce the former judgments, as we do not think it necessarily involved in the decision of this cause.

It is the opinion of the whole court, that the judgment of the court of appeals of Virginia, rendered on the mandate in this cause, be reversed, and the judgment of the district court, held at Winchester, be, and the same is hereby affirmed.

The Court relied on Article III of the Constitution that mandates the Court shall have power which "shall extend to all cases." The Court concluded that this meant that it was the nature of the case that dictated whether it could exercise its power, not the court of origin. The Supreme Court's jurisdiction and power of judicial review is not confined to cases coming up through the lower federal courts, but extends to review of cases from the highest court in each state. The Constitution operates on the states themselves, not just on the individuals within the state. To allow the state courts to determine whether a law violates the Constitution creates a likelihood that there will be conflicting decisions among the states. This is unacceptable and demonstrates the need for a single court of last resort to ensure uniformity of decisions. Finally, the Court pointed out that there was historical evidence that the Framers of the

Constitution intended the U.S. Supreme Court to be the court of last resort and also that they intended that this court review state court decisions.

The decision in *Martin v. Hunter's Lessee* is not the only time the Court has asserted its authority to judicially review cases coming from the state courts. In *Cohens v. Virginia*[103] the Court upheld its power to review state criminal cases to determine the constitutionality of the state action. More recently, the Court reasserted its power to determine the constitutionality of an action by a state legislature in the desegregation case, *Cooper v. Aaron*[104] discussed, *supra*, in Chapter 8.

The discussion of whether the Court had the power to judicially review the actions of the executive branch of the federal government was not answered until 1974 with the case of *U.S. v. Nixon.*[105] This case stemmed from the Watergate Scandal, in which several of President Nixon's top aides were indicted in a criminal conspiracy regarding the break-in at Democratic Headquarters in the Watergate office building. The federal district court ordered President Nixon to produce taped conversations between him and his aides and the President refused to comply with the order, claiming executive privilege. The district court rejected this claim of privilege, and while the case was pending appeal to the federal circuit court of appeals, the Supreme Court granted certiorari.

UNITED STATES, PETITIONER, V. RICHARD M. NIXON, PRESIDENT OF THE UNITED STATES, ET AL

RICHARD M. NIXON, PRESIDENT OF THE UNITED STATES, PETITIONER, V. UNITED STATES
418 U.S. 683 (1974)

Argued July 8, 1974.

Decided July 24, 1974.
**Mr. Chief Justice BURGER
delivered the opinion of the Court.**

This litigation presents for review the denial of a motion, filed in the District Court on behalf of the President of the United States, in the case of United States v. Mitchell et al. (D.C.Crim. No. 74–110), to quash a third-party subpoena duces tecum issued by the United States District Court for the District of Columbia, pursuant to *Fed. Rule Crim.Proc. 17(c)*. The subpoena directed the President to produce certain tape recordings and documents relating to his conversations with aides and advisers. The court rejected the President's claims of absolute executive privilege, of lack of jurisdiction, and of failure to satisfy the requirements of *Rule 17(c)*. The President appealed to the Court of Appeals. We granted both the United States' petition for certiorari before judgment (No. 73–1766), and also the President's cross-petition for certiorari before judgment (No. 73–1834), because of the public importance of the issues presented and the need for their prompt resolution.

* * *

The District Court held that the judiciary, not the President, was the final arbiter of a claim of executive privilege. The court concluded that under the circumstances of this case the presumptive privilege was overcome by the Special Prosecutor's prima facie 'demonstration of need sufficiently compelling to warrant judicial examination in chambers. . . .' The court held, finally, that the Special Prosecutor had satisfied the requirements of *Rule 17(c)*. The District Court stayed its order pending appellate review on condition that review was sought before 4 p.m., May 24. The court further provided that matters filed under seal remain under seal when transmitted as part of the record.

* * *

II

JUSTICIABILITY

In the District Court, the President's counsel argued that the court lacked jurisdiction to issue the subpoena because the matter was an intrabranch dispute between a subordinate and superior officer of the Executive Branch and hence

Continued

not subject to judicial resolution. That argument has been renewed in this Court with emphasis on the contention that the dispute does not present a 'case' or 'controversy' which can be adjudicated in the federal courts. The President's counsel argues that the federal courts should not intrude into areas committed to the other branches of Government. He views the present dispute as essentially a 'jurisdictional' dispute within the Executive Branch which he analogizes to a dispute between two congressional committees. Since the Executive Branch has exclusive authority and absolute discretion to decide whether to prosecute a case, it is contended that a President's decision is final in determining what evidence is to be used in a given criminal case. Although his counsel concedes that the President has delegated certain specific powers to the Special Prosecutor, he has not 'waived nor delegated to the Special Prosecutor the President's duty to claim privilege as to all materials . . . which fall within the President's inherent authority to refuse to disclose to any executive officer.' Brief for the President 42. The Special Prosecutor's demand for the items therefore presents, in the view of the President's counsel, a political question under *Baker v. Carr, 369 U.S. 186, 82 S.Ct. 691, 7 L.Ed.2d 663 (1962)*, since it involves a 'textually demonstrable' grant of power under Art. II.

The mere assertion of a claim of an 'intra-branch dispute,' without more, has never operated to defeat federal jurisdiction; justiciability does not depend on such a surface inquiry. In *United States v. ICC, 337 U.S. 426, 69 S.Ct. 1410, 93 L.Ed. 1451 (1949)*, the Court observed, 'courts must look behind names that symbolize the parties to determine whether a justiciable case or controversy is presented.'

* * *

Our starting point is the nature of the proceeding for which the evidence is sought—here a pending criminal prosecution. It is a judicial proceeding in a federal court alleging violation of federal laws and is brought in the name of the United States as sovereign. Under the authority of Art. II, s 2, Congress has vested in the Attorney General the power to conduct the criminal litigation of the United States Government. It has also vested in him the power to appoint subordinate officers to assist him in the discharge of his duties. Acting pursuant to those statutes, the Attorney General has delegated the authority to

represent the United States in these particular matters to a Special Prosecutor with unique authority and tenure. The regulation gives the Special Prosecutor explicit power to contest the invocation of executive privilege in the process of seeking evidence deemed relevant to the performance of these specially delegated duties. 38 Fed.Reg. 30739, as amended by 38 Fed.Reg. 32805.

So long as this regulation is extant it has the force of law.

* * *

The demands of and the resistance to the subpoena present an obvious controversy in the ordinary sense, but that alone is not sufficient to meet constitutional standards. In the constitutional sense, controversy means more than disagreement and conflict; rather it means the kind of controversy courts traditionally resolve. Here at issue is the production or nonproduction of specified evidence deemed by the Special Prosecutor to be relevant and admissible in a pending criminal case. It is sought by one official of the Executive Branch within the scope of his express authority; it is resisted by the Chief Executive on the ground of his duty to preserve the confidentiality of the communications of the President. Whatever the correct answer on the merits, these issues are 'of a type which are traditionally justiciable.' *United States v. ICC, 337 U.S., at 430, 69 S.Ct., at 1413*. The independent Special Prosecutor with his asserted need for the subpoenaed material in the underlying criminal prosecution is opposed by the President with his steadfast assertion of privilege against disclosure of the material. This setting assures there is 'that concrete adverseness which sharpens the presentation of issues upon which the court so largely depends for illumination of difficult constitutional questions'. Moreover, since the matter is one arising in the regular course of a federal criminal prosecution, it is within the traditional scope of power.

In light of the uniqueness of the setting in which the conflict arises, the fact that both parties are officers of the Executive Branch cannot be viewed as a barrier to justiciability. It would be inconsistent with the applicable law and regulation, and the unique facts of this case to conclude other than that the Special Prosecutor has standing to bring this action and that a justiciable controversy is presented for decision.

Continued

* * *

IV

THE CLAIM OF PRIVILEGE

A

Having determined that the requirements of *Rule 17(c)* were satisfied, we turn to the claim that the subpoena should be quashed because it demands 'confidential conversations between a President and his close advisors that it would be inconsistent with the public interest to produce.' The first contention is a broad claim that the separation of powers doctrine precludes judicial review of a President's claim of privilege. The second contention is that if he does not prevail on the claim of absolute privilege, the court should hold as a matter of constitutional law that the privilege prevails over the subpoena duces tecum.

In the performance of assigned constitutional duties each branch of the Government must initially interpret the Constitution, and the interpretation of its powers by any branch is due great respect from the others. The President's counsel, as we have noted, reads the Constitution as providing an absolute privilege of confidentiality for all Presidential communications. Many decisions of this Court, however, have unequivocally reaffirmed the holding of *Marbury v. Madison, 1 Cranch, 137, 2 L.Ed. 60 (1803)*, that '(i)t is emphatically the province and duty of the judicial department to say what the law is.'

No holding of the Court has defined the scope of judicial power specifically relating to the enforcement of a subpoena for confidential Presidential communications for use in a criminal prosecution, but other exercises of power by the Executive Branch and the Legislative Branch have been found invalid as in conflict with the Constitution.

* * *

In a series of cases, the Court interpreted the explicit immunity conferred by express provisions of the Constitution on Members of the House and Senate by the Speech or Debate Clause, U.S.Const. Art. I, s 6.

* * *

Since this Court has consistently exercised the power to construe and delineate claims arising under express powers, it must follow that the Court has authority to interpret claims with respect to powers alleged to derive from enumerated powers.

Our system of government 'requires that federal courts on occasion interpret the Constitution in a manner at variance with the construction given the document by another branch.' And in *Baker v. Carr, 369 U.S., at 211, 82 S.Ct., at 706*, the Court stated:

> '[D]eciding whether a matter has in any measure been committed by the Constitution to another branch of government, or whether the action of that branch exceeds whatever authority has been committed, is itself a delicate exercise in constitutional interpretation, and is a responsibility of this Court as ultimate interpreter of the Constitution.'

Notwithstanding the deference each branch must accord the others, the 'judicial Power of the United States' vested in the federal courts by *Art. III, s 1*, of the Constitution can no more be shared with the Executive Branch than the Chief Executive, for example, can share with the Judiciary the veto power, or the Congress share with the Judiciary the power to override a Presidential veto. Any other conclusion would be contrary to the basic concept of separation of powers and the checks and balances that flow from the scheme of a tripartite government. We therefore reaffirm that it is the province and duty of this Court 'to say what the law is' with respect to the claim of privilege presented in this case.

B

However, neither the doctrine of separation of powers, nor the need for confidentiality of high-level communications, without more, can sustain an absolute, unqualified Presidential privilege of immunity from judicial process under all circumstances. The President's need for complete candor and objectivity from advisers calls for great deference from the courts. However, when the privilege depends solely on the broad, undifferentiated claim of public interest in the confidentiality of such conversations, a confrontation with other values arises. Absent a claim of need to protect military, diplomatic, or sensitive national security secrets, we find it difficult to accept the argument that even the very important interest in confidentiality of Presidential communications is significantly diminished by production of such material for in camera inspection with all the protection that a district court will be obliged to provide.

Continued

The impediment that an absolute, unqualified privilege would place in the way of the primary constitutional duty of the Judicial Branch to do justice in criminal prosecutions would plainly conflict with the function of the courts under *Art. III*. In designing the structure of our Government and dividing and allocating the sovereign power among three co-equal branches, the Framers of the Constitution sought to provide a comprehensive system, but the separate powers were not intended to operate with absolute independence.

> 'While the Constitution diffuses power the better to secure liberty, it also contemplates that practice will integrate the dispersed powers into a workable government. It enjoins upon its branches separateness but interdependence, autonomy but reciprocity.'

To read the Art. II powers of the President as providing an absolute privilege as against a subpoena essential to enforcement of criminal statutes on no more than a generalized claim of the public interest in confidentiality of nonmilitary and nondiplomatic discussions would upset the constitutional balance of 'a workable government' and gravely impair the role of the courts under *Art. III*.

C

Since we conclude that the legitimate needs of the judicial process may outweigh Presidential privilege, it is necessary to resolve those competing interests in a manner that preserves the essential functions of each branch. The right and indeed the duty to resolve that question does not free the Judiciary from according high respect to the representations made on behalf of the President.

The expectation of a President to the confidentiality of his conversations and correspondence, like the claim of confidentiality of judicial deliberations, for example, has all the values to which we accord deference for the privacy of all citizens and, added to those values, is the necessity for protection of the public interest in candid, objective, and even blunt or harsh opinions in Presidential decisionmaking. A President and those who assist him must be free to explore alternatives in the process of shaping policies and making decisions and to do so in a way many would be unwilling to express except privately. These are the considerations justifying a presumptive privilege for Presidential communications. The privilege is fundamental to the operation of Government and inextricably rooted in the separation of powers under the Constitution.

* * *

We agree with Mr. Chief Justice Marshall's observation, therefore, that '(i)n no case of this kind would a court be required to proceed against the president as against an ordinary individual.'

But this presumptive privilege must be considered in light of our historic commitment to the rule of law. This is nowhere more profoundly manifest than in our view that 'the twofold aim (of criminal justice) is that guilt shall not escape or innocence suffer.' We have elected to employ an adversary system of criminal justice in which the parties contest all issues before a court of law. The need to develop all relevant facts in the adversary system is both fundamental and comprehensive.

* * *

Only recently the Court restated the ancient proposition of law, albeit in the context of a grand jury inquiry rather than a trial,

> that 'the public . . . has a right to every man's evidence,' except for those persons protected by a constitutional, common-law, or statutory privilege.

* * *

The privileges referred to by the Court are designed to protect weighty and legitimate competing interests.

* * *

In this case the President challenges a subpoena served on him as a third party requiring the production of materials for use in a criminal prosecution; he does so on the claim that he has a privilege against diclosure of confidential communications. He does not place his claim of privilege on the ground they are military or diplomatic secrets. As to these areas of Art. II duties the courts have traditionally shown the utmost deference to Presidential responsibilities.

* * *

No case of the Court, however, has extended this high degree of deference to a President's generalized interest in confidentiality. Nowhere in the Constitution, as we have noted earlier, is there any explicit reference to a privilege of

Continued

confidentiality, yet to the extent this interest relates to the effective discharge of a President's powers, it is constitutionally based.

The right to the production of all evidence at a criminal trial similarly has constitutional dimensions. The Sixth Amendment explicitly confers upon every defendant in a criminal trial the right 'to be confronted with the witnesses against him' and 'to have compulsory process for obtaining witnesses in his favor. Moreover, the Fifth Amendment also guarantees that no person shall be deprived of liberty without due process of law. It is the manifest duty of the courts to vindicate those guarantees, and to accomplish that it is essential that all relevant and admissible evidence be produced.

In this case we must weigh the importance of the general privilege of confidentiality of Presidential communications in performance of the President's responsibilities against the inroads of such a privilege on the fair administration of criminal justice of a criminal prosecution.

＊ ＊ ＊

On the other hand, the allowance of the privilege to withhold evidence that is demonstrably relevant in a criminal trial would cut deeply into the guarantee of due process of law and gravely impair the basic function of the courts.

A President's acknowledged need for confidentiality in the communications of his office is general in nature, whereas the constitutional need for production of relevant evidence in a criminal proceeding is specific and central to the fair adjudication of a particular criminal case in the administration of justice. Without access to specific facts a criminal prosecution may be totally frustrated. The President's broad interest in confidentiality of communications will not be vitiated by disclosure of a limited number of conversations preliminarily shown to have some bearing on the pending criminal cases.

We conclude that when the ground for asserting privilege as to subpoenaed materials sought for use in a criminal trial is based only on the generalized interest in confidentiality, it cannot prevail over the fundamental demands of due process of law in the fair administration of criminal justice. The generalized assertion of privilege must yield to the demonstrated, specific need for evidence in a pending criminal trial.

＊ ＊ ＊

Since this matter came before the Court during the pendency of a criminal prosecution, and on representations that time is of the essence, the mandate shall issue forthwith.

Affirmed.

President Nixon claimed that he had the power to determine the scope of the executive privilege, but the Court held that the concept of separation of powers supported the decision that it is the province of the Court to determine breadth of the executive privilege. The Court did not deny the existence of such a privilege, but such a privilege must be weighed against the interests of the criminal justice system as a whole. The Court ultimately held that the President's interest in this situation was low because the matter did not involve a national security matter, and as such, the interests of the criminal justice system as a whole outweighed those of the President. President Nixon was ultimately ordered to turn the taped conversations over to the special prosecutor. President Nixon's resignation followed shortly thereafter.

The lessons to be learned from all of these cases are that the Court has the power to review decisions from the lower federal courts, to review the legislative actions of the Congress, to review state court decisions involving federal questions and state legislation that is constitutionally questionable, as well as to review the executive branch's claim of privilege.

Summary

The history of the Supreme Court and the other federal courts is a colorful one. In the earliest days of this country's judicial history, the Court was an equal branch of the federal government in theory, but the

Court had not realized its power. With the case of *Marbury v. Madison* the Court formulated the concept of judicial review and took control of its role in the federal government. In the years that followed, the Court relied on the Constitution to define the parameters of its jurisdiction, as well as the jurisdiction of the lower federal courts. Today, the Court primarily exercises its appellate jurisdiction and continues to require that plaintiffs have standing, a case and controversy, issues ripe for decision that are not moot, and avoid becoming entangled in most political questions. It is still the Supreme Court's role to determine the constitutionality of statutes, decisions by lower federal and state courts, and issues arising from executive decisions that do not involve national security.

While experts disagree on exactly how the courts make decisions, there are many theories. It would appear that a combination of factors may go into the decision-making process, and the way the decision is made may depend on the type of case or issues involved.

Regardless of how the courts make decisions, it is still the role of the judiciary to apply the laws to real issues and determine the rights of the parties involved.

Key Terms

amicus curiae
appellate jurisdiction
balancing approach
case and controversy
certiorari
concurring opinion
declaratory judgment
dissenting opinion
diversity of citizenship

federal question
habeas corpus
judicial review
justiciable
majority opinion
moot
opinion
original jurisdiction
per curiam opinion

ratio decidendi
rational basis test
ripe
rule of four
standing
stare decisis
strict scrutiny

Review Questions

1. What is the significance of the Court's decision in *Marbury v. Madison*, and what is the impact of this decision in today's justice system?

2. What defines the power of the U.S. Supreme Court, and how does this power fit with the separation of powers in the federal system?

3. Why is it significant to understand how the Court makes its decisions?

4. What theories explain how the Court makes its decisions? How do these theories conflict and how do they seem to work together?

5. Why is it important that those justices who either disagree with the majority opinion or who reached the decision for a different reason from the majority write dissenting or concurring opinions?

Internet Connections

1. For more information about the U.S. Supreme Court, go to the Court's Web page at *http://www.supremecourtus.gov* and read "A Brief Overview of the Supreme Court."

2. For more information on the Constitution, go to *http://www.yale.edu/lawweb/avalon/avalon.htm* and access the Avalon Project at Yale Law School. You will find documents regarding the law, history of the law, and diplomacy.

3. To read more about the federal judicial system, access the Federal Judicial Center's Web site at *http://www.fjc.gov*. Two documents on that site of particular interest are "Creating the Federal Judicial System" and "Origin of the Elements of Federal Court Governance."

4. The Administrative Offices of the U.S. Courts' Web site is at *http://www.uscourts.gov* and of particular interest is a posting entitled "Understanding the Federal Courts."

End Notes

[1] U.S. Const. art. III, § 1.

[2] "The Constitution and the Federal Judiciary," *Understanding the Courts*, at http://library.lp.findlaw.com (May 25, 2003).

[3] *Id.* at 1.

[4] Judiciary Act of 1789, 1 Stat. 73.

[5] *Id.*

[6] Act of April 10, 1869, 16 Stat. 44.

[7] "The Presidents," The American Experience, Public Broadcasting System, at http://www.pub.org (May 14, 2003).

[8] *Id.*

[9] "Fireside Chat on Reorganization of the Judiciary, March 9, 1937," Oyez Oyez Oyez, a Supreme Court Resource, at http://www.hpol.org (May 14, 2003).

[10] *Id.*

[11] "Court Packing: Judicial Reorganization and the End of the New Deal," an American Studies Website, created by Paul Volpe, University of Virginia, at http://xroads.virginia.edu (May 14, 2003).

[12] *Id.*

[13] *Id.*

[14] Russell R. Wheeler & Cynthia Harrison, *Creating the Federal Judicial System*, Federal Judicial Center (2nd ed. 1994).

[15] *Id.* at 2.

[16] *Id.* at 3.

[17] *Id.* at 4.

[18] Russell R. Wheeler & Cynthia Harrison, *Creating the Federal Judicial System*, Federal Judicial Center (2nd ed. 1994).

[19] *Id.* at 4.

[20] *Id.* at 4.

[21] *Id.* at 6.

[22] *Id.* at 12–16.

[23] *Id.* at 16.

[24] Circuit Court of Appeals Act of 1891, 26 Stat. 826 (Mar. 3, 1891).

[25] Russell R. Wheeler & Cynthia Harrison, *Creating the Federal Judicial System*, Federal Judicial Center (2nd ed. 1994).

[26] *Id.* at 23.

[27] "The Constitution and the Federal Judiciary," *Understanding the Federal Courts*, at http://library.lp.findlaw.com (May 25, 2003).

[28] This power is given to the House of Representatives in art. I, §. 2, cl. 5.

[29] This power is given to the Senate in art. I, § 3, cl. 6.

[30] U.S. Const. art. III, § 1.

[31] All information in this sidebar was found at Supreme Court Justices, Constitutional Law Center, at http://supreme.lp.findlaw.com (May 14, 2003).

[32] U.S. Const. art. III, § 2.

[33] Russell R. Wheeler & Cynthia Harrison, *Creating the Federal Judicial System*, Federal Judicial Center (2nd ed. 1994).

[34] *Judicial Power and Jurisdiction—Cases and Controversies*, United States Constitution Annotated, art. III, § 2, cl.1, at http://supreme.lp.findlaw.com (May 25, 2003).

[35] *Cohens v. Virginia*, 19 U.S. 264 (1821).

[36] *Id.* at 378.

[37] *Aetna Life Insurance Company v. Haworth*, 300 U.S. 229 (1937).

[38] *Id.* at 240-241.

[39] *Chicago & G.T. Railway Company v. Wellman*, 14 U.S. 339 (1892).

[40] *Id.* at 345.

[41] *Baker v. Carr*, 369 U.S. 186, 204 (1962).

[42] *Valley Forge Christian College v. Americans United*, 454 U.S. 464, 472 (1982).

[43] *Lujan v. Defenders of Wildlife*, 504 U.S. 555 (1992).

[44] *Hunt v. Washington State Apple Advertising Commission*, 432 U.S. 333, 343 (1977).

[45] *Warth v. Seldin*, 422 U.S. 490 (1975).

[46] *Id.* at 501.

[47] *United States v. Munsingwear*, 340 U.S. 36 (1950).

[48] *Pennsylvania v. Wheeling & Belmont Bridge Company*, 54 U.S. 518 (1852).

[49] *Atherton Mills v. Johnston*, 259 U.S. 13 (1922).

[50] *Commercial Cable Company v. Burleson*, 250 U.S. 360 (1919).

[51] *Sibron v. New York*, 395 U.S. 40, 50 (1968).

[52] *United States v. W. T. Grant Company*, 345 U.S. 629, 635 (1953).

[53] *Roe v. Wade*, 410 U.S. 113 (1973).

[54] *Southern Pacific Terminal Company v. I.C.C.*, 219 U.S. 498, 515 (1911).

[55] *Weinstein v. Bradford*, 423 U.S. 147 (1975).

[56] *Younger v. Harris*, 401 U.S. 37 (1971).

[57] *United Public Workers v. Mitchell*, 330 U.S. 75 (1947).

[58] *Marbury v. Madison*, 5 U.S. 137 (1803).

[59] *Luther v. Borden*, 48 U.S. 1 (1849).

[60] *Luther v. Borden*, 48 U.S. 1, 42 (1849).

[61] *Id.*

[62] *Baker v. Carr*, 369 U.S. 186 (1962).

[63] *Id.* at 210.

[64] *Id.* at 210.

[65] *Id.* at 211.

[66] *Id.* at 217.

[67] *Powell v. McCormack*, 395 U.S. 486 (1969).

[68] *Id.* at 519.

[69] *Japan Whaling Association v. American Cetacean Society*, 478 U.S. 221, 230 (1986).

[70] *Ex parte McCardle*, 74 U.S. 506 (1869).

[71] *U.S. v. Klein*, 80 U.S. 128 (1872).

[72] Sup. Ct. R. 10.

[73] *Id.*

[74] Sup. Ct. R. 13.

[75] Sup. Ct. R. 12.

[76] Sup. Ct. R. 14.

[77] Sup. Ct. R. 16.

[78] *Id.*

[79] *Green v. United States*, 356 U.S. 165 (1958).

[80] *Id.* at 195.

[81] *Barron v. Baltimore*, 32 U.S. 243 (1833).

[82] *Id.* at 249.

[83] *Id.* at 250.

[84] *Youngstown Sheet & Tube Company v. Sawyer*, 343 U.S. 579 (1952).

[85] *Id.* at 634–635.

[86] U.S. Const. amend. IV.

[87] *Nixon v. United States*, 506 U.S. 224 (1993).

[88] *Id.* at 230.

[89] *Marbury v. Madison*, 5 U.S. 137 (1803).

[90] *Id.* at 177.

[91] Jeffrey A. Segal & Harold J. Spaeth, "The Authors Respond," *Law and Courts Newsletter*, vol. 4, 10–12, 11 (1994).

[92] Stuart S. Nagel, "Political Party Affiliation and Judges' Decisions," *The American Political Science Review*, vol. 55, 843–80 (1961).

[93] S. Sidney Ulmer, "Dissent Behavior and the Social Background of Supreme Court Justices," *The Journal of Politics*, vol. 59, 580–98 (1970).

[94] See studies by Roy B. Fleming & Dan Wood, "The Public and the Supreme Court: Individual Justice Responsiveness to American Policy Moods," *American Journal of Political Science*, vol. 41, 468–98 (1997); William Mishler & Reginald S. Sheehan, "The Supreme Court as a Countermajoritarian Institution: The Impact of Public Opinion on Supreme Court Decisions," *The American Political Science Review*, vol. 87, 87–101 (1993).

[95] Gregory A. Caldeira & John R. Wright, "Organized Interests and Agenda Setting in the U.S. Supreme Court," *The American Political Science Review*, vol. 83, 1109–27 (1988).

[96] Lee Epstein & Jack Knight, *The Choices Justices Make*, p. 72 *Congressional Quarterly Press* (1998).

[97] *Marbury v. Madison*, 5 U.S. (Cranch) 137 (1803).

[98] *Id.* at 177.

[99] *Id.* at 170.

[100] *Fletcher v. Peck*, 10 U.S. 87 (1810).

[101] *Id.* at 88.

[102] *Martin v. Hunter's Lessee*, 14 U.S. 304 (1816).

[103] *Cohens v. Virginia*, 19 U.S. 264 (1821).

[104] *Cooper v. Aaron*, 358 U.S. 1 (1958).

[105] *U.S. v. Nixon*, 418 U.S. 683 (1974).

ONLINE COMPANION For additional resources, go to *http://www.westlegalstudies.com*

CHAPTER 4

CONGRESS AND ITS POWERS

This government is acknowledged by all, to be one of enumerated powers. The principle, that it can exercise only the powers granted to it, would seem too apparent, to have required to be enforced by all those arguments, which its enlightened friends, while it was depending before the people, found it necessary to urge; that principle is now universally admitted. But the question respecting the extent of the powers actually granted, is perpetually arising, and will probably continue to arise, so long as our system shall exist.

—Chief Justice John Marshall
McCulloch v. Maryland

INTRODUCTION

The federalist system of government in the United States makes the federal legislature a coequal branch of government with the judiciary and the executive branch. But what powers, specifically, belong to this legislative branch? To answer this question, one must look at the enumerated powers given to Congress found in Article I, Section 8. It says:

The Congress shall have Power To lay and collect Taxes, Duties, Imposts and Excises, to pay the Debts and provide for the common Defence [sic] and general Welfare of the United States; but all Duties, Imposts and Excises shall be uniform throughout the United States;

To borrow Money on the credit of the United States;

To regulate Commerce with foreign Nations, and among the several States, and with the Indian Tribes;

To establish an [sic] uniform Rule of Naturalization, and uniform Laws on the subject of Bankruptcies throughout the United States;

To coin Money, regulate the Value thereof, and of foreign Coin, and fix the Standard of Weights and Measures;

To provide for the Punishment of counterfeiting the Securities and current Coin of the United States;

To establish Post Offices and post Roads;

To promote the Progress of Science and useful Arts, by securing for limited Time to Authors and Inventors the exclusive Right to their respective Writings and Discoveries;

To constitute Tribunals inferior to the supreme Court;

To define and punish Piracies and Felonies committed on the high seas, and Offences [sic] against the Law of Nations;

To declare War, grant Letters of Marque and Reprisal, and make Rules concerning Captures on Land and Water;

To raise and support Armies, but no Appropriation of Money to that Use shall be for a longer Term than two Years;

To provide and maintain a Navy;

To make Rules for the Government and Regulation of the land and naval Forces;

To provide for calling forth the Militia to execute the Laws of the Union, suppress Insurrections and repel Invasions;

To provide for organizing, arming, and disciplining, the Militia, and for governing such Part of them as may be employed in the Service of the United States, reserving to the States respectively, the Appointment of the Officers, and the Authority of training the Militia according to the discipline prescribed by Congress;

To exercise exclusive Legislation in all Cases whatsoever, over such District (not exceeding ten Miles square) as may, by Cession of Particular States, and the Acceptance of Congress, become the Seat of the Government of the United States, and to exercise like Authority over all Places purchased by the Consent of the Legislature of the State in which the Same shall be, for the Erection of Forts, Magazines, Arsenals, dock-Yards and other needful Buildings;—And

To make all Laws which shall be necessary and proper for carrying into Execution the foregoing Powers and all other Powers vested by this Constitution in the Government of the United States, or in any Department or Officer thereof.[1]

This is an extensive list of enumerated powers, but the key for this textbook is how the Court has interpreted these powers and what parameters have been set for congressional action. Some of these powers have been the subject of much litigation while others are straightforward and little interpretation is needed. In addition to the discussion of the major enumerated congressional powers, this chapter will also discuss the last power granted in Article I, § 8, commonly called the "**Necessary and Proper Clause**." One might think that this clause was the subject of much debate during the Constitutional Convention, but it was not. However, it was debated during the ratification process. Opponents of the Necessary and Proper Clause saw it as a potential way for Congress to expand its enumerated powers and, in doing so, upset the balance of power between the three branches of government. Supporters of the Necessary and Proper Clause claimed that without this clause, it would be impossible for Congress to implement the enumerated powers spelled out in Article I.

In spite of the debate during the ratification process, the clause was included and ratified in Article I, and, as will be demonstrated in the upcoming discussion, this clause allows Congress to use any method to achieve their objective so long as that method is rationally related to the objective they are trying to achieve. The only limit to this is that the method chosen by Congress may not be unconstitutional.

In addition to the enumerated powers found in Article I, other articles and clauses in the Constitution grant Congress additional powers. As discussed in Chapter 3, Article II, § 2 gives Congress the power to have some control over the jurisdiction of the Supreme Court and establish all lower federal courts. Article IV, § 3 gives Congress power over U.S. territories and federally owned

Necessary and Proper Clause   Article I, Section 8, Clause 18 of the U.S. Constitution gives *Congress* the power to pass all laws appropriate to carry out its functions.

property. Section 5 of the Fourteenth Amendment gives Congress the power to enact supporting legislation to enforce the Thirteenth, Fourteenth, and Fifteenth Amendments, also known as the Civil War Amendments. With all of these enumerated powers, there is much to discuss in this chapter.

LEGISLATIVE POWER

Article III, § 1 of the United States Constitution says, "All legislative Powers herein granted shall be vested in a Congress of the United States, which shall consist of a Senate and House of Representatives." Thus, legislative power cannot be delegated,[2] and this concept is referred to as the doctrine of nondelegability. While there are exceptions to this doctrine, the idea expressed is such an integral part of constitutional jurisprudence that the idea of nondelegability deserves discussion. The doctrine of nondelegability arises out of three sources or theories.

First, some scholars claim it arises out of the separation of powers doctrine. This doctrine is based on the fact that the federal government is divided into three distinct branches and each branch performs unique and identifiable functions. Those who argue that this is the basis of the doctrine of nondelegability contend that as the legislative powers are specifically given to the legislature, that body cannot delegate those enumerated and necessary powers.[3] Second, others argue that due process forbids the transfer of regulatory powers to agencies, commissions, or individuals.[4] Lastly, some scholars point to the concept of *delegata potestas non potest delegari* (which translates to, "a delegated power cannot be delegated") found in *J.W. Hampton Jr. & Company v. United States*, in which Chief Justice Taft wrote "[The] Federal Constitution and State Constitutions of this country divide the governmental power into three branches [and] in carrying out that constitutional division . . . it is a breach of the National fundamental law if Congress gives up its legislative power and transfers it to the President, or to the Judicial branch, or if by law it attempts to invest itself or its members with either executive power or judicial power."[5]

No matter which of these arguments makes sense, the reality is that the doctrine of nondelegability does not account for the fact that the legislature has delegated power to administrative agencies and individuals. "Delegation by Congress has long been recognized as necessary in order that the exertion of legislative power does not become a futility."[6]

The Court justified the delegation of some legislative duties and power in the case of *Wayman v. Southard*[7] when it heard a challenge to § 17 of the Judiciary Act. The defense in that case challenged the congressional delegation of authority to make rules of court to the federal courts. In the challenge, the defense argued that this was not a power that could be delegated. The Court disagreed, saying:

> "It will not be contended that Congress can delegate to the Courts, or to any other tribunals, powers which are strictly and exclusively legislative. But Congress may certainly delegate to others, powers that the legislature may rightfully exercise itself . . . The line has not been exactly drawn which separates those important subjects, which must be entirely regulated by the legislature itself, from those of less interest, in which a general provision may be made, and power given to those who are to act under such general provisions to fill up the details."[8]

In so holding, the Court found it permissible for the legislature to delegate the authority to "fill up the details," and this type of analysis was used to uphold many delegations of legislative authority.

Abandoning a strict reading of the doctrine of nondelegability was further upheld in the case of *Mistretta v. United States*, in which Mistretta and another defendant were indicted and convicted on drug charges. After conviction, the trial court sentenced Mistretta using the Federal Sentencing Guidelines that had been promulgated by the Sentencing Commission as authorized by a delegation of Congress' legislative power. Mistretta challenged these guidelines, and the Commission itself, as being an unconstitutional delegation of legislative authority.

MISTRETTA v. UNITED STATES
488 U.S. 361 (1989)

Justice BLACKMUN delivered the opinion of the Court.

In this litigation, we granted certiorari before judgment in the United States Court of Appeals for the Eighth Circuit in order to consider the constitutionality of the Sentencing Guidelines promulgated by the United States Sentencing Commission. The Commission is a body created under the Sentencing Reform Act of 1984. The United States District Court for the Western District of Missouri ruled that the Guidelines were constitutional. [Citation omitted.]

I

A

Background

For almost a century, the Federal Government employed in criminal cases a system of indeterminate sentencing. Statutes specified the penalties for crimes but nearly always gave the sentencing judge wide discretion to decide whether the offender should be incarcerated and for how long, whether he should be fined and how much, and whether some lesser restraint, such as probation, should be imposed instead of imprisonment or fine.

* * *

Both indeterminate sentencing and parole were based on concepts of the offender's possible, indeed probable, rehabilitation, a view that it was realistic to attempt to rehabilitate the inmate and thereby to minimize the risk that he would resume criminal activity upon his return to society. It obviously required the judge and the parole officer to make their respective sentencing and release decisions upon their own assessments of the offender's amenability to rehabilitation. As a result, the court and the officer were in positions to exercise, and usually did exercise, very broad discretion.

This led almost inevitably to the conclusion on the part of a reviewing court that the sentencing judge "sees more and senses more" than the appellate court; thus, the judge enjoyed the "superiority of his nether position," for that court's determination as to what sentence was appropriate met with virtually unconditional deference on appeal. The decision whether to parole was also "predictive and discretionary." [Citation omitted.] The correction official possessed almost absolute discretion over the parole decision.

Historically, federal sentencing—the function of determining the scope and extent of punishment—never has been thought to be assigned by the Constitution to the exclusive jurisdiction of any one of the three Branches of Government. Congress, of course, has the power to fix the sentence for a federal crime, and the scope of judicial discretion with respect to a sentence is subject to congressional control [citation omitted]. Congress early abandoned fixed-sentence rigidity, however, and put in place a system of ranges within which the sentencer could choose the precise punishment. Congress delegated almost unfettered discretion to the sentencing judge to determine what the sentence should be within the customarily wide range so selected. This broad discretion was further enhanced by the power later granted the judge to suspend the sentence and by the resulting growth of an elaborate probation system. Also, with the advent of parole, Congress moved toward a "three-way sharing" of sentencing responsibility by granting corrections personnel in the Executive Branch the discretion to release a prisoner before the expiration of the sentence imposed by the judge. Thus, under the indeterminate-sentence system, Congress defined the maximum, the judge imposed a sentence within the statutory range (which he usually could replace with probation), and the Executive Branch's parole official eventually determined the actual duration of imprisonment.

* * *

Continued

Serious disparities in sentences, however, were common. Rehabilitation as a sound penological theory came to be questioned and, in any event, was regarded by some as an unattainable goal for most cases.

* * *

In 1958, Congress authorized the creation of judicial sentencing institutes and joint councils, to formulate standards and criteria for sentencing. In 1973, the United States Parole Board adopted guidelines that established a "customary range" of confinement. Congress in 1976 endorsed this initiative through the Parole Commission and Reorganization Act, an attempt to envision for the Parole Commission a role, at least in part, "to moderate the disparities in the sentencing practices of individual judges." That Act, however, did not disturb the division of sentencing responsibility among the three Branches. The judge continued to exercise discretion and to set the sentence within the statutory range fixed by Congress, while the prisoner's actual release date generally was set by the Parole Commission.

This proved to be no more than a way station. Fundamental and widespread dissatisfaction with the uncertainties and the disparities continued to be expressed. Congress had wrestled with the problem for more than a decade when, in 1984, it enacted the sweeping reforms that are at issue here.

Helpful in our consideration and analysis of the statute is the Senate Report on the 1984 legislation. The Report referred to the "outmoded rehabilitation model" for federal criminal sentencing, and recognized that the efforts of the criminal justice system to achieve rehabilitation of offenders had failed. It observed that the indeterminate-sentencing system had two "unjustifi[ed]" and "shameful" consequences. The first was the great variation among sentences imposed by different judges upon similarly situated offenders. The second was the uncertainty as to the time the offender would spend in prison. Each was a serious impediment to an evenhanded and effective operation of the criminal justice system. The Report went on to note that parole was an inadequate device for overcoming these undesirable consequences. This was due to the division of authority between the sentencing judge and the parole officer who often worked at cross purposes; to the fact that the

Parole Commission's own guidelines did not take into account factors Congress regarded as important in sentencing, such as the sophistication of the offender and the role the offender played in an offense committed with others, and to the fact that the Parole Commission had only limited power to adjust a sentence imposed by the court.

Before settling on a mandatory-guideline system, Congress considered other competing proposals for sentencing reform. It rejected strict determinate sentencing because it concluded that a guideline system would be successful in reducing sentence disparities while retaining the flexibility needed to adjust for unanticipated factors arising in a particular case. The Judiciary Committee rejected a proposal that would have made the sentencing guidelines only advisory.

* * *

C

The Sentencing Commission

The Commission is established "as an independent commission in the judicial branch of the United States." It has seven voting members (one of whom is the Chairman) appointed by the President "by and with the advice and consent of the Senate." "At least three of the members shall be Federal judges selected after considering a list of six judges recommended to the President by the Judicial Conference of the United States." No more than four members of the Commission shall be members of the same political party. The Attorney General, or his designee, is an ex officio non-voting member. The Chairman and other members of the Commission are subject to removal by the President "only for neglect of duty or malfeasance in office or for other good cause shown." Except for initial staggering of terms, a voting member serves for six years and may not serve more than two full terms.

D

The Responsibilities of the Commission

In addition to the duty the Commission has to promulgate determinative-sentence guidelines, it is under an obligation periodically to "review and revise" the guidelines. It is to "consult with authorities on, and individual and institutional representatives of, various aspects of the Federal

Continued

criminal justice system." It must report to Congress "any amendments of the guidelines." It is to make recommendations to Congress whether the grades or maximum penalties should be modified. It must submit to Congress at least annually an analysis of the operation of the guidelines. It is to issue "general policy statements" regarding their application. And it has the power to "establish general policies . . . as are necessary to carry out the purposes" of the legislation; to "monitor the performance of probation officers" with respect to the guidelines; to "devise and conduct periodic training programs of instruction in sentencing techniques for judicial and probation personnel" and others; and to "perform such other functions as are required to permit Federal courts to meet their responsibilities" as to sentencing.

We note, in passing, that the monitoring function is not without its burden. Every year, with respect to each of more than 40,000 sentences, the federal courts must forward, and the Commission must review, the presentence report, the guideline worksheets, the tribunal's sentencing statement, and any written plea agreement.

* * *

III

Delegation of Power

Petitioner argues that in delegating the power to promulgate sentencing guidelines for every federal criminal offense to an independent Sentencing Commission, Congress has granted the Commission excessive legislative discretion in violation of the constitutionally based nondelegation doctrine. We do not agree.

The nondelegation doctrine is rooted in the principle of separation of powers that underlies our tripartite system of Government. The Constitution provides that "[a]ll legislative Powers herein granted shall be vested in a Congress of the United States," and we long have insisted that "the integrity and maintenance of the system of government ordained by the Constitution" mandate that Congress generally cannot delegate its legislative power to another Branch. We also have recognized, however, that the separation-of-powers principle, and the nondelegation doctrine in particular, do not prevent Congress from obtaining the assistance of its coordinate Branches. In a passage now enshrined in our jurisprudence, Chief Justice Taft, writing for the Court, explained our approach to such cooperative ventures: "In determining what [Congress] may do in seeking assistance from another branch, the extent and character of that assistance must be fixed according to common sense and the inherent necessities of the government co-ordination." So long as Congress "shall lay down by legislative act an intelligible principle to which the person or body authorized to [exercise the delegated authority] is directed to conform, such legislative action is not a forbidden delegation of legislative power."

Applying this "intelligible principle" test to congressional delegations, our jurisprudence has been driven by a practical understanding that in our increasingly complex society, replete with ever changing and more technical problems, Congress simply cannot do its job absent an ability to delegate power under broad general directives. "The Constitution has never been regarded as denying to the Congress the necessary resources of flexibility and practicality, which will enable it to perform its function." Accordingly, this Court has deemed it "constitutionally sufficient if Congress clearly delineates the general policy, the public agency which is to apply it, and the boundaries of this delegated authority."

Until 1935, this Court never struck down a challenged statute on delegation grounds.

* * *

In light of our approval of these broad delegations, we harbor no doubt that Congress' delegation of authority to the Sentencing Commission is sufficiently specific and detailed to meet constitutional requirements. Congress charged the Commission with three goals: to "assure the meeting of the purposes of sentencing as set forth" in the Act; to "provide certainty and fairness in meeting the purposes of sentencing, avoiding unwarranted sentencing disparities among defendants with similar records . . . while maintaining sufficient flexibility to permit individualized sentences," where appropriate; and to "reflect, to the extent practicable, advancement in knowledge of human behavior as it relates to the criminal justice process." Congress further specified four "purposes" of sentencing that the Commission must pursue in carrying out its mandate: "to reflect the seriousness of the offense, to promote respect for the law, and to provide just punishment for the offense"; "to afford adequate deterrence to criminal conduct";

Continued

"to protect the public from further crimes of the defendant"; and "to provide the defendant with needed . . . correctional treatment."

In addition, Congress prescribed the specific tool—the guidelines system—for the Commission to use in regulating sentencing. More particularly, Congress directed the Commission to develop a system of "sentencing ranges" applicable "for each category of offense involving each category of defendant." Congress instructed the Commission that these sentencing ranges must be consistent with pertinent provisions of Title 18 of the United States Code and could not include sentences in excess of the statutory maxima. Congress also required that for sentences of imprisonment, "the maximum of the range established for such a term shall not exceed the minimum of that range by more than the greater of 25 percent or 6 months, except that, if the minimum term of the range is 30 years or more, the maximum may be life imprisonment." Moreover, Congress directed the Commission to use current average sentences "as a starting point" for its structuring of the sentencing ranges.

To guide the Commission in its formulation of offense categories, Congress directed it to consider seven factors: the grade of the offense; the aggravating and mitigating circumstances of the crime; the nature and degree of the harm caused by the crime; the community view of the gravity of the offense; the public concern generated by the crime; the deterrent effect that a particular sentence may have on others; and the current incidence of the offense. Congress set forth 11 factors for the Commission to consider in establishing categories of defendants. These include the offender's age, education, vocational skills, mental and emotional condition, physical condition (including drug dependence), previous employment record, family ties and responsibilities, community ties, role in the offense, criminal history, and degree of dependence upon crime for a livelihood. Congress also prohibited the Commission from considering the "race, sex, national origin, creed, and socioeconomic status of offenders," and instructed that the guidelines should reflect the "general inappropriateness" of considering certain other factors, such as current unemployment, that might serve as proxies for forbidden factors.

In addition to these overarching constraints, Congress provided even more detailed guidance to the Commission about categories of offenses and offender characteristics. Congress directed that guidelines require a term of confinement at or near the statutory maximum for certain crimes of violence and for drug offenses, particularly when committed by recidivists. Congress further directed that the Commission assure a substantial term of imprisonment for an offense constituting a third felony conviction, for a career felon, for one convicted of a managerial role in a racketeering enterprise, for a crime of violence by an offender on release from a prior felony conviction, and for an offense involving a substantial quantity of narcotics. Congress also instructed "that the guidelines reflect . . . the general appropriateness of imposing a term of imprisonment" for a crime of violence that resulted in serious bodily injury. On the other hand, Congress directed that guidelines reflect the general inappropriateness of imposing a sentence of imprisonment "in cases in which the defendant is a first offender who has not been convicted of a crime of violence or an otherwise serious offense." Congress also enumerated various aggravating and mitigating circumstances, such as, respectively, multiple offenses or substantial assistance to the Government, to be reflected in the guidelines. In other words, although Congress granted the Commission substantial discretion in formulating guidelines, in actuality it legislated a full hierarchy of punishment—from near maximum imprisonment, to substantial imprisonment, to some imprisonment, to alternatives—and stipulated the most important offense and offender characteristics to place defendants within these categories.

We cannot dispute petitioner's contention that the Commission enjoys significant discretion in formulating guidelines. The Commission does have discretionary authority to determine the relative severity of federal crimes and to assess the relative weight of the offender characteristics that Congress listed for the Commission to consider. The Commission also has significant discretion to determine which crimes have been punished too leniently, and which too severely. Congress has called upon the Commission to exercise its judgment about which types of crimes and which types of criminals are to be considered similar for the purposes of sentencing.

But our cases do not at all suggest that delegations of this type may not carry with them the need to exercise judgment on matters of policy. In *Yakus v. United States*, the Court upheld a

Continued

delegation to the Price Administrator to fix commodity prices that "in his judgment will be generally fair and equitable and will effectuate the purposes of this Act" to stabilize prices and avert speculation. In *National Broadcasting Co. v. United States*, we upheld a delegation to the Federal Communications Commission granting it the authority to promulgate regulations in accordance with its view of the "public interest." In *Yakus*, the Court laid down the applicable principle:

> "It is no objection that the determination of facts and the inferences to be drawn from them in the light of the statutory standards and declaration of policy call for the exercise of judgment, and for the formulation of subsidiary administrative policy within the prescribed statutory framework. . . .

* * *

> "[O]nly if we could say that that there is an absence of standards for the guidance of the Administrator's action, so that it would be impossible in a proper proceeding to ascertain whether the will of Congress has been obeyed, would we be justified in overriding its choice of means for effecting its declared purpose. . . ."

Congress has met that standard here. The Act sets forth more than merely an "intelligible principle" or minimal standards. One court has aptly put it: "The statute outlines the policies which prompted establishment of the Commission, explains what the Commission should do and how it should do it, and sets out specific directives to govern particular situations."

Developing proportionate penalties for hundreds of different crimes by a virtually limitless array of offenders is precisely the sort of intricate, labor-intensive task for which delegation to an expert body is especially appropriate. Although Congress has delegated significant discretion to the Commission to draw judgments from its analysis of existing sentencing practice and alternative sentencing models, "Congress is not confined to that method of executing its policy which involves the least possible delegation of discretion to administrative officers." We have no doubt that in the hands of the Commission "the criteria which Congress has supplied are wholly adequate for carrying out the general policy and purpose" of the Act.

* * *

V

We conclude that in creating the Sentencing Commission—an unusual hybrid in structure and authority—Congress neither delegated excessive legislative power nor upset the constitutionally mandated balance of powers among the coordinate Branches. The Constitution's structural protections do not prohibit Congress from delegating to an expert body located within the Judicial Branch the intricate task of formulating sentencing guidelines consistent with such significant statutory direction as is present here. Nor does our system of checked and balanced authority prohibit Congress from calling upon the accumulated wisdom and experience of the Judicial Branch in creating policy on a matter uniquely within the ken of judges. Accordingly, we hold that the Act is constitutional.

The judgment of United States District Court for the Western District of Missouri is affirmed.

It is so ordered.

It seems clear that the Court is willing to allow Congress to delegate its powers so long as the delegation is to an expert body or individual whose charge is to fill in the details or to work in an area needing certain expertise that Congress as a whole does not possess.

The chart in Exhibit 4.1 demonstrates how Congress' legislative power is put to use in the passage of new legislation.[9]

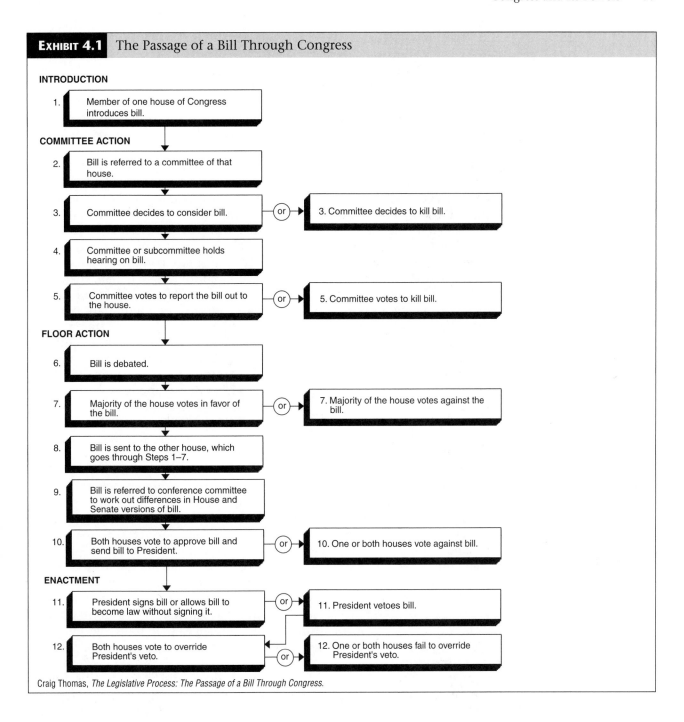

Exhibit 4.1   The Passage of a Bill Through Congress

INTRODUCTION

1. Member of one house of Congress introduces bill.

COMMITTEE ACTION

2. Bill is referred to a committee of that house.

3. Committee decides to consider bill.   or   3. Committee decides to kill bill.

4. Committee or subcommittee holds hearing on bill.

5. Committee votes to report the bill out to the house.   or   5. Committee votes to kill bill.

FLOOR ACTION

6. Bill is debated.

7. Majority of the house votes in favor of the bill.   or   7. Majority of the house votes against the bill.

8. Bill is sent to the other house, which goes through Steps 1–7.

9. Bill is referred to conference committee to work out differences in House and Senate versions of bill.

10. Both houses vote to approve bill and send bill to President.   or   10. One or both houses vote against bill.

ENACTMENT

11. President signs bill or allows bill to become law without signing it.   or   11. President vetoes bill.

12. Both houses vote to override President's veto.   or   12. One or both houses fail to override President's veto.

Craig Thomas, *The Legislative Process: The Passage of a Bill Through Congress.*

THE COMMERCE CLAUSE

One of the most litigated areas concerning congressional power involves the **Commerce Clause** found in Article I, § 8. This clause has two major purposes. First, it is the source of one of the most important powers held by the federal government and second, it limits the power of the states to regulate in a way that no other clause of the Constitution does.

The first major case to interpret the Commerce Clause and congressional power to regulate in that area was *Gibbons v. Ogden*.[10] The facts of this case are that Gibbons was a former partner of Ogden. Ogden had a monopoly granted by New York to operate steamboats on New York Harbor from New York City

Commerce Clause   the provision of the U.S. Constitution (Article I, Section 8) that gives Congress the power to control trade with foreign countries and from state to state.

to New Jersey. Gibbons began competing with his former partner. While Ogden's license was granted by New York, Gibbons' license had been granted by the federal legislature. Ogden sued to stop Gibbons from operating and the trial court granted an injunction against Gibbons ordering him to stop operating his ferry service. Gibbons brought his appeal to the Supreme Court arguing that the New York statute that had given Ogden a monopoly was unconstitutional and violated the commerce power granted to Congress under the Constitution.

The Court had to answer the question of whether the New York law was unconstitutional because it usurped Congress' power to regulate interstate **commerce**. Chief Justice Marshall wrote for the majority and concluded that the word commerce included navigation and therefore Congress had the right to regulate navigation even though the word was not expressly used when granting Congress the enumerated power to regulate interstate commerce. When Congress was given the authority to regulate commerce "among the several states" in Article I, § 8, this meant, according to Marshall, that in addition to being able to regulate commerce between states, it also included commerce beginning in one state, extending to another, and terminating back in the state of origin. Intrastate commerce begins and ends in one state without involving another state in any way. Interstate commerce can mean shipping in one state to another state, or as in this case, it can also mean that commerce begins in one state, touches one or more other states, and terminates in the original state. If the commerce power did not allow Congress to regulate the latter, it would be useless and ineffectual. States and corporations could avoid any federal regulation of their commerce activity by making sure that it always terminates back in its state in some way. Doing so would eliminate the federal power granted in the Constitution. The only limit on Congress' commerce power is the Constitution itself.

A second question the Court had to answer in this case was whether a state has the right to pass laws which concurrently affect interstate commerce. The Court's answer was no. Chief Justice Marshall wrote that while there may be some cases where a state may act concurrently with Congress to regulate interstate commerce, such was not the case here. The Court held that this power could not be shared. A state can use its police powers to require inspections, or pass other laws that may have some impact on interstate commerce, but this is different from allowing the state to regulate interstate commerce. Only Congress has the power to do so. If a state law encroaches or conflicts with Congress' ability to regulate interstate commerce, that state law must fail. The **Supremacy Clause** demands this and the law in question be held unconstitutional.

In another commerce case that followed *Gibbons* in 1837, the Court heard the case of *Mayor of the City of New York v. Miln*,[11] which focused on the conflict between Congress' commerce power and the **Tenth Amendment**. While the Court had broadly defined Congress' commerce power in *Gibbons*, the Court was not willing to defer to this congressional power in this case. In this case the State of New York argued that it had the right to regulate for the health, safety, and welfare of its citizens and that the law in question did just that. The Court agreed with New York, and this set the stage for a period of time during which the Court tried to curb the regulatory power of the federal government by holding that certain state activities were not commerce and therefore not encompassed by the Commerce Clause. This is demonstrated in *Cooley v. Board of Wardens*.[12]

In the *Cooley* case a Pennsylvania statute was challenged. The state required all riverboats to have a pilot on board in order to dock. If a boat failed to follow this requirement, the boat's captain was required to pay the state a fee. Cooley arrived without a pilot and the Board of Wardens of the Port of Philadelphia sued him to recover the fee due under the statute. At trial, the

commerce the buying, selling, transporting, or exchanging of goods or services.

Supremacy Clause the provision in Article IV of the U.S. Constitution that the U.S. Constitution, laws, and treaties take precedence over conflicting state constitutions or laws.

Tenth Amendment the U.S. constitutional amendment that says all powers not specifically given to the federal government are kept by the states and the people.

magistrate ordered Cooley to pay the fee, and Cooley appealed. The question on appeal was, Does the commerce power granted to Congress exclude the power of the States to also regulate? In a narrow decision the Court refused to hold that Congress' power to regulate interstate commerce was exclusive, but also refused to say that the States could pass laws affecting interstate commerce in all areas. The Court was clear that it was only deciding the issue of whether a state could regulate the use of pilots on navigable waters within its own borders. The Court held that Pennsylvania could do so, but in so doing, it left open the question of exactly how far state regulation of interstate commerce could extend. It was not until the 1930s and the discussion of the New Deal statutes and programs that the Court resolved this question. Up to that point, however, the Court followed a doctrine of dual federalism. Under dual federalism, Congress had the power to regulate if there was a direct effect on interstate commerce. If the effect was indirect or incidental, Congress could not regulate it as interstate commerce.

A case that demonstrates dual federalism is *Hammer v. Dagenhart.*[13] This case challenged the Child Labor Law, which attempted to prevent interstate commerce involving goods produced by manufacturers using child labor in the manufacturing process.

HAMMER V. DAGENHART
247 U.S. 251 (1918)

Mr. Justice DAY delivered the opinion of the Court.

A bill was filed in the United States District Court for the Western District of North Carolina by a father in his own behalf and as next friend of his two minor sons, one under the age of fourteen years and the other between the ages of fourteen and sixteen years, employees in a cotton mill at Charlotte, North Carolina, to enjoin the enforcement of the act of Congress intended to prevent interstate commerce in the products of child labor.

The District Court held the act unconstitutional and entered a decree enjoining its enforcement. This appeal brings the case here.

Other sections of the act contain provisions for its enforcement and prescribe penalties for its violation.

The attack upon the act rests upon three propositions: First: It is not a regulation of interstate and foreign commerce; second: It contravenes the Tenth Amendment to the Constitution; third: It conflicts with the Fifth Amendment to the Constitution.

The controlling question for decision is: Is it within the authority of Congress in regulating commerce among the states to prohibit the transportation in interstate commerce of manufactured goods, the product of a factory in which, within thirty days prior to their removal therefrom [sic] children under the age of fourteen have been employed or permitted to work, or children between the ages of fourteen and sixteen years have been employed or permitted to work more than eight hours in any day, or more than six days in any week, or after the hour of 7 o'clock p. m., or before the hour of 6 o'clock a. m.?

The power essential to the passage of this act, the government contends, is found in the commerce clause of the Constitution which authorizes Congress to regulate commerce with foreign nations and among the states. . . . [T]he power is one to control the means by which commerce is carried on, which is directly the contrary of the assumed right to forbid commerce from moving and thus destroying it as to particular commodities. But it is insisted that adjudged cases in this court establish the doctrine that the power to regulate given to Congress incidentally includes the authority to prohibit the movement of ordinary commodities and therefore that the subject is not open for discussion. The cases demonstrate the contrary. They rest upon the character of the particular subjects dealt with and the fact that the scope of governmental authority, state or national, possessed over them is

Continued

such that the authority to prohibit is as to them but the exertion of the power to regulate.

* * *

In each of these instances the use of interstate transportation was necessary to the accomplishment of harmful results. In other words, although the power over interstate transportation was to regulate, that could only be accomplished by prohibiting the use of the facilities of interstate commerce to effect the evil intended.

This element is wanting in the present case. The thing intended to be accomplished by this statute is the denial of the facilities of interstate commerce to those manufacturers in the states who employ children within the prohibited ages. The act in its effect does not regulate transportation among the states, but aims to standardize the ages at which children may be employed in mining and manufacturing within the states. The goods shipped are of themselves harmless. The act permits them to be freely shipped after thirty days from the time of their removal from the factory. When offered for shipment, and before transportation begins, the labor of their production is over, and the mere fact that they were intended for interstate commerce transportation does not make their production subject to federal control under the commerce power.

Commerce 'consists of intercourse and traffic

* * *

and includes the transportation of persons and property, as well as the purchase, sale and exchange of commodities.' The making of goods and the mining of coal are not commerce, nor does the fact that these things are to be afterwards shipped, or used in interstate commerce, make their production a part thereof.

Over interstate transportation, or its incidents, the regulatory power of Congress is ample, but the production of articles, intended for interstate commerce, is a matter of local regulation. 'When the commerce begins is determined, not by the character of the commodity, nor by the intention of the owner to transfer it to another state for sale, nor by his preparation of it for transportation, but by its actual delivery to a common carrier for transportation, or the actual commencement of its transfer to another state.' This principle has been recognized often in this court.

If it were otherwise, all manufacture intended for interstate shipment would be brought under federal control to the practical exclusion of the authority of the states, a result certainly not contemplated by the framers of the Constitution when they vested in Congress the authority to regulate commerce among the States.

It is further contended that the authority of Congress may be exerted to control interstate commerce in the shipment of childmade [sic] goods because of the effect of the circulation of such goods in other states where the evil of this class of labor has been recognized by local legislation, and the right to thus employ child labor has been more rigorously restrained than in the state of production. In other words, that the unfair competition, thus engendered, may be controlled by closing the channels of interstate commerce to manufacturers in those states where the local laws do not meet what Congress deems to be the more just standard of other states.

There is no power vested in Congress to require the states to exercise their police power so as to prevent possible unfair competition. Many causes may co-operate to give one state, by reason of local laws or conditions, an economic advantage over others. The commerce clause was not intended to give to Congress a general authority to equalize such conditions. In some of the states laws have been passed fixing minimum wages for women, in others the local law regulates the hours of labor of women in various employments. Business done in such states may be at an economic disadvantage when compared with states which have no such regulations; surely, this fact does not give Congress the power to deny transportation in interstate commerce to those who carry on business where the hours of labor and the rate of compensation for women have not been fixed by a standard in use in other states and approved by Congress.

The grant of power of Congress over the subject of interstate commerce was to enable it to regulate such commerce, and not to give it authority to control the states in their exercise of the police power over local trade and manufacture.

The grant of authority over a purely federal matter was not intended to destroy the local power always existing and carefully reserved to the states in the Tenth Amendment to the Constitution.

Continued

Police regulations relating to the internal trade and affairs of the states have been uniformly recognized as within such control.

* * *

That there should be limitations upon the right to employ children in mines and factories in the interest of their own and the public welfare, all will admit. That such employment is generally deemed to require regulation is shown by the fact that the brief of counsel states that every state in the Union has a law upon the subject, limiting the right to thus employ children. In North Carolina, the state wherein is located the factory in which the employment was had in the present case, no child under twelve years of age is permitted to work.

It may be desirable that such laws be uniform, but our federal government is one of enumerated powers; 'this principle,' declared Chief Justice Marshall in *McCulloch v. Maryland* 'is universally admitted.'

A statute must be judged by its natural and reasonable effect. The control by Congress over interstate commerce cannot authorize the exercise of authority not entrusted to it by the Constitution. The maintenance of the authority of the states over matters purely local is as essential to the preservation of our institutions as is the conservation of the supremacy of the federal power in all matters entrusted to the nation by the federal Constitution.

In interpreting the Constitution it must never be forgotten that the nation is made up of states to which are entrusted the powers of local government. And to them and to the people the powers not expressly delegated to the national government are reserved. The power of the states to regulate their purely internal affairs by such laws as seem wise to the local authority is inherent and has never been surrendered to the general government. To sustain this statute would not be in our judgment a recognition of the lawful exertion of congressional authority over interstate commerce, but would sanction an invasion by the federal power of the control of a matter purely local in its character, and over which no authority has been delegated to Congress in conferring the power to regulate commerce among the states.

We have neither authority nor disposition to question the motives of Congress in enacting this legislation. The purposes intended must be attained consistently with constitutional limitations and not by an invasion of the powers of the states. This court has no more important function than that which devolves upon it the obligation to preserve inviolate the constitutional limitations upon the exercise of authority federal and state to the end that each may continue to discharge, harmoniously with the other, the duties entrusted to it by the Constitution.

In our view the necessary effect of this act is, by means of a prohibition against the movement in interstate commerce of ordinary commercial commodities to regulate the hours of labor of children in factories and mines within the states, a purely state authority. Thus the act in a two-fold sense is repugnant to the Constitution. It not only transcends the authority delegated to Congress over commerce but also exerts a power as to a purely local matter to which the federal authority does not extend. The far reaching result of upholding the act cannot be more plainly indicated than by pointing out that if Congress can thus regulate matters entrusted to local authority by prohibition of the movement of commodities in interstate commerce, all freedom of commerce will be at an end, and the power of the states over local matters may be eliminated, and thus our system of government be practically destroyed.

For these reasons we hold that this law exceeds the constitutional authority of Congress. It follows that the decree of the District Court must be Affirmed.

As the majority opinion indicates, the Court fully recognized the evil of child labor, but was unwilling to allow Congress to use its commerce power to regulate in that area. The regulation in this statute was not directly related to interstate commerce and therefore was unconstitutional.

Perhaps the most important part of this decision is the dissent. It was this dissent, written by Justice Holmes, that eventually became the majority view in many later cases. The dissent follows:

Mr. Justice HOLMES, dissenting.

The single question in this case is whether Congress has power to prohibit the shipment in interstate or foreign commerce of any product of a cotton mill situated in the United States, in which within thirty days before the removal of the product children under fourteen have been employed, or children between fourteen and sixteen have been employed more than eight hours in a day, or more than six days in any week, or between seven in the evening and six in the morning. The objection urged against the power is that the States have exclusive control over their methods of production and that Congress cannot meddle with them, and taking the proposition in the sense of direct intermeddling I agree to it and suppose that no one denies it. But if an act is within the powers specifically conferred upon Congress, it seems to me that it is not made any less constitutional because of the indirect effects that it may have, however obvious it may be that it will have those effects, and that we are not at liberty upon such grounds to hold it void.

The first step in my argument is to make plain what no one is likely to dispute—that the statute in question is within the power expressly given to Congress if considered only as to its immediate effects and that if invalid it is so only upon some collateral ground. The statute confines itself to prohibiting the carriage of certain goods in interstate or foreign commerce. Congress is given power to regulate such commerce in unqualified terms. It would not be argued today that the power to regulate does not include the power to prohibit. Regulation means the prohibition of something, and when interstate commerce is the matter to be regulated I cannot doubt that the regulation may prohibit any part of such commerce that Congress sees fit to forbid. At all events it is established by the Lottery Case and others that have followed it that a law is not beyond the regulative power of Congress merely because it prohibits certain transportation out and out. So I repeat that this statute in its immediate operation is clearly within the Congress's constitutional power.

The question then is narrowed to whether the exercise of its otherwise constitutional power by Congress can be pronounced unconstitutional because of its possible reaction upon the conduct of the States in a matter upon which I have admitted that they are free from direct control. I should have thought that that matter had been disposed of so fully as to leave no room for doubt. I should have thought that the most conspicuous decisions of this Court had made it clear that the power to regulate commerce and other constitutional powers could not be cut down or qualified by the fact that it might interfere with the carrying out of the domestic policy of any State.

The manufacture of oleomargarine is as much a matter of State regulation as the manufacture of cotton cloth. Congress levied a tax upon the compound when colored so as to resemble butter that was so great as obviously to prohibit the manufacture and sale. In a very elaborate discussion the present Chief Justice excluded any inquiry into the purpose of an act which apart from that purpose was within the power of Congress. As to foreign commerce see *Weber v. Freed; Brolan v. United States; Buttfield v. Stranahan.* Fifty years ago a tax on state banks, the obvious purpose and actual effect of which was to drive them, or at least their circulation, out of existence, was sustained, although the result was one that Congress had no constitutional power to require. The Court made short work of the argument as to the purpose of the Act. 'The Judicial cannot prescribe to the Legislative Departments of the Government limitations upon the exercise of its acknowledged powers.' So it well might have been argued that the corporation tax was intended under the guise of a revenue measure to secure a control not otherwise belonging to Congress, but the tax was sustained, and the objection so far as noticed was disposed of by citing *McCray v. United States; Flint v. Stone Tracy Co.* And to come to cases upon interstate commerce notwithstanding *United States v. E. C. Knight Co.*, the Sherman Act has been made an instrument for the breaking up of combinations in restraint of trade and monopolies, using the power to regulate commerce as a foothold, but not proceeding because that commerce was the end actually in mind. The objection that the control of the States over production was interfered with was urged again and again but always in vain.

The Pure Food and Drug Act which was sustained in *Hipolite Egg Co. v. United States*, with the intimation that 'no trade can be carried on between the States to which it [the power of Congress to regulate commerce] does not extend,' applies not merely to articles that the changing opinions of the time condemn as intrinsically harmful but to others innocent in themselves,

Continued

simply on the ground that the order for them was induced by a preliminary fraud. It does not matter whether the supposed evil precedes or follows the transportation. It is enough that in the opinion of Congress the transportation encourages the evil. I may add that in the cases on the so-called White Slave Act it was established that the means adopted by Congress as convenient to the exercise of its power might have the character of police regulations. In *Clark Distilling Co. v. Western Maryland Ry. Co., Leisy v. Hardin*, is quoted with seeming approval to the effect that 'a subject matter which has been confided exclusively to Congress by the Constitution is not within the jurisdiction of the police power of the State unless placed there by congressional action.' I see no reason for that proposition not applying here.

The notion that prohibition is any less prohibition when applied to things now thought evil I do not understand. But if there is any matter upon which civilized countries have agreed—far more unanimously than they have with regard to intoxicants and some other matters over which this country is now emotionally aroused—it is the evil of premature and excessive child labor. I should have thought that if we were to introduce our own moral conceptions where is my opinion they do not belong, this was preeminently a case for upholding the exercise of all its powers by the United States.

But I had thought that the propriety of the exercise of a power admitted to exist in some cases was for the consideration of Congress alone and that this Court always had disavowed the right to intrude its judgment upon questions of policy or morals. It is not for this Court to pronounce when prohibition is necessary to regulation if it ever may be necessary—to say that it is permissible as against strong drink but not as against the product of ruined lives.

The Act does not meddle with anything belonging to the States. They may regulate their internal affairs and their domestic commerce as they like. But when they seek to send their products across the State line they are no longer within their rights. If there were no Constitution and no Congress their power to cross the line would depend upon their neighbors. Under the Constitution such commerce belongs not to the States but to Congress to regulate. It may carry out its views of public policy whatever indirect effect they may have upon the activities of the States. Instead of being encountered by a prohibitive tariff at her boundaries the State encounters the public policy of the United States which it is for Congress to express. The public policy of the United States is shaped with a view to the benefit of the nation as a whole. If, as has been the case within the memory of men still living, a State should take a different view of the propriety of sustaining a lottery from that which generally prevails, I cannot believe that the fact would require a different decision from that reached in *Champion v. Ames*. Yet in that case it would be said with quite as much force as in this that Congress was attempting to intermeddle with the State's domestic affairs. The national welfare as understood by Congress may require a different attitude within its sphere from that of some self-seeking State. It seems to me entirely constitutional for Congress to enforce its understanding by all the means at its command. Mr. Justice McKENNA, Mr. Justice BRANDEIS, and Mr. Justice CLARKE concur in this opinion.

As Justice Holmes argued, the Tenth Amendment should not be a limitation on federal authority if the regulatory scheme falls under an enumerated power. So long as the regulatory power being exercised by Congress is within the power specifically granted to Congress by the Constitution. The fact that there is an incidental, collateral effect is irrelevant and does not make the statute unconstitutional. Justice Holmes' argument was later accepted in the case of *U.S. v. Darby*,[14] which expressly overruled *Hammer v. Dagenhart*.[15] The *Darby* case will be discussed below, but before that discussion, the impact of President Roosevelt's New Deal on congressional commerce power is appropriate.

Following the stock market crash of 1929, the United States entered into a new era of economic recession. This era, called the Great Depression, lasted until the beginning of the United States' involvement in World War II. Between the stock market crash and the war, President Roosevelt introduced a series of government regulations and public works projects that collectively became known as the New Deal. These government regulations were the source of much litigation involving the congressional commerce powers. In light of *Hammer v. Dagenhart*, it was clear that the Court was unsettled about how to deal with commerce power questions. Throughout the period of the New Deal, the Court was given opportunities to determine how best to handle the regulation of activities that directly affected interstate commerce.

One of the most famous New Deal cases was *Schechter Poultry Corporation v. United States*.[16] The case involved the National Industrial Recovery Act (NIRA), which allowed the President to adopt codes that set minimum wages, prices, maximum hours, and collective bargaining, among other things. Schechter Poultry allegedly violated the wage and hours sections of this statute, and challenged the statute claiming that since it only bought poultry within New York City and resold it exclusively to local retailers, that it was not engaged in interstate commerce, and therefore could not be regulated by the federal government. The Court agreed saying that Schechter's business transactions were not within the stream of interstate commerce. Nor did the Court believe that Schechter's business affected interstate commerce. In order for Schechter's business to be part of interstate commerce, and thus validly regulated by Congress, the business would have to have a direct impact on interstate commerce, not an indirect or incidental one. Since the Court did not find this direct effect, the Court struck down the statute as an unconstitutional use of commerce power. In doing so, the Court struck a blow against the New Deal.

A second blow to the New Deal came a year later in *Carter v. Carter Coal Company*,[17] in which the Bituminous Coal Conservation Act of 1935 was challenged. This Act set the minimum wages and maximum hours for coal mine workers. Carter Coal Company challenged this as being an invalid use of the federal commerce power. The Court agreed with the company and held the Act unconstitutional because what Congress was attempting to regulate was the production of coal, a purely local activity. In addition, the Court rejected the alternative argument that the production of coal directly affected interstate commerce. There was no logical connection between interstate commerce and the production of the coal. The Court did not accept the argument that the purely local production of coal had an impact on interstate commerce. They acknowledged that the coal may ultimately end up in interstate commerce, however, the production process, in and of itself, did not have such an impact. It only impacted local employees, using locally owned equipment and a mine that was located in the jurisdiction.

Lastly, the Court held that the employer-employee relationship is a local relationship that is the province of the state, and the federal government did not possess the power to regulate in that area. The Court ultimately held the entire statute unconstitutional, even though Justice Cardozo argued in his dissent that at least part of the statute was valid. Justice Cardozo argued that the portion of the statute that regulated minimum and maximum prices on the coal was valid because the sales of that coal had a direct impact on interstate commerce. However, only three other Justices agreed with Justice Cardozo and that portion of the statute was held invalid as well.

The *Carter Coal* case was important because it signaled the Court's perspective that those actions determined to be local in nature would not be eligible for regulation by the federal government. It seemed to indicate that any employer-employee relationship was local in nature and not subject to federal control. President Roosevelt's response to this was to propose the infamous court-packing plan discussed in Chapter 3. This plan was to expand the number of federal judges, and more particularly, the number of Supreme Court justices. The plan ultimately failed, but it created controversy, and many resented the means chosen by the executive branch to change the balance of power in the federal government. The effect of the proposed plan and the controversy surrounding it was that the Court changed itself. Once Justice Van Devanter retired, a new majority was created on the Court. This changed alliances within the Court, setting up the opportunity for a new majority to emerge. It was this new majority that decided the case that brought the Court to the modern view of the Commerce Clause.

The case in question is *NLRB v. Jones & Laughlin Steel Corporation*.[18] In this case, Jones & Laughlin Steel Corporation was a large steelmaker that was attempting to prevent its employees from unionizing and went so far as to fire employees who were involved in union activities. When the affected employees complained to the National Labor Relations Board and that board began enforcing the National Labor Relations Act (protecting workers who wanted to organize and form a union), Jones & Laughlin challenged the Act as an unconstitutional use of the federal commerce power. Sections 8 and 9 of that Act set forth the rights of employees to organize and use collective bargaining through representatives of their own choosing, among other employee rights and benefits. Jones & Laughlin argued that the law ought to be struck down as it "is in reality a regulation of labor relations and not of interstate commerce," that its production is not subject to regulation by the federal government, and that certain provisions of the Act violate the Fifth and Seventh Amendments to the Constitution.[19]

When reviewing Jones & Laughlin's claims, the Court found the following facts: Jones & Laughlin only manufactured steel and iron in Pennsylvania, but had large holdings in several other states, used the Great Lakes shipping line to transport goods, owned iron mines in other states, owned warehouses in other states, and shipped the majority of its products through interstate commerce. The Court looked at five different issues. The first issue concerned the scope of the Act in question. It noted that the Act was being challenged in its entirety as an attempt to regulate the entire industry and this violated the reserved powers of the state to regulate intrastate commerce. The Court held in favor of the Act saying, "We think it clear that the National Labor Relations Act may be construed so as to operate within the sphere of constitutional authority."[20] In so holding, the Court paid deference to the legislative intent behind the statute, and broadly defined both the term "commerce" and the phrase "affecting commerce." The Court defined these terms as follows:

> "'The term 'commerce' means trade, traffic, commerce, transportation, or communication among the several States, or between the District of Columbia or any Territory of the United States and any state or other Territory, or between any foreign country and any State, Territory, or the District of Columbia, or within the District of Columbia or any Territory, or between points in the same State but through any other State or any Territory or the District of Columbia or any foreign country.' ✳ ✳ ✳

> 'The term 'affecting commerce' means in commerce, or burdening or obstructing commerce or the free flow of commerce, or having led or tending to lead to a labor dispute burdening or obstructing commerce or the free flow of commerce.'"[21]

The Court's definition of these terms led to the conclusion that the grant of authority to the National Labor Relations Board reaches "only what may be deemed to burden or obstruct [foreign or interstate] commerce."[22] In so doing, the power must be construed to be constitutional.

The Court went on to conclude that collective bargaining, as provided for in the challenged Act, is a fundamental right. "Employees have as clear a right to organize and select their representatives for lawful purposes as the respondent has to organize its business and select its own officers and agents."[23]

As for Jones & Laughlin's argument that their business at the factory where the alleged discrimination took place was strictly intrastate commerce and federal regulation of that business was beyond the scope of congressional commerce power, the Court disagreed. It said that, "[t]he fundamental principle is that the power to regulate commerce is the power to enact 'all appropriate legislation' for its 'protection or advancement,' adopt measures 'to promote its growth and insure its safety,' 'to foster, protect, control and restrain.' "[24] The Court went on to say that intrastate commerce, if it is closely and intimately related to interstate commerce, falls within federal control. That was the case here. The Court maintained that Jones & Laughlin's business was so closely related to interstate commerce, by virtue of its holdings in other states, its use of interstate transportation, and the nature of its business.

In holding that Congress had the authority to regulate commerce based on the "close and intimate" relationship between intrastate and interstate commerce, the Court abandoned the direct, logical relationship requirement used by the Court in earlier New Deal litigation. The new terminology used by this Court was the "substantial economic effect" test to be used by the Court in commerce cases in the future.

NLRB v. Jones & Laughlin Steel was the beginning of the Court's modern trend to expand the reach of the Commerce Clause. There are three tests used by the Court to decide cases in the modern era. While *Jones & Laughlin* demonstrates the first of these theories, the "substantial economic effect" theory, the other two theories, the "cumulative effect" and "expanded commerce-prohibiting protective" theories come with two other types of cases.

The "cumulative effect" theory provides that Congress may regulate both acts that would have a substantial economic effect on interstate commerce. An example of the Court's use of this theory is in *Wickard v. Filburn*.[25] Filburn owned and operated a small farm in Ohio. On his farm he maintained a dairy herd, sold milk, raised poultry, and sold poultry and eggs. He also raised winter wheat that he used, first, to feed his livestock and seed for the following year and second, as a cash crop. Filburn challenged the Agricultural Adjustment Act of 1938 that allowed the Secretary of Agriculture to set quotas for raising wheat on all farms in the United States. These quotas applied to all wheat production, including the amount raised to be consumed on the farmer's own property. When Filburn produced more wheat than allowed under the Act, he was fined. Filburn sued the Secretary of Agriculture, Wickard, asking for an injunction against enforcement of the Act. When the trial court gave Filburn the requested injunction, Wickard appealed. On appeal, Wickard argued that the statute does not regulate production or consumption of the wheat, but only the marketing of it. This regulation is necessary and proper to guard against the negative impact a glut of wheat would have on the market.

Filburn argued that Congress did not have the power under the Commerce Clause to regulate local activities, such as production or consumption of wheat, and that these two activities, not marketing, were the thrust of the regulation of this Act. Further, Filburn argued that at most, the challenged activities had an indirect effect on interstate commerce.

In making its decision, the Court rejected its earlier line of reasoning as found in *Gibbons v. Ogden*. It discarded the "direct-indirect effect" discussion, saying that this was only a factor to be discussed when making a decision about the ability to regulate an activity through use of the Commerce Clause. The Court held that the appropriate test to use in this instance is the substantial effect the activity would have on interstate commerce. However, instead of looking at just the effect Filburn's activity would have on interstate commerce, the Court looked instead at the cumulative effect that the production of all the small farmers throughout the country would have on interstate commerce. In doing so, the Court concluded that the cumulative activity of these farmers had a substantial effect on interstate commerce and allowed Congress to regulate through use of the Commerce Clause.

In adopting this theory, the Court opened the door for future regulation of activities, which taken alone might not have a substantial effect on interstate commerce, but if taken together with the same activities by other businesses or individuals, would substantially affect interstate commerce. In doing so, the Court extended the congressional commerce power.

The third theory, which expanded the commerce power in the modern era, is the "commerce-prohibiting theory." This theory, which allows Congress to use prohibitions on interstate commerce to further police powers or general welfare regulations, is demonstrated in *U.S. v. Darby* mentioned above. This theory substantially broadens the federal commerce power.

In *Darby* the Court was asked to determine the constitutionality of the Fair Labor Standards Act of 1938 that set the minimum wages and maximum hours for employees engaged in the production of goods to be sold in interstate commerce. The purpose of the Act was to exclude from interstate commerce goods produced which "(1) causes commerce and the channels and instrumentalities of commerce to be used to spread and perpetuate such labor conditions among the workers of the several States; (2) burdens commerce and the free flow of goods in commerce; (3) constitutes an unfair method of competition in commerce; (4) leads to labor disputes burdening and obstructing commerce and the free flow of goods in commerce; and (5) interfere with the orderly and fair marketing of goods in commerce."[26] Darby argued that Congress' motive was not so much to regulate interstate commerce but to interfere with the employer-employee relationship and that this relationship is not the province of the federal government, but is within the control of the states. The Court held, however, that the motive of Congress is not relevant to its consideration. It upheld this statute and its purpose by saying, "we conclude that the prohibition of the shipment interstate of goods produced under the forbidden substandard labor conditions is within the constitutional authority of Congress."[27]

In doing so, the Court gave Congress free rein to impose whatever conditions it wished upon the privilege of engaging in an activity that substantially affects interstate commerce. The only limitation placed on Congress by the Court was that any regulation of interstate commerce must not conflict with independent constitutional prohibitions such as those found in the Fourth Amendment or the Fourteenth Amendment. Furthermore, the Court held that the Tenth Amendment would no longer act as an independent limitation on congressional authority to regulate interstate commerce.

This view remained the majority view for many years and the Court was deferential to congressional regulation of interstate commerce. In 1995, however, the Court decided a case, which demonstrated that some limits on Congress' Commerce Clause powers still existed. The case was *U.S. v. Lopez*,[28] which was the first case in 60 years where the Court invalidated a federal statute on the grounds that it went beyond the bounds of Congress' power under the Commerce Clause.

This case involved the Gun-Free School Zones Act of 1990 that made it a crime for an individual to possess a firearm within 1,000 feet of a school. Congress justified this law by using the Commerce Clause, but there was no finding that the activity being regulated actually impacted commerce. Also, the statute banned possession of all guns in a zone that the individual in possession knew or should have known was a school zone, not just those guns that had been part of interstate commerce.

The Court noted that it was not enough to just affect interstate commerce, but held that the activity being regulated must substantially affect interstate commerce. The Court said:

> "First, Congress may regulate the use of the channels of interstate commerce . . . Second, Congress is empowered to regulate and protect the instrumentalities of interstate commerce, or persons or things in interstate commerce,

even though the threat may come only from intrastate activities . . . Finally, Congress' commerce authority includes the power to regulate those activities having a substantial relation to interstate commerce, . . . i.e., those activities that substantially affect interstate commerce."[29]

When reviewing the statute itself, the Court did not find that the possession of guns in a school zone had been shown to substantially affect interstate commerce. The activity being regulated was not, in and of itself, commerce and the Court was not persuaded by the government's argument that the use of the guns in the commission of crimes had a negative aggregate effect on interstate commerce.

"The Government argues that possession of a firearm in a school zone may result in violent crime and that violent crime can be expected to affect the function of the nation economy in two ways. First the costs of violent crimes are substantial, and, through the mechanism of insurance, those costs are spread throughout the population. Second, violent crime reduces the willingness of individuals to travel to areas within the country that are perceived to be unsafe. The Government also argues that the presence of guns in schools poses a substantial threat to the educational process by threatening the learning environment. A handicapped educational process, in turn, will result in a less productive citizenry. That, in turn, would have an adverse effect on the nation's economic well-being. As a result, the Government argues that Congress could rationally have concluded that [this section] substantially affects interstate commerce."[30]

The Court went on to say that to accept the government's argument would be to convert the Commerce Clause into an unlimited source of power. "It is difficult to perceive any limitation on federal power, even in areas such as criminal law enforcement or education where States historically have been sovereign. Thus, if we were to accept the Government's arguments, we are hard-pressed to posit any activity that Congress is without power to regulate."[31] With this, the Court rejected the government's argument and held the Gun-Free School Zones Act of 1990 to be an unconstitutional use of Congress' power to regulate commerce.

The *Lopez* case, however, was not the most recent major case in which the Court considered the constitutionality of the use of Congress' commerce power. In 2000 the Court considered the case of *U.S. v. Morrison*.[32] In *Morrison* the Court addressed the Violence Against Women Act[33] and the civil action provided in that statute for women who are victims of gender-based crimes. The case began with a sexual assault by a football player against Christy Brzonkala at Virginia Polytechnic Institute and ultimately resulted in the Court striking down the statute as an invalid exercise of the congressional commerce power.

UNITED STATES V. MORRISON
529 U.S. 598 (2000)

Chief Justice REHNQUIST delivered the opinion of the Court.

In these cases we consider the constitutionality of 42 U.S.C. § 13981, which provides a federal civil remedy for the victims of gender-motivated violence. The United States Court of Appeals for the Fourth Circuit, sitting en banc, struck down § 13981 because it concluded that Congress lacked constitutional authority to enact the section's civil remedy.

Believing that these cases are controlled by our decisions in *United States v. Lopez, United States v. Harris*, and the *In re Civil Rights Cases*, we affirm.

Continued

I

Petitioner Christy Brzonkala enrolled at Virginia Polytechnic Institute (Virginia Tech) in the fall of 1994. In September of that year, Brzonkala met respondents Antonio Morrison and James Crawford, who were both students at Virginia Tech and members of its varsity football team. Brzonkala alleges that, within 30 minutes of meeting Morrison and Crawford, they assaulted and repeatedly raped her. After the attack, Morrison allegedly told Brzonkala, "You better not have any . . . diseases." In the months following the rape, Morrison also allegedly announced in the dormitory's dining room that he "like[d] to get girls drunk and. . . ." The omitted portions, quoted verbatim in the briefs on file with this Court, consist of boasting, debased remarks about what Morrison would do to women, vulgar remarks that cannot fail to shock and offend.

Brzonkala alleges that this attack caused her to become severely emotionally disturbed and depressed. She sought assistance from a university psychiatrist, who prescribed antidepressant medication. Shortly after the rape Brzonkala stopped attending classes and withdrew from the university.

In early 1995, Brzonkala filed a complaint against respondents under Virginia Tech's Sexual Assault Policy.

* * *

After the hearing, Virginia Tech's Judicial Committee found insufficient evidence to punish Crawford, but found Morrison guilty of sexual assault and sentenced him to immediate suspension for two semesters.

Virginia Tech's dean of students upheld the judicial committee's sentence. However, in July 1995, Virginia Tech informed Brzonkala that Morrison intended to initiate a court challenge to his conviction under the Sexual Assault Policy. University officials told her that a second hearing would be necessary to remedy the school's error in prosecuting her complaint under that policy, which had not been widely circulated to students.

* * *

Following this second hearing the Judicial Committee again found Morrison guilty and sentenced him to an identical 2-semester suspension. This time, however, the description of Morrison's offense was, without explanation, changed from "sexual assault" to "using abusive language."

Morrison appealed his second conviction through the university's administrative system. On August 21, 1995, Virginia Tech's senior vice president and provost set aside Morrison's punishment. She concluded that it was " 'excessive when compared with other cases where there has been a finding of violation of the Abusive Conduct Policy,' " Virginia Tech did not inform Brzonkala of this decision. After learning from a newspaper that Morrison would be returning to Virginia Tech for the fall 1995 semester, she dropped out of the university.

In December 1995, Brzonkala sued Morrison, Crawford, and Virginia Tech in the United States District Court for the Western District of Virginia. Her complaint alleged that Morrison's and Crawford's attack violated § 13981 and that Virginia Tech's handling of her complaint violated Title IX of the Education Amendments of 1972. Morrison and Crawford moved to dismiss this complaint on the grounds that it failed to state a claim and that § 13981's civil remedy is unconstitutional. The United States, petitioner in No. 99-5, intervened to defend § 13981's constitutionality.

The District Court dismissed Brzonkala's Title IX claims against Virginia Tech for failure to state a claim upon which relief can be granted. It then held that Brzonkala's complaint stated a claim against Morrison and Crawford under § 13981, but dismissed the complaint because it concluded that Congress lacked authority to enact the section under either the Commerce Clause or § 5 of the Fourteenth Amendment.

A divided panel of the Court of Appeals reversed the District Court, reinstating Brzonkala's § 13981 claim and her Title IX hostile environment claim. The full Court of Appeals vacated the panel's opinion and reheard the case en banc. The en banc court then issued an opinion affirming the District Court's conclusion that Brzonkala stated a claim under § 13981 because her complaint alleged a crime of violence and the allegations of Morrison's crude and derogatory statements regarding his treatment of women sufficiently indicated that his crime was motivated by gender animus. Nevertheless, the court by a divided vote affirmed the District Court's conclusion that Congress lacked constitutional authority to enact § 13981's civil remedy. Because the Court of Appeals invalidated a federal statute on constitutional grounds, we granted certiorari.

Continued

Section 13981 was part of the Violence Against Women Act of 1994, § 40302. It states that "[a]ll persons within the United States shall have the right to be free from crimes of violence motivated by gender." 42 U.S.C. § 13981(b). To enforce that right, subsection (c) declares:

> "A person (including a person who acts under color of any statute, ordinance, regulation, custom, or usage of any State) who commits a crime of violence motivated by gender and thus deprives another of the right declared in subsection (b) of this section shall be liable to the party injured, in an action for the recovery of compensatory and punitive damages, injunctive and declaratory relief, and such other relief as a court may deem appropriate."

* * *

Although the foregoing language of § 13981 covers a wide swath of criminal conduct, Congress placed some limitations on the section's federal civil remedy. Subsection (e)(1) states that "[n]othing in this section entitles a person to a cause of action under subsection (c) of this section for random acts of violence unrelated to gender or for acts that cannot be demonstrated, by a preponderance of the evidence, to be motivated by gender." Subsection (e)(4) further states that § 13981 shall not be construed "to confer on the courts of the United States jurisdiction over any State law claim seeking the establishment of a divorce, alimony, equitable distribution of marital property, or child custody decree."

Every law enacted by Congress must be based on one or more of its powers enumerated in the Constitution. "The powers of the legislature are defined and limited; and that those limits may not be mistaken, or forgotten, the constitution is written." Congress explicitly identified the sources of federal authority on which it relied in enacting § 13981. It said that a "Federal civil rights cause of action" is established "[p]ursuant to the affirmative power of Congress . . . under section 5 of the Fourteenth Amendment to the Constitution, as well as under section 8 of Article I of the Constitution." We address Congress' authority to enact this remedy under each of these constitutional provisions in turn.

II

Due respect for the decisions of a coordinate branch of Government demands that we invalidate a congressional enactment only upon a plain showing that Congress has exceeded its constitutional bounds. With this presumption of constitutionality in mind, we turn to the question whether § 13981 falls within Congress' power under Article I, § 8, of the Constitution. Brzonkala and the United States rely upon the third clause of the section, which gives Congress power "[t]o regulate Commerce with foreign Nations, and among the several States, and with the Indian Tribes."

As we discussed at length in Lopez, our interpretation of the Commerce Clause has changed as our Nation has developed. We need not repeat that detailed review of the Commerce Clause's history here; it suffices to say that, in the years since *NLRB v. Jones & Laughlin Steel Corp.*, Congress has had considerably greater latitude in regulating conduct and transactions under the Commerce Clause than our previous case law permitted. Lopez emphasized, however, that even under our modern, expansive interpretation of the Commerce Clause, Congress' regulatory authority is not without effective bounds.

* * *

As we observed in Lopez, modern Commerce Clause jurisprudence has "identified three broad categories of activity that Congress may regulate under its commerce power." "First, Congress may regulate the use of the channels of interstate commerce." "Second, Congress is empowered to regulate and protect the instrumentalities of interstate commerce, or persons or things in interstate commerce, even though the threat may come only from intrastate activities." "Finally, Congress' commerce authority includes the power to regulate those activities having a substantial relation to interstate commerce, . . . i.e., those activities that substantially affect interstate commerce."

* * *

Given § 13981's focus on gender-motivated violence wherever it occurs (rather than violence directed at the instrumentalities of interstate commerce, interstate markets, or things or persons in interstate commerce), we agree that this is the proper inquiry.

* * *

Both petitioners and Justice SOUTER's dissent downplay the role that the economic nature of the regulated activity plays in our Commerce

Continued

Clause analysis. But a fair reading of Lopez shows that the noneconomic, criminal nature of the conduct at issue was central to our decision in that case.

* * *

Lopez's review of Commerce Clause case law demonstrates that in those cases where we have sustained federal regulation of intrastate activity based upon the activity's substantial effects on interstate commerce, the activity in question has been some sort of economic endeavor.

* * *

We rejected these "costs of crime" and "national productivity" arguments because they would permit Congress to "regulate not only all violent crime, but all activities that might lead to violent crime, regardless of how tenuously they relate to interstate commerce." We noted that, under this but-for reasoning:

> "Congress could regulate any activity that it found was related to the economic productivity of individual citizens: family law (including marriage, divorce, and child custody), for example. Under the[se] theories . . . , it is difficult to perceive any limitation on federal power, even in areas such as criminal law enforcement or education where States historically have been sovereign. Thus, if we were to accept the Government's arguments, we are hard pressed to posit any activity by an individual that Congress is without power to regulate."

With these principles underlying our Commerce Clause jurisprudence as reference points, the proper resolution of the present cases is clear. Gender-motivated crimes of violence are not, in any sense of the phrase, economic activity. While we need not adopt a categorical rule against aggregating the effects of any noneconomic activity in order to decide these cases, thus far in our Nation's history our cases have upheld Commerce Clause regulation of intrastate activity only where that activity is economic in nature.

* * *

The Courts of Appeals have uniformly upheld this criminal sanction as an appropriate exercise of Congress' Commerce Clause authority, reasoning that "[t]he provision properly falls within the first of Lopez's categories as it regulates the use of channels of interstate commerce—i.e., the use of the interstate transportation routes through which persons and goods move."

In contrast with the lack of congressional findings that we faced in Lopez, § 13981 is supported by numerous findings regarding the serious impact that gender-motivated violence has on victims and their families. But the existence of congressional findings is not sufficient, by itself, to sustain the constitutionality of Commerce Clause legislation.

* * *

In these cases, Congress' findings are substantially weakened by the fact that they rely so heavily on a method of reasoning that we have already rejected as unworkable if we are to maintain the Constitution's enumeration of powers. Congress found that gender-motivated violence affects interstate commerce "by deterring potential victims from traveling interstate, from engaging in employment in interstate business, and from transacting with business, and in places involved in interstate commerce; . . . by diminishing national productivity, increasing medical and other costs, and decreasing the supply of and the demand for interstate products." Given these findings and petitioners' arguments, the concern that we expressed in Lopez that Congress might use the Commerce Clause to completely obliterate the Constitution's distinction between national and local authority seems well founded. The reasoning that petitioners advance seeks to follow the but-for causal chain from the initial occurrence of violent crime (the suppression of which has always been the prime object of the States' police power) to every attenuated effect upon interstate commerce. If accepted, petitioners' reasoning would allow Congress to regulate any crime as long as the nationwide, aggregated impact of that crime has substantial effects on employment, production, transit, or consumption. Indeed, if Congress may regulate gender-motivated violence, it would be able to regulate murder or any other type of violence since gender-motivated violence, as a subset of all violent crime, is certain to have lesser economic impacts than the larger class of which it is a part.

Petitioners' reasoning, moreover, will not limit Congress to regulating violence but may, as we suggested in Lopez, be applied equally as well to

Continued

family law and other areas of traditional state regulation since the aggregate effect of marriage, divorce, and childrearing on the national economy is undoubtedly significant. Congress may have recognized this specter when it expressly precluded § 13981 from being used in the family law context.

∗ ∗ ∗

No doubt the political branches have a role in interpreting and applying the Constitution, but ever since Marbury this Court has remained the ultimate expositor of the constitutional text.

∗ ∗ ∗

We accordingly reject the argument that Congress may regulate noneconomic, violent criminal conduct based solely on that conduct's aggregate effect on interstate commerce. The Constitution requires a distinction between what is truly national and what is truly local. In recognizing this fact we preserve one of the few principles that has been consistent since the Clause was adopted. The regulation and punishment of intrastate violence that is not directed at the instrumentalities, channels, or goods involved in interstate commerce has always been the province of the States. Indeed, we can think of no better example of the police power, which the Founders denied the National Government and reposed in the States, than the suppression of violent crime and vindication of its victims.

∗ ∗ ∗

IV

Petitioner Brzonkala's complaint alleges that she was the victim of a brutal assault. But Congress' effort in § 13981 to provide a federal civil remedy can be sustained neither under the Commerce Clause nor under § 5 of the Fourteenth Amendment. If the allegations here are true, no civilized system of justice could fail to provide her a remedy for the conduct of respondent Morrison. But under our federal system that remedy must be provided by the Commonwealth of Virginia, and not by the United States. The judgment of the Court of Appeals is

Affirmed.

While the Court had some empathy for Ms. Brzonkala, it was unwilling to allow Congress to use its commerce power in this manner. The reason why the Court held the statute unconstitutional was due to the fact that the activity being regulated was a noneconomic activity. The Court held the statute invalid in spite of detailed Congressional findings showing the negative impact these gender-based crimes had on interstate commerce. "If accepted petitioners' reasoning would allow Congress to regulate any crime as long as the nationwide, aggregated impact of that crime has substantial effects on employment, production, transit, or consumption. Indeed, if Congress may regulate gender-motivated violence, it would be able to regulate murder or any other type of violence . . ."[34]

What is the significance of *Lopez* and *Morrison*? These two cases have established that in order for Congress to validly regulate interstate commerce, the activity being regulated must substantially affect interstate commerce. It is not enough that the effect of the regulation simply has an impact on interstate commerce. An incidental effect on interstate commerce will not justify congressional regulation of an activity.

Also, these cases reiterate that if an activity is commercial, Congress will always be able to use its power to regulate it using the Commerce Clause. If, in fact, the activity is noncommercial, Congress will have to establish the substantial effect noted above. In both *Lopez* and *Morrison* the Court was unable to find this substantial effect. Additionally, if the regulation by Congress is in an area that is traditionally an area regulated by the states, the Court is less likely to defer to Congress and allow federal regulation. The areas noted by the Court as those traditionally regulated by the states include education, family law, and criminal law.

IMPLIED POWERS AND THE NECESSARY AND PROPER CLAUSE

When looking at the power of Congress to regulate commerce, one must look to all 18 clauses of Article I, § 8 to determine the full extent of this authority. Specifically, it is important to read all of the enumerated powers in that section in light of Clause 18, which allows Congress to make laws that are necessary and proper for carrying out all the enumerated powers found in § 8. Discussion of exactly what this clause means started with Justice Marshall in *Gibbons v. Ogden* and continues to the present. Next we will look at the history of the "Necessary and Proper Clause," discuss how the clause was originally interpreted, and follow the Court's interpretations of this clause to the present day.

When interpreting the Necessary and Proper Clause, the Court has espoused the doctrine of implied powers also known as the **Penumbra Doctrine**. This doctrine says that the government can act in those areas where it is expressly authorized by the Constitution to do so. However, the authorization does not have to be explicitly stated in the Constitution; Congress may act in those areas that are ancillary to an enumerated power, so long as in doing so, Congress does not conflict with specific constitutional prohibitions. This doctrine is explicitly stated in the Necessary and Proper Clause and one of the most carefully drafted discussions of this doctrine is found in *McCulloch v. Maryland*.[35]

In this case, the Court heard a challenge to Congress' chartering of the Second Bank of the United States. Once the bank was chartered, it became active in the State of Maryland and the Maryland legislature passed an act to tax any bank not chartered by Maryland. McCulloch was the operator of the Second Bank of the United States and brought this action to challenge the Maryland law. The trial court and the Maryland Court of Appeals found for the state, and the appeal came to the Supreme Court on a writ of error. Upon review, the Court had to determine whether Congress had the power to incorporate a bank and whether Maryland had the power to tax said bank without violating the Constitution.

Penumbra Doctrine
(Also known as the doctrine of implied powers) the principle that the "Necessary and Proper Clause" of the U.S. Constitution allows the federal government to take all actions to carry out legitimate government purposes, even if the powers needed to carry out these purposes are only implied from other powers.

McCULLOCH V. MARYLAND
17 U.S. 316 (1819)

MARSHALL, Ch. J., delivered the opinion of the court.

In the case now to be determined, the defendant, a sovereign state, denies the obligation of a law enacted by the legislature of the Union, and the plaintiff, on his part, contests the validity of an act which has been passed by the legislature of that state. The constitution of our country, in its most interesting and vital parts, is to be considered; the conflicting powers of the government of the Union and of its members, as marked in that constitution, are to be discussed; and an opinion given, which may essentially influence the great operations of the government.

* * *

The first question made in the cause is—has congress power to incorporate a bank? It has

been truly said, that this can scarcely be considered as an open question, entirely unprejudiced by the former proceedings of the nation respecting it. The principle now contested was introduced at a very early period of our history, has been recognized by many successive legislatures, and has been acted upon by the judicial department, in cases of peculiar delicacy, as a law of undoubted obligation.

* * *

The power now contested was exercised by the first congress elected under the present constitution. The bill for incorporating the Bank of the United States did not steal upon an unsuspecting legislature, and pass unobserved. Its principle was completely understood, and was opposed with equal zeal and ability. After being resisted, first, in the fair and open field of debate, and

Continued

afterwards, in the executive cabinet, with as much persevering talent as any measure has ever experienced, and being supported by arguments which convinced minds as pure and as intelligent as this country can boast, it became a law.

* * *

From these conventions, the constitution derives its whole authority. The government proceeds directly from the people; is 'ordained and established,' in the name of the people; and is declared to be ordained, 'in order to form a more perfect union, establish justice, insure domestic tranquillity, [sic] and secure the blessings of liberty to themselves and to their posterity.' The assent of the states, in their sovereign capacity, is implied, in calling a convention, and thus submitting that instrument to the people. But the people were at perfect liberty to accept or reject it; and their act was final. It required not the affirmance, [sic] and could not be negatived,[sic] by the state governments. The constitution, when thus adopted, was of complete obligation, and bound the state sovereignties.

* * *

This government is acknowledged by all, to be one of enumerated powers. The principle, that it can exercise only the powers granted to it, would seem too apparent, to have required to be enforced by all those arguments, which its enlightened friends, while it was depending before the people, found it necessary to urge; that principle is now universally admitted. But the question respecting the extent of the powers actually granted, is perpetually arising, and will probably continue to arise, so long as our system shall exist. In discussing these questions, the conflicting powers of the general and state governments must be brought into view, and the supremacy of their respective laws, when they are in opposition, must be settled.

If any one proposition could command the universal assent of mankind, we might expect it would be this—that the government of the Union, though limited in its powers, is supreme within its sphere of action. This would seem to result, necessarily, from its nature. It is the government of all; its powers are delegated by all; it represents all, and acts for all.

* * *

Among the enumerated powers, we do not find that of establishing a bank or creating a corporation. But there is no phrase in the instrument which, like the articles of confederation, excludes incidental or implied powers; and which requires that everything granted shall be expressly and minutely described. Even the 10th amendment, which was framed for the purpose of quieting the excessive jealousies which had been excited, omits the word 'expressly,' and declares only, that the powers 'not delegated to the United States, nor prohibited to the states, are reserved to the states or to the people;' thus leaving the question, whether the particular power which may become the subject of contest, has been delegated to the one government, or prohibited to the other, to depend on a fair construction of the whole instrument. The men who drew and adopted this amendment had experienced the embarrassments resulting from the insertion of this word in the articles of confederation, and probably omitted it, to avoid those embarrassments. A constitution, to contain an accurate detail of all the subdivisions of which its great powers will admit, and of all the means by which they may be carried into execution, would partake of the prolixity of a legal code, and could scarcely be embraced by the human mind . . . Its nature, therefore, requires, that only its great outlines should be marked, its important objects designated, and the minor ingredients which compose those objects, be deduced from the nature of the objects themselves. That this idea was entertained by the framers of the American constitution, is not only to be inferred from the nature of the instrument, but from the language.

* * *

The creation of a corporation, it is said, appertains to sovereignty. This is admitted. But to what portion of sovereignty does it appertain? Does it belong to one more than to another? In America, the powers of sovereignty are divided between the government of the Union, and those of the states. They are each sovereign, with respect to the objects committed to it, and neither sovereign, with respect to the objects committed to the other.

* * *

But the constitution of the United States has not left the right of congress to employ the necessary means, for the execution of the powers

Continued

conferred on the government, to general reasoning. To its enumeration of powers is added, that of making 'all laws which shall be necessary and proper, for carrying into execution the foregoing powers, and all other powers vested by this constitution, in the government of the United States, or in any department thereof.' The counsel for the state of Maryland have urged various arguments, to prove that this clause, though, in terms, a grant of power, is not so, in effect; but is really restrictive of the general right, which might otherwise be implied, of selecting means for executing the enumerated powers. In support of this proposition, they have found it necessary to contend, that this clause was inserted for the purpose of conferring on congress the power of making laws. That, without it, doubts might be entertained, whether congress could exercise its powers in the form of legislation.

* * *

But the argument on which most reliance is placed, is drawn from that peculiar language of this clause. Congress is not empowered by it to make all laws, which may have relation to the powers conferred on the government, but such only as may be 'necessary and proper' for carrying them into execution. The word 'necessary' is considered as controlling the whole sentence, and as limiting the right to pass laws for the execution of the granted powers, to such as are indispensable, and without which the power would be nugatory. That it excludes the choice of means, and leaves to congress, in each case, that only which is most direct and simple.

Is it true, that this is the sense in which the word 'necessary' is always used? Does it always import an absolute physical necessity, so strong, that one thing to which another may be termed necessary, cannot exist without that other? We think it does not . . . To employ the means necessary to an end, is generally understood as employing any means calculated to produce the end, and not as being confined to those single means, without which the end would be entirely unattainable. Such is the character of human language, that no word conveys to the mind, in all situations, one single definite idea; and nothing is more common than to use words in a figurative sense . . . The word 'necessary' is of this description. It has not a fixed character, peculiar to itself. It admits of all degrees of comparison; and is often connected with other words, which increase or diminish the impression the mind receives of the urgency it imports. A thing may be necessary, very necessary, absolutely or indispensably necessary. To no mind would the same idea be conveyed by these several phrases. The comment on the word is well illustrated by the passage cited at the bar, from the 10th section of the 1st article of the constitution. It is, we think, impossible to compare the sentence which prohibits a state from laying 'imposts, or duties on imports or exports, except what may be absolutely necessary for executing its inspection laws,' with that which authorizes congress 'to make all laws which shall be necessary and proper for carrying into execution' the powers of the general government, without feeling a conviction, that the convention understood itself to change materially the meaning of the word 'necessary,' by prefixing the word 'absolutely.' This word, then, like others, is used in various senses; and, in its construction, the subject, the context, the intention of the person using them, are all to be taken into view.

Let this be done in the case under consideration. The subject is the execution of those great powers on which the welfare of a nation essentially depends. It must have been the intention of those who gave these powers, to insure, so far as human prudence could insure, their beneficial execution. This could not be done, by confiding the choice of means to such narrow limits as not to leave it in the power of congress to adopt any which might be appropriate, and which were conducive to the end. This provision is made in a constitution, intended to endure for ages to come, and consequently, to be adapted to the various crises of human affairs. To have prescribed the means by which government should, in all future time, execute its powers, would have been to change, entirely, the character of the instrument, and give it the properties of a legal code. It would have been an unwise attempt to provide, by immutable rules, for exigencies which, if foreseen at all, must have been seen dimly, and which can be best provided for as they occur. To have declared, that the best means shall not be used, but those alone, without which the power given would be nugatory, would have been to deprive the legislature of the capacity to avail itself of experience, to exercise its reason, and to accommodate its legislation to circumstances.

* * *

Continued

In ascertaining the sense in which the word 'necessary' is used in this clause of the constitution, we may derive some aid from that with which it is associated. Congress shall have power 'to make all laws which shall be necessary and proper to carry into execution' the powers of the government. If the word 'necessary' was used in that strict and rigorous sense for which the counsel for the state of Maryland contend, it would be an extraordinary departure from the usual course of the human mind, as exhibited in composition, to add a word, the only possible affect of which is, to qualify that strict and rigorous meaning; to present to the mind the idea of some choice of means of legislation, not strained and compressed within the narrow limits for which gentlemen contend.

But the argument which most conclusively demonstrates the error of the construction contended for by the counsel for the state of Maryland, is founded on the intention of the convention, as manifested in the whole clause. To waste time and argument in proving that, without it, congress might carry its powers into execution, would be not much less idle, than to hold a lighted taper to the sun. As little can it be required to prove, that in the absence of this clause, congress would have some choice of means. That it might employ those which, in its judgment, would most advantageously effect the object to be accomplished. That any means adapted to the end, any means which tended directly to the execution of the constitutional powers of the government, were in themselves constitutional. This clause, as construed by the state of Maryland, would abridge, and almost annihilate, this useful and necessary right of the legislature to select its means. That this could not be intended, is, we should think, had it not been already controverted, too apparent for controversy.

We think so for the following reasons: 1st. The clause is placed among the powers of congress, not among the limitations on those powers. 2d. Its terms purport to enlarge, not to diminish the powers vested in the government. It purports to be an additional power, not a restriction on those already granted. No reason has been, or can be assigned, for thus concealing an intention to narrow the discretion of the national legislature, under words which purport to enlarge it. The framers of the constitution wished its adoption, and well knew that it would be endangered by its strength, not by its weakness.

Had they been capable of using language which would convey to the eye one idea, and, after deep reflection, impress on the mind, another, they would rather have disguised the grant of power, than its limitation. If, then, their intention had been, by this clause, to restrain the free use of means which might otherwise have been implied, that intention would have been inserted in another place, and would have been expressed in terms resembling these. 'In carrying into execution the foregoing powers, and all others,' &c., 'no laws shall be passed but such as are necessary and proper.' Had the intention been to make this clause restrictive, it would unquestionably have been so in form as well as in effect.

The result of the most careful and attentive consideration bestowed upon this clause is, that if it does not enlarge, it cannot be construed to restrain the powers of congress, or to impair the right of the legislature to exercise its best judgment in the selection of measures to carry into execution the constitutional powers of the government. If no other motive for its insertion can be suggested, a sufficient one is found in the desire to remove all doubts respecting the right to legislate on that vast mass of incidental powers which must be involved in the constitution, if that instrument be not a splendid bauble.

We admit, as all must admit, that the powers of the government are limited, and that its limits are not to be transcended. But we think the sound construction of the constitution must allow to the national legislature that discretion, with respect to the means by which the powers it confers are to be carried into execution, which will enable that body to perform the high duties assigned to it, in the manner most beneficial to the people. Let the end be legitimate, let it be within the scope of the constitution, and all means which are appropriate, which are plainly adapted to that end, which are not prohibited, but consist with the letter and spirit of the constitution, are constitutional.

＊ ＊ ＊

2. Whether the state of Maryland may, without violating the constitution, tax that branch? That the power of taxation is one of vital importance; that it is retained by the states; that it is not abridged by the grant of a similar power to the government of the Union; that it is to be concurrently exercised by the two governments—are

Continued

truths which have never been denied. But such is the paramount character of the constitution, that its capacity to withdraw any subject from the action of even this power, is admitted. The states are expressly forbidden to lay any duties on imports or exports, except what may be absolutely necessary for executing their inspection laws. If the obligation of this prohibition must be conceded—if it may restrain a state from the exercise of its taxing power on imports and exports—the same paramount character would seem to restrain, as it certainly may restrain, a state from such other exercise of this power, as is in its nature incompatible with, and repugnant to, the constitutional laws of the Union. A law, absolutely repugnant to another, as entirely repeals that other as if express terms of repeal were used.

* * *

The power of congress to create, and of course, to continue, the bank, was the subject of the preceding part of this opinion; and is no longer to be considered as questionable. That the power of taxing it by the states may be exercised so as to destroy it, is too obvious to be denied. But taxation is said to be an absolute power, which acknowledges no other limits than those expressly prescribed in the constitution, and like sovereign power of every other description, is intrusted [sic] to the discretion of those who use it. But the very terms of this argument admit, that the sovereignty of the state, in the article of taxation itself, is subordinate to, and may be controlled by the constitution of the United States. How far it has been controlled by that instrument, must be a question of construction. In making this construction, no principle, not declared, can be admissible, which would defeat the legitimate operations of a supreme government. It is of the very essence of supremacy, to remove all obstacles to its action within its own sphere, and so to modify every power vested in subordinate governments, as to exempt its own operations from their own influence. This effect need not be stated in terms. It is so involved in the declaration of supremacy, so necessarily implied in it, that the expression of it could not make it more certain. We must, therefore, keep it in view, while construing the constitution.

* * *

The sovereignty of a state extends to everything which exists by its own authority, or is introduced by its permission; but does it extend to those means which are employed by congress to carry into execution powers conferred on that body by the people of the United States? We think it demonstrable, that it does not. Those powers are not given by the people of a single state. They are given by the people of the United States, to a government whose laws, made in pursuance of the constitution, are declared to be supreme. Consequently, the people of a single state cannot confer a sovereignty which will extend over them.

If we measure the power of taxation residing in a state, by the extent of sovereignty which the people of a single state possess, and can confer on its government, we have an intelligible standard, applicable to every case to which the power may be applied. We have a principle which leaves the power of taxing the people and property of a state unimpaired; which leaves to a state the command of all its resources, and which places beyond its reach, all those powers which are conferred by the people of the United States on the government of the Union, and all those means which are given for the purpose of carrying those powers into execution. We have a principle which is safe for the states, and safe for the Union. We are relieved, as we ought to be, from clashing sovereignty; from interfering powers; from a repugnancy between a right in one government to pull down, what there is an acknowledged right in another to build up; from the incompatibility of a right in one government to destroy, what there is a right in another to preserve . . . We find, then, on just theory, a total failure of this original right to tax the means employed by the government of the Union, for the execution of its powers. The right never existed, and the question whether it has been surrendered, cannot arise.

* * *

If we apply the principle for which the state of Maryland contends, to the constitution, generally, we shall find it capable of changing totally the character of that instrument. We shall find it capable of arresting all the measures of the government, and of prostrating it at the foot of the states. The American people have declared their constitution and the laws made in pursuance thereof, to be supreme; but this principle would transfer the supremacy, in fact, to the states. If the states may tax one instrument, employed by the government in the execution of its powers,

Continued

they may tax any and every other instrument. They may tax the mail; they may tax the mint; they may tax patent-rights; they may tax the papers of the custom-house; they may tax judicial process; they may tax all the means employed by the government, to an excess which would defeat all the ends of government. This was not intended by the American people. They did not design to make their government dependent on the states.

Gentlemen say, they do not claim the right to extend state taxation to these objects. They limit their pretensions to property. But on what principle, is this distinction made? Those who make it have furnished no reason for it, and the principle for which they contend denies it. They contend, that the power of taxation has no other limit than is found in the 10th section of the 1st article of the constitution; that, with respect to everything else, the power of the states is supreme, and admits of no control. If this be true, the distinction between property and other subjects to which the power of taxation is applicable, is merely arbitrary, and can never be sustained. This is not all. If the controlling power of the states be established; if their supremacy as to taxation be acknowledged; what is to restrain their exercising control in any shape they may please to give it? Their sovereignty is not confined to taxation; that is not the only mode in which it might be displayed. The question is, in truth, a question of supremacy; and if the right of the states to tax the means employed by the general government be conceded, the declaration that the constitution, and the laws made in pursuance thereof, shall be the supreme law of the land, is empty and unmeaning declamation.

* * *

The court has bestowed on this subject its most deliberate consideration. The result is a conviction that the states have no power, by taxation or otherwise, to retard, impede, burden, or in any manner control, the operations of the constitutional laws enacted by congress to carry into execution the powers vested in the general government. This is, we think, the unavoidable consequence of that supremacy which the constitution has declared. We are unanimously of opinion, that the law passed by the legislature of Maryland, imposing a tax on the Bank of the United States, is unconstitutional and void. This opinion does not deprive the states of any resources which they originally possessed. It does not extend to a tax paid by the real property of the bank, in common with the other real property within the state, nor to a tax imposed on the interest which the citizens of Maryland may hold in this institution, in common with other property of the same description throughout the state. But this is a tax on the operations of the bank, and is, consequently, a tax on the operation of an instrument employed by the government of the Union to carry its powers into execution. Such a tax must be unconstitutional.

JUDGMENT.—This cause came on to be heard, on the transcript of the record of the court of appeals of the state of Maryland, and was argued by counsel: on consideration whereof, it is the opinion of this court, that the act of the legislature of Maryland is contrary to the constitution of the United States, and void; and therefore, that the said court of appeals of the state of Maryland erred, in affirming the judgment of the Baltimore county court, in which judgment was rendered against James W. McCulloch; but that the said court of appeals of Maryland ought to have reversed the said judgment of the said Baltimore county court, and ought to have given judgment for the said appellant, McCulloch: It is, therefore, adjudged and ordered, that the said judgment of the said court of appeals of the state of Maryland in this case, be, and the same hereby is, reversed and annulled. And this court, proceeding to render such judgment as the said court of appeals should have rendered; it is further adjudged and ordered, that the judgment of the said Baltimore county court be reversed and annulled, and that judgment be entered in the said Baltimore county court for the said James W. McCulloch.

Chief Justice Marshall strongly stated that the Constitution, by its very nature, must be expressed in general terms in order for that document to adapt to unforeseen circumstances. If this were not so, the powers contained in the Constitution would be so rigid as to render the document obsolete. Therefore, some powers must be implied in order to allow Congress to exercise the broad range of express powers given to it. The language "necessary and proper" gives Congress that flexibility, especially in light of the construction the Court gave this word. The Court said that the word *necessary* should be construed to mean convenient or useful or essential and not to mean absolutely necessary. Since the necessary and proper language is among the powers listed as belonging to Congress and not as a limitation, it should be read as enlarging congressional power. Any means that is appropriate and used to institute the enumerated powers is constitutional. Therefore, the Court held, first, that Congress has the power to enact a statute to incorporate banks, and second, that Maryland may not use its police powers in a way to stand in the way of the power of the federal government to exercise its powers.

What is the modern impact of *McCulloch v. Maryland*? The ruling in *McCulloch* is still in place and affecting court decisions today. The Court, as noted in the discussion on the Commerce Clause above, will only strike down a congressional commerce action if that action is not substantially related to a valid enumerated power. Nor will the Court inquire into the legislator's motives in passing such legislation. Congress' motive in passing the law or regulation is irrelevant and the law will stand so long as the government can demonstrate the rational relationship between its commerce power and the legislation.

CIVIL RIGHTS AND LEGISLATIVE POWER

The Commerce Clause also gives Congress the power to prohibit racial discrimination in the use of interstate commerce. The Civil Rights Act of 1964 firmly established this congressional power. This Act was a comprehensive measure outlawing discrimination on basis of race, national origin, ethnicity, color, or religion, in the areas of public transportation, public accommodations and therefore, interstate commerce. Two cases came to the Court for review of the extent of Congress' power to regulate commerce and therefore, discrimination in places offering public accommodations. The first, *Heart of Atlanta Hotel v. United States*,[36] dealt with the ability of Congress to regulate a hotel in Atlanta Georgia (see Exhibit 4.2), and the second, *Katzenbach v. McClung*,[37] involved discrimination by a local restaurant in Birmingham, Alabama.

EXHIBIT 4.2   **HEART OF ATLANTA HOTEL**
(courtesy of Special Collections Dept. Georgia State Univ. Library)

HEART OF ATLANTA HOTEL V. UNITED STATES
379 U.S. 241 (1964)

Mr. Justice CLARK delivered the opinion of the Court

This is a declaratory judgment action, 28 U.S.C. s 2201 and s 2202 (1958 ed.) attacking the constitutionality of Title II of the Civil Rights Act of 1964 . . . In addition to declaratory relief the complaint sought an injunction restraining the enforcement of the Act and damages against appellees based on allegedly resulting injury in the event compliance was required.

* * *

1. The Factual Background and Contentions of the Parties.

The case comes here on admissions and stipulated facts. Appellant owns and operates the Heart of Atlanta Hotel which has 216 rooms available to transient guests. The motel is located on Courtland Street, two blocks from downtown Peachtree Street. It is readily accessible to interstate highways 75 and 85 and state highways 23 and 41. Appellant solicits patronage from outside the State of Georgia through various national advertising media, including magazines of national circulation; it maintains over 50 billboards and highway signs within the State, soliciting patronage for the motel; it accepts convention trade from outside Georgia and approximately 75% of its registered guests are from out of State. Prior to passage of the Act the motel had followed a practice of refusing to rent rooms to Negroes, and it alleged that it intended to continue to do so. In an effort to perpetuate that policy this suit was filed.

The appellant contends that Congress in passing this Act exceeded its power to regulate commerce under Art. I, s 8, cl. 3, of the Constitution of the United States; that the Act violates the Fifth Amendment because appellant is deprived of the right to choose its customers and operate its business as it wishes, resulting in a taking of its liberty and property without due process of law and a taking of its property without just compensation; and, finally, that by requiring appellant to rent available rooms to Negroes against its will, Congress is subjecting it to involuntary servitude in contravention of the Thirteenth Amendment.

The appellees counter that the unavailability to Negroes of adequate accommodations interferes significantly with interstate travel, and that Congress, under the Commerce Clause, has power to remove such obstructions and restraints; that the Fifth Amendment does not forbid reasonable regulation and that consequential damage does not constitute a 'taking' within the meaning of that amendment; that the Thirteenth Amendment claim fails because it is entirely frivolous to say that an amendment directed to the abolition of human bondage and the removal of widespread disabilities associated with slavery places discrimination in public accommodations, beyond the reach of both federal and state law.

* * *

2. The History of the Act.

Congress first evidenced its interest in civil rights legislation in the Civil Rights or Enforcement Act of April 9, 1866.

* * *

No major legislation in this field had been enacted by Congress for 82 years when the Civil Rights Act of 1957 became law. It was followed by the Civil Rights Act of 1960. Three years later, on June 19, 1963, the late President Kennedy called for civil rights legislation in a message to Congress to which he attached a proposed bill. Its stated purpose was 'to promote the general welfare by eliminating discrimination based on race, color, religion, or national origin in

* * *

public accommodations through the exercise by Congress of the powers conferred upon it

* * *

to enforce the provisions of the fourteenth and fifteenth amendments, to regulate commerce among the several States, and to make laws necessary and proper to execute the powers conferred upon it by the Constitution.'

* * *

The Act as finally adopted was most comprehensive, undertaking to prevent through peaceful and voluntary settlement discrimination in voting, as well as in places of accommodation and public facilities, federally secured programs and in employment. Since Title II is the only portion

Continued

under attack here, we confine our consideration to those public accommodation provisions.

3. Title II of the Act.

This Title is divided into seven sections beginning with s 201(a) which provides that:

> 'All persons shall be entitled to the full and equal enjoyment of the goods, services, facilities, privileges, advantages, and accommodations of any place of public accommodation, as defined in this section, without discrimination or segregation on the ground of race, color, religion, or national origin.'

There are listed in s 201(b) four classes of business establishments, each of which 'serves the public' and 'is a place of public accommodation' within the meaning of s 201(a) 'if its operations affect commerce, or if discrimination or segregation by it is supported by State action.' The covered establishments are:

'(1) any inn, hotel, motel, or other establishment which provides lodging to transient guests, other than an establishment located within a building which contains not more than five rooms for rent or hire and which is actually occupied by the proprietor of such establishment as his residence;

'(2) any restaurant, cafeteria

* * *

(not here involved);

'(3) any motion picture house

* * *

(not here involved);

'(4) any establishment

* * *

which is physically located within the premises of any establishment otherwise covered by this subsection, or

* * *

within the premises of which is physically located any such covered establishment

* * *

(not here involved).'

Section 201(c) defines the phrase 'affect commerce' as applied to the above establishments. It first declares that 'any inn, hotel, motel, or other establishment which provides lodging to transient guests' affects commerce per se. Restaurants, cafeterias, etc., in class two affect commerce only if they serve or offer to serve interstate travelers or if a substantial portion of the food which they serve or products which they sell have 'moved in commerce.' Motion picture houses and other places listed in class three affect commerce if they customarily present films, performances, etc., 'which move in commerce.' And the establishments listed in class four affect commerce if they are within, or include within their own premises, an establishment 'the operations of which affect commerce.' Private clubs are excepted under certain conditions.

* * *

A person aggrieved may bring suit, in which the Attorney General may be permitted to intervene. Thirty days' written notice before filing any such action must be given to the appropriate authorities of a State . . .

* * *

4. Application of Title II to Heart of Atlanta Motel.

It is admitted that the operation of the motel brings it within the provisions of s 201(a) of the Act and that appellant refused to provide lodging for transient Negroes because of their race or color and that it intends to continue that policy unless restrained.

The sole question posed is, therefore, the constitutionality of the Civil Rights Act of 1964 as applied to these facts. The legislative history of the Act indicates that Congress based the Act on s 5 and the Equal Protection Clause of the Fourteenth Amendment as well as its power to regulate interstate commerce under Art. I, s 8, cl. 3, of the Constitution.

The Senate Commerce Committee made it quite clear that the fundamental object of Title II was to vindicate 'the deprivation of personal dignity that surely accompanies denials of equal access to public establishments.' At the same time, however, it noted that such an objective has been and could be readily achieved 'by congressional action based on the commerce power of the Constitution.' Our study of the legislative record, made in the light of prior cases, has brought us to the conclusion that Congress possessed ample power in this regard, and we have therefore not considered the other grounds relied upon. This is not to say that the remaining authority upon which it acted was not adequate, a question upon which we do not pass, but merely that since the commerce power is sufficient for our decision

Continued

here we have considered it alone. Nor is s 201(d) or s 202, having to do with state action, involved here and we do not pass upon either of those sections.

* * *

6. The Basis of Congressional Action.

While the Act as adopted carried no congressional findings the record of its passage through each house is replete with evidence of the burdens that discrimination by race or color places upon interstate commerce. This testimony included the fact that our people have become increasingly mobile with millions of people of all races traveling from State to State; that Negroes in particular have been the subject of discrimination in transient accommodations, having to travel great distances to secure the same; that often they have been unable to obtain accommodations and have had to call upon friends to put them up overnight, and that these conditions had become so acute as to require the listing of available lodging for Negroes in a special guidebook which was itself 'dramatic testimony to the difficulties' Negroes encounter in travel. These exclusionary practices were found to be nationwide, the Under Secretary of Commerce testifying that there is 'no question that this discrimination in the North still exists to a large degree' and in the West and Midwest as well. This testimony indicated a qualitative as well as quantitative effect on interstate travel by Negroes. The former was the obvious impairment of the Negro traveler's pleasure and convenience that resulted when he continually was uncertain of finding lodging. As for the latter, there was evidence that this uncertainty stemming from racial discrimination had the effect of discouraging travel on the part of a substantial portion of the Negro community. This was the conclusion not only of the Under Secretary of Commerce but also of the Administrator of the Federal Aviation Agency who wrote the Chairman of the Senate Commerce Committee that it was his 'belief that air commerce is adversely affected by the denial to a substantial segment of the traveling public of adequate and desegregated public accommodations.' We shall not burden this opinion with further details since the voluminous testimony presents overwhelming evidence that discrimination by hotels and motels impedes interstate travel.

7. The Power of Congress Over Interstate Travel.

The power of Congress to deal with these obstructions depends on the meaning of the Commerce Clause. Its meaning was first enunciated 140 years ago by the great Chief Justice John Marshall in *Gibbons v. Ogden* . . .

* * *

That the 'intercourse' of which the Chief Justice spoke included the movement of persons through more States than one was settled as early as 1849 . . .

* * *

Nor does it make any difference whether the transportation is commercial in character. Mr. Justice Reed observed as to the modern movement of persons among the States:

> The recent changes in transportation brought about by the coming of automobiles (do) not seem of great significance in the problem. People of all races travel today more extensively than in 1878 when this Court first passed upon state regulation of racial segregation in commerce. (It but) emphasizes the soundness of this Court's early conclusion in *Hall v. De Cuir*.

* * *

That Congress was legislating against moral wrongs in many of these areas rendered its enactments no less valid. In framing Title II of this Act Congress was also dealing with what it considered a moral problem. But that fact does not detract from the overwhelming evidence of the disruptive effect that racial discrimination has had on commercial intercourse. It was this burden which empowered Congress to enact appropriate legislation, and, given this basis for the exercise of its power, Congress was not restricted by the fact that the particular obstruction to interstate commerce with which it was dealing was also deemed a moral and social wrong.

It is said that the operation of the motel here is of a purely local character. But, assuming this to be true, '(i)f it is interstate commerce that feels the pinch, it does not matter how local the operation which applies the squeeze.' As Chief Justice Stone put it in *United States v. Darby*, supra:

> The power of Congress over interstate commerce is not confined to the regulation of

Continued

commerce among the states. It extends to those activities intrastate which so affect interstate commerce or the exercise of the power of Congress over it as to make regulation of them appropriate means to the attainment of a legitimate end, the exercise of the granted power of Congress to regulate interstate commerce.

Thus the power of Congress to promote interstate commerce also includes the power to regulate the local incidents thereof, including local activities in both the States of origin and destination, which might have a substantial and harmful effect upon that commerce. One need only examine the evidence which we have discussed above to see that Congress may—as it has—prohibit racial discrimination by motels serving travelers, however 'local' their operations may appear.

Nor does the Act deprive appellant of liberty or property under the Fifth Amendment. The commerce power invoked here by the Congress is a specific and plenary one authorized by the Constitution itself. The only questions are: (1) whether Congress had a rational basis for finding that racial discrimination by motels affected commerce, and (2) if it had such a basis, whether the means it selected to eliminate that evil are reasonable and appropriate.

If they are, appellant has no 'right' to select its guests as it sees fit, free from governmental regulation. There is nothing novel about such legislation. Thirty-two States now have it on their books either by statute or executive order and many cities provide such regulation. Some of these Acts go back fourscore years. It has been repeatedly held by this Court that such laws do not violate the Due Process Clause of the Fourteenth Amendment. Perhaps the first such holding was in the Civil Rights Cases themselves, where Mr. Justice Bradley for the Court inferentially found that innkeepers, 'by the laws of all the States, so far as we are aware, are bound, to the extent of their facilities, to furnish proper accommodation to all unobjectionable persons who in good faith apply for them.'

As we have pointed out, 32 States now have such provisions and no case has been cited to us where the attack on a state statute has been successful, either in federal or state courts. Indeed, in some cases the Due Process and Equal Protection Clause objections have been specifically discarded in this Court. As a result

the constitutionality of such state statutes stands unquestioned. 'The authority of the Federal government over interstate commerce does not differ,' it was held in *United States v. Rock Royal Co-op., Inc.* 'in extent or character from that retained by the states over intrastate commerce.'

It is doubtful if in the long run appellant will suffer economic loss as a result of the Act. Experience is to the contrary where discrimination is completely obliterated as to all public accommodations. But whether this be true or not is of no consequence since this Court has specifically held that the fact that a 'member of the class which is regulated may suffer economic losses not shared by others

* * *

has never been a barrier' to such legislation. Likewise in a long line of cases this Court has rejected the claim that the prohibition of racial discrimination in public accommodations interferes with personal liberty. See *District of Columbia v. John R. Thompson Co.*, and cases there cited, where we concluded that Congress had delegated law-making power to the District of Columbia 'as broad as the police power of a state' which included the power to adopt a 'law prohibiting discriminations against Negroes by the owners and managers of restaurants in the District of Columbia.' Neither do we find any merit in the claim that the Act is a taking of property without just compensation. The cases are to the contrary.

* * *

We, therefore, conclude that the action of the Congress in the adoption of the Act as applied here to a motel which concededly serves interstate travelers is within the power granted it by the Commerce Clause of the Constitution, as interpreted by this Court for 140 years. It may be argued that Congress could have pursued other methods to eliminate the obstructions it found in interstate commerce caused by racial discrimination. But this is a matter of policy that rests entirely with the Congress not with the courts. How obstructions in commerce may be removed—what means are to be employed—is within the sound and exclusive discretion of the Congress. It is subject only to one caveat—that the means chosen by it must be reasonably adapted to the end permitted by the Constitution. We cannot say that its choice here was not so adapted. The Constitution requires no more.

Affirmed.

With this decision the Court made it possible for Congress to regulate discriminatory behavior in the hotel industry and give protection to interstate travelers. The Court agreed with the government's argument that racial discrimination discouraged travel on the part of the African American community and the aggregate effect of this substantially impacted interstate commerce. The Court was not troubled by the fact that the congressional motive was not purely economic in nature and held that the fact "[t]hat Congress was legislating against moral wrongs in many of these areas rendered its enactments no less valid."[38]

While the issue was much the same in *Katzenbach v. McClung*, the facts involved a local restaurant called Ollie's BBQ. This family owned and operated restaurant obtained meat for its business from a local vendor who had procured it from an out-of-state source. The restaurant came under fire when it continued to refuse to serve African Americans in its dining area, which the government argued violated the Civil Rights Act of 1964. The restaurant owners argued that their local business did not substantially impact interstate commerce and could not be subject to congressional regulation. Justice Clark wrote for the majority in this case, just as he had in *Heart of Atlanta Hotel*, and said, "[T]he power of Congress to promote interstate commerce also includes the power to regulate the local incidents thereof, including local activities in both the States of origin and distinction, which might have a substantial and harmful effect upon that commerce."[39] Just as it had noted in *Heart of Atlanta Hotel*, the Court noted that the unavailability of restaurant accommodations persuaded African Americans to refrain from taking part in interstate travel. Again, it was the aggregate impact caused by this reluctance to travel that persuaded the Court, in spite of the fact that neither the Court nor Congress had any evidence that this particular restaurant had any impact on interstate commerce.

Five years after the above cases were decided, the Court was once again asked to determine whether the denial of admission to African Americans to a club in Arkansas constituted discrimination that could be regulated by Congress through use of the Commerce Clause. This case, *Daniel v. Paul*,[40] involved the Lake Nixon Club just outside Little Rock, Arkansas. This club, owned by the Paul family, consisted of 232 acres that contained swimming, boating, sunbathing, picnicking, miniature golf, and dancing facilities, as well as a snack bar. The Pauls refused to allow blacks to enter the club and enjoy the amenities. The petitioners, black residents of Little Rock, brought an action in federal court to enjoin the Pauls for denying them admission and the District Court dismissed the action saying that the Lake Nixon Club was not a public accommodation covered by the Civil Rights Act of 1964. The Supreme Court first held that the club was not a private club, but "a business operated for a profit with none of the attributes of self-government and member-ownership traditionally associated with private clubs."[41] Once the Court held that this was a public accommodation, therefore, subject to regulation, it then looked to see if the activities of this club had a substantial effect on interstate commerce. The Court found that the snack bar served food that had moved in interstate commerce, the club had advertised for interstate travelers, and that this club provided entertainment that was also covered under the Act in question. For these reasons, the Court held that the club was subject to regulation and held in favor of the petitioners.

Some would argue that in light of the *Lopez* and *Morrison* cases discussed above, these cases would be decided differently today. However, in light of the importance of eliminating discrimination in the United States, the Court would probably be persuaded not to change these cases since discrimination was at issue.

CONGRESSIONAL INVESTIGATIVE POWERS

When reading Article I, § 8 it is clear that there is no specific language that gives Congress the power to conduct investigations. However, both Congress and the Supreme Court have long held that this power belongs to Congress because it is so essential to its legislative function. In 1927, the Court decided the case of *McGrain v. Daugherty*[42] in which Justice Van Devanter wrote:

> *"We are of the opinion that the power of inquiry—with process to enforce it—is an essential and appropriate auxiliary to the legislative function . . . A legislative body cannot legislate wisely or effectively in the absence of information respecting the conditions which the legislation is intended to affect or change; and where the legislative body does not itself possess the requisite information—which not infrequently is true—recourse must be had to others who possess. Experience has taught that mere requests for such information often are unavailing, and also that information which is volunteered is not always accurate or complete; so some means of compulsion are essential to obtain what is needed. All this was true before and when the Constitution was framed and adopted. In that period the power of inquiry—with enforcement process—was regarded and employed as a necessary and appropriate attribute of the power to legislate—indeed, was treated as inhering in it. Thus there is ample warrant for thinking, as we do, that the constitutional provisions which commit the legislative function to the two houses are intended to include this attribute to the end that the function may be effectively exercised."*[43]

This view of Congress' investigatory power was echoed in *Watkins v. United States*[44] when Chief Justice Warren did not question this basic power. The *Watkins* case did not question the power of Congress to investigate corruption or waste in the departments or agencies of the federal government. In fact, two years later, Justice Harlan wrote,

> *"The power of inquiry has been employed by Congress throughout our history, over the whole range of the national interests concerning which Congress might legislate or decide upon due investigation not to legislate; it has similarly been utilized in determining what to appropriate from the national purse, or whether to appropriate. The scope of the power of inquiry, in short, is as penetrating and far-reaching as the potential power to enact and appropriate under the Constitution."*[45]

This quote, from *Barenblatt*, which follows, demonstrates the investigatory power of Congress, even in educational institutions.

In *Barenblatt*, the plaintiff was a graduate student and then a professor at various educational institutions. He was called before a Subcommittee of the House Committee on Un-American Activities and asked questions about his affiliation with the Communist Party. When he refused to answer questions, he was charged with five counts of contempt of Congress, prosecuted, and convicted. Barenblatt then appealed to the Supreme Court claiming that Congress had exceeded its investigatory power.

BARENBLATT V. UNITED STATES
360 U.S. 109 (1959)

Mr. Justice HARLAN delivered the opinion of the Court.

Once more the Court is required to resolve the conflicting constitutional claims of congressional power and of an individual's right to resist its exercise. The congressional power in question concerns the internal process of Congress in moving within its legislative domain; it involves the utilization of its committees to secure 'testimony needed to enable it efficiently to exercise a legislative function belonging to it under the Constitution.' The power of inquiry has been employed by Congress throughout our history, over the whole range of the national interests concerning which Congress might legislate or decide upon due investigation not to legislate; it has similarly been utilized in determining what to appropriate from the national purse, or whether to appropriate. The scope of

Continued

the power of inquiry, in short, is as penetrating and far-reaching as the potential power to enact and appropriate under the Constitution.

Broad as it is, the power is not, however, without limitations. Since Congress may only investigate into those areas in which it may potentially legislate or appropriate, it cannot inquire into matters which are within the exclusive province of one of the other branches of the Government.

* * *

The congressional power of inquiry, its range and scope, and an individual's duty in relation to it, must be viewed in proper perspective. The power and the right of resistance to it are to be judged in the concrete, not on the basis of abstractions. In the present case congressional efforts to learn the extent of a nation-wide, indeed worldwide, problem have brought one of its investigating committees into the field of education. Of course, broadly viewed, inquiries cannot be made into the teaching that is pursued in any of our educational institutions. When academic teaching-freedom and its corollary learning-freedom, so essential to the well-being of the Nation, are claimed, this Court will always be on the alert against intrusion by Congress into this constitutionally protected domain. But this does not mean that the Congress is precluded from interrogating a witness merely because he is a teacher. An educational institution is not a constitutional sanctuary from inquiry into matters that may otherwise be within the constitutional legislative domain merely for the reason that inquiry is made of someone within its walls.

In the setting of this framework of constitutional history, practice and legal precedents, we turn to the particularities of this case.

We here review petitioner's conviction under 2 U.S.C. s 192, 2 U.S.C.A. s 192, or contempt of Congress, arising from his refusal to answer certain questions put to him by a Subcommittee of the House Committee on Un-American Activities during the course of an inquiry concerning alleged Communist infiltration into the field of education.

The case is before us for the second time. Petitioner's conviction was originally affirmed in 1957 by a unanimous panel of the Court of Appeals. This Court granted certiorari, vacated the judgment of the Court of Appeals, and remanded the case to that court for further consideration in light of *Watkins v. United States*, which had reversed a contempt of Congress conviction, and which was decided after the Court of Appeals' decision here had issued. Thereafter the Court of Appeals, sitting en banc, reaffirmed the conviction by a divided court. We again granted certiorari, to consider petitioner's statutory and constitutional challenges to his conviction, and particularly his claim that the judgment below cannot stand under our decision in the *Watkins* case.

Pursuant to a subpoena, and accompanied by counsel, petitioner on June 28, 1954, appeared as a witness before this congressional Subcommittee. After answering a few preliminary questions and testifying that he had been a graduate student and teaching fellow at the University of Michigan from 1947 to 1950 and an instructor in psychology at Vassar College from 1950 to shortly before his appearance before the Subcommittee, petitioner objected generally to the right of the Subcommittee to inquire into his 'political' and 'religious' beliefs or any 'other personal and private affairs' or 'associational activities,' upon grounds set forth in a previously prepared memorandum which he was allowed to file with the Subcommittee. Thereafter petitioner specifically declined to answer each of the following five questions:

'Are you now a member of the Communist Party? (Count One.)
'Have you ever been a member of the Communist Party? (Count Two.)
'Now, you have stated that you knew Francis Crowley. Did you know Francis Crowley as a member of the Communist Party? (Count Three.)
'Were you ever a member of the Haldane Club of the Communist Party while at the University of Michigan? (Count Four.)
'Were you a member while a student of the University of Michigan Council of Arts, Sciences, and Professions?' (Count Five.)

In each instance the grounds of refusal were those set forth in the prepared statement. Petitioner expressly disclaimed reliance upon 'the Fifth Amendment.'

Following receipt of the Subcommittee's report of these occurrences the House duly certified the matter to the District of Columbia United States Attorney for contempt proceedings. An indictment in five Counts, each embracing one of petitioner's several refusals to answer, ensued. With the consent of both sides the case was tried

Continued

to the court without a jury, and upon conviction under all Counts a general sentence of six months' imprisonment and a fine of $250 was imposed.

Since this sentence was less than the maximum punishment authorized by the statute for conviction under any one Count, the judgment below must be upheld if the conviction upon any of the Counts is sustainable. As we conceive the ultimate issue in this case to be whether petitioner could properly be convicted of contempt for refusing to answer questions relating to his participation in or knowledge of alleged Communist Party activities at educational institutions in this country, we find it unnecessary to consider the validity of his conviction under the Third and Fifth Counts, the only ones involving questions which on their face do not directly relate to such participation or knowledge.

Petitioner's various contentions resolve themselves into three propositions: First, the compelling of testimony by the Subcommittee was neither legislatively authorized nor constitutionally permissible because of the vagueness of Rule XI of the House of Representatives, Eighty-third Congress, the charter of authority of the parent Committee. Second, petitioner was not adequately apprised of the pertinency of the Subcommittee's questions to the subject matter of the inquiry. Third, the questions petitioner refused to answer infringed rights protected by the First Amendment.

Subcommittee's Authority to Compel Testimony.

At the outset it should be noted that Rule XI authorized this Subcommittee to compel testimony within the framework of the investigative authority conferred on the Un-American Activities Committee. Petitioner contends that *Watkins v. United States*, supra, nevertheless held the grant of this power in all circumstances ineffective because of the vagueness of Rule XI in delineating the Committee jurisdiction to which its exercise was to be appurtenant. This view of Watkins was accepted by two of the dissenting judges below.

The *Watkins* case cannot properly be read as standing for such a proposition. A principal contention in Watkins was that the refusals to answer were justified because the requirement of 2 U.S.C. s 192, 2 U.S.C.A. s 192 that the questions asked be 'pertinent to the question under inquiry' had not been satisfied. This Court reversed the conviction solely on that ground, holding that Watkins had not been adequately apprised of the subject matter of the Subcommittee's investigation or the pertinency thereto of the questions he refused to answer. In so deciding the Court drew upon Rule XI only as one of the facets in the total mise en scene in its search for the 'question under inquiry' in that particular investigation. The Court, in other words, was not dealing with Rule XI at large, and indeed in effect stated that no such issue was before it. That the vagueness of Rule XI was not alone determinative is also shown by the Court's further statement that aside from the Rule 'the remarks of the chairman or members of the committee, or even the nature of the proceedings themselves, might sometimes make the topic (under inquiry) clear.' In short, while Watkins was critical of Rule XI, it did not involve the broad and inflexible holding petitioner now attributes to it.

Petitioner also contends, independently of Watkins, that the vagueness of Rule XI deprived the Subcommittee of the right to compel testimony in this investigation into Communist activity. We cannot agree with this contention which in its furthest reach would mean that the House Un-American Activities Committee under its existing authority has no right to compel testimony in any circumstances. Granting the vagueness of the Rule, we may not read it in isolation from its long history in the House of Representatives. Just as legislation is often given meaning by the gloss of legislative reports, administrative interpretation, and long usage, so the proper meaning of an authorization to a congressional committee is not to be derived alone from its abstract terms unrelated to the definite content furnished them by the course of congressional actions. The Rule comes to us with a 'persuasive gloss of legislative history,' which shows beyond doubt that in pursuance of its legislative concerns in the domain of 'national security' the House has clothed the Un-American Activities Committee with pervasive authority to investigate Communist activities in this country. The essence of that history can be briefly stated. The Un-American Activities Committee, originally known as the Dies Committee, was first established by the House in 1938. The Committee was principally a consequence of concern over the activities of the German-American Bund, whose members were suspected of allegiance to Hitler Germany, and of the Communist Party, supposed by many to be under the domination of the Soviet Union.

Continued

From the beginning, without interruption to the present time, and with the undoubted knowledge and approval of the House, the Committee has devoted a major part of its energies to the investigation of Communist activities. More particularly, in 1947 the Committee announced a wide-range program in this field, pursuant to which during the years 1948 to 1952 it conducted diverse inquiries into such alleged Communist activities as espionage; efforts to learn atom bomb secrets; infiltration into labor, farmer, veteran, professional, youth, and motion picture groups; and in addition held a number of hearings upon various legislative proposals to curb Communist activities.

In the context of these unremitting pursuits, the House has steadily continued the life of the Committee at the commencement of each new Congress; it has never narrowed the powers of the Committee, whose authority has remained throughout identical with that contained in Rule XI; and it has continuingly supported the Committee's activities with substantial appropriations. Beyond this, the Committee was raised to the level of a standing committee of the House in 1945, it having been but a special committee prior to that time.

In light of this long and illuminating history it can hardly be seriously argued that the investigation of Communist activities generally, and the attendant use of compulsory process, was beyond the purview of the Committee's intended authority under Rule XI.

We are urged, however, to construe Rule XI so as at least to exclude the field of education from the Committee's compulsory authority.

* * *

We cannot follow that route here, for this is not a case where Rule XI has to 'speak for itself, since Congress put no gloss upon it at the time of its passage,' nor one where the subsequent history of the Rule has the 'infirmity of post litem motam, self-serving declarations.'

To the contrary, the legislative gloss on Rule XI is again compelling. Not only is there no indication that the House ever viewed the field of education as being outside the Committee's authority under Rule XI, but the legislative history affirmatively evinces House approval of this phase of the Committee's work. During the first year of its activities, 1938, the Committee heard testimony on alleged Communist activities at Brooklyn College, N.Y. The following year it conducted similar hearings relating to the American Student Union and the Teachers Union. The field of 'Communist influences in education' was one of the items contained in the Committee's 1947 program. Other investigations including education took place in 1952 and 1953. And in 1953, after the Committee had instituted the investigation involved in this case, the desirability of investigating Communism in education was specifically discussed during consideration of its appropriation for that year, which after controversial debate was approved.

In this framework of the Committee's history we must conclude that its legislative authority to conduct the inquiry presently under consideration is unassailable, and that independently of whatever bearing the broad scope of Rule XI may have on the issue of 'pertinency' in a given investigation into Communist activities, as in *Watkins*, the Rule cannot be said to be constitutionally infirm on the score of vagueness. The constitutional permissibility of that authority otherwise is a matter to be discussed later.

Pertinency Claim.

Undeniably a conviction for contempt under 2 U.S.C. s 192, 2 U.S.C.A. s 192 cannot stand unless the questions asked are pertinent to the subject matter of the investigation. But the factors which led us to rest decision on this ground in *Watkins* were very different from those involved here.

In *Watkins* the petitioner had made specific objection to the Subcommittee's questions on the ground of pertinency; the question under inquiry had not been disclosed in any illuminating manner; and the questions asked the petitioner were not only amorphous on their face, but in some instances clearly foreign to the alleged subject matter of the investigation— 'Communism in labor.'

In contrast, petitioner in the case before us raised no objections on the ground of pertinency at the time any of the questions were put to him. It is true that the memorandum which petitioner brought with him to the Subcommittee hearing contained the statement, 'to ask me whether I am or have been a member of the Communist Party may have dire consequences.

* * *

Continued

I might wish to challenge the pertinency of the question to the investigation,' and at another point quoted from this Court's opinion in *Jones v. Securities & Exchange Comm.*, language relating to a witness' right to be informed of the pertinency of questions asked him by an administrative agency. These statements cannot, however, be accepted as the equivalent of a pertinency objection. At best they constituted but a contemplated objection to questions still unasked, and buried as they were in the context of petitioner's general challenge to the power of the Subcommittee they can hardly be considered adequate, within the meaning of what was said in *Watkins*, to trigger what would have been the Subcommittee's reciprocal obligation had it been faced with a pertinency objection.

We need not, however, rest decision on petitioner's failure to object on this score, for here 'pertinency' was made to appear 'with undisputable clarity.' First of all, it goes without saying that the scope of the Committee's authority was for the House, not a witness, to determine, subject to the ultimate reviewing responsibility of this Court. What we deal with here is whether petitioner was sufficiently apprised of 'the topic under inquiry' thus authorized 'and the connective reasoning whereby the precise questions asked relate(d) to it.' In light of his prepared memorandum of constitutional objections there can be no doubt that this petitioner was well aware of the Subcommittee's authority and purpose to question him as it did. In addition the other sources of this information which we recognized in *Watkins*, leave no room for a 'pertinency' objection on this record. The subject matter of the inquiry had been identified at the commencement of the investigation as Communist infiltration into the field of education. Just prior to petitioner's appearance before the Subcommittee, the scope of the day's hearings had been announced as 'in the main communism in education and the experiences and background in the party by Francis X. T. Crowley.

It will deal with activities in Michigan, Boston, and in some small degree, New York.' Petitioner had heard the Subcommittee interrogate the witness Crowley along the same lines as he, petitioner, was evidently to be questioned, and had listened to Crowley's testimony identifying him as a former member of an alleged Communist student organization at the University of Michigan while they both were in attendance there. Further, petitioner had stood mute in the face of the Chairman's statement as to why he had been called as a witness by the Subcommittee. And, lastly, unlike Watkins, petitioner refused to answer questions as to his own Communist Party affiliations, whose pertinency of course was clear beyond doubt. Petitioner's contentions on this aspect of the case cannot be sustained.

Constitutional Contentions.

Our function, at this point, is purely one of constitutional adjudication in the particular case and upon the particular record before us, not to pass judgment upon the general wisdom or efficacy of the activities of this Committee in a vexing and complicated field.

The precise constitutional issue confronting us is whether the Subcommittee's inquiry into petitioner's past or present membership in the Communist Party transgressed the provisions of the First Amendment, which of course reach and limit congressional investigations.

The Court's past cases establish sure guides to decision. Undeniably, the First Amendment in some circumstances protects an individual from being compelled to disclose his associational relationships. However, the protections of the First Amendment, unlike a proper claim of the privilege against self-incrimination under the Fifth Amendment, do not afford a witness the right to resist inquiry in all circumstances. Where First Amendment rights are asserted to bar governmental interrogation resolution of the issue always involves a balancing by the courts of the competing private and public interests at stake in the particular circumstances shown. These principles were recognized in the Watkins case, where, in speaking of the First Amendment in relation to congressional inquiries, we said: 'It is manifest that despite the adverse effects which follow upon compelled disclosure of private matters, not all such inquiries are barred.

* * *

The critical element is the existence of, and the weight to be ascribed to, the interest of the Congress in demanding disclosures from an unwilling witness.' More recently in *National Association for Advancement of Colored People v. State of Alabama*, we applied the same principles in judging state action claimed to infringe rights of association assured by the Due Process Clause

Continued

of the Fourteenth Amendment, and stated that the "subordinating interest of the State must be compelling" in order to overcome the individual constitutional rights at stake. In light of these principles we now consider petitioner's First Amendment claims.

The first question is whether this investigation was related to a valid legislative purpose, for Congress may not constitutionally require an individual to disclose his political relationships or other private affairs except in relation to such a purpose.

That Congress has wide power to legislate in the field of Communist activity in this Country, and to conduct appropriate investigations in aid thereof, is hardly debatable. The existence of such power has never been questioned by this Court, and it is sufficient to say, without particularization, that Congress has enacted or considered in this field a wide range of legislative measures, not a few of which have stemmed from recommendations of the very Committee whose actions have been drawn in question here. In the last analysis this power rests on the right of self-preservation, 'the ultimate value of any society.' Justification for its exercise in turn rests on the long and widely accepted view that the tenets of the Communist Party include the ultimate overthrow of the Government of the United States by force and violence, a view which has been given formal expression by the Congress.

On these premises, this Court in its constitutional adjudications has consistently refused to view the Communist Party as an ordinary political party, and has upheld federal legislation aimed at the Communist problem which in a different context would certainly have raised constitutional issues of the gravest character. On the same premises this Court has upheld under the Fourteenth Amendment state legislation requiring those occupying or seeking public office to disclaim knowing membership in any organization advocating overthrow of the Government by force and violence, which legislation none can avoid seeing was aimed at membership in the Communist Party. Similarly, in other areas, this Court has recognized the close nexus between the Communist Party and violent overthrow of government. To suggest that because the Communist Party may also sponsor peaceable political reforms the constitutional issues before us should now be judged as if that Party were just an ordinary political party from the standpoint of national security, is to ask this Court to blind itself to world affairs which have determined the whole course of our national policy since the close of World War II, affairs to which Judge Learned Hand gave vivid expression in his opinion in *United States v. Dennis*, and to the vast burdens which these conditions have entailed for the entire Nation.

We think that investigatory power in this domain is not to be denied Congress solely because the field of education is involved.

* * *

Indeed we do not understand petitioner here to suggest that Congress in no circumstances may inquire into Communist activity in the field of education. Rather, his position is in effect that this particular investigation was aimed not at the revolutionary aspects but at the theoretical classroom discussion of communism.

In our opinion this position rests on a too constricted view of the nature of the investigatory process, and is not supported by a fair assessment of the record before us. An investigation of advocacy of or preparation for overthrow certainly embraces the right to identify a witness as a member of the Communist Party, and to inquire into the various manifestations of the Party's tenets. The strict requirements of a prosecution under the Smith Act, are not the measure of the permissible scope of a congressional investigation into 'overthrow,' for of necessity the investigatory process must proceed step by step. Nor can it fairly be concluded that this investigation was directed at controlling what is being taught at our universities rather than at overthrow. The statement of the Subcommittee Chairman at the opening of the investigation evinces no such intention, and so far as this record reveals nothing thereafter transpired which would justify our holding that the thrust of the investigation later changed. The record discloses considerable testimony concerning the foreign domination and revolutionary purposes and efforts of the Communist Party. That there was also testimony on the abstract philosophical level does not detract from the dominant theme of this investigation— Communist infiltration furthering the alleged ultimate purpose of overthrow. And certainly the conclusion would not be justified that the questioning of petitioner would have exceeded permissible bounds had he not shut off the Subcommittee at the threshold.

Continued

Nor can we accept the further contention that this investigation should not be deemed to have been in furtherance of a legislative purpose because the true objective of the Committee and of the Congress was purely 'exposure.' So long as Congress acts in pursuance of its constitutional power, the Judiciary lacks authority to intervene on the basis of the motives which spurred the exercise of that power.

＊ ＊ ＊

Thus, in stating in the *Watkins* case, that 'there is no congressional power to expose for the sake of exposure,' we at the same time declined to inquire into the 'motives of committee members,' and recognized that their 'motives alone would not vitiate an investigation which had been instituted by a House of Congress if that assembly's legislative purpose is being served.' Having scrutinized this record we cannot say that the unanimous panel of the Court of Appeals which first considered this case was wrong in concluding that 'the primary purposes of the inquiry were in aid of legislative processes.' Certainly this is not a case like *Kilbourn v. Thompson*, where 'the House of Representatives not only exceeded the limit of its own authority, but assumed a power which could only be properly exercised by another branch of the government, because it was in its nature clearly judicial.' The constitutional legislative power of Congress in this instance is beyond question.

Finally, the record is barren of other factors which in themselves might sometimes lead to the conclusion that the individual interests at stake were not subordinate to those of the state. There is no indication in this record that the Subcommittee was attempting to pillory witnesses. Nor did petitioner's appearance as a witness follow from indiscriminate dragnet procedures, lacking in probable cause for belief that he possessed information which might be helpful to the Subcommittee. And the relevancy of the questions put to him by the Subcommittee is not open to doubt.

We conclude that the balance between the individual and the governmental interests here at stake must be struck in favor of the latter, and that therefore the provisions of the First Amendment have not been offended.

We hold that petitioner's conviction for contempt of Congress discloses no infirmity, and that the judgment of the Court of Appeals must be affirmed.

Affirmed.

The Court used a **balancing test** when deciding this case. The Court balanced the individual's rights against the governmental interests. In doing so, the Court also asked whether the five questions posed by the Subcommittee were related to a valid legislative purpose. The Court concluded that the questions were related to a valid governmental interest or legislative purpose and upheld the congressional action.

This was not the last word on the investigatory power of Congress. In the 1960s, the Court began looking more closely at this congressional power and began using the more restrictive, strict scrutiny test when deciding cases involving challenges to Congress' power to investigate. In *Gibson v. Florida Legislative Committee*[46] the local president of the NAACP, Gibson, was ordered to bring the annual membership list to the hearing and use it as a reference to answer questions about the membership of certain individuals. Gibson did appear as ordered, but did not bring the membership list with him and instead volunteered to answer questions about individuals. After questioning him about 14 different individuals, none of whom were identified as members of Gibson's group, petitioner was brought into state court on contempt charges. He was convicted and sentenced, and the Florida Supreme Court affirmed this decision. Gibson then appealed to the U.S. Supreme Court, claiming that the action of the committee violated his rights under the First and Fourteenth Amendments. The Court recognized that it once again was being asked "to resolve a conflict between individual rights of free speech and association and the government's interest in conducting legislative investigations."[47]

The Court began its opinion by acknowledging that, "The First and Fourteenth Amendment rights of free speech and free association are fundamental

> **balancing test** a doctrine in constitutional law that says a court should balance constitutional rights such as free speech against the right of the government to control conduct it calls harmful.

and highly prized . . . This Court has recognized the vital relationship between freedom to associate and privacy in one's association . . . So it is here."[48] The Court then went on to acknowledge that while the legislature has broad power to investigate as part of the legislative process, the legislative power to investigate is not without limits.

> "[T]he legislative power to investigate, broad as it may be, is not without limit. The fact that the general scope of the inquiry is authorized and permissible does not compel the conclusion that the investigatory body is free to inquire into or demand all forms of information. Validation of the broad subject matter under investigation does not necessarily carry with it automatic and wholesale validation of all individual questions, subpoenas, and documentary demands."[49]

The Court then went on to say that the appropriate test to be used is the strict scrutiny test, and after reviewing the record, held that there was no compelling governmental interest that outweighed the plaintiff's First and Fourteenth Amendment rights. This decision was based on the finding that there was no "substantial relationship between the N.A.A.C.P. and subversive Communist activities."[50] Without this connection there were no grounds that justified the intrusion by the legislative committee, and Gibson's conviction was reversed.

So, while both federal and state legislatures have broad investigatory powers to assist them in making legislative decisions, this power is not unlimited. The current test used by the Court to determine whether a legislative committee has appropriately used its investigative powers is the strict scrutiny test, and the government has to demonstrate a compelling governmental interest that outweighs the individual's or organization's constitutional rights.

CONGRESSIONAL MEMBERSHIP AND PRIVILEGES

The qualification clauses of Article I of the Constitution outline the specific requirements for membership in the House of Representatives and the Senate. In order to be a member of the House of Representatives, an individual must be at least 25 years old, a citizen of the United States for at least seven years, and a resident from the state that elected that individual to office.[51] To be a member of the Senate the individual must be at least 30 years old, a national citizen for at least nine years, and a resident of the state that elected him or her.[52] These are the requirements set by the Constitution, but occasionally the legislature has attempted to set additional membership requirements. The seminal case in this area is *Powell v. McCormack*,[53] which involved a dispute between the House of Representatives and Representative Adam Clayton Powell.

This case began while Powell, a New York representative, was chairing the Committee on Education and Labor. Questions arose regarding Powell's travel expenses and an alleged illegal salary paid to Powell's wife at his direction. This took place during the 89th Congressional session, and, while no formal action was taken against Powell, when he attended the oath of office ceremony for the opening session of the 90th Congress, he was asked to step aside during the giving of the oath of office. A discussion followed during which Powell's eligibility to be seated was debated. Ultimately, the House set up a Select Committee to decide how to handle the situation.

Powell was given notice of a hearing to inquire into the usual qualifications of House membership, as well as notice that he would be asked about certain irregularities alleged to have occurred during the 89th Congress. Powell attended, but refused to answer questions except those about the standard qualifications for office. Powell was notified of a second hearing and was told that again the Select Committee would be looking at his qualifications as well as making a decision as to whether Powell would ultimately be seated. Powell did not attend this hearing, but his attorneys did and notified the committee that Powell would not be attending or answering questions beyond questions about standard qualifications for House membership.

Powell ultimately sued for **declaratory judgment**, arguing that in making a decision regarding the seating of one of its members, the House could only look at the qualifications spelled out in the Constitution. On the other hand, the House argued that Article I, § 5[54] gave it the authority to add additional qualifications as they saw fit. Chief Justice Warren wrote the majority opinion. After disposing of some initial issues, the Court ultimately held that the House could not exclude Powell by creating new or additional qualifications. The House is bound to look only at those qualifications spelled out in Article I, § 2 to determine whether a representative is eligible to be seated. Once a duly elected representative has demonstrated compliance with those qualifications, he or she must be seated. Congress does not have the right to impose additional qualifications.

Once the Court had determined that neither the House nor the Senate could impose additional qualifications on their elected members, the next question posed was whether the qualifications found in Article I for both the House and the Senate can be supplemented by the states. In the case of *U.S. Term Limits, Inc. v. Thornton*[55] the Court reviewed an amendment to the Arkansas Constitution that limited the number of terms an individual could serve in the U.S. House of Representatives to three terms and the number of terms an individual could serve in the U.S. Senate to two terms. Justice Stevens wrote the majority opinion, which held the Arkansas provision unconstitutional. The Court decided that the provision was beyond the states' police power. Justice Stevens wrote:

> *"Permitting individual States to formulate diverse qualifications for the congressional representatives would result in a patchwork of state qualifications, undermining the uniformity and the national character that the Framers envisioned and sought to ensure."*[56]

Just as the Court was unwilling to allow the federal legislature to add additional qualifications of their members, the Court was also unwilling to allow the states to do so.

declaratory judgment a judicial opinion that states the rights of the parties or answers a legal question without awarding any damages or ordering that anything be done.

TAXING AND SPENDING POWERS

Article I, Section 8, Clause 1 contains the basic enumerated taxing power. It states: "The Congress shall have Power To lay and collect Taxes, Duties, Imposts and Excises, to pay the Debts and provide for the common Defence [sic] and general Welfare of the United States; but all Duties, Imposts and Excises shall be uniform throughout the United States . . ." Because of this clause, Congress' authority is enhanced and allows Congress to tax activities or properties that it would not be authorized to regulate directly. As a matter of fact, the Court has said that the taxing power is "exhaustive,"[57] and "embraces every conceivable power of taxation."[58]

While it is true that all taxes have a regulatory effect, the Court has been unwilling to allow Congress to use this regulatory effect without restriction. When determining whether Congress has used its taxing power appropriately, the Court will examine the impact of the tax on the electorate. If the impact of the tax is one that could be achieved by Congress using another of its enumerated powers, the regulatory impact of the tax is constitutionally permissible. However, if the impact of the tax is a regulatory effect that Congress could not have accomplished using one of its enumerated powers, the tax is constitutionally invalid.[59] It is really a disguised regulation in an area in which Congress is not authorized to act.

Even when the impact of the taxing power is permissible, the congressional taxing power is not unlimited. There are three special restrictions that place parameters around it. First, if one reads Clause 1 to its conclusion, it becomes clear that Congress must tax uniformly throughout the United States. This means that Congress can only impose the same level of taxation against each state; the Congress cannot impose higher taxes on some states and lower taxes on others. What the Court requires is that Congress not show favoritism to any State by use of the taxing power, unless there is a valid basis for the classification.[60]

Second, Article I, § 2 further limits the taxing power with the statement "direct taxes shall be apportioned among the several states which may be included within this union, according to their respective numbers." In other words, direct taxes must be assessed in a manner that the revenue produced by such taxes comes from each state in proportion to that state's population. While this may seem straightforward, the question that has come up consistently is whether a particular tax is a direct tax.

The Court has consistently held that direct taxes include tax on real property, and some types of income taxes. A number of the provisions of the 1984 Income Tax Act were challenged and held to be direct taxes. Unfortunately, for the federal government, these direct taxes were not levied in accordance with the states' population, and these direct taxes were struck down as being an invalid use of the congressional taxing power.[61] In order to deal with the question of direct and indirect taxes, the Sixteenth Amendment was proposed and ratified in 1913. It says:

> *"The Congress shall have power to lay and collect taxes on incomes, from whatever source derived, without apportionment among the several States and without regard to any census or enumeration."*[62]

In doing so, the need to determine what is a direct tax and what is an indirect tax becomes moot. Now Congress can tax income earned by any citizen, no matter what state they reside in and no matter the population of that state. Third, Congress' power to lay taxes, found in Article I, § 9, denies Congress the power to tax exports. This was put in place to encourage entrepreneurs to do business abroad. However, Congress does have the power to tax imports. One of the first laws enacted by the first Congress was a tariff act that included the following purpose statement:

> *"[I]t is necessary for the support of government, for the discharge of the debts of the United States, and the encouragement and protection of manufactures, that duties be laid on goods, wares and merchandise import."*[63]

The Court in *J.W. Hampton & Company v. United States* upheld this statute[64] when Chief Justice Taft noted that the first Congress, which enacted the statute, was made up of many members of the Constitutional Convention of 1787 and those congressional members believed that they historically had promoted and upheld taxes on imports. He then wrote:

> *"Whatever we think of the wisdom of a protection policy, we cannot hold it unconstitutional. So long as the motive of Congress and the effect of its legislative action are to secure revenue for the benefit of the general government, the existence of other motives in the selection of the subject of taxes cannot invalidate Congressional action."*[65]

In spite of the parameters set on the taxing power and the discussion of the impact of the tax, the reality is that often the Court will not inquire into congressional motives in enacting the tax.[66] The rule seems to be that if a tax produces substantial revenue, the Court will, in all likelihood, sustain it. Also, when reviewing the tax, the Court will look at the regulatory provision that accompanies that tax to see if there is a reasonable relationship between the regulatory provision and the enforcement of the tax. If it appears that the regulation is reasonably related to making sure the tax is collected, the Court will uphold that regulation.

Congress' spending power is directly connected with its power to tax. Once Congress has raised revenue through taxing, then it may spend that money to "provide . . . for the general welfare."[67] This section raises two questions. First, how does Congress raise revenue for this provision? This was answered with the enumerated power to lay taxes. Second, what is meant by "the general welfare"? The Court has adopted a broad, literal view of what this phrase means, as seen in *United States v. Butler*[68] where Justice Roberts wrote:

> "Since the foundation of the Nation sharp differences of opinion have persisted as to the true interpretation of the phrase. Madison asserted it amounted to no more than a reference to the other powers enumerated in the subsequent clauses of the same section; that as the United States is a government of limited and enumerated powers, the grant of power to tax and spend for the general national welfare must be confined to the numerated legislative fields committed to the Congress. In this view the phrase is mere tautology, for taxation and appropriation are or may be necessary incidents of the exercise of any of the enumerated legislative powers. Hamilton, on the other hand, maintained the clause confers a power separate and distinct from those later enumerated, is not restricted in meaning by the grant of them, and Congress consequently has a substantive power to tax and to appropriate, limited only by the requirement that it shall be exercised to provide for the general welfare of the United States. Each contention has the support of those whose views are entitled to weight. This court has noticed the question, but has never found it necessary to decide which is the true construction. Justice Story, in his Commentaries, espouses the Hamiltonian position. We shall not review the writings of public men and commentators or discuss the legislative practice. Study of all these leads us to conclude that the reading advocated by Justice Story is the correct one. While, therefore, the power to tax is not unlimited, its confines are set in the clause which confers it, and not those of Sec. 8 which bestow and define the legislative power of the Congress. It results that the power of Congress to authorize expenditure of money for public purposes is not limited by the direct grants of legislative power found in the Constitution."[69]

With this, the Court held that the spending power is not limited by specific grants of enumerated powers, but was limited by the Tenth Amendment. This amendment held that Congress could not use tax monies to ensure state compliance with regulations in state-controlled areas over which Congress has no authority.[70] The *Butler* decision went on to say that Congress cannot regulate in areas of local control, such as agriculture, as was the case here. However, the Court's use of the Tenth Amendment in areas of local control has diminished over the last few decades, as will be discussed later in the chapter.

WAR, TREATY, AND FOREIGN AFFAIRS POWERS

War Powers

Along with all other powers discussed in this chapter, Article I, § 8, cls. 11–14 contains the **War Powers Clause** and other clauses connected to the power to declare war. Chief Justice Marshall wrote about the war powers in *McCulloch v. Maryland*[71] when he listed war powers as one of the enumerated powers held by Congress. During the Civil War era, Chief Justice Chase described the power to declare war as necessary and extending "to all legislation essential to the prosecution of war with vigor and success . . ."[72] This war power is not only the power to declare war, but also to tax and spend for national defense. In addition, Congress also has the enumerated power to raise, provide, and

War Powers Clauses the U.S. constitutional clauses (Article I, Section 8, Clauses 11–14) that give Congress the power to declare war and raise armies and give the President the power to carry on the war.

maintain an army and navy. But, why was the power given to the federal government and not left to the states? The Court addressed this question in *United States v. Curtiss-Wright Export Corporation* when Justice Sutherland wrote:

> *"As a result of the separation from Great Britain by the colonies acting as a unit, the powers of external sovereignty passed from the Crown not to the colonies severally, but to the colonies in their collective and corporate capacity as the United States of America . . . The power to declare and wage war, to conclude peace, to make treaties, to maintain diplomatic relations with other sovereignties, if they had never been mentioned in the Constitution, would have vested in the Federal Government as necessary concomitants of nationality."[73]*

Another question often asked in connection with Congress' war powers is what role the President plays in the declaration and waging of war. The traditional view of declaring war is that the President must be empowered to use the military to defend the country in case of a sudden attack. To make the President wait for congressional action might mean a critical delay resulting in loss of life and property. When it comes to waging war, it is accepted that as Commander in Chief, the President has the authority to do so. But what about situations where the President wants to commit troops without a formal declaration of war? The Court has refused to consider this issue, even when presented with the opportunity to do so during the Vietnam War.[74] The lower federal courts consider the question to be a political one and also have refused to adjudicate the question.[75] As the courts have been unwilling to settle this issue, it is incumbent on Congress and the President to work together in the interest of national security.

Several issues have arisen about the extent and use of the war powers. The war powers have been used to justify the implementation of regulations during wartime, which has led to litigation. In *Woods v. Miller Company* the Court had an opportunity to curtail Congress' use of war powers to impose economic regulations. This case involved congressional imposition of rent controls in various parts of the country. Congress imposed these controls because of a housing shortage caused by World War II. The Court found Congress' action to be a necessary and proper action under the war powers.

WOODS V. MILLER COMPANY
333 U.S. 138 (1948)

Mr. Justice DOUGLAS delivered the opinion of the Court.

The case is here on a direct appeal,

* * *

from a judgment of the District Court holding unconstitutional Title II of the Housing and Rent Act of 1947.

The Act became effective on July 1, 1947, and the following day the appellee demanded of its tenants increases of 40% and 60% for rental accommodations in the Cleveland Defense-Rental Area, and admitted violation of the Act and regulations adopted pursuant thereto. Appellant thereupon instituted this proceeding under s 206(b) of the

Act to enjoin the violations. A preliminary injunction issued. After a hearing it was dissolved and a permanent injunction denied.

The District Court, was of the view that the authority of Congress to regulate rents by virtue of the war power ended with the Presidential Proclamation terminating hostilities on December 31, 1946, since that proclamation inaugurated 'peace-in-fact' though it did not mark termination of the war. It also concluded that even if the war power continues, Congress did not act under it because it did not say so, and only if Congress says so, or enacts provisions so implying, can it be held that Congress intended to exercise such power.

Continued

That Congress did not so intend, said the District Court, follows from the provision that the Housing Expediter can end controls in any area without regard to the official termination of the war, and from the fact that the preceding federal rent control laws (which were concededly exercises of the war power) were neither amended nor extended.

The District Court expressed the further view that rent control is not within the war power because 'the emergency created by housing shortage came into existence long before the war.' It held that the Act 'lacks in uniformity of application and distinctly constitutes a delegation of legislative power not within the grant of Congress' because of the authorization to the Housing Expediter to lift controls in any area before the Act's expiration. It also held that the Act in effect provides 'low rentals for certain groups without taking the property or compensating the owner in any way.'

We conclude, in the first place, that the war power sustains this legislation. The Court said in *Hamilton v. Kentucky Distilleries and Warehouse Co.* that the war power includes the power 'to remedy the evils which have arisen from its rise and progress' and continues for the duration of that emergency. Whatever may be the consequences when war is officially terminated, the war power does not necessarily end with the cessation of hostilities. We recently held that it is adequate to support the preservation of rights created by wartime legislation. But it has a broader sweep. In *Hamilton v. Kentucky Distilleries and Warehouse Co., supra*, and *Ruppert v. Caffey*, prohibition laws which were enacted after the Armistice in World War I were sustained as exercises of the war power because they conserved manpower and increased efficiency of production in the critical days during the period of demobilization, and helped to husband the supply of grains and cereals depleted by the war effort. Those cases followed the reasoning of *Stewart v. Kahn*, which held that Congress had the power to toll the statute of limitations of the States during the period when the process of their courts was not available to litigants due to the conditions obtaining in the Civil War.

The constitutional validity of the present legislation follows a fortiori from those cases. The legislative history of the present Act makes abundantly clear that there has not yet been eliminated the deficit in housing which in considerable measure was caused by the heavy demobilization of veterans and by the cessation or reduction in residential construction during the period of hostilities due to the allocation of building materials to military projects. Since the war effort contributed heavily to that deficit, Congress has the power even after the cessation of hostilities to act to control the forces that a short supply of the needed article created. If that were not true, the Necessary and Proper Clause, Art. I, s 8, cl. 18, would be drastically limited in its application to the several war powers. The Court has declined to follow that course in the past. We decline to take it today. The result would be paralyzing. It would render Congress powerless to remedy conditions the creation of which necessarily followed from the mobilization of men and materials for successful prosecution of the war. So to read the Constitution would be to make it self-defeating.

We recognize the force of the argument that the effects of war under modern conditions may be felt in the economy for years and years, and that if the war power can be used in days of peace to treat all the wounds which war inflicts on our society, it may not only swallow up all other powers of Congress but largely obliterate the Ninth and the Tenth Amendments as well. There are no such implications in today's decision. We deal here with the consequences of a housing deficit greatly intensified during the period of hostilities by the war effort. Any power, of course, can be abused. But we cannot assume that Congress is not alert to its constitutional responsibilities. And the question whether the war power has been properly employed in cases such as this is open to judicial inquiry.

The question of the constitutionality of action taken by Congress does not depend on recitals of the power which it undertakes to exercise. Here it is plain from the legislative history that Congress was invoking its war power to cope with a current condition of which the war was a direct and immediate cause. Its judgment on that score is entitled to the respect granted like legislation enacted pursuant to the police power.

Under the present Act the Housing Expediter is authorized to remove the rent controls in any defense-rental area if in his judgment the need no longer exists by reason of new construction or satisfaction of demand in other ways. The powers thus delegated are far less extensive than

Continued

those sustained in *Bowles v. Willingham*. Nor is there here a grant of unbridled administrative discretion. The standards prescribed pass muster under our decisions. See *Bowles v. Willingham*, and cases cited.

Objection is made that the Act by its exemption of certain classes of housing accommodations violates the Fifth Amendment. A similar argument was rejected under the Fourteenth Amendment when New York made like exemptions under the rent-control statute which was here for review in *Marcus Brown Holding Co. v. Feldman*. Certainly Congress is not under greater limitations. It need not control all rents or none. It can select those areas or those classes of property where the need seems the greatest. This alone is adequate answer to the objection, equally applicable to the original Act sustained in *Bowles v. Willingham, supra*, that the present Act lacks uniformity in application.

The fact that the property regulated suffers a decrease in value is no more fatal to the exercise of the war power than it is where the police power is invoked to the same end.

* * *

Reversed.

Based on this decision, it would seem that Congress could enact legislation or regulations that have an economic impact if the problem it is seeking to remedy was caused by the waging of war. Additionally, Congress can also regulate during the war as a natural extension of the federal power to declare and wage war.

Another issue raised by the use of war powers involves time limits for military appropriations. The Framers of the Constitution placed a time limit on this in Article I that says, "no appropriation of money to [military] use shall be for a longer term than two years." The Framers placed this time limitation in the Constitution because of its experience with the British army.

The Court has also had opportunity to hear litigation regarding the power of Congress to institute the draft. The Selective Service Act of 1917 was attacked in the *Selective Draft Law Cases*,[76] when challengers claimed that Congress did not have the power to require compulsory military service, but only had the power to call up the military for the purposes specified in the Constitution. Furthermore, those challenging the act argued that compulsive service was a form of involuntary servitude that violated the Thirteenth Amendment. The Court upheld the Act when it upheld the right of Congress to require compulsory service as part of its power to raise and support the military. In holding that the Thirteenth Amendment was not violated by compulsory service, the Court followed its earlier decision in *Butler v. Perry* in which the Court held:

> "It [the 13th Amendment] introduced no novel doctrine with respect of services always treated as exceptional, and certainly was not intended to interdict enforcement of those duties which individuals owe to the State, such as services in the army, militia, on the jury, etc. The great purpose in view was liberty under the protection of effective government, not the destruction of the latter by depriving it of essential powers."[77]

While both of the above-mentioned cases looked at the draft during times of war, they did not address Congress' power to institute the draft during times of peace. The Court has not formally answered this question, but did allude to an answer in *United States v. O'Brien*.[78] This case involved a challenge to the federal act that made it a crime for an individual to destroy his selective service certificate of registration. In the majority opinion, written by Chief Justice Warren, the Court held "[t]he power of Congress to classify and conscript manpower for military service is 'beyond question.' "[79] If the authority of Congress in this area is beyond question, it is likely that the Court may someday hold that Congress has the authority to institute the draft during times of peace.

Treaty Power

Just as the war powers are divided between both the legislative and executive branches of the federal government, so too do they share the power to form a **treaty**. While the executive branch has the authority to negotiate and write a treaty, in order for that treaty to become binding, it must be **ratified** by a two-thirds vote of the Senate. The **treaty power** and its requirements are found in Article II, § 2, which says: "(2) He [the President] shall have Power, by and with the Advice and Consent of the Senate, to make Treaties, provided two thirds of the Senators present concur . . ."[80]

The power to ratify a treaty is a "necessary and proper" use of congressional power. Not only is this power affirmed in the following case, the majority also held that a validly ratified treaty is equivalent to a federal statute in authority and outlined the test for treaty power.

treaty a formal agreement between countries on a major political subject.

ratification confirmation and acceptance of a previous act done by you or by another person.

treaty power the federal power to enter into a formal agreement with a foreign country as found in the treaty clause of the U.S. Constitution.

MISSOURI v. HOLLAND
252 U.S. 416 (1920)

Mr. Justice HOLMES delivered the opinion of the Court.

This is a bill in equity brought by the State of Missouri to prevent a game warden of the United States from attempting to enforce the Migratory Bird Treaty Act, and the regulations made by the Secretary of Agriculture in pursuance of the same. The ground of the bill is that the statute is an unconstitutional interference with the rights reserved to the States by the Tenth Amendment, and that the acts of the defendant done and threatened under that authority invade the sovereign right of the State and contravene its will manifested in statutes. The State also alleges a pecuniary interest, as owner of the wild birds within its borders and otherwise, admitted by the Government to be sufficient, but it is enough that the bill is a reasonable and proper means to assert the alleged quasi sovereign rights of a State. A motion to dismiss was sustained by the District Court on the ground that the Act of Congress is constitutional. The State appeals.

On December 8, 1916, a treaty between the United States and Great Britain was proclaimed by the President. It recited that many species of birds in their annual migrations traversed many parts of the United States and of Canada, that they were of great value as a source of food and in destroying insects injurious to vegetation, but were in danger of extermination through lack of adequate protection. It therefore provided for specified closed seasons and protection in other forms, and agreed that the two powers would take or propose to their lawmaking bodies the necessary measures for carrying the treaty out. The above mentioned act of July 3, 1918, entitled an act to give effect to the convention, prohibited the killing, capturing or selling any of the migratory birds included in the terms of the treaty except as permitted by regulations compatible with those terms, to be made by the Secretary of Agriculture. Regulations were proclaimed on July 31, and October 25, 1918. It is unnecessary to go into any details, because, as we have said, the question raised is the general one whether the treaty and statute are void as an interference with the rights reserved to the States.

To answer this question it is not enough to refer to the Tenth Amendment, reserving the powers not delegated to the United States, because by Article 2, Section 2, the power to make treaties is delegated expressly, and by Article 6 treaties made under the authority of the United States, along with the Constitution and laws of the United States made in pursuance thereof, are

Continued

declared the supreme law of the land. If the treaty is valid there can be no dispute about the validity of the statute under Article 1, Section 8, as a necessary and proper means to execute the powers of the Government. The language of the Constitution as to the supremacy of treaties being general, the question before us is narrowed to an inquiry into the ground upon which the present supposed exception is placed.

It is said that a treaty cannot be valid if it infringes the Constitution, that there are limits, therefore, to the treaty-making power, and that one such limit is that what an act of Congress could not do unaided, in derogation of the powers reserved to the States, a treaty cannot do. An earlier act of Congress that attempted by itself and not in pursuance of a treaty to regulate the killing of migratory birds within the States had been held bad in the District Court. Those decisions were supported by arguments that migratory birds were owned by the States in their sovereign capacity for the benefit of their people, and that under cases like *Geer v. Connecticut* [citation omitted], this control was one that Congress had no power to displace. The same argument is supposed to apply now with equal force.

Whether the two cases cited were decided rightly or not they cannot be accepted as a test of the treaty power. Acts of Congress are the supreme law of the land only when made in pursuance of the Constitution, while treaties are declared to be so when made under the authority of the United States. It is open to question whether the authority of the United States means more than the formal acts prescribed to make the convention. We do not mean to imply that there are no qualifications to the treaty-making power; but they must be ascertained in a different way. It is obvious that there may be matters of the sharpest exigency for the national well being that an act of Congress could not deal with but that a treaty followed by such an act could, and it is not lightly to be assumed that, in matters requiring national action, 'a power which must belong to and somewhere reside in every civilized government' is not to be found. What was said in that case with regard to the powers of the States applies with equal force to the powers of the nation in cases where the States individually are incompetent to act. We are not yet discussing the particular case before us but only are considering the validity of the test proposed. With regard to that we may add

that when we are dealing with words that also are a constituent act, like the Constitution of the United States, we must realize that they have called into life a being the development of which could not have been foreseen completely by the most gifted of its begetters. It was enough for them to realize or to hope that they had created an organism; it has taken a century and has cost their successors much sweat and blood to prove that they created a nation. The case before us must be considered in the light of our whole experience and not merely in that of what was said a hundred years ago. The treaty in question does not contravene any prohibitory words to be found in the Constitution. The only question is whether it is forbidden by some invisible radiation from the general terms of the Tenth Amendment. We must consider what this country has become in deciding what that amendment has reserved.

The State as we have intimated founds its claim of exclusive authority upon an assertion of title to migratory birds, an assertion that is embodied in statute. No doubt it is true that as between a State and its inhabitants the State may regulate the killing and sale of such birds, but it does not follow that its authority is exclusive of paramount powers. To put the claim of the State upon title is to lean upon a slender reed. Wild birds are not in the possession of anyone; and possession is the beginning of ownership. The whole foundation of the State's rights is the presence within their jurisdiction of birds that yesterday had not arrived, tomorrow may be in another State and in a week a thousand miles away. If we are to be accurate we cannot put the case of the State upon higher ground than that the treaty deals with creatures that for the moment are within the state borders, that it must be carried out by officers of the United States within the same territory, and that but for the treaty the State would be free to regulate this subject itself.

As most of the laws of the United States are carried out within the States and as many of them deal with matters which in the silence of such laws the State might regulate, such general grounds are not enough to support Missouri's claim. Valid treaties of course 'are as binding within the territorial limits of the States as they are elsewhere throughout the dominion of the United States.' No doubt the great body of private relations usually fall within the control of the State, but a treaty may override its power.

Continued

We do not have to invoke the later developments of constitutional law for this proposition; it was recognized as early as *Hopkirk v. Bell*, with regard to statutes of limitation, and even earlier, as to confiscation, in *Ware v. Hylton*. It was assumed by Chief Justice Marshall with regard to the escheat of land to the State in *Chirac v. Chirac; Hauenstein v. Lynham; DeGeofroy v. Riggs; Blythe v. Hinckley*. So as to a limited jurisdiction of foreign consuls within a State [sic]. *Wildenhus' Case*. Further illustration seems unnecessary, and it only remains to consider the application of established rules to the present case.

Here a national interest of very nearly the first magnitude is involved. It can be protected only by national action in concert with that of another power. The subject matter is only transitorily within the State and has no permanent habitat therein. But for the treaty and the statute there soon might be no birds for any powers to deal with. We see nothing in the Constitution that compels the Government to sit by while a food supply is cut off and the protectors of our forests and our crops are destroyed. It is not sufficient to rely upon the States. The reliance is vain, and were it otherwise, the question is whether the United States is forbidden to act. We are of opinion that the treaty and statute must be upheld.

Decree affirmed.

The Court was clear that the treaty in question did not violate the Constitution and that Congress acted within its authority when it ratified the treaty. An important national interest was at stake, and the Court agreed that national action was necessary to ensure that the unacceptable situation was addressed. This is not to say that the executive branch, with ratification by Congress, can enter into a treaty that violates a constitutional guarantee or prohibition. The Court was clear about this in *Reid v. Covert* when it held "no agreement with a foreign nation can confer power on the Congress, or any other branch of Government, which is free from the restraints of the Constitution."[81] So while the legislative branch, along with the executive branch, has the power to enter into treaties with foreign nations, these treaties must not conflict with other constitutional provisions. In doing so, the state police power remains intact.

Foreign Affairs

The Constitution does not specifically spell out which branch of the federal government has authority over foreign affairs. However, if the Constitution is read as a whole, it becomes clear that the authority over foreign affairs rests with Congress. The Constitution gives Congress the ability to impose taxes on imports, the power to ratify treaties, and the authority to make those laws and regulations as are necessary and proper to assist the legislature in carrying out its duties. These powers, coupled with the limitation placed on the states to refrain from interfering in foreign affairs,[82] led to this conclusion. While Article I, § 10, containing the language forbidding the states to engage in foreign affairs, was once used to justify the Court's Civil War era holding that the Confederate States had no legal existence,[83] it is now viewed as the basis for holding that the states do not have the authority to act in the international arena.

Congress does share this power, much like the war and treaty powers, with the executive branch. The President, due to this high-profile position, quite often is the individual who travels to other countries and acts as the symbolic head of the country. It is also the President who nominates individuals to ambassadorships, and the Senate who must confirm the appointments of ambassadors. When examining how foreign affairs are actually conducted, it becomes clear that both Congress and the President have an important role in this arena.

OTHER CONGRESSIONAL POWERS

Coining of Money and Regulating the Value of Money

Article I, Section 8, Clauses 5 and 6 set out these congressional powers by saying: "The Congress shall have Power . . . To coin Money, regulate the Value thereof, and of foreign Coin, and fix the Standard of Weights and Measures . . . To provide for the Punishment of counterfeiting the Securities and current Coin of the United States . . ."[84] The first of these powers has been given a broad reading by the Court. *McCulloch v. Maryland, supra,* demonstrates the deference the Court pays to the congressional power to coin money and regulate its value. Congress may charter banks,[85] may authorize or forbid the circulation of notes,[86] tax the circulation of notes issued by state banks,[87] choose whether or not to use the gold standard,[88] and just about anything else to do with the regulation of money.

However, the congressional power found in Clause 6 does not include the power to prosecute counterfeiting or the regulation of equipment that might be used for that purpose. In the following early case, the Court struggled with how far the federal power to punish counterfeiting extends and how a state law punishing the use of counterfeit money to defraud someone fits within this power.

UNITED STATES V. MARIGOLD
50 U.S. 560 (1850)

Mr. Justice DANIEL delivered the opinion of the court.

This is a certificate of division of opinion from the Northern District of New York.

The case is clearly and succinctly stated in the following abstract from the record:—

'At a Circuit Court of the United States, begun and held at Albany, for the Northern District of New York, in the Second Circuit, on the third Tuesday of October, in the year of our Lord 1848, and in the seventy-third year of American Independence.

'Present, the Honorable Samuel Nelson and Alfred Conkling, Esquires.

'THE UNITED STATES OF AMERICA v. PETER MARIGOLD.

'State of the Pleadings.

'This is an indictment against the defendant, charging him, under the twentieth section of the act of Congress entitled 'An act more effectually to provide for the punishment of certain crimes against the United States, and for other purposes,' approved March 3, 1825,—

'1st. With having brought into the United States, from a foreign place, with intent to pass, utter, publish, and sell as true, certain false, forged, and counterfeit coins, made, forged, and counterfeited in the resemblance and similitude of certain gold and silver coins of the United States, coined at the mint, he knowing the same to be false, forged, and counterfeit, and intending thereby to defraud divers persons unknown.

'2d. With having uttered, published, and passed such counterfeit coins, with intent to defraud, &c.

'To this indictment the defendant demurs, and George W. Clinton, attorney of the United States for the said district, who prosecutes in this behalf, joins in demurrer.

'This cause coming on to be argued at this term, the following questions occurred:—

'First. Whether Congress, under and by the Constitution, had power and authority to enact so much of the said twentieth section of the said act as relates to bringing into the United States counterfeit coins.

'Second. Whether Congress, under and by virtue of the Constitution, had power to enact so much of the said twentieth section as relates to uttering, publishing, passing, and selling of the counterfeit coins therein specified.

'On which said several questions, the opinions of the judges were opposed.

Continued

'Whereupon, on motion of the said attorney, prosecuting for the United States in this behalf, that the points on which the disagreement has happened may, during the term be stated under the direction of the judges, and certified under the seal of the court to the Supreme Court, to be finally decided,—it is ordered, that the foregoing state of the pleadings, and statement of the points upon which the disagreement has happened, which is made under the direction of the judges, be certified, according to the request of the attorney, prosecuting as aforesaid, and the law in that case made and provided.'

The inquiry first propounded upon this record points, obviously, to the answer which concedes to Congress the power here drawn in question. Congress are, by the Constitution, vested with the power to regulate commerce with foreign nations; and however, at periods of high excitement, an application of the terms 'to regulate commerce' such as would embrace absolute prohibition may have been questioned, yet, since the passage of the embargo and non-intercourse laws, and the repeated judicial sanctions those statutes have received, it can scarcely, at this day, be open to doubt, that every subject falling within the legitimate sphere of commercial regulation may be partially or wholly excluded, when either measure shall be demanded by the safety or by the important interests of the entire nation. Such exclusion cannot be limited to particular classes or descriptions of commercial subjects; it may embrace manufactures, bullion, coin, or any other thing. The power once conceded, it may operate on any and every subject of commerce to which the legislative discretion may apply it.

But the twentieth section of the act of Congress of March 3d, 1825, or rather those provisions of that section brought to the view of this court by the second question certified, are not properly referable to commercial regulations, merely as such; nor to considerations of ordinary commercial advantage. They appertain rather to the execution of an important trust invested by the Constitution, and to the obligation to fulfill that trust on the part of the government, namely, the trust and the duty of creating and maintaining a uniform and pure metallic standard of value throughout the Union. The power of coining money and of regulating its value was delegated to Congress by the Constitution for the very purpose, as assigned by the framers of that instrument, of creating and preserving the uniformity and purity of such a standard of value; and on account of the impossibility which was foreseen of otherwise preventing the inequalities and the confusion necessarily incident to different views of policy, which in different communities would be brought to bear on this subject. The power to coin money being thus given to Congress, founded on public necessity, it must carry with it the correlative power of protecting the creature and object of that power. It cannot be imputed to wise and practical statesmen, nor is it consistent with common sense, that they should have vested this high and exclusive authority, and with a view to objects partaking of the magnitude of the authority itself, only to be rendered immediately vain and useless, as must have been the case had the government been left disabled and impotent as to the only means of securing the objects in contemplation.

If the medium which the government was authorized to create and establish could immediately be expelled, and substituted by one it had neither created, estimated, nor authorized,—one possessing no intrinsic value,—then the power conferred by the Constitution would be useless,—wholly fruitless of every end it was designed to accomplish. Whatever functions Congress are, by the Constitution, authorized to perform, they are, when the public good requires it, bound to perform; and on this principle, having emitted a circulating medium, a standard of value indispensable for the purposes of the community, and for the action of the government itself, they are accordingly authorized and bound in duty to prevent its debasement and expulsion, and the destruction of the general confidence and convenience, by the influx and substitution of a spurious coin in lieu of the constitutional currency. We admit that the clause of the Constitution authorizing Congress to provide for the punishment of counterfeiting the securities and current coin of the United States does not embrace within its language the offence of uttering or circulating spurious or counterfeited coin (the term counterfeit, both by its etymology and common intendment, signifying the fabrication of a false image or representation); nor do we think it necessary or regular to seek the foundation of the offence of circulating spurious coin, or for the origin of the right to punish that offence, either in the section of the statute before quoted, or in this clause of the Constitution. We trace both the offence and the authority to punish it to the

Continued

power given by the Constitution to coin money, and to the correspondent and necessary power and obligation to protect and to preserve in its purity this constitutional currency for the benefit of the nation. Whilst we hold it a sound maxim that no powers should be conceded to the Federal government which cannot be regularly and legitimately found in the charter of its creation, we acknowledge equally the obligation to withhold from it no power or attribute which, by the same charter, has been declared necessary to the execution of expressly granted powers, and to the fulfillment of clear and well-defined duties.

It has been argued, that the doctrines ruled in the case of *Fox v. The State of Ohio* are in conflict with the positions just stated in the case before us. We can perceive no such conflict, and think that any supposition of the kind must flow from a misapprehension of one or of both of these cases. The case of *Fox v. The State of Ohio*, involved no question whatsoever as to the powers of the Federal government to coin money and regulate its value; nor as to the power of that government to punish the offence of importing or circulating spurious coin; nor as to its power to punish for counterfeiting the current coin of the United States. That case was simply a prosecution for a private cheat practiced [sic] by one citizen of Ohio upon another, within the jurisdiction of the State, by means of a base coin in the similitude of a dollar,—an offence denounced by the law of Ohio as obnoxious to punishment by confinement in the State Penitentiary. And the question, and the only one, brought up for the examination of this court was, whether this private cheat could be punished by the State authorities, on account of the immediate instrument of its perpetration having been a base coin, in the similitude of a dollar of the coinage of the United States.

The stress of the argument of this court in that case was to show, that the right of the State to punish that cheat had not been taken from her by the express terms, nor by any necessary implication, of the Constitution. It claimed for the State neither the power to coin money nor to regulate the value of coin; but simply that of protecting her citizens against frauds committed upon them within her jurisdiction, and, indeed, as a means auxiliary thereto, of relying upon the true standard of the coin as established and regulated under the authority of Congress. In illustration of the existence of the right just mentioned in the State, and in order merely to show that it had not been taken from her, it was said that the punishment of such a cheat did not fall within the express language of those clauses of the Constitution which gave to Congress the right of coining money and of regulating its value, or of providing for the punishment of counterfeiting the current coin. It was also said by this court, that the fact of passing or putting off a base coin did not fall within the language of those clauses of the Constitution, for this fact fabricated, altered, or changed nothing, but left the coins, whether genuine or spurious, precisely as before. But this court have nowhere said, that an offence cannot be committed against the coin or currency of the United States, or against that constitutional power which is exclusively authorized for public uses to create that currency, and which for the same public uses and necessities is authorized and bound to preserve it; nor have they said, that the debasement of the coin would not be as effectually accomplished by introducing and throwing into circulation a currency which was spurious and simulated, as it would be by actually making counterfeits,—fabricating coin of inferior or base metal. On the contrary, we think that either of these proceedings would be equally in contravention of the right and of the obligation appertaining to the government to coin money, and to protect and preserve it at the regulated or standard rate of value.

With the view of avoiding conflict between the State and Federal jurisdictions, this court in the case of *Fox v. The State of Ohio* have taken care to point out, that the same act might, as to its character and tendencies, and the consequences it involved, constitute an offence against both the State and Federal governments, and might draw to its commission the penalties denounced by either, as appropriate to its character in reference to each. We think this distinction sound, as we hold to be the entire doctrines laid down in the case above mentioned, and regard them as being in no wise in conflict with the conclusions adopted in the present case.

We therefore order it to be certified to the Circuit Court of the United States for the Northern District of New York, in answer to the questions propounded by that court:—

1st. That Congress had power and authority, under the Constitution, to enact so much of the twentieth section of the act of March 3, 1825,

Continued

entitled 'An act more effectually to provide for the punishment of certain crimes against the United States, and for other purposes,' as relates to bringing into the United States counterfeit coins.

2d. That Congress, under and by virtue of the Constitution, had power to enact so much of the said twentieth section as relates to the uttering, publishing, passing, and selling of the counterfeit coin therein specified.

Order.

This cause came on to be heard on the transcript of the record from the Circuit Court of the United States for the Northern District of New York, and on the points or questions on which the judges of the said Circuit Court were opposed in opinion, and which were certified to this court for its opinion, agreeably to the act of Congress in such case made and provided, and was argued by counsel. On consideration whereof, it is the opinion of this court,—1st. That Congress had power and authority, under the Constitution, to enact so much of the twentieth section of the act of 3d March, 1825, entitled 'An act more effectually to provide for the punishment of certain crimes against the United States, and for other purposes,' as relates to bringing into the United States counterfeit coins; and 2d. That Congress, under and by virtue of the Constitution, had power to enact so much of the said twentieth section as relates to uttering, publishing, passing, and selling of the counterfeit coins therein specified. Whereupon, it is now here ordered and adjudged by this court, that it be so certified to the said Circuit Court.

The Court in *Marigold* saw the power to punish counterfeiting as a power to be shared by both the federal system and the states and upheld both the Ohio statute that punished an individual who used counterfeit coins to defraud another, and the federal statute written to punish the circulation or importation of counterfeited money. The Court was unwilling to take the power to punish counterfeiting from the states. The use of counterfeited monies to defraud another is more about the crime of fraud than it is about counterfeiting. By taking the position that counterfeiting is potentially an offense against both the federal government and the state, the Court upholds the federal power while not depriving the states of the ability to protect citizens. Thus, the power to punish for counterfeiting is not exclusive to the federal legislature.

When the two clauses discussed above are viewed in conjunction with the power to lay and collect taxes and the power to borrow money, it is clear that Congress has broad powers in monetary matters. However, sometimes these powers come in conflict, as in the case of *Perry v. United States*.[89] In this case, the congressional power to borrow money came into direct conflict with the power to set the value of money. Perry had purchased a bond from the United States in the amount of $10,000, and it was to be paid back to him with the accrued interest in United States gold coin at the then present standard rate. At the time he purchased the bond, the standard rate for a dollar was 25.8 grains of gold .9 fine. When Perry presented the bond for payment and demanded payment based on the above-noted rate, the United States refused and offered to pay instead according to the standard rate of 1934. Perry refused payment in this amount and brought suit against the United States. When the Court was called on to determine which congressional power would take precedence in this case, it held, on an 8 to 1 vote that the power to borrow money (and the obligation imposed by the use of that power) was to take precedence over the power to set the value of money.

"In authorizing the Congress to borrow money, the Constitution empowers the Congress to fix the amount to be borrowed and the terms of payment. By virtue of the power to borrow money 'on the credit of the United States,' the Congress is authorized to pledge that credit as an assurance of payment as stipulated, as the highest assurance the government can give, its plighted faith. To

say that the Congress may withdraw or ignore that pledge is to assume that the Constitution contemplates a vain promise; a pledge having no other sanction than the pleasure and convenience of the pledgor. This Court has given no sanction to such a conception of the obligations of our government."[90]

Establishing Post Offices

Clause 7 of Article I, Section 8 gives Congress the power to establish post offices and post roads.[91] In the early days of this country, the biggest question that arose under this clause was how Congress should define the word *establish*. The debate was settled in 1876 with the case of *Kohl v. United States*.[92] In *Kohl* the Court upheld the congressional power to acquire property by **eminent domain**. Congress had empowered the Treasury Department to acquire a certain parcel of land in Cincinnati for a post office and Courthouse. When this action was challenged, the Court ultimately heard the matter.

eminent domain   the government's right and power to take private land for public use by paying for it.

KOHL v. UNITED STATES
91 U.S. 367 (1975)

Mr. Justice STRONG delivered the opinion of the court.

It has not been seriously contended during the argument that the United States government is without power to appropriate lands or other property within the States for its own uses, and to enable it to perform its proper functions. Such an authority is essential to its independent existence and perpetuity. These cannot be preserved if the obstinacy of a private person, or if any other authority, can prevent the acquisition of the means or instruments by which alone governmental functions can be performed. The powers vested by the Constitution in the general government demand for their exercise the acquisition of lands in all the States. These are needed for forts, armories, and arsenals, for navy-yards and light-houses, for custom-houses, post-offices, and court-houses, and for other public uses. If the right to acquire property for such uses may be made a barren right by the unwillingness of property-holders to sell, or by the action of a State prohibiting a sale to the Federal government, the constitutional grants of power may be rendered nugatory, and the government is dependent for its practical existence upon the will of a State, or even upon that of a private citizen. This cannot be. No one doubts the existence in the State governments of the right of eminent domain,—a right distinct from and paramount to the right of ultimate ownership. It grows out of the necessities of their being, not out of the tenure by which lands are held.

But, if the right of eminent domain exists in the Federal government, it is a right which may be exercised within the States, so far as is necessary to the enjoyment of the powers conferred upon it by the Constitution. In *Ableman v. Booth*, Chief Justice Taney described in plain language the complex nature of our government, and the existence of two distinct and separate sovereignties within the same territorial space, each of them restricted in its powers, and each, within its sphere of action prescribed by the Constitution of the United States, independent of the other. Neither is under the necessity of applying to the other for permission to exercise its lawful powers. Within its own sphere, it may employ all the agencies for exerting them which are appropriate or necessary, and which are not forbidden by the law of its being. When the power to establish post-offices and to create courts within the States was conferred upon the Federal government, included in it was authority to obtain sites for such offices and for courthouses, and to obtain them by such means as were known and appropriate. The right of eminent domain was one of those means well known when the Constitution was adopted, and employed to obtain lands for public uses. Its existence, therefore, in the grantee of that power, ought not to be questioned. The Constitution itself contains an implied recognition of it beyond what may justly be implied from the express grants. The fifth amendment contains a provision that private property shall not be taken for public use without just compensation.

* * *

Continued

What is that but an implied assertion, that, on making just compensation, it may be taken? In Cooley on Constitutional Limitations, it is said,—

'So far as the general government may deem it important to appropriate lands or other property for its own purposes, and to enable it to perform its functions,—as must sometimes be necessary in the case of forts, light-houses, and military posts or roads, and other conveniences and necessities of government,—the general government may exercise the authority as well within the States as within the territory under its exclusive jurisdiction: and its right to do so may be supported by the same reasons which support the right in any case; that is to say, the absolute necessity that the means in the government for performing its functions and perpetuating its existence should not be liable to be controlled or defeated by the want of consent of private parties or of any other authority.'

* * *

It is true, this power of the Federal government has not heretofore been exercised adversely; but the non-user of a power does not disprove its existence. In some instances, the States, by virtue of their own right of eminent domain, have condemned lands for the use of the general government, and such condemnations have been sustained by their courts, without, however, denying the right of the United States to act independently of the States. Such was the ruling in *Gilmer v. Lime Point*, where lands were condemned by a proceeding in a State court and under a State law for a United States fortification. A similar decision was made in *Burt v. The Merchants' Ins. Co.*, where land was taken under a State law as a site for a post-office and subtreasury building. Neither of these cases denies the right of the Federal government to have lands in the States condemned for its uses under its own power and by its own action. The question was, whether the State could take lands for any other public use than that of the State. In *Trombley v. Humphrey*, a different doctrine was asserted, founded, we think, upon better reason. The proper view of the right of eminent domain seems to be, that it is a right belonging to a sovereignty to take private property for its own public uses, and not for those of another. Beyond that, there exists no necessity; which alone is the foundation of the right. If the United States has the power, it must be complete in itself. It can neither be enlarged nor diminished by a State. Nor can any State prescribe the manner in which it must be exercised. The consent of a State can never be a condition precedent to its enjoyment. Such consent is needed only, if at all, for the transfer of jurisdiction and of the right of exclusive legislation after the land shall have been acquired.

It may, therefore, fairly be concluded that the proceeding in the case we have in hand was a proceeding by the United States government in its own right, and by virtue of its own eminent domain. The act of Congress of March 2, 1872, gave authority to the Secretary of the Treasury to purchase a central and suitable site in the city of Cincinnati, Ohio, for the erection of a building for the accommodation of the United States courts, custom-house, United States depository, post office, internal-revenue and pension offices, at a cost not exceeding $300,000; and a proviso to the act declared that no money should be expended in the purchase until the State of Ohio should cede its jurisdiction over the site, and relinquish to the United States the right to tax the property.

The authority here given was to purchase. If that were all, it might be doubted whether the right of eminent domain was intended to be invoked. It is true, the words 'to purchase' might be construed as including the power to acquire by condemnation; for, technically, purchase includes all modes of acquisition other than that of descent. But generally, in statutes as in common use, the word is employed in a sense not technical, only as meaning acquisition by contract between the parties, without governmental interference. That Congress intended more than this is evident, however, in view of the subsequent and amendatory act passed June 10, 1872, which made an appropriation 'for the purchase at private sale or by condemnation of the ground for a site' for the building. These provisions, connected as they are, manifest a clear intention to confer upon the Secretary of the Treasury power to acquire the grounds needed by the exercise of the national right of eminent domain, or by private purchase, at his discretion. Why speak of condemnation at all, if Congress had not in view an exercise of the right of eminent domain, and did not intend to confer upon the secretary the right to invoke it?

* * *

Continued

It is argued that the assessment of property for the purpose of taking it is in its nature like the assessment of its value for the purpose of taxation. It is said they are both valuations of the property to be made as the legislature may prescribe, to enable the government, in the one case, to take the whole of it, and in the other to take a part of it for public uses; and it is argued that no one but Congress could prescribe in either case that the valuation should be made in a judicial tribunal or in a judicial proceeding, although it is admitted that the legislature might authorize the valuation to be thus made in either case. If the supposed analogy be admitted, it proves nothing. Assessments for taxation are specially provided for, and a mode is prescribed. No other is, therefore, admissible. But there is no special provision for ascertaining the just compensation to be made for land taken. That is left to the ordinary processes of the law; and hence, as the government is a suitor for the property under a claim of legal right to take it, there appears to be no reason for holding that the proper Circuit Court has not jurisdiction of the suit, under the general grant of jurisdiction made by the act of 1789.

The second assignment of error is, that the Circuit Court refused the demand of the defendants below, now plaintiffs in error, for a separate trial of the value of their estate in the property. They were lessees of one of the parcels sought to be taken, and they demanded a separate trial of the value of their interest; but the court overruled their demand, and required that the jury should appraise the value of the lot or parcel, and that the lessees should in the same trial try the value of their leasehold estate therein. In directing the course of the trial, the court required the lessor and the lessees each separately to state the nature of their estates to the jury, the lessor to offer his testimony separately, and the lessees theirs, and then the government to answer the testimony of the lessor and the lessees; and the court instructed the jury to find and return separately the value of the estates of the lessor and the lessees. It is of this that the lessees complain.

They contend, that whether the proceeding is to be treated as founded on the national right of eminent domain, or on that of the State, its consent having been given by the enactment of the State legislature of Feb. 15, 1873, it was required to conform to the practice and proceedings in the courts of the State in like cases. This requirement, it is said, was made by the act of Congress of June 1, 1872. But, admitting that the court was bound to conform to the practice and proceedings in the State courts in like cases, we do not perceive that any error was committed. Under the laws of Ohio, it was regular to institute joint proceeding against all the owners of lots proposed to be taken; but the eighth section of the State statute gave to 'the owner or owners of each separate parcel' the right to a separate trial. In such a case, therefore, a separate trial is the mode of proceeding in the State courts. The statute treats all the owners of a parcel as one party, and gives to them collectively a trial separate from the trial of the issues between the government and the owners of other parcels. It hath this extent; no more. The court is not required to allow a separate trial to each owner of an estate or interest in each parcel, and no consideration of justice to those owners would be subserved by it. The Circuit Court, therefore, gave to the plaintiffs in error all, if not more than all, they had a right to ask.

The judgment of the Circuit Court is affirmed.

Mr. Justice FIELD dissenting.

Assuming that the majority are correct in the doctrine announced in the opinion of the court,—that the right of eminent domain within the States, using those terms not as synonymous with the ultimate dominion or title to property, but as indicating merely the right to take private property for public uses, belongs to the Federal government, to enable it to execute the powers conferred by the Constitution,—and that any other doctrine would subordinate, in important particulars, the national authority to the caprice of individuals or the will of State legislatures, it appears to me that provision for the exercise of the right must first be made by legislation. The Federal courts have no inherent jurisdiction of a proceeding instituted for the condemnation of property; and I do not find any statute of Congress conferring upon them such authority.

The Judiciary Act of 1789 only invests the circuit courts of the United States with jurisdiction, concurrent with that of the State courts, of suits of a civil nature at common law or in equity; and these terms have reference to those classes of cases which are conducted by regular pleadings between parties, according to the

Continued

established doctrines prevailing at the time in the jurisprudence of England. The proceeding to ascertain the value of property which the government may deem necessary to the execution of its powers, and thus the compensation to be made for its appropriation, is not a suit at common law or in equity, but an inquisition for the ascertainment of a particular fact as preliminary to the taking; and all that is required is that the proceeding shall be conducted in some fair and just mode, to be provided by law, either with or without the intervention of a jury, opportunity being afforded to parties interested to present evidence as to the value of the property, and to be heard thereon. The proceeding by the States, in the exercise of their right of eminent domain, is often had before commissioners of assessment or special boards appointed for that purpose. It can hardly be doubted that Congress might provide for inquisition as to the value of property to be taken by similar instrumentalities; and yet, if the proceeding be a suit at common law, the intervention of a jury would be required by the seventh amendment to the Constitution.

I think that the decision of the majority of the court in including the proceeding in this case under the general designation of a suit at common law, with which the circuit courts of the United States are invested by the eleventh section of the Judiciary Act, goes beyond previous adjudications, and is in conflict with them.

Nor am I able to agree with the majority in their opinion, or at least intimation, that the authority to purchase carries with it authority to acquire by condemnation. The one supposes an agreement upon valuation, and a voluntary conveyance of the property: the other implies a compulsory taking, and a contestation as to the value. For these reasons, I am compelled to dissent from the opinion of the court.

As the Court pointed out, without the power of eminent domain, Congress' power to establish post offices would be useless. However, Justice Field dissented in this decision saying that the power to purchase property, which he felt was the power given to Congress, was the power to buy the property from a willing seller. The power was not, in his opinion, the power to condemn the property and acquire it from an unwilling property owner. Nonetheless, the majority opinion is still the view that is followed today.

In addition to the power to acquire property to establish post offices, the Court has also held that Congress has the power to take all steps necessary to ensure the speedy and secure transportation of mails as well as the prompt delivery of that mail. This power has led Congress to enact legislation that prevents tampering with the mail or using the mails to defraud or harm citizens.[93] While the power has raised some constitutional issues regarding the First Amendment Free Speech and Association rights, the Court has consistently upheld congressional power over the misuse of the mail. The 1960s and 1970s brought forth many of these types of cases, and ultimately, the Court held that so long as Congress operated the postal service, that service must be operated in a manner that did not infringe on constitutional guarantees, such as those found in the First Amendment.[94]

In short, Congress has broad powers to establish post offices, procure property for said post offices, and in regulating the mail so that it is not used for illegal, immoral, or fraudulent purposes. This power, however, must give way to specific constitutional guarantees if a conflict between the two arises.

Immigration and Naturalization

The power over **immigration, citizenship**, and **naturalization** is also an exclusive power that was given to Congress by Article I, § 8 of the Constitution. Clause 4 specifically grants this power when it states that Congress shall have the power "To establish a uniform Rule of Naturalization . . ."[95] This is an area where the courts have consistently refused to allow the states to interfere.

immigration to come into a country of which one is not a native or permanent resident.

citizenship the status of being a citizen.

naturalization the formal process of becoming a citizen of a country.

Historically Congress used this power to allow only European immigrants to become citizens,[96] but it was amended throughout the years, first to allow individuals of African descent to become citizens[97] and then to allow other minority immigrants to become citizens. Today, Congress has the power to grant citizenship to all nationalities, while barring subversives, dissidents, and radicals.[98] In addition, a person can also be denied citizenship if an appropriate federal official determines that the individual is not of good moral character.[99]

This does not mean that citizenship is automatically granted if it is found that the individual is not a subversive, dissident, or radical. In order for one to become a citizen, that individual must comply with the terms that Congress has imposed for qualification as a U.S. citizen. While a prospective citizen cannot be denied citizenship on the basis of race, ethnicity, national origin, sex, or marital status,[100] eligibility can be denied for the reasons stated above, including questions regarding character. Congress has specifically determined that an individual is not of good moral character if he or she is a drunk, commits adultery, is a polygamist, gambles, or is a convicted felon or a homosexual.[101] Congress has delegated its authority to determine citizenship matters and the eligibility of individuals for citizenship to the Bureau of Citizenship and Immigration Services. This federal agency has set out several general requirements for naturalization. Exhibit 4.3 outlines these basic requirements.

EXHIBIT 4.3 General Naturalization Requirements

Applicants must:
1. Be at least 18 years old;
2. Have been lawfully admitted to the United States for permanent residence;
3. Reside continuously as a lawful permanent resident in the U.S. for at least 5 years prior to filing with no single absence from the United States of more than one year;
4. Reside within a state or district for at least three months;
5. Be of good moral character;
6. Show that he or she is attached to the principles of the Constitution of the United States;
7. Be able to read, write, speak, and understand words in ordinary usage in the English language;
8. Demonstrate knowledge and understanding of the fundamentals of the history and the principles and form of government of the United States; and
9. Take an oath of allegiance which includes a statement in support of the Constitution and laws of the United States, a renunciation of any foreign allegiance or foreign title and a willingness to bear arms for the Armed Forces of the U.S. or perform services for the government of the U.S. when required.[102]

Once an immigrant has become a citizen, does he or she have the same rights as citizens who were born in the United States? In an early case entitled *Osborn v. Bank of the United States*[103] the Court had to decide whether the bank was entitled to sue in federal court. While this issue seems to have little to do with citizenship, Chief Justice Marshall made an interesting statement in the dicta of this case that foreshadows the Court's view of a naturalized citizen today. Chief Justice Marshall wrote:

> *"A naturalized citizen is indeed made a citizen under an act of Congress, but the act does not proceed to give, to regulate, or to prescribe his capacities. He becomes a member of the society, possessing all the rights of a native citizen, and standing, in the view of the constitution, on the footing of a native. The constitution does not authorize Congress to enlarge or abridge those rights. The simple power of the national Legislature, is to prescribe a uniform rule of naturalization, and the exercise of this power exhausts it, so far as respects the individual. The constitution then takes him up, and, among other rights, extends to him the capacity of suing in the Courts of the United States, precisely under the same circumstances under which a native might sue."[104]*

While a naturalized citizen has the same rights as any other citizen, this does not mean that these new citizens can participate in public office to the same extent as a native-born citizen. As Justice Douglas wrote in *Schneider v. Rusk*,[105]

> *"We start from the premise that the rights of citizenship of the native born and of the naturalized person are of the same dignity and are coextensive. The only difference drawn by the Constitution is that only the 'natural born' citizen is eligible to be President. While the rights of citizenship of the native born derive from s 1 of the Fourteenth Amendment and the rights of the naturalized citizen derive from satisfying, free of fraud, the requirements set by Congress, the latter, apart from the exception noted, 'becomes a member of the society, possessing all the rights of a native citizen, and standing, in the view of the constitution, on the footing of a native.' "[106]*

TENTH AMENDMENT LIMITS ON CONGRESSIONAL POWER

The Tenth Amendment says: "The powers not delegated to the United States by the Constitution, nor prohibited by it to the States, are reserved to the States respectively, or to the people."[107] While it would seem that this amendment would play a significant role in discussions concerning constitutional powers, the reality is that this amendment fell into disuse early in the twentieth century. However, it was used in *Carter v. Carter Coal Company*[108] when the Bituminous Coal Conservation Act of 1935 was challenged. The Act set maximum hours and minimum wages for coal miners, and its challengers claimed that the Act went beyond Congress' constitutionally granted powers and should be declared unconstitutional. The Court agreed, saying that the federal government had ventured into a state-controlled area under the Tenth Amendment. In doing so, the Court dealt a blow to the New Deal legislation discussed earlier. This was the last time the Tenth Amendment was used to strike down a federal statute for 40 years. It was revived however in 1976 in *National League of Cities v. Usery*.[109]

In this 5 to 4 decision, the Court used the Tenth Amendment to strike down federal legislation that set minimum wage and overtime rules for state and municipal employees. The Court agreed with the federal government's argument that the rules dictated by the legislation did, indeed, impact interstate commerce and could be applied to private employers; they could not be applied to state or municipal employers. Chief Justice Rehnquist wrote for the Court, saying,

> *"[E]ven if appellants may have overestimated the effect which the Act will have upon their current levels and patterns of governmental activity, the dispositive factor is that Congress has attempted to exercise its Commerce Clause authority to prescribe minimum wages and maximum hours to be paid by the States in their capacities as sovereign governments. In so doing, Congress has sought to wield its power in a fashion that would impair the States' "ability to function effectively in a federal system." This exercise of congressional authority does not comport with the federal system of government embodied in the Constitution. We hold that insofar as the challenged amendments operate to directly displace the States' freedom to structure integral operations in areas of traditional governmental functions, they are not within the authority granted Congress by Art. I, s 8, cl. 3."[110]*

The Court's rationale behind this holding was that the new rules violated the Constitution in two ways. First, the cost of the rules impaired the states' ability to function, as compliance would have cost both the states and the municipalities substantial amounts of money. Second, the rules deprived the states of any discretion to decide how to spend the money available for state employee salaries. In other words, to allow Congress to make and enforce these rules would be to allow Congress to make fundamental employment decisions for each state. In so deciding, the Court, in essence, revived the Tenth Amendment and once again acknowledged the sovereign power of the states in making decisions regarding its own employees.

However, the Court overruled *Usery* a few years later in *Garcia v. San Antonio Metropolitan Transit Authority*.[111] *Garcia* involved a challenge to the enforcement of federal rules found in the Fair Labor Standards Act. The transit authority had accepted monies from the federal government, and under the Act, they were also required to follow the federal rules. The Court used this controversy as an opportunity to overrule *Usery* as it believed that the standard used in that case was impossible to follow. In *Usery* the Court had distinguished between traditional government function and nontraditional functions. However, the Court in *Usery* gave no guidance as to what was traditional and what was not.

In *Garcia* the Court held in favor of the federal government and upheld the legislation. In doing so, the Court rejected the subjective approach used by courts to determine what was a traditional government function and, instead, held that "procedural safeguards inherent in the structure of the federal system" protected the states.[112] These procedural safeguards include two state-elected senators from each state and participation in the presidential election.

The significance of *Garcia* is that now Congress has the same power to regulate state and municipal employers and their employees as it does with private employers. So long as Congress is exercising its legitimate Commerce Power, the fact that it is regulating a state function is irrelevant.

Other cases seem to diminish the *Garcia* holding. For example, in 1992 the Court held that Congress cannot force the state to legislate or regulate commerce in a certain way or require state executive branch personnel to perform ministerial functions.[113] A few years later, in *Alden v. Maine*, the Court held that Congress could not force a state to waive its sovereign immunity and hear a damage case against itself in state court.[114] While the Court seems to have placed some limits on the *Garcia* holding, this holding is still viable, and works to limit the viability of the Tenth Amendment.

Summary

Congress has many enumerated powers granted to it by the Constitution. While these powers may seem to have a straightforward application, there are parameters placed around many of them. In doing so, the Court has attempted to maintain the balance of powers among the three branches of the federal government while ensuring that Congress has the ability to perform the functions given to it under the Constitution.

Key Terms

balancing test
citizenship
commerce
Commerce Clause
declaratory judgment
eminent domain

immigration
naturalization
Necessary and Proper Clause
Penumbra Doctrine
ratification
Supremacy Clause

Tenth Amendment
treaty
treaty power
War Powers Clauses

Review Questions

1. Why is the doctrine of nondelegability no longer used, and why is it important that Congress be allowed to delegate its authority under certain circumstances?

2. What is the significance of the recognized authority of Congress to use its commerce powers in the civil rights arena? Are there limitations on the use of this power?

3. What is meant by "necessary and proper" with regard to congressional powers?

4. Did the congressional investigation into Communist activity in the 1950s change the way that Americans view the congressional power to investigate? Why or why not?

5. Why was the Court so adamant that neither the Legislature itself, nor the states, be allowed to add additional qualifications for senators or representatives elected to federal office?

6. Why is the power to enter into war, form a treaty, or handle foreign affairs considered shared powers between the legislative and executive branches?

Internet Connections

1. For more information regarding immigration and naturalization, see the Bureau of Citizenship and Immigration Services' Web site at *http://www.immigration.gov.*

2. For information on your elected officials and current legislative issues, visit the Legislative Action Center's Web site at *http://gov.findlaw.com.*

3. To research legislation, legislative history, and legislative publications, visit the Law Librarian's Society's Web site to examine the LLSDC's Legislative Source Book at *http://www.llsdc.org.*

4. For information on current bills, House documents, and historical information about the House of Representatives, visit the House of Representatives Office of the Clerk's Web site at *http://www.clerkweb.house.gov.*

5. For information on the Senate, current legislation, and legislative history, visit the U.S. Senate's Web site at *http://www.senate.gov.*

End Notes

[1]U.S. Const. art. I, § 8.

[2]*United States v. Shreveport Grain & Elevator Company*, 287 U.S. 77 (1932).

[3]*Field v. Clark*, 143 U.S. 649 (1892).

[4]*Carter v. Carter Coal Company*, 298 U.S. 310 (1936).

[5]*J.W. Hampton Jr. & Company v. United States*, 276 U.S. 394, 405–406 (1928).

[6]*Sunshine Anthracite Coal Company v. Adkins*, 310 U.S. 381, 398 (1940).

[7]*Wayman v. Southard*, 23 U.S. 1 (1825).

[8]*Id.* at 42–43.

[9]Craig Thomas, *The Legislative Process: The Passage of a Bill Through Congress*, at http://thomas.senate.gov (July 2, 2003).

[10]*Gibbons v. Ogden*, 22 U.S. 1 (1824).

[11]*Mayor of the City of New York v. Miln*, 36 U.S. 102 (1837).

[12]*Cooley v. Board of Wardens*, 53 U.S. 299 (1851).

[13]*Hammer v. Dagenhart*, 247 U.S. 251 (1918).

[14]*U.S. v. Darby*, 312 U.S. 100, 116 (1941).

[15]*Id.* at 117.

[16]*Schechter Poultry Corporation v. United States*, 295 U.S. 495 (1935).

[17]*Carter v. Carter Coal Company*, 298 U.S. 238 (1936).

[18]*NLRB v. Jones & Laughlin Steel Corporation*, 301 U.S. 1 (1937).

[19]*Id.* at 25.

[20]*Id.* at 31.

[21]*Id.* at 31.

[22]*Id.* at 31.

[23]*Id.* at 33.

[24]*Id.* at 36–37.

[25]*Wickard v. Filburn*, 317 U.S. 111 (1942).

[26]*U.S. v. Darby*, 312 U.S. 100, 109–110 (1941).

[27]*Id.* at 115.

[28]*U.S. v. Lopez*, 514 U.S. 549 (1995).

[29]*Id.* at 558–559.

[30]*Id.* at 563–564.

[31]*Id.* at 564.

[32]*United States v. Morrison*, 529 U.S. 598 (2000).

[33]42 U.S.C. § 13981(a).

[34]*U.S. v. Morrison*, 529 U.S. 598, 615 (2000).

[35]*McCulloch v. Maryland*, 17 U.S. 316 (1819).

[36]*Heart of Atlanta Hotel v. United States*, 379 U.S. 241 (1964).

[37]*Katzenbach v. McClung*, 379 U.S. 294 (1964).

[38]*Heart of Atlanta Hotel v. United States*, 379 U.S. 241, 257 (1964).

[39]*Katzenbach v. McClung*, 379 U.S. 294, 301–304 (1964).

[40]*Daniel v. Paul*, 395 U.S. 298 (1969).

[41]*Id.* at 301.

[42]*McGrain v. Daugherty*, 273 U.S. 135 (1927).

[43]*Id.* at 174–175.

[44]*Watkins v. United States*, 354 U.S. 178 (1957).

[45]*Barenblatt v. United States*, 360 U.S. 109, 111 (1959).

[46]*Gibson v. Florida Legislative Committee*, 372 U.S. 539 (1963).

[47]*Id.* at 543.

[48]*Id.* at 544.

[49]*Id.* at 545.

[50]*Id.* at 555.

[51]U.S. Const. art. I, § 2, cl. 2.

[52]U.S. Const. art. I, § 3, cl. 3.

[53]*Powell v. McCormack*, 395 U.S. 486 (1969).

[54]This section of Article I says, among other things, "Each House may determine the Rules of its Proceedings, punish its Members for disorderly Behaviour, [sic] and, with the Concurrence of two thirds, expel a Member."

[55]*U.S. Term Limits, Inc. v. Thornton*, 514 U.S. 779 (1995).

[56]*Id.* at 812.

[57]*Bushaber v. Union Pacific Railroad Company*, 240 U.S. 1 (1916).

[58]*Id.* at 12.

[59]*Bailey v. Drexel Furniture Company*, 259 U.S. 20 (1922).

[60]*United States v. Ptasynski*, 462 U.S. 74 (1983).

[61]*Pollack v. Farmers Loan & Trust Company*, 157 U.S. 429 (1895).

[62]U.S. Const. amend. XVI.

[63]1 Stat. 24 (1789).

[64]*J.W. Hampton & Company v. United States*, 276 U.S. 394 (1928).

[65]*Id.* at 411–412.

[66]*McCray v. United States*, 195 U.S. 27 (1904).

[67]U.S. Const. art. I, § 8.

[68]*United States v. Butler*, 297 U.S. 1 (1936).

[69]*Id.* at 65–66.

[70]*Id.* at 84–86.

[71]*McCulloch v. Maryland*, 17 U.S. 316 (1819).

[72]Chief Justice Chase wrote about the war powers in his dissent in *Ex Parte Milligan*, 71 U.S. 2, 139 (1866).

[73]*United States v. Curtiss-Wright Export Corporation*, 299 U.S. 304, 316, 318 (1936).

[74]*Atlee v. Richardson*, 411 U.S. 911 (1973).

[75]*Massachusetts v. Laird*, 451 F.2d 26 (1st Cir. 1971).

[76]*Selective Draft Law Cases*, 245 U.S. 366 (1918).

[77]*Butler v. Perry*, 240 U.S. 328, 333 (1916).

[78]*United States v. O'Brien*, 391 U.S. 367 (1968).

[79]*Id.* at 377.

[80]U.S. Const. art. II, § 2, cl. 2.

[81]*Reid v. Covert*, 354 U.S. 1 (1957).

[82]U.S. Const. art. I, § 10.

[83]*Williams v. Bruffy*, 96 U.S. 176 (1878).

[84]U.S. Const. art. I, § 8, cls. 5–6.

[85]*McCulloch v. Maryland, supra.*

[86]*Id.* and *Veazie Bank v. Fenno*, 75 U.S. 533 (1869).

[87]*Veazie*, 75 U.S. at 533.

[88]*Nortez v. United States*, 249 U.S. 317 (1935).

[89]*Perry v. United States*, 294 U.S. 330 (1935).

[90]*Id.*

[91]U.S. Const. art. I, § 8, cl. 7.

[92]*Kohl v. United States*, 91 U.S. 367 (1876).

[93]*Ex parte Jackson*, 96 U.S. 727 (1878).

[94]*Lamont v. Postmaster General*, 381 U.S. 305 (1965).

[95]U.S. Const. art. I, § 8, cl. 4.

[96]1 Stat. 103 (1790).

[97]22 Stat. 58 (1870).

[98]8 U.S.C. § 1424(a) gives Congress the authority to deny citizenship to any person "who advocates or teaches, or who is a member of or affiliated with any organization that advocates or teaches . . . opposition to all organized government" or "who advocates or teaches or who is a member of or affiliated with any organization that advocates or teaches the overthrow by force or violence or other unconstitutional means of the government of the United States" or who is a member of or affiliated with the Communist Party, or other communist organization, or other totalitarian organizations.

[99]8 U.S.C. § 1427(a)(3).

[100]8 U.S.C. § 1422 (1952).

[101]8 U.S.C. § 1101.

[102]"General Naturalization Requirements," Bureau of Citizenship and Immigration Services, at http://www.immigration.gov (July 7, 2003).

[103]*Osborn v. Bank of the United States*, 22 U.S. 737 (1824).

[104]*Id.* at 827.

[105]*Schneider v. Rusk*, 377 U.S. 163 (1964).

[106]*Id.* at 165–166.

[107]U.S. Const. amend. X.

[108]*Carter v. Carter Coal Company*, 298 U.S. 238 (1936).

[109]*National League of Cities v. Usery*, 426 U.S. 833 (1976).

[110]*Id.* at 852.

[111]*Garcia v. San Antonio Metropolitan Transit Authority*, 469 U.S. 528 (1985).

[112]*Id.*

[113]*New York v. United States*, 505 U.S. 144 (1992).

[114]*Alden v. Maine*, 526 U.S. 1002 (1999).

CHAPTER 5

THE PRESIDENCY

*One great object of the Executive is, to control the Legislature. * * * [T]he Executive magistrate should be the guardian of the people, even the lower classes, against legislative tyranny; against the great and wealthy, who in the course of things will necessarily compose the legislative body.*

—Gouverneur Morris, N.Y. Delegate
Constitutional Convention Debate of July 19, 1787

INTRODUCTION

The executive branch is the third of the three-part governmental structure established by the Constitution. "The executive Power [is] vested in a President of the United States of America."[1] The Constitution, however, does not state with great specificity the powers granted to the President. As compared with the explicit recitation of Congress' power set forth in Article I, few powers are explicitly granted to the President. Nevertheless, the President wields a significant amount of power within the constitutional framework.

In this chapter we will consider the power of the presidency. After looking at the explicit powers granted to the Chief Executive Officer by the Constitution, a consideration of how these powers have been interpreted by the Supreme Court, first with regard to domestic affairs and then in the context of foreign affairs (as well as the President's ability to commit the armed forces of the nation) will be undertaken. Finally, the President's power of appointment and removal of executive personnel, along with impeachment, will be discussed.

THE CONSTITUTIONAL GRANT OF POWERS

As noted, the Constitution's grant of power to the President is not nearly so comprehensive as that of Congress. There are, however, a number of specifically enumerated powers of the Presidency set out in Article II, Section 2. The three separate clauses of that section constitute the only enumerated powers of the President. Clause 1 specifies that the President is Commander in Chief of the armed forces of the United States, as well as of the state militias, should they be called to serve the nation. It is also in this first clause that the President is given power over the executive departments of the government (i.e., those agencies responsible for enforcing the laws). The President is put in charge of these departments and is provided with the power to have the respective heads of departments report to him in writing on "any Subject relating to the Duties of their . . . Offices. . . ."[2] The final enumerated power set forth in Clause 1 is the power to grant pardons and reprieves for federal crimes. This power, however, does not extend to cases of impeachment.

In Clause 2, the President is given the power to make treaties. This power is conditioned upon the advice and consent of two-thirds of the Senate. The President is also specifically granted the power to nominate and appoint

"Ambassadors, other public Ministers and Consuls, Judges of the supreme Court, and all other Officers of the United States whose Appointments are not herein otherwise provided for, and which shall be established by Law"[3] with the advice and consent of the Senate. In addition, Clause 2 allows the President to appoint inferior officers where Congress has vested such authority in him.

Finally, Clause 3 vests the President with the power to fill vacancies during Senate recesses that will expire at the end of the Senate's next session.

These clauses constitute the only enumerated powers of the President under Article II that pertain to the executive power. The President is, however, endowed with one additional power. Article I, which enumerates the legislative powers, requires presentment of all bills to the President once they have passed both houses of Congress. The President has the power to veto the bill, sending it back to the Congress. Congress then has the ability to reconsider the bill and override the Presidential veto by a two-thirds vote. Thus, the President is given some limited constitutional power in the legislative process.[4]

These constitutional grants of power, though limited, provide the basis for the doctrine of implied powers. The Supreme Court may conclude that an action by the President is part of the executive sphere and is not unconstitutional simply because it does not come within the ambit of a specifically enumerated power.[5] So, it is from these enumerated powers, as well as the Court's interpretation of them, along with the executive functions that the scope of the power of the executive branch is determined.

We turn now to an in-depth discussion of how the Court has interpreted these powers and note that most of these decisions emerge from separation of powers challenges, some of which have already been discussed in Chapter 2.

THE PRESIDENT AND DOMESTIC POWER

Lawmaking

The President is without power to make law and the Court, though willing to infer broad presidential authority, has strictly limited executive power in this area.[6] At the same time, the Court has been willing to allow the President's exercise of power when circumstances indicate that Congress has implied its acquiescence in the show of presidential authority. This will be but one factor for the Court to consider, and if it is the only one, it is unlikely to persuade the Court to find the action constitutional.[7]

The Veto Power

veto   a refusal by the President or a governor to sign into law a bill that has been passed by a legislature.

pocket veto   the failure by the President to sign a bill passed within 10 days of the end of a legislative session (which has the same effect as a veto).

line-item veto   the item veto (or the *line-item veto*) is the veto by a state governor or the President of only part of an appropriations bill.

The veto power granted to the President in Article I, § 7 has been the basis for challenges to presidential authority. The President must sign or **veto** a bill within 10 days and return it to Congress so that body may attempt to override his veto. If the President does not comply with this time schedule, the bill becomes law. Article I, § 7, however, also provides that if Congress has prevented the return of the bill within the 10-day period due to adjournment, then the bill cannot become law unless the President signs the bill. This is known as the "**pocket veto**." The President's veto power in this situation is absolute.

In 1997, Congress provided the President with the ability to veto part of a particular bill—usually an item of spending. This ability is known as the **line-item veto** and was implemented by passage of the *Line Item Veto Act*.[8]

The City of New York and a farmers' cooperative challenged the Act after the President used his power under the Act to cancel two measures, arguing injury as the result of the President's actions and seeking a *declaratory judgment* that the statute was unconstitutional.[9] In *Clinton v. City of New York*, the District Court consolidated the cases and concluded that the statute violated the Presentment Clause and the separation of powers doctrine.

On direct appeal and on expedited review, in a 6 to 3 decision, the Court affirmed the District Court's ruling in an opinion by Justice John Paul Stevens. The Court found that Article I, § 7 was the only way in which legislation could be amended or repealed. Thus, the underlying premise of the Court's reasoning was that the President's ability to cancel an item from a bill constituted an amendment or repeal. Accordingly, the procedure set forth in the Line Item Veto Act violated the Constitution. Justice Stevens noted that the Court was not commenting on the wisdom of the Act, but stated that any such change in the President's role in the legislative process could only be achieved by way of a constitutional amendment.[10]

The dissenters rejected the majority's underlying premise. They maintained, in opinions by Justices Scalia and Breyer, that all Congress had done was to give the President the discretion whether to spend an appropriations item while leaving the rest of the statute fully in force.

CLINTON V. CITY OF NEW YORK
524 U.S. 417 (1998)

Justice STEVENS delivered the opinion of the Court.

We now hold . . . that the cancellation procedures set forth in the Act violate the Presentment Clause, Art. I, sec. 7, cl, 2, of the Constitution.

IV

The Line Item Veto Act gives the President the power to "cancel in whole" three types of provisions that have been signed into law: "(1) any dollar amount of discretionary budget authority; (2) any item of new direct spending; or (3) any limited tax benefit." It is undisputed that the New York case involves an "item of new direct spending" and that the Snake River case involves a "limited tax benefit" as those terms are defined in Art. II. It is also undisputed that each of those provisions had been signed into law pursuant to Art. I., sec.7, of the Constitution before it was canceled.

The Act requires the President to adhere to precise procedures whenever he exercises his cancellation authority. In identifying items for cancellation he must consider the legislative history, the purposes, and other relevant information about the items. He must determine, with respect to each cancellation, that it will "(I) reduce the Federal budget deficit; (ii) not impair any essential Government functions; and (iii) not harm the national interest." Moreover, he must transmit a special message to Congress notifying it of each cancellation within five calendar days (excluding Sundays) after the enactment of the cancelled provision. It is undisputed that the President meticulously followed these procedures in these cases.

A cancellation takes effect upon receipt by Congress of the special message from the President. If, however, a "disapproval bill" pertaining to a special message is enacted into law, the cancellations set forth in that message become "null and void." The Act sets forth a detailed expedited procedure for the consideration of a "disapproval bill", but no such bill was passed for either of the cancellations involved in these cases. A majority vote of both Houses is sufficient to enact a disapproval bill. The Act does not grant the President the authority to cancel a disapproval bill, but he does, of course, retain his constitutional authority to veto such a bill

The effect of a cancellation is plainly stated in [the statute] which defines the principal terms used in the Act. With respect to both an item of new direct spending and a limited tax benefit, the cancellation prevents the item "from having legal force or effect." Thus, under the text of the statute, the two actions of the President that are challenged in these cases prevented one section of the Balanced Budget Act of 1997 and one section of the Taxpayer Relief Act of 1997 "from having legal force or effect." The remaining provisions of those statutes, with the exception of the second canceled item in the latter, continue to have the same force and effect as they had when signed into law.

In both legal and practical effect, the President has amended two Acts of Congress by repealing a portion of each. "Repeal of statutes, no less

Continued

than enactment, must conform with Art.I." There is no provision in the Constitution that authorizes the President to enact, to amend, or to repeal statutes. Both Article I and Article II assign responsibilities to the President that directly relate to the lawmaking process, but neither addresses the issue presented by these cases. The President "shall from time to time give to Congress Information on the State of the Union, and recommend to their Consideration such Measures as he shall judge necessary and expedient. . . ." Thus, he may initiate and influence legislative proposals. Moreover, after a bill has passed both Houses of Congress, but "before it becomes a Law," it must be presented to the President. If he approves it, "he shall sign it, but if not he shall return it, with his Objections to that House in which it shall have originated, who shall enter the Objections at large on their Journal, and proceed to reconsider it." His "return" of a bill, which is usually described as a "veto," is subject to being overridden by a two-thirds vote in each House.

There are important differences between the President's "return" of a bill pursuant to Article I, sec.7, and the exercise of the President's cancellation authority pursuant to the Line Item Veto Act. The constitutional return takes place *before* the bill becomes law; the statutory cancellation occurs *after* the bill becomes law. The constitutional return is of the entire bill; the statutory cancellation is of only a part. Although the Constitution expressly authorizes the President to play a role in the process of enacting statutes, it is silent on the subject of unilateral Presidential action that either repeals or amends parts of duly enacted statutes.

There are powerful reasons for construing constitutional silence on this profoundly important issue as equivalent to an express prohibition. The procedures governing the enactment of statutes set forth in the text of Article I were the product of the great debates and compromises that produced the Constitution itself. Familiar historical materials provide abundant support for the conclusion that the power to enact statutes may only "be exercised in accord with a single, finely wrought and exhaustively considered procedure." Our first President understood the text of the Presentment Clause as requiring that he either "approve all the parts of a Bill, or reject it in toto." What has emerged in these cases from the President's exercise of his

statutory cancellation powers, however, are truncated versions of two bills that passed both Houses of Congress. They are not the product of the "finely wrought" procedure that the Framers designed.

VI

First, we express no opinion about the wisdom of the procedures authorized by the Line Item Veto Act. Many members of both major political parties who have served in the Legislative and the Executive Branches have long advocated the enactment of such procedures for the purpose of "ensuring greater fiscal accountability in Washington." The text of the Act was itself the product of much debate and deliberation in both Houses of Congress and that precise text was signed into law by the President. We do not lightly conclude that their action was unauthorized by the Constitution. We have, however, twice had full argument and briefing on the question and have concluded that our duty is clear.

Second, although appellees challenge the validity of the Act on alternative grounds, the only issue we address concerns the "finely wrought" procedure commanded by the Constitution. We have been favored with extensive debate about the scope of Congress' power to delegate lawmaking authority, or its functional equivalent, to the President. [Because] we conclude that the Act's cancellation provisions violate Article I, sec.7, of the Constitution, we find it unnecessary to consider the District Court's alternative holding that the Act "impermissibly disrupts the balance of powers among the three branches of government."

Third, our decision rests on the narrow ground that the procedures authorized by the Line Item Veto Act are not authorized by the Constitution. The Balanced Budget Act of 1997 is a 500-page document that became "Public Law 105-33" after three procedural steps were taken: (1) a bill containing its exact text was approved by a majority of the members of the House of Representatives; (2) the Senate approved precisely the same text; and (3) that text was signed into law by the President. The Constitution explicitly requires that each of those three steps be taken before a bill may "become a law." If one paragraph of that text had been omitted at any one of those three stages, Public Law 105-33 would not have been validly enacted. If the Line Item

Continued

Veto Act were valid, it would authorize the President to create a different law—one whose text was not voted on by either House of Congress or presented to the President for signature. Something that might be known as "Public Law 105-33 as modified by the President" may or may not be desirable, but it is surely not a document that may "become a law" pursuant to the procedures designed by the Framers of Article I, sec.7 of the Constitution.

If there is to be a new procedure in which the President will play a different role in determining the final text of what may "become a law," such change must come not by legislation but through the amendment procedures set forth in Article V of the Constitution.

Affirmed.

Justice KENNEDY, concurring.

A nation cannot plunder its own treasury without putting its Constitution and its survival in peril. The statute before us, then, is of first importance, for it seems undeniable the Act will tend to restrain persistent excessive spending. Nevertheless, for the reasons given by JUSTICE STEVENS in the opinion for the Court, the statute must be found invalid. Failure of political will does not justify unconstitutional remedies.

Justice BREYER, with whom Justices O'CONNOR and SCALIA join as to Part III, dissenting.

I

[I] do not agree with [the Court's] ultimate conclusion. In my view the Line Item Veto Act does not violate any specific textual constitutional command, nor does it violate any implicit Separation of Powers principle. Consequently, I believe that the Act is constitutional.

II

I approach the constitutional question before us with three general considerations in mind. *First*, this Act represents a legislative effort to provide the President with the power to give effect to some, but not to all, of the expenditure and revenue-diminishing provisions contained in a single massive appropriations bill. And this objective is constitutionally proper.

When our Nation was founded, Congress could easily have provided the President with this kind of power. In that time period, our population was less than four million, federal employees numbered fewer than 5,000, annual federal budget outlays totaled approximately $4 million. [At] that time, a Congress, wishing to give a President the power to select among appropriations, could simply have embodied each appropriation in a separate bill, each bill subject to a separate Presidential veto.

Today, however, our population is about 250 million, the Federal Government employs more than four million people, the annual federal budget is $1.5 trillion, and a typical budget appropriations bill may have a dozen titles, hundreds of sections, and spread across more than 500 pages of the Statutes at Large. Congress cannot divide such a bill into thousands, or tens of thousands, of separate appropriations bills, each one of which the President would have to sign, or to veto, separately. Thus, the question is whether the Constitution permits Congress to choose a particular novel *means* to achieve this same, constitutionally legitimate, *end*.

Second, the case in part requires us to focus upon the Constitution's generally phrased structural provisions, provisions that delegate all "legislative" power to Congress and vest all "executive" power in the President. The Court, when applying these provisions, has interpreted them generously in terms of the institutional arrangements that they permit.

Third, we need not here referee a dispute among the other two branches.

These three background circumstances mean that, when one measures the *literal* words of the Act against the Constitution's *literal* commands, the fact that the Act may closely resemble a different, literally unconstitutional arrangement is beside the point. To drive exactly 65 miles per hour on an interstate highway closely resembles an act that violates the speed limit. But it does not violate that limit, for small differences matter when the question is one of literal violation of law. No more does this Act literally violate the Constitution's words.

The background circumstances also mean that we are to interpret nonliteral Separation of Powers principles in light of the need for "workable government." If we apply those principles in light of that objective, as this Court has applied them in the past, the Act is constitutional.

Continued

III

The Court believes that the Act violates the literal text of the Constitution. A simple syllogism captures its basic reasoning:

> Major Premise: The Constitution sets forth an exclusive method for enacting, repealing,
>
> Or amending laws.
>
> Minor Premise: The Act authorizes the President to "repeal or amend" laws in a different
>
> Way, namely by announcing a cancellation of a portion of a previously enacted law.
>
> Conclusion: The Act is inconsistent with the Constitution.

I find this syllogism unconvincing, however, because its Minor Premise is faulty. When the President "canceled" the two appropriation measures now before us, he did not *repeal* any law nor did he *amend* any law. He simply *followed* the law, leaving the statutes, as they are literally written, intact.

To take a simple example, a legal document, say a will or a trust instrument, might grant a beneficiary the power (a) to appoint property "to Jones for his life, remainder to Smith for 10 years so long as Smith . . . etc. and then to Brown," or (b) to appoint the same property "to Black and the heirs of his body," or (c) not to exercise the power of appointment at all. To choose the second or third of these alternatives prevents from taking effect the legal consequences that flow from the first alternative, which the legal instrument describes in detail. Any such choice, made in the exercise of a delegated power, renders that first alternative language without "legal force or effect." But such a choice does not "repeal" or "amend" either that language or the document itself. The will or trust instrument, in delegating the power of appointment, has not delegated a power to amend or to repeal the instrument; to the contrary, it requires the delegated power to be exercised in accordance with the instrument's terms.

In fact, a power to appoint property offers a closer analogy to the power delegated here than one might at first suspect. That is because the Act contains a "lockbox" feature, which gives legal significance to the enactment of a particular appropriations item even if, and even after, the President has rendered it without "force or effect." In essence, the "lockbox" feature: (1) points to a Gramm-Rudman-Hollings Act requirement that, when Congress enacts a "budget-busting" appropriation bill, it automatically reduces authorized spending for a host of federal programs in a pro rata way; (2) notes that cancellation of an item . . . would, absent the lockbox provision, neutralize . . . the potential "budget-busting" effects of other bills (and therefore potentially the President could cancel items in order to "save" the other programs from the mandatory cuts, resulting in no net deficit reduction); and (3) says that this "neutralization" will not occur . . . so that the canceled items truly provide *additional* budget savings over and above the Gramm-Rudman-Hollings regime. That is why the Government says that the Act provides a "lockbox," and why it seems fair to say, that, despite the Act's use of the word "cancel," the Act does not delegate to the President the power, truly to cancel a line item expenditure. . . . Rather, it delegates to the President the power to decide *how* to spend the money to which the line item refers—either for the specific purpose mentioned in the item, or for general deficit reduction via the "lockbox" feature.

These features of the law do not mean that the delegated power is, or is just like, a power to appoint property. But they do mean that it is not, and it is not just like, the repeal or amendment of a law, or, for that matter, a true line item veto (despite the Act's title). Because one cannot say that the President's exercise of the power the Act grants is, literally speaking, a "repeal" or "amendment," the fact that the Act's procedures differ from the Constitution's exclusive procedures for enacting (or repealing) legislation is beside the point. The Act *itself* was enacted in accordance with these procedures and its failure to require the President to satisfy these procedures does not make the Act unconstitutional.

V

In sum, I recognize that the Act before us is novel. In a sense, it skirts a constitutional edge. But that edge has to do with means, not ends. The means chosen do not amount literally to the enactment, repeal, or amendment of a law. Nor, for that matter, do they amount literally to the "line item veto" that the Act's title announces. Those means do not violate any basic Separation of Powers principle. They do not improperly shift the constitutionally foreseen

Continued

balance of power from Congress to the President. Nor, since they comply with the Separation of Powers principles, do they threaten the liberties of individual citizens. They represent an experiment that may, or may not, help representative government work better. The Constitution, in my view authorizes Congress and the President to try novel methods in this way. Consequently, with respect, I dissent.

Justice SCALIA, with whom Justice O'CONNOR joins, and with whom Justice BREYER joins as to Part III, concurring in part and dissenting in part.

III

I do not believe that Executive cancellation of this item of direct spending violates the Presentment Clause.

The Presentment Clause requires, in relevant part, that "every Bill which shall have passed the House of Representatives and the Senate, shall, before it becomes a Law, be presented to the President of the United States; If he approve he shall sign it, but if not he shall return it." There is no question that enactment of the Balanced Budget Act complied with these requirements: the House and Senate passed the bill, and the President signed it into law. It was only *after* the requirements of the Presentment Clause had been satisfied that the President exercised this authority under the Line Item Veto Act to cancel the spending item. Thus, the Court's problem with the Act is not that it authorizes the President to veto parts of a bill and sign others into law, but rather that it authorizes him to "cancel"—prevent from "having legal force or effect"—certain parts of duly enacted statutes.

Article I, sec.7 of the Constitution obviously prevents the President from canceling a law that Congress has not authorized him to cancel. Such action cannot possibly be considered part of his execution of the law, and if it is legislative action, as the Court observes, "repeal of statutes, no less than enactment, must conform with Art.I." But that is not this case. It was certainly arguable, as an original matter, that Art. I, sec.7 also prevents the President from canceling a law which itself *authorizes* the President to cancel it. But as the Court acknowledges, that argument has long since been made and rejected. In 1809, Congress passed a law authorizing the President to cancel trade restriction against Great Britain and France if either revoked edicts directed at

the United States. Joseph Story regarded the conferral of that authority as entirely unremarkable. . . . The Tariff Act of 1890 authorized the President to "suspend, by proclamation to that effect" certain of its provisions if he determined that other countries were imposing "reciprocally unequal and unreasonable" duties. This Court upheld the constitutionality of that Act . . . reciting the history since 1798 of statutes conferring upon the President the power to, *inter alia*, "discontinue the prohibitions and restraints hereby enacted and declared," "suspend the operation of the aforesaid act," and "declare the provisions of this act to be inoperative."

As much as the Court goes on about Art. I, sec. 7, therefore, that provision does not demand the result the Court reaches. It no more categorically prohibits the Executive *reduction* of congressional dispositions in the course of implementing statutes that authorize such reduction, than it categorically prohibits the Executive *augmentation* of congressional dispositions in the course of implementing statutes that authorize such augmentation—generally known as substantive rulemaking. There are, to be sure, limits upon the former just as there are limits upon the latter—and I am prepared to acknowledge that the limits upon the former may be much more severe. Those limits are established, however, not by some categorical prohibition of Art. I. Sec. 7, which our cases conclusively disprove, but by what has come to be known as the doctrine of unconstitutional delegation of legislative authority: When authorized Executive reduction or augmentation is allowed to go too far, it usurps the nondelegable function of Congress and violates the separation of powers.

The short of the matter is this: Had the Line Item Veto Act authorized the President to "decline to spend" any item of spending contained in the Balanced Budget Act of 1997, there is not the slightest doubt that authorization would have been constitutional. What the Line Item Veto Act does instead—authorizing the President to "cancel" an item of spending—is technically different. But the technical difference does not relate to the technicalities of the Presentment Clause, which have been fully complied with; and the doctrine of unconstitutional delegation, which *is* at issue here, is preeminently *not* a doctrine of technicalities. The title of the Line Item Veto Act, which was perhaps designed to simplify for public comprehension, or perhaps merely to comply with the terms of a campaign

Continued

pledge, has succeeded in faking out the Supreme Court. The President's action it authorizes in fact is not a line-item veto and thus does not offend Art.I, sec. 7; and insofar as the substance of that action is concerned, it is no different from what Congress has permitted the President to do since the formation of the Union.

For the foregoing reasons, I respectfully dissent.

Clinton clearly illustrates the Court's inclination toward a narrow interpretation of the President's role in what is essentially a legislative function. While there may be room for a broader interpretation of presidential power in functions deemed executive, the Court appears generally unwilling to approve "novel" solutions where the Framers' words and intent can be discerned from the plain meaning of the Constitution.

FOREIGN AFFAIRS AND POWER TO COMMIT THE ARMED FORCES

The President's power is more broadly interpreted in the area of foreign affairs. This is due, in part, to the more specific enumeration of powers in Article II regarding his role in that sphere. It is also the result of the need for a singular voice to represent the nation to the world that influences the Court's interpretation.

In *United States v. Curtiss-Wright Export Corporation*,[11] The Court offers a clear explication of the President's primacy in foreign affairs. At issue, was whether a joint resolution passed by Congress authorizing the President to ban the sale of arms to nations engaging in a conflict in Bolivia constituted too broad a delegation of legislative power to the President. The Court upheld the resolution and the embargo that resulted from the President's action, setting out the reasons for allowing a broader delegation of powers in the area of foreign affairs. It should be noted that the Court ruling on the *Curtiss-Wright* matter was the very court that President Franklin Roosevelt's court-packing plan was aimed at because of the Court's reluctance to approve many of the President's programs for dealing with domestic affairs.

UNITED STATES V. CURTISS-WRIGHT EXPORT CORP.
299 U.S. 304 (1936)

Justice SUTHERLAND delivered the opinion of the Court.

Whether, if the Joint Resolution had related solely to internal affairs it would be open to the challenge that it constituted an unlawful delegation of legislative power to the executive, we find it unnecessary to determine. The whole aim of the resolution is to affect a situation entirely external to the United States, and falling within the category of foreign affairs. The determination which we are called to make, therefore, is whether the Joint Resolution, as applied to that situation, is vulnerable to attack under the rule that forbids a delegation of the law-making power. In other words, assuming (but not deciding) that the challenged delegation, if it were confined to internal affairs, would be invalid may it nevertheless be sustained on the ground that its exclusive aim is to afford a remedy for a hurtful condition within foreign territory?

It will contribute to the elucidation of the question if we first consider the differences between the powers of the federal government in respect of foreign or external affairs and those in respect of domestic or internal affairs. That there are differences between the two, and that these differences are fundamental, may not be doubted.

The two classes of powers are different, both in respect of their origin and their nature. The broad statement that the federal government

Continued

can exercise no powers except those specifically enumerated in the Constitution, and such implied powers as are necessary and proper to carry into effect the enumerated powers, is categorically true only in respect of our internal affairs. In that field, the primary purpose of the constitution was to carve from the general mass of legislative powers then possessed by the states such portions as it was thought desirable to vest in the federal government, leaving those not included in the enumeration still in the states. That this doctrine applies only to powers which the states had, is self evident. And since the states severally never possessed international powers, such powers could not have been carved from the mass of state powers but obviously were transmitted to the United States from some other source. During the colonial period, these powers were possessed exclusively by and were entirely under the control of the Crown. By the Declaration of Independence, "the Representatives of the United States of America" declared the United [not the several] Colonies to be free and independent states, and as such to have "full Power to levy War, conclude Peace, contract Alliances, establish Commerce and to do all other Acts and Things which Independent States may of right do."

As a result of the separation from Great Britain by the colonies acting as a unit, the powers of external sovereignty passed from the Crown not to the colonies severally, but to the colonies in their collective and corporate capacity as the United States of America. Even before the Declaration, the colonies were a unit in foreign affairs, acting through a common agency—namely the Continental Congress, composed of delegates from the thirteen colonies. That agency exercised the powers of war and peace, raised an army, created a navy, and finally adopted the Declaration of Independence. Rulers come and go; governments end and forms of government change; but sovereignty survives. A political society cannot endure without a supreme will somewhere. Sovereignty is never held in suspense. When, therefore, the external sovereignty of Great Britain in respect of the colonies ceased, it immediately passed to the Union. That fact was given practical application almost at once. The treaty of peace, made on September 23, 1783, was concluded between his Britannic Majesty and the "United States of America."

The Union existed before the Constitution, which was ordained and established among other things to form "a more perfect Union." Prior to that event, it is clear that the Union, declared by the Articles of Confederation to be "perpetual," was the sole possessor of external sovereignty and in the Union it remained without change save in so far as the Constitution in express terms qualified its exercise. The Framers' Convention was called and exerted upon the irrefutable postulate that though the states were several their people in respect of foreign affairs were one.

It results that the investment of the federal government with the powers of external sovereignty did not depend upon the affirmative grants of the Constitution. The powers to declare and wage war, to conclude peace, to make treaties, to maintain diplomatic relations with other sovereignties, if they had never been mentioned in the Constitution, would have vested in the federal government as necessary concomitants of nationality. Neither the Constitution nor the laws passed in pursuance of it have any force in foreign territory unless in respect of our own citizens; and operations of the nation in such territory must be governed by treaties, international understandings and compacts, and the principles of international law. As a member of the family of nations, the right and power of the United States in that field are equal to the right and power of the other members of the international family.

Not only, as we have shown, is the federal power over external affairs in origin and essential character different from that over internal affairs, but participation in the exercise of the power is significantly limited. In this vast external realm, with its important, complicated, delicate and manifold problems, the President alone has the power to speak or listen as a representative of the nation. He makes treaties with the advice and consent of the Senate; but he alone negotiates. Into the field of negotiation the Senate cannot intrude; and Congress itself is powerless to invade it. As Marshall said in his great argument of March 7, 1800, in the House of Representatives, "The President is the sole organ of the nation in its external relations, and its sole representative with foreign nations."

It is important to bear in mind that we are here dealing not alone with an authority vested in

Continued

the President by an exertion of legislative power, but with such an authority plus the very delicate, plenary and exclusive power of the President as the sole organ of the federal government in the field of international relations—a power which does not require as a basis for its exercise an act of Congress, but which, of course, like every other governmental power, must be exercised in subordination to the applicable provisions of the Constitution. It is quite apparent that if, in the maintenance of our international relations, congressional legislation which is to be made effective through negotiation and inquiry within the international field must often accord to the President a degree of discretion and freedom from statutory restriction which would not be admissible were domestic affairs alone involved. Moreover, he, not Congress, has the better opportunity of knowing the conditions which prevail in foreign countries, and especially is this true in times of war. He has his confidential sources of information. He has his agents in the form of diplomatic, consular and other officials. Secrecy in respect of information gathered by them may be highly necessary, and the premature disclosure of it productive of harmful results. Indeed, so clearly is this true that correspondence and documents relating to the negotiation of the Jay Treaty—a refusal the wisdom of which was recognized by the House itself and has never since been doubted.

When the President is to be authorized by legislation to act in respect of a matter intended to affect a situation in foreign territory, the legislator properly bears in mind the important consideration that the form of the President's action—or, indeed, whether he shall act at all—may well depend, among other things, upon the nature of the confidential information which he has or may thereafter receive, or upon the effect which his action may have upon our foreign relations. This consideration, in connection with what we have already said on the subject, discloses the unwisdom of requiring Congress in this field of governmental power to lay down narrowly definite standards by which the President is to be governed. As this court said in *Mackenzie v. Hare*, as a government, the United States is invested with all the attributes of sovereignty. As it has the character of nationality it has the powers of nationality, especially those which concern its relations and intercourse with other countries. *"We should hesitate long before limiting or embarrassing such powers."*

In the light of the foregoing observations, it is evident that this court should not be in haste to apply a general rule which will have the effect of condemning legislation like that under review as constituting an unlawful delegation of legislative power. The principles which justify such legislation find overwhelming support in the unbroken legislative practice which has prevailed almost from the inception of the national government to the present day.

Practically every volume of the United States Statutes contains one or more acts or joint resolutions of Congress authorizing action by the President in respect of subjects affecting foreign relations, which either leave the exercise of the power to his unrestricted judgment, or provide a standard far more general than that which has always been considered requisite with regard to domestic affairs.

The uniform, long-continued and undisputed legislative practice just disclosed rests upon an admissible view of the Constitution which, even if the practice found far less support in principle than we think it does, we should not feel at liberty at this late day to disturb.

We deem it unnecessary to consider, *seriatim*, the several clauses which are said to evidence the unconstitutionality of the Joint Resolution as involving an unlawful delegation of legislative power. It is enough to summarize by saying that, both upon principle and in accordance with precedent, we conclude there is sufficient warrant for the broad discretion vested in the President to determine whether the enforcement of the statute will have a beneficial effect upon the reestablishment of peace in the affected countries; whether he shall make proclamation to bring the resolution into operation; whether and when the resolution shall cease to operate and to make proclamation accordingly; and to prescribe limitations and exceptions to which the enforcement of the resolution shall be subject.

Reversed.

The Court found that the President's action in *Curtiss-Wright* was in concert with Congress' intent. This underscores the importance of the role the Court has assigned Congress in interpreting presidential powers. One must question whether the outcome would have been the same had Congress been silent on the matter, or expressed a different intent. In *Youngstown Sheet and Tube*, Justice Jackson, in his concurrence, clearly indicated the importance of Congress' rejection of seizure as a means of settling labor disputes in deciding the outcome. This raises the issue of whether President Truman might have been granted broader power under his claim that international circumstances warranted seizure had Congress not rejected that as a remedy.

Similarly, the outcome in *Dames & Moore* should be reconsidered in light of the fact that it involved a matter of foreign affairs. It can certainly be argued that the nature of the issue—that is, foreign affairs—along with Congress' implicit acquiescence were together the factors leading the Court to its result. Had one, or the other, not been present, the Court may well have come to a different conclusion.

What emerges from these discussions of delegation of power by Congress to the President are three general propositions. First, the Court will uphold a broader delegation of power in the area of foreign affairs than in that of domestic affairs. Second, today's Court, and, in fact, the Court since the 1930s, has been more willing to relax the rules of delegation even in the area of domestic issues. Third, the more precisely Congress sets out the standards to be followed by the executive branch, the more likely the Court will be to find the delegation comports with the Constitution.

The Constitution refers only to the treaty-making power of the President that requires Congress to ratify any treaties. There is no reference to any other agreements between the United States and other nations—either allowing or prohibiting such agreements. In the absence of such a prohibition, Presidents have entered into such agreements without the consent of the Senate. These agreements are known as "**executive agreements**" and are not per se constitutional, although the Court has not ruled on them. According to Lawrence Tribe, if these agreements fall within one of the powers enumerated by the Constitution, it is likely to be upheld.[12] He gives the example of an armistice agreement that would be upheld based on the President's power as Commander in Chief.[13]

The power granted the President as Commander in Chief directly relates to the President's authority to commit American armed forces abroad. It must be remembered that only Congress has the constitutional grant of power to declare war. Thus, tension is built into the Constitution with regard to these grants of authority, raising questions about how far the President's power to use the armed forces extends in the absence of a congressional declaration of war. These questions have been the focus of much debate since the 1970s.

The Court has not addressed this issue despite the fact that presidents have committed our armed forces to military action several times in our history without a declaration of war by Congress. In these situations, Congress has generally accepted the action by its tacit approval. Nevertheless, this question remains open until the circumstances are such that Congress disapproves a presidential action of this sort.

There have been instances in which Congress has delegated authority to the President to commit the armed forces without a declaration of war prior to his use of this discretionary power. This was the case with the Gulf of Tonkin Resolution in 1964, allowing the President to commit forces to aid South Vietnam pursuant to the SEATO treaty.

In the face of a secret attack, the Court, in the *Prize Cases*,[14] held that President Lincoln's blockade of Southern ports following the Confederate attack on Fort Sumter did not violate the Constitution. The Court reached this conclusion based on its analogy of this situation to one in which the President

executive agreement a document, similar to a treaty, that is signed by the President of the United States but does not require the approval of the Senate (as a treaty does).

could resist an attack by a foreign nation.[15] Since he could act to repel a sudden foreign attack, he was not stripped of that unilateral authority when the attack was undertaken by states acting in rebellion against the Union. It remains an open question whether the President has the authority to order a preemptive strike without congressional approval. It can be argued that in anticipation of an attack, there would be time to allow Congress an opportunity to consider and debate the merits of a preemptive strike prior to the President undertaking action. In light of the events of September 11, 2001, however, it remains unclear at what point it is learned an attack is to take place. In some cases, such an attack may be considered sudden, requiring immediate preemptive action, while in others, time for congressional consideration may be available. Hence, it appears that the President's ability to commit our armed forces is very much tied to the facts and circumstances of each case.

APPOINTMENT AND REMOVAL OF EXECUTIVE PERSONNEL

Article II, § 2 grants the President the power to appoint executive officers and Article I, § 2 makes it clear that Congress is without power to appoint federal officials, but the matter is not quite so clear-cut. The President clearly has the authority to select the principal officers of the executive branch. These officers have been found to include members of the President's Cabinet, Ambassadors to foreign nations, and Supreme Court nominees.[16] Congress has the power to limit the scope of the President's appointment of these officers. It may not, however, make any appointments itself. Congress has the authority to give this appointment power to the President, the judiciary, or the heads of the individual departments.[17]

Morrison v. Olson set the boundary between principal officers and inferior officers. As noted, Cabinet members, Ambassadors, and federal judges are considered principal officers. All other executive officers are inferior officers. Special prosecutors are inferior officers and Congress may delegate their appointment to the judiciary, thereby giving the judiciary the ability to name those who will investigate allegations of executive wrongdoing. Because of the nature of their work, it is not difficult to understand why the power to appoint special prosecutors is not delegated to the President.

Since Congress has no appointment power of its own, its authority in this arena is limited to designating others as agents of appointment or, in the case of inferior officers, setting the procedures under which appointments may be made. These procedures may include detailed qualifications for appointment.

Congress does, however, have authority to appoint those who will engage in investigative or informative activities. This means that Congress, or one of its committees, may appoint a staff to investigate a particular matter in which it has an interest. For example, it did not violate the Constitution for Congress to appoint the investigative staff of the Senate Watergate Committee.

The principal case involving the Appointments Clause is *Buckley v. Valeo*.[18] This case involved a challenge to the Federal Election Campaign Act.[19] The law provided for public financing of presidential election campaigns, established limits on campaign contributions, and provided for the appointment of members to the Federal Election Commission (FEC). It is the appointment of members of the Commission that is our concern here. This part of the Act was claimed to be unconstitutional based on the method of appointing the Commissioners chosen by Congress. Plaintiffs argued that this scheme violated both the separation of powers doctrine and the Appointments Clause.

The statute provided for the appointment of six voting members of the FEC. Two were to be appointed by the President. Two were to be appointed by the President pro tempore of the Senate. And, the final two were to be appointed by the Speaker of the House of Representatives. All members were subject to approval by a majority of both Houses of Congress.

The Court found that the method of appointment was violative of the Constitution since Congress was without power to appoint such federal officers. Consequently, the Commission, as then constituted, was not valid and could not exercise the powers granted to it by the statute.

BUCKLEY V. VALEO
424 U.S. 1 (1976)

PER CURIAM
IV. The Federal Election Commission

B. The Merits

[It] is . . . clear from the provisions of the Constitution itself, and from the Federalist Papers, that the Constitution by no means contemplates total separation of each of these three essential branches of Government. The President is a participant in the lawmaking process by virtue of his authority to veto bills enacted by Congress. The Senate is a participant in the appointive process by virtue of its authority to refuse to confirm persons nominated to office by the President. The men who met in Philadelphia in the summer of 1787 were practical statesmen, experienced in politics, who viewed the principle of separation of powers as a vital check against tyranny. But they likewise saw that a hermetic sealing off of the three branches of Government from one another would preclude the establishment of a Nation capable of governing itself effectively.

The principle of separation of powers was not simply an abstract generalization in the minds of the Framers: it was woven into the document that they drafted in Philadelphia in the summer of 1787. Article I section I declares: "All legislative Powers therein granted shall be vested in a Congress of the United States." Article II, section 1, vests the executive power "in a President of the United States of America," and Art. III section 1, declares that "the judicial Power of the United States, shall be vested in one supreme Court, and in such inferior Courts as the Congress may from time to time ordain and establish." The further concern of the Framers of the Constitution with maintenance of the separation of powers is found in the so-called "Ineligibility" and "Incompatibility" Clauses contained in Art. I, section 6:

"No Senator or Representative shall, during the Time for which he was elected, be appointed to any civil Office under the Authority of the United States, which shall have been created, or the Emoluments whereof shall have been increased during such time; and no Person holding any Office under the United States, shall be a Member of either House during his Continuance in Office."

It is in the context of these cognate provisions of the document that we must examine the language of Art. II, section 2, cl. 2, which appellants contend provides the only authorization for appointment of those to whom substantial executive or administrative authority is given by statute.

The Appointments Clause could, of course, be read as merely dealing with etiquette or protocol in describing "Officers of the United States," but the drafters had a less frivolous purpose in mind. This conclusion is supported by the language from *United States v. Germaine*, 99 U.S. 508 (1879):

"The Constitution for purposes of appointment very clearly divides all its officers into two classes. The primary class requires a nomination by the President and confirmation by the Senate. But foreseeing that when offices became numerous, and sudden removals necessary, this mode might be inconvenient, it was provided that, in regard to officers inferior to those specially mentioned, Congress might by law vest their appointment in the President alone, in the courts of law, or in the heads of departments. That all persons who can be said to hold an office under the government about to be established under the Constitution were intended to be included when one or the other of these modes of appointment there can be but little doubt."

We think that the term "Officers of the United States," as used in Art. II, defined to include "all persons who can be said to hold an office under the government" in *United States v. Germaine*, is a term intended to have substantive meaning. We think its fair import is that any appointee

Continued

exercising significant authority pursuant to the laws of the United States, is an "officer of the United States," and must, therefore, be appointed in the manner prescribed by section 2, cl. 2, of that Article.

If "all persons who can be said to hold an office under the government about to be established under the Constitution were intended to be included within one or the other of these modes of appointment," it is difficult to see how the members of the Commission may escape inclusion. If a Postmaster first class, and a clerk of a district court are inferior officers of the United States within the meaning of the Appointments Clause, as they are, surely the Commissioners before us are at the very least such "inferior Officers" within the meaning of the Clause.

Although two members of the Commission are initially selected by the President, his nominations are subject to confirmation not merely by the Senate, but by the House of Representatives as well. The remaining four voting members of the Commission are appointed by the President pro tempore of the Senate and by the Speaker of the House. While the second part of the Clause authorizes Congress to vest this appointment of the officers described in that part in "the Courts of Law, or in the Heads of departments," neither the Speaker of the House nor the President pro tempore of the Senate comes within this language.

The phrase "Heads of Departments," used as it is in conjunction with the phrase "Courts of Law," suggests that the Departments referred to are themselves in the executive Branch or at least have some connection with that branch. While the Clause expressly authorizes Congress to vest the appointment of certain officers in the "Courts of Law," the absence of similar language to include Congress must mean that neither Congress nor its officers were included within the language "Heads of Departments" in this part of cl. 2.

Thus with respect to four of the six voting members of the Commission, neither the President, the head of any department, nor the Judiciary has any voice in their selection.

The Appointments Clause specifies the method of appointment only for "Officers of the United States" whose appointment is not "otherwise provided for" in the Constitution. But there is no provision of the Constitution remotely providing any alternative means for the selection of the members of the Commission or for anybody like them. Appellee Commission has argued, and the Court of Appeals agreed, that the Appointments Clause of Art. II should not be read to exclude the "inherent power of congress" to appoint its own officers to perform functions necessary to that body as an institution. But there is no need to read that Appointments Clause contrary to its plain language in order to reach the result sought by the Court of Appeals. Article I, section 3, cl. 5, expressly authorizes the selection of the President pro tempore of the Senate and section 2, cl. 5, of that Article provides for the selection of the Speaker of the House. Ranking nonmembers, such as the Clerk of the House of Representatives, are elected under the internal rules of each House and are designated by statute as "officers of the Congress." There is no occasion for us to decide whether any of these member officers are "Officers of the United States" whose "appointment" is otherwise provided for within the meaning of the Appointments Clause, since even if they were such officers their appointees would not be. Contrary to the fears expressed by the majority of the Court of Appeals, nothing in our holding with respect to Art. II, section 2, cl. 2, will deny to Congress "all power to appoint its own inferior officers to carry out appropriate legislative functions."

Insofar as the powers confided in the Commission are essentially of an investigative and informative nature, falling in the same general category as those powers which Congress might delegate to one of its own committees, there can be no question that the Commission as presently constituted may exercise them.

CONCLUSION

[We] hold that most of the powers conferred by the Act upon the Federal Election Commission can be exercised only by "Officers of the United States" appointed in conformity with Article II. Section 2, cl. 2, of the Constitution, and therefore cannot be exercised by the Commission as presently constituted.

Justice WHITE, concurring in part and dissenting in part.

II

It is my view that with one exception Congress could endow a properly constituted commission with the powers and duties it has given the [Federal Election Commission] FEC.

Continued

It is apparent that none of the members of the FEC is selected in a manner Art. II specifies for the appointment of officers of the United States.

The Appointments Clause applies only to officers of the United States whose appointment is not "otherwise provided for" in the Constitution. Senators and Congressmen are officers of the United States, but the Constitution expressly provides the mode of their selection. The Constitution also expressly provides that each House of Congress is to appoint its own officers. But it is not contended here that FEC members are officers of either House selected pursuant to these express provisions, if for no other reason, perhaps, than that none of the Commissioners was selected in the manner specified by these provisions—none of them was finally selected by either House acting alone as Art. I authorizes.

The appointment power provided in Art. II also applies only to officers, as distinguished from employees, of the United States but there is no claim the Commissioners are employees of the United States rather than officers. That the Commissioners are among those officers of the United States referred to in the Appointments Clause of Art. II. is evident from the breadth of their assigned duties and the nature and importance of their assigned functions.

It is thus not surprising that the FEC, in defending the legality of its members' appointments, does not deny that they are "officers of the United States" as that term is used in the Appointments Clause of Art. II. Instead, for reasons the Court outlines, its position appears to be that even if its members are officers of the United States, Congress may nevertheless appoint a majority of the FEC without participation by the President. This position that Congress may itself appoint the members of a body that is to administer a wide-ranging statute will not withstand examination in light of either the purpose and history of the Appointments Clause or of prior cases in this Court.

The language of the Appointments Clause was not mere inadvertence. The matter of the appointment of officers of the new Federal Government was repeatedly debated by the Framers, and the final formulation of the Clause arrived at only after the most careful debate and consideration of its place in the overall design of the government. The appointment power was a major building block fitted into the constitutional structure designed to avoid the accumulation or exercise of arbitrary power by the Federal Government. The basic approach was that official power should be divided among the Executive, Legislative, and Judicial Departments. The separation of powers principle was implemented by a series of provisions, among which was the knowing decision that Congress was to have no power whatsoever to appoint federal officers, except for the power of each House to appoint its own officers serving in the strictly legislative processes and for the confirming power of the Senate alone.

The decision to give the President the exclusive power to initiate appointments was thoughtful and deliberate. The Framers were attempting to structure three departments of government so that each would have affirmative power strong enough to resist the encroachment of the others. A fundamental tenet was that the same persons should not both legislate and administer the laws. From the very outset, provision was made to prohibit members of Congress from holding office in another branch of the Government while also serving in Congress. There was little if any dispute about this incompatibility provision which survived in Art. I sec. 6, of the constitution as finally ratified. Today, no person may serve in Congress and at the same time be Attorney General, Secretary of State, a member of the judiciary, a United States attorney, or a member of the Federal Trade Commission or the National Labor Relations Board.

Under Art. II as finally adopted, law enforcement authority was not to be lodged in elected legislative officials subject to political pressures. Neither was the Legislative Branch to have the power to appoint those who were to enforce and administer the law. Also, the appointment power denied Congress and vested in the President was not limited to purely executive officers but reached officers performing purely judicial functions as well as all other officers of the United States.

I thus find singularly unpersuasive the proposition that because the FEC is implementing statutory policies with respect to the conduct of elections, which policies Congress has the power to propound, its members may be appointed by Congress. One might as well argue that the exclusive and plenary power of Congress over interstate commerce authorizes Congress to appoint the members of the Interstate Commerce Commission and of many other regulatory commissions; that its exclusive power to provide for patents and copyrights

Continued

would permit the administration of the patent laws to be carried out by a congressional committee. . . .

Congress clearly has the power to create federal offices and to define the powers and duties of those offices, but no case in this Court even remotely supports the power of Congress to appoint an officer of the United States aside from those officers each House is authorized by Art. I to appoint to assist in the legislative processes. It is apparent that the FEC is charged with the enforcement of the election laws in major respects. Indeed, except for the conduct of criminal proceedings, it would appear that the FEC has the entire responsibility for enforcement of the statutes at issue here. By no stretch of the imagination can its various functions in this respect be considered mere adjuncts to the legislative process or to the powers of Congress to judge the election and qualifications of its own members.

If the FEC members had been nominated by the President and confirmed by the Senate as provided in Art. II, nothing in the Constitution would prohibit Congress from empowering the commission to issue rules and regulations without later participation by, or consent of, the President or Congress with respect to any particular rule or regulation or initially to adjudicate questions of fact in accordance with a proper interpretation of the statute. The President must sign the statute creating the rulemaking authority of the agency or it must have been passed over his veto, and he must have nominated the members of the agency in accordance with Art. II; but agency regulations issued in accordance with the statute are not subject to his veto even though they may be substantive in character and have the force of law.

I am also of the view that the otherwise valid regulatory power of a properly created independent agency is not rendered constitutionally infirm, as violative of the President's veto power, by a statutory provision subjecting agency regulations to disapproval by either House of Congress. For a bill to become law it must pass both Houses and be signed by the President or be passed over his veto. Also, "Every Order, Resolution or Vote to which the Concurrence of the Senate and House of Representatives may be necessary . . ." is likewise subject to the veto power. Under section 438 © the FEC's regulations are subject to disapproval; but for a

regulation to become effective, neither House need approve it, pass it, or take any action at all with respect to it. The regulation becomes effective by nonaction. This no more invades the President's powers than does a regulation not required to be laid before Congress. Congressional influence over the substantive content of agency regulation may be enhanced, but I would not view the power of either House to disapprove as equivalent to legislation or to an order, resolution, or vote requiring the concurrence of both Houses.

In terms of the substantive content of regulations and the degree of congressional influence over agency lawmaking, I do not suggest that there is no difference between the situation where regulations are subject to disapproval by Congress and the situation where the agency need not run the congressional gauntlet. But the President's veto power, which gives him an important role in the legislative process, was obviously not considered an inherently executive function. Nor was its principal aim to provide another check against poor legislation. The major purpose of the veto power appears to have been to shore up the Executive Branch and to provide it with some bargaining and survival power against what the Framers feared would be the overweening power of legislators. As Hamilton said, the veto power was to provide a defense against the legislative department's intrusion on the rights and powers of other departments; without such power, "the legislative and executive powers might speedily come to be blended in the same hands."

I would be much more concerned if Congress purported to usurp the functions of law enforcement, to control the outcome of particular adjudications, or to pre-empt the President's appointment; but in the light of history and modern reality, the provision for congressional disapproval of agency regulations does not appear to transgress the constitutional design, at least where the President has agreed to legislation establishing the disapproval procedure or the legislation has been passed over his veto. It would be considerably different if Congress itself purported to adopt and propound regulations by the action of both Houses. But here no action of either House is required for the agency rule to go into effect, and the veto power of the President does not appear to be implicated.

While *Buckley* addresses the extent of the President's power of appointment, it is also necessary to consider his power of removal. The Constitution does not answer the question whether it is the President, Congress, or both who may remove federal appointees or employees. Nor does it indicate when removal may occur, although Article III § 1 sets forth the requirement that federal judges may only be removed for misconduct. The only other guideline the Constitution provides is the process for impeachment that we will consider shortly. In light of this relative lack of specific direction on the question of removal, it has been left to the Supreme Court to explicate the limits of the President's authority to remove federal officers.

In the case of quasi-judicial or quasi-legislative federal appointees, the court has made it clear that Congress may limit, but not prohibit removal by the President. In *Humphrey's Executor v. United States*,[20] the Court found that when Congress provides for the appointment of officers whose functions are not executive, but quasi-legislative or quasi-judicial, and sets limited ground for their removal, the President is without constitutional authority to remove them for any reason other than those specified by Congress.[21]

When, however, Congress is silent on whether the President may remove a quasi-judicial appointee, the President is without authority to remove such appointees.[22] Thus, it is only when Congress specifically confers the right of removal, even if the scope of that right is constrained, that the President has removal authority.

If it is purely executive officers who are going to be removed, up until *Morrison v. Olson*, it appeared that Congress could not limit the President's right of removal. But, in *Morrison*, the Court indicated that Congress may limit the presidential removal power of even purely executive officers provided the restrictions placed on removal do not impede the President's ability to conduct his constitutional duties.[23] It therefore seems that the Court endorses a position that Congress has some latitude to affect the President's control over executive matters without there being a constitutional violation.

It is not clear whether the Court would maintain the same stance if Congress sought to limit the President's power to remove principal officers. It is likely that in such a case the result would differ from that in *Morrison*. Since the Constitution specifically grants the President the power to appoint such officers, the Court might be unwilling to provide Congress with any power to dictate their removal. Moreover, Congress does not have the power to remove executive officers on its own.[24]

The Constitution provides for the removal of "[t]he President, Vice President and all civil Officers of the United States . . . from Office on **Impeachment** for and Conviction of Treason, Bribery, or other high Crimes and Misdemeanors."[25]

impeachment the first step in the removal from public office of a high public official such as a governor, judge, or president.

In our more than 200 years of being governed by the Constitution, the impeachment power has rarely been used. Articles of impeachment have been brought against only three Presidents—Andrew Johnson, Richard Nixon, and Bill Clinton. The House of Representatives impeached both Presidents Johnson and Clinton (see Exhibit 5.1). Both were found not to be guilty of the charges against them. President Nixon resigned after the Judiciary Committee of the House voted three articles of impeachment against him but before the entire House could vote.

A debate exists regarding the meaning of **high crimes and misdemeanors**. It has been argued that the phrase is vague and therefore subject to more than one interpretation. For example, President Nixon maintained that only crimes are impeachable offenses. Others argue that only "serious indictable crimes" can provide a basis for impeachment. Still others claim that any crime can provide the basis for impeachment. Some scholars assert that only serious crimes may underlie an impeachment. During President Clinton's impeachment trial those defending him argued that the minor crime of perjury in a

high crimes and misdemeanors the basis for impeachment in the U.S. Constitution (Article II, Section 4).

EXHIBIT 5.1 The Impeachment of Andrew Johnson

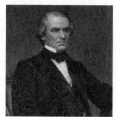

Andrew Johnson, the first of our three Presidents who became embroiled in an impeachment controversy, was a self-educated man, born in North Carolina who eventually settled in Tennessee. He entered politics and was a United States Senator from Tennessee when the Civil War broke out. Johnson refused to resign his senate seat when Tennessee seceded and, although a Southerner and slave owner, he remained a loyal Unionist.

This brought him to President Lincoln's attention and in 1862, Lincoln appointed Johnson military governor of Tennessee. Thereafter, Lincoln chose Johnson to be his running mate in the 1864 presidential election in an attempt to attract the votes of Democrats who would not otherwise vote for Lincoln, a Republican. Following Lincoln's assassination, and Johnson's ascension to the presidency, Johnson found himself at odds with the Radical Republicans over reconstruction policy.

Andrew Johnson
(Courtesy of © Stapleton Collection/Corbis)

Two different policies were advocated for reconstruction. The Radical Republicans sought total reform of Southern social and economic life. The South was viewed as a conquered territory that the federal government could rule, instituting all changes believed to be necessary to achieve their ends. Some very powerful politicians, such as Representative Thaddeus Stevens and Senator Charles Sumner were active in the Radical Republican cause. Others, including Johnson, argued for reconciliation and the opportunity for the Southern states to have some control over the changes that would lead to an amicable reconstitution of the Union.

By 1865, the Radical Republicans were in the congressional majority and had refused to seat the Southern representatives. In 1866, Congress passed the Civil Rights Act. Johnson vetoed the Act, and Congress overrode the veto. That same year Congress passed the Fourteenth Amendment despite Johnson's opposition on the grounds that the Southern states had no voice in its passage. At the urging of the President, none of the Southern states ratified the amendment other than Tennessee. The stage was set for the confrontation between the Radical Republicans and President Johnson.

The grounds for impeachment came with Congress' passage of the Tenure of Office Act in 1867. The purpose of the Act was to prevent Johnson from removing, without the concurrence of the Senate, those who needed senatorial approval for their original appointment. In particular, the Radical Republicans wanted to ensure that Secretary of War, Edwin Stanton, a Lincoln appointee, would remain in the Cabinet where he could pass along information about Johnson. This measure also passed despite Johnson's veto.

When Johnson decided to remove Stanton from office, the House voted eleven articles of impeachment against Johnson—eight of which concerned the removal of Stanton, one charging a violation of the Command of the Army Act, and two charging the President with libeling Congress in speeches he made.

The trial before the Senate began on March 5, 1868, with Chief Justice Salmon P. Chase presiding. On May 16, the vote was scheduled. There was every indication that there was a single undecided vote that could leave the Republicans one vote shy of the two-thirds necessary for conviction. That vote belonged to Edmond G. Ross, a young Radical Republican. Ross was under severe pressure from his colleagues, but when his name was called, he rose and voted not guilty. By that one vote Johnson remained in office to finish out his term.

In 1874, Johnson ran for the Senate from Tennessee and was elected. He is the only former President to serve in the Senate.[26] And, in 1926 the United States Supreme Court declared the Tenure of Office Act unconstitutional in *Myers v. United States*.

civil suit did not provide an adequate basis for impeachment. The fact that President Clinton was acquitted may be an indication that those who maintain that any crime may serve as a predicate to impeachment are not correct. Finally, it has been proposed that serious abuse of power can be an impeachable offense. The question, however, has not been before the Court, so there is, as yet, no definitive answer.

Impeachment does not protect a President from criminal liability for acts that underlie the impeachment proceedings.[27] Accordingly, a criminal prosecution may follow impeachment and it is not considered to be a constitutional violation of the Double Jeopardy Clause.[28] Neither will a pardon provide a way of avoiding subsequent criminal prosecution since Article II, Clause 1 limits the President's pardon power. Impeachment cases are specifically not included with the President's authority. Consequently, if President Nixon had been convicted by the Senate, President Ford's pardon (had he granted it under those circumstances) would not have protected Nixon from subsequent criminal liability for the offenses leading to his Senate conviction.

Another open question with regard to impeachment is whether the verdict of the Senate is open to judicial review by the Supreme Court. The traditional view is that conviction under articles of impeachment is a nonjusticiable political question. The case of *Nixon v. United States*,[29] involving federal judge Walter Nixon's challenge to his impeachment conviction indicates that this is the correct view. The Court ruled that Nixon's challenge to the procedures employed in his Senate trial—that is, what procedures constitute a valid trial—was a nonjusticiable political question. As a result, it appears that conviction in an impeachment trial is not subject to judicial review.

Summary

The powers of the Presidency, as enumerated in the Constitution, are far less specific and fewer than those vested in the legislative branch. Despite this, the Court has been willing to find presidential actions that do not fall within the particular sphere of any one of these enumerated powers to be constitutional, providing that action is considered to be clearly executive in nature.

The Court has given a wider authority to the President in the area of foreign affairs than in domestic affairs. Presidential action in foreign affairs is more likely to be found constitutional. And, over time, the Court has somewhat relaxed the standard for delegation of actions to the President by Congress even in the area of domestic affairs.

The President's power of appointment and removal of federal officers depends greatly on the nature of the job to be filled, as well as whether the appointment is one of a principal officer or an inferior officer. Another factor in determining the scope of the President's removal power is whether Congress has spoken on the issue.

Impeachment is the only means by which a President may be removed from office, and that is only if he has committed a high crime or misdemeanor. The Court has not addressed many of the questions surrounding impeachment. Although educated guesses may be made about how the Court would decide, until the Court has spoken the answers suggested are mere speculation.

Overall, the Court is less likely to interpret the President's powers broadly in the absence of a specific grant of authority in the Constitution, and these grants are limited.

Key Terms

executive agreement	impeachment	pocket veto
high crimes and misdemeanors	line-item veto	veto

Review Questions

1. The President is given the enumerated power to veto legislation enacted by Congress. Set forth the specifics of that power, as well as the arguments presented by the majority of the Court and the dissenters in *Clinton v. New York*.

2. The powers granted the President and Executive Branch are more implied than specifically enumerated than those of the other branches of government in the constitution. How has that affected the Court's interpretation of these powers in regard to domestic and foreign affairs?

3. The Court defers to Congress in cases of delegation of authority. Describe the role specificity of enumerated powers for the two branches plays in this deference.

4. The President is given the power of appointment of federal officials, while Congress has no appointment making power. What limits have been placed on each branch regarding appointment and removal of officials?

5. The President may be removed from office upon impeachment by the House of Representatives and trial by the Senate. A debate exists, however, about the meaning of "high crimes and misdemeanors" as the basis for removal. What interpretations have been offered?

Internet Connections

1. For more information on impeachment including the documents relating to the impeachment proceedings of Presidents Johnson, Nixon, and Clinton, go to *http://www.lib.auburn.edu.*

2. For information on presidential pardons addressing their constitutional basis, history and developments, and cases and proclamations, visit the University of Pittsburgh's Law School site at *http://juristlawpit.edu.*

3. The Presidents' executive orders and proclamations from 1789 to 1983 can be found at *http://www.libumichedu/govdocs.*

End Notes

[1]U.S. Const. art. II, § 1, cl. 1.

[2]U.S. Const. art. II, § 2, cl. 1.

[3]U.S. Const. art. II, § 2, cl. 2.

[4]U.S. Const. art. I, § 7.

[5]Lawrence Tribe, *American Constitutional Law* 210–11 (2d ed., Foundation Press 1988).

[6]*Youngstown Sheet & Tube Co. v. Sawyer,* 343 U.S. 579 (1952).

[7]*Dames & Moore v. Reagan,* 453 U.S. 654 (1981); *see also,* Chapter 2.

[8]2 U.S.C. § 691–692 (1997).

[9]*Clinton v. City of New York,* 524 U.S. 417 (1998).

[10]*Id.* 447, 449.

[11]*United States v. Curtiss-Wright Export Corporation,* 299 U.S. 304 (1936).

[12]Tribe, *supra,* at 170–171.

[13]Tribe at 171.

[14]*Prize Cases,* 69 U.S. 635 (1863).

[15]*Id.* at 673–674.

[16]*See Morrison v. Olson,* 487 U.S. 654 (1988).

[17]U.S. Const. art. II, § 2.

[18]424 U.S. 1 (1976).

[19]2 U.S.C. § 431–442, 451–454; 18 U.S.C. § 591–612 (1971).

[20]*Humphrey's Executor v. United States,* 295 U.S. 602 (1935).

[21]*Id.* at 626–627.

[22]*Wiener v. United States,* 357 U.S. 349 (1958).

[23]*Morrison v. Olson,* 487 U.S. at 654, 696 (1988).

[24]*Bowsher v. Synar,* 478 U.S. 714 (1986); *see also,* Chapter 2.

[25]U.S. Const. art. II, § 4.

[26]*http://www.andrewjohnson.com; http://www.law.umkc.edu/faculty/projects/ftrials/impeach /impeachmt.htm.*

[27]U.S. Const. art. I, § 3, cl. 7.

[28]U.S. Const. amend. V.

[29]*Nixon v. Fitzgerald,* 505 U.S. 224 (1993).

 For additional resources, go to *http://www.westlegalstudies.com*

CHAPTER 6

FUNDAMENTAL RIGHTS

"It has long been established that a State may not impose a penalty upon those who exercise a right guaranteed by the Constitution . . . 'Constitutional rights would be of little value if they could be . . . indirectly denied' . . ."

—*Chief Justice Earl Warren*
Harman v. Forssenius

INTRODUCTION

Are some rights more important than others? Are some more deserving of constitutional protection? Which ones would you choose? On what basis would you make the choice? Are these questions even relevant when discussing constitutional law? They are when talking about **fundamental rights**.

The Court has denominated some rights as fundamental. These rights are considered fundamental because they are independently and explicitly guaranteed by a constitutional provision other than the Fourteenth Amendment Equal Protection Clause. There are other rights that, although not granted independently and explicitly by other constitutional provisions, are fundamental if they rely on the Equal Protection Clause for their validity. The right to vote in state elections is one of these rights.

While the Court had employed the concept of fundamental rights in the past,[1] it was the Warren Court that explored the concept and made it a strong tenet of constitutional jurisprudence. Because of the fundamental nature of these rights, the Warren Court required that the strict scrutiny test be used to analyze the constitutionality of government regulation of these rights. The Warren Court used strict scrutiny analysis in three areas considered to be fundamental: access to the courts, the right to travel or interstate migration, and the right to vote. The Burger and Rehnquist Courts have refused to expand the list of fundamental rights beyond these areas. This refusal includes such important areas as education, welfare, housing, and sexual relations. This chapter will consider the Court's decisions in these areas and their implications.

fundamental rights the basic rights, such as the right to vote and right to travel, that are most strongly protected by the Constitution.

ACCESS TO THE COURTS

One of the underlying tenets of our democratic republic is that justice is available to all citizens. A means of ensuring this is to allow citizens access to the courts. While the Framers of the Constitution recognized the difference between civil and criminal matters by specifically including protections for those charged with crime against the power of the government, the issue of access was not specifically included in the Constitution. Nevertheless, there has been recognition of a right of access to the courts although it has been applied with no hard-and-fast rules. Moreover, the Court is more likely to strike down barriers that keep citizens out of court in criminal matters than in civil matters due to the seriousness of what is at stake in a criminal matter.

The Court has used two separate approaches in access challenges. The first is the equal protection approach. When this approach is employed, the Court focuses upon how to avoid disadvantaging those unable to pay for legal representation and other expert assistance. Implicit in this approach is an acknowledgement that those who are in a position to pay receive better protection. Here, the Court has determined that access must be available to all in order to avoid the inherent unfairness based on ability to pay. At other times, the Court has employed a due process analysis. In these cases the Court does not focus on one's ability to pay, but only on whether there is fundamental procedural fairness for all citizens. The equal protection approach seems to have dominated the Burger–Rehnquist Courts' decisions. The Court has generally avoided the term *fundamental* when addressing access to court issues. Instead, the Court speaks of these rights as highly important.

Judicial access cases have not generally triggered strict scrutiny analysis. It is only when the regulation contains a wealth classification (one involving the payment of a fee) along with an important interest that strict scrutiny will be applied. Most of the cases triggering strict scrutiny occurred during the Warren Court era. The first of these was *Griffin v. Illinois*,[2] involving an indigent's right to transcripts.

Having been convicted of armed robbery, Griffin and Crenshaw were entitled to an appeal by the laws of Illinois and filed a motion alleging indigence and seeking a copy of the trial record. All defendants, except those sentenced to death, were required by the state to pay for their transcripts. The state acknowledged that in order to get adequate appellate review transcripts were necessary.

The Court began its analysis noting that "[p]roviding equal justice for poor and rich, weak and powerful alike is an age old problem[,]" which was sought to be solved, at least in part, by the constitutional guarantees of due process and equal protection and their implications for ensuring equal justice before the law.[3] The Court then considered the impossibility of government denial of fair trial rights on the basis of ability to pay and analogized this to the situation being considered in *Griffin*. Discrimination on the part of the government on such a basis was impermissible. Accordingly, the Illinois scheme was found unconstitutional. The Court, however, stopped short of requiring the state to pay for transcripts for indigent defendants. Rather, all that was required was for the state to provide some measure to ameliorate access to appellate review for the poor.

Justice Harlan dissented. He argued that the state was not creating an unconstitutional classification since all defendants were required to pay the fee. The state, he asserted, was simply not alleviating the consequences of economic differences between defendants.

The Warren Court continued to address the questions concerning judicial access for the indigent in *Douglas v. California*.[4] At issue was an indigent defendant's right to state-appointed counsel in an appeal as of right, or an appeal that the court has no discretion to refuse to hear. In this case, too, the Court used equal protection and due process analysis. The Court imposed two requirements for the appointment of counsel: (1) the appeal had to be the first taken in the case and (2) the appeal had to be granted as a matter of right to all defendants. *Douglas*, however, did not give an indigent defendant a right to state-funded counsel for discretionary appeals.

In *Ross v. Moffitt*,[5] that issue came before the Court. The Burger Court refused to extend the right to state-appointed counsel to defendants for a discretionary appeal. The Court declared that lack of counsel in a discretionary appeal was only a "relative handicap" and was less of an impediment than lack of counsel during the initial appeal as of right.[6] The majority rejected both the due process and equal protection claims. In dissent Justices Douglas, Brennan, and Marshall asserted that the rationale in *Douglas* ought to be applied in discretionary appeals as well as appeals as of right.

Another topic the Court has addressed in the context of equal access to the courts is the unequal length of imprisonment. The question is whether the state may impose a longer term of incarceration because a defendant cannot afford to pay a fine. In *Williams v. Illinois,*[7] where the defendant was sentenced to the statutory maximum period in prison and was then given additional prison time because he could not afford to pay the levied fine, the Court ruled that the state cannot use imprisonment as a means of "working off" the fine. Moreover, the state may only impose a sentence for a term of incarceration up to the statutory maximum for that offense. The Court has yet to address whether additional prison time can be imposed if the defendant cannot pay the fine *and* the defendant was originally sentenced to less than the statutory maximum.

Similar challenges have been brought in the area of civil litigation. **Indigent** defendants have argued that they should be entitled to a waiver of fees in these matters as well. Generally, this argument has not been successful.

indigent a poor person. An indigent criminal defendant is entitled to a free court-appointed lawyer.

An exception has been made in family law matters. In *Boddie v. Connecticut,*[8] welfare recipients in Connecticut challenged procedural rules requiring payment of fees and costs of services in order to commence a divorce action that prevented them from obtaining a divorce due to indigence. The Supreme Court agreed that denial of access to divorce was a violation of the parties' due process rights. Two factors were critical to the decision. The first was the primacy of the marital relationship in our society. The second was the state's monopoly on the means of dissolving this relationship. Based on these factors, the Court concluded that access to the courts for divorce was different from other civil actions and required citizen access despite indigence.

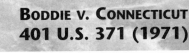

BODDIE V. CONNECTICUT
401 U.S. 371 (1971)

Mr. Justice HARLAN delivered the opinion of the Court.

Appellants, welfare recipients residing in the State of Connecticut, brought this action in the Federal Court for the District of Connecticut on behalf of themselves and others similarly situated, challenging, as applied to them, certain state procedures for the commencement of litigation, including requirements for payment of court fees and costs for service of process, that restrict their access to the courts in their effort to bring an action for divorce.

There is no dispute as to the inability of the named appellants in the present case to pay either the court fees required by the statute or the cost incurred for the service of process. The affidavits in the record establish that appellants' welfare income in each instance barely suffices to meet the costs of the daily essentials of life and includes no allotment that could be budgeted for the expense to gain access to the courts in order to obtain a divorce. Also undisputed is appellants' "good faith" in seeking a divorce.

Our conclusion is that, given the basic position of the marriage relationship in this society's hierarchy of values and the concomitant state monopolization of the means for legally dissolving this relationship, due process does prohibit a State from denying, solely because of inability to pay, access to its courts to individuals who seek judicial dissolution of their marriages.

At its core, the right to due process reflects a fundamental value in our American constitutional system. Our understanding of that value is the basis upon which we have resolved this case.

Perhaps no characteristic of an organized and cohesive society is more fundamental than its erection and enforcement of a system of rules defining the various rights and duties of its members, enabling them to govern their affairs and definitively settle their differences in an orderly, predictable manner,

It is to courts, or other quasi-judicial bodies, that we ultimately look for the implementation of a regularized, orderly process of dispute settlement. Within this framework, those who wrote our original Constitution, in the Fifth

Continued

Amendment, and later those who drafted the Fourteenth Amendment, recognized the centrality of the concept of due process in the operation of this system. Without this guarantee that one may not be deprived of his rights, neither liberty nor property, without due process of law, the State's monopoly over techniques for binding conflict resolution could hardly be said to be acceptable under our scheme of things.

Such litigation has, however, typically involved rights of defendants—not, as here, persons seeking access to the judicial process in the first instance. This is because our society has been so structured that resort to the courts is not usually the only available, legitimate means of resolving private disputes.

Recognition of this theoretical framework illuminates the precise issue presented in this case. As this Court on more than one occasion has recognized, marriage involves interests of basic importance to our society. It is not surprising, then, that the States have seen fit to oversee many aspects of that institution. Without a prior judicial imprimatur, individuals may freely enter into and rescind commercial contracts, for example, but we are unaware of any jurisdiction where private citizens may covenant for or dissolve marriages without state approval. Even where all substantive requirements are concededly met, we know of no instance where two consenting adults may divorce and mutually liberate themselves from the constraints of legal obligation that go with marriage, and more fundamentally the prohibition against remarriage, without invoking the State's judicial machinery.

Resort to the judicial process by these plaintiffs is no more voluntary in a realistic sense than that of the defendant called upon to defend his interests in court. For both groups this process is not only the paramount dispute-settlement technique, but, in fact, the only available one. In this posture we think that this appeal is properly to be resolved in light of the principles enunciated in our due process decisions that delimit rights of defendants compelled to litigate their differences in the judicial forum.

In concluding that the Due Process Clause of the Fourteenth Amendment requires that these appellants be afforded an opportunity to go into court to obtain a divorce, we wish to re-emphasize that we go no further than necessary to dispose of the case before us, a case where the bona fides of both appellants' indigency and desire for divorce are here beyond disputes. We do not decide that access for all individuals to the courts is a right that is, in all circumstances, guaranteed by the Due Process Clause of the Fourteenth Amendment so that its exercise may not be placed beyond the reach of any individual, for, as we have already noted, in the case before us this right is the exclusive precondition to the adjustment of a fundamental human relationship. The requirement that these appellants resort to the judicial process is entirely a state-created matter. Thus we hold only that a State may not, consistent with the obligations imposed on it by the Due Process Clause of the Fourteenth Amendment, pre-empt the right to dissolve this legal relationship without affording all citizens access to the means it has prescribed for doing so.

This distinction between family and other civil matters was continued in *Little v. Streater*.[9] Here, the Court held that the indigent defendant was entitled to state-subsidized blood grouping tests to determine paternity. The Court relied on the due process clause, noting the importance of the parent-child relationship as well as the "'quasi-criminal' overtones" in its decision.[10]

In *M.L.B. v. S.L.J.*,[11] the Rehnquist Court held that "the interest of parents in their relationship with their children [was] fundamental."[12] The father in this case successfully sued to terminate the mother's parental rights in order for the father's new wife to adopt the child. The mother could not afford to pay for a transcript to prepare an appeal. The Court held that the state must pay for such a transcript. While a family matter was involved, the decision seemed to turn more on the quasi-criminal nature of the allegations against the mother. Thus, it would be difficult to conclude that in any case involving a family matter the Court will uphold access.

The Court's reluctance to consider judicial access as a fundamental right becomes apparent when looking at the decisions in other civil cases claiming a right of access since the Warren years. When the Court was asked to extend the right of access established in *Boddie* to bankruptcy matters it refused. The Court maintained that the decision in *Boddie* was confined to the facts. Although failing to address the matter directly it appears that the Court tacitly accepted the government's argument that the differences between marriage and bankruptcy were sufficient to support the distinct conclusions in the two cases. The Court has also held that indigents are not entitled to a waiver of the filing fee for access to judicial review of welfare benefit termination. The Court determined that the right to welfare benefits is not fundamental and has "far less constitutional significance" than divorce or marriage.[13]

It is clear that access to the courts is a fundamental right, requiring the government to demonstrate a compelling reason before it may impede its practice. At the same time, the Court has made it readily apparent that the scope of that right is rather narrowly circumscribed, being confined largely to criminal matters and affecting those rights the Court has long-defined as fundamental.

INTERSTATE MIGRATION

For many years, interstate migration was known as the **right to travel** or the right to change residence from state to state. The terminology for this right may have changed, but its fundamental nature has not.[14] The right to interstate migration requires that a state treat new residents in substantially the same manner as established or long-term residents and if a state fails to do so, or enacts legislation that creates two classes of citizens, then judicial review (employing the strict scrutiny standard) will follow.

One of the earliest cases in this area was *Shapiro v. Thompson*.[15] In this case, the Court scrutinized welfare legislation in two states and in the District of Columbia. The legislation contained a provision that a newly arrived citizen could not file to receive welfare benefits until the applicant had resided in the state or the District of Columbia for one year. The applicants challenged the statute contending that the residency requirement created a classification that constituted discrimination, denying them equal protection. The Court agreed, saying, "This Court long ago recognized that the nature of our Federal Union and our constitutional concepts of personal liberty unite to require that all citizens be free to travel throughout the length and breadth of our land uninhibited by statutes, rules, or regulations which unreasonably burden or restrict this movement."[16] Once the Court reaffirmed that this is a fundamental right, requiring use of the strict scrutiny standard, the Court then acknowledged that there were four state interests that the states argued justified the waiting period. The states maintained that the waiting period requirement facilitated the planning of the welfare budget, provided an objective test of residency, minimized the opportunity for recipients to fraudulently receive payments from more than one jurisdiction, and encouraged early entry of new residents into the job market. One by one the Court reviewed these arguments.

The Court found the claim of using the waiting period to assist in planning the welfare budget was unfounded. Without the use of other tools, the Court found that the jurisdictions cannot know how many new residents will require welfare payments in the future. Nor did the Court accept that the waiting period was an efficient measure for determining residency. The jurisdictions actually used independent measures to determine residency, such as investigations of the applicant's employment, housing, and family situation. Similarly, the Court found that other, less drastic measures could be used to ensure that recipients did not fraudulently receive benefits from more than one jurisdiction. Lastly, the Court found that if this waiting period was justified by encouraging new residents to find jobs, that "logic would also require a similar waiting period for long-term residents of the State."[17] Thus the Court found that none of the states' interests were compelling enough to justify the statutory waiting period.

right to travel the constitutional right to be free of unreasonable restraints on personal travel.

SHAPIRO V. THOMPSON
394 U.S. 618 (1969)

Mr. Justice BRENNAN delivered the opinion of the Court.

Each [of these cases] is an appeal from a decision of a three-judge District Court holding unconstitutional a State or District of Columbia statutory provisions which denies welfare assistance to residents of the State or District who have not resided within their jurisdictions for at least one year immediately preceding their applications for such assistance. We affirm the judgments of the District Courts in the three cases.

There is no dispute that the effect of the waiting-period requirement in each case is to create two classes of needy resident families indistinguishable from each other except that one is composed of residents who have resided a year or more, and the second of residents who have resided less than a year, in the jurisdiction. On the basis of this sole difference the first class is granted and the second class is denied welfare aid upon which may depend the ability of the families to obtain the very means to subsist–food, shelter, and other necessities of life. In each case, the District Court found that appellees met the test for residence in their jurisdictions, as well as all other eligibility requirements except the requirement of residence for a full year prior to their applications.

Primarily, appellants justify the waiting-period requirement as a protective device to preserve the fiscal integrity of state public assistance programs. It is asserted that people who require welfare assistance during their first year of residence in a State are likely to become continuing burdens on state welfare programs. Therefore, the argument runs, if such people can be deterred from entering the jurisdiction by denying them welfare benefits during the first year, state programs to assist long-time residents will not be impaired by a substantial influx of indigent newcomers.

We do not doubt that the one-year waiting-period device is well suited to discourage the influx of poor families in need of assistance. An indigent who desires to migrate, resettle, find a new job, and start a new life will doubtless hesitate if he knows that he must risk making the move without the possibility of falling back on state welfare assistance during his first year of residence, when his need may be most acute. But the purpose of inhibiting migration by needy persons into the State is constitutionally impermissible.

This Court long ago recognized that the nature of our Federal Union and our constitutional concepts of personal liberty unite to require that all citizens be free to travel throughout the length and breadth of our land uninhibited by statutes, rules, or regulations which unreasonably burden or restrict this movement.

More fundamentally, a State may no more try to fence out those indigents who seek higher welfare benefits than it may try to fence out indigents generally. Implicit in any such distinction is the notion that indigents who enter a State with the hope of securing higher welfare benefits are somehow less deserving than indigents who do not take this consideration into account. But we do not perceive why a mother who is seeking to make a new life for herself and her children should be regarded as less deserving because she considers, among other factors, the level of a State's public assistance. Surely such a mother is no less deserving than a mother who moves into a particular State in order to take advantage of its better educational facilities.

We recognize that a State has a valid interest in preserving the fiscal integrity of its programs. It may legitimately attempt to limit its expenditures, whether for public assistance, public education, or any other program. But a State may not accomplish such a purpose by invidious distinctions between classes of its citizens. The saving of welfare costs cannot justify an otherwise invidious classification.

[W]e reject appellants' argument that a mere showing of a rational relationship between the waiting period and these four admittedly permissible state objectives will suffice to justify the classification. The waiting-period provision denies welfare benefits to otherwise eligible applicants solely because they have recently moved into the jurisdiction. But in moving from State to State or to the District of Columbia appellees were exercising a constitutional right, and any classification which serves to penalize the exercise of that right, unless shown to be necessary

Continued

to promote a compelling governmental interest, is unconstitutional.

The argument that the waiting-period requirement facilitates budget predictability is wholly unfounded. The records in all three cases are utterly devoid of evidence that either State or the District of Columbia in fact uses the one-year requirement as a means to predict that number of people who will require assistance in the budget year.

The argument that the waiting period serves as an administratively efficient rule of thumb for determining residency similarly will not withstand scrutiny. The residence requirement and the one-year waiting-period requirement are distinct and independent prerequisites for assistance under these three statutes, and the facts relevant to the determination of each are directly examined by the welfare authorities. Before granting an application, the welfare authorities investigate the applicant's employment, housing, and family situation and in the course of the inquiry necessarily learn the facts upon which to determine whether the applicant is a resident.

Similarly, there is no need for a State to use the one-year waiting period as a safeguard against fraudulent receipt of benefits; for less drastic means are available, and are employed, to minimize that hazard.

We conclude therefore that appellants in these cases do not use and have no need to use the one-year requirement for the governmental purposes suggested. Thus, even under traditional equal protection tests a classification of welfare applicants according to whether they have lived in the State for one year would seem irrational and unconstitutional. But, of course, the traditional criteria do not apply in these cases. Since the classification here touches on the fundamental right of interstate movement, its constitutionality must be judged by the stricter standard of whether it promotes a compelling state interest. Under this standard, the waiting-period requirement clearly violates the Equal Protection Clause.

So, what does *Shapiro* ultimately mean? It means that the right to travel is impaired whenever a penalty is attached, even if there is no actual deterrence or chilling effect. When this impairment occurs, judicial review using strict scrutiny will follow, even if there is no showing that anyone actually decided against travel or migration because of the requirement. The *Shapiro* decision sets the stage for other types of state residency requirements for other state-sponsored benefits.

The first of the post-*Shapiro* cases is *Starns v. Malkerson*.[18] In this case, the U.S. District Court in Minnesota was asked to resolve a challenge to the University of Minnesota's regulation that provides, in part, "No student is eligible for residence classification in the University . . . unless he has been a bona fide domiciliary of the state for at least a year immediately prior thereto."[19] This regulation, in effect, meant that newly arrived out-of-state students could not qualify for in-state tuition rates until they had established residency for one year. The regulations went on to say that a student admitted on a nonresident basis could qualify as an in-state student after establishing "a bona fide domicile of a year's duration within the state."[20] The Plaintiffs in the case alleged that these regulations violated their fundamental right of interstate migration, and therefore should be subject to the strict scrutiny test. Further, Plaintiffs felt that this residency requirement was like the one found in *Shapiro* and thus should fail to survive constitutional scrutiny.

The Court, however, determined that the residency requirement found here was distinguishable from that in *Shapiro* in two ways. First, the objective of that requirement was to exclude the poor who needed relief. That was not the objective here. This Court found that the one-year waiting period did not deter or exclude persons from moving into the state to attend the University. Second, the requirement in *Shapiro* denied individuals the basic necessities of life, and there was no evidence to show that the University's requirement was having this "dire" effect on the nonresidential student. The Court stated, "While we fully recognize the value of higher education, we cannot equate its attainment with food, clothing and shelter."[21] The Court then went on to conclude that the regulation was not an infringement of a fundamental right because the requirement does not constitute a penalty upon the exercise of the right to migrate or travel from state-to-state.

Another of the post-*Shapiro* cases was *Memorial Hospital v. Maricopa County*.[22] In this case, an Arizona statute required that a new, indigent citizen reside in a county for one year before that citizen was eligible for free nonemergency hospitalization or medical care at the county's expense. In deciding the constitutionality of this requirement, the Court reviewed its decision in *Shapiro*, looked at the statute, and held that the ". . . durational residence requirement for free medical care must be justified by a compelling state interest and that, such interests being lacking, the requirement is unconstitutional."[23] The appellees argued that the residency requirement was different from that found in *Shapiro* in that it penalized intrastate, not interstate, travel. The Court did not accept this argument saying, "What would be unconstitutional if done directly by the State can no more readily be accomplished by a county at the State's direction."[24]

Further, the State argued that without the residency requirement, the state-of-the-art medical facilities would be overwhelmed by the volume of new, indigent citizens wanting medical attention. This would be a severe hardship on the county and the State claimed that this was a compelling interest sufficient to justify any penalty on interstate migration. The Court found these claims to be "illusory" and rejected them. While the Court ultimately found that the ". . . durational residency requirement for eligibility for non-emergency free medical care creates an 'invidious classification' that impinges on the right of interstate travel by denying newcomers 'basic necessities of life,' [s]uch a classification can only be sustained on a showing of a compelling state interest. Appellees have not met their heavy burden of justification, or demonstrated that the State, in pursuing a legitimate objective, has chosen means which do not unnecessarily impinge on constitutionally protected interests."[25] As such, this residency requirement failed to pass the strict scrutiny test, and was struck down.

The Court next grappled with the question of whether residency requirements in the area of divorce violated the right to interstate migration. In *Sosna v. Iowa*[26] the Court reviewed a state statute requiring a person to reside in the state of Iowa for one year before being allowed to sue a nonresident for divorce. Sosna claimed that the state residency requirement denied her the opportunity to make an individualized showing of bona fide residence and therefore denied her access to the only legal method for dissolving her marriage. She also claimed cases such as *Shapiro* and *Maricopa County*, discussed *supra*, as precedent requiring the Court to strike down this residency requirement. The Court said that what those cases had in common was the fact that the residency requirement was justified on the basis of budgetary or record-keeping requirements. In *Sosna*, however, the Court maintained that Iowa had two compelling interests in establishing this residency requirement. Rather than relying on budgetary or record-keeping justifications, the Iowa residency requirement was justified on two grounds:

1. The avoidance of meddling in matters in which another State has an interest and
2. Minimizing the possibility that Iowa's divorce decrees would be susceptible to collateral attack.[27]

While the Court acknowledged that upholding the residency requirement would mean that it would take a new resident longer to obtain a divorce, ultimately, the new resident would obtain the desired divorce. Iowa's decision to avoid being labeled a "divorce mill" was a reasonable one and the residency requirement remained legitimate.

Sosna discusses a bona fide residency requirement, but this was not the first or the last case in which the Court had a discussion of this sort. The state can require that new citizens prove bona fide residency before they are eligible to receive state services, participate in an election, or enjoy state benefits. Bona fide residency requirements were discussed in *Dunn v. Blumstein*.[28] In *Dunn* the State of Tennessee required a new resident wishing to register to vote to have been a resident of the State for one year, and a resident of a Tennessee county for three months. As the challenge to this statute claimed that the fundamental rights of interstate migration and voting were being violated, the Court said that "residence laws must be measured by a strict equal protection test: they are unconstitutional unless the State can demonstrate that such laws are 'necessary to promote a compelling governmental interest.'"[29] Tennessee noted two basic purposes served by the residency requirement. First, to insure the purity of the ballot box and second, to assure that voters are knowledgeable and able to intelligently exercise the right to vote.[30] The Court looked at both of these "compelling interests" and found that while the State had compelling interest in preventing voter fraud, that there were other ways to achieve this other than the residency requirement. Specifically, the Court noted that voter registration served to prevent voter fraud. The residency requirement was not the least restrictive means for preventing voter fraud and therefore, this purpose could not withstand strict scrutiny.

As for the second purpose or interest promoted by Tennessee, the Court noted that the interest in having its citizens be residents long enough to learn the local viewpoint is an argument that the Court had previously rejected and rejected once again in this case, saying "Tennessee's hopes for voters with a 'common interest in all matters pertaining to [the community's] government' is permissible . . . we conclude that durational residence requirement cannot be justified on this basis."[31]

In *Martinez v. Bynum*,[32] the Court once again examined a bona fide residence requirement. Specifically, it examined a Texas statute that denied tuition-free admission for a minor who is not living with a parent or guardian and whose presence in the school district is for the "purpose of attending the public free schools."[33] Robert Morales was living with his sister, Oralia Martinez, and wanted to attend the McAllen Independent School District. When he was refused admission, Martinez brought an action on his behalf, claiming that the statute was an unconstitutional residency requirement. The Court noted that it has approved bona fide residency requirements in the field of public education in the past, and noted that "a bona fide residence requirement, appropriately defined and uniformly applied, furthers the substantial state interest in assuring that services provided for its residents are enjoyed only by residents . . . It does not burden or penalize the constitutional right of interstate travel, for any person is free to move to a state and to establish residence there."[34] The Court went on to say that Texas was justified in using bona fide residency requirements as a means of insuring proper planning and operation of its public schools.

It is clear from these cases that the Court will use strict scrutiny and require a compelling governmental interest whenever a state treats a new citizen differently from an established citizen. If a state can show a compelling interest, the residency requirements will be upheld. However, this is not to say that there can be no state regulation in this area. There are bona fide residence requirements that do, indeed, promote a legitimate state purpose.

THE RIGHT TO VOTE

Nothing in the Constitution places any limits on the power of the states to control local and state elections. Each state has the right to control voter qualifications for state elections. These qualifications may not violate any specific constitutional rights or prohibitions. For example, a state may not prevent a citizen from voting based on racial grounds. There are, however, a number of acceptable qualifications that may be imposed. Among these are age qualifications, citizenship and residency restrictions, and durational residency requirements. The Constitution actually gives the states the right to set voter qualifications for federal elections.

Article I, § 2 of the Constitution says that federal elections for seats to the House of Representatives are to be controlled by the same voter requirements as state elections. This provision was adopted in the Seventeenth Amendment, providing for the direct election of United States Senators. Congress does have the right to override these voter qualifications pursuant to Article 1, § 4 of the federal Constitution, but this power is limited to federal elections. The state continues to have exclusive control over voter qualifications for state elections (see Exhibit 6.1).

S I D E B A R

THE FIGHT FOR WOMEN TO VOTE: THE SUFFRAGE MOVEMENT

The idea that women deserved equality and the right to vote had its origins over two centuries ago, when the British author, Mary Wollstonecraft wrote an argument for equality of the sexes in her book, *Vindication of the Rights of Women*.[35] Over the next century, many important women were born, suffrage groups organized and campaigns waged in an effort to enfranchise women. Two of the most important women of the suffrage movement were Elizabeth Cady Stanton and Susan B. Anthony. Born within a few years of one another, these two women campaigned vigorously for the right of women to vote in the United States. Stanton, along with Lucretia Mott called for the first women's rights convention that was held on July 19–20, 1848, in Seneca Falls, New York.[36] The Seneca Falls Conference, as it became known, was attended by 300 men and women and during that conference, a Declaration of Sentiments, modeled on the Declaration of Independence, was drafted, setting forth 11 reasons why women should be treated equally, including number nine that addressed the right of women to vote.[37] One hundred men and women signed this Declaration of Sentiments, and it was published in the New York Herald.[38] This is thought by many to be the official beginning of the suffrage movement in the United States.

EXHIBIT 6.1 Susan B. Anthony and Elizabeth Cady Stanton

The Seneca Falls Conference, however, was just the beginning of the battle to gain the right to vote for women in the United States. Anthony became one of the foremost spokespeople in the movement and was often the one most visible to the American public. In 1871, Anthony and 15 other women registered and voted in the election of 1871. Later, Anthony was arrested and tried for violations of the voting laws. Upon being convicted, she was ordered to pay a $100 fine—a fine that she refused to pay and that remains unpaid to this day.[39]

Those who opposed voting rights for women had some interesting arguments to support their opposition. For instance, the anti-suffragettes argued that a woman's physical differences, specifically her 'frailty' made her unsuited to vote. This frailty made it difficult for women, first to get to the polls, and once there, the crowds that gathered would place an additional burden on her physical well being, and if a fight broke out, it was likely that a woman might get hurt.[40] A second reason given by the anti-suffragettes was the issue of morality. This idea points to the moral weakness of Eve and one anti-suffragette believed that this idea was an outgrowth of the old theory that Eve was the root of sin among humans.[41] Lastly, some arguing against suffrage believed that political involvement would place women in a vulnerable position where they could be taken advantage of and be exploited.[42] While these reasons may seem antiquated today, those who wanted to keep women from voting seriously championed them.

During most of the 19th century and into the 20th, the battle for women's equality was waged at the state level. By 1916, 11 states had given suffrage rights to women and in those states women were not only voting, but some were actually running for office. However, initial attempts to obtain suffrage at the federal level were unsuccessful. The National American Woman Suffrage Association, located in Washington, D.C., continued to lobby Congress for suffrage, and it was, at that time, the largest lobby in the nation's capital.[43] In 1918 the House of Representatives passed a resolution in favor of women's suffrage, however, the Senate rejected this resolution.[44] The next year both houses passed a joint resolution proposing the 19th Amendment to the Constitution that would give women the right to vote.[45] The amendment was sent to the states for ratification and by the end of that year, 22 states had ratified the amendment.[46]

Even before the passage of the resolution creating the 19th Amendment, the National American Woman Suffrage Association had contemplated a ratification campaign. That organization had polled every state legislature, contacted the Governors of each state, and trained individuals in each state to lobby for the ratification of the amendment.[47] It was this organization that held the key for ratification. It was not a certainty, however, but by 1920, 35 states had ratified the amendment, and only one more state was needed to complete the ratification process. Both the Republican and Democratic parties were determined that the amendment be ratified as neither wanted to be known as the party that defeated suffrage.[48] The leaders of each party began trying to influence those states that had still not acted on the amendment and ultimately, Henry Burns of Tennessee cast the vote that made Tennessee the 36th state to ratify the 19th Amendment.[49] On August 26, 1920, the 19th Amendment was adopted and women in the United States were finally entitled to vote.[50]

In spite of all this, the Court does consider the right to vote in both federal and state elections as a fundamental right. As a fundamental right, government regulations affecting the right are subject to strict scrutiny. The restriction must be necessary to achieve a compelling state interest. The issue is not whether one has the right to vote. Rather, the central question for the Court is whether a restriction of the right to vote violates the principle of equality in the distribution of the right. In other words, the question is whether all qualified voters have access to exercise their right if an election is held. The Court has considered this issue in a variety of contexts.

In *Harper v. Virginia Board of Elections,*[51] there was a challenge to Virginia's constitutional and statutory provisions requiring each person who wished to vote to personally pay a poll tax of no more than $1.50 for three years before the year in which he applies for voter registration and six months before registering for the first time at age 21. The tax was assessed with the property tax. Those who did not pay a property tax were responsible, on their own, for ensuring that the tax was assessed and paid. Failure to meet these requirements resulted in disenfranchisement. State residents sued to have the tax declared unconstitutional.

The Court acknowledged that the right to vote is fundamental and as such, could not be burdened as it was by a tax bearing no relation to one's qualification to vote. The Court held that the Equal Protection Clause precluded the state from infringing a fundamental right on the basis of wealth.[52]

HARPER V. VIRGINIA BD. OF ELECTIONS
383 U.S. 663 (1966)

Mr. Justice DOUGLAS delivered the opinion of the Court.

These are suits by Virginia residents to have declared unconstitutional Virginia's poll tax.

Long ago . . . , The Court referred to "the political franchise of voting" as a "fundamental political right, because preservative of all rights." Recently . . . we said, "Undoubtedly, the right of suffrage is a fundamental matter in a free democratic society. Especially since the right to exercise the franchise in a free and unimpaired manner is preservative of other basic civil and political rights, any alleged infringement of the right of citizens to vote must be carefully and meticulously scrutinized." There we were considering charges that voters in one part of the State had greater representation per person in the State Legislature than voters in another part of the State. We concluded:

"A citizen, a qualified voter, is no more nor no less so because he lives in the city or on the farm. The Equal Protection Clause demands no less than substantially equal state legislative representation for all citizens, of all places as well as all races."

We say the same whether the citizen, otherwise qualified to vote, has $1.50 in his pocket or nothing at all, pays the fee or fails to pay it. The principle that denies the State the right to dilute a citizen's vote on account of his economic status or other such factors by analogy bars a system which excludes those unable to pay a fee to vote or who fail to pay.

It is argued that a State may exact fees from citizens for many different kinds of licenses; that if it can demand from all an equal fee for a driver's license, it can demand from all an equal poll tax for voting. But we must remember that the interest of the State, when it comes to voting, is limited to the power to fix qualifications. Wealth, like race, creed, or color, is not germane to one's ability to participate intelligently in the electoral process.

We have long been mindful that where fundamental rights and liberties are asserted under the Equal Protection Clause, classifications which might invade or restrain them must be closely scrutinized and carefully confined.

Those principles apply here. For to repeat, wealth or fee paying has, in our view, no relation to voting qualifications; the right to vote is too precious, too fundamental to be so burdened or conditioned.

Three years later, the Court addressed another aspect of the right to vote. In some elections only those with an interest in the outcome are qualified to vote (e.g., landowners, or elections involving special boards). Where the state can prove that voters do, indeed, have a special interest or a "stake" in the election, the Court has allowed this type of special election. It is not easy for the state to meet this standard of proof because voting is a fundamental right subject to strict scrutiny analysis.

In *Kramer v. Union Free School District No. 15,*[53] New York statutorily limited the vote in school board elections to those who owned or leased property within the school district or were the parents of children in the district's schools. While the Court noted that there is a presumption of constitutionality given to state statutes, because of the importance of the franchise classifications that deny the right to some citizens and not others on a basis other than reasonable age, citizenship and residency requirements must be strictly scrutinized. Applying the strict scrutiny test, the Court struck down the statute. The Court found that the classification of those allowed to exercise the franchise was not narrowly tailored to achieve the stated goal of the government, which wanted only those "directly affected" to vote in these elections. *Kramer* clearly illustrates how difficult it is for the state to meet the standards of the strict scrutiny test where a fundamental right is involved.

As noted, the state may impose reasonable requirements to the exercise of the right to vote on the basis of residence. This means that an individual citizen may be required to live in the state for a certain period of time prior to Election Day before voting in state elections. The question then becomes whether the residency requirement infringes on the right to vote. To make this determination the Court uses the strict scrutiny analysis.

Tennessee required one year as a state resident and three months in the county before a new citizen could vote. The requirements were struck down as an infringement of the fundamental right to vote. The Court also found that the residency requirements interfered with the right of interstate migration. On the other hand, Arizona's 50-day residency requirement was upheld. The Court distinguished the two requirements on the basis of the duration as well as by noting that the Arizona requirement was necessary to prepare accurate voter lists.

In addition to age, citizenship, and residence requirements, the Court has been asked to address the constitutionality of restrictions on a felon's right to vote. In *Richardson v. Ramirez,*[54] three convicted felons sought to register to vote. They were denied on the basis of a California statute that disenfranchised those convicted of an "infamous crime." The three claimed a violation of the Equal Protection Clause.[55] The Court relied on Section 2 of the Fourteenth Amendment to uphold California's statute. After examining the legislative history of the amendment as well as the state provisions regarding disenfranchisement at the time the amendment was adopted, the majority found that it was not Congress' intent to make disenfranchisement a sanction for crime. Where, however, it is the intent of those enacting the disenfranchising statute to discriminate, invalidation is the expected result.

In *Hunter v. Underwood,*[56] the Court addressed a challenge to a section of the Alabama Constitution that disenfranchised persons convicted of certain felonies, misdemeanors and "any . . . crime involving moral turpitude." An examination of the legislative history made it clear that this section of the state constitution was adopted for the purpose of discriminating against African Americans and poor whites. The intent to discriminate in conjunction with its impact on a fundamental right provided the basis upon which to invalidate the provision.

What about those individuals who have been arrested and awaiting trial but not yet convicted? Can they be disenfranchised? The Court has not yet addressed this question. It does seem that they should be allowed to vote by absentee ballot.[57] In a country where one is presumed innocent until proven guilty, disenfranchisement prior to conviction would appear contradictory to constitutional principles.

The right to vote in this country extends to more than just general elections and those involving special boards and commissions. We also have the right to vote in primary elections, where candidates are chosen for the general elections. The Court has reviewed two plans restricting primary voting. One has survived strict scrutiny. The other has been struck down.

In *Rosario v. Rockefeller*,[58] the Court upheld the constitutionality of a New York election law that required an individual to enroll in the party of his choice 30 days before the general election in order to vote in the next party primary. In upholding the statute the Court found that it did not absolutely disenfranchise a class of voters. Moreover, it was important to the Court that the period between enrollment and the primary was not arbitrary. Rather, it was connected with an important state goal—to "inhibit party 'raiding,' whereby voters in sympathy with one party designate themselves as voters of another party so as to influence or determine the results of the other party's primary."[59]

However, an Illinois statute prohibiting a person from voting in a political party's primary election if he has voted in the primary of another party within the preceding 23 months was struck down in *Kusper v. Pontikes*.[60] The cases were specifically distinguished by the Court. The Illinois law "absolutely" precluded citizens from voting in the primary of their choice. That limitation was not the result, the Court stated, of the voters "own failure to take timely measures to enroll" as was the case in *Rosario*.[61] The situation in *Kusper* was one in which a voter who wanted to change party affiliation after one year to vote in another party's primary election was unable to do so.

In addition to the restrictions we have already considered, states have imposed restrictions to limit voters' choices. Limiting choices is "burdening" a voter's right, but not violating that right. Accordingly, strict scrutiny analysis is not applied. In these situations the Court balances the degree of the burden against the magnitude of the state's interest. The Court is slow to strike down such regulations so long as the "state election law . . . imposes only 'reasonable, nondiscriminatory restrictions' on the right to vote."[62] In *Burdick v. Takushi,* Hawaii banned all write-in votes. The Court found this restriction acceptable after balancing the proclaimed state interest in avoiding serious factionalism in the general election and "raiding" during the primaries with the burden on voters. Since voters still had reasonable access to the ballot the ban was upheld.

The right of an individual to be a candidate or the right of access to the ballot raises other issues closely tied to the fundamental right to vote. Here, we are talking about the right of an individual to be a candidate and the ability of political parties to place candidates on the ballot. There are two reasons advanced to support restricting access to the ballot by a candidate: first, the State's interest in reducing voter confusion; second, the interest in maximizing the probability that the winning candidate will have received a majority of the popular vote. There are, however, countervailing interests at stake. There is the individual's interest in being a candidate. While this is not a fundamental right it is related to the First Amendment right to free speech as well as the implicit right to participate in the political process. The second countervailing interest is that of the voters themselves in being offered a variety of candidates with a range of political views from whom to choose. There is also the countervailing interest of individuals to band together to form a political party, associated with the First Amendment guarantee of freedom of association. If the party formed cannot gain access to the ballot, then the ability to exercise the right to associate freely and participate in the political process is impaired. The Supreme Court has generally ruled that in this context freedom of association means that parties with significant support from the citizenry must be provided with reasonable opportunities to be placed on the ballot.

In cases such as *Williams v. Rhodes*[63] and *Jenness v. Fortson*,[64] the Court has addressed the popular support requirements. While indicating that states may, in order to keep ballots from becoming confusing, require parties to show a significant amount of community support, the restrictions may not be so great that minority parties or independent candidates have no realistic chance of getting on the ballot. In *Williams* the Court found that the Ohio restriction gave established parties a definite advantage over new parties. Without a compelling state interest such a burden infringed on citizens' right to vote and the guarantee of freedom of association. The Court, however, provided no clear guidance as to what constituted significant community support, although the boundaries of the Georgia statute upheld in *Jenness* stand as a minimum marker.

An issue associated with these questions is whether the state can require that candidates pay a fee to get on the ballot. This was addressed in *Lubin v. Paniish*.[65] An indigent, seeking a place on the ballot, was unable to pay the required $70 fee and brought a challenge to the California statute mandating payment of the fee. The Supreme Court recognized the importance of the state's interest in testing the seriousness of a candidate's intent. Nevertheless, the Court found the means chosen by the state impermissible, and precluded access to the ballot to those unable to pay the filing fee. The Court's decision concerned whether an indigent person could gain access to the ballot. It did not concern voters' rights to choose an indigent candidate. Thus, it appears that there is no clear right to be a candidate, although it has been asserted that there may be an independent constitutional right to be a candidate.

It seems clear that the right to vote is a fundamental right requiring application of strict scrutiny analysis. The scope of that right has been subject to challenges, which have drawn the parameters in a way that demonstrates that some aspects of the right are fundamental while others may only require a rational relationship between the government's interest in regulating voting and its associated aspects and the means by which this is done.

REFUSAL TO EXPAND

Up to this point this chapter has examined those rights that the Court has recognized as fundamental and require strict scrutiny. There are other areas that are viewed by sections of the population as also being fundamental and therefore demand the strict scrutiny analysis. Thus, challenges have been brought to the Court seeking recognition of constitutional status too. In these cases, the Court has rejected the contention that any of these claimed necessities are fundamental rights guaranteed by the Constitution. These challenges are worth noting, however.

Most citizens accept, without question, the importance of education to all sections of life. Does that importance, however, require that all citizens receive the same education? The argument that they do was made before the Court in 1973 in *San Antonio Independent School District v. Rodriguez*.[66]

A challenge was made to the manner in which elementary and secondary public schools were funded in Texas. Because the funding scheme allowed individual school districts to tax local residents to supplement state subsidies of public education, those districts with a high tax base could provide better and more personnel, materials, and services than those with a lower tax base. In a class action suit brought by the families of schoolchildren in a poor district, it was asserted that the financing scheme violated the Due Process and Equal Protection Clauses of the Fourteenth Amendment. The District Court agreed, finding that education is a fundamental right. The United States Supreme

Court disagreed. The Court stated that whether a right or interest is fundamental is determined by whether it is expressly or impliedly guaranteed by the Constitution, it is not determined by its "societal importance." Employing this standard the Court concluded that public education is not a fundamental right. The Court concluded that under the rational relationship test the financing scheme was constitutional.

Justice Thurgood Marshall dissented from the Court's opinion and proposed a different standard for determining whether a right was fundamental. The issue, he maintained, was "the extent to which constitutionally guaranteed rights are dependent on interests not mentioned in the Constitution. Marshall stated that as the nexus between the specific constitutional guarantee and the non-specified interest become closer, the interest becomes fundamental. Adopting this test would require a conclusion that education is a fundamental right since it "directly affects the ability of a child to exercise his First Amendment interest . . ."[67]

SAN ANTONIO SCHOOL DISTRICT V. RODRIGUEZ
411 U.S. 1 (1973)

Mr. Justice POWELL delivered the opinion of the Court.

This suit attacking the Texas system of financing public education was initiated by Mexican-American parents whose children attend the elementary and secondary schools in the Edgewood Independent School District, an urban school district in San Antonio, Texas. They brought a class action on behalf of schoolchildren throughout the State who are members of minority groups or who are poor and reside in school districts having a low property base.

The first Texas State Constitution, promulgated upon Texas' entry into the Union . . . provided for the establishment of a system of free schools. Early in its history, Texas adopted a dual approach to the financing of its schools, relying on mutual participation by the local school districts and the State.

Until recent times, Texas was a predominantly rural State and its population and property wealth were spread relatively evenly across the State. Sizable differences in the value of assessable property between local school districts became increasingly evident as the State became more industrialized and as rural-to-urban population shifts became more pronounced.

In due time it became apparent to those concerned with financing public education that contributions from the [state fund] were not sufficient to ameliorate this disparities.

Recognizing the need for increased state funding to help offset disparities in local spending

and to meet Texas' changing educational requirements, the state legislature undertook a thorough evaluation of public education with an eye toward major reform. [This] . . . led to . . . establishing the Texas Minimum Foundation School Program. Today, this Program accounts for approximately half of the total educational expenditures in Texas.

The Program calls for state and local contributions to a fund earmarked specifically for teacher salaries, operating expenses, and transportation costs. The State, supplying funds from its general revenues, finances approximately 80% of the Program, and the school districts are responsible—as a unit—for providing the remaining 20%. The districts' share . . . is apportioned among the school districts under a formula designed to reflect each district's relative taxpaying ability.

Texas virtually concedes that its historically rooted dual system of financing education could not withstand the strict judicial scrutiny that this Court has found appropriate in reviewing legislative judgments that interfere with fundamental constitutional rights or that involve suspect classifications. If, as previous decisions have indicated, strict scrutiny means that the State's system is not entitled to the usual presumption of validity, that the State rather than the complainants must carry a "heavy burden of justification," that the State must demonstrate that its educational system has been structured with "precision," and is "tailored" narrowly to serve legitimate objectives and that it has selected the "less drastic means" for effectuating

Continued

its objectives, the Texas financing system and its counterpart in virtually every other State will not pass muster. The State candidly admits that "[n]o one familiar with the Texas system would contend that it has yet achieved perfection." Apart from its concession that educational financing in Texas has "defects" and "imperfections," the State defends the system's rationality with vigor and disputes the District Court's finding that it lacks a "reasonable basis."

This, then, establishes the framework for our analysis. We must decide, first, whether the Texas system of financing public education operates to the disadvantage of some suspect class or impinges upon a fundamental right explicitly or implicitly protected by the Constitution, thereby requiring strict judicial scrutiny.

(After rejecting the claim that the Texas system impermissibly disadvantaged a suspect class, the Court turned to the question whether education was a fundamental right.)

In *Brown v. Board of Education,* a unanimous Court recognized that "education is perhaps the most important function of state and local governments." What was said there in the context of racial discrimination has lost none of its vitality with the passage of time. This theme, expressing an abiding respect for the vital role of education in a free society, may be found in numerous opinions of Justices of this Court writing both before and after *Brown* was decided.

Nothing this Court holds today in any way detracts from our historic dedication to public education. We are in complete agreement with the conclusion of the three-judge panel below that "the grave significance of education both to the individual and to our society" cannot be doubted. But the importance of a service performed by the State does not determine whether it must be regarded as fundamental for purposes of examination under the Equal Protection Clause.

It is not the province of this Court to create substantive constitutional rights in the name of guaranteeing equal protection of the laws. Thus, the key to discovering whether education is "fundamental" is not to be found in comparisons of the relative societal significance of education as opposed to subsistence or housing. Nor is it to be found by weighing whether there is a right to education is as important as the right to travel. Rather, the answer lies in assessing whether there is a right to education explicitly or implicitly guaranteed by the Constitution.

Education, of course, is not among the rights afforded explicit protection under our Federal Constitution. Nor do we find any basis for saying it is implicitly so protected. As we have said, the undisputed importance of education will not alone cause this Court to depart from the usual standard for reviewing a State's social and economic legislation. It is appellees' contention, however, that education is distinguishable from other services and benefits provided by the State because it bears a peculiarly close relationship to other rights and liberties accorded protection under the Constitution. Specifically, they insist that education is itself a fundamental personal right because it is essential to the effective exercise of First Amendment freedoms and to intelligent utilization of the right to vote. In asserting a nexus between speech and education, appellees urge that the right to speak is meaningless unless the speaker is capable of articulating his thoughts intelligently and persuasively. The "marketplace of ideas" is an empty forum for those lacking basic communicative tools. Likewise, they argue that the corollary right to receive information becomes little more than a hollow privilege when the recipient has not been taught to read, assimilate, and utilize available knowledge.

We need not dispute any of these propositions. The Court has long afforded zealous protection against unjustifiable governmental interference with the individual's rights to speak to vote. Yet we have never presumed to possess either the ability or the authority to guarantee to the citizenry the most effective speech or the most informed electoral choice. That these may be desirable goals of a system of freedom of expression and of a representative form of government is not to be doubted. These are indeed goals to be pursued by a people whose thoughts and beliefs are freed from governmental interference. But they are not values to be implemented by judicial intrusion into otherwise legitimate state activities.

We have carefully considered each of the arguments supportive of the District Court's finding that education is a fundamental right or liberty and have found those arguments unpersuasive. In one further respect we find this a particularly inappropriate case in which to subject state action to strict judicial scrutiny. The present case,

Continued

in another basic sense, is significantly different from any of the cases in which the Court has applied strict scrutiny to state or federal legislation touching upon constitutionally protected rights. Each of our prior cases involved legislation which "deprived," "infringed," or "interfered" with the free exercise of some such fundamental personal right or liberty.

Every step leading to the establishment of the system Texas utilizes today—including the decisions permitting localities to tax and expend locally, and creating and continuously expanding state aid—was implemented in an effort to extend public education and to improve its quality. Of course, every reform that benefits some more than others may be criticized for what it fails to accomplish. But we think it plain that, in substance, the thrust of the Texas system is affirmative and reformatory and, therefore, should be scrutinized under judicial principles sensitive to the nature of the State's efforts and to the rights reserved to the States under the Constitution.

Mr. Justice MARSHALL, with whom Mr. Justice DOUGLAS concurs, dissenting.

To avoid having the Texas financing scheme struck down because of the interdistrict variations in taxable property wealth, the District Court determined that it was insufficient for appellants to show merely that the State's scheme was rationally related to some legitimate state purpose; rather, the discrimination inherent in the scheme had to be shown necessary to promote a "compelling state interest" in order to withstand constitutional scrutiny. The basis for this determination was twofold: first, the financing scheme divides citizens on a wealth basis, a classification which the District Court viewed as highly suspect and second, the discriminatory scheme directly affects what it considered to be a "fundamental interest," namely education.

[There] are instances in which, due to the importance of interests at stake, the Court has displayed a strong concern with the existence of discriminatory state treatment. But the Court never said or indicated that these are interests which independently enjoy full-blown constitutional protection.

The majority is, of course, correct when it suggests that the process of determining which interests are fundamental is a difficult one. But I do not think the problem is insurmountable. And I certainly do not accept the view that the process need necessarily degenerate into an unprincipled, subjective "picking-and-choosing" between various interests or that it must involve this Court in creating "substantive constitutional rights in the name of guaranteeing equal protection of the laws." Although not all fundamental interests are constitutionally guaranteed, the determination of which interests are fundamental should be firmly rooted in the text of the Constitution. The task in every case should be to determine the extent to which constitutionally guaranteed rights are dependent on interests not mentioned in the Constitution. As the nexus between the specific constitutional guarantee and the nonconstitutional interest draws closer, the nonconstitutional interest becomes more fundamental and the degree of judicial scrutiny applied when the interest is infringed on a discriminatory basis must be adjusted accordingly. Thus, it cannot be denied that interests such as procreation, the exercise of the state franchise, and the access to criminal appellate processes are not fully guaranteed to the citizen by our Constitution. But these interests have nonetheless been afforded special judicial consideration in the face of discrimination because they are, to some extent, interrelated with constitutional guarantees.

Since the Court now suggests that only interests guaranteed by the Constitution are fundamental for purposes of equal protection analysis, and since it rejects the contention that public education is fundamental, it follows that the Court concludes that public education is not constitutionally guaranteed. It is true that this Court has never deemed the provision of free public education to be required by the Constitution. Indeed, it has on occasion suggested that state-supported education is a privilege bestowed by a State on its citizens. Nevertheless, the fundamental importance of education is amply indicated by the prior decisions of this Court, by the unique status accorded public education by our society, and by the close relationship between education and some of our most basic constitutional values.

[T]he majority seeks refuge in the fact that the Court has "never presumed to possess either the ability or the authority to guarantee to the citizenry the most effective speech or the most informed electoral choice." This serves only to blur what is in fact at stake. With due respect the

Continued

issue is neither provision of the most effective speech nor of the most informed vote. Appellees do not now seek the best education Texas might provide. They do seek, however, an end to state discrimination resulting from the unequal distribution of taxable district property wealth that directly impairs the ability of some districts to provide the same educational opportunity that other districts can provide with the same or even substantially less tax effort. The issue is, in other words, one of discrimination that affects the quality of the education which Texas has chosen to provide its children; and the precise question here is what importance should attach to education for purposes of equal protection analysis of that discrimination. As this Court held in *Brown v. Bd. Of Education,* the opportunity of education, "where the state has undertaken to provide it, is a right which must be made available to all on equal terms." The factors just considered, including the relationship between education and the social and political interests enshrined within the Constitution, compel us to recognize the fundamentality of education and to scrutinize with appropriate care the bases for state discrimination affecting equality of educational opportunity in Texas' school districts which is only strengthened when we consider the character of the classification in this case.

Rodriguez is significant to our understanding of the Court's fundamental rights analysis. It sets forth the test for establishing whether a right or interest is fundamental, which is determined by whether the right or interest is expressly or impliedly guaranteed by the Constitution, not whether it is important to society. This test makes it more difficult for those seeking the Court's recognition of interests or rights as fundamental under the Constitution. It should be remembered, however, that the students involved in *Rodriguez* were not being denied an education; they were challenging the quality of the education they were receiving.

Rodriguez did not address the question whether an absolute deprivation of education would violate the Constitution. In *Pyler v. Doe,*[68] the Court left the door open to an affirmative answer to that question. At issue in *Pyler* was a Texas statute that deprived local school districts of state funding for children not legally admitted to the United States. In addition, the statute authorized local school districts to deny public school enrollment to illegal alien children. While the challenge to the statute was made on the basis of an equal protection argument, the issue of entitlement to education was also of concern. The Court distinguished education from other governmental benefits finding it vital to the achievement of "one of the goals of the Equal Protection Clause: the abolition of governmental barriers presenting unreasonable obstacles to the advancement on the basis of individual merit."[69] The Court found that denial of education to an illegal alien is not a violation of a fundamental right, but the Court did not preclude the possibility that denial of education to a United States citizen would constitute such an infringement.

These cases demonstrate a general reluctance on the part of the Court to include education as a fundamental right. That reluctance is even greater in other areas. In *Pyler,* as previously noted, the Court denied education was a fundamental right, but maintained that "neither is it merely some governmental 'benefit' indistinguishable from other forms of social welfare legislation."[70] Accordingly, it should be no surprise that the Court concluded that there is no fundamental right to welfare.

Welfare schemes fall into the category of economics and social welfare and not a fundamental right. As a result, government regulations controlling welfare employ mere rationality as the standard for assessing their constitutionality. So long as a welfare scheme bears a rational relation to a legitimate state objective, it is constitutionally permissible. The Court has also declined to find that housing is a fundamental right. In *Lindsey v. Normet,*[71] a challenge to a state statute that made it less difficult for a landlord to evict a tenant for nonpayment of rent, the Court applied the rational relationship test, making it clear there is no fundamental right to housing. Finally, there is no recognition of a fundamental right of an adult to engage in sexual relations. This position was made explicit in *Bowers v. Hardwick*,[72] where the Court stated that there was no fundamental right to engage in consensual homosexual relations in the privacy of one's own home.

While one may disagree with the Court's conclusions regarding the fundamental nature of some claimed rights, we can clearly see the Court's reluctance to expand our rights too far from the interpreted boundaries of the Constitution. There is one additional area where the Court has employed a fundamental rights analysis. This is the area of privacy, which is considered in Chapter 9.

Summary

The Court has determined that certain rights are fundamental to the concept of ordered liberty, which was the underlying goal of the Framers of the Constitution. Those are the rights explicitly stated in the document itself or those implicit in the Constitution or the concept of ordered liberty. When a right is determined to be fundamental, it requires the Court to employ the strict scrutiny test to decide whether a government regulation infringes upon such a right. Even when a right has been deemed to be fundamental by the Court all aspects of exercising the right may not be fundamental. In those cases all that is required for a regulation to be sustained is a rational relationship between the regulation and its purpose. Over the years the expansion of fundamental rights begun by the Warren Court has been curtailed and narrowed, with today's Court being reluctant to find additional fundamental rights.

Key Terms

fundamental rights   indigent   right to travel

Review Questions

1. What is the difference between a fundamental and a nonfundamental right? On what basis does the Court draw this distinction?

2. What is the strict scrutiny test and how is it distinguished from the rational relationship test?

3. Does the Court's distinction between fundamental and nonfundamental rights make sense? Would you distinguish the two on another basis? What would that basis be? Why is this a better way to make the distinction?

4. What rights do you think are fundamental? Would you add or subtract any from those the Court has included?

5. Do you agree with the Court's determinations about which aspects of a right are fundamental? Explain.

Internet Connections

1. For more information on the right to vote, go to the U.S. Department of Justice, Civil Rights Division's home page and access the article "The Right to Vote, How Federal Law Protects You" at *http://www.usdoj.gov.*

2. To read Susan B. Anthony's speech on Women's Right to Vote, go to *http://www.historyplace.com.*

3. For a recent discussion on interstate migration, see Jide Nzelibe's article "Free Movement: A Federalist Reinterpretation" in the *American University Law Review,* Washington College of Law, American University at *http://www.wcl.american.edu.*

End Notes

[1]The Court has long recognized the fundamental right of parents to control decisions regarding the upbringing of their children. *See* Chapter 9.

[2]*Griffin v. Illinois,* 351 U.S. 12 (1956).

[3]*Id.* at 17.

[4]*Douglas v. California,* 372 U.S. 353 (1963).

[5]*Ross v. Moffitt,* 417 U.S. 600 (1974).

[6]*Id.* at 616.

[7]*Williams v. Illinois,* 399 U.S. 235 (1970).

[8]*Boddie v. Connecticut,* 401 U.S. 371 (1971).

[9]*Little v. Streater,* 452 U.S. 1 (1981).

[10]*Id.* at 10.

[11]*M.L.B. v. S.L.J.,* 519 U.S. 102 (1996).

[12]*Id.* The importance of the parental relationship can be seen more clearly in Chapter 9, which discusses privacy rights.

[13]*Id.*

[14]"The constitutional right to travel from one State to another . . . occupies a position fundamental to the concept of our Federal Union. It is a right that has been firmly established and repeatedly recognized." *United States v. Guest,* 383 U.S. 745, 757–758 (1966).

[15]*Shapiro v. Thompson,* 394 U.S. 618 (1969).

[16]*Id.* at 629.

[17]*Id.* at 638.

[18]*Starns v. Malkerson,* 326 F. Supp. 234 (1970).

[19]*Id.* at 235.

[20]*Id.*

[21]*Id.* at 238.

[22]*Memorial Hospital v. Maricopa County,* 415 U.S. 250 (1974).

[23]*Id.* at 254.

[24]*Id.* at 256.

[25]*Id.* at 269.

[26]*Sosna v. Iowa,* 419 U.S. 393 (1975).

[27]*Id.* at 407.

[28]*Dunn v. Blumstein,* 405 U.S. 330 (1972).

[29]*Id.* at 342.

[30]*Id.* at 345.

[31]*Id.* at 357.

[32]*Martinez v. Bynum,* 461 U.S. 321 (1983).

[33]*Id.* at 323.

[34]*Id.* at 328, 329.

[35]U.S. Suffrage Movement Timeline, ACWL, University of Rochester, at *http://www.rochester.edu* (August 5, 2003).

[36]Ibid.

[37]The Seneca Falls Conference, Suffragism Organizes, at *http://www.benet.org* (August 5, 2003).

[38]Ibid.

[39]Susan B. Anthony, "Anthony's Strong Willed Behavior in Her Fight for Suffrage," University of Rochester, at *http://www.history.rochester.edu* (August 5, 2003).

[40]"The Arguments of the Anti-Suffragists," University of Rochester, at *http://www.history.rochester.edu* (August 5, 2003).

[41]Ibid.

[42]Ibid.

[43]Carrie Chapman Catt & Nettie Rogers Shuler, *Woman Suffrage and Politics: The Inner Story of the Suffrage Movement,* 280 (C. Scribner's Publisher 1923).

[44]U.S. Suffrage Movement Timeline, ACWL, University of Rochester, at *http://www.rochester.edu* (August 5, 2003).

[45]Ibid.

[46]Ibid.

[47]Carrie Chapman Catt & Nettie Rogers Shuler, *Woman Suffrage and Politics: The Inner Story of the Suffrage Movement,* 343 (C. Scribner's Publisher 1923).

[48]*Id.* at 398.

[49]U.S. Suffrage Movement Timeline, ACWL, University of Rochester, at *http://www.rochester.edu* (August 5, 2003).

[50]Ibid.

[51]*Harper v. Virginia Board of Elections,* 383 U.S. 663 (1966).

[52]*Id.* at 664–665, 669–670.

[53]*Kramer v. Union Free School District No. 15,* 395 U.S. 621 (1969).

[54]*Richardson v. Ramirez,* 418 U.S. 24 (1974).

[55]*Id.* at 26–27.

[56]*Hunter v. Underwood,* 471 U.S. 222 (1985).

[57]Lawrence Tribe, *American Constitutional Law,* 1095 (2d ed., Foundation Press 1988).

[58]*Rosario v. Rockefeller,* 410 U.S. 752 (1973).

[59]*Id.* at 760–761.

[60]*Kusper v. Pontikes,* 414 U.S. 51 (1973).

[61]*Id.* at 60–61.

[62]*Burdick v. Takushi,* 504 U.S. 428, 434 (1992).

[63]*Williams v. Rhodes,* 393 U.S. 23 (1968).

[64]*Jenness v. Fortson,* 403 U.S. 431 (1971).

[65]*Lubin v. Paniish,* 415 U.S. 709 (1974).

[66]*San Antonio Independent School District v. Rodriguez,* 411 U.S. 1 (1973).

[67]*Id.* at 112.

[68]*Pyler v. Doe,* 457 U.S. 202 (1982).

[69]*Id.* at 221–222.

[70]*Id.* at 221.

[71]*Lindsey v. Normet,* 405 U.S. 56 (1972).

[72]*Bowers v. Hardwick,* 478 U.S. 186 (1986).

 For additional resources, go to *http://www.westlegalstudies.com*

DUE PROCESS AND EQUAL PROTECTION

[This Court has] never suggested that . . . the equal protection guarantee is less than coextensive with that entitled to due process. To the contrary, we have recognized that both provisions were fashioned to protect an identical class of persons, and to reach every exercise of state authority.

—Justice William Brennan
Plyer v. Certain Named and Unnamed Undocumented Alien Children

INTRODUCTION

With the passage of the Fourteenth Amendment following the Civil War, the guarantees of the Bill of Rights became applicable, at least by language, to the individual states. Until that time, only the federal government was bound by its guarantees and protections. The Fourteenth Amendment provided that "no State . . . shall deprive any person of life, liberty, or property, without **due process of law**; nor deny to any person within its jurisdiction the **equal protection of the laws.**"[1]

Throughout this book, you see that the Due Process Clauses of the Fifth and Fourteenth Amendments and the Equal Protection Clause have become integral in constitutional analysis. This chapter traces how this occurred and discusses the Court's interpretation of the protections and how they are used to aid the Court in its decision-making.

due process of law what constitutes due process of law under the Fifth and Fourteenth Amendments is that a person should always have notice and a real chance to present his or her side in a legal dispute and that no law or government procedure should be arbitrary or unfair.

INCORPORATION

Originally, the protections and rights guaranteed to United States citizens in the Bill of Rights were applicable only against infringement by the federal government. The individual states were bound, in this respect, only by their own constitutions and the guarantees they provided to their citizens against the state government. The Supreme Court made this clear in *Barron v. the Mayor of the City of Baltimore* by stating that the "Constitution was ordained and established by the people of the United States for themselves, for their own government, and not for the government of the individual States."[2] Accordingly, the federal courts were unable to insure that state legislators and administrators complied with constitutional requirements.

This situation began to change with the passage of the so-called Civil War Amendments—the Thirteenth, Fourteenth, and Fifteenth Amendments. In respect to due process and equal protection the Fourteenth Amendment is most relevant. This amendment was designed to protect citizens, particularly African Americans, against the power of the states to discriminate. Fairly soon after the amendment's passage, the Court seemed to reject the idea that it made the Bill of Rights applicable to the states. There have been two contradictory positions espoused by the Court and the Justices over this issue.

equal protection of laws the constitutional requirement that a state government not treat equals unequally, set up illegal categories to justify treating persons unfairly, or give unfair or unequal treatment to a person based on that person's race, religion, disability, color, sex, age, or national origin.

ExHIBIT 7.1	Selective Incorporation and the Bill of Rights

Amendment/Issue	Case	Year
Free Exercise of Religion, Amendment I	*Hamilton v. University of California,* 293 U.S. 245	1934
Separation of Church and State, Amendment I	*Everson v. Board of Education,* 220 U.S. 1	1947
Freedom of Speech, Amendment I	*Fiske v. Kansas,* 274 U.S. 380	1927
Freedom of the Press, Amendment I	*Near v. Minnesota,* 283 U.S. 697	1931
Assembly and Petition, Amendment I	*De Jonge v. Oregon,* 299 U.S. 353	1937
Unreasonable Search and Seizure, Amendment IV	*Wolf v. Colorado,* 338 U.S. 25	1949
Just Compensation, Amendment V	*Chicago, Burlington & Quincy Railroad v. Chicago,* 166 U.S. 226	1897
Compulsory Self-Incrimination, Amendment V	*Malloy v. Hogan,* 378 U.S. 1	1964
Double Jeopardy, Amendment V	*Benton v. Maryland,* 395 U.S. 784	1969
Confrontation of Hostile and Favorable Witnesses, Amendment VI	*Pointer v. Texas,* 380 U.S. 400 and *Washington v. Texas,* 388 U.S. 14	1965 1967
Impartial Jury, Amendment VI	*Parker v. Gladden,* 385 U.S. 363	1966
Right to Counsel, Amendment VI	*Gideon v. Wainwright,* 372 U.S. 335	1963
Right to a Public Trial, Amendment VI	*In re Oliver,* 333 U.S. 257	1948
Right to a Speedy Trial, Amendment VI	*Klopfer v. North Carolina,* 386 U.S. 371	1967
Jury Trial in Misdemeanor Cases, Amendment VI	*Duncan v. Louisiana,* 391 U.S. 145	1968
Cruel and Unusual Punishment, Amendment VIII	*Robinson v. California,* 370 U.S. 660	1962

selective incorporation
the principle that the Bill of Rights, which protects persons against certain actions of the federal government, also protects against most, but not all such actions by a state government because the Fourteenth Amendment requires it.

The first of these is the doctrine of **selective incorporation**. Those who take this approach argue that the term *liberty* used in the amendment should be interpreted without reference to the Bill of Rights. It should be interpreted to pertain to those aspects of liberty that are "fundamental." It is these fundamental aspects that are "selectively" incorporated into the Fourteenth Amendment and, therefore, made applicable to the states (see Exhibit 7.1).

It is this approach that Justice Cardozo used in *Palko v. Connecticut*[3] in determining whether the proscription against double jeopardy in the Federal Constitution was sufficiently fundamental to be honored by the states. The test to be employed was whether the guarantee is "implicit in the concept of ordered liberty, and through the Fourteenth Amendment, thus, become valid against the state."[4]

In addition to the doctrine that the Fourteenth Amendment does not automatically incorporate all Bill of Rights guarantees, those advocating the selective incorporation approach further maintain that the Bill of Rights does not set the standard for the concept of liberty, that is, the states may choose the level of liberty to grant their citizens. This question goes to the scope of the right. A majority of the Court has favored the position that the state right may be no less than coextensive with the scope of the right under the Bill of Rights. The individual states may, however, choose to grant their citizens greater protection than that guaranteed by the Federal Constitution.

The total incorporation doctrine is the second and opposite view of selective incorporation. Under this approach, the Fourteenth Amendment's Due Process Clause specifically makes all of the Bill of Rights guarantees applicable to the states. Justice Black favored this position, but he added an additional twist to it. Justice Black argued that the guarantees that should be made applicable to the states should be limited to those contained in the Bill of Rights and no others. This view has not been widely accepted and is not advocated by any of the current Justices.

There are weaknesses in each of the two approaches. The selective incorporation doctrine allows individual Justices to decide the scope of incorporation based on their personal views of what constitutes a fundamental right. Hence, it is unpredictable, providing states with no clear guidelines. It leaves the states uncertain as to what standards they are bound by.

Similarly, the total incorporation doctrine has its drawbacks. There is little historical support for the position. It constrains the states' ability to reform policies and legislation and, finally, it is argued that it is no less vague than the fundamental rights position. The focus is simply shifted from broad discretion on the concepts of liberty and due process to a focus on the individual guarantees of the Bill of Rights.

The selective incorporation approach continues to hold sway. The analysis, however, has changed over time. While Justice Cardozo contended that only those guarantees essential to the "scheme of ordered liberty" should be incorporated, today the Court maintains that fundamental guarantees, that is, "fundamental in the context of the [judicial] process maintained," should be incorporated.[5] This has led to most of the criminal procedural guarantees of the United States Constitution being made applicable to the states through the Fourteenth Amendment Due Process Clause. The selective incorporation approach has always been the one espoused by the Court as a body, however, over time, virtually every one of the Bill of Rights guarantees has been incorporated into the Fourteenth Amendment in a piecemeal fashion.[6]

The Fifth Amendment Due Process Clause is binding on the federal government. The Fourteenth Amendment, which employs language that is virtually identical to the Fifth Amendment, governs state action. The two clauses have been given identical interpretations by the Court. It is important, however, to understand that the Amendment which will be triggered (the Fifth or Fourteenth) is dependent on whether the challenge arises from federal or state governmental action.

SUBSTANTIVE DUE PROCESS

Due process under the Fourteenth Amendment is about more than procedures. It concerns limits on the states' substantive power to intervene in various aspects of citizens' lives in both the economic and social spheres. Where the Court does decide to intervene in the substance of state legislation its analysis is premised upon interpretation of the word **liberty**. The concept that state legislation can be found to violate the Constitution and be invalidated pursuant to the Fourteenth Amendment is known as substantive due process.

The doctrine of substantive due process has been irregularly applied over time. In the following subsections the rise of substantive due process will be considered, from the end of the nineteenth century until the 1930s, its falling into disuse in the late 1930s, and its reemergence in the 1950s and 1960s.

liberty freedom from illegal personal restraint; Personal rights under the law; a liberty interest is a right protected by due process of law.

The Early History of Substantive Due Process

Shortly after the passage of the Fourteenth Amendment, the Court was faced with its first challenge to determine whether the amendment limited state powers. Due to a variety of factors the Court reviewed the substance of state economic regulations in *The Slaughterhouse Cases*.[7]

natural law rules of conduct that are thought to be the same everywhere because they are basic to human behavior; basic moral law.

The first of these factors was widespread acceptance of the **natural law** doctrine. Certain rights, such as the right to own property and the right of **freedom of contract**, were considered fundamental and natural rights derived, not from the Constitution, but from the natural order of things. If legislators passed statutes that restricted these rights, citizens would be deprived of liberty or property without due process.

Another factor, which moved the Court toward addressing the question, was laissez-faire economic policy. At the time, it was well accepted that government interference in business should be kept to a bare minimum.

freedom of contract the constitutionally protected right to make and enforce contracts, as limited only by reasonable laws about health, safety, and consumer protection.

The third factor that moved the Court was the Fourteenth Amendment itself. The explicit guarantee of due process against state action provided a means by which substantive review of state law could be accomplished. These factors, when taken together, prodded the Court to undertake such review.

The Court was asked in *The Slaughterhouse Cases* whether the State of Louisiana could grant a monopoly on slaughterhouses to a particular company. The Court found that this did not violate due process despite an argument by one of the dissenters that a large number of citizens were deprived of liberty and property by the legislation since these citizens were unable to pursue lawful employment. Although this first consideration of substantive due process review was unsuccessful, the Court subsequently began to change its position.

The Court started to demonstrate a willingness to substantively review state legislation under particular circumstances. In *Munn v. Illinois*,[8] the Court indicated that the judiciary would not determine the reasonableness of rates charged by grain elevators. In *Mugler v. Kansas*,[9] the Court sustained a state ban on alcoholic beverages. The Court noted that such legislation was valid under the states' police powers provided it did not violate "fundamental law."[10] The Court found that the state had a legitimate interest in controlling alcohol under its police power to regulate the health and safety of its citizens. The same could not be said about the regulation of grain elevator rates. The Court also used substantive due process to invalidate a state statute in *Allegeyer v. Louisiana*.[11] Petitioner claimed his freedom to contract was impaired in violation of the Due Process Clause when he bought an insurance policy from a firm outside the state. The Court invalidated a statute that prohibited anyone from obtaining insurance on property located in Louisiana from companies that were not licensed in the state. It was found that such a statute violated due process because it interfered with citizens' freedom of contract. The Court reasoned that the Fourteenth Amendment's guarantee of liberty extended to entering into contracts to work and earn a livelihood as well as to protect physical liberty. The Court concluded that the state police power did not allow the banning of contracts that were made and were to be performed outside the state.

Between 1899 and 1937 the Court held 159 cases of state legislation to be unconstitutional. The most important of these is *Lochner v. New York*.[12] Again, the focus was on abridgment of one's freedom to contract. The statute at issue was one that limited the number of hours bakery employees could work. The state defended the law on two grounds—first, as a valid labor law and second, as a protection of the health and safety of the workers. The Court rejected both arguments. It found that the police power only extends to the protection of public welfare. Bargaining between parties in this case was not of sufficient concern to the public. The Court went on to find that the bakers were not a group endangered to the degree necessary to allow the state to intervene.

Moreover, the long hours did not affect public health. Any interest the state had in the wholesomeness of baked goods could be achieved by measures having less impact on freedom of contract. The Court expressed the belief that the legislature was acting to regulate labor conditions, not to protect health and safety and implied that the actual motive would be examined in determining substantive due process attacks. Finally, the Court refused to defer to the legislative findings of fact.

The majority's test was a stringent one. It required a "real and substantial relationship" between the statute and its objective. This test was not met in *Lochner* because less restrictive measures could have been employed to achieve the same objective. In addition, only certain legislative goals would be found acceptable. The legislature would not be permitted to readjust economic power or resources. Since the statute in question was considered a labor law that readjusted bargaining power, the so-called health regulation served an impermissible purpose. (See Exhibit 7.2 for a historical perspective of the impact of the *Lochner* decision.) The Court continues today to require strict scrutiny where fundamental interests are at issue.

Lochner was the decision of a sharply divided Court. In the 5 to 4 decision, both Justices Harlan and Holmes wrote dissents. Justice Harlan maintained that there was not enough evidence that the statute promoted health and safety such as to allow acceptance of the legislative judgment. Justice Holmes took a different tack. He argued that the Court had no right to impose its own

---

EXHIBIT 7.2   The Triangle Shirtwaist Fire

Some six years after the Court's decision in *Lochner*, an event occurred in a New York factory that would eventually have a positive impact on the States' ability to exercise their power to act for the health, safety, and welfare of their working citizens. That event was the Triangle Shirtwaist Company fire of March 25, 1911.

It was late on a Saturday afternoon. The bell signaled the end of the working day. The young women employees (mostly teenagers) and largely recent immigrants from Italy, Germany, and Eastern Europe just finished a day of overtime to increase their regular $6.00 per week pay. All of a sudden, a shout of "Fire!" rang out on the eighth floor of the building where the company occupied the eighth, ninth, and tenth floors.

The flames spread rapidly leaping from the bolts of cloth and finished garments hanging overhead. Efforts by the foreman and male employees to douse the fire with water were unsuccessful. The young women panicked. Escape routes proved problematic. There were hundreds in the building on these three floors. Only two elevators serviced the building and each could hold only ten persons. There was but a single fire escape. The door to the stairway on the ninth floor was locked. Women began jumping from the windows to save themselves.

When the Fire Department arrived they attempted to catch some of the falling bodies with their life net, but as the bodies hit the net they bounced and hit the concrete. The water from the fire hoses reached only to the seventh floor. The ladders extended only as far as a point between the sixth and seventh floors. Once the firemen entered the building, the fire was easily controlled. The building itself was fireproof.

One hundred forty-six employees, most of them young women, died in that fire. The company's owners were acquitted of charges of wrongdoing. A civil suit brought by twenty-three families against the owners resulted in recoveries of approximately $75 each.

Public outrage over the fire resulted in the appointment of a commission to investigate conditions in the city's sweatshops. The Commission was headed by Senator Robert F. Wagner, and included later to be governor and presidential candidate Alfred E. Smith and the founder of the American Federation of Labor, Samuel Gompers. The recommendations of the Commission led to changes in the states' labor laws protecting the health and safety of workers. Between 1911 and 1914 alone, thirty-six new laws aimed at reforming labor conditions were enacted.

The building where the fire occurred remains standing today. It is now a part of New York University.[13]

views about correct economic theory. He stated that one could only conclude that liberty was violated when "rational and fair men necessarily would admit that the statute . . . would infringe fundamental principles as they had been understood by the traditions of our people and our law."[14]

LOCHNER v. NEW YORK
198 U.S. 45 (1905)

Justice PECKHAM delivered the opinion of the Court.

The indictment, it will be seen, charges that the plaintiff . . . violated [the statute], in that he wrongfully and unlawfully required and permitted an employee [sic] working for him to work more than sixty hours in one week. There is nothing in any of the opinions delivered in this case, . . . which construes the section, in using the word "required," as referring to any physical force being used to obtain the labor of an employee. It is assumed that the word means nothing more than the requirement arising from voluntary contract for such labor in excess of the number of hours specified in the statute. There is no pretense in any of the opinions that the statute was intended to meet a case of involuntary labor in any form. All the opinions assume that there is no real distinction, so far as this question is concerned, between the words "required" and "permitted." The mandate of the statute that "no employee shall be required or permitted to work," is the substantial equivalent of an enactment that "no employee shall contract or agree to work," more than ten hours per day, and as there is no provision for special emergencies the statute is mandatory in all cases. It is not an act merely fixing the number of hours which shall constitute a legal day's work, but an absolute prohibition upon the employer, permitting, under circumstances more than ten hours work to be done in his establishment. The employee may desire to earn the extra money, which would arise from his working more than the prescribed time, but this statute forbids the employer from permitting the employee to earn it.

The statute necessarily interferes with the right of contract between the employer and employees, concerning the number of hours in which the latter may labor in the bakery of the employer. The general right to make a contract in relation to his business is part of the liberty of the individual by the Fourteenth Amendment of the Federal Constitution. Under that provision, no State can deprive any person of life, liberty or property without due process of law. The right to purchase or to sell labor is part of the liberty protected by this amendment, unless there are circumstances which exclude the right. There are, however, certain powers, existing in the sovereignty of each State in the Union, somewhat vaguely termed police powers, the exact description and limitation of which have not been attempted by the courts. Those powers, broadly stated and without, at present, any attempt at a more specific limitation, relate to the safety, health, morals and general welfare of the public. Both property and liberty are held on such reasonable conditions as may be imposed by the governing power of the State in the exercise of those powers, and with such conditions the Fourteenth Amendment was not designed to interfere.

The State, therefore, has power to prevent the individual from making certain kinds of contracts, and in regard to them the Federal Constitution offers no protection. If the contract be one which the State, in the legitimate exercise of its police power, has the right to prohibit, it is not prevented from prohibiting it by the Fourteenth Amendment.

This court has recognized the existence and upheld the exercise of the police powers of the States in many cases which might fairly be considered as border ones, and it has, in the course of its determination of questions regarding the asserted invalidity of such statutes, on the ground of their violation of the rights secured by the Federal Constitution, been guided by rules of a very liberal nature, the application of which has resulted, in numerous instances, in upholding the validity of state statutes thus assailed.

It must, of course, be conceded that there is a limit to the valid exercise of the police power by the State. There is no dispute concerning this general proposition. Otherwise the Fourteenth Amendment would have no efficacy and the

Continued

legislatures of the States would have unbounded power, and it would be enough to say that any piece of legislation was enacted to conserve the morals, the health or the safety of the people; such legislation would be valid, no matter how absolutely without foundation the claim might be. The claim of the police power would be a mere pretext—become another and delusive name for the supreme sovereignty of the State to be exercised free from constitutional restraint. This is not contended for. In every case that comes before this court, therefore, where legislation of this character is concerned and where the protection of the Federal Constitution is sought, the question necessarily arises: Is this a fair, reasonable and appropriate exercise of the police power of the State, or is it an unreasonable, unnecessary and arbitrary interference with the right of the individual to his personal liberty, or to enter into those contracts in relation to labor which may seem to him appropriate or necessary for the support of himself and his family? Of course the liberty of contract relating to labor includes both parties to it. The one has as much right to purchase as the other to sell labor.

The question whether this act is valid as a labor law, pure and simple, may be dismissed in a few words. There is no reasonable ground for interfering with the liberty of person or the right of free contract, by determining the hours of labor, in the occupation of a baker. There is no contention that bakers as a class are not equal in intelligence and capacity to men in other trades or manual occupations, or that they are not able to assert their rights and care for themselves without the protecting arm of the State, interfering with their independence of judgment and of action. They are in no sense wards of the State. Viewed in the light of a purely labor law, with no reference whatever, to the question of health, we think that a law like the one before us involves neither the safety, the morals nor the welfare of the public, and that the interest of the public is not in the slightest degree affected by such an act. The law must be upheld, if at all, as a law pertaining to the health of the individual engaged in the occupation of a baker. It does not affect any other portion of the public than those who are engaged in that occupation. Clean and wholesome bread does not depend upon whether the baker works but ten hours per day or only sixty hours a week. The limitation of the hours of labor does not come within the police power on that ground.

It is a question of which of two powers or rights shall prevail—the power of the State to legislate or the right of the individual to liberty of person and freedom of contract. The mere assertion that the subject relates though but in a remote degree to the public health does not necessarily render the enactment valid. The act must have a more direct relation, as a means to an end, and the end itself must be appropriate and legitimate, before an act can be held to be valid which interferes with the general right of an individual to be free in his person and in his power to contract in relation to his own labor.

We think the limit of the police power has been reached and passed in this case. There is, in our judgment, no reasonable foundation for holding this to be necessary or appropriate as a health law, to safeguard the public health or the health of the individuals who are following the trade of a baker. If this statute be valid, and if, therefore, a proper case is made out in which to deny the right of an individual, . . . as employer or employee, to make contracts for the labor of the latter, under the protection of the provisions of the Federal Constitution, there would seem to be no length to which legislation of this nature might not go.

We think that there can be no fair doubt that the trade of a baker, in and of itself, is not an unhealthy one to that degree which would authorize the legislature to interfere with the right to labor, and with the right of free contract on the part of the individual, either as employer or employee.

It is also urged, pursuing the same line of argument, that it is to the interest of the State, that its population should be strong and robust, and therefore any legislation which may be said to tend to make people healthy must be valid as health laws, enacted under the police power. If this be a valid argument and a justification for this kind of legislation, it follows that the protection of the Federal Constitution from undue interference with liberty of person and freedom of contract is visionary, wherever the law is sought to be justified as a valid exercise of the police power. Scarcely any law but might find shelter under such assumptions, and conduct, properly so called, as well as contract, would come under the restrictive sway of the legislature. [W]e think that such a law as this, although passed in the assumed exercise of the police power, and as relating to the public health, or

Continued

the health of the employees named, is not within that power, and is invalid. The act is not, within any fair meaning of the term, a health law, but is an illegal interference with the rights of individuals, both employers and employees, to make contracts regarding labor upon such terms as they may think best, or which they may agree upon with the other parties to such contracts.

It was further urged on the argument that restricting the hours of labor in the case of bakers was valid because it tended to cleanliness on the part of the workers, as a man was more apt to be cleanly when not overworked, and if cleanly then his "output" was also more likely to be so. What has already been said applies with equal force to this contention. We do not admit the reasoning to be sufficient to justify the claimed right of such interference. The interference on the part of the legislatures of the several States with the ordinary trades and occupations of the people seems to be on the increase.

It is impossible for us to shut our eyes to the fact that many of the laws of this character, while passed under what is claimed to be the police power for the purpose of protecting the public health or welfare, are, in reality, passed from other motives. We are justified in saying so when, from the character of the law and the subject upon which it legislates, it is apparent that the public health or welfare bears but the most remote relation to the law. The purpose of a statute must be determined from the natural and legal effect of the language employed; and whether it is or is not repugnant to the Constitution of the United States must be determined from the natural effect of such statutes when put into operation and not from their proclaimed purpose.

It is manifest to us that the limitation of the hours of labor as provided for in this section of the statute . . . has no such direct relation to and no such substantial effect upon the health of the employee, as to justify us in regarding the section as really a health law. It seems to us that the real object and purpose were simply to regulate the hours of labor between the master and his employees . . . in a private business, not dangerous in any degree to morals or in any real and substantial degree, to the health of employees. Under such circumstances the freedom of master and employee to contract with each other in relation to their employment, and in defining the same, cannot be prohibited or interfered with, without violating the Federal Constitution.

Reversed.

Justice HARLAN, with whom Justice WHITE and Justice DAY concurred, dissenting.

While this court has not attempted to mark the precise boundaries of what is called the police power of the State, the existence of the power has been uniformly recognized, both by Federal and state courts.

All the cases agree that this power extends at least to the protection of the lives, the health and the safety of the public against the injurious exercise by any citizen of his own rights.

Speaking generally, the State in the exercise of its powers may not unduly interfere with the right of the citizen to enter into contracts that may be necessary and essential in the enjoyment of the inherent rights belonging to every one, among which rights is the right "to be free in the enjoyment of all his faculties, to be free to use them in all lawful ways; to live and work where he will; to earn his livelihood by any lawful calling; to pursue any livelihood or avocation." But . . . it was conceded that the right to contract in relation to persons and property or to do business, within a State, may be "regulated and sometimes prohibited, when the contracts or business conflict with the policy of the State as contained in its statutes."

I take it to be firmly established that what is called the liberty of contract may, within certain limits, be subjected to regulations designed and calculated to promote the general welfare or to guard the public health, the public morals or the public safety. "The liberty secured by the Constitution of the United States to every person within its jurisdiction does not import," this court has recently said, "an absolute right in each person to be, at all times and in all circumstances, wholly freed from restraint. There are manifold restraints to which every person is necessarily subject for the common good."

Granting then that there is a liberty of contract which cannot be violated even under the sanction of direct legislative enactment, but assuming, as according to settled law we may assume, that such liberty of contract is subject to such regulations as the State may reasonably prescribe for the common good and the well-being of society, what are the conditions under which the judiciary may declare such regulations to be in excess of legislative authority and void? Upon this point there is no room for dispute; for, the

Continued

rule is universal that a legislative enactment, Federal or state, is never to be disregarded or held invalid unless it be, beyond question, plainly and palpably in excess of legislative power.

It is plain that this statute was enacted in order to protect the physical well-being of those who work in bakery and confectionery establishments. Under our systems of government the courts are not concerned with the wisdom or policy of legislation. So that in determining the question of power to interfere with liberty of contract, the court may inquire whether the means devised by the State are germane to any end which may be lawfully accomplished and have a real or substantial relation to the protection of health, as involved in the daily work of the persons, male and female, engaged in bakery and confectionery establishments. But when this inquiry is entered upon I find it impossible, in view of common experience, to say that there is here no real or substantial relation between the means employed by the State and the end sought to be accomplished by its legislation. Nor can I say that the statute has no appropriate or direct connection with that protection to health which each State owes to her citizens, or that it is not promotive of the health of the employees in question, or that the regulation prescribed by the State is utterly unreasonable and extravagant or wholly arbitrary.

It is enough for the determination of this case, and it is enough for this court to know, that the question is one about which there is room for debate and for an honest difference of opinion. There are many reasons of a weighty, substantial character, based upon the experience of mankind, in support of the theory that, all things considered, more than ten hours' steady work each day, from week to week, in a bakery or confectionery establishment, may endanger the health, and shorten the lives of the workmen, thereby diminishing their physical and mental capacity to serve the State, and to provide for those dependent upon them.

If such reasons exist that ought to be the end of this case, for the State is not amenable to the judiciary, in respect of its legislative enactments, unless such enactments are plainly, palpably, beyond all question, inconsistent with the Constitution of the United States.

Justice HOLMES dissenting.

This case is decided upon an economic theory which a large part of the country does not entertain. If it were a question whether I agreed with that theory I should desire to study it further and long before making up my mind. But I do not conceive that to be my duty, because I strongly believe that my agreement or disagreement has nothing to do with the right of a majority to embody their opinions in law. It is settled by various decisions of this court that state constitutions and state laws may regulate life in many ways which we as legislators might think as injudicious or if you like as tyrannical as this, and which equally with this interfere with the liberty to contract. Sunday laws and usury laws are ancient examples. A more modern one is the prohibition of lotteries. The liberty of the citizen to do as he likes so long as he does not interfere with the liberty of others to do the same, which has been a shibboleth for some well-known writers, is interfered with by school laws, by the Post Office, by every state or municipal institution which takes his money for purposes thought desirable, whether he likes it or not. The Fourteenth Amendment does not enact Mr. Herbert Spencer's Social Statics. It is made for people of fundamentally differing views, and the accident of our finding certain opinions natural and familiar or novel and even shocking ought not to conclude our judgment upon the question whether statutes embodying them conflict with the Constitution of the United States.

General propositions do not decide concrete cases. The decision will depend on a judgment or intuition more subtle than any articulate major premise. But I think that the proposition just stated, if it is accepted, will carry us far toward the end. Every opinion tends to become a law. I think that the word liberty in the Fourteenth Amendment is perverted when it is held to prevent the natural outcome of a dominant opinion, unless it can be said that a rational and fair man necessarily would admit that the statute proposed would infringe fundamental principles as they have been understood by the traditions of our people and our law. It does not need research to show that no such sweeping condemnation can be passed upon the statute before us. A reasonable man might think it a proper measure on the score of health. Men whom I certainly could not pronounce unreasonable would uphold it as a first installment of a general regulation of the hours of work. Whether in the latter aspect it would be open to the charge of inequality I think it unnecessary to discuss.

During this early period there was widespread invalidation of economic legislation on substantive due process grounds. All such legislation, however, was not overturned. The Court allowed legislation regulating hours where it found the need for special protection beyond that given to workers in general. For example, in *Muller v. Oregon*,[15] legislation barring women from more than 10 hours per day of employment in factories or laundries was sustained. Women were considered as a class "disadvantage[d] in the struggle for subsistence."[16] Accordingly, they were in need of special protection. Such legislation made to protect women made it harder for them to care for themselves and their children. At the same time, the Court struck down a minimum wage law for women relying on freedom to contract in *Adkins v. Children's Hospital*.[17] The two cases can be reconciled by considering the maximum hours rules in *Muller* as promoting a legitimate health objective, while the minimum wage law in *Adkins* is hard to consider as promoting anything other than a lessening of economic inequality, of which the Court had disapproved. This early reluctance to intervene would change with time.

Substantive Due Process—The Later Years

In the 30 years following *Lochner,* its philosophy and holding were subject to much criticism. With the election of Franklin Roosevelt, in the middle of the Depression, the country saw a need for legislative programs to ensure economic survival. Both the court-packing plan[18] and the turnover in Court personnel had an impact on the change from the *Lochner* doctrine to one of greater deference toward legislative intervention in economic affairs. The conditions also seemed to call for government involvement since the laissez-faire policy was called into question by the state of the economy.

In 1934, the Court upheld a state regulatory scheme for fixing the price of milk in *Nebbia v. New York*.[19] Although the Court did not explicitly reject *Lochner* it stated that the states were free "to adopt whatever economic policy may reasonably be deemed to promote public welfare, and to enforce that policy by legislation adapted to its purpose."[20] The test did not differ substantially from that in *Lochner,* but the Court made it clear that it would not impose its views about correct economic policy as it had in *Lochner.*

Not long after, the Court abandoned the degree of scrutiny imposed in *Nebbia* and *Lochner* in the case of *West Coast Hotel v. Parrish*.[21] The following year the Court made it clear that a presumption of constitutionality applied in the case of economic regulation subjected to due process attack. *U.S. v. Carolene Products Company*[22] sustained the federal prohibition on interstate shipment of milk. Congress had acted on findings of fact that demonstrated there was a public health danger. The Court ruled that even if there were no explicit findings by the legislature it must be presumed that there are facts supporting the legislature's judgment to regulate. This standard has led the Court to hypothesize reasons for supporting legislative decisions even when there was no evidence of reasons on the record. This is very different from the earlier position requiring the legislature to specifically set out its purpose in order for the statute or regulation to be upheld by the Court. In *Williamson v. Lee Optical Co.*,[23] the Court upheld a statute that prevented opticians from fitting lenses into frames in the absence of ophthalmologists' prescriptions. The Court found this to be a rational health measure because the legislature "might have concluded" that this was sometimes necessary. This sort of hypothesizing by the Court consequently put the burden on those challenging a regulation. It was necessary for them not only to rebut the reasons given by the legislature but also all those which the legislature "might have" considered. This made it difficult to succeed in a challenge because some reasons might not become clear until after the Court issued its opinion.

The degree of scrutiny was reduced even further in *Ferguson v. Skrupa*.[24] At issue was a Kansas law that prohibited nonlawyers from engaging in debt adjustment. The statute was upheld in an opinion by Justice Black. He stated that the Court had "abandoned the use of 'vague contours' of the Due Process Clause to nullify laws which the majority of the Court believed to be economically unwise."[25] In addition, he claimed that the Court would no longer sit as a "superlegislature."[26] Aside from these statements, virtually no reason for the decision was provided. This deference to the legislative authorities has continued.

Under the modern approach, the Court almost never reviews state economic regulations for substantive due process violations. The standard currently being applied in cases challenging economic regulation by the state can be considered one of minimum rationality. If the legislative goal falls within the state's police power then the state must demonstrate that there is a minimal relationship between the goal and the means of achieving it that is rational. There is a presumption of constitutionality unless it is shown that the regulation was enacted in an arbitrary and irrational way. Moreover, the Court today defines the state police power broadly. It includes essentially all health, safety, and/or general welfare goals.

The same standard that is applied to economic regulation is also used in social welfare cases. The standard, however, will not be employed if a fundamental constitutional right is impinged upon by the legislation. In such cases a significantly higher level of scrutiny is employed. Thus, when reviewing the constitutionality of state economic regulations for due process violations, the Court employs the rational relationship/basis test.

PROCEDURAL DUE PROCESS

Also contained within the provisions of the Fifth and Fourteenth Amendments is the requirement that government provide citizens with a fair procedure before depriving them of "life, liberty, or property." The requirement of due process applies only in situations where the government is intervening in a citizen's life, liberty, or property. Procedural irregularities are not unconstitutional in other situations. The government must be taking away one of these three for procedural due process to be necessary. Hence, when life, liberty, or property is not involved, the government may act in an arbitrary or unfair manner. As a result, the concern here is in those interests the Court has found to implicate liberty or property interests.

Liberty and Property Interests

Life is implicated only in rare instances—usually in capital punishment cases. Because our interest in life is so paramount, it would be difficult to argue that the government should not require procedural correctness. The particular procedural necessities associated with these cases have developed over time and a discussion of them is more appropriate to a text on criminal procedure. Here, the main interest is in the Court's varying definitions of liberty and property over time. These changes, too, will be considered in their historical context. Then, the question becomes, what procedure is due; what must the government do to ensure that the procedure is fair?

In issues of procedural due process there must be discrimination against an individual as opposed to the situation with substantive due process that concerns the state's objective. Before 1970, the Court broadly construed liberty and property interests. The view of what was included in liberty was

> not merely freedom from bodily restraint but also the right of the individual to contract, to engage in any of the common occupations of life, to acquire useful knowledge, to marry, establish a home and bring up children [and] to worship God according to the dictates of . . . conscience.[27]

During this period, however, the Court was unlikely to find that liberty or property interests existed in benefits flowing from the public sector, particularly government employment and benefits. In this area, the Court considered them as privileges rather than rights and, therefore, found they were not subject to procedural correctness. Nevertheless, privileges could not be taken for reasons that violated other constitutional protections. For example, one could not be discharged from government employment or be denied benefits for exercising First Amendment free speech and religion rights. In the 1970s the Court moved away from this stance and began to include government employment and benefits as rights subject to the requirement of due process.

Throughout the 1970s the Court offered numerous contradictory opinions regarding the scope of **entitlements**. Entitlements were expanded and contracted during that decade. This jurisprudence is best exemplified in the cases of *Board of Regents v. Roth*[28] and its companion case, *Perry v. Sinderman*.[29]

Roth brought suit against the Wisconsin Board of Regents when, after serving out a one-year nontenured contract at Wisconsin State University, the school declined to rehire him. No reasons were provided for the decision and the state law required none. Stressing that the importance of Roth's interest was not relevant, the Court maintained that the nature of the interest was the concern. Accordingly, the Court concluded that Roth's interest in being retained did not fall within the definition of liberty and property encompassed in the right to due process.

The Court reasoned that the state's decision did not damage Roth's reputation as no reasons for the decision were given, and he could obtain employment in other state institutions. Thus, the interest at stake did not amount to a liberty interest. If Roth sustained either damage to his reputation, or if he was barred from a broader category of employment, then, the Court claimed, Roth would have been entitled to procedural due process.

The Court also rejected Roth's claim that a property interest was involved. The Court found that Roth's interest in being retained did not constitute a property interest simply because he had a "need" for the job or a "unilateral expectation" of the job. Rather, an individual must have a "legitimate claim of entitlement" to be rehired in order for it to fall within the protection of procedural due process. Determination of whether one had a legitimate claim of entitlement was to be made in reference to state law. In light of the Wisconsin statute, which clearly indicated that nontenured hiring decisions were discretionary, Roth had no such claim of entitlement. The Court stated that one's interest must already have been acquired before procedural due process rights attach.

In *Perry v. Sinderman,* the Court espoused a contrary view. There, the court indicated that informal practices or customs may be sufficient to create a legitimate claim of entitlement to a benefit. *Perry* also concerned the rights of an untenured faculty member, but in this case he had taught for 10 years. The instructor maintained that the college had a **de facto** tenure program. Thus, he claimed that the administration created an understanding that he had tenure under this program. The Court found the instructor was entitled to a hearing on his claim of de facto tenure. If his claim were proven, he would be considered to have a property interest in being retained with the benefits of tenure.

In *Paul v. Davis,*[30] the Court narrowed the definition of liberty interest. The case emerged as the result of an arrest for shoplifting. Following the arrest, the individual's name was added to a flyer the police circulated to hundreds of local merchants advising them of active shoplifters. Once the charges were dropped, the individual sued the police under a federal statute permitting recovery from public officials for violations of constitutional rights. The Court held that his interest in his reputation alone did not amount to a protected liberty or property interest protected by procedural due process. The dissenters argued that this definition departed from precedent.

entitlement absolute (complete) right to something (such as Social Security) once you show that you meet the legal requirements to get it.

de facto (Latin) in fact, actual; a situation that exists in fact whether or not it is lawful.

If the holding in *Paul* is taken literally, it apparently limits those interests that are protected to:

1. Those guaranteed by specific provisions of the Constitution and
2. Interest in not being subjected to state conduct that infringes a freedom other than privacy.

The retreat from broad definitions of liberty and property has not encompassed all issues or contexts. For example, the Court has held that suspension from public school constitutes a deprivation of a constitutionally protected property interest.[31] Such decisions make it clear that the breadth of the Court's definition of what constitutes a protected interest varies with the context within which the issue arises.

In *Lawrence v. Texas*,[32] the Court struck down a Texas law criminalizing sodomy between individuals of the same sex. The Court reconsidered whether homosexuals had a liberty interest in their private sexual conduct. In an earlier case, *Bowers v. Hardwick*[33] (which is discussed *infra*, in Chapter 9), the Court framed a similar challenge to a Georgia statute that was applicable to both homosexuals and heterosexuals as "whether the Federal Constitution confers a fundamental right upon homosexuals to engage in sodomy . . ."[34] The Court in *Bowers* said no.[35] The Court in *Lawrence* reframed the question and declared that the *Bowers* Court failed "to appreciate the extent of the liberty at stake."[36]

In *Lawrence*, Justice Kennedy, writing for the majority, cited a line of cases in which the Court found that there was a liberty interest in privacy to be protected by the Due Process Clause, with regard to reproduction and sexual relations. Rejecting the historical basis upon which *Bowers* relied, the Court, in a rare incidence of overturning precedent, noted that *Bowers* had been wrongly decided.[37] The Court clearly stated that the petitioners' "right to liberty under the Due Process Clause gives them the full right to engage in their conduct without the intervention of the government." "'It is a promise of the constitution that there is a realm of personal liberty which the government may not enter.'"[38] Accordingly, the Court found that the state had no legitimate interest sufficient to allow intervention into this aspect of citizens' private lives, including private sexual conduct between consenting adults. This was a liberty interest protected by the Constitution.

LAWRENCE V. TEXAS
539 U.S. 558 (2003)

Justice KENNEDY for the Court.

Liberty protects the person from unwarranted government intrusions into a dwelling or other private places. In our tradition, the State is not omnipresent in the home. And there are other spheres of our lives and existence, outside the home, where the State should not be a dominant presence. Freedom extends beyond spatial bounds. Liberty presumes an autonomy of self that includes freedom of thought, belief, expression, and certain intimate conduct. The instant case involves liberty of the person both in its spatial and more transcendent dimensions.

I

The question before the court is the validity of a Texas statute making it a crime for two persons of the same sex to engage in certain intimate sexual conduct.

We granted certiorari . . . to consider three questions:

"1. Whether Petitioners' criminal convictions under the Texas . . . law—which criminalizes sexual intimacy by same-sex couples, but not identical behavior by different-sex couples—violate the Fourteenth Amendment guarantee of equal protection of laws?

Continued

"2. Whether Petitioners' criminal convictions for adult consensual sexual intimacy in the home violate their vital interests in liberty and privacy protected by the Due Process Clause of the Fourteenth Amendment?

"3. Whether *Bowers v. Hardwick* should be overruled?"

The petitioners were adults at the time of the alleged offense. Their conduct was in private and consensual.

II

We conclude the case should be resolved by determining whether the petitioners were free as adults to engage in the private conduct, in the exercise of their liberty under the Due Process Clause of the Fourteenth Amendment to the Constitution.

There are broad statements of the substantive reach of liberty under the Due Process Clause in earlier cases, . . . but the most pertinent beginning point is our decision in *Griswold v. Connecticut.*

After *Griswold* it was established that the right to make certain decisions regarding sexual conduct extends beyond the marital relationship.

[The cases that followed] confirmed that the reasoning of *Griswold* could not be confined to the protection of rights of married adults. This was the state of the law with respect to some of the most relevant cases when the Court considered *Bowers v. Hardwick.*

The facts in *Bowers* had some similarities to the instant case.

The Court began its substantive discussion in *Bowers* as follows: "The issue presented is whether the Federal Constitution confers a fundamental right upon homosexuals to engage in sodomy and hence invalidates the laws of the many States that still make such conduct illegal and have done so for a very long time." That statement, we now conclude discloses the Court's own failure to appreciate the extent of the liberty at stake. To say that the issue in *Bowers* was simply the right to engage in certain sexual conduct demeans the claim the individual put forward, just as it would demean a married couple were it to be said marriage is simply about the right to have sexual intercourse. The laws involved in *Bowers* and here are, to be sure, statutes that purport to do no more than prohibit a particular sexual act. Their penalties and purposes, though, have more far-reaching

consequences, touching upon the most private human conduct, sexual behavior, and in the most private of places, the home. The statutes do seek to control a personal relationship that, whether or not entitled to formal recognition in the law, is within the liberty of persons to choose without being punished as criminals.

It suffices for us to acknowledge that adults may choose to enter upon this relationship in the confines of their homes and their own private lives and still retain their dignity as free persons. When sexuality finds overt expression in intimate conduct with another person, the conduct can be but one element in a personal bond that is more enduring. The liberty protected by the Constitution allows homosexual persons the right to make this choice.

[I]t should be noted that there is no long-standing history in this country of laws directed at homosexual conduct as a distinct matter. [E]arly American sodomy laws were not directed at homosexuals as such but instead sought to prohibit non-procreative sexual activity more generally. This does not suggest approval of homosexual conduct. It does tend to show that this particular form of conduct was not thought of as a separate category from like conduct between heterosexual persons.

It was not until the 1970's that any State singled our same-sex relations for criminal prosecution, and only nine States have done so. Post-*Bowers* even some of these States did not adhere to the policy of suppressing homosexual conduct. Over the course of the last decades, States with same-sex prohibitions have moved toward abolishing them.

In summary, the historical grounds relied upon in *Bowers* are more complex than the majority opinion and the concurring opinion . . . indicate. Their historical premises are not without doubt and, at the very least, are overstated.

It must be acknowledged, of course, that the Court in *Bowers* was making the broader point that for centuries there have been powerful voices to condemn homosexual conduct as immoral. The condemnation has been shaped by religious beliefs, conceptions of right and acceptable behavior, and respect for the traditional family. For many persons these are not trivial concerns but profound deep convictions accepted as ethical and moral principles to which they aspire and which to us determine

Continued

the course of their lives. These considerations do not answer the question before us, however. The issue is whether the majority may use the power of the State to enforce these views on the whole society through operation of the criminal law. "Our obligation is to define the liberty of all, not to mandate our own moral code."

As an alternative argument in this case, counsel for the petitioners and some *amici* contend that *Romer* provides the basis for declaring the Texas statute invalid under the Equal Protection Clause. That is a tenable argument, but we conclude the instant case requires us to address whether *Bowers* itself has continuing validity. Were we to hold the statute invalid under the Equal Protection Clause some might question whether a prohibition would be valid if drawn differently, say, to prohibit the conduct both between same-sex and different-sex participants.

Equality of treatment and the due process right to demand respect for conduct protected by the substantive guarantee of liberty are linked in important respects. If protected conduct is made criminal and the law which does so remains unexamined for its substantive validity, its stigma might remain even if it were not enforceable as drawn for equal protection reasons. When homosexual conduct is made criminal by the law of the State, that declaration in and of itself is an invitation to subject homosexual persons to discrimination both in the public and in the private spheres. The central holding of *Bowers* has been brought in question by this case, and it should be addressed. Its continuance as precedent demeans the lives of homosexual persons.

The stigma this criminal statute imposes, moreover, is not trivial. The offense, to be sure, is but a class C misdemeanor, a minor offense in the Texas legal system. Still, it remains a criminal offense with all that imports for the dignity of the persons charged. The petitioners will bear on their record the history of their criminal conviction. Just this Term we rejected various challenges to state laws requiring the registration of sex offenders. We are advised that if Texas convicted an adult for private, consensual homosexual conduct under the statute here in question the convicted person would come within the registration laws of at least four States were he or she to be subject to their jurisdiction. This underscores the consequential nature of the punishment and the state-sponsored condemnation attendant to the criminal

prohibition. Furthermore, the Texas criminal conviction carries with it the other collateral consequences always following a conviction, such as notations on job application forms, to mention but one example.

The doctrine of *stare decisis* is essential to the respect accorded to the judgments of the Court and to the stability of the law. It is not, however, an inexorable command. In *Casey* we noted that when a Court is asked to overrule a precedent recognizing a constitutional liberty interest, individual or societal reliance on the existence of that liberty cautions with particular strength against reversing course. The holding in *Bowers*, however, has not induced detrimental reliance comparable to some instances where recognized individual rights are involved. Indeed, there has been no individual or societal reliance on *Bowers* of the sort that could counsel against overturning its holding once there are compelling reasons to do so. The rationale of *Bowers* does not withstand careful analysis.

Bowers was not correct when it was decided, and it is not correct today. It ought not to remain binding precedent. *Bowers v. Hardwick* should be and now is overruled.

The present case does not involve minors. It does not involve persons who might be injured or coerced or who are situated in relationships where consent might not easily be refused. It does not involve public conduct or prostitution. It does not involve whether the government must give formal recognition to any relationship that homosexual persons seek to enter. The case does involve two adults who, with full and mutual consent from each other, engaged in sexual practices common to a homosexual lifestyle. The petitioners are entitled to respect for their private lives. The State cannot demean their existence or control their destiny by making their private sexual conduct a crime. Their right to liberty under the Due Process Clause gives them the full right to engage in their conduct without intervention of the government. "It is a promise of the Constitution that there is a realm of personal liberty which the government may not enter." The Texas statute furthers no legitimate state interest which can justify its intrusion into the personal and private life of the individual.

Had those who drew and ratified the Due Process Clauses of the Fifth Amendment or the

Continued

Fourteenth Amendment known the components of liberty in its manifold possibilities, they might have been more specific. They did not presume to have this insight. They know times can blind us to certain truths and later generations can see that laws once thought necessary and proper in fact serve only to oppress. As the Constitution endures, persons in every generation can invoke its principles in their own search for greater freedom.

The judgment of the Court of Appeals for the Texas Fourteenth District is reversed, and the case is remanded for further proceedings not inconsistent with this opinion.

Justice O'CONNOR concurring in the judgment.

The Court today overrules *Bowers v. Hardwick.* I joined *Bowers,* and do not join the Court in overruling it. Nevertheless, I agree with the Court that Texas' statute banning same-sex sodomy is unconstitutional. Rather than relying on the substantive component of the Fourteenth Amendment's Due Process Clause, as the Court does, I base my conclusion on the Fourteenth Amendment's Equal Protection Clause.

The Equal Protection Clause of the Fourteenth Amendment "is essentially a direction that all persons similarly situated should be treated alike." Under our rational basis standard of review, "legislation is presumed to be valid and will be sustained if the classification drawn by the statute is rationally related to a legitimate state interest."

We have been most likely to apply rational basis review to hold a law unconstitutional under the Equal Protection Clause where, as here, the challenged legislation inhibits personal relationships.

The statute at issue here makes sodomy a crime only if a person "engages in deviate sexual intercourse with another individual of the same sex." Sodomy between opposite-sex partners, however, is not a crime in Texas. That is, Texas treats the same conduct differently based solely on the participants. Those harmed by this law are people who have a same-sex sexual orientation and thus are more likely to engage in behavior prohibited by [the law].

The Texas statute makes homosexuals unequal in the eyes of the law by making particular conduct—and only that conduct—subject to criminal sanction.

And the effect of Texas' sodomy law is not just limited to the threat of prosecution or consequence of conviction. Texas' sodomy law brands all homosexuals as criminals, thereby making it more difficult for homosexuals to be treated in the same manner as everyone else. Indeed, Texas itself has previously acknowledged the collateral effects of the law, stipulating in a prior challenge to this action that the law "legally sanctions discrimination against [homosexuals] in a variety of ways unrelated to the criminal law," including in the areas of "employment, family issues, and housing."

Texas attempts to justify the law and the effects of the law, by arguing that the statute satisfies rational basis review because it furthers the legitimate governmental interest of the promotion of morality.

This case raises a different issue than *Bowers*: whether, under the Equal Protection Clause, moral disapproval is a legitimate state interest to justify by itself a statute that bans homosexual sodomy, but not heterosexual sodomy. It is not. Moral disapproval of this group, like a bare desire to harm the group, is an interest that is insufficient to satisfy rational basis review under the Equal Protection Clause. Indeed, we have never held that moral disapproval, without any other asserted state interest, is a sufficient rationale under the Equal Protection Clause to justify a law that discriminates among groups of persons.

Moral disapproval of a group cannot be a legitimate governmental interest under the Equal Protection Clause because legal classifications must not be "drawn for the purpose of disadvantaging the group burdened by the law."

A State can of course assign certain consequences to a violation of its criminal law. But the State cannot single out one identifiable class of citizens for punishment that does not apply to everyone else, with moral disapproval as the only asserted state interest for the law. The Texas sodomy statute subjects homosexuals to "a lifelong penalty and stigma." A legislative classification that threatens the creation of an underclass . . . cannot be reconciled with the Equal Protection Clause.

Justice SCALIA with whom THE CHIEF JUSTICE and Justice THOMAS join, dissenting.

I begin with the Court's surprising readiness to reconsider a decision rendered a mere 17 years

Continued

ago . . . I do not myself believe in rigid adherence to *stare decisis* in constitutional cases, but I do believe that we should be consistent rather than manipulative in invoking the doctrine.

Today's approach to *stare decisis* invites us to overrule an erroneously decided precedent . . . *if:* (1) its foundations have been "eroded" by subsequent decision; (2) has been subject to "substantial and continuing" criticism; and (3) it has not induced "individual or societal reliance" that counsels against overturning.

II

Having decided that it need not adhere to *stare decisis,* the Court still must establish that *Bowers* was wrongly decided and that the Texas statute, as applied to petitioners, is unconstitutional.

The Court today does not overrule this holding [in *Bowers*] that the statute is not subject to heightened scrutiny because they do not implicate a "fundamental right" Instead, having failed to establish that the right to homosexual sodomy is "deeply rooted in this Nation's history and tradition," the Court concludes that the application of Texas's statute to petitioners' conduct fails the rational-basis test, and overrule *Bowers'* holding to the contrary.

IV

I turn now to the ground on which the Court squarely rests it's holding: the contention that there is no rational basis for the law here under attack. This proposition is so out of accord with our jurisprudence—indeed, with the jurisprudence of *any* society we know—that it requires little discussion.

The Texas statute undeniably seeks to further the belief of its citizens that certain forms of sexual behavior are "immoral and unacceptable."— the same interest furthered by criminal laws against fornication, bigamy, adultery, adult incest, bestiality, and obscenity. *Bowers* held that this was a legitimate state interest. The Court today reaches the opposite conclusion. The Texas statute, it says, "furthers *no legitimate state interest* which can justify its intrusion into the personal and private life of the individual." This effectively decrees the end of all morals

legislation. If, as the Court asserts, the promotion of majoritarian sexual morality is not even a *legitimate* state interest, none of the above-mentioned laws can survive rational-basis review.

V

Let me be clear that I have nothing against homosexuals, or any other group, promoting their agenda through normal democratic means. Social perceptions of sexual and other morality change over time, and every group has the right to persuade its fellow citizens that its view of such matters is the best. That homosexuals have achieved some success in that enterprise is attested to by the fact that Texas is one of the few remaining States than criminalize private, consensual homosexual acts. But persuading one's fellow citizens is one thing, and imposing one's views in absence of democratic majority will is something else. I would no more *require* a State to criminalize homosexual acts—or, for that matter, display *any* moral disapprobation of them—than I would *forbid* it to do so. What Texas has chosen to do is well within the range of traditional democratic action, and its hand should not be stayed through the invention of a brand-new "constitutional right" by a Court that is impatient of democratic change.

Justice THOMAS, dissenting.

I write separately to note that the law before the Court today "is . . . uncommonly silly." If I were a member of the Texas Legislature, I would vote to repeal it. Punishing someone for expressing his sexual preference through noncommercial consensual conduct with another adult does not appear to be a worthy way to expend valuable law enforcement resources.

Notwithstanding this, I recognize that as a member of this Court I am not empowered to help petitioners and others similarly situated. My duty, rather, is to "decide cases 'agreeably to the Constitution and laws of the United States.'" I "can find [neither in the Bill of Rights nor any other part of the Constitution a] general right of privacy," or as the Court terms it today, the "liberty of the person both in its spatial and more transcendent dimensions."

Requisite Procedures

Let us turn now to the processes that are warranted when a protected liberty or property interest is at issue. The first of these cases was *Goldberg v. Kelly.*[39] New York City residents whose welfare benefits were cut off by the government

notice . . . Formal receipt of the knowledge of certain facts.

hearing a trial-like proceeding conducted by an administrative agency or in another noncourt setting.

brought suit, arguing that doing so without prior **notice** and a **hearing** was a violation of due process. The Court found that the recipients were entitled to an evidentiary hearing before being deprived of their benefits. The Court rejected the argument that welfare benefits were a privilege, rather than a right. Justice Brennan, writing for the 5 to 4 majority reasoned that welfare payments did not constitute charity. Instead, he stated that welfare is a "right" protected by the Constitution that could not arbitrarily be cut off. Justice Brennan noted the grievous consequences resulting from the termination of benefits as well as the benefits reaped by the State in providing welfare. Accordingly, the Court found that a predetermination hearing was necessary to meet the demands of due process.

GOLDBERG v. KELLY
397 U.S. 254 (1970)

Justice BRENNAN for the Court.

I

The constitutional issue to be decided, . . . is the narrow one whether the Due Process Clause requires that the recipient be afforded an evidentiary hearing *before* the termination of benefits. Under all the circumstances, we hold that due process requires an adequate hearing before termination of welfare benefits, and the fact that there is a later constitutionally fair proceeding does not alter the result.

Relevant constitutional restraints apply as much to the withdrawal of public assistance benefits as to disqualification for unemployment compensation; or to denial of a tax exemption; or to discharge from public employment. The extent to which procedural due process must be afforded the recipient is influenced by the extent to which he may be "condemned to suffer grievous loss," and depends upon whether the recipient's interest in avoiding that loss outweighs the governmental interest in summary adjudication. Accordingly, . . . "consideration of what procedures due process may require under any given set of circumstances must begin with a determination of the precise nature of the government function involved as well as of the private interest that has been affected by governmental action."

For qualified recipients, welfare provides the means to obtain essential food, clothing, housing, and medical care. Thus the crucial factor in this context—is a factor not present in the case of the blacklisted government contractor, the discharged government employee, the taxpayer

denied a tax exemption, or virtually anyone else whose governmental entitlements are ended—is that termination of aid pending resolution of a controversy over eligibility may deprive an *eligible* recipient of the very means by which to live while he waits. Since he lacks independent resources, his situation becomes immediately desperate. His need to concentrate upon finding the means for daily subsistence, in turn, adversely affects his ability to seek redress from the welfare bureaucracy.

Moreover, important governmental interests are promoted by affording recipients a pre-termination evidentiary hearing. From its founding the Nation's basic commitment has been to foster the dignity and well-being of all persons within its borders. We have come to recognize that forces not within the control of the poor contribute to their poverty. This perception, against the background of our traditions, has significantly influenced the development of the contemporary public assistance system. Welfare, by meeting the basic demands of subsistence, can help bring within the reach of the poor the same opportunities that are available to others to participate meaningfully in the life of the community. At the same time, welfare guards against the societal malaise that may flow from a widespread sense of unjustified frustration and insecurity. Public assistance, then, is not mere charity, but a means to "promote the general Welfare, and secure the Blessings of Liberty to ourselves and our Posterity." The same governmental interests that counsel the provision of welfare, counsel as well its uninterrupted provision to those eligible to receive it; pre-termination evidentiary hearings are indispensable to that end.

Continued

Appellant does not challenge the force of these considerations but argues that they are outweighed by countervailing governmental interests in conserving fiscal and administrative resources. These interests, the argument goes, justify the delay of any evidentiary hearing until after discontinuance of the grants. Summary adjudication protects the public fisc by stopping payments promptly upon discovery of reason to believe that a recipient is no longer eligible. Since most terminations are accepted without challenge, summary adjudication also conserves both the fisc and administrative time and energy by reducing the number of evidentiary hearings actually held.

We agree with the District Court, however, that these governmental interests are not overriding in the welfare context. The requirement of a prior hearing doubtless involves some greater expense, and the benefits paid to ineligible recipients pending decision at the hearing probably cannot be recouped, since these recipients are likely to be judgment-proof. But the State is not without weapons to minimize these increased costs. Much of the drain on fiscal and administrative resources can be reduced by developing procedures for prompt pre-termination hearings and by skillful use of personnel and facilities. Indeed, the very provision for a post-termination evidentiary hearing in New York's Home Relief program is itself cogent evidence that the State recognizes the primacy of the public interest in correct eligibility determinations and therefore in the provision of procedural safeguards. Thus, the interest of the eligible recipient in uninterrupted public assistance, coupled with the State's interest that his payments not be erroneously terminated, clearly outweighs the State's competing concern to prevent any increase in its fiscal and administrative burdens. As the District Court correctly concluded, "the stakes are simply too high for the welfare recipient, and the possibility for honest error or irritable misjudgment too great, to allow termination of aid without giving the recipient a chance, if he so desires, to be fully informed of the case against him so that he may contest its basis and produce evidence in rebuttal."

II

We also agree with the District Court, however, that the pre-termination hearing need not take the form of a judicial or quasi-judicial trial. We bear in mind that the statutory "fair hearing" will provide the recipient with a full administrative review. Accordingly, the pre-termination hearing has one function only: to produce an initial determination of the validity of the welfare department's ground for discontinuance of payments in order to protect a recipient against an erroneous termination of his benefits. Thus, a complete record and a comprehensive opinion, which would serve primarily to facilitate judicial review and to guide future decisions, need not be provided at the pre-termination stage. We recognize, too, that both welfare authorities and recipients have an interest in relatively speedy resolution of questions of eligibility, that they are used to dealing with one another informally, and that some welfare departments have very burdensome caseloads. These considerations justify the limitation of the pre-termination hearing to minimum procedural safeguards, adapted to the particular characteristics of welfare recipients, and to the limited nature of the controversies to be resolved. We wish to add that we, no less than the dissenters, recognize the importance of not imposing upon the States or the Federal Government in this developing field of law any procedural requirements beyond those demanded by rudimentary due process.

"The fundamental requisite of due process of law is the opportunity to be heard." The hearing must be "at a meaningful time and in a meaningful manner." In the present context these principles require that a recipient have timely and adequate notice detailing the reasons for a proposed termination, and an effective opportunity to defend by confronting any adverse witnesses and by presenting his own arguments and evidence orally. These rights are important in cases such as those before us, where recipients have challenged proposed terminations as resting on incorrect or misleading factual premises or in misapplication of rules or policies to the facts of particular cases.

The opportunity to be heard must be tailored to the capacities and circumstances of those who are to be heard. Written submissions are an unrealistic option for most recipients, who lack the educational attainment necessary to write effectively and who cannot obtain professional assistance. [W]ritten submissions do not afford the flexibility of oral presentations. Particularly where credibility and veracity are at issue, as they must be in many termination proceedings, written submissions are a wholly unsatisfactory

Continued

basis for decision. Therefore a recipient must be allowed to state his position orally. Informal procedures will suffice, in this context due process does not require a particular order of proof or mode of offering evidence.

In almost every setting where important decisions turn on questions of fact, due process requires an opportunity to confront and cross-examine the witnesses relied on by the department.

"The right to be heard would be, in many cases, of little avail if it did not comprehend the right to be heard by counsel." We do not say that counsel must be provided at the pre-termination hearing, but only that the recipient must be allowed to retain an attorney if he so desires.

Finally, the decision maker's conclusion as to a recipient's eligibility must rest solely on the legal rules and evidence adduced at the hearing. To demonstrate compliance with this elementary requirement, the decision maker should state the reasons for his determination and indicate the evidence he relied on, though his statement need not amount to a full opinion or even formal findings of fact and conclusions of law. And, of course, an impartial decision maker is essential. We agree with the District Court that prior involvement in some aspects of a case will not necessarily bar a welfare official from acting as a decision maker. He should not, however, have participated in making the determination under review.

As the 1970s progressed, however, the Court began to move away from this broad conception of procedural protections.

The Court now engages in a balancing test to define exactly what procedural protections are warranted by due process. The test was first enunciated in *Matthews v. Eldridge*.[40]

The case concerned the termination of disability benefits and the Court ruled that benefits could be terminated without an evidentiary hearing. This was different from the conclusion in *Goldberg*. In setting forth the test, the Court enumerated the factors to be balanced. On the one hand the factors worthy of consideration included:

(1) the strength of the interest affected by the official action and
(2) "the risk of erroneous deprivation of such interest through the procedures used and the probable value, if any, of additional or substitute procedural safeguards."[41]

There was an implication that these considerations should be factored together in some way. And, on the other hand, there is the government interest that includes the function involved as well as the monetary and administrative costs and burdens entailed by additional or substitute requirements.

After setting out the balancing test, the Court applied it to the facts and circumstances in *Matthews*. The Court distinguished the disability benefits at issue here from the welfare payments in *Goldberg*, finding that the disability payments were less likely to be the only source of income. Therefore, there was less at stake for the petitioner in *Matthews*. It was also found that an evidentiary hearing was of less value than it was in *Goldberg*. The Court reasoned that because the concern was with petitioner's physical and mental condition, the evaluation of his condition could be made with written documents rather than through oral testimony, as was the case in *Goldberg*. Finally, the burden of a full administrative hearing was likely to be costly, thereby decreasing the resources available for social welfare programs. This balancing of interests led the Court to its conclusion that no hearing is required prior to termination of disability benefits.

The same balancing test used in *Matthews* was made applicable to one's interest in retaining a public sector job in *Cleveland Board of Education v. Loudermilk*.[42] When the Court balanced the interest of a tenured employee in retaining his position against the government's interest in having a quick way to fire unsatisfactory workers, the Court also considered the "risk of erroneous termination."[43] The Court concluded that some sort of hearing was necessary prior to firing a public employee but all the hearing need consist of was "oral or written notice of the charges against him, an explanation of the employer's evidence, and an opportunity to present his side of the story."[44] It was not required that the full panoply of procedures set forth in *Goldberg* be applied. The Court determined that a full adversarial hearing would "intrude to an unwarranted extent on the government's interest in quickly removing an unsatisfactory employee."[45]

The question of what procedure is due has been raised often in cases involving public education. In these cases, the Court has found that:

(1) Suspension for nontrivial amounts of time requires oral and written notice of the charges, an explanation;[46]

(2) No hearing is necessary when a student is dismissed for academic reasons;[47] and

(3) Use of corporal punishment in public schools does not require notice and an opportunity to be heard prior to infliction of the punishment.[48]

It is also clear, when one looks at the Court's decisions in the area of procedural due process, the main concern is in preventing erroneous decisions. It should be remembered, however, that procedural safeguards are an end in themselves and not only a way to arrive at correct decisions. The underlying value of fairness underscores this point.

EQUAL PROTECTION

The Fourteenth Amendment, in addition to guaranteeing that the states provide due process, also provides that "[n]o State shall make or enforce any law which shall . . . deny to any person within its jurisdiction the equal protection of the laws."[49] The underlying goal of the Equal Protection Clause was to ensure equal treatment for former slaves. Despite this underlying reason, the courts have interpreted the clause as a restraint on the use of classifications in government regulation.

The Equal Protection Clause was used mainly in cases involving classifications based on race and national origin until the advent of the Warren Court. Classifications based on grounds other than these were not subject to equal protection analysis providing the legislative means were reasonably related to the state's purpose—the rational relationship test. The legislative purpose was not a part of the analysis, that is, the courts did not consider the validity of the purpose itself. At the same time the Equal Protection Clause was being so narrowly construed, the Supreme Court was broadly interpreting the Due Process Clause. This balance changed under the Warren Court.

The rational relationship test, though most often used, gave way to strict scrutiny with the increasing reliance on the Equal Protection Clause. The Equal Protection Clause became the more favored means by which the Court would ensure individual rights against legislative interference with rights. The Warren Court employed strict scrutiny in cases of **suspect classifications** or those classifications that discriminated against politically powerless or unpopular minorities, or those having an impact on fundamental rights.

This differed from pre–Warren Court jurisprudence where strict scrutiny was employed only to classifications based on race or national origin. With the application of strict scrutiny, a statute could only be upheld if it was necessary to achieve a compelling state interest. In actuality, the Warren Court decisions only found race and national origin to be suspect classifications; nevertheless, there are indications in the opinions that other classifications might also be suspect.

suspect classification making choices (in employment, etc.) based on factors such as race or nationality. These choices, only rarely legitimate, must be strongly justified if challenged.

However, it was in the area of fundamental rights that the Warren Court had a significant effect on the use of strict scrutiny and, in turn, equal protection. Even where a classification was not suspect, if it had a substantial impact on fundamental rights, strict scrutiny was employed. The Court never made explicit what would constitute a fundamental right or interest, but their cases indicated that fundamental rights or interests were restricted to voting, criminal appeals, and interstate travel.[50] Thus, if a classification was suspect or had an impact on a fundamental right, strict scrutiny was employed. If it did not, all that was necessary for the statute to be upheld was a rational relationship between the means of achieving the legislative goal and the goal itself.

In *Harper v. Virginia Board of Elections*,[51] citizens of Virginia challenged the state's poll tax in local elections. Virginia was one of the four states still employing a poll tax at the time. Its use, the residents argued, was a violation of the Equal Protection Clause. While there was no disagreement that the right to vote is "fundamental," the more important question in the equal protection challenge was whether that right was equally distributed among the citizens.

HARPER V. VIRGINIA BOARD OF ELECTIONS
383 U.S. 663 (1966)

Justice DOUGLAS delivered the opinion of the Court.

[T]he right of suffrage "is subject to the imposition of state standards which are not discriminatory and which do not contravene any restriction that Congress, acting pursuant to constitutional powers, has imposed."

We conclude that a State violates the Equal Protection Clause of the Fourteenth Amendment whenever it makes the affluence of the voter or payment of any fee an electoral standard. Voter qualifications have no relation to wealth nor to paying or not paying this or any other tax. Our cases demonstrate that the Equal Protection Clause of the Fourteenth Amendment restrains the States from fixing voter qualifications which invidiously discriminate.

Long ago . . . the Court referred to "the political franchise of voting" as a "fundamental political because preservative of all rights." Recently . . . we said, "Undoubtedly, the right of suffrage is a fundamental matter in a free and democratic society. Especially since the right to exercise the franchise in a free and unimpaired manner is preservative of other basic civil and political rights, any alleged infringement of the right of citizens to vote must be carefully and meticulously scrutinized." There we were considering charges that voters in one part of the State had greater representation per person in the State Legislature than voters in another part of the State. We concluded: "A citizen, a qualified voter, is no more nor no less so because he lives in the city or on the farm. This is the clear and strong command of our Constitution's Equal Protection Clause. This is an essential part of the concept of a government of laws and not men. This is at the heart of Lincoln's vision of 'government of the people, by the people, [and] for the people.' The Equal Protection Clause demands no less than substantially equal state legislative representation for all citizens, of all places as well as of all races."

It is argued that a State may exact fees from citizens for many different kinds of licenses; that if it can demand from all an equal fee for a driver's license, it can demand from all an equal poll tax for voting. But we must remember that the interest of the State, when it comes to voting, is limited to the power to fix qualifications. Wealth, like race, creed, or color, is not germane to one's ability to participate intelligently in the electoral process. Lines drawn on the basis of wealth or property, like those of race are traditionally disfavored. To introduce wealth or payment of a fee as a measure of a voter's qualifications is to introduce a capricious or irrelevant factor. The degree of the discrimination is irrelevant. In this context—that is, as a condition of obtaining a ballot—the requirement of fee paying causes an "invidious" discrimination that runs afoul of the Equal Protection Clause. Levy "by the poll" . . . is an old familiar form of taxation; and we say nothing to impair its validity so long as it is not made a condition to the exercise of the franchise.

Continued

We agree, of course with Mr. Justice Holmes that the Due Process Clause of the Fourteenth Amendment "does not enact Mr. Herbert Spencer's Social Static's." Likewise, the Equal Protection Clause is not shackled to the political theory of a particular era. In determining what lines are unconstitutionally discriminatory, we have never been confined to historic notions of equality, any more than we have restricted due process to a fixed catalogue of what was at a given time deemed to be the limits of fundamental rights. Notions of what constitutes equal treatment for purposes of the Equal Protection Clause do change.

We have long been mindful that where fundamental rights and liberties are asserted under the Equal Protection Clause, classifications which might invade or restrain them must be closely scrutinized and carefully confined.

Those principles apply here. For to repeat, wealth or fee paying has, in our view, no relation to voting qualifications; the right to vote is too precious, too fundamental to be so burdened or conditioned.

Justice BLACK dissenting.

In *Breedlove v. Suttles,* a few weeks after I took my seat as a member of this Court, we unanimously upheld the right of the State of Georgia to make payment of its state poll tax a prerequisite to voting in state elections. We rejected at that time contentions that the state law violated the Equal Protection Clause of the Fourteenth Amendment because it put an unequal burden on different groups of people according to their age, sex, and ability to pay.

* * *

Believing at that time that the Court had properly respected the limitation of its power under the Equal Protection Clause and was right in rejecting the equal protection argument, I joined the Court's judgment and opinion. The Court, however, overrules *Breedlove* in part, but its opinion reveals that it does so not by using its limited power to interpret the original meaning of the Equal Protection Clause, but by giving that clause a new meaning which it believes represents a better governmental policy. From this action I dissent.

I think the interpretation that this Court gave the Equal Protection Clause in *Breedlove* was correct. The mere fact that a law results in treating some groups differently from others does not, of course, automatically amount to a violation of the Equal Protection Clause.

A study of our cases shows that this Court has refused to use the general language of the Equal Protection Clause as though it provided a handy instrument to strike down state laws which the Court feels are based on bad governmental policy. The equal protection cases carefully analyzed boil down to the principle that distinctions drawn and even discriminations imposed by state laws do not violate the Equal Protection Clause so long as these distinctions and discriminations are not "irrational," "irrelevant," "unreasonable," "arbitrary," or "invidious." These vague and indefinite terms do not, of course, provide a precise formula or an automatic mechanism for deciding cases arising under the Equal Protection Clause. The restrictive connotations of these terms, however (which in other contexts have been used to expand the Court's power inordinately), are a plain recognition of the fact that under a proper interpretation of the Equal Protection Clause States are to have the broadest kind of leeway in areas where they have a general constitutional competence to act. In view of the purpose of the terms to restrain the courts from a wholesale invalidation of state laws under the Equal Protection Clause it would be difficult to say that the poll tax requirement is "irrational" or "arbitrary" or works "invidious discriminations." State poll tax legislation can "reasonably," "rationally" and without an "invidious" or evil purpose to injure anyone be found to rest on a number of state policies including (1) the State's desire to collect its revenue, and (2) its belief that voters who pay a poll tax will be interested in furthering the State's welfare when they vote. Property qualifications existed in the Colonies and were continued by many States after the Constitution was adopted. Although I join the Court in disliking the policy of the poll tax, this is not in my judgment a justifiable reason for holding this poll tax law unconstitutional. Such a holding on my part would, in my judgment, be an exercise of power which the Constitution does not confer upon me.

Justice HARLAN, with whom Justice STEWART joins, dissenting.

The Equal Protection Clause prevents States from arbitrarily treating people differently under their laws. Whether any such differing

Continued

treatment is to be deemed arbitrary depends on whether of not it reflects an appropriate differentiating classification among those affected; the clause has never been thought to require equal treatment of all persons despite differing circumstances. The test evolved by this court for determining whether an asserted justifying classification exists is whether such a classification can be deemed to be founded on some rational and otherwise constitutionally permissible state policy. This standard reduces to a minimum the likelihood that the federal judiciary will judge state policies in terms of the individual notions and predilections of its own members, and until recently it has been followed in all kinds of "equal protection" cases.

Property and poll-tax qualification, very simply, are not in accord with current egalitarian notions of how a modern democracy should be organized. It is of course entirely fitting that the legislatures should modify the law to reflect such changes in popular attitudes. However, it is all wrong, in my view, for the Court to adopt the political doctrines popularly accepted at a particular moment of our history to declare all others to be irrational and invidious, barring them from the range of choice by reasonably minded people acting through the political process. It was not too long ago that Mr. Justice Holmes felt impelled to remind the Court that the Due Process Clause of the Fourteenth Amendment does not enact the *laissez-faire* theory of society. The times have changed, and perhaps it is appropriate to observe that neither does the Equal Protection Clause of that Amendment rigidly impose upon America an ideology of unrestrained egalitarianism.

In the era of the Burger-Rehnquist Court, the Warren Court's two-tiered approach has essentially continued in effect. The Burger-Rehnquist Court has, however, declined to expand the Warren formula. The Court has not broadened the classifications considered to be suspect, nor has it significantly altered the scope of fundamental rights. The Court has, however, changed the way it has looked at the fundamental right to vote. In *Bush v. Gore*,[52] the Court found that the right to vote is owed more protection than simply the granting of the franchise. In addition, equal protection applies to the way in which the franchise is exercised. Once the right to vote has been granted on equal protection grounds, it may not value one person's vote over another's by later imposing arbitrary or disparate treatment.

At issue was the outcome of the 2000 Presidential election. Voting irregularities in Florida caused the Democratic candidate, Al Gore, to ask for manual recounts in four counties.

The Supreme Court overturned the ruling of the Florida Supreme Court requiring the recounts in a per curiam opinion endorsed by Chief Justice Rehnquist and Justices O'Connor, Scalia, Kennedy, and Thomas. The Court, citing equal protection concerns maintained that the recount mechanism imposed by the state court did not meet the nonarbitrary treatment of voters necessary to secure the fundamental right to vote as the state legislature had prescribed. Chief Justice Rehnquist wrote a concurring opinion and each of the four dissenting Justices wrote a separate opinion.

BUSH v. GORE
531 U.S. 98 (2000)

PER CURIAM

I

The petitioner presents the following questions: whether the Florida Supreme Court established new standards for resolving Presidential election contests, thereby violating Art. II sec. 12, cl. 2, of the United States Constitution and failing to comply with 3 U.S.C. sec. 5, and whether the use of standardless manual recounts violates the Equal Protection and Due Process Clauses. With respect to the equal protection question, we find a violation of the Equal Protection Clause.

Continued

II

A

This case has shown that punch card balloting machines can produce an unfortunate number of ballots which are not punched in a clean, complete way by the voter. After the current counting, it is likely legislative bodies nationwide will examine ways to improve the mechanisms and machinery for voting.

B

The individual citizen has no federal constitutional right to vote for electors for the President of the United States unless and until the state legislature chooses a statewide election as the means to implement its power to appoint members of the Electoral College. This is the source for the statement in *McPherson v. Blacker,* 146 U.S. 1, 35 (1892), that the State legislature's power to select the manner for appointing electors is plenary; it may, if it so chooses, select the electors itself, which indeed was the manner used by State legislatures in several States for many years after the Framing of our Constitution. History has now favored the voter, and in each of the several States the citizens themselves vote for Presidential electors. When the state legislature vests the right to vote for President in its people, the right to vote as the legislature has prescribed is fundamental; and one source of its fundamental nature lies in the equal weight accorded to each vote and the equal dignity owed to each voter. The State, of course, after granting the franchise in the special context of Article II, can take back the power to appoint electors.

The right to vote is protected in more than the initial allocation of the franchise. Equal protection applies as well to the manner of its exercise. Having once granted the right to vote on equal terms, the State may not, by later arbitrary and disparate treatment, value one person's vote over that of another. It must be remembered that "the right of suffrage can be denied by a debasement or dilution of the weight of a citizen's vote just as effectively as by wholly prohibiting the free exercise of the franchise." *Reynolds v. Sims,* 377 U.S. 533,555 (1964)

There is no difference between the two sides of the present controversy on these basic propositions. Respondents say that the very purpose of vindicating the right to vote justifies the recount procedure now at issue. The question before us, however, is whether the recount procedures the Florida Supreme Court has adopted are consistent with its obligation to avoid arbitrary and disparate treatment of the members of its electorate.

Much of the controversy seems to revolve around ballot cards designed to be perforated by a stylus but which, either through error or deliberate omission, have not been perforated with sufficient precision for a machine to count them. In some cases, a piece of the card—a chad—is hanging, say by two corners. In other cases there is no separation at all, just an indentation.

The Florida Supreme Court has ordered that the intent of the voter be discerned from such ballots. For purposes of resolving the equal protection challenge, it is not necessary to decide whether the Florida Supreme Court had the authority under the legislative scheme for resolving election disputes to define what a legal vote is and to mandate a manual recount implementing that definition. The recount mechanisms implemented in response to the decisions of the Florida Supreme Court do not satisfy the minimum requirement for non-arbitrary treatment of voters necessary to secure the fundamental right. Florida's basic command for the count of legally cast votes is to consider the "intent of the voter." This is unobjectionable as an abstract proposition and a starting principle. The problem inheres in the absence of specific standards to ensure its equal application. The formulation of uniform rules to determine intent based on these recurring circumstances is practicable and, we conclude, necessary.

The law does not refrain from searching for the intent of the actor in a multitude of circumstances; and in some cases the general command to ascertain intent is not susceptible to much further refinement. In this instance, however, the question is not whether to believe a witness but how to interpret the marks or holes or scratches on an inanimate object, a piece of cardboard or paper, which, it is said, might not have registered as a vote during the machine count. The factfinder confronts a thing, not a person. The search for intent can be confined by specific rules designed to ensure uniform treatment.

The record provides some examples. A monitor in Miami-Dade County testified at trial that he observed that three members of the county canvassing board applied different standards in defining a legal vote. And testimony at trial also revealed that at least one county changed its evaluative standards during the counting

Continued

process. [This] is not a process with sufficient guarantees of equal treatment.

The recount process, . . . is consistent with the minimum procedures necessary to protect the fundamental right of each voter in the special instance of a statewide recount under the authority of a single state judicial officer. Our consideration is limited to the present circumstances, for the problem of equal protection in election processes generally presents many complexities.

The question before the Court is not whether local entities, in the exercise of their expertise, may develop different systems for implementing elections. Instead, we are presented with a situation where a state court with the power to assure uniformity has ordered a statewide recount with minimal procedural safeguards. When a court orders a statewide remedy, there must be at least some assurance that the rudimentary requirements of equal treatment and fundamental fairness are satisfied.

Upon due consideration of the difficulties identified to this point, it is obvious that the recount cannot be conducted in compliance with the requirements of equal protection and due process without substantial additional work. It would require not only the adoption (after opportunity for argument) of adequate statewide standards for determining what is a legal vote, and practicable procedures to implement them, but also orderly judicial review of any disputed matters that might arise. In addition, the Secretary of State has advised that the recount of only a portion of the ballots requires that the vote tabulation equipment be used to screen out undervotes, a function for which the machines were not designed. If a recount of overvotes were also required, perhaps even a second screening would be necessary. Use of the equipment for this purpose, and any new software developed for it, would have to be evaluated for accuracy by the Secretary of State.

The Supreme Court of Florida has said that the legislature intended the State's electors to "participate fully in the federal electoral process," as provided in 3 U.S.C. sec. 5. That statute, in turn, requires that any controversy or contest that is designed to lead to a conclusive selection of electors be completed by December 12. That date is upon us, and there is no recount procedure in place under the State Supreme Court's order that comports with minimal constitutional standards. Because it is evident that any recount seeking to meet the December 12 date will be unconstitutional for the reasons we have discussed, we reverse the judgment of the Supreme Court of Florida ordering a recount to proceed.

None are more conscious of the vital limits on judicial authority than are the members of this Court, and none stand more in admiration of the Constitution's design to leave the selection of the President to the people, through their legislatures, and to the political sphere. When contending parties invoke the process of the courts, however, it becomes our unsought responsibility to resolve the federal and constitutional issues the judicial system has been forced to confront.

Justice STEVENS, with whom Justices GINSBURG and BREYER join, dissenting.

The Constitution assigns to the States the primary responsibility for determining the manner of selecting the Presidential electors. When questions arise about the meaning of state laws, including election laws, it is our settled practice to accept the opinions of the highest courts of the States, as providing the final answers. On rare occasions, however, either federal statutes or the Federal Constitution may require federal judicial intervention in state elections. This is not such an occasion.

Even assuming that aspects of the remedial scheme might ultimately be found to violate the Equal Protection Clause, I could not subscribe to the majority's disposition of the case. As the majority explicitly holds, once a state legislature determines to select electors through a popular vote, the right to have one's vote counted is of constitutional stature. As the majority further acknowledges, Florida law holds that all ballots that reveal the intent of the voter constitute valid votes. Recognizing these principles, the majority nonetheless orders the termination of the contest proceeding before all such votes have been tabulated. Under their own reasoning, the appropriate course of action would be to remand to allow more specific procedures for implementing the legislature's uniform general standard to be established.

In the interest of finality, however, the majority effectively orders the disenfranchisement of an unknown number of voters whose ballots reveal their intent—and are therefore legal votes under state law—but were for some reason rejected by

Continued

ballot-counting machines. It does so on the basis of the deadlines set forth in Title 3 of the United States Code. But, as I have already noted, those provisions merely provide rules of decision for Congress to follow when selecting among conflicting slates of electors. They do not prohibit a State from counting what the majority concedes to be legal votes until a bona fide winner is determined. Indeed, in 1960, Hawaii appointed two slates of electors and Congress chose to count the one appointed on January 4, 1961, well after the Title 3 deadlines. Thus, nothing prevents the majority, even if it properly found an equal protection violation, from ordering relief appropriate to remedy that violation without depriving Florida voters of their right to have their votes counted. As the majority notes, "[a] desire for speed is not a general excuse for ignoring equal protection guarantees."

What must underlie petitioners' entire federal assault on the Florida election procedures is an unstated lack of confidence in the impartiality and capacity of the state judges who would make the critical decisions if the vote count were to proceed. Otherwise, their position is wholly without merit. The endorsement of that position by the majority of this Court can only lend credence to the most cynical appraisal of the work of judges throughout the land. It is confidence in the men and women who administer the judicial system that is the true backbone of the rule of law. Time will one day heal the wound to that confidence that will be inflicted by today's decision. One thing, however, is certain. Although we may never know with complete certainty the identity of the winner of this year's Presidential election, the identity of the loser is perfectly clear. It is the Nation's confidence in the judge as an impartial guardian of the rule of law.

I respectfully dissent.

Justice SOUTER, with whom Justices BREYER, STEVENS, and GINSBURG join,

The Court should not have reviewed either *Bush v. Palm Beach County Canvassing Bd.,* or this case, and should not have stopped Florida's attempt to recount all undervote ballots, by issuing a stay of the Florida Supreme Court's orders during the period of this review. If this Court had allowed the State to follow the course indicated by the opinions of its own Supreme Court, it is entirely possible that there would ultimately

have been no issue requiring our review, and political tension could have worked itself out in the Congress following the procedure provided in 3 U.S.C. sec. 15. The case being before us, however, its resolution by the majority is another erroneous decision.

[The] interpretations by the Florida court raise no substantial question under Article II. That court engaged in permissible construction in determining that Gore had instituted a contest authorized by the state statute, and it proceeded to direct the trial judge to deal with that contest in the exercise of the discretionary powers generously conferred by [state statute] to "fashion such orders as he or she deems necessary to ensure that each allegation in the complaint is investigated, examined, or checked, to prevent or correct any alleged wrong, and to provide any relief appropriate under such circumstances." As JUSTICE GINSBURG has persuasively explained in her own dissenting opinion, our customary respect for state interpretations of state law counsels against rejection of the Florida court's determinations in this case.

III

In deciding what to do about this, we should take account of the fact that electoral votes are due to be cast in six days. I would therefore remand the case to the courts of Florida with instructions to establish uniform standards for evaluating the several types of ballots that have prompted differing treatments, to be applied within and among counties when passing on such identical ballots in any further recounting (or successive recounting) that the courts might order.

Unlike the majority, I see no warrant for this Court to assume that Florida could not possibly comply with this requirement before the date set for the meeting of electors . . . Although one of the dissenting Justices of the State Supreme Court estimated that disparate standards potentially affected 170,000 votes the number at issue is significantly smaller. The 170,000 figure apparently represents all uncounted votes, both undervotes (those for which no Presidential choice was recorded by a machine) and overvotes (those rejected because of votes for more than one candidate. But as JUSTICE BREYER has pointed out, no showing has been made of legal overvotes uncounted, and counsel for Gore made an uncontradicted representation to the

Continued

Court that the statewide total of undervotes is about 60,000. To recount these manually would be a tall order, but before this Court stayed the effort to do that the courts of Florida were ready to do their best to get that job done. There is no justification for denying the State the opportunity to try to count all disputed ballots now.

I respectfully dissent.

Justice GINSBURG, with whom Justice STEVENS joins, and with whom Justices SOUTER and BREYER join as to Part I, dissenting.

I

This Court more than occasionally affirms statutory, and even constitutional, interpretations with which it disagrees.

No doubt there are cases in which the proper application of federal law may hinge on interpretations of state law. Unavoidably, this Court must sometimes examine state law in order to protect federal rights. But we have dealt with such cases ever mindful of the full measure of respect we owe to interpretations of state law by a State's highest court. In the Contract Clause case, for example, we said that although "ultimately we are bound to decide for ourselves whether a contract was made," the Court "accords respectful consideration and great weight to the views of the State's highest court." And in *Central Union Telephone Co. v. Edwardsville,* 269 U.S. 190 (1925), we upheld the Illinois Supreme Court's interpretation of a state waiver rule, even though that interpretation resulted in the forfeiture of federal constitutional rights. Refusing to supplant Illinois law with a federal definition of waiver, we explained that the state court's declaration "should bind us unless so unfair or unreasonable in its application to those asserting a federal right as to obstruct it."

The extraordinary setting of this case has obscured the ordinary principle that dictates its proper resolution: federal courts defer to state high courts' interpretations of their state's own law. This principle reflects the core of federalism, on which all agree. "The Framers split the atom of sovereignty. It was the genius of their idea that our citizens would have two political capacities, one state and one federal, each protected from incursion by the other." THE CHIEF JUSTICE's solicitude for the Florida Legislature comes at the expense of the more fundamental solicitude we owe to the legislature's sovereign.

Were the other members of this Court as mindful as they generally are of our system of dual sovereignty, they would affirm the judgment of the Florida Supreme Court.

II

I agree with JUSTICE STEVENS that petitioners have not presented a substantial equal protection claim. Ideally, perfection would be the appropriate standard for judging the recount. But we live in an imperfect world, one in which thousands of votes have not been counted. I cannot agree that the recount adopted by the Florida court, flawed as it may be, would yield a result any less fair or precise than the certification that preceded that recount.

Even if there were an equal protection violation, I would agree with JUSTICE STEVENS, JUSTICE SOUTER, and JUSTICE BREYER that the Court's concern about "the . . . deadline," is misplaced. Time is short in part because of the Court's entry of a stay . . . several hours after an able circuit judge in Leon County had begun to superintend the recount process. More fundamentally, the court's reluctance to let the recount go forward—despite its suggestion that "the search for intent can be confined by specific rules designed to ensure uniform treatment,"—ultimately turns on its own judgment about the practical realities of implementing a recount, not the judgment of those much closer to the process.

I dissent.

Justice BREYER, with whom Justices STEVENS and GINSBURG join except as to Part I-A-1, and with whom Justice SOUTER joins as to Part I, dissenting.

I

The political implications of this case for the country are momentous. But the federal legal questions presented, with one exception, are insubstantial.

A

1

The majority raises three Equal Protection problems with the Florida Supreme Court's recount order: first, the failure to include overvotes in the manual recount; second, the fact that *all* ballots, rather than simply the undervotes, were recounted in some, but not all, counties; and third, the absence of a uniform specific standard

Continued

to guide the recounts. As far as the first issue is concerned, petitioners presented no evidence to this Court or to any Florida court, that a manual recount of overvotes would identify additional legal votes. The same is true of the second, and, in addition, the majority's reasoning would seem to invalidate any state provision for a manual recount of individual counties in a statewide election.

The majority's third concern does implicate principles of fundamental fairness. The majority concludes that the Equal Protection Clause requires that a manual recount be governed not only by the uniform general standard of the "clear intent of the voter," but also by uniform subsidiary standards (for example, a uniform determination whether indented, but not perforated, "undervotes" should count). The opinion points out that the Florida Supreme Court ordered the inclusion of Broward County's undercounted "legal votes" even though those votes included ballots that were not perforated but simply "dimpled," while newly recounted ballots from other counties will likely include only votes determined to be "legal" on the basis of a stricter standard. In light of our previous remand, the Florida Supreme Court may have been reluctant to adopt a more specific standard than that provided for by the legislature for fear of exceeding its authority under Article II. However, since the use of different standards could favor one or the other of the candidates, since time was, and is, too short to permit the lower courts to iron out significant differences through ordinary judicial review, and since the relevant distinction was embodied in the order of the State's highest court, I agree that, in these very special circumstances, basic principles of fairness may well have counseled the adoption of a uniform standard to address the problem. In light of the majority's disposition, I need not decide whether, or the extent to which, as a remedial matter, the Constitution would place limits upon the content of the uniform standard.

2

Nonetheless, there is no justification for the majority's remedy, which is simply to reverse the lower court and halt the recount entirely. An appropriate remedy would be, instead, to remand this case with instructions that, even at this late date, would permit the Florida Supreme Court to require recounting *all* undercounted votes in Florida, including those from Broward,

Volusia, Palm Beach, and Miami-Dade Counties, whether or not previously recounted prior to the end of the protest period, and to do so in accordance with a single-uniform substandard.

By halting the manual recount, and thus ensuring that the uncounted legal votes will not be counted under any standard, this Court crafts a remedy out of proportion to the asserted harm. And that remedy harms the very fairness interests the Court is attempting to protect. The manual recount would itself redress a problem of unequal treatment of ballots.

II

The Constitution and federal statutes themselves make clear that restraint is appropriate. They set forth a road map of how to resolve disputes about electors, even after an election as close as this one. That road map foresees resolution of electoral disputes by state courts. But it nowhere provides for involvement by the United States Supreme Court.

To the contrary, the Twelfth Amendment commits to Congress the authority and responsibility to count electoral votes. A federal statute, the Electoral Count Act enacted after the close 1876 Hayes-Tilden Presidential election, specifies that, after States have tried to resolve disputes (through "judicial" or other means), Congress is the body primarily authorized to resolve remaining disputes.

At the same time, as I have said, the Court is not acting to vindicate a fundamental constitutional principle, such as the need to protect a basic human liberty. No other strong reason to act is present. Congressional statutes tend to obviate the need. And, above all, in the highly politicized matter, the appearance of a split decision runs the risk of undermining the public's confidence in the Court itself. That confidence is a public treasure, it has been built slowly over many years, some of which were marked by a Civil War and the tragedy of segregation. It is a vitally necessary ingredient of any successful effort to protect basic liberty and, indeed, the rule of law itself. We run no risk of returning to the day when a President (responding to this Court's efforts to protect the Cherokee Indians) might have said, "John Marshall has made this decision; now let him enforce it!" But we do risk a self-inflicted wound—a wound that may harm not just the Court, but the Nation.

Continued

I fear that in order to bring this agonizingly long election process to a definitive conclusion, we have not adequately attended to that necessary "check upon our own exercise of power," "our own sense of self-restraint." Justice Brandeis once said of the Court, "The most important thing we do is not doing." What it does today, the Court should have left undone. I would repair the damage done as best we now can, by permitting the Florida recount to continue under uniform standards.

I respectfully dissent.

At the same time the Court has expanded equal protection analysis for voting, the Burger-Rehnquist Court has moved away from the strict two-tiered analysis of the Warren Court. The Burger-Rehnquist Court has imposed a third level of scrutiny used most frequently in gender-based classifications. This third level of scrutiny, known generally as intermediate or mid-level scrutiny, has sometimes been applied in cases addressing illegitimacy and alienage-based classifications. These cases receive consideration that is less than strict scrutiny, but receive more than the mere rational relationship analysis [53]

While the Equal Protection Clause of the Fourteenth Amendment applies only to state and local governments, this does not mean that citizens have no guarantee of equal protection from the actions of the federal government. Although there is no such explicit guarantee in the Constitution, the courts have analyzed cases raising equal protection claims against the federal government to find such a requirement.

If the federal government employs a classification that would be unconstitutional if employed by a state government, the Court analogizes the situation to a Fifth Amendment due process violation. For example, *Bolling v. Sharpe*,[54] a companion case to *Brown v. Board of Education*,[55] raised the issue of segregation in the public schools of the District of Columbia for which the federal government was responsible. Chief Justice Warren, who wrote the unanimous decision in *Brown,* writing for a unanimous Court in *Bolling,* noted that while the Fifth Amendment does not contain an Equal Protection Clause, "the concepts of equal protection and due process, both stem . . . from our American ideal of fairness [and] are not mutually exclusive."[56] Thus, the Chief Justice concluded:

> *In view of our decision that the Constitution prohibits the states from maintaining racially segregated public schools, it would be unthinkable that the same Constitution would impose a lesser duty on the Federal Government. We hold that racial segregation in the public schools of the District of Columbia is a denial of the due process of law guaranteed by the Fifth Amendment to the Constitution.*[57]

As a result, the Fifth Amendment Due Process Clause is available to citizens against the federal government's actions, when a like action of the states would constitute a violation of the Fourteenth Amendment's Equal Protection Clause.

The Equal Protection Clause applies only to the making of a classification. It does not address the question of whether an individual belongs in one class or another. Rather, this question is a matter of statutory interpretation or, perhaps, the Due Process Clause.

In some cases a statute may not draw classifications on its face, but may be applied in a way that demonstrates class lines are being drawn. In such instances, the courts look at the administratively derived class as they would if the distinction had been specifically included in the statute. The classic example of such a situation is a statute requiring a literacy test for voters. The statute does not explicitly require only African Americans to take a literacy test in order to vote. The local voting officials, however, apply the statute in a way that purposely discriminates against blacks. In this case there is a violation of the Equal Protection Clause.[58]

The Equal Protection Clause guarantees that similarly situated individuals be treated similarly and that people who are not similarly situated will not be treated similarly. It is easier to establish a violation of unequal treatment of similarly situated individuals. In fact, most successful equal protection cases have involved a violation of that first principle. It is more difficult to establish a violation of equal protection when the claim is one of dissimilarly situated individuals being treated differently.

A determination whether two people are similarly situated will be made with reference to the statutory objectives being considered. This is nicely illustrated in the case of *Michael M. v. Superior Court of Sonoma County.*[59] California enacted a statute making statutory rape a criminal offense if committed by a male. Women had no liability for engaging in intercourse with persons under 18 or any other age. The question was whether this statute violated the equal protection guarantee by treating males and females differently.

The Court looked at the objective of the statute. The state established that the principal objective of the law was to discourage illegitimate pregnancies. In light of that goal, the need for, or value of, treating males and females differently can be evaluated. So, concerns like intent and causation may support the validity of a decision to treat groups differently. Today, the Court will generally defer to legislative classifications so long as neither a suspect class nor a fundamental right is concerned. Thus, claims based on wealth or poverty classifications will generally be found not to violate the Equal Protection Clause.[60]

MICHAEL M. v. SUPERIOR COURT OF SONOMA COUNTY
450 U.S. 464 (1981)

Justice REHNQUIST announced the judgment of the Court and delivered an opinion, in which THE CHIEF JUSTICE, Justice STEWART, and Justice POWELL joined.

The question presented in this case is whether California's "statutory rape" law, . . . violates the Equal Protection Clause of the Fourteenth Amendment. [The law] defines unlawful sexual intercourse as "an act of sexual intercourse accomplished with a female not the wife of the perpetrator, where the female is under the age of 18 years." The statute thus makes men alone criminally liable for the act of sexual intercourse.

As is evident from our opinions, the Court has had some difficulty in agreeing upon the proper approach and analysis in cases involving challenges to gender-based classifications. The issues posed by such challenges range from issues of standing, to the appropriate standard of judicial review for the substantive classification. Unlike the California Supreme Court, we have not held that gender-based classifications are "inherently suspect" and thus we do not apply so-called "strict scrutiny" to those classifications. Our cases have held, however, that the traditional minimum rationality test takes on a somewhat "sharper focus" when gender-based classifications are challenged. In *Reed v. Reed, 404 U.S. 71 (1971)*, for example, the Court stated that a gender-based classification will be upheld if it bears a "fair and substantial relationship" to legitimate state ends; while in *Craig v. Boren*, the Court restated the test to require the classification to bear a "substantial relationship" to "important governmental objectives."

Underlying these decisions is the principle that a legislature may not "make overboard generalizations based on sex which are entirely unrelated to any differences between men, and women, or which demean the ability or social status of the affected class." But because the Equal Protection Clause does not "demand that a statute necessarily apply equally to all persons" or require "things which are different in fact, to be treated in law as though they were the

Continued

same," this Court has consistently upheld statutes where the gender classification is not invidious, but rather realistically reflects the fact that the sexes are not similarly situated in certain circumstances. As the Court has stated, a legislature may "provide for the special problems of women."

Applying those principles to this case, the fact that the California Legislature criminalized the act of illicit sexual intercourse with a minor female is a sure indication of its intent or purpose to discourage that conduct. Precisely why the legislature desired that result is of course somewhat less clear. This Court has long recognized that "[inquiries] into congressional motives or purposes are a hazardous matter," and the search for the "actual" or "primary" purpose of a statute is likely to be illusive.

The justification for the statute offered by the State, and accepted by the Supreme Court of California, is that the legislature sought to prevent illegitimate teenage pregnancies. That finding, of course, is entitled to great deference. And although our cases establish that the State's asserted reason for the enactment of a statute may be rejected, if it "could not have been a goal of the legislation," this is not such a case.

We need not be medical doctors to discern that young men and young women are not similarly situated with respect to the problems and the risks of sexual intercourse. Only women may become pregnant, and they suffer disproportionately the profound physical, emotional, and psychological consequences of sexual activity. The statute at issue here protects women from sexual intercourse at an age when those consequences are particularly severe.

The question thus boils down to whether a State may attack the problem of sexual intercourse and teenage pregnancy directly by prohibiting a male from having sexual intercourse with a minor female. We hold that such a statute is sufficiently related to the State's objectives to pass constitutional muster.

We are unable to accept petitioner's contention that the statute is impermissibly underinclusive and must, in order to pass judicial scrutiny, be broadened so as to hold the female as criminally liable as the male. It is argued that this statute is not necessary to deter teenage pregnancy because a gender-neutral statute, where both male and female would be subject to prosecution, would serve that goal equally well. The relevant inquiry, however, is not whether the statute is drawn as precisely as it might have been, but whether the line chosen by the California Legislature is within constitutional limitations.

In any event, we cannot say that a gender-neutral statute would be as effective as the statute California has chosen to enact. The State persuasively contends that a gender-neutral statute would frustrate its interest in effective enforcement. Its view is that a female is surely less likely to report violations of the statute if she herself would be subject to criminal prosecution. In an area already fraught with prosecutorial difficulties, we decline to hold that the Equal Protection Clause requires a legislature to enact a statute so broad that it may well be incapable of enforcement.

In upholding the California statute we also recognize that this is not a case where a statute is being challenged on the grounds that it "invidiously discriminates" against females. To the contrary, the statute places a burden on males which is not shared by females. But we find nothing to suggest that men, because of past discrimination or peculiar disadvantages, are in need of the special solicitude of the courts. Nor is this a case where the gender classification is made "solely for . . . administrative convenience," or rests on the "baggage of sexual stereotypes." As we have held, the statute instead reasonably reflects the fact that the consequences of sexual intercourse and pregnancy fall more heavily on the female than on the male.

Affirmed.

Justice STEWART, concurring.

B

The Constitution is violated when government, state or federal, invidiously classifies similarly situated people on the basis of the immutable characteristics with which they were born. Thus, detrimental racial classifications by government always violate the Constitution, for the simple reason that, so far as the Constitution is concerned, people of different races are always similarly situated. By contrast, while detrimental gender classifications by government often violate the Constitution, they do not always do so, for the reason that there are differences between males and females that the Constitution necessarily recognizes. In this case we deal with the

Continued

most basic of these differences: females can become pregnant as the result of sexual intercourse, males cannot.

[W]e have recognized that in certain narrow circumstances men and women are not similarly situated; in these circumstances a gender classification based on clear differences between the sexes is not invidious, and a legislative classification realistically based upon those differences is not unconstitutional. "[Gender]-based classifications are not invariably invalid. When men and women are not in fact similarly situated in the area covered by the legislation in question, the Equal Protection Clause is not violated."

Applying these principles to the classification enacted by the California Legislature, it is readily apparent that [the law] does not violate the Equal Protection Clause. Young women and men are not similarly situated with respect to the problems and risks associated with intercourse and pregnancy, and the statute is realistically related to the legitimate state purpose of reducing those problems and risks.

* * *

E

In short, the Equal Protection Clause does not mean that the physiological differences between men and women must be disregarded. While those differences must never be permitted to become a pretext for invidious discrimination, no such discrimination is presented by this case. The Constitution surely does not require a State to pretend that demonstrable differences between men and women do not really exist.

Justice BLACKMUN, concurring in the judgment.

It is gratifying that the plurality recognizes that "[at] the risk of stating the obvious, teenage pregnancies . . . have increased dramatically over the last two decades" and "have significant social, medical, and economic consequences for both the mother and her child, and the State." There have been times when I have wondered whether the Court was capable of this perception, particularly when it has struggled with the different but not unrelated problems that attend abortion issues.

I, however, cannot vote to strike down the California statutory rape law, for I think it is a sufficiently reasoned and constitutional effort to control the problem at its inception. For me,

there is an important difference between this state action and a State's adamant and rigid refusal to face, or even to recognize, the "significant . . . consequences"—to the woman—of a forced or unwanted conception. I have found it difficult to rule constitutional, for example, state efforts to block, at that later point, a woman's attempt to deal with the enormity of the problem confronting her, just as I have rejected state efforts to prevent women from rationally taking steps to prevent that problem from arising. In contrast, I am persuaded that, although a minor has substantial privacy rights in intimate affairs connected with procreation, California's efforts to prevent teenage pregnancy, are to be viewed differently from Utah's efforts to inhibit a woman from dealing with pregnancy once it has become an inevitability.

The plurality opinion in the present case points out, the Court's respective phrasings of the applicable test in *Reed v. Reed, 404 U.S. 71,76(1971)* and in *Craig v. Boren*. I vote to affirm the judgment of the Supreme Court of California and to uphold the State's gender-based classification on that test and as exemplified by those two cases.

Justice BRENNAN, with whom Justices WHITE and MARSHALL join, dissenting.

I

It is disturbing to find the Court so splintered on a case that presents such a straightforward issue: Whether the admittedly gender-based classification . . . bears a sufficient relationship to the State's asserted goal of preventing teenage pregnancies to survive the "mid-level" constitutional scrutiny mandated by *Craig v. Boren, 429 U.S. 190 (1976)*. Applying the analytical framework provided by our precedents, I am convinced that there is only one proper resolution of this issue: the classification must be declared unconstitutional. I fear that the plurality opinion and Justices STEWART and BLACKMUN reach the opposite result by placing too much emphasis on the desirability of achieving the State's asserted statutory goal—prevention of teenage pregnancy—and not enough emphasis on the fundamental question of whether the sex-based discrimination in the California statute is substantially related to the achievement of that goal.

II

After some uncertainty as to the proper framework for analyzing equal protection challenges

Continued

to statutes containing gender-based classifications, this Court settled upon the proposition that a statute containing a gender-based classification cannot withstand constitutional challenge unless the classification is substantially related to the achievement of an important governmental objective. This analysis applies whether the classification discriminates against males or females. The burden is on the government to prove both the importance of its asserted objective and the substantial relationship between the classification and that objective. And the State cannot meet that burden without showing that a gender-neutral statute would be a less effective means of achieving that goal.

The State of California vigorously asserts that the "important governmental objective" to be served . . . is the prevention of teenage pregnancy. It claims that its statute furthers this goal by deterring sexual activity by males—the class of persons it considers more responsible for causing those pregnancies. But even assuming that prevention of teenage pregnancy is an important governmental objective and that it is in fact an objective [of the statute], California still has the burden of proving that there are fewer teenage pregnancies under its gender-based statutory rape law than there would be if the law were gender neutral. To meet this burden, the State must show that because its statutory rape law punishes only males, and not females, it more effectively deters minor females from having sexual intercourse.

The plurality assumes that a gender-neutral statute would be less effective . . . in deterring sexual activity, because a gender-neutral statute would create significant enforcement problems. However, a State's bare assertion that its gender-based statutory classifications substantially furthers an important governmental interest is not enough to meet its burden of proof. Rather, the State must produce evidence that will persuade the court that its assertion is true.

The State has not produced such evidence in this case. Moreover, there are at least two serious flaws in the State's assertion that law enforcement problems created by a gender-neutral statutory rape law would make such a statute less effective than a gender-based statute in deterring sexual activity.

First, the experience of other jurisdictions, and California, itself, belies the plurality's conclusion that a gender-neutral statutory rape law

"may well be incapable of enforcement." There are now at least 37 States that have enacted gender-neutral statutory rape laws. Although most of these laws protect young persons (of either sex) from the sexual exploitation of older individuals, the laws of Arizona, Florida, and Illinois permit prosecution of both minor females and minor males for engaging in mutual sexual conduct. California has introduced no evidence that those States have been handicapped by the enforcement problems the plurality finds so persuasive. Surely, if those States could provide such evidence, we might expect that California would have introduced it.

The second flaw in the State's assertion is that even assuming that a gender-neutral statute would be more difficult to enforce, the State has still not shown that those enforcement problems would make such a statute less effective than a gender-based statute in deterring minor females from engaging in sexual intercourse. Common sense, however, suggests that a gender-neutral statutory rape law is potentially a greater deterrent of sexual activity than a gender-based law, for the simple reason that a gender-neutral law subjects both men and women to criminal sanctions and thus arguably has a deterrent effect on twice as many potential violators. Even if fewer persons were prosecuted under the gender-neutral law, as the State suggests, it would still be true that twice as many persons would be *subject* to arrest. The State's failure to prove that a gender-neutral law would be a less effective deterrent than a gender-based law, like the State's failure to prove that a gender-neutral law would be difficult to enforce, should have led this Court to invalidate.

III

Until very recently, no California court or commentator had suggested that the purpose of California's statutory rape law was to protect young women from the risk of pregnancy. Indeed, the historical development of [the statute] demonstrates that the law was initially enacted on the premise that young women, in contrast to young men, were to be deemed legally incapable of consenting to an act of sexual intercourse. Because their chastity was considered particularly precious, those young women were felt to be uniquely in need of the State's protection. In contrast, young men were assumed to be capable of making such decisions for themselves, the law therefore did not offer them any special protection.

Continued

It is perhaps because the gender classification in California's statutory rape law was initially designed to further these outmoded sexual stereotypes, rather than to reduce the incidence of teenage pregnancies, that the State has been unable to demonstrate a substantial relationship between the classification and its newly asserted goal. But whatever the reason, the State has not shown that [the law] is any more effective than a gender-neutral law would be in deterring minor females from engaging in sexual intercourse. It has therefore not met its burden of proving that the statutory classification is substantially related to the achievement of its asserted goal.

I would hold that [the law] violates the Equal Protection Clause of the Fourteenth Amendment. . . .

Justice STEVENS, dissenting.

Local custom and belief—rather than statutory laws of venerable but doubtful ancestry—will determine the volume of sexual activity among unmarried teenagers. The empirical evidence cited by the plurality demonstrates the futility of the notion that a statutory prohibition will significantly affect the volume of that activity or provide a meaningful solution to the problems created by it. Nevertheless, as a matter of constitutional power, unlike my Brother BRENNAN, I would have no doubt about the validity of a state law prohibiting all unmarried teenagers from engaging in sexual intercourse. The societal interests in reducing the incidence of venereal disease and teenage pregnancy are sufficient, in my judgment, to justify a prohibition of conduct that increases the risk of those harms.

My conclusion that a nondiscriminatory prohibition would be constitutional does not help me answer the question whether a prohibition applicable to only half of the joint participants in the risk-creating conduct is also valid. It cannot be true that the validity of a total ban is an adequate justification for a selective prohibition; otherwise, the constitutional objection to discriminatory rules would be meaningless. The question in this case is whether the difference between males and females justifies this statutory discrimination based entirely on sex.

The fact that the Court did not immediately acknowledge that the capacity to become pregnant is what primarily differentiates the female from the male does not impeach the validity of the plurality's newly found wisdom. I think the plurality is quite correct in making the assumption that the joint act that this law seeks to prohibit creates a greater risk of harm for the female than for the male. But the plurality surely cannot believe that the risk of pregnancy confronted by the female—any more than the risk of venereal disease confronted by males as well as females—has provided an effective deterrent to voluntary female participation in the risk-creating conduct. Yet the plurality's decision seems to rest on the assumption that the California Legislature acted on the basis of that rather fanciful notion.

In my judgment, the fact that a class of persons is especially vulnerable to a risk that a statute is designed to avoid is a reason for making the statute applicable to that class. The argument that a special need for protection provides a rational explanation for an exemption is one I simply do not comprehend.

In this case, the fact that a female confronts a greater risk of harm than a male is a reason for applying the prohibition to her—not a reason for granting her a license to use her own judgment in whether or not to assume the risk. Surely, if we examine the problem from the point of view of society's interest in preventing the risk-creating conduct from occurring at all, it is irrational to exempt 50% of the potential violators. And, if we view the government's interest as that of a *parens patriae* seeking to protect its subjects from harming themselves, the discrimination is actually perverse. Would a rational parent making rules for the conduct of twin children of opposite sex simultaneously forbid the son and authorize the daughter to engage in conduct that is especially harmful to the daughter? That is the effect of this statutory classification.

If pregnancy or some other special harm is suffered by one of the two participants in the prohibited act, that special harm no doubt would constitute a legitimate mitigating factor in deciding what, if any, punishment might be appropriate in a given case. But from the standpoint of fashioning a general preventive rule—or, indeed, in determining appropriate punishment when neither party in fact has suffered any special harm—I regard a total exemption for the members of the more endangered class as utterly irrational.

Continued

In my opinion, the only acceptable justification for a general rule requiring disparate treatment of the two participants in a joint act must be a legislative judgment that one is more guilty than the other. The risk-creating conduct that this statute is designed to prevent requires the participation of two persons—one male and one female. In many situations it is probably true that one is the aggressor and the other is either an unwilling, or at least a less willing, participant in the joint act. If a statute authorized punishment of only one participant and required the prosecutor to prove that that participant had been the aggressor, I assume that the discrimination would be valid. Although the question is less clear, I also assume for the purpose of deciding this case, that it would be permissible to punish only the male participant. If one element of the offense were proof that he had been the aggressor, or at least in some respects the more responsible participant in the joint act. The statute at issue in this case, however, requires no such proof. The question raised by this statute is whether the State consistently with the Federal Constitution, may always punish the male and never the female when they are equally responsible or when the female is the more responsible of the two.

Nor do I find at all persuasive the suggestion that this discrimination is adequately justified by the desire to encourage females to inform against their male partners. Even if the concept of a wholesale informant's exemption were an acceptable enforcement device, what is the justification for defining the exempt class entirely by reference to sex rather than by reference to a more neutral criterion such as relative innocence? Indeed, if the exempt class is to be composed entirely of members of one sex, what is there to support the view that the statutory purpose will be better served by granting the informing license to females rather than to males? If a discarded male partner informs on a promiscuous female, a timely threat of prosecution might well prevent the precise harm the statute is intended to minimize.

Finally, even if my logic is faulty and there actually is some speculative basis for treating equally guilty males and females differently, I still believe that any such speculative justification would be outweighed by the paramount interest in evenhanded enforcement of the law. A rule that authorizes punishment of only one of two equally wrongdoers violates the essence of the constitutional requirement that the sovereign must govern impartially.

I respectfully dissent.

The Court's willingness to defer to the legislatures regarding classification means that the rational relationship standard applies to most economic and social welfare legislation. It is rare for the Court to strike down legislation on the ground that the legislative objective was not legitimate. In fact, as previously stated, the Court will offer possible objectives that might have motivated the legislature. Providing that the Court can find at least one conceivable, legitimate objective that is rationally related to the chosen means, the Court will ignore the possibility that an illegitimate objective may have motivated the legislature.

Despite the Court's deference to the legislature, it does not find every objective of the legislature to be legitimate in equal protection cases. In *Metropolitan Life Insurance Co. v. Ward*,[61] an Alabama statute that taxed out-of-state insurance companies more than in-state companies was found unconstitutional. The Court rejected the state's offered motivation—that it was designed to protect domestic companies. It was not a legitimate state purpose to protect domestic business by discriminating and it violated equal protection. Notice the similarity to *Allegeyer*, which was decided on due process grounds.

Before the Court can determine whether a purpose is legitimate it must first determine what the purpose is. The actual purpose of a statute may be determined by looking at the text itself. It is often included in the statute's preamble or in the legislative history. There are, however, cases where neither of these two sources is available. A number of states keep no records of a bill's history. When these sources are unavailable, the Court will look at the conceivable bases for the legislation, as noted above.

This was done in *U.S. Railroad Retirement Board v. Fritz.*[62] At issue was the modification of a prior retirement scheme. In the former scheme those who worked long enough for both the railroad and nonrailroad employers could get retirement benefits from both the railroad and the social security system. Congress eliminated the double windfall to preserve the solvency of the railroad retirement system. Four classifications depended on the number of years of service to the railroad system. The order of employment was significant in determining one's classification, that is, whether one worked first for the railroad or for another employer. The Court held that so long as a "plausible" reason for the classification existed it was not constitutionally relevant whether this was, in fact, the reason for the decision to create the classifications. Dissenting, Justices Brennan and Marshall argued that a "challenged classification, can be sustained only if it is rationally related to achievement of an actual legitimate governmental purpose."[63] Looking at the legislative history, the dissenters noted that "post hoc justifications" should be viewed skeptically.

There are instances in which the Court goes beyond its decision in *Fritz* and actually offers theoretical objectives that might have motivated the legislature. If a hypothetical purpose is adequate, the Court will uphold the statute.[64]

The Court is unwilling to uphold a claimed legitimate purpose when it finds that the classification is motivated by animus or hostility toward a politically unpopular group. This was the case in *Romer v. Evans.*[65] In addition, in *Lawrence v. Texas*[66] (discussed above), Justice O'Connor, who decided the case on equal protection grounds, found that not only was the classification employed by the state unable to meet the rational relationship test, the state's asserted interest—"moral disapproval"—was insufficient to justify a statute that proscribed homosexual, but not heterosexual sodomy. "A law branding one class of persons as criminal solely based on the State's moral disapproval of that class and the conduct associated with that class runs contrary to the values of the Constitution and the Equal Protection Clause, under any standard of review."[67]

Despite cases like *Romer,* where the state's purpose cannot withstand even the lowest level of scrutiny, overall it is clear that the Court gives great deference to the legislature where economic and social legislation is involved. The Court is willing to accept a showing that the legislature "could rationally have believed" that there was a link between the means of achieving the goal and the goal itself.[68] Moreover, this deference is underscored by the Court's willingness to find that it is sufficient for there to be only a loose fit between the means and the ends desired.[69]

Summary

The Fifth and Fourteenth Amendment Due Process Clauses restrict the government from depriving citizens of their "life, liberty, or property" without due process of law. Until the passage of the Fourteenth Amendment, only the federal government was bound by the provisions of the Bill of Rights. Through the selective incorporation doctrine, the Bill of Rights was made applicable to the individual states. Pursuant to this doctrine, each of the provisions is examined to determine whether it is fundamental to our concept of society.

The Due Process Clauses restrain the government's substantive power to infringe on our constitutional liberty. This is known as substantive due process analysis. When employing this analysis, the courts draw a distinction between fundamental and nonfundamental rights. A strict standard of scrutiny is used when fundamental rights are considered. In cases where a nonfundamental right is involved the Court merely requires that there be a rational relationship between the means chosen by the government to accomplish its goal and the goal itself. Economic regulation and, generally, all social welfare legislation come within the rational purpose test.

The courts also consider whether an individual has either a property or liberty interest in the thing being taken. If no such interest exists then due process analysis is unnecessary.

The Fifth and Fourteenth Amendment Clauses also guarantee procedural due process. This means that the government must employ fair procedures when it seeks to take a person's life, liberty, or property. The particular procedures are determined by using a balancing test that weighs the interest of the individual in specific safeguards against the state's interest in the administrative and fiscal costs of the safeguards. Most situations require a minimum of notice and an opportunity to be heard.

The Fourteenth Amendment Equal Protection Clause restrains the government from setting up classifications that result in the discriminatory treatment of individuals based on race or other characteristics that have been included over time as deserving of protection. The Fifth Amendment Due Process Clause has been held to be coextensive with the Fourteenth Amendment Equal Protection Clause, thereby preventing the federal government from treating similarly situated individuals differently.

The Court employs three different standards of review in equal protection cases. Those classifications that are considered suspect (race, national origin) are analyzed using strict scrutiny. Strict scrutiny is also applied when fundamental rights, such as voting and the right to travel, are involved. Use of strict scrutiny in equal protection cases will usually result in the statute or regulation being found unconstitutional. In cases of gender and illegitimacy, the Court applies a middle level of scrutiny that requires the government to demonstrate that its interest is important and that the classification is substantially related to its goal. For all other cases, the government must only meet the rational relationship test.

Key Terms

de facto	freedom of contract	notice
due process of law	hearing	selective incorporation
entitlement	liberty	suspect classification
equal protection of laws	natural law	

Review Questions

1. What is selective incorporation? What rights have been selectively incorporated? What do the incorporated rights have in common?

2. What is substantive due process? How has the Court changed its position on substantive due process issues over time?

3. The Fifth Amendment requires the government to provide citizens with a fair procedure before depriving them of life, liberty, or property. What have the Court's varying definitions of liberty and property been?

4. In *Goldberg v. Kelly* the Court set forth the extent of procedural due process protections. What did the Court require? How has this changed?

5. The Equal Protection Clause restrains the government from setting up classifications that result in discriminatory treatment of similarly situated individuals. Set forth the test imposed and the classifications to which each applies.

Internet Connections

1. For more information on the Fourteenth Amendment Due Process and Equal Protection Clauses, see Findlaw: United States Constitution, Fourteenth Amendment at *http://www.caselaw.findlaw.com*.

2. A worthwhile article on equal protection is "Equal Protection: An Overview" found on the Legal Information Institute's Web site at *http://www.law.cornell.edu*.

3. See WebQuest on the Supreme Court at *http://www.oncampus.richmond.edu*.

End Notes

[1]U.S. Const. amend. XIV; emphasis added.

[2]*Barron v. Mayor of the City of Baltimore*, 37 U.S. 243 (1833).

[3]*Palko v. Connecticut*, 302 U.S. 319 (1937).

[4]*Id.* at 325.

[5]Ibid.

[6]Today, the only guarantee not incorporated by the Fourteenth Amendment is the right to a grand jury proceeding.

[7]*The Slaughterhouse Cases*, 83 U.S. 36 (1873).

[8]*Munn v. Illinois*, 94 U.S. 113 (1877).

[9]*Mugler v. Kansas*, 123 U.S. 623 (1887).

[10]*Id.* at 661.

[11]*Allegeyer v. Louisiana*, 165 U.S. 578 (1897).

[12]*Lochner v. New York*, 198 U.S. 45 (1905).

[13]http://www.ilr.cornell.edu/trianglefire; David Van Drehle, Triangle, *The Fire that Changed America*, Grove Press (2004).

[14]*Id.* at 75.

[15]*Muller v. Oregon*, 208 U.S. 412 (1908).

[16]*Id.* at 421.

[17]*Adkins v. Children's Hospital*, 261 U.S. 525 (1923).

[18]*See* Chapter 3, The Courts—Jurisdiction and Judicial Review.

[19]*Nebbia v. New York*, 291 U.S. 502 (1934).

[20]*Id.* at 537.

[21]*West Coast Hotel v. Parrish*, 300 U.S. 379 (1937).

[22]*U.S. v. Carolene Products Company*, 304 U.S. 144 (1938).

[23]*Williamson v. Lee Optical Co.*, 348 U.S. 483 (1955).

[24]*Ferguson v. Skrupa*, 372 U.S. 726 (1963).

[25]*Id.* at 731.

[26]Ibid.

[27]*Meyer v. Nebraska*, 262 U.S. 390 (1923).

[28]*Board of Regents v. Roth*, 408 U.S. 564 (1973).

[29]*Perry v. Sinderman*, 408 U.S. 593 (1972).

[30]*Paul v. Davis*, 424 U.S. 693 (1976).

[31]*Goss v. Lopez*, 419 U.S. 565 (1975).

[32]*Lawrence v. Texas*, 539 U.S. 558 (2003).

[33]*Bowers v. Hardwick*, 478 U.S. 186 (1987).

[34]*Id.* at 190.

[35]*Id.* at 192.

[36]*Lawrence v. Texas, supra.*

[37]*Id.*

[38]*Id.*

[39]*Goldberg v. Kelly*, 397 U.S. 254 (1970).

[40]*Matthews v. Eldridge*, 424 U.S. 319 (1976).

[41]*Goldberg v. Kelly*, 424 U.S. at 334.

[42]*Cleveland Board of Education v. Loudermilk*, 470 U.S. 532 (1985).

[43]*Id.* at 544–545.

[44]*Id.* at 546.

[45]*Id.* at 532.

[46]*Goss v. Lopez, supra.*

[47]*Board of Curators v. Horovitz*, 419 U.S. 565 (1975).

[48]*Ingraham v. Wright*, 430 U.S. 651 (1977).

[49]U.S. Const. amend. XIV.

[50]*See* Chapter 6, Fundamental Rights.

[51]*Harper v. Virginia Board of Elections*, 383 U.S. 663 (1966).

[52]*Bush v. Gore*, 531 U.S. 98 (2000).

[53]*See* Chapter 6, Fundamental Rights.

[54]*Bolling v. Sharpe*, 347 U.S. 497 (1954).

[55]*Brown v. Board of Education*, 349 U.S. 294 (1955).

[56]*Bolling v. Sharpe*, 347 U.S. at 499.

[57]*Id.* at 500.

[58]*Lassiter v. Northhampton Election Board*, 360 U.S. 45, 51 (1959).

[59]*Michael M. v. Superior Court of Sonoma County*, 450 U.S. 464 (1981).

[60]*See, e.g., San Antonio Ind. School Dist. v. Rodriguez*, 411 U.S. 1 (1973).

[61]*Metropolitan Life Insurance Co. v. Ward*, 470 U.S. 869 (1985).

[62]*U.S. Railroad Retirement Board v. Fritz*, 449 U.S. 166 (1980).

[63]*Id.* at 188.

[64]*McDonald v. Board of Elections*, 394 U.S. 802 (1969).

[65]*Romer v. Evans*, 517 U.S. 620 (1996); *see also,* Chapter 9, The Right to Privacy.

[66]*Lawrence v. Texas, supra.*

[67]*Lawrence v. Texas, supra.*

[68]*Minnesota v. Clover Leaf Creamery Co.*, 449 U.S. 456 (1981).

[69]*Massachusetts Board of Retirement v. Murgia*, 427 U.S. 307 (1976).

 For additional resources, go to *http://www.westlegalstudies.com*

CHAPTER 8

DISCRIMINATION

"Racial discrimination in any form and in any degree has no justifiable part whatever in our democratic way of life. It is unattractive in any setting but it is utterly revolting among a free people who have embraced the principles set forth in the Constitution of the United States."

—Mr. Justice Murphy
Korematsu v. United States

INTRODUCTION

discrimination the failure to treat individuals equally; illegally unequal treatment based on race, color, religion, sex, age, handicap, or national origin.

Discrimination is not an unfamiliar concept in American society. The Civil Rights Movement of the 1960s brought the issues of disparate treatment based on race or national origin to the forefront. As a whole, U.S. citizens are very much aware of the historical perspective on discrimination in this country. Television shows and movies make us very aware of the history of discrimination against African Americans and other minority groups and the struggle to find equality in this country. In the political arena, most citizens are aware that Congress wrote the Equal Protection Clause of the Fourteenth Amendment expressly to assist African Americans in a quest for equal rights and civil liberties. Today, the Equal Protection Clause assists many groups of individuals who have suffered discrimination at the hands of the majority.

Suspect Classifications

All this is not to say that discrimination has been completely eliminated in the United States. In addition to residual historic discrimination, there are a variety of statutes and policies enacted throughout this country that have the effect of discrimination—whether it is unintentional discrimination, discrimination designed to assist those who have traditionally been discriminated against, or other, less benign forms of intentional discrimination. While discrimination has not been eliminated, the United States Supreme Court and other courts have used the Equal Protection Clause to attempt to remedy such unconstitutional treatment of minorities in this country.

In doing so, the Court has allowed some statutory classifications that give preferential treatment to groups that historically have suffered from discrimination, and made suspect classifications based on such immutable traits or characteristics as race or national origin. When examining alleged racial discrimination, the Court has traditionally used the strict scrutiny standard to determine whether the state is justified in its actions and whether there is a less intrusive means of accomplishing the state's justified action than that outlined in the statute or policy. (In gender-based discrimination cases, the appropriate standard to be used is mid-level scrutiny, as will be discussed later in this chapter.) This is a very difficult measure test to pass. Traditionally, use of the strict scrutiny test was fatal for most statutes or policies reviewed.

The last case involving race or ethnic classification that survived the strict scrutiny test was the 1944 case of *Korematsu v. The United States*[1] in which the Court quickly pointed out ". . . that all legal restrictions which curtail the civil rights of a single racial group are immediately suspect. That is not to say that all such restrictions are unconstitutional. It is to say that courts must subject them to the most rigid scrutiny."[2] The Court went on to scrutinize Executive Order

236

The Civil Rights Movement spanned the 1950s and the 1960s but one of the most important events took place between 1955 and 1956. The Montgomery Bus Boycott began on December 1, 1995,[3] however, it would be wrong to believe that this movement was the beginning. In the decade leading up to the boycott, African Americans in Montgomery, Alabama, were often called derogatory names by bus drivers, forced to enter the front of the bus to pay their fare and then made to exit the front of the bus and re-enter at the back, often being left behind by the driver who was amused by the misuse of his own power, and always being relegated to the back of the bus so that whites might have the more desirable seats. This treatment led to anger and resentment and became the fuel for the movement now known as the Montgomery Bus Boycott.

The boycott came about after the arrest of Mrs. Rosa Parks for refusing to give up her seat on one of the Montgomery buses. Mrs. Parks' story is a well-known part of the Civil Rights Movement, but she was just one of several African Americans arrested over the years for doing the same. Women such as Jo Ann Robinson, a professor at what was then Alabama State College and Claudette Colvin were among those simi-

Exhibit 8.1   The Montgomery Bus Boycott
Segregated Bus Station Montgomery Alabama

larly arrested, as was Rev. Vernon Johns. It was Mrs. Parks' arrest, however, that galvanized the movement in 1955. The night after Mrs. Parks' arrest, Jo Ann Robinson of the Women's Political Committee began planning a one-day boycott.[4] In planning the boycott, Professor Robinson printed over 50,000 flyers calling for all African Americans to boycott the city bus system for one day. As the African Americans in the 1950s Montgomery accounted for 60% of the ridership, many believed that boycotting would make a strong statement. Records show that 90% of those blacks who normally rode the buses honored the boycott.[5] This success led to a decision to extend the boycott until the old rules were abolished.

Boycotting the buses was difficult for many people. They had to utilize other forms of transportation, including taxis, car pools, and walking. For a time, the taxi drivers would only charge the boycotters a ten-cent minimum fee, instead of the usual 45-cent minimum. However, the city officials told the taxi drivers that any taxi driver caught giving a black a reduced fee would face prosecution. In addition, the city tried to stop the private car-pooling arrangements.[6] However, none of this dissuaded the boycotters. They formed organizations and met with city officials in an attempt to reach a settlement. It wasn't until the Montgomery Improvement Association (MIA), headed by Dr. Martin Luther King, Jr., sued in federal court asking the courts to extend the *Brown v. Board of Education* decision and hold that the rules governing public transportation be held unconstitutional.[7]

The court action was successful, and on December 21, 1956, the boycott was finally over. There was backlash from the victory, however. Snipers shot at the buses, while some whites attempted to start a "whites-only" bus service. In addition there were bombings of churches, and homes owned by prominent black citizens.[8] The Civil Rights Movement was far from over, but a huge victory had been won over the segregationists. Weeks after the boycott ended, ministers from the MJA joined other ministers from the Deep South and founded the Southern Christian Leadership Conference (SCLC). The SCLC led the fight for civil rights in the South. While the boycott was not the end of the quest for civil rights, it had an important role, for as Roberta Wright wrote, "It helped to launch a 10-year national struggle for freedom and justice, the Civil Rights Movement, that stimulated others to do the same at home and abroad."[9]

No. 9066 and Exclusion Order No. 34, which made it illegal for American citizens of Japanese descent to remain in certain areas of California deemed to be "military areas," while at the same time forbid these U.S. citizens from leaving those areas. While this may seem contradictory, the choice left to the affected individuals was to report to Assembly Centers (also called detention centers by some and concentration camps by others) where they were detained by the U.S. government. Mr. Korematsu refused to either leave his home or report to the Assembly Center and he was arrested for violating these orders and convicted. He ultimately appealed to the U.S. Supreme Court alleging that his constitutional rights had been violated.

KOREMATSU V. UNITED STATES 323 U.S. 214 (1944)

Mr. Justice BLACK delivered the opinion of the Court.

* * *

In the instant case prosecution of the petitioner was begun by information charging violation of an Act of congress, of March 21, 1942, 56 Stat. 173, 18 U.S.C.A. s 97a, which provides that

* * *

whoever shall enter, remain in, leave, or commit any act in any military area or military zone prescribed, under the authority of an Executive order of the President, by the Secretary of War, or by any military commander designated by the Secretary of War, contrary to the restrictions applicable to any such area or zone or contrary to the order of the Secretary of War or any such military commander, shall, if it appears that he knew or should have known of the existence and the extent of the restrictions or order and that his act was in violation thereof, be guilty of a misdemeanor and upon conviction shall be liable to a fine of not to exceed $5,000 or to imprisonment for not more than one year, or both, for each offense.'

Exclusion Order No. 34, which the petitioner knowingly and admitted violated was one of a number of military orders and proclamations, all of which were substantially based upon Executive Order No. 9066, 7 Fed. Reg. 1407. That order, issued after we were at war with Japan declared that 'the successful prosecution of the war requires every possible protection against espionage and against sabotage to national-defense material, national defense premises, and national defense utilities.'

* * *

One of the series of orders and proclamations, a curfew order . . . subjected all persons of Japanese ancestry in prescribed West Coast military areas to remain in their residences from 8 p.m. to 6 a.m. As is the case with the exclusion order here, that prior curfew order was designed as a 'protection against espionage and against sabotage. In *Kiyoshi Hirabayashi v. United States*, 320 U.S. 81, we sustained a conviction obtained for violation of the curfew order. The Hirabayashi conviction and this one thus rest on the same 1942 Congressional Act and the same basic executive and military orders, all of which orders were aimed at the twin dangers of espionage and sabotage . . .

In light of the principles we announced in the Hirabayashi case, we are unable to conclude that it was beyond the war power of Congress and the Executive to exclude those of Japanese ancestry from the West Coast war area at the time they did. True, exclusion from the area in which one's home is located is a far greater deprivation than constant confinement to the home from 8 p.m. to 6 a.m. Nothing short of apprehension by the proper military authorities of the gravest imminent danger to the public safety can constitutionally justify either. But exclusion from a threatened area, no less than curfew, has a definite and close relationship to the prevention of espionage and sabotage. The military authorities, charged with the primary responsibility of defending our shores, concluded that curfew provided inadequate protection and ordered exclusion. They did so as pointed out in our Hirabayashi opinion, in accordance with Congressional authority to the military to say who should, and who should not, remain in the threatened area.

In this case, the petitioner challenges the assumptions upon which we rested our conclusions in the Hirabayashi. He also urges that by May 1942, when Order No. 34 was promulgated, all danger of Japanese invasion of the West Coast had disappeared. After careful consideration of these contentions we are compelled to reject them.

* * *

Like curfew, exclusion of those Japanese origin was deemed necessary because of the presence of an unascertained number of disloyal members of the group, most of whom we have no doubt were loyal to this country. It was because we could not reject the finding of the military authorities that it was impossible to bring about an immediate

Continued

segregation of the disloyal from the loyal that we sustained the validity of the curfew order as applying to the whole group. In the instant case, temporary exclusion of the entire group was rested by the military on the same ground ... That there are members of the group who retained loyalties to Japan has been confirmed by investigations made subsequent to the exclusion ...

We uphold the exclusion order as of the time it was made and when the petitioner violated it ... In doing so, we are not unmindful of the hardships imposed by it upon a large group of American citizens ... But hardships are part of war, and war is an aggregation of hardships ... But when under conditions of modern warfare our shores are threatened by hostile forces, the power to protect must be commensurate with the threatened danger.

* * *

It is said that we are dealing here with the case of imprisonment of a citizen in a concentration camp solely because of his ancestry, without evidence or inquiry concerning his loyalty and good disposition towards the United States. Our task would be simple, our duty clear, were this a case involving the imprisonment of a loyal citizen in a concentration camp because of racial prejudice. Regardless of the true nature of the assembly and relocation centers—and we deem it unjustifiable to call them concentration camps with all the ugly connotations that term implies—we are dealing specifically with nothing but an exclusion order. To cast this case into outlines of racial prejudice, without reference to the real military dangers which were presented, merely confuses the issue. Korematsu was not excluded from the Military Area because of hostility to him or his race. He was excluded because we are at war with the Japanese Empire, because the properly constituted military authorities feared an invasion of our West Coast and felt constrained to take proper security measures, because they decided that the military urgency of the situation demanded that all citizens of Japanese ancestry be segregated from the West Coast temporarily, and finally, because Congress, reposing its confidence in this time of war in our military leaders—as inevitably it must—determined that they should have the power to do just this. There was evidence of disloyalty on the part of some, the military

authorities considered that the need for action was great, and time was short. We cannot—by availing ourselves of the calm perspective of hindsight—no way that at that time these actions were unjustified.

Affirmed.

Mr. Justice ROBERTS, dissenting.

I dissent, because I think the indisputable facts exhibit a clear violation of Constitutional rights.

This is not a case of keeping people off the streets at night, as was *Kiyoshi Hirabayashi v. United States*, 320 U.S. 81, nor a case of temporary exclusion of a citizen from an area for his own safety or that of the community, nor a case of offering him an opportunity to go temporarily out of an area where his presence might cause danger to himself or to his fellows. On the contrary, it is the case of convicting a citizen as a punishment for not submitting to imprisonment in a concentration camp, based on his ancestry, and solely because of his ancestry, without evidence of inquiry concerning his loyalty and good disposition towards the United States ...

The predicament in which the petitioner thus found himself was this: He was forbidden by Military Order, to leave the zone in which he lived; he was forbidden, by Military Order after a date fixed, to be found within that zone unless he were in an Assembly Center located in that zone [and I think it is clear] that an Assembly Center was a euphemism for a prison ...

In the dilemma that he dare not remain in his home, or voluntarily leave the area, without incurring criminal penalties and that the only way he could avoid punishment was to go to an Assembly Center and submit himself to military imprisonment, the petitioner did nothing.

* * *

We cannot shut our eyes to the fact that had the petitioner attempted to violate Proclamation No. 4 and leave the military area in which he lived he would have been arrested and tried and convicted for violation of Proclamation No. 4. The two conflicting orders, one which commanded him to stay and the other which commanded him to go, were nothing but a cleverly devised trap to accomplish the real purpose

Continued

of the military authority, which was to lock him up in a concentration camp. The only course by which the petitioner could avoid arrest and prosecution was to go to that camp according to instructions to be given him when he reported at a Civil Control Center. We know that is the fact. Why should we set up a figmentary and artificial situation instead of addressing ourselves to the actualities of the case?

* * *

I would reverse the judgment of conviction.

Mr. Justice MURPHY, dissenting.

The exclusion of 'all persons of Japanese ancestry, both alien and non-alien' form the Pacific Coast area on a plea of military necessity in the absence of martial law ought not to be approved. Such exclusion goes over 'the very brink of constitutional power' and falls into the ugly abyss of racism.

* * *

The judicial test of whether the Government, on a plea of military necessity, can validly deprive an individual of any of his constitutional rights is whether the deprivation is reasonably related to a public danger that is so 'immediate, imminent, and impending' as not to admit of delay and not to permit the intervention of ordinary constitutional processes to alleviate the danger . . .

The main reasons relied upon by those responsible for the forced evacuation, therefore, do not prove a reasonable relationship between the group characteristics of Japanese Americans and the dangers of invasion, sabotage and espionage. The reasons appear, instead, to be largely an accumulation of much of the misinformation, half-truths and insinuations that for years have been directed against Japanese Americans by people with racial and economic prejudices—the same people who have been among the foremost advocates of the evacuation. A military judgment based upon such racial and sociological considerations is not entitled to the great weight ordinarily given the judgment based upon strictly military considerations. Especially is this so when every charge relative to race, religion, culture, geographical local, and legal and economic status has been substantial discredited by independent studies made by experts in these matters.

* * *

I dissent, therefore, from this legalization of racism. Racial discrimination in any form and in any degree has no justifiable part whatever in our democratic way of life. It is unattractive in any setting but it is utterly revolting among a free people who have embraced the principles set forth in the Constitution of the United States.

EXHIBIT 8.2   Map of the Ten Relocation Camps

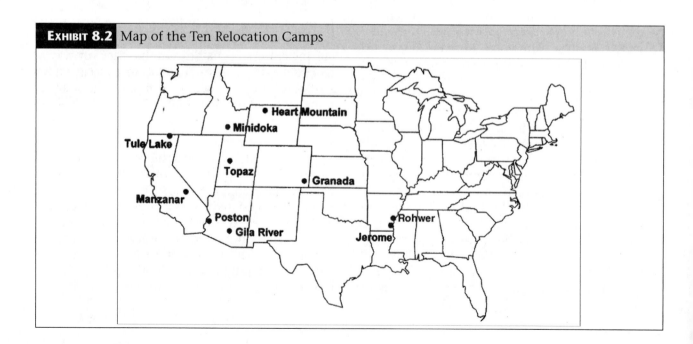

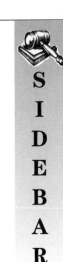

JAPANESE INTERNMENT AND THE RELOCATION CAMPS

In the aftermath of the terrorist attacks of September 11, 2001, it is much easier to understand the emotions that followed the attack by the Japanese at Pearl Harbor on December 7, 1941. The country was concerned about security and further attacks. It was these emotions that led President Franklin D. Roosevelt to issue Executive Order 9066 that authorized the War Department to evacuate many Japanese Americans and place them in internment camps. This order was given in spite of the fact that government officials were never able to prove any instance of sabotage or espionage among the West Coast Japanese population. This order virtually ensured that the affected individuals, many of whom were United States citizens would lose their homes and their businesses. However, the order was given, 10 camps were established and over 110,000 Japanese immigrants and Japanese Americans were housed in them.[10] Barbed wire fences, watchtowers, and armed guards surrounded these camps, and the barracks had no running water and each family was crowded into one room. These individuals were imprisoned without trial or any other type of due process. The government action was challenged in *Korematsu v. United States*, but as noted in the text, the Supreme Court upheld the action as a valid government function. It was not until 1976 that the United States government finally acknowledged that its actions were wrong. In Proclamation 4417, President Gerald R. Ford wrote: "We now know what we should have known then—not only was that evacuation wrong, but Japanese-Americans were and are loyal Americans."[11]

S I D E B A R

The majority in this case found that the military goal of national security and the concerns about espionage and sabotage justified the action taken against Japanese American citizens and that the means used to ensure this safety were reasonable and could not be done in a less restrictive manner. The dissents, however, indicate to us how divisive an issue this had become. There were many Americans who felt that what happened to these U.S. citizens was racism and that this was a betrayal of constitutional rights for an entire group of United States citizens. Many years later, the U.S. government compensated, or made **reparation**, to these citizens for the losses they suffered during their confinement in these Assembly Centers (see Exhibit 8.2).

reparation   payment for an injury; redress for a wrong done.

PROVING DISCRIMINATION

Based on *Korematsu* and other cases, it has become clear that the Court will use strict scrutiny when there is a legislative intent to discriminate or, in other words, purposeful discrimination. There are three ways to demonstrate purposeful discrimination. The first way is to demonstrate that the law discriminates on its face, or by the law's own explicit terms, it discriminates. An example of this is found in *Strauder v. West Virginia*[12] in which the Court reviewed a West Virginia law that allowed only white males over 21 years of age to serve as jurors. The plaintiff, an African American male, had been charged with murder and was convicted. He challenged his conviction on the grounds that he was denied his Fourteenth Amendment rights when this law was enforced and his jury was a panel of white males. The Court held that:

> "The very fact that colored people are singled out and expressly denied by a statute all right to participate in the administration of the law, as jurors, because of their color, though they are citizens, and may be in other respects fully qualified, is practically a brand upon them, affixed by the law, an assertion of their inferiority, and a stimulant to that race prejudice which is an impediment to securing to individuals of the race that equal justice which the law aims to secure to all others."[13]

The Court found, then, that this statute was discriminatory on its face, and that this is all that is required to demonstrate purposeful discrimination, therefore, that this plaintiff's conviction was unconstitutionally obtained.

A second way of demonstrating purposeful discrimination is when there is a law that does not appear to discriminate or is neutral, but the way that it is applied or administered is discriminatory. The case of *Yick Wo v. Hopkins*[14] in which the City of San Francisco enforced a city ordinance that gave the Board of Supervisors the authority to withhold permission to establish or maintain a laundry within the City and County of San Francisco. The ordinance was used by the Board of Supervisors to drive out many small laundries owned by the Chinese and give a monopoly to the larger laundries backed by Caucasian capital. The Court held that

> *"Though the law itself be fair on its face, and impartial in appearance, yet, if it is applied and administered by public authority with an evil eye and an unequal hand, so as practically to make unjust and illegal discriminations between persons in similar circumstances, material to their rights, the denial of equal justice is still within the prohibition of the constitution."*[15]

The discrimination found here against the Chinese laundry owners was thus held to be illegal. The statute looked neutral and would seem to apply to all laundries, but the Court found ample evidence to suggest that the Board of Supervisors was misusing its authority and applying the law in a manner that favored the majority. The fact that Yick Wo and the other Chinese laundry owners were not U.S. citizens did not alter the Court's finding. The Court noted that the Fourteenth Amendment applied, not just to protect citizens, but by its own words, applied to all persons within the jurisdiction, citizen or not. The Fourteenth Amendment requires that a statute be applied in an evenhanded manner, regardless of color, race, or ethnicity.

The third means of proving purposeful discrimination is a showing that while a law is neutral on its face, it was enacted with the purpose of discriminating. In doing so, the individual challenging the law can point to legislative history, statements by legislators during the enactment process, the law's **disparate impact** once it is enacted, and other circumstantial evidence of discriminatory intent. *Rogers v. Lodge*[16] demonstrates this means of proving purposeful discrimination. In this case, the plaintiff, a class of African American citizens from Burke County, Georgia, claimed that their First, Thirteenth, Fourteenth, and Fifteenth Amendment rights were violated by the county's at-large system of elections. A five-person County Board of Commissioners governed the county and all qualified voters in the county elected those individuals. In order to be elected, a candidate had to run for a specific seat and be elected by a majority vote. Under this arrangement, no African American had ever been elected to the board. The Court acknowledged that at-large voting schemes, like the one found in this case, minimized the voting strength of minority groups and generally resulted in the political majority electing those representatives that the majority felt best served their interests. The Court felt this type of scheme while appearing neutral on its face, was subject to challenge. The challenger would have to show, however, that the appearance of neutrality would be overcome with evidence that the scheme was being maintained for discriminatory purposes. The Court found that the challenger had provided such evidence and indicated by the trial court's finding that the at-large system in this county was maintained for discriminatory purposes. Specifically, the Court considered that evidence of this discriminatory purpose was supported by the fact that no African American had ever been elected to office in Burke County, that there were property ownership requirements, that there had been discrimination in the selection of grand jurors, the hiring of county employees, in the appointments to boards and committees, and the depressed socioeconomic status of blacks in the community. It was this

disparate impact
discrimination based on race, color, religion, sex, national origin, age, or disability that results from a practice that does not seem to be discriminatory and was not intended to be so.

historical discrimination that ". . . had restricted the present opportunity of blacks effectively to participate in the political process."[17] Thus, the Court upheld the District Court's finding that there was intentional discrimination on the part of Burke County and that the order dismantling the at-large election system in that county be upheld.

While *Rogers* demonstrates one way of proving the discriminatory intent behind a seemingly neutral law, this is not the best way to do so. The courts have held that using circumstantial evidence that may include de jure as well as de facto evidence of discrimination may accomplish this more effectively.

Why is the means of proving discrimination so important? The Court has held that an individual wishing to challenge the constitutionality of the law by using an equal protection discrimination claim must prove purposeful discrimination in one of the above three ways. Without this demonstration of a specific intent to discriminate and if all that was required is a showing that a disproportionate number of blacks and minorities are affected by the legislation, a significant number of laws would be invalidated just because the law places a more significant burden on minorities and the poor than on the more affluent members of society.[18] A holding of this magnitude would impact laws regarding sales tax, bridge tolls, minimum wage, and professional licensing. This would be a significant burden on the existing government structure, and the Court has been unwilling to allow this.

Occasionally, cases have been heard where there is evidence of mixed motives for the passage of a statute or regulatory scheme. These cases have questioned whether discrimination must be the sole motive for a law in order to claim an equal protection violation where the strict scrutiny standard is applied. The Court held that where there is more than one motive and one of the motives is discriminatory in nature, the statute would fail in spite of other, nondiscriminatory motives for enacting that law.

Another question that is often asked in mixed motive cases is what happens when the plaintiff is successful in showing a discriminatory motive? Once the plaintiff has done so, the burden of proof shifts to the defendant to show that the statute would have passed in spite of the discriminatory motive. If the defendant is successful in doing so, the court may find that the statute is valid in spite of the one discriminatory motive. The Court was willing to do this in *Personnel Administrator of Massachusetts v. Feeney*[19] in spite of the fact that the plaintiff in that case was able to demonstrate that there was an extreme discriminatory consequence to a statute, but was unable to demonstrate a discriminatory purpose. In that case, the plaintiff challenged a Massachusetts law that gave veterans a preference in hiring for state employment. The Court acknowledged that less than 2 percent of all veterans were female and that the impact this had on employment opportunities for women in that state had been severe. The Court pointed to the well-settled rule ". . . that the Fourteenth Amendment guarantees equal law, not equal results."[20] The Court acknowledged that the law might be the result of an unwise policy, but that plaintiff had failed to demonstrate a purpose to discriminate on the basis of sex, therefore, the Court held that the defendants had successfully overcome the constitutional challenge.

Another way to prove discriminatory intent is by the use of statistics. A statistical analysis is often the most effective tool in proving disparate impact allegations. By using statistics, it is possible to show how far reaching the disparate impact is on the minority alleging discrimination. In two cases the Court was asked to take a look at the voir dire practices of prosecutors that defendants claimed to be discriminatory. The first of these was the famous case of *Batson v. Kentucky*.[21]

BATSON V. KENTUCKY
476 U.S. 79 (1986)

Justice POWELL delivered the opinion of the Court.

I

Petitioner, a black man, was indicted in Kentucky on charges of second-degree burglary and receipt of stolen goods. On the first day of trial in Jefferson Circuit Court, the judge conducted *voir dire* examination of the venire, excused certain jurors for cause, and permitted the parties to exercise peremptory challenges. The prosecutor used his peremptory challenges to strike all four black persons in the venire, and a jury composed only of white persons was selected. Defense counsel moved to discharge the jury before it was sworn on the ground that the prosecutor's removal of the black veniremen violated petitioner's rights under the Sixth and Fourteenth Amendments to equal protection of the laws. Counsel requested a hearing on his motion. Without expressly ruling on the request for a hearing, the trial judge observed that the parties were entitled to use their peremptory challenges to "strike anybody they want to." The judge then denied petitioner's motion, reasoning that the cross-section requirement applies only to selection of the venire and not to selection of the petit jury itself.

The jury convicted petitioner on both counts. On appeal to the Supreme Court of Kentucky, petitioner pressed, among other claims, the argument concerning the prosecutor's use of peremptory challenges . . . [P]etitioner urged the court to follow decision of other States [citations omitted] and to hold that such conduct violated his rights under the Sixth Amendment and § 11 of the Kentucky Constitution . . . Petitioner also contended that the facts showed that the prosecutor had engaged in a "pattern" of discriminatory challenges in this case and established an equal protection violation . . .

The Supreme Court of Kentucky affirmed . . . We granted certiorari and now reverse.

II

In *Swain v. Alabama,* this Court recognized that a "State's purposeful or deliberate denial to Negroes on account of race of participation as jurors in the administration of justice violates the Equal Protection Clause." This principle has been "consistently and repeatedly" reaffirmed in numerous decisions of this Court both preceding and following *Swain.* We reaffirm the principle today.

* * *

III

The principles announced in *Strauder* never have been questioned in any subsequent decision of this Court. Rather, the Court has been called upon repeatedly to review the application of those principles to particular facts. A recurring question in these cases, as in any case alleging a violation of the Equal Protection Clause, was whether the defendant had met his burden of proving purposeful discrimination on the part of the State. That question also was at the heart of the portion of *Swain v. Alabama* we reexamine today.

A

Swain required the Court to decide, among other issues, whether a black defendant was denied equal protection by the State's exercise of peremptory challenges to exclude members of his race from the petit jury. The record in *Swain* showed that the prosecutor had used the State's peremptory challenges to strike the six black persons included on the petit jury venire. While rejecting the defendant's claim for failure to prove purposeful discrimination, the Court nonetheless indicated that the Equal Protection Clause placed some limits on the State's exercise of peremptory challenges.

The Court sought to accommodate the prosecutor's historical privilege of peremptory challenge free of judicial control, and the constitutional prohibition on exclusion of persons from jury service on account of race. While the Constitution does not confer a right to peremptory challenges, those challenges traditionally have been viewed as one means of assuring the selection of a qualified and unbiased jury. To preserve the peremptory nature of the prosecutor's challenge, the Court in *Swain* declined to scrutinize his actions in a particular case by relying on a presumption that he properly exercised the State's challenges.

Continued

The Court went on to observe, however, that a State may not exercise its challenges in contravention of the Equal Protection Clause. It was impermissible for a prosecutor to use his challenges to exclude blacks from the jury "for reasons wholly unrelated to the outcome of the particular case on trial" or to deny to blacks "the same right and opportunity to participate in the administration of justice enjoyed by the white population." Accordingly, a black defendant could make out a prima facie case of purposeful discrimination on proof that the peremptory challenge system was "being perverted" in that manner . . .

∗ ∗ ∗

A number of lower courts following the teaching of *Swain* reasoned that proof of repeated striking of blacks over a number of cases was necessary to establish a violation of the Equal Protection Clause. Since this interpretation of *Swain* has placed on defendants a crippling burden of proof, prosecutors' peremptory challenges are now largely immune from constitutional scrutiny. For reasons that follow, we reject this evidentiary formulation as inconsistent with standards that have developed since *Swain* for assessing a prima facie case under the Equal Protection Clause.

B

Since the decision in *Swain*, we have explained that our cases concerning selection of the venire reflect the general equal protection principle that the "invidious quality" of governmental action claimed to be racially discriminatory "must ultimately be traced to a racially discriminatory purpose." As in any equal protection case, the "burden is, of course," on the defendant who alleges discriminatory selection of the venire "to prove the existence of purposeful discrimination." In deciding if the defendant has carried his burden of persuasion, a court must undertake "a sensitive inquiry into such circumstantial and direct evidence of intent as may be available." Circumstantial evidence of invidious intent may include proof of disproportionate impact. We have observed that under some circumstances proof of discriminatory impact "may for all practical purposes demonstrate unconstitutionality because in various circumstances the discrimination is very difficult to explain on nonracial grounds." For example, "total or seriously disproportionate exclusion of

Negroes from jury venire . . . is itself such an 'unequal application of the law . . . as to show intentional discrimination,' ".

Moreover, since *Swain*, we have recognized that a black defendant alleging that members of his race have been impermissibly excluded from the venire may make out a prima facie case of purposeful discrimination by showing that the totality of the relevant facts gives rise to an inference of discriminatory purpose. Once the defendant makes the requisite showing, the burden shifts to the State to explain adequately the racial exclusion. The State cannot meet this burden on mere general assertions that its officials did not discriminate or that they properly performed their official duties. Rather, the State must demonstrate that "permissible racially neutral selection criteria and procedures have produced the monochromatic results."

The showing necessary to establish a prima facie case of purposeful discrimination in selection of the venire may be discerned in this Court's decisions. The defendant initially must show that he is a member of a racial group capable of being singled out for differential treatment. In combination with that evidence, a defendant may then make a prima facie case by proving that in the particular jurisdiction members of his race have not been summoned for jury service over an extended period of time. Proof of systematic exclusion from the venire raises an inference of purposeful discrimination because the "result bespeaks discrimination."

Since the ultimate issue is whether the State has discriminated in selecting the defendant's venire, however, the defendant may establish a prima facie case "in other way than by evidence of long-continued unexplained absence" of members of his race "from many panels." In cases involving the venire, this Court has found a prima facie case on proof that members of the defendant's race were substantially underrepresented on the venire from which his jury was drawn, and that the venire was selected under a practice providing "the opportunity for discrimination." This combination of factors raises the necessary inference of purposeful discrimination because the Court has declined to attribute to chance the absence of black citizens on a particular jury array where the selection mechanism is subject to abuse. When circumstances suggest the need, the trial court must undertake a "factual inquiry" that "takes into

Continued

account all possible explanatory factors" in the particular case.

Thus, since the decision in *Swain*, this Court has recognized that a defendant may make a prima facie showing of purposeful racial discrimination in selection of the venire by relying solely on the facts concerning its selection *in his case*. These decisions are in accordance with the proposition articulated in *Arlington Heights v. Metropolitan Housing Department Corp.,* that "a consistent pattern of official racial discrimination" is not "a necessary predicate to a violation of the Equal Protection Clause. A single invidiously discriminatory governmental act" is not "immunized by the absence of such discrimination in the making of other comparable decisions." For evidentiary requirements to dictate that "several must suffer discrimination" before one could object would be inconsistent with the promise of equal protection to all.

The standards for assessing a prima facie case in the context of discriminatory selection of the venire have been fully articulated since *Swain*. The principles support our conclusion that a defendant may establish a prima facie case of purposeful discrimination in the selection of the petit jury solely on evidence concerning the prosecutor's exercise of peremptory challenges at the defendant's trial. To establish such a case, the defendant must first show that he is a member of a cognizable racial group and that the prosecutor has exercised peremptory challenges to remove from the venire members of the defendant's race. Second, the defendant is entitled to rely on the fact, as to which there can be no dispute, that peremptory challenges constitute a jury selection practice that permits "those to discriminate who are of a mind to discriminate." Finally, the defendant must show that these facts and any other relevant circumstances raise an inference that the prosecutor used that practice to exclude the veniremen from the petit jury on account of their race. This combination of factors in the empanelling of the petit jury, as in the selection of the venire, raises the necessary inference of purposeful discrimination.

In deciding whether the defendant has made the requisite showing, the trial court should consider all relevant circumstances. For example, a "pattern" of strikes against black jurors included in a particular venire might give rise to an inference of discrimination. Similarly, the prosecutor's questions and statements during *voir dire* examination and the exercising his challenges may support or refute an inference of discriminatory purpose. These examples are merely illustrative. We have confidence that trial judges, experience in supervising *voir dire* will be able to decide if the circumstances concerning the prosecutor's use of peremptory challenges creates a prima facie case of discrimination against black jurors.

Once the defendant makes a prima facie showing, the burden shifts to the State to come forward with a neutral explanation for challenging black jurors. Though this requirement imposes a limitation in some cases on the full peremptory character of the historic challenge, we emphasize that the prosecutor's explanation need not rise to the level justifying exercise of a challenge for case. But the prosecutor may not rebut the defendant's prima facie case of discrimination by stating merely that he challenged jurors of the defendant's race on the assumption—or his intuitive judgment—that they would be partial to the defendant because of their shared race. Just as the Equal Protection Clause forbids the States to exclude black persons from the venire on the assumption that blacks as a group are unqualified to serve as jurors, so it forbids the State to strike black veniremen on the assumption that they will be biased in a particular case simply because the defendant is black. The core guarantee of equal protection, ensuring citizens that their State will not discriminate on account of race, would be meaningless were we to approve the exclusion of jurors on the basis of such assumptions, which arise solely from the jurors' race. Nor may the prosecutor rebut the defendant's case merely by denying that he had a discriminatory motive or "affirm[ing] [his] good faith in making individual selections." If these general assertions were accepted in rebutting a defendant's prima facie case, the Equal Protection Clause "would be but a vain and illusory requirement." The prosecutor therefore must articulate a neutral explanation related to the particular case to be tried. The trial court then will have the duty to determine if the defendant has established purposeful discrimination.

* * *

V

In this case, petitioner made a timely objection to the prosecutor's removal of all black persons on the venire. Because the trial court flatly rejected

Continued

> the objection without requiring the prosecutor to give an explanation for his action, we remand this case for further proceedings. If the trial court decides that the facts establish, prima facie, purposeful discrimination and the prosecutor does not come forward with a neutral explanation for his action, our precedents require that petitioner's conviction be reversed.
>
> *It is so ordered.*

In *Batson,* the defendant statistically demonstrated that the prosecutor's use of peremptory challenges discriminated against blacks. Once defendant had done so, the burden of proof shifted to the state to demonstrate that the prosecutor's actions were justified. In this case, the state was unable to do so, and the fact that the prosecutor consistently declined to seat blacks in trials with black defendants, along with the types of questions asked by the prosecutor during the **voir dire** process convinced the Court that a discriminatory practice existed, which violated the rights of the defendant as well as other potential jurors. Therefore, the rule now exists that says that, while a juror does not have an absolute right to a jury composed of individuals of his or her own race, that defendant does have a right to be tried by a jury whose members are selected by a nondiscriminatory process.

In a later case, the Court also struck down the use of gender as a reason for exclusion from serving on a jury. In *J.E.B. v. Alabama,*[22] the petitioner was named as the alleged father of a minor child. He denied this. The State of Alabama filed a complaint for paternity and child support and the matter was tried in the State trial court. When the jury was picked, the State used 9 of its 10 peremptory challenges to remove male jurors. The final jury was composed of all female jurors. Petitioner J.E.B. challenged the selection process, but the trial court rejected his challenge and empaneled the all-female jury. This jury found the petitioner to be the father and the trial court judge ordered the petitioner to pay child support. The petitioner challenged the decision and the Alabama Court of Civil Appeals affirmed the trial court decision. After the Supreme Court of Alabama denied certiorari, the Petitioner appealed to the U.S. Supreme Court.

The Petitioner argued that the same logic used by the Court in *Batson v. Kentucky* applied in this case as well. Justice Blackmun wrote the opinion and the Court affirmed that intentional discrimination on basis of race or gender violates the Equal Protection Clause. The Court found that the petitioner had demonstrated a pattern of discrimination in the manner in which the State was using peremptory challenges in these types of cases and because of the "long and unfortunate history of sex discrimination"[23] in the United States, the Court used the heightened scrutiny afforded all gender-based classifications. The State then had the burden of demonstrating that the discriminatory use of peremptory challenges furthered the legitimate state interest of providing a fair and impartial trial.

The State of Alabama argued in its Brief for Respondent

> *". . . that its decision to strike virtually all the males from the jury in this case 'may reasonably have been based upon the perception, supported by history, that men otherwise totally qualified to serve upon a jury in any case might be more sympathetic and receptive to the arguments of a man alleged in a paternity action to be the father of an out-of-wedlock child, while women equally qualified to serve upon a jury might be more sympathetic and receptive to the arguments of the complaining witness who bore the child.' "*[24]

The Court emphatically rejected this argument saying that it would not accept as a defense to gender-based discrimination "the very stereotype the law condemns."[25] The Court reaffirmed its reasoning in *Batson* and other cases which

voir dire (French) The preliminary in-court questioning of a prospective witness (or juror) to determine competency to testify (or suitability to decide a case).

followed in saying that it would not allow discrimination in the jury selection process, whether the discrimination was race- or gender-based. The Court pointed out that it was not just the litigants who would be hurt by continuing to allow this type of discrimination, but that such discrimination would impact the entire trial process. Allowing the State of Alabama or any other state to continue to use peremptory challenges in a discriminatory manner would create the impression that the judicial system is willing to suppress participation by one gender or racial group. This would violate the fundamental character of the democratic system and deny equal opportunity to participate in the process. Individual jurors have a constitutional right to be part of a voir dire process that is nondiscriminatory.

No matter which of the three ways of proving discrimination are employed, the Court has consistently used the strict scrutiny standard to decide whether the state action is constitutional. This is the standard that the Court employed in deciding other discrimination issues as well.

DISCRIMINATION IN PUBLIC ACCOMMODATIONS AND SCHOOLS

The history of discrimination in the U.S. public accommodation, transportation, and education systems is significant. By statute and by deed, discrimination was practiced daily in public life for many years and, for quite some time, the courts throughout the country condoned such discrimination. One of the earliest cases challenging discrimination in the public sector was *Plessy v. Ferguson*.[26] This case challenged the notion that it was possible to provide separate accommodations for African Americans while still providing equal accommodations. The petitioner in this case was a citizen of Louisiana. That state had a statute that provided for railway companies to provide equal but separate accommodations for whites and blacks. The petitioner was 7/8 Caucasian and 1/8 African American, and when he bought a ticket to ride the train, he was assigned to ride in the coach used for blacks. When he took a seat in the coach set aside for whites, the conductor told him that he had to vacate that seat and go to the other coach. Petitioner refused to do so, and was arrested and charged with a violation of the Louisiana law. Petitioner challenged that law claiming that it violated both the Thirteenth and the Fourteenth Amendments. The Court quickly rejected the argument that the Thirteenth Amendment applied here, however, the discussion of the Fourteenth Amendment was much longer. After discussing what the Fourteenth Amendment was enacted to do, the court said the main purpose of the amendment ". . . was to establish the citizenship of the United States and of the states, and to protect from the hostile legislation of the states the privileges and immunities of citizens of the United States, as distinguished from those of citizens of the states."[27] The Court went on to say:

> *"The object of the amendment was undoubtedly to enforce the absolute equality of the two races before the law, but, in the nature of things, it could not have been intended to abolish distinctions based upon color, or to enforce social, as distinguished from political, equality, or a commingling of the two races upon terms unsatisfactory to either. Laws permitting, and even requiring, their separation, in places where they are liable to be brought into contact, do not necessarily imply the inferiority of either race to the other, and have been generally, if not universally, recognized as within the competency of the state legislature in the exercise of their police power. The most common instance of this is connected with the establishment of separate schools for white and colored children, which have been held to be a valid exercise of the legislative power even by courts of the states where the political rights of the colored race have been longest and most earnestly enforced."[28]*

The Court concluded that it could not accept the petitioner's argument that the enforced separation of the two races indicated that the African American race was inferior. The Court held that this argument assumes that it, or the legislature of a state or the federal government, can eliminate social prejudice by forcing the races to mingle. This, the Court said, was an erroneous assumption and that such equality can only be achieved as ". . . the result of natural affinities, a mutual appreciation of each other's merits and a voluntary consent of individuals."[29] With this, the Court validated the argument that it was possible to have separate but equal accommodations based on race. This so-called **separate but equal doctrine** was used by the justice system throughout the United States from 1896 until 1954 as a means of validating this sort of discriminatory practice. In 1954, the Court decided *Brown v. The Board of Education*[30] (also known as *Brown I*) and the separate but equal doctrine espoused in *Plessy* was overturned.

separate but equal doctrine the rule, established in the 1896 Supreme Court case *Plessy v. Ferguson* and then rejected as unconstitutional in the 1954 *Brown* decision, that when races are given substantially equal facilities, they may lawfully be segregated.

BROWN ET AL. V. BOARD OF EDUCATION OF TOPEKA, SHAWNEE COUNTY, KANSAS, ET AL.
347 U.S. 483 (1954)

Mr. Chief Justice WARREN delivered the opinion of the Court.

These cases come to us from the States of Kansas, South Carolina, Virginia, and Delaware. They are premised on different facts and different local conditions, but a common legal question justifies their consideration together in this consolidated opinion.

In each of these cases, minors of the Negro race, through their legal representatives, seek the aid of the courts in obtaining admission to the public schools of their community on a nonsegregated basis. In each instance, they have been denied admission to schools attended by white children under laws requiring or permitting segregation according to race. This segregation was alleged to deprive the plaintiffs of the equal protection of the laws under the Fourteenth Amendment. In each of the cases other than the Delaware case, a three-judge federal district court denied relief to the plaintiffs on the so-called 'separate but equal' doctrine announced by this court in *Plessy v. Ferguson.* Under that doctrine, equality of treatment is accorded when the races are provided substantially equal facilities, even though these facilities be separate . . .

The plaintiffs contend that segregated public schools are not 'equal' and cannot be made 'equal' and that hence they are deprived of the equal protection of the laws. Because of the obvious importance of the question presented,

the Court took jurisdiction. Argument was heard in the 1952 Term, and reargument was heard this Term on certain questions propounded by the Court.

✳ ✳ ✳

. . . there are findings below that the Negro and white schools involved have been equalized or are being equalized, with respect to buildings, curricula, qualifications and salaries of teachers, and other 'tangible' factors. Our decision, therefore, cannot turn on merely a comparison of these tangible factors in the Negro and white schools involved in each of the cases. We must look instead to the effect of segregation itself on public education.

In approaching this problem, we cannot turn the clock back to 1868 when the Amendment was adopted, or even to 1896 when *Plessy v. Ferguson* was written. We must consider public education in the light of its full development and its present place in American life throughout the Nation. Only in this way can it be determined if segregation in public schools deprives these plaintiffs of the equal protection of the laws.

Today, education is perhaps the most important function of state and local governments. Compulsory school attendance laws and the great expenditures for education both demonstrate our recognition of the importance of education to

Continued

our democratic society. It is required in the performance of our most basic public responsibilities, even service in the armed forces. It is the very foundation of good citizenship. Today it is a principal instrument in awakening the child to cultural values, in preparing him for later professional training, and in helping him to adjust normally to his environment. In these days, it is doubtful that any child may reasonably be expected to succeed in life if he is denied the opportunity of an education. Such an opportunity, where the state has undertaken to provide it, is a right which must be made available to all on equal terms.

We come then to the question presented: Does segregation of children in public schools solely on the basis of race, even though the physical facilities and other 'tangible' factors may be equal, deprive the children of the minority group of equal educational opportunities? We believe that it does.

In *Sweatt v. Painter,* in finding that a segregated law school for Negroes could not provide them equal educational opportunities, this Court relied in large part on 'those qualities which are incapable of objective measurement but which make for greatness in a law school.' In *McLaurin v. Oklahoma State Regents,* the Court, in requiring that a Negro admitted to a white graduate school be treated like all other students, against resort to intangible considerations:

∗ ∗ ∗

his ability to study, to engage in discussions and exchange views with other students, and, in general, to learn his profession.' Such considerations apply with added force to children in grade and high schools. To separate them from others of similar age and qualifications solely because of their race generates a feeling of inferiority as to their status in the community that may affect their hearts and minds in a way unlikely ever to be undone . . .

Whatever may have been the extent of psychological knowledge at the time of *Plessy v. Ferguson,* this finding is amply supported by modern authority. Any language in *Plessy v. Ferguson* contrary to this finding is rejected. We conclude that in the field of public education the doctrine of 'separate but equal' has no place. Separate educational facilities are inherently unequal. Therefore, we hold that the plaintiffs and others similarly situated for whom the actions have been brought are, by reason of the segregation complained of, deprived of the equal protection of the laws guaranteed by the Fourteenth Amendment. This disposition makes unnecessary any discussion whether such segregation also violates the Due Process Clause of the Fourteenth Amendment.

. . . We have now announced that such segregation is a denial of equal protection of the laws. In order that we may have the full assistance of the parties in formulating degree, the cases will be restored to the docket, and the parties are requested to present further argument . . .

It is so ordered.

The Court used the findings of psychologists and educators in deciding to overturn the separate but equal doctrine and rejected the type of legislative history analysis found in *Plessy.* The Court rejected the State argument that having "tangible" factors equal was all that was required by the Constitution and found that the intangible factors kept children in the black schools from receiving an education equal to that of students in white schools. This case applied to state schools. On the same day that it decided *Brown I,* the Court also decided the case of *Bolling v. Sharpe.*[31] In this case the issue involved segregation in the Washington, D.C., public schools. The Court held that segregation was no more acceptable in the public schools of this federal district than it had been in state public schools and held: "We hold that racial segregation in the public schools of the District of Columbia is a denial of the due process of law guaranteed by the Fifth Amendment to the Constitution."[32]

The Aftermath of *Brown I*

Brown I was only the beginning of desegregation of the public schools. While the foundation for desegregation of the public schools was laid in *Brown I, Brown v. Board of Education of Topeka* (also known as *Brown II*)[33] did more to generate change in the U.S. education system. In *Brown II* the Court invited the U.S. Attorney and the Attorneys General of all states to join in oral arguments about how best to implement desegregation. After hearing these oral arguments and reading all the submitted briefs, the Court found that since the overall solution would best be met by a variety of local approaches, the Federal District Courts, which originally heard these cases, were given the authority to supervise the desegregation in public schools and therefore remanded the cases to those courts. When guiding the district courts in supervising desegregation, the Court ordered that **equitable** principles be used to effectuate a desegregation plan. The Court said: "Traditionally, equity has been characterized by a practical flexibility in shaping its remedies and by a facility for adjusting and reconciling public and private needs."[34] The Court went on to say that the district courts must take into account both public and private considerations, but that the defendants would be required to take prompt action toward compliance. The Court recognized that the required changes would take time and if additional time were necessary, in the district court's view, that would be acceptable. If a request for additional time was made, "The burden rests upon the defendants to establish that such time is necessary in the public interest and is consistent with good faith compliance at the earliest practicable date."[35] With this, the Courts not only put the district courts in a position to supervise local school districts, it gave those courts the discretion to allow more time, if needed, to effectuate those changes. This ongoing jurisdiction allowed the federal courts to maintain control and push for desegregation in those school districts where there was reluctance to comply. The Court chose this means of instituting desegregation with the hope that any public outrage or fear of desegregation would diminish as the process proceeded.

Brown II did not guarantee, however, that desegregation would go smoothly in all instances. Some school districts were so opposed to desegregation that they actively looked for ways to delay desegregation and at the time, they were outwardly hostile to the process. Most school districts tried to comply with the Court's order and often made good-faith efforts toward that goal, but other state and local officials or the general public did not always reflect this cooperation. In 1958, the Governor of Arkansas and the state legislature attempted to block the desegregation of Central High in Little Rock, Arkansas (see Exhibit 8.3). This failure to obey the Court's order is discussed in the case *Cooper v. Aaron*.

equitable just, fair, and right for a particular situation.

COOPER V. AARON
358 U.S. 1 (1958)

Opinion of the Court by The Chief Justice, Mr. Justice BLACK, Mr. Justice FRANKFURTER, Mr. Justice DOUGLAS, Mr. Justice BURTON, Mr. Justice CLARK, Mr. Justice HARLAN, Mr. Justice BRENNAN, and Mr. Justice WHITTAKER.

As this case reaches us it raises questions of the highest importance to the maintenance of our federal system of government. It necessarily involves a claim by the Governor and the Legislature of a State that there is no duty on state officials to obey federal court orders resting on this Court's considered interpretation of the United States Constitution. Specifically, it involves actions by the Governor and Legislature of Arkansas upon the premise that they are not bound by our holding in *Brown v. Board of Education*.

∗ ∗ ∗

The following are the facts and circumstances so far as necessary to show how the legal questions are presented.

On May 17, 1954, this Court decided that enforced racial segregation in the public schools of a State is a denial of the equal protection of the laws enjoined by the 14th Amendment.

Continued

In the formulation of that decree the Court recognized that good faith compliance with the principles declared in Brown might in some situations 'call for elimination of a variety of obstacles in making the transition to school systems operated in accordance with the constitutional principles set forth in our May 17, 1954, decision.'

* * *

Under such circumstances, the District Courts were directed to require 'a prompt and reasonable start toward full compliance,' and to take such action as was necessary to bring about the end of racial segregation in public schools 'with all deliberate speed.' Of course, in many locations, obedience to the duty of desegregation would require the immediate general admission of Negro children, otherwise qualified as students for their appropriate classes, at particular schools . . .

On May 20, 1954, three days after the first Brown opinion, the Little Rock District School Board adopted, and on May 23, 1954, made public, a statement of policy entitled 'Supreme Court Decisions—Segregation in Public Schools.' In this statement the Board recognized that

> 'It is our responsibility to comply with Federal Constitutional Requirements and we intend to do so when the Supreme Court of the United States outlines the method to be followed.'

Thereafter the Board undertook studies of the administrative problems confronting the transition to a desegregated public school system at Little Rock . . .

While the School Board was thus going forward with its preparation for desegregating the Little Rock school system, other state authorities, in contrast, were actively pursuing a program designed to perpetuate in Arkansas the system of racial segregation which this Court had held violated the Fourteenth Amendment . . .

The School Board and the Superintendent of Schools nevertheless continued with preparations to carry out the first stage of the desegregation program. Nine Negro children were scheduled for admission in September 1957 to Central High School, which has more than two thousand students . . .

On September 2, 1957, the date before these Negro students were to enter Central High, the school authorities were met with drastic opposing action on the part of the Governor of Arkansas who dispatched units of the Arkansas National Guard to the Central High School grounds and placed the school 'off limits' to colored students. As found by the District Court in subsequent proceedings, the Governor's action had not been requested by the school authorities, and was entirely unheralded.

* * *

. . . The Governor's action caused the School Board to request the Negro students on September 2 not attend the high school 'until the legal dilemma was solved.' The next day, September 3, 1957, the Board petitioned the District Court for instructions . . . The court determined that this was not a reason for departing from the approved plan, and ordered the School Board and Superintendent to proceed with it.

On the morning of the next day, September 4, 1957, the Negro children attempted to enter the high school but, as the District Court later found, units of the Arkansas National Guard 'acting pursuant to the Governor's order, stood shoulder to shoulder at the school grounds and thereby forcibly prevented the 9 Negro students

* * *

from entering,' as they continued to do every school day during the following three weeks.

That same day, September 4, 1957, the United States Attorney for the Eastern District of Arkansas was requested by the District Court to begin an immediate investigation in order to fix responsibility for the interference with the orderly implementation of the District Court's direction to carry out the desegregation program. Three days later, September 7, the District Court denied a petition of the School Board and Superintendent of Schools for an order temporarily suspending continuance of the program.

Upon completion of the United States Attorney's investigation, he and the Attorney General of the United States, at the District Court's request, entered the proceedings and filed a petition on behalf of the United States as *amicus curiae,* to enjoin the Governor of Arkansas and the officers of the Arkansas National Guard from further attempts to prevent obedience to the court's order. After hearings on the petition, the District Court found that the School Board's plan had been obstructed by the Governor through

Continued

the use of National Guard troops, and granted a preliminary injunction on September 20, 1957, enjoining the Governor and the officers of the Guard from preventing the attendance of Negro children at Central High School . . .

The next school day was Monday, September 23, 1957. The Negro children entered the high school that morning under the protection of the Little Rock Police Department and members of the Arkansas State Police . . . On September 25, however, the President of the United States dispatched federal troops to Central High School . . . Regular army troops continued at the high school until November 27, 1957. They were then replaced by federalized National Guardsmen who remained throughout the balance of the school year. Eight of the Negro students remained in attendance at the school throughout the school year.

We now come to the aspect of the proceeding presently before us. On February 20, 1958, the School Board and the Superintendent of Schools filed a petition in the District Court seeking a postponement of their program for desegregation. Their position in essence was that because of extreme public hostility, which they stated had been engendered largely by the official attitudes and actions of the Governor and the Legislature, the maintenance of sound educational program at Central High School, with the Negro students in attendance, would be impossible.

* * *

After a hearing the District Court granted the relief requested by the Board.

* * *

. . . The Negro respondents appealed to the Court of Appeals for the Eighth Circuit and also sought there a stay of the District Court's judgment . . . the Negro respondents, on August 23, 1958, applied to Mr. Justice Whittaker, as Circuit Justice for the Eighth Circuit, to stay the order of the Court of Appeals withholding its own mandate and also to stay the District Court's judgment . . . Recognizing the vital importance of a decision of the issues in time to permit arrangements to be made for the 1958–1959 school year, [citations omitted] we convened in Special Term on August 28, 1958, and heard oral argument on the respondents' motions and also argument of the Solicitor General, who, by invitation, appeared for the United States as *amicus curiae*, and asserted that the Court of Appeals' judgment was clearly correct on the mer-

its, and urged that we vacate its stay forthwith . . . we unanimously affirmed the judgment of the Court of Appeals in the *per curiam* opinion set forth in the margin at the outset of this opinion.

In affirming the judgment of the Court of Appeals which reversed the District Court we have accepted without reservation the position of the School Board, the Superintendent of Schools, and their counsel that they displayed entire good faith in the conduct of these proceedings and in dealing with the unfortunate and distressing sequence of events which has been outlined. We likewise accepted the findings of the District Court as to the conditions at Central High School during the 1957–1958 school year, and also the findings that the educational process of all the students, white and colored, of that school has suffered and will continue to suffer if the conditions which prevailed last year are permitted to continue.

The significance of these findings, however, is to be considered in light of the fact, indisputably revealed by the record before us, that the conditions they depict are directly traceable to the actions of legislators and executive officials of the State of Arkansas, taken in their official capacities, which reflect their own determination to resist this Court's decision in the Brown case and which have brought about violent resistance to that decision in Arkansas . . .

One may well sympathize with the position of the Board in the face of the frustrating conditions which have confronted it, but, regardless of the Board's good faith, the actions of the other state agencies responsible for those conditions compel us to reject the Board's legal position . . .

The constitutional rights of respondents are not to be sacrificed or yielded to the violence and disorder which have followed upon the actions of the Governor and Legislature . . . Thus law and order are not here to be preserved by depriving the Negro children of their constitutional rights. The record before us clearly establishes that the growth of the Board's difficulties to a magnitude beyond its unaided power to control is the product of state action.

* * *

The controlling legal principles are plain. The command of the Fourteenth Amendment is that no 'State' shall deny to any person within its

Continued

jurisdiction the equal protection of the laws. 'A State acts by its legislative, its executive, or its judicial authorities. It can act in no other way. The constitutional provision, therefore, must mean that no agency of the State, or of the officers or agents by whom its powers are exerted, shall deny to any person within its jurisdiction the equal protection of the laws. Whoever, by virtue of public position under a State government,

* * *

denies or takes away the equal protection of the laws, violates the constitutional inhibition; and as he acts in the name and for the State, and is clothed with the State's power, his act is that of the State. This must be so, or the constitutional prohibition has no meaning.' *Ex parte Virginia.* Thus the prohibitions of the Fourteenth Amendment extend to all action of the State denying equal protection of the laws; whatever the agency of the State taking the action In short, the constitutional rights of children not to be discriminated against in school admission on grounds of race or color declared by this Court in the Brown case can neither be nullified openly and directly by state legislators or state executive or judicial officers, or nullified indirectly by them through evasive schemes for segregation whether attempted 'ingeniously or ingenuously.'

* * *

No state legislator or executive or judicial officer can war against the Constitution without violating his undertaking to support it. Chief Justice Marshall spoke for a unanimous Court in saying that 'If the legislatures of the several states may, at will, annul the judgments of the courts of the United States, and destroy the rights acquired under those judgments, the constitution itself becomes a solemn mockery.'

* * *

United States v. Peters. A Governor who asserts a power to nullify a federal court order is similarly restrained. If he had such power, said Chief Justice Hughes, in 1932, also for a unanimous Court, 'it is manifest that the fiat of a state Governor, and not the Constitution of the United States, would be the supreme law of the land; that the restrictions of the Federal Constitution upon the exercise of state power would be but impotent phases.'

* * *

Sterling v. Constantin

It is, of course, quite true that the responsibility for public education is primarily the concern of the States, but it is equally true that such responsibilities, like all other state activity, must be exercised consistently with federal constitutional requirements as they apply to state action. The Constitution created a government dedicated to equal justice under law. The Fourteenth Amendment embodied and emphasized that ideal.

* * *

S I D E B A R

After the Supreme Court ordered that public schools be integrated without any undue delay, many schools worked toward that goal. The public schools in Little Rock began planning for integration, but found much resistance in the community and in the state government. In the fall of 1957, Little Rock's Central High School prepared to enroll nine African American students, but Governor Orval Faubus ordered the Arkansas National Guard to surround the school to preserve the peace. White supremacy groups had threatened to cause problems at the school, and Governor Faubus argued that the presence of the National Guard was necessary. Later, Federal District Court Judge Ronald Davies held that the Governor had used the troops to prevent integration and ordered the Governor to remove the National Guard. Finally, on September 20, 1957, the nine African American students, popularly known as the Little Rock 9, entered the school by the side door, but as they attempted to register for classes, violence broke out in the crowd surrounding the school, and the Little Rock 9 were forced to leave the school.[36]

EXHIBIT 8.3   The Little Rock Nine

Continued

Little Rock Mayor Woodrow Mann asked President Eisenhower to send federal troops to maintain order at the school and complete the integration process. President Eisenhower sent 1,000 members of the 101st Airborne Division and federalized 10,000 Arkansas National Guard. These troops escorted the Little Rock 9 back into Central High on September 25, 1957. The students were finally allowed to start classes at Central High, but that doesn't mean the violence and hatred were past. The Little Rock 9 were each given personal guards to be with them initially, but eventually those personal guards were discontinued. Guards or no guards, the white students taunted the Little Rock 9, some even physically assaulting the African American students. The families of the Little Rock 9 experienced tremendous pressure to take their children out of Central High. Three of the parents were fired from their jobs. One of the nine, Minnijean Brown, was suspended from Central High for retaliation, but the other eight remained for the entire school year.

In May 1957, Ernest Green became the first African American to graduate from Central High School. The following year, the Governor closed the public high schools in Little Rock to avoid further integration, and even though the Supreme Court later ordered the schools reopened, the battle continued. It wasn't until the fall of 1972 that all grades in the Little Rock School District became integrated. But it was the courage of the Little Rock 9 that was the first step toward the integration of that school system.

This case clearly demonstrates the hostility toward desegregation of public schools that was prevalent in many parts of the country. Attempts to maintain segregated schools took place, not just in Arkansas, but in many school districts and at the university level as well. For example, the Governor of the State of Alabama also called out the National Guard, but instead of attempting to block the desegregation of public secondary schools, he did it in an effort to prevent the desegregation of the University of Alabama. The Court was equally clear in its decision that it would not tolerate any state entity attempting to bypass the Court's decisions or ignore the Constitution.

Other Desegregation Plans and Avoiding Desegregation

Other school districts tried other plans to either slow desegregation or avoid it altogether. In 1963 the Court decided the case of *Goss v. Board of Education*[37] in which it laid down specific rules about plans which initially appeared to promote desegregation, but in reality, allowed any student in the minority at his or her school to transfer to a school where that child would be in the majority. This plan, called "minority-to-majority" transfer schemes, was held invalid by the Court because "Classification based on race for purposes of transfers between public schools, as here, violate the Equal Protection Clause of the Fourteenth Amendment."[38] In addition to the fact that race was the factor that the transfer was based upon, the Court also found that there was no provision that allowed a majority student who wished to transfer to a school where that student would be a minority. These two factors, when combined, clearly demonstrated the purely racial basis for this plan. The Court therefore held that the transfer plans were constitutionally invalid.

The plan in *Goss* was not the only plan the Court reviewed regarding desegregation. In *Griffin v. County School Board*[39] the Court reviewed a plan that closed public schools rather than comply with desegregation. In an effort to avoid sending resident children to desegregated schools, Prince Edward County in Virginia closed its public schools and gave tuition grants to those students who were enrolled in the all-white private schools opened in that county. The black families in the county refused the offer of an all-black private school and chose, instead, to bring an action asking that the courts find that Prince Edward County violated the petitioners' right to equal protection under the law as guaranteed by the Fourteenth Amendment. The Court held " . . . we agree with the District Court that, under the circumstances here, closing the Prince Edward County schools while public schools in all the other counties of Virginia were being maintained denied the petitioners and the class of Negro students they represent the equal protection of the laws guaranteed by the Fourteenth Amendment."[40] The Court found that the plan used by the County was a deliberate attempt to perpetuate racial segregation and deny minority students equal protection. It affirmed the District Court's earlier decision instituting an injunction prohibiting the County from paying the tuition grants and giving tax credits to the private school and sent the case back to the same District Court to consider how to best institute a plan to reopen the public schools and operate them without racial discrimination. The Court's work to desegregate public schools did not end with finding this plan unconstitutional. A few years later, it heard the case of *Green v. County School Board*[41] and reviewed the "Freedom of Choice" plan used by that school district.

Green, like *Griffin*, involved a school district in the state of Virginia. The School Board in this case adopted a plan that allowed the student to choose his own public school. The respondents, a group of black students and their families, challenged this plan claiming that the plan maintained the racially segregated school system that had been rejected by the Court in the *Brown I* decision. After reviewing the plan, the Court did not hold that all "freedom of choice" plans were unconstitutional, but found that the effect of this plan was to perpetuate the dual system that the Court had rejected when it rejected the "separate but equal" doctrine. The Court said:

> *"This deliberate perpetuation of the unconstitutional dual system can only have compounded the harm of such a system. Such delays are no longer tolerable, for 'the governing constitutional principles no longer bear the imprint of newly enunciated doctrine.' Moreover, a plan that at this late date fails to provide meaningful assurance of prompt and effective disestablishment of a dual system is also intolerable . . . The burden on a school board today is to come forward with a plan that promises realistically to work, and promises realistically to work now."*[42]

The Court went on to order the school board to formulate a new plan for desegregation and submit it to the District Court that had originally heard the case.

All three of these plans constituted schemes that failed to end segregation, and in fact, tended to perpetuate the status quo. In 1971, the Court heard the case of *Swann v. Charlotte-Mecklenburg*[43] in which the Court handed down more guidelines for the desegregation of public schools. The Court first differentiated between de jure and de facto segregation. Before the federal district courts can order a school board to desegregate its schools, they must first find that there is **de jure** or officially sanctioned and maintained segregation in those schools. Once the courts find de jure discrimination, several factors may be considered when deciding how to remedy the discrimination, including the school district's policies regarding faculty, staff, transportation, extracurricular activities, facilities, and, perhaps most importantly, the ratio of black students to white students in the district as a whole. To determine whether a school district has made an effort to desegregate, the Court said that the school district does not have to demonstrate that there are no "single race" schools left in the district. The Court did acknowledge that the existence of "single race" schools merits strict scrutiny by the federal courts and that the burden is on the school board to show that the racial concentration in those schools is not due to official segregation, but that another explanation, such as residential patterns, causes this segregation. If the school board is able to do so, the existence of a "single race" school will not be considered de jure discrimination.

Further, the Court in the *Swann* case noted that the federal district courts might, if warranted, order rezoning of the school district in order to eliminate the residential patterns that resulted in the "single race" schools. The plan for desegregation found in *Swann* proposed pairing or clustering schools from noncontiguous parts of the district so that African American schools could be combined with white schools to bring about a racial balance in the district.

Another potential solution for segregation found in *Swann* was a proposal for busing students from one part of the city to another to achieve racial

de jure (Latin)   of right; legitimate; lawful, whether or not true in actual fact.

balance. The Court found the busing scheme to be valid because "Bus trans-portation has been an integral part of the public education system for years . . ."[44] The busing scheme proposed in this case used direct routes for the buses, pro-vided that the students would be picked up at schools near their homes and transported to the schools they were to attend and the average commute was seven miles for the students. The Court found this was a reasonable plan, but noted, "An objection to transportation of students may have validity when the time or distance of travel is so great as to either risk the health of the children or significantly impinge on the educational process."[45]

Desegregation and Busing Plans

The court ordered school busing plans to eliminate segregation were not with-out controversy. More than one school district in more than one state passed busing schemes or amended their state constitution in response to the busing as ordered by the Court in *Swann*. The Court heard two cases involving these schemes in 1982. The first case, *Washington v. Seattle School Distict No. 1*[46] in-volved the State of Washington's challenge to a statewide initiative that was passed that was "designed to terminate the use of mandatory busing for pur-poses of racial integration."[47] This effort to nullify a court-ordered busing plan was found by the Court to be unconstitutional as the State, through an initia-tive, cannot take away the local school district's plan to bus students to achieve more of a racial balance in the Seattle schools. The initiative had the effect of reallocating governmental decision-making power, and while this is generally acceptable, the reallocation will be rejected if it is not done in a racially neu-tral manner. The reallocation here was done in such a way that it violated the Equal Protection Clause of the Fourteenth Amendment. The Court specifically said:

> "The Equal Protection Clause of the Fourteenth Amendment guarantees racial minorities the right to full participation in the political life of the community. It is beyond dispute, of course, that given racial or ethnic groups may not be de-nied the franchise, or precluded from entering into the political process in a re-liable and meaningful manner. [Citations omitted] But the Fourteenth Amendment also reaches 'a political structure that treats all individuals as equals,' [Citations omitted] yet more subtly distorts governmental processes in such a way as to place special burdens on the ability of minority groups to achieve beneficial legislation."[48]

In saying this, the Court determined that the State of Washington could not take the local school district's power to make decisions on busing, while leav-ing the local district the power to control other school matters. Such an obvi-ous attempt to avoid busing would have resulted in a more racially imbalanced school system than it was prior to the passage of the initiative. The appellants in this decision argued to the Court that there were no racial overtones to the initiative, but the Court rejected this argument saying " . . . there is little doubt that the initiative was effectively drawn for racial purposes [and] . . . the text of the initiative was carefully tailored to interfere only with desegregative busing."[49]

Another plan alleged to thwart desegregative busing was found in the sec-ond 1982 case. In *Crawford v. Los Angeles Board of Education*[50] a California state court had ordered busing of students to rid the Los Angeles schools of segre-gation. California voters later passed an amendment to the California Consti-tution that forbid any state court from ordering mandatory busing unless a Federal District Court ordered such busing to remedy a finding of de jure seg-regation. This amendment was challenged but the Court upheld the amend-ment noting that the California court that had ordered the busing had gone beyond the protection afforded by the Fourteenth Amendment to the Consti-tution, and the new amendment to the California Constitution was a return to the original federal standard. The petitioners in this case argued that the repeal of the higher standard was racially motivated. The Court rejected this saying ". . . the Equal Protection Clause is not violated by the mere repeal of race-related legislation or policies that were not required by the Federal Constitution in the first place."[51] What California had done was a modification of a desegregation law and there was no demonstrated discriminatory intent. As such, the amendment to the California Constitution was upheld.

Another question presented to the Court regarding the desegregation of public schools involved future imbalances in the racial makeup of desegregated schools. In *Swann,* the Court established that once the initial segregation had been cured, later imbalances caused by changing neighborhood demographics or other nongovernmental action would not be actionable in the federal courts. The *Swann* Court noted, however, that school boards themselves might choose to cure future imbalances, but that is a discretionary matter. In 1991, the Court heard the case of *Board of Education v. Dowell*[52] and found that the Board of Education had complied with the desegregation order for several years and their good-faith compliance had cured the initial segregation. However, several years after the federal district court had terminated the desegregation order, the community experienced demographic changes and that the resulting residential segregation impacted the local schools. The Court found, however, that the residential segregation was not a vestige of the former de jure discrimination, but was ". . . the result of private decision-making and economics . . ."[53] As such, the Court would not reinstate an order to desegregate and determined that the Board of Education could revert back to neighborhood schools so long as there were no Fourteenth Amendment, Equal Protection violations by the government.

SEGREGATION IN COLLEGES AND UNIVERSITIES

Colleges and universities have not been immune from segregation. For many years higher education institutions were subject to the same bias and prejudice as were public elementary and secondary schools. If de jure segregation is found in a college or university, the federal courts may order desegregation. Even though the courts have recognized that "separate but equal" is unacceptable at this level, just as it is in the secondary and elementary public schools, the same remedies cannot be used to achieve desegregation. For those states that had chosen to maintain dual university systems and continue to practice segregation, they must show the courts that either they have wholly abandoned their segregation policy or the policy still exists because it is necessary for a sound education.

In reviewing a dual university system, the Court decided the case of *United States v. Fordice.*[54] In this case, the Court began by noting that the State of Mississippi's university system began in 1848 with the establishment of the University of Mississippi, which was dedicated to the education of white persons. The state later established several other white-only colleges and universities, as well as three "black-only" institutions in later years. When *Brown I* was decided, no black student had ever been admitted at the University of Mississippi and in spite of that decision, no black student was admitted until 1962 and then only as a result of a court order. For 12 years the state's segregated system remained intact, and in 1975 private individuals brought an action in federal district court complaining that Mississippi had maintained its racially segregated dual university system in violation of the Fifth, Ninth, Thirteenth, and Fourteenth Amendments. In spite of a long-term attempt to reach a consensual resolution of the lawsuit, the parties were unsuccessful and the lawsuit proceeded to trial. At trial, the District Court found no violation of federal law, and the Circuit Court of Appeals affirmed that decision. When the Court reviewed the lower courts' decisions, it found that these courts had failed to take into account many factors and remanded the case for further consideration. Specifically, the Court reiterated that "Our decisions establish that a State does not discharge its constitutional obligations until it eradicates policies and practices traceable to its prior *de jure* system that continue to foster segregation."[55]

The lower courts had only looked to the race-neutral policies implemented by the State to determine that the State had completely abandoned its prior dual university system. The Court noted that there was a wide range of factors that should be examined when determining whether the State has perpetrated policies and practices that were directly traceable to its prior, segregated system. These factors included, but were not limited to, admissions standards, program duplication, institutional mission assignments, and continued operation of all eight public universities.

When examining the admissions standards of the Mississippi universities, the Court found that the standards used were originally adopted for a discriminatory purpose and that in spite of claims to the contrary, these standards still had a discriminatory effect. As such, they were constitutionally suspicious especially in light of the fact that the admissions standards looked only to ACT scores, and did not take into account the student's high school academic record. The Court held that the State failed to show that its admissions standards did not perpetuate the dual system that the State claimed to be working to eliminate.

The widespread duplication of programs was also problematic. Duplication began as an integral part of the dual university system. The Court said, ". . . the whole notion of 'separate but equal' required duplicative programs in two sets of schools—and that the present unnecessary duplication is a continuation of that practice."[56] Upon remand, this issue should be carefully considered by the lower court to determine whether the State has met its duty to dismantle the dual university system.

The third factor the Court considered was the institutional mission designations. The State had adopted the mission designations in 1981 and these designations had their roots in the de jure segregation policy. Differing missions assigned to universities impacts the students' choices as to which university to apply to for admittance. The designations tended to maintain the segregated system that was designed to limit the program scope at the historically black universities. This fact, coupled with the differential admissions practices and the unnecessary program duplication, increased the chances that the students' true choices of universities will be limited.

The final factor discussed by the court was the fact that Mississippi continued to maintain all eight universities. In the Court's words, this ". . . is wasteful and irrational."[57] The Court went on to note that a larger number of institutions means that the prospective student has different choices to make than if there were a smaller number of institutions. The closure of one or more of the eight institutions in Mississippi would decrease the discriminatory effects of the present dual system, although the Court noted that a revision of the admissions policy and elimination of program duplications might make closure of one or more institutions unnecessary. The Court concluded by saying ". . . the State may not leave in place policies rooted in its prior officially segregated system that serve to maintain the racial identifiability of its universities if those policies can practicably be eliminated without eroding sound educational policies."[58]

The Court's holding in the *Fordice* case demonstrates not only that state colleges and universities must be desegregated, but also indicates what the courts will be considering when deciding whether racial desegregation has actually been accomplished in states with historically dual university systems.

THE END OF ENFORCED DESEGREGATION IN EDUCATION

So, when does enforced desegregation end? By looking back at the cases discussed in previous sections, it becomes clear that the district courts may order the end of desegregation when the educational institution has eliminated the effects of de jure discrimination. This may be accomplished through a variety of new policies or procedures. While other factors such as private housing choices, "white-flight" from the inner cities, and other economic factors may create future imbalances, the school system's good-faith effort to desegregate will bring about an end to court-ordered desegregation. The courts encourage school systems to continue to monitor and attempt to remedy future racial imbalances in their schools, but realize that true integration may be dependent on personal choices made by the school district's citizens.

ALIENAGE AND DISCRIMINATION

alien   any person who is not a U.S. citizen, whether or not that person lives in the United States permanently; a foreigner.

While it is clear how the Court views discrimination based on race or national origin, it is not as clear what rules apply to discrimination based on alienage. The concept of alienage is often confused with national origin, however, they are distinctly different in that someone who experiences discrimination based on national origin may or may not be a citizen of the United States. One who experiences discrimination based on alienage is not a citizen and, in general, laws which purport to be discriminatory based on alienage do not focus on a particular nationality, but rather discriminate against all **aliens**, no matter their country of origin. Perhaps more significantly, aliens as a group are politically powerless, as they cannot vote. All of these factors would allow for the conclusion that aliens are, what the Court would call, a "discrete and insular minority." However, for that conclusion to hold, the classification of "alien" would have to be unchangeable or immutable. It is within the power of most aliens to become U.S. citizens and therefore change their status as aliens. It is this ability to change this status that has caused some confusion in the courts as to which standard of review should be used in cases where discrimination based on alienage is alleged.

In the 1970s, the Court was clear that strict scrutiny was the standard to be applied in alienage cases. It was the 1971 case of *Graham v. Richardson*[59] where the Court first held aliens to be a "discrete and insular minority." Further, this case established that "classifications based on alienage, like those based on nationality or race, are inherently suspect and subject to close judicial scrutiny."[60] The individuals in this case were challenging the Arizona and Pennsylvania statutes that denied them welfare benefits because they were aliens and had not resided in the state for the proscribed period of time required by the statute. They claimed their Fourteenth Amendment rights were violated by this denial, and while the states argued that they had a right to limit welfare benefits to their own citizens, the Court disagreed. The Court concluded ". . . that a State's desire to preserve limited welfare benefits for its own citizens is inadequate to justify Pennsylvania's making noncitizens ineligible for public assistance, and Arizona's restricting benefits to citizens and longtime resident aliens."[61] Therefore, without a compelling government interest to justify the denial of benefits, the statutes allowing for this were held to be unconstitutional and in violation of the Fourteenth Amendment.

Denial of welfare benefits is not the only type of challenged state action brought before the Court as a form of alienage discrimination. The Court was asked to decide whether a state could bar aliens from holding state civil service jobs. In the case of *Sugarman v. Dougall*,[62] the State of New York had a statute that flatly prohibited an alien from holding a civil service position. When four federally registered resident aliens challenged the law, the Court had to determine whether the statute was constitutionally valid. The Court began by looking at the statutory language and concluded that it prohibited any and all aliens from being civil servants and reiterated the established rule " . . . that an alien is entitled to the shelter of the Equal Protection Clause."[63] Then, using the strict scrutiny standard, the Court acknowledged that the State had an interest in having an employee of undivided loyalty, but noted that the statute designed to provide this was too broadly drawn so that it "sweeps indiscriminately" and was too imprecise. As such, the Court held that a flat ban of this sort was unconstitutional, however, the Court went on to note that they did not hold

> " . . . that, on the basis of an individualized determination, an alien may not be refused, or discharged from, public employment, even on the basis of noncitizenship, if the refusal to hire, or the discharge, rests on legitimate state interests that relate to qualifications for a particular position or to the characteristics of the employee. We hold only that a flat ban on the employment of aliens in positions that have little, if any relation to a State's legitimate interest, cannot withstand scrutiny under the Fourteenth Amendment."[64]

This is a crucial distinction. The above paragraph has come to be known as the *Sugarman* exception and recognizes that there are some civil service functions that require a citizen to perform them, specifically those functions that are part of the democratic, representative government. In reality, this "exception" has eclipsed the rule of *Sugarman*. It has allowed states to exclude aliens from employment in positions that require participation in the democratic process. Some states have used the exceptions to exclude aliens from positions as teachers,[65] probation officers,[66] and state troopers.[67]

In summary, the Court's current position allows states to ban aliens from civil service employment if it is a job that involves a political function, but will not allow such a ban when the position involves an economic purpose. In addition, the Court will also allow a ban when the position in question relates to law enforcement or education.

GENDER DISCRIMINATION

Discrimination against women is not as zealously guarded against as race discrimination, however, the courts have held that when a statute or regulatory scheme disadvantages women, that statute or regulatory scheme is subject to mid-level or intermediate scrutiny. This means that whenever there is a gender-based classification created by the statute or regulatory scheme, that classification must be substantially related to an important governmental interest.[68] But what if the classification favors women in an attempt to remedy past discrimination? The same rule applies, whether women are disadvantaged or advantaged by the classification. What the courts have done in upholding legislation that does remedy past discrimination based on gender is to acknowledge that providing a remedy for past discrimination is an important governmental interest.[69] So, in reality, the statute or regulatory scheme must then pass the aspect of the test that requires that the classification be substantially related to this important governmental interest. If it does so, it is considered benign discrimination, and the classification is allowed to stand. An example of this type of benign discrimination is found in the case of *Califano v. Webster*.[70] In this case, the Court unanimously upheld a Social Security provision that allowed an individual claiming old-age benefits to compute the benefit by using the "average monthly wage." The provision, which was later amended, allowed women to exclude three more lower-earning years than a similarly situated male. Webster, a male, challenged the provision as being discriminatory.

CALIFANO V. WEBSTER
430 U.S. 313 (1977)

PER CURIAM.

Under s 215 of the Social Security Act, as added, and amended, [citation omitted], old-age insurance benefits are computed on the basis of the wage earner's 'average monthly wage' earned during his 'benefit computation years' which are the 'elapsed years (reduced by five) during which the wage earner's covered wages were highest

* * *

Accordingly, a female wage earner could exclude from the computation of her 'average monthly wage' three more lower earning years than a similarly situated male wage earner could exclude. This would result in a slightly higher 'average monthly wage' and a correspondingly higher level of monthly old-age benefits for the retired female earner. A single-judge District Court for the Eastern District of New York . . . held that, on two grounds, the statutory scheme violated the equal protection component of the Due Process Clause of the Fifth Amendment: (1) that to give women who reached age 62 before 1975 greater benefits than men of the same age and earnings record was irrational, and (2) that in any event the 1972 amendment was to be construed to apply retroactively . . . We reverse.

To withstand scrutiny under the equal protection component of the Fifth Amendment's Due Process Clause, 'classifications by gender must serve important governmental objectives and must be substantially related to achievement of those objectives. *Craig v. Boren*. Reduction of the disparity in economic conditions between men and women caused by the long history of discrimination against women has been recognized as such an important governmental objective. *Schlesinger v. Ballard*. But 'the mere recitation of a benign, compensatory purpose is not an automatic shield which protects against any inquiry into the actual purposes underlying a statutory scheme.' *Weinberger v. Wiesenfeld*. Accordingly, we have rejected attempts to justify gender classifications as compensation for past discrimination against women when the classifications in fact penalized women wage earners, *Califano v. Goldfarb*.

. . . The more favorable treatment of the female wager earner enacted here was not the result of 'archaic and overbroad generalizations' about women, or of 'the role-typing society has long imposed 'upon women, such as casual assumptions that women are 'the weaker sex' or are more likely to be child-rearers or dependents'. Rather, 'the only discernible purpose of (s 215's more favorable treatment is) the permissible one of redressing our society's longstanding disparate treatment of women.'

The challenged statute operated directly to compensate women for past economic discrimination. Retirement benefits under the Act are based on past earnings. But as we have recognized: 'Whether from over discrimination or from the socialization process of a male-dominated culture, the job market is inhospitable to the woman seeking any but the lowest paid jobs.' Thus, allowing women, who are such have been unfairly hindered from earning as much as men, to eliminate additional low-earning years from the calculation of their retirement benefits works directly to remedy some part of the effect of past discrimination.

The legislative history of s 215(b)(3) also reveals that Congress directly addressed the justification for differing treatment of men and women in the former version of that section and purposely enacted the more favorable treatment for female wage earners to compensate for past employment discrimination against women . . .

Thus, the legislative history is clear that the differing treatment of men and women in former s 215(b)(3) was not 'the accidental byproduct of a traditional way of thinking about females,' but rather was deliberately enacted to compensate for particular economic disabilities suffered by women.

That Congress changed its mind in 1972 and equalized the treatment of men and women does not, as the District Court concluded, constitute an admission by Congress that its previous policy was invidiously discriminatory . . .

Reversed.

Thus, the Court used mid-level scrutiny to determine that the provision was indeed reasonably related to an important government interest, and upheld the provision as it applied to Mr. Webster.

While this may seem a straightforward decision, the reality is that it is often difficult to predict whether the Court will hold a classification to be benign. The same year that *Califano v. Webster* was decided, the Court also decided the case of *Califano v. Goldfarb*.[71] In this case, the Court struck down a provision of the Social Security Act that paid benefits to the widow of a covered worker, but not to a widower of a covered employee, unless that widower could prove that he was the dependent of his deceased wife. While one might predict that the Court would look at this provision the same way that it had looked at the provision in *Califano v. Webster*, that was not so. The Court stated that this was not an attempt to remedy past discrimination against women, but rather was an attempt to aid dependent spouses because the presumption was that wives are usually dependent. The Court found this to be an invalid presumption and struck the provision down.

So, how can one decide whether a classification is a form of benign discrimination aimed at remedying past wrongs done to women? There is no straightforward answer to that question. There seems to be no strong reason for the Court to strongly object to the law in *Goldfarb* while upholding the law in *Webster*. The Court may have taken this stance based on the fact that, as the Court noted in *Goldfarb,* the law was not necessarily benign. What it meant was that while on one hand the law favored the widow over the widower, on the other hand, the law disfavored the workingwoman who was supporting her husband, over the workingman who was supporting his wife. This is different from the *Webster* decision where the law favored the workingwoman and did not penalize her in any way. This may seem like a very fine line to draw, but it seems to be the only explanation for the Court's differing treatment of these statutes.

One of the reasons why it is so difficult to determine when legislation is designed to be benign and attempts to remedy past discrimination against women or when the legislation is not benign because it penalizes women, is that it is rare for a legislative body to act out of hostility toward women. Most often, the reason behind gender-based legislation is the protection of women, rather than discrimination against women. This stems from the old-fashioned idea that women should be wives, mothers, and homemakers, rather than being out in the working world. Many legislators thought that these women should be protected from the uglier aspects of life. Even when attitudes toward women began to change, new statutes were passed to undo the effects of past discrimination and in a different way were also protective of women. This is why the Court today uses the intermediate level of scrutiny demonstrated in the *Webster* case above. The rules in *Webster* remained more or less the same for almost 20 years, until the case of *U.S. v. Virginia*[72] in which the Court, with Justice Ginsburg writing, reviewed a claim that the Virginia Military Institute (VMI) violated women's rights under the Equal Protection Clause by refusing to admit women. VMI has a long and prestigious history and a reputation for graduating some of the best leaders in the United States. While some of their graduates join the military, the majority of their graduates become political and economic leaders in the private sector. VMI also has a history of being a single-sex institution of higher education. When reviewing the male-only admission policy, the Court first reviewed the history of higher education in Virginia, as well as VMI's history. After doing so, the Court noted that the initial litigation resulted in the District Court's upholding VMI's admission policy, but that the Court of Appeals reversed and remanded the action back to the lower court, ordering that Virginia be responsible for finding a remedial course to cure this discrimination. The Commonwealth did so, proposing a parallel program for women they called Virginia Women's Institute for Leadership

(VWIL). VWIL would be located at Mary Baldwin College, a private liberal arts college for women. Virginia claimed that VWIL was "substantially comparable" to the program at VMI, even though the pedagogical format for VWIL would be dramatically different, the women attending VWIL would not have the military format that students experience at VMI, and the proposed financial support for the programs was substantially different, with VWIL having far less financial support than the program at VMI.

Virginia returned to the District Court for approval of its proposed parallel plan, and that court approved the proposal. When appealed, the Court of Appeals affirmed the lower court's decision. When reviewing this case, Justice Ginsburg wrote that there were two ultimate issues:

> *"First, does Virginia's exclusion of women from the educational opportunities provided by VMI—extraordinary opportunities for military training and civilian leadership development—deny to women 'capable of all of the individual activities required of VMI cadets' [citation omitted] the equal protection of the laws guaranteed by the Fourteenth Amendment? Second, if VMI's 'unique' situation—as Virginia's sole single-sex public institution of higher education—offends the Constitution's equal protection principle, what is the remedial requirement?"*[73]

In answering the first of these questions, the Court reiterated that the standard to be used when making this type of decision can be summarized as follows: "Focusing on the differential treatment or denial of opportunity for which relief is sought, the reviewing court must determine whether the proffered justification is 'exceedingly persuasive.' The burden of justification is demanding and it rests entirely on the State."[74] When reviewing the record and the arguments by the Commonwealth, the Court concluded that Virginia had not shown an "exceedingly persuasive" justification for excluding all women from VMI and affirmed the court of appeals initial judgment that Virginia had, indeed, violated the Fourteenth Amendment's Equal Protection Clause.

That brought the Court to the second issue and in deciding this issue, the Court looked at Virginia's proposal for VWIL and the evidence submitted at trial by both the State and the federal government. The evidence showed that, historically, Virginia has tried to protect women, first from higher education in general, and that once women's colleges were instituted, women's institutions were not given equal resources. The Court concluded that based on this evidence, there was no basis for the claim that the male-only admission policy at VMI was in place to further the State's diversity policy. Further, the Court held that the State's pedagogical argument had no merit as well because it is undisputed that the VMI methodology could be used to educate women, just as it is used to educate men. The Court also acknowledged Virginia's fears that allowing women into the institution would jeopardize VMI's future. As the Court noted: "Women's successful entry into the federal military academies and their participation in the Nation's military forces, indicate that Virginia's fear for the future of VMI may not be solidly grounded."[75] Therefore, the Court concluded that Virginia had not adequately demonstrated that the need for the male-only policy is exceedingly persuasive in order to satisfy the State action.

When deciding the second issue, the Court explained "A proper remedy for an unconstitutional exclusion . . . aims to 'eliminate [so far as possible] the discriminatory effects of the past' and 'to bar like discrimination in the future.' "[76] [Citation omitted.] The Court went on to conclude that the proposal submitted by Virginia did not eliminate the past discrimination, but left the exclusionary, male-only admission policy intact. Further, the Court held that the VWIL program did not afford women an opportunity to experience the rigorous education that makes VMI famous. The Court decided that Virginia must, on behalf of women, craft ". . . a remedy that will end their exclusion from a state-supplied educational opportunity for which they are fit, a decree that will 'bar like discrimination in the future.' *Louisiana v. United States, 380 U.S. 145 at 154 (1965).*[77] In conclusion, the Court noted that VWIL is not an educational program equal to VMI's and called the VWIL program a "pale shadow" of VMI.

In making this decision, the Court strongly stated not only the intermediate level of review needed in this type of case, but also the standard to be used and the rule regarding the formation of a remedy in such cases. There are four ramifications of the *VMI* decision. First, the Court's "exceedingly persuasive justification" standard is more rigorous than the traditional intermediate level scrutiny used in the past. This standard was adopted because the Court seems suspicious of the type of stereotypical thinking exhibited by the Commonwealth of Virginia and VMI. Even though Virginia submitted evidence that most women would not want to subject themselves to the type of adversative educational method used by VMI, the Court was unwilling to accept that as justification for the male-only admission policy. So long as there are some women who wish to submit to that type of method, it is a violation of those women's constitutional rights to deny them the opportunity.

Second, there is some question about the future of single-sex public education institutions. Some judicial scholars have suggested that it would be easier to sustain or justify a single-sex institution that benefited women, but whether the Court will decide that only those single-sex institutions that exist to remedy past discrimination against women are acceptable is an unanswered question. In addition, whether a state can maintain "separate but equal" institutions for both men and women is also an unanswered question. In *VMI* the Court found that the proposed VWIL program was not equal to the VMI program, but indicated that theoretically a state could set up separate but equal programs that would not violate the Constitution. The key would be demonstrating the two programs to be truly equal, and using the exceedingly persuasive justification standard used in *VMI*, this will be very difficult.

Third, there is some question about the constitutional viability of a private single-sex educational institution if that institution receives government funding. There is an indication by the Court that financially supporting a private institution that racially discriminates is a violation of the Fourteenth Amendment,[78] but whether the Court would feel the same about a private institution that discriminates on the basis of gender remains to be seen. If the Court were to do so, tax breaks and student loans for private, same-sex institutions might become unavailable to such an institution.

Another issue the courts face with regard to gender discrimination is legislation based on biological factors. Whenever biological factors are part of a statutory or regulatory scheme, there is a possibility that that scheme will have a disparate effect on one sex or the other. If the legislators intend the disparate impact, the statute may be challenged on equal protection grounds. This principle is illustrated in the case of *Geduldig v. Aiello,*[79] where four women who were denied benefits for disabilities stemming from pregnancy challenged a state-sponsored disability insurance program. The California Unemployment Insurance Code created this disability benefit in 1946 and this program was supported entirely by employee contributions. While the disability program did not cover every type of disability, and specifically excluded ". . . any injury or illness caused by or arising in connection with pregnancy . . ."[80] the women argued that they were being discriminated against based on gender. When considering the women's challenge, the Court looked at the legislative intent of the California legislators and specifically held that the State intended to create a self-supporting benefit system that never had to draw on general state revenues. If the Court were to find for the women challenging the system, evidence indicates that it would be impossible to maintain the program through employee contributions due to the extraordinary expense of paying for coverage for pregnancy-related disabilities. Ultimately, the Court in this case had to decide whether the state interest in maintaining the disability program through self-supported funding should be sacrificed or compromised in order to uphold women's rights under the Equal Protection Clause. The Court held:

> "We cannot agree that the exclusion of this disability from coverage amounts to invidious discrimination under the Equal Protection Clause. California does not discriminate with respect to the persons or groups which are eligible for disability insurance protection under the program. The classification challenged in this case relates to the asserted underinclusiveness of the set of risks that the State has selected to insure. Although California has created a program to insure most risks of employment disability, it has not chosen to insure all such risks and this decision is reflected in the level of annual contributions exacted from participating employees."[81]

In holding that there is no intent to discriminate nor a violation of equal protection under the Fourteenth Amendment, the Court clearly demonstrated that in order to successfully challenge a statute or legislative scheme as discriminating on the basis of biological differences, the challenger will have to demonstrate an intent on the part of the State or legislature to engage in gender discrimination. Failure to do so will result in the Court upholding the statutory scheme.

In conclusion, when it comes to gender-based discrimination, the Court is not always persuaded that a statute or regulatory scheme that favors women in an effort to undo past discrimination passes constitutional scrutiny. The standard to be used in these cases is the exceedingly persuasive justification standard or mid-level scrutiny. If the state can show that there is an exceedingly persuasive interest of the state to support the discrimination, the Court will uphold it, however, if no such exceedingly persuasive interest is found, the state will be found in violation of the Equal Protection Clause.

AFFIRMATIVE ACTION

affirmative action steps to remedy past discrimination in hiring, promotion, etc., for example, by recruiting more minorities and women; any administrative action taken to right a wrong.

The phrase, **affirmative action**, often invokes opposing reactions. To some, it is a means of leveling the playing field for minorities and other disadvantaged groups in the areas of employment, housing, and other opportunities. To others, it is a means of ensuring minority opportunities at the expense of the majority. At its core, however, is the idea that affirmative action exists to remedy past discrimination, but often in an effort to do so, other groups are often treated differently, which is, of course, exactly what affirmative action was supposed to eliminate. It is a difficult and knotty problem.

When trying to sort through issues revolving around affirmative action, one of the first things the Court had to decide is what standard was to be used to determine whether an affirmative action measure was constitutional. In the landmark case of *City of Richmond v. J.A. Croson Company*,[82] the Court set the strict scrutiny standard as the applicable standard when a case involves race and the Court is deciding whether a plan is "benign" discrimination or a violation of an individual's rights under the Equal Protection Clause of the Fourteenth Amendment. This standard changes when a sex-based classification is involved, as was discussed above in the section on gender, and the mid-level standard applies.

In the *Croson* case, the majority was examining a Minority Business Utilization Plan, which required general contractors to award at least 30 percent of any contract formed with the city to minority contractors. The City of Richmond enacted this plan in an attempt to remedy past discrimination against African Americans and other minorities in the Richmond area. It was possible for a general contractor to get a waiver of this requirement if that contractor could show that there were no qualified minority subcontractors available to participate in the contract. A white-owned general contractor who was vying for a contract with the City, claimed that no minority subcontractor could be found and challenged the Minority Business Utilization Plan. The general contractor sued the City of Richmond, claiming the "set-aside" for minorities violated its right to equal protection of the law. Justice O'Connor wrote the opinion for the Court and explicitly used the strict scrutiny standard saying that Richmond must show that this race-based set-aside provision was necessary to achieve a compelling governmental purpose. Justice O'Connor then went on to give three different reasons why strict scrutiny was the appropriate standard to be used. First, she noted that there is no way to tell which racial classifications are benign and designed to remedy past discrimination against these minorities and which is, in reality, motivated by the idea that the race in question is inferior. Second, Justice O'Connor asserted that any classification based on race brings with it the possibility that the group favored by the classification will be viewed as less competent and able to be successful without special help or protection. Third, Justice O'Connor argued that allowing these classifications to exist without the benefit of strict scrutiny means that the United States may never become the race-neutral society that it aspires to be.

Once the standard to be applied was settled, the Court then went on to review the set-aside plan used by the City of Richmond. The Court struck down the plan because there was no evidence of past discrimination by the City of Richmond against anyone in the construction business, there was no evidence to support the claim that the plan would benefit minority contractors in Richmond, and evidence showed that there were not enough minority contractors in the Richmond area to actually do the work. Justice O'Connor was clear that in order for an affirmative action plan to pass constitutional scrutiny, the affirmative action measures "must identify discrimination, public and private, with some specificity."[83] In other words, if affirmative action plans are going to be used, the government entity using the plan must be able to clearly demonstrate that there was past discrimination either by that government entity or by private individuals that requires remedial action by the government. If all that can be shown is past discrimination by society as a whole, that will be insufficient to support a finding of a compelling governmental interest, and the affirmative action plan will fail.

Additionally, the second part of the strict scrutiny standard must also be met in that the compelling governmental interest must be accomplished with the least-intrusive means possible. To that end, it is unlikely that a strict quota plan will be constitutionally permissible. The Court, in *Regents of the University of California v. Bakke*,[84] struck down this type of quota plan.

In *Bakke* the Court reviewed an affirmative action admission policy at the University of California at Davis. The University's Medical School had instituted a special admissions program to assure admission of a specified number of minority students. Allen Bakke, a white male, had applied to this medical school for two years, and was rejected even though his scores were higher than many of the minority students admitted under the special admissions program. Bakke instituted a suit against the University to challenge the special admissions policy, asking that the University be enjoined from using the special admissions policy and further, that the Medical School be ordered to admit him. The trial and appellate courts in the State of California enjoined the University from using race as a factor in making admissions decisions, but did not order the University to admit Mr. Bakke. Once the California Supreme Court affirmed this decision, the case was appealed to the United States Supreme Court. The Court first held that the special admissions program was "undeniably a classification based on race and ethnic background"[85] and "Racial and ethnic distinctions of any sort are inherently suspect and thus call for the most exacting judicial examination."[86] Or, in other words, the Court applied strict scrutiny to the special admissions program used by the University.

The Court acknowledged the University's claim that the Equal Protection Clause was originally envisioned to protect African Americans and other disadvantaged groups, however, the Court pointed out that the Fourteenth Amendment was framed in universal terms and was designed to protect without regard to color, ethnic origin, or nationality. It rejected the University's argument that the Court should hold that "discrimination against members of the white 'majority' cannot be suspect if its purpose can be characterized as 'benign.' "[87] In fact, the Court noted that there are three problems connected with the idea of giving a preference to any one group over another:

"First, it may not always be clear that a so-called preference is in fact benign . . . Nothing in the Constitution supports the notion that individuals may be asked to suffer otherwise impermissible burdens in order to enhance the societal standing of their ethnic groups. Second, preferential programs may only reinforce common stereotypes holding that certain groups are unable to achieve success without special protection based on a factor having no relationship to individual worth . . . Third, there is a measure of inequity in forcing innocent persons in respondent's position to bear the burdens of redressing grievances not of their making."[88]

The Court went on to note that using a special admissions policy, such as the one in this case, may actually increase racial tension and antagonism rather than alleviate them.

The Court did go on to strictly scrutinize the policy in question as the University and the State of California argued that the special admissions policy served four particular governmental interests. The government interests allegedly being served by the policy, they argued, were "(i) reducing the historic deficit of traditionally disfavored minorities in medical schools and in the medical profession, . . . (ii) countering the effects of society discrimination; (iii) increasing the number of physicians who will practice in communities currently underserved; and (iv) obtaining the educational benefits that flow from an ethnically diverse student body."[89]

The Court rejected the first two government interests saying, "We have never approved a classification that aids persons perceived as members of a relatively victimized group at the expense of other innocent individuals . . ."[90] The Court also noted that the University had no evidence to support the claim that their policy would provide future medical care for underserved populations, so that interest failed as well.

The last government interest promoted by the University was the goal of having a diverse student body. The Court held that this was a permissible governmental interest, but also noted that ethnic diversity "is only one element in a range of factors a university properly may consider in attaining the goal . . ."[91] However, after holding that having a diverse student body was a compelling government interest, the Court then had to consider whether the special admissions policy was the appropriate method to use in order for the University to reach that goal. The University argued that this admissions policy was the only effective means of attaining this goal, but the Court disagreed. Further, the Court held that race of ethnicity ". . . may be used as a 'plus' in a particular applicant's file, yet it does not insulate the individual from comparison with all other candidates for the available seats. The file of a particular black applicant may be examined for his potential contribution to diversity without the factor of race being decisive . . ."[92] Thus, the University was required to treat each applicant as an individual, and weigh all factors, race or ethnicity included, when making admissions decisions. By doing so, the University promotes an important governmental interest by a constitutionally permissible means. However, the Court held that the set-aside plan that held seats specifically for minorities violated the Equal Protection Plan.

Ultimately, the Court overturned the injunction that kept the University and the State of California from considering race as a factor in making admissions decisions, but did direct that Mr. Bakke be admitted to the University's Medical School.

The question of how heavily the factors of race or ethnicity could be weighed in an admissions decision was left unanswered in *Bakke*. That question, however, is at the heart of the two most recent cases *Grantz v. Bollinger*[93] and *Grutter v. Bollinger*,[94] addressing discrimination in admissions. These cases involve admissions policies at the University of Michigan. The *Grantz* case involved the admissions policy for undergraduate students at that institution and the *Grutter* case involved the same type of policies in the University's Law School. In both of these cases, the Court first had to decide whether the University, as a government entity, had a compelling interest in using race as a factor in making admissions decisions and then went on to determine whether the admissions practices were narrowly tailored to meet the claimed compelling interest.

In *Grantz* the petitioners were two undergraduate students who applied for admission to the University of Michigan's College of Literature, Science and the Arts. Both are Caucasians and both were denied admission. They challenged the University's policy claiming that the use of racial preferences in undergraduate admissions violated the Equal Protection Clause of the Fourteenth Amendment, Title VI of the Civil Rights Act of 1964, and 42 U.S.C. § 1981. Chief Justice Rehnquist wrote for the Court, and Justices O'Connor, Scalia, Kennedy, and Thomas joined him in the decision. The majority reviewed the University's recent admissions policies, and specifically looked at the one used most recently. That policy, administered by the Admissions Review Committee (ARC), awarded 20 points to every applicant from an underrepresented racial or ethnic minority group. Additionally, the ARC could "flag" an applicant for special consideration if it determined "that the applicant (1) is academically prepared to succeed at the University, (2) has achieved a minimum selection index score and (3) possesses a quality or characteristic important to the University's composition of its freshman class, such as high class rank, unique life experiences, challenges, circumstances, interests or talents, socioeconomic disadvantage, and underrepresented race, ethnicity, or geography."[95] The District Court and Circuit Court of Appeals held in favor of the University, finding that the University had a compelling interest in admitting a racially and ethnically diverse freshman class, and that the policy was narrowly drawn to achieve that end.

When reviewing the lower court holdings, the Court agreed that the University's interest was compelling, but it was not convinced that the University had met the second part of the strict scrutiny test, in that the University had narrowly drawn its policy to accomplish that interest while ensuring that the policy was unnecessarily biased toward other groups. The Court said:

> *"We conclude, therefore, that because the University's use of race in its current freshman admission policy is not narrowly tailored to achieve respondents' asserted compelling interest in diversity, the admissions policy violates the Equal Protection Clause of the Fourteenth Amendment. We further find that the admissions policy also violates Title VI and 42 U.S.C. § 1981."[96]*

In reaching this conclusion, the Court specifically pointed to the fact that the policy automatically awarded 20 points to any applicant from an underrepresented group and this automatic distribution of these points meant that the University was not considering the applicant's individual background, experiences, and characteristics necessary to assess the individual's potential contribution to the diversity of the incoming freshman class.[97]

The second of the cases from the University of Michigan is *Grutter v. Bollinger*. As noted the Petitioner in this case challenged the admission policy of the University's Law School. Once again, the University was once again claiming a compelling government interest in having a diverse student body.

GRUTTER V. BOLLINGER
539 U.S. 306 (2003)

Justice O'CONNOR delivered the opinion of the Court.

This case requires us to decide whether the use of race as a factor in student admissions by the University of Michigan Law School (Law School) is unlawful.

I

A

The Law School ranks among the Nation's top law schools. It receives more than 3,500 applications each year for a class of around 350 students. Seeking to 'admit a group of students who individually and collectively are among the most capable,' the Law School looks for individuals with 'substantial promise for success in law school' and 'a strong likelihood of succeeding in the practice of law and contributing in diverse ways to the well-being of others.'

* * *

Upon the unanimous adoption of the committee's report by the Law School faculty, it became the Law School's official admissions policy.

The hallmark of that policy is its focus on academic ability coupled with a flexible assessment of applicants' talents, experiences, and potential 'to contribute to the learning of those around them.' The policy requires admissions officials to evaluate each applicant based on all the information available in the file, including a personal statement, letters of recommendation, and an essay describing the ways in which the applicant will contribute to the life and diversity of the Law School. In reviewing an applicant's file, admissions officials must consider the applicant's undergraduate grade point average (GPA) and Law School Admissions Test (LSAT) score because they are important (if imperfect) predictors of academic success in law school. The policy stresses that 'no applicant should be admitted unless we expect that applicant to do well enough to graduate with no serious academic problems.'

The policy makes clear, however, that even the highest possible score does not guarantee admission to the Law School. Nor does a low score automatically disqualify an applicant. Rather, the policy requires admissions officials to look beyond grades and test scores to other criteria that are important to the Law School's educational objectives.

* * *

The policy aspires to 'achieve that diversity which has the potential to enrich everyone's education and thus make a law school class stronger than the sum of its parts.'

* * *

The policy does, however, reaffirm the Law School's longstanding commitment to 'one particular type of diversity,' that is, 'racial and ethnic diversity with special reference to the inclusion of students from groups which have been historically discriminated against, like African-Americans, Hispanics and Native Americans, who without this commitment might not be represented in our student body in meaningful numbers.'

* * *

The policy does not define diversity 'solely in terms of racial and ethnic status.' Nor is the policy 'insensitive to the competition among all students for admission to the [L]aw [S]chool.' Ibid. Rather, the policy seeks to guide admissions officers in 'producing classes both diverse and academically outstanding, classes made up of students who promise to continue the tradition of outstanding contribution by Michigan Graduates to the legal profession.' Ibid.

B

Petitioner Barbara Grutter is a white Michigan resident who applied to the Law School in 1996 with a 3.8 grade point average and 161 LSAT score. The Law School initially placed petitioner on a waiting list, but subsequently rejected her application. In December 1997, petitioner filed suit in the United States District Court for the Eastern District of Michigan against the Law School, the Regents of the University of Michigan, Lee Bollinger (Dean of the Law School from 1987 to 1994, and President of the University of Michigan from 1996 to 2002), Jeffrey Lehman (Dean of the Law School), and Dennis Shields (Director of Admissions at the Law School from 1991 until 1998). Petitioner alleged that respondents discriminated against her on the basis of race in violation of the Fourteenth Amendment; Title VI of the Civil Rights Act of

Continued

1964, 78 Stat. 252, 42 U.S.C. §2000d; and Rev. Stat. §1977, as amended, 42 U.S.C. §1981.

Petitioner further alleged that her application was rejected because the Law School uses race as a 'predominant' factor, giving applicants who belong to certain minority groups 'a significantly greater chance of admission than students with similar credentials from disfavored racial groups.' Petitioner also alleged that respondents 'had no compelling interest to justify their use of race in the admissions process.' Petitioner requested compensatory and punitive damages, an order requiring the Law School to offer her admission, and an injunction prohibiting the Law School from continuing to discriminate on the basis of race. Petitioner clearly has standing to bring this lawsuit.

* * *

During the 15-day bench trial, the parties introduced extensive evidence concerning the Law School's use of race in the admissions process. Dennis Shields, Director of Admissions when petitioner applied to the Law School, testified that he did not direct his staff to admit a particular percentage or number of minority students, but rather to consider an applicant's race along with all other factors.

* * *

This was done, Shields testified, to ensure that a critical mass of underrepresented minority students would be reached so as to realize the educational benefits of a diverse student body. Shields stressed, however, that he did not seek to admit any particular number or percentage of underrepresented minority students.

Erica Munzel, who succeeded Shields as Director of Admissions, testified that "critical mass" means "meaningful numbers" or "meaningful representation," which she understood to mean a number that encourages underrepresented minority students to participate in the classroom and not feel isolated. Munzel stated there is no number, percentage, or range of numbers or percentages that constitute critical mass. Munzel also asserted that she must consider the race of applicants because a critical mass of underrepresented minority students could not be enrolled if admissions decisions were based primarily on undergraduate GPAs and LSAT scores.

* * *

Kent Syverud was the final witness to testify about the Law School's use of race in admissions decisions. Syverud was a professor at the Law School when the 1992 admissions policy was adopted and is now Dean of Vanderbilt Law School. In addition to his testimony at trial, Syverud submitted several expert reports on the educational benefits of diversity. Syverud's testimony indicated that when a critical mass of underrepresented minority students is present, racial stereotypes lose their force because nonminority students learn there is no "minority viewpoint" but rather a variety of viewpoints among minority students.

In an attempt to quantify the extent to which the Law School actually considers race in making admissions decisions, the parties introduced voluminous evidence at trial.

* * *

Dr. Stephen Raudenbush, the Law School's expert, focused on the predicted effect of eliminating race as a factor in the Law School's admission process. In Dr. Raudenbush's view, a race-blind admissions system would have a "very dramatic," negative effect on underrepresented minority admissions. He testified that in 2000, 35 percent of underrepresented minority applicants were admitted. Dr. Raudenbush predicted that if race were not considered, only 10 percent of those applicants would have been admitted. Under this scenario, underrepresented minority students would have comprised 4 percent of the entering class in 2000 instead of the actual figure of 14.5 percent.

In the end, the District Court concluded that the Law School's use of race as a factor in admissions decisions was unlawful. Applying strict scrutiny, the District Court determined that the Law School's asserted interest in assembling a diverse student body was not compelling because 'the attainment of a racially diverse class . . . was not recognized as such by Bakke and is not a remedy for past discrimination.' The District Court went on to hold that even if diversity were compelling, the Law School had not narrowly tailored its use of race to further that interest. The District Court granted petitioner's request for declaratory relief and enjoined the Law School from using race as a factor in its admissions decisions. The Court of Appeals entered a stay of the injunction pending appeal.

Sitting en banc, the Court of Appeals reversed the District Court's judgment and vacated the injunction. The Court of Appeals first held that Justice Powell's opinion in Bakke was binding

Continued

precedent establishing diversity as a compelling state interest.

* * *

The Court of Appeals also held that the Law School's use of race was narrowly tailored because race was merely a 'potential 'plus' factor'

* * *

We granted certiorari, to resolve the disagreement among the Courts of Appeals on a question of national importance: Whether diversity is a compelling interest that can justify the narrowly tailored use of race in selecting applicants for admission to public universities.

* * *

II

A

We last addressed the use of race in public higher education over 25 years ago. In the landmark Bakke case, we reviewed a racial set-aside program that reserved 16 out of 100 seats in a medical school class for members of certain minority groups. The decision produced six separate opinions, none of which commanded a majority of the Court.

* * *

The only holding for the Court in Bakke was that a 'State has a substantial interest that legitimately may be served by a properly devised admissions program involving the competitive consideration of race and ethnic origin.' Thus, we reversed that part of the lower court's judgment that enjoined the university 'from any consideration of the race of any applicant.'

Since this Court's splintered decision in Bakke, Justice Powell's opinion announcing the judgment of the Court has served as the touchstone for constitutional analysis of race-conscious admissions policies. Public and private universities across the Nation have modeled their own admissions programs on Justice Powell's views on permissible race-conscious policies.

* * *

We therefore discuss Justice Powell's opinion in some detail.

* * *

In Justice Powell's view, when governmental decisions 'touch upon an individual's race or ethnic background, he is entitled to a judicial determination that the burden he is asked to bear on that basis is precisely tailored to serve a compelling governmental interest.' Under this exacting standard, only one of the interests asserted by the university survived Justice Powell's scrutiny.

* * *

Justice Powell approved the university's use of race to further only one interest: 'the attainment of a diverse student body.' With the important proviso that 'constitutional limitations protecting individual rights may not be disregarded,' Justice Powell grounded his analysis in the academic freedom that 'long has been viewed as a special concern of the First Amendment.'

* * *

In seeking the 'right to select those students who will contribute the most to the "robust exchange of ideas,"' a university seeks 'to achieve a goal that is of paramount importance in the fulfillment of its mission.'

* * *

Justice Powell was, however, careful to emphasize that in his view race 'is only one element in a range of factors a university properly may consider in attaining the goal of a heterogeneous student body.'

* * *

B

The Equal Protection Clause provides that no State shall 'deny to any person within its jurisdiction the equal protection of the laws.' Because the Fourteenth Amendment 'protect[s] persons, not groups,' all 'governmental action based on race—a group classification long recognized as in most circumstances irrelevant and therefore prohibited—should be subjected to detailed judicial inquiry to ensure that the personal right to equal protection of the laws has not been infringed.'

* * *

We have held that all racial classifications imposed by government 'must be analyzed by a reviewing court under strict scrutiny.' Ibid. This means that such classifications are constitutional only if they are narrowly tailored to further compelling governmental interests. 'Absent searching judicial inquiry into the justification for such race-based measures,' we have no way to determine what 'classifications are 'benign' or 'remedial' and what

Continued

classifications are in fact motivated by illegitimate notions of racial inferiority or simple racial politics.' 'We apply strict scrutiny to all racial classifications to "smoke out" illegitimate uses of race by assuring that [government] is pursuing a goal important enough to warrant use of a highly suspect tool.'

Strict scrutiny is not 'strict in theory, but fatal in fact.' Although all governmental uses of race are subject to strict scrutiny, not all are invalidated by it. As we have explained, 'whenever the government treats any person unequally because of his or her race, that person has suffered an injury that falls squarely within the language and spirit of the Constitution's guarantee of equal protection.'

* * *

When race-based action is necessary to further a compelling governmental interest, such action does not violate the constitutional guarantee of equal protection so long as the narrow-tailoring requirement is also satisfied.

* * *

Not every decision influenced by race is equally objectionable and strict scrutiny is designed to provide a framework for carefully examining the importance and the sincerity of the reasons advanced by the governmental decisionmaker for the use of race in that particular context.

III

A

With these principles in mind, we turn to the question whether the Law School's use of race is justified by a compelling state interest. Before this Court, as they have throughout this litigation, respondents assert only one justification for their use of race in the admissions process: obtaining 'the educational benefits that flow from a diverse student body.' In other words, the Law School asks us to recognize, in the context of higher education, a compelling state interest in student body diversity.

* * *

The Law School's educational judgment that such diversity is essential to its educational mission is one to which we defer. The Law School's assessment that diversity will, in fact, yield educational benefits is substantiated by respondents and their amici.

* * *

Our holding today is in keeping with our tradition of giving a degree of deference to a university's academic decisions, within constitutionally prescribed limits.

We have long recognized that, given the important purpose of public education and the expansive freedoms of speech and thought associated with the university environment, universities occupy a special niche in our constitutional tradition. In announcing the principle of student body diversity as a compelling state interest, Justice Powell invoked our cases recognizing a constitutional dimension, grounded in the First Amendment, of educational autonomy: 'The freedom of a university to make its own judgments as to education includes the selection of its student body.' From this premise, Justice Powell reasoned that by claiming 'the right to select those students who will contribute the most to the "robust exchange of ideas,"' a university 'seek[s] to achieve a goal that is of paramount importance in the fulfillment of its mission.' Our conclusion that the Law School has a compelling interest in a diverse student body is informed by our view that attaining a diverse student body is at the heart of the Law School's proper institutional mission, and that 'good faith' on the part of a university is 'presumed' 'absent a showing to the contrary.'

As part of its goal of 'assembling a class that is both exceptionally academically qualified and broadly diverse,' the Law School seeks to 'enroll a 'critical mass' of minority students.

* * *

. . . the Law School's concept of critical mass is defined by reference to the educational benefits that diversity is designed to produce.

These benefits are substantial. As the District Court emphasized, the Law School's admissions policy promotes 'cross-racial understanding,' helps to break down racial stereotypes, and 'enables [students] to better understand persons of different races.' These benefits are 'important and laudable,' because 'classroom discussion is livelier, more spirited, and simply more enlightening and interesting' when the students have 'the greatest possible variety of backgrounds.'

The Law School's claim of a compelling interest is further bolstered by its amici, who point to the educational benefits that flow from student body diversity. In addition to the expert studies and reports entered into evidence at trial, numerous studies show that student body diversity promotes

Continued

learning outcomes, and 'better prepares students for an increasingly diverse workforce and society, and better prepares them as professionals.'

* * *

These benefits are not theoretical but real, as major American businesses have made clear that the skills needed in today's increasingly global marketplace can only be developed through exposure to widely diverse people, cultures, ideas, and viewpoints. What is more, high-ranking retired officers and civilian leaders of the United States military assert that, '[b]ased on [their] decades of experience,' a 'highly qualified, racially diverse officer corps . . . is essential to the military's ability to fulfill its principle mission to provide national security.'

* * *

We have repeatedly acknowledged the overriding importance of preparing students for work and citizenship, describing education as pivotal to 'sustaining our political and cultural heritage' with a fundamental role in maintaining the fabric of society. This Court has long recognized that 'education . . . is the very foundation of good citizenship.' For this reason, the diffusion of knowledge and opportunity through public institutions of higher education must be accessible to all individuals regardless of race or ethnicity.

* * *

B

Even in the limited circumstance when drawing racial distinctions is permissible to further a compelling state interest, government is still 'constrained in how it may pursue that end: [T]he means chosen to accomplish the [government's] asserted purpose must be specifically and narrowly framed to accomplish that purpose.' The purpose of the narrow tailoring requirement is to ensure that 'the means chosen 'fit' . . . th[e] compelling goal so closely that there is little or no possibility that the motive for the classification was illegitimate racial prejudice or stereotype.'

* * *

To be narrowly tailored, a race-conscious admissions program cannot use a quota system—it cannot 'insulat[e] each category of applicants with certain desired qualifications from competition with all other applicants.' 'Instead, a university may consider race or ethnicity only as a "plus" in a particular applicant's file,' without 'insulat[ing] the individual from comparison with all other candidates for the available seats.' In other words, an admissions program must be 'flexible enough to consider all pertinent elements of diversity in light of the particular qualifications of each applicant, and to place them on the same footing for consideration, although not necessarily according them the same weight.'

We find that the Law School's admissions program bears the hallmarks of a narrowly tailored plan.

* * *

Universities can, however, consider race or ethnicity more flexibly as a 'plus' factor in the context of individualized consideration of each and every applicant.

We are satisfied that the Law School's admissions program, like the Harvard plan described by Justice Powell, does not operate as a quota.

* * *

In contrast, 'a permissible goal . . . require[s] only a good-faith effort . . . to come within a range demarcated by the goal itself,' and permits consideration of race as a 'plus' factor in any given case while still ensuring that each candidate 'compete[s] with all other qualified applicants,'

* * *

The Law School's goal of attaining a critical mass of underrepresented minority students does not transform its program into a quota.

* * *

To the contrary, the Law School's admissions officers testified without contradiction that they never gave race any more or less weight based on the information contained in these reports.

* * *

That a race-conscious admissions program does not operate as a quota does not, by itself, satisfy the requirement of individualized consideration. When using race as a 'plus' factor in university admissions, a university's admissions program must remain flexible enough to ensure that each applicant is evaluated as an individual and not in a way that makes an applicant's race or ethnicity the defining feature of his or her application. The importance of this individualized consideration in the context of a race-conscious admissions program is paramount.

Continued

Here, the Law School engages in a highly individualized, holistic review of each applicant's file, giving serious consideration to all the ways an applicant might contribute to a diverse educational environment. The Law School affords this individualized consideration to applicants of all races. There is no policy, either de jure or de facto, of automatic acceptance or rejection based on any single 'soft' variable. Unlike the program at issue in *Gratz v. Bollinger*, ante, the Law School awards no mechanical, predetermined diversity 'bonuses' based on race or ethnicity.

* * *

(Like the Harvard plan, the Law School's admissions policy 'is flexible enough to consider all pertinent elements of diversity in light of the particular qualifications of each applicant, and to place them on the same footing for consideration, although not necessarily according them the same weight.'

We also find that, like the Harvard plan Justice Powell referenced in Bakke, the Law School's race-conscious admissions program adequately ensures that all factors that may contribute to student body diversity are meaningfully considered alongside race in admissions decisions.

* * *

The Law School does not, however, limit in any way the broad range of qualities and experiences that may be considered valuable contributions to student body diversity.

* * *

The Law School seriously considers each 'applicant's promise of making a notable contribution to the class by way of a particular strength, attainment, or characteristic—e.g., an unusual intellectual achievement, employment experience, nonacademic performance, or personal background.' All applicants have the opportunity to highlight their own potential diversity contributions through the submission of a personal statement, letters of recommendation, and an essay describing the ways in which the applicant will contribute to the life and diversity of the Law School.

What is more, the Law School actually gives substantial weight to diversity factors besides race. The Law School frequently accepts nonminority applicants with grades and test scores lower than underrepresented minority applicants (and other nonminority applicants) who are rejected. This shows that the Law School seriously weighs

many other diversity factors besides race that can make a real and dispositive difference for nonminority applicants as well. By this flexible approach, the Law School sufficiently takes into account, in practice as well as in theory, a wide variety of characteristics besides race and ethnicity that contribute to a diverse student body.

* * *

Petitioner and the United States argue that the Law School's plan is not narrowly tailored because race-neutral means exist to obtain the educational benefits of student body diversity that the Law School seeks. We disagree. Narrow tailoring does not require exhaustion of every conceivable race-neutral alternative. Nor does it require a university to choose between maintaining a reputation for excellence or fulfilling a commitment to provide educational opportunities to members of all racial groups. Narrow tailoring does, however, require serious, good faith consideration of workable race-neutral alternatives that will achieve the diversity the university seeks.

* * *

We agree with the Court of Appeals that the Law School sufficiently considered workable race-neutral alternatives.

* * *

The Law School's current admissions program considers race as one factor among many, in an effort to assemble a student body that is diverse in ways broader than race.

* * *

We are satisfied that the Law School adequately considered race-neutral alternatives currently capable of producing a critical mass without forcing the Law School to abandon the academic selectivity that is the cornerstone of its educational mission.

We acknowledge that 'there are serious problems of justice connected with the idea of preference itself.' Narrow tailoring, therefore, requires that a race-conscious admissions program not unduly harm members of any racial group.

* * *

We are satisfied that the Law School's admissions program does not. Because the Law School considers 'all pertinent elements of diversity,' it can (and does) select nonminority applicants who have greater potential to enhance student body diversity over underrepresented minority applicants.

Continued

* * *

We agree that, in the context of its individualized inquiry into the possible diversity contributions of all applicants, the Law School's race-conscious admissions program does not unduly harm nonminority applicants.

We are mindful, however, that '[a] core purpose of the Fourteenth Amendment was to do away with all governmentally imposed discrimination based on race.' Accordingly, race-conscious admissions policies must be limited in time. This requirement reflects that racial classifications, however compelling their goals, are potentially so dangerous that they may be employed no more broadly than the interest demands.

* * *

In the context of higher education, the durational requirement can be met by sunset provisions in race-conscious admissions policies and periodic reviews to determine whether racial preferences are still necessary to achieve student body diversity. Universities in California, Florida, and Washington State, where racial preferences in admissions are prohibited by state law, are currently engaged in experimenting with a wide variety of alternative approaches. Universities in other States can and should draw on the most promising aspects of these race-neutral alternatives as they develop.

* * *

The requirement that all race-conscious admissions programs have a termination point 'assure[s] all citizens that the deviation from the norm of equal treatment of all racial and ethnic groups is a temporary matter, a measure taken in the service of the goal of equality itself.'

* * *

We expect that 25 years from now, the use of racial preferences will no longer be necessary to further the interest approved today.

IV

In summary, the Equal Protection Clause does not prohibit the Law School's narrowly tailored use of race in admissions decisions to further a compelling interest in obtaining the educational benefits that flow from a diverse student body. Consequently, petitioner's statutory claims based on Title VI and 42 U.S.C. §1981 also fail.

* * *

The judgment of the Court of Appeals for the Sixth Circuit, accordingly, is affirmed.

It is so ordered.

With this decision, the Court clearly demonstrates that the use of race, as one of many factors in the decision-making process, is not unconstitutional. This case and the decision in *Grantz* clearly demonstrates two things. First, the government has a compelling interest in using policies that allow for a diverse student body in its public universities. Second, this compelling governmental interest must result in a policy that is sufficiently narrow to allow for the realization of the goal, but is not so broadly drawn that it unnecessarily discriminates against other applicants. If a public university, as was the case in *Grutter*, can institute an admission policy that uses race or ethnicity only as one factor in the individualized consideration of an applicant's suitability for admission, the Court will uphold that policy. If not, as demonstrated in *Grantz*, that admission policy will fail as a violation of the Equal Protection Clause, the Civil Rights Act, and other federal statutes.

Summary

While not every aspect of the law of discrimination can be addressed in one chapter, at this point several things should be clear. When cases arise challenging an action, plan, or statute based on claims of race, national origin, or alienage discrimination, the Court will use the strict scrutiny standard. The government will then have to show a compelling governmental interest and that the plan, action, or statute is narrowly drawn and the least-intrusive means possible to achieve this governmental interest. If the government cannot show both, its action, statute, or affirmative action plan will fail, as it will violate the Equal Protection Clause of the Fourteenth Amendment.

In cases involving gender-based discrimination claims, the Court will use a heightened, mid-level standard and require the government to demonstrate an exceedingly important justification, which bears a rational relationship to the goal the government is trying to achieve.

Affirmative action, as noted, also requires strict scrutiny, but as can be seen from the latest Supreme Court decisions, race or ethnicity as part of an overall set of considerations will not violate the constitutional rights of well-represented groups. What the Court seems to view as critical is that when decisions are being made about admissions to public institutions of higher education, the institution must look at all factors and make decisions based on individual qualifications and what that applicant may bring to the overall goal of diversity on campuses and in the classroom.

Key Terms

affirmative action	discrimination	reparation
alien	disparate impact	separate but equal doctrine
de jure	equitable	voir dire

Review Questions

1. How did the treatment of the Japanese American citizens of the 1940s differ from the treatment afforded those of Italian American and German American descent? Why were Italian Americans and German Americans not detained in Assembly Centers or their loyalty questioned during the time that the United States was at war with Italy and Germany, and either of those countries might have invaded the United States?

2. What is the justification given by the Court for the heightened, mid-level standard used in gender-based cases?

3. What are some of the factors to be reviewed when deciding whether a single-sex education program is substantially comparable to another single-sex education program?

4. Might the Supreme Court allow for the existence of a one-gender or one-race school, such as a school exclusively for African American boys, if the school district could demonstrate that these young men gained a substantial learning benefit from attending this one-gender, one-race school? If so, what would be an example of a situation that the Supreme Court might allow?

5. How is alienage different from national origin and race?

6. What are the pros and cons of affirmative action?

Internet Connections

1. For more information on gender-discrimination issues, visit the Web site for the National Women's Law Center at *http://www.nwlc.org.*

2. President John F. Kennedy requested a committee be formed to research and protect civil rights. In 1963 the Lawyer's Committee for Civil Rights Under Law, a nonpartisan, nonprofit group was formed. Visit their Web site at *http://www.lawyerscomm.org.*

3. For more information on national origin discrimination, visit the Web site for the Equal Protections Against National Origin Discrimination at *http://www.usdoj.gov/crt/legalinfo/natorigin.htm.*

4. To see more information on equal protection, visit the Web site on Equal Protection Law Materials at *http://www.law.cornell.edu/topics/equal_protection.html/.*

5. For more information on civil rights and discrimination, visit The Civil Rights Project at Harvard at *http://www.law.harvard.edu/civilrights.*

End Notes

[1]*Korematsu v. United States,* 323 U.S. 214 (1944).

[2]*Id.* at 216.

[3]Lisa Cozzens, "The Montgomery Bus Boycott," at *http://www.watson.org/~lisa_blackhistory/civilrights-55-65/montbus.html* (Nov. 6, 2004).

[4]Roberta Hughes Wright, *The Birth of the Montgomery Bus Boycott* 52–53 (Charro Press 1991).

[5]Thomas J. Gilliam "The Montgomery Bus Boycott of 1955–56," in *The Walking City: The Montgomery Bus Boycott* 191–301 (David J. Garrow, ed., Carlson Publishing 1989).

[6]Martin Luther King, Jr., *Stride Toward Freedom* 78 (Harper & Row Publishers 1958).

[7]*Id.* at 152.

[8]*Id.* at 175.

[9]Roberta Hughes Wright, *The Birth of the Montgomery Bus Boycott* 123 (Charro Press 1991).

[10]Gary Mukai, "Teaching About Japanese-American Internment," *Japan Digest,* at *http://www.indiana.edu* (January 3, 2003).

[11]President Gerald R. Ford, *An American Promise,* Proclamation 4417, at *http://www.kent.wednet.edu* (Dec. 31, 2002).

[12]*Strauder v. West Virginia,* 100 U.S. 303 (1879).

[13]*Id.* at 308.

[14]*Yick Wo v. Hopkins,* 118 U.S. 356 (1886).

[15]*Id.* at 373–374.

[16]*Rogers v. Lodge,* 458 U.S. 613 (1982).

[17]*Id.* at 625.

[18]*Washington v. Davis,* 426 U.S. 229 at 248 (1976).

[19]*Personnel Administrator of Massachusetts v. Feeney,* 442 U.S. 256 (1979).

[20]*Id.* at 273.

[21]*Batson v. Kentucky,* 476 U.S. 79 (1986).

[22]*J.E.B. v. Alabama,* 511 U.S. 127 (1994).

[23]*Id.* at 136.

[24]*Id.* at 137–138.

[25]*Id.* at 138.

[26]*Plessy v. Ferguson,* 163 U.S. 537 (1896).

[27]*Id.* at 543.

[28]*Id.* at 544.

[29]*Id.* at 551.

[30]*Brown v. The Board of Education,* 347 U.S. 483 (1954).

[31]*Bolling v. Sharpe,* 347 U.S. 497 (1954).

[32]*Id.* at 500.

[33]*Brown v. Board of Education of Topeka,* 349 U.S. 294 (1955).

[34]*Id.* at 300.

[35]*Id.* at 300.

[36]*The Little Rock Nine,* The National Park Service, at *http://www.cr.nps/gov/nr/travel/civilrights/akl,htm* (July 29, 2005).

[37]*Goss v. Board of Education,* 373 U.S. 683 (1963).

[38]*Id.* at 687.

[39]*Griffin v. County School Board,* 377 U.S. 218 (1964).

[40]*Id.* at 225.

[41]*Green v. County School Board,* 391 U.S. 430 (1968).

[42]*Id.* at 438–439.

[43]*Swann v. Charlotte-Mecklenburg,* 402 U.S. 1 (1971).

[44]*Id.* at 29.

[45]*Id.* at 30.

[46]*Washington v. Seattle School District No. 1,* 458 U.S. 457 (1982).

[47]*Id.* at 462.

[48]*Id.* at 467.

[49]*Id.* at 471.

[50]*Crawford v. Los Angeles Board of Education,* 458 U.S. 527 (1982).

[51]*Id.* at 538.

[52]*Board of Education v. Dowell,* 498 U.S. 237 (1991).

[53]*Id.* at 635.

[54]*United States v. Fordice,* 505 U.S. 717 (1992).

[55]*Id.* at 728.

[56]*Id.* at 738.

[57]*Id.* at 742.

[58]*Id.* at 743.

[59]*Graham v. Richardson,* 403 U.S. 365 (1971).

[60]*Id.* at 372.

[61]*Id.* at 374.

[62]*Sugarman v. Dougall,* 413 U.S. 634 (1973).

[63]*Id.* at 641.

[64]*Id.* at 646–647.

[65]*Ambach v. Norwick,* 441 U.S. 68 (1979).

[66]*Cabell v. Chavez-Salido,* 454 U.S. 432 (1982).

[67]*Foley v. Connelie,* 435 U.S. 291 (1978).

[68]*Craig v. Boren,* 429 U.S. 190 (1976).

[69]*Schlesinger v. Ballard,* 419 U.S. 498 (1975).

[70]*Califano v. Webster,* 430 U.S. 313 (1977).

[71]*Califano v. Goldfarb,* 430 U.S. 199 (1977).

[72]*U.S. v. Virginia,* 518 U.S. 515 (1986).

[73]*Id.* at 530–531.

[74]*Id.* at 532–533.

[75]*Id.* at 544–545.

[76]*Id.* at 547.

[77]*Id.* at 551.

[78]*Bob Jones University v. United States,* 461 U.S. 574 (1983).

[79]*Geduldig v. Aiello,* 417 U.S. 484 (1974).

[80]*Id.* at 489.

[81]*Id.* at 494–495.

[82]*City of Richmond v. J.A. Croson Company,* 488 U.S. 469 (1989).

[83]*Id.*

[84]*Regents of the University of California v. Bakke,* 438 U.S. 265 (1978).

[85]*Id.* at 289.

[86]*Id.* at 290.

[87]*Id.* at 294.

[88]*Id.* at 298.

[89]*Id.* at 306.

[90]*Id.* at 307.

[91]*Id.* at 314.

[92]*Id.* at 315.

[93]*Grantz v. Bollinger,* 539 U.S. 244 (2003).

[94]*Grutter v. Bollinger,* 539 U.S. 306 (2003).

[95]*Grantz v. Bollinger,* 539 U.S. 244 (2003).

[96]*Id.* at 265.

[97]*Id.* at 264.

THE RIGHT TO PRIVACY

"[The Constitution] is made for people of fundamentally differing views, and the accident of our finding certain opinions natural and familiar or novel and even shocking ought not to conclude our judgment upon the question whether statutes embodying them conflict with the Constitution of the United States."

—Oliver Wendell Holmes
Lochner v. New York

INTRODUCTION

Nowhere does the Constitution mention a citizen's right to privacy. Thus, there is often debate regarding which section or amendment of the Constitution guarantees citizens their right to privacy. While there is no consensus about where this right originates, there is little doubt of its existence. The Framers of the Constitution included provisions throughout the Constitution to minimize government interference. This chapter will examine the derivation of the right and the extent to which it has been applied.

RIGHT TO PRIVACY

A right of personal **privacy** has been recognized as implicit in the liberty protected by the Due Process Clause. However, legal scholars debate the origin of this right in a variety of amendments in the Constitution. In 1928, Supreme Court Justice Louis Brandeis discussed the Right to Privacy in his dissenting opinion in *Olmstead v. United States*.[1] Justice Brandeis found that the Fourth and Fifth Amendments protected a citizen's privacy right against wiretapping and asserted "the right to be let alone [is] the most comprehensive of rights and the right most valued by civilized men."[2] While Brandeis' position was not adopted by a majority of the Court for several decades, it became a part of constitutional jurisprudence in the plurality opinion in *Griswold v. Connecticut*.[3]

In *Griswold*, the first case to discuss the right to privacy, Justice William O. Douglas wrote for the Court, which found that the right to privacy "emanates" or flows from specific guarantees in the Bill of Rights. These specific guarantees create a "**zone of privacy**" protected by the Constitution. Douglas then gave examples, including the Fourth Amendment's ban on unreasonable search and seizure based on an **expectation of privacy**, the Third Amendment prohibition against quartering soldiers in citizens' homes during times of peace, the Fifth Amendment right against self-incrimination, and the Ninth Amendment. Douglas supported his argument by using the analogy of the First Amendment Right to Association. While the Right to Association is not specifically named in the First Amendment, the Court has long held that such a right exists.[4]

Other justices in their concurring opinions discussed the right to privacy found by the *Griswold* majority. In Justice Arthur Goldberg's concurring

privacy describes the right to be left alone; the *right to privacy* is sometimes "balanced" against other rights.

zone of privacy a place or activity protected against government intrusion by the Constitution.

expectation of privacy the belief that you (or your possessions) are in a place, or engaged in an activity, where you have a right to expect privacy.

279

opinion he emphasized the Ninth Amendment's support of the protection of all fundamental rights, including the right to privacy, whether or not that right is explicitly listed in the Bill of Rights. The Ninth Amendment says, in part, "[t]he enumeration in the Constitution of certain rights shall not be construed to deny or disparage others retained by the people."[5] Justice John Marshall Harlan argued in his concurring opinion that the Fourteenth Amendment Due Process Clause does not merely incorporate the specific Bill of Rights guarantees, but instead stands on its own to protect the basic rights implicit in the concept of ordered liberty.

It is obvious that no matter which of these Amendments one looks to, the right of privacy has been recognized and has become an integral part of constitutional jurisprudence, as well as part of the public consciousness. Constitutional scholars, practitioners, and the general public all recognize the right to privacy. The Supreme Court has used the right to privacy to analyze cases concerning marriage, childbearing, abortion, birth control, sex and sexuality, child rearing, and the right to die. The right to privacy implicitly concerns the freedom of an individual to make fundamental choices and protects individuals from unwarranted government interference in intimate personal relationships or activities.

These applications of the right of privacy have occurred because the Court has found them to be fundamental rights. The Court has consistently held that the right to privacy applies only to cases in which a fundamental right is at issue. The question then becomes, how does the Court decide which rights are fundamental and which are not.

The Court's reasoning in *Griswold* establishes that each individual has a zone of privacy that the government may not easily invade. Any government action that invades that zone of privacy violates the individual's substantive due process rights unless there is a compelling governmental interest. The rights within that zone of privacy are fundamental rights due to their intimate nature. This is clear when considering sexual acts of married couples in private. States may not place an undue burden on these fundamental rights. A state regulation will be an undue burden if it places a substantial obstacle in the path of exercising a fundamental right.

Those rights that the Court has held to be fundamental in nature must be reviewed using the strict scrutiny test and in doing so, the Court has consistently held that a state's objective must be "compelling" in order to regulate a fundamental right. In addition, the state must also show that its objective cannot be achieved by use of a less burdensome method of regulation.

In contrast to the fundamental rights mentioned, are the nonfundamental, economic rights. In the last 50 years, the Court has not found one economic right to be fundamental in nature. These nonfundamental rights are reviewed using a different standard, the rational relationship or basis test, rather than strict scrutiny. With the rational basis test, any legitimate state objective that has a rational means to achieve the desired objective is acceptable and does not violate a citizen's right to privacy. These two tests, depending on whether it is a fundamental or a nonfundamental right, have been applied when petitioners to the Supreme Court have raised the issue of governmental interference in a claimed zone of privacy.

RIGHT TO MARRY

The Court has declared that marriage is a fundamental right. Accordingly, the strict scrutiny standard is the proper one for analysis of these cases. This does not mean, however, that the state is precluded from regulating marriage. Some regulation of marriage is valid, however, the regulation may not significantly interfere with the decision to marry.

In *Loving v. Virginia*,[6] one of the first cases in which the Court addressed the question of state regulation of marriage, the challenged regulation was an antimiscegenation law (see Exhibit 9.1). One was not permitted to marry a person of another race. While the Court essentially employed a Fourteenth Amendment equal protection analysis, it was clearly stated that marriage is a fundamental right. As such, Virginia was required to demonstrate a compelling interest in legislating against interracial marriage. The Court could find no such compelling interest in that case.[7]

EXHIBIT 9.1   The Lovings and Interracial Marriage
(The Lovings courtesy of Corbis)

S I D E B A R

In Virginia during the 1950s it was illegal for blacks and whites to marry because of a law entitled the Racial Integrity Act, which said that a white person was prohibited from marrying "any save a[nother] white person." Virginia was not alone in its stance on interracial marriage. It was one of 16 states of that era that had laws prohibiting marriage between blacks and whites. Interestingly enough, the law did not prohibit marriage between blacks and races other than the white race.

During this time, Richard Loving, a white man, met and fell in love with Mildred Jeter, a black woman. When Loving and Jeter could not marry in Virginia, they married in Washington, D.C., where it was not illegal. However, when the Lovings returned to their home in Caroline County, Virginia, both were ultimately arrested and tried for violating the Racial Integrity Act. The law carried with it a penalty of imprisonment from one to five years. When the Lovings were convicted, the Virginia judge sentenced them to one year in prison, but suspended the sentence when the Lovings agreed to leave Virginia and not return for 25 years. Judge Leon Bazile justified the conviction and sentence by summarizing his belief that if God had created different races and placed them on different continents and if humans had not interfered, that arrangement would still exist and interracial marriage would not be an issue This, Judge Bazile believed showed that God did not intend for the different races to marry.[8]

The Lovings moved to Washington, D.C., but in 1963 they brought a lawsuit in the Virginia courts challenging the constitutionality of the Racial Integrity Act. The state courts, including the Virginia Supreme Court upheld the law, and the Lovings appealed the case to the U.S. Supreme Court. In 1967 the Court heard the appeal, and struck down the law in a 9-0 decision. Chief Justice Earl Warren, writing for the Court, stated that the Virginia Racial Integrity Act violated the Equal Protection Clause of the Fourteenth Amendment. To justify this decision, Chief Justice Warren wrote, "Marriage is one of the 'basic civil rights of man,' 'fundamental to our very existence and survival.' To deny this fundamental freedom on so unsupportable a basis as the racial classifications embodied in these statutes, classifications so directly subversive of the principle of equality at the heart of the Fourteenth Amendment is surely to deprive all the State's citizens of liberty without due process of law. The Fourteenth Amendment requires that the freedom of choice to marry not be restricted by invidious racial discriminations. Under our Constitution, the freedom to marry, or not marry, a person of another race resides with the individual and cannot be infringed by the State."[9] Further, Chief Justice Warren explicitly stated that neither Virginia nor any of the other 15 states that had such laws could prohibit and punish marriages on the basis of racial classifications any longer.

With this decision, Virginia and 15 other states were ordered to eliminate these antimiscegenation laws. However, the last of these laws, an Alabama law, was only removed from the books in November 2000.[10]

This same reasoning was also used to strike down a Wisconsin statute that prohibited divorced, noncustodial parents to marry if behind in their child support.[11] In the case of *Zablocki v. Redhail*, the state interest claimed was a need to protect the health, morality, and welfare of children, as well as the integrity of marriage. Again, the Court stressed that marriage was a fundamental right and the claimed interest did not meet the strict scrutiny standard. The Court held that the state had less restrictive collection devices such as civil contempt proceedings, wage garnishment, or attachment procedures to ensure compliance with child support orders. Therefore, the state was unable to satisfy either part of the strict scrutiny test. The Court did indicate in *Zablocki*, however, that if a regulation has some incidental effect upon the ability to marry, while not significantly interfering with the right, the mere rationality test would be the appropriate standard. The use of the rational relationship test should be used where there is no direct, legal obstacle put in the path of the person who wants to marry and the regulation does not significantly discourage marriage, as demonstrated in *Califano v. Jobst*.[12]

ZABLOCKI V. REDHAIL
434 U.S. 374 (1978)

Mr. Justice Marshall delivered the opinion of the Court.

At issues in this case is the constitutionality of a Wisconsin statute, which provides that members of a certain class of Wisconsin residents may not marry, within the State or elsewhere, without first obtaining a court order granting permission to marry . . . The statute specifies that court permission cannot be granted unless the marriage applicant submits proof of compliance with the support obligation and, in addition, demonstrates that the children covered by the support order "are not then and are not likely thereafter to become public charge." No marriage license may lawfully be issued in Wisconsin to a person covered by the statute, except upon court order; any marriage entered into without compliance with § 245.10 is declared void; and persons acquiring marriage licenses in violation of the section are subject to criminal penalties . . .

Appellee Redhail is a Wisconsin resident, who, under the terms of § 245.10, is unable to enter into a lawful marriage in Wisconsin or elsewhere so long as he maintains his Wisconsin residency. The facts, according to the stipulation filed by the parties in the District Court, are as follows. In January 1972, when appellee was a minor and a high school student, a paternity action was instituted against him in Milwaukee County Court, alleging that he was the father of a baby girl born out of wedlock on July 5, 1971. After he appeared and admitted that he was the child's father, the court entered an order on May 12, 1972, adjudging appellee the father and ordering him to pay $109 per month as support for the child until she reached 18 years of age. From May 1972 until August 1974, appellee was unemployed and indigent, and consequently was unable to make any support payments.

On September 27, 1974, appellee filed an application for a marriage license with appellant Zablocki, the County Clerk of Milwaukee County, and a few days later the application was denied on the sole ground that appellee had not obtained a court order granting him permission to marry, as required by § 245.10 . . .

In evaluating §§ 245.10(1), (4), (5) under the Equal Protection Clause, "we must first determine what burden or justification the classification created thereby must meet, by looking to the nature of the classification and the individual interests affected." Since our past decisions make clear that the right to marry is of fundamental importance, and since the classification at issue here significantly interferes with the exercise of that right, we believe that "critical examination" of the state interests advanced in support of the classification is required. The leading decision of this Court on the right to marry is *Loving v. Virginia*. In that case, an interracial couple who had been convicted of violating Virginia's miscegenation laws challenged the statutory scheme on both equal protection and due process grounds. The Court's opinion could have rested solely on the ground that the statutes discriminated on the basis of race in violation of the Equal Protection Clause. But the Court went on to hold that the laws arbitrarily deprived the couple of a fundamental liberty protected by the Due Process Clause, the freedom to marry. The Court's language on the latter point bears repeating:

"The freedom to marry has long been recognized as one of the vital personal rights essential to the orderly pursuit of happiness by free men. Marriage is one of the 'basic civil rights of man,' fundamental to our very existence and survival."

Although *Loving* arose in the context of racial discrimination, prior and subsequent decisions of this Court confirm that the right to marry is of fundamental importance for all individuals. Long ago, in *Maynard v. Hill*, the Court characterized marriage as "the most important relation in life," and as "the foundation of the family and of society, without which there would be neither civilization nor progress . . ." In *Meyer v. Nebraska* the Court recognized that the right "to marry, establish a home and bring up children" is a central part of the liberty protected by the Due Process Clause and in *Skinner v. Oklahoma* marriage was described as "fundamental to the very existence and survival of the race . . ."

It is not surprising that the decision to marry has been placed on the same level of importance as decisions relating to procreation, childbirth, child rearing and family relationships. As the facts of this case illustrate, it would make little

Continued

sense to recognize a right of privacy with respect to other matters of family life and not with respect to the decision to enter the relationship that is the foundation of the family in our society. The woman whom appellee desired to marry had a fundamental right to seek an abortion of their expected child, or to bring the child into life to suffer the myriad social, if not economic, disabilities that the status of illegitimacy brings. Surely, a decision to marry and raise the child in a traditional family setting must receive equivalent protection. And, if appellee's right to procreate means anything at all, it must imply some right to enter the only relationship in which the State of Wisconsin allows sexual relations legally to take place.

By reaffirming the fundamental character of the right to marry, we do not mean to suggest that every state regulation, which relates in any way to the incidents of or prerequisites for marriage must be subjected to rigorous scrutiny. To the contrary, reasonable regulations that do not significantly interfere with decisions to enter into the marital relationship may legitimately be imposed. The statutory classification here, however, clearly does interfere directly and substantially with the right to marry. Under the challenged statute, no Wisconsin resident in the affected class may marry in Wisconsin or elsewhere without a court order, and marriages contracted in violation of the statute are both void and punishable as criminal offenses. Some of these in the affected class, like appellee, will never be able to obtain the necessary court order, because they either lack the financial means to meet their support obligations or cannot prove that their children will not become public charges. These persons are absolutely prevented from getting married. Many others, able in theory to satisfy the statute's requirements, will be sufficiently burdened by having to do so that they will in effect be coerced into forgoing their right to marry. And even those who can be persuaded to meet the statute's requirements suffer a serious intrusion into their freedom of choice in an area in which we have held such freedom to be fundamental . . .

When a statutory classification significantly interferes with the exercise of a fundamental right, it cannot be upheld unless it is supported by sufficiently important state interests and is closely tailored to effectuate only those interests. Appellant asserts that two interests are served by the challenged statute: the permission to marry proceeding furnishes an opportunity to counsel the applicant as to the necessity of fulfilling his prior support obligations; and the welfare of the out-of-custody children is protected. We may accept for present purposes that these are legitimate and substantial interest, but, since the means selected by the State for achieving these interests unnecessarily impinge on the right to marry, the statute cannot be sustained.

At issue in *Califano* was a Social Security benefit that accrued to the minor child of a deceased, qualified parent. The Social Security regulation in question terminated that child's benefit upon marriage. This regulation was challenged as an undue burden or deterrent to a decision to marry. The Court disagreed saying, " [t]hat general rule is not rendered invalid simply because some persons who might otherwise have married were deterred by the rule or because some who did marry were burdened thereby."[13]

Perhaps even clearer examples of the state's ability to regulate marriage without impinging upon an individual's right to privacy would be state regulation of age and the requirement of a blood test. Neither significantly impairs choice of partner or decision to marry.

RIGHT TO PROCREATE

The Court has long recognized the importance of marriage and procreation. In 1942, the Court decided the case of *Skinner v. Oklahoma*.[14] In that case the Court struck down an Oklahoma statute that required sterilization of individuals who had been convicted three times of felonies involving "**moral turpitude**," but not white-collar crimes. In the majority opinion, the Court emphasized "marriage and procreation are fundamental to the very existence and survival of the race," and then went on to decide this case on equal protection grounds.[15] This sets the stage for the Court's decision in *Griswold*.

moral turpitude
describes any crime, such as larceny, that involves immorality or dishonesty.

GRISWOLD V. CONNECTICUT
381 U.S. 479 (1965)

Mr. Justice DOUGLAS delivered the opinion of the Court.

Appellant Griswold is Executive Director of the Planned Parenthood League of Connecticut. Appellant Buxton is a licensed physician and a professor at the Yale Medical School who served as Medical Director for the League at its Center in New Haven—a center open and operating from November 1 to November 10, 1961, when appellants were arrested.

They gave information, instruction, and medical advice to married persons as to the means of preventing conception. They examined the wife and prescribed the best contraceptive device or material for her use. Fees were usually charged, although some couples were served free.

The statutes whose constitutionality is involved in this appeal are 53-32 and 54-196 of the General Statutes of Connecticut (1958 rev.). The former provides:

> "Any person who uses any drug, medicinal article or instrument for the purpose of preventing conception shall be fined not less than fifty dollars or imprisoned not less than sixty days nor more than one year or be both fined and imprisoned."

Section 54-196 provides:

> "Any person who assists, abets, counsels, causes, hires or commands another to commit any offense may be prosecuted and punished as if he were the principal offender."

The appellants were found guilty as accessories and fined $100 each, against the claim that the accessory statute as so applied violated the Fourteenth Amendment. The Appellate Division of the Circuit Court affirmed. The Supreme Court of Errors affirmed that judgment. We noted Probable jurisdiction . . .

The association of people is not mentioned in the Constitution or the Bill of Rights. The right to educate a child in a school of the parents' choice—whether public or private or parochial—is also not mentioned. Nor is the right to study any particular subject of any foreign language. Yet the First Amendment has been construed to include certain of those rights.

By *Pierce v. Society of Sisters*, supra, the right to educate one's children as one chooses is made applicable to the States by the force of the First and Fourteenth Amendments. By *Meyer v. Nebraska*, supra, the same dignity is given the right to study the German language in a private school. In other words, the State may not, consistently with the spirit of the First Amendment, contract the spectrum of available knowledge. The right of freedom of speech and press includes not only the right to utter or to print, but the right to distribute, the right to receive, the right to read and freedom of inquiry, freedom of thought, and freedom to teach—indeed the freedom of the entire university community. Without those peripheral rights the specific rights would be less secure. And so we reaffirm the principle of the *Pierce* and the *Meyer* cases.

In *NAACP v. Alabama*, we protected the "freedom to associate and privacy in one's associations," noting that freedom of association was a peripheral First Amendment right. Disclosure of membership lists of a constitutionally valid association, we held, was invalid "as entailing the likelihood of a substantial restraint upon the exercise by petitioner's members of their right to freedom of association." In other words, the First Amendment has a penumbra where privacy is protected from governmental intrusion. In like context, we have protected forms of "association" that are not principal in the customary sense but pertain to the social, legal, and economic benefit of the members. In *Schware v. Board of Bar Examiners* we held it not permissible to bar a lawyer from practice, because he had once been a member of the Communist Party. The man's "association with that Party" was not shown to be "anything more than a political faith in a political party" and not action of a kind proving bad moral character.

Those cases involved more than the "right of assembly"—a right that extends to all irrespective of their race or ideology. The right of "association," like the right of belief is more than the right to attend a meeting; it includes the right to express one's attitudes or philosophies by membership in a group or by affiliation with it or by

Continued

other lawful means. Association in that context is a form of expression of opinion; and while it is not expressly included in the First Amendment its existence is necessary in making the express guarantees fully meaningful.

The foregoing cases suggest that specific guarantees in the Bill of Rights have penumbras, formed by emanations from those guarantees that help give them life and substance. Various guarantees create zones of privacy. The right of association contained in the penumbra of the First Amendment is one, as we have seen. The Third Amendment in its prohibition against the quartering of soldiers "in any house" in time of peace without the consent of the owner is another facet of that privacy. The Fourth Amendment explicitly affirms the "right of the people to be secure in their persons, houses, papers, and effects, against unreasonable searches and seizures." The Fifth Amendment in its Self-Incrimination Clause enables the citizen to create a zone of privacy which government may not force him to surrender to his detriment. The Ninth Amendment provides: "The enumeration in the Constitution, of certain rights, shall not be construed to deny or disparage others retained by the people."

The Fourth and Fifth Amendments were described in *Boyd v. United States* as protection against all governmental invasions "of the sanctity of a man's home and the privacies of life." We recently referred in *Mapp v. Ohio* to the Fourth Amendment as creating a "right to privacy, no less important than any other right carefully and particularly reserved to the people." . . .

The present case then concerns a relationship lying within the zone of privacy created by several fundamental constitutional guarantees. And it concerns a law which, in forbidding the use of contraceptives rather than regulating their manufacture or sale, seeks to achieve its goals by means having a maximum destructive impact upon that relationship. Such a law cannot stand in light of the familiar principle, so often applied by this Court, that a "governmental purpose" to control or prevent activities constitutionally subject to state regulation may not be achieved by means which sweep unnecessarily broadly and thereby invade the area of protected freedoms. Would we allow the police to search the sacred precincts of marital bedrooms for telltale signs of the use of contraceptives?

The very idea is repulsive to the notions of privacy surrounding the marriage relationship.

We deal with a right of privacy older than the Bill of Rights—older than our political parties, older than our school system. Marriage is a coming together for better or for worse, hopefully enduring, and intimate to the degree of being sacred. It is an association that promotes a way of life, not causes; a harmony in living, not political faiths; a bilateral loyalty, not commercial or social projects. Yet it is an association for as noble a purpose as any involved in our prior decisions.

Mr. Justice GOLDBERG, whom The Chief Justice and Mr. Justice BRENNAN join, concurring.

I agree with the Court that Connecticut's birth-control law unconstitutionally intrudes upon the right of marital privacy, and I join in its opinion and judgment. I do agree that the concept of liberty protects those personal rights that are fundamental, and is not confined to the specific terms of the Bill of Rights. My conclusion that the concept of liberty is not so restricted and that it embraces the right of marital privacy though that right is not mentioned explicitly in the Constitution is supported both by numerous decisions of this Court, referred to in the Court's opinion, and by the language and history of the Ninth Amendment. In reaching the conclusion that the right of marital privacy is protected, as being within the protected penumbra of specific guarantees of the Bill of Rights, the Court refers to the Ninth Amendment. I add these words to emphasize the relevance of that Amendment to the Court's holding.

While this Court has had little occasion to interpret the Ninth Amendment, "[I]t cannot be presumed that any clause in the constitution is intended to be without effect." In interpreting the Constitution, "real effect should be give to all the words it uses." The Ninth Amendment to the Constitution may be regarded by some as a recent discovery and may be forgotten by others, but since 1791 it has been a basic part of the Constitution which we are sworn to uphold. To hold that a right so basic and fundamental and so deep-rooted in our society as the right of privacy in marriage may be infringed because that right is not guaranteed in so many words by the first eight amendments to the Constitution is to ignore the Ninth Amendment and to give it no effect whatsoever. Moreover, a judicial

Continued

construction that this fundamental right is not protected by the Constitution because it is not mentioned in explicit terms by one of the first eight amendments or elsewhere in the Constitution would violate the Ninth Amendment, which specifically states that "[t]he enumeration in the Constitution, of certain rights, shall not be construed to deny or disparage others retained by the people."

Mr. Justice HARLAN, concurring in the judgment.

I fully agree with the judgment of reversal, but find myself unable to join the Court's opinion. The reason is that it seems to me to evince an approach to this case very much like that taken by my Brothers BLACK and STEWART in dissent, namely: the Due Process Clause of the Fourteenth Amendment does not touch this Connecticut statute unless the enactment is found to violate some right assured by the letter or penumbra of the Bill of Rights.

In my view, the proper constitutional inquiry in this case is whether this Connecticut statute infringes the Due Process Clause of the Fourteenth Amendment because the enactment violates basic values "implicit in the concept of ordered liberty." For reasons stated at length in my dissenting opinion in *Poe v. Ullman*, I believe that it does. While the relevant inquiry may be aided by resort to one or more of the provisions of the Bill of Rights, it is not dependent on them or any of their radiations. The Due Process Clause of the Fourteenth Amendment stands, in my opinion, on its own bottom.

The appellants in *Griswold* challenged a Connecticut statute that prohibited the use of any drug, medicinal article, or instrument for the prevention of pregnancy. The appellants were found guilty of violating this statute, and fined $100.00 each. They appealed, claiming the law unconstitutionally intruded on an individual's right of marital privacy. The Court agreed, and for the first time, discussed the concept of "penumbra of rights." Justice Douglas, writing for the Court, explained that each of the specific rights guaranteed to the people in the Bill of Rights was more than that explicated by the particular words. Rather, protections were embraced within these words extending them beyond their plain meanings. These additional concepts and protections were contained within the words, emanating from them and embracing the full scope of the Framers' intentions. Douglas called these "penumbras."[16] When taken as a whole, these penumbras make up the "zone of privacy" within marriage.[17]

In applying these concepts to the facts in *Griswold*, the Court seemed particularly concerned with the invasion of privacy required to gather proof of the use of contraceptives. Douglas wrote that the case here dealt with a relationship falling within the zone of privacy and asked the rhetorical question "Would we allow the police to search the sacred precincts of marital bedrooms for telltale signs of the use of contraceptives? The very idea is repulsive to the notions of privacy surrounding the marriage relationship."[18]

Since *Griswold*, the Court has made it very clear that no person, married or single, can be prevented from using contraceptives or making individual decisions about procreation. In *Eisenstadt v. Baird*,[19] the Court expanded *Griswold* when striking down a Massachusetts statute that prohibited anyone, other than a registered physician or registered pharmacist from providing contraceptives to any unmarried person. Justice William Brennan, in his opinion for the majority, noted that while *Griswold* concerned privacy in the marital relationship, the marital couple is a union of individuals. "If the right of privacy means anything, it is the right of the individual, married or single, to be free from unwarranted governmental intrusion into matters so fundamentally affecting a person . . ."[20] Thus, the court shifted the relevant consideration from the place (the marital bedroom) to the intimate relationship.

The expansion of privacy rights in the area of procreation and birth control continued in *Carey v. Population Services International*.[21] At issue was a New York statute that limited the distribution of contraceptives to those under sixteen by licensed pharmacists and proscribed the sale and distribution of contraceptives to minors (those under sixteen) without a prescription. Reiterating that the decision whether to procreate was a fundamental right and applying strict scrutiny, the Court struck down that part of the statute permitting only pharmacists from distributing contraceptives to adults. A plurality of the Court agreed that the state did not meet its burden of demonstrating a "significant state interest" regarding the ban on contraceptive devices for minors.[22] *Carey* thus ensured that not only all adults, married or single, have a fundamental right to control procreation but also that minors are protected from government interference in purchasing contraceptives.

ABORTION

Abortion is one of the most controversial areas in which the Court has addressed privacy issues. In fact, the Court has noted that it is a unique situation that can be compared with no other.[23] In *Roe v. Wade*, the Court acknowledged its "awareness of the sensitive and emotional nature of the abortion controversy, of the vigorous opposing views . . . and of the deep and seemingly absolute conviction that the subject inspires."[24] Not unlike the death penalty where the Court has also acknowledged the uniqueness of the issue, the Court's decisions in the area of abortion have been among those most affected by the political, cultural and historical climate. Nevertheless, the Court has used the well-established principles of constitutional law and statutory interpretation to set forth a comprehensive jurisprudence around this issue.

After an extensive discussion of the history of abortion, the Court in *Roe* finally arrived at the central question—whether a Texas statute prohibiting abortion violates a woman's right to privacy. While a woman certainly has the fundamental right to make decisions regarding her own body, this is not an absolute right. The Court found that this right might be regulated by the states if a compelling state interest exists. At some point, the state's interest in the health of the mother and the potential life must be balanced against the woman's right to privacy. In order to strike this balance, the Court formulated the infamous trimester analysis.

In the first trimester of a pregnancy, the state may not ban or closely regulate abortions. As the fetus is not considered to be a person under the law until it is a **viable child**, the state's interest is not compelling. The Court also examined the mortality rates for pregnant women having abortions during this trimester and found them to be lower than those for full-term pregnancies. Therefore, the state has no valid or compelling interest in protecting the pregnant woman's health by banning or restricting abortions during this trimester. During the first trimester, the decision regarding abortion is left to the pregnant woman in consultation with her physician.

viable child a child developed enough to live outside the womb.

During the second trimester, the state may regulate the abortion procedure so long as the regulations are reasonably related to the health and welfare of the pregnant woman. The state's compelling interest during this trimester is the pregnant woman's health. The Court also noted that the maternal health risk through abortion during this trimester is notably higher than during the first trimester. There is still no legal protection given to the fetus during the second trimester.

The Court held that the fetus is viable during the third trimester. The Court defined viability as "potentially able to live outside the mother's womb, albeit with artificial aid. . . ."[25] Thus, with viability, the state's interest in the health and welfare of that fetus becomes compelling. Once the state's interest becomes compelling, the state may regulate or prohibit abortion during this trimester, although an abortion must be permitted where necessary to preserve the life or health of the pregnant woman.

The trimester analysis was based on medical technology as it existed in 1973, and scientific knowledge has advanced the Court's understanding in this area over the years. Relying on the state of medical knowledge, rather than constitutional principles, leaves the Court's decision open to criticism and questioning in later cases. This is much like the Court's reliance on social science evidence in *Brown v. The Board of Education*.[26]

The trimester system later came under fire in *Planned Parenthood of Southeastern Pennsylvania v. Casey*.[27] In that case, the Court ultimately discarded the trimester analysis. There were a number of factors, along with the change in medical knowledge in the period between *Roe* and *Casey*, which had an impact upon the Court's view of abortion. Aside from a change in Court personnel, which resulted in a less united Court, the public outcry against the decision in *Roe* put the issue before the Court in numerous cases. In *Casey*, the Court took the opportunity to revisit *Roe*.

PLANNED PARENTHOOD OF SOUTHEASTERN PA. v. CASEY
505 U.S. 833 (1992)

Justice O'CONNOR, Justice KENNEDY, and Justice SOUTER announced the judgment of the Court.

Liberty finds no refuge in a jurisprudence of doubt. Yet, 19 years after our holding that the Constitution protects a women's right to terminate her pregnancy in its early stages, that definition of liberty is still questioned. Joining the respondents as amicus curiae, the United States, as it has done in five other cases in the last decade, again asks us to overrule *Roe*.

After considering the fundamental constitutional questions resolved by Roe, principles of institutional integrity, and the rule of stare decisis, we are led to conclude this: the essential holding of *Roe v. Wade* should be retained and once again reaffirmed.

Constitutional protection of the woman's decision to terminate her pregnancy derives from the Due Process Clause of the Fourteenth Amendment. It declares that no State shall "deprive any person of life, liberty, or property, without due process of law." The controlling word in the cases before us is "liberty." Although a literal reading of the Clause might suggest that it governs only the procedures by which a State may deprive persons of liberty, for at least 100 years . . . the Clause has been understood to contain a substantive component as well, one "barring certain government actions regardless of the fairness of the procedures used to implement them." As Justice Brandeis observed . . . it is settled that the due process clause of the Fourteenth Amendment applies to matters of substantive law as well as to matters of procedure. Thus all fundamental rights comprised within the term liberty are protected by the Federal Constitution from invasion by the States.

Neither the Bill of Rights nor the specific practices of States at the time of the adoption of the Fourteenth Amendment marks the outer limits of the substantive sphere of liberty which the Fourteenth Amendment protects. This "liberty" is not a series of isolated points pricked out in terms of the taking of property, the freedom of speech, press, and religion, the right to keep and bear arms; the freedom from unreasonable searches and seizures; and so on. It is a rational continuum which, broadly speaking, includes a freedom from all substantial arbitrary impositions and purposeless restraints . . . and which also recognizes, what a reasonable and sensitive judgment must, that certain interests require particularly careful scrutiny of the state needs asserted to justify their abridgment.

Our law affords constitutional protection to personal decisions relating to marriage, procreation, contraception, family relationships, child rearing, and education. Our cases recognize the right of the individual, married or single, to be free from unwarranted governmental intrusion into matters so fundamentally affecting a person as the decision whether to bear or beget a child. Our precedents "have respected the private realm of family life which the state cannot enter." These matters, involving the most intimate and personal choices a person may make in a lifetime, choices central to personal dignity and autonomy, are central to the liberty

Continued

protected by the Fourteenth Amendment. At the heart of liberty is the right to define one's own concept of existence, of meaning, of the universe, and of the mystery of human life. Beliefs about these matters could not define the attributes of personhood were they formed under compulsion of the State.

These considerations begin our analysis of the woman's interest in terminating her pregnancy, but cannot end it, for this reason: though the abortion decision may originate within the zone of conscience and belief, it is more than a philosophic exercise. Abortion is a unique act. It is an act fraught with consequences for others: for the woman who must live with the implications of her decision; for the persons who perform and assist in the procedure; for the spouse, family, and society which must confront the knowledge that these procedures exist, procedures some deem nothing short of an act of violence against innocent human life; and, depending on one's beliefs, for the life or potential life that is aborted. Though abortion is conduct, it does not follow that the State is entitled to proscribe it in all instances. That is because the liberty of the woman is at stake in a sense unique to the human condition, and so, unique to the law. The mother who carries a child to full term is subject to anxieties, to physical constraints, to pain that only she must bear. That these sacrifices have from the beginning of the human race been endured by woman with pride that ennobles her in the eyes of others and give to the infant a bond of love cannot alone be grounds for the State to insist she make the sacrifice. Her suffering is too intimate and personal for the State to insist, without more, upon its own vision of the woman's role, however dominant that vision has been in the course of our history and our culture. The destiny of the woman must be shaped to a large extent on her own conception of her spiritual imperatives and her place in society.

The obligation to follow precedent begins with necessity, and a contrary necessity marks its outer limit. With Cardozo, we recognize that no judicial system could do society's work if it eyed each issue afresh in every case that raised it. Indeed, the very concept of the rule of law underlying our own Constitution requires such continuity over time that a respect for precedent is, by definition, indispensable. At the other extreme, a different necessity would make itself felt if a prior judicial ruling should come to be seen so clearly as error that its enforcement was, for that very reason, doomed.

Although Roe has engendered opposition, it has in no sense proven "unworkable," representing as it does a simple limitation beyond which a state is unenforceable. While *Roe* has, of course, required judicial assessment of state laws affecting the exercise of the choice guaranteed against government infringement, and although the need for such review will remain as a consequence of today's decision, the required determinations fall within judicial competence.

From what we have said so far, it follows that it is a constitutional liberty of the woman to have some freedom to terminate her pregnancy. We conclude that the basic decision in *Roe* was based on a constitutional analysis which we cannot now repudiate. The woman's liberty is not so unlimited, however, that, from the outset, the State cannot show its concern for the life of the unborn, and, at a later point in fetal development, the State's interest in life has sufficient force so that the right of the woman to terminate the pregnancy can be restricted.

We conclude that the line should be drawn at viability, so that, before that time, the woman has a right to choose to terminate her pregnancy. We adhere to this principle for two reasons. First, as we have said, is the doctrine of stare decisis.

The second reason is that the concept of viability, . . . is the time at which there is a realistic possibility of maintaining and nourishing a life outside the womb, so that the independent existence of the second life can, in reason and all fairness, be the object of state protection that now overrides the rights of the woman. [T]here is no line other than viability which is more workable.

The woman's right to terminate her pregnancy before viability is the most central principle of *Roe v. Wade*. It is a rule of law and a component of liberty we cannot renounce.

[I]t must be remembered that Roe v. Wade speaks with clarity in establishing not only the woman's liberty but also the State's "important and legitimate interest in potential life." That portion of the decision in *Roe* has been given too little acknowledgment and implementation by the Court in its subsequent cases.

Continued

Roe established a trimester framework to govern abortion regulations. Under this elaborate but rigid construct, almost no regulation at all is permitted during the first trimester of pregnancy; regulations designed to protect the woman's health, but not to further the State's interest in potential life, are permitted during the second trimester; and, during the third trimester, when the fetus is viable, prohibitions are permitted provided the life or health of the mother is not at stake.

We reject the trimester framework, which we do not consider to be part of the essential holding of *Roe*. Measures aimed at ensuring that a woman's choice contemplates consequences for the fetus do not necessarily interfere with the right recognized in *Roe*, although those measures have been found to be inconsistent with the rigid trimester framework announced in that case. A logical reading of the central holding in *Roe* itself, and a necessary reconciliation of the liberty of the woman and the interest of the State in promoting prenatal life, require, in our view, that we abandon the trimester framework as a rigid prohibition on all pre-viability regulation aimed at the protection of fetal life. The trimester framework suffers from these basic flaws in its formulation, it misconceives the nature of the pregnant woman's interest, and in practice, it undervalues the State's interest in potential life, as recognized in *Roe*.

As our jurisprudence relating to all liberties save perhaps abortion has recognized, not every law which makes a right more difficult to exercise is . . . an infringement of that right.

The abortion right is similar. Numerous forms of state regulation might have the incidental effect of increasing the cost or decreasing the availability of medical care, whether for abortion or any other medical procedure. The fact that a law which serves a valid purpose, one not designed to strike at the right itself, has the incidental effect of making it more difficult or more expensive to procure an abortion cannot be enough to invalidate it. Only where state regulation imposes an undue burden on a woman's ability to make this decision does the power of the State reach into the heart of the liberty protected by the Due Process Clause.

A finding of an undue burden is a shorthand for the conclusion that a state regulation has the purpose or effect of placing a substantial obstacle in the path of a woman seeking an abortion of a nonviable fetus. A statute with this purpose is invalid because the means chosen by the State to further the interest in potential life must be calculated to inform the woman's free choice, not hinder it. And a statute which, while furthering the interest in potential life or some other valid state interest, has the effect of placing a substantial obstacle in the path of a woman's choice cannot be considered a permissible means of serving its legitimate ends. Understood another way, we answer the question, left open in previous opinions discussing the undue burden formulation, whether a law designed to further the State's interest in fetal life which imposes an undue burden on the woman's decision before fetal viability could be constitutional. The answer is no.

Some principles should emerge. What is at stake is the woman's right to make the ultimate decision, not a right to be insulated from all others in doing so. Regulations which do no more than create a structural mechanism by which the State, or the parent or guardian of a minor, may express profound respect for the life of the unborn are permitted, if they are not a substantial obstacle to the woman's exercise of the right to choose. Unless it has that effect on her right of choice, a state measure designed to persuade her to choose childbirth over abortion will be upheld if reasonably related to that goal. Regulations designed to foster the health of a woman seeking an abortion are valid if they do not constitute an undue burden.

The Court of Appeals applied what it believed to be the undue burden standard, and upheld each of the provisions except for the husband notification requirement. We agree generally with this conclusion, but refine the undue burden analysis in accordance with the principles articulated above.

Our Constitution is a covenant running from the first generation of Americans to us, and then to future generations. It is a coherent succession. Each generation must learn anew that the Constitution's written terms embody ideas and aspirations that must survive more ages than one. We accept our responsibility not to retreat from interpreting the full meaning of the covenant in light of all of our precedents. We invoke it once again to define the freedom guaranteed by the Constitution's own promise, the promise of liberty.

Continued

Justice BLACKMUN, concurring in part, concurring in the judgment in part, and dissenting in part.

Three years ago, in *Webster v. Reproductive Health Services*, four Members of this Court appeared poised to "cas[t] into darkness the hopes and visions of every woman in this country" who had come to believe that the Constitution guaranteed her the right to reproductive choice. All that remained between the promise of *Roe* and the darkness of the plurality was a single, flickering flame. Decisions since *Webster* gave little reason to hope that this flame would cast much light. But now, just when so many expected the darkness to fall, the flame has grown bright.

I do not underestimate the significance of today's joint opinion. Yet I remain steadfast in my belief that the right to reproductive choice is entitled to the full protection afforded by this Court before *Webster*. And I fear for the darkness as four Justices anxiously await the single vote necessary to extinguish the light.

Chief Justice REHNQUIST, with whom Justice WHITE, Justice SCALIA, and Justice THOMAS join, concurring in the judgment in part and dissenting in part.

The joint opinion, following its newly minted variation on stare decisis, retains the outer shell of *Roe v. Wade*, but beats a wholesale retreat from the substance of that case. We believe that Roe was wrongly decided, and that it can and should be overruled consistently with our traditional approach to stare decisis in constitutional cases. We would adopt the approach of the plurality in *Webster v. Reproductive Health Services*, and uphold the challenged provision of the Pennsylvania statute in their entirely.

A woman's interest in having an abortion is a form of liberty protected by the Due Process Clause, but States may regulate abortion procedures in ways rationally related to a legitimate state interest.

Justice SCALIA, with whom The Chief Justice, Justice WHITE, and Justice THOMAS join, concurring in the judgment in part and dissenting in part.

The States may, if they wish, permit abortion on demand, but the Constitution does not require them to do so. The permissibility of abortion, and limitations upon it, are to be resolved like most important questions in our democracy: by citizens trying to persuade one another and then voting. As the Court acknowledges, "where reasonable people disagree, the government can adopt one position or the other." The Court is correct in adding the qualification that this "assumes a state of affairs in which the choice does not intrude upon a protected liberty,"—but the crucial part of that qualification is the penultimate word. A State's choice between two positions on which reasonable people can disagree is constitutional even when (as is often the case) it intrudes upon a "liberty" in the absolute sense. Laws against bigamy, for example—with which entire societies of reasonable people disagree—intrude upon men and women's liberty to marry and live with one another. But bigamy happens not to be a liberty specially "protected" by the Constitution.

That is, quite simply, the issue in this case: not whether the power of a woman to abort her unborn child is a "liberty" in the absolute sense, or even whether it is a liberty of great importance to many women. Of course it is both. The issue is whether it is a liberty protected by the Constitution of the United States. I am sure it is not. I reach that conclusion not because of anything so exalted as my views concerning the "concept of existence, of meaning, of the universe, and of the mystery of human life." Rather, I reach it for the same reason I reach the conclusion that bigamy is not constitutionally protected—because of two simple facts: (1) the Constitution says absolutely nothing about it, and (2) the longstanding traditions of American society have permitted it to be legally proscribed.

The Court's acknowledgement of a state's ability to regulate abortion in the second and third trimesters of pregnancy led Pennsylvania to pass a statute containing five provisions challenged by five abortion clinics and a doctor. These sections of the law required informed consent by a woman and a 24-hour waiting period before the abortion could be performed; the informed consent of one parent in order for a minor to obtain an abortion or a judicial bypass procedure; and, in the absence of certain exceptions being applicable, the notification of a married woman's husband of the abortion. The statute also defined "medical emergency," which provided a basis for excusing compliance with these provisions.[28] Moreover, reporting requirements were imposed on facilities that provided abortions.

Before addressing the challenged regulations, the plurality opinion considered the appropriateness of overturning *Roe*. The Court reexamined the principles on which *Roe* was decided and reaffirmed *Roe*'s essential holding of a woman's fundamental right of privacy in the abortion decision. Justice Sandra Day O'Connor stated that changes in scientific knowledge did not affect this central holding of *Roe* and that the principle of *stare decisis* was important enough to those joining the opinion to make them unwilling to overturn *Roe*. The majority maintained that the legitimacy of the Court would be undermined if, in the absence of a compelling reason, the opposite result were reached. There was also concern that to do otherwise would leave the impression that the Court surrendered to public pressure. The dissenters adamantly rejected this argument.

Recognizing the personal nature of the abortion decision, the Court altered the *Roe* analysis. As noted, the trimester scheme was jettisoned and in its place the Court substituted an "undue burden" standard.[29] Any previability restriction on abortion must survive the undue burden test. A state regulation will constitute an undue burden if the state regulation places a substantial obstacle in the path of the woman who wants an abortion. The state can create a structural mechanism to express a respect for the life of the unborn. It may not, however, place a substantial impediment to a woman's choice. Pursuant to the undue burden test the state has greater latitude in regulating abortion than was the case when *Roe* was controlling. This is clear from the Court's analysis of the regulations in question here.

The Court upheld several of the challenged regulations in *Casey*. The Court accepted the statutory definition of "medical emergency" addressing this issue first because of its importance to the other challenged regulations. The Court went on to uphold the 24-hour waiting period. The Court rejected the claim that this requirement, which included receiving information about the procedure, associated health risks, and consequences to the fetus, violated a woman's privacy rights. The Court found that this was a reasonable means to ensure a woman's informed consent. However, the Court maintained that the more difficult question was whether this regulation constituted "a substantial obstacle" to a woman's choice. Acknowledging that the 24-hour waiting period has an impact on those with the least resources, the Court nevertheless concluded that it did not amount to an undue burden.

The Court also upheld the parental notification provision. In a number of cases between *Roe* and *Casey* the Court considered parental notification provisions. In *Planned Parenthood of Missouri v. Danforth*,[30] the Court struck down an absolute veto of a daughter's right to choose by both parents. Following *Danforth* the Court reviewed the circumstances under which the state may require parental consent to a minor's abortion. As part of that review, the Court found that there is no automatic right to an abortion for a minor. The state may require parental consent; it must also allow for the "judicial bypass" or an exception to the requirement of parental consent to the abortion, in situations where the parents object. The *Casey* Court noted this and other decisions regarding parental consent, and said that there was nothing new in this particular challenge.[31]

PLANNED PARENTHOOD OF CENTRAL MISSOURI V. DANFORTH
428 U.S. 52 (1976)

Mr. Justice Blackmun delivered the opinion of the Court.

This case is a logical and anticipated corollary to *Roe v. Wade* and *Doe v. Bolton* for it raises issues secondary to those that were then before the Court. Indeed, some of the questions now presented were forecast and reserved in *Roe* and *Doe*.

In *Roe v. Wade* the Court concluded that the "right of privacy, whether it be founded in the Fourteenth Amendment's concept of personal liberty and restrictions upon state action, as we feel it is, or, as the District Court determined, in the Ninth Amendment's reservation of rights to the people, is broad enough to encompass a woman's decision whether or not to terminate her pregnancy." It emphatically rejected, however, the proffered argument "that the woman's right is absolute and that she is entitled to terminate her pregnancy at whatever time, in whatever way, and for whatever reason she alone chooses." Instead, this right 'must be considered against important state interests in regulation.' The Court went on to say that the "pregnant woman cannot be isolated in her privacy," for "she carries an embryo and, later, a fetus." It was therefore "reasonable and appropriate for a State to decide that at some point in time another interest, that of health of the mother or that of potential human life, becomes significantly involved. The woman's privacy is no longer sole and any right of privacy she possesses must be measured accordingly." The Court stressed the measure of the State's interest in "the light of present medical knowledge."

[5] Parental consent. Section 3(4) requires, with respect to the first 12 weeks of pregnancy, where the woman is unmarried and under the age of 18 years, the written consent of a parent or person *in loco parentis* unless, again, "the abortion is certified by a licensed physician as necessary in order to preserve the life of the mother." It is to be observed that only one parent need consent. The appellees defend the statute in several ways. They point out that the law properly may subject minors to more stringent limitations than are permissible with respect to adults, . . . Certain decisions are considered by the State to be outside the scope of a minor's ability to act in his own best interest or in the interest of the public, citing statutes proscribing the sale of firearms and deadly weapons to minors without parental consent, and other statutes relating to minors' exposure to certain types of literature, the purchase by pawnbrokers of property from minors, and the sale of cigarettes and alcoholic beverages to minors. It is pointed out that the record contains testimony to the effect that children of tender years (even ages 10 and 11) have sought abortions. Thus, a State's permitting a child to obtain an abortion without the counsel of an adult "who has responsibility or concern for the child would constitute an irresponsible abdication of the State's duty to protect the welfare of minors." Parental discretion, too, has been protected from unwarranted or unreasonable interference from the State. Finally, it is said that s [sic] 3(4) imposes no additional burden on the physician because even prior to the passage of the Act the physician would require parental consent before performing an abortion on a minor.

The appellants, in their turn, emphasize that no other Missouri statute specifically requires the additional consent of a minor's parent for medical or surgical treatment, and that in Missouri a minor legally may consent to medical services for pregnancy (excluding abortion), venereal disease, and drug abuse. Mo. Rev. Stat. Ss [sic] 431.061-431.063 (Supp. 1975).

The District Court majority recognized that, in contrast to s [sic] 3(3), the State's interest in protecting the mutuality of a marriage relationship is not present with respect to s [sic] 3(4). It found "a compelling basis," however, in the State's interest "in safeguarding the authority of the family relationship."

We agree with the appellants . . . that the State may not impose a blanket provision, such as s [sic] 3(4), requiring the consent of a parent or person *in loco parentis* as a condition for abortion of an unmarried minor during the first 12 weeks of her pregnancy. Just as with the requirement of consent from a spouse, so here, the State does not have the constitutional authority to give a third party an absolute, and possibly arbitrary, veto over the decision of the physician and his patient to terminate the patient's pregnancy,

Continued

regardless of the reason for withholding the consent.

[6] Constitutional rights do not mature and come into being magically only when one attains the state-defined age of majority. Minors, as well as adults, are protected by the Constitution and possess constitutional rights . . .

The Court indeed, however, long has recognized that the State has somewhat broader authority to regulate the activities of children than adults. It remains, then to examine whether there is any significant state interest in conditioning an abortion on the consent of a parent or person *in loco parentis* that is not present in the case of an adult. One suggested interest is the safeguarding of the family unit and of parental authority. It is difficult, however, to conclude that providing a parent with absolute power to overrule a determination, made by the physician and minor patient, to terminate the patient's pregnancy will serve to strengthen the family unit. Neither is it likely that such veto power will enhance parental authority or control where the minor and the nonconsenting parent are so fundamentally in conflict and the very existence of the pregnancy already has fractured the family structure. Any independent interest the parent may have in the termination of the minor daughter's pregnancy is no more weighty than the right of privacy of the competent minor mature enough to have become pregnant . . .

The fault with s [sic] 3(4) is that it imposes a special-consent provision, exercisable by a person other than the woman and her physician, as a prerequisite to a minor's termination of her pregnancy and does so without a sufficient justification for the restriction. It violates the strictures of *Roe* and *Doe*.

Lastly, the *Casey* Court examined the majority of the record-keeping regulations. Of the reporting provisions the Court found that all, except one, were constitutional. The Court overturned the provision that required the abortion facility to report a married woman's reason for failing to provide spousal notice. The Court asserted that this provision was clearly contrary to its determination that spousal notification places an undue burden on a woman's right to choose. The Court noted that requiring a woman to give a reason for failing to notify her husband was putting the woman in the position of justifying her reason for exercising her constitutional right and this the Court was unwilling to do. Addressing the spousal notification provision, the Court reviewed evidence regarding domestic abuse and the effect of a spousal notification provision on preventing a woman's decision to terminate her pregnancy. The Court also considered the husband's interest in the abortion decision and found that such interest reflected an earlier view of women and marriage. The Court determined that women do not lose their right to constitutional liberty when married. Hence, the spousal notification provision was struck down.

While the previous discussion sets forth the constitutional principles and analysis of the majority of the Court, it does not capture the extent of disagreement among court personnel in *Casey* or regarding the abortion issues in general. In addition to Justices O'Connor, Kennedy, and Souter's majority opinion, Justices Stevens and Blackmun agreed to portions of that opinion, while each filed opinions concurring in part and dissenting in part. Chief Justice Rehnquist and Justice Scalia also filed opinions concurring in part and dissenting in part. Justices White and Thomas also joined the Rehnquist-Scalia opinions.

Since the Court's decision in *Casey*, Justices Blackmun and White have departed the Court to be replaced by Justices Breyer and Ginsburg. No significant abortion case has been before the Court since they have been appointed. This raises questions about the direction of the Court's future opinions on abortion.

Before turning to other post-*Roe* abortion cases, the importance of *Casey* should be emphasized. Abortion continues to have constitutional protection, although it would appear that it has been downgraded from a fundamental right, as the test now being used is undue burden and not strict scrutiny. The Court did not specifically state that abortion was no longer a fundamental right, but such an implication is present. Regulations are easier to sustain under *Casey* than in the past when strict scrutiny was used. *Casey* has led to further regulation by the states.

As already noted, *Casey* and *Roe* do not constitute the Court's only pronouncements on abortion. Other questions surrounding the abortion decision including funding, the use of public facilities, counseling, and the permissible medical procedures were considered in the years between the two landmark cases and continue to be addressed today.

In 1980, the Court was asked whether the state or federal government could refuse to pay for medically necessary abortions in *Harris v. McRae*.[32] At issue was the constitutionality of the Hyde Amendment, an act of Congress severely limiting the use of federal funds to reimburse abortion costs to the states as part of Title XIX of the Social Security Act establishing Medicaid. The relevant claim was that the Hyde Amendment interfered with a woman's fundamental right. Before addressing this substantive claim, the Court first considered whether a state had an obligation to fund medically necessary abortions on its own after Congress withdrew federal funding pursuant to the amendment. The Court, examining the legislative history of both the amendment and Title XIX, concluded that there was no obligation to do so. Once that determination was made, the Court then turned to the question of whether a woman's constitutional rights were violated by the Hyde Amendment. The Court found that the Hyde Amendment did not impinge upon a woman's liberty interest protected in *Roe* since it placed no governmental obstacle in the path of a woman seeking an abortion but instead, encouraged childbirth, an alternative activity deemed in the public interest. "[R]egardless of whether the freedom of a woman to choose to terminate her pregnancy for health reasons lies at the core or the periphery of the due process liberty recognized in [*Roe*] it simply does not follow that a woman's freedom of choice carries with it a constitutional entitlement to the financial resources to avail herself of a full range of protected choices."[33]

In arriving at the decision in *Harris*, the Court relied on its decision in *Maher v. Roe* in which the question of funding for nontherapeutic abortions was undertaken.[34] The Court rejected the claim of two indigent women that their inability to obtain a doctor's certification of medical necessity in order to receive medical benefits for their abortions was a violation of a fundamental right. The Court maintained that the regulation involved here was different from the Texas statute considered in *Roe*. It was determined that unlike the statute in *Roe*, the challenged regulation was not a direct interference with a protected activity and did not place an obstacle in the path of a woman's freedom of choice. Justice Powell, writing for the majority claimed that the decision in *Maher* did not signal a retreat from *Roe* and its progeny. A review of these post-*Roe* cases raises some questions concerning this statement.

In *Webster v. Reproductive Health Services*,[35] the Court moved from the funding questions raised in *Harris* and *Maher* to the issue of the use of public facilities and publicly employed staff for abortions not necessary to save the life of the mother. The Court found the regulations constitutional using the same reasoning as in *Maher* and *Harris*. The position of the five-Justice majority was that a woman retained the same choice whether to obtain an abortion as she had if the state had no publicly funded hospitals. It was found that the government is under no obligation to provide resources to facilitate abortion.

Another aspect of the funding question was addressed in *Rust v. Sullivan*.[36] A regulation pursuant to Title X of the Public Health Service Act that provided federal funds for family planning was challenged. The regulation proscribed physicians at clinics receiving federal funding from counseling women about abortion as a method of family planning. This precluded recommendation of an abortion and referral to an abortion provider. The Court rejected the claim that the regulations violated a woman's right to choose. The Court found the state had "no affirmative duty" to facilitate abortion and could constitutionally choose to support childbirth rather than abortion without "impermissibly" burdening due process rights.[37]

The most recent case in the area of abortion rights is *Stenberg v. Carhart*[38] in which the Nebraska statute banning "partial birth abortions" was challenged. Justice Breyer began the majority opinion by reiterating the woman's right to an abortion as discussed in *Roe* and *Casey*, saying, "We shall not revisit those legal principles. Rather, we apply them to the circumstances of this case."[39] The discussion of whether the Nebraska statute constitutes an undue burden on a woman's right to choose an abortion then turned to a graphic discussion of the types of procedures the Nebraska legislature intended to ban with this statute. After discussing these procedures, the Court answered the question whether the total ban of the procedures, known as D & E and D & X, violated the Constitution since banning these methods created significant health risks to a woman, and therefore placed an undue burden on the right to choose. Nebraska argued that the law needed no "health exception" because the procedures are rarely used. The court rejected this argument saying, "[a] rarely used treatment might be necessary to treat a rarely occurring disease that could strike anyone—the State cannot prohibit a person from obtaining treatment simply by pointing out that most people do not need it."[40] The Court went on to hold that the Nebraska law must have a health exception because "the absence of a health exception will place women at an unnecessary risk of tragic health consequences."[41] Requiring a health exception does not depart from the Court's reasoning in *Casey* and "where substantial medical authority supports the proposition that banning a particular abortion procedure could endanger women's health, *Casey* include[s] a health exception when the procedure is 'necessary . . . for the preservation of the life or health of the mother.' "[42] Therefore, the Court struck down the Nebraska statute as, in the words of Justice O'Connor in her concurring opinion, "[the] Nebraska statute cannot be reconciled with our decision in *Planned Parenthood of Southeastern Pa. v. Casey . . .*"[43] Nebraska's statute imposed an undue burden on a woman's right to terminate her pregnancy before viability.

While the Court has consistently held that the state may regulate in the area of abortion so long as there is no undue burden imposed on the woman making the decision regarding the termination of her pregnancy, the basic right of a woman to choose an abortion prior to the viability of a fetus still exists. It seems clear that the Court still supports its basic decision in *Roe*, but as Court personnel changes in the future, so may the right to choose an abortion. A signal that this change may be coming in the near future was foreshadowed during President George W. Bush's first week in office. On January 22, 2001, President Bush signed an executive order to ban the use of federal funds by international family planning groups that offer abortions or abortion counseling.[44] How far the Bush administration is willing to go to overturn *Roe* is unclear.

SEX AND SEXUALITY

Griswold suggests that the zone of privacy protects individuals from state interference with a married couple's sexual intimacy; however, it stops short of extending this zone of privacy to sexual relations in general. The Court was very specific in finding this protection for sexual relations within marriage. Currently, there is no constitutionally recognized privacy interest in committing fornication. Nor is there any constitutional protection of sexual acts committed by married couples in public places. In fact, apart from issues of procreation or family, it is unclear whether a person's sexual conduct has any general protection under the constitution. In the area of adult consensual sexual activity, there are two cases worth noting.

The first case, *Bowers v. Hardwick*, involves a challenge to the sodomy laws of Georgia.[45] Hardwick, a practicing homosexual, brought suit to challenge the law claiming that it violated his fundamental right to engage in consensual sex in his own home. The Court looked at all the other rights of privacy found to be encompassed in the Constitution, and then looked at the claimed right in this case. The Court said that the Constitution would not "extend a fundamental right to homosexuals to engage in acts of consensual sodomy."[46] The Court said that none of the constitutional rights discussed in cases such as *Griswold, Roe, Casey, Eisenstadt,* or *Skinner,* "bears any resemblance to the claimed right of homosexuals to engage in acts of sodomy . . ."[47] The Court concluded by looking at the rights that are part of the concept of "ordered liberty" as set forth in *Palko v. Connecticut,*[48] or deeply rooted in U.S. history and tradition as in *Moore v. East Cleveland,*[49] and found neither aspect of this concept applied in this case.

The dissent in *Bowers v. Hardwick* emphasized the way that the majority framed the issue. Justice Blackmun, joined by Justices Brennan, Marshall, and Stevens, wrote the dissent and said, "this case is about 'the most comprehensive of rights and the right most valued by civilized men,' namely, 'the right to be let alone.' "[50] The dissent went on to say that the majority has distorted the real question in this case by focusing on homosexual activity. Blackmun looked at the language of the Georgia statute, and noted that the Georgia legislature did not focus on homosexuals but rather used broader language that makes the sex or status of the person engaged in the act irrelevant. The dissenting opinion pointed out that the Court had, in the past, construed the right to privacy to include not only certain types of individual decisions (e.g. *Roe v. Wade*) but also include certain places without regard to the types of activities which might occur in those places. As such, the dissent concludes that the majority in this case has "refused to recognize . . . the fundamental interest all individuals have in controlling the nature of their intimate associations with others."[51] Had Blackmun and his colleagues been in the majority, they would have couched the issue in this case in terms of the right of privacy in one's home, and concluded by expressing the hope that "the Court soon will reconsider its analysis and conclude that depriving individuals of the right to choose for themselves how to conduct their intimate relationships poses a far greater threat to the values most deeply rooted in our Nation's history than tolerance of nonconformity could ever do."[52]

This hope may have been echoing in the ears of the Court in 1996 when it decided *Romer v. Evans.*[53] The citizens of the State of Colorado passed a constitutional amendment, known as Amendment 2, that precluded all legislative, executive, or judicial action designed to protect individuals based on their status as homosexual, lesbian, or bisexual or to protect their conduct, practices, or relationships. This was passed as a reaction to ordinances extending this protection to individuals in several Colorado municipalities. The State argued that the amendment put homosexuals in the same position as all other individuals in Colorado, or, to put it another way, the amendment denied homosexuals any special rights. The Court did not buy this argument saying, "Homosexuals, by state decree, are put in a solitary class with respect to transactions and relations in both the private and governmental spheres. The amendment withdraws from homosexuals, but no others, specific legal protection from the injuries caused by discrimination, and forbids reinstatement of these laws and policies."[54]

The amendment did two things that the Court found objectionable. First, it allowed for discrimination against homosexuals in the private sphere and second, it operated to repeal all laws or policies forbidding discrimination by all levels of Colorado government. The consequences of the amendment were to deprive homosexuals of the rights enjoyed by all other citizens of Colorado and "impose[d] a special disability upon those persons alone."[55]

The Court also rejected the State's argument that Amendment 2 was passed to support other citizens' freedom of association. It did not accept that the liberties of landlords or employers who have personal and religious objections to homosexuality should have the right to discriminate against homosexuals. As a matter of fact, the Court did not find any identifiable legitimate purpose or objective that was forwarded by Amendment 2. In conclusion, the Court said "that Amendment 2 classifies homosexuals not to further a proper legislative end but to make them unequal to everyone else. This Colorado cannot do."[56]

The dissent in *Romer*, written by Justice Scalia, said that the issue of discrimination against homosexuals was a "cultural debate" and "[s]ince the Constitution of the United States says nothing about this subject, it is left to be resolved by normal democratic means, including the democratic adoption of provisions in state constitution."[57] Justice Scalia went on to say that the Court had no business imposing on the American public the pronouncement that "animosity" toward homosexuality is evil.

The conclusion that can be drawn from *Romer* is that this may be the first indication from the Court that it will use equal protection to review any government action that discriminates against homosexuals or other politically unpopular groups. Whether this meant that someday *Bowers* might be overturned was unclear, until the Court decided the case of *Lawrence v. Texas*, which was discussed in Chapter 7, *supra*. In *Lawrence*, with Justice Kennedy writing for the Court, the Texas statute outlawing consensual sex between same-sex adults was overturned on due process grounds.[58] The Court explicitly found that *Bowers* was wrongly decided.[59] Justice O'Connor, in her concurrence, maintained that equal protection was the proper basis for overturning the *Bowers* decision.[60]

CHILD REARING

Child rearing is also included under the umbrella of the right to privacy. Government interference in parents' direction of their children's upbringing is to be limited. The Court has long supported this proposition and continues to do so today.

In 1925, the Court was asked to review an Oregon statute requiring parents and others with custody of children, aged 8 to 16, to send the child to public school. Failure to do so constituted a misdemeanor. The government sought to ensure that children attend school.[61]

Two private educational institutions challenged the statute, one a religious school, the other a military academy. The institutions maintained that the statute interfered in a parent's right to choose a school that provided mental or religious training that the parent determined appropriate for the child.

The Court acknowledged that the state could reasonably regulate schools and enumerated the various sorts of regulations that were constitutionally permissible. The Court went on to note that these private schools were doing nothing "inherently harmful" and that there was no evidence which "demand[ed] extraordinary measures relative to primary education."[62] Then, relying on the earlier case of *Meyer v. Nebraska*,[63] the Court ruled that the statute unconstitutionally abridged parents' rights to direct the education and rearing of their children. The Court asserted that it was the duty, as well as the obligation of parents to prepare children for aspects of life that encompass more than just citizenship.

The Court, however, did not give parents unlimited rights to direct their children's upbringing. As noted, the Court maintained that there would be instances in which the state had a legitimate interest in limiting parental freedom where a child's welfare is at stake. This is clearly demonstrated in *Prince v. Massachusetts.*[64] Sarah Prince, the aunt and custodian of a nine-year-old girl was convicted of violating the state's child labor law[65] because she provided her niece, Betty, with magazines knowing that they would be sold on a street corner. Because the magazines in question were Jehovah's Witness publications, Ms. Prince claimed the statute violated her First Amendment religious freedom guarantees. In addition, she claimed a parental right under the Fifth Amendment to raise her child according to her conscience.

The Court discussed the tension between the state's interest in protecting child welfare and the parent's authority over child rearing, noting that where issues of religious training are concerned the conflict is more serious than it would be were there only secular matters of concern. Nevertheless, the Court stated that the state's authority was not negated simply because parental and religious rights were at issue. Moreover, the authority of the state over children is greater than that over adults particularly in the areas of employment and public activities. The Court set out the dangers to children associated with the activities undertaken by Betty and other children in similar situations. Thus, it was determined that the state had not reached beyond its authority in this statute.

The Court most recently addressed the right of parents to direct their children's upbringing in *Troxel v. Granville.*[66] The Washington State legislature passed a bill allowing "any person" to petition for visitation rights at any time and authorized the courts to grant such visitation when in the child's best interest. In the case before the U.S. Supreme Court, grandparents had petitioned for extended visitation rights with their granddaughters following their son's death. The children's mother had allowed visitation and had not indicated that she would prevent the visitation even though she was marrying and her spouse was intending to adopt the children. The grandparents were unsatisfied with the amount of time they would have with their granddaughters. When the case reached the U.S. Supreme Court, a majority found the Washington statute too broad. Relying on a long line of cases in which the Court recognized a fundamental right of parents to make decisions regarding the upbringing of their children, the majority again found a Fourteenth Amendment liberty interest. Even in light of the changing nature of the American family and the importance of grandparents to children's growth and development and the fact that it might be in the child's interest to have a relationship with grandparents, the Court ruled that the statute violated a parent's fundamental right to make decisions concerning a child's care and custody without government interference when the parent is fit.

RIGHT TO DIE AND COMMIT SUICIDE

By now it should be clear that the right to privacy has an impact on many aspects of our lives, from the decisions concerning birth to ones affecting our upbringing and marriage. The right to privacy has also provided the context for analysis of our rights surrounding decisions about our deaths.

In the 1970s and 1980s the Court first considered the right to die free of governmental interference in the context of whether and under what circumstances a family member or guardian of an incapacitated individual could make a decision to end life. Throughout this period, courts allowed a standard of substituted judgment, which allows the relatives or guardians to decide what the patient would want or what would be in the patient's best interest. In jurisdictions that have substituted judgment, the courts will allow the relatives or guardian to control decisions regarding medical care and treatment or the withholding of such care or treatment.

The best example of this standard was set forth in *In re Quinlan.*[67] The father of Karen Quinlan sought to disconnect the respirator that was keeping his daughter, in a persistent vegetative state, alive. The New Jersey Supreme Court found that Quinlan had a constitutional right to privacy that would allow her to terminate treatment for herself. While recognizing that this right was not absolute due to the state's interest the Court found that the state's interest diminished as the "degree of bodily invasion increases and the prognosis dims."[68] The Court concluded that the only way in which Quinlan's right could be preserved in her state was by allowing her family or guardian to determine whether Quinlan would decide to exercise her right. In decisions following *Quinlan*, most state courts relied on the right of informed consent, which provided a basis for refusing treatment, the right to privacy, or a combination of the two. These cases never addressed the question of what procedural standard was appropriate for someone to be designated the surrogate who would make the judgment in the patient's stead. The United States Supreme Court did not get an opportunity to address the issue until 1990 in *Cruzan v. Director, Missouri Department of Health.*[69]

In 1983, Nancy Cruzan lost control of her car and was found lying face down in a ditch by paramedics who restored her breathing and heartbeat before taking her, unconscious, to the hospital. Cruzan did not regain consciousness but was given hydration and feeding tubes to sustain life. It was determined by medical personnel that she was in a persistent vegetative state from which she would not recover. Once her parents recognized the nature of her condition they asked the hospital to remove the tubes, knowing that the removal would result in Cruzan's death.

After much litigation the matter reached the Missouri Supreme Court, which acknowledged a right to refuse treatment but did not accept a broad right of privacy under the Missouri Constitution. The court found that the state had a strong policy of preserving life under the living will statute and found that Cruzan's statements to her roommate concerning her desire to live or die did not, under the statute, constitute clear and convincing evidence of her intent. As a result, the court declined her parents' request for an order terminating treatment.

The United States Supreme Court accepted the case to consider whether Nancy had a federal constitutional right to have treatment terminated under these conditions. Chief Justice Rehnquist, writing for the five-Justice majority stated that a competent person has a Fourteenth Amendment liberty interest in refusing medical treatment. That statement, however, did not address the issue of an incompetent patient. The Court maintained that the situation was distinct from that in which the patient was competent because in the case of an incompetent patient a surrogate must of necessity, make the decision. Missouri required that the surrogate must present clear and convincing evidence of the incompetent's wishes when competent. This left the Court with the question whether Missouri's requirement for clear and convincing evidence was unconstitutional. The majority found it was not. To arrive at this decision the Court reviewed the state's interests in this situation and found those interests substantial. The Court mentioned the serious consequences that would result from erroneous decisions about the wishes of the incompetent. In conclusion, Justice Rehnquist stated that the Constitution does not require the state to grant decision-making power in these situations with anyone but the patient.

CRUZAN V. DIRECTOR, MISSOURI DEPARTMENT OF HEALTH
497 U.S. 261 (1990)

Chief Justice Rehnquist delivered the opinion of the Court.

[Nancy Cruzan was involved in a serious automobile accident on January 11, 1983. While she sur-

vived, she was left in a permanent, vegetative state. Her life functions were being maintained by artificial means, and her parents, upon accepting that she had no chance of regaining her mental faculties, asked that such life support be terminated. The State of Missouri refused, and Cruzan's parents appealed.]

Continued

We granted certiorari to consider the question of whether Cruzan has a right under the United States Constitution which would require the hospital to withdraw life-sustaining treatment from her under these circumstances . . .

Before the turn of the century, this Court observed that "[n]o right is held more sacred, or is more carefully guarded by the common law, than the right of every individual to the possession and control of his own person, free from all restraint or interference of others, unless by clear and unquestionable authority of law." This notion of bodily integrity has been embodied in the requirement that informed consent is generally required for medical treatment.

The logical corollary of the doctrine of informed consent is that the patient generally possesses the right not to consent, that is, to refuse treatment. Until about 15 years ago and the seminal decision in *In re Quinlan*, the number of right-to-refuse-treatment decisions were relatively few. Most of the earlier cases involved patients who refused medical treatment forbidden by their religious belief, thus implicating First Amendment rights as well as common law rights of self-determination. More recently, however, with the advance of medical technology capable of sustaining life well past the point where natural forces would have brought certain death in earlier times, cases involving the right to refuse life-sustaining treatment have burgeoned.

As these cases demonstrate, the common law doctrine of informed consent is viewed as generally encompassing the right of a competent individual to refuse medical treatment. Beyond that, these decisions demonstrate both similarity and diversity in their approach to decision of what all agree is a perplexing question with unusually strong moral and ethical overtones. State courts have available to them for decision a number of sources—state constitutions, statutes, and common law—which are not available to us. In this Court, the question is simply and starkly whether the United States Constitution prohibits Missouri from choosing the rule of decision which it did. This is the first case in which we have been squarely presented with the issue of whether the United States Constitution grants what is in common parlance referred to as a "right to die." We follow the judicious counsel of our decision in *Twin City Bank v. Nebeker* where we said that, in deciding "a question of such magnitude and importance . . . it is the [better] part of wisdom not to attempt, by any

general statement, to cover every possible phase of the subject."

The Fourteenth Amendment provides that no State shall "deprive any person of life, liberty, or property, without due process of law." The principle that a competent person has a constitutionally protected liberty interest in refusing unwanted medical treatment may be inferred from our prior decisions. In *Jacobson v. Massachusetts*, for instance, the Court balanced an individual's liberty interest in declining an unwanted smallpox vaccine against the State's interest in preventing disease. Decisions prior to the incorporation of the Fourth Amendment into the Fourteenth Amendment analyzed searches and seizures involving the body under the Due Process Clause and were thought to implicate substantial liberty interests.

But determining that a person has a "liberty interest" under the Due Process Clause does not end the inquiry, "whether respondent's constitutional rights have been violated must be determined by balancing his liberty interests against the relevant state interests." *Youngberg v. Romeo.*

Petitioner insists that under the general holding of our cases, the forced administration of life-sustaining medical treatment, and even of the artificially-delivered food and water essential to life, would implicate a competent person's liberty interest. Although we think the logic of the cases discussed above would embrace such a liberty interest, the dramatic consequences involved in refusal of such treatment would inform the inquiry as to whether the deprivation of that interest is constitutionally permissible. But for purposes of this case, we assume that the United States Constitution would grant a competent person a constitutionally protected right to refuse lifesaving hydration and nutrition.

Petitioners go on to assert that an incompetent person should possess the same right in this respect as is possessed by a competent person . . .

The difficulty with petitioners' claim is that, in a sense, it begs the question: an incompetent person is not able to make an informed and voluntary choice to exercise a hypothetical right to refuse treatment or any other right. Such a "right" must be exercised for her, if at all, by some sort of surrogate. Here, Missouri has in effect recognized that, under certain circumstances, a surrogate may act for the patient in electing to have hydration and nutrition withdrawn in

Continued

such a way as to cause death, but it has established a procedural safeguard to assure that the action of the surrogate conforms as best it may to the wishes expressed by the patient while competent. Missouri requires that evidence of the incompetent's wishes as to the withdrawal of treatment be proved by clear and convincing evidence. The question, then, is whether the United States Constitution forbids the establishment of this procedural requirement by the State. We hold that it does not.

Whether or not Missouri's clear and convincing evidence requirement comports with the United States Constitution depends in part on what interests the State may properly seek to protect in this situation. Missouri relies on its interest in the protection and preservation of human life, and there can be no gainsaying this interest. As a general matter, the States—indeed, all civilized nations—demonstrate their commitment to life by treating homicide as a serious crime. Moreover, the majority of States in this country have laws imposing criminal penalties on one who assists another to commit suicide. We do not think a State is required to remain neutral in the face of an informed and voluntary decision by a physically able adult to starve to death.

But in the context presented here, a State has more particular interests at stake. The choice between life and death is a deeply personal decision of obvious and overwhelming finality. We believe Missouri may legitimately seek to safeguard the personal element of this choice through the imposition of heightened evidentiary requirements. [W]e think a State may properly decline to make judgments about the "quality" of life that a particular individual may enjoy, and simply assert an unqualified interest in the preservation of human life to be weighed against the constitutionally protected interests of the individual.

In our view, Missouri has permissibly sought to advance these interests through the adoption of a "clear and convincing" standard of proof to govern such proceedings. "The function of a standard of proof, as that concept is embodied in the Due Process Clause and in the realm of factfinding, is to 'instruct the factfinder concerning the degree of confidence our society thinks he should have in the correctness of factual conclusions for a particular adjudication.' "

In sum, we conclude that a State may apply a clear and convincing evidence standard in proceedings where a guardian seeks to discontinue nutrition and hydration of a person diagnosed to be in a persistent vegetative state. We note that many courts which have adopted some sort of substituted judgment procedure in situations like this, whether they limit consideration of evidence to the prior expressed wishes of the incompetent individual, or whether they allow a more general proof of what the individual's decision would have been, require a clear and convincing standard of proof for such evidence.

The judgment of the Supreme Court of Missouri is

Affirmed.

Justice BRENNAN, with whom Justice MARSHALL and Justice BLACKMUN join, dissenting.

"Medical technology has effectively created a twilight zone of suspended animation where death commences while life, in some form, continues. Some patients, however, want no part of a life sustained only by medical technology. Instead, they prefer a plan of medical treatment that allows nature to take its course and permits them to die with dignity."

Nancy Cruzan has dwelt in that twilight zone for six years. She is oblivious to her surroundings and will remain so. Her body twitches only reflexively, without consciousness. The areas of her brain that once thought, felt, and experienced sensations have degenerated badly, and are continuing to do so. The cavities remaining are filling with cerebrospinal fluid. The "cerebral cortical atrophy is irreversible, permanent, progressive and ongoing." "Nancy will never interact meaningfully with her environment again. She will remain in a persistent vegetative state until her death."

Today the Court, while tentatively accepting that there is some degree of constitutionally protected liberty interest in avoiding unwanted medical treatment, including life-sustaining medical treatment such as artificial nutrition and hydration, affirms the decision of the Missouri Supreme Court. The majority opinion, as I read it, would affirm that decision on the ground that a State may require "clear and convincing" evidence of Nancy Cruzan's prior decision to forgo life-sustaining treatment under circumstances such as hers in order to ensure that her actual wishes are honored. Because I believe that Nancy Cruzan has a fundamental

Continued

right to be free of unwanted artificial nutrition and hydration, which right is not outweighed by any interests of the State, and because I find that the improperly biased procedural obstacles imposed by the Missouri Supreme Court impermissibly burden that right, I respectfully dissent. Nancy Cruzan is entitled to choose to die with dignity.

Cruzan establishes two major propositions: (1) a competent adult has a constitutionally protected Fourteenth Amendment liberty interest in declining unwanted medical procedures and (2) where a patient is incompetent, a state may constitutionally refuse to allow medical procedures to be terminated except where there is clear and convincing evidence that this is what the patient would want. Where the patient is incompetent, the first question is whether the patient previously expressed clear wishes that in these types of circumstances, treatment was unwanted. This raises questions about what evidence would establish the patient's intent. The Court's pronouncements indicate that a living will would constitute an expression of that intent and if it does, the state is constitutionally required to accept it as such. In *Cruzan* the Court also indicated that an incompetent patient could express her wishes by designating someone to make decisions in the event of incapacity. Although it is not clear whether a state must accept documents designating someone to make decisions for an incompetent patient, many states have explicitly recognized health proxies in response to the *Cruzan* decision.

Related to the issue of one's right to die are the questions whether one has a right to commit suicide and whether the state may prohibit another person from assisting in a suicide. These questions came before the Court in *Washington v. Glucksberg.*[70]

The State of Washington passed a statute in 1979 that declared those who withheld or withdrew "life sustaining treatment" at the direction of a patient would participate in a suicide. Thus, the state, in effect, banned assisted suicide. In 1994 physicians treating terminally ill patients, and the patients themselves, challenged the statute as unconstitutional claiming that it placed an undue burden on a protected liberty interest.

The Court began its analysis by reviewing history and legal tradition. The Court also considered the debate over assisted suicide. While acknowledging that attitudes had changed since colonial times, the Court maintained that our laws "consistently condemned, and continue to prohibit, assisted suicide."[71] Arriving at the merits of this case, Chief Justice Rehnquist framed the question under consideration as whether one had a right to commit suicide with assistance from another. The instant case was distinguished from *Cruzan* and *Casey*, on which plaintiffs relied. The Court stated that the right to refuse medical treatment found in *Cruzan* (which was based in the common law and viewed in light of history and legal tradition) was different from a right to help in committing suicide, which had no similar history or support. On much the same basis reliance on *Casey* was also rejected. Since the Court found no fundamental liberty interest, the only question remaining was whether the statute was rationally related to a legitimate state interest. The Court found that the state's ban on assisted suicide met a legitimate state interest in preserving human life as well as other legitimate interests. The Court concluded that the statute was reasonably related to the legitimate state interests and noted that the decisions would allow the debate about "the morality, legality and practicability of physician assisted suicide" to continue. It does.

Summary

The right to privacy, found only implicitly in the Constitution, has been recognized by the courts to come within the concept of ordered liberty guaranteed by the Fifth and Fourteenth Amendments Due Process Clauses. It is the right to be free of government interference in making intimate choices about one's life. A balancing test is employed to weigh the individual interest in privacy against the government interest in regulation. Where a fundamental right to privacy is found, the courts will apply the strict scrutiny test requiring a stronger government interest. The Court has long recognized the right of parents to control and care for their children. Other privacy rights were recognized in the 1960s and 1970s. Since that time, however, the Court has been reluctant to find decisions surrounding privacy issues to be fundamental rights. Thus, there is a greater willingness on the part of the Court to allow government regulation of personal aspects of citizens' rights. Recent decisions appear to indicate the Court's retreat from a fundamental right to privacy, but this trend may change over time.

Key Terms

expectation of privacy   privacy   zone of privacy
moral turpitude   viable child

Review Questions

1. From where does the constitutional right to privacy originate and to what areas has it been applied?

2. Please define "zone of privacy" and explain its use in the analysis of cases regarding a right to privacy.

3. How did *Planned Parenthood of Southeastern Pennsylvania v. Casey* change the Court's abortion rights analysis as set forth in *Roe v. Wade*?

4. How has the Court's analysis of a homosexual's right to privacy changed from *Bowers* to *Romer* to *Lawrence v. Texas*?

5. What does a court look to when determining whether life support ought to be terminated for an individual who is in a persistent vegetative state?

Internet Connections

1. To learn more about the state laws on the right to die, see "The Legalities of the Right to Live or Die" at *http://public.findlaw.com*.

2. For a discussion on the U.S. Attorney General's decision on assisted suicide, see J. Paul Oetken's article "Assisted Suicide and Democracy: Why an Oregon Federal Judge Was Right to Overturn Attorney General Ashcroft's Assisted Suicide Decision," FindLaw, Corporate Counsel Center at *http://writ.corporate.findlaw.com*.

3. For commentary on abortion and free speech, see Andrew Hyman's article "Abortion and Free Speech: Applying the 'Prior Restraint' Doctrine to Abortion Law," FindLaw's Legal Commentary at *http://writ.news.findlaw.com*.

4. For the most recent U.S. Supreme Court decision regarding sexual orientation, see *Lawrence v. Texas*, Docket Number 02-102, 71 USLW 4574 at *http://news.findlaw.com*.

End Notes

[1]*Olmstead v. United States*, 277 U.S. 438, 478 (1928).

[2]*Id.*

[3]*Griswold v. Connecticut*, 381 U.S. 479 (1965).

[4]*NAACP v. Alabama*, 357 U.S. 449, 462 (1958).

[5]U.S. Const. amend. IX.

[6]*Loving v. Virginia*, 388 U.S. 1 (1967).

[7]A discussion of the Fourteenth Amendment aspects of *Loving v. Virginia* can be found in Chapter 8, *supra*.

[8]Randall Kennedy, "Loving v. Virginia at Thirty," Speakout.com, at *http://speakout.com* (Aug. 6, 2003).

[9]*Loving v. Virginia*, 388 U.S. 1 (1967).

[10]Lane Harill, "A Brief History of Interracial Marriage," *Christian Science Monitor* (July 25, 2001).

[11]*Zablocki v. Redhail*, 434 U.S. 374 (1978).

[12]*Califano v. Jobst*, 434 U.S. 47 (1977).

[13]*Id.* at 55.

[14]*Skinner v. Oklahoma ex rel. Williamson*, 316 U.S. 535 (1942).

[15]*Id.* at 541.

[16]*Griswold v. Connecticut*, 381 U.S. 479, 484 (1965).

[17]*Id.* at 485.

[18]*Id.* at 486–487.

[19]*Eisenstadt v. Baird*, 405 U.S. 438 (1972).

[20]*Id.* at 453.

[21]*Carey v. Population Services International*, 431 U.S. 678 (1977).

[22]*Id.* at 689.

[23]*Planned Parenthood of Southeastern Pennsylvania v. Casey*, 505 U.S. 883 (1992).

[24]*Roe v. Wade*, 410 U.S. 113, 116 (1973).

[25]*Id.* at 160.

[26]*Brown v. The Board of Education*, 347 U.S. 483 (1954).

[27]*Planned Parenthood of Southeastern Pennsylvania v. Casey*, 505 U.S. 833 (1992).

[28]*Id.* at 880, 885, 887, 893, 900.

[29]*Id.* at 879.

[30]*Planned Parenthood of Missouri v. Danforth*, 428 U.S. 52 (1976).

[31]*Casey v. Population Services International*, 505 U.S. at 895 (1972).

[32]*Harris v. McRae*, 448 U.S. 287 (1980).

[33]*Id.* at 316.

[34]*Maher v. Roe*, 402 U.S. 464 (1977).

[35]*Webster v. Reproductive Health Services*, 492 U.S. 490 (1989).

[36]*Rust v. Sullivan*, 500 U.S. 173 (1991).

[37]*Id.* at 201.

[38]*Stenberg v. Carhart*, 530 U.S. 914 (2000).

[39]*Id.* at 921.

[40]*Id.* at 934.

[41]*Id.* at 937.

[42]*Id.* at 938.

[43]*Id.* at 947.

[44]"Bush Reinstates Ban on International Family Planning," CNN.com, at *http://www.cnn.com/2001/ALLPOLITICS* (Jan. 22, 2001).

[45]*Bowers v. Hardwick*, 478 U.S. 186 (1986).

[46]*Id.* at 192.

[47]*Id.* at 191.

[48]*Palko v. Connecticut*, 302 U.S. 319 (1937).

[49]*Moore v. East Cleveland*, 431 U.S. 494 (1977).

[50]*Bowers v. Hardwick*, 478 U.S. at 199 (1986).

[51]*Id.* at 206.

[52]*Id.* at 214.

[53]*Romer v. Evans*, 517 U.S. 620 (1996).

[54]*Id.* at 627.

[55]*Id.* at 631.

[56]*Id.* at 636.

[57]*Id.* at 636.

[58]*Lawrence v. Texas*, 539 U.S. 558 (2003).

[59]*Id.* at 578.

[60]*Id.* at 580.

[61]*Pierce v. Society of the Sisters of the Holy Names of Jesus and Mary*, 268 U.S. 510, 529 (1925).

[62]*Id.* at 534.

[63]*Meyer v. Nebraska*, 262 U.S. 390 (1923).

[64]*Prince v. Massachusetts*, 321 U.S. 158 (1944).

[65]The law provided that "[n]o boy under twelve and no girl under eighteen shall sell, expose or offer for sale any newspapers, magazines, periodicals or any other articles of merchandise of any description . . . in any street or public place."

[66]*Troxel v. Granville*, 530 U.S. 57 (2000).

[67]*In re Quinlan*, 70 N.J. 10, 355 A.2d 647, *cert. denied sub nom. Garger v. New Jersey*, 429 U.S. 922 (1976).

[68]*Cruzan v. Director, Missouri Department of Health*, 497 U.S. 261 (1990).

[69]*Washington v. Glucksberg*, 521 U.S. 702 (1997).

[70]*Id.*

[71]*Id.* at 711.

 For additional resources, go to *http://www.westlegalstudies.com*

10 CHAPTER

FREEDOM OF EXPRESSION

"Of [freedom of speech] one may say that it is the matrix, the indispensable condition, of nearly every other form of freedom. With aberrations a pervasive recognition of that truth can be traced in our history, political and legal."

—Justice Benjamin Nathan Cardozo
Palko v. Connecticut

INTRODUCTION

freedom of speech the First Amendment right to say what you want as long as you do not interfere with others' rights.

freedom of expression the First Amendment freedoms of religion, speech, and press combined.

The guarantee of **freedom of speech** is at the heart of American society; a primary value shared by all. **Freedom of expression** is a hallmark of a democratic society, serving to encourage a dialogue among citizens in the free marketplace of ideas. While all citizens agree on the value of free speech they do not always agree on what categories of speech and expression are guaranteed protection under the First Amendment nor do they always agree on the extent of that protection. There are those who take literally the language of the First Amendment that "Congress shall make no law . . . abridging the freedom of speech . . ." Others, including the majority of the Supreme Court, see a more limited scope to the protection as we shall see in Chapter 11 on unprotected speech.

Until the twentieth century, the Supreme Court did not address First Amendment expression issues. This was in part because the rights guaranteed in our Bill of Rights had not yet been made applicable to state and local governments. The situation changed in 1925, when in *Gitlow v. New York*,[1] the Court needed to address the scope of free speech protection in the context of political dissent. In *Gitlow* the Court found that the First Amendment free speech guarantee was applicable to the states through the Fourteenth Amendment. Since that time, the Court has frequently been faced with determining the nature and extent of the First Amendment protection of speech and expression. Before these issues can be addressed, however, the concepts that direct First Amendment speech and expression analysis must be understood, as well as how the Court has drawn the lines between protected and unprotected speech.

BASIC PRINCIPLES OF FIRST AMENDMENT ANALYSIS

The Content/Content-Neutral Distinction

The government's reasons for abridging First Amendment speech rights fall into two main categories:

1. The nature of the speech itself or restricting speech based on its content; those situations in which the government wishes to preclude the dissemination of particular ideas or information or a general subject matter of speech, and
2. Situations in which the government is attempting to avoid the by-products of speech.

In this second category, the government's reason for regulation is unconnected to the content of the speech. Rather, the government is concerned with some evil that is an incidental result of the speech. An example of this sort of regulation could be a ban on the use of sound trucks outside a hospital to prevent noise disturbances for patients.

Based on these two different categories, the Court applies different analyses. This is because each category entails different dangers. The dangers related to the first category are more serious than the second because they undermine the very nature of the free speech guarantee. This sort of regulation is aimed at the communicative impact of the speech. In the category of content-neutral regulation, the aim is something other than control of the communicative impact.

For those cases where the government is aiming to regulate content, the Court employs a rigid analytical framework using the strict scrutiny standard. This standard allows for only the narrowest suppression of content and in so doing respects the Framers' ideal of the free marketplace of ideas.

The Framers believed that truth emerges from a full and fair discussion of ideas. To ensure this goal, the Court will allow interference with communication and discussion of ideas only when there is insufficient time within which to bring to light the evil of the ideas expressed before the harm may occur. In any other circumstance, it is believed that the harm may be avoided by more speech, rather than less.

Aside from those areas of communication that the Court has ruled are not protected by the First Amendment because they do not fall within the Framers' intent to protect these categories, the government may not argue that the content of speech is harmful and should be suppressed or punished. If a content-based regulation is imposed on protected First Amendment speech there is a strong presumption that it is unconstitutional.

When the government attempts to regulate speech because of its content, the government must demonstrate that the regulation is necessary to serve a compelling state interest and is narrowly drawn to achieve that interest.[2] Use of this strict scrutiny standard results in the regulation being stricken if more speech will prevent the asserted evil. Therefore, any government argument that others have adequately expressed the position or viewpoints contained in the speech it is attempting to regulate will not prevail. Similarly, a government argument that another time, place, or manner of expression will be just as adequate will also fail.[3]

Nevertheless, strict scrutiny is not always fatal to content-based regulations. There are instances in which the government can establish a compelling state interest as well as demonstrating that its aim cannot be achieved by less restrictive means. These cases are best exemplified by restrictions on electioneering within specified distances from the polls. In cases challenging these distance restrictions, the Court has consistently upheld the restrictions because the government has a compelling interest in free and fair elections.

In *Burson v. Freeman*[4] the state statute banning solicitation of votes and distribution or display of campaign literature within 100 feet of a polling place was challenged on First Amendment and Fourteenth Amendment grounds. The Court found that the restriction was content based and affected protected political speech in the public forum. As such, strict scrutiny analysis was required under either of the two Amendments. The state had to demonstrate that it had a compelling interest and that the statute was narrowly tailored to achieve that interest. The Court found that the state's interest in preventing voter intimidation and election fraud was such a compelling interest. Moreover, the state met its burden of demonstrating that the regulation was reasonable and that it did not significantly infringe on protected rights. The 100-foot boundary did not, according to the Court, constitute a significant infringement. The Court found that the state has a compelling interest in the right of citizens to vote freely in elections conducted with reliability and integrity. Accordingly, the Court held that a 100-foot limit from the polls for electioneering was a narrowly tailored regulation that could withstand strict scrutiny.

The need for content-neutrality in regulation means that the government may not endorse one point of view over another. Nor may the government remove particular issues from public discussion while allowing others to be discussed.[5] This point is nicely illustrated by the Court's decision in *Simon & Schuster, Inc. v. Members of the New York State Crime Victims Board.*

New York State passed a statute to prevent criminals from profiting from their notoriety while crime victims remained uncompensated. The statute required that any funds earned by those who had committed a crime were to be paid to the Crime Victims Board, and that the board use those monies to compensate crime victims. This meant that anytime a convicted criminal wrote a book about the crime, sold the motion picture rights, or otherwise made money, that convicted criminal had to turn the monies over to the state. The Court found the statute violated the First Amendment in that it was a content-based regulation. According to the Court, the statute singled out speech on a particular subject for a financial burden that was not placed on other speech, despite the state's compelling interest in compensating victims from the fruits of the crime.[6]

Until recently the requirement of content-neutral regulation was not applicable to categories of speech deemed unprotected by the First Amendment. Thus, in unprotected categories all the government needed to show was a rational relationship between the regulation and a legitimate state interest for the regulation to be upheld. In other words, a regulation of unprotected speech did not have to be content-neutral. It appears this has changed.[7] Now, unprotected categories may be regulated only if the government acts in a content-neutral manner.

It appears that the content neutrality restriction may no longer be as viable as was previously the case. However, the government's right to discriminate on the basis of categories of speech is subject to other First Amendment principles of analysis. The Public Forum Doctrine Regulations that are not aimed at the content of expression will be analyzed in part on the basis of where the speech occurs. The Supreme Court has drawn a distinction between speech that takes place in a public forum and speech that does not. This raises the question, what is a public forum?

The Public Forum

The Court has defined two types of public forum: (1) traditional and (2) designated. The traditional, or true, public forum consists of places that by custom have been open to the public. These include the streets, parks, and sidewalks of a community.[8] Designated public forums are those places and activities that the government specifically denominates as such. These are facilities the government has chosen to open to a broad range of expressive activities. For example, a meeting of the government that is open to the public is considered a designated public forum and, as such, cannot exclude a particular group of speakers.[9] Once a place has been designated as a public forum it is subject to the same constitutional protection and analyses as traditional public forums. The question of what constitutes a public forum has been one the Court has been faced with on numerous occasions due to the changes society has experienced in the way its citizens lead their daily lives, and the places at which they congregate.

As a result of these changes the Court has been asked to consider whether shopping malls and airports fall within the public forum. In deciding what constitutes nonpublic forums, the Court has increasingly found that some publicly owned facilities are not public forums. The analysis turns on whether the government intended to create a general right of access for speakers.[10] Employing this analysis, the Court has found that airport terminals do not constitute public forums.

In *International Society for Krishna Consciousness v. Lee,*[11] the Court was faced with a challenge to a regulation promulgated by the Port Authority of New York and New Jersey. The Port Authority operated the area airport terminals that were open to the public and contained commercial establishments such as restaurants and newsstands. The regulation banned repetitive solicitation for money. Solicitation was permitted on the sidewalks outside the terminals. The Krishna Society, a religious corporation, wanted to solicit in the terminals and sued for a declaratory judgment and an injunction on the grounds that the regulation violated First Amendment rights. The District Court granted summary judgment holding that the terminals were public forums. The Court of Appeals for the Second Circuit reversed, refusing to find the terminals were public forums. The United States Supreme Court, in a plurality opinion, affirmed the appellate court's holding.

INTERNATIONAL SOCIETY FOR KRISHNA CONSCIOUSNESS, INC. V. LEE
505 U.S. 672 (1992)

Chief Justice REHNQUIST delivered the opinion of the Court.

In this case we consider whether an airport terminal operated by a public authority is a public forum and whether a regulation prohibiting solicitation in the interior of an airport terminal violates the First Amendment.

The Port Authority owns and operates three major airports in the greater New York City area . . . The three airports collectively form one of the world's busiest metropolitan airport complexes. They serve approximately 8% of this country's domestic airline market and more than 50% of the trans-Atlantic market. By decade's end they are expected to serve at least 110 million annually.

The airports are funded by user fees and operated to make a regulated profit. Most space at the three airports is leased to commercial airlines, which bear primary responsibility for the leasehold. The Port Authority retains control over unleased portions, including LaGuardia's Central Terminal Building, portions of Kennedy's International Arrivals Building, and Newark's North Terminal Building (we refer to these collectively as the "terminals"). The terminals are generally accessible to the general public and contain various commercial establishments such as restaurants, snack stands, bars, newsstands, and stores of various types. Virtually all who visit the terminals do so for purposes related to air travel. These visitors principally include passengers, those meeting or seeing off passengers, flight crews and terminals employees.

The Port Authority has adopted a regulation forbidding within the terminals the repetitive solicitation of money or distribution of literature.

The regulations govern only the terminals; the Port Authority permits solicitation and distribution on the sidewalks outside the terminal buildings. The regulation effectively prohibits ISKCON [the Krishna Society] from performing *sankitran* in the terminals. As a result, ISKCON brought suit seeking declaratory and injunctive relief . . . alleging that the regulation worked to deprive its members of rights guaranteed under the First Amendment. The District Court analyzed the claim under the "traditional public forum" doctrine. It concluded that the terminals were akin to public streets, the quintessential traditional public fora. This conclusion in turn meant that the Port Authority's terminal regulation could be sustained only if it was narrowly tailored to support a compelling state interest. In the absence of any arguments that the blanket prohibition constituted such narrow tailoring, the District Court granted ISKCON summary judgment.

The Court of Appeals . . . concluded that the terminals are not public fora.

It is uncontested that the solicitation at issue in this case is a form of speech protected under the First Amendment. But it is also well settled that the government need not permit all forms of speech on property that it owns and controls. Where the government is acting as a proprietor, managing its internal operations, rather than acting as lawmaker with the power to regulate or

Continued

license, its action will not be subjected to the heightened review to which its actions as a lawmaker may be subject. Thus, we have upheld a ban on political advertisements in city-operated transit vehicles, even though the city permitted other types of advertising on those vehicles. Similarly, we have permitted a school district to limit access to an internal mail system used to communicate with teachers employed by the district.

These cases reflect, either implicitly or explicitly, a "forum based" approach for assessing restrictions that the government seeks to place on the use of its property. Under this approach, regulation of speech on government property that has traditionally been available for public expression is subject to the highest scrutiny. Such regulations survive only if they are narrowly drawn to achieve a compelling state interest. The second category of public property is the designated public forum, whether of a limited or unlimited character—property that the State has opened for expressive activity by part or all of the public. Regulation of such property is subject to the same limitations as that governing a traditional public forum. Finally, there is all remaining public property. Limitations on expressive activity conducted on this last category of property must survive only a much more limited review. The challenged regulation need only be reasonable, as long as the regulation is not an effort to suppress the speaker's activity due to disagreement with the speaker's view.

[The parties] disagree whether the airport terminals are public fora or nonpublic fora.

The suggestion that the government has a high burden in justifying speech restrictions relating to traditional public fora made its first appearance in *Hague v. Committee for Industrial Organization*. Justice Roberts, concluding that individuals have a right to use "streets and parks for communication of views," reasoned that such a right flowed from the fact that "streets and parks . . . have immemorially been held in trust for the use of the public and, time out of mind, have been used for purposes of assembly, communicating thoughts between citizens, and discussing public questions." We confirmed this observation in *Frisby v. Schultz*, . . . where we held that a residential street was a public forum.

Our recent cases provide additional guidance on the characteristics of a public forum. In *Cornelius* we noted that a traditional public forum is property that has as "a principal purpose . . . the free exchange of ideas." Moreover, consistent with the notion that the government—like other property owners—"has power to preserve the property under its control for the use to which it is lawfully dedicated," the government does not create a public forum by inaction. Nor is a public forum created "whenever members of the public are permitted freely to visit a place owned or operated by the Government." The decision to create a public forum must instead be made "by intentionally opening a nontraditional forum for public discourse." Finally, we have recognized that the location of property also has bearing because separation from acknowledged public areas may serve to indicate that the separated property is a special enclave, subject to greater restriction.

These precedents foreclose the conclusion that airport terminals are public fora. Reflecting the general growth of the air travel industry, airport terminals have only recently achieved their contemporary size and character. But given the lateness with which the modern air terminal has made its appearance, it hardly qualifies for the description of having "immemorially . . . time out of mind" been held in the public trust and used for purposes of expressive activity. Moreover, even within the rather short history of air transport, it is only "in recent years [that] it has become a common practice for various religious and nonprofit organizations to use commercial airports as a forum for the distribution of literature, the solicitation of funds, the proselytizing of new members, and other similar activities." Thus the tradition of airport activity does not demonstrate that airports have historically been made available for speech activity. Nor can we say that these particular terminals, or airport terminals generally, have been intentionally opened by their operators to such activity; the frequent and continuing litigation evidencing the operators' objections belies any such claim. In short, there can be no argument that society's time-tested judgment, expressed through acquiescence in a continuing practice, has resolved the issue in petitioners' favor.

Petitioners attempt to circumvent the history and practice governing airport activity by pointing our attention to the variety of speech activity that they claim historically occurred at various "transportation nodes" such as rail stations, bus stations, wharves, and Ellis Island. Even if we were inclined to accept petitioners'

Continued

historical account describing speech activity at these locations, an account respondent contests, we think that such evidence is of little import for two reasons. First, much of the evidence is irrelevant to public fora analysis, because sites such as bus and rail terminals traditionally had private ownership. Second, the relevant unit for our inquiry is an airport, not "transportation nodes" generally. When new methods of transportation develop, new methods for accommodating that transportation are also likely to be needed. And, with each new step, it therefore will be a new inquiry whether the transportation necessities are comparable with various kinds of expressive activity. To make a category of "transportation nodes," therefore, would unjustifiably elide what may prove to be critical differences of which we should rightfully take account.

The differences among such facilities are unsurprising since, as the Court of Appeals noted, airports are commercial establishments funded by users fees and designed to make a regulated profit, and where nearly all who wish do so for some travel related purpose. As commercial enterprises, airports must provide services attractive to the marketplace. In light of this, it cannot fairly be said that an airport terminal has as a principal purpose promoting "the free exchange of ideas." Although many airports have expanded their functions beyond merely contributing to efficient air travel, few have included among their purposes the designation of a forum for solicitation and distribution activities. Thus, we think that neither by tradition nor purpose can the terminals be described as satisfying the standard we have previously set out for identifying a public forum. The restrictions here challenged, therefore, need only satisfy a requirement of reasonableness. We reiterate what we stated in *Kokinda:* The restriction "need only be *reasonable;* it need not be the most reasonable or the only reasonable limitation." We have no doubt that under this standard the prohibition on solicitation passes muster.

Affirmed.

The Court has also found that other publicly owned properties do not constitute public forums. Jails have not been found public forums,[12] since their function is housing prisoners and expressive conduct is not compatible with that purpose. Military bases also do not constitute public forums because their purpose is to train soldiers.[13] The same may be said for courthouses that are not traditionally open for expressive activity.[14] School mail systems are also not public forums.[15] And, although the Court has not directly ruled on whether post offices constitute a public forum, the Court has ruled that sidewalks in front of a post office are not a public forum when the sidewalk only links the parking lot to the building,[16] since its opening was not intended as a site for public discourse.

By definition, it is also clear that private places do not fall within the parameters of the public forum doctrine. In such places, the right of access is denied if the owner of the property objects. It has been argued, however, that some private places should be designated public forums by the government thereby granting access to speakers. This argument usually pertains to two particular forums to which access is sought: shopping centers and media. The argument is made in light of the changes that have occurred in the American lifestyle over the years.

Many of our downtown areas have been essentially abandoned as places to shop and engage in community activities. Today, a great many of these activities occur at local shopping malls. By precluding access to these areas, the ability to reach large numbers of our citizens is denied to speakers. For this same reason, access to the media becomes more necessary. One is no longer able to take up a downtown corner to hand out leaflets or address passersby and have one's message reach a widespread sector of the population. The success of these arguments has, however, been minimal.

Initially there was some success in gaining access to shopping centers. In *Amalgamated Food Employees Local 500 v. Logan Valley Plaza*,[17] the Court found that where a privately owned shopping center constituted the functional equivalent of a usual business district, those seeking to exercise their First Amendment expression rights could not constitutionally be prevented from doing so by using trespass laws.

Only four years later, in 1972, however, the case was overturned in *Lloyd Corporation v. Tanner*,[18] when the Court overturned *Logan Valley*. When *Lloyd* was decided, the Court distinguished it from *Logan Valley* on the basis that the speech in *Lloyd* did not relate to the shopping center's operation. At issue in *Lloyd* was whether antiwar activists could be barred from distributing leaflets at the shopping center, whereas the issue in *Logan Valley* was whether store employees could picket the store where they worked.

In *Hudgens v. National Labor Relations Board*,[19] the Court found that the distinction between the two previous cases was not a valid one because the right of access then depended on the content of the expression. The decision in *Hudgens* remains the law to date. That is, citizens have no right of expression in shopping centers if the property owner objects.

The success of the free speech argument with regard to the media depends on the medium to which access is sought. When access is sought to the print media it is generally clear that no right exists. In *Miami Herald Publishing Co. v. Tornillo*,[20] the Court found a Florida statute requiring newspapers to print the replies of political candidates who had been attacked in print unconstitutional. A unanimous court found a First Amendment violation of First Amendment freedom of press.

In *Pacific Gas and Electric Co. v. Public Utilities Commission of California*,[21] another access case, the Court ruled that a utility company could not constitutionally be compelled to include, with its bill, the position of a group of ratepayers it disagreed with. Although the reasoning in these two cases was different, both represent a clear rejection of the right of access to print media.

Turning now to the question of broadcast media, the result is essentially the same, but for a very different reason. The Court distinguishes between print media and broadcast media in its analysis of right of access questions. The distinction rests on the fact that access to broadcast media is difficult due to their scarcity, while print media abound. Thus, the Court has granted a limited right of access to the public in the broadcast arena. It is clear that an individual has the right of reply to personal attacks broadcast by a particular station.[22] The limits on other aspects of the right of access in the context of broadcast media have not yet been defined.

In general, where speech occurs in a public forum any regulation must be content-neutral. Additionally, the regulation must leave adequate alternative channels open. Finally, the regulation must be narrowly tailored to serve a significant government interest. In these situations, the Court employs a balancing test. The individual's interest in free speech is weighed against the government's interest in regulating the speech. That interest must be equally as important as the individual's. Further, the government must demonstrate that its interest cannot be achieved in a less restrictive way.

Speech in a nonpublic forum is also analyzed using a balancing test. The test, however, is less strict than that employed for speech in the public forum. If the interference in an individual's interest in free speech is not substantial, the government need only meet the rational relationship standard, demonstrating that there is a rational relationship between the government's legitimate interest and the regulation employed to achieve that interest. In such cases, the government may exclude some speakers and some subject matters. The basis upon which this is done must be reasonable in light of the Framers' purpose and must not be premised upon viewpoint.[23]

In determining what constitutes a significant state interest, the Court has found that mere administrative convenience will not meet the significant state interest standard. But, it has found that crowd control in the interest of preventing physical danger will constitute a significant interest.[24] Similarly, the need to protect an unwilling listener will also meet the standard,[25] as will the need to provide access to public and private buildings,[26] and the need to keep streets clear for ordinary traffic.[27] The Court has even upheld a regulation prohibiting the posting of all signs on public property in pursuit of aesthetic objectives as a significant interest.[28]

It is not necessary for the government to demonstrate the availability of other channels in nonpublic forum cases, as it is when speech occurs in the public forum. However, the state can prove that a regulation has an insubstantial effect by demonstrating that alternative channels exist allowing the speaker to reach the audience. Thus, it makes it easier for the government to regulate speech in nonpublic forums.

Overbreadth and Vagueness

To ensure that speech and expression get the protection intended by the Framers, the Court employs two different doctrines in its analyses. These are the doctrines of **overbreadth** and **vagueness**. Each will be considered separately, although they are related.

Overbreadth

The overbreadth doctrine is employed in determining whether a statute covers constitutionally protected speech or conduct at the same time it proscribes expression that is not protected.[29]

In overbreadth cases, a challenger may prevail if it can be shown that the regulation, as applied according to its terms, would violate the rights of those not before the court. This differs from the usual application of the standing doctrine that prevents an individual from challenging a statute on constitutional grounds if he or she cannot demonstrate that his or her own rights are being violated. Moreover, the application of the overbreadth doctrine will lead the Court to find a challenged statute void on its face, thereby striking the entire statute. Usually, the Court will excise those portions of a statute that are unconstitutional in their application, leaving the remainder of the statute in force.

There are two main reasons for employing the overbreadth doctrine. First is the concern that statutes that cover too broad an area may have a "chilling effect" on the freedom of expression. There is a concern that citizens will be afraid that conduct, which is constitutionally protected, is proscribed and will refrain from conduct they may have otherwise engaged in. Citizens will, in effect, have been intimidated from exercising their rights.[30]

The second reason the Court has for employing the overbreadth doctrine is the ease with which it can be selectively enforced. In these cases, the Court is concerned that law enforcement will focus on only certain categories of conduct by certain individuals who engage in it. The result would be discriminatory enforcement. While this may be the case in many situations, it is more of a danger in overbreadth cases. Overbroad statutes give law enforcement officers an opportunity to violate the constitutional rights of one person and not another.

The Burger-Rehnquist Court has narrowed the overbreadth doctrine. The Court now requires a challenger to demonstrate "substantial" overbreadth before finding a statute unconstitutional. This change was first made by the Court in *Broadrick v. Oklahoma*,[31] and remains in effect to date. At issue was a statute preventing civil servants from engaging in certain political activities. Included among these were management of any political party or campaign

overbreadth   a law will be declared void for overbreadth if it attempts to punish speech or conduct that is protected by the Constitution and if it is impossible to eliminate the unconstitutional part of the law without invalidating the whole law.

vague   The vagueness doctrine is the rule that a criminal law may be unconstitutional if it does not clearly say what is required or prohibited, what punishment may be imposed, or what persons may be affected; a law that violates due process of law in this way is void for vagueness.

and soliciting campaign contributions. Broadrick took part in activities proscribed and then challenged the statute on overbreadth and vagueness grounds. He argued that some of the activities covered by the statute were constitutionally protected.

In a 5 to 4 decision the Court rejected Broadrick's claims. The majority drew a distinction between speech and conduct upon which it rested its new standard in overbreadth cases. The Court decided that where a statute pertained directly to speech, the traditional standard for overbreadth applied. Where conduct was being regulated, however, the Court concluded that prior to declaring a statute facially invalid on overbreadth grounds, the statute should be substantially overbroad in relation to its legitimate overage. Applying this standard to *Broadrick*, the Court found that the statute was primarily directed at conduct. In addition, the statute clearly applied to the wide range of conduct that could be constitutionally regulated. Accordingly, it was not substantially overbroad. There has been no indication from the Court that the traditional standard will change in pure speech cases.

In dissent, Justice Brennan rejected the newly found requirement of substantiality, arguing that it broke with prior decisions. He also took issue with the Court's distinction between speech and conduct when considering overbreadth.

Vagueness

We turn now to the vagueness doctrine. A statute will be found void for vagueness when it is unclear what conduct Congress meant to proscribe. The standard to be used is whether the conduct proscribed is so unclearly defined that a person, of common intelligence must necessarily guess at its meaning and differ as to its application.[32]

The rationale here, as it was with overbreadth, is concern with the chilling effect of the legislation. The Fifth Amendment Due Process Clause requires that people receive fair notice of what conduct is proscribed. A vague statute, by its very terms, cannot adequately provide fair notice. Without such notice citizens may curb their constitutional speech and expression because they are not certain if these activities are banned under the statute. Thus, the vagueness doctrine protects First Amendment speech guarantees by ensuring that citizens have fair notice of what they can and cannot do under the statute.

The other rationale for the vagueness doctrine is also shared with the overbreadth doctrine. The vagueness doctrine also seeks to curb the discretion of law enforcement.

Despite the similarity of the underlying rationales and purposes, it should not be forgotten that the two are distinct from one another. They are designed to deal with different problems that can result in the same unconstitutional outcomes.

The Speech and Conduct Distinction

The First Amendment protects more than just the spoken or written word. It also protects conduct that is meant to communicate a message to an audience. As we have seen, the Court draws a distinction between speech and conduct. That distinction is not always helpful in deciding whether a regulation is constitutional or not since virtually all speech includes some component of conduct or action. For example, students protesting the war in Vietnam burned their draft cards while speaking out against the war. To aid the Court in determining whether a regulation is valid the Court uses a two-part test to determine if the communicative element of the conduct is sufficient to entitle the expression to protection under the First Amendment. The conduct must clearly demonstrate intent to convey a message and the likelihood that the audience will understand the message. This was the test employed by the Court in *Spence v. Washington*.[33]

Spence displayed an American flag upside down in his apartment window. Affixed to the flag with tape was a peace symbol. Based upon this action he was found guilty of violating the state statute proscribing exhibition of the flag with "superimposed figures, symbols or other extraneous material" attached.[34] The flag was a protest against the United States' incursion into Cambodia and the killing of student protestors at Kent State University. Spence claimed, at trial, that his reason for displaying the flag in this manner was to proclaim the flag's association with peace rather than violence.

In a per curiam opinion, the Court reversed his conviction using the standard previously set forth. It was determined that Spence's display of the flag was a communicative act. The Court then addressed the issue of whether the activity "was significantly imbued with elements of communication" to fall within the protection of the First and Fourteenth Amendments.[35] The Court noted that it is important to look at the context within which the symbol is used, as that may provide a meaning to the symbol. Spence's action was, according to the Court, "a prosecution for the expression of an idea through activity."[36] The Court reviewed the various state interests offered in support of sustaining Spence's conviction including breach of the peace and preserving the flag as a symbol of our nation. Although the Court did not directly determine that these interests were insufficient to overturn the conviction, the Court found that the statute, as applied, violated Spence's right of expression. Nevertheless, the Court indicated its view of the relative weight of the interests involved by concluding that, "[g]iven the protected character of [Spence's] expression and in light of the fact that no interest the State may have in preserving the physical integrity of a privately owned flag was significantly impaired on these facts, the conviction must be invalidated."[37]

In *Spence,* it is clear that appellants demonstrated an intent to convey a message. And, in the context of the period in which that conduct occurred, a likelihood existed that the message would be understood. Accordingly, the communicative element was sufficient to entitle appellant to protection under the First Amendment.

TIME, PLACE, AND MANNER ORDINANCES

Simply because U.S. citizens have the right to express themselves freely, does not mean that they can do it wherever, whenever, and however they want. The state may regulate the "**time, place, or manner**" in which they exercise their First Amendment free expression rights.

As discussed earlier, whether or not the expression occurs in a public forum will be a factor in determining the standard the Court will apply in analyzing the regulation. In public forum cases a higher standard must be met, while in nonpublic forums all the state must demonstrate is a rational relationship between the regulation and its object. In this section what constitutes a valid time, place, and manner regulation will be considered.

The Court employs a three-part test to determine if the regulation infringes upon constitutionally protected rights. In order for the regulation to be found valid, all three parts of the test must be met. The initial requirement is that the regulation be content-neutral. Regulations aimed at the communicative impact of the expression will not be found valid. In addition to content neutrality, the regulation must be narrowly drawn in a way that serves a significant government interest. The final requirement for a valid time, place, and manner regulation is that it leaves alternative channels open for the speaker to communicate his or her message. The last two requirements will be applied more stringently when the speech occurs in a public forum (see Exhibit 10.1).

time, place, or manner restriction government restriction of when, where, or how a speech may be made or a group may assemble in public; the restriction does not violate First Amendment rights if it serves a legitimate government purpose, permits reasonable alternate speech or assembly, and does not restrict the subject matter.

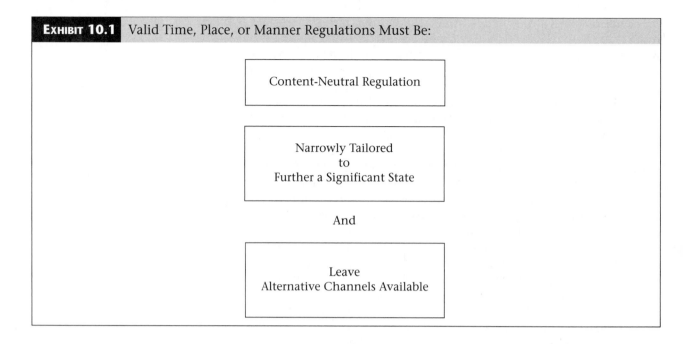

EXHIBIT 10.1   Valid Time, Place, or Manner Regulations Must Be:

Content-Neutral Regulation

Narrowly Tailored
to
Further a Significant State

And

Leave
Alternative Channels Available

As previously noted, the Court will consider whether the regulation is aimed at pure speech or speech plus conduct. Where the latter is the case, a stricter standard will be employed.[38] This distinction, however, is of little value since virtually all speech has some component of conduct. The more helpful analysis would be to consider the harm that is believed to flow from the impact of the expression, such as whether the expression is a peaceful protest march, or involves throwing rocks at the plant of an arms manufacturer to demonstrate against a war. In the first case, the perceived harm resulting from the expression that can justify the regulation is of a different quality from that of the second. Both contain elements of speech and conduct, but an analysis based on harm will be better able to predict outcome than one based on a speech and conduct distinction.

When we look at the test for a valid time, place, and manner regulation, it is important to understand what the Court means when it requires a regulation to be "narrowly tailored" to serve the state's interest. The Court has made it clear that the state is not required to choose the least-restrictive or the least-intrusive means. In *Ward v. Rock Against Racism*,[39] the Court ruled that the requirement is satisfied when the following two conditions are met:

(1) The government interest would be less effectively achieved in the absence of the regulation; and
(2) The means chosen are not substantially broader than necessary to achieve the goal.[40]

At issue in *Ward* was a Use Guideline for the band shell in New York City's Central Park. The band shell was near an area in the park designated for passive recreation. The city had received numerous noise complaints during Rock Against Racism concerts, and on other occasions audiences complained when other concerts were not sufficiently amplified to be heard. To solve these problems the Use Guideline was adopted. The guideline stated that the city would furnish high-quality equipment and retain an independent, experienced sound technician for all performances. Rock Against Racism sued for damages and a declaratory judgment that the guideline was invalid on its face because it violated the First Amendment. The District Court, applying the three-part test for determining the validity of time, place, and manner regulations, found the guideline met constitutional standards. On appeal the Second Circuit reversed, finding that such regulations must employ the means that are least restrictive and least intrusive and that was not the case with the guideline.

The Supreme Court also used the three-part test. It was found that the guideline was content-neutral and that noise control was a significant state interest. As noted, the Court agreed that the guideline was narrowly tailored. Lastly, the Court found that the guideline left open an ample number of alternative channels.[41]

The question of what constitutes leaving open alternative channels of communication must also be considered as seen in *Ward*. It is not always necessary for this question to be considered since it will usually be met if the first two elements are met. On occasion, however, it will make a difference in the outcome of a case. This will occur when the regulation eliminates access to an entire medium or method of expression. In these cases, when that medium or method is inexpensive and easy to use, other channels will not fulfill the alternative channel requirement.

For example, in *City of Ladue v. Gilleo*,[42] the Court found that the city's prohibition of all signs on residential property with the exception of "For Sale" signs and signs of identification violated residents' First Amendment rights. The Court maintained that although the city had a valid interest in limiting visual assault by the clutter of unrestricted signs, the ordinance virtually foreclosed an entire medium. While it was acknowledged that the ordinance was content-neutral, Justice Stevens, writing for a unanimous Court, noted that such a measure could suppress too much speech. Getting to the heart of the question, the Court rejected the city's argument that this was a valid time, place, and manner ordinance because residents could communicate their messages by other means. The city pointed to "letters, handbills, flyers, telephone calls, newspaper advertisements, bumper stickers, speeches and neighborhood community meetings" as alternative channels.[43] The Court was "unpersuaded" by the adequacy of these alternatives.

> Displaying a sign from one's own residence often carries a message quite distinct from placing the same sign someplace else, or conveying the same text or picture by other means. Precisely because of their location, such signs provide information about the identity of the speaker. * * * A sign advocating "Peace in the Gulf" in the front lawn of a retired general or decorated war veteran may provoke a different reaction than the same sign in a 10-year-old child's bedroom window or the same message on a bumper sticker of a passing automobile. An espousal of socialism may carry different implications when displayed on the grounds of a stately mansion than when pasted on a factory wall or an ambulatory sandwich board.[44]

The Court then turned to the inexpensive nature and convenience of signs, noting the particular importance of these factors to "persons of modest means or limited mobility."[45] Justice Stevens also noted that some of the alternative means suggested by the city entailed added costs and time, which could mean "the difference between participating and not participating in public debate."[46] Since the Court was "confident" that less restrictive measures would allow the city to achieve its goal without infringing free expression, the city was enjoined from enforcing the ordinance.[47]

Licensing is another way by which government may seek to regulate speech through time, place, and manner restrictions. The government requires that permission be obtained in advance of events where public expression is involved (e.g., rallies and marches). In protecting First Amendment expression guarantees, the Court looks at a variety of factors when analyzing the regulation. Not surprisingly, the first factor is consideration of whether the permit or licensing requirement is content-neutral. It is only in situations where the nature of the speech is unprotected (see Chapter 11) that the content may be considered. When the First Amendment protects speech, the regulation must be content-neutral. This means that requiring a different fee for the permit or license based on content is impermissible. This is the case even when the increased fee is based on the costs of additional security.[48]

The Court also looks at whether the ordinance sets forth the grounds for denial of the permit. These must be narrow and specific. The reason for this requirement is that the official charged with making the decision about issuance of the permit will have limited discretion. A grant of too much discretion will leave the ordinance open to challenge as overbroad, vague, or both.[49]

Courts tend to disfavor permit regulations. These regulations are viewed as prior restraints on expression—speech is prevented rather than being punished after it has occurred.[50] This flies in the face of the Framers' intent to keep restrictions in the free marketplace of ideas as unrestricted as possible.

Essentially, the Court will uphold permit or licensing ordinances if they are content-neutral, narrowly circumscribe discretion, and are a reasonable means of ensuring public order. *Cox v. New Hampshire,*[51] nicely illustrates this. The Court upheld a municipal ordinance that required a permit for all parades and public meetings. The state statute under which the ordinance was enacted set forth the procedural requirements for granting or denying permit requests. The Court relied heavily on the state court's interpretation of the statute. The state court found that the statutes required content neutrality, that there was no impermissibly wide grant of discretion and that the government interest in having advance notice to ensure public safety was sufficient to justify the permit requirement.[52]

It is also necessary to consider what happens when a permit requirement is ignored and the speaker attacks that requirement after he has spoken and been convicted of violating the regulation. The answer is dependent upon whether the permit requirement is invalid on its face or as it is applied. If the permit requirement is facially unconstitutional due to overbreadth or vagueness, then the speaker is not required to either obtain or apply for the permit. But, if the regulation is unconstitutional as applied, then the result changes.

In such a situation, the speaker is arguing, in essence, that he is constitutionally entitled to a permit. Thus, the speaker is in no position to ignore the application procedure. If he does so, he loses the right to challenge the constitutionality of the scheme, since it has not been applied to him.[53]

A speaker who has been enjoined not to speak may not ignore the injunction. Such speaker is required to go to the courts for judicial relief. This was the case in *Walker v. Birmingham,*[54] where defendants, charged with contempt of court for violating an injunction, could not defend against the contempt charge by arguing that the injunction was based on an unconstitutionally overbroad regulation. The Court maintained that the defendants were required to first obtain judicial review of the regulation before violating the injunction.

Time, place, and manner regulations may also run afoul of the Constitution when the government seeks to protect citizens against the unwanted intrusions of speakers and their right to communicate. We highly value our privacy and do not want to be bombarded with people, messages, and other stimuli that we have not invited into our space. The Constitution, however, provides no right to be let alone. In a variety of contexts the government has argued for just such a right when ordinances have been passed to protect against being forced to listen. The most recent attempt is one against telemarketers that allows citizens to have their names placed on "do not call" lists and provides penalties for violations. While the Court has not yet had the opportunity to address this specific issue, it has generally held that government attempts to protect unwilling listeners are not constitutional. Rather, it is the Court's position that it is up to the unwilling listener to avoid the unwanted expression. This general proposition has emerged from cases raising the rights of the unwilling listener in a variety of contexts.

Efforts by the government to place restrictions on the use of loudspeakers and sound trucks have been carefully considered by the Court. In these cases, the

Court sees the question of discretion granted by the ordinance to the official as analogous to that in permit requirements. Where an ordinance gives unlimited discretion to officials, the ordinances will not pass constitutional muster.

In *Saia v. New York*,[55] the Court held that an ordinance requiring permission from the police chief in order to use amplification systems constituted a prior restraint on speech and one that was without any standards. The Court in *Saia* also noted that less restrictive alternatives were available to accomplish the same purpose. Thus, the ordinance should have been drawn more narrowly—focusing instead on the level of unacceptable noise and the hours and locations where sound devices could be used.[56]

Where discretion is restricted and issues of vagueness and overbreadth are not present, the Court will uphold amplification systems, as was the case in *Kovacs v. Cooper*.[57] There, the Court upheld an ordinance banning sound trucks and instruments attached to vehicles that emitted "loud and raucous noises" on the city's streets. At the outset, the Court found that there was no vagueness issue present. Although it was argued that "loud and raucous" violated the vagueness standard, the Court maintained that, "[w]hile these are abstract words they have through daily use acquired a content that conveys to any interested person a sufficiently accurate concept of what is forbidden."[58] The Court distinguished this case from *Saia*. *Saia* was unconstitutional on its face because it constituted a "prior restraint" on speech. The Court asserted that the ordinance in *Kovacs* was "not of that character."[59] The Court found that there was neither a previous restraint on speech nor an impermissible grant of discretion and, in conformance with settled principles of constitutional law, adopted the New Jersey Supreme Court's construction of the statute.[60] In conclusion, the Court stated:

> There is no restriction upon the communication of ideas or discussion of issues by the human voice, by newspapers, by pamphlets, by dodgers. We think that the need for reasonable protection in the homes or business houses from the distracting noises of vehicles equipped with such sound amplifying devices justifies the ordinance.[61]

It is clear that the Court is demonstrating some sympathy for the unwilling listener, but that sympathy will only be indulged if it does not infringe on the speakers' right of expression protected by the First Amendment.

When we deal with the unwilling listener, we must also consider the captive audience. There are situations in which the unwilling listener cannot simply walk away or close his window. Who has not encountered this situation? The Court is not without sympathy for the captive audience. Thus, it has upheld restrictions on print advertising on city-owned buses,[62] picketing in front of a particular individual's residence,[63] and state-created buffer zones between pickets and abortion/health care facilities.[64]

In *Hill v. Colorado,* an ordinance limiting protestors at an abortion clinic to remain 100 feet from the facility was upheld by a majority of the Court. The decision was based on a right to be left alone. It was also important to the Court that the statute was narrowly tailored so as to reduce infringement on expression.[65] Other relevant factors supporting the Court's decision were the statute's content neutrality, no vagueness or overbreadth problems, and no imposed prior restraint on speech. Thus, once again we see the Court's sympathy will be held in check unless the guarantees of free speech and expression are met.

The question of the right to be let alone also arises in cases involving canvassing and soliciting. The right to be left alone is one factor in balancing the state's interest in regulating expression against the speaker's First Amendment rights. Another consideration in this balancing is the place where the activity occurs. The Court is more concerned about activities occurring in public than those in private homes. Nevertheless some protection has been given to the occupants of private dwellings. For example, in *Rowan v. Post Office Department*,[66] the Court upheld a postal regulation that required a mailer to remove a homeowner's name from its mailing list when the homeowner received sexually provocative or erotic material. The Court has also limited a mailer's right of access by upholding a statute that prohibited putting unstamped materials in home mailboxes, finding that such were not part of the public forum.[67]

The Court has also addressed time, place, and manner ordinances when regulating in-person canvassing and soliciting. In general, the Court has protected those who solicit or canvas by making home visits. The general position has been that it is for the homeowner to indicate a desire to be left alone.[68] This position was reinforced in *Watchtower Bible and Tract Society of New York, Inc. v. Village of Stratton,*[69] when striking down a regulation requiring a permit, the Court noted that "the posting of 'No Solicitation' signs . . . coupled with the resident's unquestioned right to refuse to engage in conversation with unwelcome visitors, provides ample protection for the unwilling listener."[70]

Heightened scrutiny of regulations directed at canvassing and soliciting are required before they can be found constitutional. A regulation will not be found constitutional if it directly and substantially impairs free speech guarantees and is not substantially related to a "strong, subordinating interest of the state."[71] The same constitutional requirements for door-to-door personal solicitation also apply to solicitation in public places. This means that the regulation must be content-neutral, not grant officials too much discretion, serve a significant government interest, and leave alternative channels open. The Court, however, will be less tolerant of regulations of speech in the public forum. The reason for this is that there is a stronger governmental interest in having citizens protected against unwarranted incursions in the public sphere. Thus, the particular nature of the public place will play an important role in determining the outcome for a challenged regulation.

Despite this stronger governmental interest in regulation of expression in public places, there are instances in which the right of expression will be protected, even in private places and even if the regulation is content neutral. This will occur when no alternative channels are appropriate or available for disseminating the message.[72] There is no clear guidance for determining when this will be the case and it seems clear that the Burger-Rehnquist Court has not rushed to find an absence of alternative channels. In *Members of the City Council of the City of Los Angeles v. Taxpayers for Vincent,*[73] the Court upheld a complete ban on posting signs on public property. The Court found that speaking and passing out literature were sufficient alternative channels to keep the regulation from impermissible First Amendment infringement.[74]

In the nonpublic forum the issue of viewpoint neutrality has an impact on the analysis of time, place, and manner regulations. The government may not regulate speech in a way that prefers some messages to others. This is particularly true in cases involving religious viewpoints. For example, the Court found that a New York school policy that allowed public use of school buildings for various activities, but precluded use for religious purposes, constituted viewpoint discrimination, violating First Amendment expression guarantees.[75] The government must also maintain viewpoint neutrality when inviting candidates to a debate or forum.[76] And, activities funded by the government must also reflect viewpoint neutrality.[77]

A distinction is made, however, between viewpoint neutrality and subject neutrality. A speaker may be excluded from a nonpublic forum on the basis of the topic he or she wishes to address, if that topic does not come within the purpose of the forum.[78]

Overall, it is clear that the basic considerations in all First Amendment expression issues appear in the case of time, place, and manner ordinances. Concern with content neutrality, location, overbreadth, and vagueness all have a place in the analysis of ordinances that set limits on where, when, and how expression may be regulated by the government.

SYMBOLIC EXPRESSION

So far, both pure speech and expression, that is, a combination of speech and conduct, have been considered. Sometimes expression may only consist of nonverbal action, and it is to this area of expression the discussion turns.

The Court recognizes that the First Amendment protects certain nonverbal conduct. The cases that involve symbolic expression today follow the same analytical rules as speech cases. Where the conduct is regulated on the basis of content, strict scrutiny will be applied to determine outcome. If the regulation is content neutral, the state need only show a rational relationship between the regulation and its object.

One of the areas in which the Court has addressed symbolic expression arose in the context of protests against the Vietnam War (see Exhibit 10.2). Young men protesting against the war took to publicly burning their draft cards. In *United States v. O'Brien*,[79] one such young man was arrested and convicted of violating an amendment to the draft law.[80] O'Brien argued that the amendment was unconstitutional. He maintained that its purpose was to infringe on First Amendment guarantees and was without a legitimate legislative purpose.

WAR PROTESTORS

There are conflicting dates as to the beginning of the United States' involvement in Vietnam, just as there are conflicting reasons given for why the United States got involved in the civil war between North and South Vietnam. There are those who claim that the involvement started as far back as 1845 with the arrest of a French Missionary by the people of Da Nang.[81] Others point to a later time when the OSS (the predecessor to the CIA) began covert intelligence operations in Vietnam in 1944.[82] Still others claim that the war's genesis was the 1963 military coup that toppled Ngo Dinh Diem's government in Vietnam.[83] No matter which date or incident is used as the starting point for American involvement in Southeast Asia, the American people, as a whole, did not start taking the military action in Vietnam seriously until President Lyndon Johnson began a massive bombing campaign against North Vietnam in 1965. It was also in this year that the Antiwar Movement began in the United States. While many were questioning the reasons for the war and watching the bloody guerilla war on their television sets, it wasn't until the draft was instituted that young people all around the country began organizing and protesting against the war.

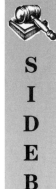

EXHIBIT 10.2   Vietnam Veterans Against the War Button

While many think that these war protestors were "hippies" or "radicals," many celebrities, musicians, academics, politicians, and even veterans themselves were protesting the war.

One of the most significant groups protesting the Vietnam War was the Vietnam Veterans Against the War (VVAW) that formed in 1967 after six Vietnam vets marched together in a peace demonstration.[84] VVAW was instrumental in exposing the truth about the American involvement in Southeast Asia and its members related their firsthand experiences in Vietnam that helped many Americans left at home to understand the nature of that war.[85] In addition to protesting the war, this group is also credited with fighting for amnesty for war resisters, and exposing the negative health effects of the chemical defoliants used in Vietnam. During the presidential campaign of 1972, VVAW brought 1,500 Vietnam vets to protest Richard Nixon's renomination for president.[86]

Another significant event in the history of Vietnam War protests was a day in 1969 known as M-day, which was celebrated on October 15. M-day or Moratorium day was a nationwide protest against the Vietnam War. Various types of ceremonies and protests were held from Brunswick, Maine, to Spokane, Washington,[87] and while the forms of protest were diverse, the participants from different religions, political parties, and socioeconomic levels, the unifying factor was "exhaustion of patience with the war, doubts about the pace of Richard Nixon's efforts to end it."[88] This day was a signal to the government that the American people were unhappy with the war and wanted to see it end.

In May 1970 another significant event in the protest against the Vietnam War occurred. On that day, a group of young people were demonstrating on the campus of Kent State University in Ohio. As the young people protested, National Guardsmen fired into the crowd, killing four students and injuring others. This outraged people across the country, and added to the nationwide feeling that the Vietnam War was no longer a war that the general public could support. It wasn't until January 1973, however, that a pact among the United States and South and North Vietnam was signed. By March of that year, the last of the American troops were removed from Vietnam and all sides exchanged prisoners of war.

Some may argue that the war protestors were not instrumental in bringing the Vietnam War to a close, however, others believe that the Antiwar Movement had a significant impact on the length and outcome of the Vietnam War. Whatever perspective is advanced, the war protestors and their Antiwar Movement had a lasting impact on the United States and particularly on that generation of Americans.

S I D E B A R

The Court dismissed O'Brien's contention that the passage of the amendment was intended to abridge freedom of expression and declared that the purpose of the amendment was irrelevant to the question of constitutionality if there was a legitimate state interest to support its enactment. The Court noted that expression (even protected expression) could be regulated if there was an important government interest at stake even if it involved incidental limits on expression no greater than essential to that interest. Moreover, if the regulation was within the government's constitutional power, and the regulatory interest was unrelated to suppression of free expression it did not violate the Constitution. The Court then went on to consider the interests served by the amendment. The Court found many interests unrelated to communication. Included among these were the state's interest in making sure all males had possession of a document demonstrating availability for induction in case of emergency; the interest in facilitating communication between registrants and local draft boards; and the interest in providing a reminder that registrants must advise local boards of changes in address or status. The Court found these interests to be important and substantial ones that could not be achieved with less impact on expressive rights. In sum, this regulation was narrowly tailored. Accordingly, the amendment was constitutional and O'Brien's conviction was affirmed.

Another symbolic expression case from the Vietnam War era involved a protest by students at an elementary school in Iowa. In *Tinker v. Des Moines Independent Community School District*,[89] the Court found that a regulation prohibiting the wearing of black armbands by students to demonstrate their opposition to the war and suspending those who did not comply was unconstitutional.

After determining that the wearing of black armbands was symbolic expression and entitled to First Amendment protection, the Court, relying on a long line of precedents, found that neither students nor teachers shed their First Amendment rights at the schoolhouse door.[90] The Court stated that fear of controversy did not provide a valid justification for the regulation's infringement on expression. It went on to note the lack of any evidence of "interference . . . with the school's work or collision with the rights of other students to be secure and to be let alone."[91] "In the circumstances, our Constitution does not permit officials of the State to deny their form of expression."[92] As noted, a lower level of scrutiny applies when regulations are content-neutral.

Determining whether a regulation is content-neutral is not always easy. Sometimes, there is disagreement among the members of the Court on this subject. Addressing a very different sort of symbolic expression, the Court faced this situation in *Erie v. Pap's A.M.*[93] At issue was a city regulation banning nude dancing and requiring any dancer to wear pasties and a g-string. The city, which was found to have violated First Amendment rights by the Pennsylvania Supreme Court, claimed in the United States Supreme Court that the object of the regulation was to eliminate the undesirable effects of nude dancing, such as increased crime. The Court found the regulation to be content-neutral, as it addressed only conduct not its expressive content. Once this question was answered, the Court applied the standard set out in *O'Brien* and determined that it was met. The city, pursuant to its police power, could constitutionally enact the regulation to protect citizens' health, safety, and welfare. An important governmental interest was furthered by the regulation. The government interest was unrelated to the suppression of expression, and the restriction was narrowly tailored so that the restriction on expression was no greater than that essential to achieve the governmental interest. Thus, it becomes apparent that once the Court determines the question of content neutrality, the outcome is no longer in doubt; that is, the degree of scrutiny employed will usually indicate how the Court will rule.

One of the most important questions the Court has dealt with in the area of symbolic expression is the desecration of the American flag. The Court's decisions in this area have been ones that appear out of step with the thinking of many of our citizens, in light of yearly attempts by Congress to amend the Constitution to make it unlawful to burn the flag. Such attempts invariably fail to pass the Senate.

The policy in most states and the federal government is to criminalize flag mutilation or desecration. If the statute applies to some flag-related conduct and not others based on the message conveyed, the Court applies a strict scrutiny analysis and will probably strike down the statute. This was the case in *Texas v. Johnson*.[94]

During the 1984 Republican National Convention in Dallas, a political demonstration against the President's policies was staged. At the demonstration, an American flag was doused with kerosene and set on fire. The protesters were charged with burning the flag and were convicted of violating the statute that prohibited flag desecration. Desecration was defined as "defac[ing], damag[ing], or otherwise physically mistreat[ing] in a way that the actor knows will seriously offend one or more persons likely to observe or discover his action."[95]

A sharply divided Court rejected the state's assertion that its interest was unrelated to expression and that the interests asserted by the state were sufficient to justify conviction.

TEXAS V. JOHNSON
491 U.S. 397 (1989)

Justice BRENNAN delivered the opinion of the Court.

II

Johnson was convicted of flag desecration for burning the flag rather than for uttering insulting words. This fact somewhat complicates our consideration of his conviction under the First Amendment. We must first determine whether Johnson's burning of the flag constituted expressive conduct, permitting him to invoke the First Amendment in challenging his conviction. If his conduct was expressive, we next decide whether the State's regulation is related to the suppression of free expression. If the State's regulation is not related to expression, then the less stringent standard we announced in *United States v. O'Brien* for regulations of non-communicative conduct controls. If it is, then we are outside of *O'Brien's* test, and we must ask whether this interest justifies Johnson's conviction under a more demanding standard. A third possibility is that the State's asserted interest is simply not implicated on these facts.

The First Amendment literally forbids the abridgment only of "speech," but we have long recognized that its protection does not end at the spoken or written word. While we have rejected "the view that an apparently limitless variety of conduct can be labeled 'speech' whenever the person engaging in the conduct intends thereby to express an idea," *United States v. O'Brien*, we have acknowledged that conduct may be "sufficiently imbued with elements of communication to fall within the scope of the First and Fourteenth Amendments. . . ."

Especially pertinent to the case are our decisions recognizing the communicative nature of conduct relating to flags. Attaching a peace sign to the flag; refusing to salute the flag; and displaying a red flag, we have held, all may find shelter under the First Amendment. That we have had little difficulty identifying an expressive element in conduct relating to flags should not be surprising. The very purpose of a national flag is to serve as a symbol of our country; it is, one might say, "the one visible manifestation of two hundred years of nationhood."

Pregnant with expressive content, the flag as readily signifies this Nation as does the combination of letters found in "America."

Continued

III

The government generally has a freer hand in restricting expressive conduct than it has in restricting the written or spoken word. It may not, however, proscribe particular conduct *because* it has expressive elements. "[W]hat might be termed the more generalized guarantee of freedom of expression makes the communicative nature of conduct an inadequate basis for singling out that conduct for proscription. A law *directed* at the communicative nature of conduct must, like a law directed at speech itself, be justified by the substantial showing of need that the First Amendment requires . . ." It is, in short, not simply the verbal or nonverbal nature of the expression, but the governmental interest at stake, that helps to determine whether a restriction on that expression is valid.

Thus, although we have recognized that where "'speech' and 'non-speech' elements are combined in the same course of conduct, a sufficiently important governmental interest in regulating the non-speech element can justify incidental limitations on First Amendment freedoms," we have limited the applicability of *O'Brien's* relatively lenient standard to those cases in which "the governmental interest is unrelated to the suppression of free expression." In stating, moreover, that *O'Brien's* test "in the last analysis is little, if any, different from the standard applied to time, place, or manner restrictions," we have highlighted the requirement that the governmental interest in question be unconnected to expression in order to come under *O'Brien's* less demanding rule.

In order to decide whether *O'Brien's* test applies here, therefore, we must decide whether Texas has asserted an interest in support of Johnson's conviction that is unrelated to the suppression of expression. If we find that an interest asserted by the State is simply not implicated on the facts before us, we need not ask whether *O'Brien's* test applies. The State offers two separate interests to justify this conviction: preventing breaches of the peace and preserving the flag as a symbol of nationhood and national unity. We hold that the first interest is not implicated on this record and that the second is related to the suppression of expression.

A

Texas claims that its interest in preventing breaches of the peace justifies Johnson's conviction

for flag desecration. However, no disturbance of the peace actually occurred or threatened to occur because of Johnson's burning of the flag. Although the State stresses the disruptive behavior of the protestors during their march toward City Hall, it admits that "no actual breach of the peace occurred at the time of the flag burning or in response to the flag burning." The State's emphasis on the protestors' disorderly actions prior to arriving at City Hall is not only somewhat surprising given that no charges were brought on the basis of this conduct, but it also fails to show that a disturbance of the peace was a likely reaction to Johnson's conduct. The only evidence offered by the State at trial to show the reaction to Johnson's actions was the testimony of several persons who had been seriously offended by the flag burning.

Thus, we have not permitted the government to assume that every expression of a provocative idea will invite a riot, but have instead required careful consideration of the actual circumstances surrounding such expression, asking whether the expression "is directed to inciting or producing imminent lawless action and is likely to incite or produce such action." To accept Texas' arguments that it need only demonstrate "the potential for a breach of the peace," and that every flag burning necessarily possesses that potential, would be to eviscerate our holding in *Brandenburg*. This we decline to do.

Nor does Johnson's expressive conduct fall within that small class of "fighting words" that are "likely to provoke the average person to retaliation, and thereby cause a breach of the peace."

We thus conclude that the State's interest in maintaining order is not implicated on these facts. The State need not worry that our holding will disable it from preserving the peace. We do not suggest that the First Amendment forbids a State to prevent "imminent lawless action." And, in fact, Texas already has a statute specifically prohibiting breaches of the peace, which tends to confirm that Texas need not punish this flag desecration in order to keep the peace.

B

The State also asserts an interest in preserving the flag as a symbol of nationhood and national unity. In *Spence,* we acknowledged that the government's interest in preserving the flag's special symbolic value "is directly related to expression,

Continued

in the context of activity," such as affixing a peace symbol to the flag. We are equally persuaded that this interest is related to expression in the case of Johnson's burning of the flag. The State, apparently, is concerned that such conduct will lead people to believe either that the flag does not stand for nationhood and national unity, but instead reflects other, less positive concepts, or that the concepts reflected in the flag do not in fact exist, that is, that we do not enjoy unity as a Nation. These concerns blossom only when a person's treatment of the flag communicates some message, and thus are related "to the suppression of free expression" within the meaning of *O'Brien*'s test altogether.

IV

It remains to consider whether the State's interest in preserving the flag as a symbol of nationhood and national unity justifies Johnson's conviction.

As in *Spence,* "[w]e are confronted with a case of prosecution for the expression of an idea through activity," and "[a]ccordingly, we must examine with particular care the interests advanced by [petitioner] to support its prosecution." Johnson was not, we add, prosecuted for the expression of just any idea; he was prosecuted for his expression of dissatisfaction with the policies of this country, expression situated at the core of our First Amendment values.

Moreover, Johnson was prosecuted because he knew that his politically charged expression would cause "serious offense." If he had burned the flag as a means of disposing of it because it was dirty or torn, he would not have been convicted of flag desecration under the Texas law. * * * The Texas law is thus not aimed at protecting the physical integrity of the flag in all circumstances, but is designed instead to protect it only against impairments that would cause serious offense to others.

Whether Johnson's treatment of the flag violated Texas law thus depended on the likely communicative impact of his expressive conduct. Our decision in *Boos v. Barry,* tells us that this restriction on Johnson's expression is content based.

Johnson's political expression was restricted because of the content of the message he conveyed. We must therefore subject the State's asserted interest in preserving the special symbolic character of the flag to "the most exacting scrutiny."

Texas argues that its interest in preserving the flag as a symbol of nationhood and national unity survives this close analysis. * * * The State's argument is not that it has an interest simply in maintaining the flag as a symbol of *something,* no matter what it symbolizes; indeed, if that were the State's position, it would be difficult to see how that interest is endangered by highly symbolic conduct such as Johnson's. Rather, the State's claim is that it has an interest in preserving the flag as a symbol of *nationhood* and *national unity,* a symbol with a determinate range of meanings.

If there is a bedrock principle underlying the First Amendment, it is that the government may not prohibit expression of an idea simply because society finds the idea itself offensive or disagreeable.

We have not recognized an exception to this principle even where our flag has been involved. * * * Nor may the government, we have held, compel conduct that would evince respect for the flag.

In short, nothing in our precedents suggests that a State may foster its own view of the flag by prohibiting expressive conduct. To bring its argument outside our precedents, Texas attempts to convince us that even if its interest in preserving the flag's symbolic role does not allow it to prohibit words or some expressive conduct critical of the flag, it does permit it to forbid the outright destruction of the flag. The State's argument cannot depend here on the distinction between written or spoken words and nonverbal conduct. That distinction, we have shown, is of no moment where the nonverbal conduct is expressive, as it is here, and where the regulation of that conduct is related to expression, as it is here. In addition, both *Barnette* and *Spence* involved expressive conduct, not only verbal communications, and both found that conduct protected.

We never before have held that the Government may ensure that a symbol be used to express only one view of that symbol or its referents.

To conclude that the government may permit designated symbols to be used to communicate only a limited set of messages would be to enter territory having no discernible or defensible boundaries. Could the government, on this

Continued

theory, prohibit the burning of state flags? Of copies of the Presidential seal? Of the Constitution? In evaluating these choices under the First Amendment, how would we decide which symbols were sufficiently special to warrant this unique status? To do so, we would be forced to consult our own political references, and impose them on citizenry, in the very way that the First Amendment forbids us to do.

There is, moreover, no indication—either in the text of the Constitution or in our cases interpreting it—that a separate juridical category exists for the American flag alone. Indeed, we would not be surprised to learn that the persons who framed our Constitution and wrote the Amendment that we now construe were not known for their reverence for the Union Jack. The First Amendment does not guarantee that other concepts virtually sacred to our Nation as a whole—such as the principle that discrimination on the basis of race is odious and destructive—will go unquestioned in the market place of ideas. We decline, therefore, to create for the flag an exception to the joust of principles protected by the First Amendment.

It is not the State's ends, but its means, to which we object. It cannot be gainsaid that there is a special place reserved for the flag in this Nation, and thus we do not doubt that the government has a legitimate interest in making efforts to "preserv[e] the national flag as an unalloyed symbol of our country."

* * *

To say that the government has an interest in encouraging proper treatment of the flag, however, is not to say that it may criminally punish a person for burning a flag as a means of political protest. National unity as an end which officials may foster, by persuasion and example is not in question. The problem is whether under our Constitution compulsion as here employed is a permissible means for its achievement.

We are tempted to say, in fact, that the flag's deservedly cherished place in our community will be strengthened, not weakened, by our holding today. Our decision is a reaffirmation of the principles of freedom and inclusiveness that the flag best reflects, and of the conviction that our toleration of criticism such as Johnson's is a sign and source of our strength. Indeed, one of the proudest images of our flag, the one immortalized in our own national anthem, is of the bom-

bardment it survived at Fort McHenry. It is the Nation's resilience, not its rigidity, that Texas sees reflected in the flag—and it is that resilience that we reassert today.

The way to preserve the flag's special role is not to punish those who feel differently about these matters. It is to persuade them that they are wrong. "To courageous, self-reliant men, with confidence in the power of free and fearless reasoning applied through the processes of popular government, no danger flowing from speech can be deemed clear and present, unless the incidence of the evil apprehended is so imminent that it may befall before there is opportunity for full discussion. If there be time to expose through discussion the falsehood and fallacies, to avert the evil by the processes of education, the remedy to be applied is more speech, not enforced silence." And, precisely because it is our flag that is involved, one's response to the flag burner may exploit the uniquely persuasive power of the flag itself. We can imagine no more appropriate response to burning a flag than waving one's own, no better way to counter a flag burner's message than by saluting the flag that burns, no surer means of preserving the dignity even of the flag that burned than by—as one witness here did—according its remains a respectful burial. We do not consecrate the flag by punishing its desecration, for in doing so we dilute the freedom that this cherished emblem represents.

Affirmed.

Justice KENNEDY, concurring.

The case before us illustrates better than most that the judicial power is often difficult in its exercise. We cannot here ask another Branch to share responsibility, as when the argument is made that a statue is flawed or incomplete. For we are presented with a clear and simple statute to be judged against a pure command of the Constitution. The outcome can be laid at no door but ours.

The hard fact is that sometimes we must make decisions we do not like. We make them because they are right, right in the sense that the law and the Constitution, as we see them, compel the result. And so great is our commitment to the process that, except in the rare case, we do not pause to express distaste for the result, perhaps for fear of undermining a valued principle that dictates the decision. This is one of those rare cases.

Continued

I do not believe the Constitution gives us the right to rule as the dissenting Members of the Court urge, however, painful this judgment is to announce. Though symbols often are what we ourselves make of them, the flag is constant in expressing beliefs Americans share, beliefs in law and peace and that freedom which sustains the human spirit. The case here today forces recognition of the costs to which these beliefs commit us. It is poignant but fundamental that the flag protects those who hold it in contempt.

Chief Justice REHNQUIST, with whom Justices WHITE and O'CONNOR join, dissenting.

In holding this Texas statute unconstitutional, the Court ignores Justice Holmes' familiar aphorism that "a page of history is worth a volume of logic." For more than 200 years, the American flag has occupied a unique position as the symbol of our Nation, a uniqueness that justifies a governmental prohibition against flag burning in the way respondent Johnson did here.

The flag symbolizes the Nation in peace as well as in war. It signifies our national presence on battleships, airplanes, military installations, and public buildings from the United States Capitol to the thousands of county courthouses and city halls throughout the country. Two flags are prominently placed in our courtroom. Countless flags are placed by the graves of loved ones each year on what was first called Decoration Day, and is now called Memorial Day. The flag is traditionally placed on the casket of deceased members of the Armed Forces, and it is later given to the deceased's family. Congress has provided that the flag be flown at half-staff upon the death of the President, Vice President, and other government officials "as a mark of respect to their memory." The flag identifies United States merchant ships and "[t]he laws of the Union protect our commerce wherever the flag of the country may float."

No other symbol has been as universally honored as the flag.

The American flag, then, throughout more than 200 years of our history, has come to be the visible symbol embodying our Nation. It does not represent the views of any particular political party, and it does not represent any particular political philosophy. The flag is not simply another "idea" or "point of view" competing for recognition in the marketplace of ideas. Millions and millions of Americans regard it with an almost mystical reverence regardless of what sort of social, political, or philosophical beliefs they may have. I cannot agree that the First Amendment invalidates the Act of Congress, and the laws of 48 or 50 States, which make criminal the public burning of the flag.

Here it may . . . well be said that the public burning of the American flag by Johnson was no essential part of any exposition of ideas, and at the same time it had a tendency to incite a breach of the peace. Johnson was free to make any verbal denunciation of the flag that he wished; indeed, he was free to burn the flag in private. He could publicly burn other symbols of the Government or effigies of political leaders. He did lead a march through the streets of Dallas, and conducted a rally in front of the Dallas City Hall. He engaged in a "die-in" to protest nuclear weapons. He shouted out various slogans during the march. . . . For none of these acts was he arrested or prosecuted; it was only when he proceeded to burn publicly an American flag stolen from its rightful owner that he violated the Texas statute.

Our Constitution wisely places limits on powers of legislative majorities to act, but the declaration of such limits by the Court "is, at all times, a question of much delicacy, which ought seldom, if ever, to be decided in the affirmative, in a doubtful case." Uncritical extension of constitutional protection to the burning of the flag risks the frustration of the very purpose for which organized governments are instituted. The Court decides that the American flag is just another symbol, about which not only must opinions pro and con be tolerated, but for which the most minimal public respect may not be enjoined. The government may conscript men into the Armed Forces where they must fight and perhaps die for the flag, but the government may not prohibit the public burning of the banner under which they fight. I would uphold the Texas statute as applied in this case.

Justice STEVENS, dissenting.

As the Court analyzes this case, it presents the question whether the State of Texas, or indeed the Federal Government, has the power to prohibit the public desecration of the American flag. The question is unique. In my judgment rules that apply to a host of other symbols, such as state flags, armbands, or various privately promoted emblems or political or

Continued

commercial identity, are not necessarily controlling. Even if flag burning could be considered just another species of symbolic speech under the logical application of the rules that the Court has developed in its interpretation of the First Amendment in other contexts, this case has an intangible dimension that makes those rules inapplicable.

A country's flag is a symbol of more than "nationhood and national unity." It also signifies the ideas that characterize the society that has chosen that emblem as well as the special history that has animated the growth and power of those ideas.

[T]he American flag . . . is more than a proud symbol of the courage, the determination, and the gifts of nature that transformed 13 fledgling Colonies into a world power. It is a symbol of freedom, of equal opportunity, of religious tolerance, and of good will for other peoples who share our aspirations. The symbol carries its message to dissidents both at home and abroad who may have no interest at all in our national unity or survival.

The value of the flag as a symbol cannot be measured. Even so, I have no doubt that the interest in preserving that value for the future is both significant and legitimate.

The Court is . . . quite wrong in blandly asserting that respondent "was prosecuted for his expression of dissatisfaction with the policies of this country, expression situated at the core of our First Amendment values." Respondent was prosecuted because of the method he chose to express his dissatisfaction with those policies. Had he chosen to spray-paint—or perhaps convey with a motion picture projector—his message of dissatisfaction on the façade of the Lincoln Memorial, there would be no question about the power of the Government to prohibit his means of expression. The prohibition would be supported by the legitimate interest in preserving the quality of an important national asset. Though the asset at stake in this case is intangible given its unique value, the same interest supports a prohibition on the desecration of the American flag.

The ideas of liberty and equality have been an irresistible force in motivating leaders like Patrick Henry, Susan B. Anthony, and Abraham Lincoln, schoolteachers like Nathan Hale and Booker T. Washington, the Philippine Scouts who fought at Bataan, and the soldiers who scaled the bluff at Omaha Beach. If those ideas are worth fighting for—and our history demonstrates that they are—it cannot be true that the flag that uniquely symbolizes their power is not itself worthy of protection from unnecessary desecration.

Justice Kennedy was, indeed, correct when he noted that the decision would not be one easily accepted. Following immediately upon the Court's decision in *Johnson*, Congress passed the Flag Protection Act of 1989,[96] in an attempt to ban flag burning while not running afoul of the roadblocks to a finding of constitutionality that derailed the Texas statute. Thus, the federal statute applied to those who "knowingly mutilate[ ], deface[ ], physically defile[ ], burn, maintain[ ] on the floor or ground, or trample[ ] upon any flag of the United States. . . ." It made no reference to the "offend" language of the Texas statute that troubled the Court in *Johnson*. Despite this, the Court found the statute unconstitutional with the same split on the decision when it was challenged in *United States v. Eichman*.[97]

This statute was also found to be content-based. While the Court determined that there was no specific content-based limitation in the statute, the state's interest was related to suppressing expression.[98] That interest was to preserve the flag as a symbol of certain principles and this was related to content. Consequently, the statute could not pass strict scrutiny.

In its most recent pronouncement on symbolic speech and the extent of the limits that may be placed on it, the Court addressed a Virginia statute that made it a felony "for any person . . . with the intent of intimidating any person or group . . . to burn . . . a cross on the property of another, a highway or other public place . . ."[99] The statute made it explicit that any such burning constituted "**prima facie** evidence" of such an intent.

In *Virginia v. Black,*[100] the Supreme Court of Virginia consolidated the appeals of three individuals convicted of violating the cross-burning statute. The Court reversed the convictions finding the statute violative of the First

prima facie (Latin) describes something that will be considered to be true unless disproved by contrary evidence, for example, a *prima facie case* is a case that will win unless the other side comes forward with evidence to disprove it.

Amendment on its face. The Court reasoned that the statute was content-based since it only banned cross burning and was overbroad as a result of the prima facie evidence provision. The United States Supreme Court affirmed in part, vacated in part, and remanded.

VIRGINIA V. BLACK
538 U.S. 343 (2003)

Justice O'CONNOR announced the judgment of the Court and delivered the opinion of the Court with respect to Parts I, II, and III, and an opinion with respect to Parts IV and V, in which Chief Justice REHNQUIST and Justices STEVENS and BREYER join.

II

Cross burning originated in the 14th century as a means for Scottish tribes to signal each other. Sir Walter Scott used cross burnings for dramatic effect in *The Lady of the Lake*, where the burning cross signified both a summons and a call to arms. Cross burning in this country, however, long ago became unmoored from its Scottish ancestry. Burning a cross in the United States is inextricably intertwined with the history of the Ku Klux Klan.

From the inception of the second Klan, cross burnings have been used to communicate both threats of violence and messages of shared ideology.

Often, the Klan used cross burnings as a tool of intimidation and a threat of impending violence. For example, in 1939 and 1940, the Klan burned crosses in front of synagogues and churches. After one cross burning at a synagogue, a Klan member noted that if the cross burning did not "shut the Jews up, we'll cut a few throats and see what happens." In Miami in 1941, the Klan burned four crosses in front of a proposed housing project, declaring, "We are here to keep niggers out of your town . . . . When the law fails you, call on us." And in Alabama in 1942, in "a whirlwind climax to weeks of flogging and terror," the Klan burned crosses in front of a union hall and in front of a union leader's home on the eve of a labor election. These cross burnings embodied threats to people whom the Klan deemed antithetical to its goals. And these threats had special force given the long history of Klan violence.

The Klan continued to use cross burnings to intimidate after World War II.

The decision of this Court in *Brown v. Board of Education,* . . . along with the civil rights movement of the 1950's and 1960's, sparked another outbreak of Klan violence. These acts of violence included bombings, beatings, shootings, stabbings, and mutilations. Members of the Klan burned crosses on the lawns of those associated with the civil rights movement, assaulted the Freedom Riders, bombed churches, and murdered blacks as well as whites whom the Klan viewed as sympathetic toward the civil rights movement.

Throughout the history of the Klan, cross burnings have also remained potent symbols of shared group identity and ideology. The burning cross became a symbol of the Klan itself and a central feature of Klan gatherings. According to the Klan constitution . . . the "fiery cross" was the "emblem of that sincere, unselfish devotedness of all Klansmen to the sacred purpose and principles we have espoused."

To this day, regardless of whether the message is a political one or whether the message is also meant to intimidate, the burning of a cross is a "symbol of hate." And while cross burning sometimes carries a not intimidating message, at other times the intimidating message is the only message conveyed. For example, when a cross burning is directed at a particular person not affiliated with the Klan, the burning cross often serves as a message of intimidation, designed to inspire in the victim a fear of bodily harm. Moreover, the history of violence associated with the Klan shows that the possibility of injury or death is not just hypothetical. The person who burns a cross directed at a particular person often is making a serious threat, meant to coerce the victim to comply with the Klan's wishes unless the victim is willing to risk the wrath of the Klan. Indeed, as the cases of respondents . . . indicate, individuals without

Continued

Klan affiliation who wish to threaten or menace another person sometimes use cross burning because of this association between a burning cross and violence.

In sum, while a burning a cross does not inevitably convey a message of intimidation, often the cross burner intends that the recipients of the message fear for their lives. And when a cross burning is used to intimidate, few if any messages are more powerful.

III

A

The First Amendment applicable to the States through the Fourteenth Amendment, provides that "Congress shall make no law . . . abridging the freedom of speech." The hallmark of the protection of free speech is to allow "free trade in ideas"—even ideas that the overwhelming majority of people might find distasteful or discomforting. Thus, the First Amendment "ordinarily" denies a State "the power to prohibit dissemination of social, economic and political doctrine which a vast majority of its citizens believes to be false and fraught with evil consequence." The First Amendment affords protection to symbolic or expressive conduct as well as to actual speech.

The protections afforded by the First Amendment, however, are not absolute, and we have long recognized that the government may regulate certain categories of expression consistent with the Constitution. The First Amendment permits "restrictions upon the content of speech in a few limited areas, which are of such slight social value as a step to truth that any benefit that may be derived from them is clearly outweighed by the social interest in order and morality."

Thus, for example, a State may punish those words "which by their very utterance inflict injury or tend to incite an immediate breach of the peace." We have consequently held that fighting words—"those personally abusive epithets which when addressed to the ordinary citizen, are, as a matter of common knowledge, inherently likely to provoke violent reaction"—are generally proscribable under the First Amendment. Furthermore, "the constitutional guarantees of free speech and free press do not permit a State to forbid or proscribe advocacy of the use of force or of law violation except where such advocacy is directed to inciting or producing imminent lawless action and is likely to incite or produce such action." And the First Amendment also permits a State to ban a "true threat."

"True threats" encompass those statements where the speaker means to communicate a serious expression of an intent to commit an act of unlawful violence to a particular individual or a group of individuals. The speaker need not actually intend to carry out the threat. Rather, a prohibition on true threats "protects individuals from the fear of violence" and "from the disruption that fear engenders," in addition to protecting people "from the possibility that the threatened violence will occur." Intimidation in the constitutionally proscribable sense of the word is a type of true threat, where a speaker directs a threat to a person or group of persons with the intent of placing the victim in fear of bodily harm or death. Respondents do not contest that some cross burnings fit within the meaning of intimidating speech, and rightly so. As noted in Part II, . . . the history of cross burning in this country shows that cross burning is often intimidating, intended to create a pervasive fear in victims that they are a target of violence.

B

The Supreme Court of Virginia ruled that in light of *R.A.V. v. City of St. Paul,* even if it is constitutional to ban cross burning in a content-neutral manner, the Virginia cross-burning statute is unconstitutional because it discriminates on the basis of content and viewpoint. It is true, as the Supreme Court of Virginia held, that the burning of a cross is symbolic expression.

The fact that cross burning is symbolic expression, however, does not resolve the constitutional question. The Supreme Court of Virginia relied upon *R.A.V. v. City of St. Paul,* to conclude that once a statute discriminates on the basis of this type of content, the law is unconstitutional. We disagree.

We did not hold in *R.A.V.* that the First Amendment prohibits *all* forms of content-based discrimination within a proscribable area of speech. Rather, we specifically stated that some types of content discrimination did not violate the First Amendment.

Consequently, while the holding of *R.A.V.* does not permit a State to ban only obscenity based

Continued

on "offensive *political* messages," or "only those threats against the President that mention his policy on aid to inner cities," the First Amendment permits content discrimination "based on the very reasons why the particular class of speech at issue . . . is proscribable."

Similarly, Virginia's statute does not run afoul of the First Amendment insofar as it bans cross burning with intent to intimidate. Unlike the statute at issue in *R.A.V.* the Virginia statute does not single out for opprobrium only that speech directed toward "one of the specified disfavored topics." It does not matter whether an individual burns a cross with intent to intimidate because of the victim's race, gender, or religion, or because of the victim's "political affiliation, union membership, or homosexuality." Moreover, as a factual matter, it is not true that cross burners direct their intimidating conduct solely to racial or religious minorities.

The First Amendment permits Virginia to outlaw cross burnings done with the intent to intimidate because burning a cross is a particularly virulent form of intimidation. Instead of prohibiting all intimidating messages, Virginia may choose to regulate this subset of intimidating messages in light of cross burnings' long and pernicious history as a signal of impending violence. Thus, just as a State may regulate only that obscenity which is the most obscene due to its prurient content, so too may a State choose to prohibit only those forms of intimidation that are most likely to inspire fear of bodily harm. A ban on cross burning carried out with the intent to intimidate is fully consistent with our holding in *R.A.V.* and is proscribable under the First Amendment.

IV

The Supreme Court of Virginia ruled in the alternative that Virginia's cross-burning statute was unconstitutionally overbroad due to its provision stating that "any such burning of a cross shall be prima facie evidence of an intent to intimidate a person or group of persons." The Commonwealth added the prima facie provision to the statute in 1968. The court below did not reach whether this provision is severable from the rest of the cross-burning statute under Virginia law. In this Court, as in the Supreme Court of Virginia, respondents do not argue that the prima facie evidence provision is unconstitutional as applied to any one of them. Rather,

they contend that the provision is unconstitutional on its face.

The prima facie evidence provision, as interpreted by the jury instruction, renders the statute unconstitutional. Because this jury instruction is the Model Jury Instruction, and because the Supreme Court of Virginia had the opportunity to expressly disavow the jury instruction, the jury instruction's construction of the prima facie provision "is a ruling on a question of state law that is as binding on us as though the precise words had been written into" the statute. As construed by the jury instruction, the prima facie provision strips away the very reason why a State may ban cross burning with the intent to intimidate. The prima facie evidence provision permits a jury to convict in every cross-burning case in which defendants exercise their constitutional right not to put on a defense. And even where a defendant like Black presents a defense, the prima facie evidence provision makes it more likely that the jury will find an intent to intimidate regardless of the particular facts of the case. The provision permits the Commonwealth to arrest, prosecute, and convict a person based solely on the fact of cross burning itself.

It is apparent that the provision as so interpreted "would create an unacceptable risk of the suppression of ideas." The act of burning a cross may mean that a person is engaging in constitutionally proscribable intimidation. But that same act may mean only that the person is engaged in core political speech. The prima facie evidence provision in this statute blurs the line between these two meanings of a burning cross. As interpreted by the jury instruction, the provision chills constitutionally protected political speech because of the possibility that a State will prosecute—and potentially convict—somebody engaging only in lawful political speech at the core of what the First Amendment is designed to protect.

The prima facie provision makes no effort to distinguish among these different types of cross burnings. It does not distinguish between a cross burning done with the purpose of creating anger or resentment and a cross burning done with the purpose of threatening or intimidating a victim. It does not distinguish between a cross burning at a public rally or a cross burning on the neighbor's lawn. It does not treat the cross burning directed at an individual differently

Continued

from the cross burning directed at a group of like-minded believers. It allows a jury to treat a cross burning on the property of another with the owner's acquiescence in the same manner as a cross burning on the property of another without the owner's permission. To this extent I agree with Justice Souter that the prima facie evidence provision can "skew jury deliberations toward conviction in cases where the evidence of intent to intimidate is relatively weak and arguably consistent with a solely ideological reason for burning."

It may be true that a cross burning, even at a political rally, arouses a sense of anger or hatred among the vast majority of citizens who see a burning cross. But this sense of anger or hatred is not sufficient to ban all cross burnings. As Gerald Gunther has stated, "The reason I have drawn from my childhood in Nazi Germany and my happier adult life in this country is the need to walk the sometimes difficult path denouncing the bigot's hateful ideas by force of law." The prima facie evidence provision in this case ignores all of the contextual factors that are necessary to decide whether a particular cross burning is intended to intimidate. The First Amendment does not permit such a shortcut.

Justice STEVENS, concurring.

Cross burning with "an intent to intimidate," unquestionably qualifies as the kind of threat that is unprotected by the First Amendment. For the reasons stated in the separate opinions that Justice White and I wrote in *R.A.V. v. St. Paul,* that simple proposition provides a sufficient basis for upholding the basic prohibition in the Virginia statute even though it does not confer other types of threatening expressive conduct. With this observation, I join in Justice O'Connor's opinion.

Justice THOMAS, dissenting.

In every culture, certain things acquire meaning well beyond what outsiders can comprehend. That goes for both the sacred and the profane. I believe that cross burning is the paradigmatic example of the latter.

I

Although I agree with the majority's conclusion that it is constitutionally permissible to "ban . . . cross burning carried out with intent to intimidate," I believe that the majority errs in imputing an expressive component to the activity in question. In my view, whatever expressive value cross burning has, the legislature simply wrote it out by banning only intimidating conduct undertaken by a particular means. A conclusion that the statute prohibiting cross burning with intent to intimidate sweeps beyond a prohibition on certain conduct into the zone of expression overlooks not only the words of the statute but also reality.

A

To me, the majority's brief history of the Ku Klux Klan only reinforces this common understanding of the Klan as a terrorist organization, which, in its endeavor to intimidate, or even eliminate those it dislikes, uses the most brutal of methods.

Such methods typically include cross burning— "a tool for the intimidation and harassment of racial minorities, Catholics, Jews, Communists, and any other groups hated by the Klan." For those not easily frightened, cross burning has been followed by more extreme measures, such as beatings and murder. As the Solicitor General points out, the association between acts of intimidating cross burning and violence is well documented in recent American history. Indeed, the connection between cross burning and violence is well ingrained, and lower courts have so recognized.

But the perception that a burning cross is a threat and a precursor of worse things to come is not limited to blacks. Because the modern Klan expanded the list of its enemies beyond blacks and "radicals," to include Catholics, Jews, most immigrants, and labor unions, a burning cross is now widely viewed as a signal of impending terror and lawlessness.

In our culture, cross burning has almost invariably meant lawlessness and understandably instills in its victims well-grounded fear of physical violence.

B

The ban on cross burning with intent to intimidate demonstrates that even segregationists understood the difference between intimidating and terroristic conduct and racist expression. It is simply beyond belief that, in passing the statute now under review, the Virginia legislature was concerned with anything but penalizing conduct it must have viewed as particularly vicious.

Continued

Accordingly, the statute prohibits only conduct, not expression. And, just as one cannot burn down someone's house to make a political point and then seek refuge in the First Amendment, those who hate cannot terrorize and intimidate to make their point. In light of my conclusion that the statute here addresses only conduct, there is no need to analyze it under any of our First Amendment tests.

II

B

The plurality, . . . is troubled by the presumption because this is a First Amendment case. The plurality laments the fate of an innocent cross-burner who burns a cross, but does so without an intent to intimidate. The plurality fears the chill on expression because, according to the plurality, the inference permits "the Commonwealth to arrest, prosecute and convict a person based solely on the fact of cross burning itself." First, it is, at the very least, unclear that the inference comes into play during arrest and initiation of a prosecution, that is, prior to the instructions stage of an actual trial. Second, as I explained above, the inference is rebuttable and, as the jury instructions given in this case demonstrate, Virginia law still requires the jury to find the existence of each element, including intent to intimidate, beyond a reasonable doubt.

Moreover, even in the First Amendment context, the Court has upheld such regulations where conduct that initially appears culpable, ultimately results in dismissed charges. A regulation of pornography is one such example. While possession of child pornography is illegal, possession of adult pornography, as long as it is not obscene, is allowed. As a result, those pornographers trafficking in images of adults who look like minors, may be not only deterred, but also arrested and prosecuted for possessing what a jury might find to be legal materials. This "chilling" effect has not, however, been a cause for grave concern with respect to overbreadth of such statutes among the members of the Court.

That the First Amendment gives way to other interests is not a remarkable proposition. What is remarkable is that, under the plurality's analysis, the determination of whether an interest is sufficiently compelling depends not on the harm a regulation in question seeks to prevent, but on the area of society at which it aims. For instance, in *Hill v. Colorado,* the Court upheld a restriction on protests near abortion clinics, explaining that the State had a legitimate interest, which was sufficiently narrowly tailored, in protecting those seeking services of such establishments "from unwanted advice" and "unwanted communication. . . ." In so concluding, the Court placed heavy reliance on the "vulnerable physical and emotional conditions" of patients. Thus, when it came to the rights of those seeking abortions, the Court deemed restrictions on "unwanted advice," which notably, can be given only from a distance of at least 8 feet from a prospective patient, justified by the countervailing interest in obtaining abortion. Yet, here, the plurality strikes down the statute because one day an individual might wish to burn a cross, but might do so without an intent to intimidate anyone. That cross burning subjects its targets, and sometimes, an unintended audience, to extreme emotional distress, and is virtually never viewed merely as "unwanted communication," but rather, as a physical threat, is of no concern to the plurality. Henceforth, under the plurality's view, physical safety will be valued less than the right to be free from unwanted communications.

III

Because I would uphold the validity of this statute, I respectfully dissent.

Justice SOUTER, with whom Justices KENNEDY and GINSBURG join, concurring in the judgment in part and dissenting in part.

I agree with the majority that the Virginia statute makes a content-based distinction within the category of punishable intimidating or threatening expression, the very type of distinction we considered in *R.A.V. v. St. Paul.* I disagree that any exception should save Virginia's law from unconstitutionality under the holding in *R.A.V.* or any acceptable variation of it.

I

The issue is whether the statutory prohibition restricted to this symbol falls within one of the exceptions to *R.A.V.'s* general condemnation of limited content-based proscription within a broader category of expression proscribed generally. Because of the burning cross's extraordinary force as a method of intimidation, the *R.A.V.* exception most likely to cover the statute is the first of the three mentioned there, which the *R.A.V.* opinion called an exception for

Continued

content discrimination on a basis that "consists entirely of the very reason the entire class of speech at issue is proscribable." This is the exception the majority speaks of here as covering statutes prohibiting "particularly virulent" proscribable expression.

I do not think that the Virginia statute qualifies for this virulence exception as *R.A.V.* explained it. The statute fits poorly with the illustrative examples given in *R.A.V.*, none of which involves communication generally associated with a particular message, and in fact, the majority's discussion of a special virulence exception here moves that exception toward a more flexible conception than the version in *R.A.V.* I will reserve judgment on that doctrinal development, for even on a pragmatic conception of *R.A.V.* and its exceptions the Virginia statute could not pass muster, the most obvious hurdle being the statute's prima facie evidence provision. That provision is essential to understanding why the statute's tendency to suppress a message disqualifies it from any rescue by exception from *R.A.V.*'s general rule.

II

R.A.V. defines the special virulence exception to the rule barring content-based subclasses of categorically proscribable expression this way: prohibition by subcategory is nonetheless constitutional if it is made "entirely" on the "basis" of "the very reason" that "the entire class of speech at issue is proscribable" at all. The Court explained that when the subcategory is confined to the most obviously proscribable instances, "no significant danger of idea or viewpoint discrimination exists," and the explanation was rounded out with some illustrative example. None of them, however, resembles the case before us.

I thus read *R.A.V.*'s examples of the particular virulence exception as covering prohibitions that are not clearly associated with a particular viewpoint, and that are consequently different from the Virginia statute. On that understanding of things, I necessarily read the majority opinion as treating *R.A.V.*'s virulence exception in a more flexible, pragmatic manner than the original illustrations would suggest. Actually, another way of looking at today's decision would see it as a slight modification of *R.A.V.*'s third exception, which allows content-based discrimination within a proscribable category when its "nature" is such "that there is no realistic possibility that official suppression of ideas is afoot." The majority's approach could be taken as recognizing an exception to *R.A.V.* when circumstances show that the statute's ostensibly valid reason for punishing particularly serious proscribable expression probably is not a ruse for message suppression, even though the statute may have a greater (but not exclusive) impact on adherents of one ideology than on others.

III

[N]o content-based statute should survive even under a pragmatic recasting of *R.A.V.* without a high probability that no "official suppression of ideas is afoot."

IV

I conclude that the statute under which all three of the respondents were prosecuted violates the First Amendment, since the statute's content-based distinction was invalid at the time of the charged activities, regardless of whether the prima facie evidence provision was given any effect in any respondent's individual case.

The rules used to analyze cases of symbolic speech are the same as those the Court employs in pure speech and speech plus conduct cases. The only difference in symbolic speech is that no pure speech is involved; the messages sought to be expressed are done through conduct alone.

SPECIAL CONTEXTS

There are some areas in which First Amendment rights conflict with important public policy interests that have allowed a body of constitutional law to develop around them. These include not just the particular interest involved, but also sometimes a particular arena. When thinking of the former instances, the concern focuses on the interest in a fair political process. The school comes to mind when thinking of a particular arena. Discussion of these topics follows.

Schools

The conflict between First Amendment rights and public policy arises in the school arena as a result of the primary purpose of the public schools. This purpose is to socialize students in the norms and values of our society as well as to transmit the knowledge that will allow students, as citizens, to be productive. As such, schools necessarily teach students how to think as well as what to think about some things. Because of this, the things that are taught can run headlong into students' First Amendment rights, which are not abandoned altogether at the schoolhouse door. The Court must, therefore, balance the rights of students against the importance of the state's interest in socializing our children in the public schools when faced with these conflicts.

The Court demonstrates a general reluctance to intervene in school authorities' decision in dealing with such issues. There are, however, cases involving basic constitutional values that are directly implicated when the Court will not only intervene, but also find that the authorities have crossed the line and violated constitutional rights. For example, in *West Virginia Board of Education v. Barnette*,[101] the Court held that students could not be required to salute the flag, and in *Meyer v. Nebraska*,[102] schools were not permitted to forbid the teaching of foreign languages. And, as noted earlier in this chapter, school authorities could not ban a student protest that entailed the wearing of black armbands as a statement against the Vietnam War.[103] Generally, however, the Court will uphold authorities' actions designed to ensure discipline, protect the rights of other students and preserve the educational function of the school.

In the school arena another First Amendment issue that arises is the extent of school authorities' power to control curriculum and teaching materials. Of particular interest in this area is the right of authorities to remove books from school libraries. The Court addressed this issue in *Board of Education, Island Trees Union Free School District Number 26 v. Pico*.[104]

In *Pico* members of the Board of Education attended a conference held by a politically conservative organization of parents concerned with education issues. The board members obtained lists of books at the conference of "objectionable books." Thereafter the members found that a number of the books on the lists were in the high school library and that one was in the junior high school library. Among the books were *Slaughter House Five* by Kurt Vonnegut, Jr.; *The Naked Ape* by Desmond Morris; *Black Boy* by Richard Wright; and *Soul on Ice* by Eldridge Cleaver. At a meeting among the Board, the school superintendent, and the principals of the two schools, the Board indicated unofficially that the books should be removed from the libraries and provided to the Board for review. When the community learned of the action, the Board issued a press release to justify its action. The books that were removed were characterized as "anti-American, anti-Christian, anti-[Semitic], and just plain filthy."[105] The Board justified its action by asserting that "[it] is our duty, our moral obligation, to protect the children in our schools from this moral danger as surely as from physical and medical dangers."[106]

Not long after, the Board appointed a committee of parents and school staff to review the books and make a recommendation whether the books should be retained. The committee agreed that five books should be retained and two should be removed. The members of the committee were unable to agree on four of the books. The Board substantially rejected the recommendation of the committee and found that nine of the books should permanently be removed from the libraries. Only one book was to be returned to the library on an unrestricted basis and another would be available if parental approval was obtained.

High school and junior high students challenged the Board's determination in a suit, claiming that the books were removed " 'because particular passages in the books offended their social, political and moral tastes and not because the books, taken as a whole, were lacking in educational value.'"[107] The Board's actions, they asserted, infringed their First Amendment rights. The students sought injunctive relief to have the books permanently returned to the libraries and prevent the Board "from interfering with the use of those books in the school's curricula."[108]

The Board brought a motion for summary judgment, which the District Court granted. The appellate court reversed and the Supreme Court granted certiorari, noting that the question before the Court was a narrow one; one solely about library books, not one that intruded into the classroom or the courses taught.[109] The Court framed the substantive question as whether "the First Amendment imposes any limitations upon the discretion of [the Board] to remove library books from [the high school and junior high school]."

Seven separate opinions emerged from the nine justices. No majority opinion could be reached, although five agreed that summary judgment was inappropriate since a material issue of fact existed. It is the opinions regarding the substantive question, however, that speak to the conflict between school authorities' power and students' First Amendment rights.

Justice Brennan, writing for four members of the Court noted the Board had broad discretion to determine school management issues but that discretion was limited when the First Amendment rights of students were implicated, particularly when the school library was the focus.[110] Justice Brennan stated that there was a distinction between the Board's discretion regarding issues of curriculum, where it was absolute, and the school library. In fact, Justice Brennan recognized a duty to inculcate community values in school but found that duty was misplaced when it extended beyond the classroom environment into the realm of the library.[111] He acknowledged that the Board did have some discretion in determining the content of the school library and that discretion could not be exercised in a manner that was narrowly partisan or political. Students have the right to receive information and ideas and they need such for meaningful exercise of their rights as citizens. Other valid grounds existed for removal of books from school libraries, for example, educational suitability, but the grounds asserted here violated constitutional rights.[112]

Justice Rehnquist's dissent clearly stated that in the context of education, the government's actions were to be considered in a different light, such as First Amendment concerns from its role as a sovereign. Justice Rehnquist also stated that there were no precedents to support the plurality's determination that high school and junior high school students have a right to receive information. Finally, he contended that the plurality was incorrect to find that the Constitution does not permit the official suppression of ideas.[113]

These opposing views might, however, come together when the Court is asked to determine the extent of authorities' discretion to choose curriculum and textbooks. It is clear from Justice Brennan's opinion in *Pico* that the members of the plurality believed that the removal of books already acquired by the libraries presented a very different sort of question from that of what should be taught and how. This position, along with the dissenters' explicit contention that school authorities' discretion was very broad and that students' First Amendment rights were very limited, points to a very different outcome for curriculum and textbook issues.

This conclusion is only buttressed when we look at the Court's pronouncements about student speech and student publications. The Court has upheld the school authorities' decision to discipline a student despite the student's claim that such action violated his right of expression.[114] The Court has also found that school authorities can exercise editorial control over student newspapers if such control is reasonably related to teaching concerns.[115] These cases make it clear that the Court will exercise little restraint on school officials' actions in the context of school-related activities.

Political Processes

Our concern with ensuring a fair political process and its impact on First Amendment expression rights has largely centered on campaign financing. It has been argued that in today's world access to the media is inextricably intertwined with the election process. To gain access to the media it takes a great deal of money, so that politicians must find effective ways to raise funds for their campaigns. At the same time, this has generated a concern over the kind of impact/control contributors of large sums of money may have on the making of public policy. Accordingly, the Court has been asked to determine the constitutionality of statutes regulating campaign financing.

The seminal case in this area is *Buckley v. Valeo*,[116] where the Court addressed the constitutionality of the Federal Election Campaign Act of 1971, as amended in 1974, and the provision of Subtitle H of the Internal Revenue Code.[117] Various provisions of the law were attacked as violating First Amendment speech and association rights. The challenged provisions concerned specific limits placed on campaign contributions to federal elections. They were those that addressed the limits on campaign contributions and expenditures.

In a per curiam opinion, five justices found those provisions of the Act imposing ceilings on contributions did not violate the First Amendment; seven justices agreed that those provisions limiting independent political expenditures by individuals and groups, and that fixed ceilings on overall campaign expenditures by candidates were violative of the First Amendment. In addition, six members of the Court found that the provisions limiting personal expenditures by a candidate were unconstitutional pursuant to the First Amendment. Six justices also found that the reporting requirements of the Act were neither vague, nor overbroad. Similarly, the public funding provision did not violate the First Amendment according to seven members of the Court. Five separate opinions were written and only three justices joined in the per curiam opinion in its entirety.

BUCKLEY V. VALEO
424 U.S. 1 (1975)

PER CURIAM

In this Court, appellants argue that the Court of Appeals failed to give this legislation the critical scrutiny demanded under accepted First Amendment and equal protection principles. In appellants' view, limiting use of money for political purposes constitutes a restriction on communication violative of the First Amendment, since virtually all-meaningful political communications in the modern setting involve the expenditure of money.

I. CONTRIBUTION AND EXPENDITURE LIMITATIONS

The intricate statutory scheme adopted by Congress to regulate federal election campaigns includes restrictions on political contributions and expenditures that apply broadly to all phases of and all participants in the election process.

[T]he critical constitutional questions presented here go not to the basic power of Congress to legislate in this area, but to whether the specific legislation that Congress has enacted interferes with First Amendment freedoms.

A. General Principles

The Act's contribution and expenditure limitations operate in an area of the most fundamental First Amendment activities. Discussion of public issues and debate on the qualifications of candidates are integral to the operation of the system of government established by our Constitution. The First Amendment affords the broadest protection to such political expression in order "to assure [the] unfettered interchange

Continued

of ideas for the bringing about of political and social changes desired by the people." Although First Amendment protections are not confined to "the exposition of ideas," "there is practically universal agreement that a major purpose of that Amendment was to protect the free discussion of government affairs . . . of course include[ing] discussion of candidates . . . ." This no more than reflects our "profound national commitment to the principle that debate on public issues should be uninhibited, robust, and wide-open." In a republic where the people are sovereign, the ability of the citizenry to make informed choices among candidates for office is essential for the identities of those who are elected will inevitably shape the course that we follow as a nation. As the Court observed in *Monitor Patriot Co. v. Roy,* "it can hardly be doubted that the constitutional guarantee has its fullest and most urgent application precisely to the conduct of campaigns for political office."

It is with these principles in mind that we consider the primary contentions of the parties with respect to the Act's limitations upon the giving and spending of money in political campaigns. Those conflicting contentions could not more sharply define the basic issues before us. Appellees contend that what the Act regulates is conduct, and that its effect on speech and association is incidental at most. Appellants respond that contributions and expenditures are at the very core of political speech, and that the Act's limitations thus constitute restraints on First Amendment liberty that are both gross and direct.

In upholding the constitutional validity of the Act's contribution and expenditure provisions on the ground that those provisions should be viewed as regulating conduct not speech, the Court of Appeals relied upon *United States v. O'Brien.*

We cannot share the view that the present Act's contribution and expenditure limitations are comparable to the restriction on conduct upheld in *O'Brien.* The expenditure of money simply cannot be equated with such conduct as destruction of a draft card. Some forms of communication made possible by the giving and spending of money involve speech alone, some involve conduct primarily, and some involve a combination of the two. Yet this Court has never suggested that the dependence of a communication on the expenditure of money operates itself to introduce a non-speech ele-

ment or to reduce the exacting scrutiny required by the First Amendment.

Even if the categorization of the expenditure of money as conduct were accepted, the limitations challenged here would not meet the *O'Brien* test because the governmental interests advanced in support of the Act involve "suppressing communication." The interests served by the Act include restricting the voices of people and interest groups who have money to spend and reducing the overall scope of federal election campaigns. Although the Act does not focus on the ideas expressed by persons or groups subjected to its regulations, it is aimed in part at equalizing the relative ability of all voters to affect electoral outcomes by placing a ceiling on expenditures for political expression by citizens and groups.

* * *

[I]t is beyond dispute that the interest in regulating the alleged "conduct" of giving or spending money "arises in some measure because the communication allegedly integral to the conduct is itself thought to be harmful."

Nor can the Act's contribution and expenditure limitations be sustained, as some of the parties suggest, by reference to the constitutional principles reflected in such decisions as . . . *Kovacs v. Cooper.* Those cases stand for the proposition that the government may adopt reasonable time, place, and manner regulations, which do not discriminate among speakers or ideas, in order to further an important governmental interest unrelated to the restriction of communication.

* * *

The critical difference between this case and those time, place and manner cases is that the present Act's contribution and expenditure limitations impose direct quantity restrictions on political communication and association by persons, groups, candidates, and political parties in addition to any reasonable time, place, and manner regulations otherwise imposed.

A restriction on the amount of money a person or group can spend on political communication during a campaign necessarily reduces the quantity of expression by restricting the number of issues discussed, the depth of their exploration, and the size of the audience reached. This is because virtually every means of communicating ideas in today's mass society requires the expenditure of

Continued

money. The distribution of the humblest handbill or leaflet entails printing, paper, and circulation costs. Speeches and rallies generally necessitate hiring a hall and publicizing the event. The electorate's increasing dependence on television, radio, and other mass media for news and information has made these expensive modes of communication indispensable instruments of effective political speech.

The expenditure limitations contained in the Act represent substantial rather than merely theoretical restraints on the quantity and diversity of political speech.

By contrast with a limitation upon expenditures for political expression, a limitation upon the amount that any one person or group may contribute to a candidate or political committee entails only a marginal restriction upon the contributor's ability to engage in free communication.

Given the important role of contributions in financing political campaigns, contribution restrictions could have a severe impact on political dialogue if the limitations prevented candidates and political committees from amassing the resources necessary for effective advocacy. There is no indication, however, that the contribution limitations imposed by the Act would have any dramatic adverse effect on the funding of campaigns and political associations. The overall effect of the Act's contribution ceilings is merely to require candidates and political committees to raise funds from a greater number of persons and to compel people who would otherwise contribute amounts greater than the statutory limits to expend such funds on direct political expression, rather than to reduce the total amount of money potentially available to promote political expression.

In sum, although the Act's contribution and expenditure limitations both implicate fundamental First Amendment interests, its expenditure ceilings impose significantly more severe restriction on protected freedoms of political expression and association than do its limitations on financial contributions.

B. Contribution Limitations

(a)
Appellants contend that the $1,000 contribution ceiling unjustifiably burdens First Amendment freedoms, [and] employs overbroad dollar limits . . .

It is unnecessary to look beyond the Act's primary purpose—to limit the actuality and appearance of corruption resulting from large individual financial contributions—in order to find a constitutionally sufficient justification for the . . . limitation. Under a system of private financing of elections, a candidate lacking immense personal or family wealth must depend on financial contributions from others to provide the resources necessary to conduct a successful campaign. The increasing importance of the communications media and sophisticated mass-mailing and polling operations to effective campaigning make the raising of large sums of money an even more essential ingredient of an effective candidacy. To the extent that large contributions are given to secure political quid pro quo's from current and potential office holders, the integrity of our system of representative democracy is undermined. Although the scope of such pernicious practices can never be reliably ascertained, the deeply disturbing examples surfacing after the election demonstrates that the problem is not an illusory one.

Of almost equal concern as the danger of actual quid pro quo arrangement is the impact of the appearance of corruption stemming from public awareness of the opportunities for abuse inherent in a regime of large individual financial contributions.

Significantly, the Act's contribution limitations in themselves do not undermine, to any material degree, the potential for robust and effective discussion of candidates and campaign issues by individual citizens, associations, the institutional press, candidates, and political parties. We find that under the rigorous standard of review established by our prior decisions, the weighty interests served by restricting the size of financial contributions to political candidates are sufficient to justify the limited effect upon First Amendment freedoms caused by the . . . contribution ceiling.

(b)
Appellants' first overbreadth challenge to the contribution ceilings rests on the proposition that most large contributions do not seek improper influence over a candidate's position or an officeholder's action. Although the truth of that proposition may be assumed, it does not undercut the validity of the . . . contribution limitation. Not only is it difficult to isolate suspect contributions but, more importantly,

Continued

Congress was justified in concluding that the interest in safeguarding against the appearance of impropriety requires that the opportunity for abuse inherent in the process of raising large monetary contributions be eliminated.

A second, related overbreadth claim is that the . . . restriction is unrealistically low because much more than that amount would still not be enough to enable an unscrupulous contributor to exercise improper influence over a candidate or officeholder, especially in campaigns for statewide or national office. While the contribution limitation provisions might well have been structured to take account of the graduated expenditure limitations for Congressional and Presidential campaigns, Congress' failure to engage in such fine-tuning does not invalidate the legislation. As the Court of Appeals observed, "[if] it is satisfied that some limit on contributions is necessary, a court has no scalpel to probe, whether, say, a $2,000 ceiling might not serve as well as $1,000." Such distinctions in degree become significant only when they can be said to amount to differences in kind.

C. Expenditure Limitations

The Act's expenditure ceilings impose direct and substantial restraints on the quantity of political speech. The most drastic of the limitations restricts individuals and groups, including political parties that fail to place a candidate on the ballot, to an expenditure of $1,000 "relative to a clearly identified candidate during a calendar year." Other expenditure ceilings limit spending by candidates, their campaigns, and political parties in connection with election campaigns. It is clear that a primary effect of these expenditure limitations is to restrict the quantity of campaign speech by individuals, groups and candidates. The restrictions, while neutral as to the ideas expressed, limit political expression "at the core of our electoral process and, of the First Amendment freedoms."

Before examining the interests advanced in support of section 608 (e) (1)'s expenditure ceiling, consideration must be given to appellants' contention that the provision is unconstitutionally vague. Close examination of the specificity of the statutory limitation is required where, as here, the legislation imposes criminal penalties in an area permeated by First Amendment interests. The test is whether the language of section 608 (e)(1) affords the "[p]recision of regulation

[that] must be the touchstone in an area so closely touching our most precious freedoms."

We agree that in order to preserve the provision against invalidation on vagueness grounds, section 608 (e)(1) must be construed to apply only to expenditures for communications that in express terms advocate the election or defeat of a clearly identified candidate for federal office.

We turn then to the basic First Amendment question—whether section 608 (e)(1) . . . impermissibly burdens the constitutional right of free expression. The Court of Appeals summarily held the provision constitutionally valid. . . . We cannot agree.

We find that the governmental interest in preventing corruption and the appearance of corruption is inadequate to justify section 608 (e)(1)'s ceiling on independent expenditures. First, assuming arguendo, that large independent expenditures pose the same dangers of actual or apparent quid pro quo arrangements as do large contributions, section 608 (e)(1) does not provide an answer that sufficiently relates to the elimination of those dangers.

Second, quite apart from the shortcomings of section 608 (e)(1) in preventing any abuses generated by large independent expenditures, the independent advocacy restricted by the provision does not presently appear to pose dangers of real or apparent corruption comparable to those identified with large campaign contributions.

While the independent expenditure ceiling thus fails to serve any substantial governmental interest in stemming the reality or appearance of corruption in the electoral process, it heavily burdens core First Amendment expression. For the First Amendment right to "speak one's mind . . . on all public institutions" includes the right to engage in "vigorous advocacy" no less than "abstract discussion." Advocacy of the election or defeat of candidates for federal office is no less entitled to protection under the First Amendment than the discussion of political policy generally or advocacy of the passage or defeat of legislation.

It is argued, however, that the ancillary governmental interest in equalizing the relative ability of individuals and groups to influence the outcome of elections serves to justify the limitation on express advocacy of the election or defeat of candidates imposed by section 608 (e)(1)'s

Continued

expenditure ceiling. But the concept that government may restrict the speech of some elements of our society in order to enhance the relative voice of others is wholly foreign to the First Amendment, which was designed "to secure" the widest possible dissemination of information from diverse and antagonistic sources,' " and "to assure unfettered interchange of ideas for the bringing about of political and social changes desired by the people." The First Amendment's protection against governmental abridgment of free expression cannot properly be made to depend on a person's financial ability to engage in public discussion.

For the reasons stated, we conclude that section 608 (e)(1)'s independent expenditure limitation is unconstitutional under the First Amendment.

2. Limitation on Expenditures by Candidates from Personal or Family Resources

The Act also sets limits on expenditures by a candidate "from his personal funds, or the personal funds of his immediate family, in connection with his campaigns during any calendar year." These ceilings vary (depending on the office sought).

The ceiling on personal expenditures by candidates on their own behalf, like limitations on independent expenditures contained in section 608 (e)(1), imposes a substantial restraint on the ability of persons to engage in protected First Amendment expression. The candidate, no less than any other person, has a First Amendment right to engage in the discussion of public issues and vigorously and tirelessly to advocate his own election and election of other candidates. Indeed, it is of particular importance that candidates have the unfettered opportunity to make their views known so that the electorate may intelligently evaluate the candidates' personal qualities and their positions on vital public issues before choosing among them on Election Day. Mr. Justice Brandeis' observation that in our country "public discussion is a political duty," applies with special force to candidates for public office. Section 608 (a)'s ceiling on personal expenditures by a candidate in furtherance of his own candidacy thus clearly and directly interferes with constitutionally protected freedoms. The primary governmental interest served by the Act—prevention of actual and apparent corruption of the political process—does not support the limitation on the candidate's expenditure of his own personal

funds. * * * Indeed, the use of personal funds reduces the candidate's dependence on outside contributions and thereby counteracts the coercive pressures and attendant risks of abuse to which the Act's contribution limitations are directed.

The ancillary interest in equalizing the relative financial resources of candidates competing for elective office, therefore, provides the sole relevant rationale for section 608 (a)'s expenditure ceiling. That interest is clearly not sufficient to justify the provision's encouragement of fundamental First Amendment rights. First, the limitation may fail to promote financial equality among candidates. A candidate who spends less of his personal resources on his campaign may nonetheless outspend his rival as a result of more successful fundraising efforts. Indeed a candidate's personal wealth may impede his efforts to persuade others that he needs their financial contributions or volunteer efforts to conduct an effective campaign. Second, and more fundamentally, the First Amendment simply cannot tolerate section 608 (a)'s restriction upon the freedom of a candidate to speak without legislative limit on behalf of his own candidacy. We therefore hold that section 608 (a)'s restriction on a candidate's personal expenditures is unconstitutional.

3. Limitations on Campaign Expenditures

Section 608 places limitations on overall campaign expenditures by candidates seeking nomination for election and election to federal office.

No governmental interest that has been suggested is sufficient to justify the restriction on the quantity of political expression imposed by section 608©'s campaign expenditure limitations. The major evil associated with rapidly increasing campaign expenditures is the danger of candidate dependence on large contributions. The interest in alleviating the corrupting influence of large contributions is served by the Act's contribution limitations and disclosure provisions rather than by section 608©'s campaign expenditure ceilings. The Court of Appeals' assertion that the expenditure restrictions are necessary to reduce the incentive to circumvent direct contribution limits is not persuasive. There is no indication that the substantial criminal penalties for violating the contribution ceilings combined with the political repercussion of

Continued

such violations will be insufficient to police the contribution provisions. Extensive reporting, auditing and disclosure requirements applicable to both contributions and expenditures by political campaigns are designed to facilitate the detection of illegal contributions. Moreover, as the Court of Appeals noted, the Act permits an officeholder or successful candidate to retain contributions in excess of the expenditure ceiling and to use these funds for "any other lawful purpose." This provision undercuts whatever marginal role the expenditure limitations might otherwise play in enforcing the contribution ceilings.

The interest in equalizing the financial resources of candidates competing for federal office is not more convincing a justification for restricting the scope of federal election campaigns. Given the limitation on the size of outside contributions, the financial resources available to a candidate's campaign, like the number of volunteers recruited, will normally vary with the size and intensity of the candidate's support. There is nothing invidious, improper, or unhealthy in permitting such funds to be spent to carry the candidate's message to the electorate. Moreover, the equalization of permissible campaign expenditures might serve not to equalize the opportunities of all candidates but to handicap a candidate who lacked substantial name recognition or exposure of his views before the start of the campaign.

The campaign expenditure ceilings appear to be designed primarily to serve the governmental interests in reducing the allegedly skyrocketing costs of political campaigns.

* * *

[T]he mere growth in the cost of federal election campaigns in and of itself provides no basis for governmental restrictions on the quantity of campaign spending and the resulting limitation on the scope of federal campaigns. The First Amendment denies government the power to determine that spending to promote one's political views is wasteful, excessive, or unwise. In the free society ordained by our Constitution it is not the government but the people—individually as citizens and candidates and collectively as associations and political committees—who must retain control over the quantity and range of debate on public issues in a political campaign.

For these reasons we hold that section 608© is constitutionally invalid.

In sum, the provisions of the Act that impose . . . limitation[s] on contributions . . . are constitutionally valid. These limitations, along with the disclosure provisions, constitute the Act's primary weapon against the reality or appearance of improper influence stemming from the dependence of candidates on large campaign contributions. The contribution ceilings thus serve the basic governmental interest in safeguarding the integrity of the electoral process without directly impinging upon the rights of individual citizens and candidates to engage in political debate and discussion. By contrast, the First Amendment requires the invalidation of the Act's independent expenditure ceiling, its limitation on a candidate's expenditures from his own personal funds, and its ceilings on overall campaign expenditures. These provisions place substantial and direct restrictions on the ability of candidates, citizens, and associations to engage in protected political expression, restrictions that the First Amendment cannot tolerate.

In sum, the per curiam opinion makes it clear that *Buckley* is distinguishable from *O'Brien*. The statute at issue in *Buckley* is not a time, place, or manner ordinance. Strict scrutiny was employed since a strong governmental interest in limiting actual corruption, as well as the appearance of corruption could not be achieved by a less restrictive means. As to expenditures by individuals the provisions imposed "direct and substantial" restraints on the quantity of political speech.[118] This limited political expression in the absence of a sufficient state interest. The Court also struck down limits on total campaign spending by candidates finding a First Amendment right to spend as much as one wants to promote his own political views. Thus, the Court rejected the government's contention that its interest in preventing runaway campaign costs was sufficient to outweigh First Amendment rights.

One of the most contentious issues was whether money was synonymous with speech.

Justice WHITE, concurring in part and dissenting in part.

I

I dissent . . . from the Court's view that the expenditure limitations of 18 U.S.C. sections 608 (c) and (e) violate the First Amendment.

The Court . . . accepts the congressional judgment that the evils of unlimited contributions are sufficiently threatening to warrant restriction regardless of the impact of the limits on the contributor's opportunity for effective speech and in turn on the total volume of the candidate's political communications by reason of his inability to accept large sums from those willing to give.

It would make little sense to me, and apparently made none to Congress, to limit the amounts an individual may give to a candidate or spend with his approval but fail to limit the amounts that could be spent on his behalf. Yet the Court permits the former while striking down the latter limitation. No more than $1,000 may be given to a candidate or spent at his request or with his approval or cooperation; but otherwise, apparently, a contributor is to be constitutionally protected in spending unlimited amounts of money in support of his chosen candidate or candidates.

In sustaining the contribution limits, the Court recognizes the importance of avoiding public misapprehension about a candidate's reliance on large contributions. It ignores that consideration in invalidating section 608 (e). In like fashion, it says that Congress was entitled to determine that the criminal provisions against bribery and corruption, together with the disclosure provisions, would not in themselves be adequate to combat the evil and that limits on contributions should be provided. Here, the Court rejects the identical kind of judgment made by Congress as to the need for and utility of expenditure limits. I would not do so.

The Court also rejects Congress' judgment manifested in section 608 that the federal interest in limiting total campaign expenditures by individual candidates justifies the incidental effect on their opportunity for effective political speech. I disagree both with the Court's assessment of the impact on speech and with its narrow view of the values the limitations will serve.

As an initial matter, the argument that money is speech and that limiting the flow of money to the speaker violates the First Amendment proves entirely too much. Compulsory bargaining and the right to strike, both provided for or protected by federal law, inevitably have increased the labor costs of those who publish newspapers, which are in turn an important factor in the recent disappearance of many daily papers. Federal and state taxation directly removes from company coffers large amounts of money that might be spent on larger and better newspapers. The antitrust laws are aimed at preventing monopoly profits and price fixing, which gouge the consumer. It is also true that general price controls have from time to time existed and have been applied to the newspapers or other media. But it has not been suggested, nor could it be successfully, that these laws, and many others, are invalid because they siphon off or prevent the accumulation of large sums that would otherwise be available for communicative activities.

In any event, as it should be unnecessary to point out, money is not always equivalent to or used for speech, even in the context of political campaigns. I accept the reality that communicating with potential voters is the heart of an election campaign and that widespread communication has become very expensive. There are, however, many expensive campaign activities that are not themselves communicative or remotely related to speech. Furthermore, campaigns differ among themselves. Some seem to spend much less money than others and yet communicate as much or more than those supported by enormous bureaucracies with unlimited financing. The record before us no more supports the conclusion that the communicative efforts of congressional and Presidential candidates will be crippled by the expenditure limitations than it supports the contrary. The judgment of Congress was that reasonably effective campaigns could be conducted within the limits established by the Act and that the communicative efforts of these campaigns would not seriously suffer. In this posture of the case, there is no sound basis for invalidating the expenditure limitations, so long as the purposes they serve are legitimate and sufficiently substantial, which in my view they are.

I have little doubt in addition that limiting the total that can be spent will ease the candidate's understandable obsession with the fundraising function. There is nothing objectionable—indeed it seems to me a weighty interest in favor of the provision—in the attempt to insulate the political expression of federal candidates from the influence inevitably exerted by the endless

Continued

job of raising increasingly large sums of money. I regret that the Court has returned them all to the treadmill.

The ceiling on candidate expenditures represents the considered judgment of Congress that elections are to be decided among candidates none of whom has overpowering advantage by reason of a huge campaign war chest. At least so long as the ceiling placed upon the candidates is not plainly too low, elections are not to turn on the difference in the amounts of money that candidates have to spend. This seems an acceptable purpose and the means chosen a commonsense way to achieve it. The Court nevertheless holds that a candidate has a constitutional right to spend unlimited amounts of money, mostly that of other people, in order to be elected. The holding perhaps is not that federal candidates have the constitutional right to purchase their election, but many will so interpret the Court's conclusion in this case. I cannot join the Court in this respect.

I also disagree with the Court's judgment that section 608 (a), which limits the amount of money that a candidate or his family may spend on his campaign, violates the Constitution. Although it is true that the provision does not promote any interest in preventing the corruption of candidates, the provision does, nevertheless, serve salutary purposes related to the integrity of federal campaigns. By limiting the importance of personal wealth, section 608 (a) helps to assure that only individuals with a modicum of support from others will be viable candidates. This in turn would tend to discourage any notion that the outcome of elections is primarily a function of money. Similarly, section 608 (a) tends to equalize access to the political arena, encouraging the less wealthy, unable to bankroll their own campaigns, to run for political office.

As with the campaign expenditure limits, Congress was entitled to determine that personal wealth ought to play a less important role in political campaigns than it has in the past. Nothing in the First Amendment stands in the way of that determination.

For these reasons I respectfully dissent from the Court's answers [to these issues].

Justice MARSHALL, concurring in part and dissenting in part.

I join in all of the Court's opinion except [that] which deals with 18 U.S.C. section 608 (a). That section limits the amount a candidate may spend from his personal funds, or family funds under his control, in connection with his campaigns during any calendar year. The Court invalidates section 608 (a) as violative of the candidate's First Amendment rights. "[T]he First Amendment," the Court explains, "simply cannot tolerate section 608 (a)'s restriction upon the freedom of a candidate to speak without legislative limit on behalf of his own candidacy." I disagree.

To be sure, section 608 (a) affects the candidate's exercise of his First Amendment rights. But unlike the other expenditure limitations contained in the Act and invalidated by the Court—the limitation on independent expenditures relative to a clearly identified candidate, and the limitations on overall candidate expenditures—the limitations on expenditures by candidates from personal resources contained in section 608 (a) need never prevent the speaker from spending another dollar to communicate his ideas. Section 608 (a) imposes no overall limit on the amount a candidate can spend; it simply limits the "contribution" a candidate may make to his own campaign. The candidate remains free to raise an unlimited amount in contributions from others. So long as the candidate does not contribute to his campaign more than the amount specified . . . and so long as he does not accept contributions from others in excess of the limitations imposed by section 608 (b), he is free to spend without limit on behalf of his campaign.

It is significant, moreover, that the ceilings imposed by section 608 (a) on candidate expenditures from personal resources are substantially higher than the $1,000 limit imposed by section 608 (e) on independent expenditures by noncandidates.

* * *

But they will admittedly limit the availability of personal funds for some candidates and the question is whether that limitation is justified.

The concern that candidacy for public office not become, or appear to become, the exclusive province of the wealthy assumes heightened significance when one considers the impact of section 608 (b), which the Court today upholds. That provision prohibits contributions from individuals and groups to candidates in excess of $1,000 and contributions from political committees in excess of $5,000. While the limitations on contributions are neutral in the sense that all candidates are foreclosed from accepting large contributions, there can be no question

Continued

that large contributions generally mean more to the candidate without a substantial personal fortune to spend on his campaign. Large contributions are the less wealthy candidate's only hope of countering the wealthy candidate's immediate access to substantial sums of money. With that option removed, the less wealthy candidate is without the means to match the large initial expenditures of money of which the wealthy candidate is capable. In short, the limitations on contributions put a premium on a candidate's personal wealth.

In addition to section 608 (a), section 608 (c) which limits overall candidate expenditures in a campaign, also provides a check on the advantage of the wealthy candidate. But we today invalidate that section, which unlike section 608 (a) imposes a flat prohibition on a candidate's expenditures above a certain level, and which is less tailored to the interest in equalizing access than section 608 (a). The effect of invalidating both section 608 (c) and section 608 (a) is to enable the wealthy candidate to spend his personal resources without limit, while the less wealthy opponent is forced to make do with whatever amount he can accumulate through relatively small contributions.

In the 28 years since *Buckley,* the Court has addressed other campaign contribution/free expression controversies. In *Nixon v. Shrink Missouri Political Action Committee,*[119] the Court not only made it clear that *Buckley* was still good law, it also stated that limitations on spending may be restricted so long as the amount of the limitation does not "render contributions pointless."[120] Moreover, states as well as the federal government could impose limits.

In early September 2003, the Court sat in a special session for expedited review, on a challenge to the first campaign finance reform statute to be passed by Congress since *Buckley.* The Bipartisan Campaign Reform Act, also known as the McCain-Feingold Act was being challenged on First Amendment grounds. From the cases heard since *Buckley,* it appeared that Justices Kennedy, Scalia, and Thomas viewed campaign finance regulations as violative of First Amendment rights of expression and association, with Justices Stevens, Souter, Ginsburg, and Breyer being likely supporters. When the Court heard *McConnell v. Federal Election Commission,*[121] as predicted the Court was widely divided. Amidst a plethora of concurring and dissenting opinions, the Court affirmed the judgment of the District Court which upheld those parts of the statute regulating "soft money" and prohibited corporations and unions from using general treasury funds for communications intended to, or having an effect upon, election outcomes. Both sides of the Court claimed to be upholding the principles of *Buckley.* What is clear from the opinion is that the Court is willing to place some limits on First Amendment speech when elections are at stake.

Miscellaneous

There is one final context within which to consider the interpretation of First Amendment rights of expression. This is when the government wishes to speak or fund the speech of another rather than regulate speech. In these situations it appears that the government's ability to select among messages and speakers is greater than in the regulatory context.

In those situations where the government chooses to speak, it seems that it is relatively free to say what it chooses. This means that the rule of viewpoint neutrality, in essence, is not applicable. Although there is little case law directly on point there has been some indication that this is true. For example, in *Rust v. Sullivan,*[122] the government could condition a grant on the parties' agreement not to recommend abortion and, in a dissent in *National Endowment for the Arts v. Finley,*[123] Justice Souter stated that the government may condemn smoking in an advertising campaign without the need "to show a cowboy taking a puff on the opposite page."[124]

The question becomes more complicated when the government seeks to fund a speaker—one expressing his own beliefs, not those of the government. In these situations, it appears that the government must maintain viewpoint neutrality. In *Rosenberger v. University of Virginia*,[125] it was held that once the university funds student publications it cannot exclude some and include others. The need for viewpoint neutrality in these situations is underscored by the Court's decision in *Legal Service Corp. v. Velazquez*.[126] There, the Court found that Congress violated the First Amendment by placing limits on the positions Legal Services attorneys could take in litigation. This was the same type of viewpoint-based restriction as that in *Rosenberger*.

The majority rejected the government's position that this was not the government's own speech, finding that the Legal Services program was designed to "facilitate private speech, not to promote a governmental message."[127] As such, the regulation required application of a strict scrutiny standard that it could not meet. Thus, it appears that when the government chooses to fund private speech it is bound to maintain viewpoint neutrality.

Summary

The Framers of the Constitution sought to encourage the exchange of ideas in a free society. Their aim was to place as few limits on this ability as possible. Consequently, they added a constitutional guarantee of free expression in the First Amendment.

When the government seeks to regulate speech, and/or conduct that has an expressive component, First Amendment free expression issues arise. Analysis of these challenges involves consideration of numerous factors. Of primary concern is whether the government is seeking to regulate the speech on the basis of its content, that is, whether there is something in the message itself that the government is seeking to suppress. If this is the case, the Court will generally apply a strict scrutiny analysis. The government must be able to demonstrate that the regulation is necessary to achieve a compelling state interest and that it impinges on free expression no more than it is essential to do so in order to achieve that interest.

Where the government's regulation is not directed at the content of the speech itself, but rather at where, when, and how the expression occurs, the Court employs a somewhat different analysis. After demonstrating that these "time, place, and manner ordinances" are content-neutral, the government must show that a significant government interest is involved; that the regulation has been narrowly drawn to achieve that interest; and that alternative channels of communication have been left open for the speaker.

It is also of concern in analyzing First Amendment expression cases whether the expression takes place in a traditional public forum; those areas historically open to the people for communicating ideas, such as the parks and sidewalks, or elsewhere. If a nonpublic forum is involved, the Court will interpret the requirements for narrowly drawn regulations and alternative channels less strictly than would be the case were the expression to occur in a public forum.

In those situations where criminal penalties are being imposed for exercise of free expression rights, the Court looks at whether the regulations are overbroad or encompass protected speech as well as that which is unprotected, or vague, not giving the speaker sufficient notice of what is proscribed. If either of these situations occurs, the Court will find the statute unconstitutional.

Finally, in considering First Amendment expression rights we must be aware that there are some contexts in which they may come into conflict with strong public policy concerns. For example, this may be the case in ensuring a fair political process.

Where to draw the line in a society that prizes freedom of expression is one of the thorniest problems the Court faces.

Key Terms

freedom of expression
freedom of speech

overbreadth
prima facie

time, place, or manner restriction
vagueness

Review Questions

1. What is a public forum and how does the concept effect the Court's analysis of First Amendment expression rights?

2. Discuss the distinction between true speech and symbolic expression. What is the speech/conduct distinction and how does it contribute or detract from analysis of First Amendment expression cases?

3. Time, place, and manner ordinances allow the government to regulate where and when speech/expression may occur. How may they permissibly regulate speech?

4. Define the overbreadth and vagueness doctrines. What are the major concerns associated with each?

5. The Court draws a distinction between regulations based on the content of speech and those regulations that are content-neutral. What is this distinction? Why is it relevant to our concept of freedom of expression?

Internet Connections

1. For more information on free speech issues and cases, go to the American Civil Liberties Union Web site at *http://www.aclu.org.*

2. The Freedom Forum is a nonpartisan foundation dedicated to freedom of speech, available at *http://www.freedomforum.org.*

3. For information on protecting your freedom of expression rights, go to the Web site of the Thomas Jefferson Center for the Protection of Free Expression at *http://www.tjcenter.org.*

End Notes

[1] *Gitlow v. New York,* 268 U.S. 652 (1925).

[2] *Widmar v. Vincent,* 454 U.S. 263 (1981).

[3] *Metromedia, Inc. v. San Diego,* 453 U.S. 490 (1981).

[4] *Burson v. Freeman,* 504 U.S. 191 (1992).

[5] *Simon & Schuster, Inc. v. New York State Crime Victims' Board,* 502 U.S. 105 (1991).

[6] *Id.* at 115, 119.

[7] *See* Chapter 11, Unprotected Speech; *R.A.V. v. City of St. Paul,* 505 U.S. 377 (1992).

[8] *Hayes v. C.I.O.,* 307 U.S. 496 (1939).

[9] *Madison Joint School District v. Wisconsin Employment Relations Comm'n,* 429 U.S. 167 (1976).

[10] *Arkansas Educational Television Commission v. Forbes,* 523 U.S. 666 (1998).

[11] *International Society for Krishna Consciousness v. Lee,* 505 U.S. 672 (1992).

[12] *Adderly v. Florida,* 385 U.S. 118 (1966).

[13] *Greer v. Spock,* 424 U.S. 828 (1976).

[14] *United States v. Grance,* 461 U.S. 171 (1983).

[15] *Perry Educational Association v. Perry Local Educators Association,* 460 U.S. 37 (1983).

[16] *United States v. Kokinda,* 497 U.S. 720 (1990).

[17] *Amalgamated Food Employees Local 500 v. Logan Valley Plaza,* 391 U.S. 308 (1968).

[18] *Lloyd Corporation v. Tanner,* 407 U.S. 551 (1972).

[19] *Hudgens v. National Labor Relations Board,* 424 U.S. 507 (1976).

[20] *Miami Herald Publishing Co. v. Tornillo,* 418 U.S. 241 (1974).

[21] *Pacific Gas and Electric Co. v. Public Utilities Commission of California,* 475 U.S. 1 (1986).

[22] *Red Lion Broadcasting Co. v. Federal Communications Commission,* 395 U.S. 367 (1969).

[23] *Cornelius v. NAACP Legal Defense Fund,* 473 U.S. 788 (1985).

[24] *Cox v. Louisiana,* 379 U.S. 536 (1965).

[25] *Frisby v. Schultz,* 487 U.S. 474 (1988).

[26] *Madsen v. Women's Health Center,* 512 U.S. 753 (1994).

[27]*Cox v. Louisiana,* 379 U.S. 536 (1965).

[28]*Los Angeles v. Taxpayers for Vincent,* 466 U.S. 789 (1984).

[29]*Thornhill v. Alabama,* 310 U.S. 88 (1940).

[30]*Arnette v. Kennedy,* 416 U.S. 134 (1974).

[31]*Broadrick v. Oklahoma,* 413 U.S. 601 (1973).

[32]*Connally v. General Construction Co.,* 269 U.S. 385 (1926).

[33]*Spence v. Washington,* 418 U.S. 405 (1974).

[34]*Id.* at 406.

[35]*Id.* at 409.

[36]*Id.* at 411.

[37]*Id.* at 415.

[38]*Cox v. Alabama,* 379 U.S. 559 (1965).

[39]*Ward v. Rock Against Racism,* 491 U.S. 781 (1989).

[40]*Id.* at 798–799.

[41]*Id.* at 802.

[42]*City of Ladue v. Gilleo,* 512 U.S. 43 (1994).

[43]*Id.* at 56.

[44]*Id.* at 56–57.

[45]*Id.* at 57.

[46]*Id.* at 57.

[47]*Id.* at 59.

[48]*Forsyth Company v. The Nationalist Movement,* 505 U.S. 123 (1992).

[49]*Lakewood v. Plain Dealer Publishing,* 468 U.S. 750 (1989); *Lovell v. Griffin,* 303 U.S. 444 (1939).

[50]*Kunz v. New York,* 340 U.S. 290 (1951).

[51]*Cox v. New Hampshire,* 312 U.S. 569 (1941).

[52]*Id.* at 575–576.

[53]*Poulous v. New Hampshire,* 345 U.S. 395 (1953).

[54]*Walker v. Birmingham,* 388 U.S. 307 (1967).

[55]*Saia v. New York,* 334 U.S. 558 (1948).

[56]*Id.* at 562.

[57]*Kovacs v. Cooper,* 336 U.S. 77 (1949).

[58]*Id.* at 79.

[59]*Id.* at 82–83.

[60]*Id.* at 83.

[61]*Id.* at 89.

[62]*Lehman v. Shaker Heights,* 418 U.S. 298 (1984).

[63]*Frisby v. Schultz,* 487 U.S. 474 (1988).

[64]*Hill v. Colorado,* 530 U.S. 703 (2000).

[65]*Id.* at 717–718; 729–730.

[66]*Rowan v. Post Office Department,* 397 U.S. 728 (1970).

[67]*U.S. Postal Service v. Greenburgh Civic Association,* 453 U.S. 114 (1981).

[68]*Martin v. Struthers,* 319 U.S. 141 (1943).

[69]*Watchtower Bible and Tract Society of New York, Inc. v. Village of Stratton,* 536 U.S. 150 (2002).

[70]*Id.* at 168.

[71]*Shaumberg v. Citizens for a Better Environment,* 444 U.S. 620 (1980).

[72]*Metromedia, Inc. v. San Diego,* 453 U.S. 490 (1981).

[73]*Members of the City Council of the City of Los Angeles v. Taxpayers for Vincent,* 466 U.S. 789 (1984).

[74]*Id.* at 812.

[75]*Good News Club v. Milford Central School,* 533 U.S. 98 (2001); *see also, Lamb's Chapel v. Central Moriches Union Free School District,* 508 U.S. 384 (1993); *Rosenberger v. Rector and Visitors of the University of Virginia,* 515 U.S. 819 (1995); Chapter 15.

[76]*Arkansas Educational Television Commission v. Forbes,* 523 U.S. 666 (1998).

[77]*Rosenberger,* Rector and Visitor of the University of Virginia, 515 U.S. 819 (1995); *Legal Services Corporation v. Velazquez,* 531 U.S. 533 (2001).

[78]*Cornelius v. NAACP Legal Defense and Education Fund, Inc.* 473 U.S. 788 (1985).

[79]*United States v. O'Brien,* 391 U.S. 367 (1968).

[80]50 U.S.C. app. § 463(b).

[81]Romo, Zastrow, & Miller, "History of the U.S. War in Vietnam," Vietnam Veterans Against the War, 2002, at *http://www.vvaw.org* (Sept. 15, 2003).

[82]*Id.*

[83]Martina Bexte, "The Vietnam War Protest," PageWise, at *http://ohoh/essortment/coa/vietnamwarprot_rlcz.htm* (Sept. 15, 2003).

[84]*Id.*

[85]"Strike Against the War," excerpts from an article published in TIME Magazine on October 17, 1969, at *http://www.cnn.com/SPECIALS/cold.war/episodes/13/1st.draft/* (Sept. 15, 2003).

[86]*Id.*

[87]*Id.*

[88]*Id.*

[89]*Tinker v. Des Moines Independent Community School District,* 393 U.S. 303 (1969).

[90]*Id.* at 505–507.

[91]*Id.* at 508.

[92]*Id.* at 514.

[93]*Erie v. Pap's A.M.,* 529 U.S. 277 (2000).

[94]*Texas v. Johnson,* 491 U.S. 397 (1989).

[95]Tex. Penal Code Ann. § 42.09 (1989).

[96]18 U.S.C. § 700 (Supp. 1990).

[97]*United States v. Eichman,* 496 U.S. 310 (1990).

[98]*Id.* at 315–316.

[99]*Virginia v. Black,* 538 U.S. 343 (2003).

[100]*Id.* at 343.

[101]*West Virginia Board of Education v. Barnette,* 319 U.S. 624 (1943).

[102]*Meyer v. Nebraska,* 262 U.S. 390 (1923).

[103]*Tinker v. Des Moines School District,* 393 U.S. 503 (1969).

[104]*Board of Education, Island Trees Union Free School District No. 26 v. Pico,* 457 U.S. 853 (1982).

[105]*Id.* at 873.

[106]*Id.* at 856.

[107]*Id.* at 858–859.

[108]*Id.* at 859.

[109]*Id.* at 861.

[110]*Id.* at 869.

[111]*Id.* at 869.

[112]*Id.* at 871.

[113]*Id.* at 910.

[114]*Bethel School District Number 403 v. Fraser,* 478 U.S. 675 (1986).

[115]*Hazelwood School District v. Kuhlmeier,* 484 U.S. 260 (1988).

[116]*Buckley v. Valeo,* 424 U.S. 1 (1975).

[117]2 U.S.C. § 431 *et seq*; 18 U.S.C. § 591 *et seq*; 26 U.S.C. § 9001 *et seq.*

[118]*Id.* at 48.

[119]*Nixon v. Shrink Missouri Political Action Committee,* 523 U.S. 666 (2000).

[120]*Id.* at 672.

[121]*McConnell v. Federal Election Commission,* 540 U.S. 93 (2003).

[122]*Rust v. Sullivan,* 500 U.S. 173 (1991).

[123]*National Endowment for the Arts v. Finley,* 524 U.S. 569 (1998).

[124]*Id.* at 610–611.

[125]*Rosenberger v. University of Virginia,* 515 U.S. 819 (1995).

[126]*Legal Service Corp. v. Velazquez,* 531 U.S. 533 (2001).

[127]*Id.* at 542.

 For additional resources, go to *http://www.westlegalstudies.com*

11 Chapter

Unprotected Speech

"It is a fundamental principle, long established, that the freedom of speech and of the press which is secured by the Constitution, does not confer an absolute right to speak or publish, without responsibility, whatever one may choose, or an unrestricted and unabridged license that gives immunity for every possible use of language and prevents the punishment of those who abuse this freedom."

—Justice Edward T. Sanford
Gitlow v. New York

INTRODUCTION

advocacy forceful persuasion; arguing a cause, right, or position.

fighting words speech that is not protected by the First Amendment to the U.S. Constitution because it is likely to cause violence by the person to whom the words are spoken.

obscene lewd and offensive to accepted standards of decency.

defamation transmission to others of false statements that harm the reputation, business, or property rights of a person.

commercial speech expression, such as newspaper ads, related solely to the economic interest of the "speaker" and the audience.

Previous chapters discussed First Amendment protection of speech and expression. This chapter addresses speech that does not directly fall within the First Amendment and can, therefore, be regulated. As previously noted, the Framers were concerned with the free exchange of ideas. They believed that through such an exchange truth would emerge from discussion. The First Amendment protections are not absolute, however. The Supreme Court has protected certain categories of speech. Speech that is considered harmful or valueless and that cannot be cured by more speech falls into this unprotected area. Included among the unprotected categories of speech are:

- **Advocacy** of illegal conduct
- **Fighting words**
- **Obscenity**
- **Defamation**
- **Commercial speech**

Speech falling within these categories is not completely without protection. Over time the Court has expanded the scope of the First Amendment to limit regulation in these areas. Today, at the very least, regulation must be accomplished in a content-neutral manner. Until recently, this was not the case. These categories of speech allowed for non-content-neutral regulations and were subjected only to a mere rationality standard. As we shall see, the distinction between protected and unprotected speech has been blurred and, as a result, restrictions that are premised on content will be subject to judicial scrutiny. Today it could be argued that there is little distinction between protected and unprotected speech. The answer appears to be that speech falling within the unprotected categories may be completely proscribed so long as the regulation is content-neutral. Moreover, time, place, and manner ordinances regarding speech in the public forum will be presumptively valid when they address speech in unprotected categories.

ADVOCACY OF ILLEGAL CONDUCT

As noted, it is political speech that is given the greatest First Amendment protection. Underlying First Amendment speech protection was the idea that suppression of such speech is dangerous to our democratic form of government. This idea is premised on the belief that peaceful change will emerge from public discussion. Nevertheless, some types of political speech pose the greatest threat to the democratic form of government that free speech was designed to protect. Once the government is allowed to ban or punish some types of political speech, however, the potential for banning legitimate dissent arises. This poses a problem for the courts in distinguishing between the two types of speech. The Court has had great difficulty in deciding where the line should be drawn. Where that line is drawn seems to depend largely on the historical context and the perceived nature of the threat. An examination of the Court's decisions throughout the twentieth century will lead us to the current standard enunciated by the Court in *Brandenburg v. Ohio*.[1]

Throughout most of the twentieth century, the Supreme Court has employed the clear and present danger test in determining where the line should be drawn between protected and unprotected speech. This approach allowed punishment of speech that created a **clear and present danger** that the advocated illegal act would occur even if it never did.

Justice Holmes set forth this standard in *Schenck v. United States*.[2] The issue of concern was the extent to which citizens had the right to oppose World War I. In 1917, Congress passed the Espionage Act making it a crime to willfully cause or attempt to cause insubordination or disloyalty, or refusal to serve in the armed forces of the United States, or to willfully obstruct recruiting or enlistment in the service of the United States. Defendants who did so were charged with conspiracy to violate the Act. Schenck and others sent a document opposing the draft to two individuals, calling the draft despotism and urging draftees not to submit. The document did not advocate illegal resistance to the draft in explicit terms. Rather, it advocated peaceful measures such as petitioning for repeal of the draft.

The Supreme Court, in an opinion by Justice Holmes, unanimously found the defendants' conspiracy conviction constitutional. Justice Holmes stated that whether particular speech was protected depended on the surrounding circumstances. He framed the issue as "whether the words used are used in such circumstances and are of such a nature as to create a clear and present danger that they will bring about the substantive evils that Congress has a right to prevent."[3]

It was for the fact-finder to decide whether a defendant's conduct posed such a danger. To make the point clear, Holmes gave an example that one had no constitutional right to falsely yell "fire" in a crowded theater. While this is a graphic illustration and one that has been repeated often enough to become a part of our culture, it can be argued that the two acts—defendants' documents and falsely crying fire in a confined space—are clearly distinguishable. There is a difference between the false cry that is understood to be a statement of fact by those who hear it and an opinion or encouragement to act in a particular manner, as was the case with the document. There is also a temporal difference between the two acts. The false cry of "fire" does not provide time to challenge its truth whereas there is time to combat defendants' argument as set forth in the document. This point is particularly important in the face of the underlying concept of the free marketplace of ideas that serves as the basis for the First Amendment.

Schenck was not the only case that came before the Court as a result of Espionage Act convictions. That same year, the Court heard *Frohwerk v. United States*[4] and *Debs v. United States*.[5] *Frohwerk* concerned editorial writers criticizing the draft in a German-language newspaper. Again Holmes wrote for the Court upholding defendants' convictions, using the same reasoning found in *Schenck*. The *Debs* defendant was a well-known socialist and presidential candidate. He made a speech opposing World War I and was convicted of obstructing military recruitment. Holmes enunciated the standard to be whether the speech had a "natural tendency and reasonably probable effect" of obstructing recruitment. Accordingly, Debs' conviction was also upheld. While

clear and present danger test a test of whether or not speech may be restricted or punished; it may be if it will probably lead to violence soon or if it threatens a serious, immediate weakening of national safety and security.

Holmes claimed that he was employing the clear and present danger test, his language weakened the test, making it easier for the government to sustain a conviction. There was no evidence that the speech resulted in any obstruction of recruitment. Holmes also failed to draw a distinction between the direct mailing in *Schenck* and Debs' speech to a general audience.

Later in that same year, the unanimous front of the Court on these cases began to crumble. In *Abrams v. United States*,[6] Holmes, the author of the previous decisions and the standard that had been applied dissented, joined by Justice Brandeis. In the *Abrams* decision, Holmes put some teeth in the clear and present danger test so that it offered some protection for political dissenters.

The defendants in *Abrams* were American socialists of Russian birth. They were convicted of violating a new section of the Espionage Act. The section proscribed urging curtailment of war production with intent to hinder prosecution of the war.[7] Defendants published two leaflets that expressed their pro-Bolshevik sentiments and attacked United States production and supplying of arms that could be used against Russia. The leaflets were not pro-German (our enemy at the time), but they urged workers not to make bullets that could be used against Russians as well as Germans. The issue before the Court was whether defendants had the intent required by the statute to interfere with the war effort against Germany. The majority acknowledged that the primary purpose may have been only to aid the Russian Revolution but indicated that men should be held to intend the effects that their acts were "likely to produce."[8] The Court noted that curtailing production to help the Russians could not be accomplished without impeding the war effort. Thus, the majority concluded that the intent element was established.

Holmes, in dissent, also focused on intent. He maintained that one does not intend the consequences of his act "unless that consequence is the aim of the deed."[9] This standard demanded the conclusion that defendants did not have the requisite intent. While it is unclear how the clear and present danger standard was employed in Holmes' dissent, it is in this dissent that Holmes addresses the value of free speech. He advocated "free trade in ideas"[10] and stated that "[t]he best test of truth is the power of the thought to get itself accepted in the competition of the market . . ."[11] This competition, Holmes asserted, was so important that it should not be suppressed "unless [the ideas] so imminently threaten immediate interference with the lawful and pressing purposes of the law that an immediate check is required to save the country."[12] This is clearly a stricter view of the clear and present danger test than had previously been employed by Holmes himself in earlier cases.

The clear and present danger test provided little protection for speech in the earliest cases. Moreover, its reliance on the fact-finder's opinion regarding the immediacy of threat makes political speech vulnerable to public fears in times of national crisis. There are parallels in today's reaction to September 11, 2001. In addition, the standard is so vague that the ability to overturn a verdict resulting from a fact-finder's determination is difficult if not impossible. It can be inferred from the standard that speech is permissible as long as it does not succeed in its objective. This inference is clearly at odds with the First Amendment goal of political change through discourse and not violence.

Judge Learned Hand articulated a different test for determining the extent to which political speech can be curtailed. Hand set forth his test in *Masses Publishing Co. v. Patten*.[13] Judge Hand focused on the words themselves, not the circumstances under which they were spoken. Judge Hand maintained that words could be punished when they urged others to violate the law, as it existed at the time. Words that were merely critical of the current state of the law were not subject to punishment. At issue in this case were antiwar cartoons and text critical of World War I and the draft, which expressed sympathy for draft resisters. Judge Hand determined that all this constituted only abstract advocacy and was not a direct call to violate the law. Accordingly, the convictions went beyond the government's ability to punish. Under Hand's test, the likely effects of the speech are not relevant. It is only if the publication/speech was a direct call to violate the law that it could be punished even if it was ineffectual. Hand's test found no acceptance by other courts. In fact, the federal appeals court rejected it. This rejection left the clear and present danger test in effect for the next 50 years until the Court adapted its main tenets.

Up to this point, the statutes of interest did not proscribe speech, only acts. Speech was relevant because the government argued that speech amounted to an attempt or conspiracy to bring about an act. In time, legislatures passed statutes that prohibited certain types of speech. The Court was then faced with resolving whether the clear and present danger standard applied to these statutes as well.

Initially, those on the Court who agreed that the test had no applicability to statutes directly proscribing speech were in control of the majority. The Court adopted the position that the legislative conclusion that certain types of speech were inherently dangerous deserved respect. Consequently, in *Gitlow v. New York*[14] the Court found that the statute banning advocacy of overthrowing the government by assassination or other violent means was constitutional.

The defendant in *Gitlow* advocated establishing a dictatorship of the proletariat through strikes and revolutionary action by the masses. The Court stated that the clear and present danger test was only applicable to proscribing acts "without any reference to language itself. . . ."[15] It was not for the Court to take issue with the legislative judgment that language of a certain kind posed a risk that certain substantive harms would result. In addition, there was no requirement that only such speech that posed a definite or immediate action be prohibited. Justice Holmes, in concert with Justice Brandeis, dissented and took the position that the clear and present danger test should be the appropriate standard in addressing these cases. Employing that test, Justice Holmes found that the speech at issue "had no chance of starting a present conflagration."[16] Accordingly, Justice Holmes believed the convictions violated defendants' constitutional right to free speech.

Two years later the Court revisited the issue in *Whitney v. California.*[17] This was a time when there was much fear generated by the Communist Revolution in Russia. The California legislature enacted a statute prohibiting the knowing membership in any organization advocating the use of force or violence to bring about political change. Defendant Whitney, an acknowledged member of the Communist Party, was convicted under the act despite the fact that she did not agree with the party's advocacy of violent change and voted against that plank. The majority of the Court declined to overturn her conviction reasoning that the legislative conclusion that knowing membership in an organization advocating criminal syndicalism was, in itself, a sufficiently substantive danger. Justice Brandeis, joined by Justice Holmes, wrote an opinion that disagreed with the majority on how the statute should be evaluated. In essence, Brandeis argued that the legislature itself could not establish the facts of a law's validity. The correct standard was the clear and present danger test and it was the Court alone that could make such a determination. As Holmes had done in *Abrams,* Brandeis now did in *Whitney.* He wrote about the value of free speech. He argued that the way to preserve an orderly society was not by enacting repressive measures that breed hate. Bad ideas, he asserted, should be combated by good ones and it is only in situations where the danger is imminent that speech should be suppressed or punished. Brandeis went on to say that even in the face of imminent danger suppression should not be used unless the danger is "relatively serious."[18] Fifty-two years later, the majority decision in *Whitney* would be explicitly overruled, and Justice Brandeis' view vindicated.

Fear of political dissent reared its head again during and following World War II. Again the fear was of a Communist threat to American democracy. That perceived threat prompted the passage of the Smith Act[19] that paralleled the terms of the New York law that was upheld in *Gitlow*. Many cases arose from the passage of the Smith Act. *Dennis v. United States*[20] was one of the most important. It marked the high-water mark in the Court's suppression of political dissent and the broadest reading of the clear and present danger test.

In *Dennis* the defendants were convicted under the statute of conspiring to advocate the overthrow of government and conspiracy to reorganize the Communist Party, a group that advocated violent overthrow, the government claimed. The majority claimed to be applying the clear and present danger test and upheld the conviction. The Court found that under the test the government did not have to wait until the overthrow was about to take place, in other words, the danger did not have to be imminent. Rather, the majority employed the test fashioned by Learned Hand, which was "whether the gravity of the 'evil' discounted by its improbability,"[21] justified abridging free speech in order to avoid the danger. Employing this standard, the Court found that danger of violent overthrow was so great that even a minor chance of success supported controls on speech. The Court went further than it had in the past stating that the issue of whether danger existed was to be determined by the trial judge, not the jury. This determination, the Court held, was one of constitutional law and not fact.

DENNIS V. UNITED STATES
341 U.S. 494 (1951)

Chief Justice VINSON for the Court.

II

The obvious purpose of the statute is to protect existing Government, not from change by peaceable, lawful and constitutional means, but from change by violence, revolution and terrorism. That it is within the *power* of the Congress to protect the Government of the United States from armed rebellion is a proposition which requires little discussion. Whatever theoretical merit there may be to the argument that there is a "right" to rebellion against dictatorial government is without force where the existing structure of the government provides for peaceful and orderly change. We reject any principle of governmental helplessness in the face of preparation for revolution, which principle, carried to its logical conclusion, must lead to anarchy. No one could conceive that it is not within the power of Congress to prohibit acts intended to overthrow the Government by force and violence. The question with which we are concerned here is not whether Congress has such *power*, but whether the *means* which it has employed conflict with the First and Fifth Amendments to the Constitution.

One of the bases for the contention that the means which Congress has employed are invalid takes the form of an attack on the face of the statute on the grounds that by its terms it prohibits academic discussion of the merits of Marxism-Leninism, that it stifles ideas and is contrary to all concepts of a free speech and a free press. Although we do not agree that the language itself has that significance, we must bear in mind that it is the duty of the federal courts to interpret federal legislation in a manner not inconsistent with the demands of the Constitution. . . . This is a federal statute which we must interpret as well as judge. Herein lies the fallacy of reliance upon the manner in which this Court has treated judgments of state courts. Where the statute as construed by the state court transgressed the First Amendment, we could not but invalidate the judgments of conviction.

The very language of the Smith Act negates the interpretation which petitioners would have us impose on the Act. It is directed at advocacy, not discussion. Thus, the trial judge properly charged the jury that they could not convict if they found that petitioners did "no more than pursue peaceful studies and discussions or teaching and advocacy in the realm of ideas." He further charged that it was not unlawful "to

Continued

conduct in an American college or university a course explaining the philosophical theories set forth in the books which have been placed in evidence." Such a charge is in strict accord with the statutory language, and illustrates the meaning to be placed on those words. Congress did not intend to eradicate the free discussion of political theories, to destroy the traditional rights of Americans to discuss and evaluate ideas without fear of governmental sanction. Rather Congress was concerned with the very kind of activity in which the evidence showed these petitioners engaged.

III

But, although the statute is not directed at the hypothetical cases which petitioners have conjured, its application in this case has resulted in convictions for the teaching and advocacy of the overthrow of the Government by force and violence, which, even though coupled with the intent to accomplish that overthrow, contains an element of speech. For this reason, we must pay special heed to the demands of the First Amendment marking [out the] boundaries of speech.

We pointed out . . . that the basis of the First Amendment is the hypothesis that speech can rebut speech, propaganda will answer propaganda, free debate of ideas will result in the wisest governmental policies. It is for this reason that this Court has recognized the inherent value of free discourse. An analysis of the leading cases in this Court which have involved direct limitations on speech, however, will demonstrate that both the majority of the Court and the dissenters in particular cases have recognized that this is not an unlimited, unqualified right, but that the societal value of speech must, on occasion, be subordinated to other values and considerations.

The rule we deduce . . . is that where an offense if specified by a statute in nonspeech or nonpress terms, a conviction relying upon speech or press as evidence of violation may be sustained only when the speech or publication created a "clear and present danger" of attempting or accomplishing the prohibited crime. . . .

In this case we are squarely presented with the application of the "clear and present danger" test, and must decide what that phrase imports. We first note that many of the cases in which this Court has reversed convictions by use of this or similar tests have been based on the fact that the interest which the State was attempting to protect was itself too insubstantial to warrant restriction of speech.

The argument that there is no need for Government to concern itself, for Government is strong, it possesses ample powers to put down a rebellion, it may defeat the revolution with ease needs no answer. For that is not the question. Certainly an attempt to overthrow the Government by force, even though doomed from the outset because of inadequate numbers or power of the revolutionists, is a sufficient evil for Congress to prevent. The damage which such attempts create physically and politically to a nation makes it impossible to measure the validity in terms of the probability of success, or the immediacy of a successful attempt. In the instant case the trial judge charged the jury that they could not convict unless they found that petitioners intended to overthrow the Government "as speedily as circumstances would permit." This does not mean, and could not properly mean, that they would not strike until there was certainty of success. What was meant was that the revolutionists would strike when they thought the time was ripe. We must therefore reject the contention that success or probability of success is the criterion.

Chief Judge Learned Hand . . . interpreted the phrase as follows: "In each case [courts] must ask whether the gravity of the 'evil,' discounted by its improbability, justifies such invasion of free speech as is necessary to avoid the danger." We adopt this statement of the rule. As articulated by Chief Judge Hand, it is as succinct and inclusive as any other we might devise at this time. It takes into consideration those factors which we deem relevant, and relates their significance. More we cannot expect from words.

IV

When facts are found that establish the violation of a statute, the protection against conviction afforded by the First Amendment is a matter of law. The doctrine that there must be a clear and present danger of a substantive evil that Congress has a right to prevent is a judicial rule to be applied as a matter of law by the courts. The guilt is established by proof of facts. Whether the First Amendment protects the activity which constitutes the violation of the statute must depend upon a judicial determination of

Continued

the scope of the First Amendment applied to the circumstances of the case.

The question in this case is whether the statute which the legislature has enacted may be constitutionally applied. In other words, the Court must examine judicially the application of the statute to the particular situation, to ascertain if the Constitution prohibits the conviction. We hold that the statute may be applied where there is a "clear and present danger" of the substantive evil which the legislature had the right to prevent. Bearing, as it does, the marks of a "question of law," the issue is properly one for the judge to decide.

V

We hold that [sections] 2(a)(1), 2(a)(3) and 3 of the Smith Act do not inherently, or as construed or applied in the instant case, violate the First Amendment and other provisions of the Bill of Rights, or the First and Fifth Amendments because of indefiniteness. Petitioners intended to overthrow the Government of the United States as speedily as the circumstances would permit. Their conspiracy to organize the Communist Party and to teach and advocate the overthrow of the Government of the United States by force and violence created a "clear and present danger" of an attempt to overthrow the Government by force and violence. They were properly and constitutionally convicted for violation of the Smith Act. The judgments of conviction are

Affirmed.

Justice BLACK dissenting

[M]y basic disagreement with the Court is not as to how we should explain or reconcile what was said in prior decisions but springs from a fundamental difference in constitutional approach. Consequently, it would serve no useful purpose to state my position at length.

At the outset I want to emphasize what the crime involved in this case is, and what it is not. These petitioners were not charged with an attempt to overthrow the Government. They were not charged with overt acts of any kind designed to overthrow the Government. They were not even charged with saying anything or writing anything designed to overthrow the Government. The charge was that they agreed to assemble and to talk and publish certain ideas at a later date: The indictment is that they conspired to organize the Communist Party and to use speech or newspapers and other publications in the future to teach and advocate the forcible overthrow of the Government. No matter how it is worded, this is a virulent form of prior censorship of speech and press, which I believe the First Amendment forbids. I would hold [section]3 of the Smith Act authorizing this prior restraint unconstitutional on its face and as applied.

Public opinion being what it now is, few will protest the conviction of these Communist petitioners. There is hope, however, that in calmer times, when present pressures, passions and fears subside, this or some later Court will restore the First Amendment liberties to the high preferred place where they belong in a free society.

Justice DOUGLAS dissenting

The First Amendment provides that "Congress shall make no law . . . abridging the freedom of speech." The Constitution provides no exception. This does not mean, however, that the Nation need hold its hand until it is in such weakened condition that there is no time to protect itself from incitement to revolution. Seditious conduct can always be punished. But the command of the First Amendment is so clear that we should not allow Congress to call a halt to free speech except in the extreme case of peril from the speech itself. The First Amendment makes confidence in the common sense of our people and in their maturity of judgment the great postulate of our democracy. Its philosophy is that violence is rarely, if ever, stopped by denying civil liberties to those advocating resort to force. The First Amendment reflects the philosophy of Jefferson "that it is time enough for the rightful purposes of civil government, for its officers to interfere when principles break out into overt acts against peace and good order." The political censor has no place in our public debates. Unless and until extreme and necessitous circumstances are shown, our aim should be to keep speech unfettered and to allow the process of law to be invoked only when the provocateurs among us move from speech to action.

Justice Frankfurter concurred but maintained that the proper standard was not whether a clear and present danger existed. Instead, he suggested, that Congress and not the judiciary should use a balancing test. If, and only if, the

Court found that Congress acted in the absence of a reasonable basis, should the Court overrule the determination. Applying this standard, Justice Frankfurter maintained that Congress could have concluded that recruiting members to the Communist Party posed a danger to national security.

Justices Black and Douglas dissented. Justice Black believed that the Court's reasoning undermined the preferred place of First Amendment guarantees. Justice Douglas accepted the use of the clear and present danger test but claimed that the majority misapplied it. He asserted that only in the absence of time within which to avoid the threatened evil of the speech could limits be placed on speech. The majority interpretation and application of the clear and present danger test replaced the immediacy of the threatened danger with its seriousness. As a result, speech could be curtailed no matter how remote the anticipated consequences.

The test in *Dennis* was criticized for the narrowness of its protection of political dissent. Another criticism was also leveled at this interpretation. It was charged that the balance had become one between the seriousness of the evil against the probability that it would occur from any cause, not just the speech. In the cases following *Dennis* the Court retreated somewhat from its stance, finding means to more fully protect free speech in the context of political dissent.

In *Yates v. United States,*[22] the Court interpreted the Smith Act in a manner more consistent with Judge Hand's perspective in *Masses Publishing*. It found only the counseling of illegal acts, not advocacy of abstract theory, alone should be proscribed. The Court found that Congress' intent was to prohibit advocacy of unlawful action. The Court expanded the protection afforded speech in *Yates* with its decision in *Scales v. United States.*[23] There the Court found that the Smith Act allowed convictions based on party membership only where it was defendant's specific intent to carry out the aims of the party by illegal means. Pursuant to this interpretation, mere membership was not sufficient to trigger a conviction under the statute. If membership were punished, the statute would violate the First Amendment guarantee of free association. Congress' attempt to achieve its goal of controlling communist organization through requiring registration of those joining the party was undermined by the Court's invocation of the overbreadth doctrine to narrow Congress' control.

The standard used today for determining the boundaries of political speech was enunciated in *Brandenburg v. Ohio.*[24] This standard constitutes the most expansive interpretation of political dissent. The Court wove together elements of the clear and present danger test and the advocacy/incitement test of Hand that were the most protective of speech to articulate a new test. This new test requires that the statute prohibiting speech could withstand constitutional challenge only when advocacy was "directed to inciting or producing imminent lawless action" and such advocacy was "likely to incite or produce such action."[25] This standard emerged as a result of defendant's conviction for violating Ohio's criminal syndicalism statute that was similar to the statute sustained in *Whitney*. In this case, defendant was the leader of a Ku Klux Klan group. The Court found that the language of the statute was sufficiently broad to cover advocacy of abstract doctrines of political change in addition to imminent unlawful action. As such it was unconstitutional.

The test fails to explicitly address the severity of the harm threatened. Accordingly, it may ban speech that incites listeners to engage in conduct that threatens minimal danger while allowing speech advocating future action that may threaten serious harm. *Brandenburg* specifically overruled *Whitney*.

Other cases decided in the late 1960s clearly demonstrate the two requirements set forth in *Brandenburg* of incitement and imminent harm. The same year *Brandenburg* was decided, the Court had another opportunity to address the issue in *Watts v. United States.*[26] Defendant, who was an African American antiwar activist, was convicted pursuant to a statute making it a crime to intentionally threaten the life of the President. Defendant stated that "[I]f they ever make me carry a rifle, the first man I want to get in my sights is L [yndon] B[aines] J[ohnson]."[27] The Court reversed defendant's conviction finding defendant's statement not to be a true threat but a means by which to set forth his opposition to the President's policy of pursuing war.[28] The Court relied heavily on the fact that defendant's statement was conditional and the fact that the audience responded with laughter. In *Bond v. Floyd*,[29] the Court found that the exclusion of Julian Bond from the Georgia House of Representatives violated Bond's First Amendment rights. As a consequence of his opposition to the Vietnam War Bond signed a statement of "sympathy and support" for those unwilling to respond to the draft. The Georgia House concluded that Bond could not swear to the oath to support the Constitution. The Supreme Court ruled that Bond could not be penalized since his action did not amount to a call to unlawfully resist the draft but was a general abstract declaration of his opposition to the war.

Brandenburg, Bond, and *Watts* were all decided during the years of the Warren Court, and this may be one way of explaining the Court's willingness to expand First Amendment protection of political dissent. The Court, however, has signaled its adherence to the *Brandenburg* standard in the post–Warren Court era. In *Hess v. Indiana*,[30] a defendant's conviction resulting from a statement that antiwar demonstrators who had been moved by police for blocking a street would "take the . . . streets later" was reversed. The Court found the statement to be protected speech not incitement to illegal action. Only words intended to produce imminent disorder could be punished. Continued use of the *Brandenburg* standard was underscored by the Court's decision in *NAACP v. Claiborne Hardware Company*.[31] At issue was a speech by one of the NAACP leaders made in conjunction with black citizens' boycott of white merchants until demands for racial equality were met. The statement leading to conviction was that African Americans who violated the boycott would be "disciplined" by their own people. The Court reversed the verdict against the defendants holding that the statement was not incitement and therefore was deserving of First Amendment protection. At the same time, the Court recognized that the speaker "must be free to stimulate the audience."[32] The Court's conclusion was based, in part, on the fact that unlawful acts did not result from the speech. The Court implied that if such acts did follow speech it was more likely that intent to incite may be found.

It is clear that protection of political speech is narrowed in times that danger is perceived. When this is not the case, the Court is more willing to expand the boundaries of political dissent. In general, wars and the threat of wars trigger the narrowing of protections. The exception was the Vietnam War. It will be interesting to watch what happens in the wake of September 11, 2001, and the conflict with Iraq. It has already been demonstrated that anyone speaking out against a narrowing of constitutional protections against government power in investigating and prosecuting crime faces charges of being unpatriotic, but not criminal. Will it go further?

FIGHTING WORDS

Another of the unprotected areas is known as "fighting words." This refers to words that are likely to provoke an act of violence by the listener. Speech of this sort is unprotected because it does not necessarily fall into that communication of ideas intended to be protected. The Court first addressed this issue in *Chaplinsky v. New Hampshire*[33] where a Jehovah's Witness called the city marshal a "god-damned racketeer" and "a damned fascist." Following this the Jehovah's Witness got into a fight with the marshal on the sidewalk. He was convicted under a statute that proscribed "offensive, derisive or annoying" words addressed to anyone lawfully on the streets or in public places.[34] The Supreme Court upheld the Jehovah's Witness' conviction. The Court found that the words were likely to provoke the average person into retaliating. The Court went on to rule that fighting words were not among the classes of speech the First Amendment was designed to protect. The Court defined fighting words as "those by which by their very utterance inflict injury or tend to incite an immediate breach of the peace."[35] The Court declared that the words did not constitute an "essential part of any exposition of ideas and are of such slight social value as a step to the truth that any benefit that may be derived from them is clearly outweighed by the social interest in order and morality."[36]

The Court began to narrow its definition of fighting words as it became clear that the definition as those that may inflict injuries was so broad as to include speech that should be protected under the First Amendment. In *Terminello v. Chicago,*[37] defendant's speech drew an angry crowd that the speaker then called "snakes" and "slimy scum." Defendant was convicted of violating a breach of the peace ordinance that was interpreted as including speech that encouraged public anger and/or encouraged dispute. The Supreme Court reversed the ruling, reasoning that the most important speech may be that which produces an emotional response. The Court found that speech which stirs the audience to anger or invites dispute is protected by the First Amendment speech guarantees. The Court determined that the ordinance was overbroad because it included protected speech.

If such speech is protected, then what is the obligation of the authorities when one is exercising First Amendment rights that provoke the audience? This question was answered in *Cox v. Alabama.*[38] There, a large crowd of approximately 2,000 people, demonstrating for their civil rights, picketed the local courthouse. Some 75 law enforcement personnel separated some demonstrators from other demonstrators on the opposite side of the street. The leader of the demonstration was arrested for violating the breach of the peace ordinance. The Court reversed the conviction stating that where the police can physically control an angry crowd as a means of preventing threatened violence, they are obligated to do so rather than arresting the speaker for use of fighting words. Thus, the Court rejected the state's argument that the arrest was justified since violence was imminent. The decision was based, in part, on the Court's finding that the police could have controlled the crowd.

Where police cannot control a crowd they must still have more than a generalized concern that violence may ensue before the fighting words doctrine applies. Police must be able to point to specific words or acts by the speaker or audience that threaten violence.[39] Further, police must rely on more than the speaker's identification. Action must be prompted by his threatening words or deeds. In *Garner v. Louisiana,*[40] this point was brought home when state authorities attempted to justify concern of imminent violence by arguing that the use of segregated facilities by civil rights activists would lead to attacks by whites. The Court rejected this.

With these specifications it becomes clearer when the fighting words doctrine is applied. It is applicable in situations where (1) imminent audience violence, (2) which cannot be controlled through the use of ordinary crowd control tactics, and (3) the speech itself constitutes the seeming cause of imminent violence. This is best illustrated in *Feiner v. New York,*[41] the last case in which the Court upheld a fighting words conviction.

On a city street corner, petitioner addressed a crowd of approximately 75 to 80 African Americans and whites. Using a loudspeaker, he made derogatory comments about the President, the American Legion, and various politicians. The crowd filled the sidewalk and spilled over into the street. When police first arrived on the scene they took no action but simply observed. They then attempted to get the spillover crowd back on the sidewalk. As the police listened, petitioner's tone changed and it seemed to the officers that he was attempting to arouse the African Americans against the whites—urging them to take up arms and fight for equal rights. At least one member of the crowd threatened violence if the police did not act. Passions were flaring. The officers approached petitioner to ask him to break up the crowd, not to arrest him. Asked twice to stop talking, petitioner refused. The crowd pressed closer to the speaker and the officers. It was at this point that the officers told petitioner that he was under arrest for violating the city's breach of the peace ordinance. Petitioner had been speaking for more than a half hour.

The Court found that the officers acted to prevent disorder and interference with traffic—legitimate government interests. The Court noted with approval the lower courts' findings that the officers acted reasonably and without an intent to suppress petitioner's views.[42]

OFFENSIVE SPEECH

Another issue concerns the government's ability to ban or punish speech found offensive by the audience although it is insufficient to provoke violence. In general, the Court has found that speech that is merely profane and consequently offensive to the audience may not be punished. Most illustrative of the Court's approach to such cases is the decision in *Cohen v. California*.[43]

In the Los Angeles courthouse Cohen wore a jacket with the legend "F--- the Draft" emblazoned on the back. Women and children were present. Cohen was arrested and convicted of violating a "disturbing the peace" ordinance by his offensive conduct. The Supreme Court reversed the conviction rejecting the government's arguments to sustain it. Justice Harlan, writing for the majority, began by rejecting the contention that the legend was obscene. He asserted that to be obscene, speech must have an element of eroticism. In response to the state's argument that Cohen "thrust" his message upon a captive audience, Harlan noted that those in the courthouse could simply have averted their eyes. Harlan also rejected the state's contention that the state could ban certain language to insure that a "stable level of discourse" be maintained. In response to that argument, Harlan proclaimed that the underlying purpose of the First Amendment was to limit governmental restraints in the arena of public discussion. Harlan went on to state that under the Constitution matters of taste are properly left to the individual and not the government.

That offensiveness to the audience does not provide a basis for suppressing speech was also underlined in *Collin v. Smith*,[44] where survivors of the Holocaust in a predominantly Jewish neighborhood sought to prevent a demonstration of neo-Nazis (see Exhibit 11.1). In response to the outcry against the

EXHIBIT 11.1   The Nazi March in Skokie and the ACLU

In early October of 1976, Frank Collin, the leader of the Nationalist Socialist Party in America, wrote to the Director of Skokie, Illinois' Parks and Recreation district requesting a permit to hold a rally in one of the community's parks. Collin knew that approximately one-half of the suburban community's population was Jewish and many had survived the Nazi concentration camps in Germany. Collin could easily have surmised the reaction to his request would be negative and that much media publicity would attach to any struggle that might result from even the possibility of a Nazi rally in this location. Indeed, Collin could not have been disappointed by the ensuing controversy.

The first response Collin received informed him that he was required to post a $350,000 insurance bond and that he would have to comply with an ordinance (passed on October 25), which required that a permit be obtained at least 30 days prior to the march. The ordinance also prohibited demonstrators from parading in "military-style" dress or displaying offensive symbols. First Amendment issues were clearly raised by this law. Consequently, Collin went out to find counsel to represent his organization.

Collin obtained the services of the Illinois branch of the American Civil Liberties Union, and the legal and social battle was on. Thousands of Jewish members of the ACLU, an organization dedicated to protecting citizens' civil rights, resigned from the group to demonstrate their opposition to supporting these particular speakers. The militant Jewish Defense League indicated its intent to be present in the event the march took place. One could predict the likelihood of a

Continued

confrontation. Skokie's Jews offered two opposing positions. The first was to ignore Collin and his sympathizers should they succeed in obtaining the March permit. The other position was that it was necessary to take a stand against the Nazis.

Meanwhile, throughout 1977 and 1978 the case wended its way through the state and federal courts. On May 22, 1978, the United States Court of Appeals for the Seventh Circuit ruled that Skokie's ordinances violated the First Amendment rights of the Nazis. Three days later Skokie issued a permit allowing Collin and his band to demonstrate before the city hall.

The demonstration, however, never took place. On June 23, 1978, Collin announced that the demonstration was cancelled. Collin withdrew from Skokie, he claimed, because he was given a permit to hold a demonstration in Chicago's Marquette Park, which was his primary goal.

The ACLU lost approximately 15 percent of its members in the clash over the Nazi march in Skokie, but its goal of protecting free speech was upheld in the courts.[45]

demonstration the city passed ordinances drafted to neutralize the demonstration. The federal courts at the trial and appellate levels found the ordinances unconstitutional. The Seventh Circuit, while recognizing that the demonstration might be shocking, determined that the shock was directly tied to the content of the speech and ruled that expression of ideas in public may not be prohibited merely because the ideas are themselves offensive to some of their listeners. The court also noted that this was not a case in which the residents constituted a captive audience.

To succeed in regulating speech on the basis of its offensive content, the state must face the evaluation of courts employing the strict scrutiny standard. The strict scrutiny standard will be employed even when the state's intention is simply to burden offensive speech and not only prohibit it. In *United States v. Playboy Entertainment Group, Inc.,*[46] the Court struck down Congress' attempt to limit access to sexually explicit material after applying the strict scrutiny test and finding that less restrictive alternatives were available.

HATE SPEECH

There is yet another type of speech that the government has made efforts to control. This is what is known as "hate speech." Advocates of efforts to control such speech argue that speech directed against citizens that is based on race, ethnicity, gender, and sexual orientation should be subject to governmental regulation. Hate crime statutes were enacted by legislatures across the country, but when one of these ordinances came before the Supreme Court, the Court made it clear that the constitutionality of such statutes was questionable.

In *R.A.V. v. City of St. Paul,*[47] the Court was faced with determining the constitutionality of a city ordinance. A group of teenagers who made a cross from taping together broken chair legs burned the cross in the yard of an African American family living across the street from one of the teens. R.A.V., a juvenile, was convicted under the city ordinance that provided that

> [w]hoever places on public or private property a symbol, object, appellation, characterization or graffiti, including, but not limited to, a burning cross or Nazi swastika, which one knows or has reasonable grounds to know arouses anger, alarm or resentment in others on the basis of race, color, creed, religion or gender commits disorderly conduct and shall be guilty of a misdemeanor.[48]

The members of the Court all agreed that the ordinance was unconstitutional, but the Court split 5 to 4 on the reasoning. Justice Scalia, writing for five members of the Court, found that the ordinance was overly broad and was not content-neutral.

R.A.V. v. City of St. Paul
505 U.S. 377 (1992)

Justice SCALIA for the Court.

I

In construing the St. Paul ordinance, we are bound by the construction given to it by the Minnesota court. Accordingly, we accept the Minnesota Supreme Court's authoritative statement that the ordinance reaches only those expressions that constitute "fighting words" within the meaning of *Chaplinsky*. Petitioner and his *amici* urge us to modify the scope of the *Chaplinsky* formulation, thereby invalidating the ordinance as "substantially overbroad. . . ." We find it unnecessary to consider this issue. Assuming, *arguendo*, that all of the expression reached by the ordinance is proscribable under the "fighting words" doctrine, we nonetheless conclude that the ordinance is facially unconstitutional in that it prohibits otherwise permitted speech solely on the basis of the subject the speech addresses.

The First Amendment generally prevents government from proscribing speech, or even expressive conduct, because of disapproval of the ideas expressed. Content-based regulations are presumptively invalid. From 1791 to the present, however, our society, like other free but civilized societies, has permitted restrictions upon the content of speech in a few limited areas, which are "of such slight social value as a step to truth that any benefit that may be derived from them is clearly outweighed by the social interest in order and morality." We have recognized that "the freedom of speech" referred to by the First Amendment does not include a freedom to disregard these traditional limitations. Our decisions since the 1960s have narrowed the scope of the traditional categorical exceptions for defamation, and for obscenity, but a limited categorical approach has remained an important part of our First Amendment jurisprudence.

[T]he exclusion of "fighting words" from the scope of the First Amendment simply means that, for purposes of that Amendment, the unprotected features of the words, are, despite their verbal character, essentially a "nonspeech" element of communication. Fighting words are thus analogous to a noisy sound truck: Each is . . . a "mode of speech", used to convey an idea; but neither has, in and of itself, a claim upon the First Amendment. As with the sound truck, however, so also with fighting words: The government may not regulate use based on hostility—or favoritism—towards the underlying message expressed.

II

What we have here, it must be emphasized, is not a prohibition of fighting words that are directed at certain persons or groups (which would be facially valid if it met the requirements of the Equal Protection Clause); but rather, a prohibition of fighting words that contain . . . messages of "bias motivated" hatred and in particular, as applied to this case, messages "based on virulent notions of racial supremacy." One must wholeheartedly agree with the Minnesota Supreme Court that "it is the responsibility, even the obligation, of diverse communities to confront such notions in whatever form they appear," but the manner of that confrontation cannot counsel of selective limitations upon speech. St. Paul's brief asserts that a general "fighting words" law would not meet the city's needs because only a content-specific measure can communicate to minority groups that the "group hatred" aspect of such speech "is not condoned by the majority." The point of the First Amendment is that majority preferences must be expressed in some fashion other than silencing speech on the basis of its content.

The dispositive question in this case, therefore, is whether content discrimination is reasonably necessary to achieve St. Paul's compelling interests; it plainly is not. An ordinance not limited to the favored topics, for example, would have precisely the same beneficial effect. In fact the only interest distinctively served by the content limitation is that of displaying the city council's special hostility towards the particular biases thus singled out. That is precisely what the First Amendment forbids. The politicians of St. Paul are entitled to express that hostility—but not through the means of imposing unique limitations upon speakers who (however benightedly) disagree.

Justice STEVENS concurring

Conduct that creates special risks or causes special harms may be prohibited by special rules. Lighting a fire near an ammunition dump or a

Continued

gasoline storage tank is especially dangerous; such behavior may be punished more severely than burning trash in a vacant lot. Threatening someone because of her race or religious beliefs may cause particularly severe trauma or touch off a riot, and threatening a high public official may cause substantial social disruption; such threats may be punished more severely than threats against someone based on, say, his support of a particular athletic team. There are legitimate, reasonable, and neutral justification for such special rules.

This case involves the constitutionality of one such ordinance. Because the regulated conduct has some communicative content—a message of racial, religious, or gender hostility—the ordinance raises two quite different First Amendment questions. Is the ordinance "overbroad" because it prohibits too much speech? If not, is it "underbroad" because it does not prohibit enough speech?

In answering these questions, my colleagues today wrestle with two broad principles: first, that certain "categories of expression [including 'fighting words'] are 'not within the area of constitutionally protected speech;'" and second, that "content-based speech regulations [of expression] are presumptively invalid. . . ." Although in past opinions the Court has repeated both of these maxims, it has—quite rightly—adhered to neither with the absolutism suggested by my colleagues. Thus, while I agree that the St. Paul ordinance is unconstitutionally overbroad, I write separately to suggest how the allure of absolute principles has skewed the analysis of both the majority and Justice White's opinions.

I

The Court attempts to bolster its argument by likening its novel analysis to that applied to restrictions on the time, place, or manner of expression or on expressive conduct. It is true that loud speech in favor of the Republican Party can be regulated because it is loud, but not because it is pro-republican; and it is true that the public burning of the American flag can be regulated because it involves public burning and not because it involves the flag. But these analogies are inapposite. In each of these examples, the two elements (e.g., loudness and pro-Republican orientation) can coexist; in the case of "obscene antigovernment" speech, however, the presence of one element ("obscenity") by definition means the absence of the other. To my mind, it is unwise and unsound to craft a new doctrine based on such highly speculative hypotheticals.

I am, however, even more troubled by the second step of the Court's analysis—namely, its conclusion that the St. Paul ordinance is an unconstitutional content-based regulation of speech. Drawing on broadly worded dicta, the Court establishes a near-absolute ban on content-based regulations of expression and holds that the First Amendment prohibits the regulation of fighting words by subject matter. Thus, while the Court rejects the "all-or-nothing-at-all" nature of the categorical approach, it promptly embraces an absolutism of its own: Within a particular "proscribable" category of expression, the Court holds, a government must either proscribe *all* speech or no speech at all. This aspect of the Court's ruling fundamentally misunderstands the role and constitutional status of content-based regulations on speech, conflicts with the very nature of First Amendment jurisprudence, and disrupts well-settled principles of First Amendment law.

In essence, the decision extends the content neutrality requirement to speech in the unprotected category of hate speech. The majority rejected the argument that the ordinance should still pass the strict scrutiny standard because it was necessary to serve a compelling state interest. Justice Scalia maintained that the legislation was not necessary because there were adequate content-neutral alternatives. The result of *R.A.V.* is to invalidate statutes that created a new and separate crime for activities that are motivated by the actors' dislike for certain categories of persons.

In 2003, the Court once again heard and decided a case involving a First Amendment challenge to a state statute that proscribed hate speech or expressive conduct. In *Virginia v. Black*, the Court had to determine the constitutionality of the Virginia statute that bans the burning of an object when done "with the intent of intimidating any person or group of persons."[49]

VIRGINIA V. BLACK
538 U.S. 343 (2003)

Justice O'CONNOR announced the judgment of the Court and delivered the opinion of the Court with respect to Parts I, II, and III, and an opinion with respect to Parts IV and V, in which THE CHIEF JUSTICE, Justice STEVENS, and Justice BREYER join.

In this case we consider whether the Commonwealth of Virginia's statute banning cross burning with "an intent to intimidate a person or group of persons" violates the First Amendment. Va.Code Ann. § 18.2-423 (1996). We conclude that while a State, consistent with the First Amendment, may ban cross burning carried out with the intent to intimidate, the provision in the Virginia statute treating any cross burning as prima facie evidence of intent to intimidate renders the statute unconstitutional in its current form.

I

Respondents Barry Black, Richard Elliott, and Jonathan O'Mara were convicted separately of violating Virginia's cross-burning statute, § 18.2-423. That statute provides:

"It shall be unlawful for any person or persons, with the intent of intimidating any person or group of persons, to burn, or cause to be burned, a cross on the property of another, a highway or other public place. Any person who shall violate any provision of this section shall be guilty of a Class 6 felony.

"Any such burning of a cross shall be prima facie evidence of an intent to intimidate a person or group of persons."

On August 22, 1998, Barry Black led a Ku Klux Klan rally in Carroll County, Virginia. Twenty-five to thirty people attended this gathering, which occurred on private property with the permission of the owner, who was in attendance.

* * *

When the sheriff of Carroll County learned that a Klan rally was occurring in his county, he went to observe it from the side of the road. During the approximately one hour that the sheriff was present, about 40 to 50 cars passed the site, a "few" of which stopped to ask the sheriff what was happening on the property. Eight to ten houses were located in the vicinity of the rally. Rebecca Sechrist, who was related to the owner of the property where the rally took place, "sat and watched to see wha[t][was] going on" from the lawn of her in-laws' house. She looked on as the Klan prepared for the gathering and subsequently conducted the rally itself.

* * *

At the conclusion of the rally, the crowd circled around a 25- to 30-foot cross. The cross was between 300 and 350 yards away from the road. According to the sheriff, the cross "then all of a sudden . . . went up in a flame." As the cross burned, the Klan played Amazing Grace over the loudspeakers. Sechrist stated that the cross burning made her feel "awful" and "terrible."

When the sheriff observed the cross burning, he informed his deputy that they needed to "find out who's responsible and explain to them that they cannot do this in the State of Virginia." The sheriff then went down the driveway, entered the rally, and asked, "Who was responsible for burning the cross." Black responded, "I guess I am because I'm the head of the rally." The sheriff then told Black, "[T]here's a law in the State of Virginia that you cannot burn a cross and I'll have to place you under arrest for this."

Black was charged with burning a cross with the intent of intimidating a person or group of persons, in violation of § 18.2-423.

* * *

The jury found Black guilty, and fined him $2,500. The Court of Appeals of Virginia affirmed Black's conviction.

On May 2, 1998, respondents Richard Elliott and Jonathan O'Mara, as well as a third individual, attempted to burn a cross on the yard of James Jubilee. Jubilee, an African-American, was Elliott's next-door neighbor in Virginia Beach, Virginia.

* * *

Before the cross burning, Jubilee spoke to Elliott's mother to inquire about shots being fired from behind the Elliott home. Elliott's mother explained to Jubilee that her son shot firearms as

Continued

a hobby, and that he used the backyard as a firing range.

On the night of May 2, respondents drove a truck onto Jubilee's property, planted a cross, and set it on fire. Their apparent motive was to "get back" at Jubilee for complaining about the shooting in the backyard. Respondents were not affiliated with the Klan. The next morning, as Jubilee was pulling his car out of the driveway, he noticed the partially burned cross approximately 20 feet from his house. After seeing the cross, Jubilee was "very nervous" because he "didn't know what would be the next phase," and because "a cross burned in your yard . . . tells you that it's just the first round."

Elliott and O'Mara were charged with attempted cross burning and conspiracy to commit cross burning. O'Mara pleaded guilty to both counts, reserving the right to challenge the constitutionality of the cross-burning statute. The judge sentenced O'Mara to 90 days in jail and fined him $2,500. The judge also suspended 45 days of the sentence and $1,000 of the fine.

* * *

The jury found Elliott guilty of attempted cross burning and acquitted him of conspiracy to commit cross burning. It sentenced Elliott to 90 days in jail and a $2,500 fine. The Court of Appeals of Virginia affirmed the convictions of both Elliott and O'Mara.

Each respondent appealed to the Supreme Court of Virginia, arguing that § 18.2-423 is facially unconstitutional. The Supreme Court of Virginia consolidated all three cases, and held that the statute is unconstitutional on its face. It held that the Virginia cross-burning statute "is analytically indistinguishable" from the ordinance found unconstitutional in *R.A.V.*

* * *

II

Cross burning originated in the 14th century as a means for Scottish tribes to signal each other. Sir Walter Scott used cross burnings for dramatic effect in *The Lady of the Lake,* where the burning cross signified both a summons and a call to arms. Cross burning in this country, however, long ago became unmoored from its Scottish ancestry. Burning a cross in the United States is inextricably intertwined with the history of the Ku Klux Klan.

The first Ku Klux Klan began in Pulaski, Tennessee, in the spring of 1866. Although the Ku Klux Klan started as a social club, it soon changed into something far different. The Klan fought Reconstruction and the corresponding drive to allow freed blacks to participate in the political process. Soon the Klan imposed "a veritable reign of terror" throughout the South. The Klan employed tactics such as whipping, threatening to burn people at the stake, and murder. The Klan's victims included blacks, southern whites who disagreed with the Klan, and "carpetbagger" northern whites.

The activities of the Ku Klux Klan prompted legislative action at the national level. In 1871, "President Grant sent a message to Congress indicating that the Klan's reign of terror in the Southern States had rendered life and property insecure." In response, Congress passed what is now known as the Ku Klux Klan Act. See "An Act to enforce the Provisions of the Fourteenth Amendment to the Constitution of the United States, and for other Purposes," 17 Stat. 13 (now codified at 42 U.S.C. §§ 1983, 1985, and 1986). President Grant used these new powers to suppress the Klan in South Carolina, the effect of which severely curtailed the Klan in other States as well. By the end of Reconstruction in 1877, the first Klan no longer existed.

The genesis of the second Klan began in 1905, with the publication of Thomas Dixon's *The Clansmen: An Historical Romance of the Ku Klux Klan.* Dixon's book was a sympathetic portrait of the first Klan, depicting the Klan as a group of heroes "saving" the South from blacks and the "horrors" of Reconstruction. Although the first Klan never actually practiced cross burning, Dixon's book depicted the Klan burning crosses to celebrate the execution of former slaves. Cross burning thereby became associated with the first Ku Klux Klan. When D.W. Griffith turned Dixon's book into the movie "The Birth of a Nation" in 1915, the association between cross burning and the Klan became indelible. In addition to the cross burnings in the movie, a poster advertising the film displayed a hooded Klansman riding a hooded horse, with his left hand holding the reins of the horse and his right hand holding a burning cross above his head. Soon thereafter, in November 1915, the second Klan began.

From the inception of the second Klan, cross burnings have been used to communicate both threats of violence and messages of shared

Continued

ideology. The first initiation ceremony occurred on Stone Mountain near Atlanta, Georgia. While a 40-foot cross burned on the mountain, the Klan members took their oaths of loyalty. This cross burning was the second recorded instance in the United States. The first known cross burning in the country had occurred a little over one month before the Klan initiation, when a Georgia mob celebrated the lynching of Leo Frank by burning a "gigantic cross" on Stone Mountain that was "visible throughout" Atlanta.

The new Klan's ideology did not differ much from that of the first Klan. As one Klan publication emphasized, "We avow the distinction between [the] races, . . . and we shall ever be true to the faithful maintenance of White Supremacy and will strenuously oppose any compromise thereof in any and all things." Violence was also an elemental part of this new Klan. By September 1921, the New York World newspaper documented 152 acts of Klan violence, including 4 murders, 41 floggings, and 27 tar-and-featherings.

Often, the Klan used cross burnings as a tool of intimidation and a threat of impending violence. For example, in 1939 and 1940, the Klan burned crosses in front of synagogues and churches. After one cross burning at a synagogue, a Klan member noted that if the cross burning did not "shut the Jews up, we'll cut a few throats and see what happens." In Miami in 1941, the Klan burned four crosses in front of a proposed housing project, declaring, "We are here to keep niggers out of your town. . . . When the law fails you, call on us." And in Alabama in 1942, in "a whirlwind climax to weeks of flogging and terror," the Klan burned crosses in front of a union hall and in front of a union leader's home on the eve of a labor election. These cross burnings embodied threats to people whom the Klan deemed antithetical to its goals. And these threats had special force given the long history of Klan violence.

The Klan continued to use cross burnings to intimidate after World War II. In one incident, an African-American "school teacher who recently moved his family into a block formerly occupied only by whites asked the protection of city police . . . after the burning of a cross in his front yard." And after a cross burning in Suffolk, Virginia during the late 1940's, the Virginia Governor stated that he would "not allow any of our people of any race to be subjected to terrorism or intimidation in any form by the Klan or any other organization." These incidents of cross burning, among others, helped prompt Virginia to enact its first version of the cross-burning statute in 1950.

The decision of this Court in *Brown v. Board of Education,* along with the civil rights movement of the 1950's and 1960's, sparked another outbreak of Klan violence. These acts of violence included bombings, beatings, shootings, stabbings, and mutilations. Members of the Klan burned crosses on the lawns of those associated with the civil rights movement, assaulted the Freedom Riders, bombed churches, and murdered blacks as well as whites whom the Klan viewed as sympathetic toward the civil rights movement.

Throughout the history of the Klan, cross burnings have also remained potent symbols of shared group identity and ideology. The burning cross became a symbol of the Klan itself and a central feature of Klan gatherings. According to the Klan constitution (called the kloran), the "fiery cross" was the "emblem of that sincere, unselfish devotedness of all Klansmen to the sacred purpose and principles we have espoused." And the Klan has often published its newsletters and magazines under the name The Fiery Cross.

At Klan gatherings across the country, cross burning became the climax of the rally or the initiation. Posters advertising an upcoming Klan rally often featured a Klan member holding a cross. Typically, a cross burning would start with a prayer by the "Klavern" minister, followed by the singing of Onward Christian Soldiers. The Klan would then light the cross on fire, as the members raised their left arm toward the burning cross and sang The Old Rugged Cross.

Throughout the Klan's history, the Klan continued to use the burning cross in their ritual ceremonies.

For its own members, the cross was a sign of celebration and ceremony. During a joint Nazi-Klan rally in 1940, the proceeding concluded with the wedding of two Klan members who "were married in full Klan regalia beneath a blazing cross." In response to antimasking bills introduced in state legislatures after World War II, the Klan burned crosses in protest. On March 26, 1960, the Klan engaged in rallies and cross burnings throughout the South in an attempt to recruit 10 million members. Later in 1960, the Klan became an issue in the third debate between Richard Nixon and John Kennedy, with both candidates renouncing the Klan. After this debate, the Klan reiterated its support for Nixon

Continued

by burning crosses. And cross burnings featured prominently in Klan rallies when the Klan attempted to move toward more nonviolent tactics to stop integration. In short, a burning cross has remained a symbol of Klan ideology and of Klan unity.

To this day, regardless of whether the message is a political one or whether the message is also meant to intimidate, the burning of a cross is a "symbol of hate." And while cross burning sometimes carries no intimidating message, at other times the intimidating message is the only message conveyed. For example, when a cross burning is directed at a particular person not affiliated with the Klan, the burning cross often serves as a message of intimidation, designed to inspire in the victim a fear of bodily harm. Moreover, the history of violence associated with the Klan shows that the possibility of injury or death is not just hypothetical. The person who burns a cross directed at a particular person often is making a serious threat, meant to coerce the victim to comply with the Klan's wishes unless the victim is willing to risk the wrath of the Klan. Indeed, as the cases of respondents Elliott and O'Mara indicate, individuals without Klan affiliation who wish to threaten or menace another person sometimes use cross burning because of this association between a burning cross and violence.

In sum, while a burning cross does not inevitably convey a message of intimidation, often the cross burner intends that the recipients of the message fear for their lives. And when a cross burning is used to intimidate, few if any messages are more powerful.

III

A

The First Amendment, applicable to the States through the Fourteenth Amendment, provides that "Congress shall make no law . . . abridging the freedom of speech." The hallmark of the protection of free speech is to allow "free trade in ideas"—even ideas that the overwhelming majority of people might find distasteful or discomforting. Thus, the First Amendment "ordinarily" denies a State "the power to prohibit dissemination of social, economic and political doctrine which a vast majority of its citizens believes to be false and fraught with evil consequence." The First Amendment affords protection to symbolic or expressive conduct as well as to actual speech.

The protections afforded by the First Amendment, however, are not absolute, and we have long recognized that the government may regulate certain categories of expression consistent with the Constitution. The First Amendment permits "restrictions upon the content of speech in a few limited areas, which are 'of such slight social value as a step to truth that any benefit that may be derived from them is clearly outweighed by the social interest in order and morality.'"

Thus, for example, a State may punish those words "which by their very utterance inflict injury or tend to incite an immediate breach of the peace." We have consequently held that fighting words—"those personally abusive epithets which, when addressed to the ordinary citizen, are, as a matter of common knowledge, inherently likely to provoke violent reaction"—are generally proscribable under the First Amendment. Furthermore, "the constitutional guarantees of free speech and free press do not permit a State to forbid or proscribe advocacy of the use of force or of law violation except where such advocacy is directed to inciting or producing imminent lawless action and is likely to incite or produce such action." And the First Amendment also permits a State to ban a "true threat."

"True threats" encompass those statements where the speaker means to communicate a serious expression of an intent to commit an act of unlawful violence to a particular individual or group of individuals. The speaker need not actually intend to carry out the threat. Rather, a prohibition on true threats "protect[s] individuals from the fear of violence" and "from the disruption that fear engenders," in addition to protecting people "from the possibility that the threatened violence will occur." Intimidation in the constitutionally proscribable sense of the word is a type of true threat, where a speaker directs a threat to a person or group of persons with the intent of placing the victim in fear of bodily harm or death. Respondents do not contest that some cross burnings fit within this meaning of intimidating speech, and rightly so.

* * *

B

The Supreme Court of Virginia ruled that in light of *R.A.V. v. City of St. Paul, supra,* even if it is constitutional to ban cross burning in a

Continued

content-neutral manner, the Virginia cross-burning statute is unconstitutional because it discriminates on the basis of content and viewpoint. It is true, as the Supreme Court of Virginia held, that the burning of a cross is symbolic expression. The reason why the Klan burns a cross at its rallies, or individuals place a burning cross on someone else's lawn, is that the burning cross represents the message that the speaker wishes to communicate. Individuals burn crosses as opposed to other means of communication because cross burning carries a message in an effective and dramatic manner.

The fact that cross burning is symbolic expression, however, does not resolve the constitutional question. The Supreme Court of Virginia relied upon *R.A.V. v. City of St. Paul, supra,* to conclude that once a statute discriminates on the basis of this type of content, the law is unconstitutional. We disagree.

In *R.A.V.,* we held that a local ordinance that banned certain symbolic conduct, including cross burning, when done with the knowledge that such conduct would " 'arouse anger, alarm or resentment in others on the basis of race, color, creed, religion or gender' " was unconstitutional. We held that the ordinance did not pass constitutional muster because it discriminated on the basis of content by targeting only those individuals who "provoke violence" on a basis specified in the law. The ordinance did not cover "[t]hose who wish to use 'fighting words' in connection with other ideas—to express hostility, for example, on the basis of political affiliation, union membership, or homosexuality." This content-based discrimination was unconstitutional because it allowed the city "to impose special prohibitions on those speakers who express views on disfavored subjects."

We did not hold in *R.A.V.* that the First Amendment prohibits all forms of content-based discrimination within a proscribable area of speech. Rather, we specifically stated that some types of content discrimination did not violate the First Amendment:

"When the basis for the content discrimination consists entirely of the very reason the entire class of speech at issue is proscribable, no significant danger of idea or viewpoint discrimination exists. Such a reason, having been adjudged neutral enough to support exclusion of the entire class of speech from First Amendment

protection, is also neutral enough to form the basis of distinction within the class."

Indeed, we noted that it would be constitutional to ban only a particular type of threat: "[T]he Federal Government can criminalize only those threats of violence that are directed against the President . . . since the reasons why threats of violence are outside the First Amendment . . . have special force when applied to the person of the President." And a State may "choose to prohibit only that obscenity which is the most patently offensive in its prurience—i.e., that which involves the most lascivious displays of sexual activity." Consequently, while the holding of *R.A.V.* does not permit a State to ban only obscenity based on "offensive political messages," or "only those threats against the President that mention his policy on aid to inner cities," the First Amendment permits content discrimination "based on the very reasons why the particular class of speech at issue . . . is proscribable, . . ."

Similarly, Virginia's statute does not run afoul of the First Amendment insofar as it bans cross burning with intent to intimidate. Unlike the statute at issue in *R.A.V.,* the Virginia statute does not single out for opprobrium only that speech directed toward "one of the specified disfavored topics." It does not matter whether an individual burns a cross with intent to intimidate because of the victim's race, gender, or religion, or because of the victim's "political affiliation, union membership, or homosexuality." Moreover, as a factual matter it is not true that cross burners direct their intimidating conduct solely to racial or religious minorities. Indeed, in the case of Elliott and O'Mara, it is at least unclear whether the respondents burned a cross due to racial animus.

The First Amendment permits Virginia to outlaw cross burnings done with the intent to intimidate because burning a cross is a particularly virulent form of intimidation. Instead of prohibiting all intimidating messages, Virginia may choose to regulate this subset of intimidating messages in light of cross burning's long and pernicious history as a signal of impending violence. Thus, just as a State may regulate only that obscenity which is the most obscene due to its prurient content, so too may a State choose to prohibit only those forms of intimidation that are most likely to inspire fear of bodily harm. A ban on cross burning carried out with the intent to intimidate is fully consistent with

Continued

our holding in *R.A.V.* and is proscribable under the First Amendment.

IV

The Supreme Court of Virginia ruled in the alternative that Virginia's cross-burning statute was unconstitutionally overbroad due to its provision stating that "[a]ny such burning of a cross shall be prima facie evidence of an intent to intimidate a person or group of persons." The Commonwealth added the prima facie provision to the statute in 1968. The court below did not reach whether this provision is severable from the rest of the cross-burning statute under Virginia law. See § 1-17.1 In this Court, as in the Supreme Court of Virginia, respondents do not argue that the prima facie evidence provision is unconstitutional as applied to any one of them. Rather, they contend that the provision is unconstitutional on its face.

The Supreme Court of Virginia has not ruled on the meaning of the prima facie evidence provision. It has, however, stated that "the act of burning a cross alone, with no evidence of intent to intimidate, will nonetheless suffice for arrest and prosecution and will insulate the Commonwealth from a motion to strike the evidence at the end of its case-in-chief." The jury in the case of Richard Elliott did not receive any instruction on the prima facie evidence provision, and the provision was not an issue in the case of Jonathan O'Mara because he pleaded guilty. The court in Barry Black's case, however, instructed the jury that the provision means: "The burning of a cross, by itself, is sufficient evidence from which you may infer the required intent." This jury instruction is the same as the Model Jury Instruction in the Commonwealth of Virginia.

The prima facie evidence provision, as interpreted by the jury instruction, renders the statute unconstitutional. Because this jury instruction is the Model Jury Instruction, and because the Supreme Court of Virginia had the opportunity to expressly disavow the jury instruction, the jury instruction's construction of the prima facie provision "is a ruling on a question of state law that is as binding on us as though the precise words had been written into" the statute. As construed by the jury instruction, the prima facie provision strips away the very reason why a State may ban cross burning with the intent to intimidate. The prima facie evidence provision permits a jury to convict in

every cross-burning case in which defendants exercise their constitutional right not to put on a defense. And even where a defendant like Black presents a defense, the prima facie evidence provision makes it more likely that the jury will find an intent to intimidate regardless of the particular facts of the case. The provision permits the Commonwealth to arrest, prosecute, and convict a person based solely on the fact of cross burning itself.

It is apparent that the provision as so interpreted "'would create an unacceptable risk of the suppression of ideas.'" The act of burning a cross may mean that a person is engaging in constitutionally proscribable intimidation. But that same act may mean only that the person is engaged in core political speech. The prima facie evidence provision in this statute blurs the line between these two meanings of a burning cross. As interpreted by the jury instruction, the provision chills constitutionally protected political speech because of the possibility that a State will prosecute—and potentially convict—somebody engaging only in lawful political speech at the core of what the First Amendment is designed to protect.

As the history of cross burning indicates, a burning cross is not always intended to intimidate. Rather, sometimes the cross burning is a statement of ideology, a symbol of group solidarity. It is a ritual used at Klan gatherings, and it is used to represent the Klan itself. Thus, "[b]urning a cross at a political rally would almost certainly be protected expression." Indeed, occasionally a person who burns a cross does not intend to express either a statement of ideology or intimidation. Cross burnings have appeared in movies such as "Mississippi Burning", and in plays such as the stage adaptation of Sir Walter Scott's *The Lady of the Lake.*

The prima facie provision makes no effort to distinguish among these different types of cross burnings. It does not distinguish between a cross burning done with the purpose of creating anger or resentment and a cross burning done with the purpose of threatening or intimidating a victim. It does not distinguish between a cross burning at a public rally or a cross burning on a neighbor's lawn. It does not treat the cross burning directed at an individual differently from the cross burning directed at a group of likeminded believers. It allows a jury to treat a cross burning on the property of another with the owner's acquiescence in the same manner as a

Continued

cross burning on the property of another without the owner's permission. To this extent I agree with Justice SOUTER that the prima facie evidence provision can "skew jury deliberations toward conviction in cases where the evidence of intent to intimidate is relatively weak and arguably consistent with a solely ideological reason for burning." It may be true that a cross burning, even at a political rally, arouses a sense of anger or hatred among the vast majority of citizens who see a burning cross. But this sense of anger or hatred is not sufficient to ban all cross burnings. As Gerald Gunther has stated, "The lesson I have drawn from my childhood in Nazi Germany and my happier adult life in this country is the need to walk the sometimes difficult path of denouncing the bigot's hateful ideas with all my power, yet at the same time challenging any community's attempt to suppress hateful ideas by force of law." The prima facie evidence provision in this case ignores all of the contextual factors that are necessary to decide whether a particular cross burning is intended to intimidate. The First Amendment does not permit such a shortcut.

For these reasons, the prima facie evidence provision, as interpreted through the jury instruction and as applied in Barry Black's case, is unconstitutional on its face. We recognize that the Supreme Court of Virginia has not authoritatively interpreted the meaning of the prima facie evidence provision. Unlike Justice SCALIA, we refuse to speculate on whether any interpretation of the prima facie evidence provision would satisfy the First Amendment. Rather, all we hold is that because of the interpretation of the prima facie evidence provision given by the jury instruction, the provision makes the statute facially invalid at this point. We also recognize the theoretical possibility that the court, on remand, could interpret the provision in a manner different from that so far set forth in order to avoid the constitutional objections we have described. We leave open that possibility. We also leave open the possibility that the provision is severable, and if so, whether Elliott and O'Mara could be retried under § 18.2-423.

V

With respect to Barry Black, we agree with the Supreme Court of Virginia that his conviction cannot stand, and we affirm the judgment of the Supreme Court of Virginia. With respect to Elliott and O'Mara, we vacate the judgment of the Supreme Court of Virginia, and remand the case for further proceedings.

It is so ordered.

The Court in this opinion distinguishes between its decision in *R.A.V.* and this case. The Court agreed that the cross burning is symbolic expression, however, this is not the only determining factor to be considered in determining the constitutionality of a statute. The Court noted that the statute in *R.A.V.* was unconstitutional because it allowed the city of St. Paul to impose restrictions on certain types of speech based on the fact that the speech involved unpopular political subjects. However, the First Amendment does not prohibit the state from outlawing cross burning that is done with the intent to intimidate a particular individual or group when the type of intimidation that it is prohibiting has the history of signaling impending violence.

Neither the result in *Virginia v. Black* nor *R.A.V.* invalidate those laws that provided for enhanced penalties based on defendants' motives. In *Wisconsin v. Mitchell*,[50] the Court ruled on the speech and conduct distinction to uphold an enhanced penalty statute.

Pursuant to a state statute that provided longer maximum sentences for offenses where the accused intentionally selected a victim based on race, religion, color, disability, sexual orientation, national origin, or ancestry, Mitchell was sentenced to an enhanced term for his conviction for aggravated battery. His conviction arose from encouraging a group of African American males to attack a young white boy. The group beat the boy severely, rendering him unconscious, and then stole his sneakers. Mitchell challenged the conviction on the ground that the enhanced penalty violated his First Amendment rights. A unanimous Court rejected his claim finding that the statute was not aimed at speech protected by the First Amendment. Moreover, the statute was aimed at conduct rather than speech. The Court noted that the statute was aimed at redressing societal harm and extended beyond disagreement with an accused's beliefs—it focused on the way one acted upon those beliefs.

The ruling in *R.A.V.* has had an impact on university codes that sought to eliminate speech that was harassing or insulting to others on the basis of categories. Where public universities are concerned *R.A.V.* must be seen to limit those codes aimed at preventing this speech. The most significant effect of *R.A.V.* is that the Court has now provided some measure of protection for speech that has been considered to fall within a restricted category. It imposes a requirement that states must act in a content-neutral manner for previously unprotected speech. The possible results of limiting speech can fly in the face of the policy of open debate. Consequences can include such speech going underground where it cannot be met and challenged; and a chilling effect on speech in general when citizens are afraid that what they say may be subject to penalties. Nevertheless, the Court has not completely abandoned the distinction between forms of speech, making it apparent that some speech is more valuable than others.[51]

OBSCENITY

The Court has also been asked to determine whether speech that is labeled obscene is entitled to First Amendment protection. In the first of these cases, *Roth v. United States,*[52] the court considered the issue in depth. The protagonists offered two very different arguments to the Court.

Roth, who was convicted of violating federal and state obscenity laws for sending out circulars advertising an obscene book, urged the Court to find that obscene speech could not be punished unless it was found to present a clear and present danger. There was no evidence of danger as required by the clear and present danger standard. Roth also argued that obscene thoughts were not a subject that was within the legitimate province of the legislature. On the other hand the government argued that the Court should employ a balancing test that considered the value of the speech involved.

The Court held that obscenity was not a protected category of speech but also ruled that First Amendment concerns limited what could legitimately be considered obscene. In *Roth* the Court set out the first of its definitions of obscenity. Obscene material was defined as that which the "average person, applying contemporary community standards [would find] the dominant theme of the material, taken as a whole, appeals to [one's] prurient interest."[53] The Court went on to define "prurient" as material "having the tendency to excite lustful thoughts."[54] Having set these limits, the Court then distinguished between obscenity and material that had redeeming social value. Included in this second category was the "portrayal of sex . . . in art, literature and scientific works."[55] While the Court indicated that materials falling within this second category were protected under the First Amendment, it did not make clear what was to be done when work had some redeeming social value and also fell within the definition of prurient.

Following *Roth* the Court was presented with numerous cases in which it was asked to decide whether particular materials fell within the case's dictates. The Court continued in its attempt to provide specific guidelines for what could be punished as obscene within the confines of the First Amendment. Yet it failed to provide a standard that legislatures could consistently apply leaving the Court in the position of deciding on a case-by-case basis whether material could constitutionally be punished. For a period of time in the 1950s and 1960s the members of the Court spent a good deal of time viewing films to determine whether they were obscene and could, therefore, be legitimately suppressed. It was during this period that Justice Steward declared "I know it [obscenity] when I see it. . . ."[56] However, no agreement on rationale emerged form these cases until 1973 when the Court decided *Miller v. California*.[57]

In *Miller,* five members of the Court agreed on a three-part test that would allow for the identification of material that could be prohibited as obscene. *Miller* required that the "average person, applying contemporary community standards" would conclude that "the work, taken as a whole, appeals to prurient interest."[58] Further, the contested material had to "depict[ ] or describe[ ], in a patently offensive way, sexual conduct specifically defined by the applicable state law" and which lacks "serious literary, artistic, political or scientific value."[59] All three parts of the test must be satisfied to allow the government to ban material.

The Court made it clear that material was to be judged by local community standards. This means that something which might be acceptable in more sophisticated metropolitan areas (for example, New York City or San Francisco) might be controlled in a smaller, rural community. *Miller* also limited a state's ability to ban material only to the extent that is was considered "hard core" sexual conduct. States were required to be specific about what could be banned in order to give fair notice and prevent a chilling effect on speech.

The Court included several examples of materials that could be banned in order to minimize any confusion in legislatures. Here, the Court employed a "patently offensive" standard. Despite this seemingly broad guideline, the Court placed limits on local communities' ability to interpret this standard and the prurient interest standard. It would not be permissible to employ a concept of "lust" that included "only normal, healthy sexual desires."[60]

In its continuing efforts to set limits of First Amendment protection or lack thereof for obscene materials, the Court went beyond mere definition to look at other relevant issues. In *Stanley v. Georgia*[61] the Court ruled that the simple possession of obscene materials by an adult could not constitutionally be criminalized. In essence, the Court applied a balancing test that weighed the state's interest in controlling private possession of obscenity against the individual's interest in having such materials. The Court found that the state's interest was weak, but the citizen's interest in avoiding control of his or her thoughts was considerably stronger. The Court stated this quite forcefully, noting that "if the First Amendment means anything, it means that the State has no business telling a man, sitting alone in his own house what books he may read or what films he may watch."[62] *Stanley,* did, however, place one limit on citizens' rights to possess obscene material. The Court allowed that states had an interest in preventing possession of **child pornography**. Consequently, states could constitutionally criminalize possession of such materials.[63] This determination is part of the Court's continued policy of protecting children from **pornography**.

The Court is concerned about two particular dangers associated with child pornography. First is the danger that children may read, view, or listen to pornography. Second is the concern that children may be induced to participate in sexual conduct to be filmed for pornographic films and photographs.

In regard to the first concern, the Court has found that a state may prohibit the distribution of sexually explicit material to children even if these materials would not be obscene if distributed to an adult.[64] Some First Amendment protection is arguably retained by the publisher in distributing these materials but that interest may be outweighed by the state's compelling interest in protecting minors. Nevertheless, the state must not exercise its compelling interest in a way that substantially impairs adult access to the forbidden materials.[65]

As to the second legitimate state interest, that of ensuring that children are not used to create child pornography, the state is given wider control of material depicting children engaged in sexual conduct. States may ban the distribution of these materials even through they may not fall within the definition of legal obscenity. In *New York v. Ferber,*[66] the Court found the state had a

child pornography pornography showing children engaged in sexual activity.

pornography depicting sexual behavior to cause sexual excitement. Nonobscene pornography is protected by the First Amendment, but child pornography is not.

"compelling interest" in preventing sexual exploitation and abuse of children in producing these materials.

The Court, in recent years, has been asked to place more regulation on pornography on the grounds that pornography promotes the degradation and subordination of women. Feminists groups have advocated for antipornography ordinances around the country and have been successful in some cities. The ordinances make a distinction between materials that subordinate and degrade women.

The Seventh Circuit Court of Appeals in *American Booksellers Assoc., Inc. v. Hudnut* considered the Indianapolis ordinance.[67] The ordinance treated pornography as a practice that discriminated against women and was to be treated as other forms of discrimination. Pornography was defined as "graphic sexually explicit subordination of women" and included the presentation of women as "sexual objects."[68] The appellate court found the ordinance was not content-neutral and stated

> *We do not try to balance the arguments for and against an ordinance such as this. The ordinance discriminates on the ground of the content of the speech. Speech treating women in the approved way—in sexual encounters 'premised on equality'—is lawful no matter how sexually explicit. Speech treating women in the disapproved way—as submissive in matters sexual or as enjoying humiliation—is unlawful no matter how significant the literary, artistic, or political qualities of the work taken as a whole. The state may not ordain preferred viewpoints in this way. The Constitution forbids the state to declare one perspective right and silence opponents.[69]*

Accordingly, the ordinance was struck down. The Supreme Court summarily affirmed the Seventh Circuit's decision[70] signaling its agreement that such ordinances are unconstitutional.

The Court's concern with obscenity has not ended here. There are other issues surrounding the regulation of obscenity that have been considered by the Court. The Court revisited the community standards question in *Jenkins v. Georgia*[71] and *Hamling v. United States*.[72] The Court rejected the argument that standards of determining patently offensive materials should be statewide. The Court indicated that a town standard might be the relevant community in determining whether the materials fall within the category of those that may be regulated. The implication of this is that national distribution may open a publisher to prosecution if the materials pass through an area where they may be considered patently offensive. This is because the Court has ruled that a government may criminalize the mailing of obscene materials even to consenting adults.[73] The Court reasoned that *Stanley* did not provide any right to acquire obscene materials. Rather, it was limited to freedom of thought and the privacy of one's home.

The value of a work is not determined in reference to community standards, however. In such cases, the applicable standard is whether a reasonable person would find that the work, as a whole, has social value.[74] The way in which the work is advertised may be considered in determining whether it appeals primarily to **prurient interest**. Works marketed to underline a sexually provocative nature are considered pandering and, consequently, may constitute obscene materials. The result is that such materials may not be distributed through the mails.[75]

prurient interest   a shameful or obsessive interest in immoral or sexual things.

The Court has also imposed some particular procedural rules in obscenity cases providing additional protection for freedom of expression while at the same time indicating that obscene materials warrant less protection than other types of expression. The Court has been antagonistic to regulations that constitute a prior restraint on expression. In obscenity cases, the Court has curbed this antagonism allowing some measure of prior restraint and it is in these cases that procedural rules are important. In cases dealing with film licensing requirements, the film must be submitted to an official censor before it may be exhibited. The Court has ruled that these requirements will not be struck down merely because they constitute a prior restraint.[76] These provisions must, however, include certain procedural safeguards to protect First Amendment rights of the exhibitor and future audience. In *Freedman v. Maryland,*[77] the Court set forth these requirements that include the following:

- The burden of proof must be on the government
- The administrative agency must act within a time period specified by the regulation
- That time period must be brief
- Denial of a license may not become effective unless the administration goes to court for an injunction
- A court hearing on an injunction application must also be decided within a short time.

These requirements are applicable in dealing with films. In the case of printed material, an injunction may also be sought. If procedural safeguards are adhered to, no First Amendment violation will be found even though the procedure constitutes a prior restraint.[78] The Court reasons that this will have a smaller chilling effect than a criminal proceeding.

Finally, the Court has found that the seller of obscene works must be shown to have knowledge of the contents of the material before being convicted.[79] This does not mean, however, that the seller knew the materials, as a matter of law, were obscene. Thus, the Court has acted to limit the chilling effect on materials prior to a determination that they are obscene.

DEFAMATION AND INVASION OF PRIVACY

For most of our history the Supreme Court took the position that defamatory language was unprotected by the First Amendment. Thus, it was an area that could be regulated by each state without interference from the federal courts. The Supreme Court in *Beauharnais v. Illinois* made the exclusion of defamation from First Amendment protection clear.[80]

At issue was a statute that proscribed the public exhibition of publications that portrayed "depravity, criminality, unchastity or lack of virtue of a class of citizens of any race, color, creed or religion" that would open those citizens to "contempt, derision, or obloquy or which is productive of breach of the peace or riots."[81] Petitioners to the Supreme Court were convicted under this statute for distributing a leaflet, which called for Chicago city officials to stop the "invasion" of African Americans into white neighborhoods, and declared that

> *if persuasion and the need to prevent the white race from becoming mongrelized by the negro [sic] will not unite us, then the aggressions . . . rapes, robberies, knives, guns and marijuana of the negro [sic], surely will.*[82]

The Supreme Court, in a 5 to 4 decision, indicated that states could define libel in any way they wished within the confines of the federal Constitution. In the instant case that meant that even groups could be considered victims. The only limit that was placed upon the states was that the definition of libel must be related to the state's "peace and well-being."[83] The dissenters maintained that such an extension of libel law impeded First Amendment expression in those cases where there was no clear and present danger resulting from the libel. Some 12 years after *Beauharnais* the Court was asked to revisit the libel question.

In *New York Times v. Sullivan,*[84] the newspaper was being sued by Alabama officials for having run an advertisement that stated that Montgomery police had attempted to terrorize Martin Luther King and his followers. Some of the statements in the advertisement were untrue.

Alabama's libel law provided for strict liability. This meant that a publisher could not avoid liability if he reasonably believed the statements were true even if they were, in fact, untrue. No liability would attach if the statement was true but it was the publisher's burden to prove that this was the case. Thus, despite the fact that the errors in the advertisement were minor and there was no showing at trial that the *New York Times* knew or should have known that there were untruths in the ad, the *Times* was found liable.

The Supreme Court reversed the judgment against the *Times* and in doing so made state libel laws subject to First Amendment principles. To reach this decision, the Court viewed the case as one in which the issue was about government criticism. Clearly, the First Amendment was designed to insure citizens the ability to criticize the government and to engage in public debate. Consequently, if those seeking to engage in debate and to criticize government action were required to guarantee the truth of their claims, debate would be constrained. There would, in effect, be a chilling effect on speech that was intended to be protected. The Court enunciated a standard that would serve as a guide to speakers in circumstances similar to those in *Sullivan*. **Public figures** would be unable to recover damages for libel when falsehoods relating to official conduct were made unless it could be proven that the statement was "made with knowledge that it was false" or "with reckless disregard of whether it was false or not."[85] If the statement fell within either of these two categories, it was considered to have been made with "actual malice" and would then subject the publisher to liability.[86]

> **public figure** anyone who is famous (or infamous) for what he or she has done or who has come forward to take part in a public controversy.

Not long after the Court's decision in *Sullivan*, the standard was modified. While the *Sullivan* standard was applicable in cases involving public officials, *Curtis Publishing Co. v. Butts*[87] and *Associated Press v. Walker*[88] extended the standard to public figures. Over time, the Court supplied a narrow definition of public figure. Public figures could be persons who fell within one of three categories.

First, a public figure is one who has "general fame and notoriety in the community."[89] These individuals are considered public figures for all purposes. Second, public figures are those who have "voluntarily injected themselves into a public controversy in order to influence the resolution of the issues involved."[90] Individuals who fall into this category are public figures only with regard to the issue from which the controversy arises. The third category includes those who are "involuntarily public figures."[91] The Court has narrowly construed the class of those falling within this involuntary category.

The requirements of *Sullivan* are not applicable to private figures. An individual who is neither a public official nor a public figure does not have to prove that the defendant acted with actual malice. In such situations the state can set the standard at any one of three levels—(1) negligence, (2) recklessness, or (3) knowing falsity. Strict liability, however, cannot be the standard since it violates First Amendment guarantees. The Court reached this conclusion in *Gertz v. Robert Welch*.[92] There the Court reasoned that private citizens are more entitled to protection and more deserving of recovery. This is because private citizens have limited access to media to remedy damage to their reputations incurred by false statements and do not voluntary place themselves in a position of risk of such statements as do public figures and public officials. The Court also made it clear in *Gertz* that damages in such cases would be limited to actual injury. It did, however, define actual injury broadly. Actual injury would include "impairment of reputation," "personal humiliation," and "mental anguish and suffering."[93]

Sullivan has since been held to apply to actions where an individual sues for intentional infliction of emotional distress. In *Hustler Magazine v. Falwell*,[94] the Court ruled that a public figure or public official could recover damages if a publisher caused distress only when it could be proved that the statement was false or made with reckless disregard of its falsity.

The Court found that an advertisement that portrayed the Reverend Jerry Falwell as a drunken hypocrite was a parody and would not support an award for intentional infliction of emotional distress consistently with the First Amendment. Rather, the Court found that the First Amendment protected political parody and that it could not distinguish between this publication and political speech that was protected. Thus, political speech was given primacy over harm resulting to a political official or public figure by its publication.

Issues similar to these in defamation actions are also raised in claims against the media for invasion of privacy. One concern in deciding these cases is the extent to which the standards of *Sullivan* and *Gertz* are applicable. The issues raised most often in these cases are known as "false light" actions. In such cases, the individual claims that she or he has been presented in public in a misleading way and that such presentation will be highly offensive to the reasonable person. These actions are different from defamation cases because it is not necessary for the plaintiff to demonstrate that her or his reputation has been damaged. All that is necessary is for the plaintiff to show that there has been substantial misstatement of the facts. In cases where a public figure or public official sues for invasion of privacy it appears that the *Sullivan* standard is still applicable.

COMMERCIAL SPEECH

Commercial speech has traditionally fallen within the categories of unprotected speech. As the Court has extended limited protection to such areas as obscenity and libel over time, so too has it included commercial speech. In fact, commercial speech has received the greatest protection of the traditionally unprotected categories.

As has been apparent with the areas of libel and obscenity, the change has concerned definitions. Before the 1970s, once speech met the definition of commercial then the government was free to regulate without any concern for First Amendment principles. Today, commercial speech is deemed to have some First Amendment protection. The exception is speech that misleads or encourages illegal transactions. While some First Amendment protection has been extended to commercial speech, it is important to keep in mind that this protection is not as extensive as that afforded to political speech that is considered to be at the core of First Amendment guarantees.

Traditionally commercial advertising was precluded from any protection. This allowed the government to regulate it the same way as any business activity.[95] As was clear from *Sullivan* this approach was problematic. Despite the fact that the offending speech in that case was part of a paid advertisement, because it was political in nature, the Court ruled that it was entitled to First Amendment protection.

The Court confronted this problem in *Virginia Pharmacy Board v. Virginia Consumer Council.*[96] The Virginia legislature passed a statute that made advertising prescription drug prices unprofessional conduct. Pharmacists violating the statute could lose their licenses or have them revoked. The Consumer Council argued that the advertisement was outside the protection of the First Amendment because it was commercial speech. The Court rejected the argument even though it accepted the fact that the speech was purely commercial in nature. The Court reasoned that society had a strong interest in the "free flow of commercial information."[97] The Court went on to employ a balancing test weighing the consumers' interest against the state interest. Poor consumers had a compelling interest in learning who charged how much for drugs. Against this interest, the Court weighed the state's asserted interest in maintaining a high degree of professionalism by pharmacies. The State claimed that without the ban aggressive price competition would result, so, in order to protect consumers, prices could not be advertised. In essence, the

State's argument was that it was necessary to keep consumers ignorant. The Court emphatically rejected this position, stating that

> [w]hat is at issue is whether a State may completely suppress the dissemination of concededly truthful information about entirely lawful activity, fearful of that information's effect upon its disseminators and recipients. [W]e conclude that the answer to this one [question] is in the negative."[98]

It can be inferred from the decision that the protection guaranteed was not coextensive with other types of speech. Commercial speech that is false or deceptive may, consistently with the First Amendment, be regulated by the states. Justice Rehnquist, the sole dissenter, argued that the First Amendment was designed to protect political speech and was not, therefore, applicable to commercial speech.

The Court applied the *Virginia Pharmacy* reasoning that the state could not consistently ban speech because it might harm the audience in *Linmark Associates Inc. v. Willingboro*.[99] In response to fears of "white flight," the town council passed an ordinance that banned "For Sale" signs. In a unanimous decision the Court rejected the town's argument that the ordinance was necessary to prevent citizens from acting irrationally. It found that the government did not establish the necessity of this measure to ensure an integrated community. Moreover, the Court found that the ordinance, which only banned "For Sale" signs, was not content-neutral.

First Amendment protection of commercial speech was also extended to regulation of the means by which attorneys acquire clients. Traditionally lawyers have been prevented from actively soliciting clients. A challenge to this policy came before the Supreme Court in *Bates v. State Bar of Arizona*.[100] There, the Court ruled that states might not prohibit all newspaper advertising of legal services. The Court has also considered whether lawyers could be prevented from engaging in in-person solicitation of clients. The Court found that such solicitation engaged in for monetary gain, more commonly known as "ambulance chasing," could be proscribed.[101] However, the Court has indicated that some in-person solicitation will be allowed. In *Edenfield v. Fane*,[102] the Court struck down Florida's ban on direct, in-person, uninvited solicitation of business owners by Certified Public Accountants, but has yet to extend this ruling to attorneys.

While *Virginia Pharmacy* opened some commercial speech to First Amendment protection, it should not be read too broadly. In subsequent cases, the Court has indicated that commercial speech is not entitled to the full panoply of protections, as is the case for more core aspects of speech. In *Ohralik v. Ohio*,[103] the Court noted that commercial speech is only entitled to a "limited measure of protection, commensurate with its subordinate position in the scale of First Amendment values. . . ."[104] And, in *Central Hudson Gas v. Public Service Commission*,[105] the Court set forth a test to be employed in determining whether a regulation of commercial speech violates the First Amendment.

Under the test in *Central Hudson*, courts must proceed in the following manner to reach a determination. Initially, a determination must be made as to whether the commercial speech at issue is entitled to any First Amendment protection. If the speech is misleading or concerns illegal activity it is not deserving of any protection. Next, a court must look to whether the asserted government interest is substantial. Only if the interest meets this criterion may a court go on to the next two parts. If the government interest is deemed substantial, a court will then consider the question of whether the regulation advances the asserted government interest. If it does, the court then goes on to the fourth and final consideration. A court must then determine whether the regulation is narrowly tailored to the government interest. This final prong has been modified to require only that the regulation be reasonably tailored to meet the government interest. In sum, today commercial speech that is entitled to First Amendment protection can be regulated in a content-neutral manner if the state can demonstrate that the regulation directly advances a substantial government interest in a manner that is reasonably tailored to achieve that interest.

The First Amendment provides no protection to misleading or deceptive commercial speech. Nor is any protection afforded to commercial speech proposing illegal transactions. Similarly, advertising promoting unlawful products can be regulated. The question then arises whether advertisement of legal but harmful products may be regulated. Addressing a Rhode Island statute that prohibited all advertising of liquor prices, a unanimous Court agreed that the statute could not stand. The Court's members, however, could not agree on the rationale for that conclusion. In *44 Liquormart v. Rhode Island*,[106] most of the Court did agree that the statute could not pass the fourth prong of *Central Hudson*. Justice Stevens went further, indicating that a stricter test could be used, but this position did not gain majority support. Justice Thomas advocated giving commercial speech the same protection as political speech but found no other supporters for his stance. Since then the Court has indicated that the power to regulate particular conduct does not necessarily include the power to regulate speech about that conduct.[107]

Currently, the state's justification for regulating lawful but harmful products will determine the standard to be employed. If the government's justification is that the regulation will limit consumption of the product, it must demonstrate the regulation "significantly reduces consumption and no means that are significantly less intrusive can be employed."[108] This is a difficult test to meet because the government has the ability to tax as well as to regulate how and where a product can be sold. Where the government seeks to justify the limitation as a means of preventing minors from gaining access to the product, the government must tailor its methods so as to prevent undue interference with the rights of adults to obtain the product. This is necessary because we do not want a society that treats all its citizens as if they were children.

Summary

There are five areas of speech that traditionally were considered unprotected by the First Amendment's free expression guarantees. The underlying reason for this is that these areas were not considered to be central to the free exchange of ideas.

The first of these areas is the advocacy of illegal conduct. In such cases, the courts will generally consider three factors in determining whether government regulation is appropriate. Initially, the court will ask whether the perceived illegality (e.g., a riot) is imminent. Only if the answer to this question is yes, may the speech or conduct be punished. Next, the court will inquire into whether the speech or conduct was intended to produce the illegality. If there was no intention to produce an illegality then the speech may not be punished. The last question for the court is whether the speech or conduct is likely to produce the illegality. If the speaker's efforts are ineffectual then punishment does not follow.

The second area of speech traditionally considered unprotected is fighting words—those words that by their very nature are likely to result in an act of violence on the part of those to whom they are addressed. The government can prohibit such words or punish them once they have been uttered. In situations where fighting words are employed, it is the responsibility of the police to control the crowd if they can and to protect the speaker. Further, simply because listeners may find speech offensive, does not mean that the speech may be forbidden. A distinction is drawn between fighting words and offensive speech.

The third traditional area of unprotected speech is obscenity. The relevant standard in determining what obscene speech and conduct may be regulated is the particular community standard. Moreover, a court must consider whether that standard applies when the work is considered as a whole, in light of its artistic, scientific, or political merit. Possession of obscene material may not be punished, but the sale of such material may be.

Defamation has also been considered to be unprotected by First Amendment expression guarantees. Today, when the government regulates defamation, some First Amendment limits do apply. Public officials and public figures may recover only if they can demonstrate that the statements about them were made with knowledge of their falsity or reckless disregard of truth or falsity.

Finally, there is the area of commercial speech. Commercial speech is that related to a sale or commercial transaction. When the speech is truthful and does not propose an illegal act, the courts will apply a mid-level scrutiny. The government's regulation will be upheld if a substantial government interest is directly advanced in a manner that is no more expansive than necessary. The government may prohibit false or deceptive speech as well as that which proposes illegal transactions.

Today the lines between protected and unprotected speech have been blurred. They are no longer as clear-cut as they were at the beginning—or even the middle—of the twentieth century.

Key Terms

advocacy

child pornography

clear and present danger test

commercial speech

defamation

fighting words

obscene

pornography

prurient interest

public figure

Review Questions

1. What reasons support a hierarchy of speech protection? What categories of speech were traditionally unprotected by the First Amendment expression guarantees?

2. What distinction does the Court currently draw between protected and unprotected speech in its analyses of these cases?

3. What tests has the Court employed in determining which political speech is unprotected by First Amendment guarantees? Describe each in terms of what speech is precluded by each of these tests.

4. What is the Court's test for obscenity? How has it changed over time? What interpretations have the Court put on its definition with regard to community standards?

5. What test does the Court apply in defamation cases and what does it require the plaintiff to demonstrate? Explain the difference in standards for public officials, public figures, and private figures?

Internet Connections

For more information on the question of protected and unprotected speech, you can visit the following sites:

The First Amendment Lawyers Association at *http://www.fala.org.*

The Thomas Jefferson Center for the Protection of Free Expression at *http://www.tjcenter.org.*

The American Civil Liberties Union at *http://www.aclu.org.*

End Notes

[1]*Brandenburg v. Ohio*, 395 U.S. 444 (1969).

[2]*Schenck v. United States*, 249 U.S. 47 (1919).

[3]*Id.* at 52.

[4]*Frohwerk v. United States*, 249 U.S. 204 (1919).

[5]*Debs v. United States*, 249 U.S. 211 (1919).

[6]*Abrams v. United States*, 250 U.S. 616 (1919).

[7]Sec.3, tit. 1 (as amended, 40 Stat. 553).

[8]*Abrams v. United States*, 250 U.S. at 621 (1919).

[9]*Id.* at 627.

[10]*Id.* at 630.

[11]*Id.* at 630.

[12]*Id.* at 630.

[13]*Masses Publishing Co. v. Patten,* 244 F. 535 (S.D.N.Y. 1917).

[14]*Gitlow v. New York,* 268 U.S. 652 (1925).

[15]*Id.* at 670.

[16]*Id.* at 673.

[17]*Whitney v. California,* 274 U.S. 357 (1927).

[18]*Id.* at 377.

[19]18 U.S.C. § 2385.

[20]*Dennis v. United States,* 341 U.S. 494 (1951).

[21]*Id.* at 510.

[22]*Yates v. United States,* 354 U.S. 298 (1957).

[23]*Scales v. United States,* 367 U.S. 203 (1961).

[24]*Brandenburg v. Ohio,* 395 U.S. 444 (1969).

[25]*Id.* at 447.

[26]*Watts v. United States,* 394 U.S. 705 (1969).

[27]*Id.* at 706.

[28]*Id.* at 705.

[29]*Bond v. Floyd,* 385 U.S. 116 (1966).

[30]*Hess v. Indiana,* 414 U.S. 105 (1973).

[31]*NAACP v. Claiborne Hardware Company,* 458 U.S. 886 (1982).

[32]*Id.* at 928.

[33]*Chaplinsky v. New Hampshire,* 315 U.S. 568 (1942).

[34]*Id.* at 569.

[35]*Id.* at 572.

[36]*Id.* at 572.

[37]*Terminello v. Chicago,* 337 U.S. 1 (1949).

[38]*Cox v. Alabama,* 379 U.S. 536 (1965).

[39]*Edwards v. South Carolina,* 372 U.S. 229 (1963).

[40]*Garner v. Louisiana,* 368 U.S. 157 (1961).

[41]*Feiner v. New York,* 340 U.S. 315 (1951).

[42]*Id.* at 320–321.

[43]*Cohen v. California,* 403 U.S. 15 (1971).

[44]*Collin v. Smith,* 578 F.2d 1197 (7th Cir. 1978).

[45]*http://www.skokiehistory.info/chrono/nazis.html; http://www.lib.niu.edu/ipo*

[46]*United States v. Playboy Entertainment Group, Inc.,* 529 U.S. 803 (2000).

[47]*R.A.V. v. City of St. Paul,* 505 U.S. 377 (1992).

[48]*Id.* at 379.

[49]*Virginia v. Black,* 538 U.S. 343 (2003).

[50]*Wisconsin v. Mitchell,* 508 U.S. 476 (1993).

[51]*Young v. American Mini Theaters, Inc.,* 427 U.S. 50 (1976).

[52]*Roth v. United States,* 354 U.S. 476 (1957).

[53]*Id.* at 489.

[54]*Id.* at 489.

[55]*Id.* at 489.

[56]*Jacobellis v. Ohio,* 378 U.S. 184 (1964).

[57]*Miller v. California,* 413 U.S. 15 (1973).

[58]*Id.* at 24–25.

[59]*Id.* at 24–25.

[60]*Brockett v. Spokane Arcades, Inc.,* 472 U.S. 491 (1985).

[61]*Stanley v. Georgia,* 394 U.S. 557 (1969).

[62]*Id.* at 565.

[63]*Osborne v. Ohio,* 495 U.S. 103 (1990).

[64]*Ginsburg v. New York,* 390 U.S. 629 (1968).

[65]*Ashcroft v. The Free Speech Coalition,* 535 U.S. 234 (2002).

[66]*New York v. Ferber,* 458 U.S. 747 (1982).

[67]*American Booksellers Assoc., Inc. v. Hudnut,* 771 F.2d 323 (7th Cir. 1985).

[68]*Id.* at 324.

[69]*Id.* at 325.

[70]*American Booksellers Assoc., Inc. v. Hudnut,* 475 U.S. 1001 (1986).

[71]*Jenkins v. Georgia,* 418 U.S. 153 (1974).

[72]*Hamling v. United States,* 418 U.S. 87 (1974).

[73]*Stanley v. Reidel,* 402 U.S. 351 (1971).

[74]*Pope v. Illinois,* 481 U.S. 497 (1987).

[75]*Ginzburg v. United States,* 383 U.S. 463 (1966).

[76]*Times Film Corp. v. Chicago,* 365 U.S. 43 (1961).

[77]*Freedman v. Maryland,* 380 U.S. 51 (1965).

[78]*Kingsley Books v. Brown,* 354 U.S. 436 (1957).

[79]*Smith v. California,* 361 U.S. 147 (1959).

[80]*Beauharnais v. Illinois,* 343 U.S. 250 (1952).

[81]*Id.* at 251.

[82]*Id.* at 252.

[83]*Id.* at 258.

[84]*New York Times v. Sullivan,* 376 U.S. 254 (1964).

[85]*Id.* at 54–55.

[86]*Id.* at 55.

[87]*Curtis Publishing Co. v. Butts,* 388 U.S. 130 (1967).

[88]*Associated Press v. Walker,* 389 U.S. 28 (1967).

[89]*Id.* at 30.

[90]*Id.* at 31.

[91]*Gertz v. Robert Welch,* 418 U.S. 323 (1974). *See* n.87.

[92]*Id.* at 350.

[93]*Id.* at 352.

[94]*Hustler Magazine v. Falwell,* 485 U.S. 46 (1988).

[95]*Valentine v. Christensen,* 316 U.S. 52 (1942).

[96]*Virginia Pharmacy Board v. Virginia Consumer Council,* 425 U.S. 748 (1976).

[97]*Id.* at 765.

[98]*Id.* at 773.

[99]*Linmark Associates Inc. v. Willingboro,* 431 U.S. 85 (1977).

[100]*Bates v. State Bar of Arizona,* 433 U.S. 353 (1977).

[101]*Ohralik v. Ohio State Bar Ass'n,* 436 U.S. 447 (1978).

[102]*Edenfield v. Fain,* 307 U.S. 761 (1993).

[103]*Bates v. State Bar of Arizona,* 433 U.S. 353 (1977).

[104]*Id.* at 456.

[105]*Central Hudson Gas v. Public Service Commission,* 447 U.S. 557 (1980).

[106]*44 Liquormart v. Rhode Island,* 517 U.S. 484 (1996).

[107]*Id.* at 527–528.

[108]*Greater New Orleans Broadcasting Ass'n, Inc. v. United States,* 527 U.S. 173 (1999).

 For additional resources, go to *http://www.westlegalstudies.com*

FREEDOM OF ASSOCIATION

"It is beyond debate that freedom to engage in association for the advancement of beliefs and ideas is an inseparable aspect of the 'liberty' assured by the Due Process Clause of the Fourteenth Amendment . . ."

—*Justice John M. Harlan II*
National Association for the Advancement of Colored People v. State of Alabama

INTRODUCTION

The issue of an individual's right to freely associate with individuals who share common religious, political, and expressive beliefs was at the heart of one of the most infamous political periods of United States history. During the 1950s, Senator Joseph McCarthy was in the spotlight with his investigation of Communism in America (see Exhibit 12.1). The famous question of that era was "Are you now, or have you ever been, a member of the Communist Party?" It is that kind of question that brings to mind the right of **freedom of association**, which this chapter addresses.

freedom of association
the First Amendment right to gather together in groups for any lawful purpose.

THE BASIC LAW OF FREEDOM OF ASSOCIATION

While not explicitly mentioned in the First Amendment, the right of freedom of association has nonetheless been upheld by the U.S. Supreme Court. The Court has said that this right is implicitly derived from the explicitly **enumerated rights** of free speech, free press, free assembly, and the right to petition the government for redress. In spite of this recognition this is not a broadly construed right, but there is little doubt that the Court recognizes an individual's right to join other individuals or organizations to pursue common goals explicitly protected by the First Amendment.

enumerated rights
those rights, held by the federal government or the U.S. citizens, which are mentioned specifically or listed one by one in the U.S. Constitution.

Joseph Raymond McCarthy was a little-known Senator from Wisconsin until he gave a speech in Wheeling, West Virginia, in 1950. He gained national attention when he claimed that members of the Communist Party had infiltrated the State Department. During that speech, he held papers that he claimed listed 205 individuals who were Communists. Later, these charges were labeled a fraud and a hoax. However, McCarthy refused to abandon his search for Communists in the federal government and in 1953 he became the chair of the Senate permanent investigations subcommittee, also known as the Government Operations Committee. In the months that followed, McCarthy and his aides continued their search for Communists and subversives and often ruined careers with their innuendo and smear tactics. In 1954, the Senate censured McCarthy for contempt of a Senate elections subcommittee that had investigated his conduct and financial affairs, abuse of certain Senators, and insults to the Senate itself. With the Democrats gaining control of the Senate in 1954, McCarthy's influence and power began to wane. McCarthy's dogged attacks based on rumor and innuendo gave rise to the term "McCarthyism," which has come to mean attacks based on unsubstantiated rumor.[1]

EXHIBIT 12.1 Joseph McCarthy (courtesy of © Bettmann/Corbis)

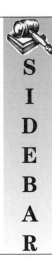

S I D E B A R

In various cases, the Court has indicated that the protected common goals include freedom of expression, political advocacy, religious worship, and also litigation. The Court in *NAACP v. Button* discussed the latter right.[2] In recounting the history of the NAACP, the Court noted that while the organization engaged in educational and lobbying activities, it also had a program of assisting individuals engaged in litigation when the individual was pursuing an issue that coincided with the overall goals of the NAACP. The NAACP's Defense Fund lawyers were drawn into the litigation in a variety of ways, including meeting prospective litigants at educational meetings designed to eliminate desegregation. This activity allegedly violated the Virginia Code which forbid ". . . solicitation of legal business by a 'runner' or 'capper' to include, in the definition of 'runner' or 'capper' an agent for an individual or organization which retains a lawyer in connection with an action to which it is not a party and in which it has no pecuniary right or liability."[3]

The NAACP challenged this statute, and while the statute was upheld in the Virginia courts, the Supreme Court reversed holding that the activities of the NAACP and its Defense Fund lawyers were **lawful advocacy** protected by the First Amendment as modes of expression and association.[4] The Court rejected the State of Virginia's argument that the solicitation scheme was outside the protection of the First Amendment, saying the state cannot prohibit the exercise of a constitutional right by labeling the activity in a certain way and additionally, that the First Amendment protects lawful advocacy. The Court emphasized that the orderly type of activity found in this case was a means of advocating the vindication of legal rights and both the First and the Fourteenth Amendments protect this advocacy.

While the Court has upheld the right to associate when First Amendment expression is involved, this does not mean that individuals have a general right of association for every purpose. An individual does not have a constitutionally protected right to engage in a social activity such as attending a sporting event. There is no First Amendment protection of expression in purely social association. Nor does the existence of the right of freedom of association mean that the state can never regulate expressive activity. The government may interfere in an individual's or organization's freedom of association. To do so, however, the government must show two things, first, that a compelling governmental interest was being pursued and second, that this compelling interest cannot be achieved by a less restrictive method. In other words, the Court will apply the strict scrutiny standard when reviewing government regulation of the freedom of association.[5] This was the standard applied by the Court in two associational cases in which the government claimed the compelling interest of ending discrimination on the basis of one of the constitutionally suspect classifications. The two cases, *Board of Directors of Rotary International v. Rotary Club of Duarte*[6] and *Roberts v. United States Jaycees*,[7] involved the refusal of the two named organizations to admit women as members.

In *Roberts*, the Jaycees challenged the Minnesota Human Rights Act, which provided that it was discriminatory "To deny any person the full and equal enjoyment of the goods, services, facilities, privileges, advantages, and accommodations of a place of public accommodation because of race, color, creed, religion, disability, national origin or sex."[8] The Jaycees allowed women to have associational memberships in its organization, but refused to allow them to be admitted as regular members who have the right to vote, hold local or national office, or participate in leadership training or awards. Two Jaycee chapters, one in Minneapolis and one in St. Paul, began admitting women as regular members and when the national organization learned of this, the national organization voted to revoke the charters of these chapters. The

lawful advocacy forceful persuasion authorized by law or the arguing of a cause, right, or position by a means not forbidden by law.

Minneapolis and St. Paul chapters filed an action with the Minnesota Department of Human Rights, while the national organization filed an action in federal district court. *Roberts* eventually made its way to the U.S. Supreme Court, which discussed, as part of its opinion, that there are two lines of decisions upholding freedom of association.

The first line of decisions involves those where the Court has concluded that there are certain types of relationships that an individual has a right to enter into and maintain without government intrusion. These decisions are based on the belief that such relationships are necessary to guarantee individual freedoms that are constitutionally essential.[9] In the second line of decisions, the Court has recognized freedom of association for the purpose of the individual's right to exercise First Amendment rights such as speech, assembly, religion and petition for redress.[10]

The type of association discussed in *Roberts* falls under the first line of cases. The Court noted that it has long recognized the value that individuals gain from being closely tied to others and noted: "Protecting these relationships from unwarranted state interference therefore safeguards the ability independently to define one's identity that is central to any concept of liberty."[11] The Court then went on to say that even though there are broad ranges of relationships that deserve constitutional protection, there are several characteristics of the Jaycees that make that organization fall outside the category of relationships warranting constitutional protection. The right to associate for expressive purposes, such as the right asserted by the Jaycees in this case, is not absolute and the state may have a compelling interest in regulating the activities of such an organization. In this case, "Minnesota's compelling interest in eradicating discrimination against its female citizens justifies the impact that application of the statute to the Jaycees may have on the male members' associational freedoms."[12] Minnesota had a long history of regulating to ensure equal access to publicly available organizations, services, and goods, and the law challenged here was the means of protecting Minnesota citizens. In doing so, Minnesota has used "the least restrictive means of achieving its ends."[13]

In *Board of Directors of Rotary International v. Rotary Club of Duarte*[14] the Court once again looked at a state statute that required a club to admit women as members. The California statute, the Unruh Civil Rights Act, required the California Rotary Clubs to admit women as active members. This was in violation of the Standard Rotary Club Constitution and the international organization brought suit claiming that the California statute violated the constitutional right of freedom of association. The Court cited the *Roberts* case and once again noted that some private relationships are protected by the constitution and held that "In determining whether a particular association is sufficiently personal or private to warrant constitutional protection, we consider factors such as size, purpose, selectivity, and whether others are excluded from critical aspects of the relationship."[15] When applying this test to the current facts, the Court held that the relationship among Rotary members is not the type of relationship warranting constitutional protection and concluded that the Unruh Act does not unduly interfere with the right of Freedom of Association. This conclusion was based on the fact that the plaintiffs in this case failed to provide any evidence that admitting women would affect the current members' ability to continue with their various projects. This lack of interference, coupled with California's compelling interest in eliminating discrimination combined to make this a constitutionally permissible statute.[16] So, once again, the Court has upheld a state's right to regulate freedom of association so long as there is a compelling governmental interest and this interest is achieved using the least-restrictive means available.

BOARD OF DIRECTORS OF ROTARY INTERNATIONAL, ET AL., APPELLANTS V. ROTARY CLUB OF DUARTE, ET AL. 481 U.S. 537 (1987)

Mr. Justice POWELL delivered the opinion of the Court.

We must decide whether a California statute that requires California Rotary Clubs to admit women members violates the First Amendment.

I

A

. . . Individuals are admitted to membership in a Rotary Club according to a "classification system." The purpose of this system is to insure "that each Rotary Club includes a representative of every worthy and recognized business, professional, or institutional activity in the community." Each active member must work in a leadership capacity in his business or profession. The general rule is that "one active member is admitted for each classification, but he, in turn, may propose an additional active member, who must be in the same business or professional classification." Thus, each classification may be represented by two active members. In addition, "senior active" and "past service" members may represent the same classifications as active members.

Subject to these requirements, each local Rotary Club is free to adopt its own rules and procedures for admitting new members. International has promulgated Recommended Club By-laws providing that candidates for membership will be considered by both a "classifications committee" and a "membership committee . . ."

Membership is open only to men . . . Although women are not admitted to membership, they are permitted to attend meeting, give speeches, and receive awards. Women relatives or Rotary members may form their own associations, and are authorized to wear the Rotary lapel pin. Young women between 14 and 28 years of age may join Interact or Rotaract, organizations sponsored by Rotary International.

B

In 1977 the Rotary Club of Duarte, California, admitted Dona Bogart, Mary Lou Elliott, and Rosemary Freitag to active membership. International notified the Duarte Club that admitting women members is contrary to the Rotary Constitution. After an internal hearing, International's board of directors revoked the charter of the Duarte Club and terminated its membership in Rotary International. The Duarte Club's appeal to the International Convention was unsuccessful.

The Duarte Club and two of its women members filed a complaint in the California Superior Court for the County of Los Angeles. The complaint alleged, *inter alia*, that appellants' actions violated the Unruh Civil Rights Act, Cal. Civ. Code Ann. § 51. Appellees sought to enjoin International from enforcing its restrictions against admitting women members, revoking the Duarte club's charter, or compelling delivery of the charter to any representative of International. Appellees also sought a declaration that appellants' actions and violated the Unruh Act. After a bench trial, the court concluded that neither Rotary International nor the Duarte Club is a "business establishment" within the meaning of the Unruh Act . . . it found that ". . . the principal purposes of the association . . . to promote fellowship . . . and . . . 'service' activities." The court also found that Rotary clubs do not provide their members with goods, services, or facilities. On the basis of these finding and conclusions, the court entered judgment for International.

The California Court of Appeal reversed . . . The California Supreme Court denied appellants' petition for review.

II

In *Roberts v. United States Jaycees,* we upheld against First Amendment challenge a Minnesota statute that required the Jaycees to admit women as full voting members. *Roberts* provides the framework for analyzing appellants' constitutional claims. As we observed in *Roberts,* our cases have afforded constitutional protection to freedom of association in two distinct senses. First, the Court has held that the Constitution protects against unjustified government interference with an individual's choice to enter into and maintain certain intimate or private relationships. Second, the Court has upheld the freedom of individuals to associate for the purpose of engaging in protected speech or religious activities . . .

Continued

A

The Court has recognized that the freedom to enter into and carry on certain intimate or private relationships is a fundamental element of liberty protected by the Bill of Rights. Such relationships may take various forms, including the most intimate . . . Of course, we have held that constitutional protection is restricted to relationships among family members. We have emphasized that the First Amendment protects those relationships, including family relationships that presuppose "deep attachments and commitments to the necessarily few other individuals with whom one shares not only a special community of thoughts, experiences, and beliefs but also distinctively person aspects of one's life." *Roberts v. United States Jaycees*, 468 U.S., at 619-620 . . . In determining whether a particular association is sufficiently personal or private to warrant constitutional protection, we consider factors such as size, purpose, selectivity, and whether others are excluded from critical aspects of the relationship.

The evidence in this case indicates that the relationship among Rotary Club members is not the kind of intimate or private relation that warrants constitutional protection. The size of local Rotary Clubs ranges from fewer than 20 and to more than 900 . . . The membership undertakes a variety of service projects designed to aid the community, to raise the standards of the members' businesses and professions, and to improve international relations . . .

Many of the Rotary Clubs' central activities are carried on in the presence of strangers. Rotary Clubs are required to admit any members of any other Rotary Club to their meeting. Members are encouraged to invite business associates and competitors to meetings . . . We therefore conclude that application of the Unruh Act to local Rotary Clubs does not interfere unduly with the members' freedom of private association.

The Court also has recognized that the right to engage in activities protected by the First Amendment implies "a corresponding right to associate with others in pursuit of a wide variety of political, social, economic, education, religious, and cultural end." *Roberts v. United States Jaycees*, 468 U.S. at 622 . . . In this case, however, the evidence fails to demonstrate that admitting women to Rotary Clubs will affect in any significant way the existing members' ability to carry out their purposes . . . Indeed, by opening membership to leading business and professional women in the community, Rotary Clubs are likely to obtain a more representative cross section of community leaders with a broadened capacity for service.

Even if the Unruh Act does work some slight infringement on Rotary members' right of expressive association, that infringement is justified because it serves the State's compelling interest in eliminating discrimination against women . . . Moreover, public accommodations laws "plainly serv[e] compelling state interests of the highest order." 468 U.S., at 624. In *Roberts* we recognized that the State's compelling interest in assuring equal access to women extends to the acquisition of leadership skills and business contacts as well as tangible goods and services. The Unruh Act plainly serves this interest. We therefore hold that application of the Unruh Act to California Rotary Clubs does not violate the right of expressive association afforded by the First Amendment . . .

IV

The judgment of the Court of Appeals of California is affirmed.

It is so ordered.

In addition to the freedom to associate, the Court has also recognized the right not to associate. In the case of *Abood v. Detroit Board of Education*[17] the Court decided the issue of whether an individual can be compelled to support or join an organization involuntarily. The Court used the same strict scrutiny test that it used in the cases discussed above.

The facts of *Abood* involved a statute enacted by the Michigan legislature authorizing union representation for local government employees. The law provided for an "**agency shop**" arrangement where every employee represented by the union is compelled to pay union dues, whether or not that employee is actually a member of the union or wants to be a member of the union. Plaintiffs in this action challenged the agency shop clause of their contract under

agency shop   a business in which workers are not required to join a union but are required to pay the equivalent of union dues and fees.

both federal and state law alleging that the statute violates plaintiffs' freedom of association. In answering this challenge, the Court looked to two previous decisions, *Railway Employees' Department v. Hanson*[18] and *Machinists v. Street*.[19] In both of these cases, the Court looked at similar circumstances as those found in the *Abood* case. In the *Hanson* case, however, the assessed union dues were not used for any purpose other than for collective bargaining and ". . . the Court squarely held that 'the requirement for financial support of the collective-bargaining agency by all who receive the benefits of its work . . . does not violate . . . the First . . . Amendmen(t).' "[20] The Court went on to say that the agency shop arrangement fairly distributes the cost of collective bargaining activities among all who benefit from it. To hold otherwise would allow those who wished to opt out, for whatever reason, to refuse to contribute while enjoying the benefits of collective bargaining. Further, so long as the union is acting to promote the interests of all its members during the bargaining process, no member can withdraw financial support simply because that individual disagrees with the union's strategy.[21] These are important government interests, says the Court, and the agency shop arrangement contained in the Michigan statute did not unduly infringe on the plaintiffs' constitutional rights. The Court did recognize that the union members do have a right to refuse to support political activities of the union with which that member disagrees.

> *"[T]he Constitution requires only that such expenditures be financed from charges, dues or assessments paid by employees who do not object to advancing those ideas and who are not coerced into doing so against their will by the threat of loss of governmental employment."[22]*

Ultimately, then, the Court held that the union had to devise a means to separate the use of a member's contribution for political activity if that member has an ideological objection, while still using that member's contribution for collective bargaining activities. In order to do this, the Court vacated the judgment of the lower court and remanded this matter to allow for the parties to find an internal remedy to this problem that was in keeping with the Court's holding.

A twist on this issue was once again presented to the Court in the recent case of *Board of Regents of the University of Wisconsin System v. Southworth*.[23] In *Southworth* a group of students sued the university over mandatory student activity fees. The students claimed that their First Amendment right to freedom of association was violated by the mandatory fees because some of the fees were used to support groups or organizations that represent a point of view objectionable to the students. While both the District Court and the Court of Appeals sided with the students, the Supreme Court reversed, supporting the University's contention that these mandatory fees to support all types of speech furthers its educational mission. The Court said:

> *"The First Amendment permits a public university to charge its students an activity fee used to fund a program to facilitate extracurricular student speech if the program is viewpoint neutral."[24]*

The Court did recognize the students' right to expect safeguards regarding the expressive activities that the students, through their fees, supported, but the University's important interest in facilitating a wide range of ideas and perspectives outweighs the students' objection to the infringement on their constitutional rights. Again, the Court is using strict scrutiny and balancing the University's compelling interest in fostering many viewpoints during the education process against the students' constitutional rights of association and expression.

In spite of these cases, it does not mean that the Court will force an organization to accept members who would interfere with that organization's overall message. In 2000, the Court heard the case of *Boy Scouts of America v. Dale*,[25]

James Dale, a longtime member of and leader for the Boy Scouts, was also a gay man involved in the Rutgers University Lesbian/Gay Alliance. When his sexual orientation became public, Dale received a letter from the Boys Scouts telling him that the Boy Scouts forbid membership to homosexuals. Dale brought an action arguing that the Boy Scouts had violated New Jersey's public accommodation statute. The Boy Scouts countered by arguing that the First Amendment freedom of expressive association protected them from being forced to accept individuals as members who hold differing views from the organization. The trial court granted relief in favor of the Boy Scouts, the appellate division affirmed this, but the New Jersey Supreme Court held that the Boy Scouts did not have the type of personal or private organization that would warrant protection under the First Amendment. The United States Supreme Court granted certiorari and found in favor of the Boy Scouts. The Court specifically looked back at *Roberts, supra,* and said, "This right [freedom of association] is crucial in preventing the majority from imposing its views on groups that would rather express other, perhaps unpopular, ideas."[26] If a group is forced to accept a member who represents a view that is different from the organization's view it may interfere with the organization's ability to express "only those views that it intends to express."[27] The majority believed that the position of the Boy Scouts on the issue of homosexuality, as evidenced by internal rules and position statements, was that homosexuals were not to be Scout leaders. The majority felt that Dale's presence as a Boy Scout leader would send a message to the general public, as well as the young members, that the organization did support Dale's "lifestyle." "The Boy Scouts has a First Amendment right to choose to send one message but not the other."[28] In reaching its conclusion, the Court held that the Boy Scouts were an expressive organization and in finding so, forcing the Boy Scouts to comply with the New Jersey statute violated the organization's First Amendment right to freedom of association.

The dissent, written by Justice Stevens who was joined in this dissent by Justices Souter, Ginsburg, and Breyer, is worth noting in this case. The dissent first looked at the New Jersey statute and its legislative intent and found that the State of New Jersey had given its citizens more expansive rights against discrimination than most states, and that this was proper and that the majority was mistaken in holding that the New Jersey law violated the constitutional rights of the Boy Scouts. With this background, Justice Stevens then looked at the values of the Boy Scouts, which the majority relied on as a reason for the decision. The dissent contends that the only Boy Scout statements that might be construed to condemn homosexuality were the phrases "morally straight" and "clean." After reading all of the policies and documents supplied by the Boy Scouts, Justice Stevens concluded:

> "It is plain as the light of day that neither one of these principles—"morally straight" and "clean"—says the slightest thing about homosexuality. Indeed, neither term in the Boy Scouts' Law and Oath expresses any position whatsoever on sexual matters."[29]

In addition, Justice Stevens stated four other reasons to disagree with the majority and they are:

1. The Boy Scout literature does not encourage members to ask their Scoutmasters about matters of a sexual nature and expressly tells them to ask their parents, ministers, or teachers about these things before asking the Scoutmaster;
2. The Boy Scouts are ecumenical in nature and as some religious groups do not view homosexuality as wrong, the Boy Scouts should not now be allowed to claim that it has adopted a particular religious philosophy on this particular interest;

3. The Boy Scouts' claimed policy, as outlined in an internal memo, is only a letter that adopts an exclusionary policy and this has never been held by the Court to be sufficient to support a right to association claim;

4. The case law itself, in Justice Stevens's opinion, does not support the majority's opinion. He points specifically to cases discussed in this chapter, *Roberts v. United States Jaycees* and *Board of Directors of Rotary International v. Rotary Club of Duarte* and notes that the right to freedom of association is not absolute and that the Court has held in the past that a state's action to prohibit discrimination is enough to outweigh an organization's right to exclude a group of individuals from membership.

Justice Stevens then concludes,

"The only apparent explanation for the majority's holding, then, is that homosexuals are simply so different from the rest of society that their presence alone—unlike any other individual's—should be singled out for special First Amendment treatment."[30]

It would appear from the 5 to 4 split decision that the Court itself is unsettled on this issue and that future cases might bring a different decision.

In addition to simple membership or leadership in an organization, the right to freedom of association also extends to other activities, such as parades, as found in *Hurley v. Irish-American Gay, Lesbian and Bisexual Group of Boston*.[31] This case was decided five years prior to the *Dale* case, but also involved the expressive nature of freedom of association. In this case, a group of Irish-American homosexuals (GLIB) wanted to participate in a St. Patrick's Day parade in Boston. This parade, organized by private individuals, included a variety of groups with differing political views, lifestyles, and ideologies. When GLIB asked to join the parade, the parade organizers refused to allow their participation. GLIB then filed an action in the Massachusetts courts alleging constitutional violations. After the state trial court found that GLIB was entitled to participate in the parade, the decision was then affirmed by the Supreme Judicial Court of Massachusetts. The U.S. Supreme Court granted certiorari to decide whether requiring the organizers to admit a group whose message was not condoned by the organizers violates the First Amendment rights of the parade organizers.

To decide this issue, the Court first had to determine whether a parade is a form of expression. The Court first looked at the historical definition of a parade and found that "[p]arades are public dramas of social relations, and in them performers define who can be a social actor and what subjects and ideas are available for communication and consideration."[32] With this in mind, the Court decided that parades are a form of expression protected by the Constitution. The Court then went on to discuss the fact that the parade organizers were willing to let other groups with diverse messages into the parade does not mean that the organizers had given up their right to exclude a group's message with which the organizers disagreed. The general rule, says the Court, is ". . . that the speaker has the right to tailor the speech [and this] applies not only to expressions of value, opinion, or endorsement, but equally to statements of fact the speaker would rather avoid."[33] To order the parade organizers to include GLIB in the parade would result in a perception that the organizers approved or supported the message that they clearly did not support. This is not acceptable, and the Supreme Court reversed the state court holding.

GOVERNMENTAL INTERFERENCE THAT HAS BEEN CHALLENGED

There are governmental regulatory schemes that have been challenged; some of them have been upheld while others have been struck down. Included among those regulatory schemes are: laws making it illegal to be a member of an organization, withholding governmental benefits or jobs from members of a particular group or organization, and governmentally required disclosure of an individual's organizational affiliations.

The Court has consistently held that the government cannot make membership in a particular organization illegal. If the right to freely associate means anything, it means that the individual may choose to belong to an organization—even if it is an unpopular organization. Any regulatory scheme that attempts to make it illegal to become a member or maintain a membership in an organization will be struck down.

The Court has also not looked favorably on attempts to withhold a government job or benefit based on an individual's organizational membership. Today, it is unconstitutional to withhold a public job or benefit solely because an individual belongs to a particular organization. This has not always been so. In the past, the courts viewed an individual's job as a privilege, not a right. It could therefore be withdrawn at will without violating the employee's legal rights under the **at-will doctrine**, which was prevalent in most U.S. jurisdictions. As the at-will doctrine began to be questioned and replaced, the more recent view is that the government may not ask a citizen to forego a constitutional right or privilege in order to obtain employment with the government.

Two cases were decided in the mid-1960s that spoke directly to this constitutionality of withholding public employment due to an individual's organizational association. *Elfbrandt v. Russell*[34] was decided in 1966 and the following year the Court decided *Keyishian v. Board of Regents*.[35] The *Elfbrandt* case arose when an Arizona teacher was legally required to take a loyalty oath. The teacher challenged the oath because she did not know what the oath meant nor was she given a hearing at which the meaning of the oath could be determined. In the *Keyishian* case, faculty members of a New York university refused to sign a loyalty oath as well, and challenged the state statute that required such a signing.

at-will doctrine a common law doctrine that allows an employer to terminate the employment of an employee for good cause, bad cause, or no cause at all.

HARRY KEYISHIAN, ET AL., APPELLANTS V. THE BOARD OF REGENTS OF THE UNIVERSITY OF THE STATE OF NEW YORK, ET AL.
385 U.S. 589 (1967)

Mr. Justice BRENNAN delivered the opinion of the Court.

Appellants were members of the faculty of the privately owned and operated University of Buffalo, and became state employees when the University was merged in 1962 into the State University of New York, an institution of higher education owned and operated by the State of New York. As faculty members of the State University their continued employment was conditioned upon their compliance with a New York plan, formulated partly in statutes and partly in administrative regulations, which the State utilizes to prevent the appointment or retention of 'subversive' persons in state employment.

Appellants Hochfield and Maud were Assistant Professors of English, appellant Keyishian an instructor in English, and appellant Garver, a lecturer in Philosophy. Each of them refused to sign, as regulations then in effect required, a certificate that he was not a Communist and that if he had ever been a Communist, he had communicated that fact to the President of the State University of New York. Each was notified that his failure to sign the certificate would require his dismissal. Keyishian's one-year term contract was not renewed because of his failure to sign the certificate. Hochfield and Garver, whose contracts still had time to run, continue to teach, but subject to proceedings for their dismissal if the constitutionality of the New York plan is sustained. Maud has voluntarily resigned and therefore no longer has standing in this suit. . . .

Appellants brought this action for declaratory and injunctive relief, alleging that the state program violated the Federal Constitution in various respects. A three-judge federal court held that the program was constitutional. We reverse . . .

Continued

II

A 1953 amendment extended the application of the Feinberg Law to personnel of any college or other institution of higher education owned and operated by the State or its subdivisions. In the same year, the Board of Regents, after notice and hearing, listed the Communist Party of the United States and of the State of New York as 'subversive organizations.' In 1965 each applicant for an appointment or the renewal of an appointment was required to sign the so-called 'Feinberg Certificate' declaring that he had read the Regents Rules and understood that the Rules and the statutes constituted terms of employment, and declaring further that he was not a member of the Communist Party, and that if he had ever been a member he had communicated that fact to the President of the State University. This was the certificate that appellants Hochfield, Maud, Keyishian, and Garver refused to sign.

In June 1965, shortly before the trial of this case, the Feinberg Certificate was rescinded and it was announced that no person then employed would be deemed ineligible for continued employment 'solely' because he refused to sign the certificate. In lieu of the certificate, it was provided that each applicant be informed before assuming his duties that the statutes . . . constituted part of his contract. He was particularly to be informed of the disqualification which flowed from membership in a listed 'subversive' organization . . .

The change in procedure in no wise moots appellants' constitutional questions raised in the context of their refusal to sign the now abandoned Feinberg Certificate. The substance of the statutory and regulatory complex remains and from the outset appellants' basic claim has been that they are aggrieved by its application.

III

. . . Our experience under the Sedition Act of 1798 taught us that dangers fatal to First Amendment freedoms inhere in the word 'seditious.' As the word 'treasonable,' if left undefined, is no less dangerously uncertain. Thus it becomes important whether, despite the omission of a similar reference to the Penal Law . . . the words as used in that section are to be read . . . Or are they to be read more broadly and to constitute utterances or acts 'seditious' and 'treasonable' which would not be so regarded for the purposes [of the act]?

We do not have the benefit of a judicial gloss by the New York courts enlightening us as to the scope of this complicated plan. In light of the intricate administrative machinery for its enforcement, this is not surprising. The very intricacy of the plan and the uncertainty as to the scope of its proscriptions make it highly efficient in theorem mechanism. It would be a bold teacher who would not stay as far as possible from utterances or acts which might jeopardize his living by enmeshing him in this intricate machinery. The uncertainty as to the utterances and acts proscribed increases that causation in 'those who believe the written law means what it says.' *Baggett v. Bullitt*. The result must be to stifle 'that free play of the spirit which all teachers ought especially to cultivate and practice . . .' That probability is enhanced by the provisions requiring an annual review of every teacher to determine whether any utterance or act of his, inside the classroom or out, came within the sanctions of the laws . . .

There can be no doubt of the legitimacy of New York's interest in protecting its education system from subversion. But 'even though the governmental purpose be legitimate and substantial, that purpose cannot be pursued by means that broadly stifle fundamental personal liberties when the end can be more narrowly achieved.' *Shelton v. Tucker*. The principle is not inapplicable because the legislation is aimed at keeping subversives out of the teaching ranks. In *De Jonge v. State of Oregon* the Court said:

> 'The greater the importance of safeguarding the community from incitements to the overthrow of our institutions by force and violence, the more imperative is the need to preserve inviolate the constitutional rights of free speech, free press and free assembly in order to maintain the opportunity for free political discussion, to the end that government may be responsive to the will of the people and that changes, if desired, may be obtained by peaceful means. Therein lies the security of the Republic, the very foundation of constitutional government.'

Our Nation is deeply committed to safeguarding academic freedom, which is of transcendent value to all of us and not merely to the teachers

Continued

concerned. That freedom is therefore a special concern of the First Amendment, which does not tolerate laws that cast a pall of orthodoxy over the classroom. 'The vigilant protection of constitutional freedoms is nowhere more vital than in the community of American schools.' *Shelton v. Tucker*. The classroom is peculiarly the 'marketplace of ideas.' The Nation's future depends upon leaders trained through wide exposure to that robust exchange of ideas which discovers truth 'out of a multitude of tongues, (rather) than through any kind of authoritative selection.' *United States v. Associated Press* . . .

We emphasize once again that '(p)recision of regulation must be the touchstone in an area so closely touching our most precious freedoms.' *NAACP v. Button* . . . New York's complicated and intricate scheme plainly violates that standard. When one must guess what conduct or utterance may lose him his position, one necessarily will 'steer far wider of the unlawful zone . . .' *Speiser v. Randall*.

The regulatory maze created by New York is wholly lacking in 'terms susceptible of objective measurement.' *Cramp v. Board of Public Instruction* [citation omitted]. It has the quality of 'extraordinary ambiguity' found to be fatal to the oaths considered in *Cramp and Baggett v. Bullitt* . . . Vagueness of wording is aggravated by prolixity and profusion of statutes, regulations, and administrative machinery, and by manifold cross-references to interrelated enactments and rules . . .

VI

Appellants have also challenged the constitutionality of the discrete provisions . . . of the Feinberg Law, which make Communist Party membership, as such, prima facie evidence of disqualification. The provision was added . . . after the Board of Regents, following notice and hearing, listed the Communist Party of the United States and the Communist Party of New York as 'subversive' organizations. Subdivision 2 of the Feinberg Law was, however, before the Court in Adler and its constitutionality was sustained. But constitutional doctrine which has emerged since that decision has rejected its major premise. That premise was that public employment, including academic employment, may be conditioned upon the surrender of constitutional rights which could not be abridged by direct government action. Teachers, the Court said in Adler, 'may work for the school system upon the reasonable terms laid down by the proper authorities of New York. If they do not choose to work on such terms, they are at liberty to retain their beliefs and associations and go elsewhere.' The Court also stated that a teacher denied employment because of membership in a listed organization 'is not thereby denied the right of free speech and assembly. His freedom of choice between membership in the organization and employment in the school system might be limited, but not his freedom of speech or assembly, except in the remote sense that limitation is inherent in every choice.'

However, the Court of Appeals for the Second Circuit correctly said in an earlier stage of this case, '. . . the theory that public employment which may be denied altogether may be subjected to any conditions, regardless of how unreasonable, has been uniformly rejected.' Indeed, that theory was expressly rejected in a series of decisions following Adler. In *Sherbert v. Verner* we said: 'It is too late in the day to doubt that the liberties of religion and expression may be infringed by the denial of or placing conditions upon a benefit or privilege.'

We proceed then to the question of the validity of the provision of [the Feinberg Law] barring employment to members of listed organizations. Here again constitutional doctrine has developed since Adler. Mere knowing membership without a specific intent to further the unlawful aims of an organization is not a constitutionally adequate basis for exclusion from such positions as those held by appellants.

In *Elfbrandt v. Russell* we said, 'Those who join an organization but do not share its unlawful purposes and who do not participate in its unlawful activities surely pose no threat, either as citizens or as public employees.' We therefor struck down a statutorily required oath binding the state employee not to become a member of the Communist Party with knowledge of its unlawful purpose, on threat of discharge and perjury prosecution if the oath were violated. We found that '(a)ny lingering doubt that proscription of mere knowing membership, without any showing of 'specific intent' would run afoul of the Constitution was set at rest by our decision in *Aptheker v. Secretary of State*. In *Aptheker* we held that Party; membership, without knowledge of the Party's unlawful purposes and specific intent to further its unlawful aims, could not constitutionally warrant deprivation of the right to

Continued

travel abroad. As we said in *Schneiderman v. United States* 'Under our traditions beliefs are personal and not a matter of mere association, and . . . men in adhering to a political party or other organization . . . do not subscribe unqualifiedly to all of its platforms or asserted principles.' 'A law which applies to membership without the 'specific intent' to further the illegal aims of the organization infringes unnecessarily on protected freedoms. It rests on the doctrine of 'guilt by association' which has no place here.' *Elfbrandt, supra.* Thus mere Party membership, even with knowledge of the Party's unlawful goals, cannot suffice to justify criminal punishment, see *Scales v. United States* . . . nor may it warrant a finding of moral unfitness justifying disbarment. *Schware v. Board of Bar Examiners.*

These limitations clearly apply to a provision like [those found in the Fienberg Law], which blankets all state employees, regardless of the 'sensitivity' of their positions. But even the Feinberg Law provision, applicable primarily to activities of teachers, who have captive audiences of young minds, are subject to these limitations in favor of freedom of expression and association; the stifling effect on the academic mind from curtailing freedom of association in such manner is manifest, and has been documented in recent studies. *Elfbrandt* and *Aptheker* state the government standard: legislation which sanctions membership unaccompanied by specific intent to further the unlawful goals of the organization or which is not active membership violates constitutional limitations . . . Thus proof of nonactive membership or a showing of the absence of intent to further unlawful aims will not rebut the presumptions and defeat dismissal. This is emphasized in official and administrative interpretations. For example, it is said in a letter addressed to prospective appointees by the President of the State University, 'You will note that . . . both the Law and regulations are very specifically directed toward the elimination and nonappointment of 'Communist' from or to our teaching ranks . . .'

The Feinberg Certificate was even more explicit: 'Anyone who is a member of the Communist Party or of any organization that advocates the violent overthrow of the Government of the United States or of the State of New York or any political subdivision thereof cannot be employed by the State University.' (Emphasis supplied.) This official administrative interpretation is supported by the legislative preamble to the Feinberg Law, s 1, in which the legislature concludes as a result of its findings that 'it is essential that the laws prohibiting persons who are members of subversive groups, such as the communist party and its affiliated organizations, from obtaining or retaining employment in the public schools, be rigorously enforced.' (Emphasis supplied.)

Thus s 105, subd. 1(c), and s 3022, subd. 2, [of the Feinberg Law] suffer from impermissible 'overbreadth.' *Elfbrandt v. Russell.* They seek to bar employment both for association which legitimately may be proscribed and for association which may not be proscribed consistently with the First Amendment rights. Where statutes have an overbroad sweep, just as where they are vague, 'the hazard of loss or substantial impairment of those precious rights may be critical.' *Dombrowski v. Pfister,* since those covered by the statute are bound to limit their behavior to that which is unquestionably safe. As we said in *Shelton v. Tucker,* 'The breadth of legislative abridgment must be viewed in the light of less drastic means for achieving the same basic purpose.'

We therefore hold that [the laws in question] are invalid insofar as they proscribe mere knowing membership without any showing of specific intent to further the unlawful aims of the Communist Party of the United States or of the State of New York.

The judgment of the District Court is reversed and the case is remanded for further proceedings consistent with this opinion.

Reversed and remanded.

The Court, in both of these cases, was concerned with the vagueness of the statutes. If an individual is unable to discern whether his or her action will violate the law, that law is too vague. Such vagueness was found by the *Keyishian* Court to have a chilling effect in that it would likely result in citizens avoiding perfectly legal activities on the chance that such activity might fall within the scope of the vague law. The Court found this unacceptable.

In addition to concerns about vagueness, the *Elfbrandt* Court was concerned that Arizona act "threatens the cherished freedom of association protected by the First Amendment."[36] While the Court acknowledged that states may pass laws that touch on associational rights, they must do so by first narrowly defining the conduct prohibited and second, by passing such a law only when there is "conduct . . . constituting a clear and present danger to a substantial interest of the State."[37] In order for an individual to be held accountable for mere membership, that individual would have to have the specific intent to further the illegal aims of an organization. Barring that, any law that makes it illegal to be a member of an organization is using the old adage, guilt by association, and that is not acceptable in this country.

The Court once again looked at the issue of loyalty oaths in the 1972 case, *Cole v. Richardson*.[38] In this case, Cole, an employee at a state hospital, refused to take a loyalty oath required by Massachusetts law. Cole was ultimately discharged and brought an action challenging the law. The Court reaffirmed three major rules that it had laid down about loyalty oaths in the past. They are: (1) that neither federal nor state government can condition employment on the taking of an oath that infringes on a right guaranteed by the U.S. Constitution; (2) that employment may not be conditioned on the taking of an oath that one has not and will not engage in protected speech activities; and (3) that an oath may not be so vague that individuals of common intelligence cannot ascertain its meaning.[39] The Court did not, however, eliminate loyalty oaths altogether. The Court was clear that "[s]ince there is no constitutionally protected right to overthrow a government by force, violence, or illegal or unconstitutional means, no constitutional right is infringed by an oath to abide by the constitutional system in the future."[40] Therefore, so long as the oath looks to the future, it is permissible.

So, if loyalty oaths are permissible under those circumstances, what happens when an employee criticizes a superior and is perceived to be disloyal? Can the employee be discharged for that? In deciding this issue, the Court distinguished between speech that discusses a matter of public concern, and that which does not. In two cases, *Connick v. Myers*[41] and *Rankin v. McPherson*,[42] the Court discussed this difference and used the strict scrutiny standard to make the decisions. The Court struck a balance between the right of free speech and the governmental interest in promoting efficiency and harmony in the workplace. The Court held:

> *"This balancing is necessary; in order to accommodate the dual role of the public employer as a provider of public services and as a government entity operating under the constraints of the First Amendment. On the one hand, public employers are employers, concerned with the efficient function of their operation; review of every personnel decision made by a public employer could, in the long run, hamper the performance of public functions. On the other hand, 'the threat of dismissal from public employment is . . . a potent means of inhibiting speech.' Vigilance is necessary to ensure that public employers do not use authority over employees to silence discourse, not because it hampers public functions but simply because superiors disagree with the content of employees' speech."*[43]

When the matter is of public concern, the strict scrutiny standard applies, and the government must show a compelling governmental interest in enforcing a policy prohibiting speech critical of the government or its agents. If the matter is not of public concern, the Court will be deferential to the government/employer's policies. In the *Rankin* case, the employee was discharged for making remarks critical of President Reagan's administration. She challenged

public interest a broad term for anything that can affect the general public's finances, health, rights, etc.

the termination and upon review, the Supreme Court held that first, the remarks were of public concern or **public interest** in that every U.S. citizen has the right to question and discuss their views of the government, its officials, and its actions, even if others perceive the remarks to be disloyal. The Court then balanced Rankin's right to make these remarks against the state's interest. While the Court recognized that some speech might detract from the speaker's job performance and therefore from the efficient workplace, the Court did not find that interest to outweigh Rankin's right of free speech, her right to adopt a particular point of view, or right to associate with a particular political point of view. As a matter of fact, the Court found that a reduction of efficiency in the workplace was not part of the consideration when the decision to discharge Rankin was made, but rather it was the content of the statements that motivated her supervisor. Ultimately, the Court found the discharge improper.

Independent contractors have the same rights as employees when it comes to speech that is critical of a public employer. This was settled in the case of *Board of County Commissioners v. Umbehr*.[44] In this case, the Court first noted that the similarities between public employees and government contractors was obvious and acknowledged that the government had the same need to be free to terminate both, so long as it was not in retaliation for the exercise of a constitutional right. While the Court acknowledged ". . . that the First Amendment does not create property or tenure rights, and does not guarantee absolute freedom of speech . . . The First Amendment's guarantee of freedom of speech protects government employees from termination *because of* their speech on matters of public concern."[45] With this, the Court held that the same balancing test used for government employees must be used in determining whether the termination or nonrenewal of a contract with an independent governmental contractor is legitimate. The Court will still look to see whether the speech is on a matter of public concern, and if it is, will balance the government contractors right of free speech against the government's interest in maintaining control and efficiency in the workplace.

Another government regulatory scheme that has been challenged is the requirement that an individual employee disclose his or her organizational affiliations to the government. In the 1950s, the Court viewed this type of inquiry as acceptable. The 1951 case, *Garner v. Los Angeles Board of Public Works*[46] exemplified the attitude of that era. Fear of Communism was rampant in the United States and many government entities had laws that prohibited individuals who were or had been members of the Communist Party from holding public office, or having public employment. Los Angeles County was one of these. The petitioners, civil service employees, refused to comply with the county ordinance and were discharged. They brought an action challenging the statute and suing for reinstatement and unpaid salaries. The Court rejected all of petitioner's arguments and held that the statute did not violate the employees' rights and in fact, refusal to answer questions about one's affiliations was a perfect reason for terminating employment. Failure to answer was seen as evidence of insubordination.

Much has changed in the years since the *Garner* case. While there is no strict prohibition against governmental inquiry into one's associational ties, the government's ability to delve into that area is narrow. As mentioned earlier in this section, the Court uses the strict scrutiny standard when determining whether the government's need to know information related to one's associational ties is greater than the individual's rights under the First Amendment. In *NAACP v. Alabama*,[47] the State of Alabama claimed that the NAACP was "doing business" within the state without complying with the Alabama statute which required that a business file its charter and name a resident agent for the business. When the NAACP argued that it was a nonprofit organization that was not required to meet the mandates of the statute, the State of Alabama demanded that the NAACP disclose, among other documents, its membership list. When the NAACP refused and challenged the state action, the Court held that compulsory disclosure of membership lists would have a chilling effect on a citizen's First Amendment rights, including associational freedom. Organizations, particularly those that espouse unpopular views, must be able to protect the privacy of its members, if freedom of association is to be preserved. In this case, the Court looked to see if Alabama had a compelling governmental interest in having the names of the NAACP members living in Alabama and found that the state did not have such an interest.

Eighteen years after *NAACP v. Alabama,* the Court heard another case challenging compulsory disclosure of a political organization's list of contributors. In the case of *Buckley v. Valeo*[48] many issues surrounding the Federal Election Campaign Act were raised, discussed, and decided. Among the issues was whether this federal statute violated an individual's right to freedom of association. In deciding this issue, the Court once again used the strict scrutiny standard to weigh the interest of the government against the rights of the individual. The federal government argued that it had several compelling interests. First and foremost was a compelling interest in preserving the integrity of the electoral process. To do this, the government argued it must be able to have access to records concerning contributors and the amounts they contribute. With regard to freedom of association, the government argued specifically that there were three compelling reasons for allowing the government to have access to such information. First, allowing access gives voters the information needed to assess the candidate and ascertain the candidate's political views on a variety of topics. Second, disclosure would deter corruption or the appearance of corruption by large contributors and third, the record-keeping process is essential to enforce the law as written. The Court agreed with these arguments and found them compelling enough to outweigh the individual's right to freedom of association and other First Amendment rights.

The last discussion of the regulatory schemes that have been challenged and reviewed involves the compulsory disclosure of information during legislative investigations. These legislative committees have the power to compel testimony through the use of subpoena and contempt powers. One of the earliest cases in this area is the result of the work of the House Un-American Activities Committee's investigation into Communism in the United States during the 1950s. When Professor Barenblatt of Vassar College appeared before the House Un-American Activities Committee, he refused to answer questions about his alleged affiliation with the Communist Party. Because of his refusal, Professor Barenblatt was indicted on five contempt charges in U.S. District Court. Barenblatt challenged his conviction, claiming that his associational rights under the First Amendment were violated.[49] When the U.S. Supreme Court decided the case, it showed deference to the Committee by holding that so long as the questions were related to a valid governmental interest, the Committee was free to ask questions and hold someone in contempt that refused to cooperate. This power rests on the governmental interest of self-preservation and at that time, the official view of the Communist Party included the desire to overthrow the United States government by force. The governmental interest in protecting itself was more important than any asserted First Amendment right in this case.

In the 1960s, this view began to change and instead of the simple test to see if the government's action was more important than the individual's asserted right, the Court began to use the strict scrutiny standard. In *Gibson v. Florida Legislative Investigation Committee,*[50] Gibson, the Miami NAACP's President, refused to disclose the organization's membership list to the Florida Legislative Investigation Committee. His failure to do so resulted in a contempt conviction and Gibson's challenge to the committee's action. The Court first held that "The First and Fourteenth Amendment rights of free speech and free association are fundamental and highly prized, and 'need breathing space to survive.'"[51] The Court then went on to reiterate its holding that there is a direct relationship between associational freedom and an individual's privacy. In balancing this fundamental right against the state's interest in maintaining its investigative power, the Court looked to see if the state's interest was compelling enough to overcome this fundamental right. While the Court recognized the state's interest, it did not find it compelling enough, under the facts of the case, to override the individual's right to freedom of association. So in this case, the Court moves from a lesser balancing standard to recognition that freedom of association under the First Amendment is a fundamental right and that the proper test for evaluating state infringement on this right is strict scrutiny. This continues to be the standard used to evaluate state action that impacts one's right to freedom of association today.

Summary

While the Court recognizes the right of freedom of association, it is not explicitly stated in the Constitution. The Court has found that this right to associate with others of like mind and philosophy can be implied from the explicit First Amendment guarantees of freedom of religion, freedom of speech, and freedom of assembly. These explicit rights bring with them common, shared goals that cause individuals to form groups to promote, exercise, and protect. Without the freedom to associate in groups to exercise these common goals, these explicit rights would be severely curtailed.

However, this right to associate is not an unlimited or unfettered right. There is no right of association in a purely social event or organization and under certain situations, a State can curtail or regulate an individual's right to associate. While the State's regulation of this right will trigger a strict scrutiny analysis in the courts, if that State can show a compelling governmental interest that cannot be achieved by a less restrictive means, that regulation will stand.

The Court, however, will not support any regulation or decision that would force an organization to accept members who might interfere with the organization's overall goals or message. Nor will the Court tolerate any attempts to make membership in a particular organization illegal.

Overall, the Court recognizes that protecting the freedom to freely associate is crucial in upholding other inalienable rights and unless the government can show that its statutes or regulations can withstand the strict scrutiny test, the government cannot interfere with this right.

Key Terms

agency shop	enumerated rights	lawful advocacy
at-will doctrine	freedom of association	public interest

Review Questions

1. Where does the right to freedom of association originate?

2. Why is this an important constitutional right?

3. The Court has consistently held that there are two lines of decisions with regard to freedom of association. What are these two lines, and how do they differ?

4. Is the right to associate freely an absolute right? If not, when may the government interfere with this right?

5. After reviewing organizations to which you belong, answer the following:
    a. Why is it important to you to belong to this organization?
    b. Is this an organization that would warrant protection under the First Amendment?
    c. Once you have categorized each organization, what case supports your conclusion?

Internet Connections

1. The following Web sites can provide more information about the House Un-American Activities Committee and those involved in the investigation:
    a. CNN Cold War: Excerpts from HUAC Hearings, including testimony of SAG Presidents Ronald Reagan, Gary Cooper, Walt Disney, and Ayn Rand at *http://www.cnn.com/SPECIALS/cold.war/episodes.*
    b. The history of the HUAC from its origin in the 1930s to its dissolution in the 1970s, including links for some individuals investigated by the HUAC at *http://www.spartacus.schoolnet.co.uk/USAhuac.htm.*
2. More information on freedom of association can be found at:
    a. Legal Information Institution (LII), a search engine allowing access to articles and organizations on many constitutional law topics, including freedom of association at *http://www.law.cornell.edu.*
    b. FindLaw Constitutional Law Center: US Constitution, a search engine allowing access to annotated articles and summaries of constitutional issues, including the First Amendment freedom of association at *http://supreme.lp.findlaw.com.*

End Notes

[1]"McCarthy, Joseph Raymond." *The Columbia Electronic Encyclopedia,* at *http://www.Infoplease.com* (Aug. 1, 2002).

[2]*NAACP v. Button,* 371 U.S. 415 (1963).

[3]*Id.* at 423.

[4]*Id.* at 427.

[5]*NAACP v. Alabama,* 357 U.S. 449, 461 (1958).

[6]*Board of Directors of Rotary International v. Rotary Club of Duarte,* 481 U.S. 537 (1987).

[7]*Roberts v. United States Jaycees,* 468 U.S. 609 (1984).

[8]Minn. Stat. § 363.03, subd. 3 (1982).

[9]*Roberts v. United States Jaycees,* 468 U.S. 609, 617–618 (1984).

[10]*Id.* at 618.

[11]*Id.* at 619.

[12]*Id.* at 623.

[13]*Id.* at 626.

[14]*Board of Directors of Rotary International v. Rotary Club of Duarte,* 481 U.S. 537 (1987).

[15]*Id.* at 546.

[16]*Id.* at 549.

[17]*Abood v. Detroit Board of Education,* 431 U.S. 209 (1977).

[18]*Railway Employees' Dept. v. Hanson,* 351 U.S. 225 (1956).

[19]*International Association of Machinists v. Street,* 367 U.S. 740 (1961).

[20]*Abood v. Detroit Board of Education,* 431 U.S. 209, 219 (1977).

[21]*Id.* at 222–223.

[22]*Id.* at 236.

[23]*Board of Regents of the University of Wisconsin System v. Southworth,* 529 U.S. 217 (2000).

[24]*Id.* at 221.

[25]*Boy Scouts of America v. Dale,* 530 U.S. 640 (2000).

[26]*Id.* at 648.

[27]*Id.* at 648.

[28]*Id.* at 656.

[29]*Id.* at 668–669.

[30]*Id.* at 696.

[31]*Hurley v. Irish-American Gay, Lesbian and Bisexual Group of Boston,* 515 U.S. 557 (1995).

[32]*Id.* at 568.

[33]*Id.* at 573, citing *McIntyre v. Ohio Elections Commission,* 514 U.S. 334 (1995).

[34]*Elfbrandt v. Russell,* 384 U.S. 11 (1966).

[35]*Keyishian v. Board of Regents,* 385 U.S. 589 (1967).

[36]*Elfbrandt v. Russell,* 384 U.S. 11, 18 (1966).

[37]*Id.*

[38]*Cole v. Richardson,* 405 U.S. 676 (1972).

[39]*Id.* at 680–681.

[40]*Id.* at 686.

[41]*Connick v. Myers,* 461 U.S. 138 (1983).

[42]*Rankin v. McPherson,* 483 U.S. 378 (1987).

[43]*Id.* at 384.

[44]*Board of County Commissioners v. Umbehr,* 518 U.S. 668 (1966).

[45]*Id.* at 677.

[46]*Garner v. Los Angeles Board of Public Works,* 341 U.S. 716 (1951).

[47]*Id.* fn4. *See* n.5.

[48]*Buckley v. Valeo,* 424 U.S. 1 (1976).

[49]*Barenblatt v. U.S.,* 360 U.S. 109 (1959).

[50]*Gibson v. Florida Legislative Investigation Committee,* 372 U.S. 539 (1963).

[51]*Id.* at 544.

 For additional resources, go to *http://www.westlegalstudies.com*

CHAPTER 13

FREEDOM OF PRESS AND OTHER MEDIA-RELATED ISSUES

"In the First Amendment the Founding Fathers gave the free press the protection it must have to fulfill its essential role in our democracy. The press was to serve the governed, not the governors. The Government's powers to censor the press was abolished so that the press would remain forever free to censure the Government. The press was protected so that it could bare the secrets of government and inform the people. Only a free and unrestrained press can effectively expose deception in government. And paramount among the responsibilities of a free press is the duty to prevent any part of the government from deceiving the people and sending them off to distant lands to die of foreign fevers and foreign shot and shell."

—*Justice Hugo Black*
New York Times v. United States

INTRODUCTION

The First Amendment's **freedom of the press** is a right that the Framers of the Constitution took very seriously. Often this right is mixed in with the discussion of freedom of speech or expression that is also found in that amendment. In this textbook, the discussion on freedom of expression is contained in Chapter 10, but there are special issues surrounding the press or media that need to be discussed in this chapter.

The First Amendment says:

> *Congress shall make no law respecting an establishment of religion, or prohibiting the free exercise thereof; or abridging the freedom of speech or of the press: or the right of the people peaceably to assemble, and to petition the Government for a redress of grievances.*[1]

It is this language that has given rise to much litigation through the years. The courts have been called on to determine what freedom of the press means, whether the media has special rights or privileges that ordinary citizens do not enjoy, how and when the government may restrain the publication of information, what governmental information must be made available to the public through the press or media, when members of the press or media can be compelled to divulge the source of information that is published, and exactly what is meant by the public's "right to know." These are the issues to be discussed in this chapter.

freedom of the press
the First Amendment right of the press to publish most things "without censorship or prior restraint," to be free from unreasonable attempts to punish what has already been published, and other rights.

HISTORY OF FREEDOM OF THE PRESS

The right to freedom of the press has an interesting history. In pre-Revolutionary times, the first residents of this country suffered from the types of prior restraints upon publications that the Framers of the Constitution hoped to avoid in the future. The British government was persistent in its attempt to prevent or abridge free expression when it came to criticism of the government or its agencies. The British government went so far as to pass tax laws that were intended to suppress the publication of comments and criticisms of the King and his policies. It was one type of taxation that stirred the colonists to revolt and declare their independence.

In spite of the experience the colonists had with the British, the first Massachusetts legislature passed a stamp tax on all newspapers and magazines, which had the same effect as the British taxes that had caused the colonists to revolt. This stamp tax, along with an advertisement tax, which was imposed the following year, caused violent protests and eventually both tax laws were repealed. This was prior to the passage of the First Amendment, but the Framers of the Constitution were very familiar not only with the British experience, but also with the struggle in Massachusetts. It was these experiences that prompted the Framers to include the specific right of freedom of the press in the First Amendment and made it unconstitutional for the federal government to use most types of prior restraints to keep individuals from publishing unpopular ideas.

Freedom of the press was selectively incorporated or became applicable to the states with the case of *Gitlow v. New York*[2] and that holding was reaffirmed in the case of *Near v. Minnesota*.[3] In the *Near* case, the Court heard a challenge to a Minnesota law, which made it illegal for anyone to publish obscene, malicious, scandalous, or defamatory magazines, newspapers, and periodicals. Near, a publisher, was prosecuted under the statute and he claimed the law violated his rights under the First Amendment freedom of the press and the Fourteenth Amendment Due Process Clause. While the Court reaffirmed that freedom of the press is applicable to the states as well as the federal government, it went on to note that this right is not absolute and, under certain circumstances, the state can punish the abuse of this right. "The security of the community life may be protected against incitement to acts of violence and the overthrow by force of orderly government. The constitutional guaranty of free speech does not 'protect a man from an injunction against uttering words that may have all the effect of force. *Gompers v. Buck's Stove & Range Co.*, 221 U.S. 418.'"[4] Near claimed that this statute did not qualify as a justification for state action against him and his publication, and what he had published could not be construed as advocating violence or the overthrow of the government by force.

The Court agreed with Near and further noted that the statute was not intended to punish Near or others in a similar situation, but the purpose of the law was to act as a restraint on publication, and stated that "it has generally, if not universally, considered that it is the chief purpose of the guaranty to prevent previous restraints upon publication."[5] The Court agreed with the famous jurist, Blackstone, who wrote that liberty of the press is essential to having a free society. However, in the Court's view, there will always be some abuse associated with the right of freedom of the press, and as such, the state may have the right to restrain publication under the circumstances noted above. The Court cautioned, however, that to eliminate all potential or perceived abuse would allow for unacceptable **prior restraints** and noted that "[t]he general principle that the constitutional guaranty of the liberty of the press gives immunity from previous restraints has been approved in many decisions under the provisions of state constitutions. The importance of this immunity has not lessened."[6] While the Court was not in favor of reckless attacks on individuals through use of the press, it asserted that the fact that these potential abuses exist does not change the fact that prior restraints are constitutionally impermissible. The constitutional guarantee of freedom of the press exists because an "even more serious public evil would be caused by authority to prevent publication."[7] In saying this, the Court reversed the Minnesota Court's decision to grant an injunction prohibiting Near from publishing his newspaper.

prior restraint   the government stopping someone from saying, publishing, or otherwise communicating something; prior restraint of speech is unconstitutional under the First Amendment unless the speech is a "clear and present danger" to the country or is obscene or violates a person's legally recognized right to privacy.

Thus, while the Court will strictly scrutinize any state action that acts as a prior restraint on freedom of the press, they also hold that this right is not absolute. Over the years the Court has looked at many state actions that have been alleged to have acted as a prior restraint on publication. It is this basic principle and the acknowledgement of the state's right to restrain publication under certain circumstances that has led to the many issues and interesting cases discussed below.

SPECIAL PRIVILEGES OF THE MEDIA

Members of the media often suggest that, as the First Amendment mentions freedom of the press, logic dictates that the media has special rights or privileges under this amendment. While the argument may seem to make sense on the surface, because, after all, specifically mentioning freedom of the press must be significant, the Court has never recognized special privileges for the media. On the other hand, the Court has never held that the freedom of the press clause is simply a part or clarification of the overall right of free speech. This ambiguity has left the question of special privileges for the press open to debate. The Court has certainly had many opportunities to clear up this question and while we have a general rule, there are still some questions in this area.

The first case to raise the question of special privileges for the media is the case of *Garland v. Torre*[8] where it was argued that the First Amendment protected a reporter from having to reveal confidential information pursuant to a subpoena in a civil action. The Second Circuit Court of Appeals rejected this argument and held that the reporter must appear pursuant to the subpoena and answer questions accordingly. The Supreme Court denied certiorari in that case, but in the cases that followed this type of argument has routinely been rejected.

Generally, the Court has said the "publisher of a newspaper has no special immunity from the applications of general laws. He has no special privilege to invade the rights and liberties of others."[9] While the Court does recognize that a publisher does have the right to print almost anything, there are restrictions such as being forbidden to publish or circulate information known to be false and damaging to another's reputation.[10] It is also well established that a journalist may be punished for contempt of court under certain circumstances,[11] and that the First Amendment does not guarantee the press special access to information that is not generally available to the public.[12]

With these general rules as a backdrop, there are specific issues relating to the press that are worth noting specifically. In 1972, the Court combined two freedom of the press cases that raised the same issue regarding the power of the state to compel a publisher or journalist to appear in front of a grand jury to answer questions regarding a confidential source. The cases, *Branzburg v. Hayes* and *United States v. Caldwell*,[13] brought the issue of whether it is a violation of the First Amendment freedom of the press to require a journalist to appear and testify before a state or federal grand jury. In both of these cases, the journalists reported on cases involving individuals who were committing illegal acts, but were careful not to reveal the names of the individuals involved. The journalists were subsequently subpoenaed by grand juries in their respective jurisdictions and asked to answer questions about the source of the information each had reported. The journalists refused to answer questions, claiming that the First Amendment freedom of the press clause protected them from being compelled to answer these types of questions. Specifically, the journalists argued that in order to gather news it is necessary for them to agree not to identify the source of that information and if they are forced to reveal these sources to a grand jury, those sources, as well as future sources, will not agree to give information. This would be detrimental to the free flow of information protected by the First Amendment.[14] In deciding the issue, the Court first recognized the importance of protecting free speech, press and assembly, but ultimately held that compelling a journalist to answer questions about sources when appearing in front of a grand jury is not a violation of any of the First Amendment rights. The Court said that:

> [T]he great weight of authority is that newsmen are not exempt from the normal duty of appearing before a grand jury and answering questions relevant to a criminal investigation. At common law, courts consistently refused to recognize the existence of any privilege authorizing a newsman to refuse to reveal confidential information to a grand jury.[15]

The Court went on to acknowledge that in order for a grand jury to do the tasks assigned to it, namely to determine whether criminal activity has occurred, the powers of the grand jury must be broad in scope. To grant the journalists the type of privilege they requested would be to undermine the grand jury's authority and ability to accomplish the tasks assigned to it.

In spite of the Court's unwillingness to grant the privilege requested by the journalists, it does acknowledge that several states have given journalists such a privilege. The Court declines to grant such a privilege on the federal level. The Court's opinion suggests that the history of the First Amendment is part of the reason for its decision, but also notes that if it were to do as the journalists requested, it would be creating a privilege that is not enjoyed by other citizens and one that would place a significant burden on the government's ability to enforce the laws. The Court held that it was in the public interest to ensure an effective grand jury process and that this public interest outweighed any burden placed on the press that results from requiring journalists to respond to a grand jury subpoena and answer questions asked of them during the grand jury's investigation.[16]

The Court also noted that the desire of informants to remain anonymous rests on the fact that those informants want to escape criminal prosecution. Granting the privilege requested by the journalists supports this desire, and the Court held that this desire to escape criminal prosecution is not deserving of constitutional protection. Lastly, the journalists did not persuade the Court that refusing to give journalists the privilege requested would diminish the flow of news. The Court held that the journalists had failed to offer sufficient evidence to demonstrate the claimed outcome. It was "unclear how often and to what extent informers are actually deterred from furnishing information when newsmen are forced to testify before a grand jury."[17] For all of these reasons, the Court reaffirmed the prior common-law and constitutional rules that require journalists to appear before and answer questions posed by grand juries.

Other issues regarding special privileges for journalists persisted, even after *Branzburg*. In 1978, the Court heard the case of *Zurcher v. The Stanford Daily*.[18] A photojournalist for the *Stanford Daily* (the *Daily*) attended a demonstration at a local hospital. The demonstrators had seized the hospital's administrative offices and the police were called. While the police attempted to end the standoff with the demonstrators, a number of the demonstrators attacked some of the police officers, injuring nine of them. The *Daily's* photojournalist took pictures of the altercation and later published them in the *Daily*. When the police saw the publication, they obtained a warrant from the local court giving them permission to search the *Daily's* office for negatives, photographs, and films or other evidence relevant to identifying the individuals who assaulted the police officers. This warrant was executed, but no new evidence, beyond that already published in the paper, was found, and no materials were removed from the *Daily's* offices. The *Daily* and several of its staff brought a civil action in federal court a month later, claiming the search had violated their

First, Fourth, and Fourteenth Amendment rights. While much of the opinion focused on the Fourth Amendment, it is worth noting that the *Daily* and its staff claimed that such a search of a newspaper office should only be allowed in rare circumstances and that two things must be shown in order to get such a search warrant. The two things are (1) a showing that it is likely that important materials will be destroyed or removed from the jurisdiction if a search warrant is not issued and executed and (2) the danger of destruction or removal cannot be guarded against by the issuance of a restraining order.[19] While other courts have accepted this, the Supreme Court did not, holding "Neither the Fourth Amendment nor the cases requiring consideration of First Amendment values in issuing search warrants, however, call for imposing the regime ordered by the District Court."[20] The Court went on to say that the ordinary conditions for obtaining a search warrant are sufficient to insure that the First Amendment rights are not violated. The Court said:

> There is no reason to believe . . . that magistrates cannot guard against searches of the type, scope, and intrusiveness that would actually interfere with the timely publication of a newspaper. Nor, of the requirement of specificity and reasonableness are properly applied, policed, and observed, will there be any occasion or opportunity for officers to rummage at large in newspaper files or to intrude into or to deter normal editorial and publication decisions.[21]

The Court also noted that the *Daily* was alleging that the police action was a prior restraint and yet another violation of the First Amendment. When specifically reviewing the facts of this particular case, the Court first noted that not all searches and seizures are automatically a prior restraint as the *Daily* urged. In addition, the Court held that a search warrant issued to search for photographs made in a public place and that have already been published could not be seen as a "realistic threat of prior restraint or of any direct restraint whatsoever."[22] Therefore, the Court concluded, their was no violation of either the Fourth or the First Amendment as it was demonstrated that the magistrate signing the search warrant had used all the appropriate standards in deciding whether such a warrant was justified, the police had acted appropriately when executing the warrant and there was no prior restraint.

Another case involving an alleged violation of the Freedom of the Press Clause of the First Amendment is the case of *Minneapolis Star and Tribune Company v. Minnesota Commissioner of Revenue*.[23] This case involved a challenge to a Minnesota tax law that required publishers to pay a tax on paper and ink products used in the production of their publication.

MINNEAPOLIS STAR AND TRIBUNE COMPANY V. MINNESOTA COMMISSIONER OF REVENUE
460 U.S. 575 (1983)

Justice O'CONNOR delivered the opinion of the Court.

This case presents the question of a State's power to impose a special tax on the press and, by enacting exemptions, to limit its effect to only a few newspapers.

I

Since 1967, Minnesota has imposed a sales tax on most sales of goods for a price in excess of a nominal sum. In general, the tax applies only to retail sales. An exemption for industrial and agricultural users shields from the tax sales of components to be used in the production of goods that will themselves be sold at retail.

* * *

The appellant, Minneapolis Star and Tribune Company "Star Tribune", is the publisher of a morning newspaper and an evening newspaper in Minneapolis. From 1967 to 1971, it enjoyed an

Continued

exemption from the sales and use tax provided by Minnesota for periodic publications. In 1971, however, while leaving the exemption from the sales tax in place, the legislature amended the scheme to impose a "use tax" on the cost of paper and ink products consumed in the production of a publication. Ink and paper used in publications became the only items subject to the use tax that were components of goods to be sold at retail. In 1974, the legislature again amended the statute, this time to exempt the first $100,000 worth of ink and paper consumed by a publication in any calendar year, in effect giving each publication an annual tax credit of $4,000. Publications remained exempt from the sales tax.

After the enactment of the $100,000 exemption, 11 publishers, producing 14 of the 388 paid circulation newspapers in the State, incurred a tax liability in 1974. Star Tribune was one of the 11, and, of the $893,355 collected, it paid $608,634, or roughly two-thirds of the total revenue raised by the tax. In 1975, 13 publishers, producing 16 out of 374 paid circulation papers, paid a tax. That year, Star Tribune again bore roughly two-thirds of the total receipts from the use tax on ink and paper.

Star Tribune instituted action to seek a refund of the use taxes it paid from January 1, 1974 to May 31, 1975. It challenged the imposition of the use tax on ink and paper used in publications as a violation of the guarantees of freedom of the press and equal protection in the First and Fourteenth Amendments. The Minnesota Supreme Court upheld the tax against the federal constitutional challenge. We noted probable jurisdiction, and we now reverse.

* * *

III

Clearly, the First Amendment does not prohibit all regulation of the press. It is beyond dispute that the States and the Federal Government can subject newspapers to generally applicable economic regulations without creating constitutional problems. Minnesota, however, has not chosen to apply its general sales and use tax to newspapers. Instead, it has created a special tax that applies only to certain publications protected by the First Amendment. Although the State argues now that the tax on paper and ink is part of the general scheme of taxation, the use tax provision . . . is facially discriminatory,

singling out publications for treatment that is, to our knowledge, unique in Minnesota tax law.

Minnesota's treatment of publications differs from that of other enterprises in at least two important respects: it imposes a use tax that does not serve the function of protecting the sales tax, and it taxes an intermediate transaction rather than the ultimate retail sale. A use tax ordinarily serves to complement the sales tax by eliminating the incentive to make major purchases in States with lower sales taxes; it requires the resident who shops out-of-state to pay a use tax equal to the sales tax savings. Minnesota designed its overall use tax scheme to serve this function. As the regulations state, "The 'use tax' is a compensatory or complementary tax."

Thus, in general, items exempt from the sales tax are not subject to the use tax, for, in the event of a sales tax exemption, there is no "complementary function" for a use tax to serve. But the use tax on ink and paper serves no such complementary function; it applies to all uses, whether or not the taxpayer purchased the ink and paper in-state, and it applies to items exempt from the sales tax.

Further the ordinary rule in Minnesota, as discussed above, is to tax only the ultimate, or retail, sale rather than the use of components like ink and paper . . . Publishers, however, are taxed on their purchase of components, even though they will eventually sell their publications at retail. By creating this special use tax, which, to our knowledge, is without parallel in the State's tax scheme, Minnesota has singled out the press for special treatment. We then must determine whether the First Amendment permits such special taxation. A tax that burdens rights protected by the First Amendment cannot stand unless the burden is necessary to achieve an overriding governmental interest. Any tax that the press must pay, of course, imposes some "burden." But, as we have observed this Court has long upheld economic regulation of the press. The cases approving such economic regulation, however, emphasized the general applicability of the challenged regulation to all businesses, suggesting that a regulation that has singled out the press might place a heavier burden of justification on the Sate, and we now conclude that the special problems created by differential treatment do indeed impose such a burden.

Continued

There is substantial evidence that differential taxation of the press would have troubled the Framers of the First Amendment. The role of the press in mobilizing sentiment in favor of independence was critical to the Revolution. When the Constitution was proposed without an explicit guarantee of freedom of the press, the Antifederalists objected.

*** *** ***

The fears of the Antifederalists were well-founded. A power to tax differentially, as opposed to a power to tax generally, gives a government a powerful weapon against the taxpayer selected. When the State imposes a generally applicable tax, there is little cause for concern. We need not fear that a government will destroy a selected group of taxpayers by burdensome taxation if it must impose the same burden on the rest of its constituency. When the State singles out the press, though, the political constraints that prevent a legislature from passing crippling taxes of general applicability are weakened, and the threat of burdensome taxes becomes acute. That threat can operate as effectively as a censor to check critical comment by the press, undercutting the basic assumption of our political system that the press will often serve as an important restraint in government.

Further, differential treatment, unless justified by some special characteristic of the press, suggests that the goal of the regulation is not unrelated to suppression of expression, and such a goal is presumptively unconstitutional. Differential taxation of the press, then, places such a burden on the interests protected by the First Amendment that we cannot countenance such treatment unless the State asserts a counterbalancing interest of compelling importance that it cannot achieve without differential taxation.

IV

The main interest asserted by Minnesota in this case is the raising of revenue. Of course that interest is critical to any government. Standing alone, however, it cannot justify the special treatment of the press, for an alternative means of achieving the same interest without raising concerns under the First Amendment is clearly available: the State could raise the revenue by taxing businesses generally, avoiding the censorial threat implicit in a tax that singles out the press.

Addressing the concern with differential treatment, Minnesota invites us to look beyond the form of the tax to its substance. The tax is, according to the State, merely a substitute for the sales tax, which, as a generally applicable tax, would b constitutional as applied to the press. There are two fatal flaws in this reasoning. First, the State has offered no explanation of why it chose to use a substitute for the sales tax rather than the sales tax itself. The court below speculated that the State might have been concerned that collection of a tax on such small transactions would be impractical. That suggestion is unpersuasive, for sales of other low-priced goods are not exempt. If the real goal of this tax is to supplicate the sales tax, it is difficult to see why the State did not achieve that goal by the obvious and effective expedient of applying the sales tax.

Further, even assuming the legislature did have valid reasons for substituting another tax for the sales tax, we are not persuaded that this tax does serve as a substitute. The State asserts that this scheme actually favors the press over other businesses, because the same rate of tax is applied, but, for the press, the rate applies to the cost of components rather than to the sales price. We would be hesitant to fashion a rule that automatically allowed the State to single out the press for a different method of taxation as long as the effective burden was no different from that on other taxpayers or the burden on the press was lighter than that on other businesses. One reason for this reluctance is that the very selection of the press for special treatment threatens the press not only with the current differential treatment, but with the possibility of subsequent differentially more burdensome treatment. Thus, even without actually imposing an extra burden on the press, the government might be able to achieve censorial effects for "[t]he threat of sanctions may deter [the] exercise of [First Amendment] rights almost as potently as the actual application of sanctions." *NAACP v. Button*, 371 U.S. 415, 433, 83 S. Ct. 328, 338 9 L. Ed. 2d 405 (1963).

A second reason to avoid the proposed rule is that courts as institutions are poorly equipped to evaluate with precision the relative burdens of various methods of taxation. The complexities of factual economic proof always present a certain potential for error, and courts have little

Continued

familiarities with the process of evaluating the relative economic burden of taxes. In sum, the possibility of error inherent in the proposed rule poses too great a threat to concerns at the heart of the First Amendment, and we cannot tolerate that possibility. Minnesota, therefore has offered no adequate justification for the special treatment of newspapers.

V

Minnesota's ink and paper tax violates the First Amendment not only because it singles out the press, but also because it targets a small group of newspapers. The effect of the $100,000 exemption enacted in 1974 is that only a handful of publishers pay any tax at all, and even fewer pay any significant amount of tax. The State explains this exemption as part of a policy favoring an "equitable" tax system, although there are no comparable exemptions for small enterprises outside the press. Again, there is no legislative history supporting the State's view of the purpose of the amendment. Whatever the motive of the legislature in this case, we think that recognizing a power in the State not only to single out the press but also to tailor the tax so that it singles out a few members of the press presents such a potential for abuse that no interest suggested by Minnesota can justify the scheme. It has asserted no interest, other than its desire to have an "equitable" tax system. The current system, it explains, promotes equity because it places the burden on large publications that impose more social costs than do smaller publications and that are more likely to be able to bear the burden of the tax. Even if we were willing to accept the premise that large businesses are more profitable and therefore better able to bear the burden of the tax, the State's commitment to this "equity" is questionable, for the concern has not led the State to grant benefits to small businesses in general. And when the exemption selects such a narrowly defined group to bear the full burden of the tax, the tax begins to resemble more a penalty for a few of the largest newspapers than an attempt to favor struggling enterprises.

We need not and do not impugn the motives of the Minnesota legislature in passing the ink and paper tax. Illicit legislative intent is not the sine qua non of a violation of the First Amendment. We have long recognized that even regulations aimed at proper governmental concerns can restrict unduly the exercise of rights protected by the First Amendment. A tax that singles out the press, or that targets individual publications within the press, places a heavy burden on the State to justify its action. Since Minnesota has offered no satisfactory justification for its tax on the use of ink and paper, the tax violates the First Amendment, and the judgment below is

Reversed.

With this case, the Court made it clear that neither federal nor state government can single out the press, whether it is singling out the press for special privileges or for special burdens. The Court held in this manner in spite of the fact that there was no reason to believe that the Minnesota legislature was attempting to censor the *Star Tribune* or any of the other newspapers affected by the use tax. In reaching its conclusion, the Court used the strict scrutiny standard that it uses in most situations involving fundamental or explicitly granted rights under the constitution. Minnesota was not able to give a compelling governmental interest that could be accomplished only through use of the paper and ink tax. The state's failure to give this compelling reason guaranteed the failure of the use tax.

Lastly, in the area of special privileges for the media, the Courts have held that newspapers and other publications can be civilly sued for damages arising out of violations of confidentiality agreements. In *Cohen v. Cowles Media Company*,[24] Dan Cohen sued the publishers of the *St. Paul Pioneer Press Dispatch* and the *Minneapolis Star and Tribune* when those newspapers published his name in connection with information he had given them as a confidential source. Cohen had approached the newspapers and offered to supply information about a candidate in an upcoming election. The reporters working for the newspapers agreed to Cohen's demand that his identity not be revealed and once this agreement was in place Cohen turned over the information to the reporters. Once the reporters had looked at the documents and investigated the candidate named in the documents, they, along with the editorial staffs of the two newspapers, decided to name Cohen as the source of the information, in spite of the agreement. Cohen was fired from his job as a result of being named as a source and he sued in the Minnesota courts. After appeals to both the Minnesota Court of Appeals and the Minnesota Supreme Court, the case was appealed to the U.S. Supreme Court for a decision on the question of "whether the First Amendment prohibits a plaintiff from recovering damages, under state **promissory estoppel** law, for a newspaper's breach of a promise of confidentiality given to the plaintiff in exchange for information."[25] After a discussion of promissory estoppel in general, the Court noted that there is a well-established line of cases that hold that laws which apply to the general population also apply to the press and do not violate the First Amendment simply because the laws have an incidental effect on the ability to gather and report the news. The Court specifically quoted *Associated Press v. NLRB* where it was written "It is, therefore, beyond dispute that 'the publisher of a newspaper has no special immunity from the application of general laws. He has no special privilege to invade the rights and liberties of others.'"[26] As this is so, the enforcement of the law against the press is no different from the enforcement against the general population. The Court went on to say that even though the dissenting opinions in this case suggest that the press should not be subject to any law that limits the press' ability to gather and report the news. The Court rejected this saying "The First Amendment does not grant the press such limitless protection."[27] With regard to the specific question about promissory estoppel, the Court concluded that the First Amendment does not give the press the right to disregard promises and held that this general law does, indeed, apply to the press just as it would to anyone else.

While there may be questions concerning specific law in the future, the Court's holdings indicate that it steadfastly adheres to the principle that rules of general applicability apply to the press as well as the general population. It appears that so long as a law does not single out the press and treat it differently from the general population, the press will not be successful in asserting that the First Amendment gives it special privileges.

promissory estoppel the principle that when Person A makes a promise and expects Person B to do something in reliance upon that promise, then Person B does act in reliance upon that promise, the law will usually help Person B enforce the promise because Person B has *relied* upon the promise to his or her *detriment;* person A is "stopped" from breaking the promise even when there is no consideration to make the promise binding as part of a contract.

GOVERNMENT ATTEMPTS TO RESTRAIN THE PRESS

Prior Restraints in General

Attempts have been made over the years, using legislation and court-ordered injunctions, to keep the press from publishing or disseminating information or opinions. These attempts to use prior restraints have been held to be unconstitutional and in the Court's words, "Any system of prior restraints of expression comes to this Court bearing a heavy presumption against its constitutional validity."[28]

One of the two classic cases dealing with prior restraints is the *Near* case discussed earlier in this chapter. The other classic case is most popularly known as the Pentagon Papers Case, whose true title is *New York Times Co. v. United States.*[29] This case began on June 13, 1971, when the *New York Times* published its first story on the Pentagon Papers entitled "Vietnam Archive: Pentagon

Study Traces 3 Decades of Growing U.S. Involvement" (see Exhibit 13.1). A day later, the Attorney General of the United States, John Mitchell, warned the *New York Times* not to publish any future articles on the Pentagon Papers. The day after that, the United States went to federal court to get an injunction against the *New York Times* as well as the *Washington Post* to keep both newspapers from publishing any further information about the Pentagon Papers. By June 26, 1971, the case was before the Supreme Court, which handed down its decision on June 30, 1971. In its per curiam opinion, the Court simply stated the general rule that prior restraints were presumed unconstitutional and that the government had the burden of demonstrating a compelling governmental interest sufficient enough to warrant the issuing of an injunction. The concurring opinions that followed indicated that a majority of six agreed that the government had failed to adequately demonstrate a compelling governmental interest and that no injunction should have been issued, but the six could not all agree as to the reasoning behind the decision. Three justices, Chief Justice Burger, Justice Blackmun, and Justice Harlan, dissented from the majority stating they believed that the government was entitled to an injunction because the need to protect national security justified the use of prior restraints in this case.

Of the six in the majority, there were two schools of thought. One group, Justices Black and Douglas, argued that there should never be prior restraints imposed on the press. The other group, Justices White, Stewart, Brennan, and Marshall, wrote that there could be prior restraints under some extreme circumstances, but none of them believed extreme circumstances were proven in this case.

If one is to look at the number of votes in an effort to determine the attitude toward prior restraints in this case, the conclusion could be drawn that prior restraints would be available in cases involving circumstances demonstrating grave damage to national security. Justice Brennan wrote: "there is a single, extremely narrow class of cases in which the First Amendment's ban on prior judicial restraint may be overridden. Our cases have thus far indicated that such cases may arise only when the Nation 'is at war' . . ."[30] Therefore, the Court would enjoin the press from publishing the information in this case only if the government could demonstrate, in Justice Stewart's words, that the publication would "surely result in direct, immediate, and irreparable damage to our Nation or its people."[31] Several of the justices noted in their opinions that the government failed to demonstrate any irreparable harm to national security and because of this failure the government was not entitled to the injunction it sought.

Another issue that seemed to haunt the justices in this case was the fact that the government was not attempting to obtain an injunction based on any statutory authority. Instead, the executive branch was asking for assistance from the judicial branch without giving any real justification for its request. As Justice Stewart wrote,

> [T]he only effective restraint upon executive policy and power in the areas of national defense and international affairs may lie in an enlightened citizenry—in an informed and critical public opinion which alone can here protect the values of democratic government. For this reason, it is perhaps here that a press that is alert, aware, and free most vitally serves the basic purpose of the First Amendment. For without an informed and free press there cannot be an enlightened people.[32]

Without disclosure and statutory authority to support it, the Court was further justified in refusing to act as the executive branch of the government requested.

EXHIBIT 13.1   Pentagon Papers

In 1967, Secretary of Defense Robert S. McNamara commissioned a study of the United States' involvement in the ongoing war in Southeast Asia. The result was a 47-volume study that the government classified as "top secret" when in reality, the information was historical in nature and contained no operational information that would impact the United States' ongoing war effort.[33]

Daniel Ellsberg, who had worked for the Rand Corporation researching and writing studies on defense policies, disclosed the Pentagon Papers to the *New York Times*. Ellsberg, along with Anthony Russo, was later arrested for disclosing these "top secret" papers. The *Times* reporter Neil Sheehan used the disclosed information and wrote an article, published on June 13, 1971. This article told of the study done by the government and reported that the study showed that four administrations had gradually increased U.S. involvement in Southeast Asia and that the Johnson administration in particular had lied to both the public and Congress about the extent of the U.S. involvement.[34] This was the first of a 10-part series that would specifically show that the government had resisted full disclosure of its involvement and that there were air strikes over Laos, raids along the coast of North Vietnam, and offensive actions by U.S. Marines taking place long before such actions were disclosed to the public.

On Monday evening, June 14, 1971, Attorney General John Mitchell called the *New York Times* and demanded that the publication of the 10-part series on the Pentagon Papers be halted. This phone call was followed by a telegram that said:

"Arthur Ochs Sulzberger
President and Publisher
The New York Times
New York New York

I have been advised by the Secretary of Defense that the material published in The New York Times on June 13, 1971 captioned "Key Texts From Pentagon's Vietnam Study" contains information relating to the national defense of the United States and bears a top secret classification.

As such, publication of this information is directly prohibited by the provisions of the Espionage law, Title 18, United States Code, Section 793.

Moreover further publication of information of this character will cause irreparable injury to the defense interests of the United States.

Accordingly, I respectfully request that you publish no further information of this character and advise me that you have made arrangements for the return of these documents to the Department of Defense.

John W. Mitchell
Attorney General"[35]

The *New York Times* refused the demand and on June 15, 1971, the U.S. Attorney General's office went to the Federal District Court where Judge Murray L. Gurfein issued a temporary restraining order requiring the *New York Times* to halt publication for four days. The lower federal courts continued to prohibit the publication of the *New York Times* articles and similar articles by other newspapers. Ultimately, the U.S. Supreme Court heard the matter approximately two weeks after the conflict had begun. On June 30, 1971, the Supreme Court held, on a 9-0 vote, to lift the prior restraints imposed by the lower courts.

The men responsible for the leak, Daniel Ellsberg and Anthony Russo, were later tried on charges of conspiracy and espionage, but were acquitted.

Fair Trial versus Freedom of the Press

It is the conflict between the First Amendment's freedom of the press and the Sixth Amendment's right to a fair trial that is most troublesome to the courts. On the one hand, the First Amendment indicates that the public has the right to information brought to them through the press. On the other hand, the Sixth Amendment gives the defendant a variety of rights connected to the idea of a "fair" trial, such as the right to a speedy trial, the right to a public trial, and the right to be tried by a jury of one's peers. If the press is given free rein to publish unlimited information about a defendant, particularly information about a confession, prior convictions, and other bad acts, it will diminish the justice system's ability to provide a fair trial for that defendant. An example of this conflict arises in the 1935 case involving Bruno Hauptmann, the defendant in the infamous kidnapping and murder case known as the Lindbergh Baby Trial (see Exhibit 13.2). There were so many journalists and filmmakers in the courtroom that many questioned whether Hauptmann had been given a fair trial. Following the Hauptmann case, a series of cases regarding the conflict between a fair trial and a free press were decided.

EXHIBIT 13.2   The Lindbergh Baby Trial

On March 1, 1932, the son of the famous aviator, Charles Lindbergh, was kidnapped from the Lindbergh home in New Jersey. The kidnapper entered the nursery through a window, using a homemade extension ladder. The kidnapper left a ransom note and then exited the home with the child. The ladder was found broken outside the house and there were large footprints leading away from the home. After a month of notes and other developments, Dr. John F. Condon paid the ransom on behalf of the Lindberghs and received information from the individual accepting the ransom money that the child was on a boat called *Nelly* that was anchored between Horseneck Beach and Elizabeth Island. A search for the boat proved fruitless. On May 12, 1932, a truck driver came across the remains of a child's body about two miles from the Lindbergh home. The autopsy proved that the child was Charles A. Lindbergh, Jr. and that he had died the night he was kidnapped.

The case remained open and no progress was made on the case until November 27, 1933, when a cashier at the Loew's Theater took a gold note, which had been part of the ransom, from a man who matched the description of the man who had taken the ransom money from Condon. Several months later, the head teller at the Corn Exchange Bank found another gold note with numbers penciled in the margin that proved to be a license plate number. The gas station attendant who had taken it from a male customer driving a blue Dodge van had written the number on it. The New York Motor Vehicle Bureau traced the number and found that the vehicle belonged to Bruno Richard Hauptmann. Hauptmann was arrested and searches of his home and garage uncovered over $1800 in gold notes that had been part of the $50,000 paid by Lindbergh to the kidnapper. Hauptmann claimed that the money had belonged to his friend, Isidor Fisch, who had died a few months earlier from tuberculosis. Hauptmann never confessed, his fingerprints were never matched to those at the scene of the kidnapping, but Hauptmann was charged with the kidnapping and murder of the Lindbergh baby. He was tried in New Jersey.

The trial began on January 2, 1935, and over 700 journalists and technicians were on hand for the event. In addition, celebrities such as Walter Winchell and Jack Benny attended, as well as thousands of curious spectators. Vendors pandered to the crowds by selling miniature kidnap ladders, locks of the child's hair and photographs of Charles Lindbergh. The publicity, both before and during the trial, was overwhelming, but a jury was impaneled, and the trial began. In all, 162 witnesses were called including the child's parents, the defendant's spouse and the defendant. Hauptmann offered many alibi witnesses, but these individuals were found to be less than credible on cross-examination. Hauptmann was convicted on February 13, 1935 and sentenced to die. On April 3, 1936, Hauptmann was put to death in the electric chair. He was offered large sums of money for his family if he would confess and give details of the crime and he was also told that he might avoid the electric chair if he would confess, but Hauptmann steadfastly maintained his innocence to the end.[36]

EXHIBIT 13.2   Wanted Poster

EXHIBIT 13.2   The Courthouse, Hunterdon, NJ, 1935 (courtesy of © Bettman/Corbis)

The first of the cases was *Bridges v. California*, a 1941 case in which the Court held that prior restraints on pretrial coverage were unconstitutional unless the government could show that there was a clear and present danger to the administration of justice.[37] In 1951 the Court decided another case involving free press and fair trials. That case was *Shepherd v. Florida*[38] and in that case, the Court reviewed the conviction of four African Americans convicted of raping a 17-year-old white girl.

SHEPHERD V. FLORIDA
341 U.S. 50 (1951)

PER CURIAM.

On the 16th of July, 1949, a seventeen-year-old white girl in Lake County, Florida, reported that she had been raped, at the point of a pistol, by four Negroes. Six days later petitioners were indicted and, beginning September 1, were tried for the offense, convicted without recommendation of mercy, and sentenced to death. The

Continued

Supreme Court of Florida, in reviewing evidence of guilt, said, "As we study the testimony, the only question presented here is which set of witnesses would the jury believe, that is, the State's witnesses or the testimony as given by the defendant-appellants."

But prejudicial influences outside the courtroom, becoming all too typical of a highly publicized trial, were brought to bear on this jury with such force that the conclusion is inescapable that these defendants were prejudged as guilty and the trial was but a legal gesture to register a verdict already dictated by the press and the public opinion which it generated.

Newspapers published as a fact, and attributed the information to the sheriff, that these defendants had confessed. No one, including the sheriff, repudiated the story. Witnesses and persons called as jurors said they had read or heard of this statement. However, no confession was offered at the trial. The only rational explanations for its nonproduction in court are that the story was false or that the confession was obtained under circumstances which made it inadmissible or its use inexpedient.

If the prosecutor in the courtroom had told the jury that the accused had confessed but did not offer to prove the confession, the court would undoubtedly have declared a mistrial and cited the attorney for contempt. If a confession had been offered in court, the defendant would have had the right to be confronted by the persons who claimed to have witnessed it, to cross-examine them, and to contradict their testimony. If the court had allowed an involuntary confession to be placed before the jury, we would not hesitate to consider it a denial of due process of law and reverse. When such events take place in the courtroom, defendant's counsel can meet them with evidence, arguments, and requests for instructions, and can at least preserve his objections on the record.

But neither counsel nor court can control the admission of evidence if unproven, and probably unprovable, "confessions" are put before the jury by newspapers and radio. Rights of the defendant to be confronted by witness against him and to cross-examine them are thereby circumvented. It is hard to imagine a more prejudicial influence than a press release by the officer of the court charged with defendants' custody stating that they had confessed, and here just such a statement, unsworn to, unseen, uncross-examined and uncontradicted was conveyed by the press to the jury.

* * *

No doubt this trial judge felt helpless to give the accused any real protection against this out-of-court campaign to convict. But if freedoms of press are so abused as to make fair trial in the locality impossible, the judicial process must be protected by removing the trial to a forum beyond its probable influence. Newspapers, in the enjoyment of their constitutional rights, may not deprive accused persons of their right to fair trial. These convictions, accompanied by such events, do not meet any civilized conceptions of due process of law. That alone, is sufficient, to my mind, to warrant reversal.

But that is not all. Of course, such a crime stirred deep feeling and was exploited to the limit by the press. These defendants were first taken to the county jail of Lake County. A mob gathered and demanded that defendants be turned over to it. By order of court, they were quickly transferred for safekeeping to the state prison, where they remained until about two weeks before the trial. Meanwhile, a mob burned the home of defendant Shepherd's father and mother and two other Negro houses. Negroes were removed from the community to prevent their being lynched. The National Guard was called out on July 17 and 18 and, on July 19, the 116th Field Artillery was summoned from Tampa. The Negroes of the community abandoned their homes and fled.

Every detail of these passion-arousing events was reported by the press under such headlines as, "Night Riders Burn Lake Negro Homes" and "Flames From Negro Homes Light Night Sky in Lake County." These and many other articles were highly prejudicial, including a cartoon published at the time of the grand jury, picturing four electric chairs and headed, "No Compromise-Supreme Penalty."

Counsel for defendants made two motions, one to defer the trial until the passion had died out and the other for a change of venue. These were denied. The Supreme Court of Florida, in affirming the conviction, observed that "The inflamed public sentiment was against the crime with which the appellants were charged rather than defendants' race." Such an estimate seems more charitable than realistic, and I cannot agree that the prejudice had subsided at the time of trial.

Continued

The trial judge . . . promulgated special rules which limited the number of visitors to those that could be seated, allowed no one to stand or loiter in hallways, stairways, and parts of the courthouse for thirty minutes before court convened and after it recessed, closed the elevators except to officers of the court or individuals to whom the sheriff gave special permit, required each person entering the courtroom to submit to search, prohibited any person from taking a "valise, satchel, bag, basket, bottle, jar, jug, bucket, package, bundle, or other such item" to the courtroom floor of the courthouse, allowed crutches, canes and walking sticks only after inspection by the sheriff showed them to be necessary aids, prohibited demonstrations of any nature and made various other regulations, all of which the sheriff was charged to enforce and to that end was authorized to employ such number of deputies as might be necessary. Such precautions, however commendable, show the reaction to the atmosphere which permeated the trial created in the mind of the trial judge.

[T]his trial took place under conditions and was accompanied by events which would deny defendants a fair trial before any kind of jury. I do not see, as a practical matter, how any Negro on the jury would have dared to cause a disagreement or acquittal. The only chance these Negroes had of acquittal would have been in the courage and decency of some sturdy and forthright white person of sufficient standing to face and live down the odium among his white neighbors that such a vote, if required, would have brought . . . The case presents one of the best examples of one of the worst menaces to American justice.

Reversed.

This case demonstrates the Court's view of the importance of a fair trial overriding the press's right to report the news. The defendant's right to confront any witness who makes a statement regarding the charges against him cannot be undermined by pre-trial statements or reports from the media. In addition, this case also demonstrates the trial court's power to take steps to insure that a fair and safe trial is possible. The Court upheld the trial judge's special rules such as the number of observers allowed into the courtroom during the trial, controlling access to the courtroom and the requirement that individuals entering the courtroom be subject to search by law enforcement. In spite of favorably noting the trial judge's efforts, however, the Court still ultimately held that the defendant's right to a fair trial was violated due to the "confession" that was broadcast, but was not subject to cross-examination.

The tension between the First and Sixth Amendments was also explored in the famous case of *Sheppard v. Maxwell*.[39] This case was the basis for the television show and movie, "The Fugitive" and involved a prominent Cleveland, Ohio, doctor. Sam Sheppard was sleeping on the couch in his home when he heard his wife cry out. When he went to the bedroom, he saw someone standing next to the bed. He struggled with the man and was knocked unconscious. When he awoke, he found his wife mortally injured. He heard a noise in another part of the house and once again, saw someone running out the door. Sheppard pursued this man and he was once again knocked unconscious. When Sheppard recounted the events of the evening to friends, family, and the local police, there were some discrepancies in his story. Ultimately, Sheppard was arrested for the murder; the publicity leading up to the arrest and post-arrest was intense. The press freely interviewed potential witnesses, intruded on the investigation, and published many speculative stories. Publicity increased at trial with the press taking photographs of and publishing the names and addresses of jurors, causing a constant commotion in the courtroom, having free access to every part of the courthouse, and publishing testimony of witnesses with editorials interpreting their testimony. Sheppard was convicted, and ultimately appealed to the Supreme Court claiming that all of the publicity and the inability or unwillingness of the judge to curtail publicity and take control of the courtroom was a violation of his right to a fair and impartial trial.

The Court thoroughly reviewed the record of this case and concluded that Sheppard was correct in his assertion that he had not received a fair trial. The press's actions before and during the trial, combined with the trial judge's mistaken belief that he could do nothing to control the publicity led to the Court's conclusion. In addition, the Court listed several safeguards that trial judges could use in the future to avoid the types of problems found in *Sheppard*. These safeguards include:

1. Taking control of the courthouse, courtroom, and the proceedings to avoid a circus-like atmosphere;
2. Controlling the number of reporters allowed in the courtroom during the trial;
3. Controlling the conduct of the reporters in the courtroom;
4. Insulating the witnesses from the press prior to trial and ordering the witnesses to refrain from reading newspapers or listening to the media via television or radio;
5. Granting a continuance or change of venue when circumstances warrant such a decision;
6. Sequestering the jury to insulate them from continuing publicity;
7. Making an ". . . effort to control the release of leads, information, and gossip to the press by police officers, witnesses, and the counsel for both sides."[40]

These safeguards would ensure that the courts would have done all they could to ensure a fair and impartial trial for a defendant. However, for Sam Sheppard, he spent 10 years in prison leading up to the Court's decision to grant him a new trial and was ultimately acquitted. The murder of his wife has never been solved.

Gag Orders

The *Sheppard* case and the safeguards spelled out by the Court bring up another topic to be discussed when looking at the issue of governmental attempts to restrain the press. The question to be answered is whether **gag orders**, also known as **gag rules**, or the ability of the courts to forbid the press to report on certain legal matters before that court, are constitutional. Justice Clark, who wrote the *Sheppard* decision, alluded to this issue when saying that the judge should have made an effort to control the release of information to the press. He was alluding to gag orders; these orders may be used to keep attorneys, parties, or witnesses from discussing their judicial proceedings with the press. The concern, of course, is that extensive pretrial publicity will make it difficult to find impartial jurors and thus interfere with a defendant's right to a fair trial, as discussed above. While it would seem that the Court in *Sheppard* was promoting the idea of using gag orders, in reality, there is only one case that has reached the Court involving a gag order, and in that case, the Court held that the gag order would rarely be held to be constitutional. That case is *Nebraska Press Association v. Stuart*.[41]

Justice Burger wrote the majority opinion in this case. The case involved the murder of six members of a family in a small Nebraska town. Charles Simants was arrested and charged with these murders and the crime attracted attention from the local, regional, and national press. Three days after the crime, both the county prosecutor and the defense council went to the County Court asking for a restrictive order that would prohibit the press from publishing any information heard at the arraignment or preliminary exam in this matter. It also required the press to observe the Nebraska Bar-Press Guidelines. The order applied only until the jury was impaneled and prohibited the press from reporting five specific subjects: "(1) the existence or contents of a confession Simants had made to law enforcement officers, which had been introduced in open court at arraignment; (2) the fact or nature of statements Simants had

gag order a judge's order that a wildly disruptive defendant be bound and gagged during a trial; a judge's order to lawyers and witnesses that they discuss the trial with no outsiders, reporters in particular; a judge's order, usually held unconstitutional, to reporters that they not report certain court proceedings.

gag rule a gag order; any law or rule that prohibits the expression of ideas or that cuts off debate.

made to other persons; (3) the contents of a note he had written the night of the crime; (4) certain aspects of the medical testimony at the preliminary hearing; and (5) the identity of the victims of the alleged sexual assault and the nature of the assault."[42] The Nebraska Press Association appealed, first asking the District Court to stay its order and then bringing the matter to the Nebraska Supreme Court. The Nebraska Supreme Court balanced Simants' right to a fair trial against the First Amendment claim of the Nebraska Press Association. That court found that Simants' right to a fair trial was in jeopardy due to the publicity surrounding the crime. The Nebraska Supreme Court upheld the order in general, but modified it to prohibit reporting on three matters, "(a) the existence and nature of any confessions or admissions made by the defendant to law enforcement officers, (b) any confessions or admissions made to any third parties, except members of the press, and (c) other facts 'strongly implicative' of the accused."[43] The U.S. Supreme Court granted certiorari to consider the First Amendment/Sixth Amendment issue raised by this order.

The Court acknowledged that the conflict between the First Amendment freedom of the press and the Sixth Amendment right to a fair trial has been in existence since the birth of the country. It also noted that the Framers of the Constitution had not indicated which of these interests was to take precedent over the other. In considering this dilemma, the Court acknowledged that the conflict had risen to new heights as technology has given the press the ability to broadcast the news faster and further than ever before. After reviewing the precedents in this area of the law, this Court concluded that:

> *Taken together, these cases demonstrate that pretrial publicity even pervasive, adverse publicity does not inevitably lead to an unfair trial. The capacity of the jury eventually impaneled to decide the case fairly is influenced by the tone and extent of the publicity, which is in part, and often in large part, shaped by what attorneys, police, and other officials do to precipitate news coverage. The trial judge has a major responsibility. What the judge says about a case, in or out of the courtroom, is likely to appear on newspapers and broadcasts. More important, the measures a judge takes or fails to take to mitigate the effects of pretrial publicity . . . may well determine whether the defendant receives a trial consistent with the requirements of due process . . .*

> *The costs of failure to afford a fair trial are high. In the most extreme cases . . . the risk of injustice was avoided when the convictions were reversed. But a reversal means that justice has been delayed for both the defendant and the state; in some cases, because of lapse of time retrial is impossible or further prosecution is gravely handicapped.[44]*

While the Court believed that the trial court judge had acted responsibly and out of a legitimate concern for the defendant's right to a fair trial, the Court was unwilling to allow what it believed to be a prior restraint to stand in this case. The Court noted that "[a] prior restraint . . . has an immediate and irreversible sanction"[45] that "chills," if not "freezes" speech for a time. This is not to say that the Court held that such an order can never be constitutional, but the Court provided a stringent test to be used in these situations. The Court looked to former Justice Learned Hand who wrote in *United States v. Dennis*[46] "the gravity of the 'evil,' discounted by its improbability, justifies such invasion of free speech as is necessary to avoid the danger."[47] This test was first written for those cases involving subversive advocacy, but was used by this Court to determine whether the trial court was correct in its decision to issue the gag order in question. In applying this test, the Court found that the trial court had not met this standard because that judge's assessment that the pretrial publicity would harm the defendant's chance for a fair trial was speculative in nature, and that other alternatives could have been used by the trial judge to ensure a fair trial for the defendant. In the Court's mind, there was a question as to whether the gag order would be effective in protecting prospective jurors from speculation and rumor surrounding this notorious case.

The conclusion to be drawn from this case is that courts should use gag orders sparingly, as the barriers protecting the freedom of the press remain high and difficult to overcome. If a court decides to use a gag order, that court may wish to consider using a gag order limited to prohibiting what "contending lawyers, the police, and witnesses may say to anyone,"[48] or be prepared to demonstrate the nature and extent of pretrial news coverage. The Court must also find that no other measure would be likely to mitigate the effects of the pretrial publicity and the effectiveness of the gag order in preventing the threat to the defendant's right to a fair trial. If these things can be shown, then it can be successfully argued that "the gravity of the 'evil,' discounted by its improbability, justifies such invasion of free speech as is necessary to avoid the danger."[49]

The *Nebraska Press Association v. Stuart* case discusses the above requirements for a gag order and implies that a trial judge has the ability to issue a gag order effective against the attorneys involved in the case, the police, and witnesses in a case. However, it is not as easy as it may sound. A court may issue a gag order when, as seen in the case of *Seattle Times Co. v. Rhinehart*,[50] the gag order furthers ". . . an important or substantial governmental interest unrelated to the suppression of expression and whether the limitation of First Amendment freedoms [is] no greater than is necessary or essential to the protection of the particular government interest involved."[51] In this particular case, the Court approved a gag order that kept the parties from publishing information obtained through the civil discovery process. The Court did so because to do otherwise would have a "chilling" effect on a plaintiff's right to bring a lawsuit.

A court's ability to successfully use a gag order against an attorney was further demonstrated in the case of *Gentile v. State Bar Association of Nevada*[52] in 1991. Gentile was an attorney practicing in the State of Nevada who held a press conference in an attempt to offset the negative publicity the prosecutor and police were releasing about Gentile's client. Gentile was disciplined under the State Bar of Nevada's Rule 177 that prohibits an attorney from making "an extra-judicial statement that a reasonable person would expect to be disseminated by means of public communication if the lawyer knows or reasonably should know that it will have a substantial likelihood of materially prejudicing an adjudicative proceeding."[53] The Court found that Rule 177 was vague and overbroad and thus struck it down because no reasonable individual could predict what was a violation and therefore be able to comply with said rule. However, the Court reaffirmed the decision of *Seattle Times Co. v. Rhinehart*. The Court continued to uphold gag orders that kept attorneys from disseminating information obtained during civil discovery. This very limited use of gag orders indicates that the Court, while willing to allow their use, is very concerned that they not be misused and violate First Amendment rights.

Closure Orders

This limit on gag orders does not exhaust the trial court's options. It is still permissible for the trial judge to close pretrial proceedings to the public and the press in an effort to ensure that the potential jury pool is not contaminated. In *Gannett Company v. DePasquale*,[54] the case involved the press's perceived right to access the pretrial proceedings in a murder case and the defendant's right to a fair trial, which the trial court safeguarded by means of a closure order.

GANNETT COMPANY, INC. v. DEPASQUALE
443 U.S. 368 (1979)

Mr. Justice STEWART delivered the opinion of the Court.

The question presented in this case is whether members of the public have an independent constitutional right to insist upon access to a pretrial judicial proceeding, even though the accused, the prosecutor, and the trial judge all have agreed to closure of that proceeding in order to assure a fair trial.

I

Wayne Clapp, aged 42 and residing in Henrietta, Rochester, N.Y., suburb, disappeared in July 1976. He was last seen on July 16 when, with two male companions, he went out on his boat to fish in Seneca Lake, about 40 miles from Rochester. The two companions returned the boat the same day and drove away in Clapp's pickup truck. Clapp was not with them. When he failed to return home by July 19, his family reported his absence to the police. An examination of the boat, laced with bulletholes, seemed to indicate that Clapp had met a violent death aboard it. Police then began an intensive search for the two men.

The petitioner, Gannett Co., Inc., publishes two Rochester newspapers, the morning Democrat & Chronicle and the evening Times-Union. On July 20, each paper carried its first story about Clapp's disappearance. Each reported that Clapp had been shot on his boat and his body dumped overboard. Each stated that the body was missing. The Times-Union mentioned the names of respondents Greathouse and Jones and said that Greathouse "was identified as one of the two companions who accompanied Clapp Friday" on the boat; said that the two were aged 18 and 21 respectively; and noted that the police were seeking the two men and Greathouse's wife, also 16 . . .

Michigan police apprehended Greathouse, Jones and the woman on July 21. This came about when an interstate bulletin describing Clapp's truck led to their discovery in Jackson County, Mich., by police who observed the truck parked at a local motel. The petitioner's two Rochester papers on July 22 reported the details of the capture.

* * *

Both papers carried stories on July 23. These revealed that Jones, the adult, had waived extradition and that New York police had traveled to Michigan and were questioning the suspects.

* * *

The Democrat & Chronicle carried another story on the morning of July 24. It stated that Greathouse had led the Michigan police to the spot where he had buried a .357 magnum revolver belonging to Clapp and that the gun was being returned to New York with the three suspects. It also stated that the police had found ammunition at the motel where Greathouse and the woman were believed to have stayed before they were arrested.

* * *

On July 25, the Democrat and Chronicle reported that Greathouse and Jones had been arraigned before a Seneca County Magistrate on second-degree murder charges shortly after their arrival from Michigan . . .

Greathouse, Jones and the woman were indicted by a Seneca County grand jury on August 2 . . . Both the Democrat & Chronicle and the Times-Union on August 3 reported the filing of the indictments. Each story stated that the murder charges specified that the two men had shot Clapp with his own gun, had weighted his body with anchors and tossed it into the lake, and then had made off with Clapp's credit card, gun, and truck.

* * *

On August 6, each paper carried a story reporting the details of the arraignments of Greathouse and Jones the day before. The papers stated both men had pleaded not guilty to all charges. Once again, each story repeated the basic facts of the accusations against the men . . . The stories noted that defense attorneys had been given 90 days in which to file pretrial motions.

During this 90-day period, Greathouse and Jones moved to suppress statements made to the police.

* * *

Continued

The motions to suppress came in before Judge DePasquale on November 4. At this hearing, defense attorneys argued that the unabated buildup of adverse publicity had jeopardized the ability of the defendant to receive a fair trial. They thus requested that the public and the press be excluded from the hearing. The District Attorney did not oppose the motion. Although Carol Ritter, a reporter employed by the petitioner, was present in the courtroom, no objection was made at the time of the closure motion. The trial judge granted the motion.

The next day, however, Ritter wrote a letter to the trial judge asserting a "right to cover this hearing," and requesting that "we . . . be given access to the transcript." The judge responded later the same day. He stated that the suppression hearing had concluded and that any decision on immediate release of the transcript had been reserved. The petitioner moved the court to set aside its exclusionary order.

The trial judge scheduled a hearing on this motion for November 16 . . . At this proceeding, the trial judge stated that, in his view, the press had a constitutional right of access although he deemed it "unfortunate" that no representative of the petitioner had objected at the time of the closure motion. Despite his acceptance of the existence of this right, however, the judge emphasized that it had to be balanced against the constitutional right of the defendants to a fair trial. After finding on the record that an open suppression hearing would pose a "reasonable probability of prejudice to these defendants," the judge ruled that the interest of the press and the public was outweighed in this case by the defendant's right to a fair trial . . .

The following day, an original proceeding the nature of prohibition and mandamus, challenging the closure order on First, Sixth, and Fourteenth Amendments grounds, was commenced by the petition in the supreme Court of the State of New York, Appellate Division, Fourth Department.

* * *

. . . Thus, the Court of Appeals upheld the exclusion of the press and the public from the pretrial proceeding. Because of the significance of the constitutional questions involved, we granted certiorari.

* * *

III

This court has long recognized that adverse publicity can endanger the ability of a defendant to receive a fair trial. To safeguard the due process rights of the accused, a trial judge has an affirmative constitutional duty to minimize the effects of prejudicial pretrial publicity. And because of the Constitution's pervasive concern for these due process rights, a trial judge may surely take protective measures even when they are not strictly and inescapably necessary.

Publicity concerning pretrial suppression hearing such as the one involved in the present case poses special risks of unfairness. The whole purpose of such hearings is to screen out unreliable or illegally obtained evidence and insure that this evidence does not become known to the jury. Publicity concerning the proceedings at a pretrial hearing, however, could influence public opinion against a defendant and inform potential jurors of inculpatory information wholly inadmissible at the actual trial.

The danger of publicity concerning pretrial suppression hearings is particularly acute, because it may be difficult to measure with any degree of certainty the effects of such publicity on the fairness of the trial . . . Closure of pretrial proceedings is often one of the most effective methods that a trial judge can employ to attempt to insure that the fairness of a trial will not be jeopardized by the dissemination of such information throughout the community before the trial itself has even begun.

* * *

IV

* * *

B

While the Sixth Amendment guarantees to a defendant in a criminal case the right to a public trial, it does not guarantee the right to compel a private trial. "The ability to waive a constitutional right does not ordinarily carry with it the right to insist upon the opposite of that right." But the issue here is not whether the defendant can compel a private trial. Rather the issue is whether members of the public have an enforceable right to a public trial that can be asserted independently of the parties in the litigation.

Continued

There can be no blinking the fact that there is a strong societal interest in public trials. Openness in court proceedings may improve the quality of testimony, induce unknown witnesses to come forward with relevant testimony, cause all trial participants to perform their duties more conscientiously, and generally give the public an opportunity to observe the judicial system. . . . In an adversary system of criminal justice, the public interest in the administration of justice is protected by the participants in the litigation. Thus, because of the great public interest in jury trials as the preferred mode of fact-finding in criminal cases, a defendant cannot waive a jury trial without the consent of the prosecutor and judge. But if the defendant waives his right to a jury trial, and the prosecutor and the judge consent, it could hardly be seriously argued that a member of the public could demand a jury trial because of the societal interest in that mode of fact-finding . . . In short, our adversary system of criminal justice is premised on the proposition that the public interest is fully protected by the participants in the litigation.

* * *

V

* * *

B

But even if the Sixth and Fourteenth Amendments could properly be viewed as embodying the common-law right of the public to attend criminal trials, it would not necessarily follow that the petitioner would have a right to attend pretrial proceedings; indeed, there is substantial evidence to the contrary. By the time of the adoption of the Constitution, public trials were clearly associated with the protection of the defendant. And pretrial proceedings, precisely because of the same concern for a fair trial, were never characterized by the same degree of openness as were actual trials.

* * *

Closed pretrial proceedings have been a familiar part of the judicial landscape in this country . . . The original New York Field Code of Criminal Procedure published in 1850, for example, provided that pretrial hearings should be closed to the public "upon request of a defendant." The explanatory report made clear that this provision was designed to protect defendants from prejudicial pretrial publicity . . .

Indeed, eight of the States that have retained all or part of the Field Code have kept the explicit provision relating to closed pretrial hearings.

For these reasons, we hold that members of the public have no constitutional right under the Sixth and Fourteenth Amendments to attend criminal trials.

VI

The petitioner also argues that members of the press and the public have a right of access to the pretrial hearing by reason of the First and Fourteenth Amendments.

* * *

Several factors lead to the conclusion that the actions of the trial judge here were consistent with any right of access the petitioner may have had under the First and Fourteenth Amendments. First, none of the spectators present in the courtroom, including the reporter employed by the petitioner, objected when the defendants made the closure motion. Despite this failure to make a contemporaneous objection, counsel for the petitioner was given an opportunity to be heard at a proceeding where he was allowed to voice the petitioner's objections to closure of the pretrial hearing. At this proceeding, which took place after the filing of the briefs, the trial court balanced the "constitutional rights of the press and the public" against the "defendants' right to a fair trial." The trial judge concluded after making this appraisal that the press and the public could be excluded from the suppression hearing and could be denied immediate access to a transcript, because an open proceeding would pose a "reasonable probability of prejudice to these defendants." Thus, the trial court found that the representatives of the press did have a right of access of constitutional dimension, but held, under the circumstances of this case, that this right was outweighed by the defendants' right to a trial. In short, the closure decision was based "on an assessment of the competing societal interests involved . . . rather than on any determination that First Amendment freedoms were not implicated."

Furthermore, any denial of access in this case was not absolute but only temporary. Once the

Continued

danger of prejudice had dissipated, a transcript of the suppression hearing was made available. The press and the public then had a full opportunity to scrutinize the suppression hearing. Unlike the case of an absolute ban on access, therefore, the press here had the opportunity to inform the public of the details of the pretrial hearing accurately and completely. Under these circumstances, any First and Fourteenth Amendment right of the petitioner to attend a criminal trial was not violated.

* * *

For all of the reasons discussed in this opinion, we hold that the Constitution provides no such right. Accordingly, the judgment of the New York Court of Appeals is affirmed.

It is so ordered.

The Court, then, settled the issue of whether a pretrial proceeding could be closed to the public, as well as the press. It is clear that if a trial judge balances the competing constitutional interests of the public/press's right of access and the defendant's right to a fair trial, and finds that the defendant's right is the weightier of the two, it is acceptable for the trial judge to deny public access to the pretrial proceedings. While this case seems to have settled the matter of closing pretrial proceedings if the above test can be met, it does not answer the question of whether a court can close a criminal trial to the public. This question was answered in the case of *Richmond Newspapers, Inc. v. Virginia.*[55]

In *Richmond Newspapers, Inc. v. Virginia,* the Court had to decide a very narrow issue: "whether the right of the public and press to attend criminal trials is guaranteed under the United States Constitution."[56] In late 1975 a hotel manager had been murdered, and a man named Stevenson was arrested and tried for this murder. Stevenson was convicted, but his conviction was reversed because the Virginia Supreme Court held that certain evidence had been improperly admitted at trial. Stevenson's second and third trials ended in mistrials, and when Stevenson was to be tried for the fourth time, the defense counsel moved to have the trial closed to the public so that the witnesses could not be privy to the testimony they were going to give. The trial judge asked the prosecutor if he had any objections to this motion, and when the prosecutor expressed none, the trial judge granted the motion. Even though reporters were present in the courtroom, including reporters who worked for the Richmond Newspapers, Inc., no one objected to the closure order. Later, the newspaper company asked for a hearing on a motion to vacate, which the trial judge granted. At the hearing, however, the trial judge held that the proceedings were part of the trial, and ordered the reporters to leave the courtroom. Ultimately, the trial judge denied the **motion to vacate** and ordered that the trial continue to be closed to the public and the press. The newspaper appealed to the Virginia Supreme Court and that court held that there was no reversible error and denied the petition for appeal. The newspapers then appealed to the U.S. Supreme Court.

In deciding whether a criminal trial can be closed to the public and the press, the Court first looked at the history of public trials both in England and colonial America. History proved that there has been a tradition of public trials coming from England to the United States. Thus, the Court concluded "the historical evidence demonstrates conclusively that at the time when our organic laws were adopted, criminal trials both here and in England had long been presumptively open. This is no quirk of history; rather, it has long been recognized as an indispensable attribute of an Anglo-American trial."[57] There are four reasons why an open trial is important, it assures

> **motion to vacate** a request that a judge make a ruling or take some other action to annul; for example, when a judge vacates a judgment, it is wiped out completely.

1. The proper function of a trial;
2. That the proceedings are conducted fairly;
3. The proper conduct of witnesses and discourages perjury;
4. No decision is based on secret bias or partiality.[58]

Based on these reasons and the unbroken historical precedent for open trials, the Court stated: "we are bound to conclude that a presumption of openness inhere in the very nature of a criminal trial under our system of justice."[59]

Nor was the Court persuaded by the State of Virginia's claim that because neither the Constitution nor the Bill of Rights explicitly guarantees the right of the public to attend a criminal trial, no such right exists. The Court discussed several rights that, while implicit in the Constitution, have been recognized as being rights enjoyed by citizens of the United States. These rights include the right of privacy, the right of association, the right to be presumed innocent, and the right to be found guilty beyond a reasonable doubt. In spite of the absence of explicit language, these rights do exist and have constitutional protection.

In addition, the Court also discussed its prior decision in *Gannett*, which allowed for a closure order for a pretrial proceeding if it can be shown that the potential prejudice to the defendant outweighs the right of freedom of the press. This Court reiterated that decision and distinguished it from the case at hand. In *Gannett* the trial judge balanced the rights of the defendant and the rights of the press or public and determined that, in that case, the defendant's right to a fair trial outweighed the other claimed rights. That did not happen in this case. The Court discussed ways that the trial judge in this case might have handled things in order to insure a fair trial for the defendant, while not going so far as to close the trial to the public. Because the trial judge did not look for other alternatives or attempt to balance the competing rights here, the Court found no overriding state interest and said "[a]bsent an overriding interest articulated in finding, the trial of a criminal case must be open to the public."[60] In so saying the Court reversed the lower court's decision.

The conclusion to be drawn after reading both the *Gannett* and the *Richmond Newspapers, Inc.* cases is twofold: First, that if a trial judge balances the competing interests and finds that the state interest in providing a fair trial outweighs freedom of the press, a pretrial proceeding may be closed to the public. Second, there is a heavy presumption that criminal trials must be open to the public and if a trial judge wishes to close a criminal trial, that judge should engage in the same balancing of rights used by the court in *Gannett*. This balancing test will determine whether there is an overriding state interest to be served by closing the case because no other means of preserving the right to a fair trial exists. If this can be done, then the trial court will be justified in closing the criminal trial in spite of the long history and constitutionally backed right to a public trial.

ACCESSING GOVERNMENT-HELD INFORMATION

As many of the holdings discussed in this chapter have indicated, the Court has not recognized that the press has a right to information that is generally inaccessible to the public. While some might argue that this might be changing since the Court recognized that a criminal trial must be open to the public, as seen in *Richmond Newspapers, Inc.*, it is too early to make such a bold statement. It is still safe to say that while the press has broad First Amendment rights to publish information, there is no recognized constitutional right to have the government's assistance in obtaining information for publication.

An example of this principle can be found in the case of *Pell v. Procunier*.[61] In this case, the petitioners were three prison inmates and three professional journalists. The defendant was the Director of the California Department of Corrections and several of his subordinates. The suit challenged a specific policy found in the California Department of Corrections Manual. Section 415.071 provides that face-to-face interviews of specific, press selected, inmates, as requested by the media, would not be permitted. This policy was put into place in 1971 as a response to a violent episode that the Department of

Corrections felt was partially attributable to a former face-to-face interview policy that was much more liberal. The prior policy allowed for the face-to-face interviews, and the result of allowing these interviews was to make certain inmates notorious among the other inmates and give them greater influence. The record indicated, "Because of this notoriety and influence, these inmates often became the source of severe disciplinary problems."[62] The petitioners, however, saw the new policy as an infringement on their First and Fourteenth Amendment rights.

The Court looked at the petitioner inmates' claim first. The Court noted "[l]awful incarceration brings about the necessary withdrawal or limitation of many privileges and rights, a retraction justified by the considerations underlying our penal system,"[63] and then went on to outline the goals of the correction system. There are four such goals noted and they include deterrence of crime, protection of society from inmates, rehabilitation, and internal security of the correctional facility. It is the final goal, internal security, that the Court said was central to all other corrections goals but noted that even that goal must be viewed along with all other considerations. In other words, the Court held that it must balance the petitioners' claim against all legitimate governmental interests. When the Court weighed the legitimate governmental interest of security, rehabilitation, protection, and deterrence, it concluded that these interests outweighed the inmates' First Amendment claims. Perhaps the most persuasive reason the Court found to support its holding was the fact that the inmates had alternative channels of communication. The Court noted that there were no restrictions keeping the inmates from communicating with the media via written correspondence. Also, "inmates have an unrestricted opportunity to communicate with the press or any other member of the public through their families, friends, clergy, or attorneys who are permitted to visit them in prison."[64] In addition, the Court noted its extensive precedent for allowing time, place, and manner regulations of free speech. The Court said:

> Although [we] would not permit prison officials to prohibit all expression or communication by prison inmates, security considerations are sufficiently paramount in the administration of the prison to justify the imposition of some restrictions on the entry of outsiders into prison for face-to-face contact with inmates.[65]

Thus, the Court found that the inmates' claim was unfounded, and so long as the Department of Corrections applied the policy in a neutral manner, the policy was an appropriate exercise of the government's authority over inmates.

The Court next turned to the journalists' claim that their First and Fourteenth Amendment rights had been violated. The journalists claimed that they had a constitutional right to interview any willing inmate unless it could be demonstrated that the interview constituted a clear and present danger to the prison security or some other substantial governmental interest. The Court reviewed this claim and noted that the regulation in question was not an attempt by the State of California to hide problems within its prisons or to keep the reporters from discovering such problems, but was clearly an attempt to maintain security within the prisons. Further, the Court did not accept the journalists' argument that denying them face-to-face interviews was to deny them a superior method of newsgathering, which violated their constitutional rights. The Court said:

> The Constitution does not . . . require government to accord the press special access to information not shared by members of the public generally. It is one thing to say that a journalist is free to seek out sources of information not available to members of the general public, that he is entitled to some constitutional protection of the confidentiality of such sources, and the government cannot restrain the publication of news emanating from such sources. It is

quite another thing to suggest that the Constitution imposes upon government the affirmative duty to make available to journalists sources of information not available to members of the public generally. That proposition finds no support in the words of the Constitution or in any decision of this Court. Accordingly, since 415.071 does not deny the press access to sources of information available to members of the general public, we hold that it does not abridge the protections that the First and Fourteenth Amendments guarantee.[66]

For this reason, the Court upheld the policy and rejected both the journalists' and inmates' constitutional claims.

The question of media access to inmates was revisited in 1977 in the case of *Houchins v. KQED, Inc.*[67] In this case, the media argued that they have a right to gather news in general, and this gives them an implied right of access to government-controlled information. This access, they argued, was necessary to prevent the government officials from concealing problems and unsuitable prison conditions.

The Court agreed that the media was correct when saying that prison conditions were a matter of public interest, that the public should have access to information about inappropriate prison conditions, and that the media had an important role to play in bringing about positive change when needed. However, the Court remained unconvinced that

The public importance of conditions in penal facilities and the media's role of providing information afford no basis for reading into the Constitution a right of the public or the media to enter these institutions, with camera equipment, and take moving and still pictures of inmates for broadcast purposes. This Court has never intimated a First Amendment guarantee of a right of access to all sources of information within government control.[68]

The Court once again discussed the ability of the press to use alternative means for communicating with inmates about problematic conditions in jails and prisons and remained unconvinced that it should alter its former holdings. As such, the Court continued the general rule that the media has no constitutional right to information that is not available to the general public.

DIFFERING RULES FOR BROADCAST MEDIA

Is there a legal significance between the broadcast media and the print media? The Court has held that there is and bases its decision on the fact that the broadcast airwaves are a limited resource and, therefore, must be regulated by the government. Prior to 1927, the airwaves were not regulated and the ensuing chaos caused Congress to pass the first act to regulate broadcasting when it passed the Radio Act of 1927. The Act was designed to eliminate broadcasters attempting to broadcast on the same frequency and during the same hours. The competition was in response to the limited number of frequencies. In 1939, Congress further acted in this area when it created the Federal Communications Commission, which allocates the broadcast frequencies and promulgates rules and regulations for the broadcast industry. While there have been many challenges regarding this regulation, many of which claim First Amendment, freedom of the press violations, the Court has consistently held that it is in the public's interest to regulate in this area.

This stands in contrast to the Court's attitude toward the print media. The distinction is that there can be an unlimited number of newspapers and only the marketplace will control how many newspapers will be financially viable. When it comes to radio and television, however, the limited number of frequencies available makes it a limited commodity that must be accessible for a variety of ideas and viewpoints. Even though this distinction is less viable today with the advent of cable television and other innovations in the broadcast industry, it is still a distinction that the Court has been willing to utilize.

One of the most well-known cases regarding this distinction with regard to the broadcast media is the 1969 case of *Red Lion Broadcasting Company, Inc. v. FCC*.[69] This case involved a challenge to the FCC's fairness doctrine that imposed on radio and television stations the requirement that both sides of a discussion of public issues must be given fair coverage. Specifically, the FCC required an equal opportunity for an individual who has his or her views or life questioned or discussed during the course of a discussion on a public issue, that individual must be given the opportunity to respond to that previous discussion. Fred Cook's career and political views had been discussed on a radio program broadcast by WGCB radio in Pennsylvania. When Cook learned of the broadcast, he asked for free reply time, and after a discussion between Red Lion, Cook, and the FCC, the FCC found that Cook was entitled to this free reply time and that Red Lion's refusal to give this time was a violation of the fairness doctrine. The lower courts upheld the FCC's position and Red Lion appealed, claiming that the fairness doctrine violated its First Amendment rights.

When reviewed by the Court, another case, which began after the Red Lion litigation had begun, was consolidated with *Red Lion*. This case, *FCC v. Radio Television News Directors Association*, involved a challenge to a new FCC rule passed to make the fairness doctrine more precise and enforceable. The Radio Television News Directors Association (RTNDA) challenged the new rule and as this case also challenged the fairness doctrine, the Court heard arguments from the attorney representing the parties from both cases.

In deciding these cases, the Court first looked at the history of the regulation of the broadcast media and reaffirmed its previous holding that "Without government control, the medium would be of little use because of the cacophony of competing voices, none of which could be clear and predictably heard. Consequently, the Federal Radio Commission was established to allocate frequencies among competing applicants in a manner responsible to the public 'convenience, interest or necessity.'"[70]

From there, the Court then looked at the fairness doctrine and found that there is a twofold duty required by the doctrine. First, the broadcaster must give coverage to public issues and second, the coverage must be fair by allowing for opposing viewpoints. These two requirements mean that when a personal attack is made on someone who is involved in a public issue, that individual must be given an opportunity to respond to the attack. While this is slightly different from allowing time for competing views, the requirement of time to respond for personal attacks was held by the Court to be substantially the same as the fairness doctrine. As such, the Court held that its decision applied to both the personal attack doctrine and the fairness doctrine.

Ultimately, the Court held that the FCC had the statutory authority to **promulgate** the fairness doctrines and that its authority was broad enough to encompass these regulations. This doctrine served the public interest and was supported by 30 years of precedent. The Court specifically noted:

> *Without the fairness doctrine, then, a licensee could ban all campaign appearances by candidates themselves from the air and proceed to deliver over his station entirely to the supporters of one slate of candidates to the exclusion of others. In this way the broadcaster could have a far greater impact on the favored candidacy than he could by simply allowing a spot appearance by the candidate himself. It is the fairness doctrine as an aspect of the obligation to operate in the public interest, rather than s[ection] 315, which prohibits the broadcaster from taking such a step.[71]*

promulgate publish; announce officially; put out formally.

The Court went on to say that the fairness doctrine, and its component personal attack and political editorializing regulations, are a legitimate exercise of the FCC's authority and that "rather than abridge the freedoms of speech and press protected by the First Amendment, we hold them valid and constitutional . . ."[72]

Not only did the Court reject the petitioner's arguments regarding the First Amendment rights, it noted, "[w]here there are substantially more individuals who want to broadcast than there are frequencies to allocate, it is idle to posit an unabridgeable First Amendment right to broadcast comparable to the right of every individual to speak, write, or publish."[73] This is because it is the right of the viewers and listeners that is of utmost importance here, not the right of the broadcasters.

The *Red Lion* case thus upholds the FCC's ability to regulate the broadcast media in ways that would be unacceptable if the regulations were impacting the print media. It is in the public's best interest for the FCC to have this authority and the best use of a limited resource.

This case, however, was not the last challenge to the FCC's authority and while the Court has upheld the FCC's authority to make and enforce regulations that do not impact the content of the broadcast, or are content-neutral in their impact, it is more reluctant to allow FCC regulation when the regulation is content-based, or has an impact on the content of the broadcast. The test used by the Court when reviewing a content-neutral regulation is the "mere rationality" test or in other words, the Court looks to see whether the regulation is rationally related to a legitimate government interest. When the regulation is content-based, however, the Court has consistently used a middle-level scrutiny test that is more stringent than mere rationality.

The Court used the middle-level of scrutiny in *FCC v. League of Women Voters*.[74] This case involved a challenge to a congressional ban on editorializing by broadcasters who received federal funding. Specifically, the case was a challenge to § 399 of the Public Broadcasting Act of 1967. The lower appellate court had used the strict scrutiny standard when looking at the appeal, but the Court noted that it had never applied this stringent a standard in this type of case. Instead, the Court has consistently used a balancing approach and required that the competing interests be weighed against one another and required the regulation be upheld only where the government interest outweighs the broadcasters constitutional rights. In addition, the regulation must be narrowly tailored and these competing interests must be decided on the particular circumstances of each case.

With this in mind, the Court looked at § 399, considered the respondent's argument and noted, ". . . the restriction imposed by § 399 is specifically directed at a form of speech—namely, the expression of editorial opinion—that lies at the head of First Amendment protection."[75] The regulation ignored the fact that the broadcast media, as well as the rest of the press, has a responsibility to not only report information but to also bring forth viewpoints that are often critical of public affairs. This role, and the fact that § 399 banned speech solely on the basis of its content, was the source of the Court's decision that this section is constitutionally indefensible. This section was also too broadly tailored so that it not only banned the type of speech it presumably was written to regulate, but also interfered with a "potentially infinite variety of speech, most of it unconnected to governmental affairs, political candidacies or elections."[76] As such, this section cannot survive the middle-level of scrutiny even though the government argued a substantial government interest. The means chosen by the government to promote its interest was too broad and sweeping and thus violated the broadcasters' free speech and free press rights.

The *League of Women Voters* case was decided at the beginning of the cable-TV era. Has the Court treated cable-TV any differently? Yes, over the last decade, the Court has had an opportunity to look at issues involving cable-TV and has treated it differently from the regular broadcast media. It has used strict scrutiny when looking at issues involving cable-TV and content-based regulations. When content-neutral regulations are at issue in cases involving cable-TV, the Court has used the middle-level of scrutiny[77] applied in the *League of Women Voters.*

The most recent cable-TV/free press case is *U.S. v. Playboy Entertainment Group, Inc.,*[78] which challenged § 505 of the Telecommunications Act of 1996, which required cable television operators to scramble or block sexually explicit programming or limit their broadcast to the hours of 10 P.M. and 6 A.M. when children were less likely to be watching. While the majority of cable operators chose to limit the programming to the time frame mentioned above, the Playboy Entertainment Group challenged the statute as a restrictive content-based regulation that violated its First Amendment rights. Playboy argued that the statute could not pass the strict scrutiny test because there were less restrictive means of regulation available to the government than implementing that section, which required scrambling or blocking or time limitations. The District Court agreed with this assessment and found that there were two less-restrictive alternatives available to the government. The government argued that the less-restrictive means, specifically parental requests that the cable channel broadcasting the sexually explicit materials be blocked so that it did not come into their home, was ignored or underutilized by the public and thus was ineffective. The Court said:

> It is no response that voluntary blocking requires a consumer to take action, or may be inconvenient, or may not go perfectly every time. A court should not assume a plausible, less restrictive alternative would be ineffective; and a court should not presume parents, given full information, will fail to act.[79]

The Court concluded that the statute did violate Playboy's free speech and free press rights under the First Amendment and affirmed the District Court's judgment striking the statute down.

Summary

While newspapers and television broadcasts often regale the public with the "right to know" and imply that the press somehow has some constitutional protections not available to the general public, this chapter demonstrates that, in general, this is not so. While the press does enjoy constitutional protection, that protection is not absolute and the government may regulate the press under certain circumstances. The discussion in this chapter has demonstrated that while the Court generally will not uphold a prior restraint on publication, it does recognize that the press may not operate unfettered by other considerations. Freedom of the press sometimes interferes with a defendant's right to a fair trial, and in doing so must, under some circumstances, take a backseat to that right.

The cases and discussion in this chapter also demonstrate that with the print media, the standard used most often when looking at the constitutional viability of a government regulation is the strict scrutiny standard. This standard changes, however, when looking at the traditional broadcast media, where the mere rationality test is applied when discussing content-neutral–based regulations, and the middle-level of scrutiny applies when discussing content-based regulations. When discussing cable-TV, the standards change once again. The most recent case decided by the Court indicates that the appropriate standard to be used when the issue involves a content-neutral regulation and cable-TV is the middle-level of scrutiny, but when a content-based regulation is challenged, the strict scrutiny standard must be applied.

Key Terms

freedom of the press	motion to vacate	promulgate
gag orders	prior restraints	
gag rule	promissory estoppel	

Review Questions

1. What role does the press play in our society, and why is freedom of the press such an important concept in our legal system?
2. Should the press have greater access to information than an individual citizen?
3. Why is the regular broadcast media treated differently from the print media?
4. What is the difference between content-neutral and content-based regulations, and what standards of review are used for both?

Internet Connections

1. For more information on the media's perspective on free press, visit the home page of the Society of Professional Journalists. This organization is dedicated to the perpetuation of freedom of the press and can be found at *http://www.spj.org.*

2. For a list of cases discussing freedom of the press issues, go to the home page of the Legal Information Institute (LII) at Cornell Law School. It can be found at *http://www2.law.cornell.edu.*

3. To find journal articles discussing freedom of the press, see the U.S. Information Agency Electronic Journal, Vol. 2, No. 1, February 1997, which includes the USIS Bibliography of Journal Articles at *http://www.usinfo.state.gov/journals.*

4. For a country-by-country survey of press freedom, see the Press Freedom Survey 2000 at *http://www.freedomhouse.org/pfs2000/.*

End Notes

[1] U.S. Const. amend. I.

[2] *Gitlow v. New York*, 268 U.S. 652 (1925).

[3] *Near v. Minnesota*, 283 U.S. 697 (1931).

[4] *Id.* at 716.

[5] *Id.* at 713.

[6] *Id.* at 719.

[7] *Id.* at 722.

[8] *Garland v. Torre*, 259 F.2d 545 (2nd Cir. 1958).

[9] *Associated Press v. NLRB*, 301 U.S. 103, 132–133 (1937).

[10] *See New York Times Co. v. Sullivan*, 376 U.S. 64 (1964).

[11] *See Craig v. Harney*, 331 U.S. 367 (1947).

[12] *Zemel v. Rusk*, 381 U.S. 1 (1965).

[13] *Branzburg v. Hayes*, 405 U.S. 665 (1972).

[14] *Id.* at 679–680.

[15] *Id.* at 687.

[16] *Id.* at 690–691.

[17] *Id.* at 693.

[18] *Zurcher v. The Stanford Daily*, 436 U.S. 547 (1978).

[19] *Id.* at 552.

[20] *Id.* at 565.

[21] *Id.* at 566.

[22] *Id.* at 567.

[23] *Minneapolis Star and Tribune Company v. Minnesota Commissioner of Revenue*, 460 U.S. 575 (1983).

[24] *Cohen v. Cowles Media Company*, 501 U.S. 663 (1991).

[25] *Id.* at 665.

[26] *Id.* at 670.

[27] *Id.* at 671.

[28] *Bantam Books, Inc. v. Sullivan*, 372 U.S. 58 (1963).

[29] *New York Times Co. v. United States*, 403 U.S. 713 (1971).

[30] *Id.* at 726.

[31] *Id.* at 730.

[32] *Id.* at 729.

[33] Max Frankel, "Top Secret," *New York Times*, at http://www.nytimes.com/books (Feb. 15, 2003).

[34] R.W. Apple, "Lessons From the Pentagon Papers," *New York Times*, at http://www.nytimes.com (Feb. 15, 2003).

[35] *Id.* at 3.

[36] Douglas Linder, *The Trial of Bruno Hauptmann: An Account*, at http://www.law.umkc.edu (Feb. 15, 2003).

[37] *Bridges v. California*, 314 U.S. 252 (1941).

[38] *Shepherd v. Florida*, 341 U.S. 50 (1951).

[39] *Sheppard v. Maxwell*, 384 U.S. 333 (1966).

[40] *Id.* at 18–20.

[41] *Nebraska Press Association v. Stuart*, 427 U.S. 539 (1976).

[42] *Id.* at 553.

[43]*Id.* at 545.

[44]*Id.* at 555.

[45]*Id.* at 559.

[46]*United States v. Dennis*, 341 U.S. 494 (1951).

[47]*Nebraska Press Association v. Stuart*, 427 U.S. 539, 562 (1976).

[48]*Id.* at 564.

[49]*Id.* at 562.

[50]*Seattle Times Company v. Rhinehart*, 467 U.S. 20 (1984).

[51]*Id.* at 38.

[52]*Gentile v. State Bar Association of Nevada*, 501 U.S. 1030 (1991).

[53]*Id.* at 1033.

[54]*Gannett Company v. DePasquale*, 443 U.S. 368 (1979).

[55]*Richmond Newspapers, Inc. v. Virginia*, 448 U.S. 555 (1980).

[56]*Id.* at 558.

[57]*Id.* at 555, 569.

[58]*Id.* at 569.

[59]*Id.* at 573.

[60]*Id.* at 581.

[61]*Pell v. Procunier*, 417 U.S. 817 (1974).

[62]*Id.* at 832.

[63]*Id.* at 822, quoting *Price v. Johnson*, 334 U.S. 266, 285 (1948).

[64]*Id.* at 825.

[65]*Id.* at 826.

[66]*Id.* at 834–835.

[67]*Houchins v. KQED, Inc.*, 438 U.S. 1 (1977).

[68]*Id.* at 9.

[69]*Red Lion Broadcasting Company, Inc. v. FCC*, 395 U.S. 367 (1969).

[70]*Id.* at 376–377.

[71]*Id.* at 383.

[72]*Id.* at 385.

[73]*Id.* at 389.

[74]*FCC v. League of Women Voters*, 468 U.S. 364 (1984).

[75]*Red Lion Broadcasting Company, Inc. v. FCC*, 395 U.S. at 381 (1969).

[76]*Id.* at 393.

[77]*See Turner Broadcasting System, Inc. v. FCC*, 512 U.S. 622 (1994).

[78]*United States v. Playboy Entertainment Group, Inc.*, 529 U.S. 803 (2000).

[79]*Id.* at 824.

 For additional resources, go to *http://www.westlegalstudies.com*

14 CHAPTER

FREEDOM OF RELIGION: THE FREE EXERCISE CLAUSE

"[N]o liberty is more essential to the continued vitality of the free society which Our Constitution guarantees than is the religious liberty protected by the Free Exercise Clause. . . ."

—Justice Potter Stewart
Sherbert v. Verner

INTRODUCTION

freedom of religion the First Amendment right to hold any religious beliefs and to practice these beliefs in any way that does not infringe on public safety or infringe on important rights of others; also, the right of all citizens to be free of the government control in the exercise of these beliefs.

Religion is a hallmark of American society. People in the United States are likely to hold religious beliefs and attend religious services. In addition to being a religious nation, the United States is also a nation of religious diversity. This country is more religiously diverse than most nations in the world. At the same time, this is a nation where all these diverse groups exist in harmony with one another. The answer, in part, lies in our Constitution and the way in which the Supreme Court has interpreted it.

The Framers of the Constitution were aware of the excesses that could result from religious belief, particularly when supported by the government. Many of our earliest citizens came to escape religious persecution in the countries of their birth. Despite this flight from governmental interference in their religious practices, nine of the 13 original colonies established official churches. To avoid the excess that could result from the confluence of religion and government, protections were included in the Bill of Rights. In James Madison's first draft proposal for a **freedom of religion** amendment, he included a prohibition against establishment of religion by both the states and the federal government. This was rejected and the Constitution only prohibited the establishment of religion by the federal government until the 1940s when the religious protections of the First Amendment were made applicable to the states through the Fourteenth Amendment.[1]

The First Amendment provides that "Congress shall make no law respecting an establishment of religion or prohibiting the free exercise thereof." There are two separate provisions to the amendment and each is subject to its own analysis by the Court. The first of the two provisions is the Establishment Clause, which prohibits the government from setting up an official religion. The second is the Free Exercise Clause, which is designed to prevent the government from outlawing or seriously burdening the practice of one's chosen religion. The amendment strives to keep government from constraining people's choice of religious belief. Occasionally, there will be a conflict between the two provisions. An example is the government's provision of military chaplains. While the Establishment Clause would usually preclude the government from providing the means for religious practice, if the government did not provide religious personnel, the ability of military personnel to practice their religion would be impaired. Thus, the Court has found inclusion of chaplains in the military to be constitutional.[2]

This chapter will consider the development of constitutional law surrounding the Free Exercise Clause. In Chapter 15, the Establishment Clause jurisprudence will be examined. While at first blush the two provisions seem clear, the range of subjects and situations to which they apply is complex and has required the Court to continually interpret the simple words of the First Amendment. There are always new challenges, and religious freedom continues to be an expanding area of constitutional law. The Court changes its approach over time while using the familiar tests. Before the actual provisions can be addressed, the first question to be answered is: What constitutes a religion?

WHAT IS RELIGION?

To arrive at a decision whether protection is warranted under the Free Exercise Clause, it is necessary to first consider what constitutes religious belief. This question is intimately connected with the question of what constitutes a religion. Are all claims that one is acting on the basis of religious belief sufficient to trigger First Amendment protection? If the answer were affirmative, then assertion of a professed doctrine of religious belief would "in effect . . . permit every citizen to become a law unto himself. Government could exist only in name under such circumstance."[3]

Since a valid free exercise claim must involve a religious belief, the starting point, one would assume, would be a definition of religion. This means that a court must determine whether a belief is religious. The Court, however, has never set forth a definition of either religion or religious belief. This does not mean that it has not articulated certain principles to be used to determine whether or not a belief is religious in nature.

The belief does not necessarily have to be premised upon a belief in a Supreme Being. This means that nontheistic, as well as theistic, religions may be entitled to free exercise protection.[4] In a nation with a high degree of religious diversity, protection is afforded to a wider range of beliefs than a strict adherence to a theistic view would allow. If the narrower view were the accepted standard then such religious beliefs as Buddhism would not be deserving of First Amendment protection. Moreover, limits would be placed on those who sought to engage in religious beliefs that were not practiced or recognized by the mainstream. An individual who did not believe in a Supreme Being would be denied the opportunities available to other citizens.

The Court has also sought to avoid the preference of organized religions above new or unconventional ones. In this sense, an organized religion is one that is well established, with large numbers of adherents and generally conventional practices. Would a religious belief professed by a single individual be deserving of free exercise protection? The Court has held that it is not necessary for one to be part of a group or sect to warrant protection of his beliefs. In *Frazee v. Illinois Department of Employment Security,*[5] the Court ruled that "membership in an organized religious denomination, especially one with a specific tenet forbidding members to work on Sunday would simplify the problem of identifying sincerely held religious beliefs, but we reject the notion that to claim the protection of the Free Exercise Clause, one must be responding to the commands of a particular religious organization."[6]

Courts must also be concerned with the sincerity of one's belief. Consider, for example, a prisoner who claims to have converted to Judaism once incarcerated to take advantage of the better diet provided to Orthodox Jews due to their religious dietary rules. Should one professing religious belief for this reason be afforded the benefits of a free exercise claim? The notion of sustaining a free exercise claim where the belief is not genuine and is claimed only to obtain a benefit is rejected. The Court has striven, however, to avoid a consideration of the truth or reasonableness of the belief in making a determination on the genuineness of the belief. Addressing the question of the truth of one's religious conviction to determine the validity of a free exercise claim the Court has stated that, "[m]en may believe what they cannot prove. They may not be put to the proof of their religious doctrines or beliefs."[7] The Court has further asserted that "[w]ith relations to his Maker and the obligations he may think they impose . . . no interference can be permitted, provided always the laws of society, designed to secure its peace and prosperity, and the morals of its people, are not interfered with."[8] Nevertheless, while the truth of religious beliefs was not a legitimate area of inquiry, the sincerity of claims can be considered. It is difficult, however, to evaluate sincerity without some consideration of truth or falsity.

Finally, the claimed belief must be central to the religion in order to establish a free exercise claim. The test has a subjective element. If the individual feels that the conflict between the government regulations and the belief is central to him, then a free exercise claim can be established even in the absence of support from other members of the religion. The Court has upheld free exercise relief for a Jehovah's Witness who refused to work in a munitions factory but was collecting unemployment insurance even though other members of the sect were willing to work in the same factory.[9]

These four factors—no requirement to believe in a Supreme Being; no requirement for an organized religion; sincerity of belief; and centrality of belief—are considerations in determining whether a religious belief exists. If such a belief exists then a valid free exercise claim may be established. Let us now look at how the Court handles such claims.

FREE EXERCISE

The First Amendment provides virtually absolute protection to individual conviction and belief. The government may not question your beliefs, nor may it impose penalties or disabilities solely on the basis of those beliefs. If, however, belief were all that need be considered, the Free Exercise Clause would provide little basis for constitutional challenges. But, the Free Exercise Clause extends beyond belief into the realm of action. It is in this realm that the Court addresses the meaning of free exercise. The question is whether the government may regulate actions when the actions are intimately tied to religious beliefs.

If the Court took a literalist approach to free exercise, then the practice of religion would be free of any governmental interference. If that were the case, citizens could lawfully engage in animal sacrifice, polygamy, and snake handling free of government regulation. That is not the case. When it comes to religious practices, First Amendment rights are limited. The government may regulate action and some activities lie outside the First Amendment. Whether the First Amendment protects a specific action depends on the nature of the action and the government's rationale for regulating it. The Court will engage in a balancing test using the same considerations it employs in the constitutional analysis of our individual rights as against the purpose for government regulation.

There is no clear test for determining whether a violation occurs, but there are general principles. When the purpose of a government action has a negative impact on the conduct dictated by religion, the Court will almost certainly find a violation of religious guarantees. Where the interference is purposeful, that is, when the government intends to interfere in religious practice, the state's action will be strictly scrutinized. This is rarely the case. When it does occur, however, the Court will find a violation and strike the regulation. Where the regulation is not motivated by an intent to interfere in religious practice or conduct, but has the effect of doing so, the Court will apply a heightened scrutiny. This means the state must demonstrate that the regulation is premised upon a "particularly important governmental goal" and that "an exemption would substantially hinder" achievement of that goal.[10] In these cases an exemption from the regulation must be granted if the government goal can be accomplished. As we look at the cases we will see that the Court may be modifying its stand on exemptions, being less willing to require them today, than in the past. Where a generally applicable criminal prohibition incidentally burdens free exercise, the Court will not find a free exercise violation. It is upon these principles that free exercise jurisdiction turns.

INTENTIONAL IMPACTS ON FREE EXERCISE

The Court applies the strictest level of scrutiny to those rare cases in which the government intends to interfere in religious practices—where its object is impermissible. In a 1993 case, *Church of the Lukumi Babalu Aye v. City of Hialeah*,[11] the Court made clear that intentional interference is not consistent with First Amendment religious freedom.

The City of Hialeah was faced with a large influx of Cuban refugees practicing Santeria. Santeria is a religion with African roots brought to Cuba by slaves. The religion has absorbed significant elements of Roman Catholicism. Santeria includes animal sacrifice as part of its religious rituals. This aspect of the religion was upsetting to the citizens of Hialeah. When plans were announced to open a Santeria church in the city, the council held an emergency meeting. From that meeting, and others that followed, a number of ordinances were adopted which prohibited animal sacrifice. The church and its members sued alleging a violation of free exercise rights.

EXHIBIT 14.1   Santeria

When West Africans were captured in what is today known as Nigeria and Benin, and taken as slaves to the Caribbean Islands they were prevented from practicing their native Yoruba religion. In fact, almost immediately after landing in the islands they were baptized into the Catholic Church. The slaves were forced to follow Catholic ritual that was largely in opposition to their native beliefs. The slaves, however, noticed that there were parallels between their Yoruba religion and Catholicism. They used these parallels to create their own secret religion, one that would please the slave owners, by appearing to be Catholic, while at the same time fulfilling their own religious needs. Santeria is that religion. It blends the Yoruba beginnings with Spanish Catholicism.

Santerians believe in a single, supreme god known as Olorun who is the source of all spiritual energy that constitutes the universe. This god coincides with the Catholic Jesus Christ and interacts with the world through his agents the Orisha. In Santeria, the Catholic saints are used to represent the Orisha, with each saint a substitute for its corresponding Orisha. Each Orisha guards or protects a certain aspect of human life. For example, Babalue Aye is associated with disease and it is to him that Santerians pray for recovery when someone is ill. Saint Lazarus represents him.

Santeria is a religion without a sacred book. However, Olorun has given them eleven commandments to live by which are very similar to the Judeo-Christian Ten Commandments.

Sacrifice to the Orisha is an integral part of the religion and has caused conflict between Santerians and others in their communities. Sacrifice is considered central to human well-being because it is through sacrifice that general well-being is maintained or restored in the face of negative events. Sacrifices run the gamut from candles and candy to doves and chickens. It is only in cases of serious illness or misfortune that animal sacrifice is called for. When it is, the animals are humanely killed, with as little pain as possible, and those attending eat the meat.

During the controversy leading to the Supreme Court's decision, mainstream religions supported the Santerians' position albeit for their own religious freedom. Jewish organizations were concerned about the impact of a decision against Santeria sacrifice on their own laws of ritual slaughter. Christian groups were concerned about government encroachments on religious freedom.

Today, it is estimated that there are approximately five million practitioners of Santeria in the United States. Most live in Florida, New York City, Puerto Rico, and Los Angeles. There are also worldwide communities ranging from Central and South America to France and the Netherlands.[12]

S I D E B A R

The Court first considered the neutrality of the statute by examining its object and its operation. From the plain language of the statute, as well as the way in which the ordinances were designed to operate, the Court concluded that the object of the statute was to target the practice of animal sacrifice by the Santerians. After looking at the statements made at the hearings the Court noted that they "disclose[d] animosity to Santeria adherents and their religious practices."[13]

CHURCH OF THE LUKUMI BABALU AYE, INC. V. CITY OF HIALEAH
508 U.S. 520 (1993)

Mr. Justice KENNEDY for the Court.

At a minimum, the protections of the Free Exercise Clause pertain if the law at issue discriminates against some or all religious beliefs or regulates or prohibits conduct because it is undertaken for religious reasons.

Although a law targeting religious beliefs as such is never permissible, if the object of a law is to infringe upon or restrict practices because of their religious motivation, the law is not neutral, and it is invalid unless it is justified by a compelling interest and is narrowly tailored to advance that interest. There are, of course, many ways of demonstrating that the object or purpose of a law is the suppression of religion or religious conduct. To determine the object of a law, we must begin with its text, for the minimum requirement of neutrality is that a law not discriminate on its face. A law lacks facial neutrality if it refers to a religious practice without a secular meaning discernable from the language or context. Petitioners contend that three of the ordinances fail this test of facial neutrality because they use the words "sacrifice" and "ritual," words with strong religious connotations. We agree that these words are consistent with the claim of facial discrimination, but the argument is not conclusive. The words "sacrifice" and "ritual" have a religious origin, but current use admits also of secular meanings. The ordinances, furthermore, define "sacrifice" in secular terms, without referring to religious practices.

We reject the contention advanced by the city that our inquiry must end with the text of the laws at issue. Facial neutrality is not determinative. The Free Exercise Clause, like the Establishment Clause, extends beyond facial discrimination. The Clause "forbids subtle departures from neutrality," and "covert suppression of particular religious beliefs. . . ." Official action that targets religious conduct for distinctive treatment cannot be shielded by mere compliance with the requirement of facial neutrality. The Free Exercise Clause protects against governmental hostility that is masked, as well as overt. "The Court must survey meticulously the circumstances of governmental categories to eliminate, as it were, religious gerrymanders."

The record in this case compels the conclusion that suppression of the central element of the Santeria worship service was the object of the ordinances. First, though use of the words "sacrifice" and "ritual" does not compel a finding of improper targeting of the Santeria religion, the choice of these words is support for our conclusion. There are further respects in which the text of the city council's enactments discloses the improper attempt to target Santeria. Resolution 87-66 . . . recited that "residents and citizens of the City of Hialeah have expressed their concern that certain religions may propose to engage in practices which are inconsistent with public morals, peace or safety," and "reiterate[d]" the city's commitment to prohibit "any and all [such] acts of any and all religious groups." No one suggests, and on this record it cannot be maintained, that city officials had in mind a religion other than Santeria.

It becomes evident that these ordinances target Santeria sacrifice when the ordinances' operation is considered. Apart from the text, the effect of a law in its real operation is strong evidence of its object. To be sure, adverse impact will not always lead to a finding of impermissible targeting. For example, a social harm may have been a legitimate concern of government for reasons quite apart from discrimination. The subject at hand does implicate, of course, multiple concerns unrelated to religious animosity, for example, the suffering or mistreatment visited upon the sacrificed animals and health hazards from improper disposal. But the ordinances when considered together disclose an object remote from these legitimate concerns. The design of these laws accomplishes instead a "religious gerrymander," an impermissible attempt to target petitioners and their religious practices.

It is a necessary conclusion that almost the only conduct subject to Ordinances 87-40, 87-52, and 87-71 is the religious exercise of Santeria church members.

We also find significant evidence of the ordinances' improper targeting of Santeria sacrifice in the fact that they proscribe more religious conduct than is necessary to achieve their stated ends. It is not unreasonable to infer, at least

Continued

when there are no persuasive indications to the contrary, that law which visits "gratuitous restrictions" on religious conduct, seeks not to effectuate the stated governmental interests, but to suppress the conduct because of its religious motivation.

The legitimate governmental interests in protecting the public health and preventing cruelty to animals could be addressed by restrictions stopping far short of a flat prohibition of all Santeria sacrificial practice.

A law burdening religious practice that is not neutral or not of general application must undergo the most rigorous of scrutiny. To satisfy the commands of the First Amendment, a law restrictive of religious practice must advance "'interests of the highest order'" and must be narrowly tailored in pursuit of those interests. The compelling interest standard that we apply once a law fails to meet the *Smith* requirements is not water[ed] . . . down but "really means what it says." A law that targets religious conduct for distinctive treatment or advances legitimate governmental interests only against conduct with a religious motivation will survive strict scrutiny only in rare cases. It follows from what we have already said that these ordinances cannot withstand this scrutiny.

The Free Exercise Clause commits government itself to religious tolerance, and upon even slight suspicion that proposals for state intervention stem from animosity to religion or distrust of its practices, all officials must pause to remember their own high duty to the Constitution and to the rights it secures. Those in office must be resolute in resisting importunate demands and must ensure that the sole reasons for imposing the burdens of law and regulation are secular. Legislators may not devise mechanisms, overt or disguised, designed to persecute or oppress a religion or its practices. The laws here in question were enacted contrary to these constitutional principles, and they are void.

Reversed.

The Court also found that the general applicability requirement was not met due to the underinclusiveness of the ordinances. Where a law fails to meet the standards of neutrality and general applicability strict scrutiny must, of necessity, be employed. The Court stated that even assuming a compelling interest, the failure to narrowly tailor the ordinances to protect religious freedom would call for a decision to overrule the ordinances. At any rate, the Court rejected any claim of a compelling purpose to the ordinance and struck the legislation.

UNINTENDED IMPACTS ON RELIGIOUS CONDUCT

Lukumi is the only modern case dealing with intentional government interference in religious exercise. This points up the rarity of these actions and underscores the principles of religious freedom that guide our nation. The more likely type of challenge occurs when the state incidentally burdens religious practice while pursuing a legitimate state interest. The way in which the Court has handled these challenges has changed over time. Before the 1960s the Court reasoned that as long as the state was not acting to interfere with religion and was regulating only conduct not belief, then the First Amendment Free Exercise Clause was not implicated.

Reynolds v. U.S[14] makes this clear. At issue was a statute making bigamy a crime. Reynolds, who was convicted pursuant to the statute, maintained that he should have been acquitted since he was fulfilling his religious duty. Reynolds was a Mormon and polygamy was a doctrine of the church. The Court stated, at the outset, that Congress could not pass legislation prohibiting free exercise of religion, but questioned whether this was such a law. To answer the question it was necessary to determine what religious freedom had been guaranteed by the Constitution.

The Court examined the history of the amendment and the context within which it was adopted. It also considered the acceptance of polygamy and the application of laws punishing it in England and the United States up to the time of the Constitution. In view of the historical rejection of polygamy in England and the Colonies, the Court concluded that the government was within its right in passing the statute.

The Court then turned to the question of whether one who makes the practice of polygamy part of his beliefs may be punished for his actions. "To permit this would make the professed doctrine of religious belief superior to the law of the land, and in effect permit every citizen to become a law unto himself. Government could exist only in name under such circumstance."[15] The Court concluded that Reynolds knowingly engaged in an action contrary to law because of his religious belief and that allowing him to avoid punishment would be "dangerous" to society.[16]

The Court's reluctance to imply a strict scrutiny standard during the period before the 1960s is underscored in *Cantwell v. Connecticut*,[17] where the Court ruled that the First Amendment Free Exercise Clause was applicable to the states through the Fourteenth Amendment. At the same time, the Court rejected petitioner's claim that an ordinance requiring a license to distribute literature violated her free exercise rights since she was distributing religious tracts. Employing the rational relationship test, the Court ruled that the state might regulate action in a nondiscriminatory way. The Court found a valid interest in prohibiting fraudulent solicitation, a legitimate, nonreligious interest with a secular purpose.

Use of the rational relationship test also dictated the result in *Minersville School District v. Gobitis*.[18] There, the Court rejected a free exercise claim by Jehovah's Witnesses based on a government regulation requiring students to recite the flag salute in school each day or be penalized with expulsion from school. The Court found a legitimate secular purpose to the statute and an unintended effect on religion. Accordingly, it was held that the ordinance was constitutional.

Four years later, when faced with deciding the constitutionality of a similar statute the Court did not abandon the secular purpose test, it merely shifted its analysis away from free exercise to free speech. The result was to overrule *Gobitis*, an action rarely taken by the Court. It is important to understand the reasons surrounding the change in the Court's view before we examine the shift in analysis.

Following the decision in *Gobitis*, violence against Jehovah's Witnesses occurred. This prompted the search for a new challenge to the flag salute regulations. The opportunity came in *West Virginia Board of Education v. Barnette*.[19] The discrimination against Jehovah's Witnesses was only one of the factors that led to the overruling of *Gobitis*; other **extrajudicial** factors contributed to the *Barnette* decision. State courts were not following the dictates of *Gobitis* In addition, the political climate had changed. World War II had begun and requiring a flag salute that entailed a straight-arm salute to the American flag appeared antidemocratic and fascistic. Moreover, there was a change in court personnel. Chief Justice Stone, who was in the minority in *Gobitis*, became a leading member of the majority by the time *Barnette* reached the Court. These factors explain the change in the Court's view of the flag salute regulations and point up the importance of societal factors in explaining evolving constitutional law.

The change in analysis demonstrates that whatever protection the Court would afford to religious conduct resided in the Free Speech Clause of the First Amendment rather than the Free Exercise Clause. Until the 1960s the Court continued to adhere to the rational relationship test for free exercise claims.

In *Barnette*, while noting that the petitioners were motivated by religious beliefs, "many citizens who do not share these religious views hold such a

extrajudicial
unconnected with court business; outside of court. Beyond the proper scope of court business; not having legal effect, though said or done by a judge.

compulsory rite [the required flag salute] to infringe constitutional liberty of the individual."[20] The issue was framed as one of opinion and political attitude—free speech considerations. On this basis, the Court concluded the regulations could not be found unconstitutional and, thus, avoided the free exercise issue.

Free speech analysis was also used to address a free exercise claim in *Wooley v. Maynard*[21] Maynard, a Jehovah's Witness, refused to comply with a state statute that required motor vehicles to display a license plate containing the state motto "Live Free or Die." Maynard objected on religious and moral grounds to the motto, covered it on his license plate, and was convicted of violating the statute. The Court framed the issue as "whether the State may constitutionally require an individual to participate in the disseminating of an ideological message by displaying it on his private property in a manner and for the express purpose that it be observed and read by the public."[22] Relying on *Barnette* the Court determined that the State could not and did not address the question of whether the legislation infringed on the free exercise rights of Maynard.

In 1961 the Court was still adhering to its restrictive analysis of free exercise claims. At that time the Court was asked to decide a free exercise issue regarding Sunday closing laws in *Braunfeld v. Brown*.[23] It is important to look closely at *Braunfeld* to see, in the context of one particular issue, how the Court's analysis changed in a two-year period from offering relatively little protection to free exercise claims to affording significantly expanded protection to individuals who faced the impact of unintentional infringement on their religious practices.

The Pennsylvania statute challenged in *Braunfeld* made it a crime to engage in retail sales of clothing and home furnishings on Sundays. The merchants who sought a permanent injunction against enforcement of the statute were Orthodox Jews who, in order to comply with their religious dictates, were required to close their businesses from sundown Friday through sundown Saturday. By opening on Sunday the merchants could recover the losses incurred by closing for religious observance on Saturday. The statute precluded this action. The merchants maintained that "serious disadvantage" to their livelihood would result if they continued to adhere to the dictates of their religion. Consequently, they maintained that the statute infringed upon their free exercise rights by forcing them to choose between their religion and their livelihood.

Addressing these claims, the Court reiterated the proposition that the state could not constitutionally infringe upon a citizen's religious beliefs and found that this statute did not do so. Actions are not necessarily free from governmental regulation, the Court stated. As to actions, the statute at issue did not proscribe any religious practices. Rather, the Court asserted, the statue "simply regulates a secular activity and, as applied to [the merchants], operates so as to make practice of their religious beliefs more expensive."[24]

The Court spelled out the standard for deciding free exercise claims when the regulation made religious observance more costly: when the regulation had a secular purpose and effect, and was general in its applicability, then the statute would be valid despite any undue burden on religious practices. The Court's pronouncements on the underlying purposes of such laws were central in arriving at the decision in *Braunfeld*. The secular purpose found by the Court in *Braunfeld* was providing a uniform day of rest for all citizens. This was considered a legitimate and substantial state interest that the government could pursue. The Court also went on to reject any proposed accommodation for Orthodox Jews, by noting that such an accommodation would provide an unfair advantage by eliminating competition from those bound by the statute. Accordingly, the Court found the statute valid on its face and as applied.

In a partial concurrence and dissent by Justice Brennan, the Court's standard of analysis was rejected. Justice Brennan argued for strict scrutiny in light of the importance of religious freedom in our society. He argued for continued use of the standard set forth in *Barnette* that allowed restriction of religious freedom "only to prevent grave and immediate danger to interests that the state may lawfully protect."[25] This standard, Justice Brennan maintained, was different from the Court's adoption of the substantial state interest standard in the majority opinion.

Two years later, the Court was faced with a similar challenge in *Sherbert v. Verner*[26] and reached a decision quite the opposite of that in *Braunfeld*. Justice Brennan wrote the majority decision.

The appellant, a Seventh Day Adventist was fired from her job because she would not work on Saturday, her Sabbath. Her determination to comply with her religion's practices by not accepting employment on Saturday prevented her from finding new employment. Consequently, she sought unemployment compensation under the state statute that required availability for Saturday work for eligibility.

The Court turned first to the question whether refusal of employment benefits imposed a burden on Sherbert's free exercise rights and answered that question affirmatively. While the Court found that the burden was only indirect, it was recognized that the regulation "forces her to choose between following the precepts of her religion and forfeiting benefits, on the one hand and abandoning one of the precepts of her religion in order to accept work on the other hand. Governmental imposition of such a choice puts the same kind of burden upon the free exercise as would a fine imposed against [Sherbert] for her Saturday worship."[27]

From here, the Court turned to the issue of determining whether a compelling state interest was at issue. Justice Brennan made it clear that the rational relationship test was inappropriate for First Amendment analysis. Freedom of religion may be abridged only when necessary to protect a compelling state interest and none existed in this case. The asserted state interest—that only those involuntarily employed received benefits—even if compelling, would require the state to demonstrate that there was no alternative means of achieving this purpose without infringing First Amendment rights. The Court stated its holding narrowly as "only that South Carolina may not consistently apply the eligibility provisions so as to constrain a worker to abandon his religious convictions respecting the day of rest."[28] This was the only effort the Court made to distinguish the result in *Sherbert* and *Braunfeld*.

This did not satisfy Justice Stewart who dissented in *Braunfeld* but concurred in the result in *Sherbert*. He asserted that there was no distinction between this case and *Braunfeld* because both asked whether the government could ask a citizen to choose between his livelihood and his religious beliefs. Justice Stewart concluded, "in order to reach [the conclusion here] the court must explicitly reject the reasoning of *Braunfeld v. Brown*"[29] As we see, the Court did not do this and one must still wonder how the two cases can be reconciled since both ask the individual to decide between following the dictates of religion or suffering financial hardship.

OTHER FREE EXERCISE CLAIMS

Accommodations for the Sabbath are not the only areas in which the Court has faced free exercise challenges resulting from unintended consequences of government regulation. These cases focus on the necessity of granting an exemption to those claiming interference with their religious practices. The central concern for the Court in making a determination will be the asserted state interest and the ability of the state to achieve the goal if an exemption is granted.

Sherbert indicates that there are situations in which the government must accommodate religious practices. The Establishment Clause, however, limits the extent of government accommodation. If the state accommodates religious practice it may conflict with the proscription against the establishment of religion. Thus, a clear tension exists between the two clauses.[30] In these cases the Court will focus on the Establishment Clause and be less willing to support an exemption. The state may be required to grant an exemption only in situations where there are no less restrictive means to achieve its goals but also in some situations where the grant of an exemption would almost allow the state to accomplish its purposes, that is, where there is only a minimal sacrifice of state objectives.

In *Wisconsin v. Yoder*,[31] parents who were members of the Old Order Amish and Mennonite religions challenged the state compulsory school attendance statute. The law mandated school attendance to age 16 and imposed a fine or imprisonment for failure to comply. The parents claimed that the statute was contrary to their way of life and would "endanger their own salvation and that of their children."[32] Amish children attended school through the eighth grade, usually until age 14 and then were schooled informally at home in farming and the activities of daily life in the Amish community.

The trial court accepted the validity of the parents' claim but found that the state was acting reasonably and within its power by enacting the statute. Thus, the convictions were upheld. The Wisconsin Supreme Court reversed the lower court decision, finding that the state's interest in education was not sufficient to overcome the parents' free exercise rights.

The Court also accepted the sincerity and legitimacy of the parents' claim and found the impact on religious practice severe. Before turning to the state's asserted interests, the Court noted that the statue, while neutral on its face, could not survive strict scrutiny on that basis alone, if in its applicability it unduly burdened free exercise rights. Employing strict scrutiny, the Court found that the state's interest in promoting education to ensure productive and economically self-sufficient citizens was not sufficient to overcome the impact on freedom of exercise. The Court reached this determination after examining the lifestyle of the Amish and determining that an additional two years of education would not deter Amish youth from taking their rightful and productive place in the rural Amish communities in which they lived. The closed nature of Amish society and the fact that most Amish children remained in the Amish community for their lifetime was important to the Court's decision.

WISCONSIN V. YODER
406 U.S. 205 (1972)

Chief Justice BURGER, for the Court.

There is no doubt as to the power of a State, having a high responsibility for education of its citizens, to impose reasonable regulations for the control and duration of basic education. Providing public schools ranks at the very apex of the function of a State. Yet even this paramount responsibility was, in *Pierce*, made to yield to the right of parents to provide an equivalent education in a privately operated system. There the Court held that Oregon's statute compelling attendance in a public school from age eight to age 16 unreasonably interfered with the interest of parents in directing the rearing of their off-spring, including their education in church-operated schools. As that case suggests, the values of parental direction of the religious upbringing and education of their children in their early and formative years have a high place in our society. Thus, a State's interest in universal education, however highly we rank it, is not totally free from a balancing process when it impinges on fundamental rights and interests, such as those specifically protected by the Free

Continued

Exercise Clause of the First Amendment, and the traditional interest of parents with respect to the religious upbringing of their children so long as they, in the words of Pierce, 'prepare (them) for additional obligations.'

It follows that in order for Wisconsin to compel school attendance beyond the eighth grade against a claim that such attendance interferes with the practice of a legitimate religious belief, it must appear either that the State does not deny the free exercise of religious belief by its requirement, or that there is a state interest of sufficient magnitude to override the interest claiming protection under the Free Exercise Clause. Long before there was general acknowledgement of the need for universal formal education, the Religion Clauses had specifically and firmly fixed the right to free exercise of religious beliefs, and buttressing this fundamental right was an equally firm, even if less explicit, prohibition against the establishment of any religion by government. These values underlying these two provisions relating to religion have been zealously protected, sometimes even at the expense of other interests of admittedly high social importance.

The essence of all that has been said and written on the subject is that only those interests of the highest order and those not otherwise served can overbalance legitimate claims to the free exercise of religion. We can accept it as settled, therefore, that, however strong the State's interest in universal compulsory education, it is by no means absolute to the exclusion or subordination of all other interests.

II

We come then to the quality of the claims of the respondents concerning the alleged encroachment of Wisconsin's compulsory school-attendance statute on their rights and the rights of their children to the free exercise of the religious beliefs they and their forbears have adhered to for almost three centuries. In evaluating those claims we must be careful to determine whether the Amish religious faith and their mode of life are, as they claim, inseparable and interdependent. A way of life, however virtuous and admirable, may not be interposed as a barrier to reasonable state regulation of education if it is based on purely secular considerations; to have the protection of the Religion Clauses, the claims must be rooted in religious belief.

Although a determination of what is a 'religious' belief or practice entitled to constitutional protection may present a most delicate question, the very concept of ordered liberty precludes allowing every person to make his own standards on matters of conduct in which society as a whole has important interests. Thus, if the Amish asserted their claims because of their subjective evaluation and rejection of the contemporary secular values accepted by the majority, much as Thoreau rejected the social values of his time and isolated himself at Walden Pond, their claims would not rest on a religious basis. Thoreau's choice was philosophical and personal rather than religious, and such belief does not rise to the demands of the Religion Clauses.

Giving no weight to such secular considerations, however, we see that the record in this case abundantly supports the claim that the traditional way of life of the Amish is not merely a matter of personal preference, but one of deep religious conviction, shared by an organized group, and intimately related to daily living. That the Old Order Amish daily life and religious practice stem from their faith is shown by the fact that it is in response to their literal interpretation of the Biblical injunction from the Epistle of Paul to the Romans, 'be not conformed to this world. . . .' This command is fundamental to the Amish faith. Moreover, for the Old Order Amish, religion is not simply a matter of theocratic belief. As the expert witnesses explained, the Old Order Amish religion pervades and determines virtually their entire way of life, regulating it with the detail of the Talmudic diet through the strictly enforced rules of the church community.

The impact of the compulsory-attendance law on respondents' practice of the Amish religion is not only severe, but inescapable, for the Wisconsin law affirmatively compels them, under threat of criminal sanction, to perform acts undeniably at odds with fundamental tenets of their religious beliefs. Nor is the impact of the compulsory-attendance law confined to grave interference with important Amish religious tenets from a subjective point of view. It carries with it precisely the kind of objective danger to the free exercise of religion that the First Amendment was designed to prevent. As the record shows, compulsory school attendance to age 16 for Amish children carries with it a very real threat of undermining the Amish community and religious practice as they exist

Continued

today; they must either abandon belief and be assimilated into society at large, or be forced to migrate to some other more tolerant region.

Nor can this case be disposed of on the grounds that Wisconsin's requirement for school attendance to age 16 applies uniformly to all citizens of the State and does not, on its face, discriminate against religions or a particular religion, or that it is motivated by legitimate secular concerns. A regulation neutral on its face may, in its application, nonetheless offend the constitutional requirement for governmental neutrality if it unduly burdens the free exercise of religion.

We turn, then, to the State's broader contention that its interest in its system of compulsory education is so compelling that even the established religious practices of the Amish must give way. Where fundamental claims of religious freedom are at stake, however, we cannot accept such a sweeping claim; despite its admitted validity in the generality of cases, we must searchingly examine the interests that the State seeks to promote by its requirement for compulsory education to age 16, and the impediment to those objectives that would flow from recognizing the claimed Amish exemption.

Insofar as the State's claim rests on the view that a brief additional period of formal education is imperative to enable the Amish to participate effectively and intelligently in our democratic process, it must fall.

For the reasons stated we hold, . . . that the First and Fourteenth Amendments prevent the State from compelling respondents to cause their children to attend formal high school to age 16. Our disposition of this case, however, in no way alters our recognition of the obvious fact that courts are not school boards or legislatures, and are ill-equipped to determine the 'necessity' of discrete aspects of a State's program of compulsory education. This should suggest that courts must move with great circumspection in performing the sensitive and delicate task of weighing a State's legitimate social concern when faced with religious claims for exemption from generally applicable education requirements. It cannot be overemphasized that we are not dealing with a way of life and mode of education by a group claiming to have recently discovered some 'progressive' or more enlightened process for rearing children for modern life.

Nothing we hold is intended to undermine the general applicability of the State's compulsory school-attendance statutes or to limit the power of the State to promulgate reasonable standards that, while not impairing the free exercise of religion, provide for continuing agricultural vocational education under parental and church guidance by the Old Order Amish or others similarly situated.

Affirmed.

Yoder demonstrates that the need for an exemption will be recognized not only when the state has no other means for achieving its goal but also when its goal might almost be achieved with the exemption. The state's interest was read broadly to limit the governmental interference in religious freedom without doing significant damage to the state's goals.

An exemption will not always be required even when strict scrutiny is applied. There are situations in which the Court has found that an exemption would significantly impair the achievement of the government's objective. This was the case in *U.S. v. Lee*.[33] There, a member of the Amish religion, who employed other Amish, claimed an exemption from the payment of social security taxes because it infringed on his religious freedom and that of his employees. The Court accepted that the payment of the tax and receipt of benefits was proscribed by the Amish religion. Nevertheless, the Court reiterated that all conflicts between faith and government regulation were not unconstitutional. Where the state demonstrates a compelling interest the regulation may stand. The Court found that the "[g]overnment's interest in assuring mandatory and continuous participation in and contribution to the social security system is very high."[34] Moreover, accommodation to the Amish belief was determined to interfere in securing that goal. The Court distinguished this case from *Yoder* asserting that "the broad public interest in maintaining a sound tax system is of such a high order, religious belief in conflict with the payment of taxes affords no basis for resisting the tax."[35] The Court noted that Congress had made accommodations for self-employed Amish, but further accommodation would undermine the system. Thus, it was made clear that there are instances in which the grant of an exemption is unwarranted in order for the state to achieve a compelling interest even if religious freedom is infringed.

The integrity of the tax system is not the only state interest that is sufficiently compelling to prevent the granting of an exemption. The state's interest in preventing discrimination is deemed to be so compelling and so unlikely to be achieved if exemptions are granted that racial discrimination may be prohibited even when it conflicts with religious belief.

In 1983, the Court directly addressed this issue in *Bob Jones University v. U.S*[36] Bob Jones University is a nonprofit institution of learning dedicated to promoting Christian ethics in teaching. Fundamentalist Christian beliefs, as derived from the Bible, underlie all teaching at the University. The sponsors of the university believe that the Bible forbids interracial dating and marriage. At one time, the university did not admit African American students. Later, in the face of Supreme Court rulings, the University first began to admit African Americans married within their race (no unmarried African Americans were accepted) and then went on to accept all African Americans. The University, however, maintained a disciplinary rule that prohibited interracial dating and marriage. Students who engaged in these activities, encouraged them, advocated them, or belonged to any group that did so were expelled. Based on this policy the Internal Revenue Service, consistent with its mandate from Congress to determine tax-exempt status for charitable institutions, revoked the university's tax-exempt status.

Underlying the tax code is the intent to provide exemptions to organizations that engage in charitable activities that "supplement or take the place of public institutions of the same kind."[37] Such exemptions are warranted because they confer a benefit on the public by offering services that would otherwise be unavailable or paid for by the taxpayers. The organizations receiving the exemptions must not engage in an activity that is contrary to public policy.

With this background, the Court considered the public policy of interest in this case—racial discrimination. The Court reviewed the various judicial, legislative, and executive decisions following *Brown v. Board of Education* and found that all three branches of government had acted consistently to eliminate racial discrimination in education. Accordingly, the Court found that a racially discriminatory school was not a charitable institution warranting an exemption.

The University maintained that revocation of its tax-exempt status violated free exercise rights. Even if the policy of denying tax exemptions to nonreligious schools engaging in discrimination was proper, because the University was acting in accordance with religious beliefs while conceding that there would be an impact on the school's operation, denial of tax-exempt status would not prevent observance of the University's practice of its religious tenets. The Court determined that the religiously held tenets were incompatible with the state's compelling interest in preventing racial discrimination. In addition, the Court asserted that there was no way in which an accommodation could be granted that would allow the state to achieve its interest.

BOB JONES UNIVERSITY V. UNITED STATES
461 U.S. 574 (1983)

Chief Justice BURGER delivered the opinion of the Court.

We granted certiorari to decide whether petitioners, nonprofit private schools that prescribe and enforce racially discriminatory admissions standards on the basis of religious doctrine, qualify as tax-exempt organizations under sec. 501 § (3) of the Internal Revenue Code of 1954.

Section 501 § (3) . . . must be analyzed and construed within the framework of the Internal Revenue Code and against the background of the Congressional purposes. Such an examination reveals unmistakable evidence that, underlying all relevant parts of the Code, is the intent that entitlement to tax exemption depends on meeting certain common law standards of charity—namely, that an institution seeking tax-exempt status must serve a public purpose and not be contrary to established public policy.

This "charitable" concept appears explicitly in sec. 170 of the Code. That section contains a list of organizations virtually identical to that contained in section 501 § (3). It is apparent that Congress intended that list to have the same meaning in both sections. In sec. 170, Congress used the list of organizations in defining the term "charitable contributions." On its face, therefore, sec.170 reveals that Congress' intention was to provide tax benefits to organizations serving charitable purposes. The form of sec. 170 simply makes plain what common sense and history tell us: in enacting both sec. 170 and sec. 501 § (3), Congress sought to provide tax benefits to charitable organizations, to encourage the development of private institutions that serve a useful public purpose or supplement or take the place of public institutions of the same kind.

Tax exemptions for certain institutions thought beneficial to the social order of the country as a whole, or to a particular community, are deeply rooted in our history, as in that of England. The origins of such exemptions lie in the special privileges that have long been extended to charitable trusts.

When the Government grants exemptions or allows deductions all taxpayers are affected; the very fact of the exemption or deduction for the donor means that other taxpayers can be said to be indirect and vicarious "donors." Charitable exemptions are justified on the basis that the exempt entity confers a public benefit—a benefit which the society or the community may not itself choose or be able to provide, or which supplements and advances the work of public institutions already supported by tax revenues. History buttresses logic to make clear that, to warrant exemption under sec. 501 § (3), an institution must fall within a category specified in that section and must demonstrably serve and be in harmony with the public interest. The institution's purpose must not be so at odds with the common community conscience as to undermine any public benefit that might otherwise be conferred.

B

We are bound to approach these questions with full awareness that determinations of public benefit and public policy are sensitive matters with serious implications for the institutions affected; a declaration that a given institution is not "charitable" should be made only where there can be no doubt that the activity involved is contrary to a fundamental public policy. But there can no longer be any doubt that racial discrimination in education violates deeply and widely accepted views of elementary justice. Prior to 1954, public education in many places still was conducted under the pall of *Plessy v. Ferguson*; racial segregation in primary and secondary education prevailed in many parts of the country. This Court's decision in *Brown v. Board of Education* signaled an end to that era. Over the past quarter of a century, every pronouncement of this Court and myriad Acts of Congress and Executive Orders attest a firm national policy to prohibit racial segregation and discrimination in public education.

An unbroken line of cases following *Brown v. Board of Education* establishes beyond doubt this Court's view that racial discrimination in education violates a most fundamental national public policy, as well as rights of individuals.

"The right of a student not to be segregated on racial grounds in schools . . . is indeed so fundamental and pervasive that it is embraced in the concept of due process of law."

Continued

Congress, in Titles IV and VI of the Civil Rights Act of 1964, clearly expressed its agreement that racial discrimination in education violates fundamental public policy. Other sections of the Act, and numerous enactments since then, testify to the public policy against racial discrimination.

The Executive Branch has consistently placed its support behind eradication of racial discrimination.

Few social or political issues in our history have been more vigorously debated and more extensively ventilated than the issue of racial discrimination, particularly in education. Given the stress and anguish of the history of efforts to escape from the shackles of the "separate but equal" doctrine of *Plessy v. Ferguson*, it cannot be said that educational institutions that, for whatever reasons, practice racial discrimination, are institutions exercising "beneficial and stabilizing influences in community life," or should be encouraged by having all taxpayers share in their support by way of special tax status.

On the record before us, there can be no doubt as to the national policy. In 1970, when the IRS first issued the ruling challenged here, the position of all three branches of the Federal Government was unmistakably clear. The correctness of the Commissioner's conclusion that a racially discriminatory private school "is not 'charitable' within the common law concepts reflected in . . . the Code," is wholly consistent with what Congress, the Executive and the courts had repeatedly declared before 1970. Indeed, it would be anomalous for the Executive, Legislative and Judicial Branches to reach conclusions that add up to a firm public policy on racial discrimination, and at the same time have the IRS blissfully ignore what all three branches of the Federal Government had declared. Clearly an educational institution engaging in practices affirmatively at odds with this declared position of the whole government cannot be seen as exercising a "beneficial and stabilizing influenc[e] in community life," and is not "charitable," within the meaning of sec. 170 and sec. 501 § (3). We therefore hold that the IRS did not exceed its authority . . .

Affirmed.

There are also situations in which an exemption will be denied based on the particular circumstances of the individual claiming the exemption. The Court has found that prisoners and those who are in the military may have their free exercise rights infringed upon due to the nature of their status. In these cases the Court applies a different standard of review.

In *Goldman v. Weinberger*,[38] an Orthodox Jewish rabbi who was on active service in the United States Armed Forces sued the government claiming that a regulation preventing him form wearing his yarmulke, as required by his religion, violated his free exercise rights. The Court began its analysis by stating that it would be more deferential to military regulations than would be the case of similar civilian regulations. "The military need not encourage debate or tolerate protest to the extent that such tolerance is required of the civilian state by the First Amendment; to accomplish its mission the military must foster instinctive obedience, unity, commitment, and esprit de corps."[39] This deference foreshadowed the ultimate decision to uphold the regulation. There was, however, some disagreement as to the reason the regulation should be upheld. The government asserted an interest in the use of standardized uniforms to "encourage the subordination of personal preferences and identities in favor of the overall group mission."[40] The majority accepted this. In a concurrence signed by three Justices, however, the problem was seen as one of the need for treating all members of the service, no matter what their religious preference, uniformly.

In *Daniels v. City of Arlington*, a Texas police officer, who was fired for wearing a crucifix pin on his uniform, failed to get the four votes necessary to obtain a full hearing before the United States Supreme Court. The Court let stand a Fifth Circuit Court of Appeals decision to uphold the firing. The City of

Arlington, for which the officer worked, claimed that the restriction was based on the alteration of the uniform and that the officer would have been free to wear the symbol on another piece of jewelry that did not alter the appearance of his uniform.[41]

The same level of deference is given to correctional authorities in determining the extent of free exercise claims for prisoners. Islamic prisoners challenged prison policies that prevented them from attending religious services in *O'Lone v. Shabazz*.[42] The prisoners were assigned to a detail that worked outside the prison gates and would have to have special arrangements to return them to the prison for Jumu'ah service, a weekly service commanded by the Koran (the Moslem holy book) to be held every Friday afternoon and before afternoon prayer. Jumu'ah is considered a central practice of Islam.

The authorities argued that returning the prisoners for the service "resulted in security risks and administrative burdens that prison officials found unacceptable."[43] Based on the assertion of the authorities, the Court upheld the policies that prevented the prisoners from attending service. The Court recognized the sincerity of the prisoners' beliefs and the fact that prisoners retain some of their constitutional rights upon entering the institution. It was asserted that those rights, however, had to be balanced against the authorities' interests in achieving legitimate penal objectives. The Court stressed the importance of giving significant deference to prison authorities in determining how best to achieve these objectives, citing the judiciary's lack of knowledge about prison administration. Accordingly, the Court found that the standard for determining the prisoners' claim was one of reasonableness. The Court determined that the regulations in question here met that standard and was "justified by concerns of institutional order and security . . ."[44]

Although the Court acknowledged that there were no alternative means available for the prisoners to attend Jumu'ah, the Court "was unwilling to hold that prison officials are required by the Constitution to sacrifice legitimate penological objectives to that end."[45] The Court stated that since the prisoners were not completely deprived of their religious observance the regulation was reasonable. Thus, since the prisoners could practice their religion in other ways, the interference with regard to Jumu'ah was not unconstitutional.

The four dissenters maintained that the correct standard for determination was whether the prison officials could show that the policies preventing the prisoners from attending religious services were "necessary to further an important government interest, and that these restrictions are no greater than necessary to achieve prison objectives."[46] At the same time the dissenters took issue with the standard the Court employed, they also argued that the application of the standard still demanded a contrary result. Justice Brennan wrote, "Jumu'ah is the central religious ceremony of Muslims. . . . Jumu'ah therefore cannot be regarded as one of several essentially fungible religious practices. The ability to engage in other religious activities cannot obscure the fact that the denial at issue in this case is absolute; respondents are completely foreclosed from participating in the core ceremony that reflects their membership in a particular religious community. If a Catholic prisoner were prevented from attending Mass on Sunday, few would regard that deprivation as anything but absolute, even if the prisoner were afforded other opportunities to pray, to discuss the Catholic faith with others, and even to avoid eating meat on Friday if that were a preference. Prison officials in this case therefore cannot show that 'other avenues' remain available for the exercise of the asserted right."[47]

Goldman and *O'Lone* make clear that when the individual challenging a regulation, as an infringement of free exercise, is not a civilian who retains all constitutional rights, the analysis of a free exercise claim is different and the Court applies a less stringent standard (see Exhibit 14.1).

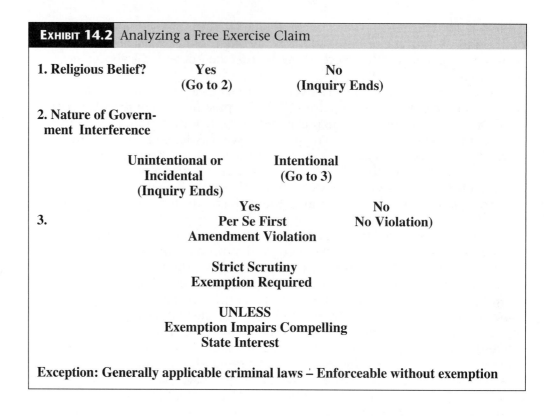

EXHIBIT 14.2 Analyzing a Free Exercise Claim

1. Religious Belief?   **Yes**   **No**
                                  (Go to 2)   (Inquiry Ends)

**2. Nature of Govern-
   ment Interference**

              Unintentional or   Intentional
                  Incidental   (Go to 3)
               (Inquiry Ends)
                                    Yes   **No**
3.   **Per Se First**   **No Violation)**
                          Amendment Violation

                            Strict Scrutiny
                         Exemption Required

                               UNLESS
                    Exemption Impairs Compelling
                           State Interest

Exception: Generally applicable criminal laws – Enforceable without exemption

Since *O' Lone* and *Goldman* the Congress has attempted to provide greater protection of free exercise to those in the military and institutionalized individuals, including prisoners. For those in the uniform unless it would interfere in work performance. In 2005, after the Court found that Congress' first attempt to protect prisoners' free exercise rights failed, the court heard a challenge to the Religious Land Use and Institutionalized Persons Act of 2000.[48] The Court upheld the statute that applies when a substantial burden is imposed on religious practice in programs or activities receiving federal assistance or affecting commerce. It protects people unable to "attend to their religious needs" when they are dependent on government to provide for those needs.[49]

At the moment it is unclear whether this will have an impact upon the way in which the Court analyzes these cases by including the claimants who are civilian and retain all their constitutional rights, rather than applying a less stringent standard.

Another area of free exercise challenges occurs when a generally applicable criminal statute has an unintended impact upon citizens' free exercise rights. In this situation the Court has recently enunciated a new rule for analyzing these cases. In *Employment Division v. Smith*,[50] the Court held that such generally applicable criminal laws were automatically enforceable regardless of the degree of burden imposed on an individual's religious practices.

Alfred Smith and co-worker Galen Black were fired from their jobs because they used peyote, a hallucinogenic, as part of their religious observance at the Native American Church to which they belonged. When the two applied for unemployment insurance benefits, they were denied because they were fired for "misconduct." Before the Supreme Court, Smith argued that the denial of benefits was unconstitutional because it forced him to give up conduct required by his religion. The Court rejected his argument. The Court found that the First Amendment did not require exemptions from compliance with valid laws that prohibited conduct that the State could legitimately regulate. So long as the law is neutral (i.e., not intended to burden religious practices), there is a requirement to comply with that law. The Court stated that it was only in cases where the generally applicable law burdened some other constitutional right along with the right to free exercise that it had held to the contrary. The Court also considered whether it was necessary to grant an exemption in this case and found that it was not. Noting that the *Sherbert* test was essentially limited to unemployment cases, the Court found that even when the test was applied to generally applicable criminal statutes it had never resulted in the statute's invalidation. Consequently, the Court ruled that the test was not applicable to such challenges. The government's ability to enforce generally applicable prohibitions of socially harmful conduct, like its ability to carry out other aspects of public policy "cannot depend on measuring the effects of a governmental action on religious objector's spiritual development."[51] Thus, the Court rejected the use of the "compelling state interest" standard. It was the Court's position that accommodation should be properly left to the political process, although it was recognized that this would put those who engaged in religious practices that were not widely adopted at a disadvantage. The Court concluded, however, that this was an "unavoidable consequence of democratic government [and] must be preferred to a system in which each conscience is a law unto itself or in which judges weigh the social importance of all laws against the centrality of all religious beliefs."[52]

The Court has thus circumscribed the circumstances under which exemptions to accommodate free exercise claims are necessary. Those cases we have discussed so far have involved situations in which the government specifically prescribes or proscribes conduct that conflicts with a citizen's religious practices. There is another class of cases that must also be considered. These are cases in which government regulation makes the practice of one's religion more difficult. In light of the Court's direction in *Smith* we should not be surprised that the Court is less likely to uphold free exercise claims in these less restrictive situations.

In *Lyng v. Northwest Indian Cemetery Protective Association*,[53] the Court addressed such a claim. At issue was whether the government could construct a road through federal land that would cause an impact on sacred areas of land integral to Native American culture and religion. Native Americans sought to halt the construction. Despite the acknowledgement by the government that damage to Native American religious practices would be great and that the government's interest was small, the Court found that there was no constitutional basis for halting construction. As in *Smith* the Court noted the tension between government regulation and free exercise and concluded that the government could not operate if it was constrained by every citizen's claim of religious freedom and again noted that the proper forum for deciding on the appropriate balance between these interests lay in the legislature.

Lyng makes clear that the Court will not find a constitutional violation where the effect of a government regulation merely makes exercise of one's religious beliefs more difficult. It appears that only in situations where the government's actions preclude practice of one's religion will the Court find a violation. And, the Court is narrowing those situations.

The Court has continued to narrow those situations in which government regulation is found to interfere with free exercise rights. In the area of public health, individuals raising free exercise claims have not succeeded in challenging regulations affecting health and welfare. The Court has ruled that one may be required to be vaccinated despite religious convictions to the contrary.[54] In situations where a parent objects to medical treatment for a child based on the parent's religious beliefs, most courts will compel treatment, although competent adults are free to refuse medical treatment on their own behalf.

There is one final area in which there have been challenges to government regulation on the basis of the First Amendment Free Exercise Clause. Citizens have sought to be relieved of the obligation for military service on the basis of their beliefs that all war is evil. Exemptions for those who hold such beliefs are available. During the Vietnam War, however, there were those who sought conscientious objector status on the basis of their opposition to this particular war. In *Gilette v. U.S.*, [55] the Court found that the section of the Military Selective Service Act, which provided exemption from military service for those who objected on the basis of conscience to all wars, did not violate the Free Exercise Clause by requiring service of those who opposed a particular war.

Summary

To protect against the problems that could arise from state-endorsed religion, the Framers included two provisions in the Bill of Rights guaranteeing that government could not establish a state religion and that citizens were free to exercise their religious beliefs.

This guarantee of free exercise virtually ensures that government may not regulate citizens' beliefs. A distinction, however, is drawn between belief and activity. The government may regulate, under certain circumstances, citizens' activities associated with religious beliefs.

The Court engages in a balancing test, weighing the state's purpose in regulating conduct against the individual's free exercise rights. When the state purposefully intends to have an impact on religious practice, the courts will almost certainly find a violation of First Amendment religious guarantees. Where the impact is not purposeful, but results in infringing on religious practices, the determination is not as clear-cut.

Until the 1960s the Court used the rational relationship test to determine the constitutionality of the regulation. Any protection offered to citizens claiming a violation of free exercise rights was the result of the Court employing a free speech analysis. In the 1960s the Court began to employ strict scrutiny to determine whether a government regulation violated free exercise. Under this standard the state was required to demonstrate a compelling interest. Exemptions from compliance with the regulation had to be granted by the government, when there was no less restrictive means to accomplish the governmental purpose and the regulation infringed upon citizens' rights. Nevertheless, situations exist where exemptions will not be required even when strict scrutiny is applied where the accommodation would so seriously undermine public policy.

There are also situations where the Court is more tolerant of government regulation. The Court will grant greater deference to military and prison authorities to regulate conduct even when religious freedom is infringed. In addition, generally applicable criminal statutes will be upheld regardless of their impact on religious practices.

The Court's recent decisions display a return to a less rigid scrutiny of government regulations that burden religious practices.

Key Terms

extrajudicial   freedom of religion

Review Questions

1. The Court employs four factor in considering whether a religious belief exists that will give rise to a First Amendment free exercise claim. What are these factors and what interpretation is given to each by the court?

2. The court reached opposite conclusions about the need for exemptions in *Braunfeld* and *Sherbert*. What analysis was used by the Court in each of these cases? How do the analyses differ?

3. A distinction is drawn by the Court between religious belief and religious practice. On what basis does the Court maintain the government has a right/obligation to intervene in religious practice?

4. *Sherbert* indicated that there are situations in which the government must accommodate religious practices but such accommodation may cause tension with the Establishment Clause. Under what conditions will an exemption be granted?

5. The court grants deference to military and corrections authorities in their decisions which may impinge upon individuals free exercise rights when they are in these authorities custody and care. What standard of review is used in these cases? How does the standard differ for military and corrections personnel?

Internet Connections

1. To read any of the cases mentioned in this chapter, you can obtain the full text from *http://www.findlaw.com.*

2. The American Civil Liberties Union, the foremost protector of civil rights and civil liberties, maintains a Web site at *http://www.aclu.org.*

3. The First Amendment Lawyers Association, which provides for defense of First Amendment claims, also has a Web site at *http://www.fala.org.*

End Notes

[1] The Establishment Clause was incorporated in *Everson v. Board of Education*, 330 U.S. 1 (1947), and the Free Exercise Clause was incorporated in *Cantwell v. Connecticut*, 310 U.S. 296 (1940).

[2] Under this reasoning, the Court has also found that religious personnel must be made available to those in prison.

[3] *Reynolds v. U.S.*, 98 U.S. 145,167 (1879). In *Reynolds*, the Court was considering a challenge to a state statute making polygamy a crime. Reynolds was convicted and challenged the conviction on the ground that he was acting in conformity with his duty as a member of the Mormon Church.

[4] In 1961 the Court struck down a state requirement that public officeholders must declare their belief in the existence of God. *Torasco v. Watkins*, 367 U.S. 488 (1961).

[5] *Frazee v. Illinois Department of Employment Security*, 489 U.S. 829 (1989).

[6] *Id.* at 834.

[7] *U.S. v. Ballard*, 322 U.S. 78 (1944). Defendants in *Ballard* were charged with using the mails to defraud based on their religious movement. The Court agreed that the lower court rightly withheld the question of the truth of defendants' beliefs from the jury.

[8] *Davis v. Beason*, 133 U.S. 333, 342 (1890).

[9] *Thomas v. Review Bd. Ind. Empl. Sect. Div.*, 450 U.S. 707 (1981).

[10] Lawrence Tribe, *American Constitutional Law*, 1215 (2d ed., Foundation Press 1988).

[11] *Church of Lukumi Babalu Aye v. City of Hialeah*, 508 U.S. 520 (1993).

[12] http://sparta.rice.edu/~

[13] *Id. Church of Lukumi Babalu v. City of Hialeah*, 520 U.S. 520, 538 (1993).

[14] *Reynolds v. United States*, 98 U.S. 145 (1878).

[15] *Id.* at 167.

[16] Ibid.

[17] *Cantwell v. Connecticut*, 310 U.S. 296 (1940).

[18] *Minersville School District v. Gobitis*, 310 U.S. 586 (1940).

[19] *West Virginia Board of Education v. Barnette*, 319 U.S. 624 (1943).

[20] *Id.* at 634–635.

[21] *Wooley v. Maynard*, 430 U.S. 705 (1977).

[22] *Id.* at 713.

[23] *Braunfeld v. Brown*, 366 U.S. 599 (1961). *Braunfeld* was decided the same day as *McGowan v. Maryland*, 366 U.S. 420 (1961), which raided the Sunday closing law issue in terms of the Establishment Clause.

[24] *Braunfeld v. Brown*, 366 U.S. at 605 (1961).

[25] *Id.* at 612, citing *West Virginia Board of Education v. Barnette*, 440 U.S. 973 (1943).

[26] *Sherbert v. Verner*, 374 U.S. 398 (1963).

[27] *Id.* at 410.

[28] *Id.* at 418.

[29] Ibid.

[30] See *Thornton v. Caldor, Inc.*, 472 U.S. 703 (1985).

[31] *Wisconsin v. Yoder*, 406 U.S. 205 (1972).

[32] *Id.* at 209.

[33] *United States v. Lee*, 455 U.S. 252 (1982).

[34] *Id.* at 258–259.

[35] *Id.* at 260.

[36] *Bob Jones University v. United States*, 461 U.S. 574 (1983).

[37] *Id.* at 588.

[38] *Goldman v. Weinberger*, 475 U.S. 503 (1986).

[39] *Id.* at 505.

[40] *Id.* at 508.

[41]*Daniels v. City of Arlington*, 246 F.3d 500, (5th cir.) cert. denied, 534 U.S. 951 (2001) U.S. App. LEXIS 6018 (5th cir.2001), *cert. denied.*

[42]*O'Lone v. Shabazz*, 492 U.S. 342 (1987).

[43]*Id.* at 346.

[44]*Id.* at 350.

[45]*Id.* at 350–351.

[46]*Id.* at 354.

[47]*Id.* at 360.

[48]*Cutter v. Washington*, (2005) slip op.

[49]*Id.* at slip op.

[50]*Employment Division v. Smith*, 494 U.S. 872 (1990).

[51]*Id.* at 885.

[52]*Id.* at 890.

[53]*Lyng v. Northwest Indian Cemetery Protective Association*, 485 U.S. 439 (1988).

[54]*Jacobson v. Massachusetts*, 197 U.S. 11 (1905).

[55]*Gillette v. United States*, 401 U.S. 437 (1971).

 For additional resources, go to *http://www.westlegalstudies.com*

CHAPTER 15

FREEDOM OF RELIGION: THE ESTABLISHMENT CLAUSE

"Believing with you that religion is a matter which lies solely between man and his God; that he owes account to none other for his faith or his worship; that the legislative powers of the government reach actions only, and not opinions,—I contemplate with sovereign reverence that act of the whole American people which declared that their legislature should 'make no law respecting an establishment of religion or prohibiting the free exercise thereof,' thus building a wall of separation between church and State."

—Thomas Jefferson
Reynolds v. United States

INTRODUCTION

As discussed in the previous chapter, there are two clauses in the First Amendment that discuss freedom of religion. The **Establishment Clause** states, "Congress shall make no law respecting an establishment of religion . . ."[1]

The purpose of the Establishment Clause is quite simple: to keep the government from establishing or becoming involved in the promotion of religion. In the words of Thomas Jefferson, noted above, the clause was to establish "a wall of separation between church and state."[2] It is this wall, and how it has been applied in a variety of circumstances that will be the topic of discussion in this chapter.

While it was always understood that the Establishment Clause applied to the federal government, it was not always so clear that it had application to the states. In the case of *Murdock v. Commonwealth of Pennsylvania*[3] the Court selectively incorporated this First Amendment right and made it applicable to the states as well. In doing so, the Court reflected the mind-set of the early Americans who wanted to stamp out religious oppression. The historical perspective behind this amendment was carefully outlined by the Court in *Everson v. Board of Education of Ewing Township.*[4] The Court noted that many of the early settlers in this country came here from Europe to escape the oppressive laws that compelled them to support and attend churches favored by the government. In spite of this, many of these same practices were instituted in the new world. It became commonplace for the colonies to impose taxes to pay the salaries of ministers or to build and maintain church buildings and rectories. As the colonists became more and more indignant about this, the Founding Fathers reached the conclusion that individual religious freedom could only be achieved if the government no longer had the power to tax, support or assist any or all religions or interfere with an individual's religious beliefs.[5]

In spite of these convictions, and the attempts by the courts to uphold the Establishment Clause, there is difficulty in drawing the line between legislation that provides for the welfare of the general public and legislation that is designed to promote religion. In *Everson,* the Court was reviewing a New Jersey statute authorizing local school districts to make rules and contracts for the transportation of children to and from schools. The Board of Education of Ewing Township acted pursuant to this statute and authorized reimbursement to parents who had spent money for the public bus transportation of their children to Catholic parochial schools. When a lawsuit was filed challenging the

Establishment Clause
that part of the First Amendment to the U.S. Constitution that states "Congress shall make no law respecting an *establishment* of religion."

constitutionality of the statute, one argument was that this constituted an unconstitutional "establishment" of religion. When outlining what the Establishment Clause means, the Court said that it means at least five things:

1. Neither federal nor state governments may establish an official church;
2. The government may not "force or influence a person to go to or remain away from church against his will or force him to profess a belief or disbelief in any religion . . .
3. No individual may be "punished for entertaining or professing religious beliefs or disbeliefs, for church attendance or non-attendance . . .
4. The federal or state governments may not prefer one religion over another, including preferring religion over non-religion;
5. The government may not participate in the affairs of a religious organization nor can such organization participate in the affairs of government.[6]

In reviewing the specific statute, the *Everson* Court went on to say that it had to be careful to protect the citizens from state-established churches and at the same time, extend the general state law benefits to all citizens without regard to their religious beliefs. Ultimately, the Court held that the Establishment Clause of the First Amendment does not prohibit the state from spending tax-raised funds to pay the bus fares of parochial school pupils as part of a general program that allows for the reimbursement of fares for public and other parochial school students.

THE LEMON TEST

Since *Everson*, situations have arisen and the Court has had to decide when a government action is in violation of the Establishment Clause. In order to give guidance in this area, the Court came up with a three-prong test in the case of *Lemon v. Kurtzman* (see Exhibit 15.1).[7] In this case, which was combined with the companion case of *Early v. DiCenso*,[8] the Court reviewed statutes from Pennsylvania and Rhode Island that provided for state aid to church-related elementary and secondary schools. The Court again said that the First Amendment was designed to protect against three "main evils" and they are the sponsorship, financial support, and active involvement in religious activities.[9] The Court went on to say that legislation that meets all three prongs of the test would be valid. However, if the legislation fails any part, it will be held unconstitutional. In order for a statute to be constitutional it must have a secular legislative purpose, its primary or principal effect must neither advance nor inhibit religion, and it must not foster an excessive governmental entanglement with religion. This final prong would include avoidance of the creation of an excessive degree of political division along religious or denominational lines.[10] In these cases, the Court held that the statutes were unconstitutional

---

EXHIBIT 15.1 The Lemon Test

A three-prong test used to test the validity of state or federal statutes that allegedly establish or promote religion. If the statute or regulatory scheme demonstrates the following, it will be upheld under the Lemon Test:

1. The legislation or statute must have a secular purpose,
2. Its primary goal must neither promote nor inhibit religion, and
3. The legislation or statute may not promote excessive entanglement between religion and the government.

All three prongs must be met in order for the law to be upheld under this test.

because "[t]he substantial religious character of these church-related schools gives rise to entangling church-state relationships of the kind that the Religion Clause sought to avoid."[11]

While the Lemon Test has been used for years, there is some indication that the Court is unhappy with it. A 1989 case, *Texas Monthly, Inc. v. Bullock*,[12] brought an indication from the Court that they may be moving to a simpler, more straightforward test. In *Texas Monthly, Inc.*, the Court looked at a Texas statute that exempted religious periodicals from the collection of the state sales tax. The question was whether this exemption violated the Establishment Clause because only religious periodicals, and no others, were exempted. The Court held that since the statute was confined exclusively to "publications advancing the tenets of a religious faith, the exemption runs afoul of the Establishment Clause . . ."[13] The Court mentioned the *Lemon* case and its three-prong test, but instead, used an "endorsement of religion" test. The Court said, "In proscribing all laws 'respecting an establishment of religion,' the Constitution prohibits, at the very least, legislation that constitutes an endorsement of one or another set of religious beliefs or of religion generally."[14] The state of Texas claimed a **compelling interest** in avoiding any free exercise violations and that without the statute, an individual's free exercise rights would be trammeled. The Court rejected this argument and struck down the statute.

A more current example of the Court's unhappiness with the Lemon Test is found in the *Board of Education of Kiryas Joel v. Grumet*.[15] In this case, a New York statute was challenged. The statute created a special school district for an enclave of Satner Masidim, a strict form of Judaism. An association of school boards and taxpayers brought an action alleging that the statute was a violation of the Establishment Clause. Justice Souter wrote on behalf of the Court saying that the statute creating the Kiryas Joel Village School District violated the constitutional command that the government favor neither one religion over another nor religious adherents over nonreligious adherents. In deciding this, the Court again mentioned the Lemon Test, but did not apply it. Instead, the Court found that the Religion Clauses "commanded" neutrality and said that there is "ample room under the Establishment Clause for 'benevolent neutrality' which will permit religious exercise to exist without sponsorship and without interference."[16]

The most recent case to discuss the Lemon Test is *Mitchell v. Helms*.[17] In that decision, written by Justice Thomas, the Court attempted to sort out the confusion over the Lemon Test. Justice Thomas wrote:

> "... Whereas in Lemon we had considered whether a statute (1) has a secular purpose, (2) has a primary effect of advancing or inhibiting religion, or (3) creates an excessive entanglement between government and religion, [citation omitted] in Agostini we modified Lemon for purposes of evaluating aid to schools and examined only the first and second factors, [citation omitted]. We acknowledged that our cases discussing excessive entanglement had applied many of the same considerations as had our cases discussing primary effect, and we therefore recast Lemon's entanglement inquiry as simply one criterion relevant to determining a statute's effect ... We also acknowledged that our cases had pared somewhat the factors that could justify a finding of excessive entanglement."[18]

Once again we see the Court modifying the Lemon Test, but not overruling it. Whether the Court continues to use the Lemon Test, overrules it, just ignores it, as it has in *Texas Monthly, Inc.* and *Board of Education of Kiryas Joel*, or modifies it as it did in *Mitchell v. Helms*, remains to be seen. Whichever test is used, the Court continues to draw lines preventing the establishment of a state-sponsored or -supported religion in a variety of contexts. Those contexts will be discussed in the following pages.

compelling interest a strong enough reason for a state law to make the law constitutional even though the law classifies persons on the basis of race, sex, [religion], etc, or uses the state's police powers to limit an individual's constitutional right.

SUNDAY CLOSING LAWS

Throughout the history of this country, there have been laws requiring businesses to be closed on Sunday. In general, these Sunday Closing Laws do not violate the Establishment Clause. In 1961, the Court had the occasion to review a Sunday Closing Law in the case of *McGowan v. Maryland*.[19] The Maryland statute in this case proscribed all labor, business, and other commercial activities on Sunday. The appellants were seven employees of a large discount store and they were indicted for retail sales made on Sunday, convicted under the statute, and fined five dollars plus costs. The appellants challenged the statute claiming that, among other things, it violated the guarantee of separation of church and state.

The Court looked at this Maryland statute, reviewed the history of Sunday Closing Laws in this country and reaffirmed that the purpose of the Establishment Clause was not only to protect the free exercise of religion, but also to prevent the "establishment of a religion . . . because of its [state sponsored religion] tendencies to political tyranny and subversion of civil authority."[20] The Court went on to say that nonreligious reasons for Sunday Closing laws exist and that such statutes had "begun to lose some of their totally religious flavor."[21] In conclusion, the Court held that the Establishment Clause does not ban legislation that happens to have some or all of the same goals as a religion and that the state's goals of the improvement of the health, safety and well-being of its citizens is a secular goal which does not violate any constitutional provisions. The Court went on to hold that the purpose of the law was to set aside a day of rest and recreation. The fact that the state chose Sunday as that day of rest and relaxation was not constitutionally impermissible, either, as the Court found that:

> ". . . it is common knowledge that the first day of the week has come to have special significance as a rest day in this country. People of all religions and people with no religion regard Sunday as a time for family activity, for visiting friends and relatives, for late sleeping, for passive and active entertainments, for dining out, and the like."[22]

Thus, any statute which has overlapping secular and religious purposes, but whose primary purpose is secular in nature, is not in violation of the Establishment Clause.

Fourteen years later, the Court once again heard a case involving Sunday Closing Laws; this case involved a Connecticut statute that gave Connecticut citizens an absolute right to refuse to work on their day of religious observance or worship.[23] Donald Thornton was a manager for a Connecticut store owned by Caldor, Inc. When Thornton refused to work Sundays (his day of worship), Caldor first offered to transfer him to another store that was not open on Sunday, and then, when Thornton refused this transfer, demoted Thornton to a clerical position in the Connecticut store. Thornton resigned and then brought an action against Caldor claiming that Caldor violated the Connecticut statute.

Caldor argued that the Connecticut statute violated the Establishment Clause by arming "Sabbath observers with an absolute and unqualified right not to work on whatever day they designate as their Sabbath."[24] While this may seem like a way to avoid promoting one religion over another, it does impose on employers a duty to conduct their businesses according to the observance of the Sabbath day that the employee unilaterally chooses. In doing so, the State places employers under the control of religious concerns, as the statute does not allow for the interests of the employers or even other nonreligious employees to be taken into account. In doing so, the statute's primary effect is to advance a religious practice. In holding that this statute violates the

Establishment Clause, this Court quoted Judge Learned Hand who wrote in *Otten v. Baltimore & Ohio Railroad Company*:

> *"The First Amendment . . . gives no one the right to insist that in pursuit of their own interests others must conform their conduct to his own religious necessities."*[25]

With this holding, the Court noted that an employer should make a reasonable attempt to accommodate an employee's observance of the Sabbath. It was the absolute right given by the statute that the Court held to be an impermissible advancement of a religions practice. This case clearly demonstrates the tension between the Establishment Clause and the Free Exercise Clause. To give an absolute right to observe the Sabbath is to violate the Establishment Clause. On the other hand, failure to make reasonable accommodation could put the employer in the position of violating the Free Exercise Clause. When called on to make a decision, the Court's analysis often rests on the "reasonableness" of the accommodation.

CHURCH AND GOVERNMENT INVOLVEMENT

Introduction

Often the Court has been called upon to review statutes that allow churches and other religious organizations to be involved in the exercise of governmental powers. When this happens, the Court generally uses the Lemon Test and looks at the antientanglement principle found in that case. One case, which demonstrates the Court's reasoning in this area, is *Larkin v. Grendel's Den, Inc.*[26] *Larkin* is a review of a Massachusetts statute, known as Section 16C, which allowed churches and schools to file written objections to applications for liquor licenses, and in doing so, veto the application. When Grendel's Den applied for a liquor license, Holy Cross Church objected because Grendel's Den was located next to the church's school and based on this objection, the License Commission denied the application. While it is recognized that the State may enforce zoning laws and ". . . regulate the environment in the vicinity of schools, churches, hospitals and the like . . ."[27] the Court found that this was not an exercise of zoning power, but a delegation of legislative power to a private, non-governmental entity. As such, the deference generally given to legislative zoning judgment was not given here.

Having decided this, the Court went on to do a *Lemon* analysis of the facts in this case. The Court reasserted that the statute must satisfy the three requirements of *Lemon*. First, the State must demonstrate that the statute has a valid secular purpose. The Court agreed that it did, but thought that these objectives could be accomplished by means other than allowing churches and schools to have veto power.

Second, the State must show that the statute neither advances nor inhibits religion. The State in this case argued that the statute had only incidentally advanced religion, but because the power conferred on churches and schools was "standard less" and, theoretically, could be used for "explicitly religious goals," the Court held that "the statute could be seen as having a 'primary' and 'principal' effect of advancing religion."[28]

Lastly, the State would have to demonstrate that the statute does not unduly entangle or enmesh the government in religious affairs. The Court held:

> *"Section 16C substitutes the unilateral and absolute power of a church for the reasoned decision making of a public legislative body acting on evidence and guided by standards, on issues with significant economic and political implications. The challenged statute thus enmeshes churches in the process of*

government and creates the danger of 'political fragmentation and divisiveness along religious lines.' "[29]

For these reasons, the Court struck down the Massachusetts statute, and indicated how it would deal with cases when government and church become entangled.

Ceremonies

Over the years, the Court has had to make decisions related to religion and government ceremonies or displays. The key here seems to be the "entanglement" of the government in religious affairs, and the Court had to look at the facts and circumstances of the following cases in order to determine whether the government has gotten impermissibly entangled with religion. For the most part, a mere mention of God or a reference to religion is not enough to trigger the Establishment Clause. An example of this is found in *Marsh v. Chambers*[30] when the Court had to decide whether a Nebraska legislative practice of opening each legislative day with a prayer by a paid chaplain is a violation of the Establishment Clause. In deciding this case, the Court looked at the history of such practices in the United States. The practice dates back to colonial days, and in 1774, the Continental Congress adopted the tradition of opening its sessions with a prayer.[31] The Court noted that this decision was not lightly entered into, and brought with it discussion of whether this was appropriate. The Court concluded that:

> *"This unique history leads us to accept the interpretation of the First Amendment draftsmen who saw no real threat to the Establishment Clause arising from a practice of prayer similar to that now challenged. We conclude that legislative prayer presents no more potential for establishment than the provision of school transportation [citation omitted], beneficial grants for higher education [citation omitted], or tax exemptions for religious organizations [citation omitted]."[32]*

The Court further noted that the prayer, as had been traditionally given, did not attempt to proselytize or advance any religion, and that the justices saw no threat to the Establishment Clause.

Justice Brennan dissented in this decision, writing that he believed that if the majority were to look at this practice with an "unsentimental" eye, it would strike down this practice as a "clear violation of the Establishment Clause."[33] He believed that the claim of nonsecular purposes, that is, "formally opening the legislative session, getting the members of the body to quiet down, and imbuing them with a sense of seriousness and high purpose"[34] could have been achieved without using prayer. Justice Brennan wrote that the practice was an excessive entanglement of government and religion and that if *Lemon* were to be properly applied, the practice would be found unconstitutional.

The Court has considered other cases involving ceremonies and public schools. These cases will be discussed below.

Displays

In many communities across the country it was common to have a religious display placed on government property during the Christmas holiday season. While this may be a long-standing tradition, it has raised the question, "Is this a violation of the Establishment Clause?" There is no pat answer. Whether a display violates the Establishment Clause depends on whether a reasonable person, seeing the display, would conclude that the government was endorsing a specific religion or religion in general. If the display seems to be endorsing a specific religion, it would be a violation, however, under other circumstances that includes a secular purpose, it would not be considered a violation. If the display is part of a display with other nonreligious symbols or a sign nearby indicating that a private group or individual has erected the display or if it is common knowledge in the community that the government make space available to private parties who want to put up a display, the display may pass constitutional scrutiny, so long as the reasonable person would understand that a religion is not getting government endorsement.

What is important here is context. If the government has put up the display, it is more likely that the Court will find that it is a violation of the Establishment Clause. If it is a holiday display that includes nonreligious or secular symbols of the holiday season, it is easier for the Court to find no violation. The test used by the Court to make such a decision is confusing. A five-Justice majority has adopted the Reasonable Observer Test, while seven justices would join together to allow a display. Of those seven, three justices would look at history and context and the other four justices would look to be sure that there is equal access to all groups, religious and nonreligious. Perhaps the only way a government entity can be assured that it does not violate the Establishment Clause is to close the public property to all private displays, both religious and nonreligious. However, after reading the three major cases in this area, the Court's reasoning may become clearer.

The first of these cases is *Lynch v. Donnelly*.[35] This case involved a holiday display in the city of Pawtucket, Rhode Island. The display, wholly owned by the city and located in a park owned by a nonprofit organization, included a crèche or Nativity Scene, a Santa Clause house, Santa's sleigh and reindeers, a Christmas tree, carolers, a clown, a teddy bear, an elephant, a banner which read "Seasons Greetings," and many colored lights. The display had been used for 40 or more years, and was erected by the city each year. Several residents of Pawtucket felt that the display was violating their rights under the Establishment Clause, and brought an action to challenge the government involvement in the display. The residents claimed that the display gave the "appearance of official sponsorship" and conferred "more than a remote and incidental benefit on Christianity."[36] The District Court held that there was a violation of the Establishment Clause saying that there was an endorsement of a particular religious belief. The Circuit Court of Appeals affirmed the lower court decision and the City of Pawtucket appealed to the Supreme Court, which granted *certiorari*.

In deciding this case, the Court acknowledged past decisions regarding the Establishment Clause and reaffirmed that total separation between church and state is not absolute and that there is an "inescapable tension between the objective of preventing unnecessary intrusion of either the church or the state upon the other . . ."[37] The Court went on to say that context was the important aspect of its decision. It looked at the history of government involvement in religious holiday celebrations and found that this involvement dated back to 1789. The Court noted that not all government involvement equated to a violation of the Establishment Clause. The Court declined to take an absolute approach and said that each challenged action must be scrutinized to determine whether it, in fact, establishes a religion or a particular religious faith. The Court then went on to reiterate the three-part Lemon Test.

When looking at the first prong of the test, the Court found that there were secular purposes behind the display, such as to celebrate the holiday season and to depict the origins of the holiday. Just because the effect of the display happened to harmonize with the beliefs of a particular religion did not make it a violation of the Establishment Clause.

The Court then turned to the second-prong of the Lemon Test and held that the "display of the crèche is no more an advancement or endorsement of religion than the Congressional and Executive recognition of the origins of the Holiday itself as 'Christ's Mass,' or the exhibition of literally hundreds of religious paintings in governmentally supported museums."[38] Lastly, the Court looked at the third-prong of the test and considered the government's entanglement with this religious display. In doing so, the Court noted the District Court holding that the entanglement was not excessive. This was based on the fact that the government did not own the park where the display was located, and spent little money putting the display out each holiday season. In conclusion, the Court held that there were secular purposes for the display and as the display served the commercial interests of the community by drawing people to the downtown shopping area, there was no violation of the Establishment Clause in this case.

Five years later, the Court again heard a case involving two holiday displays, located in the City of Pittsburgh, in the case of *County of Allegheny v. ACLU*.[39] One display was in the Allegheny County Courthouse and the second display was just outside the City-County Building.

The display in the courthouse was a crèche located on the Grand Staircase of that building, and the second display was of a Chanukah menorah, Christmas tree, and a sign saluting liberty just outside the above-mentioned building. The crèche had been on display every holiday season since 1981 and put there each year by the Holy Name Society, a Roman Catholic group. There was a sign on the display noting Holy Name Society's sponsorship. The city did add a Christmas tree and some poinsettia plants to the display and used it as part of their annual Christmas Carol program.

The Chanukah menorah display had been at the City-County Building each year since 1982. Prior to this, the city had annually placed a Christmas tree at the entrance of the building. The menorah display, owned by Chabad, a Jewish group, was put in place and removed by the city each year. In addition to the Christmas tree and the Chanukah menorah, the city had also placed a sign saluting liberty.

The Greater Pittsburgh Chapter of the American Civil Liberties Union claimed the displays violated the Establishment Clause, and brought an action asking that the city be permanently enjoined from displaying these items. The Federal District Court denied the request for an injunction, relying on *Lynch v. Donnelly*. The Court of Appeals reversed the District Court's decision holding, and the Court granted *certiorari* and ultimately held that the crèche display violated the Establishment Clause while the second display did not.

When discussing the crèche display, the court held that "nothing in the context of the display detracts from the crèche's religious message."[40] This is different from the crèche in *Lynch v. Donnelly* where the crèche was displayed along with many other nonreligious symbols of the holiday season. As the Court noted, the crèche in this case is the only element of the display on the Grand Staircase. This being so, the Court went on to say that:

> *"No viewer could reasonably think that it occupies this location without the support and approval of the government . . . the county sends an unmistakable message that it supports and promotes the Christian praise to God that is the crèche's religious message."*[41]

As the Establishment Clause prohibits the endorsement of religion by the government, it prohibits exactly what occurred with this particular display.

As for the display that included the Chanukah menorah, the Court felt that this was a more difficult decision than the other display. While the menorah is a religious symbol, it was part of a display with two other symbols, and the Court held that the overall result was to create an "overall holiday setting" that represented two holidays.[42] However, as the Court noted, this does not end the discussion; it is no more permissible to allow the endorsement or advancement of two religions over all others than it is to endorse or advance one religion over all others. So, was this display an endorsement of Christian and Jewish faiths, or recognition of the larger, holiday season?

The Court held that the more plausible explanation is that this display was part of the overall winter-holiday season. The Christmas tree is a nonreligious symbol and its presence in the display served to emphasize the secular message being communicated by the holiday display.

The sign proclaiming the value of liberty placed in the display by the mayor's office "further diminishes the possibility that the tree and the menorah will be interpreted as a dual endorsement of Christianity and Judaism."[43] In conclusion, the Court held that this display did not endorse religion. The Court did not address the other two prongs of the Lemon Test, as these issues were not considered by the Court of Appeals and therefore not part of this appeal.

A more recent display case involves the display of a religious symbol in a public forum. Unlike the two previous cases, the display in *Capitol Square Review and Advisory Board v. Pinette*[44] is not part of a holiday observance. Capitol Square is a public forum used for speeches, gatherings, festivals, and other religious and nonreligious celebrations. In order to use the square, the group or individual must fill out an application and meet the criteria, which concerns safety, sanitation, and other requirements that are neutral toward the content of speech or use. The Ku Klux Klan applied for a permit to erect a Latin cross on the square near the state capitol and when they were denied the permit, they brought an action asking for an injunction requiring the Capitol Square Review and Advisory Board to issue a permit allowing them to do so. The Klan argued that their display was a private expression and the Board argued that they rejected the Klan's application because of the interest in complying with the Establishment Clause and because they feared that an observer might mistake the private expression for a state-endorsed religious expression.

The Court rejected the Board's argument saying:

> *"By its terms [the Establishment] Clause applies only to the words and acts of government. It was never meant, and has never been read by this Court, to serve as an impediment to purely private religious speech connected to the State only through its occurrence in a public forum."*[45]

The Court further held that the Capitol Square is, and is widely known to be, a public forum and that the State of Ohio, through the Board, cannot ban all private religious speech from this public forum. In conclusion, the Court held that

> *"Religious expression cannot violate the Establishment Clause where it (1) is purely private and (2) occurs in a traditional or designated public forum, publicly announced and open to all on equal terms."*[46]

Thus, the Court allowed the display of the Latin cross, even though the group advocating the display has a message that is repugnant to many individuals.

The Court decided the most recent of the religious display cases in June 2005. Both of these cases involved the display of the Ten Commandments in a courthouse. The facts of the cases, *McCreary County, Kentucky v. ACLU*[47] and *Van Order v. Perry*,[48] are similar. However, there are some important differences that lead to opposing holdings.

In *McCreary* two counties in Kentucky posted large, readily visible copies of the Ten Commandments in their courthouses. The ACLU challenged the displays on the grounds that they violated the Establishment Clause. After having consulted legal counsel, the counties then adopted a resolution that allowed for a broader, more extensive exhibit. The purpose of the resolution was to show that the Ten Commandments were Kentucky's precedent legal code. There were no secular or historical documents to provide context for this display and the result was a display whose sole common element was religion.

The ACLU filed in federal district court to enjoin the displays. The district court entered a preliminary injunction, using the Lemon Test to make its decision, and concluded "that the original display 'lacked any secular purpose' because the Commandments 'are a distinctly religious document, believed by many Christians and Jews to be the direct and revealed word of God.'"[49] The counties appealed, but dropped the appeal and came up with a third version of the display that included the Ten Commandments as well as the Magna Carta, the Declaration of Independence, the Bill of Rights, the lyrics of the Star Spangled Banner, the Mayflower Compact, the National Motto, the Preamble of the Kentucky Constitution and a picture of Lady Justice. The ACLU then moved to supplement the preliminary injunction previously granted to include the counties' third display. The district court granted the extension of the injunction and the counties appealed to the Sixth Circuit Court of Appeals.

A divided circuit court affirmed the district court's decision, noting, "Displaying the Commandments bespeaks a religious object unless they are integrated with other materials so as to carry 'a secular message.'"[50] This court found that there was no integration with this display because there was no analytical or historical connection made between the various documents. The counties then appealed to the U.S. Supreme Court.

Upon review, the counties asked that the Supreme Court overrule the Lemon Test but the Court refused to do so. The counties argued that it was impossible to know the purpose behind a piece of legislation and as such, one of the three prongs of the Lemon Test could never be met. While the Court respected this argument, it held, "When the government acts with the ostensible and predominant purpose of advancing religion, it violates that central Establishment Clause value of official religious neutrality, there being no neutrality when the government's ostensible object is to take sides."[51] The Court went on to say that scrutinizing purpose does make practical sense and used the **objective observer standard**. The objective observer standard has been used by the Court in previous cases such as *Wallace v. Jaffree,*[52] *Santa Fe Independent School District v. Doe*[53] and *Edwards v. Aguillard.*[54]

The Court held that when using the objective observer standard to scrutinize the legislative purpose, deference should be given to the legislature's stated reason, but it is required that the purpose be genuine and not a sham. In other words, the secular purpose given must not be secondary to a religious objective. The Court held that changing the display twice gives insight into the original purpose of the display. The Court went on to say:

> *"The display's unstinting focus was on religious passages, showing that the Counties were posting the Commandments precisely because of their sectarian content. That demonstration of the government's objective was enhanced by serial religious references and the accompanying resolution's claim about the embodiment of ethics in Christ. Together, the display and resolution presented an indisputable and undisputed, showing of an impermissible purpose."[55]*

The Court stated that an objective observer could conclude, as did this Court, that the counties were looking for any way to keep a religious document on the walls of the courthouse. The Court affirmed the District Court's decision that the predominant purpose behind the display was a religious purpose and continued the injunction.

This, like many recent Supreme Court decisions, was decided by a 5–4 vote. There had been much dissention between members of the Court over various issues, and the questions regarding religion are among those issues. Justice Scalia wrote the dissent in the *McCreary* case, claiming that the deity that the Farmers had in mind when writing the Constitution was the God of monotheism and that the government may espouse such a tenant on publicly-owned property. Justice Souter responds to this in the majority opinion saying

> *"Today's dissent, however, apparently means that government should be free to approve the core beliefs of a favored religion over the tenets of others, a view that should trouble anyone who prizes religious liberty. Certainly, history cannot justify it; on the contrary, history shows that the religion of concern to the Farmers was not that of the monotheistic faiths generally, but Christianity in*

objective observer standard   a standard for reviewing the legislative purpose of a new statute by looking at the legislative history and other supporting documents to see whether the average, objective person would conclude that there was a religious purpose behind the new statute.

*particular, a fact that no member of this Court takes as a premise for constru-
ing the Religion Clauses."*[56]

It was this difference of opinion that led to a different decision in the second of the Ten Commandment display cases, *Van Orden v. Perry.*[57] This case, too, involved a display of the Ten Commandments on publicly owned property. Chief Justice Rehnquist wrote the opinion and was joined by Justices Scalia, Kennedy, Thomas and Breyer. In this case, the State of Texas displayed a monolith that has the Ten Commandments as its predominant text. This monolith is located on the ground of the Texas State Capital that consists of 22 acres and also has 17 other monuments and 21 historical markers. The monolith in question was presented to the State by the Fraternal Order of the Eagles of Texas, which is a national, social, civic, and patriotic organization, not a religious organization. The petitioner, Thomas Van Order, sued state officials, asking that the monument be declared in violation of the Establishment Clause of the First Amendment. The district court found in favor of the State and the Fifth Circuit Court of Appeals affirmed that judgment. The Supreme Court granted certiorari and again, in deciding this case, the Court refused to use the Lemon Test, but instead looked at the monument's nature and the legislative history of the display using the objective observer standard.

The issue decided by the Court in this case was whether the Establishment Clause of the First Amendment allows the display of a monument inscribed with the Ten Commandments on publicly owned property and the Court held that it was permissible.

The Court acknowledged that Establishment Clause challenges present a difficult dilemma. On one hand, government institutions recognize a Supreme Being, but on the other, these same institutions may not show a preference for one religion over another, or even religion over nonreligion. The Court agreed with the *McCreary* decision that the issue should be decided using the objective observer standard. The Court in this case held that this was the appropriate standard, rather than the Lemon Test, noting that in the case of *Hunt v. McNair*[58] the Court held that "the factors identified in Lemon serve as 'no more than helpful signposts.'"[59]

The Court then went on to note that there are many monuments on both state and federally owned land that contain religious references, and these monuments merely recognize the role religion plays in America's legal heritage. The Court acknowledged limits to the display or religious icons and messages and reviewed cases where the Ten Commandments were removed from public school rooms and also noted the decision in the *McCreary* case. The Court then turned to this case in particular and held that the passive use of the Ten Commandments, the history of the display and the inclusion of secular symbols and documents as part of the overall display made this display acceptable when the display in *McCreary* was not.

The conclusion that the Texas display did not violate the Establishment Clause was not reached without dissent. Justices Stevens, Ginsberg, O'Connor and Souter dissented in this decision. Justice Stevens wrote, "Viewed on its face, Texas' display has no purported connection to God's role in the formation of Texas or the founding of our nation; nor does it provide the reasonable observer with any basis to guess that it was erected to honor any individual or organization. The message transmitted by Texas' chosen display is quite plain: This State endorses the divine code of the 'Judeo-Christian' God."[60] This is obviously an issue that remains controversial and it is likely that new cases involving the display of the Ten Commandments may arise in the future. For now, the Court seems consistent in its use of the objective observer standard and had made it clear that the secular purpose as evidence by the legislative intent and the connection between the display and other secular, historical objects are the critical factors to determine the constitutionality of such displays.

In conclusion, these display cases are clear that a religious display with government ownership or on government property will not automatically violate the Establishment Clause. What government entities should avoid is the endorsement or advancement of a particular religion, as well as favoring or discriminating against unpopular groups or messages. It will be the objective observer standard that will determine whether or not a display violates the Establishment Clause.

Avoiding Favoritism

An issue that was alluded to in *Capitol Square Review and Advisory Board v. Pinette* was the notion that an unpopular group or idea might be treated differently under the law from a group or idea that reflected the mainstream belief. It has long been held by the Court that religion may not be favored over nonreligion. Therefore, a religious group cannot be given greater access to a public forum over a nonreligious group. The Court will use the Lemon Test when determining whether a religious group is being favored over a nonreligious group and vice versa. What happens, however, when one religion is favored over another? Is there a different standard used by the Court?

This very issue was presented in *Larson v. Valente*.[61] In this case, the Court reviewed the Minnesota Charitable Solicitation Act[62] that required the registration and disclosure of fund-raising from charitable organizations in that state. The statute was designed to protect the public from fraudulent solicitation practices and it gave the State the authority to deny or withdraw the registration of any charitable organization if it finds that it would be in the public interest to do so. Part of the Act includes the "fifty percent rule" which "provided that only those religious organizations that received more than half of their total contributions from members or affiliated organizations would remain exempt from the reporting requirements of the Act."[63]

The appellee, Holy Spirit Association for the Unification of World Christianity (Unification Church), was notified that it was required to register under the Act. The church brought an action, first asking for a preliminary injunction, and then asking that the statute be held unconstitutional because it discriminated among religious organizations. After the Supreme Court held that the Unification Church did have standing to challenge the statute, it then went on to decide whether the statute violated the Establishment Clause by giving preferential treatment to one religion over another. The Court looked at the writings of James Madison and said that Madison had "naturally assumed that every denomination would be equally at liberty to exercise and propagate its beliefs. But such equality would be impossible in an atmosphere of official denominational preference."[64] The Court then held that "The fifty percent rule of § 309.515, subd. 1(b), clearly grants denominational preference of the sort consistently and firmly deprecated in our precedents."[65] However, rather than just strike down the statute at this point, the Court refused to use the Lemon Test and instead used the strict scrutiny test to review the statute. This was the first time the Supreme Court used strict scrutiny in an establishment case. It would seem that the Court uses the Lemon Test when determining whether there is a preference given to a religion or a religious organization over a nonreligious group, but when examining a case to see if it involves a preference of one religion or denomination over another, the Court will use strict scrutiny to determine whether there is a compelling government interest to justify the law. If the government has a compelling interest and has narrowly tailored the statute to resolve the situation, the law will withstand strict scrutiny and will be held constitutional. If not, the Court will strike the law down as being unconstitutional.

In this case, the State argued that it had three compelling interests. The State's first argument was that if a religious organization gets at least 50 percent of its support from its members, that organization will be controlled and supervised by the members, thus reducing the possibility of fraudulent solicitation or deception. The Court held that there was nothing to justify this assumption, noting that the appellants had offered no evidence to support this claim, and that the legislative history of the statute itself suggested that this argument had no merit.

Nor did the Court find merit in the appellant's second and third arguments. The second argument was that membership control is an adequate safeguard against abusive solicitations. This flies in the face of the central premise of the Act that claims that the state cannot rely on such groups to regulate themselves, and so state regulation is necessary.

The third argument was that there is a need for public disclosure of information regarding the raising of funds and solicitation practices. The State's way of dealing with this was to look at the percentage of funds that were generated from nonmembers. The Court found that what was more important than the percentage was the actual amount of money generated by nonmember contributions. Minnesota's use of a percentage was also not consistent with other laws regarding charitable contributions. Other sections of the Minnesota law exempted organizations from registration under the Act if the nonmember contributions were less than $10,000.00. This inconsistency indicated to the court that there was a narrower, less discriminatory way to regulate effectively.

As all of Minnesota's arguments were found to be invalid, the Court found that there was no compelling governmental interest and that the 50 percent rule imposes "burdens and advantages upon particular denominations."[66] Section 309.515, subd. 1(b) was therefore in violation of the Establishment Clause.

FINANCIAL AID TO RELIGIOUS SCHOOLS

Over the years, the Court has had many opportunities to decide cases involving the granting of financial aid to religious or parochial schools. Whenever these cases have come up, the Court has used the Lemon Test to review the government action. The Court has looked at the secular purpose of the action, whether the action advances or inhibits religion and whether there is excessive entanglement between the government and the religious organization. In addition to this or perhaps as part of the entanglement discussion, the Court also looks to see whether the government action is politically divisive. If the plan to give financial aid to religious schools can pass this three-prong test, the financial aid will be permissible. If not, there is a violation of the Establishment Clause.

Aid to Colleges and Universities

Before looking at some of the cases involving financial aid to religious schools at the elementary and secondary levels, it is worth noting that the Court views financial aid and government involvement with elementary and secondary education differently from those cases of involvement with higher education. The Court is more likely to allow financial assistance to colleges and universities because, in general, they are autonomous entities capable of separating secular and religious functions, college students are adults and less susceptible to the influence of religious teachings, academic freedom allows professors to teach and expose the students to a variety of perspectives and theories, and in situations where the Court has found that there is no violation of the Establishment Clause, there are safeguards in place to assure that the financial aid is used for secular purposes. The types of safeguard used and the extent of the government entanglement have been the basis of the discussion in a series of cases involving higher education and government financial aid.

The first such case is *Tilton v. Richardson*[67] in which the Court reviewed the Higher Education Facilities Act of 1963.[68] This Act authorizes government grants for the construction of academic facilities at colleges and universities, including church-related colleges and universities. Taxpayers, who asked that the Court hold this Act to be unconstitutional, challenged this Act. The Court declined to do so saying that all colleges and universities, no matter their affiliation with a religions organization or denomination, were included as potential recipients under the Act. The secular goal of the Act was to provide appropriate facilities so that more individuals had access to a college education, there was no discrimination against, or advancement of a religious goal, and that, for the most part, there was no excessive government entanglement. The Court did find, however, that one section of the Act was unconstitutional. This section allowed the U.S. Government to maintain an interest in the facilities built with government money for 20 years. The Court held that this was excessive entanglement, but that this section could easily be separated and negated from the rest of the Act.

The second case involving financial aid to religiously affiliated colleges and universities was *Roemer v. Board of Public Works of Maryland*[69] in which four Maryland citizens challenged the constitutionality of grants given by the State of Maryland to eligible colleges and universities. Unlike the grants in *Tilton*, the grants in this case were noncategorical, which means that the institution can use the money as it wishes, so long as the money is not used for sectarian purposes. The State of Maryland established an administrative oversight board, the Maryland Council for Higher Education, whose job it was to establish and follow a "two-step screening process" to "insure compliance with the statutory restrictions on the grants."[70] The first step of the process was to assure that the institution was an eligible institution. An ineligible institution was defined by statute as one "awarding primarily theological or seminary degrees."[71] The second step of the process was to require an eligible institution to submit an application outlining the nonsectarian uses for the requested monies. The application had to be accompanied by an affidavit, signed by the institution's chief executive officer verifying that the funds would not be used for sectarian purposes.

Once the institution was given the grants, the statutory scheme further requires that the institution file a "Utilization of Funds Report" describing how the money was spent. Again, this document has to be accompanied by an affidavit by the chief executive officer. In spite of this scheme, the four citizens challenging the statutory scheme alleged that this was a violation of the Establishment Clause.

When reviewing the statutory scheme, the Court said that a complete separation of church and state is impossible and that so long as a plan for financial aid is neutral and the aid is available to both secular and nonsecular colleges and universities, the scheme is constitutional. The Court maintained that the two-step process, as well as the post-grant accounting for how the monies were spent, safeguarded the process and made sure that all three prongs of the Lemon Test were met. The first prong of the Lemon Test was met when the Court found that the purpose of the Maryland statute was to provide support to all private higher education institutions. The second prong of the test was met when the Court found that the primary effect of the statutory scheme was to support private educational activities, not religious activities, with state funds. Lastly, the entanglement prong was the most difficult part of the test for the Court to decide. While in *Tilton*, the Court held that the 20-year interest held by the government led to excessive entanglement; that Court favored the "one-time, single-purpose" type of grants. The present scheme calls for annual review of the grants and continuing supervision by the Council. The Court asserted that the ongoing contacts ". . . are not likely to be any more entangling than the inspects and audits incident to the normal process of the colleges' accreditations by the State."[72] The Court also mentioned the potential problem of political divisiveness and found that since the grants were available to private institutions that had no religious affiliation, as well as those who were religiously affiliated, the political divisiveness was diminished.[73] As all three prongs of the Lemon Test were met, the Court upheld the Maryland statute and affirmed the judgment of the lower Court.

In 1995, the Court once again had a case come before it regarding the use of state funds being used by a university-sponsored religious activity. The University of Virginia, a state institution, authorized the disbursement of university monies to outside contractors for the printing costs of a variety of student publications. It denied funding for the publication of the student newspaper, which had a Christian editorial viewpoint, however, this is not the only type of activity that may result in a denial of student activity funds. Excluded activities include "religious activities, philanthropic contributions and activities, political activities, activities that would jeopardize the University's tax-exempt status, those which involve payment of honoraria or similar fees, or social entertainment or related expenses."[74] The petitioners in this case, Rosenberger and Wide Awake Productions wanted funding to publish a magazine of philosophical and religious expression and were denied funds because this was a "religious activity." The U.S. District Court held for the university saying that the university's concern about violating the Establishment Clause justified the denial of payment for publishing the magazine.

The Court first discussed the issues raised by the petitioners regarding free speech (as that topic is discussed in Chapter 10 these issues will not be addressed here), and then moved on to discuss "[w]hether the Establishment Clause compels a state university to exclude an otherwise eligible student publication from participation in the student activities fund, solely on the basis of its religious viewpoint, where such exclusion would violate the Speech and Press Clauses if the viewpoint of the publication were nonreligious."[75] To begin this discussion, the Court first looked at the purpose and object of the university's action. Central to this decision is whether the university's action is neutral toward religion. The state can no more discriminate against a religious activity than it can promote one. There is no violation of the Establishment Clause if a public university allows access to its facilities by religious groups on the same religion-neutral basis as the university uses for all groups. This may mean that a religious organization is given a benefit, but it is incidental to the primary, secular activity of the university. The fact that this organization recognized the incidental benefit of a routine university activity (i.e., printing) is just part of student life and not a violation of the Establishment Clause.

With these two cases, the Court has clearly established that it would use the Lemon Test when looking at challenged governmental activity involving postsecondary education. So long as the governmental action has a secular purpose, maintains neutrality, and avoids excessive government entanglement, the Court will uphold the action. This was clear in *Widmar v. Vincent*[76] when the Court heard a challenge to a University of Missouri at Kansas City policy that denied access to university facilities to organizations that wanted to use the facilities for religious worship or teaching. The students challenging this policy claimed that it violated their rights under the First Amendment. The District Court found that there was no violation, and said the Establishment Clause required the policy. The Eleventh Circuit Court of Appeals reversed and the U.S. Supreme Court granted *certiorari*.

The Court held the university's policy had a secular purpose, and allowed the university to avoid excessive entanglement, but was not neutral toward religious groups. The university argued that to allow the religious groups to use university facilities would advance a religious belief or ideology. The Court disagreed, saying that the benefit to the religious groups was "incidental" and did not advance religion. The Court maintained the benefit was incidental because simply supplying an open forum on university property does not give the group or its message university approval. Further, as the facilities were open to more than 100 groups, many of them nonreligious, a broad spectrum of ideologies and beliefs benefited; a strong indication of the secular effect of the policy.[77] The Court also said that if the religious groups dominated the use of the facilities, this case would have been decided differently as dominance would have the effect of advancing religion. Once again, the Court relied on the Lemon Test to resolve an issue regarding a university policy and a claimed violation of the Establishment Clause.

Aid to Elementary and Secondary Schools

When it comes to government funding of private, religious elementary and secondary schools, there are several general conclusions that can be drawn. First, the Court does not always find financial aid to religiously affiliated schools to be a violation of the Establishment Clause. Second, the Court will more likely uphold aid, which assists students of both public and private schools. Third, aid given directly to parents of private school students is more likely to be constitutional, and finally, financial aid that has a secular effect is also more likely to be constitutional.

Through the years, there have been several cases involving direct financial aid to elementary and secondary education. In 1947, the Court decided *Everson v. Board of Education of Ewing Township*,[78] previously discussed in this chapter. That case involved the use of tax dollars to support transportation of school children, both private and public. The Court upheld this statute because the justices found it to have a valid secular purpose, in that all students were being transported to school.

Other cases have followed, including state-supported textbook programs that provide textbooks to students in private schools.[79] The Court held that it was constitutional for schools to provide textbooks for private school students so long as the textbooks were nonreligious in nature and that students of both private and public schools are given the same type of state support. Most recently, the Court decided the case of *Mitchell v. Helms*,[80] discussed briefly above. In *Mitchell* the Court decided on the constitutionality of state and federal school aid programs that supplied computers and non-textbook, educational materials to private and public schools. The challenge involved the aid given to private schools, and the Court upheld this program, so long as the materials were nonreligious in nature, not used for religious purposes, and if the private schools are eligible for the aid on the same basis as the public schools.

Governmental salary supplements for private school teachers are also an issue decided in the area of aid to private elementary and secondary schools. The initial case involving this issue was *Lemon v. Kurtzman* discussed at several points in this chapter. In *Lemon*, Rhode Island and Pennsylvania were providing salary supplements to teachers of secular subjects in nonpublic, elementary schools. This practice was challenged as a violation of the Establishment Clause. Even though the teachers were teaching secular subjects, the Court with Chief Justice Burger writing, held that the statutes were unconstitutional. The Court did so by using the test discussed in Exhibit 15.1. The Court found that the first prong of the test was met when it found that the legislative intent was "to enhance the quality of the secular education in all schools covered by the [state] compulsory attendance laws."[81] The second prong of the test was met by the states in that there was "no basis for a conclusion that the legislative intent was to advance religion."[82] Then the Court looked at the final prong of the test, the excessive entanglement prong. In order to determine this, the Court examined the types of institutions benefited by the aid, the nature of the aid provided by the state, and the relationship that results between the state and the religious institutions. When the *Lemon* Court completed its examination, it found that there was "an impermissible degree of entanglement."[83] The Court held that the state may not subsidize salaries, even if the teacher in question was teaching a secular subject, because there was no mechanism in place to assure that the funds provided would not be used for religious purposes. Careful government control or surveillance is needed to ensure that the funds would not be misused or would amount to excessive entanglement. Thus, the statutes fail constitutional scrutiny.

In *Agostini v. Felton*[84] the Court examined a related state program that involved sending public school teachers into parochial schools to provide remedial education to disadvantaged students. The Court had examined this practice 10 years earlier in the case of *Aguilar v. Felton*[85] and the Court held that this violated the Establishment Clause because the plan necessitated excessive entanglement between the parochial schools and the State. A permanent injunction had been issued reflecting the Court's decision, and in *Agostini* the parties bound by the injunction were seeking relief. Justice O'Connor wrote for the Court, which held the program to be constitutional. As the Court had indicated in previous holdings, not all direct aid to parochial or sectarian schools is unconstitutional. If the funds aid the educational function of the institution, the Court may uphold it. The Court found that assigning public school teachers to teach remedial courses in parochial schools does not indicate a union between church and state or any type of excessive entanglement. The Court further noted that the remedial courses being taught by public school teachers was no different from the constitutionally upheld practice of the State providing sign-language interpreters for parochial schools.[86] As noted previously in this chapter, the Court did not use the traditional Lemon Test, but focused instead on only the first two prongs of the test.

Justice Souter dissented in *Agostini*, writing that the program amounted to a subsidy for parochial schools. The public employees might teach only remedial courses, which in fact, freed parochial employees, who might otherwise be engaged in teaching the remedial classes, to teach religion courses. This, according to Justice Souter, is an advancement of religion. Further, Justice Souter wrote that the presence of public employees in the parochial schools does, indeed, give the impression that the state is endorsing the parochial school's religious mission.

When looking at these cases, it would appear that the Court will only use the first two prongs of the Lemon Test when determining the constitutional validity of direct aid to private, parochial schools. However, this is not the latest word on aid to private schools. In June, 2002, the Court decided the case of *Zelman v. Simmons-Harris*[87] which challenged an Ohio scheme establishing a "voucher" system in the Cleveland City School District. The program was enacted after the Cleveland City School District schools failed to meet any of the 18 standards required by the State of Ohio. The aid or voucher went directly to the parents of school-age children who, in turn, choose a public, private, community, or magnet school, for their children. The parents then signed the aid check or voucher over to the school chosen. Statistically speaking, 96 percent of the choices made were to send the student to a religious, private school. This scheme was challenged as a violation of the Establishment Clause, but upon review, the Court held that the program was neutral and did not violate the Establishment Clause. Chief Justice Rehnquist wrote for the Court, which used the Reasonable Observer Test in making its decision. The rule established in this case is

"... where a government program is neutral with respect to religion, and provides assistance directly to a broad class of citizens who, in turn, direct government aid to religious school wholly as a result of their own genuine and independent private choice, the program is not readily subject to challenge under the Establishment Clause."[88]

The Court goes on to discuss how this case is consistent with some of its previous decisions and concludes that since this is a program of true private choice, it does not violate the Establishment Clause. Four justices dissented in this case, but this does not change the fact that the Court will be using the Reasonable Observer Test when determining whether financial aid benefiting public as well as nonpublic schools violates the Establishment Clause.

ZELMAN V. SIMMONS-HARRIS
2002 WL 1378554

June 27, 2002

Chief Justice REHNQUIST
delivered the opinion of the Court.

The state of Ohio has established a pilot program designed to provide educational choices to families with children who reside in the Cleveland City School District. The question presented is whether this program offends the Establishment Clause of the United States Constitution. We hold that it does not.

There are more than 75,000 children enrolled in the Cleveland City School District. The majority of these children are from low-income and minority families. Few of these families enjoy the means to send their children to any school other than an inner-city public school. For more than a generation, however, Cleveland's public schools have been among the worst performing public schools in the nation. In 1995, a Federal District Court declared a "crisis of magnitude" and placed the entire Cleveland school district under state control. Shortly thereafter, the state auditor found that Cleveland's public schools were in the midst of a "crisis unprecedented in the history of American education." The district had failed to meet any of the 18 state standards for minimal acceptable performance. Only 1 in 10 ninth graders could pass a basic proficiency examination, and students at all levels performed at a dismal rate compared with students in other Ohio public schools . . .

It is against this backdrop that Ohio enacted, among other initiatives, its Pilot Project Scholarship Program . . . The program provides financial assistance to families in any Ohio school district that is or has been "under federal court order requiring supervision and operational management of the district by the state superin-

tendent." Cleveland is the only Ohio school district to fall within that category.

* * *

The tuition aid portion of the program is designed to provide educational choices to parents who reside in a covered district. Any private school, whether religious or nonreligious, may participate in the program and accept program students so long as the school is located within the boundaries of a covered district and meets statewide educational standards.

* * *

Tuition aid is distributed to parents according to financial need . . . Where tuition aid is spent depends solely upon where parents who receive tuition aid choose to enroll their child. If parents choose a private school, checks are made payable to parents who then endorse the checks over to the chosen school.

* * *

The program has been in operation within the Cleveland City School District since the 1996–1997 school year.

* * *

The program is part of a broader undertaking by the State to enhance the education options of Cleveland's schoolchildren in response to the 1995 takeover. That undertaking includes program governing community and magnet schools. Community schools are funded under state law but are run by their own school boards . . . These schools enjoy academic independence to hire their own teachers and to determine their own curriculum. They can have no religious

Continued

affiliation and are required to accept students by lottery . . .

Magnet schools are public schools operated by a local school board that emphasize a particular subject area, teaching method, or service to students.

* * *

In July 1999, respondents filed this action in United States District Court, seeking to enjoin the reacted program on the ground that it violated the Establishment Clause of the United States Constitution. In August 1999, the District Court issued a preliminary injunction barring further implementation of the program, which we stayed pending review by the Court of Appeals . . . we granted certiorari . . . and now reverse the Court of Appeals.

. . . There is no dispute that the program challenged here was enacted for the valid secular purpose of providing educational assistance to poor children in a demonstrably failing public school system. Thus the question presented is whether the Ohio program nonetheless has the forbidden "effect" of advancing or inhibiting religion.

To answer that question, our decisions have drawn a consistent distinction between government programs that provide aid directly to religious schools, and programs of true private choice, in which government aid reaches religious schools only as a result of the genuine and independent choices of private individuals. While our jurisprudence with respect to the constitutionality of direct aid programs has "changed significantly" over the past two decades . . . our jurisprudence with respect to true private choice programs has remained consistent and unbroken. Three times we have confronted Establishment Clause challenges to neutral government programs that provide aid directly to a broad class of individuals, who, in turn, direct the aid to religious schools or institutions of their own choosing. Three times we have rejected such challenges.

* * *

. . . Then, viewing the program as a whole, we emphasized the principle of private choice, noting that public funds were made available to religious schools "only as a result of numerous,

private choices of individual parents of school-age children.

* * *

That the program was one of true private choice, with no evidence that the State deliberately skewed incentives toward religious schools, was sufficient for the program to survive scrutiny under the Establishment Clause.

* * *

. . . Our holding thus rested not on whether few or many recipients chose to expend government aid at a religious school but, rather, on whether recipients generally were empowered to direct the aid to schools or institutions of their own choosing.

* * *

Mueller, Witters, and *Zobrest* thus make clear that where a government aid program is neutral with respect to religion, and provides assistance directly to a broad class of citizens who, in turn, direct government aid to religious schools wholly as a result of their own genuine and independent private choice, the program is not readily subject to challenge under the Establishment Clause. A program that shares these features permits government aid to reach religious institutions only by way of the deliberate choices of numerous individual recipients. The incidental advancement of a religious mission, or the perceived endorsement of a religious message, is reasonably attributable to the individual recipient, not to the government, whose role ends with the disbursement of benefits . . .

* * *

We believe that the program challenged here is a program of true private choice, consistent with *Mueller, Witters,* and *Zobrest,* and thus constitutional. As was true in those cases, the Ohio program is neutral in all respects toward religion. It is part of a general and multifaceted undertaking by the State of Ohio to provide educational opportunities to the children of a failed school district. It confers educational assistance directly to a broad class of individuals defined without reference to religion, i.e., any parents of a school-age child who resides in the Cleveland City School District. The program permits the participation of all schools within the district,

Continued

religious or nonreligious. Adjacent public schools also may participate and have a financial incentive to do so. Program benefits are available to participating families on neutral terms, with no reference to religion. The only preference stated anywhere in the program is a preference for low-income families, who receive greater assistance and are given priority for admission at participating schools.

* * *

. . . The program here in fact creates financial *dis*incentives for religious schools, with private schools receiving only half the government assistance given to community schools and one-third the assistance given to magnet schools . . . Families too have a financial disincentive to choose a private religious school over other schools. Parents that choose to participate in the scholarship program and then to enroll their children in a private school (religious or nonreligious) must copay a portion of the school's tuition. Families that choose a community school, magnet school, or traditional public school pay nothing. Although such features of the program are not necessary; to its constitutionality, they clearly dispel the claim that the program "creates financial incentive[s] for parents to choose a sectarian school."

Respondents suggest that even without a financial incentive for parents to choose a religious school, the program creates a "public perception that the State is endorsing religious practices and belief." But we have repeatedly recognized that no reasonable observer would think a neutral program of private choice, where state aid reaches religious schools solely as a result of the numerous independent decisions of private individuals, carries with it the *imprimatur* of government endorsement, . . .

There is also no evidence that the program fails to provide genuine opportunities for Cleveland parents to select secular educational options for their school-age children. Cleveland schoolchildren enjoy a range of educational choices: They may remain in public school as before, remain in public school with publicly funded tutoring aid, obtain a scholarship and choose a religious school, obtain a scholarship and choose a nonreligious private school, enroll in a community school, or enroll in a magnet school. That 46 of the 56 private schools now

participating in the program are religious schools does not condemn it as a violation of the Establishment Clause. The Establishment Clause question is whether Ohio is coercing parents into sending their children to religious schools, and that question must be answered by evaluating all options Ohio provides Cleveland schoolchildren, only one of which is to obtain a program scholarship and then choose a religious school.

* * *

Respondents and Justice SOUTER claim that even if we do not focus on the number of participating schools that are religious schools, we should attach constitutional significance to the fact that 96% of scholarship recipients have enrolled in religious schools. They claim that this alone proves parents lack genuine choice, even if no parent has ever said so. We need not consider this argument in detail, since it was flatly rejected in *Mueller*, where we found it irrelevant that 96% of parents taking deductions for tuition expenses paid tuition at religious schools . . . The constitutionality of a neutral educational aid program simply does not turn on whether and why, in a particular area, at a particular time, most private schools are run by religious organizations, or most recipients choose to use the aid at a religious school . . .

* * *

Respondents finally claim that we should look to *Committee for Public Ed. & Religious Liberty v. Nyquist*, to decide these cases. We disagree for two reasons. First, the program in *Nyquist* was quite different from the program challenged here. *Nyquist* involved a New York program that gave a package of benefits exclusively to private schools and the parents of private school enrollees. Although the program was enacted for ostensibly secular purposes . . . we found that its "function" was "*unmistakably* to provide desired financial support for nonpublic, sectarian institutions," . . .

* * *

Second, were there any doubt that the program challenged in *Nyquist* is far removed from the program challenged here, we expressly reserved judgment with respect to "a case involving some form of public assistance (e.g., scholarships)

Continued

made available generally without regard to the sectarian-nonsectarian, or public-nonpublic nature of the institution benefited." That, of course, is the very question now before us, and it has since been answered . . . To the extent the scope of *Nyquist* has remained an open question in light of these later decisions, we now hold that *Nyquist* does not govern neutral educational assistance programs that, like the program here, offer aid directly to a broad class of individual recipients defined without regard to religion.

In sum, the Ohio program is entirely neutral with respect to religion. It provides benefits directly to a wide spectrum of individuals, defined only by financial need and residence in a particular school district. It permits such individuals to exercise genuine choice among options public and private, secular and religious. The program is therefore a program of true private choice. In keeping with an unbroken line of decisions rejecting challenges to similar programs, we hold that the program does not offend the Establishment Clause.

The judgment of the Court of Appeals is reversed.

It is so ordered.

Justices O'Connor, Thomas, Scalia and Kennedy concurred.

Justices Stevens, Souter, Ginsburg and Breyer dissented.

Religion and Other Public School Issues

1. Religious Instruction

One of the earliest issues discussed by the Court with regard to the Establishment Clause was whether to allow religious instruction on public school property during school hours. The Court decided this issue in *People of the State of Illinois ex rel. McCollum v. Board of Education of School District No. 71.*[89] McCollum brought this action against the school district as a resident and tax-paying parent whose child was compelled by state law to attend the local public school. McCollum alleged that religious teachers, employed by private religious groups, were allowed to hold classes in the local public school during regular school hours and that this joint program violated the Establishment Clause of the First Amendment. The Court held the program unconstitutional, saying:

> "For the First Amendment rests upon the premise that both religion and government can best work to achieve their lofty aims if each is left free from the other within its respective sphere . . . Here not only are the state's tax supported public school buildings used for the dissemination of religious doctrine. The State also affords sectarian groups an invaluable aid in that it helps to provide pupils for their religious classes through use of the state's compulsory public school machinery. This is not separation of Church and State."[90]

This case was followed a few years later by the case of *Zorch v. Clauson*[91] in which the Court was asked to determine the constitutional validity of a program in which New York City public schools allowed their students to be released during regular school hours in order to attend classes and devotional programs at churches and other religious centers. Unlike the *McCollum* case, this program did not involve the use of the school building or public funds to support this religious instruction. The appellants, however, filed this action arguing that the authority of the public schools was promoting this program, that the public school teachers were given the responsibility to monitor the program and the students attending it, and that the regular educational activities of the school came to a stop. The Court was not convinced by these arguments and held that this type of release program did not constitute an establishment of religion within the meaning of the First Amendment. The Court went on to say "When the state encourages religious instruction or co-operates with religious authorities by adjusting the schedule of public events to sectarian needs, it follows the best of our traditions."[92] The Court was careful to say that the State could not finance religious training or blend the sectarian and secular educational programs, but the government did not have to be hostile toward religion and there was no constitutional prohibition making it necessary for the government to refuse to cooperate in a released-time program such as found in this case.

As noted, the Court in *Zorch* found it significant that the public school facilities were not used in the challenged released-time program. However, since that case, Congress passed the Education for Economic Security Act, which included the Equal Access subchapter. This statute provides, in part:

> "It shall be unlawful for any public secondary school which receives Federal financial assistance and which has a limited open forum to deny equal access or a fair opportunity to, or discriminate against, any students who wish to conduct a meeting within that limited open forum on the basis of religious, political, philosophical, or other content of the speech at such meeting."[93]

This statutory mandate makes the rule discussed above in the *Widmar*[94] case applicable to public high schools. The statute goes on to establish parameters for equal access. It provides that the access to the school forum must not interfere with "the orderly conduct of educational activities," and this has been construed to mean that the access must take place before and after regular school hours. In addition, the statute only applies if the school allows other extracurricular groups to use the facilities as well. The meetings must be voluntary, student initiated, and with no sponsorship of the meeting by the school, the government, or any government agent or employee. Any school or government employees present at the meeting may not participate and "non-school persons may not direct, conduct, control, or regularly attend activities of student groups."[95]

ZORCH V. CLAUSON
343 U.S. 306 (1952)

Justice DOUGLAS delivered the opinion of the Court.

New York City has a program which permits its public schools to release students during the school day so that they may leave the school buildings and school grounds and go to religious centers for religious instruction or devotional exercises. A student is released on written request of his parents. Those not released stay in the classrooms. The churches make weekly reports to the schools, sending a list of children who have been released from public school but who have not reported for religious instruction.

This 'release time' program involves neither instruction in public school classrooms nor the expenditure of public funds. All costs, including the application blanks, are paid by the religious organizations. The case is therefore unlike *McCollum v. Board of Education* which involved a 'released time' program from Illinois. In that case the classrooms were turned over to religious instructors. We accordingly held that the program violated the First Amendment which (by reason of the Fourteenth Amendment) prohibits the states from establishing religion or prohibiting its free exercise.

Appellants, who are taxpayers and residents of New York City and whose children attend its public schools, challenge the present law, contending it is in essence not different from the one involved in the *McCollum* case. Their argument, stated elaborately in various ways, reduces itself to this: the weight and influence of the school is put behind a program for religious instruction; public school teachers police it,

Continued

keeping tabs on students who are released; the classroom activities come to a halt while the students who are released for religious instruction are on leave; the school is a crutch on which the churches are leaning for support in their religious training; without the cooperation of the schools this 'released time' program, like the one in the *McCollum* case, would be futile and ineffective. The New York Court of Appeals sustained the law against this claim of unconstitutionality. The case is here on appeal.

The briefs and arguments are replete with data bearing on the merits of this type of 'released time' program. Views pro and con are expressed, based on practical experience with these programs and with their implications. We do not stop to summarize these materials nor to burden the opinion with an analysis of them . . . Those matters are of no concern here, since our problem reduces itself to whether New York by this system has either prohibited the 'free exercise' of religion or has made a law 'respecting an establishment of religion' within the meaning of the First Amendment.

* * *

. . . we do not see how New York by this type of 'released time' program has made a law respecting an establishment of religion within the meaning of the First Amendment. There is much talk of the separation of Church and State in the history of the Bill of Rights and in the decisions clustering around the First Amendment . . . The First Amendment, however, does not say that in every and all respects there shall be a separation of Church and State. Rather, it studiously defines the manner, the specific ways, in which there shall be no concert or union or dependency one on the other. That is the common sense of the matter. Otherwise the state and religion would be aliens to each other—hostile, suspicious, and even unfriendly . . .

We would have to press the concept of separation of Church and State to these extremes to condemn the present law on constitutional grounds. The nullification of this law would have wide and profound effects . . .

We are a religious people whose institutions presuppose a Supreme Being. We guarantee the freedom to worship as one chooses. We make room for as wide a variety of beliefs and creeds as the spiritual needs of man deem necessary. We sponsor an attitude on the part of government that shows no partiality to any one group and that lets each flourish according to the zeal of its adherents and the appeal of its dogma. When the state encourages religious instruction or cooperates with religious authorities by adjusting the schedule of public events to sectarian needs, it follows the best of our traditions. For it then respects the religious nature of our people and accommodates the public service to their spiritual needs. To hold that it may not would be to find the Constitution a requirement that the government show a callous indifference to religious groups. That would be preferring those who believe in no religion over those who do believe. Government may not finance religious groups nor undertake religious instruction nor blend secular and sectarian education nor use secular institutions to force one or some religion on any person. But we find no constitutional requirement which makes it necessary for government to be hostile to religion and to throw its weight against efforts to widen the effective scope of religious influence. The government must be neutral when it comes to competition between sects. It may not thrust any sect on any person. It may not make a religious observance compulsory. It may not coerce anyone to attend church, to observe a religious holiday, or to take religious instruction . . .

In the *McCollum* case the classrooms were used for religious instruction and the force of the public school was used to promote that instruction. Here, as we have said, the public schools do no more than accommodate their schedules to a program of outside religious instruction. We follow the *McCollum* case. But we cannot expand it to cover the present released time program unless separation of Church and State means that public institutions can make no adjustments of their schedules to accommodate the religious needs of the people. We cannot read into the Bill of Rights such a philosophy of hostility to religion.

Affirmed.

This statute was used by high school students who challenged a school policy they felt violated their right to equal access. In *Board of Education of the Westside Community Schools v. Mergens*[96] the Court had to decide whether the students' rights under the statute were violated and whether the statute itself violated the Establishment Clause of the First Amendment.

In summary, the Court found that, just as in *Widmar*, this equal access policy did not violate the Establishment Clause. The Court used the Lemon Test and found that the policy had a secular purpose, would not advance religion and would not involve excessive entanglement between government and religious organizations. Currently, then, both universities and secondary schools must provide equal access if the institution accepts financial aid from the federal government.

Prayer in Schools

The issue of prayer in schools has arisen in a variety of contexts over the years. While strong feelings exist on both sides of this issue, the Court has attempted to remain consistent in its decisions. The first case to challenge prayer in schools came in 1962 with *Engel v. Vitale*.[97] In this case, the Board of Education of Union Free School District in New Hyde, New York, asked the principal of the school to write a prayer, which was to be recited at the opening of each school day in the classrooms of that school district. The prayer was written, approved by the State Board of Regents, and recitation began in the classroom. Shortly thereafter, the parents of 10 students brought an action in the New York State Court challenging the use of this official prayer as a violation of the Establishment Clause. The prayer in question was:

> *"Almighty God, we acknowledge our dependence upon Thee, and we beg Thy blessings upon us, our parents, our teachers and our Country."*[98]

The Court began its analysis by looking at religious history of this country. Due to the persecution suffered at the hands of a state-sponsored religion, the Colonists endeavored to establish a new government, which forbid government involvement with religion. The Constitution and the First Amendment to that Constitution were designed "to stand as a guarantee that neither the power nor the prestige of the Federal Government would be used to control, support or influence the kinds of prayer the American people can say . . ."[99]

The State of New York argued that the prayer did not violate the Establishment Clause because the prayer was nondenominational. It was approved by the New York courts and the students were not required to participate, but could stand silent while other students recited the prayer. The Court found none of these arguments convincing, saying that the argument "ignores the essential nature of the program's constitutional defects."[100] The Court found the daily recitation of the prayer to be a religious activity that violated the Establishment Clause, as it was "no part of the business of government to compose official prayers for any group of the American people to recite as part of a religious program carried on by the government."[101]

The Court also disagreed with New York's contention that to apply the Constitution in this manner was to indicate hostility toward religion or prayer. To the contrary, the Court said that:

> *"It is neither sacrilegious nor antireligious to say that each separate government in this country should stay out of the business of writing or sanctioning official prayers and leave that purely religious function to the people themselves and to those the people choose to look to for religious guidance."*[102]

A year later, the Court once again looked at another state-sponsored activity that required schools to start each school day with Bible readings. In the case of *School District of Abington Township, Pennsylvania v. Schempp*,[103] the Court reviewed the constitutionality of a Pennsylvania statute which required "'At least ten verses from the Holy Bible shall be read, without comment, at the opening of each public school on each school day. Any child shall be excused from such Bible reading, or attending such Bible reading, upon the written request of his parent or guardian.'"[104] The appellant school district conducted these readings pursuant to the statute by broadcasting them into each classroom in the school building. The readings were followed by a recitation of the Lord's Prayer. The appellees, parents of two school-age students, challenged the statute. The parents testified at trial that they had considered having their children excused from the reading, but decided against it as they believed that the children's relationships with their fellow students and their teachers would be adversely affected. The trial court struck down the statute as the Bible reading practice "possess[ed] a devotional and religious character and constitut[ed] in effect a religious observance."[105] On appeal, Justice Clark wrote for the Supreme Court and began by looking at the history of religious freedom in the United States, including how the Establishment Clause and the Free Exercise Clause work together. The Court quoted its opinion in *Engel v. Vitale* and reminded the reader that the Court in that case had written:

> *"Although these two clauses may in certain instances overlap, they forbid two quite different kinds of governmental encroachment upon religious freedom. The Establishment Clause, unlike the Free Exercise Clause, does not depend upon any showing of direct governmental compulsion and is violated by the enactment of laws which establish an official religion whether those laws operate directly to coerce non-observing individuals or not. This is not to say, of course, that laws officially prescribing a particular form of religious worship do not involve coercion of such individuals. When the power, prestige and financial support of government is placed behind a particular religious belief, the indirect coercive pressure upon religious minorities to conform to the prevailing officially approved religion is plain."[106]*

The Court then applied the Establishment Clause to this case and agreed with the trial court that this means of opening each school day was a religious ceremony. Further, the Court found that the State intended this ceremony to be religious in nature. In doing so, the Court ultimately held that the statute requiring this Bible reading was in violation of the Establishment Clause.[107] In reaching the conclusion, the Court rejected the State's argument that to eliminate the opening exercise of Bible reading was to allow the government to establish the "religion of secularism." The Court agreed that allowing an establishment of "secularism" would also violate the Establishment Clause, but rejected the idea that their decision in this case was tantamount to establishing any form of religion, but rather, the decision was maintaining neutrality and neither opposed nor promoted religion.[108]

In reaching its conclusion in *Abington*, Justice Clark used two of the three prongs of the Lemon Test. First, the purpose of the statutory action must be secular and, second, it must neither promote nor oppose religion. The Court clearly felt that the statutory requirement of daily Bible reading in the public schools did not meet either of these prongs of the Lemon Test, leading to its decision that this statute was unconstitutional.

More than 20 years later, the Court had another opportunity to discuss an alleged religious exercise in the public school setting. In *Wallace v. Jaffree*,[109] a series of Alabama statutes authorizing one minute of silence at the beginning of each school day for prayer or meditation was challenged. Justice Stevens wrote for the Court, which examined the statute challenged by the parent of three school-age children. The District Court, after a trial, held that Alabama had the power to establish a state religion if it chose to do so. The Court of Appeals reversed the District Court decision and the case was appealed to the U.S. Supreme Court for the sole purpose of answering the question of whether the Alabama statute, which authorized a period of silence for meditation or voluntary prayer, was a law in violation of the Establishment Clause of the First Amendment. Even though the statutes authorized the period of silence, the appellee alleged that his children had been subject to various types of religious instruction at the local public school. Further, he alleged that the teachers led students in daily prayer, said in unison, and that if his children did not participate, their peers ostracized them. Appellee, therefore, challenged the religious activities of the school, as well as the Alabama statutes in question.

When the Court looked at the purpose of the statutes, the legislative history showed that it was intended to return prayer to public schools. The Court also looked at the District Court's decision, which was based on what that court believed to be new historical evidence, that nothing in the Establishment Clause prohibited Alabama from establishing a state religion. The Court reaffirmed that the ". . . States have no greater power to restrain the individual freedoms protected by the First Amendment than does the Congress of the United States."[110] The Court went on to discuss this case in light of the Lemon Test. The Court noted that there was no secular purpose for the Alabama statute in question. The Court went on to note that the very text of the statute indicated its religious purpose. The Court found that:

> *"The well-supported concurrent finding of the District Court and the Court of Appeals—that §16-1-20.1 was intended to convey a message of state approval of prayer activities in the public schools—make it unnecessary, and indeed inappropriate to evaluate the practical significance of the addition of the words 'or voluntary prayer' to the statute. Keeping in mind, as we must, 'both the fundamental place held by the Establishment Clause in our constitutional scheme and the myriad, subtle ways in which Establishment Clause values can be eroded,' we much conclude that §16-1-20.1 violates the First Amendment."[111]*

Thus, the Court held that Alabama did not have the right to establish a state-sponsored religion, nor did it have the right to enact statutes that had an expressly religious purpose. In doing so, the Court acted consistently with its prior decisions regarding prayer in the public schools.

School Ceremonies

Governmental ceremonies were discussed earlier in this chapter, but the Supreme Court takes a different approach when it comes to school ceremonies. The Court has been very aware that with school ceremonies, underage students are involved, and a need for a more restrictive approach exists when it comes to mixing religious observations with school ceremonies. There are several cases in which the Court has struck down religious observations in school ceremonies, but this chapter will only address two.

In 1992, the Court decided the case of *Lee v. Weisman*,[112] which involved prayer at a graduation ceremony at Nathan Bishop Middle School in Providence, Rhode Island. The principal of that school invited members of the clergy to give the invocation and benediction at the graduation ceremony. The Weismans, whose daughter, Deborah, was to graduate at the ceremony in question, challenged the school's action and got a temporary restraining order to prohibit the school from including the prayers in the ceremony. In spite of the order, the prayers were recited at the ceremony, and the Weismans brought this action to permanently bar this school and other Providence schools from including such prayers in future graduation ceremonies. The trial court granted a permanent injunction and the appellate court affirmed.

In making its appeal to the Supreme Court, the school district, joined by the federal government, argued that they had made a good-faith effort to ensure the prayers would be nonsectarian and thus, not offensive to any particular religion. Further, they argued that attendance was voluntary, so the student who objected to the prayers could simply not attend. Lastly, the school district argued that for many graduates and their families, an important occasion such as a graduation would not be complete without an acknowledgment of the significance of religion in their lives. The Court found none of the arguments compelling.

The first argument was not persuasive when the Court took a look at the dominant facts that controlled the school district's decision. It was the principal, an agent of the state and local governments, who decided to include an invocation and benediction in the ceremony; it was the principal who gave the clergy guidelines for composition of the prayers. In doing so, the principal controlled the content of the prayers.[113] The fact that the principal did so in a good-faith attempt to ensure that the prayers were sectarian was not compelling. The good faith of the government ". . . does not resolve the dilemma caused by its participation. The question is not the good faith of the school in attempting to make the prayer acceptable to most persons, but the legitimacy of its undertaking that enterprise at all when the object is to produce a prayer to be used in a formal religious exercise which students, for all practical purposes, are obliged to attend."[114]

The Court was also not persuaded that attendance was voluntary and so no student was required to participate if that student objected. In responding to this argument, the Court said that the ". . . effort to monitor prayer will be perceived by the students as inducing participation they might otherwise reject."[115] The Court further held that the student is not free to refuse to attend graduation and therefore, attendance is not, in "any real sense of the term 'voluntary,' for absence would require forfeiture of those intangible benefits which have motivated the student through youth and all her high school years."[116] Further, graduation is a time for students and their families and friends to celebrate their accomplishments and is a symbolic passage into adulthood and adult responsibilities.

Lastly, the Court found that the school district and government's argument that for many individuals, the inclusion of prayer in such a ceremony was essential to underscore the importance of the occasion was not persuasive, but was, in fact, inconsistent. To do so

> ". . . fails to acknowledge that . . . While in some societies the wishes of the majority might prevail, the Establishment Clause of the First Amendment is addressed to this contingency and rejects the balance urged upon us."[117]

In conclusion, the Court in *Lee v. Weisman* held that the school's action violated the Establishment Clause and affirmed the lower court's decision, in spite of a vehement dissent written by Justice Scalia. Justice Scalia argued that there was no official compulsion to attend the graduation ceremony and therefore, there was no violation of the Establishment Clause. Furthermore, he said, the inclusion of an invocation and benediction at a graduation ceremony is a long-held tradition in this country. Justice Scalia argued that the secular purpose and this historical tradition keep this practice from being a violation of the Establishment Clause.[118] In spite of this dissent, the decision in *Lee v. Weisman* stands, and the Court cites this case in a more recent decision regarding ceremonies in public schools.

In *Santa Fe Independent School District v. Doe*[119] the Texas school district initially had a policy that allowed a student, elected by popular vote, to give a nonsectarian, nonproselytizing prayer before every home football game. Before the policy could be used, the Does, who asked to remain anonymous to protect them from intimidation or harassment, brought an action asking for a temporary restraining order to prevent the district from using the policy. The Does argued that the policy violated the Establishment Clause. The Supreme Court accepted this appeal as there was a conflict between cases with similar issues, which had been decided by the Fifth Circuit Court of Appeals. To resolve the conflict, the Court had to decide the issue: "Whether petitioner's policy permitting student-led, student-initiated prayer at football games violates the Establishment Clause."[120] The Court cited the *Lee v. Weisman* case throughout its decision noting that the right to the free exercise of religion does not supersede the limits imposed by the Establishment Clause.[121]

The petitioner argued four things on appeal: first that the Establishment Clause is inapplicable because the messages given during the prayers are private speech, not public speech. Private speech is protected by the Free Speech and Free Exercise Clauses. Second, the petitioner argued that the challenged policy had the secular purposes of fostering free expression of private persons, solemnizing sporting events, and promoting good sportsmanship. Third, that there was a difference between prayer at a graduation ceremony (as was the case in *Lee*) and an invocation at a school football game in that a football game is an extracurricular activity and attendance is voluntary. The latter, the petitioner claims, does not coerce students to participate in a religious observance. Lastly, the petitioner argued that this case involves a facial challenge, based on a possibility or likelihood of an unconstitutional application, and facial challenges of potential future harm must fail.

The Court looked at the private speech argument first. The Court agreed with the petitioner's distinction between private and public speech, but found that the invocations were authorized by a government policy and that the prayers would take place on government property during a government-sponsored, extracurricular activity. In addition, the petitioner did not divorce itself from the religious content of the prayers and the election process virtually ensured that only a student, whose views reflected the beliefs of the majority of the students, would be elected to give the prayers. All of this led to the conclusion that the policy "involve[ed] both perceived and actual endorsement of religion"[122] and that the prayers were not private speech.

In speaking to the argument regarding the policy's secular purpose, the Court did not find the petitioner's argument persuasive and held that an invocation is not the proper mechanism to use to accomplish the alleged purposes. Further, the Court found that, in spite of what the petitioner claimed, the "specific purpose of the policy was to preserve a popular 'state-sponsored' religious practice."[123] This true purpose was impermissible as it sends a message to nonbelievers that they are outsiders in their own community.

The Court responded to petitioner's third argument by looking first at the mechanism used to choose the student who would lead the invocation at all the home football games. The Court noted that the mechanism encouraged divisiveness among the students; divisiveness along religious lines. The Court held that this was at odds with the Establishment Clause.[124] Further, the Court said that while attendance may be voluntary from one perspective, "[t]here are some students, however, such as cheerleaders, members of the band, and of course, team members themselves, for whom seasonal commitments mandate their attendance, sometimes for class credit.[125] Football games are a tradition in high schools and they bring the community together. While these games are more important to some students and community members than others, the Constitution . . . demands that the school may not force this difficult choice upon these students for '[i]t is a tenet of the First Amendment that the State cannot require one of its citizens to forfeit his or her rights and benefits as the price of resisting conformance to state-sponsored religious practice.'"[126] The Court was unwilling to force a student to conform to a religious belief in order to join classmates at a football game.

Petitioner's last argument was that this was a facial challenge, which was being decided prematurely. The policy had not yet been used, and until a student had actually delivered an invocation under the policy, there was no way to be sure that the message given would be religious in nature. The Court rejected the argument that a facial challenge could not be entertained, saying,

> *"Our Establishment Clause cases involving facial challenges, however, have not focused solely on the possible applications of the statute, but rather have considered whether the statute has an unconstitutional purpose."[127]*

It is this alleged unconstitutional purpose that the Court then addresses, holding that the purpose of the policy was understood by the school administration, student body and the community to be religious in nature. This is an unconstitutional purpose, and there is no need to wait until the actual violation occurs before holding it unconstitutional. In responding to this argument, the Court said:

> *"This policy . . . does not survive a facial challenge because it impermissibly imposes upon the student body a majoritarian election on the issue of prayer.*

Through its election scheme, the District has established a governmental electoral mechanism that turns the school into a forum for religious debate. It further empowers the student body majority with the authority to subject students of minority views to constitutionally improper messages. The award of that power alone, regardless of the students' ultimate use of it is not acceptable . . . No further injury is required for the policy to fail a facial challenge."[128]

With this decision, the Court reaffirms *Lee v. Weisman*, resolves the conflict in the lower court, and confirms that it is unwilling to let the Establishment Clause be subverted by use of the First Amendment Free Speech or Free Exercise Clauses. While the Court continues to support private, student prayer before, during, and after school, it is not willing to impose the religious beliefs of the majority by use of a government-sponsored school event. Even though Chief Justice Rehnquist argued in his dissent that the prayer was a form of private speech controlled by the students, this was firmly rejected by the majority.

School Curriculum

For over 30 years, schools have been involved in legal challenges to curriculum perceived to promote religious over nonreligious views or one religion over another. While the Court has always supported the idea that it is permissible to study the Bible as part of an academic curriculum, this may not become a "Bible Study" per se. In addition to the famous Scopes Monkey Trial of 1927,[129] in which the Tennessee Supreme Court upheld the constitutionality of that state's antievolution statute, the U.S. Supreme Court addressed curriculum issues in two cases of note. The first of these cases is *Epperson v. Arkansas* (see Exhibit 15.2).[130]

While *Epperson v. Arkansas* was the case that ultimately struck down the anti-evolution statutes that had been passed in a great many states and thus prohibited the government from forbidding the teaching of evolution in the public schools, the debate about this issue began in the 1920s and was at the center of one of the most infamous cases of the 20th Century. In 1925, the case, popularly entitled the Scopes Monkey Trial, came about because of an ACLU announcement, placed in a Tennessee paper, asking for individuals who wanted to challenge the new Tennessee anti-evolution statute. George Rappalyea of Dayton, Tennessee who believed that involvement in such a challenge would give Dayton national exposure read this announcement. Rappalyea and other community leaders approached John Scopes, a high school teacher and football coach, and asked if he had ever taught the theory of evolution in his classes. When Scopes admitted that he had, they asked if he would participate in a test case challenging the anti-evolution statute. Scopes agreed and Rappalyea swore out a complaint against Scopes, asking that he be charged with a violation of the anti-evolution statute.

Exhibit 15.2 Scopes Trial Cartoon
(www.msu/edu/course/mc/112/1920s/Scopes)

The trial that followed took on a circus-like atmosphere and two famous attorneys, Clarence Darrow and William Jennings Bryan became involved. Darrow represented Scopes, while Bryan joined the prosecution. The trial spanned twelve long, hot summer days, during which the prosecution brought forth students in Scopes' class, the superintendent of schools and other witnesses, who had heard Scopes admit to teaching evolution, to testify. After the prosecution rested, the defense began by putting a zoologist from Johns Hopkins University to testify about the theory of evolution. While the presiding judge allowed the testimony initially, he ultimately ruled the testimony inadmissible. Darrow then asked to read excerpts from prepared statements of scientists and religious experts who had been prepared to testify, but were now disqualified by the judge. He did so in an effort to prepare a record for appellate review and to forward his ultimate goal of having the statute declared unconstitutional. After reading these statements, Darrow then made a surprising move. He asked that he be allowed to call William Jennings Bryan to the stand as an expert on the Bible. The judge and Bryan agreed and what followed was an interrogation that left Bryan's reputation in tatters. Bryan's testimony was embarrassing to his supporters as well as the others on the prosecution team. At the end of Bryan's testimony, Darrow moved for a directed verdict of guilty. Darrow's request was granted, and Scopes was found guilty and the judge fined Scopes $100.

While this trial did not end with the statute being held unconstitutional, as Darrow and the ACLU had hoped, the Tennessee Supreme Court overturned Scopes' conviction in 1927. That Court overturned the conviction on a technicality. Tennessee law dictated that the jury, not the judge, must set a fine if it is over $50. The Tennessee anti-evolution law remained untested. It was not until 1968, with the *Epperson* case, that the U.S. Supreme Court finally overturned this type of anti-evolution statute.[131]

S I D E B A R

In *Epperson* an antievolution statute prohibited anyone from teaching the theory of evolution in public schools and universities. To do so was a misdemeanor. Epperson taught biology in a Little Rock high school. The first year that she taught, the textbook used by the school did not include any information about evolution, but the following year, a new textbook was adopted by the school system, and it did contain such information. Ms. Epperson faced a dilemma; should she teach according to the new textbook and violate the statute, or should she ignore the chapter in the textbook and refuse to include the information in her curriculum. Rather than make this decision on her own, Epperson instituted an action in the Chancery Court of Arkansas asking that the statute be held void and in the alternative, that the State of Arkansas be enjoined from dismissing her for any future violations of the law. The Chancery Court held that the statute violated the Fourteenth Amendment to the U.S. Constitution. The Arkansas Supreme Court reversed, and ultimately the U.S. Supreme Court reversed the decision holding that the statute was vague and conflicted with the constitutional prohibition of state laws respecting the establishment of religion as it was not neutral toward both secular and sectarian beliefs. The Court, with Justice Fortas writing, said "There is and can be no doubt that the First Amendment does not permit the State to require that teaching and learning must be tailored to the principles or prohibitions of any religious sect or dogma."[132] The Court reiterated its holding from previous cases that the State may not aid or oppose any religion, but must maintain religious neutrality. The State's sole purpose in this statute was to bar the teaching of a theory that was at odds with a religious doctrine. In effect, the statute promoted the religious belief of creation. This was unacceptable.

Another case worth noting in this area is the case of *Edwards v. Aguillard*[133] in which a Louisiana statute requiring that if evolution was taught, creationism must also be taught. Parents of students attending Louisiana public schools challenged this statute as a violation of the Establishment Clause. The Federal District Court agreed and held that the act violated the Establishment Clause because it promoted a particular religious doctrine. The Court of Appeals affirmed, and the Supreme Court accepted the petition for a Writ of Certiorari.

The Supreme Court once again used the three-prong Lemon Test to determine whether the statute was valid. In applying the test, the Court noted that if the State action failed to pass the first prong of the test, which deals with the purpose of the statute, there was no need to discuss the last two prongs. The statute in question failed the first prong of the Lemon Test as the Court held that the statute did not promote a valid secular purpose. The State had argued that the statute was to promote academic freedom by providing a more comprehensive science curriculum. The Court was not swayed by this argument, and said:

> *"If the Louisiana Legislature's purpose was solely to maximize the comprehensiveness and effectiveness of science instruction, it would have encouraged the teaching of all scientific theories about the origins of humankind. But under the Act's requirements, teachers who were once free to teach any and all facets of this subject are now unable to do so. Moreover, the Act fails even to ensure that creation science will be taught, but instead require the teaching of this theory only when the theory of evolution is taught. Thus we agree with the Court of Appeals' conclusion that the Act does not serve to protect academic freedom, but has the distinctly different purpose of discrediting 'evolution by counterbalancing its teaching at every turn with the teaching of creationism . . .[134]*

The Court went on to hold that the primary purpose of this statute was to advance the religious doctrine of creationism, and thus the statute fails the first prong of the Lemon Test and violates the Establishment Clause of the First Amendment.

Once again, in discussing curriculum, the Court has consistently demonstrated that it is concerned about the actions of public schools that expose minors to religious doctrines in the classroom. While the Court has demonstrated that it is not always enthusiastic about the Lemon Test, it is the test that the Justices used in these cases.

Summary

When discussing the Establishment Clause, there is no one rule used by the Court in making its decisions. The test used is determined by the type of Establishment Clause challenge being heard by the Court. While the Lemon Test has not been overruled, often it is disregarded in favor of the Reasonable Observer Test—a test in favor with the current Supreme Court Justices. It is clear that the Court continues to afford more protection when minor children are involved and emphasizes neutrality toward all religious denominations. When examining challenges to see if the wall separating church and state has been breached, the Court will not tolerate hostility toward religion any more than it will tolerate an endorsement of any religion.

Key Terms

compelling interest   Establishment Clause   objective observer standard

Review Questions

1. Is there or should there be a wall separating church and state, and on what do you base your answer?
2. What is the difference between the Lemon Test and the Reasonable Observer Test?
3. Does the line in the Pledge of Allegiance, ". . . one nation, under God, indivisible . . ." violate the Establishment Clause? What test would you use in reaching your conclusion, and how would that test work?

Internet Connections

1. Visit the following Web site for an introduction to the Establishment Clause, its history, and the original intent of the Framers of the Constitution when writing this clause at *http://www.law. umkc.edu/faculty/projects/ftrials/conlaw/estabinto.htm.*

2. To read an article on the Establishment Clause and the public schools see http://www.aclu.org/ issues/religion/pr3.html. For other articles on this and other constitutional law topics, see the ACLU home page at *http://www.aclu.org.*

3. For more information on the Scopes Monkey Trial, visit the following Web sites at *http://www.law. umkc.edu/faculty/projects/ftrials/scopes/evolut.htm or http://www.dimensional.com.*

End Notes

[1] U.S. Const. amend. I.

[2] *Reynolds v. United States*, 98 U.S. 145 (1878).

[3] *Murdock v. Commonwealth of Pennsylvania*, 319 U.S. 105 (1943).

[4] *Everson v. Board of Education of Ewing Township*, 330 U.S. 1 (1947).

[5] *Id.* at 11.

[6] *Id.* at 16.

[7] *Lemon v. Kurtzman*, 403 U.S. 602 (1970).

[8] *Early v. DiCenso*, 403 U.S. 602 (1970).

[9] *Lemon v. Kurtzman*, 403 U.S. 602 (1970).

[10] *Id.* at 612.

[11] *Id.* at 616.

[12] *Texas Monthly, Inc. v. Bullock*, 489 U.S. 1 (1989).

[13] *Id.* at 5.

[14] *Id.* at 8.

[15] *Board of Education of Kiryas Joel v. Grumet*, 512 U.S. 687 (1994).

[16] *Id.* at 705.

[17] *Mitchell v. Helms*, 530 U.S. 793 (2000).

[18] *Id.* at 807–808.

[19] *McGowan v. Maryland*, 366 U.S. 420 (1961).

[20] *Id.* at 430.

[21] *Id.* at 433.

[22] *Id.* at 451–452.

[23] *Estate of Thornton v. Caldor, Inc.*, 472 U.S. 703 (1985).

[24] *Id.* at 709.

[25] *Otten v. Baltimore & Ohio Railroad Company*, 205 F.2d 58, 61 (2d Cir. 1953).

[26] *Larkin v. Grendel's Den, Inc.*, 459 U.S. 116 (1982).

[27] *Id.* at 121.

[28] *Id.* at 126.

[29] *Id.* at 127.

[30] *March v. Chambers*, 463 U.S. 783 (1983).

[31] *Id.* at 787.

[32] *Id.* at 791.

[33] *Id.* at 796.

[34] *Id.* at 797.

[35] *Lynch v. Donnelly*, 465 U.S. 668 (1984).

[36] *Id.* at 672.

[37] *Id.* at 673.

[38] *Id.* at 683.

[39] *County of Allegheny v. ACLU*, 492 U.S. 573 (1989).

[40] *Id.* at 598.

[41] *Id.* at 600.

[42] *Id.* at 614.

[43] *Id.* at 619.

[44] *Capitol Square Review and Advisory Board v. Pinette*, 515 U.S. 753 (1995).

[45] *Id.* at 767.

[46] *Id.* at 770.

[47] *McCreary County, Kentucky v. ACLU*, 125 S. Ct. 2722 (2005).

[48] *Van Orden v. Perry*, 125 S. Ct. 2854 (2005).

[49] *McCreary County, Kentucky v. ACLU*, 125 S. Ct. 2722, 2730 (2005).

[50] *Id.* at 2731.

[51] *Id.* at 2733.

[52] *Wallace v. Jaffree*, 472 U.S. 38 (1985).

[53] *Santa Fe Independent School District v. Doe*, 530 U.S. 290 (2000).

[54] *Edwards v. Aguillard*, 482 U.S. 578 (1987).

[55] *McCreary County, Kentucky v. ACLU*, 125 S. Ct. 2722, 2739 (2005).

[56] *Id.* at 2745.

[57] *Van Orden v. Perry*, 125 S. Ct. 2854 (2005).

[58] *Hunt v. McNair*, 413 U.S. 734 (1973).

[59] *Ibid.*

[60] *Van Orden v. Perry*, 125 U.S. 2854, 2874 (2005).

[61] *Larson v. Valente*, 456 U.S. 228 (1982).

[62] Minnesota Charitable Solicitation Act, Minn. Stat. § 309.515(1)(b) (1969 & Supp. 1982).

[63] *Larson v. Vincent*, 456 U.S. 228 (1982).

[64] *Id.* at 246.

[65] *Id.* at 247.

[66] *Id.* at 254.

[67] *Tilton v. Richardson*, 403 U.S. 672 (1971).

[68] 20 U.S.C. §§ 711–721.

[69] *Roemer v. Board of Public Works of Maryland*, 426 U.S. 736 (1976).

[70] *Id.* at 743.

[71] *Id.* at 744.

[72] *Id.* at 764.

[73] *Id.* at 765.

[74] *Rosenberger v. Rector and Visitors of the University of Virginia*, 515 U.S. 819, 825 (1995).

[75] *Id.* at 837.

[76] *Widmar v. Vincent*, 454 U.S. 263 (1981).

[77] *Id.* at 276–277.

[78] *Iverson v. Board of Education of Ewing Township*, 330 U.S. 1 (1947).

[79] *Board of Education of Central School District No. 1 v. Allen*, 392 U.S. 236 (1968).

[80] *Mitchell v. Helms*, 530 U.S. 793 (2000).

[81] *Lemon v. Kurtzman*, 403 U.S. 602, 613 (1971).

[82] *Id.* at 613.

[83] *Id.* at 615.

[84] *Agostini v. Felton*, 521 U.S. 203 (1997).

[85] *Aguilar v. Felton*, 473 U.S. 402 (1987).

[86] The Court discussed the constitutionality of a state program that provided a sign-language interpreter for a deaf parochial student in the case of *Zobrest v. Catalina Foothills School District*, 509 U.S. 1 (1993). The Court held in that case that it was permissible because the only public aid provided was the interpreter who knew the parameters of the position and was

not indoctrinating the student with religious beliefs. Further, the Court held that there is no longer a presumption that the presence of a public employee in a parochial school was a symbolic link between the church and State.

[87]*Zelman v. Simmons-Harris*, 536 U.S. 639 (2002).

[88]*Id.* at 652.

[89]*People of the State of Illinois ex rel. McCollum v. Board of Education of District No. 71*, 333 U.S. 203 (1948).

[90]*Id.* at 212.

[91]*Zorch v. Clauson*, 343 U.S. 306 (1952).

[92]*Id.* at 314.

[93]Education for Economic Security Act, Subchapter VIII, Equal Access, 20 U.S.C.A. §§ 4071–4074 (1984).

[94]*Supra*, n.76.

[95]Education for Economic Security Act, Subchapter VIII, Equal Access, 20 U.S.C.A. § 4071(c)(1)–(5) (1984).

[96]*Board of Education of the Westside Community Schools v. Mergens*, 496 U.S. 226 (1990).

[97]*Engel v. Vitale*, 370 U.S. 421 (1962).

[98]*Id.* at 422.

[99]*Id.* at 429.

[100]*Id.* at 430.

[101]*Id.* at 425.

[102]*Id.* at 435.

[103]*School District of Abington Township, Pennsylvania v. Schempp*, 374 U.S. 203 (1963).

[104]*Id.* at 205.

[105]*Id.* at 210.

[106]*Engel v. Vitale*, 370 U.S. 430, 431 (1962).

[107]*School District of Abington Township, Pennsylvania v. Schempp*, 374 U.S. 203, 223 (1963).

[108]*Id.* at 225.

[109]*Wallace v. Jaffree*, 472 U.S. 38 (1985).

[110]*Id.* at 49.

[111]*Id.* at 61.

[112]*Lee v. Weisman*, 505 U.S. 577 (1992).

[113]*Id.* at 588.

[114]*Id.* at 589.

[115]*Id.* at 590.

[116]*Id.* at 595.

[117]*Id.* at 596.

[118]*Id.* at 632.

[119]*Santa Fe Independent School District v. Doe*, 530 U.S. 290 (2000).

[120]*Id.* at 301.

[121]*Lee v. Weisman*, 505 U.S. 577, 587 (1992).

[122]*Santa Fe Independent School District v. Doe*, 530 U.S. 290, 303 (2000).

[123]*Id.* at 309.

[124]*Id.* at 311.

[125]*Id.* at 311.

[126]*Id.* at 312.

[127]*Id.* at 314.

[128]*Scopes v. State of Tennessee*, 154 Tenn. 105, 289 S. W. 363 (1927).

[129]*Epperson v. Arkansas*, 363 U.S. 97 (1968).

[130]Information in Exhibit 15.2 was found in *An Introduction to the John Scopes (Monkey) Trial*, at http://www.law.umkc.edu (Aug. 14, 2002) and *The Scopes 'Monkey Trial'—July 10, 1925–July 25, 1925*, at http://www.xroads.virginia.edu (Aug. 14, 2002).

[131]*Epperson v. Arkansas*, 363 U.S. 97, 106 (1968).

[132]*Edwards v. Aguillard*, 482 U.S. 578 (1987).

[133]*Id.* at 588–589.

 For additional resources, go to *http://www.westlegalstudies.com*

APPENDIX A

THE UNITED STATES CONSTITUTION

Articles

Preamble

We the People of the United States, in Order to form a more perfect Union, establish Justice, insure domestic Tranquillity, provide for the common defence, promote the general Welfare, and secure the Blessings of Liberty to ourselves and our Posterity, do ordain and establish this Constitution for the United States of America.

Article I

Section 1

All legislative Powers herein granted shall be vested in a Congress of the United States, which shall consist of a Senate and House of Representatives.

Section 2

The House of Representatives shall be composed of Members chosen every second Year by the People of the several States, and the Electors in each State shall have the Qualifications requisite for Electors of the most numerous Branch of the State Legislature.

No Person shall be a Representative who shall not have attained to the age of twenty five Years, and been seven Years a Citizen of the United States, and who shall not, when elected, be an Inhabitant of that State in which he shall be chosen.

Representatives and direct Taxes shall be apportioned among the several States which may be included within this Union, according to their respective Numbers, which shall be determined by adding to the whole Number of free Persons, including those bound to Service for a Term of Years, and excluding Indians not taxed, three fifths of all other Persons. The actual Enumeration shall be made within three Years after the first Meeting of the Congress of the United States, and within every subsequent Term of ten Years, in such Manner as they shall by Law direct. The Number of Representatives shall not exceed one for every thirty Thousand, but each State shall have at Least one Representative; and until such enumeration shall be made, the State of New Hampshire shall be entitled to chuse three, Massachusetts eight, Rhode Island and Providence Plantations one, Connecticut five, New York six, New Jersey four, Pennsylvania eight, Delaware one, Maryland six, Virginia ten, North Carolina five, South Carolina five, and Georgia three.

When vacancies happen in the Representation from any State, the Executive Authority thereof shall issue Writs of Election to fill such Vacancies.

The House of Representatives shall chuse their Speaker and other Officers; and shall have the sole Power of Impeachment.

Section 3

The Senate of the United States shall be composed of two Senators from each State, chosen by the Legislature thereof, for six Years; and each Senator shall have one Vote.

Immediately after they shall be assembled in Consequence of the first Election, they shall be divided as equally as may be into three Classes. The Seats of the Senators of the first Class shall be vacated at the Expiration of the second Year, of the second Class at the Expiration of the fourth Year, and of the third Class at the Expiration of the sixth Year, so that one third may be chosen every second Year; and if Vacancies happen by Resignation, or otherwise, during the Recess of the Legislature of any State, the Executive thereof may make temporary Appointments until the next Meeting of the Legislature, which shall then fill such Vacancies.

No Person shall be a Senator who shall not have attained to the Age of thirty Years, and been nine Years a Citizen of the United States, and who shall not, when elected, be an Inhabitant of that State for which he shall be chosen.

The Vice President of the United States shall be President of the Senate but shall have no Vote, unless they be equally divided.

The Senate shall chuse their other Officers, and also a President pro tempore, in the Absence of the Vice President, or when he shall exercise the Office of President of the United States.

The Senate shall have the sole Power to try all Impeachments. When sitting for that Purpose, they shall be on Oath or Affirmation. When the President of the United States is tried the Chief Justice shall preside: And no Person shall be convicted without the Concurrence of two thirds of the Members present.

Judgment in Cases of Impeachment shall not extend further than to removal from Office, and disqualification to hold and enjoy any Office of honor, Trust or Profit under the United States: but the Party convicted shall nevertheless be liable and subject to Indictment, Trial, Judgment and Punishment, according to Law.

Section 4

The Times, Places and Manner of holding Elections for Senators and Representatives, shall be prescribed in each State by the Legislature thereof; but the Congress may at any time by Law make or alter such Regulations, except as to the Places of chusing Senators.

The Congress shall assemble at least once in every Year, and such Meeting shall be on the first Monday in December, unless they shall by Law appoint a different Day.

Section 5

Each House shall be the Judge of the Elections, Returns and Qualifications of its own Members, and a Majority of each shall constitute a Quorum to do Business; but a smaller Number may adjourn from day to day, and may be authorized to compel the Attendance of absent Members, in such Manner, and under such Penalties as each House may provide.

Each House may determine the Rules of its Proceedings, punish its Members for disorderly Behaviour, and, with the Concurrence of two thirds, expel a Member.

Each House shall keep a Journal of its Proceedings, and from time to time publish the same, excepting such Parts as may in their Judgment require Secrecy; and the Yeas and Nays of the Members of either House on any question shall, at the Desire of one fifth of those Present, be entered on the Journal.

Neither House, during the Session of Congress, shall, without the Consent of the other, adjourn for more than three days, nor to any other Place than that in which the two Houses shall be sitting.

Section 6

The Senators and Representatives shall receive a Compensation for their Services, to be ascertained by Law, and paid out of the Treasury of the United States. They shall in all Cases, except Treason, Felony and Breach of the Peace, be privileged from Arrest during their Attendance at the Session of their respective Houses, and in going to and returning from the same; and for any Speech or Debate in either House, they shall not be questioned in any other Place.

No Senator or Representative shall, during the Time for which he was elected, be appointed to any civil Office under the Authority of the United States, which shall have been created, or the Emoluments whereof shall have been encreased during such time; and no Person holding any Office under the United States, shall be a Member of either House during his Continuance in Office.

Section 7

All Bills for raising Revenue shall originate in the House of Representatives; but the Senate may propose or concur with amendments as on other Bills.

Every Bill which shall have passed the House of Representatives and the Senate, shall, before it becomes a law, be presented to the President of the United States: If he approve he shall sign it, but if not he shall return it, with his Objections to that House in which it shall have originated, who shall enter the Objections at large on their Journal, and proceed to reconsider it. If after such Reconsideration two thirds of that House shall agree to pass the Bill, it shall be sent, together with the Objections, to the other House, by which it shall likewise be reconsidered, and if approved by two thirds of that House, it shall become a Law. But in all such Cases the Votes of both Houses shall be determined by Yeas and Nays, and the Names of the Persons voting for and against the Bill shall be entered on the Journal of each House respectively. If any Bill shall not be returned by the President within ten Days (Sundays excepted) after it shall have been presented to him, the Same shall be a Law, in like Manner as if he had signed it, unless the Congress by their Adjournment prevent its Return, in which Case it shall not be a Law.

Every Order, Resolution, or Vote to which the Concurrence of the Senate and House of Representatives may be necessary (except on a question of Adjournment) shall be presented to the President of the United States; and before the Same shall take Effect, shall be approved by him, or being disapproved by him, shall be repassed by two thirds of the Senate and House of Representatives, according to the Rules and Limitations prescribed in the Case of a Bill.

Section 8

The Congress shall have Power To lay and collect Taxes, Duties, Imposts and Excises, to pay the Debts and provide for the common Defence and general Welfare of the United States; but all Duties, Imposts and Excises shall be uniform throughout the United States;

To borrow Money on the credit of the United States;

To regulate Commerce with foreign Nations, and among the several States, and with the Indian Tribes;

To establish Rule of Naturalization, and uniform Laws on the subject of Bankruptcies throughout the United States;

To coin Money, regulate the Value thereof, and of foreign Coin, and fix the Standard of Weights and Measures;

To provide for the Punishment of counterfeiting the Securities and current Coin of the United States;

To establish Post Offices and post Roads;

To promote the Progress of Science and useful Arts, by securing for limited Times to Authors and Inventors the exclusive Right to their respective Writings and Discoveries;

To constitute Tribunals inferior to the supreme Court;

To define and punish Piracies and Felonies committed on the high Seas, and Offences against the Law of Nations;

To declare War, grant Letters of Marque and Reprisal, and make Rules concerning Captures on Land and Water;

To raise and support Armies, but no Appropriation of Money to that Use shall be for a longer Term than two Years;

To provide and maintain a Navy;

To make Rules for the Government and Regulation of the land and naval Forces;

To provide for calling forth the Militia to execute the Laws of the Union, suppress Insurrections and repeal Invasions;

To provide for organizing, arming, and disciplining, the Militia, and for governing such Part of them as may be employed in the Service of the United States, reserving to the States respectively, the Appointment of the Officers, and the Authority of training the Militia according to the discipline prescribed by Congress;

To exercise exclusive Legislation in all Cases whatsoever, over such District (not exceeding ten Miles square) as may, by Cession of Particular States, and the Acceptance of Congress, become the Seat of the Government of the United States, and to exercise like Authority over all Places purchased by the Consent of the Legislature of the State in which the Same shall be, for the Erection of Forts, Magazines, Arsenals, dock-Yards and other needful Buildings;—And

To make all Laws which shall be necessary and proper for carrying into Execution the foregoing Powers and all other Powers vested by this Constitution in the Government of the United States, or in any Department or Officer thereof.

Section 9

The Migration or Importation of such Persons as any of the States now existing shall think proper to admit, shall not be prohibited by the Congress prior to the Year one thousand eight hundred and eight, but a Tax or duty may be imposed on such Importation, not exceeding ten dollars for each Person.

The Privilege of the Writ of Habeas Corpus shall not be suspended, unless when in Cases of Rebellion or Invasion the public Safety may require it.

No Bill of Attainder or ex post facto Law shall be passed.

No Capitation, or other direct, Tax shall be laid, unless in Proportion to the Census of Enumeration herein before directed to be taken.

No Tax or Duty shall be laid on Articles exported from any State.

No Preference shall be given by any Regulation of Commerce or Revenue to the Ports of one State over those of another: nor shall Vessels bound to, or from, one State, be obliged to enter, clear or pay Duties in another.

No Money shall be drawn from the Treasury, but in Consequence of Appropriations made by Law; and a regular Statement and Account of the Receipts and Expenditures of all public Money shall be published from time to time.

No Title of Nobility shall be granted by the United States: And no Person holding any Office of Profit or Trust under them, shall, without the Consent of the Congress, accept of any present, Emolument, Office, or Title, of any kind whatever, from any King, Prince or foreign State.

Section 10

No State shall enter into any Treaty, Alliance, or Confederation; grant Letters of Marque and Reprisal; coin Money; emit Bills of Credit; make any Thing but gold and silver Coin a Tender in Payment of Debts; pass any Bill of Attainder, ex post facto Law, or Law impairing the Obligation of Contracts, or grant any Title of Nobility.

No State shall, without the Consent of the Congress, lay any Imposts or Duties on Imports or Exports, except what may be absolutely necessary for executing its inspection Laws: and the net Produce of all Duties and Imposts, laid by any State on Imports or Exports, shall be for the Use of the Treasury of the United States; and all such Laws shall be subject to the Revision and Controul of the Congress.

No State shall, without the Consent of Congress, lay any Duty of Tonnage, keep Troops, or Ships of War in time of Peace, enter into any Agreement or Compact with another State, or with a foreign Power, or engage in War, unless actually invaded, or in such imminent Danger as will not admit of delay.

Article II

Section 1

The executive Power shall be vested in a President of the United States of America. He shall hold his Office during the Term of four Years, and, together with the Vice President, chosen for the same Term, be elected, as follows:

Each State shall appoint, in such Manner as the Legislature thereof may direct, a Number of Electors, equal to the whole Number of Senators and Representatives to which the State may be entitled in the Congress: but no Senator or Representative, or Person holding an Office of Trust or Profit under the United States, shall be appointed an Elector.

The Electors shall meet in their respective States, and vote by Ballot for two Persons, of whom one at least shall not be an Inhabitant of the same State with themselves. And they shall make a List of all the Persons voted for, and of the Number of Votes for each; which List they shall sign and certify, and transmit sealed to the Seat of the Government of the United States, directed to the President of the Senate. The President of the Senate shall, in the Presence of the Senate and House of Representatives, open all the Certificates, and the Votes shall then be counted. The Person having the greatest Number of Votes shall be the President, if such Number be a Majority of the whole Number of Electors appointed; and if there be more than one who have such Majority, and have an equal Number of Votes, then the House of Representatives shall immediately chuse by Ballot one of them for President; and if no Person has a Majority, then from the five highest on the List the said House shall in like Manner chuse the President. But in chusing the President, the Votes shall be taken by States, the Representatives from each State having one Vote; a quorum for this Purpose shall consist of a Member or Members from two thirds of the States, and a Majority of all the States shall be necessary to a Choice. In every Case, after the Choice of the President, the Person having the greatest Number of Votes of the Electors shall be the Vice President. But if there should remain two or more who have equal Votes, the Senate shall chuse from them by Ballot the Vice President.

The Congress may determine the Time of chusing the Electors, and the Day on which they shall give their Votes; which Day shall be the same throughout the United States.

No Person except a natural born Citizen, or a Citizen of the United States, at the time of the Adoption of this Constitution, shall be eligible to the Office of President; neither shall any person be eligible to that Office who shall not have attained to the Age of thirty five Years, and been fourteen Years a Resident within the United States.

In Case of the Removal of the President from Office, or of his Death, Resignation, or Inability to discharge the Powers and Duties of the said Office, the Same shall devolve on the Vice President, and the Congress may by Law provide for the Case of Removal, Death, Resignation or Inability, both of the President and Vice President, declaring what Officer shall then act as President, and such Officer shall act accordingly, until the Disability be removed, or a President shall be elected.

The President shall, at stated Times, receive for his Services, a Compensation, which shall neither be encreased nor diminished during the Period for which he shall have been elected, and he shall not receive within that Period any other Emolument from the United States, or any of them.

Before he enters on the Execution of his Office, he shall take the following Oath or Affirmation:—"I do solemnly swear (or affirm) that I will faithfully execute the Office of President of the United States, and will to the best of my Ability, preserve, protect and defend the Constitution of the United States."

Section 2
The President shall be Commander in Chief of the Army and Navy of the United States, and of the Militia of the several States, when called into the actual Service of the United States; he may require the Opinion, in writing, of the principal Officer in each of the executive Departments, upon any Subject relating to the Duties of their respective Offices, and he shall have Power to Grant Reprieves and Pardons for Offences against the United States, except in Cases of Impeachment.

He shall have Power, by and with the Advice and Consent of the Senate, to make Treaties, provided two thirds of the Senators present concur; and he shall nominate, and by and with the Advice and Consent of the Senate, shall appoint Ambassadors, other public Ministers and Consuls, Judges of the supreme Court, and all other Officers of the United States, whose Appointments are not herein otherwise provided for, and which shall be established by Law: but the Congress may by Law vest the Appointment of such inferior Officers, as they think proper, in the President alone, in the Courts of Law, or in the Heads of Departments.

The President shall have Power to fill up all Vacancies that may happen during the Recess of the Senate, by granting Commissions which shall expire at the End of their next Session.

Section 3

He shall from time to time give to the Congress Information on the State of the Union, and recommend to their Consideration such Measures as he shall judge necessary and expedient; he may, on extraordinary Occasions, convene both Houses, or either of them, and in Case of Disagreement between them, with Respect to the Time of Adjournment, he may adjourn them to such Time as he shall think proper; he shall receive Ambassadors and other public Ministers; he shall take Care that the Laws be faithfully executed, and shall Commission all the Officers of the United States.

Section 4

The President, Vice President and all Civil Officers of the United States, shall be removed from Office on Impeachment for and Conviction of, Treason, Bribery, or other high Crimes and Misdemeanors.

Article III

Section 1

The judicial Power of the United States, shall be vested in one supreme Court, and in such inferior Courts as the Congress may from time to time ordain and establish. The Judges, both of the supreme and inferior Courts, shall hold their Offices during good Behaviour, and shall, at stated Times, receive for their Services, a Compensation, which shall not be diminished during their Continuance in Office.

Section 2

The judicial Power shall extend to all Cases, in Law and Equity, arising under this Constitution, the Laws of the United States, and Treaties made, or which shall be made, under their Authority;—to all Cases affecting Ambassadors, other public ministers and Consuls;—to all Cases of admiralty and maritime Jurisdiction;—to Controversies to which the United States shall be a Party;—to Controversies between two or more States;—between a State and Citizens of another State;—between Citizens of different States;—between Citizens of the same State claiming Lands under Grants of different States, and between a State, or the Citizens thereof, and foreign States, Citizens or Subjects.

In all Cases affecting Ambassadors, other public Ministers and Consuls, and those in which a State shall be Party, the supreme Court shall have original Jurisdiction. In all the other Cases before mentioned, the supreme Court shall have appellate Jurisdiction, both as to Law and Fact, with such Exceptions, and under such Regulations as the Congress shall make.

The Trial of all Crimes, except in Cases of Impeachment, shall be by Jury; and such Trial shall be held in the State where the said Crimes shall have been committed; but when not committed within any State, the Trial shall be at such Place or Places as the Congress may by Law have directed.

Section 3

Treason against the United States, shall consist only in levying War against them, or in adhering to their Enemies, giving them Aid and Comfort.

No Person shall be convicted of Treason unless on the Testimony of two Witnesses to the same overt Act, or on Confession in open Court.

The Congress shall have Power to declare the Punishment of Treason, but no Attainder of Treason shall work Corruption of Blood, or Forfeiture except during the Life of the Person attainted.

Article IV

Section 1
Full Faith and Credit shall be given in each State to the public Acts, Records, and judicial Proceedings of every other State. And the Congress may by general Laws prescribe the Manner in which such Acts, Records and Proceedings shall be proved, and the Effect thereof.

Section 2
The Citizens of each State shall be entitled to all Privileges and Immunities of Citizens in the several States.

A Person charged in any State with Treason, Felony, or other Crime, who shall flee from Justice, and be found in another State, shall on Demand of the executive Authority of the State from which he fled, be delivered up, to be removed to the State having Jurisdiction of the Crime.

No Person held to Service or Labour in one State, under the Laws thereof, escaping into another, shall, in Consequence of any Law or Regulation therein, be discharged from such Service or Labour, but shall be delivered up on Claim of the Party to whom such Service or Labour may be due.

Section 3
New States may be admitted by the Congress into this Union; but no new State shall be formed or erected within the Jurisdiction of any other State; nor any State be formed by the Junction of two or more States, or Parts of States, without the Consent of the Legislatures of the States concerned as well as of the Congress.

The Congress shall have Power to dispose of and make all needful Rules and Regulations respecting the Territory or other Property belonging to the United States; and nothing in this Constitution shall be so construed as to Prejudice any Claims of the United States, or of any particular State.

Section 4
The United States shall guarantee to every State in this Union a Republican Form of Government, and shall protect each of them against Invasion; and on Application of the Legislature, or of the Executive (when the Legislature cannot be convened) against domestic Violence.

Article V

The Congress, whenever two thirds of both Houses shall deem it necessary, shall propose Amendments to this Constitution, or, on the Application of the Legislatures of two thirds of the several States, shall call a Convention for proposing Amendments, which, in either Case, shall be valid to all Intents and Purposes, as Part of this Constitution, when ratified by the Legislatures of three fourths of the several States, or by Conventions in three fourths thereof, as the one or the other Mode of Ratification may be proposed by the Congress; Provided that no Amendment which may be made prior to the Year One thousand eight hundred and eight shall in any Manner affect the first and fourth Clauses in the Ninth Section of the first Article; and that no State, without its Consent, shall be deprived of its equal Suffrage in the Senate.

Article VI

All Debts contracted and Engagements entered into, before the Adoption of this Constitution, shall be as valid against the United States under this Constitution, as under the Confederation.

This Constitution, and the Laws of the United States which shall be made in Pursuance thereof; and all Treaties made, or which shall be made, under the Authority of the United States, shall be the supreme Law of the Land; and the Judges in every State shall be bound thereby, any Thing in the Constitution or Laws of any state to the Contrary notwithstanding.

The Senators and Representatives before mentioned, and the Members of the several State Legislatures, and all executive and judicial Officers, both of the United States and of the several States, shall be bound by Oath or Affirmation, to support this Constitution; but no religious Test shall ever be required as a Qualification to any Office or public Trust under the United States.

Article VII

The Ratification of the Conventions of nine States, shall be sufficient for the Establishment of this Constitution between the States so ratifying the same.

Amendments

Amendments to the Constitution of the United States of America
Articles in addition to, and amendment of, the Constitution of the United States of America, proposed by Congress, and ratified by the several states, pursuant to the Fifth Article of the original Constitution.

Amendment I

Congress shall make no law respecting an establishment of religion, or prohibiting the free exercise thereof; or abridging the freedom of speech, or of the press; or the right of the people peaceably to assemble, and to petition the Government for a redress of grievances.

Amendment II

A well regulated Militia, being necessary to the security of a free State, the right of the people to keep and bear Arms, shall not be infringed.

Amendment III

No Soldier shall, in time of peace be quartered in any house, without the consent of the Owner, nor in time of war, but in a manner to be prescribed by law.

Amendment IV

The right of the people to be secure in their persons, houses, papers, and effects, against unreasonable searches and seizures, shall not be violated, and no Warrants shall issue, but upon probable cause, supported by Oath or affirmation, and particularly describing the place to be searched, and the persons or things to be seized.

Amendment V

No person shall be held to answer for a capital, or otherwise infamous crime, unless on a presentment or indictment of a Grand Jury, except in cases arising in the land or naval forces, or in the Militia, when in actual service in time of War or public danger; nor shall any person be subject for the same offence to be twice put in jeopardy of life or limb; nor shall be compelled in any criminal case to be a witness against himself, nor be deprived of life, liberty, or property, without due process of law; nor shall private property be taken for public use, without just compensation.

Amendment VI

In all criminal prosecutions, the accused shall enjoy the right to a speedy and public trial, by an impartial jury of the State and district wherein the crime shall have been committed, which district shall have been previously ascertained by law, and to be informed of the nature and cause of the accusation; to be confronted with the witnesses against him; to have compulsory process for obtaining witnesses in his favor, and to have the Assistance of Counsel for his defence.

Amendment VII

In Suits at common law, where the value in controversy shall exceed twenty dollars, the right of trial by jury shall be preserved, and no fact tried by a jury, shall be otherwise re-examined in any Court of the United States, than according to the rules of the common law.

Amendment VIII

Excessive bail shall not be required, nor excessive fines imposed, nor cruel and unusual punishments inflicted.

Amendment IX

The enumeration in the Constitution, of certain rights, shall not be construed to deny or disparage others retained by the people.

Amendment X

The powers not delegated to the United States by the Constitution, nor prohibited by it to the States, are reserved to the States respectively, or to the people.

Amendment XI

The Judicial power of the United States shall not be construed to extend to any suit in law or equity, commenced or prosecuted against one of the United States by Citizens of another State, or by Citizens or Subjects of any Foreign State.

Amendment XII

The Electors shall meet in their respective states and vote by ballot for President and Vice President, one of whom, at least, shall not be an inhabitant of the same state with themselves; they shall name in their ballots the person voted for as President, and in distinct ballots the person voted for as Vice President, and they shall make distinct lists of all persons voted for as President, and of all persons voted for as Vice President, and of the number of votes for each, which lists they shall sign and certify, and transmit sealed to the seat of the government of the United States, directed to the President of the Senate;—The President of the Senate shall, in the presence of the Senate and House of Representatives, open all the certificates and the votes shall then be counted;—The person having the greatest Number of votes for President, shall be the President, if such number be a majority of the whole number of Electors appointed; and if no persons have such majority, then from the persons having the highest numbers not exceeding three on the list of those voted for as President, the House of Representatives shall choose immediately, by ballot, the President. But in choosing the President, the votes shall be taken by states, the representation from each state having one vote; a quorum for this purpose shall consist of a member or members from two-thirds of the states, and a majority of all the states shall be necessary to a choice. And if the House of Representatives shall not choose a President whenever the right of choice shall devolve upon them, before the fourth day of March next following, then the Vice President shall act as President, as in the case of the death or other constitutional disability of the President—The person having the greatest number of votes as Vice President, shall be the Vice President, if such number be a majority of the whole number of Electors appointed, and if no persons have a majority, then from the two highest numbers on the list, the Senate shall choose the Vice President; a quorum for the purpose shall consist of two-thirds of the whole number of Senators, and a majority of the whole number shall be necessary to a choice. But no person constitutionally ineligible to the office of President shall be eligible to that of Vice President of the United States.

Amendment XIII

Section 1. Neither slavery nor involuntary servitude, except as a punishment for crime whereof the party shall have been duly convicted, shall exist within the United States, or any place subject to their jurisdiction.

Section 2. Congress shall have power to enforce this article by appropriate legislation.

Amendment XIV

Section 1. All persons born or naturalized in the United States and subject to the jurisdiction thereof, are citizens of the United States and of the State wherein they reside. No State shall make or enforce any law which shall abridge the privileges or immunities of citizens of the United States; nor shall any State deprive any person of life, liberty, or property, without due process of law; nor deny to any person within its jurisdiction the equal protection of the laws.

Section 2. Representatives shall be apportioned among the several States according to their respective numbers, counting the whole number of persons in each State, excluding Indians not taxed. But when the right to vote at any election for the choice of electors for President and Vice President of the United States, Representatives in Congress, the Executive and Judicial officers of a State, or the members of the Legislature thereof, is denied to any of the male inhabitants of such State, being twenty-one years of age, and citizens of the United States, or in any way abridged, except for participation in rebellion, or other crime, the basis of representation therein shall be reduced in the proportion which the number of such male citizens shall bear to the whole number of male citizens twenty-one years of age in such State.

Section 3. No person shall be a Senator or Representative in Congress, or elector of President and Vice President, or hold any office, civil or military, under the United States, or under any State, who, having previously taken an oath, as a member of Congress, or as an officer of the United States, or as a member of any State legislature, or as an executive or judicial officer of any State, to support the Constitution of the United States, shall have engaged in insurrection or rebellion against the same, or given aid or comfort to the enemies thereof. But Congress may by a vote of two-thirds of each House, remove such disability.

Section 4. The validity of the public debt of the United States, authorized by law, including debts incurred for payment of pensions and bounties for services in suppressing insurrection or rebellion, shall not be questioned. But neither the United States nor any State shall assume or pay any debt or obligation incurred in aid of insurrection or rebellion against the United States, or any claim for the loss or emancipation of any slave; but all such debts, obligations and claims shall be held illegal and void.

Section 5. The Congress shall have power to enforce, by appropriate legislation, the provisions of this article.

Amendment XV

Section 1. The right of citizens of the United States to vote shall not be denied or abridged by the United States or by any State on account of race, color, or previous condition of servitude.

Section 2. The Congress shall have power to enforce this article by appropriate legislation.

Amendment XVI

The Congress shall have power to lay and collect taxes on incomes, from whatever source derived, without apportionment among the several States, and without regard to any census or enumeration.

Amendment XVII

The Senate of the United States shall be composed of two Senators from each State, elected by the people thereof, for six years; and each Senator shall have one vote. The electors in each State shall have the qualifications requisite for electors of the most numerous branch of the State legislatures.

When vacancies happen in the representation of any State in the Senate, the executive authority of such State shall issue writs of election to fill such vacancies: Provided, That the legislature of any State may empower the executive thereof to make temporary appointments until the people fill the vacancies by election as the legislature may direct.

This amendment shall not be so construed as to affect the election or term of any Senator chosen before it becomes valid as part of the Constitution.

Amendment XVIII

Section 1. After one year from the ratification of this article the manufacture, sale, or transportation of intoxicating liquors within, the importation thereof into, or the exportation thereof from the United States and all territory subject to the jurisdiction thereof for beverage purposes is hereby prohibited.

Section 2. The Congress and the several States shall have concurrent power to enforce this article by appropriate legislation.

Section 3. This article shall be inoperative unless it shall have been ratified as an amendment to the Constitution by the legislatures of the several States, as provided in the Constitution, within seven years from the date of the submission hereof to the States by the Congress.

Amendment XIX

The right of citizens of the United States to vote shall not be denied or abridged by the United States or by any State on account of sex.

Congress shall have power to enforce this article by appropriate legislation.

Amendment XX

Section 1. The terms of the President and Vice President shall end at noon on the 20th day of January, and the terms of Senators and Representatives at noon on the 3d day of January, of the years in which such terms would have ended if this article had not been ratified; and the terms of their successors shall then begin.

Section 2. The Congress shall assemble at least once in every year, and such meeting shall begin at noon on the 3d day of January, unless they shall by law appoint a different day.

Section 3. If, at the time fixed for the beginning of the term of the President, the President elect shall have died, the Vice President elect shall become President. If a President shall not have been chosen before the time fixed for the beginning of his term, or if the President elect shall have failed to qualify, then the Vice President elect shall act as President until a President shall have qualified; and the Congress may by law provide for the case wherein neither a President elect nor a Vice President elect shall have qualified, declaring who shall then act as President, or the manner in which one who is to act shall be selected, and such person shall act accordingly until a President or Vice President shall have qualified.

Section 4. The Congress may by law provide for the case of the death of any of the persons from whom the House of Representatives may choose a President whenever the right of choice shall have devolved upon them, and for the case of the death of any of the persons from whom the Senate may choose a Vice President whenever the right of choice shall have devolved upon them.

Section 5. Sections 1 and 2 shall take effect on the 15th day of October following the ratification of this article.

Section 6. This article shall be inoperative unless it shall have been ratified as an amendment to the Constitution by the legislatures of three-fourths of the several States within seven years from the date of its submission.

Amendment XXI

Section 1. The eighteenth article of amendment to the Constitution of the United States is hereby repealed.

Section 2. The transportation or importation into any State, Territory, or possession of the United States for delivery or use therein of intoxicating liquors, in violation of the laws thereof, is hereby prohibited.

Section 3. This article shall be inoperative unless it shall have been ratified as an amendment to the Constitution by conventions in the several States, as provided in the Constitution, within seven years from the date of the submission hereof to the States by the Congress.

Amendment XXII

Section 1. No person shall be elected to the office of the President more than twice, and no person who has held the office of President, or acted as President, for more than two years of a term to which some other person was elected President shall be elected to the office of the President more than once. But this Article shall not apply to any person holding the office of President, when this Article was proposed by the Congress, and shall not prevent any person who may be holding the office of President, or acting as President, during the term within which this Article becomes operative from holding the office of President or acting as President during the remainder of such term.

Section 2. This article shall be inoperative unless it shall have been ratified as an amendment to the Constitution by the legislatures of three-fourths of the several States within seven years from the date of its submission to the States by the Congress.

Amendment XXIII

Section 1. The District constituting the seat of Government of the United States shall appoint in such manner as the Congress may direct: A number of electors of President and Vice President equal to the whole number of Senators and Representatives in Congress to which the District would be entitled if it were a State, but in no event more than the least populous State; they shall be in addition to those appointed by the States, but they shall be considered, for the purposes of the election of President and Vice President, to be electors appointed by a State; and they shall meet in the District and perform such duties as provided by the twelfth article of amendment.

Section 2. The Congress shall have power to enforce this article by appropriate legislation.

Amendment XXIV

Section 1. The right of citizens of the United States to vote in any primary or other election for President or Vice President, for electors for President or Vice President, or for Senator or Representative in Congress, shall not be denied or abridged by the United States or any State by reason of failure to pay any poll tax or other tax.

Section 2. The Congress shall have power to enforce this article by appropriate legislation.

Amendment XXV

Section 1. In case of the removal of the President from office or of his death or resignation, the Vice President shall become President.

Section 2. Whenever there is a vacancy in the office of the Vice President, the President shall nominate a Vice President who shall take office upon confirmation by a majority vote of both Houses of Congress.

Section 3. Whenever the President transmits to the President pro tempore of the Senate and the Speaker of the House of Representatives his written declaration that he is unable to discharge the powers and duties of his office, and until he transmits to them a written declaration to the contrary, such powers and duties shall be discharged by the Vice President as Acting President.

Section 4. Whenever the Vice President and a majority of either the principal officers of the executive departments or of such other body as Congress may by law provide, transmit to the President pro tempore of the Senate and the Speaker of the House of Representatives their written declaration that the President is unable to discharge the powers and duties of his office, the Vice President shall immediately assume the powers and duties of the office as Acting President.

Thereafter, when the President transmits to the President pro tempore of the Senate and the Speaker of the House of Representatives his written declaration that no inability exists, he shall resume the powers and duties of his office unless the Vice President and a majority of either the principal officers of the executive department or of such other body as Congress may by law provide, transmit within four days to the President pro tempore of the Senate and the Speaker of the House of Representatives their written declaration that the President is unable to discharge the powers and duties of his office. Thereupon Congress shall decide the issue, assembling within forty-eight hours for that purpose if not in session. If the Congress, within twenty-one days after receipt of the latter written declaration, or, if Congress is not in session, within twenty-one days after Congress is required to assemble, determines by two-thirds vote of both Houses that the President is unable to discharge the powers and duties of his office, the Vice President shall continue to discharge the same as Acting President; otherwise, the President shall resume the powers and duties of his office.

Amendment XXVI

Section 1. The right of citizens of the United States, who are eighteen years of age or older, to vote shall not be denied or abridged by the United States or by any State on account of age.

Section 2. The Congress shall have power to enforce this article by appropriate legislation.

Amendment XXVII

No law varying the compensation for the services of the Senators and Representatives shall take effect, until an election of Representatives shall have intervened.

APPENDIX B

SELECTED FEDERAL STATUTES

42 U.S.C.A. § 2000a

UNITED STATES CODE ANNOTATED
TITLE 42. THE PUBLIC HEALTH AND WELFARE
CHAPTER 21—CIVIL RIGHTS
SUBCHAPTER II—PUBLIC ACCOMMODATIONS

§ 2000a. Prohibition against discrimination or segregation in places of public accommodation

(a) Equal access

All persons shall be entitled to the full and equal enjoyment of the goods, services, facilities, privileges, advantages, and accommodations of any place of public accommodation, as defined in this section, without discrimination or segregation on the ground of race, color, religion, or national origin.

(b) Establishments affecting interstate commerce or supported in their activities by State action as places of public accommodation; lodgings; facilities principally engaged in selling food for consumption on the premises; gasoline stations; places of exhibition or entertainment; other covered establishments

Each of the following establishments which serves the public is a place of public accommodation within the meaning of this subchapter if its operations affect commerce, or if discrimination or segregation by it is supported by State action:

(1) any inn, hotel, motel, or other establishment which provides lodging to transient guests, other than an establishment located within a building which contains not more than five rooms for rent or hire and which is actually occupied by the proprietor of such establishment as his residence;

(2) any restaurant, cafeteria, lunchroom, lunch counter, soda fountain, or other facility principally engaged in selling food for consumption on the premises, including, but not limited to, any such facility located on the premises of any retail establishment; or any gasoline station;

(3) any motion picture house, theater, concert hall, sports arena, stadium or other place of exhibition or entertainment; and

(4) any establishment (A)(i) which is physically located within the premises of any establishment otherwise covered by this subsection, or (ii) within the premises of which is physically located any such covered establishment, and (B) which holds itself out as serving patrons of such covered establishment.

(c) Operations affecting commerce; criteria; "commerce" defined

The operations of an establishment affect commerce within the meaning of this subchapter if (1) it is one of the establishments described in paragraph (1) of subsection (b) of this section; (2) in the case of an establishment described in paragraph (2) of subsection (b) of this section, it serves or offers to serve interstate travelers or a substantial portion of the food which it serves, or gasoline or other products which it sells, has moved in commerce; (3) in the case of an establishment described in paragraph (3) of subsection (b) of this section, it customarily presents films, performances, athletic teams, exhibitions, or other sources of entertainment which move in commerce; and (4) in the case of an establishment described in paragraph (4) of subsection (b) of this section, it is physically located within the premises of, or there is physically located within its premises, an establishment the operations of which affect commerce within the meaning of this subsection. For purposes of this section, "commerce" means travel, trade, traffic, commerce, transportation, or communication among the several States, or between the District of Columbia and any State, or between any foreign country or any territory or possession and any State or the District of Columbia, or between points in the same State but through any other State or the District of Columbia or a foreign country.

(d) Support by State action

Discrimination or segregation by an establishment is supported by State action within the meaning of this subchapter if such discrimination or segregation (1) is carried on under color of any law, statute, ordinance, or regulation; or (2) is carried on under color of any custom or usage required or enforced by officials of the State or political subdivision thereof; or (3) is required by action of the State or political subdivision thereof.

(e) Private establishments

The provisions of this subchapter shall not apply to a private club or other establishment not in fact open to the public, except to the extent that the facilities of such establishment are made available to the customers or patrons of an establishment within the scope of subsection (b) of this section.

42 U.S.C.A. § 2000b

UNITED STATES CODE ANNOTATED
TITLE 42. THE PUBLIC HEALTH AND WELFARE
CHAPTER 21—CIVIL RIGHTS
SUBCHAPTER III—PUBLIC FACILITIES
§ 2000b. Civil actions by the Attorney General

(a) Complaint; certification; institution of civil action; relief requested; jurisdiction; impleading additional parties as defendants

Whenever the Attorney General receives a complaint in writing signed by an individual to the effect that he is being deprived of or threatened with the loss of his right to the equal protection of the laws, on account of his race, color, religion, or national origin, by being denied equal utilization of any public facility which is owned, operated, or managed by or on behalf of any State or subdivision thereof, other than a public school or public college as defined in section 2000c of this title, and the Attorney General believes the complaint is meritorious and certifies that the signer or signers of such complaint are unable, in his judgment, to initiate and maintain appropriate legal proceedings for relief and that the institution of an action will materially further the orderly progress of desegregation in public facilities, the Attorney General is authorized to institute for or in the name of the United

States a civil action in any appropriate district court of the United States against such parties and for such relief as may be appropriate, and such court shall have and shall exercise jurisdiction of proceedings instituted pursuant to this section. The Attorney General may implead as defendants such additional parties as are or become necessary to the grant of effective relief hereunder.

(b) Persons unable to initiate and maintain legal proceedings

The Attorney General may deem a person or persons unable to initiate and maintain appropriate legal proceedings within the meaning of subsection (a) of this section when such person or persons are unable, either directly or through other interested persons or organizations, to bear the expense of the litigation or to obtain effective legal representation; or whenever he is satisfied that the institution of such litigation would jeopardize the personal safety, employment, or economic standing of such person or persons, their families, or their property.

42 U.S.C.A. § 2000b-1

UNITED STATES CODE ANNOTATED
TITLE 42. THE PUBLIC HEALTH AND WELFARE
CHAPTER 21—CIVIL RIGHTS
SUBCHAPTER III—PUBLIC FACILITIES
§ 2000b-1. Liability of United States for costs and attorney's fee

In any action or proceeding under this subchapter the United States shall be liable for costs, including a reasonable attorney's fee, the same as a private person.

42 U.S.C.A. § 2000b-2

UNITED STATES CODE ANNOTATED
TITLE 42. THE PUBLIC HEALTH AND WELFARE
CHAPTER 21—CIVIL RIGHTS
SUBCHAPTER III—PUBLIC FACILITIES
§ 2000b-2. Personal suits for relief against discrimination in public facilities

Nothing in this subchapter shall affect adversely the right of any person to sue for or obtain relief in any court against discrimination in any facility covered by this subchapter.

42 U.S.C.A. § 2000b-3

UNITED STATES CODE ANNOTATED
TITLE 42. THE PUBLIC HEALTH AND WELFARE
CHAPTER 21—CIVIL RIGHTS
SUBCHAPTER III—PUBLIC FACILITIES
§ 2000b-3. "Complaint" defined

A complaint as used in this subchapter is a writing or document within the meaning of section 1001, Title 18.

42 U.S.C.A. § 2000c

UNITED STATES CODE ANNOTATED
TITLE 42. THE PUBLIC HEALTH AND WELFARE
CHAPTER 21—CIVIL RIGHTS
SUBCHAPTER IV—PUBLIC EDUCATION
§ 2000c. Definitions

As used in this subchapter—

(a) "Secretary" means the Secretary of Education.

(b) "Desegregation" means the assignment of students to public schools and within such schools without regard to their race, color, religion, sex or national origin, but "desegregation" shall not mean the assignment of students to public schools in order to overcome racial imbalance.

(c) "Public school" means any elementary or secondary educational institution, and "public college" means any institution of higher education or any technical or vocational school above the secondary school level, provided that such public school or public college is operated by a State, subdivision of a State, or governmental agency within a State, or operated wholly or predominantly from or through the use of governmental funds or property, or funds or property derived from a governmental source.

(d) "School board" means any agency or agencies which administer a system of one or more public schools and any other agency which is responsible for the assignment of students to or within such system.

42 U.S.C.A. § 2000c-2

UNITED STATES CODE ANNOTATED
TITLE 42. THE PUBLIC HEALTH AND WELFARE
CHAPTER 21—CIVIL RIGHTS
SUBCHAPTER IV—PUBLIC EDUCATION
§ 2000c-2. Technical assistance in preparation, adoption, and implementation of plans for desegregation of public schools

The Secretary is authorized, upon the application of any school board, State, municipality, school district, or other governmental unit legally responsible for operating a public school or schools, to render technical assistance to such applicant in the preparation, adoption, and implementation of plans for the desegregation of public schools. Such technical assistance may, among other activities, include making available to such agencies information regarding effective methods of coping with special educational problems occasioned by desegregation, and making available to such agencies personnel of the Department of Education or other persons specially equipped to advise and assist them in coping with such problems.

42 U.S.C.A. § 2000c-3

UNITED STATES CODE ANNOTATED
TITLE 42. THE PUBLIC HEALTH AND WELFARE
CHAPTER 21—CIVIL RIGHTS
SUBCHAPTER IV—PUBLIC EDUCATION
§ 2000c-3. Training institutes; stipends; travel allowances

The Secretary is authorized to arrange, through grants or contracts, with institutions of higher education for the operation of short-term or regular session institutes for special training designed to improve the ability of teachers, supervisors, counselors, and other elementary or secondary school personnel to deal effectively with special educational problems occasioned by desegregation. Individuals who attend such an institute on a full-time basis may be paid stipends for the period of their attendance at such institute in amounts specified by the Secretary in regulations, including allowances for travel to attend such institute.

42 U.S.C.A. § 2000c-4

UNITED STATES CODE ANNOTATED
TITLE 42. THE PUBLIC HEALTH AND WELFARE

CHAPTER 21—CIVIL RIGHTS
SUBCHAPTER IV—PUBLIC EDUCATION
§ 2000c-4. Grants for inservice training in dealing with and for employment of specialists to advise in problems incident to desegregation; factors for consideration in making grants and fixing amounts, terms, and conditions

(a) The Secretary is authorized, upon application of a school board, to make grants to such board to pay, in whole or in part, the cost of—

> (1) giving to teachers and other school personnel inservice training in dealing with problems incident to desegregation, and

> (2) employing specialists to advise in problems incident to desegregation.

(b) In determining whether to make a grant, and in fixing the amount thereof and the terms and conditions on which it will be made, the Secretary shall take into consideration the amount available for grants under this section and the other applications which are pending before him; the financial condition of the applicant and the other resources available to it; the nature, extent, and gravity of its problems incident to desegregation; and such other factors as he finds relevant.

42 U.S.C.A. § 2000c-5

UNITED STATES CODE ANNOTATED
TITLE 42. THE PUBLIC HEALTH AND WELFARE
CHAPTER 21—CIVIL RIGHTS
SUBCHAPTER IV—PUBLIC EDUCATION
§ 2000c-5. Payments; adjustments; advances or reimbursement; installments

Payments pursuant to a grant or contract under this subchapter may be made (after necessary adjustments on account of previously made overpayments or underpayments) in advance or by way of reimbursement, and in such installments, as the Secretary may determine.

42 U.S.C.A. § 2000c-6

UNITED STATES CODE ANNOTATED
TITLE 42. THE PUBLIC HEALTH AND WELFARE
CHAPTER 21—CIVIL RIGHTS
SUBCHAPTER IV—PUBLIC EDUCATION
§ 2000c-6. Civil actions by the Attorney General

(a) Complaint; certification; notice to school board or college authority; institution of civil action; relief requested; jurisdiction; transportation of pupils to achieve racial balance; judicial power to insure compliance with constitutional standards; impleading additional parties as defendants

Whenever the Attorney General receives a complaint in writing—

> (1) signed by a parent or group of parents to the effect that his or their minor children, as members of a class of persons similarly situated, are being deprived by a school board of the equal protection of the laws, or

> (2) signed by an individual, or his parent, to the effect that he has been denied admission to or not permitted to continue in attendance at a public college by reason of race, color, religion, sex or national origin, and the Attorney General believes the complaint is meritorious and certifies that the signer or signers of such complaint are unable, in his judgment, to initiate and maintain appropriate legal proceedings for relief and that the institution of an action will materially further the orderly achievement of desegregation in public education, the Attorney General is authorized, after giving notice of such complaint to the appropriate school board or college

authority and after certifying that he is satisfied that such board or authority has had a reasonable time to adjust the conditions alleged in such complaint, to institute for or in the name of the United States a civil action in any appropriate district court of the United States against such parties and for such relief as may be appropriate, and such court shall have and shall exercise jurisdiction of proceedings instituted pursuant to this section, provided that nothing herein shall empower any official or court of the United States to issue any order seeking to achieve a racial balance in any school by requiring the transportation of pupils or students from one school to another or one school district to another in order to achieve such racial balance, or otherwise enlarge the existing power of the court to insure compliance with constitutional standards. The Attorney General may implead as defendants such additional parties as are or become necessary to the grant of effective relief hereunder.

(b) Persons unable to initiate and maintain legal proceedings

The Attorney General may deem a person or persons unable to initiate and maintain appropriate legal proceedings within the meaning of subsection (a) of this section when such person or persons are unable, either directly or through other interested persons or organizations, to bear the expense of the litigation or to obtain effective legal representation; or whenever he is satisfied that the institution of such litigation would jeopardize the personal safety, employment, or economic standing of such person or persons, their families, or their property.

(c) "Parent" and "complaint" defined

The term "parent" as used in this section includes any person standing in loco parentis. A "complaint" as used in this section is a writing or document within the meaning of section 1001, Title 18.

42 U.S.C.A. § 2000d

UNITED STATES CODE ANNOTATED
TITLE 42. THE PUBLIC HEALTH AND WELFARE
CHAPTER 21—CIVIL RIGHTS
SUBCHAPTER V—FEDERALLY ASSISTED PROGRAMS

§ 2000d. Prohibition against exclusion from participation in, denial of benefits of, and discrimination under Federally assisted programs on ground of race, color, or national origin

No person in the United States shall, on the ground of race, color, or national origin, be excluded from participation in, be denied the benefits of, or be subjected to discrimination under any program or activity receiving Federal financial assistance.

42 U.S.C.A. § 2000d-1

UNITED STATES CODE ANNOTATED
TITLE 42. THE PUBLIC HEALTH AND WELFARE
CHAPTER 21—CIVIL RIGHTS
SUBCHAPTER V—FEDERALLY ASSISTED PROGRAMS

§ 2000d-1. Federal authority and financial assistance to programs or activities by way of grant, loan, or contract other than contract of insurance or guaranty; rules and regulations; approval by President; compliance with requirements; reports to Congressional committees; effective date of administrative action

Each Federal department and agency which is empowered to extend Federal financial assistance to any program or activity, by way of grant, loan, or contract other than a contract of insurance or guaranty, is authorized and directed to effectuate the provisions of section 2000d of this title with respect to such program or activity by issuing rules, regulations, or orders of general applicability which shall be consistent with achievement of the objectives of the statute authorizing the financial assistance in connection with which the action is taken. No such rule, regulation, or order shall become effective unless and until approved by the President. Compliance with any requirement adopted pursuant to this section may be effected (1) by the termination of or refusal to grant or to continue assistance under such program or activity to any recipient as to whom there has been an express finding on the record, after opportunity for hearing, of a failure to comply with such requirement, but such termination or refusal shall be limited to the particular political entity, or part thereof, or other recipient as to whom such a finding has been made and, shall be limited in its effect to the particular program, or part thereof, in which such noncompliance has been so found, or (2) by any other means authorized by law: Provided, however, That no such action shall be taken until the department or agency concerned has advised the appropriate person or persons of the failure to comply with the requirement and has determined that compliance cannot be secured by voluntary means. In the case of any action terminating, or refusing to grant or continue, assistance because of failure to comply with a requirement imposed pursuant to this section, the head of the Federal department or agency shall file with the committees of the House and Senate having legislative jurisdiction over the program or activity involved a full written report of the circumstances and the grounds for such action. No such action shall become effective until thirty days have elapsed after the filing of such report.

42 U.S.C.A. § 2000d-2

UNITED STATES CODE ANNOTATED
TITLE 42. THE PUBLIC HEALTH AND WELFARE
CHAPTER 21—CIVIL RIGHTS
SUBCHAPTER V—FEDERALLY ASSISTED PROGRAMS
§ 2000d-2. Judicial review; administrative procedure provisions

Any department or agency action taken pursuant to section 2000d-1 of this title shall be subject to such judicial review as may otherwise be provided by law for similar action taken by such department or agency on other grounds. In the case of action, not otherwise subject to judicial review, terminating or refusing to grant or to continue financial assistance upon a finding of failure to comply with any requirement imposed pursuant to section 2000d-1 of this title, any person aggrieved (including any State or political subdivision thereof and any agency of either) may obtain judicial review of such action in accordance with chapter 7 of Title 5, and such action shall not be deemed committed to unreviewable agency discretion within the meaning of that chapter.

42 U.S.C.A. § 2000d-3

UNITED STATES CODE ANNOTATED
TITLE 42. THE PUBLIC HEALTH AND WELFARE
CHAPTER 21—CIVIL RIGHTS
SUBCHAPTER V—FEDERALLY ASSISTED PROGRAMS
§ 2000d-3. Construction of provisions not to authorize administrative action with respect to employment practices except where primary objective of Federal financial assistance is to provide employment

Nothing contained in this subchapter shall be construed to authorize action under this subchapter by any department or agency with respect to any employment practice of any employer, employment agency, or labor organization except where a primary objective of the Federal financial assistance is to provide employment.

42 U.S.C.A. § 2000d-4

UNITED STATES CODE ANNOTATED
TITLE 42. THE PUBLIC HEALTH AND WELFARE
CHAPTER 21—CIVIL RIGHTS
SUBCHAPTER V—FEDERALLY ASSISTED PROGRAMS
§ 2000d-4. Federal authority and financial assistance to programs or activities by way of contract of insurance or guaranty

Nothing in this subchapter shall add to or detract from any existing authority with respect to any program or activity under which Federal financial assistance is extended by way of a contract of insurance or guaranty.

42 U.S.C.A. § 2000d-5

UNITED STATES CODE ANNOTATED
TITLE 42. THE PUBLIC HEALTH AND WELFARE
CHAPTER 21—CIVIL RIGHTS
SUBCHAPTER V—FEDERALLY ASSISTED PROGRAMS
§ 2000d-5. Prohibited deferral of action on applications by local educational agencies seeking federal Funds for alleged noncompliance with Civil Rights Act

The Secretary of Education shall not defer action or order action deferred on any application by a local educational agency for funds authorized to be appropriated by this Act, by the Elementary and Secondary Education Act of 1965 [20 U.S.C.A. § 6301 et seq.], by the Act of September 30, 1950 (Public Law 874, Eighty-first Congress), or by the Cooperative Research Act [20 U.S.C.A. § 331 et seq.], on the basis of alleged noncompliance with the provisions of this subchapter for more than sixty days after notice is given to such local agency of such deferral unless such local agency is given the opportunity for a hearing as provided in section 2000d-1 of this title, such hearing to be held within sixty days of such notice, unless the time for such hearing is extended by mutual consent of such local agency and the Secretary, and such deferral shall not continue for more than thirty days after the close of any such hearing unless there has been an express finding on the record of such hearing that such local educational agency has failed to comply with the provisions of this subchapter: Provided, That, for the purpose of determining whether a local educational agency is in compliance with this subchapter, compliance by such agency with a final order or judgment of a Federal court for the desegregation of the school or school system operated by such agency shall be deemed to be compliance with this subchapter, insofar as the matters covered in the order or judgment are concerned.

42 U.S.C.A. § 2000d-6

UNITED STATES CODE ANNOTATED
TITLE 42. THE PUBLIC HEALTH AND WELFARE
CHAPTER 21—CIVIL RIGHTS
SUBCHAPTER V—FEDERALLY ASSISTED PROGRAMS
§ 2000d-6. Policy of United States as to application of nondiscrimination provisions in schools of local educational agencies

(a) Declaration of uniform policy

It is the policy of the United States that guidelines and criteria established pursuant to title VI of the Civil Rights Act of 1964 [42 U.S.C.A. § 2000d et seq.] and section 182 of the Elementary and Secondary Education Amendments of 1966 [42 U.S.C.A. § 2000d-5] dealing with conditions of segregation by race, whether de jure or de facto, in the schools of the local educational agencies of any State shall be applied uniformly in all regions of the United States whatever the origin or cause of such segregation.

(b) Nature of uniformity

Such uniformity refers to one policy applied uniformly to de jure segregation wherever found and such other policy as may be provided pursuant to law applied uniformly to de facto segregation wherever found.

(c) Prohibition of construction for diminution of obligation for enforcement or compliance with nondiscrimination requirements

Nothing in this section shall be construed to diminish the obligation of responsible officials to enforce or comply with such guidelines and criteria in order to eliminate discrimination in federally assisted programs and activities as required by title VI of the Civil Rights Act of 1964 [42 U.S.C.A. § 2000d et seq.].

(d) Additional funds

It is the sense of the Congress that the Department of Justice and the Secretary of Education should request such additional funds as may be necessary to apply the policy set forth in this section throughout the United States.

42 U.S.C.A. 1981

UNITED STATES CODE ANNOTATED
TITLE 42. THE PUBLIC HEALTH AND WELFARE
CHAPTER 21—CIVIL RIGHTS
GENERALLY
§ 1981. Equal Rights Under the Law

(a) Statement of equal rights

All persons within the jurisdiction of the United States shall have the same right in every State and Territory to make and enforce contracts, to sue, be parties, give evidence, and to the full and equal benefit of all laws and proceedings for the security of persons and property as is enjoyed by white citizens, and shall be subject to like punishment, pains, penalties, taxes, licenses, and exactions of every kind, and to no other.

(b) "Make and enforce contracts" defined

For purposes of this section, the term "make and enforce contracts" includes the making, performance, modification, and termination of contracts, and the enjoyment of all benefits, privileges, terms, and conditions of the contractual relationship.

(c) Protection against impairment

The rights protected by this section are protected against impairment by non-governmental discrimination and impairment under color of State law.

42 U.S.C.A. 1983

SUBCHAPTER I—GENERALLY
§ 1983. Civil action for deprivation of rights
Every person who, under color of any statute, ordinance, regulation, custom, or usage, of any State or Territory or the District of Columbia, subjects, or

causes to be subjected, any citizen of the United States or other person within the jurisdiction thereof to the deprivation of any rights, privileges, or immunities secured by the Constitution and laws, shall be liable to the party injured in an action at law, suit in equity, or other proper proceeding for redress, except that in any action brought against a judicial officer for an act or omission taken in such officer's judicial capacity, injunctive relief shall not be granted unless a declaratory decree was violated or declaratory relief was unavailable. For the purposes of this section, any Act of Congress applicable exclusively to the District of Columbia shall be considered to be a statute of the District of Columbia.

42 U.S.C.A. § 1985

UNITED STATES CODE ANNOTATED
TITLE 42. THE PUBLIC HEALTH AND WELFARE
CHAPTER 21—CIVIL RIGHTS
SUBCHAPTER I—GENERALLY
§ 1985. Conspiracy to interfere with civil rights

(1) Preventing officer from performing duties

If two or more persons in any State or Territory conspire to prevent, by force, intimidation, or threat, any person from accepting or holding any office, trust, or place of confidence under the United States, or from discharging any duties thereof; or to induce by like means any officer of the United States to leave any State, district, or place, where his duties as an officer are required to be performed, or to injure him in his person or property on account of his lawful discharge of the duties of his office, or while engaged in the lawful discharge thereof, or to injure his property so as to molest, interrupt, hinder, or impede him in the discharge of his official duties;

(2) Obstructing justice; intimidating party, witness, or juror

If two or more persons in any State or Territory conspire to deter, by force, intimidation, or threat, any party or witness in any court of the United States from attending such court, or from testifying to any matter pending therein, freely, fully, and truthfully, or to injure such party or witness in his person or property on account of his having so attended or testified, or to influence the verdict, presentment, or indictment of any grand or petit juror in any such court, or to injure such juror in his person or property on account of any verdict, presentment, or indictment lawfully assented to by him, or of his being or having been such juror; or if two or more persons conspire for the purpose of impeding, hindering, obstructing, or defeating, in any manner, the due course of justice in any State or Territory, with intent to deny to any citizen the equal protection of the laws, or to injure him or his property for lawfully enforcing, or attempting to enforce, the right of any person, or class of persons, to the equal protection of the laws;

(3) Depriving persons of rights or privileges

If two or more persons in any State or Territory conspire or go in disguise on the highway or on the premises of another, for the purpose of depriving, either directly or indirectly, any person or class of persons of the equal protection of the laws, or of equal privileges and immunities under the laws; or for the purpose of preventing or hindering the constituted authorities of any State or Territory from giving or securing to all persons within such State or Territory the equal protection of the laws; or if two or more persons conspire to prevent by force, intimidation, or threat, any citizen who is lawfully entitled to vote, from giving his support or advocacy in a legal manner, toward or in favor of the election of any lawfully qualified person as an elector for President or Vice President, or as a Member of Congress of the United States; or to injure any citizen in person or property on account of such support or advocacy; in any case of conspiracy set forth in this section, if one or more persons engaged therein do, or cause to be done, any act in furtherance of the object of such conspiracy, whereby another is injured in his person or property, or deprived of having and exercising any right or privilege of a citizen of the United States, the party so injured or deprived may have an action for the recovery of damages occasioned by such injury or deprivation, against any one or more of the conspirators.

28 U.S.C.A. § 1251

UNITED STATES CODE ANNOTATED
TITLE 28. JUDICIARY AND JUDICIAL PROCEDURE
PART IV—JURISDICTION AND VENUE
CHAPTER 81—SUPREME COURT
§ 1251. Original jurisdiction

(a) The Supreme Court shall have original and exclusive jurisdiction of all controversies between two or more States.

(b) The Supreme Court shall have original but not exclusive jurisdiction of:

(1) All actions or proceedings to which ambassadors, other public ministers, consuls, or vice consuls of foreign states are parties;

(2) All controversies between the United States and a State;

(3) All actions or proceedings by a State against the citizens of another State or against aliens.

28 U.S.C.A. § 1253

UNITED STATES CODE ANNOTATED
TITLE 28. JUDICIARY AND JUDICIAL PROCEDURE
PART IV—JURISDICTION AND VENUE
CHAPTER 81—SUPREME COURT
§ 1253. Direct appeals from decisions of three-judge courts

Except as otherwise provided by law, any party may appeal to the Supreme Court from an order granting or denying, after notice and hearing, an interlocutory or permanent injunction in any civil action, suit or proceeding required by any Act of Congress to be heard and determined by a district court of three judges.

28 U.S.C.A. § 1254

UNITED STATES CODE ANNOTATED
TITLE 28. JUDICIARY AND JUDICIAL PROCEDURE
PART IV—JURISDICTION AND VENUE
CHAPTER 81—SUPREME COURT
§ 1254. Courts of appeals; certiorari; certified questions

Cases in the courts of appeals may be reviewed by the Supreme Court by the following methods:

(1) By writ of certiorari granted upon the petition of any party to any civil or criminal case, before or after rendition of judgment or decree;

(2) By certification at any time by a court of appeals of any question of law in any civil or criminal case as to which instructions are desired, and upon such certification the Supreme Court may give binding instructions

or require the entire record to be sent up for decision of the entire matter in controversy.

28 U.S.C.A. § 1257

UNITED STATES CODE ANNOTATED
TITLE 28. JUDICIARY AND JUDICIAL PROCEDURE
PART IV—JURISDICTION AND VENUE
CHAPTER 81—SUPREME COURT
§ 1257. State courts; certiorari
(a) Final judgments or decrees rendered by the highest court of a State in which a decision could be had, may be reviewed by the Supreme Court by writ of certiorari where the validity of a treaty or statute of the United States is drawn in question or where the validity of a statute of any State is drawn in question on the ground of its being repugnant to the Constitution, treaties, or laws of the United States, or where any title, right, privilege, or immunity is specially set up or claimed under the Constitution or the treaties or statutes of, or any commission held or authority exercised under, the United States.

(b) For the purposes of this section, the term "highest court of a State" includes the District of Columbia Court of Appeals.

29 U.S.C.A. § 141

UNITED STATES CODE ANNOTATED
TITLE 29. LABOR
CHAPTER 7—LABOR-MANAGEMENT RELATIONS
SUBCHAPTER I—GENERAL PROVISIONS
§ 141. Short title; Congressional declaration of purpose and policy

(a) This chapter may be cited as the "Labor Management Relations Act, 1947".

(b) Industrial strife which interferes with the normal flow of commerce and with the full production of articles and commodities for commerce, can be avoided or substantially minimized if employers, employees, and labor organizations each recognize under law one another's legitimate rights in their relations with each other, and above all recognize under law that neither party has any right in its relations with any other to engage in acts or practices which jeopardize the public health, safety, or interest.

It is the purpose and policy of this chapter, in order to promote the full flow of commerce, to prescribe the legitimate rights of both employees and employers in their relations affecting commerce, to provide orderly and peaceful procedures for preventing the interference by either with the legitimate rights of the other, to protect the rights of individual employees in their relations with labor organizations whose activities affect commerce, to define and proscribe practices on the part of labor and management which affect commerce and are inimical to the general welfare, and to protect the rights of the public in connection with labor disputes affecting commerce.

18 U.S.C.A. § 3551

UNITED STATES CODE ANNOTATED
TITLE 18. CRIMES AND CRIMINAL PROCEDURE
PART II—CRIMINAL PROCEDURE
CHAPTER 227—SENTENCES
SUBCHAPTER A—GENERAL PROVISIONS
§ 3551. Authorized sentences

(a) In general.—Except as otherwise specifically provided, a defendant who has been found guilty of an offense described in any Federal statute, including sections 13 and 1153 of this title, other than an Act of Congress applicable exclusively in the District of Columbia or the Uniform Code of Military Justice, shall be sentenced in accordance with the provisions of this chapter so as to achieve the purposes set forth in subparagraphs (A) through (D) of section 3553(a)(2) to the extent that they are applicable in light of all the circumstances of the case.

(b) Individuals.—An individual found guilty of an offense shall be sentenced, in accordance with the provisions of section 3553, to—

> (1) a term of probation as authorized by subchapter B;

> (2) a fine as authorized by subchapter C; or

> (3) a term of imprisonment as authorized by subchapter D.

A sentence to pay a fine may be imposed in addition to any other sentence. A sanction authorized by section 3554, 3555, or 3556 may be imposed in addition to the sentence required by this subsection.

(c) Organizations.—An organization found guilty of an offense shall be sentenced, in accordance with the provisions of section 3553, to—

> (1) a term of probation as authorized by subchapter B; or

> (2) a fine as authorized by subchapter C.

A sentence to pay a fine may be imposed in addition to a sentence to probation. A sanction authorized by section 3554, 3555, or 3556 may be imposed in addition to the sentence required by this subsection.

28 U.S.C.A. § 991

UNITED STATES CODE ANNOTATED
TITLE 28. JUDICIARY AND JUDICIAL PROCEDURE
PART III—COURT OFFICERS AND EMPLOYEES
CHAPTER 58—UNITED STATES SENTENCING COMMISSION
§ 991. United States Sentencing Commission; establishment and purposes

(a) There is established as an independent commission in the judicial branch of the United States a United States Sentencing Commission which shall consist of seven voting members and one nonvoting member. The President, after consultation with representatives of judges, prosecuting attorneys, defense attorneys, law enforcement officials, senior citizens, victims of crime, and others interested in the criminal justice process, shall appoint the voting members of the Commission, by and with the advice and consent of the Senate, one of whom shall be appointed, by and with the advice and consent of the Senate, as the Chair and three of whom shall be designated by the President as Vice Chairs. Not more than 3 of the members shall be Federal judges selected after considering a list of six judges recommended to the President by the Judicial Conference of the United States. Not more than four of the members of the Commission shall be members of the same political party, and of the three Vice Chairs, no more than two shall be members of the same political party. The Attorney General, or the Attorney General's designee, shall be an ex officio, nonvoting member of the Commission. The Chair, Vice Chairs, and members of the Commission shall be subject to removal from the Commission by the President only for neglect of duty or malfeasance in office or for other good cause shown.

(b) The purposes of the United States Sentencing Commission are to—

> (1) establish sentencing policies and practices for the Federal criminal justice system that—

(A) assure the meeting of the purposes of sentencing as set forth in section 3553(a)(2) of title 18, United States Code;

(B) provide certainty and fairness in meeting the purposes of sentencing, avoiding unwarranted sentencing disparities among defendants with similar records who have been found guilty of similar criminal conduct while maintaining sufficient flexibility to permit individualized sentences when warranted by mitigating or aggravating factors not taken into account in the establishment of general sentencing practices; and

(C) reflect, to the extent practicable, advancement in knowledge of human behavior as it relates to the criminal justice process; and

(2) develop means of measuring the degree to which the sentencing, penal, and correctional practices are effective in meeting the purposes of sentencing as set forth in section 3553(a)(2) of title 18, United States Code.

28 U.S.C.A. § 992

UNITED STATES CODE ANNOTATED
TITLE 28. JUDICIARY AND JUDICIAL PROCEDURE
PART III—COURT OFFICERS AND EMPLOYEES
CHAPTER 58—UNITED STATES SENTENCING COMMISSION
§ 992. Terms of office; compensation

(a) The voting members of the United States Sentencing Commission shall be appointed for six-year terms, except that the initial terms of the first members of the Commission shall be staggered so that—

(1) two members, including the Chair, serve terms of six years;

(2) three members serve terms of four years; and

(3) two members serve terms of two years.

(b)(1) Subject to paragraph (2)—

(A) no voting member of the Commission may serve more than two full terms; and

(B) a voting member appointed to fill a vacancy that occurs before the expiration of the term for which a predecessor was appointed shall be appointed only for the remainder of such term.

(2) A voting member of the Commission whose term has expired may continue to serve until the earlier of—

(A) the date on which a successor has taken office; or

(B) the date on which the Congress adjourns sine die to end the session of Congress that commences after the date on which the member's term expired.

(C) The Chair and Vice Chairs of the Commission shall hold full-time positions and shall be compensated during their terms of office at the annual rate at which judges of the United States courts of appeals are compensated. The voting members of the Commission, other than the Chair and Vice Chairs, shall hold full-time positions until the end of the first six years after the sentencing guidelines go into effect pursuant to section 235(a)(1)(B)(ii) of the Sentencing Reform Act of 1984, and shall be compensated at the annual rate at which judges of the United States courts of appeals are compensated. Thereafter, the voting members of the Commission, other than the Chair and Vice Chairs shall hold part-time positions and shall be paid at the daily rate at which judges of the United States courts of appeals are compensated. A Federal judge may serve as a member of the Commission without resigning the judge's appointment as a Federal judge.

(D) Sections 44(c) and 134(b) of this title (relating to the residence of judges) do not apply to any judge holding a full-time position on the Commission under subsection (c) of this section.

28 U.S.C.A. § 993

UNITED STATES CODE ANNOTATED
TITLE 28. JUDICIARY AND JUDICIAL PROCEDURE
PART III—COURT OFFICERS AND EMPLOYEES
CHAPTER 58—UNITED STATES SENTENCING COMMISSION
§ 993. Powers and duties of Chair

The Chair shall—

(a) call and preside at meetings of the Commission, which shall be held for at least two weeks in each quarter after the members of the Commission hold part-time positions; and

(b) direct—

(1) the preparation of requests for appropriations for the Commission; and

(2) the use of funds made available to the Commission.

28 U.S.C.A. § 994

UNITED STATES CODE ANNOTATED
TITLE 28. JUDICIARY AND JUDICIAL PROCEDURE
PART III—COURT OFFICERS AND EMPLOYEES
CHAPTER 58—UNITED STATES SENTENCING COMMISSION
§ 994. Duties of the Commission

(a) The Commission, by affirmative vote of at least four members of the Commission, and pursuant to its rules and regulations and consistent with all pertinent provisions of any Federal statute shall promulgate and distribute to all courts of the United States and to the United States Probation System—

(1) guidelines, as described in this section, for use of a sentencing court in determining the sentence to be imposed in a criminal case, including—

(A) a determination whether to impose a sentence to probation, a fine, or a term of imprisonment;

(B) a determination as to the appropriate amount of a fine or the appropriate length of a term of probation or a term of imprisonment;

(C) a determination whether a sentence to a term of imprisonment should include a requirement that the defendant be placed on a term of supervised release after imprisonment, and, if so, the appropriate length of such a term;

(D) a determination whether multiple sentences to terms of imprisonment should be ordered to run concurrently or consecutively; and

(E) a determination under paragraphs (6) and (11) of section 3563(b) of title 18;

(2) general policy statements regarding application of the guidelines or any other aspect of sentencing or sentence implementation that in the view of the Commission would further the purposes set forth in section 3553(a)(2) of title 18, United States Code, including the appropriate use of—

(A) the sanctions set forth in sections 3554, 3555, and 3556 of title 18;

(B) the conditions of probation and supervised release set forth in sections 3563(b) and 3583(d) of title 18;

(C) the sentence modification provisions set forth in sections 3563(c), 3564, 3573, and 3582(c) of title 18;

(D) the fine imposition provisions set forth in section 3572 of title 18;

(E) the authority granted under rule 11(e)(2) of the Federal Rules of Criminal Procedure to accept or reject a plea agreement entered into pursuant to rule 11(e)(1); and

(F) the temporary release provisions set forth in section 3622 of title 18, and the prerelease custody provisions set forth in section 3624(c) of title 18; and

(3) guidelines or general policy statements regarding the appropriate use of the provisions for revocation of probation set forth in section 3565 of title 18, and the provisions for modification of the term or conditions of supervised release and revocation of supervised release set forth in section 3583(e) of title 18.

(b) (1) The Commission, in the guidelines promulgated pursuant to subsection (a)(1), shall, for each category of offense involving each category of defendant, establish a sentencing range that is consistent with all pertinent provisions of title 18, United States Code.

(2) If a sentence specified by the guidelines includes a term of imprisonment, the maximum of the range established for such a term shall not exceed the minimum of that range by more than the greater of 25 percent or 6 months, except that, if the minimum term of the range is 30 years or more, the maximum may be life imprisonment.

(c) The Commission, in establishing categories of offenses for use in the guidelines and policy statements governing the imposition of sentences of probation, a fine, or imprisonment, governing the imposition of other authorized sanctions, governing the size of a fine or the length of a term of probation, imprisonment, or supervised release, and governing the conditions of probation, supervised release, or imprisonment, shall consider whether the following matters, among others, have any relevance to the nature, extent, place of service, or other incidents of an appropriate sentence, and shall take them into account only to the extent that they do have relevance—

(1) the grade of the offense;

(2) the circumstances under which the offense was committed which mitigate or aggravate the seriousness of the offense;

(3) the nature and degree of the harm caused by the offense, including whether it involved property, irreplaceable property, a person, a number of persons, or a breach of public trust;

(4) the community view of the gravity of the offense;

(5) the public concern generated by the offense;

(6) the deterrent effect a particular sentence may have on the commission of the offense by others; and

(7) the current incidence of the offense in the community and in the Nation as a whole.

(d) The Commission in establishing categories of defendants for use in the guidelines and policy statements governing the imposition of sentences of probation, a fine, or imprisonment, governing the imposition of other authorized sanctions, governing the size of a fine or the length of a term of probation, imprisonment, or supervised release, and governing the conditions of probation, supervised release, or imprisonment, shall consider whether the following matters, among others, with respect to a defendant, have any relevance to the nature, extent, place of service, or other incidents of an appropriate sentence, and shall take them into account only to the extent that they do have relevance—

(1) age;

(2) education;

(3) vocational skills;

(4) mental and emotional condition to the extent that such condition mitigates the defendant's culpability or to the extent that such condition is otherwise plainly relevant;

(5) physical condition, including drug dependence;

(6) previous employment record;

(7) family ties and responsibilities;

(8) community ties;

(9) role in the offense;

(10) criminal history; and

(11) degree of dependence upon criminal activity for a livelihood.

The Commission shall assure that the guidelines and policy statements are entirely neutral as to the race, sex, national origin, creed, and socioeconomic status of offenders.

(e) The Commission shall assure that the guidelines and policy statements, in recommending a term of imprisonment or length of a term of imprisonment, reflect the general inappropriateness of considering the education, vocational skills, employment record, family ties and responsibilities, and community ties of the defendant.

(f) The Commission, in promulgating guidelines pursuant to subsection (a)(1), shall promote the purposes set forth in section 991(b)(1), with particular attention to the requirements of subsection 991(b)(1)(B) for providing certainty and fairness in sentencing and reducing unwarranted sentence disparities.

(g) The Commission, in promulgating guidelines pursuant to subsection (a)(1) to meet the purposes of sentencing as set forth in section 3553(a)(2) of title 18, United States Code, shall take into account the nature and capacity of the penal, correctional, and other facilities and services available, and shall make recommendations concerning any change or expansion in the nature or capacity of such facilities and services that might become necessary as a result of the guidelines promulgated pursuant to the provisions of this chapter. The sentencing guidelines prescribed under this chapter shall be formulated to minimize the likelihood that the Federal prison population will exceed the capacity of the Federal prisons, as determined by the Commission.

(h) The Commission shall assure that the guidelines specify a sentence to a term of imprisonment at or near the maximum term authorized for categories of defendants in which the defendant is eighteen years old or older and—

(1) has been convicted of a felony that is—

(A) a crime of violence; or

(B) an offense described in section 401 of the Controlled Substances Act (21 U.S.C. 841), sections 1002(a), 1005, and 1009 of the Controlled Substances Import and Export Act (21 U.S.C. 952(a), 955, and 959), and the Maritime Drug Law Enforcement Act (46 U.S.C. App. 1901 et seq.); and

(2) has previously been convicted of two or more prior felonies, each of which is—

(A) a crime of violence; or

(B) an offense described in section 401 of the Controlled Substances Act (21 U.S.C. 841), sections 1002(a), 1005, and 1009 of the Controlled Substances Import and Export Act (21 U.S.C. 952(a), 955, and 959), and the Maritime Drug Law Enforcement Act (46 U.S.C. App. 1901 et seq.).

(i) The Commission shall assure that the guidelines specify a sentence to a substantial term of imprisonment for categories of defendants in which the defendant—

(1) has a history of two or more prior Federal, State, or local felony convictions for offenses committed on different occasions;

(2) committed the offense as part of a pattern of criminal conduct from which the defendant derived a substantial portion of the defendant's income;

(3) committed the offense in furtherance of a conspiracy with three or more persons engaging in a pattern of racketeering activity in which the defendant participated in a managerial or supervisory capacity;

(4) committed a crime of violence that constitutes a felony while on release pending trial, sentence, or appeal from a Federal, State, or local felony for which he was ultimately convicted; or

(5) committed a felony that is set forth in section 401 or 1010 of the Comprehensive Drug Abuse Prevention and Control Act of 1970 (21 U.S.C. 841 and 960), and that involved trafficking in a substantial quantity of a controlled substance.

(j) The Commission shall insure that the guidelines reflect the general appropriateness of imposing a sentence other than imprisonment in cases in which the defendant is a first offender who has not been convicted of a crime of violence or an otherwise serious offense, and the general appropriateness of imposing a term of imprisonment on a person convicted of a crime of violence that results in serious bodily injury.

(k) The Commission shall insure that the guidelines reflect the inappropriateness of imposing a sentence to a term of imprisonment for the purpose of rehabilitating the defendant or providing the defendant with needed educational or vocational training, medical care, or other correctional treatment.

(l) The Commission shall insure that the guidelines promulgated pursuant to subsection (a)(1) reflect—

(1) the appropriateness of imposing an incremental penalty for each offense in a case in which a defendant is convicted of—

(A) multiple offenses committed in the same course of conduct that result in the exercise of ancillary jurisdiction over one or more of the offenses; and

(B) multiple offenses committed at different times, including those cases in which the subsequent offense is a violation of section 3146 (penalty for failure to appear) or is committed while the person is released pursuant to the provisions of section 3147 (penalty for an offense committed while on release) of title 18; and

(2) the general inappropriateness of imposing consecutive terms of imprisonment for an offense of conspiring to commit an offense or soliciting commission of an offense and for an offense that was the sole object of the conspiracy or solicitation.

(m) The Commission shall insure that the guidelines reflect the fact that, in many cases, current sentences do not accurately reflect the seriousness of the offense. This will require that, as a starting point in its development of the initial sets of guidelines for particular categories of cases, the Commission ascertain the average sentences imposed in such categories of cases prior to the creation of the Commission, and in cases involving sentences to terms of imprisonment, the length of such terms actually served. The Commission shall not be bound by such average sentences, and shall independently develop a sentencing range that is consistent with the purposes of sentencing described in section 3553(a)(2) of title 18, United States Code.

(n) The Commission shall assure that the guidelines reflect the general appropriateness of imposing a lower sentence than would otherwise be imposed, including a sentence that is lower than that established by statute as a minimum sentence, to take into account a defendant's substantial assistance in the investigation or prosecution of another person who has committed an offense.

(o) The Commission periodically shall review and revise, in consideration of comments and data coming to its attention, the guidelines promulgated pursuant to the provisions of this section. In fulfilling its duties and in exercising its powers, the Commission shall consult with authorities on, and individual and institutional representatives of, various aspects of the Federal criminal justice system. The United States Probation System, the Bureau of Prisons, the Judicial Conference of the United States, the Criminal Division of the United States Department of Justice, and a representative of the Federal Public Defenders shall submit to the Commission any observations, comments, or questions pertinent to the work of the Commission whenever they believe such communication would be useful, and shall, at least annually, submit to the Commission a written report commenting on the operation of the Commission's guidelines, suggesting changes in the guidelines that appear to be warranted, and otherwise assessing the Commission's work.

(p) The Commission, at or after the beginning of a regular session of Congress, but not later than the first day of May, may promulgate under subsection (a) of this section and submit to Congress amendments to the guidelines and modifications to previously submitted amendments that have not taken effect, including modifications to the effective dates of such amendments. Such an amendment or modification shall be accompanied by a statement of the reasons therefore and shall take effect on a date specified by the Commission, which shall be no earlier than 180 days after being so submitted and no later than the first day of November of the calendar year in which the amendment or modification is submitted, except to the extent that the effective date is revised or the amendment is otherwise modified or disapproved by Act of Congress.

(q) The Commission and the Bureau of Prisons shall submit to Congress an analysis and recommendations concerning maximum utilization of resources to deal effectively with the Federal prison population. Such report shall be based upon consideration of a variety of alternatives, including—

(1) modernization of existing facilities;

(2) inmate classification and periodic review of such classification for use in placing inmates in the least restrictive facility necessary to ensure adequate security; and

(3) use of existing Federal facilities, such as those currently within military jurisdiction.

(r) The Commission, not later than two years after the initial set of sentencing guidelines promulgated under subsection (a) goes into effect, and thereafter whenever it finds it advisable, shall recommend to the Congress that it raise or lower the grades, or otherwise modify the maximum penalties, of those offenses for which such an adjustment appears appropriate.

(s) The Commission shall give due consideration to any petition filed by a defendant requesting modification of the guidelines utilized in the sentencing of such defendant, on the basis of changed circumstances unrelated to the defendant, including changes in—

(1) the community view of the gravity of the offense;

(2) the public concern generated by the offense; and

(3) the deterrent effect particular sentences may have on the commission of the offense by others.

(t) The Commission, in promulgating general policy statements regarding the sentencing modification provisions in section 3582(c)(1)(A) of title 18, shall describe what should be considered extraordinary and compelling reasons for sentence reduction, including the criteria to be applied and a list of specific examples. Rehabilitation of the defendant alone shall not be considered an extraordinary and compelling reason.

(u) If the Commission reduces the term of imprisonment recommended in the guidelines applicable to a particular offense or category of offenses, it shall specify in what circumstances and by what amount the sentences of prisoners serving terms of imprisonment for the offense may be reduced.

(v) The Commission shall ensure that the general policy statements promulgated pursuant to subsection (a)(2) include a policy limiting consecutive terms of imprisonment for an offense involving a violation of a general prohibition and for an offense involving a violation of a specific prohibition encompassed within the general prohibition.

(w)(1) The Chief Judge of each district court shall ensure that, within 30 days following entry of judgment in every criminal case, the sentencing court submits to the Commission a written report of the sentence, the offense for which it is imposed, the age, race, sex of the offender, and information regarding factors made relevant by the guidelines. The report shall also include—

(A) the judgment and commitment order;

(B) the statement of reasons for the sentence imposed (which shall include the reason for any departure from the otherwise applicable guideline range);

(C) any plea agreement;

(D) the indictment or other charging document;

(E) the presentence report; and

(F) any other information as the Commission finds appropriate.

(2) The Commission shall, upon request, make available to the House and Senate Committees on the Judiciary, the written reports and all underlying records accompanying those reports described in this section, as well as other records received from courts.

(3) The Commission shall submit to Congress at least annually an analysis of these documents, any recommendations for legislation that the Commission concludes is warranted by that analysis, and an accounting of those districts that the Commission believes have not submitted the appropriate information and documents required by this section.

(4) The Commission shall make available to the Attorney General, upon request, such data files as the Commission may assemble or maintain in electronic form that include any information submitted under paragraph (1). Such data files shall be made available in electronic form and shall include all data fields requested, including the identity of the sentencing judge.

(x) The provisions of section 553 of title 5, relating to publication in the Federal Register and public hearing procedure, shall apply to the promulgation of guidelines pursuant to this section.

(y) The Commission, in promulgating guidelines pursuant to subsection (a)(1), may include, as a component of a fine, the expected costs to the Government of any imprisonment, supervised release, or probation sentence that is ordered.

28 U.S.C.A. § 995

UNITED STATES CODE ANNOTATED
TITLE 28. JUDICIARY AND JUDICIAL PROCEDURE
PART III—COURT OFFICERS AND EMPLOYEES
CHAPTER 58—UNITED STATES SENTENCING COMMISSION
§ 995. Powers of the Commission
(a) The Commission, by vote of a majority of the members present and voting, shall have the power to—

(1) establish general policies and promulgate such rules and regulations for the Commission as are necessary to carry out the purposes of this chapter;

(2) appoint and fix the salary and duties of the Staff Director of the Sentencing Commission, who shall serve at the discretion of the Commission and who shall be compensated at a rate not to exceed the highest rate now or hereafter prescribed for Level 6 of the Senior Executive Service Schedule (5 U.S.C. 5382);

(3) deny, revise, or ratify any request for regular, supplemental, or deficiency appropriations prior to any submission of such request to the Office of Management and Budget by the Chair;

(4) procure for the Commission temporary and intermittent services to the same extent as is authorized by section 3109(b) of title 5, United States Code;

(5) utilize, with their consent, the services, equipment, personnel, information, and facilities of other Federal, State, local, and private agencies and instrumentalities with or without reimbursement therefor;

(6) without regard to 31 U.S.C. 3324, enter into and perform such contracts, leases, cooperative agreements, and other transactions as may be necessary in the conduct of the functions of the Commission, with any public agency, or with any person, firm, association, corporation, educational institution, or non- profit organization;

(7) accept and employ, in carrying out the provisions of this title, voluntary and uncompensated services, notwithstanding the provisions of 31 U.S.C. 1342, however, individuals providing such services shall not be considered Federal employees except for purposes of chapter 81 of title 5, United States Code, with respect to job-incurred disability and title 28, United States Code, with respect to tort claims;

(8) request such information, data, and reports from any Federal agency or judicial officer as the Commission may from time to time require and as may be produced consistent with other law;

(9) monitor the performance of probation officers with regard to sentencing recommendations, including application of the Sentencing Commission guidelines and policy statements;

(10) issue instructions to probation officers concerning the application of Commission guidelines and policy statements;

(11) arrange with the head of any other Federal agency for the performance by such agency of any function of the Commission, with or without reimbursement;

(12) establish a research and development program within the Commission for the purpose of—

(A) serving as a clearinghouse and information center for the collection, preparation, and dissemination of information on Federal sentencing practices; and

(B) assisting and serving in a consulting capacity to Federal courts, departments, and agencies in the development, maintenance, and coordination of sound sentencing practices;

(13) collect systematically the data obtained from studies, research, and the empirical experience of public and private agencies concerning the sentencing process;

(14) publish data concerning the sentencing process;

(15) collect systematically and disseminate information concerning sentences actually imposed, and the relationship of such sentences to the factors set forth in section 3553(a) of title 18, United States Code;

(16) collect systematically and disseminate information regarding effectiveness of sentences imposed;

(17) devise and conduct, in various geographical locations, seminars and workshops providing continuing studies for persons engaged in the sentencing field;

(18) devise and conduct periodic training programs of instruction in sentencing techniques for judicial and probation personnel and other persons connected with the sentencing process;

(19) study the feasibility of developing guidelines for the disposition of juvenile delinquents;

(20) make recommendations to Congress concerning modification or enactment of statutes relating to sentencing, penal, and correctional matters that the Commission finds to be necessary and advisable to carry out an effective, humane and rational sentencing policy;

(21) hold hearings and call witnesses that might assist the Commission in the exercise of its powers or duties;

(22) perform such other functions as are required to permit Federal courts to meet their responsibilities under section 3553(a) of title 18, United States Code, and to permit others involved in the Federal criminal justice system to meet their related responsibilities;

(23) retain private attorneys to provide legal advice to the Commission in the conduct of its work, or to appear for or represent the Commission in any case in which the Commission is authorized by law to represent itself, or in which the Commission is representing itself with the consent of the Department of Justice; and the Commission may in its discretion pay reasonable attorney's fees to private attorneys employed by it out of its appropriated funds. When serving as officers or employees of the United States, such private attorneys shall be considered special government employees as defined in section 202(a) of title 18; and

(24) grant incentive awards to its employees pursuant to chapter 45 of title 5, United States Code.

(b) The Commission shall have such other powers and duties and shall perform such other functions as may be necessary to carry out the purposes of this chapter, and may delegate to any member or designated person such powers as may be appropriate other than the power to establish general policy statements and guidelines pursuant to section 994(a)(1) and (2), the issuance of general policies and promulgation of rules and regulations pursuant to subsection (a)(1) of this section, and the decisions as to the factors to be considered in establishment of categories of offenses and offenders pursuant to section 994(b). The Commission shall, with respect to its activities under subsections (a)(9), (a)(10), (a)(11), (a)(12), (a)(13), (a)(14), (a)(15), (a)(16), (a)(17), and (a)(18), to the extent practicable, utilize existing resources of the Administrative Office of the United States Courts and the Federal Judicial Center for the purpose of avoiding unnecessary duplication.

(c) Upon the request of the Commission, each Federal agency is authorized and directed to make its services, equipment, personnel, facilities, and information available to the greatest practicable extent to the Commission in the execution of its functions.

(d) A simple majority of the membership then serving shall constitute a quorum for the conduct of business. Other than for the promulgation of guidelines and policy statements pursuant to section 994, the Commission may exercise its powers and fulfill its duties by the vote of a simple majority of the members present.

(e) Except as otherwise provided by law, the Commission shall maintain and make available for public inspection a record of the final vote of each member on any action taken by it.

28 U.S.C.A. § 996

UNITED STATES CODE ANNOTATED
TITLE 28. JUDICIARY AND JUDICIAL PROCEDURE
PART III—COURT OFFICERS AND EMPLOYEES
CHAPTER 58—UNITED STATES SENTENCING COMMISSION
§ 996. Director and staff

(a) The Staff Director shall supervise the activities of persons employed by the Commission and perform other duties assigned to the Staff Director by the Commission.

(b) The Staff Director shall, subject to the approval of the Commission, appoint such officers and employees as are necessary in the execution of the functions of the Commission. The officers and employees of the Commission shall be exempt from the provisions of part III of title 5, except the following: chapters 45 (Incentive Awards), 63 (Leave), 81 (Compensation for Work Injuries), 83 (Retirement), 85 (Unemployment Compensation), 87 (Life Insurance), and 89 (Health Insurance), and subchapter VI of chapter 55 (Payment for accumulated and accrued leave).

28 U.S.C.A. § 997

UNITED STATES CODE ANNOTATED
TITLE 28. JUDICIARY AND JUDICIAL PROCEDURE
PART III—COURT OFFICERS AND EMPLOYEES
CHAPTER 58—UNITED STATES SENTENCING COMMISSION
§ 997. Annual report

The Commission shall report annually to the Judicial Conference of the United States, the Congress, and the President of the United States on the activities of the Commission.

28 U.S.C.A. § 998

UNITED STATES CODE ANNOTATED
TITLE 28. JUDICIARY AND JUDICIAL PROCEDURE

PART III—COURT OFFICERS AND EMPLOYEES
CHAPTER 58—UNITED STATES SENTENCING COMMISSION
§ 998. Definitions

As used in this chapter—

(a) "Commission" means the United States Sentencing Commission;

(b) "Commissioner" means a member of the United States Sentencing Commission;

(c) "guidelines" means the guidelines promulgated by the Commission pursuant to section 994(a) of this title; and

(d) "rules and regulations" means rules and regulations promulgated by the Commission pursuant to section 995 of this title.

Appendix C

Reading and Briefing Cases

Introduction

Learning a few things about the case and its various components will assist the student in understanding how to read and brief the case. Since case briefing is an integral part of studying the law, it is important for the student to understand what the components of a case are and why they are part of the overall case. To begin, it is important to understand the title and citation of the case. Consider the following:

Loving v. Virginia, 388 U.S. 1 (1967).

This is called the **style** or the name of the case. It consists of the last name of the first plaintiff (if there is more than one) and the last name of the first defendant. In this instance, the plaintiffs were Richard Loving and Mildred Loving and the defendant was the State of Virginia. Following the names of the parties is the citation of the case. The citation consists of a combination of numbers and letters. The first number, 388 in this example, is the volume number of the set of books in which this case can be found. Following the volume number is the abbreviation for the name of the set of books containing the opinion. In this example, the letters, U.S., stand for the *United States Reports,* the official, government-published set of books containing the opinions of the United States Supreme Court. After the abbreviation for the reporter is another number, which refers to the page number where the case can be found, or in this case, page 1. So, to summarize, the case of *Loving v. Virginia* can be found in volume 388 of the *United States Reports,* page 1.

Components of the Case

The case begins with some supplementary material that is not binding or authoritative. The first component after the style is the **caption**. This is a second reciting of the parties to the case, but this time, instead of just the last names of the first plaintiff and defendant, the caption contains the full names of all parties, including multiple plaintiffs and defendants. The caption indicates not only who are plaintiffs and defendants, but also notes which party is the appellant (the party who is appealing the case) and which party is the appellee (the party who is responding to the appeal). The following example demonstrates this:

Supreme Court of the United States
Richard Perry LOVING et ux., Appellants,
v.
COMMONWEALTH OF VIRGINIA.
No. 395.
Argued April 10, 1967.
Decided June 12, 1967.

This example indicates that Loving was not only the plaintiff who brought the action originally, but is also the appellant who requested the appeal to the Supreme Court of the United States.

The next component of the case is the **syllabus** or brief summary of the case. It immediately follows the caption of the case and briefly informs the reader of the basic conflict in the case and a simple stating of the Court's decision in the case. This syllabus is often prepared by a court clerk and is not authoritative or binding. It is simply information to assist the reader in understanding the underlying conflict in the case. The following is an example of a syllabus from the *Loving* case:

> *Proceeding on motion to vacate sentences for violating state ban on interracial marriages. The Circuit Court of Caroline County, Virginia, denied motion, and writ of error was granted. The Virginia Supreme Court of Appeals, 206 Va. 924, 147 S.E.2d 78, affirmed the convictions, and probable jurisdiction was noted. The United States Supreme Court, Mr. Chief Justice Warren, held that miscegenation statutes adopted by Virginia to prevent marriages between persons solely on basis of racial classification violate equal protection and due process clauses of Fourteenth Amendment.*

> *Convictions reversed.*

The next component of the case is the **headnotes**. These are prepared by the editors of the reporter in which the case is appearing, and not by the Court itself. For this reason, headnotes are not considered authoritative but do assist the reader and researcher to understand the major points of law to be found in the case, or in finding that part of the case that is relevant to his or her research. The headnotes are numbered, and the editors also include these numbers in brackets in the part of the opinion that is discussing the point of law noted in each headnote. Thus, if the headnote is labeled "[1]," the reader can skim the opinion itself and find an analogous paragraph also labeled [1] and immediately find the portion of the opinion that discusses the relevant point of law. The following is an example of one of the headnotes to be found in the *Loving* case:

> West Headnotes
> [1] KeyCite this headnote
> 253 Marriage
> 253k2 k. Power to Regulate and Control.
> Marriage is social relation subject to state's police power.

Following the headnotes is a paragraph indicating who represented the parties during the appeal. This paragraph indicates the **attorneys of record** and the following is an example, again from the *Loving* case:

> Philip J. Hirschkop, pro hac vice, by special leave of Court, Bernard S. Cohen, Alexandria, Va., for appellants.
> R. D. McIlwaine, III, Richmond, Va., for appellee.
> William M. Marutani, Philadelphia, Pa., for Japanese American Citizens League, as amicus curiae, by special leave of Court.

Immediately following the names of the attorneys is the beginning of the opinion. The opinion always begins with a sentence indicating the *author of the opinion* for the Court. This will be evident because the justice's name will be in all capital letters:

> Mr. Chief Justice WARREN delivered the opinion of the Court.

This sentence introduces the *opinion* of the Court, and this is the official, authoritative decision handed down. It is written by the justice on behalf of the majority of the Court, and contains the rule of law that is binding on all lower courts. This *majority opinion* is often followed by *concurring opinions* to the majority (if any), and these are followed by *dissenting opinions* and possibly opinions concurring with the dissent.

Reading the Case

Reading a case is not the same as briefing a case, but often students attempt to both read and brief a case together. It is important, especially as a student is engaging in this exercise for the first few times, that these two activities occur separately. A student new to the analysis of case law should begin by reading the case in its entirety without taking notes. This is the student's opportunity to get a feel for the facts of the case and the major thrust of the decision. It may not be immediately clear what the Court is deciding and the Court may even discuss preliminary matters, such as jurisdiction or procedural matters, before discussing the central issue of the case. Students should not be discouraged if they feel somewhat at a loss when reading a case for the first time.

Cases generally are organized using the following format. The case usually begins by giving an *overview of the process* by which the case reached the appellate court. It begins by outlining what took place at the trial court level, including any major procedural issues and the outcome of that trial.

The author of the case generally follows this overview with a recitation of the *facts*. Even though an appellate decision is traditionally concerned with an issue of law, rather than an issue of fact, it is important that the author sets the stage by telling the story of the underlying dispute. While it is the trial court that places the most emphasis on the facts of the case, no appellate decision would be complete without summarizing the facts.

While there is no guarantee, generally the author follows the facts by stating the question or questions to be decided by the Court, more commonly called the **issue(s).** Traditionally the justice writing the opinion often indicates the statement of the issue(s) by using language, such as "The question to be decided is . . ." or "The issue before the court is . . ." However, some authors are not so accommodating and in those instances, the reader will have to search the opinion for the issue. It is important for the student to remember that the issue(s) is the most important aspect of the case and only with practice will the student be able to quickly identify the issue and get to the heart of the case.

Following the recitation of facts and the issues, the author then launches into the *discussion* of the law and how it relates to the facts and the issue. This is the portion of the case that looks at precedent and explains not only the decision, but also the reasons the Court has reached that decision. It is this application of the law that explains the Court's conclusion in that particular case. It is this part of the case that gives the Court's justification for their ultimate holding.

The **holding**, or **rule of law**, is the Court's conclusion in the case. It is this conclusion that answers the question presented by the issue and declares the rights or responsibilities of the parties to the litigation. It is also that part of the case that is binding as precedent on the lower courts within the same jurisdiction.

After having initially read the case and sorted out these elements of the case, the student should begin again with an eye toward briefing the case.

How to Brief

Briefing a case means preparing a brief summary of the important aspects of the case. The important elements of a brief include the *facts*, the *issue(s)*, the *holding*, and the *reasoning*. If there are concurring or dissenting opinions, these, too, should be summarized and included in the brief.

In writing the brief, the student should begin by sorting out the relevant facts from those that have no direct bearing on the decision of the Court. It would be convenient if the Court would place all the facts at the beginning of the case so that the reader could quickly sort through them, but the student should be aware that the author of the opinion may well scatter facts throughout the opinion. In addition to the relevant facts, the student should include the lower trial or appellate court decisions as part of the factual history of the case.

Once the student has sorted through the facts, the next step is for the student to state the issue(s). As noted above, it may not be easy to sort out the issues unless the author of the opinion is helpful enough to include language indicating the question(s) to be answered by the Court. The issue should always be presented by a question that can be answered with either a simple "yes" or "no." Remember, not only may a case have more than one issue, it may have more than one type of issue. It may have procedural issues concerning the mechanics of the previous litigation in the case, or it may have substantive issues that concern the law as it applies to the certain set of facts presented in the case. The student should also remember that the issue is one of the two most important aspects of the case brief.

After stating the issue(s), the next step in briefing is to answer the issue(s). Stating the holding of the case does this. The holding actually has three parts. First, the issue should be answered with a simple "yes" or "no." Second, the student should include an indication of which of the parties won, such as J/P for judgment for the prosecution or plaintiff, or J/D for judgment for the defendant. The third part of the holding is an indication of whether the lower court decision was affirmed, reversed, or reversed and remanded.

The last major aspect of a brief is the *reasoning*. This part of the brief will tell the reader why the Court decided as it did. Some opinion authors are very specific and clear about why the Court took the action that it did, but some are not. If the reasons are unclear, the student may have to read the case again to discern the reasons.

If there are *concurring* or *dissenting* opinions, these, too, should be noted in the brief. The reasons why a judge or justice decides to concur with the majority opinion or dissent from the majority holding should be outlined in the brief.

As the student briefs the case, he or she should remember that every person's briefing style may be a bit different, but no matter the person's style, the issue(s) and the reasoning are the two most important elements of the brief. While it is important to know the facts and the holding, the issue(s) outlines the important questions to be answered by the Court and the reasoning tells future readers why the Court decided as it did. Briefs are a tool to help the students or researcher understand the law as they organize their notes for studying or writing for their employer.

APPENDIX D

RESEARCHING THE CONSTITUTION

Introduction

When researching the United States Constitution, it is relatively easy to find a copy of the document itself. Many textbooks, including this one, will include a copy for the students' convenience. Some political entities, including senators' and representatives' offices, have the Constitution in booklet form and will often send copies to their constituents upon request. However, in order to effectively research the Constitution, it is necessary to look at the official and commercially prepared versions of the Constitution in the statute books. The purpose of this appendix is to give the student some ideas on resources that can be tapped to find cases, commentary, and case information regarding the various constitutional provisions.

Statutory Treatment of the Constitution

The official publication source for the United States Constitution is the *United States Code* (U.S.C.), which is published by the U.S. Government Printing Office. This publication contains the text of the Constitution and all the amendments thereto, but does not include research aids, such as annotations to cases, commentary, references to other library sources, etc. In order to have access to these tools, a researcher may choose to access the text of the Constitution in one of the other commercial statutory publications. They are: the *United States Code Annotated* (U.S.C.A.), published by West Publishing Company, or the *United States Code Service* (U.S.C.S.), published by Lawyer's Cooperative Publishing Company. Both of these versions contain many helpful research tools as well as references to cases that have interpreted the relevant constitutional provision. By using these commercial versions, the student can quickly find supporting materials for the research project.

All three of these statutory collections are accessed by a subject-matter index. The student need only to look up a relevant word or phrase to find out which volume of the set contains the information sought. These collections also contain cross-indexing tools such as the Popular Names Table that allows the student to look up the well-known name of a statute and find where that statute is located in the collection.

In addition to offering these statutory collections in the traditional book form, the publishers also offer the collections on CD-ROM. The CD-ROM versions contain the same statutory information, referencing tools, and research materials as the printed versions. Libraries that choose to have the CD-ROM versions often do so because of their space-saving qualities and ease of updating. Although the book versions are updated regularly, the librarian must actually go to the stacks, locate the appropriate book, and insert the update in a pocket provided for such updates on the back cover of the book. It is much easier just to add an additional updating CD to the collection. And, needless to say, CDs take up far less space than a set of books.

Legal Encyclopedias

In addition to the official and commercial versions of the statutes, there are legal encyclopedias that can be of great assistance to a researcher. Two of the more prominent legal encyclopedias are *American Jurisprudence* or Am. Jur. and *Corpus Juris Secundum* or C.J.S. Both of these legal encyclopedias offer commentary written by legal experts that explains the various provisions of the Constitution, the cases that have interpreted the constitutional provisions, and cross-references to related publications. Both are accessed via a subject-matter index, or an alphabetical listing of the various topics discussed in the publication.

The *American Law Reports* or A.L.R. is another excellent source for researching the Constitution. Like the other legal encyclopedias discussed, this resource is accessed via a subject-matter index, allowing the student to look up the topic being researched.

Textbooks, Hornbooks, and Nutshells

There are many textbooks written on constitutional law. These textbooks often contain valuable information about the court opinions written on the various constitutional topics. A good textbook gives the student an introduction to the topic at hand, as well as case names and citations.

In addition to traditional textbooks, there are many hornbooks on the market. While law students most often use these hornbooks to assist them in the study of law, they are also excellent overviews of the topic being researched.

Another publication offering an overview of particular topics is the Nutshell series. These small books contain a vast amount of information regarding the constitutional topic, the cases interpreting the topic, and references to academic discourse on the topic.

Other Research Tools

In addition to the above research tools, the student will also need to access information from other publications such as legal dictionaries and legal thesauruses. There are a variety of each of these on the market, and the authors used *Oran's Dictionary of the Law* to prepare this textbook. No matter what type of legal research one is engaged in, it is a good investment to have both a good legal dictionary and legal thesaurus.

Once You Find the Information You Need

Finding the information you need is only the beginning of the research process. While it is important to find the constitutional provision that is relevant to your research and the cases interpreting that provision, it is just as important to make sure that the information you have found is relevant, timely, and still good law. The updating process is crucial. When updating the statutory or constitutional provision, the first step in updating is to check the pocket part updates or the later CD-ROM updates. Once you are sure that the provision has not been repealed or amended, you will probably want to look at the cases interpreting that provision.

Physically locating the cases that interpret the Constitution in the library will involve looking at one of three versions of the printed cases. The official version of the Supreme Court cases are found in the *United States Reports,* abbreviated U.S. Two commercial versions are also available and they are: the

Supreme Court Reporter by West Publishing Company, abbreviated S. Ct. and the *Lawyer's Cooperative Supreme Court Reporter* by Lawyer's Cooperative Publishing, abbreviated L. Ed. Accessing these cases via the Internet or using computer-assisted legal research will be discussed shortly. To find the appropriate volume containing the sought after case, the student need only to look at the citation of the case. The citation includes a volume number, followed by the abbreviation for the appropriate publication, and ends with the page number. Thus, the citation 157 U.S. 45 can be found in volume 157 of the *United States Reports* on page 45.

After the student has found and read the case, it is once again imperative for that student to update or make sure the case has not been modified, explained, or reversed. This process is referred to as "Shepardizing" after the individual who invented the process using *Shepard's Citators*. These citators allow the student to use a series of books or CD-ROMs to look at the subsequent history of the case. When done properly, the student can be confident that the case is still good law.

Computer-Assisted Legal Research and the Internet

In addition to the already mentioned CD-ROM technology, the student may also have access to legal research databases such as WESTLAW and LEXIS. These commercially available research services are available through many law firms and law libraries, but may not be available to undergraduate students at their college or university library, and few local libraries have these rather expensive on-line services. If the student has access to these on-line services, the student will find that both contain the full-text of all state and federal statutes, Supreme Court and other federal court cases, cases coming from the state court systems, and a variety of legal research tools.

It is possible for a student to access many legal resources on the Internet. Throughout this book the authors have directed the students to various Web sites that contain information relevant to the constitutional topic being discussed. While the student must ascertain the credibility of the Web site, there are many legitimate Web sites containing accurate and valuable information. Many of the best Web Sites are government agency Web sites, law school library holdings, access to legal periodicals, and various legal search engines.

Finding the End

The number of legal resources available both in printed form and via various types of technology can be overwhelming. Students often become anxious and overwhelmed by the amount of information available to them. The often-asked question is, "How do I know when I'm finished?" That is a good question and while there are no hard-and-fast indicators that you have reached the end, a good rule of thumb is that you are "finished" when you begin seeing the same cases and statutes over and over, no matter which research tool you are using. While this may not add a great deal to the student's comfort level, as the researcher gains experience in the area of legal research, the answer to this question will be easier and easier to determine.

APPENDIX E

AN ALPHABETICAL LISTING OF THE JUSTICES OF THE UNITED STATES SUPREME COURT

Name	Years of Service
Justice Henry Baldwin	1830–1844
Justice Phillip B. Barbour	1836–1841
Justice Hugo Black	1937–1971
Justice Harry Blackmun	1970–1994
Justice John Blair	1789–1796
Justice Samuel Blatchford	1882–1893
Justice Joseph Bradley	1870–1892
Justice Louis D. Brandeis	1916–1939
Justice William Brennan, Jr.	1956–1990
Justice David J. Brewer	1889–1910
Justice Steven Breyer	1994–present
Justice Henry B. Brown	1890–1906
Chief Justice Warren Burger	1969–1986
Justice Pierce Butler	1922–1939
Justice Harold H. Burton	1945–1958
Justice James F. Byrnes	1941–1942
Justice John Campbell	1853–1861
Justice Benjamin N. Cardozo	1932–1938
Justice John Catron	1837–1865
Chief Justice Salmon P. Chase	1864–1873
Justice Samuel Chase	1796–1811
Justice Tom C. Clark	1949–1967
Justice John H. Clarke	1916–1922
Justice Nathan Clifford	1858–1881
Justice Benjamin Curtis	1851–1857
Justice William Cushing	1789–1810
Justice Peter V. Daniel	1841–1860
Justice David Davis	1862–1877
Justice William R. Day	1903–1922
Justice William O. Douglas	1939–1975
Justice Gabriel Duval	1811–1835
Chief Justice Oliver Ellsworth	1796–1800
Justice Stephen J. Field	1863–1897
Justice Abe Fortas	1965–1970
Justice Felix Frankfurter	1939–1962
Chief Justice Melville W. Fuller	1888–1910
Justice Ruth Bader Ginsburg	1993–present

Justice Arthur Goldberg	1961–1965
Justice Horace Gray	1881–1902
Justice Robert C. Grier	1846–1870
Justice John M. Harlan I	1877–1911
Justice John M. Harlan II	1955–1971
Justice Oliver Wendall Holmes	1902–1932
Chief Justice Charles E. Hughes	1930–1941
Justice Charles E. Hughes	1910–1916
Justice Ward Hunt	1872–1882
Justice James Iredell	1790–1799
Chief Justice John Jay	1789–1795
Justice Howell E. Jackson	1893–1895
Justice Robert H. Jackson	1941–1954
Justice Thomas Johnson	1791–1793
Justice William Johnson	1804–1834
Justice Anthony Kennedy	1988–present
Justice Joseph R. Lamar	1910–1916
Justice Lucias Q. C. Lamar	1888–1893
Justice Henry B. Livingston	1806–1823
Justice Horace L. Lurton	1909–1914
Chief Justice John Marshall	1801–1835
Justice Thurgood Marshall	1967–1991
Justice Stanley Matthews	1881–1889
Justice Joseph McKenna	1898–1925
Justice John McKinley	1837–1852
Justice John McLean	1829–1861
Justice James McReynolds	1914–1941
Justice Samuel F. Miller	1862–1890
Justice Sherman Minton	1949–1956
Justice William H. Moody	1906–1910
Justice Alfred Moore	1799–1804
Justice Frank Murphy	1940–1949
Justice Samuel Nelson	1845–1872
Justice Sandra Day O'Connor	1981–present
Justice William Paterson	1793–1806
Justice Rufus W. Peckham	1895–1909
Justice Mahlon Pitney	1912–1922
Justice Lewis F. Powell, Jr.	1972–1987
Justice Stanley F. Reed	1938–1957
Chief Justice William H. Rehnquist	1972–2005
Chief Justice John G. Roberts, Jr	2005–present
Justice Owen Roberts	1930–1945
Chief Justice John Rutledge	1795 (unconfirmed)
Justice John Rutledge	1789–1791
Justice Wiley B. Rutledge	1943–1949

Justice Edward T. Sanford	1923–1930
Justice Antonin Scalia	1986–present
Justice George Shiras, Jr.	1892–1903
Justice David H. Souter	1990–present
Justice John Paul Stevens	1975–present
Justice Potter Stewart	1958–1981
Chief Justice Harlan F. Stone	1925–1946
Justice Joseph Story	1811–1845
Justice William Strong	1870–1880
Justice George Sutherland	1922–1938
Justice Noah H. Swayne	1862–1881
Chief Justice William H. Taft	1921–1930
Chief Justice Roger B. Taney	1836–1864
Justice Clarence Thomas	1991–present
Justice Smith Thompson	1823–1843
Justice Thomas Todd	1807–1826
Justice Robert Trimble	1826–1828
Justice Willis Van Devanter	1910–1937
Chief Justice Fred M. Vinson	1946–1953
Chief Justice Morrison R. Waite	1874–1888
Chief Justice Earl Warren	1953–1969
Justice Bushrod Washington	1798–1829
Justice James M. Wayne	1835–1867
Justice Byron R. White	1962–1993
Chief Justice Edward D. White	1894–1921
Justice Charles E. Whittaker	1957–1962
Justice James Wilson	1789–1798
Justice Levi Woodbury	1845–1851
Justice William B. Woods	1880–1887

APPENDIX F

GENERAL TIMETABLE FOR THE UNITED STATES SUPREME COURT

Court Term Begins	First Monday in October
Public Sessions	Mondays, Tuesdays, and Wednesdays, October through May
Research and Writing	Thursdays, October through May
Meeting of Justices	Fridays, October through May
Last of Term's Decisions Handed Down	June and July
Summer Recess	July and August
Review of Summer Petitions	September

GLOSSARY

–A–

advocacy
forceful persuasion; arguing a cause, right, or position.

affirmative action
steps to remedy past discrimination in hiring, promotion, etc., for example, by recruiting more minorities and women. Any administrative action taken to right a wrong, rather than to punish anyone for causing it.

agency shop
a business in which workers are not required to join a union but are required to pay the equivalent of union dues and fees. Agency shops are not permitted under certain state right to work laws.

alien
any person who is not a U.S. citizen, whether or not the person lives in the United States permanently. A foreigner.

amendment
A change made to a bill during its passage through a legislature or to a law already passed. One of the provisions of the U.S. Constitution enacted since the original Constitution became law. A change made to a pleading that is already before a court.

amicus curiae
(Latin) "Friend of the court." A person allowed to give argument or appear in a lawsuit (usually to file a brief, but sometimes to take an active part) who is not a party to the lawsuit.

appellate jurisdiction
the power and authority of a higher court to take up cases that have already been in a lower court and the power to make decisions about these cases. The process is called *appellate review*. Also, a trial court may have appellate jurisdiction over cases from an administrative agency.

attachment
formally seizing property (or a person) in order to bring it under the control of the court. This is usually done by getting a court order to have a law enforcement officer take control of the property. A document added onto another document. A security interest, such as a mortgage, attaches if it is valid and can be enforced by the person who has it against the person who holds the attached property.

at-will-doctrine
a common law doctrine that allows an employer to terminate the employment of an employee for good cause, bad cause, or no cause at all.

Articles of Confederation
the document that held together the thirteen original American colonies before the adoption of the Constitution.

attorney of record
the lawyer listed in the court papers as representing a person and who is responsible to the person and the court for all work done (and not done) in the lawsuit. The attorney of record is empowered to receive all legal papers from the court and from the other side in the case.

–B–

balancing approach or test

a doctrine in constitutional law that says a court should balance constitutional rights such as free speech against the right of the government to control conduct it calls harmful. The court should decide for the side with more important needs in each individual situation. The doctrine says that no rights are absolute. Any judicial decision-making principle that "balances" rights or responsibilities.

bicameral

having two chambers. A two-part legislature, such as the U.S. Congress, is bicameral: composed of the Senate (the "upper house" or "upper chamber") and the House of Representatives (the "lower house" or "lower chamber").

Bill of Rights

the first ten amendments (or changes or additions) to the U.S. Constitution.

–C–

caption

the heading or introductory section of a legal paper usually contains the names of the parties, the court, and the case number.

cases and controversies

real (not hypothetical or faked) disputes that turn into lawsuits. The U.S. Constitution gives the federal courts the power to decide certain "cases and controversies."

certiorari

(Latin) "To make sure." A request for certiorari (or "cert." for short) is like an appeal, but one which the higher court is not required to take for decision. It is literally a writ from the higher court asking the lower court for the record of the case.

child pornography

pornography showing children engaged in sexual activity.

citizen

a person born in the United States, a person who goes through the formal process of naturalization, or most children born abroad to a U.S. citizen. A person is a citizen of the state where he or she has permanent residence, and a corporation is a citizen of the state where it was legally created.

clear and present danger test

a test of whether or not speech may be restricted or punished. It may be if it will probably lead to violence soon or if it threatens a serious, immediate weakening of national safety and security. The test was first stated in *Schenck v. U.S.* (249 U.S. 47 (1919)), applied in *Dennis v. U.S.* (341 U.S. 494 (1951)) to punish advocacy of the forcible overthrow of the U.S. government, and revised in *Yates v. U.S.* (354 U.S. 298 (1957)) to permit such advocacy in the abstract, but not coupled with action.

commerce

the buying, selling, transporting, or exchanging of goods or services. Short for the Department of Commerce, the cabinet department that promotes U.S. trade, economic development, and technology. It includes the patent office and many scientific and business-development branches.

Commerce Clause

the provision of the U.S. Constitution (Article I, Section 8) that gives Congress the power to control trade with foreign countries and from state to state. This is called the *commerce power*. Congress can regulate anything that "affects interstate commerce" or that uses the "instrumentalities of interstate commerce" (and can keep the states from regulating interstate commerce) because the federal government has the power under the Supremacy Clause.

commercial speech

expression, such as newspaper ads, related solely to the economic interest of the "speaker" and the audience. Commercial speech is entitled to First Amendment protection but not to the extent that personal or political expression is protected.

compelling state interest

a strong enough reason for a state law to make the law constitutional even though the law classifies persons on the basis of race, sex, etc., or uses the state's police power to limit an individual's constitutional rights.

concurring opinion

opinion in which a judge agrees with the result reached in an opinion by another judge in the same case but not necessarily with the reasoning that the other judge used to reach the conclusion.

constitution

a document that sets out the basic principles and most general laws of a country, state, or organization. The U.S. Constitution is the basic law of the country, on which most other laws are based, and to which all other laws must yield. Often abbreviated "Const." or "Con."

constitutional convention

representatives of the people of a country who meet to write or change a constitution. Article V of the U.S. Constitution (which was written and adopted in the Philadelphia Constitutional Convention of 1787) allows a convention if two-thirds of the state legislatures call for one.

–D–

de facto

(Latin) in fact; actual; a situation that exists in fact whether or not it is lawful. For example, a de facto corporation is a company that has failed to follow some of the technical legal requirements to become a legal corporation, but carries on business as one in good faith, and a de facto government is one that has at least temporarily overthrown the rightful, legal one.

de jure

(Latin) of right; legitimate; lawful, whether or not true in actual fact. For example, a president may still be the de jure head of a government even if the army takes actual power by force. De jure segregation is a separation of races that is the result of governmental action while de facto segregation is caused by social, geographic, or economic conditions only.

declaratory judgment

a judicial opinion that states the rights of the parties or answers a legal question without awarding any damages or ordering that anything be done. A person may ask a court for a declaratory judgment only if there is a real, not theoretical, problem that involves real legal consequences.

defamation

transmission to others of false statements that harm the reputation, business, or property rights of a person. Spoken defamation is slander and written defamation is libel.

discrimination

the failure to treat individuals equally. The setting up of sham or irrelevant categories to justify treating individuals unfairly. Illegally unequal treatment based on race, color, religion, sex, age, handicap, or national origin. This is often called *invidious discrimination*.

disparate impact

discrimination based on race, color, religion, sex, national origin, age, or disability that results from a practice that does not seem to be discriminatory and was not intended to be so.

dissenting opinion

a judge's formal disagreement with the decision of the majority of the judges in a lawsuit.

diversity of citizenship

the situation that occurs when persons on one side of a case in federal court come from a different state from persons on the other side. *Complete diversity* (all the plaintiffs are from a different state from all the defendants) allows the court to accept and decide the case based on the court's diversity jurisdiction, provided that certain other criteria are met. Only *minimal diversity* (at least one plaintiff comes from a different state from at least one defendant) is needed for interpleader between states. *Manufactured diversity* (improperly creating diversity for the sake of obtaining federal jurisdiction) is prohibited. Diversity of citizenship also applies to suits between citizens and foreign nationals.

due process of law

the Due Process Clauses of the Fifth and Fourteenth Amendments to the U.S. Constitution require that no person be deprived of life, liberty, or property without due process of law. What constitutes due process of law varies from situation to situation, but the core of the idea is that a person should always have notice and a real chance to present his or her side in a legal dispute ("procedural due process") and that no law or government procedures should be arbitrary or unfair ("substantive due process"). Some of the specifics of due process include the right to a transcript of court proceedings, the right to question adverse witnesses, etc.

–E–

electoral college

a name for the persons chosen by voters to elect the president and vice president of the United States. The electoral college is now almost a formality, and the vote of the general public in each state directly controls the election. Theoretically, however, some electors might decide to vote differently from their instructions, a choice that could change the result of a close election.

eminent domain

the government's right and power to take private land for public use by paying for it.

entitlement

absolute (complete) right to something (such as Social Security) once you show that you meet the legal requirements to get it.

enumerated powers

those powers specifically granted to the three branches of government in the U.S. Constitution.

enumerated rights

those rights specifically granted to the citizens of the United States in the U.S. Constitution.

equal protection of the laws

the constitutional requirement that a state government not treat equals unequally, set up illegal categories to justify treating persons unfairly, or give unfair or unequal treatment to a person based on that person's race, religion, disability, color, sex, age, or national origin. This is based on the Equal Protection Clause of the Fourteenth Amendment.

equitable

just, fair, and right for a particular situation, for example, an equitable distribution of money or property is a fair division, but not necessarily an equal one. An equitable election is choosing between two things when it is not fair to have both. The doctrine of equitable election is the rule that a person cannot accept something given in a will and also challenge the validity of the will for other purposes. Also, whenever something should exist but does not exist under a strict interpretation of the law, a court may decide in fairness that it does exist.

Establishment Clause

that part of the First Amendment to the U.S. Constitution that states "Congress shall make no law respecting an establishment of religion."

executive agreement

a document similar to a treaty that is signed by the president of the United States but does not require the approval of the Senate (as a treaty does).

executive privilege

the right of the president of the United States and subordinates to keep some information (primarily documents) from public disclosure. The privilege is used most often for military and diplomatic secrets.

exemption

freedom from a general burden, duty, service, or tax. The subtraction from income for tax purposes of a certain amount of money for yourself, your spouse, and each dependent (such as a child living at home). Each exemption lowers the income on which a person must pay taxes. Property that must be kept by a debtor when property is taken away from the debtor by a court order such as in a judgment debt or bankruptcy.

expectation of privacy

the belief that you (or your possessions) are in a place, or engaged in an activity, where you have a right to expect privacy. This belief is required to challenge the Fourth Amendment reasonableness, and thus the validity, of a search or seizure.

extrajudicial

unconnected with court business; outside of court. Beyond the proper scope of court business. Not having legal effect, though said or done by a judge.

–F–

federal question

a legal issue directly involving the U.S. Constitution, statutes, or treaties. Federal courts have jurisdiction in cases involving a federal question.

federalism

a system of political organization with several different levels of government (for example, city, state, and national) coexisting in the same area with the lower levels having some independent powers.

fighting words

speech that is not protected by the First Amendment to the U.S. Constitution because it is likely to cause violence by the person to whom the words are spoken.

freedom of association (or assembly)

the First Amendment right to gather together in groups for any lawful purpose.

freedom of contract

the constitutionally protected right to make and enforce contracts, as limited only by reasonable laws about health, safety, and consumer protection.

freedom of expression
the First Amendment freedoms of religion, speech, and press combined.

freedom of the press
the First Amendment right of the press to publish most things "without censorship or prior restraint," to be free from unreasonable attempts to punish what has already been published, and other rights.

freedom of religion
the First Amendment right to hold any religious beliefs in any way that does not infringe on public safety or infringe on important rights of others. Also, the right of all citizens to be free of government control in the exercise of these beliefs.

freedom of speech
the First Amendment right to say what you want as long as you do not interfere with others' rights. These other rights are protected by the laws of defamation, public safety, etc.

Free Exercise Clause
that part of the First Amendment to the U.S. Constitution that states, "Congress shall make no law . . . prohibiting the free exercise of religion."

fundamental rights
basic or crucial rights. Fundamental rights are the basic rights, such as the right to vote and right to travel, which are most strongly protected by the Constitution.

–G–

gag order
a judge's order that a wildly disruptive defendant be bound and gagged during a trial. A judge's order to lawyers and witnesses that they discuss the trial with no outsiders, reporters in particular. A judge's order, usually held unconstitutional, to reporters that they not report certain court proceedings.

gag rule
a gag order. Any law or rule that prohibits the expression of ideas or that cuts off debate.

–H–

habeas corpus
(Latin) "You have the body." A judicial order to someone holding a person to bring that person to court. It is most often used to get a person out of the unlawful imprisonment by forcing the captor and the person being held to come to court for a decision on the legality of the imprisonment or other holding (such as keeping a child when someone else claims custody).

headnote
a summary of a case, or of an important legal point made in the case, placed at the beginning of the case when it is published. A case may have several headnotes.

hearing
a court proceeding. A trial-like proceeding conducted by an administrative agency or in another noncourt setting. A meeting of a legislative committee to gather information. A "public hearing" may involve an agency's showing a new plan or proposed action to the public and allowing public comment and criticism.

high crimes and misdemeanors

the basis for impeachment in the U.S. Constitution (Article II, Section 4). Opinions differ as to the exact meaning of the phrase. It may include felonies; it may include offenses against the United States that have serious governmental or political consequences; or it may be whatever the U.S. Congress decides it is.

Holding

the core of a judge's decision in a case. It is that part of the judge's written opinion that applies the law to the facts of the case and about which could be said the case means no more and no less than this. When later cases rely on a case as precedent, it is only the holding that should be used to establish the precedent. A holding may be less than the judge said it was. If the judge made broad, general statements, the holding is limited to only that part of the generalization that directly apply to the facts of that particular case.

–I–

immigrant

a foreigner who comes into a country. A foreigner who comes into a country with the intention of living there permanently. In U.S. law, a foreigner who comes to the United States to live permanently and who meets several specific requirements of the Immigration and Naturalization Act.

immunity

an exemption from a legally imposed duty, freedom from a duty, or freedom from a penalty. The freedom from prosecution (based on anything the witness says) that is given by the government to a witness who is forced to testify in a trial; before a grand jury, before a legislature, etc. *Transactional immunity*, the broadest form, is freedom from prosecution for all crimes related to the compelled testimony, so long as the witness tells the truth. *Use immunity*, less broad, is freedom from prosecution based on the compelled testimony and on anything the government learns from following up on the testimony. *Testimonial immunity*, the narrowest form, is freedom from prosecution based on the compelled testimony only. The freedom of a national, state, or local government from all taxes and from most tort lawsuits. The freedom of national, state, and local government officials from prosecution for, or arrest during, most official acts, and their freedom from most tort lawsuits resulting from their official duties.

impeachment

showing that a witness is untruthful, either by evidence of past conduct, or by showing directly that the witness is not telling the truth. When you do this, you impeach the witness. The first step in the removal from public office of a high public official such as a governor, judge, or president. In the case of the President of the United States, the House of Representatives makes an accusation by drawing up "articles of impeachment," voting on them, and presenting them to the Senate. This is impeachment. But impeachment is popularly thought to include the process that may take place after impeachment: the trial of the President in the Senate and conviction by two-thirds of the senators.

indeterminate

with the exact time period not set. For example, an indeterminate sentence is a criminal sentence with a maximum or minimum set, but not the exact amount of time. Some states allow judges to set only indeterminate sentences, and have special boards to decide the exact sentence later.

indigent

a poor person. An indigent criminal defendant is entitled to a free court-appointed lawyer.

injunction

a judge's order to a person to do or to refrain from doing a particular thing. For example, a court might issue an injunction to "enjoin" (prevent) a company from dumping wastes into a river. An injunction may be preliminary or temporary (until the issue can be fully tried in court) or it may be final or permanent.

issue

one single point in the dispute between two sides in a lawsuit. An issue may be of law (a dispute about how the law applies to the case) or of fact (about the truth of the fact).

–J–

judicial review

a court's power to declare a statute unconstitutional and to interpret laws. An appeal from an administrative agency decision. In the federal government the general rules governing this are in the Judicial Review Act. A higher court's examination of a lower court's decision.

justiciable

proper to be decided by a particular court. For example, a "justiciable controversy" is a real, rather than hypothetical, dispute. Federal courts may handle only cases that present a justiciable controversy.

–L–

lawful advocacy

legal or authorized forceful persuasion.

liberty

freedom from illegal personal restraint. Personal rights under law. A liberty interest is a right protected by due process of law.

line-item veto

the veto by the President or a state governor of only part of an appropriations bill.

–M–

majority opinion

a majority opinion is written when over half of the judges in a case agree about both the result and the reasoning used to reach that result.

moot

moot has several conflicting and overlapping definitions, including: no longer important or no longer needing a decision because already decided. For example, a federal court will not take a case if it is moot in this sense. For the sake of argument or practice. For example, moot court is a mock court in which law students practice by arguing appellate cases. Abstract. Not a real case involving a real dispute. A subject for argument; undecided; unsettled. In this sense moot means roughly the opposite of the first definition.

moral turpitude

describes any crime, such as larceny, that involves immorality or dishonesty.

motion to vacate

a request that a judge make a ruling or take some other action to annul; set aside; take back. For example, when a judge vacates a judgment, it is wiped out completely.

–N–

natural law
rules of conduct that are thought to be the same everywhere because they are basic to human behavior. Basic moral law.

naturalization
the formal process of becoming a citizen of a country.

Necessary and Proper Clause
(Article I, Section 8, Clause 18) that section of the U.S. Constitution giving Congress the power to pass all laws appropriate to carry out its functions.

notice
knowledge of certain facts. "Constructive notice" means a person is treated as if he or she knew certain facts. Formal receipt of the knowledge of certain facts. For example, "notice" of a lawsuit usually means that formal papers have been delivered to a person (personal notice) or to the person's agent (imputed notice). Various trial notices include notice: of motion, of orders, of judgments, of trial, to appear, to plead, etc.

–O–

objective observer standard
a standard for reviewing the legislative purpose of a new statute by looking at the legislative history and other supporting documents to see whether this average, objective person would conclude that there was a religious purpose behind the new statute.

obscene
lewd and offensive to accepted standards of decency. The "test" of whether something is obscene (as stated in the 1973 U.S. Supreme Court case of *Miller v. California*, 413 U.S. 15) includes such things as whether a book, movie, etc., "violates contemporary community standards," "appeals primarily to prurient interest," "describes sexual conduct in a patently offensive way," "is without redeeming social importance," etc. If a court finds speech to be obscene, it loses its protection under the freedom of speech and freedom of the press clauses of the First Amendment to the Constitution and may be banned, regulated, or prosecuted under state law.

opinion
a judge's statement of the decision he or she has reached in a case. A *memorandum opinion* is unanimous and briefly states only the result. A document prepared by a lawyer for a client that gives the lawyer's conclusions about how the law applies to a set of facts in which the client is interested.

original jurisdiction
the power of a court to take a case, try it, and decide it (as opposed to appellate jurisdiction, the power of a court to hear and decide an appeal).

overbreadth
a law will be declared void for overbreadth if it attempts to punish speech or conduct that is protected by the Constitution and if it is impossible to eliminate the unconstitutional part of the law without invalidating the whole law.

–P–

Penumbra Doctrine
the principle that the "Necessary and Proper Clause" of the U.S. Constitution allows the federal government to take all actions to carry out legitimate government purposes, even if the powers needed to carry out these purposes are only implied from other powers (which themselves are not specifically mentioned in the Constitution, but only implied). The principle that specific constitutional rights have less clear, but still real, implied rights, such as the right to privacy.

per curiam

(Latin) "By the court." Describes an opinion backed by all the judges in a particular court and usually with no one judge's name on it.

pocket veto

the failure by the President to sign a bill passed within 10 days of the end of a legislative session (which has the same effect as a veto).

police power

the government's right and power to set up and enforce laws to provide for the safety, health, and general welfare of the people; for example, police power to license occupations such as hair cutting.

pornography

books, movies, etc., that depict sexual behavior to cause sexual excitement. Nonobscene pornography is protected by the First Amendment, but child pornography is not.

prima facie

(Latin) At first sight; on the face of it; presumably. Describes something that will be considered to be true unless disproved by contrary evidence. For example, a prima facie case is a case that will win unless the other side comes forward with evidence to disprove it.

prior restraint

the government stopping someone from saying, publishing, or otherwise communicating something. Prior restraint of speech is unconstitutional under the First Amendment unless the speech is a "clear and present danger" to the country or is obscene or violates a person's legally recognized right to privacy.

privacy

describes the right to be left alone. The right to privacy is sometimes "balanced" against other rights, such as freedom of the press.

promissory estoppel

the principle that when Person A makes a promise and expects Person B to do something in reliance upon that promise, then Person B does act in reliance upon that promise, the law will usually help Person B enforce the promise because Person B has relied upon the promise to his or her detriment. Person A is "estopped" from breaking the promise even when there is no consideration to make the promise binding as part of a contract.

promulgate

publish; announce officially; put out formally.

prurient interest

a shameful or obsessive interest in immoral or sexual things. "Appealing to prurient interest" is one of many factors involved in deciding whether speech is obscene.

public figure

anyone who is famous (or infamous) for what he or she has done or who has come forward to take part in a public controversy. A public figure is given less legal protection against defamation and invasion of privacy than is an ordinary person.

public interest

a broad term for anything that can affect the general public's finances, health, rights, etc. For example, a business that is on public property and that the public must deal with is called "affected with," or "clothed by" a public interest. The practice of public interest law is often done on a nonprofit basis for a public cause such as protection of the environment.

–R–

ratification

confirmation and acceptance of a previous act done by you or by another person. For example, when the President signs a treaty, the Senate must ratify it (make it valid from the moment it was signed). Also, if a child makes a contract it is probably not enforceable against the child, but if the child ratifies it after becoming an adult it becomes a binding contract.

ratio decidendi

(Latin) "Reason for decision." The rationale for a judge's holding; the basic ideas a judge uses to come to a decision in a case.

rational basis (or purpose) test

the principle that a court should not second-guess a legislature (or an administrative agency) about the wisdom of a law (or of an administrative decision) if the law (or decision) has some rational basis.

reparation

payment for an injury; redress for a wrong done.

ripe

a case is ripe for selection and decision by the U.S. Supreme Court if the legal issues involved are clear enough and well enough evolved and presented so that a clear decision can come out of the case. Any court or agency that has the power to turn down cases may use ripeness as a way of deciding whether to take a case. Ripeness also includes the idea that the case involves a real controversy, not merely potential harm. A case is ripe for decision by a trial court if everything is completed and in order, and nothing remains but the decision itself.

rule of law

a general legal principle, often stated as a maxim or rule of thumb, that is used as a guide in deciding legal issues. A general statement that is intended to guide conduct, applied by government officials, and supported by an authoritative source. The principle that the highest authority is the law, not the government or its leaders.

rule of four

the principle that if at least four of the nine U.S. Supreme Court Justices vote to take a case, the court will hear the case. The Court uses the rule of four for cases that reach the Court by certiorari.

–S–

selective incorporation

the principle that the Bill of Rights, which protects persons against certain actions of the federal government, also protects against most, but not all such actions by a state government because the Fourteenth Amendment requires it.

separate but equal doctrine

the rule, established in the 1896 Supreme Court case *Plessy v. Ferguson* and then rejected as unconstitutional in the 1954 *Brown* decision, that when races are given substantially equal facilities, they may lawfully be segregated.

separation of powers

the division of the federal government (and state governments) into legislative (lawmaking), judicial (law interpreting), and executive (law carrying-out) branches. Each acts to prevent the others from becoming too powerful.

standing

a person's right to bring (start) a lawsuit because the issue directly affects him or her. This is called "standing to sue." Reputation. A standing committee of a house of a legislature is a regular committee, with full power to act within a subject area.

stare decisis

(Latin) "Let the decision stand." The rule that when a court has decided a case by applying a legal principle to a set of facts, the court should stick by the principle and apply it to all later cases with clearly similar facts, unless there is a strong reason not to, and that courts below must apply the principle in similar cases. This rule helps promote fairness and reliability in judicial decision-making.

strict scrutiny test

the principle that a state law (or an administrative agency regulation) that affects fundamental individual rights is valid only if it accomplishes important state objectives in the least-restrictive way possible.

style

official name.

Supremacy Clause

the provision in Article IV of the U.S. Constitution that the U.S. Constitution, laws, and treaties take precedence over conflicting state constitutions or laws.

suspect classification

making choices (in employment, etc.) based on factors such as race or nationality. These choices, only rarely legitimate, must be strongly justified if challenged. (Gender is a quasi-suspect classification that must be justified, but not as strongly, if challenged.)

syllabus

a headnote, summary, or abstract of a case.

–T–

Taft-Hartley Act

(29 U.S.C. § 141) a 1947 federal law that added several employers' rights to the union rights in the Wagner Act. It established several union "unfair labor practices" (such as attempting to force an employee to join a union).

Tenth Amendment

the U.S. constitutional amendment that says all powers not specifically given to the federal government are kept by the states and the people.

time, place, or manner restriction

government restriction of when, where, or how a speech may be made or a group may assemble in public. The restriction does not violate First Amendment rights if it serves a legitimate government purpose, permits reasonable alternate speech or assembly, and does not restrict the subject matter.

travel rights

the constitutional right to be free of unreasonable restraints on personal travel. These rights range from absolute rights (such as the absence of a passport requirement to travel between states of the United States) to relatively more fragile Penumbra Doctrine rights (such as the restriction on unreasonable state residency requirements for receipt of welfare benefits).

treaty

a formal agreement between countries on a major political subject. The Treaty Clause of the U.S. Constitution requires the approval of two-thirds of the Senate for any treaty made by the President.

treaty power

the power of the president of the U.S. to enter into a treaty which is a formal agreement between countries on major political subjects. The treaty clause of the U.S. Constitution requires the approval of two-thirds of the Senate.

–V–

vague

indefinite; uncertain; imprecise. The vagueness doctrine is the rule that a criminal law may be unconstitutional if it does not clearly say what is required or prohibited, what punishment may be imposed, or what persons may be affected. A law that violates due process of law in this way is void for vagueness.

veto

a refusal by the President or a governor to sign into law a bill that has been passed by a legislature. In the case of a presidential veto, the bill can still become a law if two-thirds of each house of Congress votes to override the veto.

viable child

a child developed enough to live outside the womb.

voir dire

(French) "To see, to say"; "to state the truth." The preliminary in-court questioning of a prospective witness (or juror) to determine competency to testify (or suitability to decide a case).

–W–

War Powers Clauses

the U.S. constitutional clauses (Article I, Section 8, Clauses 11–14) that give Congress the power to declare war and raise armies and give the President the power to carry on the war.

–Z–

zone of privacy

a place or activity protected against government intrusion by the Constitution.

INDEX